BRIDGES

Literature across Cultures

Gilbert H. Muller
The City University of New York
LaGuardia

John A. Williams
Rutgers University

McGraw-Hill, Inc.
New York   St. Louis   San Francisco   Auckland   Bogotá
Caracas   Lisbon   London   Madrid   Mexico City   Milan   Montreal
New Delhi   San Juan   Singapore   Sydney   Tokyo   Toronto

This book was developed by STEVEN PENSINGER, Inc.

This book was set in New Baskerville by ComCom, Inc.
The editors were Steve Pensinger and James R. Belser;
the designer was Karen K. Quigley;
the production supervisor was Denise L. Puryear.
The photo editor was Deborah Bull/Photosearch.
R. R. Donnelley & Sons Company was printer and binder.

Cover credit: "Our Bread" by Diego Rivera. Fresco, 1928. Ministry of Education, Court of the Fiestas, Mexico City. Photo, Bob Schalkwijk.

BRIDGES
Literature across Cultures

Permissions acknowledgments appear on pages 1025–1037, and on this page by reference.

1 2 3 4 5 6 7 8 9 0 DOC DOC 9 0 9 8 7 6 5 4 3

ISBN 0-07-044216-9

Library of Congress Cataloging-in-Publication Data

Bridges: literature across cultures / [compiled by] Gilbert H.
   Muller, John A. Williams.
          p.   cm.
   Includes index.
   ISBN 0-07-044216-9
      1. Literature—Collections.   I. Muller, Gilbert H., (date).
   II. Williams, John Alfred, (date).
   PQ6014.B75   1994
   808.8—dc20   93-3954

About the Authors

Gilbert H. Muller, who received a Ph.D. in English and American literature from Stanford University, is currently professor of English and special assistant to the president at the LaGuardia campus of the City University of New York. He has also taught at Stanford, Vassar, and several universities overseas. Dr. Muller is the author of the award-winning *Nightmares and Visions: Flannery O'Connor and the Catholic Grotesque, Chester Himes,* and other critical studies. His essays and reviews have appeared in *The New York Times, The New Republic, The Nation, The Sewanee Review, The Georgia Review,* and elsewhere. He is also a noted author and editor of textbooks in English and composition, including *The Short Prose Reader* with Harvey Wiener and, with John A. Williams, *The McGraw-Hill Introduction to Literature* and *Ways In: Approaches to Reading and Writing about Literature.* Among Dr. Muller's awards are National Endowment for the Humanities Fellowships, a Fulbright Fellowship, and a Mellon Fellowship.

John A. Williams, the Paul Robeson Professor of English at Rutgers University, is the author of twelve novels, among them *The Man Who Cried I Am* (1967), *!Click Song* (1982), *Jacob's Ladder* (1987), and *Trio: Clifford's Blues* (1994); ten nonfiction works that include studies on Richard Wright and Martin Luther King, Jr. (1970), Richard Pryor (1991), and Malcolm X (1993). In addition, he has edited or co-edited ten books, among them *The McGraw-Hill Introduction to Literature* (1985). A former journalist, Williams is also a poet and playwright and a recipient of the Rutgers University Lindback Foundation Award for Distinguished Teaching.

To
Laleh, Parisa, and Darius
And to
Lori, Greg, Dennis, and Adam
And as well to
Margo, John Gregory, Nancy, and David

Contents

Children & Families

Fiction

Poetry

Drama

Women & Men

Fiction

Poetry

viii   Contents

Caste & Class

Drama

War & Peace

Fiction

Poetry

Drama

Faith & Doubt

Fiction

Poetry

Drama

Preface

Writing and reading are not all that distinct for a writer. Both exercises require being alert and reading for unaccountable beauty, for the intricateness or simple elegance of the writer's imagination, for the world that the imagination evokes.

Toni Morrison
Playing in the Dark

Bridges, an anthology of literature from the many American cultures as well as cultures around the world, is suited ideally for today's composition and introductory literature courses. Offering a blend of classic favorites and selections from other cultures, the text contains some 300 stories, poems, and plays from the six habitable continents of our world. Among the authors are twelve Nobel Laureates, twelve Pulitzer Prize designees, twenty-six National Book Award recipients, twenty-two American Book Award winners, and many other prize-winning writers. These superlative authors, together with other outstanding talents, many of them minority and women writers, celebrate the diversity of our expanded literary canon.

We have created a mix of writers who have been world standard-bearers of literature as well as those relatively less well known. These authors, ranging from Sophocles to Sandra Cisneros, span classic to contemporary times, illustrating just how diverse yet at the same time how similar we are. Literature, of course, is a reflection of humanity. It transcends national and international borders. It allows us to understand, as we certainly must, that we truly are one people, alone as far as we know, in this "distant corner of the sky." Literature, when we read enough of it, can be discovery.

Once, the literature we studied was classified as "Western." With few exceptions the designation excluded the greater portion of the world and the literatures its various peoples produced. Our own national literature was shaped frequently by Western or Eurocentric imperatives, but here, too, many important literary viewpoints are over-looked.

Perhaps more than any other country, the United States reflects the cultures of the world, and for this reason *Bridges* offers a rich presentation of writing by African Americans, Latinos, Asian Americans, and Native Americans. These cultures, framed by ethnic history and custom, have in turn been reshaped by mainstream forces creating what has been called the "American experience," even as they have influenced and modified that experience, making our literature far richer.

Ultimately, *Bridges* is both an American and a global anthology. The text is organized around five themes that relate to situations people share universally: children and families, women and men, caste and class, war and peace, faith and doubt. We find these universal themes expressed by writers of every period, from ancient Egyptians and Greeks to those of contemporary times—each experience colored by place, custom, and point of view.

Within each thematic chapter readers will encounter sections on fiction, poetry, and drama. Each of these subsections contains the work of authors presenting culturally discrete but also shared experiences of the human condition. Questions for discussion and writing follow all fiction and drama selections and many poems; end-of-section apparatus permits comparative assessment of authors. With chapter introductions, a glossary of literary terms, and a biographical dictionary, *Bridges* is a complete literary anthology alerting students to the many imaginative worlds that major authors invite them to share. This, to us, is the finest definition of cultural literacy.

Supplementing this anthology is a companion text, *Ways In: Approaches to Reading and Writing about Literature*. This succinct guide contains six chapters on critical reading; the writing process; the elements of fiction, poetry, and drama; and approaches to the research paper. Numerous literary examples correlated with *Bridges*, along with sample student essays, make *Ways In* a valuable ancillary text for teachers who want to stress literary appreciation *and* critical writing in their classrooms.

Instructor's guides are available for both texts.

In *A Room of One's Own*, Virginia Woolf speaks of the collaborative effort—the marriage of opposites—that men and women must bring to the creative process if literary artists are to communicate experience "with perfect fullness." Such literature invites careful readings and excited rereadings, and ultimately the reconciliation of diverse viewpoints. This is the sort of literature we seek to present in *Bridges*—literature that is luminous, provocative, and culturally complete.

ACKNOWLEDGMENTS

We wish to thank several individuals who have helped in the development of this text. We owe a special debt to our editor and publisher Steve Pensinger, who has skillfully guided this project and our related text, *Ways In: Approaches to Reading and Writing about Literature*. Our thanks also to our agent John Wright; to James R. Belser for exceptional help in nursing the text through production; to Wesley Hall for permissions assistance; to Alan Gerstel and Cecilia Macheski for research; and to Susan Haines for preparing the manuscript. We are grateful for the comments and suggestions offered by the following teachers: Rosalie Hewitt, Northern Illinois University; Jodi Johnson, Los Angeles Pierce College; Mary LaMattery, City College of San Francisco; Gratia Murphy, Youngstown State University; and Merritt W. Stark, Henderson State University.

Gilbert H. Muller
John A. Williams

Children

&

Families

"Our Bread" by Diego Rivera. Fresco, 1928. Ministry of Education, Court of the Fiestas, Mexico City. Photo, Bob Schalkwijk.

INTRODUCTION

The family has always been the basic unit of cultures in the world, from the least to the most developed nations. And it has been the strongest and most influential unit in human history. The family existed long before the state, and therein lies its power, accumulated over the centuries. Certain families, literature and history tell us, even became the state in various societies. The works of Sophocles and Shakespeare include depictions of family history. In ancient Egypt and elsewhere, dynasties were built in part from the succession of children to their parents' throne. In our own time, we see the remnants of royal (or state) families in England, Spain, Holland, and elsewhere, but they exist concurrently with democratic, representative bodies such as the British Parliament or the Spanish Cortes.

In the average family, however, power is derived from interdependency and closeness—the familiar and obligatory interactions that become, up to a time, the norm. This unit extends not only to the immediate parents and children, but to grandparents and sometimes relatives somewhat further distant. In short, the extended family is made up of lesser related people who choose to assume a function within the family unit.

It is not surprising that much literature focuses on children, their parents, and the conflicts and relationships that inevitably develop between them. Literature helps us, as the state does not, to recognize that the interaction among family members is universal; and that it is in microcosm the interaction among larger groups and even nations. Literature can also help those of us who are past childhood to reexperience the emotions, perceptions, and thought processes peculiar to that time of life.

Early in this section, we can see the universality of childhood experience in two short stories written by authors from diverse cultural backgrounds. Yasunari Kawabata's "Up in the Tree" depicts a young Japanese boy acting upon his wishes and desires. In this brief story, the boy awakens to his longing for contact with the opposite sex, which is realized when he persuades a neighborhood girl to climb up a tree with him to share an honest, benign intimacy. Through simple description and dialogue, Kawabata allows us to peer into the inchoate world of youth, where much of the interaction involves probing, risking, and exploring.

James Joyce, the Irish writer, explores a similar theme of exploration and discovery—albeit with a much more embellished style—in his classic short story "Araby." The story takes us on a fanciful journey, seen through the eyes of a young man who is beguiled by a girl his own age. Through subtle imagery and symbolism, Joyce reproduces the consciousness of a boy whose vision transforms everyday life into a world where it is difficult to distinguish the actual from the imaginary, owing to his powerful desire to make a strong impression on the object of his attention.

Perhaps because poetry has had a tradition of addressing the personal, it too is an excellent vehicle for depicting the consciousness and self-consciousness of childhood. In Margaret Atwood's "Game After Supper," Robert Hayden's "Those Winter Sundays," Sylvia Plath's "Daddy," Theodore Roethke's "My Papa's Waltz," and Dylan Thomas's "Fern Hill," various versions of childhood perception are described, ranging from the spiritual—in the work of Dylan Thomas, for example—to images of abuse and abandonment, as in the work of Sylvia Plath.

But even more common among literary themes are family relationships. A majority of the stories, poems, and plays in this section describe the interaction and communication *between* family and child. And just as each family has its unique characteristics, relationships, and networks, so too do the families depicted here. David Leavitt's "Gravity" and Grace Paley's "A Conversation with My Father," for example, depict a parent's relationship with his or her child. But that is as far as the comparison goes; both stories focus on a parent-child relationship centered on illness. While Paley's story describes the bond between a daughter and her sick, aging father, Leavitt's focuses on the link between a mother and her son, who has AIDS. While conflict seems inherent between parents and their children, the added variable of illness makes these two stories particularly dramatic and poignant, as we see father and daughter and mother and son, respectively, grapple with issues of love, understanding, hope, pathos, communication, and ultimately communion, despite extraordinary circumstances.

Even without this added dimension of illness, however, anger, disappointment, hurt, and forgiveness are prominent themes in much of the work, just as they are in real-life family relationships. Take, for example, Raymond Carver's poem "Photograph of My Father in His Twenty-Second Year." Carver expresses the mixed emotions of sympathy and antagonism he feels upon viewing the photograph in the title. And we see that even when removed from the actual presence of our parents, our relationships with them continue to have a profound effect on our consciousness. Lucille Clifton's poem "Forgiving My Father" also deals with a parent whose physical absence in no way reduces the impact or presence of the parent-child relationship. Clifton describes the bitterness of having had an absent father; through her poem, we see her attempt to reconcile her own disappointment over this fact. This type of poem—wherein the poet uses the poem as a form of catharsis—has often been labeled confessional, and is a popular genre in today's literary world, perhaps owing to the deep influence psychiatry and psychoanalysis have had on the writers of our era.

Nonetheless, we should not assume that *all* literature about families and children deals with the tragic, discomforting side of life. There are examples in this section on family life that contain elements of pleasure, adventure, serenity, and fun. Such moods occur in poems such as "Grandfather and Grandmother in Love" and "Danse Russe." These poems as well as others show the wide range of positive experiences that family life provides.

Since the time of ancient Greece, drama has focused on what we now call nuclear and extended families, and many contemporary plays have revived this tradition. Two plays in this section—Hansberry's *A Raisin in the Sun* and Hwang's *Family Devotions*—are notable for their complex depiction of family life, as well as for revealing the powerful influence of society's biases against the family. The former reveals the Younger family's strength and courage in the face of degradation and oppression aimed at black Americans, while the latter shows the compromises and intergenerational conflicts a Chinese-American family undergoes as a result of adopting the values of the American Dream.

The personal, the interpersonal, and society-at-large—all are significant parts of the family network. And because these factors have a strong effect on all of us, writers continue to address family issues, while readers continue to seek understanding, enlightenment, sympathy, and empathy through reading about them.

Fiction

James Joyce

ARABY

North Richmond Street, being blind, was a quiet street except at the hour when the Christian Brothers School set the boys free. An uninhabited house of two stories stood at the blind end, detached from its neighbors in a square ground. The other houses of the street, conscious of decent lives within them, gazed at one another with brown imperturbable faces.

The former tenant of our house, a priest, had died in the back drawing-room. Air, musty from having been long enclosed, hung in all the rooms, and the waste room behind the kitchen was littered with old useless papers. Among these, I found a few paper-covered books, the pages of which were curled and damp: *The Abbott,* by Walter Scott, *The Devout Communicant* and *The Memoirs of Vidocq.* I liked the last best because its leaves were yellow. The wild garden behind the house contained a central apple-tree and a few straggling bushes under one of which I found the late tenant's rusty bicycle-pump. He had been a very charitable priest; in his will he had left all his money to institutions and the furniture of his house to his sister.

When the short days of winter came dusk fell before we had well eaten our dinners. When we met in the street the houses had grown somber. The space of sky above us was the color of ever-changing violet and towards it the lamps of the street lifted their feeble lanterns. The cold air stung us and we played till our bodies glowed. Our shouts echoed in the silent street. The career of our play brought us through the dark muddy lanes behind the houses where we ran the gauntlet of the rough tribes from the cottages, to the back doors of the dark dripping gardens where odors arose from the ashpits, to the dark odorous stables where a coachman smoothed and combed the horse or shook music from the buckled harness. When we returned to the street light from the kitchen windows had filled the areas. If my uncle was seen turning the corner we hid in the shadow until we had seen him safely housed. Or if Mangan's sister came out on the doorstep to call her brother in to his tea we watched her from our shadow peer up and down the street. We waited to see whether she would remain or go in and, if she remained, we left our shadow and walked up to Mangan's steps resignedly. She was waiting for us, her figure defined by the light from the half-opened door. Her brother always teased her before he obeyed and I stood by the railings looking at her. Her dress swung as she moved her body and the soft rope of her hair tossed from side to side.

Every morning I lay on the floor in the front parlor watching her door. The blind was pulled down to within an inch of the sash so that I could not be seen. When she came out on the doorstep my heart leaped. I ran to the hall, seized my books and followed her. I kept her brown figure always in my eye and, when we came near the point at which our ways diverged, I quickened my pace and passed her. This happened morning after morning. I had never spoken to her, except for a few casual words, and yet her name was like a summons to all my foolish blood.

Her image accompanied me even in places the most hostile to romance. On Saturday evenings when my aunt went marketing I had to go to carry some of the parcels. We walked through the flaring streets, jostled by drunken men and bargaining women, amid the curses of laborers, the shrill litanies of shopboys who stood on guard by the barrels of pigs' cheeks, the nasal chanting of street-singers, who sang a *come-all-you* about O'Donovan Rossa, or a ballad about the troubles in our native land. These noises converged in a single sensation of life for me: I imagined that I bore my chalice safely through a throng of foes. Her name sprang to my lips at moments in strange prayers and praises which I myself did not understand. My eyes were often full of tears (I could not tell why) and at times a flood from my heart seemed to pour itself out into my bosom. I thought little of the future. I did not know whether I would ever speak to her or not or, if I spoke to her, how I could tell her of my confused adoration. But my body was like a harp and her words and gestures were like fingers running upon the wires.

One evening I went into the back drawing-room in which the priest had died. It was a dark rainy evening and there was no sound in the house. Through one of the broken panes I heard the rain impinge upon the earth, the fine incessant needles of water playing in the sodden beds. Some distant lamp or lighted window gleamed below me. I was thankful that I could see so little. All my senses seemed to desire to veil themselves and, feeling that I was about to slip from them, I pressed the palms of my hands together until they trembled, murmuring: *"Oh love! O love!"* many times.

At last she spoke to me. When she addressed the first words to me I was so confused that I did not know what to answer. She asked me was I going to *Araby*. I forgot whether I answered yes or no. It would be a splendid bazaar, she said she would love to go.

"And why can't you?" I asked.

While she spoke she turned a silver bracelet round and round her wrist. She could not go, she said, because there would be a retreat that week in her convent. Her brother and two other boys were fighting for their caps and I was alone at the railings. She held one of the spikes, bowing her head towards me. The light from the lamp opposite our door caught the white curve of her neck, lit up her hair that rested there and, falling, lit up the hand upon the railing. It fell over one side of her dress and caught the white border of a petticoat, just visible as she stood at ease.

"It's well for you," she said.

"If I go," I said, "I will bring you something."

What innumerable follies laid waste my waking and sleeping thoughts after that evening! I wished to annihilate the tedious intervening days. I chafed against the work of school. At night in my bedroom and by day in the classroom her image came between me and the page I strove to read. The syllables of the word *Araby* were called to me through the silence in which my soul luxuriated and cast an Eastern enchantment over me. I asked for leave to go to the bazaar on Saturday night. My aunt was surprised and hoped it was not some Freemason affair. I answered few questions in class. I watched my master's face pass from amiability to sternness; he hoped I was not beginning to idle. I could not call my wandering thoughts together. I had hardly any patience with the serious work of life which, now that it stood between me and my desire, seemed to me child's play, ugly monotonous child's play.

On Saturday morning I reminded my uncle that I wished to go to the bazaar in the evening. He was fussing at the hallstand, looking for the hat-brush, and answered me curtly:

"Yes, boy, I know."

As he was in the hall I could not go into the front parlor and lie at the window. I left the house in bad humor and walked slowly towards the school. The air was pitilessly raw and already my heart misgave me.

When I came home to dinner my uncle had not yet been home. Still it was early. I sat staring at the clock for some time and, when its ticking began to irritate me, I left the room. I mounted the staircase and gained the upper part of the house. The high cold empty gloomy rooms liberated me and I went from room to room singing. From the front window I saw my companions playing below in the street. Their cries reached me weakened and indistinct and, leaning my forehead against the cool glass, I looked over at the dark house where she lived. I may have stood there for an hour, seeing nothing but the brown-clad figure cast by my imagination, touched discreetly by the lamplight at the curved neck, at the hand upon the railings and at the border below the dress.

When I came downstairs again I found Mrs. Mercer sitting at the fire. She was an old garrulous woman, a pawnbroker's widow, who collected used stamps for some pious purpose. I had to endure the gossip of the tea-table. The meal was prolonged beyond an hour and still my uncle did not come. Mrs. Mercer stood up to go: she was sorry she couldn't wait any longer, but it was after eight o'clock and she did not like to be out late, as the night air was bad for her. When she had gone I began to walk up and down the room, clenching my fists. My aunt said:

"I'm afraid you may put off your bazaar for this night of Our Lord."

At nine o'clock I heard my uncle's latchkey in the halldoor. I heard him talking to himself and heard the hallstand rocking when it had received the weight of his overcoat. I could interpret these signs. When he was midway through his dinner I asked him to give me the money to go to the bazaar. He had forgotten.

"The people are in bed and after their first sleep now," he said.

I did not smile. My aunt said to him energetically:

"Can't you give him the money and let him go? You've kept him late enough as it is."

My uncle said he was very sorry he had forgotten. He said he believed in the old saying: "All work and no play makes Jack a dull boy." He asked me where I was going and, when I had told him a second time he asked me did I know *The Arab's Farewell to his Steed*. When I left the kitchen he was about to recite the opening lines of the piece to my aunt.

I held a florin tightly in my hand as I strode down Buckingham Street towards the station. The sight of the streets thronged with buyers and glaring with gas recalled to me the purpose of my journey. I took my seat in a third-class carriage of a deserted train. After an intolerable delay the train moved out of the station slowly. It crept onward among ruinous houses and over the twinkling river. At Westland Row Station a crowd of people pressed to the carriage doors; but the porters moved them back, saying that it was a special train for the bazaar. I remained alone in the bare carriage. In a few minutes the train drew up beside an improvised wooden platform. I passed out on to the road and saw by the lighted dial of a clock that it was ten minutes to ten. In front of me was a large building which displayed the magical name.

I could not find any sixpenny entrance and, fearing that the bazaar would be closed, I passed in quickly through a turnstile, handing a shilling to a weary-looking man. I found myself in a big hall girdled at half its height by a gallery. Nearly all the stalls were closed and the greater part of the hall was in darkness. I recognized a silence like that which pervades a church after a service. I walked into the center of the bazaar timidly. A few people were gathered about the stalls which were still open. Before a curtain, over which the words *Café Chantant* were written in colored lamps, two men were counting money on a salver. I listened to the fall of the coins.

Remembering with difficulty why I had come I went over to one of the stalls and examined porcelain vases and flowered tea-sets. At the door of the stall a young lady was talking and laughing with two young gentlemen. I remarked their English accents and listened vaguely to their conversation.

"O, I never said such a thing!"

"O, but you did!"

"O, but I didn't!"

"Didn't she say that?"

"Yes. I heard her."

"O, there's a . . . fib!"

Observing me the young lady came over and asked me did I wish to buy something. The tone of her voice was not encouraging; she seemed to have spoken to me out of a sense of duty. I looked humbly at the great jars that stood like eastern guards at either side of the dark entrance to the stall and murmured:

"No, thank you."

The young lady changed the position of one of the vases and went back to the two young men. They began to talk of the same subject. Once or twice the young lady glanced at me over her shoulder.

I lingered before her stall, though I knew my stay was useless, to make my interest in her wares seem the more real. Then I turned away slowly and walked down the middle of the bazaar. I allowed the two pennies to fall against the sixpence in my pocket.

I heard a voice call from one end of the gallery that the light was out. The upper part of the hall was now completely dark.

Gazing up into the darkness I saw myself as a creature driven and derided by vanity; and my eyes burned with anguish and anger.

QUESTIONS

1. Does the first-person narrator seem like a child, an adult, or both? Why?
2. Examine Joyce's description of Dublin, especially in the first five paragraphs. What details stand out? What dominant impression emerges? What nationalist statement might Joyce be making?
3. What is the importance of Mangan's sister? How does she contrast with the boy's uncle? How does she contrast with the women whom the boy encounters at the bazaar?
4. The Irish fiction writer and critic Sean O'Faolain states that a story "must lead toward its point of illumination." (Joyce termed this moment of illumination an *epiphany*.) What is the point of illumination in "Araby"? How does it dictate the theme?
5. Explore the "dreams" of the children in "Araby" and in "Up in the Tree." How do they come in conflict with the realities of the adult world?

Yasunari Kawabata

UP IN THE TREE

Keisuke's house was on the shore where the great river began to enter the sea. Although the river ran alongside the garden, because of the somewhat elevated embankment it could not be seen from the house. The old shore, lined with pines and slightly lower than the embankment, seemed part of the garden, its pines the garden pines. This side of the pines, there was a hedge of Chinese black pine.

Michiko, forcing her way through the hedge, came to play with Keisuke. No, she came just to be with him. Both Michiko and Keisuke were fourth graders. This ducking through the hedge, instead of coming in by the front gate or by the garden gate in back, was a secret between them. For a girl, it wasn't easy. Shielding her head and face with both arms, bent over from the waist, she would plunge into the hedge. Tumbling out into the garden, she would often be caught up in Keisuke's arms.

Shy about letting the people in the house know that Michiko came every day, Keisuke had taught her this way through the hedge.

"I like it. My heart pounds and pounds like anything," Michiko said.

One day, Keisuke climbed up into a pine tree. While he was up there, along came

Michiko. Looking neither right nor left, she hurried along by the shore. Stopping at the hedge where she always went through, she looked all around her. Bringing her long, triple-braided pigtails in front of her face, she put them into her mouth halfway along their length. Bracing herself, she threw herself at the hedge. Up in the tree, Keisuke held his breath. When she'd popped out of the hedge into the garden, Michiko did not see Keisuke, whom she had thought would be there. Frightened, she shrank back into the shadow of the hedge, where Keisuke could not see her.

"Mitchan, Mitchan," Keisuke called. Michiko, coming away from the hedge, looked around the garden.

"Mitchan, I'm in the pine tree. I'm up in the pine tree." Looking up toward Keisuke's voice, Michiko did not say a word. Keisuke said, "Come out. Come out of the garden."

When Michiko had come back out through the hedge, she looked up at Keisuke. "You come down."

"Mitchan, climb up here. It's nice up here in the tree."

"I can't climb it. You're making fun of me, just like a boy. Come down."

"Come up here. The branches are big like this, so even a girl can do it."

Michiko studied the branches. Then she said, "If I fall, it's your fault. If I die, I won't know anything about it."

First dangling from a lower branch, she began to climb.

By the time she'd gotten up to Keisuke's branch, Michiko was gasping for breath. "I climbed it, I climbed it." Her eyes sparkled. "It's scary. Hold me."

"Hmm." Keisuke firmly drew Michiko to him.

Michiko, her arms around Keisuke's neck, said, "You can see the ocean."

"You can see everything. Across the river, and even up the river . . . It's good you climbed up here."

"It *is* good. Keichan, let's climb up here tomorrow."

"Hmm." Keisuke was silent a while. "Mitchan, it's a secret. Climbing up the tree and being up here in the tree—it's a secret. I read books and do homework up here. It's no good if you tell anyone."

"I won't tell." Michiko bowed her head in assent. "Why have you become like a bird?"

"Since it's you, Mitchan, I'll tell you. My father and mother had an awful quarrel. My mother said she was going to take me and go back to her parents' house. I didn't want to look at them, so I climbed a tree in the garden and hid at the top. Saying, 'Where's Keisuke gone to?' they looked all over for me. But they couldn't find me. From the tree, I saw my father go all the way to the ocean to look. This was last spring."

"What were they quarreling about?"

"Don't you know? My father has a woman."

Michiko said nothing.

"Since then, I've been up in this tree a lot. My father and mother still don't know. It's a secret," Keisuke said again, just to make sure. "Mitchan, starting tomorrow, bring your schoolbooks. We'll do our homework up here. We'll get good grades. The trees in the garden are all those big camellia trees with lots of leaves, so nobody can see us from the ground or anywhere."

The "secret" of their being up in the tree had continued for almost two years now. Where the thick trunk branched out near the top, the two could sit comfortably. Michiko, straddling one branch, leaned back against another. There were days when little birds came and days when the wind sang through the pine needles. Although they weren't that high off the ground, these two little lovers felt as if they were in a completely different world, far away from the earth.

Translated by Lane Dunlop

QUESTIONS

1. Kawabata, a Nobel Prize–winning writer, offers a clear description of setting. What is distinctive about the landscape? How do Michiko and Keisuke relate to it? Why do they hide in the pine tree?
2. What words best describe the mood or atmosphere of this story? Point out passages that convey this mood.
3. Adults are in the background of both "Araby" and "Up in the Tree." What is their function in both stories? How do they intensify certain conflicts?

Jamaica Kincaid

GIRL

Wash the white clothes on Monday and put them on the stone heap; wash the color clothes on Tuesday and put them on the clothes-line to dry; don't walk barehead in the hot sun; cook pumpkin fritters in very hot sweet oil; soak your little cloths right after you take them off; when buying cotton to make yourself a nice blouse, be sure that it doesn't have gum on it, because that way it won't hold up well after a wash; soak salt fish overnight before you cook it; is it true that you sing benna in Sunday school?; always eat your food in such a way that it won't turn someone else's stomach; on Sundays try to walk like a lady and not like the slut you are so bent on becoming; don't sing benna in Sunday school; you mustn't speak to wharf-rat boys, not even to give directions; don't eat fruits on the street—flies will follow you; *but I don't sing benna on Sundays at all and never in Sunday school;* this is how to sew on a button; this is how to make a buttonhole for the button you have just sewed on; this is how to hem a dress when you see the hem coming down and so to prevent yourself from looking like the slut I know you are so bent on becoming; this is how you iron your father's khaki shirt so that it doesn't have a crease; this is how you iron your father's khaki pants so that they don't have a crease; this is how you grow okra—far from the house, because okra tree harbors red ants; when you are growing dasheen, make sure it gets plenty of water or else it makes your throat itch when you are eating it; this is how you sweep a corner; this is how you sweep a whole house; this is how you sweep a yard; this is how you smile to someone you don't like too much; this is how you smile to someone you don't like at all; this is how you smile to someone you like completely; this is how you set a table for tea; this is how you set a table for dinner; this is how you set a table for dinner with an important guest; this is how you set a table for lunch; this is how you set a table for breakfast; this is how to behave in the presence of men who don't know you very well, and this way they won't recognize immediately the slut I have warned you against becoming; be sure to wash every day, even if it is with your own spit; don't squat down to play marbles—you are not a boy, you know; don't pick people's flowers—you might catch something; don't throw stones at blackbirds, because it might not be a blackbird at all; this is how to make a bread pudding; this is how to make doukona; this is how to make pepper pot; this is how to make a good medicine for a cold; this is how to make a good medicine to throw away a child before it even becomes a child; this is how to catch a fish; this is how to throw back a fish you don't like, and that way something bad won't fall on you; this is how to bully a man; this is how a man bullies you; this is how to love a man, and if this doesn't work there are other ways, and if they don't work don't feel too bad about giving up; this is how to spit up in the air if you feel like it, and this is how to move quick so that it doesn't fall on you; this is how to make ends meet; always squeeze bread to make sure it's fresh; *but what if the baker won't let me feel the bread?;* you mean to say that after all you are really going to be the kind of woman who the baker won't let near the bread?

QUESTIONS

1. Who is speaking in this sketch, and to whom? Does it matter that the girl has no name? What must the girl learn? What kind of person will she turn out to be?
2. The author was born in Saint Johns, the capital of the West Indian island nation of Antigua. What do we learn in the story about the culture of this Caribbean island?
3. This is a very short story. Does a theme emerge? Why or why not?

David Leavitt

GRAVITY

Theo had a choice between a drug that would save his sight and a drug that would keep him alive, so he chose not to go blind. He stopped the pills and started the injections— these required the implantation of an unpleasant and painful catheter just above his heart—and within a few days the clouds in his eyes started to clear up; he could see again. He remembered going into New York City to a show with his mother, when he was twelve and didn't want to admit he needed glasses. "Can you read that?" she'd shouted, pointing to a Broadway marquee, and when he'd squinted, making out only one or two letters, she'd taken off her own glasses—harlequins with tiny rhinestones in the corners—and shoved them onto his face. The world came into focus, and he gasped, astonished at the precision around the edges of things, the legibility, the hard, sharp, colorful landscape. Sylvia had to squint through *Fiddler on the Roof* that day, but for Theo, his face masked by his mother's huge glasses, everything was as bright and vivid as a comic book. Even though people stared at him, and muttered things, Sylvia didn't care; he could *see*.

Because he was dying again, Theo moved back to his mother's house in New Jersey. The DHPG injections she took in stride—she'd seen her own mother through *her* dying, after all. Four times a day, with the equanimity of a nurse, she cleaned out the plastic tube implanted in his chest, inserted a sterilized hypodermic and slowly dripped the bag of sight-giving liquid into his veins. They endured this procedure silently, Sylvia sitting on the side of the hospital bed she'd rented for the duration of Theo's stay—his life, he sometimes thought—watching reruns of *I Love Lucy* or the news, while he tried not to think about the hard piece of pipe stuck into him, even though it was a constant reminder of how wide and unswimmable the gulf was becoming between him and the ever-receding shoreline of the well. And Sylvia was intricately cheerful. Each day she urged him to go out with her somewhere—to the library, or the little museum with the dinosaur replicas he'd been fond of as a child—and when his thinness and the cane drew stares, she'd maneuver him around the people who were staring, determined to shield him from whatever they might say or do. It had been the same that afternoon so many years ago, when she'd pushed him through a lobbyful of curious and laughing faces, determined that nothing should interfere with the spectacle of his seeing. What a pair they must have made, a boy in ugly glasses and a mother daring the world to say a word about it!

This warm, breezy afternoon in May they were shopping for revenge. "Your cousin Howard's engagement party is next month," Sylvia explained in the car. "A very nice girl from Livingston. I met her a few weeks ago, and really, she's a superior person."

"I'm glad," Theo said. "Congratulate Howie for me."

"Do you think you'll be up to going to the party?"

"I'm not sure. Would it be okay for me just to give him a gift?"

"You already have. A lovely silver tray, if I say so myself. The thank-you note's in the living room."

"Mom," Theo said, "why do you always have to—"

Sylvia honked her horn at a truck making an illegal left turn. "Better they should get something than no present at all, is what I say," she said. "But now, the problem is, *I* have to give Howie something, to be from me, and it better be good. It better be very, very good."

"Why?"

"Don't you remember that cheap little nothing Bibi gave you for your graduation? It was disgusting."

"I can't remember what she gave me."

"Of course you can't. It was a tacky pen-and-pencil set. Not even a real leather box. So naturally, it stands to reason that I have to get something truly spectacular for Howard's engagement. Something that will make Bibi blanch. Anyway, I think I've found just the thing, but I need your advice."

"Advice? Well, when my old roommate Nick got married, I gave him a garlic press. It cost five dollars and reflected exactly how much I felt, at that moment, our friendship was worth."

Sylvia laughed. "Clever. But my idea is much more brilliant, because it makes it possible for me to get back at Bibi *and* give Howard the nice gift he and his girl deserve." She smiled, clearly pleased with herself. "Ah, you live and learn."

"You live," Theo said.

Sylvia blinked. "Well, look, here we are." She pulled the car into a handicapped-parking place on Morris Avenue and got out to help Theo, but he was already hoisting himself up out of his seat, using the door handle for leverage. "I can manage myself," he said with some irritation. Sylvia stepped back.

"Clearly one advantage to all this for you," Theo said, balancing on his cane, "is that it's suddenly so much easier to get a parking place."

"Oh Theo, please," Sylvia said. "Look, here's where we're going."

She leaned him into a gift shop filled with porcelain statuettes of Snow White and all seven of the dwarves, music boxes which, when you opened them, played "The Shadow of Your Smile," complicated-smelling potpourris in purple wallpapered boxes, and stuffed snakes you were supposed to push up against drafty windows and doors.

"Mrs. Greenman," said an expansive, gray-haired man in a cream-colored cardigan sweater. "Look who's here, Archie, it's Mrs. Greenman."

Another man, this one thinner and balding, but dressed in an identical cardigan, peered out from the back of the shop. "Hello there!" he said, smiling. He looked at Theo, and his expression changed.

"Mr. Sherman, Mr. Baker. This is my son, Theo."

"Hello," Mr. Sherman and Mr. Baker said. They didn't offer to shake hands.

"Are you here for that item we discussed last week?" Mr. Sherman asked.

"Yes," Sylvia said. "I want advice from my son here." She walked over to a large ridged crystal bowl, a very fifties sort of bowl, stalwart and square-jawed. "What do you think? Beautiful, isn't it?"

"Mom, to tell the truth, I think it's kind of ugly."

"Four hundred and twenty-five dollars," Sylvia said admiringly. "You have to feel it."

Then she picked up the big bowl and tossed it to Theo, like a football.

The gentlemen in the cardigan sweaters gasped and did not exhale. When Theo caught it, it sank his hands. His cane rattled as it hit the floor.

"That's heavy," Sylvia said, observing with satisfaction how the bowl had weighted Theo's arms down. "And where crystal is concerned, heavy is impressive."

She took the bowl back from him and carried it to the counter. Mr. Sherman was mopping his brow. Theo looked at the floor, still surprised not to see shards of glass around his feet.

Since no one else seemed to be volunteering, he bent over and picked up the cane.

"Four hundred and fifty-nine, with tax," Mr. Sherman said, his voice still a bit shaky, and a look of relish came over Sylvia's face as she pulled out her checkbook to pay. Behind the counter, Theo could see Mr. Baker put his hand on his forehead and cast his eyes to the ceiling.

It seemed Sylvia had been looking a long time for something like this, something heavy enough to leave an impression, yet so fragile it could make you sorry.

They headed back out to the car.

"Where can we go now?" Sylvia asked, as she got in. "There must be someplace else to go."

"Home," Theo said. "It's almost time for my medicine."

"Really? Oh. All right." She pulled on her seat belt, inserted the car key in the ignition and sat there.

For just a moment, but perceptibly, her face broke. She squeezed her eyes shut so tight the blue shadow on the lids cracked.

Almost as quickly she was back to normal again, and they were driving. "It's getting hotter," Sylvia said. "Shall I put on the air?"

"Sure," Theo said. He was thinking about the bowl, or more specifically, about how surprising its weight had been, pulling his hands down. For a while now he'd been worried about his mother, worried about what damage his illness might secretly be doing to her that of course she would never admit. On the surface things seemed all right. She still broiled herself a skinned chicken breast for dinner every night, still swam a mile and a half a day, still kept used teabags wrapped in foil in the refrigerator. Yet she had also, at about three o'clock one morning, woken him up to tell him she was going to the twenty-four-hour supermarket, and was there anything he wanted. Then there was the gift shop: She had literally pitched that bowl toward him, pitched it like a ball, and as that great gleam of flight and potential regret came sailing his direction, it had occurred to him that she was trusting his two feeble hands, out of the whole world, to keep it from shattering. What was she trying to test? Was it his newly regained vision? Was it the assurance that he was there, alive, that he hadn't yet slipped past all her caring, a little lost boy in rhinestone-studded glasses? There are certain things you've already done before you even think how to do them—a child pulled from in front of a car, for instance, or the bowl, which Theo was holding before he could even begin to calculate its brief trajectory. It had pulled his arms down, and from that apish posture he'd looked at his mother, who smiled broadly, as if, in the war between heaviness and shattering, he'd just helped her win some small but sustaining victory.

QUESTIONS

1. Leavitt has been termed a "poet of the affections." Apply this insight to the complex relationship between Theo and his mother.
2. Why is Sylvia "shopping for revenge"? Explain the significance of the bowl that she tosses to Theo.
3. Why does the author call his story "Gravity"?

Doris Lessing

FLIGHT

Above the old man's head was the dovecote, a tall wire-netted shelf on stilts, full of strutting, preening birds. The sunlight broke on their gray breasts into small rainbows. His ears were lulled by their crooning; his hands stretched up toward his favorite, a homing pigeon, a young plump-bodied bird, which stood still when it saw him and cocked a shrewd bright eye.

"Pretty, pretty, pretty," he said, as he grasped the bird and drew it down, feeling the cold coral claws tighten around his finger. Content, he rested the bird lightly on his chest and leaned against a tree, gazing out beyond the dovecote into the landscape of a late afternoon. In folds and hollows of sunlight and shade, the dark red soil, which was broken into great dusty clods, stretched wide to a tall horizon. Trees marked the course of the valley; a stream of rich green grass the road.

His eyes traveled homeward along this road until he saw his granddaughter swinging on the gate underneath a frangipani tree. Her hair fell down her back in a wave of sunlight; and her long bare legs repeated the angles of the frangipani stems, bare, shining brown stems among patterns of pale blossoms.

She was gazing past the pink flowers, past the railway cottage where they lived, along the road to the village.

His mood shifted. He deliberately held out his wrist for the bird to take flight, and caught it again at the moment it spread its wings. He felt the plump shape strive and strain under his fingers; and, in a sudden access of troubled spite, shut the bird into a small box and fastened the bolt. "Now you stay there," he muttered and turned his back on the shelf of birds. He moved warily along the hedge, stalking his granddaughter, who was now looped over the gate, her head loose on her arms, singing. The light happy sound mingled with the crooning of the birds, and his anger mounted.

"Hey!" he shouted, and saw her jump, look back, and abandon the gate. Her eyes veiled themselves, and she said in a pert, neutral voice, "Hullo, Grandad." Politely she moved toward him, after a lingering backward glance at the road.

"Waiting for Steven, hey?" he said, his fingers curling like claws into his palm.

"Any objection?" she asked lightly, refusing to look at him.

He confronted her, his eyes narrowed, shoulders hunched, tight in a hard knot of pain that included the preening birds, the sunlight, the flowers, herself. He said, "Think you're old enough to go courting, hey?"

The girl tossed her head at the old-fashioned phrase and sulked, "Oh, Grandad!"

"Think you want to leave home, hey? Think you can go running around the fields at night?"

Her smile made him see her, as he had every evening of this warm end-of-summer month, swinging hand in hand along the road to the village with that red-handed, red-throated, violent-bodied youth, the son of the postmaster. Misery went to his head and he shouted angrily: "I'll tell your mother!"

"Tell away!" she said, laughing, and went back to the gate.

He heard her singing, for him to hear:

"I've got you under my skin,
I've got you deep in the heart of . . ."

"Rubbish," he shouted. "Rubbish. Impudent little bit of rubbish!"

Growling under his breath, he turned toward the dovecote, which was his refuge from the house he shared with his daughter and her husband and their children. But now the house would be empty. Gone all the young girls with their laughter and their squabbling and their teasing. He would be left, uncherished and alone, with that square-fronted, calm-eyed woman, his daughter.

He stopped, muttering, before the dovecote, resenting the absorbed, cooing birds.

From the gate the girl shouted: "Go and tell! Go on, what are you waiting for?"

Obstinately he made his way to the house, with quick, pathetic, persistent glances of appeal back at her. But she never looked around. Her defiant but anxious young body stung him into love and repentance. He stopped. "But I never meant. . . ." he muttered, waiting for her to turn and run to him. "I didn't mean. . . ."

She did not turn. She had forgotten him. Along the road came the young man Steven, with something in his hand. A present for her? The old man stiffened as he watched the gate swing back and the couple embrace. In the brittle shadows of the frangipani tree his granddaughter, his darling, lay in the arms of the postmaster's son, and her hair flowed back over his shoulder.

"I see you!" shouted the old man spitefully. They did not move. He stumped into the little whitewashed house, hearing the wooden veranda creak angrily under his feet. His daughter was sewing in the front room, threading a needle held to the light.

He stopped again, looking back into the garden. The couple were now sauntering among the bushes, laughing. As he watched he saw the girl escape from the youth with a sudden mischievous movement and run off through the flowers with him in pursuit. He heard shouts, laughter, a scream, silence.

"But it's not like that at all," he muttered miserably. "It's not like that. Why can't you see? Running and giggling, and kissing and kissing. You'll come to something quite different."

He looked at his daughter with sardonic hatred, hating himself. They were caught and finished, both of them, but the girl was still running free.

"Can't you *see*?" he demanded of his invisible granddaughter, who was at that moment lying in the thick green grass with the postmaster's son.

His daughter looked at him and her eyebrows went up in tired forbearance.

"Put your birds to bed?" she asked, humoring him.

"Lucy," he said urgently. "Lucy. . . ."

"Well, what is it now?"

"She's in the garden with Steven."

"Now you just sit down and have your tea."

He stumped his feet alternately, thump, thump, on the hollow wooden floor and shouted: "She'll marry him. I'm telling you, she'll be marrying him next!"

His daughter rose swiftly, brought him a cup, set him a plate.

"I don't want any tea. I don't want it, I tell you."

"Now, now," she crooned. "What's wrong with it? Why not?"

"She's eighteen. Eighteen!"

"I was married at seventeen, and I never regretted it."

"Liar," he said. "Liar. Then you should regret it. Why do you make your girls marry? It's you who do it. What do you do it for? Why?"

"The other three have done fine. They've three fine husbands. Why not Alice?"

"She's the last," he mourned. "Can't we keep her a bit longer?"

"Come, now, Dad. She'll be down the road, that's all. She'll be here every day to see you."

"But it's not the same." He thought of the other three girls, transformed inside a few months from charming, petulant, spoiled children into serious young matrons.

"You never did like it when we married," she said. "Why not? Every time, it's the same. When I got married you made me feel like it was something wrong. And my girls the same. You get them all crying and miserable the way you go on. Leave Alice alone. She's happy." She sighed, letting her eyes linger on the sunlit garden. "She'll marry next month. There's no reason to wait."

"You've said they can marry?" he said incredulously.

"Yes, Dad. Why not?" she said coldly and took up her sewing.

His eyes stung, and he went out on to the veranda. Wet spread down over his chin, and he took out a handkerchief and mopped his whole face. The garden was empty.

From around the corner came the young couple; but their faces were no longer set against him. On the wrist of the postmaster's son balanced a young pigeon, the light gleaming on its breast.

"For me?" said the old man, letting the drops shake off his chin. "For me?"

"Do you like it?" The girl grabbed his hand and swung on it. "It's for you, Grandad. Steven brought it for you." They hung about him, affectionate, concerned, trying to charm away his wet eyes and his misery. They took his arms and directed him to the shelf of birds, one on each side, enclosing him, petting him, saying wordlessly that nothing would be changed, nothing could change, and that they would be with him always. The bird was proof of it, they said, from their lying happy eyes, as they thrust it on him. "There, Grandad, it's yours. It's for you."

They watched him as he held it on his wrist, stroking its soft, sun-warmed back, watching the wings lift and balance.

"You must shut it up for a bit," said the girl intimately, "until it knows this is its home."

"Teach your grandmother to suck eggs," growled the old man.

Released by his half-deliberate anger, they fell back, laughing at him. "We're glad you like it." They moved off, now serious and full of purpose, to the gate, where they hung, backs to him, talking quietly. More than anything could, their grown-up serious-ness shut him out, making him alone; also, it quietened him, took the sting out of their tumbling like puppies on the grass. They had forgotten him again. Well, so they should, the old man reassured himself, feeling his throat clotted with tears, his lips trembling. He held the new bird to his face, for the caress of its silken feathers. Then he shut it in a box and took out his favorite.

"*Now* you can go," he said aloud. He held it poised, ready for flight, while he looked down the garden toward the boy and the girl. Then, clenched in the pain of loss, he lifted the bird on his wrist and watched it soar. A whirr and a spatter of wings, and a cloud of birds rose into the evening from the dovecote.

At the gate Alice and Steven forgot their talk and watched the birds.

On the veranda, that woman, his daughter, stood gazing, her eyes shaded with a hand that still held her sewing.

It seemed to the old man that the whole afternoon had stilled to watch his gesture of self-command, that even the leaves of the trees had stopped shaking.

Dry-eyed and calm, he let his hands fall to his sides and stood erect, staring up into the sky.

The cloud of shining silver birds flew up and up, with a shrill cleaving of wings, over the dark ploughed land and the darker belts of trees and the bright folds of grass, until they floated high in the sunlight, like a cloud of motes of dust.

They wheeled in a wide circle, tilting their wings so there was flash after flash of light, and one after another they dropped from the sunshine of the upper sky to shadow, one after another, returning to the shadowed earth over trees and grass and field, returning to the valley and the shelter of night.

The garden was all a fluster and a flurry of returning birds. Then silence, and the sky was empty.

The old man turned, slowly, taking his time; he lifted his eyes to smile proudly down the garden at his granddaughter. She was staring at him. She did not smile. She was wide-eyed and pale in the cold shadow, and he saw the tears run shivering off her face.

QUESTIONS

1. How does the relationship between the grandfather, his daughter, and his grand-daughter define the many conflicts in this story?
2. Why does Lessing devote so much attention to a description of the setting—and especially to the birds? What do the birds symbolize?
3. Compare the final episode in "Flight" with the last scene in "Gravity."

R. K. Narayan

MOTHER AND SON

Ramu's mother waited till he was halfway through dinner and then introduced the subject of marriage. Ramu merely replied, "So you are at it again!" He appeared more amused than angry, and so she brought out her favourite points one by one: her brother's daughter was getting on to fourteen, the girl was good-looking and her brother was prepared to give a handsome dowry; she (Ramu's mother) was getting old and wanted a holiday from housekeeping: she might die any moment and then who would cook Ramu's food and look after him? And the most indisputable argument: a man's luck changed with marriage. "The harvest depends not on the hand that holds the plough but on the hand which holds the pot." Earlier in the evening Ramu's mother had decided that if he refused again or exhibited the usual sullenness at the mention of marriage, she would leave him to his fate; she would leave him absolutely alone even if she saw him falling down before a coming train. She would never more interfere in his affairs. She realized what a resolute mind she possessed, and felt proud of the fact. That was the kind of person one ought to be. It was all very well having a mother's heart and so on, but even a mother could have a limit to her feelings. If Ramu thought he could do what he pleased just because she was only a mother, she would show him he was mistaken. If he was going to slight her judgement and feelings, she was going to show how indifferent she herself could be. . . .

With so much preparation she broached the subject of marriage and presented a formidable array of reasons. But Ramu just brushed them aside and spoke slightingly of the appearance of her brother's daughter. And then she announced, "This is the last time I am speaking about this. Hereafter I will leave you alone. Even if I see you drowning I will never ask why you are drowning. Do you understand?"

"Yes." Ramu brooded. He could not get through his Intermediate even at the fourth attempt; he could not get a job, even at twenty rupees a month. And here was Mother worrying him to marry. Of all girls, his uncle's! That protruding tooth alone would put off any man. It was incredible that he should be expected to marry that girl. He had always felt that when he married he would marry a girl like Rezia, whom he had seen in two or three Hindi films. Life was rusty and sterile, and Ramu lived in a stage of perpetual melancholia and depression; he loafed away his time, or slept, or read old newspapers in a free reading room. . . .

He now sat before his dining leaf and brooded. His mother watched him for a moment and said, "I hate your face. I hate anyone who sits before his leaf with that face. A woman only ten days old in widowhood would put on a more cheerful look."

"You are saying all sorts of things because I refuse to marry your brother's daughter," he replied.

"What do I care? She is a fortunate girl and will get a really decent husband." Ramu's mother hated him for his sullenness. It was this gloomy look that she hated in people. It was unbearable. She spoke for a few minutes, and he asked, "When are you going to shut up?"

"My life is nearly over," said the mother. "You will see me shutting up once and for all very soon. Don't be impatient. You ask me to shut up! Has it come to this?"

"Well, I only asked you to give me some time to eat."

"Oh, yes. You will have it soon, my boy. When I am gone you will have plenty of time, my boy."

Ramu did not reply. He ate his food in silence. "I only want you to look a little more human when you eat," she said.

"How is it possible with this food?" asked Ramu.

"What do you say?" screamed the mother. "If you are so fastidious, work and earn like all men. Throw down the money and demand what you want. Don't command when you are a pauper."

When the meal was over, Ramu was seen putting on his sandals. "Where are you going?" asked the mother.

"Going out," he curtly replied, and walked out, leaving the street door ajar.

Her duties for the day were over. She had scrubbed the floor of the kitchen, washed the vessels and put them in a shining row on the wooden shelf, returned the short scrubbing broom to its corner and closed the kitchen window.

Taking the lantern and closing the kitchen door, she came to the front room. The street door stood ajar. She became indignant at her son's carelessness. The boy was indifferent and irresponsible and didn't feel bound even to shut the street door. Here she was wearing out her palm scrubbing the floor night after night. Why should she slave if he was indifferent? He was old enough to realize his responsibilities in life.

She took out her small wooden box and put into her mouth a clove, a cardamom and a piece of areca nut. Chewing these, she felt more at peace with life. She shut the door without bolting it and lay down to sleep.

Where could Ramu have gone? She began to feel uneasy. She rolled her mat, went out, spread it on the *pyol* and lay down. She muttered to herself the holy name of Sri Rama in order to keep out disturbing thoughts. She went on whispering, "Sita Rama Rama . . ." But she ceased unconsciously. Her thoughts returned to Ramu. What did he say before going out? "I am just going out for a stroll, Mother. Don't worry. I shall be back soon." No, it was not that. Not he. Why was the boy so secretive about his movements? That was impudent and exasperating. But, she told herself, she deserved no better treatment with that terrible temper and cutting tongue of hers. There was no doubt that she had conducted herself abominably during the meal. All her life this had been her worst failing: this tendency, while in a temper, to talk without restraint. She even felt that her husband would have lived for a few more years if she had spoken to him less. . . . Ramu had said something about the food. She would include more vegetables and cook better from tomorrow. Poor boy . . .

She fell asleep. Somewhere a gong sounded one, and she woke up. One o'clock? She called, "Ramu, Ramu."

She did not dare to contemplate what he might have done with himself. Gradually she came to believe that her words during the meal had driven him to suicide. She sat up and wept. She was working herself up to a hysterical pitch. When she closed her eyes to press out the gathering tears, the vision of her son's body floating in Kukanahalli Tank came before her. His striped shirt and mill dhoti were sodden and clung close to his body. His sandals were left on one of the tank steps. His face was bloated beyond all recognition.

She screamed aloud and jumped down from the *pyol*. She ran along the whole length of Old Agrahar Street. It was deserted. Electric lights twinkled here and there. Far away a *tonga* was rattling on, the *tonga*-driver's song faintly disturbing the silence; the blast of a night constable's whistle came to her ears, and she stopped running. She realized that after all it might be only her imagination. He might have gone away to the drama, which didn't usually close before three in the morning. She rapidly uttered the holy name of Sri Rama in order to prevent the picture of Kukanahalli Tank coming before her mind.

She had a restless night. Unknown to herself, she slept in snatches and woke up with a start every time the gong boomed. The gong struck six through the chill morning.

Tears streaming down her face, she started for Kukanahalli Tank. Mysore was just waking to fresh life. Milkmen with slow cows passed along. Municipal sweepers were busy with their long brooms. One or two cycles passed her.

She reached the tank, not daring even once to look at the water. She found him sleeping on one of the benches that lined the bund. For just a second she wondered if it might be his corpse. She shook him vigorously, crying "Ramu!" She heaved a tremendous sigh of relief when he stirred.

He sat up, rubbing his eyes. "Why are you here, Mother?"

"What a place to sleep in!"

"Oh, I just fell asleep," he said.

"Come home," she said. She walked on and he followed her. She saw him going down the tank steps. "Where are you going?"

"Just for a wash," Ramu explained.

She clung to his arm and said vehemently, "No, don't go near the water."

He obeyed her, though he was slightly baffled by her vehemence.

QUESTIONS

1. Describe the lives of Ramu and his mother in this story. Where do they live? What are their social and economic backgrounds? What cultural implications about family life and marriage are advanced?
2. How might the last sentence predict whether or not Ramu will marry his first cousin?
3. Compare and contrast the preoccupation with marriage on the part of the grandfather in "Flight" and the mother in "Mother and Son."

Grace Paley

A CONVERSATION WITH MY FATHER

My father is eighty-six years old and in bed. His heart, that bloody motor, is equally old and will not do certain jobs any more. It still floods his head with brainy light. But it won't let his legs carry the weight of his body around the house. Despite my metaphors, this muscle failure is not due to his old heart, he says, but to a potassium shortage. Sitting on one pillow, leaning on three, he offers last-minute advice and makes a request.

"I would like you to write a simple story just once more," he says, "the kind de Maupassant wrote, or Chekhov, the kind you used to write. Just recognizable people and then write down what happened to them next."

I say, "Yes, why not? That's possible." I want to please him, though I don't remember writing that way. I *would* like to try to tell such a story, if he means the kind that begins: "There was a woman . . ." followed by plot, the absolute line between two points which I've always despised. Not for literary reasons, but because it takes all hope away. Everyone, real or invented, deserves the open destiny of life.

Finally I thought of a story that had been happening for a couple of years right across the street. I wrote it down, then read it aloud. "Pa," I said, "how about this? Do you mean something like this?"

Once in my time there was a woman and she had a son. They lived nicely, in a small apartment in Manhattan. This boy at about fifteen became a junkie, which is not unusual in our neighborhood. In order to maintain her close friendship with him, she became a junkie too. She said it was part of the youth culture, with which she felt very much at home. After a while, for a number of reasons, the boy gave it all up and left the city and his mother in disgust. Hopeless and alone, she grieved. We all visit her.

"O.K., Pa, that's it," I said, "An unadorned and miserable tale."

"But that's not what I mean," my father said. "You misunderstood me on purpose. You know there's a lot more to it. You know that. You left everything out. Turgenev wouldn't do that. Chekhov wouldn't do that. There are in fact Russian writers you never heard of, you don't have an inkling of, as good as anyone, who can write a plain ordinary story, who would not leave out what you have left out. I object not to facts but to people sitting in trees talking senselessly, voices from who knows where. . . ."

"Forget that one, Pa, what have I left out now? In this one?"

"Her looks, for instance."

"Oh. Quite handsome, I think. Yes."

"Her hair?"

"Dark, with heavy braids, as though she were a girl or a foreigner."

"What were her parents like, her stock? That she became such a person. It's interesting, you know."

"From out of town. Professional people. The first to be divorced in their county. How's that? Enough?" I asked.

"With you, it's all a joke," he said. "What about the boy's father? Why didn't you mention him? Who was he? Or was the boy born out of wedlock?"

"Yes," I said. "He was born out of wedlock."

"For Godsakes, doesn't anyone in your stories get married? Doesn't anyone have the time to run down to City Hall before they jump into bed?"

"No," I said. "In real life, yes. But in my stories, no."

"Why do you answer me like that?"

"Oh, Pa, this is a simple story about a smart woman who came to N.Y.C. full of interest love trust excitement very up to date, and about her son, what a hard time she had in this world. Married or not, it's of small consequence."

"It is of great consequence," he said.

"O.K.," I said.

"O.K. O.K. yourself," he said, "but listen. I believe you that she's good-looking, but I don't think she was so smart."

"That's true," I said. "Actually that's the trouble with stories. People start out fantastic. You think they're extraordinary, but it turns out as the work goes along, they're just average with a good education. Sometimes the other way around, the person's kind of dumb innocent, but he outwits you and you can't even think of an ending good enough."

"What do you do then?" he asked. He had been a doctor for a couple of decades and he's still interested in details, craft, technique.

"Well, you just have to let the story lie around till some agreement can be reached between you and the stubborn hero."

"Aren't you talking silly now?" he asked. "Start again," he said. "It so happens I'm not going out this evening. Tell the story again. See what you can do this time."

"O.K.," I said. "But it's not a five-minute job." Second attempt:

Once, across the street from us, there was a fine handsome woman, our neighbor. She had a son whom she loved because she'd known him since birth (in helpless chubby infancy, and in the wrestling, hugging ages, seven to ten, as well as earlier and later). This boy, when he fell into the fist of adolescence, became a junkie. He was not a hopeless one. He was in fact hopeful, an ideologue and successful converter. With his busy brilliance, he wrote persuasive articles for his high-school newspaper. Seeking a wider audience, using important connections, he drummed into Lower Manhattan newsstand distribution a periodical called *Oh! Golden Horse!*

In order to keep him from feeling guilty (because guilt is the stony heart of nine tenths of all clinically diagnosed cancers in America today, she said), and because she had always believed in giving bad habits room at home where one could keep an eye on them, she too became a junkie. Her kitchen was famous for a while—a center for intellectual addicts who knew what they were doing. A few felt artistic like Coleridge and others were scientific and revolutionary like Leary. Although she was often high herself, certain good mothering reflexes remained, and she saw to it that there was lots of orange juice around and honey and milk and vitamin pills. However, she never cooked anything but chili, and that no more than once a week. She explained, when we talked to her, seriously, with neighborly concern, that it was her part in the youth culture and she would rather be with the young, it was an honor, than with her own generation.

One week, while nodding through an Antonioni film, this boy was severely jabbed by the elbow of a stern and proselytizing girl, sitting beside him. She offered immediate apricots and nuts for his sugar level, spoke to him sharply, and took him home.

She had heard of him and his work and she herself published, edited, and wrote a competitive journal called *Man Does Live by Bread Alone*. In the organic heat of her continuous presence he could not help but become interested once more in his muscles, his arteries, and nerve connections. In fact he began to love them, treasure them, praise them with funny little songs in *Man Does Live*. . . .

> the fingers of my flesh transcend
> my transcendental soul
> the tightness in my shoulders end
> my teeth have made me whole

To the mouth of his head (that glory of will and determination) he brought hard apples, nuts, wheat germ, and soybean oil. He said to his old friends, From now on, I guess I'll keep my wits about me. I'm going on the natch. He said he was about to begin a spiritual deep-breathing journey. How about you too, Mom? he asked kindly.

His conversion was so radiant, splendid, that neighborhood kids his age began to say that he had never been a real addict at all, only a journalist along for the smell of the story. The mother tried several times to give up what had become without her son and his friends a lonely habit. This effort only brought it to supportable levels. The boy and his girl took their electronic mimeograph and moved to the bushy edge of another borough. They were very strict. They said they would not see her again until she had been off drugs for sixty days.

At home alone in the evening, weeping, the mother read and reread the seven issues of *Oh! Golden Horse!* They seemed to her as truthful as ever. We often crossed the street to visit and console. But if we mentioned any of our children who were at college or in the hospital or dropouts at home, she would cry out, My baby! My baby! and burst into terrible, face-scarring, time-consuming tears. The End.

First my father was silent, then he said, "Number One: You have a nice sense of humor. Number Two: I see you can't tell a plain story. So don't waste time." Then he said sadly, "Number Three: I suppose that means she was alone, she was left like that, his mother. Alone. Probably sick?"

I said, "Yes."

"Poor woman. Poor girl, to be born in a time of fools, to live among fools, The end. The end. You were right to put that down. The end."

I didn't want to argue, but I had to say, "Well, it is not necessarily the end, Pa."

"Yes," he said, "what a tragedy. The end of a person."

"No, Pa," I begged him. "It doesn't have to be. She's only about forty. She could be a hundred different things in this world as time goes on. A teacher or a social worker. An ex-junkie! Sometimes it's better than having a master's in education."

"Jokes," he said. "As a writer that's your main trouble. You don't want to recognize it. Tragedy! Plain tragedy! Historical tragedy! No hope. The end."

"Oh, Pa," I said. "She could change."

"In your own life, too, you have to look it in the face." He took a couple of nitroglycerin. "Turn to five," he said, pointing to the dial on the oxygen tank. He inserted the tubes into his nostrils and breathed deep. He closed his eyes and said, "No."

I had promised the family to always let him have the last word when arguing, but in this case I had a different responsibility. That woman lives across the street. She's my knowledge and my invention. I'm sorry for her. I'm not going to leave her there in that house crying. (Actually neither would Life, which unlike me has no pity.)

Therefore: She did change. Of course her son never came home again. But right now, she's the receptionist in a storefront community clinic in the East Village. Most of the customers are young people, some old friends. The head doctor has said to her, "If we only had three people in this clinic with your experiences. . . ."

"The doctor said that?" My father took the oxygen tubes out of his nostrils and said, "Jokes. Jokes again."

"No, Pa, it could really happen that way, it's a funny world nowadays."

"No," he said. "Truth first. She will slide back. A person must have character. She does not."

"No, Pa," I said. "That's it. She's got a job. Forget it. She's in that storefront working."

"How long will it be?" he asked. "Tragedy! You too. When will you look it in the face?"

QUESTIONS

1. The author has written: "Everyone, real or invented, deserves the open destiny of life." How is this observation reflected in the story?
2. Why does the father believe his daughter should write stories like Maupassant, Chekhov, and Turgenev? Who were these writers? How do they reflect the father's philosophy?
3. Why is "filling out" the story important to the father? Why does the daughter refuse to do more with the story? What does the struggle between father and daughter actually represent?

Amy Tan

TWO KINDS

My mother believed you could be anything you wanted to be in America. You could open a restaurant. You could work for the government and get good retirement. You could buy a house with almost no money down. You could become rich. You could become instantly famous.

"Of course, you can be prodigy, too," my mother told me when I was nine. "You can be best anything. What does Auntie Lindo know? Her daughter, she is only best tricky."

America was where all my mother's hopes lay. She had come to San Francisco in 1949 after losing everything in China: her mother and father, her family home, her first husband, and two daughters, twin baby girls. But she never looked back with regret. Things could get better in so many ways.

We didn't immediately pick the right kind of prodigy. At first my mother thought I could be a Chinese Shirley Temple. We'd watch Shirley's old movies on TV as though they were training films. My mother would poke my arm and say, *"Ni kan.* You watch." And I would see Shirley tapping her feet, or singing a sailor song, or pursing her lips into a very round O while saying "Oh, my goodness."

"Ni kan," my mother said, as Shirley's eyes flooded with tears. "You already know how. Don't need talent for crying!"

Soon after my mother got this idea about Shirley Temple, she took me to the beauty training school in the Mission District and put me in the hands of a student who could barely hold the scissors without shaking. Instead of getting big fat curls, I emerged with an uneven mass of crinkly black fuzz. My mother dragged me off to the bathroom and tried to wet down my hair.

"You look like Negro Chinese," she lamented, as if I had done this on purpose.

The instructor of the beauty training school had to lop off these soggy clumps to make my hair even again. "Peter Pan is very popular these days," the instructor assured my mother. I now had hair the length of a boy's, with curly bangs that hung at a slant two inches above my eyebrows. I liked the haircut, and it made me actually look forward to my future fame.

In fact, in the beginning I was just as excited as my mother, maybe even more so. I pictured this prodigy part of me as many different images, and I tried each one on for size. I was a dainty ballerina girl standing by the curtain, waiting to hear the music that would send me floating on my tiptoes. I was like the Christ child lifted out of the straw manger, crying with holy indignity. I was Cinderella stepping from her pumpkin carriage with sparkly cartoon music filling the air.

In all of my imaginings I was filled with a sense that I would soon become perfect. My mother and father would adore me. I would be beyond reproach. I would never feel the need to sulk, or to clamor for anything.

But sometimes the prodigy in me became impatient. "If you don't hurry up and get me out of here, I'm disappearing for good," it warned. "And then you'll always be nothing."

Every night after dinner my mother and I would sit at the Formica-topped kitchen table. She would present new tests, taking her examples from stories of amazing children that she had read in *Ripley's Believe It or Not* or *Good Housekeeping, Reader's Digest,* or any of a dozen other magazines she kept in a pile in our bathroom. My mother got these magazines from people whose houses she cleaned. And since she cleaned many houses each week, we had a great assortment. She would look through them all, searching for stories about remarkable children.

The first night she brought out a story about a three-year-old boy who knew the capitals of all the states and even of most of the European countries. A teacher was quoted as saying that the little boy could also pronounce the names of the foreign cities correctly. "What's the capital of Finland?" my mother asked me, looking at the story.

All I knew was the capital of California, because Sacramento was the name of the street we lived on in Chinatown. "Nairobi!" I guessed, saying the most foreign word I could think of. She checked to see if that might be one way to pronounce *Helsinki* before showing me the answer.

The tests got harder—multiplying numbers in my head, finding the queen of hearts in a deck of cards, trying to stand on my head without using my hands, predicting the daily temperatures in Los Angeles, New York, and London. One night I had to look at a page from the Bible for three minutes and then report everything I could remember. "Now Jehoshaphat had riches and honor in abundance and . . . that's all I remember, Ma," I said.

And after seeing, once again, my mother's disappointed face, something inside me began to die. I hated the tests, the raised hopes and failed expectations. Before going to bed that night I looked in the mirror above the bathroom sink, and when I saw only my face staring back—and understood that it would always be this ordinary face—I began to cry. Such a sad, ugly girl! I made high-pitched noises like a crazed animal, trying to scratch out the face in the mirror.

And then I saw what seemed to be the prodigy side of me—a face I had never seen before. I looked at my reflection, blinking so that I could see more clearly. The girl staring back at me was angry, powerful. She and I were the same. I had new thoughts, willful thoughts—or, rather, thoughts filled with lots of won'ts. I won't let her change me, I promised myself. I won't be what I'm not.

So now when my mother presented her tests, I performed listlessly, my head propped on one arm. I pretended to be bored. And I was. I got so bored that I started counting the bellows of the foghorns out on the bay while my mother drilled me in other areas. The sound was comforting and reminded me of the cow jumping over the moon. And the next day I played a game with myself, seeing if my mother would give up on me before eight bellows. After a while I usually counted only one bellow, maybe two at most. At last she was beginning to give up hope.

Two or three months went by without any mention of my being a prodigy. And then one day my mother was watching the *Ed Sullivan Show* on TV. The TV was old and the sound kept shorting out. Every time my mother got halfway up from the sofa to adjust the set, the sound would come back on and Sullivan would be talking. As soon as she sat down, Sullivan would go silent again. She got up—the TV broke into loud piano music. She sat down—silence. Up and down, back and forth, quiet and loud. It was like a stiff, embraceless dance between her and the TV set. Finally, she stood by the set with her hand on the sound dial.

She seemed entranced by the music, a frenzied little piano piece with a mesmerizing quality, which alternated between quick, playful passages and teasing, lilting ones.

"*Ni kan,*" my mother said, calling me over with hurried hand gestures. "Look here."

I could see why my mother was fascinated by the music. It was being pounded out by a little Chinese girl, about nine years old, with a Peter Pan haircut. The girl had the sauciness of a Shirley Temple. She was proudly modest, like a proper Chinese child. And she also did a fancy sweep of a curtsy, so that the fluffy skirt of her white dress cascaded to the floor like the petals of a large carnation.

In spite of these warnings signs, I wasn't worried. Our family had no piano and we couldn't afford to buy one, let alone reams of sheet music and piano lessons. So I could be generous in my comments when my mother bad-mouthed the little girl on TV.

"Play note right, but doesn't sound good!" my mother complained. "No singing sound."

"What are you picking on her for?" I said carelessly. "She's pretty good. Maybe she's not the best, but she's trying hard." I knew almost immediately that I would be sorry I had said that.

"Just like you," she said. "Not the best. Because you not trying." She gave a little huff as she let go of the sound dial and sat down on the sofa.

The little Chinese girl sat down also, to play an encore of "Anitra's Tanz," by Grieg. I remember the song, because later on I had to learn how to play it.

Three days after watching the *Ed Sullivan Show* my mother told me what my schedule would be for piano lessons and piano practice. She had talked to Mr. Chong, who lived on the first floor of our apartment building. Mr. Chong was a retired piano teacher, and my mother had traded housecleaning services for weekly lessons and a piano for me to practice on every day, two hours a day, from four to six.

When my mother told me this, I felt as though I had been sent to hell. I whined, and then kicked my foot a little when I couldn't stand it anymore.

"Why don't you like me the way I am?" I cried. "I'm *not* a genius! I can't play the piano. And even if I could, I wouldn't go on TV if you paid me a million dollars!"

My mother slapped me. "Who ask you to be genius?" she shouted. "Only ask you be your best. For your sake. You think I want you to be genius? Hnnh! What for! Who ask you!"

"So ungrateful," I heard her mutter in Chinese. "If she had as much talent as she has temper, she'd be famous now."

Mr. Chong, whom I secretly nicknamed Old Chong, was very strange, always tapping his fingers to the silent music of an invisible orchestra. He looked ancient in my eyes. He had lost most of the hair on the top of his head, and he wore thick glasses and had eyes that always looked tired. But he must have been younger than I thought, since he lived with his mother and was not yet married.

I met Old Lady Chong once, and that was enough. She had a peculiar smell, like a baby that had done something in its pants, and her fingers felt like a dead person's, like an old peach I once found in the back of the refrigerator; its skin just slid off the flesh when I picked it up.

I soon found out why Old Chong had retired from teaching piano. He was deaf. "Like Beethoven!" he shouted to me. "We're both listening only in our head!" And he would start to conduct his frantic silent sonatas.

Our lessons went like this. He would open the book and point to different things, explaining their purpose: "Key! Treble! Bass! No sharps or flats! So this is C major! Listen now and play after me!"

And then he would play the C scale a few times, a simple chord, and then, as if inspired by an old unreachable itch, he would gradually add more notes and running trills and a pounding bass until the music was really something quite grand.

I would play after him, the simple scale, the simple chord, and then just play some nonsense that sounded like a cat running up and down on top of garbage cans. Old Chong would smile and applaud and say, "Very good! But now you must learn to keep time!"

So that's how I discovered that Old Chong's eyes were too slow to keep up with the wrong notes I was playing. He went through the motions in half time. To help me keep rhythm, he stood behind me and pushed down on my right shoulder for every beat. He balanced pennies on top of my wrists so that I would keep them still as I slowly played the scales and arpeggios. He had me curve my hand around an apple and keep that shape when playing chords. He marched stiffly to show me how to make each finger dance up and down, staccato, like an obedient little soldier.

He taught me all these things, and that was how I also learned I could be lazy and get away with mistakes, lots of mistakes. If I hit the wrong notes because I hadn't practiced enough, I never corrected myself. I just kept playing in rhythm. And Old Chong kept conducting his own private reverie.

So maybe I never really gave myself a fair chance. I did pick up the basics pretty quickly, and I might have become a good pianist at that young age. But I was so determined not to try, not to be anybody different, that I learned to play only the most ear-splitting preludes, the most discordant hymns.

Over the next year I practiced like this, dutifully in my own way. And then one day I heard my mother and her friend Lindo Jong both talking in a loud, bragging tone of voice so that others could hear. It was after church, and I was leaning against a brick wall, wearing a dress with stiff white petticoats. Auntie Lindo's daughter, Waverly, who was my age, was standing farther down the wall, about five feet away. We had grown up together and shared all the closeness of two sisters, squabbling over crayons and dolls. In other words, for the most part, we hated each other. I thought she was snotty. Waverly Jong had gained a certain amount of fame as "Chinatown's Littlest Chinese Chess Champion."

"She bring home too many trophy," Auntie Lindo lamented that Sunday. "All day she play chess. All day I have no time do nothing but dust off her winnings." She threw a scolding look at Waverly, who pretended not to see her.

"You lucky you don't have this problem," Auntie Lindo said with a sigh to my mother.

And my mother squared her shoulders and bragged: "Our problem worser than yours. If we ask Jing-mei wash dish, she hear nothing but music. It's like you can't stop this natural talent."

And right then I was determined to put a stop to her foolish pride.

A few weeks later Old Chong and my mother conspired to have me play in a talent show that was to be held in the church hall. By then my parents had saved up enough to buy me a secondhand piano, a black Wurlitzer spinet with a scarred bench. It was the showpiece of our living room.

For the talent show I was to play a piece called "Pleading Child," from Schumann's *Scenes From Childhood*. It was a simple, moody piece that sounded more difficult than it was. I was supposed to memorize the whole thing. But I dawdled over it, playing a few bars and then cheating, looking up to see what notes followed. I never really listened to what I was playing. I daydreamed about being somewhere else, about being someone else.

The part I liked to practice best was the fancy curtsy: right foot out, touch the rose on the carpet with a pointed foot, sweep to the side, bend left leg, look up, and smile.

My parents invited all the couples from their social club to witness my debut. Auntie Lindo and Uncle Tin were there. Waverly and her two older brothers had also come. The first two rows were filled with children either younger or older than I was. The littlest ones got to go first. They recited simple nursery rhymes, squawked out tunes on miniature violins, and twirled hula hoops in pink ballet tutus, and when they bowed or curtsied, the audience would sigh in unison, *"Awww,"* and then clap enthusiastically.

When my turn came, I was very confident. I remember my childish excitement. It was as if I knew, without a doubt, that the prodigy side of me really did exist. I had no fear whatsoever, no nervousness. I remember thinking, This is it! This is it! I looked out over the audience, at my mother's blank face, my father's yawn, Auntie Lindo's stiff-lipped smile, Waverly's sulky expression. I had on a white dress, layered with sheets of lace, and a pink bow in my Peter Pan haircut. As I sat down, I envisioned people jumping to their feet and Ed Sullivan rushing up to introduce me to everyone on TV.

And I started to play. Everything was so beautiful. I was so caught up in how lovely I looked that I wasn't worried about how I would sound. So I was surprised when I hit the first wrong note. And then I hit another, and another. A chill started at the top of my head and began to trickle down. Yet I couldn't stop playing, as though my hands were bewitched. I kept thinking my fingers would adjust themselves back, like a train switching to the right track. I played this strange jumble through to the end, the sour notes staying with me all the way.

When I stood up, I discovered my legs were shaking. Maybe I had just been nervous, and the audience, like Old Chong, had seen me go through the right motions and had not heard anything wrong at all. I swept my right foot out, went down on my knee, looked up, and smiled. The room was quiet, except for Old Chong, who was beaming and shouting, "Bravo! Bravo! Well done!" But then I saw my mother's face, her stricken face. The audience clapped weakly, and as I walked back to my chair, with my whole face quivering as I tried not to cry, I heard a little boy whisper loudly to his mother, "That was awful," and the mother whispered back, "Well, she certainly tried."

And now I realized how many people were in the audience—the whole world, it seemed. I was aware of eyes burning into my back. I felt the shame of my mother and father as they sat stiffly through the rest of the show.

We could have escaped during intermission. Pride and some strange sense of honor must have anchored my parents to their chairs. And so we watched it all: the eighteen-year-old boy with a fake moustache who did a magic show and juggled flaming hoops while riding a unicycle. The breasted girl with white makeup who sang an aria from *Madame Butterfly* and got an honorable mention. And the eleven-year-old boy who won first prize playing a tricky violin song that sounded like a busy bee.

After the show the Hsus, the Jongs, and the St. Clairs, from the Joy Luck Club, came up to my mother and father.

"Lots of talented kids," Auntie Lindo said vaguely, smiling broadly.

"That was somethin' else," my father said, and I wondered if he was referring to me in a humorous way, or whether he even remembered what I had done.

Waverly looked at me and shrugged her shoulders. "You aren't a genius like me," she said matter-of-factly. And if I hadn't felt so bad, I would have pulled her braids and punched her stomach.

But my mother's expression was what devastated me: a quiet, blank look that said she had lost everything. I felt the same way, and everybody seemed now to be coming up, like gawkers at the scene of an accident, to see what parts were actually missing.

When we got on the bus to go home, my father was humming the busy-bee tune and my mother was silent. I kept thinking she wanted to wait until we got home before shouting at me. But when my father unlocked the door to our apartment, my mother walked in and went straight to the back, into the bedroom. No accusations. No blame. And in a way, I felt disappointed. I had been waiting for her to start shouting, so that I could shout back and cry and blame her for all my misery.

I had assumed that my talent-show fiasco meant that I would never have to play the piano again. But two days later, after school, my mother came out of the kitchen and saw me watching TV.

"Four clock," she reminded me, as if it were any other day. I was stunned, as though she were asking me to go through the talent-show torture again. I planted myself more squarely in front of the TV.

"Turn off TV," she called from the kitchen five minutes later.

I didn't budge. And then I decided. I didn't have to do what my mother said anymore. I wasn't her slave. This wasn't China. I had listened to her before, and look what happened. She was the stupid one.

She came out from the kitchen and stood in the arched entryway of the living room. "Four clock," she said once again, louder.

"I'm not going to play anymore," I said nonchalantly. "Why should I? I'm not a genius."

She stood in front of the TV. I saw that her chest was heaving up and down in an angry way.

"No!" I said, and I now felt stronger, as if my true self had finally emerged. So this was what had been inside me all along.

"No! I won't!" I screamed.

She snapped off the TV, yanked me by the arm, and pulled me off the floor. She was frighteningly strong, half pulling, half carrying me toward the piano as I kicked the throw rugs under my feet. She lifted me up and onto the hard bench. I was sobbing by now, looking at her bitterly. Her chest was heaving even more and her mouth was open, smiling crazily as if she were pleased that I was crying.

"You want me to be someone that I'm not!" I sobbed. "I'll never be the kind of daughter you want me to be!"

"Only two kinds of daughters," she shouted in Chinese. "Those who are obedient and those who follow their own mind! Only one kind of daughter can live in this house. Obedient daughter!"

"Then I wish I weren't your daughter. I wish you weren't my mother," I shouted. As I said these things I got scared. It felt like worms and toads and slimy things crawling out of my chest, but it also felt good, that this awful side of me had surfaced, at last.

"Too late change this," my mother said shrilly.

And I could sense her anger rising to its breaking point. I wanted to see it spill over. And that's when I remembered the babies she had lost in China, the ones we never talked about. "Then I wish I'd never been born!" I shouted. "I wish I were dead! Like them."

It was as if I had said magic words. Alakazam!—her face went blank, her mouth closed, her arms went slack, and she backed out of the room, stunned, as if she were blowing away like a small brown leaf, thin, brittle, lifeless.

• • •

It was not the only disappointment my mother felt in me. In the years that followed, I failed her many times, each time asserting my will, my right to fall short of expectations. I didn't get straight As. I didn't become class president. I didn't get into Stanford. I dropped out of college.

Unlike my mother, I did not believe I could be anything I wanted to be. I could only be me.

And for all those years we never talked about the disaster at the recital or my terrible declarations afterward at the piano bench. Neither of us talked about it again, as if it were a betrayal that was now unspeakable. So I never found a way to ask her why she had hoped for something so large that failure was inevitable.

And even worse, I never asked her about what frightened me the most: Why had she given up hope? For after our struggle at the piano, she never mentioned my playing again. The lessons stopped. The lid to the piano was closed, shutting out the dust, my misery, and her dreams.

So she surprised me. A few years ago she offered to give me the piano, for my thirtieth birthday. I had not played in all those years. I saw the offer as a sign of forgiveness, a tremendous burden removed.

"Are you sure?" I asked shyly. "I mean, won't you and Dad miss it?"

"No, this your piano," she said firmly. "Always your piano. You only one can play."

"Well, I probably can't play anymore," I said. "It's been years."

"You pick up fast," my mother said, as if she knew this was certain. "You have natural talent. You could be genius if you want to."

"No, I couldn't."

"You just not trying," my mother said. And she was neither angry nor sad. She said it as if announcing a fact that could never be disproved. "Take it," she said.

But I didn't, at first. It was enough that she had offered it to me. And after that, every time I saw it in my parents' living room, standing in front of the bay window, it made me feel proud, as if it were a shiny trophy that I had won back.

Last week I sent a tuner over to my parents' apartment and had the piano reconditioned, for purely sentimental reasons. My mother had died a few months before, and I had been getting things in order for my father, a little bit at a time. I put the jewelry in special silk pouches. The sweaters she had knitted in yellow, pink, bright orange—all the colors I hated—I put in moth-proof boxes. I found some old Chinese silk dresses, the kind with little slits up the sides. I rubbed the old silk against my skin, and then wrapped them in tissue and decided to take them home with me.

After I had the piano tuned, I opened the lid and touched the keys. It sounded even richer than I remembered. Really, it was a very good piano. Inside the bench were the same exercise notes with handwritten scales, the same secondhand music books with their covers held together with yellow tape.

I opened up the Schumann book to the dark little piece I had played at the recital. It was on the left-hand page, "Pleading Child." It looked more difficult than I remembered. I played a few bars, surprised at how easily the notes came back to me.

And for the first time, or so it seemed, I noticed the piece on the right-hand side. It was called "Perfectly Contented." I tried to play this one as well. It had a lighter melody but with the same flowing rhythm and turned out to be quite easy. "Pleading Child" was shorter but slower; "Perfectly Contented" was longer but faster. And after I had played them both a few times, I realized they were two halves of the same song.

QUESTIONS

1. The writer Alice Walker (whose work appears later in this anthology) states that Amy Tan's fiction illuminates "the mystery of the mother-daughter bond in ways that we have not experienced before." Apply this assessment to "Two Kinds," with specific reference to the cross-cultural conflicts in the story.
2. Do you find this story witty and humorous? Why or why not?
3. How do you interpret the conclusion of the story?

Children & Families

Fiction

TOPICS FOR WRITING

1. Select your favorite story from this section and explain why you relate to it so well, why you like it, and what it means to you. Feel free to connect your appreciation of this story to your own family, or to recount one or two personal memories that reflect the situation or conflict in the story you have chosen.
2. Compare and contrast the ways in which the mothers are presented in "Girl," "Gravity," and "Two Kinds." What images of these mothers emerge? What is their attitude toward their children? What problems must they deal with? Are their conflicts resolved?
3. Several stories depict the initiation of children into adult realities. Explain the ways in which they come of age. Exactly what are they being initiated into? Who seems more mature and why?
4. Several ethnic and cultural groups appear in these stories. Analyze the impact of cultural background on the characters in "Mother and Son," "Two Kinds," and one other story of your choice.
5. Analyze the types of families that we witness in these stories. Which stories contain nuclear families? Which project extended or kinship families? Which involved single-parent families? Concern yourself with the issue of "typical" families as you examine these questions.
6. Do you agree or disagree with the proposition that mothers are more influential than fathers in raising children? How do these stories support your position?

Poetry

Margaret Atwood

GAME AFTER SUPPER

This is before electricity,
it is when there were porches.

On the sagging porch an old man
is rocking. The porch is wooden,

the house is wooden and grey;   5
in the living room which smells of
smoke and mildew, soon
the woman will light the kerosene lamp.

There is a barn but I am not in the barn;
there is an orchard too, gone bad,   10
its apples like soft cork
but I am not there either.

I am hiding in the long grass
with my two dead cousins,
the membrane grown already   15
across their throats.

We hear crickets and our own hearts
close to our ears;
though we giggle, we are afraid.

From the shadows around   20
the corner of the house
a tall man is coming to find us:

He will be an uncle,
if we are lucky.

QUESTIONS

1. Is the poet describing a memory, a dream, a fantasy, or something that really happened? On what do you base your view?
2. How does Atwood establish the time and place of the poem?
3. What is the significance of the title?
4. How does the author use details to evoke the senses of sight, smell, touch, and hearing?

Ulli Beier

PRAISE-NAMES OF TWINS

Those who are woken up with a drum.
Those who have beautiful eyes.
I am glad to receive you.
You meet one who prepared cloth for you.
Two in a day!   5
Uncountable in the eyes of the co-wives,
Though only two in the eyes of the mother,
They walk together.
They do not leave one another behind.
Two joined on top of a tree.   10
Something sweet on top of the tree.
                              from the Yoruba

John Berryman

THE BALL POEM

What is the boy now, who has lost his ball,
What, what is he to do? I saw it go
Merrily bouncing, down the street, and then
Merrily over—there it is in the water!
No use to say 'O there are other balls':   5
An ultimate shaking grief fixes the boy
As he stands rigid, trembling, staring down
All his young days into the harbour where
His ball went. I would not intrude on him,
A dime, another ball, is worthless. Now   10
He senses first responsibility
In a world of possessions. People will take balls,
Balls will be lost always, little boy,
And no one buys a ball back. Money is external.
He is learning, well behind his desperate eyes,   15
The epistemology of loss, how to stand up
Knowing what every man must one day know
And most know many days, how to stand up
And gradually light returns to the street,
A whistle blows, the ball is out of sight,   20
Soon part of me will explore the deep and dark
Floor of the harbour . . . I am everywhere,
I suffer and move, my mind and my heart move
With all that move me, under the water
Or whistling, I am not a little boy.   25

Elizabeth Bishop

SESTINA

September rain falls on the house.
In the failing light, the old grandmother
sits in the kitchen with the child
beside the Little Marvel Stove,
reading the jokes from the almanac,   5
laughing and talking to hide her tears.

She thinks that her equinoctial tears
and the rain that beats on the roof of the house
were both foretold by the almanac,
but only known to a grandmother.   10
The iron kettle sings on the stove.
She cuts some bread and says to the child,

It's time for tea now; but the child
is watching the teakettle's small hard tears
dance like mad on the hot black stove,   15
the way the rain must dance on the house.
Tidying up, the old grandmother
hangs up the clever almanac

on its string. Birdlike, the almanac
hovers half open above the child,   20
hovers above the old grandmother
and her teacup full of dark brown tears.
She shivers and says she thinks the house
feels chilly, and puts more wood in the stove.

It was to be, says the Marvel Stove.   25
I know what I know, says the almanac.
With crayons the child draws a rigid house
and a winding pathway. Then the child
puts in a man with buttons like tears
and shows it proudly to the grandmother.   30

But secretly, while the grandmother
busies herself about the stove,
the little moons fall down like tears
from between the pages of the almanac
into the flower bed the child   35
has carefully placed in the front of the house.

Time to plant tears, says the almanac.
The grandmother sings to the marvellous stove
and the child draws another inscrutable house.

Anne Bradstreet

BEFORE THE BIRTH OF ONE OF HER CHILDREN

All things within this fading world hath end,
Adversity doth still our joyes attend;
No tyes so strong, no friends so dear and sweet,
But with deaths parting blow is sure to meet.
The sentence past is most irrevocable,   5
A common thing, yet oh inevitable;
How soon, my Dear, death may my steps attend,
How soon't may be thy Lot to lose thy friend,
We both are ignorant, yet love bids me
These farewell lines to recommend to thee,   10
That when that knot's unty'd that made us one,
I may seem thine, who in effect am none.
And if I see not half my dayes that's due,
What nature would, God grant to yours and you;
The many faults that well you know I have,   15
Let be interr'd in my oblivious grave;
If any worth or virtue were in me,
Let that live freshly in thy memory
And when thou feel'st no grief, as I no harms,
Yet love thy dead, who long lay in thine arms: 20
And when thy loss shall be repaid with gains
Look to my little babes my dear remains.
And if thou love thy self, or loved'st me
These O protect from step Dames injury.
And if chance to thine eyes shall bring this verse,   25
With some sad sighs honour my absent Herse;
And kiss this paper for thy loves dear sake,
Who with salt tears this last Farewel did take.

IN MEMORY OF MY DEAR GRAND-CHILD ELIZABETH BRADSTREET, WHO DECEASED AUGUST, 1665, BEING A YEAR AND A HALF OLD

Farewel dear babe, my hearts too much content.
Farewel sweet babe, the pleasure of mine eye,
Farewel fair flower that for a space was lent,
Then ta'en away unto Eternity.
Blest babe why should I once bewail thy fate,   5
Or sigh thy dayes so soon were terminate;
Sith thou art settled in an Everlasting state.

By nature Trees do rot when they are grown.
And Plumbs and Apples throughly ripe do fall,
And Corn and grass are in their season mown,   10
And time brings down what is both strong and tall.
But plants new set to be eradicate,
And buds new blown, to have so short a date,
Is by His hand alone that guides nature and fate.

QUESTIONS

1. What is the poem's main argument? In which lines is it most clearly expressed?
2. Where is repetition used in the poem? What is its function and effect?
3. The poem is composed of two stanzas. What makes each stanza stand as a separate unit of expression?
4. What is the mood of the poem? How does the author create this mood?

Gwendolyn Brooks

A SONG IN THE FRONT YARD

I've stayed in the front yard all my life.
I want a peek at the back
Where it's rough and untended and hungry weed grows.
A girl gets sick of a rose.

I want to go in the back yard now   5
And maybe down the alley,
To where the charity children play.
I want a good time today.

They do some wonderful things.
They have some wonderful fun.   10
My mother sneers, but I say it's fine
How they don't have to go in at quarter to nine.
My mother, she tells me that Johnnie Mae
Will grow up to be a bad woman.
That George'll be taken to Jail soon or late   15
(On account of last winter he sold our back gate).

But I say it's fine. Honest, I do.
And I'd like to be a bad woman, too,
And wear the brave stockings of night-black lace
And strut down the streets with paint on my face.   20

Raymond Carver

PHOTOGRAPH OF MY FATHER IN HIS TWENTY-SECOND YEAR

October. Here in this dank, unfamiliar kitchen
I study my father's embarrassed young man's face.
Sheepish grin, he holds in one hand a string
Of spiny yellow perch, in the other
A bottle of Carlsbad beer.   5

In jeans and denim shirt, he leans
Against the front fender of a Ford *circa* 1934.
He would like to pose bluff and hearty for his posterity,
Wear his old hat cocked over his ear, stick out his
tongue . . .   10
All his life my father wanted to be bold.

But the eyes give him away, and the hands
That limply offer the string of dead perch
And the bottle of beer. Father, I loved you,
Yet how can I say thank you,   15
  I who cannot hold my liquor either
And do not even know the places to fish?

Cho Chi-Hun

ANCIENT TEMPLE

Overcome by a stealthy slumber,
A blue boy in the upper seat,

With the wooden fish in his hands,
Closes his eyes and nods.

While Amitabha and Bodhisattva   5
Smile, smile without words,

Along the western borders,
Under the blinding red sky,
Peonies fall, peonies fall.

translated by Peter H. Lee

Sandra Cisneros

HIS STORY

I was born under a crooked star.
So says my father.
And this perhaps explains his sorrow.

An only daughter
whom no one came for   5
and no one chased away.

It is an ancient fate.
A family trait we trace back
to a great aunt no one mentions.

Her sin was beauty.   10
She lived mistress.
Died solitary.

There is as well
the cousin with the famous
how shall I put it?   15
profession.

She ran off with the colonel.
And soon after,
the army payroll.

And, of course,   20
grandmother's mother
who died a death of voodoo.
There are others.

For instance,
my father explains,   25

in the Mexican papers
a girl with both my names
was arrested for audacious crimes
that began by disobeying fathers.

Also, and here he pauses,   30
the Cubano who sells him shoes
says he too knew a Sandra Cisneros
who was three times cursed a widow.

You see.
An unlucky fate is mine   35
to be born woman in a family of men.

Six sons, my father groans,
all home.
And one female,
gone.   40

Lucille Clifton

FORGIVING MY FATHER

it is friday. we have come
to the paying of the bills.
all week you have stood in my dreams
like a ghost, asking for more time
but today is payday, payday old man;   5
my mother's hand opens in her early grave
and i hold it out like a good daughter.

there is no more time for you. there will
never be time enough daddy daddy old lecher
old liar. i wish you were rich so i could take it all   10
and give the lady what she was due
but you were the son of a needy father,
the father of a needy son;
you gave her all you had
which was nothing. you have already given her   15
all you had.

you are the pocket that was going to open
and come up empty any friday.
you were each other's bad bargain, not mine.
daddy old pauper   old prisoner,   old dead man   20
what am i doing here collecting?
you lie side by side in debtors' boxes
and no accounting will open them up.

QUESTIONS

1. What are the primary family relationships described in the poem? How are they depicted?
2. Describe the significance of the mother's hand.
3. Why has the poet written the poem in lowercase letters?
4. What is the mood of the poem? What is the significance of the words *friday* and *payday* in the creation of this mood?

Emily Dickinson

FROM ALL THE JAILS

From all the Jails the Boys and Girls
Ecstatically leap—
Beloved only Afternoon
That Prison doesn't keep

They storm the Earth and stun the Air,   5
A Mob of solid Bliss—
Alas—that Frowns should lie in wait
For such a Foe as this—

Rita Dove

FIFTH GRADE
AUTOBIOGRAPHY

I was four in this photograph fishing
with my grandparents at a lake in Michigan.
My brother squats in poison ivy.
His Davy Crockett cap
sits squared on his head so the raccoon tail   5
flounces down the back of his sailor suit.

My grandfather sits to the far right
in a folding chair,
and I know his left hand is on
the tobacco in his pants pocket   10
because I used to wrap it for him
every Christmas. Grandmother's hips
bulge from the brush, she's leaning
into the ice chest, sun through the trees
printing her dress with soft   15
luminous paws.

I am staring jealously at my brother;
the day before he rode his first horse, alone.
I was strapped in a basket
behind my grandfather.   20
He smelled of lemons. He's died—

but I remember his hands.

Nikki Giovanni

KNOXVILLE, TENNESSEE

I always like summer
best
you can eat fresh corn
from daddy's garden
and okra   5

and greens
and cabbage
and lots of
barbecue
and buttermilk   10
and homemade ice cream
at the church picnic
and listen to
gospel
music   15
outside
at the church
homecoming
and go to the mountains with
your grandmother   20
and go barefooted
and be warm
all the time
not only when you go to bed
and sleep   25

MOTHERS

the last time i was home
to see my mother we kissed
exchanged pleasantries
and unpleasantries pulled a warm
comforting silence around   5
us and read separate books

i remember the first time
i consciously saw her
we were living in a three room
apartment on burns avenue   10
mommy always sat in the dark
i don't know how i knew that but she did

that night i stumbled into the kitchen
maybe because i've always been
a night person or perhaps because i had wet the bed   15
she was sitting on a chair
the room was bathed in moonlight diffused through

those thousands of panes landlords who rented
to people with children were prone to put in windows

she may have been smoking but maybe not   20
her hair was three-quarters her height
which made me a strong believer in the samson myth
and very black

i'm sure i just hung there by the door
i remember thinking: what a beautiful lady   25

she was very deliberately waiting
perhaps for my father to come home
from his night job or maybe for a dream
that had promised to come by
"come here" she said "i'll teach you   30
a poem: *i see the moon*
> *the moon sees me*
> *god bless the moon*
> *and god bless me"*
i taught it to my son   35
who recited it for her
just to say we must learn
to bear the pleasures ·
as we have borne the pains

Robert Hayden

THOSE WINTER SUNDAYS

Sundays too my father got up early
and put his clothes on in the blueblack cold,
then with cracked hands that ached
from labor in the weekday weather made
banked fires blaze. No one ever thanked him.   5

I'd wake and hear the cold splintering, breaking.
When the rooms were warm, he'd call,
and slowly I would rise and dress,
fearing the chronic angers of that house,

Speaking indifferently to him,   10
who had driven out the cold
and polished my good shoes as well.
What did I know, what did I know
of love's austere and lonely offices?

Langston Hughes

MOTHER TO SON

Well, Son, I'll tell you
Life for me ain't been no crystal stair
It's had tacks in it,
And splinters,
And boards torn up,   5
And places with no carpets on the floor,

Bare.
But all the time
I'se been climbin' on
and reachin' landin's   10
And turning corners
And sometimes goin' on in the dark
Where there ain't been no light.
So, Boy, don't you turn back.
Don't you set down on the steps   15
'Cause you find it's kinder hard.
Don't you fall now—
For I'se still goin', Honey,
I'se still climbin'
And life for me ain't been   20
                    no crystal stair.

Ben Jonson

ON MY FIRST DAUGHTER

Here lies, to each her parents' ruth,
Mary, the daughter of their youth;
Yet all heaven's gifts being heaven's due,
It makes the father less to rue.
At six months' end she parted hence   5
With safety of her innocence;
Whose soul heaven's queen, whose name she bears,
In comfort of her mother's tears,
Hath placed amongst her virgin train:
Where, while that severed doth remain,   10
This grave partakes the fleshly birth;
Which cover lightly, gentle earth!

ON MY FIRST SON

Farewell, thou child of my right hand, and joy;
My sin was too much hope of thee, loved boy:
Seven years thou wert lent to me, and I thee pay,
Exacted by thy fate, on the just day.
O could I lose all father now! for why   5
Will man lament the state he should envy,
To have so soon 'scaped world's and flesh's rage,
And, if no other misery, yet age?
Rest in soft peace, and asked, say, "Here doth lie
Ben Jonson his best piece of poetry."   10
For whose sake henceforth all his vows be such
As what he loves may never like too much.

D. H. Lawrence

PIANO

Softly, in the dusk, a woman is singing to me;
Taking me back down the vista of years, till I see
A child sitting under the piano, in the boom of the tingling strings
And pressing the small, poised feet of a mother who smiles as she sings

In spite of myself, the insidious mastery of song   5
Betrays me back, till the heart of me weeps to belong
To the old Sunday evenings at home, with winter outside
And hymns in the cosy parlour, the tinkling piano our guide.

So now it is vain for the singer to burst into clamour
With the great black piano appassionato. The glamour   10
Of childish days is upon me, my manhood is cast
Down in the flood of remembrance, I weep like a child for the past.

Audre Lorde

OYA

God of my father discovered at midnight
my mother asleep on her thunders
my father
returning at midnight
out of tightening circles of anger   5
out of days' punishment
the inelegant safety of power
Now midnight empties your house of bravado
and passion sleeps like a mist
outside desire   10
your strength splits like a melon
dropped on our prisoners floor
midnight glows
like a jeweled love
at the core of the broken fruit.   15

My mother is sleeping.
Hymns of dream lie like bullets
in her nights weapons
the sacred steeples
of nightmare are secret and hidden   20
in the disguise of fallen altars
I too shall learn how to conquer yes
Yes yes god
damned
I love you   25
now free me
quickly
before I destroy us.

Janice Mirikitani

SING WITH YOUR BODY

To my daughter, Tianne Tsukiko

We love with great difficulty
spinning in one place
afraid to create
                    spaces
                              new/rhythm   5

the beat of a child
dangled by her own inner ear
takes Aretha with her
                    upstairs,   somewhere.

go quickly, Tsukiko,   10
                    into your circled dance
go quickly
                    before your steps are
                    halted by who you are not

go quickly   15
                    to learn the mixed
                    rhythm of your tongue,

go quickly

to who you are

before   20

your mother swallows
what she has lost.

David Mura

GRANDFATHER AND GRANDMOTHER IN LOVE

Now I will ask for one true word beyond
betrayal, that creaks and buoys like the bedsprings
used by the bodies that begot the bodies that begot me.
Now I will think of the moon bluing the white
sheets soaked in sweat, that heard him whisper   5
haiku of clover, azaleas, the cry of the cuckoo:
complaints of moles and beetles,
blight and bad debts, as the *biwa*'s[1] spirit
bubbled up between them, its song quavering.
Now I take this word and crack it, like a seed   10
between the teeth, spit it out into the world,
and let it seek the loam that nourished his greenhouse
roses, sputtering petals of chrysanthemum:
let it leave the sweet taste of *teriyaki*,
and a grain of rice lodges in my molars,   15
and the faint breath of *sake*, hot in the nostrils.
Now the drifting before writhing, now Buddha
stand back, now he bumps beside her,
otoo-san,[2] *okaa-san*,[3] calling each other.
Now there reverberates the *ran* of lovers,   20
and the bud of the past has burst through
into the other world,

[1] *biwa*—a Japanese stringed instrument
[2] *otoo-san*—grandfather
[3] *okaa-san*—grandmother

where she, teasing, pushes him away, swats
his hand, like a pesky, tickling fly,
and then turns to his face that cries out   25
laughing, and he is hauling her in, trawling
the caverns of her flesh, gathering gift
after gift from a sea that seems endless,
depths a boy dreams of, where dolphins
and fluorescent fins and fish with wings   30
suddenly spill their glittering scales
before him, and he, who was always baffled by beauty,
lets slip the net and dives under, and the night
washes over them, slipping from sight,
just the soft shushing of waves, drifting ground   35
swells, echoing the knocking tide of morning.

QUESTIONS

1. What does the poet mean by the "one true word beyond/betrayal"?
2. How does the poet use alliteration (the repetition of consonantal sounds) and what
   is its intended effect?
3. Images of nature abound in the poem. What are they, and how could you classify
   them according to type?
4. Upon whom is the poem focused—the grandfather, the grandmother, or both
   equally? How did you arrive at your conclusion?
5. The poet is a *Sansei*, a third-generation Japanese American. Explain how this might
   influence the poem.

Simon J. Ortiz

SPEAKING

I take him outside
under the trees,
have him stand on the ground.
We listen to the crickets,
cicadas, million years old sound.   5
Ants come by us.
I tell them,

"This is he, my son.
This boy is looking at you.
I am speaking for him."   10

The crickets, cicadas,
the ants, the millions of years
are watching us,
hearing us.
My son murmurs infant words,   15
speaking, small laughter
bubbles from him.
Tree leaves tremble.
They listen to this boy
speaking for me.   20

Sylvia Plath

DADDY

You do not do, you do not do
Any more, black shoe
in which I have lived like a foot
For thirty years, poor and white,
Barely daring to breathe or Achoo.   5

Daddy, I have had to kill you.
You died before I had time—
Marble-heavy, a bag full of God,
Ghastly statue with one grey toe
Big as a Frisco seal   10

And a head in the freakish Atlantic
Where it pours bean green over blue
In the waters off beautiful Nauset.
I used to pray to recover you.
Ach, du.   15

In the German tongue, in the Polish town
Scraped flat by the roller
Of wars, wars, wars.

But the name of the town is common.
My Polack friend   20

Says there are a dozen or two.
So I never could tell where you
Put your foot, your root,
I never could talk to you.
The tongue stuck in my jaw.   25

It stuck in a barb wire snare.
Ich, ich, ich, ich,
I could hardly speak.
I thought every German was you.
And the language obscene   30

An engine, an engine
Chuffing me off like a Jew.
A Jew to Dachau, Auschwitz, Belsen.
I began to talk like a Jew.
I think I may well be a Jew.   35

The snows of the Tyrol, the clear beer of Vienna
Are not very pure or true.
With my gypsy ancestress and my weird luck
And my Taroc pack and my Taroc pack
I may be a bit of a Jew.   40

I have always been scared of *you,*
With your Luftwaffe, your gobbledygoo.
And your neat moustache
And your Aryan eye, bright blue.
Panzer-man, panzer-man, O You—   45

Not God but a swastika
So black no sky could squeak through.
Every woman adores a Fascist,
The boot in the face, the brute
Brute heart of a brute like you.   50

You stand at the blackboard, daddy,
In the picture I have of you,
A cleft in your chin instead of your foot
But no less a devil for that, no not
Any less the black man who   55

Bit my pretty red heart in two.
I was ten when they buried you.
At twenty I tried to die
And get back, back, back at you.
I thought even the bones will do.   60

But they pulled me out of the sack,
And they stuck me together with glue.
And then I knew what to do.
I made a model of you,
A man in black with a Meinkampf look   65

And a love of the rack and the screw.
And I said I do, I do.
So daddy, I'm finally through.
The black telephone's off at the root,
The voices just can't worm through.   70

If I've killed one man, I've killed two—
The vampire who said he was you
And drank my blood for a year,
Seven years, if you want to know.
Daddy, you can lie back now.   75

There's a stake in your fat black heart
And the villagers never liked you.
They are dancing and stamping on you.
They always *knew* it was you,
Daddy, daddy, you bastard, I'm through.   80

Alexander Pushkin

TO MY OLD NURSE

Faithful friend in years of sorrow,
Frail and aged nurse of mine,
Expecting me with every morrow,
Lonely in the woods of pine.
Waiting in your attic lowly,   5
Sadly watching, as on guard.

Knitting needles clicking slowly,
Fingers wrinkled, withered, hard.
Peering at deserted portal—
Dark and distant is the road—   10
Grief and care, unhappy mortal,
These are now thy bosom's load.
And still you dream. . . . .
Interpreted by Henry Jones

Theodore Roethke

MY PAPA'S WALTZ

The whiskey on your breath
Could make a small boy dizzy;
But I hung on like death:
Such waltzing was not easy.

We romped until the pans   5
Slid from the kitchen shelf;
My mother's countenance
Could not unfrown itself.

The hand that held my wrist
Was battered on one knuckle;   10
At every step you missed
My right ear scraped a buckle.

You beat time on my head
With a palm caked hard by dirt,
Then waltzed me off to bed   15
Still clinging to your shirt.

Muriel Rukeyser

MYTH

Long afterward, Oedipus, old and blinded, walked the
roads.   He smelled a familiar smell.   It was
the Sphinx.   Oedipus said, "I want to ask one question.
Why didn't I recognize my mother?"   "You gave the
wrong answer," said the Sphinx.   "But that was what   5
made everything possible," said Oedipus.   "No," she said.
"When I asked, What walks on four legs in the morning,
two at noon, and three in the evening, you answered,
Man.   You didn't say anything about woman."
"When you say Man," said Oedipus, "you include women   10
too. Everyone knows that."   She said, "That's what
you think."

QUESTIONS

1. What makes this piece of writing a poem and not a work of prose?
2. The last line is ironic for several reasons. What are they?
3. The title of the poem is "Myth." What makes the poem resemble a myth?
4. Rukeyser's poetry has often addressed themes of oppression. How does this poem
   represent this choice of theme?

Sonia Sanchez

POEM AT THIRTY

it is midnight
no magical bewitching
hour for me
i know only that
i am here waiting   5
remembering that
once as a child
i walked two
miles in my sleep.
did I know   10

then where i
was going?
traveling. i'm
always traveling.
i want to tell   15
you about me
about nights on a
brown couch when
i wrapped my
bones in lint and   20
refused to move.
no one touches
me anymore.
father do not
send me out   25
among strangers.
you you black man
stretching scraping
the mold from your body
here is my hand.   30
i am not afraid
of the night.

Gary Snyder

NOT LEAVING THE HOUSE

When Kai is born
I quit going out

Hang around the kitchen—make cornbread
Let nobody in.
Mail is flat.   5
    Masa lies on her side, Kai sighs,
    Non washes and sweeps
We sit and watch
    Masa nurse, and drink green tea.

Navajo turquoise beads over the bed   10
A peacock tail feather at the head

A badger pelt from Nagano-ken
For a mattress; under the sheet;
A pot of yogurt setting
Under the blankets, at his feet.   15

Masa, Kai,
And Non, our friend
In the green garden light reflected in
Not leaving the house.
From dawn til late at night   20
        making a new world of ourselves
        around this life.

Gary Soto

LEARNING TO BARGAIN

Summer. Flies knitting
Filth on the window,
A mother calling a son home . . .
I'm at that window, looking
Onto the street: dusk,   5
A neighbor kid sharpening
A stick at the curb.
I go outside and sit
Next to him without saying
A word. When he looks   10
Up, his eyes dark as flies,
I ask about the cat, the one
Among weeds in the alley.
"It's mine," he admits
And stares down at his feet,   15
Then my feet. "What do you want?"
"A dime," I say. Without
Looking at me, he gets
Up, goes behind his house,
And returns with two coke bottles.   20
"These make a dime." He sits
At the curb, his shoulders

So bony they could be wings
To lift him so far. "Don't tell."
He snaps a candy in halves 25
And we eat in silence.

Wallace Stevens

THE IRISH CLIFFS OF MOHER

Who is my father in this world, in this house,
At the spirit's base?

My father's father, his father's father, his—
Shadows like winds

Go back to a parent before thought, before speech, 5
At the head of the past.

They go to the cliffs of Moher rising out of the mist,
Above the real,

Rising out of present time and place, above
The wet, green grass. 10

This is not landscape, full of the somnambulations
Of poetry

And the sea. This is my father or, maybe,
It is as he was,

A likeness, one of the race of fathers: earth 15
And sea and air.

Dylan Thomas

FERN HILL

Now as I was young and easy under the apple boughs
About the lilting house and happy as the grass was green,
     The night above the dingle starry,
        Time let me hail and climb
     Golden in the heydays of his eyes,   5
And honoured among wagons I was prince of the apple towns
And once below a time I lordly had the trees and leaves
        Trail with daisies and barley
     Down the rivers of the windfall light.

And as I was green and carefree, famous among the barns   10
About the happy yard and singing as the farm was home,
     In the sun that is young once only,
        Time let me play and be
     Golden in the mercy of his means,
And green and golden I was huntsman and herdsman, the calves   15
Sang to my horn, the foxes on the hills barked clear and cold,
        And the sabbath rang slowly
     In the pebbles of the holy streams.

All the sun long it was running, it was lovely, the hay
Fields high as the house, the tunes from the chimneys, it was air   20
     And playing, lovely and watery
        And fire green as grass.
     And nightly under the simple stars
As I rode to sleep the owls were bearing the farm away,
All the moon long I heard, blessed among stables, the night-jars   25
     Flying with the ricks, and the horses
     Flashing into the dark.

And then to awake, and the farm, like a wanderer white
With the dew, come back, the cock on his shoulder: it was all
     Shining, it was Adam and maiden,   30
        The sky gathered again
     And the sun grew round that very day.
So it must have been after the birth of the simple light
In the first, spinning place, the spellbound horses walking warm
     Out of the whinnying green stable   35
     On to the fields of praise.

QUESTIONS

1. This poem is filled with religious terms such as *mercy, sabbath,* and *holy.* What do they tell us about the youth of the narrator?
2. Identify the passages in which the narrator discusses his relationship to nature. How many of the images are possible? How many are pure fantasy? How does the mixing of the two contribute to the tone of the poem?
3. How is the concept of Time treated in the poem—as an abstraction, as something concrete, or both? Explain.
4. Nearly every line begins with a conjunction or preposition. How does this structural device relate to the theme of the poem?

Joyce Carol Thomas

BLACK CHILD

My mother says I am
Still honey in sassafras tea
My father calls me the
Brown sugar of his days
Yet they warn   5
There are those who
Have brewed a
Bitter potion for
Children kissed long by the sun
Therefore I approach   10
The cup slowly
But first I ask
Who has set this table

Cesar Vallejo

TO MY BROTHER MIGUEL

in memoriam.

Brother, today I'm sitting on the bench outside our house.
Where you are missed so deeply!
I remember how we used to play at this hour, and that mama
would hug and caress us: "But, boys . . ."

Now I hide,   5
just like before, all those evening
prayers, and I hope you can't find me.
Through the living room, the entryway, the halls.
Then, you hide, and I can't find you.
I remember we made each other cry,   10
brother, in that game.

Miguel, you hid
one night in August, just before dawn;
but, instead of hiding laughing, you were sad.
And your twin heart of those extinct evenings   15
has gotten tired of not finding you. And now
shadow falls across the soul.

Hey, brother, don't take so long
coming out. Okay? Mama might get worried.

> Translated by Richard Scharf and Kathleen Ross

Gerald Vizenor

FAMILY PHOTOGRAPH

among trees
my father was a spruce

corded for tribal pulp
he left the white earth reservation
colonial genealogies   5
taking up the city at twenty-three

telling stories
sharing dreams from a mason jar
running
low through the stumps at night   10
was his line

at twenty-three
he waited with the old men
colorless
dressed in their last uniforms   15
reeling on the nicollet island bridge

arm bands adrift
wooden limbs
men too civilized by war
thrown back to evangelists and charity   20

no reservation superintendents there
no indian agents
pacing off allotments twenty acres short
only family photographs ashore

no catholics on the wire   25
tying treaty money to confirmations

in the city
my father was an immigrant
hanging paper flowers
painting ceilings white for a union boss   30
disguising saint louis park

his weekend women
listened to him measuring my blood at night

downtown rooms were cold
half truths   35
peeling like blisters of history
two sizes too small

he smiles
holding me in a photograph then
the new spruce   40
half white
half immigrant
taking up the city and losing at cards

Margaret Walker

LINEAGE

My grandmothers were strong.
They followed plows and bent to toil.
They moved through fields sowing seed.

They touched earth and grain grew.
They were full of sturdiness and singing.   5
My grandmothers were strong.

My grandmothers are full of memories.
Smelling of soap and onions and wet clay
With veins rolling roughly over quick hands
They have many clean words to say.   10
My grandmothers were strong.
Why am I not as they?

Walt Whitman

THERE WAS A CHILD
WENT FORTH

There was a child went forth every day,
And the first object he look'd upon, that object he became,
And that object became part of him for the day or a certain part of the day,
Or for many years or stretching cycles of years.

The early lilacs became part of this child,   5
And grass and white and red morning-glories, and white and red clover,
    and the song of the phœbe-bird,
And the Third-month lambs and the sow's pink-faint litter,
    and the mare's foal and the cow's calf,
And the noisy brood of the barnyard or by the mire of the pond-side,   10
And the fish suspending themselves so curiously below there,
    and the beautiful curious liquid,
And the water-plants with their graceful flat heads, all became part of him.

The field-sprouts of Fourth-month and Fifth-month became part of him,
Winter-grain sprouts and those of the light-yellow corn,   15
    and the esculent roots of the garden,
And the apple-trees cover'd with blossoms and the fruit afterward,
    and wood-berries, and the commonest weeds by the road,
And the old drunkard staggering home from the outhouse of the tavern
    whence he had lately risen,   20
And the schoolmistress that pass'd on her way to the school,
And the friendly boys that pass'd, and the quarrelsome boys,
And the tidy and fresh-cheek'd girls, and the barefoot negro boy and girl,
And all the changes of city and country wherever he went.

His own parents, he that had father'd him and she that had conceiv'd him   25
    in her womb and birth'd him,
They give this child more of themselves than that,
They gave him afterward every day, they became part of him.

The mother at home quietly placing the dishes on the supper-table,
The mother with mild words, clean her cap and gown,   30
    a wholesome odor falling off her person and clothes as she walks by,
The father, strong, self-sufficient, manly, mean, anger'd, unjust,
The blow, the quick loud word, the tight bargain, the crafty lure,
The family usages, the language, the company, the furniture,
    the yearning and swelling heart,   35
Affection that will not be gainsay'd, the sense of what is real,
    the thought if after all it should prove unreal,
The doubts of day-time and the doubts of night-time,
    the curious whether and how,
Whether that which appears so is so, or is it all flashes and specks?   40
Men and women crowding fast in the streets,
    if they are not flashes and specks what are they?
The streets themselves and the façades of houses, and goods in the windows,
Vehicles, teams, the heavy-plank'd wharves, the huge crossing at the ferries,
The village on the highland seen from afar at sunset, the river between,   45
Shadows, aureola and mist, the light falling on roofs and gables
    of white or brown two miles off,
The schooner near by sleepily dropping down the tide,
    the little boat slack-tow'd astern,
The hurrying tumbling waves, quick-broken crests, slapping,   50
The strata of color'd clouds, the long bar of maroon-tint away solitary
    by itself, the spread of purity it lies motionless in,
The horizon's edge, the flying sea-crow, the fragrance of salt marsh and
    shore mud,
These became part of that child who went forth every day,   55
    and who now goes, and will always go forth every day.

William Carlos Williams

DANSE RUSSE

If when my wife is sleeping
and the baby and Kathleen
are sleeping
and the sun is a flame-white disc
in silken mists   5
above shining trees,—
if I in my north room
dance naked, grotesquely
before my mirror
waving my shirt round my head   10
and singing softly to myself:
"I am lonely, lonely.
I was born to be lonely,
I am best so!"
If I admire my arms, my face,   15
my shoulders, flanks, buttocks
against the yellow drawn shades,—

Who shall say I am not
the happy genius of my household?

QUESTIONS

1. The title is an early twentieth-century term in ballet that connoted scandal and exoticism. How do the narrator's behavior and the poet's imagery make this title apt?
2. What pleasure does the poet derive from his dance? Why is it only possible for him to feel this pleasure when he is alone?
3. How can the poet be "lonely" and happy at the same time?
4. Concentrate on the line structure of the poem and the rhythm it creates as you read the poem aloud. How does its rhythm contribute to the mood of the poem?

James Wright

MUTTERINGS OVER THE CRIB OF A DEAF CHILD

"How will he hear the bell at school
Arrange the broken afternoon,
And know to run across the cool
Grasses where the starlings cry,
Or understand the day is gone?"   5

Well, someone lifting cautious brows
Will take the measure of the clock.
And he will see the birchen boughs
Outside the sagging dark from the sky,
And the shade crawling upon the rock.   10

"And how will he know to rise at morning?
His mother has other sons to waken,
She has the stove she must build to burning
Before the coals of the night-time die,
And he never stirs when he is shaken."   15

I take it the air affects the skin,
And you remember, when you were young,
Sometimes you could feel the dawn begin,
And the fire would call you, by and by,
Out of the bed and bring you along.   20

"Well, good enough. To serve his needs
All kinds of arrangements can be made.
But what will you do if his finger bleeds?
Or a bobwhite whistles invisibly
And flutes like an angel off in the shade?"   25

He will learn pain. And, as for the bird,
It is always darkening when that comes out.
I will putter as though I had not heard,
And lift him into my arms and sing
Whether he hears my song or not.   30

Judith Wright

TO ANOTHER HOUSEWIFE

Do you remember how we went,
on duty bound, to feed the crowd
of hungry dogs your father kept
as rabbit-hunters? Lean and loud,
half-starved and furious, how they leapt   5
against their chains, as though they meant
in mindless rage for being fed,
to tear our childish hands instead!

With tomahawk and knife we hacked
the flyblown tatters of old meat,   10
gagged at their carcass-smell, and threw
the scraps and watched the hungry eat.
Then turning faint, we made a pact,
(two greensick girls), crossed hearts and swore
to touch no meat forever more.   15

How many cuts of choice and prime
our housewife hands have dressed since then—
these hands with love and blood imbrued—
for daughters, sons, and hungry men!
How many creatures bred for food   20
we've raised and fattened for the time
they met at last the steaming knife
that serves the feast of death-in-life!

And as the evening meal is served
we hear the turned-down radio   25
begin to tell the evening news
just as the family joint is carved.
O murder, famine, pious wars. . . .
Our children shrink to see us so,
in sudden meditation, stand   30
with knife and fork in either hand.

C h i l d r e n & F a m i l i e s

Poetry

TOPICS FOR WRITING

1. Family memories often contain feelings of loss and/or lack of fulfillment. Compare and contrast these themes as they are portrayed in "Photograph of My Father in His Twenty-Second Year," "Forgiving My Father," and a third poem of your own choice.

2. In both "My Papa's Waltz" and "Those Winter Sundays," a son reflects upon the relationship between himself and his father. Compare and contrast the two relationships.

3. Gender obviously has a lot to do with one's experiences of childhood and family. After studying the poems in this section, select three written by men and three by women, and use selected passages from each to illustrate differences the two sexes experience in terms of childhood, family, and maturation.

4. Reread "Learning to Bargain." Then select a season, a place, and a group of people. Compose a poem or a narrative essay using these three elements as its base.

5. Reread "Fern Hill." Select a time and place in your life when you were so happy you lost sense of time itself. Using the method of freewriting, jot down everything you remember of that time. Then shape your notes into a poem or a narrative essay.

6. Select a poem from the "Children and Families" section that describes an aspect of family life you most identify with. Examine and explain the similarities you find, using details and events from your own family life to compare and contrast with those in the poems.

7. Several of the poems in this section describe experiences in the life of a child. Based on your own childhood and your observations of others, write an essay explaining what you believe to be the major differences between childhood and adulthood.

8. Do you agree or disagree with the proposition that children grow up much faster in contemporary society than they did in the past? Provide illustrations to support your view.

9. As a research project, go to the library and read a biography of one of the poets included in this section (your librarian can help you discover which ones are available). Write an essay discussing how the poem presented in this section reflects actual issues or events in the poet's childhood.

D r a m a

Lorraine Hansberry

A RAISIN IN THE SUN

———— CHARACTERS ————

RUTH YOUNGER   JOSEPH ASAGAI
TRAVIS YOUNGER   GEORGE MURCHISON
WALTER LEE YOUNGER (Brother)   KARL LINDNER
BENEATHA YOUNGER   BOBO
LENA YOUNGER (Mama)   MOVING MEN

The action of the play is set in Chicago's Southside, sometime between World War II and the present.

ACT I
SCENE 1: *Friday morning.*
SCENE 2: *The following morning.*

ACT II
SCENE 1: *Later, the same day.*
SCENE 2: *Friday night, a few weeks later.*
SCENE 3: *Moving day, one week later.*

ACT III
An hour later.

76

What happens to a dream deferred?
Does it dry up
Like a raisin in the sun?
Or fester like a sore—
And then run?
Does it stink like rotten meat?
Or crust and sugar over—
Like a syrupy sweet?

Maybe it just sags
Like a heavy load.

Or does it explode?
—Langston Hughes

ACT I

SCENE 1

The YOUNGER *living room would be a comfortable and well-ordered room if it were not for a number of indestructible contradictions to this state of being. Its furnishings are typical and undistinguished and their primary feature now is that they have clearly had to accommodate the living of too many people for too many years—and they are tired. Still, we can see that at some time, a time probably no longer remembered by the family [except perhaps for* MAMA*], the furnishings of this room were actually selected with care and love and even hope—and brought to this apartment and arranged with taste and pride.*

That was a long time ago. Now the once loved pattern of the couch upholstery has to fight to show itself from under acres of crocheted doilies and couch covers which have themselves finally come to be more important than the upholstery. And here a table or a chair has been moved to disguise the worn places in the carpet: but the carpet has fought back by showing its weariness, with depressing uniformity, elsewhere on its surface.

Weariness has, in fact, won in this room. Everything has been polished, washed, sat on, used, scrubbed too often. All pretenses but living itself have long since vanished from the very atmosphere of this room.

Moreover, a section of this room, for it is not really a room unto itself, though the landlord's lease would make it seem so, slopes backward to provide a small kitchen area, where the family prepares the meals that are eaten in the living room proper, which must also serve as dining room. The single window that has been provided for these "two" rooms is located in this kitchen area. The sole natural light the family may enjoy in the course of a day is only that which fights its way through this little window.

At left, a door leads to a bedroom which is shared by MAMA *and her daughter,* BENEATHA*. At right, opposite, is a second room (which in the beginning of the life of this apartment was probably a breakfast room) which serves as a bedroom for* WALTER *and his wife,* RUTH*.*

Time: Sometime between World War II and the present.
Place: Chicago's Southside.

At Rise: It is morning dark in the living room. WALTER *is asleep on the make-down bed at center. An alarm clock sounds from within the bedroom at right, and presently* RUTH *enters from that room and closes the door behind her. She crosses sleepily toward the window. As she passes her sleeping son she reaches down and shakes him a little. At the window she raises the shade and a dusky Southside morning light comes in feebly. She fills a pot with water and puts it on to boil. She calls to the boy between yawns, in a slightly muffled voice.*

RUTH *is about thirty. We can see that she was a pretty girl, even exceptionally so, but now it is apparent that life has been little that she expected, and disappointment has already begun to hang in her face. In a few years, before thirty-five even, she will be known among her people as a "settled woman."*

She crosses to her son and gives him a good, final, rousing shake.

RUTH: Come on now, boy, it's seven thirty! [*Her son sits up at last, in a stupor of sleepiness.*] I say hurry up, Travis! You ain't the only person in the world got to use a bathroom! [*The child, a sturdy, handsome little boy of ten or eleven, drags himself out of the bed and almost blindly takes his towels and "today's clothes" from drawers and a closet and goes out to the bathroom, which is in an outside hall and which is shared by another family or families on the same floor.* RUTH *crosses to the bedroom door at right and opens it and calls in to her husband.*] Walter Lee! . . . It's after seven thirty! Lemme see you do some waking up in there now! [*She waits.*] You better get up from there, man! It's after seven thirty I tell you. [*She waits again.*] All right, you just go ahead and lay there and next thing you know Travis be finished and Mr. Johnson'll be in there and you'll be fussing and cussing round here like a mad man! And be late too! [*She waits, at the end of patience.*] *Walter Lee*—it's time for you to get up!

[*She waits another second and then starts to go into the bedroom, but is apparently satisfied that her husband has begun to get up. She stops, pulls the door to, and returns to the kitchen area. She wipes her face with a moist cloth and runs her fingers through her sleep-disheveled hair in a vain effort and ties an apron around her housecoat. The bedroom door at right opens and her husband stands in the doorway in his pajamas, which are rumpled and mismated. He is a lean, intense young man in his middle thirties, inclined to quick nervous movements and erratic speech habits—and always in his voice there is a quality of indictment.*]

WALTER: Is he out yet?

RUTH: What you mean *out?* He ain't hardly got in there good yet.

WALTER [*wandering in, still more oriented to sleep than to a new day*]: Well, what was you doing all that yelling for if I can't even get in there yet? [*Stopping and thinking.*] Check coming today?

RUTH: They *said* Saturday and this is just Friday and I hopes to God you ain't going to get up here first thing this morning and start talking to me 'bout no money—'cause I 'bout don't want to hear it.

WALTER: Something the matter with you this morning?

RUTH: No—I'm just sleepy as the devil. What kind of eggs you want?

WALTER: Not scrambled. [RUTH *starts to scramble eggs.*] Paper come? [RUTH *points impatiently to the rolled up* Tribune *on the table, and he gets it and spreads it out and vaguely reads the front page.*] Set off another bomb yesterday.

RUTH [*maximum indifference*]: Did they?

WALTER [*looking up*]: What's the matter with you?

RUTH: Ain't nothing the matter with me. And don't keep asking me that this morning.

WALTER: Ain't nobody bothering you. [*Reading the news of the day absently again.*] Say Colonel McCormick is sick.

RUTH [*affecting tea-party interest*]: Is he now? Poor thing.

WALTER [*sighing and looking at his watch*]: Oh, me. [*He waits.*] Now what is that boy doing in that bathroom all this time? He just going to have to start getting up earlier. I can't be being late to work on account of him fooling around in there.

RUTH [*turning on him*]: Oh, no he ain't going to be getting up no earlier no such thing! It ain't his fault that he can't get to bed no earlier nights 'cause he got a bunch of crazy good-for-nothing clowns sitting up running their mouths in what is supposed to be his bedroom after ten o'clock at night . . .

WALTER: That's what you mad about, ain't it? The things I want to talk about with my friends just couldn't be important in your mind, could they?

[*He rises and finds a cigarette in her handbag on the table and crosses to the little window and looks out, smoking and deeply enjoying this first one.*]

RUTH [*almost matter of factly, a complaint too automatic to deserve emphasis*]: Why you always got to smoke before you eat in the morning?

WALTER [*at the window*]: Just look at 'em down there . . . Running and racing to work . . . [*He turns and faces his wife and watches her a moment at the stove, and then, suddenly.*] You look young this morning, baby.

RUTH [*indifferently*]: Yeah?

WALTER: Just for a second—stirring them eggs. It's gone now—just for a second it was—you looked real young again. [*Then, drily.*] It's gone now—you look like yourself again.

RUTH: Man, if you don't shut up and leave me alone.

WALTER [*looking out to the street again*]: First thing a man ought to learn in life is not to make love to no colored woman first thing in the morning. You all some evil people at eight o'clock in the morning.

[TRAVIS *appears in the hall doorway, almost fully dressed and quite wide awake now, his towels and pajamas across his shoulders. He opens the door and signals for his father to make the bathroom in a hurry.*]

TRAVIS [*watching the bathroom*]: Daddy, come on!

[WALTER *gets his bathroom utensils and flies out to the bathroom.*]

RUTH: Sit down and have your breakfast, Travis.

TRAVIS: Mama, this is Friday. [*Gleefully.*] Check coming tomorrow, huh?

RUTH: You get your mind off money and eat your breakfast.

TRAVIS [*eating*]: This is the morning we supposed to bring the fifty cents to school.

RUTH: Well, I ain't got no fifty cents this morning.

TRAVIS: Teacher say we have to.

RUTH: I don't care what teacher say. I ain't got it. Eat your breakfast, Travis.

TRAVIS: I *am* eating.

RUTH: Hush up now and just eat!

[*The boy gives her an exasperated look for her lack of understanding, and eats grudgingly.*]

TRAVIS: You think Grandmama would have it?

RUTH: No! And I want you to stop asking your grandmother for money, you hear me?

TRAVIS [*outraged*]: Gaaaleee! I don't ask her, she just gimme it sometimes!

RUTH: Travis Willard Younger—I got so much on me this morning to be—

TRAVIS: Maybe Daddy—

RUTH: *Travis!*

[*The boy hushes abruptly. They are both quiet and tense for several seconds.*]

TRAVIS [*presently*]: Could I maybe go carry some groceries in front of the supermarket for a little while after school then?

RUTH: Just hush, I said. [TRAVIS *jabs his spoon into his cereal bowl viciously, and rests his head in anger upon his fists.*] If you through eating, you can get over there and make up your bed.

[*The boy obeys stiffly and crosses the room, almost mechanically, to the bed and more or less carefully folds the covering. He carries the bedding into his mother's room and returns with his books and cap.*]

TRAVIS [*sulking and standing apart from her unnaturally*]: I'm gone.

RUTH [*looking up from the stove to inspect him automatically*]: Come here. [*He crosses to her and she studies his head.*] If you don't take this comb and fix this here head, you better! [TRAVIS *puts down his books with a great sigh of oppression, and crosses to the mirror. His mother mutters under her breath about his "slubbornness".*] 'Bout to march out of here with that head looking just like chickens slept in it! I just don't know where you get your slubborn ways . . . And get your jacket, too. Looks chilly out this morning.

TRAVIS [*with conspicuously brushed hair and jacket*]: I'm gone.

RUTH: Get carfare and milk money—[*Waving one finger.*]—and not a single penny for no caps, you hear me?

TRAVIS [*with sullen politeness*]: Yes'm.

[*He turns in outrage to leave. His mother watches after him as in his frustration he approaches the door almost comically. When she speaks to him, her voice has become a very gentle tease.*]

RUTH [*mocking; as she thinks he would say it*]: Oh, Mama makes me so mad sometimes, I don't know what to do! [*She waits and continues to his back as he stands stock-still in front of the door.*] I wouldn't kiss that woman good-bye for nothing in this world this morning! [*The boy finally turns around and rolls his eyes at her, knowing the mood has changed and he is vindicated; he does not, however, move toward her yet.*] Not for nothing in this world! [*She finally laughs aloud at him and holds out her arms to him and we see that it is a way between them, very old and practiced. He crosses to her and allows her to embrace him warmly but keeps his face fixed with masculine rigidity. She holds him back from her presently and looks at him and runs her fingers over the features of his face. With utter gentleness—.*] Now—whose little old angry man are you?

TRAVIS [*the masculinity and gruffness start to fade at last*]: Aw gaalee—Mama . . .

RUTH [*mimicking*]: Aw—gaaaaalleeeee, Mama! [*She pushes him, with rough playfulness and finality, toward the door.*] Get on out of here or you going to be late.

TRAVIS [*in the face of love, new aggressiveness*]: Mama, could I *please* go carry groceries?

RUTH: Honey, it's starting to get so cold evenings.

WALTER [*coming in from the bathroom and drawing a make-believe gun from a make-believe holster and shooting at his son*]: What is it he wants to do?

RUTH: Go carry groceries after school at the supermarket.

WALTER: Well, let him go . . .

TRAVIS [*quickly, to the ally*]: I *have* to—she won't gimme the fifty cents . . .

WALTER [*to his wife only*]: Why not?

RUTH [*simply, and with flavor*]: 'Cause we don't have it.

WALTER [*to* RUTH *only*]: What you tell the boy things like that for? [*Reaching down into his pants with a rather important gesture.*] Here, son—

[*He hands the boy the coin, but his eyes are directed to his wife's.* TRAVIS *takes the money happily.*]

TRAVIS: Thanks, Daddy.

[*He starts out.* RUTH *watches both of them with murder in her eyes.* WALTER *stands and stares back at her with defiance, and suddenly reaches into his pocket again on an afterthought.*]

WALTER [*without even looking at his son, still staring hard at his wife*]: In fact, here's another fifty cents . . . Buy yourself some fruit today—or take a taxi cab to school or something!

TRAVIS: Whoopee—

[*He leaps up and clasps his father around the middle with his legs, and they face each other in mutual appreciation; slowly* WALTER LEE *peeks around the boy to catch the violent rays from his wife's eyes and draws his head back as if shot.*]

WALTER: You better get down now—and get to school, man.

TRAVIS [*at the door*]: O.K. Good-bye. [*He exits.*]

WALTER [*after him, pointing with pride*]: That's *my* boy. [*She looks at him in disgust and turns back to her work.*] You know what I was thinking 'bout in the bathroom this morning?

RUTH: No.

WALTER: How come you always try to be so pleasant!

RUTH: What is there to be pleasant 'bout!

WALTER: You want to know what I was thinking 'bout in the bathroom or not!

RUTH: I know what you was thinking 'bout.

WALTER [*ignoring her*]: 'Bout what me and Willy Harris was talking about last night.

RUTH [*immediately—a refrain*]: Willy Harris is a good-for-nothing loud mouth.

WALTER: Anybody who talks to me has got to be a good-for-nothing loud mouth, ain't he? And what you know about who is just a good-for-nothing loud mouth? Charlie Atkins was just a "good-for-nothing loud mouth" too, wasn't he! When he wanted me to go in the dry-cleaning business with him. And now—he's grossing a hundred thousand a year. A hundred thousand dollars a year! You still call *him* a loud mouth!

RUTH [*bitterly*]: Oh, Walter Lee . . .

[*She folds her head on her arms over on the table.*]

WALTER [*rising and coming to her and standing over her*]: You tired, ain't you? Tired of everything. Me, the boy, the way we live—this beat-up hole—everything. Ain't you? [*She doesn't look up, doesn't answer.*] So tired—moaning and groaning all the time, but you wouldn't do nothing to help, would you? You couldn't be on my side that long for nothing, could you?

RUTH: Walter, please leave me alone.

WALTER: A man needs for a woman to back him up . . .

RUTH: Walter—

WALTER: Mama would listen to you. You know she listen to you more than she do me and Bennie. She think more of you. All you have to do is just sit down with her when you drinking your coffee one morning and talking 'bout things like you do and—[*He sits down beside her and demonstrates graphically what he thinks her methods and tone should be.*]—you just sip your coffee, see, and say easy like that you been thinking 'bout that deal Walter Lee is so interested in, 'bout the store and all, and sip some more coffee, like what you saying ain't really that important to you—And the next thing you know, she be listening good and asking you questions and when I come home—I can tell her the details. This ain't no fly-by-night proposition, baby. I mean we figured it out, me and Willy and Bobo.

RUTH [*with a frown*]: Bobo?

WALTER: Yeah. You see, this little liquor store we got in mind cost seventy-five thousand and we figured the initial investment on the place be 'bout thirty thousand, see. That be ten thousand each. Course, there's a couple of hundred you got to pay so's you don't spend your life just waiting for them clowns to let your license get approved—

RUTH: You mean graft?

WALTER [*frowning impatiently*]: Don't call it that. See there, that just goes to show you what women understand about the world. Baby, don't *nothing* happen for you in this world 'less you pay *somebody* off!

RUTH: Walter, leave me alone! [*She raises her head and stares at him vigorously—then says, more quietly.*] Eat your eggs, they gonna be cold.

WALTER [*straightening up from her and looking off*]: That's it. There you are. Man say to his woman: I got me a dream. His woman say: Eat your eggs. [*Sadly, but gaining in power.*] Man say: I got to take hold of this here world, baby! And a woman will say: Eat your eggs and go to work. [*Passionately now.*] Man say: I got to change my life,

I'm choking to death, baby! And his woman say—[*In utter anguish as he brings his fists down on his thighs.*]—Your eggs is getting cold!

RUTH [*softly*]: Walter, that ain't none of our money.

WALTER [*not listening at all or even looking at her*]: This morning, I was lookin' in the mirror and thinking about it . . . I'm thirty-five years old; I been married eleven years and I got a boy who sleeps in the living room—[*Very, very quietly.*]—and all I got to give him is stories about how rich white people live . . . .

RUTH: Eat your eggs, Walter.

WALTER: *Damn my eggs . . . damn all the eggs that ever was!*

RUTH: Then go to work.

WALTER [*looking up at her*]: See—I'm trying to talk to you 'bout myself—[*Shaking his head with the repetition.*]—and all you can say is eat them eggs and go to work.

RUTH [*wearily*]: Honey, you never say nothing new. I listen to you every day, every night and every morning and you never say nothing new. [*Shrugging.*] So you would rather *be* Mr. Arnold than be his chauffeur. So—I would *rather* be living in Buckingham Palace.

WALTER: That is just what is wrong with the colored woman in this world . . . Don't understand about building their men up and making 'em feel like they somebody. Like they can do something.

RUTH [*drily, but to hurt*]: There *are* colored men who do things.

WALTER: No thanks to the colored woman.

RUTH: Well, being a colored woman, I guess I can't help myself none.

[*She rises and gets the ironing board and sets it up and attacks a huge pile of rough-dried clothes, sprinkling them in preparation for the ironing and then rolling them into tight fat balls.*]

WALTER [*mumbling*]: We one group of men tied to a race of women with small minds.

[*His sister* BENEATHA *enters. She is about twenty, as slim and intense as her brother. She is not as pretty as her sister-in-law, but her lean, almost intellectual face has a handsomeness of its own. She wears a bright-red flannel nightie, and her thick hair stands wildly about her head. Her speech is a mixture of many things; it is different from the rest of the family's insofar as education has permeated her sense of English—and perhaps the Midwest rather than the South has finally—at last—won out in her inflection; but not altogether, because over all of it is a soft slurring and transformed use of vowels which is the decided influence of the Southside. She passes through the room without looking at either* RUTH *or* WALTER *and goes to the outside door and looks, a little blindly, out to the bathroom. She sees that it has been lost to the Johnsons. She closes the door with a sleepy vengeance and crosses to the table and sits down a little defeated.*]

BENEATHA: I am going to start timing those people.

WALTER: You should get up earlier.

BENEATHA [*her face in her hands. She is still fighting the urge to go back to bed*]: Really—would you suggest dawn? Where's the paper?

WALTER [*pushing the paper across the table to her as he studies her almost clinically, as though he has never seen her before*]: You a horrible-looking chick at this hour.

BENEATHA [*drily*]: Good morning everybody.

WALTER [*senselessly*]: How is school coming?

BENEATHA [*in the same spirit*]: Lovely. Lovely. And you know, biology is the greatest. [*Looking up at him.*] I dissected something that looked just like you yesterday.

WALTER: I just wondered if you've made up your mind and everything.

BENEATHA [*gaining in sharpness and impatience*]: And what did I answer yesterday morning—and the day before that?

RUTH [*from the ironing board, like someone disinterested and old*]: Don't be so nasty, Bennie.

BENEATHA [*still to her brother*]: And the day before that and the day before that!

WALTER [*defensively*]: I'm interested in you. Something wrong with that? Ain't many girls who decide—

WALTER *and* BENEATHA [*in unison*]: —"to be a doctor."

[*Silence.*]

WALTER: Have we figured out yet just exactly how much medical school is going to cost?

RUTH: Walter Lee, why don't you leave that girl alone and get out of here to work?

BENEATHA [*exits to the bathroom and bangs on the door*]: Come on out of there, please! [*She comes back into the room.*]

WALTER [*looking at his sister intently*]: You know the check is coming tomorrow.

BENEATHA [*turning on him with a sharpness all her own*]: That money belongs to Mama, Walter, and it's for her to decide how she wants to use it. I don't care if she wants to buy a house or a rocket ship or just nail it up somewhere and look at it. It's hers. Not ours—*hers*.

WALTER [*bitterly*]: Now ain't that fine! You just got your mother's interest at heart, ain't you, girl? You such a nice girl—but if Mama got that money she can always take a few thousand and help you through school too—can't she?

BENEATHA: I have never asked anyone around here to do anything for me!

WALTER: No! And the line between asking and just accepting when the time comes is big and wide—ain't it!

BENEATHA [*with fury*]: What do you want from me, Brother—that I quit school or just drop dead, which!

WALTER: I don't want nothing but for you to stop acting holy 'round here. Me and Ruth done made some sacrifices for you—why can't you do something for the family?

RUTH: Walter, don't be dragging me in it.

WALTER: You are in it—Don't you get up and go work in somebody's kitchen for the last three years to help put clothes on her back?

RUTH: Oh, Walter—that's not fair . . .

WALTER: It ain't that nobody expects you to get on your knees and say thank you, Brother; thank you, Ruth; thank you Mama—and thank you, Travis, for wearing the same pair of shoes for two semesters—

BENEATHA [*dropping to her knees*]: Well—I *do*—all right?—thank everybody . . . and forgive me for ever wanting to be anything at all . . . forgive me, forgive me!

RUTH: Please stop it! Your mama'll hear you.

WALTER: Who the hell told you you had to be a doctor? If you so crazy 'bout messing 'round with sick people—then go be a nurse like other women—or just get married and be quiet . . .

BENEATHA: Well—you finally got it said . . . It took you three years but you finally got it said. Walter, give up; leave me alone—it's Mama's money.

WALTER: *He was my father, too!*

BENEATHA: So what? He was mine, too—and Travis' grandfather—but the insurance money belongs to Mama. Picking on me is not going to make her give it to you to invest in any liquor stores—[*Underbreath, dropping into a chair.*]—and I for one say, God bless Mama for that!

WALTER [*to* RUTH]: See—did you hear? Did you hear!

RUTH: Honey, please go to work.

WALTER: Nobody in this house is ever going to understand me.

BENEATHA: Because you're a nut.

WALTER: Who's a nut?

BENEATHA: You—you are a nut. Thee is mad, boy.

WALTER [*looking at his wife and his sister from the door, very sadly*]: The world's most backward race of people, and that's a fact.

BENEATHA [*turning slowly in her chair.*]: And then there are all those prophets who would lead us out of the wilderness—[WALTER *slams out of the house.*]—into the swamps!

RUTH: Bennie, why you always gotta be pickin' on your brother? Can't you be a little sweeter sometimes? [*Door opens.* WALTER *walks in.*]

WALTER [*to* RUTH]: I need some money for carfare.

RUTH [*looks at him, then warms; teasing, but tenderly*]: Fifty cents? [*She goes to her bag and gets money.*] Here, take a taxi.

[WALTER *exits.* MAMA *enters. She is a woman in her early sixties, full-bodied and strong. She is one of those women of a certain grace and beauty who wear it so unobtrusively that it takes a while to notice. Her dark-brown face is surrounded by the total whiteness of her hair, and, being a woman who has adjusted to many things in life and overcome many more, her face is full of strength. She has, we can see, wit and faith of a kind that keep her eyes lit and full of interest and expectancy. She is, in a word, a beautiful woman. Her bearing is perhaps most like the noble bearing of the women of the Hereros of Southwest Africa—rather as if she imagines that as she walks she still bears a basket or a vessel upon her head. Her speech, on the other hand, is as careless as her carriage is precise—she is inclined to slur everything—but her voice is perhaps not so much quiet as simply soft.*]

MAMA: Who that 'round here slamming doors at this hour?

[*She crosses through the room, goes to the window, opens it, and brings in a feeble little plant growing doggedly in a small pot on the window sill. She feels the dirt and puts it back out.*]

RUTH: That was Walter Lee. He and Bennie was at it again.

MAMA: My children and they tempers. Lord, if this little old plant don't get more sun than it's been getting it ain't never going to see spring again. [*She turns from the window.*]

What's the matter with you this morning, Ruth? You looks right peaked. You aiming to iron all them things? Leave some for me. I'll get to 'em this afternoon. Bennie honey, it's too drafty for you to be sitting 'round half dressed. Where's your robe?

BENEATHA: In the cleaners.

MAMA: Well, go get mine and put it on.

BENEATHA: I'm not cold, Mama, honest.

MAMA: I know—but you so thin . . .

BENEATHA [*irritably*]: Mama, I'm not cold.

MAMA [*seeing the make-down bed as* TRAVIS *has left it*]: Lord have mercy, look at that poor bed. Bless his heart—he tries, don't he? [*She moves to the bed* TRAVIS *has sloppily made up.*]

RUTH: No—he don't half try at all 'cause he knows you going to come along behind him and fix everything. That's just how come he don't know how to do nothing right now—you done spoiled that boy so.

MAMA: Well—he's a little boy. Ain't supposed to know 'bout housekeeping. My baby, that's what he is. What you fix for his breakfast this morning?

RUTH [*angrily*]: I feed my son, Lena!

MAMA: I ain't meddling—[*Underbreath; busybodyish.*]I just noticed all last week he had cold cereal, and when it starts getting this chilly in the fall a child ought to have some hot grits or something when he goes out in the cold—

RUTH [*furious*]: I gave him hot oats—is that all right!

MAMA: I ain't meddling. [*Pause.*] Put a lot of nice butter on it? [RUTH *shoots her an angry look and does not reply.*] He likes lots of butter.

RUTH [*exasperated*]: Lena—

MAMA [*to* BENEATHA. MAMA *is inclined to wander conversationally sometimes*]: What was you and your brother fussing 'bout this morning?

BENEATHA: It's not important, Mama. [*She gets up and goes to look out at the bathroom, which is apparently free, and she picks up her towels and rushes out.*]

MAMA: What was they fighting about?

RUTH: Now you know as well as I do.

MAMA [*shaking her head*]: Brother still worrying hisself sick about that money?

RUTH: You know he is.

MAMA: You had breakfast?

RUTH: Some coffee.

MAMA: Girl, you better start eating and looking after yourself better. You almost thin as Travis.

RUTH: Lena—

MAMA: Uh-hunh?

RUTH: What are you going to do with it?

MAMA: Now don't you start, child. It's too early in the morning to be talking about money. It ain't Christian.

RUTH: It's just that he got his heart set on that store—

MAMA: You mean that liquor store that Willy Harris want him to invest in?

RUTH: Yes—

MAMA: We ain't no business people, Ruth. We just plain working folks.

RUTH: Ain't nobody business people till they go into business. Walter Lee say colored people ain't never going to start getting ahead till they start gambling on some different kinds of things in the world—investments and things.

MAMA: What done got into you, girl? Walter Lee done finally sold you on investing.

RUTH: No. Mama, something is happening between Walter and me. I don't know what it is—but he needs something—something I can't give him any more. He needs this chance, Lena.

MAMA [*frowning deeply*]: But liquor, honey—

RUTH: Well—like Walter say—I spec people going to always be drinking themselves some liquor.

MAMA: Well—whether they drinks it or not ain't none of my business. But whether I go into business selling it to 'em *is,* and I don't want that on my ledger this late in life. [*Stopping suddenly and studying her daughter-in-law.*] Ruth Younger, what's the matter with you today? You look like you could fall over right there.

RUTH: I'm tired.

MAMA: Then you better stay home from work today.

RUTH: I can't stay home. She'd be calling up the agency and screaming at them, "My girl didn't come in today—send me somebody! My girl didn't come in!" Oh, she just have a fit . . .

MAMA: Well, let her have it. I'll just call her up and say you got the flu—

RUTH [*laughing*]: Why the flu?

MAMA: 'Cause it sounds respectable to 'em. Something white people get, too. They know 'bout the flu. Otherwise they think you been cut up or something when you tell 'em you sick.

RUTH: I got to go in. We need the money.

MAMA: Somebody would of thought my children done all but starved to death the way they talk about money here late. Child, we got a great big old check coming tomorrow.

RUTH [*sincerely, but also self-righteously*]: Now that's your money. It ain't got nothing to do with me. We all feel like that—Walter and Bennie and me—even Travis.

MAMA [*thoughtfully, and suddenly very far away*]: Ten thousand dollars—

RUTH: Sure is wonderful.

MAMA: Ten thousand dollars.

RUTH: You know what you should do, Miss Lena? You should take yourself a trip somewhere. To Europe or South America or someplace—

MAMA [*throwing up her hands at the thought*]: Oh child!

RUTH: I'm serious. Just pack up and leave! Go on away and enjoy yourself some. Forget about the family and have yourself a ball for once in your life—

MAMA [*drily*]: You sound like I'm just about ready to die. Who'd go with me? What I look like wandering 'round Europe by myself?

RUTH: Shoot—these here rich white women do it all the time. They don't think nothing of packing up they suitcases and piling on one of them big steamships and—swoosh!—they gone, child.

MAMA: Something always told me I wasn't no rich white woman.

RUTH: Well—what are you going to do with it then?

MAMA: I ain't rightly decided. [*Thinking. She speaks now with emphasis.*] Some of it got to be put away for Beneatha and her schoolin'—and ain't nothing going to touch that part of it. Nothing. [*She waits several seconds, trying to make up her mind about something, and looks at* RUTH *a little tentatively before going on.*] Been thinking that we maybe could meet the notes on a little old two-story somewhere, with a yard where Travis could play in the summertime, if we use part of the insurance for a down payment and everybody kind of pitch in. I could maybe take on a little day work again, few days a week—

RUTH [*studying her mother-in-law furtively and concentrating on her ironing, anxious to encourage without seeming to*]: Well, Lord knows, we've put enough rent into this here rat trap to pay for four houses by now . . .

MAMA [*looking up at the words "rat trap" and then looking around and leaning back and sighing—in a suddenly reflective mood—*]: "Rat trap"—yes, that's all it is. [*Smiling.*] I remember just as well the day me and Big Walter moved in here. Hadn't been married but two weeks and wasn't planning on living here no more than a year. [*She shakes her head at the dissolved dream.*] We was going to set away, little by little, don't you know, and buy a little place out in Morgan Park. We had even picked out the house. [*Chuckling a little.*] Looks right dumpy today. But Lord, child, you should know all the dreams I had 'bout buying that house and fixing it up and making me a little garden in the back—[*She waits and stops smiling.*] And didn't none of it happen. [*Dropping her hands in a futile gesture.*]

RUTH [*keeps her head down, ironing*]: Yes, life can be a barrel of disappointments, sometimes.

MAMA: Honey, Big Walter would come in here some nights back then and slump down on that couch there and just look at the rug, and look at me and look at the rug and then back at me—and I'd know he was down then . . . really down. [*After a second very long and thoughtful pause; she is seeing back to times that only she can see.*] And then, Lord, when I lost that baby—little Claude—I almost thought I was going to lose Big Walter too. Oh, that man grieved hisself! He was one man to love his children.

RUTH: Ain't nothin' can tear at you like losin' your baby.

MAMA: I guess that's how come that man finally worked hisself to death like he done. Like he was fighting his own war with this here world that took his baby from him.

RUTH: He sure was a fine man, all right. I always liked Mr. Younger.

MAMA: Crazy 'bout his children! God knows there was plenty wrong with Walter Younger—hard-headed, mean, kind of wild with women—plenty wrong with him. But he sure loved his children. Always wanted them to have something—be something. That's where Brother gets all these notions, I reckon. Big Walter used to say, he'd get right wet in the eyes sometimes, lean his head back with the water standing in his eyes and say, "Seem like God didn't see fit to give the black man nothing but dreams—but He did give us children to make them dreams seem worth while." [*She smiles.*] He could talk like that, don't you know.

RUTH: Yes, he sure could. He was a good man, Mr. Younger.

MAMA: Yes, a fine man—just couldn't never catch up with his dreams, that's all.

[BENEATHA *comes in, brushing her hair and looking up to the ceiling, where the sound of a vacuum cleaner has started up.*]

BENEATHA: What could be so dirty on that woman's rugs that she has to vacuum them every single day?

RUTH: I wish certain young women 'round here who I could name would take inspiration about certain rugs in a certain apartment I could also mention.

BENEATHA [*shrugging*]: How much cleaning can a house need, for Christ's sakes.

MAMA [*not liking the Lord's name used thus*]: Bennie!

RUTH: Just listen to her—just listen!

BENEATHA: Oh, God!

MAMA: If you use the Lord's name just one more time—

BENEATHA [*a bit of a whine*]: Oh, Mama—

RUTH: Fresh—just fresh as salt, this girl!

BENEATHA [*drily*]: Well—if the salt loses its savor—

MAMA: Now that will do. I just ain't going to have you 'round here reciting the scriptures in vain—you hear me?

BENEATHA: How did I manage to get on everybody's wrong side by just walking into a room?

RUTH: If you weren't so fresh—

BENEATHA: Ruth, I'm twenty years old.

MAMA: What time you be home from school today?

BENEATHA: Kind of late. [*With enthusiasm.*] Madeline is going to start my guitar lessons today.

[MAMA *and* RUTH *look up with the same expression.*]

MAMA: Your *what* kind of lessons?

BENEATHA: Guitar.

RUTH: Oh, Father!

MAMA: How come you done taken it in your mind to learn to play the guitar?

BENEATHA: I just want to, that's all.

MAMA [*smiling*]: Lord, child, don't you know what to do with yourself? How long it going to be before you get tired of this now—like you got tired of that little play-acting group you joined last year? [*Looking at* RUTH.] And what was it the year before that?

RUTH: The horseback-riding club for which she bought that fifty-five-dollar riding habit that's been hanging in the closet ever since!

MAMA [*to* BENEATHA]: Why you got to flit so from one thing to another, baby?

BENEATHA [*sharply*]: I just want to learn to play the guitar. Is there anything wrong with that?

MAMA: Ain't nobody trying to stop you. I just wonders sometimes why you has to flit so from one thing to another all the time. You ain't never done nothing with all that camera equipment you brought home—

BENEATHA: I don't flit! I—I experiment with different forms of expression—

RUTH: Like riding a horse?

BENEATHA: —People have to express themselves one way or another.

MAMA: What is it you want to express?

BENEATHA [*angrily*]: Me! [MAMA *and* RUTH *look at each other and burst into raucous laughter.*] Don't worry—I don't expect you to understand.

MAMA [*to change the subject*]: Who you going out with tomorrow night?

BENEATHA [*with displeasure*]: George Murchison again.

MAMA [*pleased*]: Oh—you getting a little sweet on him?

RUTH: You ask me, this child ain't sweet on nobody but herself—[*Underbreath.*] Express herself!

[*They laugh.*]

BENEATHA: Oh—I like George all right, Mama. I mean I like him enough to go out with him and stuff, but—

RUTH [*for devilment*]: What does *and stuff* mean?

BENEATHA: Mind your own business.

MAMA: Stop picking at her now, Ruth. [*A thoughtful pause, and then a suspicious sudden look at her daughter as she turns in her chair for emphasis.*] What *does* it mean?

BENEATHA [*wearily*]: Oh, I just mean I couldn't ever really be serious about George. He's—he's so shallow.

RUTH: Shallow—what do you mean he's shallow? He's *Rich!*

MAMA: Hush, Ruth.

BENEATHA: I know he's rich. He knows he's rich, too.

RUTH: Well—what other qualities a man got to have to satisfy you, little girl?

BENEATHA: You wouldn't even begin to understand. Anybody who married Walter could not possibly understand.

MAMA [*outraged*]: What kind of way is that to talk about your brother?

BENEATHA: Brother is a flip—let's face it.

MAMA [*to* RUTH, *helplessly*]: What's a flip?

RUTH [*glad to add kindling*]: She's saying he's crazy.

BENEATHA: Not crazy. Brother isn't really crazy yet—he—he's an elaborate neurotic.

MAMA: Hush your mouth!

BENEATHA: As for George. Well. George looks good—he's got a beautiful car and he takes me to nice places and, as my sister-in-law says, he is probably the richest boy I will ever get to know and I even like him sometimes—but if the Youngers are sitting around waiting to see if their little Bennie is going to tie up the family with the Murchisons, they are wasting their time.

RUTH: You mean you wouldn't marry George Murchison if he asked you someday? That pretty, rich thing? Honey, I knew you was odd—

BENEATHA: No I would not marry him if all I felt for him was what I feel now. Besides, George's family wouldn't really like it.

MAMA: Why not?

BENEATHA: Oh, Mama—the Murchisons are honest-to-God-real-*live*-rich colored people, and the only people in the world who are more snobbish than rich white people are rich colored people. I thought everybody knew that. I've met Mrs. Murchison. She's a scene!

MAMA: You must not dislike people 'cause they well off, honey.

BENEATHA: Why not? It makes just as much sense as disliking people 'cause they are poor, and lots of people do that.

RUTH [*a wisdom-of-the-ages manner. To* MAMA]: Well, she'll get over some of this—

BENEATHA: Get over it? What are you talking about, Ruth? Listen, I'm going to be a doctor. I'm not worried about who I'm going to marry yet—if I ever get married.

MAMA *and* RUTH: *If!*

MAMA: Now, Bennie—

BENEATHA: Oh, I probably will . . . but first I'm going to be a doctor, and George, for one, still thinks that's pretty funny. I couldn't be bothered with that. I am going to be a doctor and everybody around here better understand that!

MAMA [*kindly*]: 'Course you going to be a doctor, honey, God willing.

BENEATHA [*drily*]: God hasn't got a thing to do with it.

MAMA: Beneatha—that just wasn't necessary.

BENEATHA: Well—neither is God. I get sick of hearing about God.

MAMA: Beneatha!

BENEATHA: I mean it! I'm just tired of hearing about God all the time. What has He got to do with anything? Does He pay tuition?

MAMA: You 'bout to get your fresh little jaw slapped!

RUTH: That's just what she needs, all right!

BENEATHA: Why? Why can't I say what I want to around here, like everybody else?

MAMA: It don't sound nice for a young girl to say things like that—you wasn't brought up that way. Me and your father went to trouble to get you and Brother to church every Sunday.

BENEATHA: Mama, you don't understand. It's all a matter of ideas, and God is just one idea I don't accept. It's not important. I am not going out and be immoral or commit crimes because I don't believe in God. I don't even think about it. It's just that I get tired of Him getting credit for all the things the human race achieves through its own stubborn effort. There simply is no blasted God—there is only man and it is he who makes miracles!

[MAMA *absorbs this speech, studies her daughter and rises slowly and crosses to* BENEATHA *and slaps her powerfully across the face. After, there is only silence and the daughter drops her eyes from her mother's face, and* MAMA *is very tall before her.*]

MAMA: Now—you say after me, in my mother's house there is still God. [*There is a long pause and* BENEATHA *stares at the floor wordlessly.* MAMA *repeats the phrase with precision and cool emotion.*] In my mother's house there is still God.

BENEATHA: In my mother's house there is still God. [*A long pause.*]

MAMA [*walking away from* BENEATHA, *too disturbed for triumphant posture. Stopping and turning back to her daughter*]: There are some ideas we ain't going to have in this house. Not long as I am at the head of this family.

BENEATHA: Yes, ma'am.

[MAMA *walks out of the room.*]

RUTH [*almost gently, with profound understanding*]: You think you a woman, Bennie—but you still a little girl. What you did was childish—so you got treated like a child.

BENEATHA: I see. [*Quietly.*] I also see that everybody thinks it's all right for Mama to be a tyrant. But all the tyranny in the world will never put a God in the heavens!

[*She picks up her books and goes out.*]

RUTH [*goes to* MAMA'*s door*]: She said she was sorry.

MAMA [*coming out, going to her plant*]: They frightens me, Ruth. My children.

RUTH: You got good children, Lena. They just a little off sometimes—but they're good.

MAMA: No—there's something come down between me and them that don't let us understand each other and I don't know what it is. One done almost lost his mind thinking 'bout money all the time and the other done commence to talk about things I can't seem to understand in no form or fashion. What is it that's changing, Ruth?

RUTH [*soothingly, older than her years*]: Now . . . you taking it all too seriously. You just got strong-willed children and it takes a strong woman like you to keep 'em in hand.

MAMA [*looking at her plant and sprinkling a little water on it*]: They spirited all right, my children. Got to admit they got spirit—Bennie and Walter. Like this little old plant that ain't never had enough sunshine or nothing—and look at it . . .

[*She has her back to* RUTH, *who has had to stop ironing and lean against something and put the back of her hand to her forehead.*]

RUTH [*trying to keep* MAMA *from noticing*]: You . . . sure . . . loves that little old thing, don't you? . . .

MAMA: Well, I always wanted me a garden like I used to see sometimes at the back of the houses down home. This plant is close as I ever got to having one. [*She looks out of the window as she replaces the plant.*] Lord, ain't nothing as dreary as the view from this window on a dreary day, is there? Why ain't you singing this morning, Ruth? Sing that "No Ways Tired." That song always lifts me up so—[*She turns at last to see that* RUTH *has slipped quietly into a chair, in a state of semiconsciousness.*] Ruth! Ruth honey—what's the matter with you . . . Ruth!

SCENE 2

It is the following morning; a Saturday morning and house cleaning is in progress at the YOUNGERS. *Furniture has been shoved hither and yon and* MAMA *is giving the kitchen-area walls a washing down.* BENEATHA, *in dungarees, with a handkerchief tied around her face, is spraying insecticide into the cracks in the walls. As they work, the radio is on and a Southside disk-jockey program is inappropriately filling the house with a rather exotic saxophone blues.* TRAVIS, *the sole idle one, is leaning on his arms, looking out of the window.*

TRAVIS: Grandmama, that stuff Bennie is using smells awful. Can I go downstairs, please?

MAMA: Did you get all them chores done already? I ain't seen you doing much.

TRAVIS: Yes'm—finished early. Where did Mama go this morning?

MAMA [*looking at* BENEATHA]: She had to go on a little errand.

TRAVIS: Where?

MAMA: To tend to her business.

TRAVIS: Can I go outside then?

MAMA: Oh, I guess so. You better stay right in front of the house, though . . . and keep a good lookout for the postman.

TRAVIS: Yes'm [*He starts out and decides to give his* AUNT BENEATHA *a good swat on the legs as he passes her.*] Leave them poor little old cockroaches alone, they ain't bothering you none.

[*He runs as she swings the spray gun at him both viciously and playfully.* WALTER *enters from the bedroom and goes to the phone.*]

MAMA: Look out there, girl, before you be spilling some of that stuff on that child!

TRAVIS [*teasing*]: That's right—look out now!

[*He exits.*]

BENEATHA [*drily*]: I can't imagine that it would hurt him—it has never hurt the roaches.

MAMA: Well, little boys' hides ain't as tough as Southside roaches.

WALTER [*into phone*]: Hello—Let me talk to Willy Harris.

MAMA: You better get over there behind the bureau. I seen one marching out of there like Napoleon yesterday.

WALTER: Hello, Willy? It ain't come yet. It'll be here in a few minutes. Did the lawyer give you the papers?

BENEATHA: There's really only one way to get rid of them, Mama—

MAMA: How?

BENEATHA: Set fire to this building.

WALTER: Good. Good. I'll be right over.

BENEATHA: Where did Ruth go, Walter?

WALTER: I don't know. [*He exits abruptly.*]

BENEATHA: Mama, where did Ruth go?

MAMA [*looking at her with meaning*]: To the doctor, I think.

BENEATHA: The doctor? What's the matter. [*They exchange glances.*] You don't think—

MAMA [*with her sense of drama*]: Now I ain't saying what I think. But I ain't never been wrong 'bout a woman neither.

[*The phone rings.*]

BENEATHA [*at the phone*]: Hay-lo . . . [*Pause, and a moment of recognition.*] Well—when did you get back! . . . And how was it? . . . Of course I've missed you—in my way . . . This morning? No . . . house cleaning and all that and Mama hates it if I let people come over when the house is like this . . . You *have?* Well, that's different . . . What is it—Oh, what the hell, come on over . . . Right, see you then. [*She hangs up.*]

MAMA [*who has listened vigorously, as is her habit*]: Who is that you inviting over here with this house looking like this? You ain't got the pride you was born with!

BENEATHA: Asagai doesn't care how houses look, Mama—he's an intellectual.

MAMA: *Who?*

BENEATHA: Asagai—Joseph Asagai. He's an African boy I met on campus. He's been studying in Canada all summer.

MAMA: What's his name?

BENEATHA: Asagai, Joseph. Ah-sah-guy . . . He's from Nigeria.

MAMA: Oh, that's the little country that was founded by slaves way back . . .

BENEATHA: No, Mama—that's Liberia.

MAMA: I don't think I never met no African before.

BENEATHA: Well, do me a favor and don't ask him a whole lot of ignorant questions about Africans. I mean, do they wear clothes and all that—

MAMA: Well, now, I guess if you think we so ignorant 'round here maybe you shouldn't bring your friends here—

BENEATHA: It's just that people ask such crazy things. All anyone seems to know about when it comes to Africa is Tarzan—

MAMA [*indignantly*]: Why should I know anything about Africa?

BENEATHA: Why do you give money at church for the missionary work?

MAMA: Well, that's to help save people.

BENEATHA: You mean save them from *heathenism*—

MAMA [*innocently*]: Yes.

BENEATHA: I'm afraid they need more salvation from the British and the French.

[RUTH *comes in forlornly and pulls off her coat with dejection. They both turn to look at her.*]

RUTH [*dispiritedly*]: Well, I guess from all the happy faces—everybody knows.

BENEATHA: You pregnant?

MAMA: Lord have mercy, I sure hope it's a little old girl. Travis ought to have a sister.

[BENEATHA *and* RUTH *give her a hopeless look for this grandmotherly enthusiasm.*]

BENEATHA: How far along are you?

RUTH: Two months.

BENEATHA: Did you mean to? I mean did you plan it or was it an accident?

MAMA: What do you know about planning or not planning?

BENEATHA: Oh, Mama.

RUTH [*wearily*]: She's twenty years old, Lena.

BENEATHA: Did you plan it, Ruth?

RUTH: Mind your own business.

BENEATHA: It is my business—where is he going to live, on the *roof?* [*There is silence following the remark as the three women react to the sense of it.*] Gee—I didn't mean that, Ruth, honest. Gee, I don't feel like that at all. I—I think it is wonderful.

RUTH [*dully*]: Wonderful.

BENEATHA: Yes—really.

MAMA [*looking at* RUTH, *worried*]: Doctor say everything going to be all right?

RUTH [*far away*]: Yes—she says everything is going to be fine . . .

MAMA [*immediately suspicious*]: "She"—What doctor you went to?

[RUTH *folds over, near hysteria.*]

MAMA [*worriedly hovering over* RUTH]: Ruth honey—what's the matter with you—you sick?

[RUTH *has her fists clenched on her thighs and is fighting hard to suppress a scream that seems to be rising in her.*]

BENEATHA: What's the matter with her, Mama?

MAMA [*working her fingers in* RUTH'S *shoulder to relax her*]: She be all right. Women gets right depressed sometimes when they get her way. [*Speaking softly, expertly, rapidly.*] Now you just relax. That's right . . . just lean back, don't think 'bout nothing at all . . . nothing at all—

RUTH: I'm all right . . .

[*The glassy-eyed look melts and then she collapses into a fit of heavy sobbing. The bell rings.*]

BENEATHA: Oh, my God—that must be Asagai.

MAMA [*To* RUTH]: Come on now, honey. You need to lie down and rest awhile . . . then have some nice hot food.

[*They exit,* RUTH'S *weight on her mother-in-law.* BENEATHA, *herself profoundly disturbed, opens the door to admit a rather dramatic-looking young man with a large package.*]

ASAGAI: Hello, Alaiyo—

BENEATHA [*holding the door open and regarding him with pleasure*]: Hello . . . [*Long pause.*] Well—come in. And please excuse everything. My mother was very upset about my letting anyone come here with the place like this.

ASAGAI [*coming into the room*]: You look disturbed too . . . Is something wrong?

BENEATHA [*still at the door, absently*]: Yes . . . we've all got acute ghetto-itus. [*She smiles and comes toward him, finding a cigarette and sitting.*] So—sit down! How was Canada?

ASAGAI [*a sophisticate*]: Canadian.

BENEATHA [*looking at him*]: I'm very glad you are back.

ASAGAI [*looking back at her in turn*]: Are you really?

BENEATHA: Yes—very.

ASAGAI: Why—you were quite glad when I went away. What happened?

BENEATHA: You went away.

ASAGAI: Ahhhhhhhh.

BENEATHA: Before—you wanted to be so serious before there was time.

ASAGAI: How much time must there be before one knows what one feels?

BENEATHA [*stalling this particular conversation; her hands pressed together, in a deliberately childish gesture*]: What did you bring me?

ASAGAI [*handing her the package*]: Open it and see.

BENEATHA [*eagerly opening the package and drawing out some records and the colorful robes of a Nigerian woman*]: Oh, Asagai! . . . You got them for me! . . . How beautiful . . . and the records too! [*She lifts out the robes and runs to the mirror with them and holds the drapery up in front of herself.*]

ASAGAI [*coming to her at the mirror*]: I shall have to teach you how to drape it properly. [*He flings the material about her for the moment and stands back to look at her.*] Ah—*Oh-pay-pay-day oh-gbah-mu-shay.* [*A Yoruba exclamation for admiration.*] You wear it well . . . very well . . . mutilated hair and all.

BENEATHA [*turning suddenly*]: My hair—what's wrong with my hair?

ASAGAI [*shrugging*]: Were you born with it like that?

BENEATHA [*reaching up to touch it*]: No . . . of course not. [*She looks back to the mirror, disturbed.*]

ASAGAI [*smiling*]: How then?

BENEATHA: You know perfectly well how . . . as crinkly as yours . . . that's how.

ASAGAI: And it is ugly to you that way?

BENEATHA [*quickly*]: Oh, no—not ugly . . . [*More slowly, apologetically.*] But it's so hard to manage when it's well—raw.

ASAGAI: And so to accommodate that—you mutilate it every week?

BENEATHA: It's not mutilation!

ASAGAI [*laughing aloud at her seriousness*]: Oh . . . please! I am only teasing you because you are so very serious about these things. [*He stands back from her and folds his arms across his chest as he watches her pulling at her hair and frowning in the mirror.*] Do you remember the first time you met me at school? . . . [*He laughs.*] You came up to me and you said—and I thought you were the most serious little thing I had ever seen—you said: [*He imitates her.*] "Mr. Asagai—I want very much to talk with you. About Africa. You see, Mr. Asagai, I am looking for my *identity!*" [*He laughs.*]

BENEATHA [*turning to him, not laughing*]: Yes—[*Her face is quizzical, profoundly disturbed.*]

ASAGAI [*still teasing and reaching out and taking her face in his hands and turning her profile to him*]: Well . . . it is true that this is not so much a profile of a Hollywood queen as perhaps a queen of the Nile—[*A mock dismissal of the importance of the question.*] But what does it matter? Assimilationism is so popular in your country.

BENEATHA [*wheeling, passionately, sharply*]: I am not an assimilationist!

ASAGAI [*the protest hangs in the room for a moment and* ASAGAI *studies her, his laughter fading*]: Such a serious one. [*There is a pause.*] So—you like the robes? You must take excellent care of them—they are from my sister's personal wardrobe.

BENEATHA [*with incredulity*]: You—you sent all the way home—for me?

ASAGAI [*with charm*]: For you—I would do much more . . . Well, that is what I came for. I must go.

BENEATHA: Will you call me Monday?

ASAGAI: Yes . . . We have a great deal to talk about. I mean about identity and time and all that.

BENEATHA: Time?

ASAGAI: Yes. About how much time one needs to know what one feels.

BENEATHA: You never understood that there is more than one kind of feeling which can exist between a man and a woman—or, at least, there should be.

ASAGAI [*shaking his head negatively but gently*]: No. Between a man and a woman there need be only one kind of feeling. I have that for you . . . Now even . . . right this moment . . .

BENEATHA: I know—and by itself—it won't do. I can find that anywhere.

ASAGAI: For a woman it should be enough.

BENEATHA: I know—because that's what it says in all the novels that men write. But it isn't. Go ahead and laugh—but I'm not interested in being someone's little episode in America or—[*With feminine vengeance.*]—one of them! [ASAGAI *has burst into laughter again.*] That's funny as hell, huh!

ASAGAI: It's just that every American girl I have known has said that to me. White—black—in this you are all the same. And the same speech, too!

BENEATHA [*angrily*]: Yuk, yuk, yuk!

ASAGAI: It's how you can be sure that the world's most liberated women are not liberated at all. You all talk about it too much!

[MAMA *enters and is immediately all social charm because of the presence of a guest.*]

BENEATHA: Oh—Mama—this is Mr. Asagai.

MAMA: How do you do?

ASAGAI [*total politeness to an elder*]: How do you do, Mrs. Younger. Please forgive me for coming at such an outrageous hour on a Saturday.

MAMA: Well, you are quite welcome. I just hope you understand that our house don't always look like this. [*Chatterish.*] You must come again. I would love to hear all about—[*Not sure of the name.*]—your country. I think it's so sad the way our American Negroes don't know nothing about Africa 'cept Tarzan and all that. And all that money they pour into these churches when they ought to be helping you people over there drive out them French and Englishmen done taken away your land. [*The mother flashes a slightly superior look at her daughter upon completion of the recitation.*]

ASAGAI [*taken aback by this sudden and acutely unrelated expression of sympathy*]: Yes . . . yes . . .

MAMA [*smiling at him suddenly and relaxing and looking him over*]: How many miles is it from here to where you come from?

ASAGAI: Many thousands.

MAMA [*looking at him as she would* WALTER]: I bet you don't half look after yourself, being away from your mama either. I spec you better come 'round here from time to time and get yourself some decent home-cooked meals . . .

ASAGAI [*moved*]: Thank you. Thank you very much. [*They are all quiet, then—.*] Well . . . I must go. I will call you Monday, Alaiyo.

MAMA: What's that he call you?

ASAGAI: Oh—"Alaiyo." I hope you don't mind. It is what you would call a nickname, I think. It is a Yoruba word. I am a Yoruba.

MAMA [*looking at* BENEATHA]: I—I thought he was from—

ASAGAI [*understanding*]: Nigeria is my country. Yoruba is my tribal origin—

BENEATHA: You didn't tell us what Alaiyo means . . . for all I know, you might be calling me Little Idiot or something . . .

ASAGAI: Well . . . let me see . . . I do not know how just to explain it . . . The sense of a thing can be so different when it changes languages.

BENEATHA: You're evading.

ASAGAI: No—really it is difficult . . . [*Thinking.*] It means . . . it means One for Whom Bread—Food—Is Not Enough. [*He looks at her.*] Is that all right?

BENEATHA [*understanding, softly*]: Thank you.

MAMA [*looking from one to the other and not understanding any of it*]: Well . . . that's nice . . . You must come see us again—Mr.—

ASAGAI: Ah-sah-guy . . .

MAMA: Yes . . . Do come again.

ASAGAI: Good-bye. [*He exits.*]

MAMA [*after him*]: Lord, that's a pretty thing just went out here! [*Insinuatingly, to her daughter.*] Yes, I guess I see why we done commence to get so interested in Africa 'round here. Missionaries my aunt Jenny! [*She exits.*]

BENEATHA: Oh, Mama! . . . [*She picks up the Nigerian dress and holds it up to her in front of the mirror again. She sets the headdress on haphazardly and then notices her hair again and clutches at it and then replaces the headdress and frowns at herself. Then she starts to wriggle in front of the mirror as she thinks a Nigerian woman might.* TRAVIS *enters and regards her.*]

TRAVIS: You cracking up?

BENEATHA: Shut up. [*She pulls the headdress off and looks at herself in the mirror and clutches at her hair again and squinches her eyes as if trying to imagine something. Then, suddenly, she gets her raincoat and kerchief and hurriedly prepares for going out.*]

MAMA [*coming back into the room*]: She's resting now. Travis, baby, run next door and ask Miss Johnson to please let me have a little kitchen cleanser. This here can is empty as Jacob's kettle.

TRAVIS: I just came in.

MAMA: Do as you told. [*He exits and she looks at her daughter.*] Where you going?

BENEATHA [*halting at the door*]: To become a queen of the Nile! [*She exits in a breathless blaze of glory.* RUTH *appears in the bedroom doorway.*]

MAMA: Who told you to get up?

RUTH: Ain't nothing wrong with me to be lying in no bed for. Where did Bennie go?

MAMA [*drumming her fingers*]: Far as I could make out—to Egypt. [RUTH *just looks at her.*] What time is it getting to?

RUTH: Ten twenty. And the mailman going to ring that bell this morning just like he done every morning for the last umpteen years.

[TRAVIS *comes in with the cleanser can.*]

TRAVIS: She say to tell you that she don't have much.

MAMA [*angrily*]: Lord, some people I could name sure is tight-fisted! [*Directing her grandson.*] Mark two cans of cleanser down on the list there. If she that hard up for kitchen cleanser, I sure don't want to forget to get her none!

RUTH: Lena—maybe the woman is just short on cleanser—

MAMA [*not listening*]: —Much baking powder as she done borrowed from me all these years, she could of done gone into the baking business!

[*The bell sounds suddenly and sharply and all three are stunned—serious and silent—mid-speech. In spite of all the other conversations and distractions of the morning, this is what they have been waiting for, even* TRAVIS, *who looks helplessly from his mother to his grandmother.* RUTH *is the first to come to life again.*]

RUTH [*to* TRAVIS]: Get down them steps, boy!

[TRAVIS *snaps to life and flies out to get the mail.*]

MAMA [*her eyes wide, her hand to her breast*]: You mean it done really come?

RUTH [*excited*]: Oh, Miss Lena!

MAMA [*collecting herself*]: Well . . . I don't know what we all so excited about 'round here for. We known it was coming for months.

RUTH: That's a whole lot different from hoping it come and being able to hold it in your hands . . . a piece of paper worth ten thousand dollars . . . [TRAVIS *bursts back into the room. He holds the envelope high above his head, like a little dancer, his face is radiant and he is breathless. He moves to his grandmother with sudden slow ceremony and puts the envelope into her hands. She accepts it, and then merely holds it and looks at it.*] Come on! Open it . . . Lord have mercy, I wish Walter Lee was here!

TRAVIS: Open it, Grandmama!

MAMA [*staring at it*]: Now you all be quiet. It's just a check.

RUTH: Open it . . .

MAMA [*still staring at it*]: Now don't act silly . . . We ain't never been no people to act silly 'bout no money—

RUTH [*swiftly*]: We ain't never had none before—open it!

[MAMA *finally makes a good strong tear and pulls out the thin blue slice of paper and inspects it closely. The boy and his mother study it raptly over* MAMA's *shoulders.*]

MAMA: *Travis!* [*She is counting off with doubt.*] Is that the right number of zeros?

TRAVIS: Yes'm . . . ten thousand dollars. Gaalee, Grandmama, you rich.

MAMA [*she holds the check away from her, still looking at it; slowly her face sobers into a mask of unhappiness*]: Ten thousand dollars. [*She hands it to* RUTH.] Put it away somewhere, Ruth. [*She does not look at* RUTH; *her eyes seem to be seeing something somewhere very far off.*] Ten thousand dollars they give you. Ten thousand dollars.

TRAVIS [*to his mother, sincerely*]: What's the matter with Grandmama—don't she want to be rich?

RUTH [*distractedly*]: You go on out and play now, baby. [TRAVIS *exits.* MAMA *starts wiping dishes absently, humming intently to herself.* RUTH *turns to her, with kind exasperation.*] You've gone and got yourself upset.

MAMA [*not looking at her*]: I spec if it wasn't for you all . . . I would just put that money away or give it to the church or something.

RUTH: Now what kind of talk is that. Mr. Younger would just be plain mad if he could hear you talking foolish like that.

MAMA [*stopping and staring off*]: Yes . . . he sure would. [*Sighing.*] We got enough to do with that money, all right. [*She halts then, and turns and looks at her daughter-in-law hard;* RUTH *avoids her eyes and* MAMA *wipes her hands with finality and turns to speak firmly to* RUTH.] Where did you go today, girl?

RUTH: To the doctor.

MAMA [*impatiently*]: Now, Ruth . . . you know better than that. Old Doctor Jones is strange enough in his way but there ain't nothing 'bout him make somebody slip and call him "she"—like you done this morning.

RUTH: Well, that's what happened—my tongue slipped.

MAMA: You went to see that woman, didn't you?

RUTH [*defensively, giving herself away*]: What woman you talking about?

MAMA [*angrily*]: That woman who—

[WALTER *enters in great excitement.*]

WALTER: Did it come?

MAMA [*quietly*]: Can't you give people a Christian greeting before you start asking about money?

WALTER [*to* RUTH]: Did it come? [RUTH *unfolds the check and lays it quietly before him, watching him intently with thoughts of her own.* WALTER *sits down and grasps it close and counts off the zeros.*] Ten thousand dollars—[*He turns suddenly, frantically to his mother and draws some papers out of his breast pocket.*] Mama—look. Old Willy Harris put everything on paper—

MAMA: Son—I think you ought to talk to your wife . . . I'll go on out and leave you alone if you want—

WALTER: I can talk to her later—Mama, look—

MAMA: Son—

WALTER: WILL SOMEBODY PLEASE LISTEN TO ME TODAY!

MAMA [*quietly*]: I don't 'low no yellin' in this house, Walter Lee, and you know it—[WALTER *stares at them in frustration and starts to speak several times.*] And there ain't going to be no investing in no liquor stores. I don't aim to have to speak on that again.

[*A long pause.*]

WALTER: Oh   so you don't aim to have to speak on that again? So *you* have decided . . . [*Crumpling his papers.*] Well, *you* tell that to my boy tonight when you put him to sleep on the living-room couch . . . [*Turning to* MAMA *and speaking directly to her.*] Yeah—and tell it to my wife, Mama, tomorrow when she has to go out of here to look after somebody else's kids. And tell it to *me*, Mama, every time we need a new pair of curtains and I have to watch *you* go out and work in somebody's kitchen. Yeah, you tell me then! [WALTER *starts out.*]

RUTH: Where you going?

WALTER: I'm going out!

RUTH: Where?

WALTER: Just out of this house somewhere—

RUTH [*getting her coat*]: I'll come too.

WALTER: I don't want you to come!

RUTH: I got something to talk to you about, Walter.

WALTER: That's too bad.

MAMA [*still quietly*]: Walter Lee—[*She waits and he finally turns and looks at her.*] Sit down.

WALTER: I'm a grown man, Mama.

MAMA: Ain't nobody said you wasn't grown. But you still in my house and my presence. And as long as you are—you'll talk to your wife civil. Now sit down.

RUTH [*suddenly*]: Oh, let him go on out and drink himself to death! He makes me sick to my stomach! [*She flings her coat against him.*]

WALTER [*violently*]: And you turn mine too, baby! [RUTH *goes into their bedroom and slams the door behind her.*] That was my greatest mistake—

MAMA [*still quietly*]: Walter, what is the matter with you?

WALTER: Matter with me? Ain't nothing the matter with *me!*

MAMA: Yes there is. Something eating you up like a crazy man. Something more than me not giving you this money. The past few years I been watching it happen to you. You get all nervous acting and kind of wild in the eyes—[WALTER *jumps up impatiently at her words.*] I said sit there now, I'm talking to you!

WALTER: Mama—I don't need no nagging at me today.

MAMA: Seem like you getting to a place where you always tied up in some kind of knot about something. But if anybody ask you 'bout it you just yell at 'em and bust out the house and go out and drink somewheres. Walter Lee, people can't live with that. Ruth's a good, patient girl in her way—but you getting to be too much. Boy, don't make the mistake of driving that girl away from you.

WALTER: Why—what she do for me?

MAMA: She loves you.

WALTER: Mama—I'm going out. I want to go off somewhere and be by myself for a while.

MAMA: I'm sorry 'bout your liquor store, son. It just wasn't the thing for us to do. That's what I want to tell you about—

WALTER: I got to go out, Mama—[*He rises.*]

MAMA: It's dangerous, son.

WALTER: What's dangerous?

MAMA: When a man goes outside his home to look for peace.

WALTER [*beseechingly*]: Then why can't there never be no peace in this house then?

MAMA: You done found it in some other house?

WALTER: No—there ain't no woman! Why do women always think there's a woman somewhere when a man gets restless. [*Coming to her.*] Mama—Mama—I want so many things . . .

MAMA: Yes, son—

WALTER: I want so many things that they are driving me kind of crazy . . . Mama— look at me.

MAMA: I'm looking at you. You a good-looking boy. You got a job, a nice wife, a fine boy and—

WALTER: A job. [*Looks at her.*] Mama, a job? I open and close car doors all day long. I drive a man around in his limousine and I say, "Yes, sir; no, sir; very good, sir; shall I take the Drive, sir?" Mama, that ain't no kind of job . . . that ain't nothing at all. [*Very quietly.*] Mama, I don't know if I can make you understand.

MAMA: Understand what, baby?

WALTER [*quietly*]: Sometimes it's like I can see the future stretched out in front of me—just plain as day. The future, Mama. Hanging over there at the edge of my days. Just waiting for me—a big, looming blank space—full of *nothing.* Just waiting for *me.* [*Pause.*] Mama—sometimes when I'm downtown and I pass them cool, quiet-looking restaurants where them white boys are sitting back and talking 'bout things . . . sitting there turning deals worth millions of dollars . . . sometimes I see guys don't look much older than me—

MAMA: Son—how come you talk so much 'bout money?

WALTER [*with immense passion*]: Because it is life, Mama!

MAMA [*quietly*]: Oh—[*Very quietly.*] So now it's life. Money is life. Once upon a time freedom used to be life—now it's money. I guess the world really do change . . .

WALTER: No—it was always money, Mama. We just didn't know about it.

MAMA: No. . . . something has changed. [*She looks at him.*] You something new, boy. In my time we was worried about not being lynched and getting to the North if we could and how to stay alive and still have a pinch of dignity too . . . Now here come you and Beneatha—talking 'bout things we ain't never even thought about hardly, me and your daddy. You ain't satisfied or proud of nothing we done. I mean that you had a home; that we kept you out of trouble till you was grown; that you don't have to ride to work on the back of nobody's streetcar—You my children—but how different we done become.

WALTER: You just don't understand, Mama, you just don't understand.

MAMA: Son—do you know your wife is expecting another baby? [WALTER *stands, stunned, and absorbs what his mother has said.*] That's what she wanted to talk to you about. [WALTER *sinks down into a chair.*] This ain't for me to be telling—but you ought to know. [*She waits.*] I think Ruth is thinking 'bout getting rid of that child.

WALTER [*slowly understanding*]: No—no—Ruth wouldn't do that.

MAMA: When the world gets ugly enough—a woman will do anything for her family. *The part that's already living.*

WALTER: You don't know Ruth, Mama, if you think she would do that.

[RUTH *opens the bedroom door and stands there a little limp.*]

RUTH [*beaten*]: Yes I would too, Walter. [*Pause.*] I gave her a five-dollar down payment.

[*There is total silence as the man stares at his wife and the mother stares at her son.*]

MAMA [*presently*]: Well—[*Tightly.*] Well—son, I'm waiting to hear you say something . . . I'm waiting to hear how you be your father's son. Be the man he was . . . [*Pause.*] Your wife say she going to destroy your child. And I'm waiting to hear you talk like him and say we a people who give children life, not who destroys them—[*She rises.*] I'm waiting to see you stand up and look like your daddy and say we done give up one baby to poverty and that we ain't going to give up nary another one . . . I'm waiting.

WALTER: Ruth—

MAMA: If you a son of mine, tell her! [WALTER *turns, looks at her and can say nothing. She continues, bitterly.*] You . . . you are a disgrace to your father's memory. Somebody get me my hat.

ACT II

SCENE 1

Time: Later the same day.

At rise: RUTH *is ironing again. She has the radio going. Presently* BENEATHA'S *bedroom door opens and* RUTH'S *mouth falls and she puts down the iron in fascination.*

RUTH: What have we got on tonight!

BENEATHA [*emerging grandly from the doorway so that we can see her thoroughly robed in the costume Asagai brought*]: You are looking at what a well-dressed Nigerian woman wears—[*She parades for* RUTH, *her hair completely hidden by the headdress; she is coquettishly fanning herself with an ornate oriental fan, mistakenly more like Butterfly than any Nigerian that ever was.*] Isn't it beautiful? [*She promenades to the radio and, with an arrogant flourish, turns off the good loud blues that is playing.*] Enough of this assimilationist junk! [RUTH *follows her with her eyes as she goes to the phonograph and puts on a record and turns and waits ceremoniously for the music to come up. Then, with a shout—*] OCOMOGOSIAY!

[RUTH *jumps. The music comes up, a lovely Nigerian melody.* BENEATHA *listens, enraptured, her eyes far away—"back to the past." She begins to dance.* RUTH *is dumbfounded.*]

RUTH: What kind of dance is that?
BENEATHA: A folk dance.
RUTH [*Pearl Bailey*]: What kind of folks do that, honey?
BENEATHA: It's from Nigeria. It's a dance of welcome.
RUTH: Who you welcoming?
BENEATHA: The men back to the village.
RUTH: Where they been?

BENEATHA: How should I know—out hunting or something. Anyway, they are coming back now . . .

RUTH: Well, that's good.

BENEATHA [*with the record*]:

Alundi, alundi
Alundi alunya
Jop pu a jeepua
Ang gu sooooooooooo

Ai yai yae . . .
Ayehaye—alundi . . .

[WALTER *comes in during this performance; he has obviously been drinking. He leans against the door heavily and watches his sister, at first with distaste. Then his eyes look off—"back to the past"—as he lifts both his fists to the roof, screaming.*]

WALTER: YEAH . . . AND ETHIOPIA STRETCH FORTH HER HANDS AGAIN! . . .

RUTH [*drily, looking at him*]: Yes—and Africa sure is claiming her own tonight. [*She gives them both up and starts ironing again.*]

WALTER [*all in a drunken, dramatic shout*]: Shut up! . . . I'm digging them drums . . . them drums move me! . . . [*He makes his weaving way to his wife's face and leans in close to her.*] In my *heart of hearts*— [*He thumps his chest.*]—I am much warrior!

RUTH [*without even looking up*]: In your heart of hearts you are much drunkard.

WALTER [*coming away from her and starting to wander around the room, shouting*]: Me and Jomo . . . [*Intently, in his sister's face. She has stopped dancing to watch him in this unknown mood.*] That's my man, Kenyatta. [*Shouting and thumping his chest.*] FLAMING SPEAR! HOT DAMN! [*He is suddenly in possession of an imaginary spear and actively spearing enemies all over the room.*] OCOMOGOSIAY . . . THE LION IS WAKING . . . OWIMOWEH! [*He pulls his shirt open and leaps up on a table and gestures with his spear. The bell rings.* RUTH *goes to answer.*]

BENEATHA [*to encourage* WALTER, *thoroughly caught up with this side of him*]: OCOMOGO-SIAY, FLAMING SPEAR!

WALTER [*on the table, very far gone, his eyes pure glass sheets. He sees what we cannot, that he is a leader of his people, a great chief, a descendant of Chaka, and that the hour to march has come*]: Listen, my black brothers—

BENEATHA: OCOMOGOSIAY!

WALTER: —Do you hear the waters rushing against the shores of the coastlands—

BENEATHA: OCOMOGOSIAY!

WALTER: —Do you hear the screeching of the cocks in yonder hills beyond where the chiefs meet in council for the coming of the mighty war—

BENEATHA: OCOMOGOSIAY!

WALTER: —Do you hear the beating of the wings of the birds flying low over the mountains and the low places of our land—

[RUTH *opens the door.* GEORGE MURCHISON *enters.*]

BENEATHA: OCOMOGOSIAY!

WALTER: —Do you hear the singing of the women, singing the war songs of our fathers to the babies in the great houses . . . singing the sweet war songs? OH, DO YOU HEAR, MY BLACK BROTHERS!

BENEATHA [*completely gone*]: We hear you, Flaming Spear—

WALTER: Telling us to prepare for the greatness of the time—[*To* GEORGE.] Black Brother! [*He extends his hand for the fraternal clasp.*]

GEORGE: Black Brother, hell!

RUTH [*having had enough, and embarrassed for the family*]: Beneatha, you got company— what's the matter with you? Walter Lee Younger, get down off that table and stop acting like a fool . . .

[WALTER *comes down off the table suddenly and makes a quick exit to the bathroom.*]

RUTH: He's had a little to drink . . . I don't know what her excuse is.

GEORGE [*to* BENEATHA]: Look honey, we're going *to* the theatre—we're not going to be *in* it . . . so go change, huh?

RUTH: You expect this boy to go out with you looking like that?

BENEATHA [*looking at* GEORGE]: That's up to George. If he's ashamed of his heritage—

GEORGE: Oh, don't be so proud of yourself, Bennie—just because you look eccentric.

BENEATHA: How can something that's natural be eccentric?

GEORGE: That's what being eccentric means—being natural. Get dressed.

BENEATHA: I don't like that, George.

RUTH: Why must you and your brother make an argument out of everything people say?

BENEATHA: Because I hate assimilationist Negroes!

RUTH: Will somebody please tell me what assimila-whoever means!

GEORGE: Oh, it's just a college girl's way of calling people Uncle Toms—but that isn't what it means at all.

RUTH: Well, what does it mean?

BENEATHA [*cutting* GEORGE *off and staring at him as she replies to* RUTH]: It means someone who is willing to give up his own culture and submerge himself completely in the dominant, and in this case, *oppressive* culture!

GEORGE: Oh, dear, dear, dear! Here we go! A lecture on the African past! On our Great West African Heritage! In one second we will hear all about the great Ashanti empires; the great Songhay civilizations; and the great sculpture of Benth—and then some poetry in the Bantu—and the whole monologue will end with the word *bondage!* [*Nastily*] Let's face it, baby, your heritage is nothing but a bunch of raggedy-assed spirituals and some grass huts!

BENEATHA: *Grass huts!* [RUTH *crosses to her and forcibly pushes her toward the bedroom.*] See there . . . you are standing there in your splendid ignorance talking about people who were the first to smelt iron on the face of the earth! [RUTH *is pushing her through the door.*] The Ashanti were performing surgical operations when the English—[RUTH *pulls the door to, with* BENEATHA *on the other side, and smiles graciously at* GEORGE. BENEATHA *opens the door and shouts the end of the sentence defiantly at* GEORGE.]—were still tatooing themselves with blue dragons . . . [*She goes back inside.*]

RUTH: Have a seat, George. [*They both sit.* RUTH *folds her hands rather primly on her lap, determined to demonstrate the civilization of the family.*] Warm, ain't it? I mean for September. [*Pause.*] Just like they always say about Chicago weather: If it's too hot or cold for you, just wait a minute and it'll change. [*She smiles happily at this cliché of clichés.*] Everybody say it's got to do with them bombs and things they keep setting off. [*Pause.*] Would you like a nice cold beer?

GEORGE: No, thank you. I don't care for beer. [*He looks at his watch.*] I hope she hurries up.

RUTH: What time is the show?

GEORGE: It's an eight-thirty curtain. That's just Chicago though. In New York standard curtain time is eight forty. [*He is rather proud of this knowledge.*]

RUTH [*properly appreciating it*]: You get to New York a lot?

GEORGE [*offhand*]: Few times a year.

RUTH: Oh—that's nice. I've never been to New York.

[WALTER *enters. We feel he has relieved himself, but the edge of unreality is still with him.*]

WALTER: New York ain't got nothing Chicago ain't. Just a bunch of hustling people all squeezed up together—being "Eastern." [*He turns his face into a screw of displeasure.*]

GEORGE: Oh—you've been?

WALTER: *Plenty* of times.

RUTH [*shocked at the lie*]: Walter Lee Younger!

WALTER [*staring her down*]: Plenty! [*Pause.*] What we got to drink in this house? Why don't you offer this man some refreshment. [*To* GEORGE.] They don't know how to entertain people in this house, man.

GEORGE: Thank you—I don't really care for anything.

WALTER [*feeling his head; sobriety coming*]: Where's Mama?

RUTH: She ain't come back yet.

WALTER [*looking* MURCHISON *over from head to toe, scrutinizing his carefully casual tweed sports jacket over cashmere V-neck sweater over soft eyelet shirt and tie, and soft slacks, finished off with white buckskin shoes*]: Why all you college boys wear them fairyish-looking white shoes?

RUTH: Walter Lee!

[GEORGE MURCHISON *ignores the remark.*]

WALTER [*to* RUTH]: Well, they look crazy as hell—white shoes, cold as it is.

RUTH [*crushed*]: You have to excuse him—

WALTER: No he don't! Excuse me for what? What you always excusing me for! I'll excuse myself when I needs to be excused! [*A pause.*] They look as funny as them black knee socks Beneatha wears out of here all the time.

RUTH: It's the college *style*, Walter.

WALTER: Style, hell. She looks like she got burnt legs or something!

RUTH: Oh, Walter—

WALTER [*an irritable mimic*]: Oh, Walter! Oh, Walter! [*To* MURCHISON.] How's your old man making out? I understand you all going to buy that big hotel on the Drive? [*He finds a beer in the refrigerator, wanders over to* MURCHISON, *sipping and wiping his lips with the back of his hand, and straddling a chair backwards to talk to the other man.*] Shrewd move. Your old man is all right, man. [*Tapping his head and half winking for emphasis.*] I mean he knows how to operate. I mean he thinks *big*, you know what I mean, I mean for a *home*, you know? But I think he's kind of running out of ideas now. I'd like to talk to him. Listen, man, I got some plans that could turn this city upside down. I mean I think like he does. *Big*. Invest big, gamble big, hell, lose *big* if you have to, you know what I mean. It's hard to find a man on this whole Southside who understands my kind of thinking—you dig? [*He scrutinizes* MURCHISON *again, drinks his beer, squints his eyes and leans in close, confidential, man to man.*] Me and you ought to sit down and talk sometimes, man. Man, I got me some ideas . . .

MURCHISON [*with boredom*]: Yeah—sometimes we'll have to do that, Walter.

WALTER [*understanding the indifference, and offended*]: Yeah—well, when you get the time, man. I know you a busy little boy.

RUTH: Walter, please—

WALTER [*bitterly, hurt*]: I know ain't nothing in this world as busy as you colored college boys with your fraternity pins and white shoes . . .

RUTH [*covering her face with humiliation*]: Oh, Walter Lee—

WALTER: I see you all the time—with the books tucked under your arms—going to your [*British A—a mimic.*] "clahsses." And for what! What the hell you learning over there? Filling up your heads—[*Counting off on his fingers.*]—with the sociology and the psychology—but they teaching you how to be a man? How to take over and run the world? They teaching you how to run a rubber plantation or a steel mill? Naw—just to talk proper and read books and wear white shoes . . .

GEORGE [*looking at him with distaste, a little above it all*]: You're all wacked up with bitterness, man.

WALTER [*intently, almost quietly, between the teeth, glaring at the boy*]: And you—ain't you bitter, man? Ain't you just about had it yet? Don't you see no stars gleaming that you can't reach out and grab? You happy?—you contented son-of-a-bitch—you happy? You got it made? Bitter? Man, I'm a volcano. Bitter? Here I am a giant—surrounded by ants! Ants who can't even understand what it is the giant is talking about.

RUTH [*passionately and suddenly*]: Oh, Walter—ain't you with nobody!

WALTER [*violently*]: No! 'Cause ain't nobody with me! Not even my own mother!

RUTH: Walter, that's a terrible thing to say!

[BENEATHA *enters, dressed for the evening in a cocktail dress and earrings.*]

GEORGE: Well—hey, you look great.

BENEATHA: Let's go, George. See you all later.

RUTH: Have a nice time.

GEORGE: Thanks. Good night. [*To* WALTER, *sarcastically.*] Good night, *Prometheus*.

[BENEATHA *and* GEORGE *exit.*]

WALTER [*to* RUTH]: Who is Prometheus?

RUTH: I don't know. Don't worry about it.

WALTER [*in fury, pointing after* GEORGE]: See there—they get to a point where they can't insult you man to man—they got to go talk about something ain't nobody never heard of!

RUTH: How you know it was an insult? [*To humor him.*] Maybe Prometheus is a nice fellow.

WALTER: Prometheus! I bet there ain't even no such thing! I bet that simple-minded clown—

RUTH: Walter—[*She stops what she is doing and looks at him.*]

WALTER [*yelling*]: Don't start!

RUTH: Start what?

WALTER: Your nagging! Where was I? Who was I with? How much money did I spend?

RUTH [*plaintively*]: Walter Lee—why don't we just try to talk about it . . .

WALTER [*not listening*]: I been out talking with people who understand me. People who care about the things I got on my mind.

RUTH [*wearily*]: I guess that means people like Willy Harris.

WALTER: Yes, people like Willy Harris.

RUTH [*with a sudden flash of impatience*]: Why don't you all just hurry up and go into the banking business and stop talking about it!

WALTER: Why? You want to know why? 'Cause we all tied up in a race of people that don't know how to do nothing but moan, pray and have babies! [*The line is too bitter even for him and he looks at her and sits down.*]

RUTH: Oh, Walter . . . [*Softly*] Honey, why can't you stop fighting me?

WALTER [*without thinking*]: Who's fighting you? Who even cares about you? [*This line begins the retardation of his mood.*]

RUTH: Well—[*She waits a long time, and then with resignation starts to put away her things.*] I guess I might as well go on to bed . . . [*More or less to herself.*] I don't know where we lost it . . . but we have . . . [*Then, to him.*] I—I'm sorry about this new baby, Walter. I guess maybe I better go on and do what I started . . . I guess I just didn't realize how bad things was with us . . . I guess I just didn't really realize—[*She starts out to the bedroom and stops.*] You want some hot milk?

WALTER: Hot milk?

RUTH: Yes—hot milk.

WALTER: Why hot milk?

RUTH: 'Cause after all that liquor you come home with you ought to have something hot in your stomach.

WALTER: I don't want no milk.

RUTH: You want some coffee then?

WALTER: No, I don't want no coffee. I don't want nothing hot to drink. [*Almost plaintively.*] Why you always trying to give me something to eat?

RUTH [*standing and looking at him helplessly*]: What else can I give you, Walter Lee Younger?

[*She stands and looks at him and presently turns to go out again. He lifts his head and watches her going away from him in a new mood which began to emerge when he asked her "Who cares about you?"*]

WALTER: It's been rough, ain't it, baby? [*She hears and stops but does not turn around and he continues to her back.*] I guess between two people there ain't never as much understood as folks generally thinks there is. I mean like between me and you—[*She turns to face him.*] How we gets to the place where we scared to talk softness to each other. [*He waits, thinking hard himself.*] Why you think it got to be like that? [*He is thoughtful, almost as a child would be.*] Ruth, what is it gets into people ought to be close?
RUTH: I don't know, honey. I think about it a lot.
WALTER: On account of you and me, you mean? The way things are with us. The way something done come down between us.
RUTH: There ain't so much between us, Walter . . . Not when you come to me and try to talk to me. Try to be with me . . . a little even.
WALTER [*total honesty*]: Sometimes . . . sometimes . . . I don't even know how to try.
RUTH: Walter—
WALTER: Yes?
RUTH [*coming to him, gently and with misgiving, but coming to him*]: Honey . . . life don't have to be like this. I mean sometimes people can do things so that things are better . . . You remember how we used to talk when Travis was born . . . about the way we were going to live . . . the kind of house . . . [*She is stroking his head.*] Well, it's all starting to slip away from us . . .

[MAMA *enters, and* WALTER *jumps up and shouts at her.*]

WALTER: Mama, where have you been?
MAMA: My—them steps is longer than they used to be. Whew! [*She sits down and ignores him.*] How you feeling this evening, Ruth?

[RUTH *shrugs, disturbed some at having been prematurely interrupted and watching her husband knowingly.*]

WALTER: Mama, where have you been all day?
MAMA [*still ignoring him and leaning on the table and changing to more comfortable shoes*]: Where's Travis?
RUTH: I let him go out earlier and he ain't come back yet. Boy, is he going to get it!
WALTER: Mama!
MAMA [*as if she has heard for the first time*]: Yes, son?
WALTER: Where did you go this afternoon?
MAMA: I went down town to tend to some business that I had to tend to.

WALTER: What kind of business?

MAMA: You know better than to question me like a child, Brother.

WALTER [*rising and bending over the table*]: Where were you, Mama? [*Bringing his fists down and shouting.*] Mama, you didn't go do something with that insurance money, something crazy?

[*The front door opens slowly, interrupting him, and* TRAVIS *peeks his head in, less than hopefully.*]

TRAVIS [*to his mother*]: Mama, I—

RUTH: "Mama I" nothing! You're going to get it, boy! Get on in that bedroom and get yourself ready!

TRAVIS: But I—

MAMA: Why don't you all never let the child explain hisself.

RUTH: Keep out of it now, Lena.

[MAMA *clamps her lips together, and* RUTH *advances toward her son menacingly.*]

RUTH: A thousand times I have told you not to go off like that—

MAMA [*holding out her arms to her grandson*]: Well—at least let me tell him something. I want him to be the first one to hear . . . Come here, Travis. [*The boy obeys, gladly.*] Travis—[*She takes him by the shoulders and looks into his face.*]—you know that money we got in the mail this morning?

TRAVIS: Yes'm—

MAMA: Well—what you think your grandmama gone and done with that money?

TRAVIS: I don't know, Grandmama.

MAMA [*putting her finger on his nose for emphasis*]: She went out and she bought you a house! [*The explosion comes from* WALTER *at the end of the revelation and he jumps up and turns away from all of them in a fury.* MAMA *continues, to* TRAVIS.] You glad about the house? It's going to be yours when you get to be a man.

TRAVIS: Yeah—I always wanted to live in a house.

MAMA: All right, gimme some sugar then—[TRAVIS *puts his arms around her neck as she watches her son over the boy's shoulder. Then, to* TRAVIS, *after the embrace.*] Now when you say your prayers tonight, you thank God and your grandfather—'cause it was him who give you the house—in his way.

RUTH [*taking the boy from* MAMA *and pushing him toward the bedroom*]: Now you get out of here and get ready for your beating.

TRAVIS: Aw, Mama—

RUTH: Get on in there—[*Closing the door behind him and turning radiantly to her mother-in-law.*] So you went and did it!

MAMA [*quietly, looking at her son with pain*]: Yes, I did.

RUTH [*raising both arms classically*]: *Praise God!* [*Looks at* WALTER *a moment, who says nothing. She crosses rapidly to her husband.*] Please, honey—let me be glad . . . you be glad too. [*She has laid her hands on his shoulders, but he shakes himself free of her roughly, without turning to face her.*] Oh, Walter . . . a home . . . a home. [*She comes back to* MAMA.] Well—where is it? How big is it? How much it going to cost?

MAMA: Well—

RUTH: When we moving?

MAMA [*smiling at her*]: First of the month.

RUTH [*throwing back her head with jubilance*]: *Praise God!*

MAMA [*tentatively, still looking at her son's back turned against her and* RUTH]: It's—it's a nice house too . . . [*She cannot help speaking directly to him. An imploring quality in her voice, her manner, makes her almost like a girl now.*] Three bedrooms—nice big one for you and Ruth. . . . Me and Beneatha still have to share our room, but Travis have one of his own—and—[*With difficulty.*] I figures if the—new baby—is a boy, we could get one of them double-decker outfits . . . And there's a yard with a little patch of dirt where I could maybe get to grow me a few flowers . . . And a nice big basement . . .

RUTH: Walter honey, be glad—

MAMA [*still to his back, fingering things on the table*]: 'Course I don't want to make it sound fancier than it is . . . It's just a plain little old house—but it's made good and solid—and it will be *ours*. Walter Lee—it makes a difference in a man when he can walk on floors that belong to *him* . . .

RUTH: Where is it?

MAMA [*frightened at this telling*]: Well—well—it's out there in Clybourne Park—

[RUTH's *radiance fades abruptly, and* WALTER *finally turns slowly to face his mother with incredulity and hostility.*]

RUTH: Where?

MAMA [*matter-of-factly*]: Four o six Clybourne Street, Clybourne Park.

RUTH: Clybourne Park? Mama, there ain't no colored people living in Clybourne Park.

MAMA [*almost idiotically*]: Well, I guess there's going to be some now.

WALTER [*bitterly*]: So that's the peace and comfort you went out and bought for us today!

MAMA [*raising her eyes to meet his finally*]: Son—I just tried to find the nicest place for the least amount of money for my family.

RUTH [*trying to recover from the shock*]: Well—well—'course I ain't one never been 'fraid of no crackers, mind you—but—well, wasn't there no other houses nowhere?

MAMA: Them houses they put up for colored in them areas way out all seem to cost twice as much as other houses. I did the best I could.

RUTH [*struck senseless with the news, in its various degrees of goodness and trouble, she sits a moment, her fists propping her chin in thought, and then she starts to rise, bringing her fists down with vigor, the radiance spreading from cheek to cheek again*]: Well—well!—All I can say is—if this is my time in life—*my time*—to say good-bye—[*and she builds with momentum as she starts to circle the room with an exuberant, almost tearfully happy release*]—to these God-damned cracking walls!—[*she pounds the walls*]—and these marching roaches!—[*she wipes at an imaginary army of marching roaches*]—and this cramped little closet which ain't now or never was no kitchen! . . . then I say it loud and good, *Hallelujah!* and good-bye misery . . . I don't never want to see your ugly face again! [*She laughs joyously, having practically destroyed the apartment, and flings her arms up and lets them come down happily, slowly, reflectively, over her*

abdomen, *aware for the first time perhaps that the life therein pulses with happiness and not despair.*]
Lena?

MAMA [*moved, watching her happiness*]: Yes, honey?

RUTH [*looking off*]: Is there—is there a whole lot of sunlight?

MAMA [*understanding*]: Yes, child, there's a whole lot of sunlight.

[*Long pause.*]

RUTH [*collecting herself and going to the door of the room* TRAVIS *is in*]: Well—I guess I better see 'bout Travis. [*To* MAMA.] Lord, I sure don't feel like whipping nobody today! [*She exits.*]

MAMA [*the mother and son are left alone now and the mother waits a long time, considering deeply, before she speaks*]: Son—you—you understand what I done, don't you? [WALTER *is silent and sullen.*] I—I just seen my family falling apart today . . . just falling to pieces in front of my eyes . . . We couldn't of gone on like we was today. We was going backwards 'stead of forwards—talking 'bout killing babies and wishing each other was dead . . . When it gets like that in life—you just got to do something different, push on out and do something bigger . . . [*She waits.*] I wish you say something, son . . . I wish you'd say how deep inside you you think I done the right thing—

WALTER [*crossing slowly to his bedroom door and finally turning there and speaking measuredly*]: What you need me to say you done right for? *You* the head of this family. You run our lives like you want to. It was your money and you did what you wanted with it. So what you need for me to say it was all right for? [*Bitterly, to hurt her as deeply as he knows is possible.*] So you butchered up a dream of mine—you—who always talking 'bout your children's dreams . . .

MAMA: Walter Lee—

[*He just closes the door behind him.* MAMA *sits alone, thinking heavily.*]

SCENE 2

Time: Friday night. A few weeks later.

At rise: Packing crates mark the intention of the family to move. BENEATHA *and* GEORGE *come in, presumably from an evening out again.*

GEORGE: O.K. . . . O.K., whatever you say . . . [*They both sit on the couch. He tries to kiss her. She moves away.*] Look, we've had a nice evening; let's not spoil it, huh? . . .

[*He again turns her head and tries to nuzzle in and she turns away from him, not with distaste but with momentary lack of interest; in a mood to pursue what they were talking about.*]

BENEATHA: I'm *trying* to talk to you.

GEORGE: We always talk.

BENEATHA: Yes—and I love to talk.

GEORGE [*exasperated; rising*]: I know it and I don't mind it sometimes . . . I want you to cut it out, see—The moody stuff, I mean. I don't like it. You're a nice-looking girl . . . all over. That's all you need, honey, forget the atmosphere. Guys aren't going to go for the atmosphere—they're going to go for what they see. Be glad for that. Drop the Garbo routine. It doesn't go with you. As for myself, I want a nice— [*Groping.*]—simple—[*Thoughtfully.*]—sophisticated girl . . . not a poet—O.K.?

[*She rebuffs him again and he starts to leave.*]

BENEATHA: Why are you angry?
GEORGE: Because this is stupid! I don't go out with you to discuss the nature of "quiet desperation" or to hear all about your thoughts—because the world will go on thinking what it thinks regardless—
BENEATHA: Then why read books? Why go to school?
GEORGE [*with artificial patience, counting on his fingers*]: It's simple. You read books—to learn facts—to get grades—to pass the course—to get a degree. That's all—it has nothing to do with thoughts.

[*A long pause.*]

BENEATHA: I see. [*A longer pause as she looks at him.*] Good night, George.

[GEORGE *looks at her a little oddly, and starts to exit. He meets* MAMA *coming in.*]

GEORGE: Oh—hello, Mrs. Younger.
MAMA: Hello, George, how you feeling?
GEORGE: Fine—fine, how are you?
MAMA: Oh, a little tired. You know them steps can get you after a day's work. You all have a nice time tonight?
GEORGE: Yes—a fine time. Well, good night.
MAMA: Good night. [*He exits.* MAMA *closes the door behind her.*] Hello, honey. What you sitting like that for?
BENEATHA: I'm just sitting.
MAMA: Didn't you have a nice time?
BENEATHA: No.
MAMA: No? What's the matter?
BENEATHA: Mama, George is a fool—honest. [*She rises.*]
MAMA [*hustling around unloading the packages she has entered with; she stops*]: Is he, baby?
BENEATHA: Yes. [BENEATHA *makes up* TRAVIS' *bed as she talks.*]
MAMA: You sure?
BENEATHA: Yes.
MAMA: Well—I guess you better not waste your time with no fools.

[BENEATHA *looks up at her mother, watching her put groceries in the refrigerator. Finally she gathers up her things and starts into the bedroom. At the door she stops and looks back at her mother.*]

BENEATHA: Mama—

MAMA: Yes, baby—

BENEATHA: Thank you.

MAMA: For what?

BENEATHA: For understanding me this time.

[*She exits quickly and the mother stands, smiling a little, looking at the place where* BENEATHA *just stood.* RUTH *enters.*]

RUTH: Now don't you fool with any of this stuff, Lena—

MAMA: Oh, I just thought I'd sort a few things out.

[*The phone rings.* RUTH *answers.*]

RUTH [*at the phone*]: Hello—Just a minute. [*Goes to door.*] Walter, it's Mrs. Arnold. [*Waits. Goes back to the phone. Tense.*] Hello. Yes, this is his wife speaking . . . He's lying down now. Yes . . . well, he'll be in tomorrow. He's been very sick. Yes—I know we should have called, but we were so sure he'd be able to come in today. Yes—yes, I'm very sorry. Yes . . . Thank you very much. [*She hangs up.* WALTER *is standing in the doorway of the bedroom behind her.*] That was Mrs. Arnold.

WALTER [*indifferently*]: Was it?

RUTH: She said if you don't come in tomorrow that they are getting a new man . . .

WALTER: Ain't that sad—ain't that crying sad.

RUTH: She said Mr. Arnold has had to take a cab for three days . . . Walter, you ain't been to work for three days! [*This is a revelation to her.*] Where you been, Walter Lee Younger? [WALTER *looks at her and starts to laugh.*] You're going to lose your job.

WALTER: That's right . . .

RUTH: Oh, Walter, and with your mother working like a dog every day—

WALTER: That's sad too—Everything is sad.

MAMA: What you been doing for these three days, son?

WALTER: Mama—you don't know all the things a man what got leisure can find to do in this city . . . What's this—Friday night? Well—Wednesday I borrowed Willy Harris' car and I went for a drive . . . just me and myself and I drove and drove . . . Way out . . . way past South Chicago, and I parked the car and I sat and looked at the steel mills all day long. I just sat in the car and looked at them big black chimneys for hours. Then I drove back and I went to the Green Hat. [*Pause.*] And Thursday—Thursday I borrowed the car again and I got in it and I pointed it the other way and I drove the other way—four hours—way, way up to Wisconsin, and I looked at the farms. I just drove and looked at the farms. Then I drove back and I went to the Green Hat. [*Pause.*] And today—today I didn't get the car. Today I just walked. All over the Southside. And I looked at the Negroes and they looked at me and finally I just sat down on the curb at Thirty-ninth and South Parkway and I just sat there and watched the Negroes go by. And then I went to the Green Hat. You all sad? You all depressed? And you know where I am going right now—

[RUTH *goes out quietly.*]

MAMA: Oh, Big Walter, is this the harvest of our days?

WALTER: You know what I like about the Green Hat? [*He turns the radio on and a steamy, deep blues pours into the room.*] I like this little cat they got there who blows a sax . . . He blows. He talks to me. He ain't but 'bout five feet tall and he's got a conked head and his eyes is always closed and he's all music—

MAMA [*rising and getting some papers out of her handbag*]: Walter—

WALTER: And there's this other guy who plays the piano . . . and they got a sound. I mean they can work on some music . . . They got the best little combo in the world in the Green Hat . . . You can just sit there and drink and listen to them three men play and you realize that don't nothing matter worth a damn, but just being there—

MAMA: I've helped do it to you, haven't I, son? Walter, I been wrong.

WALTER: Naw—you ain't never been wrong about nothing, Mama.

MAMA: Listen to me, now. I say I been wrong, son. That I been doing to you what the rest of the world been doing to you. [*She stops and he looks up slowly at her and she meets his eyes pleadingly.*] Walter—what you ain't never understood is that I ain't got nothing, don't own nothing, ain't never really wanted nothing that wasn't for you. There ain't nothing as precious to me . . . There ain't nothing worth holding on to, money, dreams, nothing else—if it means—if it means it's going to destroy my boy. [*She puts her papers in front of him and he watches her without speaking or moving.*] I paid the man thirty-five hundred dollars down on the house. That leaves sixty-five hundred dollars. Monday morning I want you to take this money and take three thousand dollars and put it in a savings account for Beneatha's medical schooling. The rest you put in a checking account—with your name on it. And from now on any penny that come out of it or that go in it is for you to look after. For you to decide. [*She drops her hands a little helplessly.*] It ain't much, but it's all I got in the world and I'm putting in your hands. I'm telling you to be the head of this family from now on like you supposed to be.

WALTER [*stares at the money*]: You trust me like that, Mama?

MAMA: I ain't never stop trusting you. Like I ain't never stop loving you.

[*She goes out, and* WALTER *sits looking at the money on the table as the music continues in its idiom, pulsing in the room. Finally, in a decisive gesture, he gets up, and, in mingled joy and desperation, picks up the money. At the same moment,* TRAVIS *enters for bed.*]

TRAVIS: What's the matter, Daddy? You drunk?

WALTER [*sweetly, more sweetly than we have ever known him*]: No, Daddy ain't drunk. Daddy ain't going to never be drunk again. . . .

TRAVIS: Well, good night, Daddy.

[*The* FATHER *has come from behind the couch and leans over, embracing his son.*]

WALTER: Son, I feel like talking to you tonight.

TRAVIS: About what?

WALTER: Oh, about a lot of things. About you and what kind of man you going to be when you grow up. . . . Son—son, what do you want to be when you grow up?

TRAVIS: A bus driver.

WALTER [*laughing a little*]: A what? Man, that ain't nothing to want to be!

TRAVIS: Why not?

WALTER: 'Cause, man—it ain't big enough—you know what I mean.

TRAVIS: I don't know then. I can't make up my mind. Sometimes Mama asks me that too. And sometimes when I tell you I just want to be like you—she says she don't want me to be like that and sometimes she says she does. . . .

WALTER [*gathering him up in his arms*]: You know what, Travis? In seven years you going to be seventeen years old. And things is going to be very different with us in seven years, Travis. . . . One day when you are seventeen I'll come home—home from my office downtown somewhere—

TRAVIS: You don't work in no office, Daddy.

WALTER: No—but after tonight. After what your daddy gonna do tonight, there's going to be offices—a whole lot of offices. . . .

TRAVIS: What you gonna do tonight, Daddy?

WALTER: You wouldn't understand yet, son, but your daddy's gonna make a transaction . . . a business transaction that's going to change our lives. . . . That's how come one day when you 'bout seventeen years old I'll come home and I'll be pretty tired, you know what I mean, after a day of conferences and secretaries getting things wrong the way they do . . . 'cause an executive's life is hell, man—[*The more he talks the farther away he gets.*] And I'll pull the car up on the driveway . . . just a plain black Chrysler, I think, with white walls—no—black tires. More elegant. Rich people don't have to be flashy . . . though I'll have to get something a little sportier for Ruth—maybe a Cadillac convertible to do her shopping in. . . . And I'll come up the steps to the house and the gardener will be clipping away at the hedges and he'll say, "Good evening, Mr. Younger." And I'll say, "Hello, Jefferson, how are you this evening?" And I'll go inside and Ruth will come downstairs and meet me at the door and we'll kiss each other and she'll take my arm and we'll go up to your room to see you sitting on the floor with the catalogues of all the great schools in America around you. . . . All the great schools in the world! And—and I'll say, all right son—it's your seventeenth birthday, what is it you've decided? . . . Just tell me where you want to go to school and you'll *go*. Just tell me, what it is you want to be—and you'll *be* it. . . . Whatever you want to be—Yessir! [*He holds his arms open for* TRAVIS.] You just name it, son . . . [TRAVIS *leaps into them.*] and I hand you the world! [WALTER's *voice has risen in pitch and hysterical promise and on the last line he lifts* TRAVIS *high.*]

SCENE 3

Time: Saturday, moving day, one week later.

   Before the curtain rises, RUTH's *voice, a strident, dramatic church alto, cuts through the silence.*

   It is, in the darkness, a triumphant surge, a penetrating statement of expectation: "Oh, Lord, I don't feel no ways tired! Children, oh, glory hallelujah!"

As the curtain rises we see that RUTH *is alone in the living room, finishing up the family's packing. It is moving day. She is nailing crates and tying cartons.* BENEATHA *enters, carrying a guitar case, and watches her exuberant sister-in-law.*

RUTH: Hey!

BENEATHA [*putting away the case*]: Hi.

RUTH [*pointing at a package*]: Honey—look in that package there and see what I found on sale this morning at the South Center. [RUTH *gets up and moves to the package and draws out some curtains.*] Lookahere—hand-turned hems!

BENEATHA: How do you know the window size out there?

RUTH [*who hadn't thought of that*]: Oh—Well, they bound to fit something in the whole house. Anyhow, they was too good a bargain to pass us. [RUTH *slaps her head, suddenly remembering something.*] Oh, Bennie—I meant to put a special note on that carton over there. That's your mama's good china and she wants 'em to be very careful with it.

BENEATHA: I'll do it. [BENEATHA *finds a piece of paper and starts to draw large letters on it.*]

RUTH: You know what I'm going to do soon as I get in that new house?

BENEATHA: What?

RUTH: Honey—I'm going to run me a tub of water up to here . . . [*With her fingers practically up to her nostrils.*] And I'm going to get in it—and I am going to sit . . . and sit . . . and sit in that hot water and the first person who knocks to tell *me* to hurry up and come out—

BENEATHA: Gets shot at sunrise.

RUTH [*laughing happily*]: You said it, sister! [*Noticing how large* BENEATHA *is absent-mindedly making the note.*] Honey, they ain't going to read that from no airplane.

BENEATHA [*laughing herself*]: I guess I always think things have more emphasis if they are big, somehow.

RUTH [*looking up at her and smiling*]: You and your brother seem to have that as a philosophy of life. Lord, that man—done changed so 'round here. You know—you know what we did last night? Me and Walter Lee?

BENEATHA: What?

RUTH [*smiling to herself*]: We went to the movies. [*Looking at* BENEATHA *to see if she understands.*] We went to the movies. You know the last time me and Walter went to the movies together?

BENEATHA: No.

RUTH: Me neither. That's how long it been. [*Smiling again.*] But we went last night. The picture wasn't much good, but that didn't seem to matter. We went—and we held hands.

BENEATHA: Oh, Lord!

RUTH: We held hands—and you know what?

BENEATHA: What?

RUTH: When we come out of the show it was late and dark and all the stores and things was closed up . . . and it was kind of chilly and there wasn't many people on the streets . . . and we was still holding hands, me and Walter.

BENEATHA: You're killing me.

[WALTER *enters with a large package. His happiness is deep in him; he cannot keep still with his newfound exuberance. He is singing and wiggling and snapping his fingers. He puts his package in a corner and puts a phonograph record, which he has brought in with him, on the record player. As the music comes up he dances over to* RUTH *and tries to get her to dance with him. She gives in at last to his raunchiness and in a fit of giggling allows herself to be drawn into his mood and together they deliberately burlesque an old social dance of their youth.*]

BENEATHA [*regarding them a long time as they dance, then drawing in her breath for a deeply exaggerated comment which she does not particularly mean*]: Talk about—olddddddddddd-fashioned-dddddd—Negroes!

WALTER [*stopping momentarily*]: What kind of Negroes?

[*He says this in fun. He is not angry with her today, nor with anyone. He starts to dance with his wife again.*]

BENEATHA: Old-fashioned.

WALTER [*as he dances with* RUTH]: You know, when these *New Negroes* have their convention—[*pointing at his sister*]—that is going to be the chairman of the Committee on Unending Agitation. [*He goes on dancing, then stops.*] Race, race, race! . . . Girl, I do believe you are the first person in the history of the entire human race to successfully brainwash yourself. [BENEATHA *breaks up and he goes on dancing. He stops again, enjoying his tease.*] Damn, even the N double A C P takes a holiday sometimes! [BENEATHA *and* RUTH *laugh. He dances with* RUTH *some more and starts to laugh and stops and pantomimes someone over an operating table.*] I can just see that chick someday looking down at some poor cat on an operating table before she starts to slice him, saying . . . [*Pulling his sleeves back maliciously.*] "By the way, what are your views on civil rights down there? . . ." [*He laughs at her again and starts to dance happily. The bell sounds.*]

BENEATHA: Sticks and stones may break my bones but . . . words will never hurt me! [BENEATHA *goes to the door and opens it as* WALTER *and* RUTH *go on with the clowning.* BENEATHA *is somewhat surprised to see a quiet-looking middle-aged white man in a business suit holding his hat and a briefcase in his hand and consulting a small piece of paper.*]

MAN: Uh—how do you do, miss. I am looking for a Mrs.—[*He looks at the slip of paper.*] Mrs. Lena Younger?

BENEATHA [*smoothing her hair with slight embarrassment*]: Oh—yes, that's my mother. Excuse me. [*She closes the door and turns to quiet the other two.*] Ruth! Brother! Somebody's here. [*Then she opens the door. The man casts a curious quick glance at all of them.*] Uh—come in please.

MAN [*coming in*]: Thank you.

BENEATHA: My mother isn't here just now. Is it business?

MAN: Yes . . . well, of a sort.

WALTER [*freely, the Man of the House*]: Have a seat. I'm Mrs. Younger's son. I look after most of her business matters.

[RUTH *and* BENEATHA *exchange amused glances.*]

MAN [*regarding* WALTER, *and sitting*]: Well—My name is Karl Lindner . . .

WALTER [*stretching out his hand*]: Walter Younger. This is my wife—[RUTH *nods politely.*]—and my sister.

LINDNER: How do you do.

WALTER [*amiably, as he sits himself easily on a chair, leaning with interest forward on his knees and looking expectantly into the newcomer's face*]: What can we do for you, Mr. Lindner!

LINDNER [*some minor shuffling of the hat and briefcase on his knees*]: Well—I am a representative of the Clybourne Park Improvement Association—

WALTER [*pointing*]: Why don't you sit your things on the floor?

LINDNER: Oh—yes. Thank you. [*He slides the briefcase and hat under the chair.*] And as I was saying—I am from the Clybourne Park Improvement Association and we have had it brought to our attention at the last meeting that you people—or at least your mother—has bought a piece of residential property at—[*He digs for the slip of paper again.*]—four o six Clybourne Street . . .

WALTER: That's right. Care for something to drink? Ruth, get Mr. Lindner a beer.

LINDNER [*upset for some reason*]: Oh—no, really. I mean thank you very much, but no thank you.

RUTH [*innocently*]: Some coffee?

LINDNER: Thank you, nothing at all.

[BENEATHA *is watching the man carefully.*]

LINDNER: Well, I don't know how much you folks know about our organization. [*He is a gentle man; thoughtful and somewhat labored in his manner.*] It is one of these community organizations set up to look after—Oh, you know, things like block upkeep and special projects and we also have what we call our New Neighbors Orientation Committee . . .

BENEATHA [*drily*]: Yes—and what do they do?

LINDNER [*turning a little to her and then returning the main force to* WALTER]: Well—it's what you might call a sort of welcoming committee, I guess. I mean they, we, I'm the chairman of the committee—go around and see the new people who move into the neighborhood and sort of give them the lowdown on the way we do things out in Clybourne Park.

BENEATHA [*with appreciation of the two meanings, which escape* RUTH *and* WALTER]: Un-huh.

LINDNER: And we also have the category of what the association calls—[*He looks elsewhere.*]—uh—special community problems . . .

BENEATHA: Yes—and what are some of those?

WALTER: Girl, let the man talk.

LINDNER [*with understated relief*]: Thank you. I would sort of like to explain this thing in my own way. I mean I want to explain to you in a certain way.

WALTER: Go ahead.

LINDNER: Yes. Well. I'm going to try to get right to the point. I'm sure we'll all appreciate that in the long run.

BENEATHA: Yes.

WALTER: Be still now!

LINDNER: Well—

RUTH [*still innocently*]: Would you like another chair—you don't look comfortable.

LINDNER [*more frustrated than annoyed*]: No, thank you very much. Please. Well—to get right to the point I—[*A great breath, and he is off at last.*] I am sure you people must be aware of some of the incidents which have happened in various parts of the city when colored people have moved into certain areas—[BENEATHA *exhales heavily and starts tossing a piece of fruit up and down in the air.*] Well—because we have what I think is going to be a unique type of organization in American community life—not only do we deplore that kind of thing—but we are trying to do something about it. [BENEATHA *stops tossing and turns with a new and quizzical interest to the man.*] We feel—[*Gaining confidence in his mission because of the interest in the faces of the people he is talking to.*]—we feel that most of the trouble in this world, when you come right down to it—[*He hits his knee for emphasis.*]—most of the trouble exists because people just don't sit down and talk to each other.

RUTH [*nodding as she might in church, pleased with the remark*]: You can say that again, mister.

LINDNER [*more encouraged by such affirmation*]: That we don't try hard enough in this world to understand the other fellow's problem. The other guy's point of view.

RUTH: Now that's right.

[BENEATHA *and* WALTER *merely watch and listen with genuine interest.*]

LINDNER: Yes—that's the way we feel out in Clybourne Park. And that's why I was elected to come here this afternoon and talk to you people. Friendly like, you know, the way people should talk to each other and see if we couldn't find some way to work this thing out. As I say, the whole business is a matter of *caring* about the other fellow. Anybody can see that you are a nice family of folks, hard working and honest I'm sure. [BENEATHA *frowns slightly, quizzically, her head tilted regarding him.*] Today everybody knows what it means to be on the outside of *something*. And of course, there is always somebody who is out to take the advantage of people who don't always understand.

WALTER: What do you mean?

LINDNER: Well—you see our community is made up of people who've worked hard as the dickens for years to build up that little community. They're not rich and fancy people; just hardworking, honest people who don't really have much but those little homes and a dream of the kind of community they want to raise their children in. Now, I don't say we are perfect and there is a lot wrong in some of the things they want. But you've got to admit that a man, right or wrong, has the right to want to have the neighborhood he lives in a certain kind of way. And at the moment the overwhelming majority of our people out there feel that people get along better, take more of a common interest in the life of the community, when they share a common background. I want you to believe me when I tell you that race prejudice simply doesn't enter into it. It is a matter of the people of Clybourne Park believing, rightly or wrongly, as I say, that for the happiness of all concerned that our Negro families are happier when they live in their *own* communities.

BENEATHA [*with a grand and bitter gesture*]: This, friends, is the Welcoming Committee!

WALTER [*dumfounded, looking at* LINDNER]: Is this what you came marching all the way over here to tell us?

LINDNER: Well, now we've been having a fine conversation. I hope you'll hear me all the way through.

WALTER [*tightly*]: Go ahead, man.

LINDNER: You see—in the face of all things I have said, we are prepared to make your family a very generous offer . . .

BENEATHA: Thirty pieces and not a coin less!

WALTER: Yeah?

LINDNER [*putting on his glasses and drawing a form out of the briefcase*]: Our association is prepared, through the collective effort of our people, to buy the house from you at a financial gain to your family.

RUTH: Lord have mercy, ain't this the living gall!

WALTER: All right, you through?

LINDNER: Well, I want to give you the exact terms of the financial arrangement—

WALTER: We don't want to hear no exact terms of no arrangements. I want to know if you got any more to tell us 'bout getting together?

LINDNER [*taking off his glasses*]: Well—I don't suppose that you feel . . .

WALTER: Never mind how I feel—you got any more to say 'bout how people ought to sit down and talk to each other? . . . Get out of my house, man. [*He turns his back and walks to the door.*]

LINDNER [*looking around at the hostile faces and reaching and assembling his hat and briefcase*]: Well—I don't understand why you people are reacting this way. What do you think you are going to gain by moving into a neighborhood where you just aren't wanted and where some elements—well—people can get awful worked up when they feel that their whole way of life and everything they've ever worked for is threatened.

WALTER: Get out.

LINDNER [*at the door, holding a small card*]: Well—I'm sorry it went like this.

WALTER: Get out.

LINDNER [*almost sadly regarding* WALTER]: You just can't force people to change their hearts, son. [*He turns and puts his card on a table and exits.* WALTER *pushes the door to with stinging hatred, and stands looking at it.* RUTH *just sits and* BENEATHA *just stands. They say nothing.* MAMA *and* TRAVIS *enter.*]

MAMA: Well—this all the packing got done since I left out of here this morning. I testify before God that my children got all the energy of the dead. What time the moving men due?

BENEATHA: Four o'clock. You had a caller, Mama. [*She is smiling, teasingly.*]

MAMA: Sure enough—who?

BENEATHA [*her arms folded saucily*]: The Welcoming Committee.

[WALTER *and* RUTH *giggle.*]

MAMA [*innocently*]: Who?

BENEATHA: The Welcoming Committee. They said they're sure going to be glad to see you when you get there.

WALTER [*devilishly*]: Yeah, they said they can't hardly wait to see your face.

[*Laughter.*]

MAMA [*sensing their facetiousness*]: What's the matter with you all?

WALTER: Ain't nothing the matter with us. We just telling you 'bout the gentleman who came to see you this afternoon. From the Clybourne Park Improvement Association.

MAMA: What he want?

RUTH [*in the same mood as* BENEATHA *and* WALTER]: To welcome you, honey.

WALTER: He said they can't hardly wait. He said the one thing they don't have, that they just *dying* to have out there is a fine family of colored people! [*To* RUTH *and* BENEATHA.] Ain't that right!

RUTH *and* BENEATHA [*mockingly*]: Yeah! He left his card in case—[*They indicate the card, and* MAMA *picks it up and throws it on the floor—understanding and looking off as she draws her chair up to the table on which she has put her plant and some sticks and some cord.*]

MAMA: Father, give us strength. [*Knowingly—and without fun.*] Did he threaten us?

BENEATHA: Oh—Mama—they don't do it like that any more. He talked Brotherhood. He said everybody ought learn how to sit down and hate each other with good Christian fellowship.

[*She and* WALTER *shake hands to ridicule the remark.*]

MAMA [*Sadly*]: Lord, protect us . . .

RUTH: You should hear the money those folks raised to buy the house from us. All we paid and then some.

BENEATHA: What they think we going to do—eat 'em?

RUTH: No, honey, marry 'em.

MAMA [*shaking her head*]: Lord, Lord, Lord . . .

RUTH: Well—that's the way the crackers crumble. Joke.

BENEATHA [*laughingly noticing what her mother is doing*]: Mama, what are you doing?

MAMA: Fixing my plant so it won't get hurt none on the way . . .

BENEATHA: Mama, you going to take *that* to the new house?

MAMA: Un-huh—

BENEATHA: That raggedy-looking old thing?

MAMA [*stopping and looking at her*]: It expresses me.

RUTH [*with delight, to* BENEATHA]: So, there, Miss Thing!

[WALTER *comes to* MAMA *suddenly and bends down behind her and squeezes her in his arms with all his strength. She is overwhelmed by the suddenness of it and, though delighted, her manner is like that of* RUTH *with* TRAVIS.]

MAMA: Look out now, boy! You make me mess up my thing here!

WALTER [*his face lit, he slips down on his knees beside her, his arms still about her*]: Mama . . . you know what it means to climb up in the chariot?

MAMA [*gruffly, very happy*]: Get on away from me now . . .

RUTH [*near the gift-wrapped package, trying to catch* WALTER's *eye*]: Psst—

WALTER: What the old song say, Mama . . .

RUTH: Walter—Now? [*She is pointing at the package.*]

WALTER [*speaking the lines, sweetly, playfully, in his mother's face*]:
I got wings . . . you got wings . . .
All God's children got wings . . .

MAMA: Boy—get out of my face and do some work . . .

WALTER:
When I get to heaven gonna put on my wings,
Gonna fly all over God's heaven . . .

BENEATHA [*teasingly, from across the room*]: Everybody talking 'bout heaven ain't going there!

WALTER [*to* RUTH, *who is carrying the box across to them*]: I don't know, you think we ought to give her that . . . Seems to me she ain't been very appreciative around here.

MAMA [*eyeing the box, which is obviously a gift*]: What is that?

WALTER [*taking it from* RUTH *and putting it on the table in front of* MAMA]: Well—what you all think. Should we give it to her?

RUTH: Oh—she was pretty good today.

MAMA: I'll good you—[*She turns her eyes to the box again.*]

BENEATHA: Open it, Mama.

[*She stands up, looks at it, turns and looks at all of them, and then presses her hands together and does not open the package.*]

WALTER [*sweetly*]: Open it, Mama. It's for you. [MAMA *looks in his eyes. It is the first present in her life without its being Christmas. Slowly she opens her package and lifts out, one by one, a brand-new sparkling set of gardening tools.* WALTER *continues, prodding.*] Ruth made up the note—read it . . .

MAMA [*picking up the card and adjusting her glasses*]: "To our own Mrs. Miniver—Love from Brother, Ruth and Beneatha." Ain't that lovely . . .

TRAVIS [*tugging at his father's sleeve*]: Daddy, can I give her mine now?

WALTER: All right, son. [TRAVIS *flies to get his gift.*] Travis didn't want to go in with the rest of us, Mama. He got his own. [*Somewhat amused.*] We don't know what it is . . .

TRAVIS [*racing back in the room with a large hatbox and putting it in front of his grandmother*]: Here!

MAMA: Lord have mercy, baby. You done gone and bought your grandmother a hat?

TRAVIS [*very proud*]: Open it!

[*She does and lifts out an elaborate, but very elaborate, wide gardening hat, and all the adults break up at the sight of it.*]

RUTH: Travis, honey, what is that?

TRAVIS [*who thinks it is beautiful and appropriate*]: It's a gardening hat! Like the ladies always have on in the magazines when they work in their gardens.

BENEATHA [*giggling fiercely*]: Travis—we were trying to make Mama Mrs. Miniver—not Scarlett O'Hara!

MAMA [*indignantly*]: What's the matter with you all! This here is a beautiful hat! [*Absurdly.*] I always wanted me one just like it! [*She pops it on her head to prove it to her grandson, and the hat is ludicrous and considerably oversized.*]

RUTH: Hot dog! Go, Mama!

WALTER [*doubled over with laughter*]: I'm sorry, Mama—but you look like you ready to go out and chop you some cotton sure enough!

[*They all laugh except* MAMA, *out of deference to* TRAVIS' *feelings.*]

MAMA [*gathering the boy up to her*]: Bless your heart—this is the prettiest hat I ever owned—[WALTER, RUTH *and* BENEATHA *chime in—noisily, festively and insincerely congratulating* TRAVIS *on his gift.*] What are we all standing around here for? We ain't finished packin' yet. Bennie, you ain't packed one book.

[*The bell rings.*]

BENEATHA: That couldn't be the movers . . . it's not hardly two good yet—

[BENEATHA *goes into her room.* MAMA *starts for door.*]

WALTER [*turning, stiffening*]: Wait—wait—I'll get it. [*He stands and looks at the door.*]

MAMA: You expecting company, son?

WALTER [*just looking at the door*]: Yeah—yeah . . .

[MAMA *looks at* RUTH, *and they exchange innocent and unfrightened glances.*]

MAMA [*not understanding*]: Well, let them in, son.

BENEATHA [*from her room*]: We need some more string.

MAMA: Travis—you run to the hardware and get me some string cord.

[MAMA *goes out and* WALTER *turns and looks at* RUTH. TRAVIS *goes to a dish for money.*]

RUTH: Why don't you answer the door, man?

WALTER [*suddenly bounding across the floor to her*]: 'Cause sometimes it hard to let the future begin! [*Stooping down in her face.*]

I got wings! You got wings!
All God's children got wings!

[*He crosses to the door and throws it open. Standing there is a very slight little man in a not too prosperous business suit and with haunted frightened eyes and a hat pulled down tightly, brim up, around his forehead.* TRAVIS *passes between the men and exits.* WALTER *leans deep in the man's face, still in his jubilance.*]

When I get to heaven gonna put on my wings,
Gonna fly all over God's heaven . . .

[*The little man just stares at him.*]

Heaven—

[*Suddenly he stops and looks past the little man into the empty hallway.*]

Where's Willy, man?
BOBO: He ain't with me.
WALTER [*not disturbed*]: Oh—come on in. You know my wife.
BOBO [*dumbly, taking off his hat*]: Yes—h'you, Miss Ruth.
RUTH [*quietly, a mood apart from her husband already, seeing* BOBO]: Hello, Bobo.
WALTER: You right on time today . . . Right on time. That's the way! [*He slaps* BOBO
   on his back.] Sit down . . . lemme hear.

[RUTH *stands stiffly and quietly in back of them, as though somehow she senses death, her eyes fixed
   on her husband.*]

BOBO [*his frightened eyes on the floor, his hat in his hands*]: Could I please get a drink a water,
   before I tell you about it, Walter Lee?

[WALTER *does not take his eyes off the man,* RUTH *goes blindly to the tap and gets a glass of water
   and brings it to* BOBO.]

WALTER: There ain't nothing wrong, is there?
BOBO: Lemme tell you—
WALTER: Man—didn't nothing go wrong?
BOBO: Lemme tell you—Walter Lee. [*Looking at* RUTH *and talking to her more than to*
   WALTER.] You know how it was. I got to tell you how it was. I mean first I got to
   tell you how it was all the way . . . I mean about the money I put in, Walter
   Lee . . .
WALTER [*with taut agitation now*]: What about the money you put in?
BOBO: Well—it wasn't much as we told you—me and Willy—[*He stops.*] I'm sorry,
   Walter. I got a bad feeling about it. I got a real bad feeling about it . . .
WALTER: Man, what you telling me about all this for? . . . Tell me what happened in
   Springfield . . .
BOBO: Springfield.
RUTH [*like a dead woman*]: What was supposed to happen in Springfield?
BOBO [*to her*]: This deal that me and Walter went into with Willy—Me and Willy was
   going to go down to Springfield and spread some money 'round so's we wouldn't
   have to wait so long for the liquor license . . . That's what we were going to do.
   Everybody said that was the way you had to do, you understand, Miss Ruth?

WALTER: Man—what happened down there?

BOBO [*a pitiful man, near tears*]: I'm trying to tell you, Walter.

WALTER [*screaming at him suddenly*]: THEN TELL ME, GODDAMNIT . . . WHAT'S THE MATTER WITH YOU?

BOBO: Man . . . I didn't go to no Springfield, yesterday.

WALTER [*halted, life hanging in the moment*]: Why not?

BOBO [*the long way, the hard way to tell*]: 'Cause I didn't have no reasons to . . .

WALTER: Man, what are you talking about!

BOBO: I'm talking about the fact that when I got to the train station yesterday morning—eight o'clock like we planned . . . Man—*Willy didn't never show up.*

WALTER: Why . . . where was he . . . where is he?

BOBO: That's what I'm trying to tell you . . . I don't know . . . I waited six hours . . . I called his house . . . and I waited . . . six hours . . . I waited in that train station six hours . . . [*Breaking into tears.*] That was all the extra money I had in the world . . . [*Looking up at* WALTER *with the tears running down his face.*] Man, *Willy is gone.*

WALTER: Gone, what you mean Willy is gone? Gone where? You mean he went by himself. You mean he went off to Springfield by himself—to take care of getting the license—[*Turns and looks anxiously at* RUTH.] You mean maybe he didn't want too many people in on the business down there? [*Looks to* RUTH *again, as before.*] You know Willy got his own ways. [*Looks back to* BOBO.] Maybe you was late yesterday and he just went on down there without you. Maybe—maybe—he's been callin' you at home tryin' to tell you what happened or something. Maybe—maybe—he just got sick. He's somewhere—he's got to be somewhere. We just got to find him—me and you got to find him. [*Grabs* BOBO *senselessly by the collar and starts to shake him.*] We got to!

BOBO [*in sudden angry, frightened agony*]: What's the matter with you, Walter! *When a cat take off with your money he don't leave you no maps!*

WALTER [*turning madly, as though he is looking for* WILLY *in the very room*]: Willy! . . . Willy . . . don't do it . . . Please don't do it . . . Man, not with that money . . . Man, please, not with that money . . . Oh, God . . . Don't let it be true . . . [*He is wandering around, crying out for Willy and looking for him or perhaps for help from God.*] Man . . . I trusted you . . . Man, I put my life in your hands . . . [*He starts to crumple down on the floor as* RUTH *just covers her face in horror.* MAMA *opens the door and comes into the room, with* BENEATHA *behind her.*] Man . . . [*He starts to pound the floor with his fists, sobbing wildly.*] *That money is made out of my father's flesh* . . .

BOBO [*standing over him helplessly*]: I'm sorry, Walter . . . [*Only* WALTER'S *sobs reply.* BOBO *puts on his hat.*] I had my life staked on this deal, too . . . [*He exits.*]

MAMA [*to* WALTER]: Son—[*She goes to him, bends down to him, talks to his bent head.*] Son . . . Is it gone? Son, I gave you sixty-five hundred dollars. Is it gone? All of it? Beneatha's money too?

WALTER [*lifting his head slowly*]: Mama . . . I never . . . went to the bank at all . . .

MAMA [*not wanting to believe him*]: You mean . . . your sister's school money . . . you used that too . . . Walter? . . .

WALTER: Yessss! . . . All of it . . . It's all gone . . .

[*There is total silence.* RUTH *stands with her face covered with her hands;* BENEATHA *leans forlornly against a wall, fingering a piece of red ribbon from the mother's gift.* MAMA *stops and looks at her son without recognition and then, quite without thinking about it, starts to beat him senselessly in the face.* BENEATHA *goes to them and stops it.*]

BENEATHA: Mama!

[MAMA *stops and looks at both of her children and rises slowly and wanders vaguely, aimlessly away from them.*]

MAMA: I seen . . . him . . . night after night . . . come in . . . and look at that rug . . . and then look at me . . . the red showing in his eyes . . . the veins moving in his head . . . I seen him grow thin and old before he was forty . . . working and working and working like somebody's old horse . . . killing himself . . . and you—you give it all away in a day . . .
BENEATHA: Mama—
MAMA: Oh, God . . . [*She looks up to Him.*] Look down here—and show me the strength.
BENEATHA: Mama—
MAMA [*folding over*]: Strength . . .
BENEATHA [*plaintively*]: Mama . . .
MAMA: Strength!

ACT III

An hour later.

    At curtain, there is a sullen light of gloom in the living room, gray light not unlike that which began the first scene of Act One. At left we can see WALTER *within his room, alone with himself. He is stretched out on the bed, his shirt out and open, his arms under his head. He does not smoke, he does not cry out, he merely lies there, looking up at the ceiling, much as if he were alone in the world.*

    In the living room BENEATHA *sits at the table, still surrounded by the now almost ominous packing crates. She sits looking off. We feel that this is a mood struck perhaps an hour before, and it lingers now, full of the empty sound of profound disappointment. We see on a line from her brother's bedroom the sameness of their attitudes. Presently the bell rings and* BENEATHA *rises without ambition or interest in answering. It is* ASAGAI, *smiling broadly, striding into the room with energy and happy expectation and conversation.*

ASAGAI: I came over . . . I had some free time. I thought I might help with the packing. Ah, I like the look of packing crates! A household in preparation for a journey! It depresses some people . . . but for me . . . it is another feeling. Something full of the flow of life, do you understand? Movement, progress . . . It makes me think of Africa.
BENEATHA: Africa!
ASAGAI: What kind of a mood is this? Have I told you how deeply you move me?
BENEATHA: He gave away the money, Asagai . . .

ASAGAI: Who gave away what money?

BENEATHA: The insurance money. My brother gave it away.

ASAGAI: Gave it away?

BENEATHA: He made an investment! With a man even Travis wouldn't have trusted.

ASAGAI: And it's gone?

BENEATHA: Gone!

ASAGAI: I'm very sorry . . . And you, now?

BENEATHA: Me? . . . Me? . . . Me I'm nothing . . . Me. When I was very small . . . we used to take our sleds out in the wintertime and the only hills we had were the ice-covered stone steps of some houses down the street. And we used to fill them in with snow and make them smooth and slide down them all day . . . and it was very dangerous you know . . . far too steep . . . and sure enough one day a kid named Rufus came down too fast and hit the sidewalk . . . and we saw his face just split open right there in front of us . . . And I remember standing there looking at his bloody open face thinking that was the end of Rufus. But the ambulance came and they took him to the hospital and they fixed the broken bones and they sewed it all up . . . and the next time I saw Rufus he just had a little line down the middle of his face . . . I never got over that . . .

ASAGAI: What?

BENEATHA: That that was what one person could do for another, fix him up—sew up the problem, make him all right again. That was the most marvelous thing in the world . . . I wanted to do that. I always thought it was the one concrete thing in the world that a human being could do. Fix up the sick, you know—and make them whole again. This was truly being God. . . .

ASAGAI: You wanted to be God?

BENEATHA: No—I wanted to cure. It used to be so important to me. I wanted to cure. It used to matter. I used to care. I mean about people and how their bodies hurt . . .

ASAGAI: And you've stopped caring?

BENEATHA: Yes—I think so.

ASAGAI: Why?

[WALTER *rises, goes to the door of his room and is about to open it, then stops and stands listening, leaning on the door jamb.*]

BENEATHA: Because it doesn't seem deep enough, close enough to what ails mankind—I mean this thing of sewing up bodies or administering drugs. Don't you understand? It was a child's reaction to the world. I thought that doctors had the secret to all the hurts. . . . That's the way a child sees things—or an idealist.

ASAGAI: Children see things very well sometimes—and idealists even better.

BENEATHA: I know that's what you think. Because you are still where I left off—you still care. This is what you see for the world, for Africa. You with the dreams of the future will patch up all Africa—you are going to cure the Great Sore of colonialism with Independence—

ASAGAI: Yes!

BENEATHA: Yes—and you think that one word is the penicillin of the human spirit: "Independence!" But then what?

ASAGAI: That will be the problem for another time. First we must get there.

BENEATHA: And where does it end?

ASAGAI: End? Who even spoke of an end? To life? To living?

BENEATHA: An end to misery!

ASAGAI [*smiling*]: You sound like a French intellectual.

BENEATHA: No! I sound like a human being who just had her future taken right out of her hands! While I was sleeping in my bed in there, things were happening in this world that directly concerned me—and nobody asked me, consulted me—they just went out and did things—and changed my life. Don't you see there isn't any real progress, Asagai, there is only one large circle that we march in, around and around, each of us with our own little picture—in front of us—our own little mirage that we think is the future.

ASAGAI: That is the mistake.

BENEATHA: What?

ASAGAI: What you just said—about the circle. It isn't a circle—it is simply a long line—as in geometry, you know, one that reaches into infinity. And because we cannot see the end—we also cannot see how it changes. And it is very odd but those who see the changes are called "idealists"—and those who cannot, or refuse to think, they are the "realists." It is very strange, and amusing too, I think.

BENEATHA: You—you are almost religious.

ASAGAI: Yes . . . I think I have the religion of doing what is necessary in the world— and of worshipping man—because he is so marvelous, you see.

BENEATHA: Man is foul! And the human race deserves its misery!

ASAGAI: You see: *you* have become the religious one in the old sense. Already, and after such a small defeat, you are worshipping despair.

BENEATHA: From now on, I worship the truth—and the truth is that people are puny, small and selfish. . . .

ASAGAI: Truth? Why is it that you despairing ones always think that only you have the truth? I never thought to see *you* like that. Your brother made a stupid, childish mistake—and you are grateful to him. So that now you can give up the ailing human race on account of it. You talk about what good is struggle; what good is anything? Where are we all going? And why are we bothering?

BENEATHA: *And you cannot answer it!* All your talk and dreams about Africa and Independence. Independence and then what? What about all the crooks and petty thieves and just plain idiots who will come into power to steal and plunder the same as before—only now they will be black and do it in the name of the new Independence—You cannot answer that.

ASAGAI [*shouting over her*]: *I live the answer!* [*Pause.*] In my village at home it is the exceptional man who can even read a newspaper . . . or who ever *sees* a book at all. I will go home and much of what I will have to say will seem strange to the people of my village . . . But I will teach and work and things will happen, slowly and swiftly. At times it will seem that nothing changes at all . . . and then again . . . the sudden dramatic events which make history leap into the future. And then quiet again.

Retrogression even. Guns, murder, revolution. And I even will have moments when I wonder if the quiet was not better than all that death and hatred. But I will look about my village at the illiteracy and disease and ignorance and I will not wonder long. And perhaps . . . perhaps I will be a great man . . . I mean perhaps I will hold on to the substance of truth and find my way always with the right course . . . and perhaps for it I will be butchered in my bed some night by the servants of empire . . .

BENEATHA: *The martyr!*

ASAGAI: . . . or perhaps I shall live to be a very old man respected and esteemed in my new nation . . . And perhaps I shall hold office and this is what I'm trying to tell you, Alaiyo; perhaps the things I believe now for my country will be wrong and outmoded, and I will not understand and do terrible things to have things my way or merely to keep my power. Don't you see that there will be young men and women, not British soldiers then, but my own black countrymen . . . to step out of the shadows some evening and slit my then useless throat? Don't you see they have always been there . . . that they always will be. And that such a thing as my own death will be an advance? They who might kill me even . . . actually replenish me!

BENEATHA: Oh, Asagai, I know all that.

ASAGAI: Good! Then stop moaning and groaning and tell me what you plan to do.

BENEATHA: Do?

ASAGAI: I have a bit of a suggestion.

BENEATHA: What?

ASAGAI [*rather quietly for him*]: That when it is all over—that you come home with me—

BENEATHA [*slapping herself on the forehead with exasperation born of misunderstanding*]: Oh— Asagai—at this moment you decide to be romantic!

ASAGAI [*quickly understanding the misunderstanding*]: My dear, young creature of the New World—I do not mean across the city—I mean across the ocean; home—to Africa.

BENEATHA [*slowly understanding and turning to him with murmured amazement*]: To—to Nigeria?

ASAGAI: Yes! . . . [*Smiling and lifting his arms playfully.*] Three hundred years later the African Prince rose up out of the seas and swept the maiden back across the middle passage over which her ancestors had come—

BENEATHA [*unable to play*]: Nigeria?

ASAGAI: Nigeria. Home. [*Coming to her with genuine romantic flippancy.*] I will show you our mountains and our stars; and give you cool drinks from gourds and teach you the old songs and the ways of our people—and, in time, we will pretend that—[*Very softly.*]—you have only been away for a day—

[*She turns her back to him, thinking. He swings her around and takes her full in his arms in a long embrace which proceeds to passion.*]

BENEATHA [*pulling away*]: You're getting me all mixed up—

ASAGAI: Why?

BENEATHA: Too many things—too many things have happened today. I must sit down and think. I don't know what I feel about anything right this minute. [*She promptly sits down and props her chin on her fist.*]

ASAGAI [*charmed*]: All right, I shall leave you. No—don't get up. [*Touching her, gently sweetly.*] Just sit awhile and think . . . Never be afraid to sit awhile and think. [*He goes to door and looks at her.*] How often I have looked at you and said, "Ah—so this is what the New World hath finally wrought . . ."

[*He exits. BENEATHA sits on alone. Presently WALTER enters from his room and starts to rummage through things, feverishly looking for something. She looks up and turns in her seat.*]

BENEATHA [*hissingly*]: Yes—just look at what the New World hath wrought! . . . Just look! [*She gestures with bitter disgust.*] There he is! *Monsieur le petit bourgeois noir*—himself! There he is—Symbol of a Rising Class! Entrepreneur! Titan of the system! [WALTER *ignores her completely and continues frantically and destructively looking for something and hurling things to floor and tearing things out of their place in his search. BENEATHA ignores the eccentricity of his actions and goes on with the monologue of insult.*] Did you dream of yachts on Lake Michigan, Brother? Did you see yourself on that Great Day sitting down at the Conference Table, surrounded by all the mighty baldheaded men in America? All halted, waiting, breathless, waiting for your pronouncements on industry? Waiting for you—Chairman of the Board? [WALTER *finds what he is looking for—a small piece of white paper—and pushes it in his pocket and puts on his coat and rushes out without ever having looked at her. She shouts after him.*] I look at you and I see the final triumph of stupidity in the world!

[*The door slams and she returns to just sitting again. RUTH comes quickly out of MAMA's room.*]

RUTH: Who was that?
BENEATHA: Your husband.
RUTH: Where did he go?
BENEATHA: Who knows—maybe he has an appointment at U.S. Steel.
RUTH [*anxiously, with frightened eyes*]: You didn't say nothing bad to him, did you?
BENEATHA: Bad? Say anything bad to him? No—I told him he was a sweet boy and full of dreams and everything is strictly peachy keen, as the ofay kids say!

[MAMA *enters from her bedroom. She is lost, vague, trying to catch hold, to make some sense of her former command of the world, but it still eludes her. A sense of waste overwhelms her gait; a measure of apology rides on her shoulders. She goes to her plant, which has remained on the table, looks at it, picks it up and takes it to the window sill and sits it outside, and she stands and looks at it a long moment. Then she closes the window, straightens her body with effort and turns around to her children.*]

MAMA: Well   ain't it a mess in here, though? [*A false cheerfulness, a beginning of something.*] I guess we all better stop moping around and get some work done. All this unpacking and everything we got to do. [RUTH *raises her head slowly in response to the sense of the line; and* BENEATHA *in similar manner turns very slowly to look at her mother.*] One of you all better call the moving people and tell 'em not to come.
RUTH: Tell 'em not to come?
MAMA: Of course, baby. Ain't no need in 'em coming all the way here and having to

go back. They charges for that too. [*She sits down, fingers to her brow, thinking.*] Lord, ever since I was a little girl, I always remembers people saying, "Lena—Lena Eggleston, you aims too high all the time. You needs to slow down and see life a little more like it is. Just slow down some." That's what they always used to say down home— "Lord, that Lena Eggleston is a high-minded thing. She'll get her due one day!"

RUTH: No, Lena . . .

MAMA: Me and Big Walter just didn't never learn right.

RUTH: Lena, no! We gotta go. Bennie—tell her . . . [*She rises and crosses to* BENEATHA *with her arms outstretched.* BENEATHA *doesn't respond.*] Tell her we can still move . . . the notes ain't but a hundred and twenty five a month. We got four grown people in this house—we can work . . .

MAMA [*to herself*]: Just aimed too high all the time—

RUTH [*turning and going to* MAMA *fast—the words pouring out with urgency and desperation*]: Lena—I'll work . . . I'll work twenty hours a day in all the kitchens in Chicago . . . I'll strap my baby on my back if I have to and scrub all the floors in America and wash all the sheets in America if I have to—but we got to move . . . We got to get out of here.

[MAMA *reaches out absently and pats* RUTH's *hand.*]

MAMA: No—I sees things differently now. Been thinking 'bout some of the things we could do to fix this place up some. I seen a second-hand bureau over on Maxwell Street just the other day that could fit right there. [*She points to where the new furniture might go.* RUTH *wanders away from her.*] Would need some new handles on it and then a little varnish and then it look like something brand-new. And—we can put up them new curtains in the kitchen . . . Why this place be looking fine. Cheer us all up so that we forget trouble ever came . . . [*To* RUTH.] And you could get some nice screens to put up in your room round the baby's basinet . . . [*She looks at both of them, pleadingly.*] Sometimes you just got to know when to give up some things . . . and hold on to what you got.

[WALTER *enters from the outside, looking spent and leaning against the door, his coat hanging from him.*]

MAMA: Where you been, son?

WALTER [*breathing hard*]: Made a call.

MAMA: To who, son?

WALTER: To The Man.

MAMA: What man, baby?

WALTER: The Man, Mama. Don't you know who The Man is?

RUTH: Walter Lee?

WALTER: *The Man.* Like the guys in the streets say—The Man. Captain Boss—Mistuh Charley . . . Old Captain Please Mr. Bossman . . .

BENEATHA [*suddenly*]: Lindner!

WALTER: That's right! That's good. I told him to come right over.

BENEATHA [*fiercely, understanding*]: For what? What do you want to see him for!

WALTER [*looking at his sister*]: We going to do business with him.

MAMA: What you talking 'bout, son?

WALTER: Talking 'bout life, Mama. You all always telling me to see life like it is. Well—I laid in there on my back today . . . and I figured it out. Life just like it is. Who gets and who don't get. [*He sits down with his coat on and laughs.*] Mama, you know it's all divided up. Life is. Sure enough. Between the takers and the "tooken." [*He laughs.*] I've figured it out finally. [*He looks around at them.*] Yeah. Some of us always getting "tooken." [*He laughs.*] People like Willy Harris, they don't never get "tooken." And you know why the rest of us do? 'Cause we all mixed up. Mixed up bad. We get to looking 'round for the right and the wrong; and we worry about it and cry about it and stay up nights trying to figure out 'bout the wrong and the right of things all the time . . . And all the time, man, them takers is out there operating, just taking and taking. Willy Harris? Shoot—Willy Harris don't even count. He don't even count in the big scheme of things. But I'll say one thing for old Willy Harris . . . he's taught me something. He's taught me to keep my eye on what counts in this world. Yeah—[*Shouting out a little.*] Thanks, Willy!

RUTH: What did you call that man for, Walter Lee?

WALTER: Called him to tell him to come on over to the show. Gonna put on a show for the man. Just what he wants to see. You see, Mama, the man came here today and he told us that them people out there where you want us to move—well they so upset they willing to pay us not to move out there. [*He laughs again.*] And—and oh, Mama—you would of been proud of the way me and Ruth and Bennie acted. We told him to get out . . . Lord have mercy! We told the man to get out. Oh, we was some proud folks this afternoon, yeah. [*He lights a cigarette.*] We were still full of that old-time stuff . . .

RUTH [*coming toward him slowly*]: You talking 'bout taking them people's money to keep us from moving in that house?

WALTER: I ain't just talking 'bout it, baby—I'm telling you that's what's going to happen.

BENEATHA: Oh, God! Where is the bottom! Where is the real honest-to-God bottom so he can't go any farther!

WALTER: See—that's the old stuff. You and that boy that was here today. You all want everybody to carry a flag and a spear and sing some marching songs, huh? You wanna spend your life looking into things and trying to find the right and the wrong part, huh? Yeah. You know what's going to happen to that boy someday—he'll find himself sitting in a dungeon, locked in forever—and the takers will have the key! Forget it, baby! There ain't no causes—there ain't nothing but taking in this world, and he who takes most is smartest—and it don't make a damn bit of difference *how*.

MAMA: You making something inside me cry, son. Some awful pain inside me.

WALTER: Don't cry, Mama. Understand. That white man is going to walk in that door able to write checks for more money than we ever had. It's important to him and I'm going to help him . . . I'm going to put on the show, Mama.

MAMA: Son—I come from five generations of people who was slaves and sharecroppers—but ain't nobody in my family never let nobody pay 'em no money that was a way of telling us we wasn't fit to walk the earth. We ain't never been that poor. [*Raising her eyes and looking at him.*] We ain't never been that dead inside.

BENEATHA: Well—we are dead now. All the talk about dreams and sunlight that goes on in this house. All dead.

WALTER: What's the matter with you all! I didn't make this world! It was give to me this way! Hell, yes, I want me some yachts someday! Yes, I want to hang some real pearls 'round my wife's neck. Ain't she supposed to wear no pearls? Somebody tell me—tell me, who decides which women is suppose to wear pearls in this world. I tell you I am a *man*—and I think my wife should wear some pearls in this world!

[*This last line hangs a good while and* WALTER *begins to move about the room. The word "Man" has penetrated his consciousness; he mumbles it to himself repeatedly between strange agitated pauses as he moves about.*]

MAMA: Baby, how you going to feel on the inside?

WALTER: Fine! . . . Going to feel fine . . . a man . . .

MAMA: You won't have nothing left then, Walter Lee.

WALTER [*coming to her*]: I'm going to feel fine, Mama. I'm going to look that son-of-a-bitch in the eyes and say—[*He falters.*]—and say, "All right, Mr. Lindner—[*He falters even more.*]—that's your neighborhood out there. You got the right to keep it like you want. You got the right to have it like you want. Just write the check and—the house is yours." And, and I am going to say—[*His voice almost breaks.*] And you—you people just put the money in my hand and you won't have to live next to this bunch of stinking niggers! . . . [*He straightens up and moves away from his mother, walking around the room.*] Maybe—maybe I'll just get down on my black knees . . . [*He does so;* RUTH *and* BENNIE *and* MAMA *watch him in frozen horror.*] Captain, Mistuh, Bossman. [*He starts crying.*] A-hee-hee-hee! [*Wringing his hands in profoundly anguished imitation.*] Yasssssuh! Great White Father, just gi' ussen de money, fo' God's sake, and we's ain't gwine come out deh and dirty up yo' white folks neighborhood . . . [*He breaks down completely, then gets up and goes into the bedroom.*]

BENEATHA: That is not a man. That is nothing but a toothless rat.

MAMA: Yes—death done come in this here house. [*She is nodding, slowly, reflectively.*] Done come walking in my house. On the lips of my children. You what supposed to be my beginning again. You—what supposed to be my harvest. [*To* BENEATHA.] You—you mourning your brother?

BENEATHA: He's no brother of mine.

MAMA: What you say?

BENEATHA: I said that that individual in that room is no brother of mine.

MAMA: That's what I thought you said. You feeling like you better than he is today? [BENEATHA *does not answer.*] Yes? What you tell him a minute ago? That he wasn't a man? Yes? You give him up for me? You done wrote his epitaph too—like the rest of the world? Well, who give you the privilege?

BENEATHA: Be on my side for once! You saw what he just did, Mama! You saw him—down on his knees. Wasn't it you who taught me—to despise any man who would do that? Do what he's going to do.

MAMA: Yes—I taught you that. Me and your daddy. But I thought I taught you something else too . . . I thought I taught you to love him.

BENEATHA: Love him? There is nothing left to love.

MAMA: There is always something left to love. And if you ain't learned that, you ain't learned nothing. [*Looking at her.*] Have you cried for that boy today? I don't mean for yourself and for the family 'cause we lost the money. I mean for him; what he been through and what it done to him. Child, when do you think is the time to love somebody the most; when they done good and made things easy for everybody? Well then, you ain't through learning—because that ain't the time at all. It's when he's at his lowest and can't believe in hisself 'cause the world done whipped him so. When you starts measuring somebody, measure him right, child, measure him right. Make sure you done taken into account what hills and valleys he come through before he got to wherever he is.

[TRAVIS *bursts into the room at the end of the speech, leaving the door open.*]

TRAVIS: Grandmama—the moving men are downstairs! The truck just pulled up.

MAMA [*turning and looking at him*]: Are they, baby? They downstairs?

[*She sighs and sits. Lindner appears in the doorway. He peers in and knocks lightly, to gain attention, and comes in. All turn to look at him.*]

LINDNER [*hat and briefcase in hand*]: Uh—hello . . .

[RUTH *crosses mechanically to the bedroom door and opens it and lets it swing open freely and slowly as the lights come up on* WALTER *within, still in his coat, sitting at the far corner of the room. He looks up and out through the room to* LINDNER.]

RUTH: He's here.

[*A long minute passes and* WALTER *slowly gets up.*]

LINDNER [*coming to the table with efficiency, putting his briefcase on the table and starting to unfold papers and unscrew fountain pens*]: Well, I certainly was glad to hear from you people. [WALTER *has begun the trek out of the room, slowly and awkwardly, rather like a small boy, passing the back of his sleeve across his mouth from time to time.*] Life can really be so much simpler than people let it be most of the time. Well—with whom do I negotiate? You, Mrs. Younger, or your son here? [MAMA *sits with her hands folded on her lap and her eyes closed as* WALTER *advances.* TRAVIS *goes close to* LINDNER *and looks at the papers curiously.*] Just some official papers, sonny.

RUTH: Travis, you go downstairs.

MAMA [*opening her eyes and looking into* WALTER'S]: No. Travis, you stay right here. And you make him understand what you doing, Walter Lee. You teach him good. Like Willy Harris taught you. You show where our five generations done come to. Go ahead, son—

WALTER [*looks down into his boy's eyes.* TRAVIS *grins at him merrily and* WALTER *draws him beside him with his arm lightly around his shoulder*]: Well, Mr. Lindner. [BENEATHA *turns away.*] We called you—[*There is a profound, simple groping quality in his speech.*]—because, well, me and my family [*He looks around and shifts from one foot to the other.*] Well—we are very plain people . . .

LINDNER: Yes—

WALTER: I mean—I have worked as a chauffeur most of my life—and my wife here, she does domestic work in people's kitchens. So does my mother. I mean—we are plain people . . .

LINDNER: Yes, Mr. Younger—

WALTER [*really like a small boy, looking down at his shoes and then up at the man*]: And—uh—well, my father, well, he was a laborer most of his life.

LINDNER [*absolutely confused*]: Uh, yes—

WALTER [*looking down at his toes once again*]: My father almost beat a man to death once because this man called him a bad name or something, you know what I mean?

LINDNER: No, I'm afraid I don't.

WALTER [*finally straightening up*]: Well, what I mean is that we come from people who had a lot of pride. I mean—we are very proud people. And that's my sister over there and she's going to be a doctor—and we are very proud—

LINDNER: Well—I am sure that is very nice, but—

WALTER [*starting to cry and facing the man eye to eye*]: What I am telling you is that we called you over here to tell you that we are very proud and that this is—this is my son, who makes the sixth generation of our family in this country, and that we have all thought about your offer and we have decided to move into our house because my father—my father—he earned it. [MAMA *has her eyes closed and is rocking back and forth as though she were in church, with her head nodding the amen yes.*] We don't want to make no trouble for nobody or fight no causes—but we will try to be good neighbors. That's all we got to say. [*He looks the man absolutely in the eyes.*] We don't want your money. [*He turns and walks away from the man.*]

LINDNER [*looking around at all of them*]: I take it then that you have decided to occupy.

BENEATHA: That's what the man said.

LINDNER [*to* MAMA *in her reverie*]: Then I would like to appeal to you, Mrs. Younger. You are older and wiser and understand things better I am sure . . .

MAMA [*rising*]: I am afraid you don't understand. My son said we was going to move and there ain't nothing left for me to say. [*Shaking her head with double meaning.*] You know how these young folks is nowadays, mister. Can't do a thing with 'em. Good-bye.

LINDNER [*folding up his materials*]: Well—if you are that final about it . . . There is nothing left for me to say. [*He finishes. He is almost ignored by the family, who are concentrating on* WALTER LEE. *At the door* LINDNER *halts and looks around.*] I sure hope you people know what you're doing. [*He shakes his head and exits.*]

RUTH [*looking around and coming to life*]: Well, for God's sake—if the moving men are here—LET'S GET THE HELL OUT OF HERE!

MAMA [*into action*]: Ain't it the truth! Look at all this here mess. Ruth put Travis' good jacket on him . . . Walter Lee, fix your tie and tuck your shirt in, you look just like somebody's hoodlum. Lord have mercy, where is my plant? [*She flies to get it amid the general bustling of the family, who are deliberately trying to ignore the nobility of the past moment.*] You all start on down . . . Travis child, don't go empty-handed . . . Ruth, where did I put that box with my skillets in it? I want to be in charge of it myself . . . I'm going to make us the biggest dinner we ever ate tonight . . . Beneatha, what's the matter with them stockings? Pull them things up, girl . . .

[*The family starts to file out as two moving men appear and begin to carry out the heavier pieces of furniture, bumping into the family as they move about.*]

BENEATHA: Mama, Asagai—asked me to marry him today and go to Africa—
MAMA [*in the middle of her getting-ready activity*]: He did? You ain't old enough to marry nobody—[*Seeing the moving men lifting one of her chairs precariously.*] Darling, that ain't no bale of cotton, please handle it so we can sit in it again. I had that chair twenty-five years . . .

[*The movers sigh with exasperation and go on with their work.*]

BENEATHA [*girlishly and unreasonably trying to pursue the conversation*]: To go to Africa, Mama—be a doctor in Africa . . .
MAMA [*distracted*]: Yes, baby—
WALTER: Africa! What he want you to go to Africa for?
BENEATHA: To practice there . . .
WALTER: Girl, if you don't get all them silly ideas out your head! You better marry yourself a man with some loot . . .
BENEATHA [*angrily, precisely as in the first scene of the play*]: What have you got to do with who I marry!
WALTER: Plenty. Now I think George Murchison—

[*He and* BENEATHA *go out yelling at each other vigorously;* BENEATHA *is heard saying that she would not marry* GEORGE MURCHISON *if he were Adam and she were Eve, etc. The anger is loud and real till their voices diminish.* RUTH *stands at the door and turns to* MAMA *and smiles knowingly.*]

MAMA [*fixing her hat at last*]: Yeah—they something all right, my children . . .
RUTH: Yeah—they're something. Let's go, Lena.
MAMA [*stalling, starting to look around at the house*]: Yes—I'm coming. Ruth—
RUTH: Yes?
MAMA [*quietly, woman to woman*]: He finally come into his manhood today, didn't he? Kind of like a rainbow after the rain . . .
RUTH [*biting her lip lest her own pride explode in front of* MAMA]: Yes, Lena.

[WALTER'S *voice calls for them raucously.*]

MAMA [*waving* RUTH *out vaguely*]: All right, honey—go on down. I be down directly.

[RUTH *hesitates, then exits.* MAMA *stands, at last alone in the living room, her plant on the table before her as the lights start to come down. She looks around at all the walls and ceilings and suddenly, despite herself, while the children call below, a great heaving thing rises in her and she puts her fist to her mouth, takes a final desperate look, pulls her coat about her, pats her hat and goes out. The lights dim down. The door opens and she comes back in, grabs her plant, and goes out for the last time.*]

Curtain

QUESTIONS

1. The playwright introduces her description of the Younger home by saying it has a "number of indestructible contradictions." Explain what she means by this. Select one of the characters introduced in Act I, and explain his or her "contradictions."

2. What is the first major conflict that occurs in Act I? How does it foreshadow a major event that occurs in the latter part of the play?

3. Based on Act I, which of the characters do you find most appealing? Least appealing? Explain why.

4. What is the chief conflict between George Murchison and Beneatha? Between George Murchison and Walter?

5. Compare Walter's feelings at the end of Act II, scene II, with his reaction to what Bobo reveals to him at the end of Act II, scene III. How does the contrast between these two dramatic moments contribute to the dramatic tension of the play?

6. Asagai and Beneatha have an argument at the beginning of Act III. What is each one's main contention? Do you take sides with either of them? If so, which one, and why?

7. In Act III, Walter explains to Mama what he plans to tell Lindner about moving into the new house. But what he actually tells him when he arrives is quite different. How do you account for this change of heart? How does it heighten the intensity of the drama?

Langston Hughes

SOUL GONE HOME

———— CHARACTERS ————

THE MOTHER
THE SON
TWO MEN

Night.

A tenement room, bare, ugly, dirty. An unshaded electric-light bulb. In the middle of the room a cot on which the body of a Negro youth is lying. His hands are folded across his chest. There are pennies on his eyes. He is a soul gone home.

As the curtain rises, his mother, a large, middle-aged woman in a red sweater, kneels weeping beside the cot, loudly simulating grief.

MOTHER: Oh, Gawd! Oh Lawd! Why did you take my son from me? Oh, Gawd, why did you do it? He was all I had! Oh, Lawd, what am I gonna do? [*Looking at the dead boy and stroking his head.*] Oh, son! Oh, Ronnie! Oh, my boy, speak to me! Ronnie, say something to me! Son, why don't you talk to your mother? Can't you see she's bowed down in sorrow? Son, speak to me, just a word! Come back from the spirit-world and speak to me! Ronnie, come back from the dead and speak to your mother!

SON [*lying there dead as a doornail, speaking loudly*]: I wish I wasn't dead, so I could speak to you. You been a hell of a mama!

MOTHER [*falling back from the cot in astonishment, but still on her knees*]: Ronnie! Ronnie! What's that you say? What you sayin' to your mother? [*Wild-eyed.*] Is you done opened your mouth and spoke to me?

SON: I said you a hell of a mama!

MOTHER [*rising suddenly and backing away, screaming loudly*]: Awo-oo-o! Ronnie, that ain't you talkin'!

SON: Yes, it is me talkin', too! I say you been a no-good mama.

MOTHER: What for you talkin' to me like that, Ronnie? You ain't never said nothin' like that to me before.

SON: I know it, but I'm dead now—and I can say what I want to say. [*Stirring.*] You done called on me to talk, ain't you? Lemme take these pennies off my eyes so I can see. [*He takes the coins off his eyes, throws them across the room, and sits up in bed. He is a very dark boy in a torn white shirt. He looks hard at his mother.*] Mama, you know you ain't done me right.

MOTHER: What you mean, I ain't done you right? [*She is rooted in horror.*] What you mean, huh?

SON: You know what I mean.

MOTHER: No, I don't neither. [*Trembling violently.*] What you mean comin' back to haunt your poor old mother? Ronnie, what does you mean?

SON [*leaning forward*]: I'll tell you just what I mean! You been a bad mother to me.

MOTHER: Shame! Shame! Shame, talkin' to your mama that away. Damn it! Shame! I'll slap your face. [*She starts toward him, but he rolls his big white eyes at her, and she backs away.*] Me, what borned you! Me, what suffered the pains o' death to bring you into this world! Me, what raised you up, what washed your dirty didies. [*Sorrowfully.*] And now I'm left here mighty nigh prostrate 'cause you gone from me! Ronnie, what you mean talkin' to *me* like that—what brought you into this world?

SON: You never did feed me good, that's what I mean! Who wants to come into the world hongry, and go out the same way?

MOTHER: What you mean hongry? When I had money, ain't I fed you?

SON [*sullenly*]: Most of the time you ain't had no money.

MOTHER: Twarn't my fault then.

SON: Twarn't *my* fault neither.

MOTHER [*defensively*]: You always was so weak and sickly, you couldn't earn nothin' sellin' papers.

SON: I know it.

MOTHER: You never was no use to me.

SON: So you just lemme grow up in the street, and I ain't had no manners nor morals, neither.

MOTHER: Manners and morals? Ronnie, where'd you learn all them big words?

SON: I learnt 'em just now in the spirit-world.

MOTHER [*coming nearer*]: But you ain't been dead no more'n an hour.

SON: That's long enough to learn a lot.

MOTHER: Well, what else did you find out?

SON: I found out you was a hell of a mama puttin' me out in the cold to sell papers soon as I could even walk.

MOTHER: What? You little liar!

SON: If I'm lyin', I'm dyin'! And lettin' me grow up all bowlegged and stunted from undernourishment.

MOTHER: Under-nurse-mint?

SON: Undernourishment. You heard what the doctor said last week?

MOTHER: Naw, what'd he say?

SON: He said I was dyin' o' undernourishment, that's what he said. He said I had TB 'cause I didn't have enough to eat never when I were a child. And he said I couldn't get well, nohow eating nothin' but beans ever since I been sick. Said I needed milk and eggs. And you said you ain't got no money for milk and eggs, which I know you ain't. [*Gently.*] We never had no money, mama, not even since you took up hustlin' on the streets.

MOTHER: Son, money ain't everything.

SON: Naw, but when you got TB you have to have milk and eggs.

MOTHER [*advancing sentimentally*]: Anyhow, I love you, Ronnie!

SON [*rudely*]: Sure you love me—but here I am dead.

MOTHER [*angrily*]: Well, damn your hide, you ain't even decent dead. If you was, you wouldn't be sittin' there jawin' at your mother when she's sheddin' every tear she's got for you tonight.

SON: First time you ever did cry for me, far as I know.

MOTHER: Tain't! You's a liar! I cried when I borned you—you was such a big child—ten pounds.

SON: Then *I* did the cryin' after that, I reckon.

MOTHER [*proudly*]: Sure, I could of let you die, but I didn't. Naw, I kept you with me—off and on. And I lost the chance to marry many a good man, too—if it weren't for you. No man wants to take care o' nobody else's child. [*Self-pityingly.*] You been a burden to me, Randolph.

SON [*angrily*]: What did you have me for then, in the first place?

MOTHER: How could I help havin' you, you little bastard? Your father ruint me— and you's the result. And I been worried with you for sixteen years. [*Disgustedly.*] Now, just when you get big enough to work and do me some good, you have to go and die.

SON: I sure am dead!

MOTHER: But you ain't decent dead! Here you come back to haunt your poor old mama, and spoil her cryin' spell, and spoil the mournin'. [*There is the noise of an ambulance going outside. The mother goes to the window and looks down into the street. Turns to son.*] Ronnie, lay down quick! Here comes the city's ambulance to take you to the undertaker's. Don't let them white men see you dead, sitting up here quarrelin' with your mother. Lay down and fold your hands back like I had 'em.

SON [*passing his hand across his head*]: All right, but gimme that comb yonder and my stocking cap. I don't want to go out of here with my hair standin' straight up in front, even if I is dead. [*The mother hands him a comb and his stocking cap. The son combs his hair and puts the cap on. Noise of men coming up the stairs.*]

MOTHER: Hurry up, Ronnie, they'll be here in no time.

SON: Aw, they got another flight to come yet. Don't rush me, ma!

MOTHER: Yes, but I got to put these pennies back on your eyes, boy! [*She searches in a corner for the coins as her son lies down and folds his hands, stiff in death. She finds the coins and puts them nervously on his eyes, watching the door meanwhile. A knock.*] Come in.

[*Enter two men in the white coats of city health employees.*]

MAN: Somebody sent for us to get the body of Ronnie Bailey? Third floor, apartment five.

MOTHER: Yes, sir, here he is! [*Weeping loudly.*] He's my boy! Oh, Lawd, he's done left me! Oh, Lawdy, he's done gone home! His soul's gone home! Oh, what am I gonna do? Mister! Mister! Mister, the Lawd's done took him home! [*As the men unfold the stretchers, she continues to weep hysterically. They place the boy's thin body on the stretchers and cover it with a rubber cloth. Each man takes his end of the stretchers. Silently, they walk out the door as the mother wails.*] Oh, my son! Oh, my boy! Come back, come back, come back! Ronnie, come back! [*One loud scream as the door closes.*] Awo-ooo-o!

[*As the footsteps of the men die down on the stairs, the mother becomes suddenly quiet. She goes to a broken mirror and begins to rouge and powder her face. In the street the ambulance gong sounds fainter and fainter in the distance. The mother takes down an old fur coat from a nail and puts it*] *on. Before she leaves, she smooths back the quilts on the cot from which the dead boy has been removed. She looks into the mirror again, and once more whitens her face with powder. She dons a red hat. From a handbag she takes a cigarette, lights it, and walks slowly out the door. At the door she switches off the light. The hallway is dimly illuminated. She turns before closing the door, looks back into the room, and speaks.*]

MOTHER: Tomorrow, Ronnie, I'll buy you some flowers—if I can pick up a dollar tonight. You was a hell of a no-good son, I swear!

Curtain.

QUESTIONS

1. Would you characterize the tone of the play as comic, tragic, tragicomic, or something else? Explain your answer.
2. Hughes describes the mother as "loudly simulating grief." What does this imply about the relationship of the mother to her son? What might Hughes be implying in this stage direction about the black experience in America in general?
3. The son makes the ironic remark that "I'm dead now—and I can say what I want to say." What does he mean by this? Find other ironies in the characters' actions and statements, and explain their meaning.
4. Why does the author write in "stock" black dialect? For naturalism? To make a statement? For humor? Explain.

David Henry Hwang

FAMILY DEVOTIONS

CHARACTERS

JOANNE, late thirties, Chinese American raised in the Philippines.
WILBUR, her husband, Japanese American, nisei (second generation).
JENNY, their daughter, seventeen.
AMA, Joanne's mother, born in China, emigrated to the Philippines, then to America.
POPO, Ama's younger sister.
HANNAH, Popo's daughter and Joanne's cousin, slightly older than Joanne.
ROBERT, Hannah's husband, Chinese American, first generation.
DI-GOU, Ama and Popo's younger brother, born and raised in China, still a resident of the People's Republic of China (P.R.C.).
CHESTER, Hannah and Robert's son, early twenties.

```
              AMA ———————— POPO ——————— DI-GOU

  WILBUR — m — JOANNE        HANNAH — m — ROBERT

         JENNY                     CHESTER
```

SYNOPSIS OF SCENES

ACT I. *Late afternoon, the lanai/sunroom and tennis court of a home in Bel Air, California.*

ACT II. *Same scene, immediately following.*

ACT I

The sunroom and backyard of a home in Bel Air. Everywhere is glass—glass roof, glass walls. Upstage of the lanai/sunroom is a patio with a barbecue and a tennis court. The tennis court leads offstage. As the curtain rises, we see a single spotlight on an old Chinese face and hear Chinese music or chanting. Suddenly, the music becomes modern-day funk or rock 'n' roll, and the lights come up to reveal the set.

The face is that of DI-GOU, *an older Chinese man wearing a blue suit and carrying an old suitcase. He is peering into the sunroom from the tennis court, through the glass walls. Behind him, a stream of black smoke is coming from the barbecue.*

JOANNE: [*Offstage*] Wilbur! Wilbur!

[DI-GOU *exits off the tennis court. Enter* JOANNE, *from the house. She is a Chinese American woman, attractive, in her mid-thirties. She sees the smoke coming from the barbecue.*]

JOANNE: Aiii-ya! [*She heads for the barbecue, and on her way notices that the sunroom is a mess.*] Jenny! [*She runs out to the barbecue, opens it up. Billows of black smoke continue to pour out.*] Oh, gosh. Oh, golly. [*To offstage*] Wilbur! [*She begins pulling burnt objects out of the barbecue.*] Sheee! [*She pulls out a chicken, dumps it onto the ground.*] Wilbur! [*She pulls out another chicken, does the same.*] Wilbur, the heat was too high on the barbecue! [*She begins pulling out burnt objects and tossing them all over the tennis court.*] You should have been watching it! It could have exploded! We could all have been blown up! [*She picks up another chicken, examines it.*] You think we can have some of this? [*She pauses, tosses it onto the court.*] We'll get some more chickens. We'll put barbecue sauce on them and stick them into the microwave. [*She exits into the house holding a chicken on the end of her fork.*] Is this okay, do you think?

[WILBUR *appears on the tennis court. He is a Japanese American man, nisei, in his late thirties. His hair is permed. He wears tennis clothes.*]

WILBUR: Hon? [*He looks around.*] What's up? [*He picks a burnt chicken off the tennis court.*] Hon? [*He walks over to the barbecue.*] Who—? Why's the heat off? [*He walks around the tennis court picking up chickens.*] Jesus! [*He smears grease on his white tennis shirt, notices it.*] Aw, shit! [*He dumps all the chickens except one, which he has forgotten to pick up, back into the barbecue.*

He walks into the sunroom, gets some ice, and tries to dab at the stain.] Hon? Will you come here a sec? [*He exits into the house.*]

[JENNY *appears on the tennis court. She is seventeen,* WILBUR *and* JOANNE's *daughter. She carries a large wire-mesh box.*]

JENNY: Chickie! [*Looking around*] Chickie? Chickie, where the hell did you go? You know, it's embarrassing. It's embarrassing being this old and still having to chase a chicken all over the house. [*She sees the lone burnt chicken on the court. She creeps over slowly, then picks it up.*] Blaagh! Who cooked this? See, Chickie, this is what happens—what happens when you're a bad chickie.

[CHESTER, *a young Chinese American male in his early twenties, appears on the tennis court. He tries to sneak up on* JENNY.]

JENNY: [*To chicken*] Look, if you bother Popo and Ama, I'm gonna catch shit, and you know what that means for you—chicken soccer. You'll be sorry. [CHESTER *is right behind* JENNY.] You'll be sorry if you mess with me. [*She turns around, catching* CHESTER.] Oh, good. You have to be here, too.

CHESTER: No, I don't. I've gotta pack.

JENNY: They'll expect you to be here when that Chinese guy gets here. What's name? Dar-gwo?

CHESTER: I dunno. Dah-gim?

JENNY: Doo-goo? Something.

CHESTER: Yeah. I'm not staying.

JENNY: So what else is new?

CHESTER: I don't have time.

JENNY: You luck out 'cause you don't live here. Me—there's no way I can get away. When you leaving?

CHESTER: Tomorrow.

JENNY: Tomorrow? And you're not packed?

CHESTER: Don't rub it in. Listen, you still have my green suitcase?

JENNY: Yeah. I wish *I* had an excuse not to be here. All I need is to meet another old relative. Another goon.

CHESTER: Yeah. Where's my suitcase?

JENNY: First you have to help me find Chickie.

CHESTER: Jesus!

AMA: [*Offstage*] Joanne!

CHESTER: [*To* JENNY] All right. I don't want them to know I'm here.

[CHESTER *and* JENNY *exit.* POPO *and* AMA *enter. They are* JOANNE's *aunt and mother, respectively.*]

AMA: Joanne! Joanne! Jenny! Where is Joanne?

POPO: Probably busy.

AMA: Where is Jenny? Joanne?

POPO: Perhaps you can find, ah, Wilbur.

AMA: Joanne!

POPO: Ah, you never wish to see Wilbur.

AMA: I see him at wedding. That is enough. He was not at church again today.

POPO: Ah?

AMA: He will be bad influence when Di-gou arrive. Wilbur—holy spirit is not in him.

POPO: Not matter. He can perhaps eat in kitchen.

AMA: Outside!

POPO: This is his house.

AMA: All heart must join as one—

POPO: He may eat inside!

AMA: only then, miracles can take place.

POPO: But in kitchen.

AMA: Wilbur—he never like family devotions.

POPO: Wilbur does not come from Christian family.

AMA: He come from Japanese family.

POPO: I mean to say, we—ah—very fortunate. Mama teach us all Christianity. Not like Wilbur family.

AMA: When Di-gou arrive, we will remind him. What Mama tells us.

POPO: Di-gou can remember himself.

AMA: No.

POPO: But we remember.

AMA: You forget—Di-gou, he lives in China.

POPO: So?

AMA: Torture, Communists. Make him work in rice fields.

POPO: I no longer think so.

AMA: In rice field, all the people wear wires in their heads—yes! Wires force them work all day and sing Communist song. Like this! [*She mimes harvesting rice and singing.*]

POPO: No such thing!

AMA: Yes! You remember Twa-Ling? Before we leave China, before Communist come, she say, "I will send you a picture. If Communists are good, I will stand—if bad, I will sit."

POPO: That does not mean anything!

AMA: In picture she sent, she was lying down!

POPO: Picture was not sent for ten years. Probably she forget.

AMA: You wait till Di-gou arrive. You will see.

POPO: See what?

AMA: Brainwash! You watch for little bit of wires in his hair.

[POPO *notices the lone burnt chicken on the tennis court.*]

POPO: What's there?

AMA: Where?

POPO: There—on cement.

AMA: Cannot see well.

POPO: There. Black.

AMA: Oh. I see.
POPO: Looks like *gao sai.*
AMA: They sometimes have problem with the dog.
POPO: Ha!
AMA: Very bad dog.
POPO: At home, dog do that?—we shoot him.
AMA: Should be punish.
POPO: Shot! [*Pause*] That no *gao sai.*
AMA: No? What then?
POPO: I don't know.
AMA: Oh, I know.
POPO: What?
AMA: That is Chickie.
POPO: No. That no Chickie.
AMA: They have a chicken—"Chickie."

[*They get up, head toward the chicken.*]

POPO: No. That one, does not move.
AMA: Maybe sick. [*They reach the chicken.*] Aiii-ya! What happen to Chickie!
POPO: [*Picking it up*] This chicken very sick! [*She laughs.*]
AMA: Wilbur.
POPO: Huh?
AMA: Wilbur—his temper is very bad.
POPO: No!
AMA: Yes. Perhaps Chickie bother him too much.
POPO: No—this is only a chicken.
AMA: "Chickie" *is* chicken.
POPO: No—this—another chicken.
AMA: How you know?
POPO: No matter now. Like this, all chicken look same. Here. Throw away. No
    good.
AMA: Very bad temper. Japanese man. [AMA *sees* POPO *looking for a trash can.*] Wait.
POPO: Huh?
AMA: Jenny—might want to keep it.
POPO: This?
AMA: Leave here until we know. [*She takes the chicken from* POPO.]
POPO: No, throw away. [*She takes it back.*] Stink up whole place soon.
AMA: Don't want to anger Wilbur!
POPO: You pig-head!
AMA: He do this to Chickie—think what he will do to us?
POPO: *Zin gao tza!* [Always so much trouble!]
AMA: You don't know Japanese man!

[AMA *knocks the chicken from* POPO's *hands; they circle around it like boxers sparring.*]

POPO: *Pah-di!* [Spank you!]

AMA: Remember? During war? Pictures they show us? Always—Japanese man kill Chinese!

POPO: Go away, pig-head!

AMA: In picture—Japanese always kill and laugh, kill and laugh.

POPO: If dirty, should throw away!

AMA: Sometimes—torture and laugh, too.

POPO: Wilbur not like that! Hardly even laugh!

AMA: When he kill Chickie, then he laugh!

[*They both grab the chicken;* JOANNE *enters, sees them.*]

JOANNE: Hi, Mom, Auntie. Who cleaned up the chicken?

AMA: Huh? This is not Chickie?

POPO: [*To* AMA] Tell you things, you never listen. *Gong-gong-ah!* [Idiot!]

JOANNE: When's Hannah getting here?

POPO: Hannah—she is at airport.

JOANNE: We had a little accident and I need help programming the microwave. Last time, I put a roast inside and it disintegrated. She should be here already.

AMA: Joanne, you prepare for family devotions?

JOANNE: Of course, Mom. I had the maid set up everything just like you said. [*She exits.*]

AMA: Good. Praise to God will bring Di-gou back to family. Make him rid of Communist demon.

POPO: He will speak in tongue of fire. Like he does when he is a little boy with See-goh-poh.

[WILBUR *enters the tennis court with an empty laundry basket. He heads for the barbecue.* JOANNE *follows him.*]

JOANNE: [*To* WILBUR] Hon, what are you going to do with those?

WILBUR: [*Referring to the burnt chicken*] I'm just going to give them to Grizzly. [*He piles the chickens into the basket.*]

JOANNE: All right. [*She notices that the mess in the lanai has not been touched.*] Jenny! [*To* WILBUR] But be careful not to give Grizzly any bones! [JOANNE *exits.*]

WILBUR: [*To* AMA *and* POPO] How you doin', Mom, Auntie?

AMA: [*To* POPO, *sotto voce*] Kill and laugh.

WILBUR: Joanne tells me you're pretty excited about your brother's arrival—pretty understandable, after all these years—what's his name again? Di-ger, Di-gow, something . . .

AMA: Di-gou!

WILBUR: Yeah, right. Gotta remember that. Be pretty embarrassing if I said the wrong name. Di-gou.

POPO: Di-gou is not his name.

WILBUR: What? Not his—? What is it again? Di-gow? De—?

AMA: Di-gou!

WILBUR: Di-gou.

POPO: That is not his name.

WILBUR: Oh. It's the tones in Chinese, isn't it? I'm saying the wrong tone: Di-gou? or Di-gou? Or—

POPO: Di-gou meaning is "second brother."

WILBUR: Oh, I see. It's not his name. Boy, do I feel ignorant in these situations. If only there were some way I could make sure I don't embarrass myself tonight.

AMA: Eat outside.

WILBUR: Outside?

POPO: Or in kitchen.

WILBUR: In the kitchen? That's great! You two are real jokers, you know?

AMA: No. We are not.

WILBUR: C'mon. I should bring you down to the club someday. The guys never believe it when I tell them how much I love you two.

AMA: [*To* POPO] *Gao sai.*

[JENNY *enters the sunroom.*]

WILBUR: Right. *"Gao sai"* to you, too. [*He starts to leave, sees* JENNY.] Wash your hands before you play with your grandmother.

JENNY: [*To* WILBUR] Okay, Dad. [*To* AMA] Do I have to, Ama?

AMA: No. Of course not.

JENNY: Can I ask you something personal?

AMA: Of course.

JENNY: Did Daddy just call you "dog shit"?

AMA: Jenny!

POPO: Yes. Very good!

JENNY: Doesn't that bother you?

POPO: [*To* AMA] Her Chinese is improving!

JENNY: We learned it in Chinese school.

AMA: Jenny, you should not use this American word.

JENNY: Sorry. It just slipped out.

AMA: You do not use such word at school, no?

JENNY: Oh, no. Of course not.

AMA: You should not use anyplace.

JENNY: Right.

POPO: Otherwise—no good man wants marry you.

JENNY: You mean, no rich man.

AMA: No—money is not important.

POPO: As long as he is good man.

[*Pause*]

AMA: Christian.

POPO: Chinese.

AMA: Good education.

POPO: Good school.

AMA: Princeton.

POPO: Harvard.

AMA: Doctor.

POPO: Surgeon.

AMA: Brain surgeon.

POPO: Surgeon general.

AMA: Otherwise—you marry anyone that you like.

JENNY: Ama, Popo—look, I'm only seventeen.

POPO: True. But you can develop the good habits now.

JENNY: I don't want to get married till I'm at least thirty or something.

POPO: Thirty! By that time we are dead!

AMA: Gone to see God!

POPO: Lie in ground, arms cross!

JENNY: Look at it this way: how can I be a good mother if I have to follow my career around?

AMA: Your career will not require this.

JENNY: Yeah, it will. What if I have to go on tour?

AMA: Dental technicians do not tour.

JENNY: Ama!

POPO: Only tour—one mouth to next mouth: "Hello. Clean your teeth?"

JENNY: Look, I'm telling you, I'm going to be a dancer.

AMA: We say—you can do both. Combine skills.

JENNY: That's ridiculous.

POPO: Be first dancing dental technician.

JENNY: I don't wanna be a dental technician!

POPO: Dancing dental technician very rare. You will be very popular.

JENNY: Why can't I be like Chester?

AMA: You cannot be like Chester.

JENNY: Why not!

POPO: You do not play violin. Chester does not dance. No hope.

JENNY: I know, but, I mean, he's a musician. Why can't I be a dancer?

AMA: Chester—his work very dangerous.

JENNY: Dangerous?

AMA: He just receive new job—play with Boston Symphony.

JENNY: Yeah. I know. He's leaving tomorrow. So? What's so bad about Boston?

AMA: Conductor—Ozawa—he is Japanese.

JENNY: Oh, no. Not this again.

AMA: Very strict. If musicians miss one note, they must kill themself!

JENNY: Don't be ridiculous. That's no reason why I can't be like Chester.

POPO: But Chester—he makes plenty money.

JENNY: Yeah. Right. Now. But he has to leave home to do it, see? I want a career, too. So what if I never get married?

AMA: Jenny! You must remember—you come from family of See-goh-poh. She was a great evangelist.

JENNY: I know about See-goh-poh. She was your aunt.

AMA: First in family to become Christian.

POPO: She make this family chosen by God.

JENNY: To do what? Clean teeth?

AMA: Jenny!

JENNY: Look, See-goh-poh never got married because of her work, right?

AMA: See-goh-poh was marry to God.

POPO: When Di-gou arrive, he will tell you his testimony. How See-goh-poh change his life.

AMA: Before, he is like you. [*To* POPO] You remember?

POPO: Yes. He is always so fussy.

JENNY: I'm not fussy.

AMA: Stubborn.

POPO: Complain this, complain that.

JENNY: I'm not complaining!

AMA: He will be very happy to meet you. Someone to complain with.

JENNY: I'm just telling you, there's no such thing as a dancing dental technician.

AMA: Good. You will be new discovery.

POPO: When Di-gou is a little boy, he never play with other children. He only read the books. Read books—and play tricks.

AMA: He is very naughty.

POPO: He tell other children there are ghosts hide inside the tree, behind the bush, in the bathroom at night.

AMA: One day, he feed snail poison to gardener.

POPO: Then, when he turns eight year old, See-goh-poh decide she will bring him on her evangelism tour. When he return, he has the tongue of fire.

JENNY: Oh, c'mon—those kind of things only happened in China.

AMA: No—they can happen here as well.

POPO: Di-gou at eight, he goes with See-goh-poh on her first evangelism tour—they travel all around Fukien—thirty day and night, preach to all villages. Five hundred people accept Christ on these thirty day, and See-goh-poh heal many sick, restore ear to deaf, put tongue in mouth of dumb, all these thing and cast out the demon. Perhaps even one dead man—dead and wither—he rise up from his sleep. Di-gou see all this while carry See-goh-poh's bag and bring her food, ah? After thirty day, they return home. We have large banquet—perhaps twelve different dish that night—outside—underneath—ah—cloth. After we eat, See-goh-poh say, "Now is time for Family Devotions, and this time, he will lead." See-goh-poh point to Di-gou, who is still a boy, but he walk up in front of table and begin to talk and flame begin to come from his mouth, over his head. Fire. Fire, all around. His voice—so loud—praise and testify the miracle of God. Louder and louder, more and more fire, till entire sky fill with light, does not seem to be night, like middle of day, like twelve noon. When he finish talk, sun has already rise, and cloth over our head, it is all burn, gone, ashes blow away.

[JOANNE *enters, pulling* CHESTER *behind. He carries a suitcase.*]

JOANNE: Look who's here!

POPO: Chester—good you decide to come.

JOANNE: He looked lost. This house isn't that big, you know. [*Exits.*]

AMA: [*To* CHESTER] You come for reunion with Di-gou. Very good.

CHESTER: Uh—look, I really can't stay. I have to finish packing.

AMA: You must stay—see Di-gou!

CHESTER: But I'm leaving tomorrow.

[*Doorbell*]

CHESTER: Oh, no.

JOANNE: Can somcone gct that? } [*Simultaneously*]

JENNY: Too late!

POPO: Di-gou!

AMA: [*To* CHESTER] You must! This will be Di-gou!

[WILBUR *crosses with basket, now full of chicken bones.*]

WILBUR: I'll get it. Chester, good to see you made it. [*Exits.*]

JENNY: He almost didn't.

CHESTER: I'm really short on time. I gotta go. I'll see you tomorrow at the airport.

POPO: Chester! When Di-gou arrive, he must see whole family! You stay!

[CHESTER *pauses, decides to stay.*]

CHESTER: [*To* JENNY] This is ridiculous. I can't stay.

JENNY: I always have to. Just grin a lot when you meet this guy. Then everyone will be happy.

CHESTER: I don't wanna meet this guy!

[WILBUR *enters with* HANNAH *and* ROBERT, *who are* CHESTER's *parents.* HANNAH *is* POPO's *daughter. They are five to ten years older than* JOANNE *and* WILBUR.]

WILBUR: [*To* ROBERT] What? What do you mean?

AMA: [*Stands up on a chair; a speech*] Di-gou, thirty year have pass since we last see you—

WILBUR: [*To* AMA] Not now, Ma.

AMA: Do you still love God?

ROBERT: What do you mean, "What do you mean?" That's what I mean.

HANNAH: He wasn't there, Wilbur. [*To* AMA] Auntie! Di-gou isn't with us.

AMA: What? How can this be?

ROBERT: Those Chinese airliners—all junk stuffs—so inefficient.

AMA: Where is he?

POPO: [*To* ROBERT] You sure you look close?

ROBERT: What "look close"? We just waited for everyone to get off the plane.

AMA: Where is he?

HANNAH: [*To* AMA] We don't know, Auntie! [*To* CHESTER] Chester, are you packed?
AMA: Don't know?
CHESTER: [*To* HANNAH] No, I'm not. And I'm really in a hurry.
HANNAH: You're leaving tomorrow! Why aren't you packed?
CHESTER: I'm trying to, Mom.

[ROBERT *pulls out a newspaper clipping, shows it to* CHESTER.]

ROBERT: Look, son, I called the Chinese paper, used a little of my influence—they did
  a story on you—here.
CHESTER: [*Looks at clipping*] I can't read this, Dad! It's in Chinese!
ROBERT: [*Takes back clipping*] Little joke, there.
AMA: [*To anyone who will listen*] Where is he?
HANNAH: [*To* AMA] Auntie, ask Wilbur. [*To* CHESTER] Get packed!
CHESTER: All right!
WILBUR: [*Trying to explain to* AMA] Well, Mom, they said he wasn't at—
AMA: [*Ignoring* WILBUR *totally*] Where is he?!

[ROBERT *continues to study the newspaper clipping, points a section out to* CHESTER.]

ROBERT: Here—this is where it talks about my bank.
CHESTER: I'm going to pack.
HANNAH: [*To* CHESTER] Going?
CHESTER: [*To* HANNAH] You said I should—
HANNAH: [*To* CHESTER] You have to stay and see Di-gou!

[WILBUR *makes another attempt to explain the situation to* AMA.]

WILBUR: [*To* AMA] See, Mom, I guess—
AMA: [*Ignoring him again*] Where is he?

[ROBERT *continues studying his clipping, oblivious.*]

ROBERT: [*Translating, to* CHESTER] It says, "Great Chinese violinist will conduct and
  solo with New York Philharmonic."
CHESTER: What? It says what?
HANNAH: [*To* CHESTER] You came without being packed?

[AMA *decides to look for* DI-GOU *on her own, and starts searching the house.*]

AMA: Di-gou! Di-gou!
WILBUR: [*Following* AMA] Ma, listen. I'll explain.
HANNAH: [*To* CHESTER] How can you be so inefficient?
CHESTER: [*To* ROBERT] Dad, I just got a job playing in the violin section in Boston.
AMA: Di-gou! Di-gou!

CHESTER: [*To* ROBERT] I'm not conducting, and—

ROBERT: [*To* CHESTER] Ssssh! I know. But good publicity—for the bank.

HANNAH: [*To* CHESTER] Well, I'll help you pack later. But you have to stay till Di-gou arrives. Sheesh!

CHESTER: I can't believe this!

AMA: [*Continuing her search*] Di-gou! Are you already in bathroom? [*Exits.*]

HANNAH: [*To* AMA] Auntie, he wasn't at the airport! [*To* WILBUR] Why didn't you tell her?

WILBUR: [*Following* AMA] I'm trying! I'm trying! [*Exits.*]

ROBERT: It's those Communist airlines, I'm telling you. Inefficient.

HANNAH: We asked at the desk. They didn't have a flight list.

AMA: [*Entering*] Then where is he?

WILBUR: [*Entering, in despair*] Joanne, will you come here?

ROBERT: They probably left him in Guam.

POPO: [*To* ROBERT] We give you that photograph. You remember to bring it?

ROBERT: Of course I remembered.

HANNAH: [*To* POPO] Mom, it's not Robert's fault.

POPO: [*To* HANNAH] Should leave him [*Refers to* ROBERT] in car.

HANNAH: I tried.

ROBERT: In the car?

HANNAH: He wanted to come in.

ROBERT: It's hot in the car!

AMA: [*To* ROBERT] Suffer, good for you.

POPO: [*To* HANNAH] You cannot control your husband.

ROBERT: I suffer enough.

HANNAH: He said he could help.

POPO: He is wrong again.

AMA: What to do now?

[JENNY *exits in the confusion;* JOANNE *enters.*]

JOANNE: What's wrong now?

WILBUR: They lost your uncle.

JOANNE: Who lost him?

HANNAH: We didn't lose him.

AMA: [*To* ROBERT] You ask at airport desk?

ROBERT: I'm telling you, he's in Guam.

JOANNE: [*To* HANNAH] How could you lose a whole uncle?

HANNAH: We never had him to begin with!

JOANNE: So where is he?

ROBERT: Guam, I'm telling—!

POPO: [*To* ROBERT] Guam, Guam! Shut mouth or go there yourself!

HANNAH: [*A general announcement*] We don't know where he is!

JOANNE: Should I call the police?

WILBUR: You might have looked longer at the airport.

HANNAH: That's what I said, but he [*Refers to* ROBERT] said, "Aaah, too much trouble!"

POPO: [*To* ROBERT] See? You do not care about people from other province besides Shanghai.

ROBERT: [*To* POPO] Mom, I care. It's just that—

POPO: [*To* ROBERT] Your father trade with Japanese during war.

WILBUR: Huh?

ROBERT: Mom, let's not start that—

POPO: Not like our family. We die first!

WILBUR: What's all this about?

ROBERT: Hey, let's not bring up all this other junk, right?

POPO: [*To* ROBERT] You are ashamed.

ROBERT: The airport is a big place.

WILBUR: [*To* ROBERT] Still, you should've been able to spot an old Chinese man!

ROBERT: Everyone on that plane was an old Chinese man.

AMA: True. All Communist look alike.

HANNAH: Hold it, everybody! [*Pause*] Listen, Di-gou has this address, right?

AMA: No.

HANNAH: No? [*To* POPO] Mom, you said he did.

POPO: Yes. He does.

AMA: [*To* POPO] Yes? But I did not write to him.

POPO: I did.

AMA: Now, Communist—they will know this address.

POPO: Never mind.

AMA: No safety. Bomb us.

HANNAH: Okay, he has this address, and he can speak English—after all, he went to medical school here, right? So he shouldn't have any problem.

JOANNE: What an introduction to America.

HANNAH: All we can do is wait.

ROBERT: We went up to all these old Chinese men at the airport, asked them, "Are you our Di-gou?" They all said yes. What could we do? They all looked drunk, bums.

JOANNE: Maybe they're all still wandering through the metal detectors, looking for their families, and will continue till they die.

[CHESTER *wanders onto the tennis court, observes the following section from far upstage.*]

JOANNE: I must have been only about seven the last time Di-gou visited us in the Philippines.

AMA: Less.

JOANNE: Maybe less.

WILBUR: Honey, I'm sure everyone here has a memory, too. You don't see them babbling about it, do you?

JOANNE: The last thing I remember about Di-gou, he was trying to convince you grown-ups to leave the Philippines and return to China. There was a terrible fight—one of the worst that ever took place in our complex. I guess he wanted you to join the Revolution. The fight was so loud that all our servants gathered around the windows to watch.

AMA: They did this?

POPO: Shoot them.

JOANNE: I guess this was just around 1949. Finally, Di-gou left, calling you all sorts of terrible names. On his way out, he set fire to one of our warehouses. All us kids sat around while the servants tried to put it out.

POPO: No. That was not a warehouse.

HANNAH: Yeah, Joanne—the warehouses were concrete, remember?

JOANNE: [*To* HANNAH] But don't you remember a fire?

HANNAH: Yes.

POPO: I think he burn a pile of trash.

ROBERT: [*To* WILBUR] I know how you feel. They're always yap-yap-yapping about their family stories—you'd think they were the only family in China. [*To* HANNAH] I have memories, too.

HANNAH: You don't remember anything. You have a terrible memory.

ROBERT: Look, when I was kidnapped, I didn't know—

HANNAH: Sssssh!

JOANNE: Quiet, Robert!

POPO: Like broken record—ghang, ghang, ghang.

WILBUR: [*To* ROBERT] I tell you what: you wanna take a look at my collection of tax shelters?

ROBERT: Same old stuff?

WILBUR: No. Some new ones.

[*They exit.* DI-GOU *appears on the tennis court; only* CHESTER *sees him, but* CHESTER *says nothing.* CHESTER *watches* DI-GOU *watching the women.*]

JOANNE: Anyway, he set fire to something and the flames burned long into the night. One servant was even killed in it, if I remember correctly. I think Matthew's nursemaid was trying to put it out when her dress caught fire and, like a fool, she ran screaming all over the complex. All the adults were too busy to hear her, I guess, and all the kids just sat there and watched this second fire, moving in circles and screaming. By morning, both fires were out, and our tutors came as usual. But that day, nothing functioned just right—I think the water pipes broke in Sah-Zip's room, the cars wouldn't start—something—all I remember is servants running around all day with one tool or another. And that was how Di-gou left Manila for the last time. Left Manila and returned to China—in two fires—one which moved—and a great rush of handymen.

[DI-GOU *is now sitting in their midst in the sunroom. He puts down his suitcase. They turn and see him. He sticks his thumb out, as if for hitchhiking, but it is pointed in the wrong direction.*]

DI-GOU: "Going my way?"

AMA: Di-gou!

DI-GOU: "Hey, baby, got a lift?"

POPO: You see? Our family members will always return.

JOANNE: [*To* DI-GOU] Are you—? Oh, you're—? Well, nice—How did you get here?

DI-GOU: [*Pulls a book out of his jacket*] Our diplomacy handbook. Very useful.

POPO: Welcome to America!

DI-GOU: [*Referring to the handbook*] It says, "When transportation is needed, put your thumb as if to plug a hole."

AMA: [*On chair*] Di-gou, thirty year have passed—

DI-GOU: [*Still reading*] "And say, 'Going my way?'"

AMA: Do you still believe in God?

DI-GOU: "Or, 'Hey, baby, got a lift?'"

AMA: Do you?

HANNAH: [*To* AMA] Auntie, he's explaining something.

DI-GOU: It worked! I am here!

AMA: [*Getting down off chair*] Still as stubborn as before.

DI-GOU: Hello, my sisters.

POPO: Hello, Di-gou. This is my daughter, Hannah.

HANNAH: [*To* DI-GOU] Were you at the airport? We were waiting for you.

DI-GOU: Hannah. Oh, last time, you were just a baby.

AMA: [*Introducing* JOANNE] And Joanne, remember?

JOANNE: Hello, Di-gou. How was your flight?

DI-GOU: Wonderful, wonderful.

POPO: Where is Chester? Chester! [CHESTER *enters the lanai.*] Him—this is number one grandson.

DI-GOU: Oh, you are Chester. You are the violinist, yes?

CHESTER: You're Di-gou?

DI-GOU: Your parents are so proud of you.

HANNAH: We are not. He's just a kid who needs to pack.

AMA: Where is Jenny? Jenny!

HANNAH: [*To* DI-GOU] We figured you'd be able to get here by yourself.

DI-GOU: Oh, yes. [*He sticks out his thumb.* JENNY *enters.*]

JOANNE: Jenny! Say, "Hi, Di-gou."

JENNY: Hi, Di-gou.

DI-GOU: [*To* JOANNE] This is your daughter?

JOANNE: Yes. Jenny. [*Pause*] Jenny, say, "Hi, Di-gou."

JENNY: Mom, I just did!

JOANNE: Oh. Right.

JENNY: Will you cool out?

DI-GOU: Jenny, the last time I saw your mother, she was younger than you are now.

JENNY: He's kinda cute.

JOANNE: Jenny, your granduncle is not cute.

DI-GOU: Thank you.

JENNY: [*To* JOANNE] Can I go now?

AMA: Why you always want to go?

JENNY: Sorry, Ama. Busy.

JOANNE: [*Allowing* JENNY *to leave*] All right.

DI-GOU: [*To* JENNY] What are you doing?

JENNY: Huh? Reading.

DI-GOU: Oh. Schoolwork.

JENNY: Nah. *Vogue.* [*Exits.*]

JOANNE: I've got to see about dinner. [*To* HANNAH] Can you give me a hand? I want to use my new Cuisinart.

HANNAH: All right. What do you want to make?

JOANNE: I don't know. What does a Cuisinart do?

[HANNAH *and* JOANNE *exit;* DI-GOU, AMA, POPO, *and* CHESTER *are left in the sunroom.*]

AMA: Di-gou, thirty year have pass. Do you still love God?

DI-GOU: Thirty-three.

AMA: Ah?

POPO: 1949 to 1982. Thirty-three. He is correct.

AMA: Oh. But you do still love God? Like before?

DI-GOU: You know, sisters, after you left China, I learned that I never did believe in God. [*Pause*]

AMA: What!

POPO: How can you say this?

CHESTER: Ama, Popo, don't start in on that—he just got here.

POPO: You defend him?

AMA: [*Chasing* CHESTER *out to tennis court*] You both are influence by bad people.

POPO: Spend time with bums! Communist bum, musician bum, both same.

DI-GOU: Just to hear my sisters after all these years—you may speak whatever you like.

AMA: Do you still love God?

DI-GOU: I have much love.

AMA: For God?

DI-GOU: For my sisters. [*Pause*]

POPO: You are being very difficult.

AMA: You remember when you first become Christian?

POPO: You travel with See-goh-poh on her first evangelism tour? Before we move to Philippines and you stay in China? Remember? You speak in tongues of fire.

DI-GOU: I was only eight years old. That evening is a blur to me.

AMA: Tonight—we have family devotions. You can speak again. Miracles. You still believe in miracles?

DI-GOU: It is a miracle that I am here again with you!

POPO: Why you always change subject? You remember Ah Hong? Your servant? How See-goh-poh cast out his opium demon?

DI-GOU: I don't think that happened.

AMA: Yes! Remember? After evangelism tour—she cast out his demon.

POPO: Ah Hong tell stories how he eats opium, then he can see everything so clear, like—uh—glass. He can see even through wall, he say, and can see—ah—all the way through floor. Yes! He say he can see through ground, all the way to hell. And he talk with Satan and demon who pretend to be Ah Hong's dead uncles. You should remember.

DI-GOU: I vaguely recall some such stories.

[DI-GOU *opens up his suitcase during* POPO's *following speech and takes out two small Chinese toys and a small Chinese flag. He shows them to* POPO, *but she tries to ignore them.*]

POPO: Demon pretend to be ghost, then show himself everyplace to Ah Hong—in kitchen, in well, in barn, in street of village. Always just sit there, never talk, never move, just sit. So See-goh-poh come, call on God, say only, "Demon begone."

AMA: And from then on, no more ghost, no more opium.

POPO: You—you so happy, then. You say, you will also cast out the demon.

DI-GOU: We were all just children. [*He lines the toys up on the floor.*]

AMA: But you have faith of a child.

DI-GOU: Ah Hong didn't stop eating opium, though. He just needed money. That's why two years later, he was fired.

AMA: Ah Hong never fired!

POPO: I do not think so.

DI-GOU: Yes, my tenth, eleventh birthday, he was fired.

AMA: No—remember? Ah Hong die many year later—just before you come to America for college.

DI-GOU: No, he was fired before then.

POPO: No. Before you leave, go to college, you must prepare your own suitcase. [*To* AMA] Bad memory.

AMA: Brainwash.

[ROBERT *and* WILBUR *enter;* CHESTER *exits off the tennis court.* ROBERT *and* WILBUR *surround* DI-GOU.]

ROBERT *and* WILBUR: Welcome!

WILBUR: How you doing, Di-gow?

ROBERT: [*Correcting* WILBUR] Di-gou!

WILBUR: Oh, right. "Di-gou."

ROBERT: [*To* DI-GOU] We tried to find you at the airport.

WILBUR: [*To* DI-GOU] That means "second brother."

ROBERT: So, you escaped the Communists, huh?

WILBUR: Robert and I were just—

ROBERT: Little joke, there.

WILBUR: —looking at my collection of tax shelters.

ROBERT: China's pretty different now, huh?

WILBUR: You care to take a look?

ROBERT: I guess there's never a dull moment—

WILBUR: Probably no tax shelters, either.

ROBERT: —waiting for the next cultural revolution.

WILBUR: Oh, Robert!

ROBERT: Little joke, there.

WILBUR: [*To* DI-GOU] That's how he [*Refers to* ROBERT] does business.

ROBERT: Of course, I respect China.

WILBUR: He says these totally outrageous things.

ROBERT: But your airlines—so inefficient.

WILBUR: And people remember him.

ROBERT: How long were you in Guam?

WILBUR: [*To* ROBERT] He wasn't in Guam!

ROBERT: No?

WILBUR: [*To* DI-GOU] Well, we're going to finish up the tour.

ROBERT: My shelters are all at my house.

WILBUR: Feel welcome to come along.

ROBERT: His [*Refers to* WILBUR] are kid stuff. Who wants land in Montana?

WILBUR: [*To* ROBERT] Hey—I told you. I need the loss.

[WILBUR *and* ROBERT *exit, leaving* DI-GOU *with* AMA *and* POPO. *There is a long silence.*]

DI-GOU: Who are they?

POPO: Servants.

AMA: Don't worry. They will eat outside. In America, servants do not take over their masters' house.

DI-GOU: What are you talking about?

AMA: We know. In China now, servants beat their masters.

DI-GOU: Don't be ridiculous. I have a servant. A chauffeur.

[ROBERT *reenters.*]

ROBERT: Hey, Di-gou—we didn't even introduce ourselves.

DI-GOU: Oh, my sisters explained it to me.

ROBERT: I'm Robert. Hannah's my wife. [ROBERT *puts his arm around* DI-GOU.] When we married, I had nothing. I was working in grocery stores, fired from one job after another. But she could tell—I had a good heart.

DI-GOU: It is good to see servants marrying into the moneyed ranks. We are not aware of such progress by even the lowest classes.

[*Pause*]

ROBERT: Huh?

DI-GOU: To come to this—from the absolute bottom of society.

ROBERT: Wait, wait, I mean, sure, I made progress, but "the bottom of society"? That's stretching it some, wouldn't you say?

DI-GOU: Did you meet Hannah while preparing her food?

ROBERT: Huh? No, we met at a foreign students' dance at UCLA.

DI-GOU: Oh. You attended university?

ROBERT: Look, I'm not a country kid. It's not like I was that poor. I'm from Shanghai, you know.

POPO: [*To* ROBERT] Ssssh! Neighbors will hear!

ROBERT: I'm cosmopolitan. So when I went to college, I just played around at first. That's the beauty of the free-enterprise system, Di-gou. If you wanna be a bum, it lets you be a bum. I wasted my time, went out with all those American girls.

POPO: One girl.

ROBERT: Well, one was more serious, a longer commitment . . .

POPO: Minor.

DI-GOU: What?

POPO: He go out with girl—only fifteen year old.

ROBERT: I didn't know!

POPO: [*To* ROBERT] How come you cannot ask?

ROBERT: I was just an FOB. This American girl—she talked to me—asked me out—
kissed me on first date—and I thought, "Land of opportunity!" Anyway, I decided
to turn my back on China.

POPO: [*To* DI-GOU] He cannot even ask girl how old.

ROBERT: This is my home. When I wanted to stop being a bum, make money, it let
me. That's America!

DI-GOU: I also attended American university. Columbia Medical School.

ROBERT: Right. My wife told me.

POPO: [*To* ROBERT] But he does not date the minor!

ROBERT: [*To* POPO] How was I supposed to know? She looked fully developed!

[AMA *and* POPO *leave in disgust, leaving* ROBERT *alone with* DI-GOU.]

ROBERT: [*To* DI-GOU] Well, then, you must understand American ways.

DI-GOU: It has been some time since I was in America.

ROBERT: Well, it's improved a lot, lemme tell you. Look, I have a friend who's an
immigration lawyer. If you want to stay here, he can arrange it.

DI-GOU: Oh, no. The thought never even—

ROBERT: I know, but listen. I did it. Never had any regrets. We might be able to get
your family over, too.

DI-GOU: Robert, I cannot leave China.

ROBERT: Huh? Look, Di-gou, people risk their lives to come to America. If only you
could talk to—to the boat people.

DI-GOU: Uh—the food here looks very nice.

ROBERT: Huh? Oh, help yourself. Go ahead.

DI-GOU: Thank you. I will wait.

ROBERT: No, go on!

DI-GOU: Thank you, but—

ROBERT: Look, in America, there's so much, we don't have to be polite at all!

DI-GOU: Please—I'm not yet hungry.

ROBERT: Us Chinese, we love to eat, right? Well, here in America, we can be pigs!

DI-GOU: I'm not hungry.

ROBERT: I don't see why you can't—? Look. [*He picks up a piece of food, a* bao.] See?
[*He stuffs the whole thing into his mouth.*] Pigs!

DI-GOU: Do you mind? I told you, I'm not—

ROBERT: I know. You're not hungry. Think I'm hungry? No, sir! What do I have to
do to convince you? Here. [*He drops a tray of* guo-tieh *on the ground, begins stomping them.*]
This is the land of plenty!

DI-GOU: Ai! Robert!

[ROBERT *continues stomping them like roaches.*]

ROBERT: There's one next to your foot! [*He stomps it.*] Gotcha!
DI-GOU: Please! It is not right to step on food!
ROBERT: "Right"? Now, see, that's your problem in the P.R.C.—lots of justice, but you don't produce.

[WILBUR *enters, catching* ROBERT *in the act.*]

WILBUR: Robert? What are you—? What's all this?
ROBERT: [*Stops stomping*] What's the big deal? You got a cleaning woman, don't you?

[JENNY *enters.*]

JENNY: Time to eat yet? [*She sees the mess.*] Blaagh.

[HANNAH *enters.*]

HANNAH: What's all this?
JENNY: Never mind.

[JENNY *exits;* WILBUR *points to* ROBERT, *indicating to* HANNAH *that* ROBERT *is responsible for the mess.* AMA *and* POPO *also enter at this moment, and see* WILBUR's *indication.*]

DI-GOU: In China, the psychological problems of wealth are a great concern.
POPO: Ai! Who can clean up after man like this!
WILBUR: Robert, I just don't think this is proper.
AMA: Wilbur—not clean himself.
ROBERT: Quiet! You all make a big deal out of nothing!
DI-GOU: I am a doctor. I understand.
POPO: But Robert—he also has the fungus feet.
ROBERT: Shut up, everybody! Will you all just shut up? I was showing Di-gou American ways!

[WILBUR *takes* DI-GOU's *arm.*]

WILBUR: [*To* DI-GOU] Uh—come out here. I'll show you some American ways.

[WILBUR *and* DI-GOU *go out to the tennis court.*]

ROBERT: [*To* WILBUR] What do you know about American ways? You were born here!
POPO: [*To* AMA] Exercise—good for him.

ROBERT: Only us immigrants really know American ways!

POPO: [*To* AMA, *pinching her belly*] Good for here.

HANNAH: [*To* ROBERT] Shut up, dear. You've done enough damage today.

[WILBUR *gets* DI-GOU *a racket.*]

AMA: [*To* POPO] In China, he [*Refers to* DI-GOU] receives plenty exercise. Whenever Communists, they come torture him.

WILBUR: [*On tennis court, to* DI-GOU] I'll set up the machine. [*He goes* OFF.]

ROBERT: [*In sunroom, looking at tennis court*] What's so American about tennis?

HANNAH: [*To* ROBERT] Yes, dear.

ROBERT: You all ruined it!

HANNAH: You ruined the *guo-tieh*, dear.

ROBERT: What's a few *guo-tieh* in defense of America?

DI-GOU: [*To* WILBUR] I have not played tennis since my college days at Columbia.

ROBERT: [*To* HANNAH] He [*refers to* DI-GOU] was being so cheap! Like this was a poor country!

HANNAH: He's lived in America before, dear.

ROBERT: That was years ago. When we couldn't even buy a house in a place like this.

HANNAH: We still can't.

ROBERT: What?

HANNAH: Let's face it. We still can't afford—

ROBERT: That's not what I mean, stupid! I mean, when we wouldn't be able to because we're Chinese! He doesn't know the new America. I was making a point and you all ruined it!

HANNAH: Yes, dear. Now let's go in and watch the Betamax.

ROBERT: No!

HANNAH: C'mon!

[ROBERT *and* HANNAH *exit. On the tennis court,* DI-GOU *and* WILBUR *stand next to each other, facing offstage. A machine offstage begins to shoot tennis balls at them, each ball accompanied by a small explosive sound. A ball goes by;* DI-GOU *tries to hit it, but it is too high for him. Two more balls go by, but they are also out of* DI-GOU'S *reach. A fourth ball is shot out, which hits* WILBUR.]

WILBUR: Aaaah!

[*Balls are being shot out much faster now, pummeling* WILBUR *and* DI-GOU. AMA *and* POPO *continue to sit in the sunroom, staring away from the tennis court, peaceful and oblivious.*]

DI-GOU: Aaah!

WILBUR: I don't—! This never happened—!

DI-GOU: Watch out!

WILBUR: I'll turn off the machine.

DI-GOU: Good luck! Persevere! Overcome! Oh! Watch—!

[*A volley of balls drives* WILBUR *back.* AMA *and* POPO *hear the commotion, look over to the tennis court. The balls stop shooting out.*]

ROBERT: Tennis.
AMA: A fancy machine.

[*They return to looking downstage. The balls begin again.*]

WILBUR: Oh no!
AMA: Wilbur—he is such a bad loser.
POPO: Good exercise, huh? His age—good for here. [*She pinches her belly.*]
DI-GOU: I will persevere! [DI-GOU *tries to get to the machine, is driven back.*]
WILBUR: No! Di-gow!
DI-GOU: I am overcome!
WILBUR: Joanne! [*He begins crawling like a guerrilla toward the machine and finally makes it offstage. The balls stop, presumably because* WILBUR *reached the machine.* DI-GOU *runs off the court.*]
DI-GOU: [*Breathless*] Is it time yet . . . that we may cease to have . . . such enjoyment?

[WILBUR *crosses back onto the tennis court and into the lanai.*]

WILBUR: [*To offstage*] Joanne! This machine's too fast. I don't pay good money to be attacked by my possessions! [*Exits.*]

[AMA *and* POPO *get up, exit into the house, applauding* DI-GOU *as they go, for his exercise.*]

AMA *and* POPO: [*Clapping*] Good, good, very good!

[DI-GOU *is left alone on the tennis court. He is hit by a lone tennis ball.* CHESTER *enters, with a violin case. It is obvious that he has thrown that ball.*]

CHESTER: Quite a workout, there.
DI-GOU: America is full of surprises—why do all these products function so poorly?
CHESTER: Looks like "Made in U.S." is gonna become synonymous with defective workmanship. [*Pause*] You wanna see my violin?
DI-GOU: I would love to.
CHESTER: I thought you might. Here. [*He removes the violin from its case.*] See? No "Made in U.S." label.
DI-GOU: It is beautiful.
CHESTER: Careful! The back has a lacquer which never dries—so don't touch it, or you'll leave your fingerprints in it forever.
DI-GOU: Imagine that. After I die, someone could be playing a violin with my fingerprint.
CHESTER: Funny, isn't it?
DI-GOU: You know, I used to play violin.

CHESTER: Really?

DI-GOU: Though I never had as fine an instrument as this.

CHESTER: Try it. Go ahead.

DI-GOU: No. Please. I get more pleasure looking at it than I would playing it. But I would get the most pleasure hearing you play.

CHESTER: No.

DI-GOU: Please?

CHESTER: All right. Later. How long did you play?

DI-GOU: Some years. During the Cultural Revolution, I put it down.

CHESTER: Must've been tough, huh? [CHESTER *directs* DI-GOU's *attention to the back of his violin.*] Look—the back's my favorite part.

DI-GOU: China is my home, my work. I had to stay there. [DI-GOU *looks at the back of the violin.*] Oh—the way the light reflects—look. And I can see myself in it.

CHESTER: Yeah. Nice, huh?

DI-GOU: So you will take this violin and make music around the world.

CHESTER: Around the world? Oh, you probably got a misleading press clipping. See, my dad . . .

DI-GOU: Very funny.

CHESTER: [*Smiling*] Yeah. See, I'm just playing in the Boston Symphony. I'm leaving tomorrow.

DI-GOU: I am fortunate, then, to come today, or perhaps I would never meet you.

CHESTER: You see, I wasn't even planning to come here.

DI-GOU: That would be terrible. You know, in China, my wife and I had no children—for the good of the state. [DI-GOU *moves to where he left the Chinese toys earlier in the act. He picks them up and studies them.*] All these years, I try to imagine—what does Hannah look like? What does her baby look like? Now, I finally visit and what do I find? A young man. A violinist. The baby has long since disappeared. And I learn I'll never know the answer to my question.

[*Silence*]

CHESTER: Di-gou, why did you come here?

DI-GOU: My wife has died, I'm old. I've come for my sisters.

CHESTER: Well, I hope you're not disappointed to come here and see your sisters, your family, carry on like this.

DI-GOU: They are still my sisters.

CHESTER: I'm leaving here. Like you did.

DI-GOU: But, Chester, I've found that I cannot leave the family. Today—look!—I follow them across an ocean.

CHESTER: You know, they're gonna start bringing you to church.

DI-GOU: No. My sisters and their religion are two different things.

CHESTER: No, they're not. You've been away. You've forgotten. This family breathes for God. Ever since your aunt, See-goh-poh.

DI-GOU: See-goh-poh is not the first member of this family.

CHESTER: She's the first Christian.

DI-GOU: There are faces back further than you can see. Faces long before the white missionaries arrived in China. Here. [*He holds* CHESTER's *violin so that its back is facing* CHESTER, *and uses it like a mirror.*] Look here. At your face. Study your face and you will see—the shape of your face is the shape of faces back many generations—across an ocean, in another soil. You must become one with your family before you can hope to live away from it.

CHESTER: Oh, sure, there're faces. But they don't matter here. See-goh-poh's face is the only one that has any meaning here.

DI-GOU: No. The stories written on your face are the ones you must believe.

CHESTER: Stories? I see stories, Di-gou. All around me. This house tells a story. The days of the week tell a story—Sunday is service, Wednesday and Friday are fellowship, Thursday is visitation. Even the furniture tells stories. Look around. See-goh-poh is sitting in every chair. There's nothing for me here.

DI-GOU: I am here.

CHESTER: You? All right. Here. [CHESTER *turns the back of the violin toward* DI-GOU, *again using it like a mirror.*] You look. You wanna know what I see? I see the shape of your face changing. And with it, a mind, a will, as different as the face. If you stay with them, your old self will go, and in its place will come a new man, an old man, a man who'll pray.

DI-GOU: Chester, you are in America. If you deny those who share your blood, what do you have in this country?

AMA: [*From offstage*] All right? Ready?

CHESTER: Your face is changing, Di-gou. Before you know it, you'll be praying and speaking in tongues.

AMA: [*Still offstage*] One, two, three, four!

[*The "Hallelujah Chorus" begins. The choir enters, consisting of* WILBUR, JOANNE, ROBERT, HANNAH, *and* POPO. *They are led by* AMA, *who stands at a movable podium which is being pushed into the room by* ROBERT *and* WILBUR *as they sing. (The choir heads for the center of the room, where the podium comes to rest, with* AMA *still on it, and the "Hallelujah Chorus" ends.)* ROBERT *begins singing the tenor aria "Every Valley Shall Be Exalted," from Handel's* Messiah.]

ROBERT: "Every valley, every valley . . ."

HANNAH: Quiet, Robert!

ROBERT: But I want my solo!

JOANNE: [*To* ROBERT] Ssssh! We already decided this.

ROBERT: [*Continuing to sing*] ". . . shall be exalted . . ."

JOANNE: [*Yelling offstage*] Jenny!

AMA: [*To* ROBERT] Time for Family Devotions! Set up room!

[*They begin to arrange the room like a congregation hall, with the pulpit up front.*]

ROBERT: But it's a chance to hear my beautiful voice.

JENNY: [*From offstage*] Yeah! What?

POPO: [*To* ROBERT] Hear at home, hear in car. Now set up room.

JOANNE: [*Yelling offstage*] Jenny! Devotions!

JENNY: [*From offstage*] Aw, Mom.

JOANNE: [*Yelling offstage*] Devotions!

JENNY: [*Entering*] All right.

ROBERT: [*To* HANNAH] You know what this is? This is the breakdown of family authority.

HANNAH: [*To* ROBERT] You have all the authority, dear. Now shut up.

[JENNY *goes over to* CHESTER.]

JENNY: Hey, you still here? I thought for sure you'd have split by now.

CHESTER: I will.

JENNY: You gotta take it easier. Do like me. I act all lotus blossom for them. I say, "Hi, uncle this and auntie that." It's easy.

ROBERT: Look—all this free time. [*Sings*] "Every valley . . ."

POPO: Shoot him!

[*The room is set up.*]

AMA: We begin! Family Devotions! [AMA *flips a switch. A neon cross is lit up.*]

JENNY: [*To* CHESTER] Looks like a disco.

[*Everyone is seated except* DI-GOU. *The rest of the family waits for him. He walks over and sits down.* AMA *bows down to pray. Everyone bows except* CHESTER *and* DI-GOU, *but since all other eyes are closed, no one notices their noncompliance.* AMA *begins to pray.*]

AMA: Dear Father, when we think of your great mercy to this family, we can only feel so grateful, privilege to be family chose for your work. You claim us to be yours, put your mark on our heart.

[CHESTER *gets up, picks up his violin, gets* DI-GOU's *attention.*]

AMA: Your blessing begin many year ago in China.

[CHESTER *begins playing; his music serves as underscoring to* AMA's *prayer.*]

AMA: When See-goh-poh, she hear your word—from missionary. Your spirit, it touch her heart, she accept you, she speak in tongue of fire.

[CHESTER *begins to move out of the room as he plays.*]

AMA: You continue, bless See-goh-poh. She become agent of God, bring light to whole family, until we are convert, we become shining light for you all through Amoy.

[CHESTER *stops playing, looks at* DI-GOU, *waves good-bye, and exits.* DI-GOU *gets up, walks to where* CHESTER *was standing before he left, and waves good-bye.*]

AMA: Let us praise your victory over Satan. Praise your power over demon. Praise miracle over our own sinful will. Praise your victory over even our very hearts. Amen.

[AMA *conducts the choir in the ending of the "Hallelujah Chorus." As they sing, she notices* DI-GOU's *chair is empty. She turns and sees him waving. They look at each other as the "Hallelujah Chorus" continues.* CURTAIN.]

ACT II

A moment later. As the curtain rises, all are in the same positions they occupied at the end of Act I. AMA *and* DI-GOU *are looking at each other. The choir ends the "Hallelujah Chorus."* DI-GOU *walks back toward his chair, and sits.* AMA *notices that* CHESTER's *seat is empty.*

AMA: Where is Chester?
HANNAH: I heard his violin.
AMA: This is family devotions.
ROBERT: The kid's got a mind of his own.
HANNAH: He probably went home to pack, Auntie. He's really in a hurry.
JENNY: Can I go look?
AMA: Why everyone want to go?
JENNY: But he forgot his suitcase. [*She points to the green suitcase, which* CHESTER *has left behind.*]
POPO: [*To* JENNY] Di-gou, he will want to hear you give testimony.

[JENNY *sits back down.*]

AMA: Now—Special Testimony. Let us tell of God's blessing! Who will have privilege? Special Testimony! Who will be first to praise? [*Silence*] He is in our presence! Open His arms to us! [*Silence*] He is not going to wait forever—you know this! He is very busy!

[ROBERT *stands up, starts to head for podium.* POPO *notices that* ROBERT *has risen, points to him.*]

POPO: No! Not him!
AMA: [*To* ROBERT] He is very bored with certain people who say same thing over and over again.
WILBUR: Why don't we sit down, Robert?
JENNY: C'mon, Uncle Robert.
HANNAH: Dear, forget it, all right?
ROBERT: But she needed someone to start. I just—

POPO: [*To* ROBERT] She did not include you.

WILBUR: Can't you see how bored they are with that, Robert?

ROBERT: Bored.

WILBUR: Everybody else has forgotten it.

ROBERT: Forgotten it? They can't.

JOANNE: We could if you'd stop talking about it.

ROBERT: But there's something new!

WILBUR: Of course. There always is.

ROBERT: There is!

JOANNE: [*To* WILBUR] Don't pay attention, dear. It just encourages him.

WILBUR: [*To* JOANNE] Honey, are you trying to advise *me* on how to be diplomatic?

JOANNE: I'm only saying, if you let Hannah—

WILBUR: You're a real stitch, you know that? You really are.

JOANNE: Hannah's good at keeping him quiet.

ROBERT: Quiet?

WILBUR: [*To* JOANNE] Look, who was voted "Mr. Congeniality" at the club last week—you or me?

ROBERT: Hannah, who are you telling to be quiet?

HANNAH: Quiet, Robert.

WILBUR: [*To* JOANNE] Afraid to answer? Huh? Who? Who was "Mr. Congeniality"? Tell me—were you "Mr. Congeniality"?

JENNY: [*To* WILBUR] I don't think she stood a chance, Dad.

WILBUR: [*To* JENNY] Who asked you, huh?

JENNY: "Mr. Congeniality," I think.

WILBUR: Don't be disrespectful.

AMA: We must begin Special Testimony! Who is first?

POPO: I talk.

JOANNE: Good.

POPO: Talk from here. [*She stands.*] Long time since we all come here like this. I remember long ago, family leave China—the boat storm, storm, storm, storm, all around, Hannah cry. I think, "Aaah, why we have to leave China, go to Philippines?" But I remember Jonah, when he did not obey God, only then seas become—ah—dangerous. And even after, after Jonah eaten by whale, God provide for him. So if God has plan for us, we live; if not [*She looks at* DI-GOU.] we die. [*She sits.*] Okay. That's all.

[*Everyone applauds.*]

AMA: Very good! Who is next?

ROBERT: I said, I'd be happy to—

HANNAH: How about Jenny?

JENNY: Me?

JOANNE: Sure, dear, c'mon.

JENNY: Oh . . . well . . .

POPO: [*To* DI-GOU] You see—she is so young, but her faith is old.

JENNY: After I do this, can I go see what's happened to Chester?

POPO: [*To* JENNY] First, serve God.

ROBERT: Let her go.

POPO: Then, you may see about Chester.

JENNY: All right. [*She walks to the podium.*]

POPO: [*To* DI-GOU] I will tell you what each sentence meaning.

DI-GOU: I can understand quite well.

POPO: No. You are not Christian. You need someone—like announcer at baseball game—except announce for God.

JENNY: [*At podium, she begins testimony.*] First, I want to say that I love you all very much. I really do.

POPO: [*To* DI-GOU] That meaning is, she love God.

JENNY: And I appreciate what you've done for me.

POPO: [*To* DI-GOU] She loves us because we show her God.

JENNY: But I guess there are certain times when even love isn't enough.

POPO: [*To* DI-GOU] She does not have enough love for you. You are not Christian.

JENNY: Sometimes, even love has its dark side.

POPO: [*To* DI-GOU] That is you.

JENNY: And when you find that side, sometimes you have to leave in order to come back in a better way.

POPO: [*To* DI-GOU] She cannot stand to be around you.

JENNY: Please. Remember what I said, and think about it later.

POPO: [*To* DI-GOU] You hear? Think!

JENNY: Thank you.

[*Everyone applauds.*]

AMA: Good, good.

JENNY: Can I go now?

ROBERT: [*To* HANNAH] What was she talking about?

AMA: [*To* JENNY] Soon, you can be best testifier—do testimony on TV.

JENNY: Can I go now?

JOANNE: All right, Jenny.

JENNY: Thanks. [*Exits.*]

ROBERT: [*To* POPO] Why don't you interpret for *me?* I didn't understand what she was talking about. Not a bit.

POPO: Good.

ROBERT: Good? Don't you want me to be a better Christian?

POPO: No. Not too good. Do not want to live in same part of Heaven as you.

ROBERT: Why not? It'll be great, Popo. We can tell stories, sing—

POPO: In Heaven, hope you live in basement.

ROBERT: Basement? C'mon, Popo, I'm a celebrity. They wouldn't give me the basement. They'll probably recognize my diplomacy ability, make me ambassador.

JOANNE: To Hell?

ROBERT: Well, if that's the place they send ambassadors.

POPO: Good. You be ambassador.

AMA: Special Testimony! Who is next?

ROBERT: [*Asking to be recognized*] Ama?

AMA: [*Ignoring him*] Who is next?

ROBERT: Not me. I think Wilbur should speak.

AMA: [*Disgusted*] Wilbur?

WILBUR: Me?

ROBERT: Yeah.

WILBUR: Well, I don't really . . .

ROBERT: Tell them, Wilbur. Tell them what kind of big stuffs happen to you. Tell them how important you are.

WILBUR: Well, I . . .

AMA: Would you . . . like to speak . . . Wilbur?

WILBUR: Well, I'd be honored, but if anyone else would rather . . .

ROBERT: We want to hear what you have to be proud of.

WILBUR: All right. [WILBUR *takes the podium;* AMA *scurries away.*] Uh—well, it's certainly nice to see this family reunion. Uh—last week, I was voted "Mr. Congeniality" at the club.

ROBERT: What papers was it in?

WILBUR: Huh?

ROBERT: Was it in the L.A. *Times?* Front page? Otis Chandler's paper?

HANNAH: [*A rebuff*] Robert!

POPO: [*To* ROBERT] Devotions is not question-and-answer for anyone except God.

ROBERT: God sometimes speaks through people, doesn't He?

POPO: He has good taste. Would not speak through you.

ROBERT: [*Undaunted, to* WILBUR] Show me one newspaper clipping. Just one!

WILBUR: Well, besides the *Valley Green Sheet* . . .

ROBERT: The *Valley Green Sheet?* Who pays for that? Junk. People line their birdcages with it.

WILBUR: Well, I suppose from a media standpoint, it's not that big a deal.

AMA: [*To* JOANNE] What means "congeniality"?

JOANNE: It means "friendly," sort of.

ROBERT: [*To* WILBUR] So why are you talking about it? Waste our time?

WILBUR: Look, Robert, it's obviously a token of their esteem.

ROBERT: Junk stuffs. Little thing. Who cares?

AMA: [*To herself*] "Mr. Friendly"?

ROBERT: It's embarrassing. What if clients say to me, "You're a bank president but your relatives can only get into the *Valley Green Sheet?*" Makes me lose face. They think my relatives are bums.

AMA: [*To* JOANNE] He is "Mr. Friendly"?

WILBUR: Look, Robert, the business is doing real well. It's not like that's my greatest accomplishment.

AMA: [*To* JOANNE] How can he be "Mr. Friendly"? He always kill and laugh.

JOANNE: Mom!

ROBERT: [*To* WILBUR] Does your business get in the paper?

WILBUR: Computer software happens to be one of the nation's fastest-growing—
ROBERT: So what? Lucky guess. Big deal.
WILBUR: It was an educated choice, not luck!

[ROBERT *gets up, starts to head for the podium.*]

ROBERT: Anyone can make money in America. What's hard is to become . . . a celebrity.
WILBUR: You're not a celebrity!
ROBERT: Yes, I am. That's the new thing. See, I just wanted to say that—[*He nudges* WILBUR *off the podium, takes his place.*]—when I was kidnapped, I didn't know if I would live or die.
POPO: [*Turns and sees* ROBERT *at the podium*] Huh?
JOANNE: Robert, forget it!
POPO: How did he get up there?
WILBUR: [*To* JOANNE] I'm perfectly capable of handling this myself.
POPO: He sneak up there while we are bored!
WILBUR: [*To* POPO] I'm sorry you found my testimony boring.
ROBERT: [*To* WILBUR] It was. [*To the assemblage*] Now hear mine.
JOANNE: We've all heard it before.
HANNAH: [*To* ROBERT] They're tired, dear. Get down.
ROBERT: Why? They listened to Wilbur's stuff. Boring. Junk.
JOANNE: "I didn't know if I would live or die." "I didn't know if I would live or die."
ROBERT: Di-gou, he hasn't heard. Have you, Di-gou?
DI-GOU: Is this when you didn't know if you would live or die?
ROBERT: How did—? Who told him?
POPO: I cannot think of enough ways to shoot him! Rifle! Arrows!
HANNAH: [*To* ROBERT] Sit down!
ROBERT: But there's something new!
HANNAH: I think we better let him speak, or he'll never shut up.
ROBERT: She's right. I won't.
JOANNE: All right. Make it quick, Robert.
ROBERT: All right. As I was saying, I didn't know if I would live or die.
JOANNE: You lived.
ROBERT: But the resulting publicity has made me a celebrity. Every place I go, people come up to me—"Aren't you the one that got kidnapped?" When I tell them how much the ransom was, they can hardly believe it. They ask for my autograph. Now—here's the new thing. I met these clients last week, told them my story. Now these guys are big shots and they say it would make a great movie. Yeah. No kidding. They made movies before. Not just regular movie, that's junk stuffs. We want to go where the big money is—we want to make a miniseries for TV. Like "Shogun." I told them, they should take the story, spice it up a little, you know? Add some sex scenes—we were thinking that I could have some hanky-panky with one of my kidnappers—woman, of course—just for audience sake—like Patty Hearst. I told them I should be played by Marlon Brando. And I have the greatest title: "Not a

Chinaman's Chance." Isn't that a great title? "Not a Chinaman's Chance." Beautiful. I can see the beginning already: I'm walking out of my office. I stop to help a
man fixing a flat tire.

HANNAH: All right, dear. That's enough.

ROBERT: Meanwhile, my secretary is having sex with my kidnapper.

HANNAH: Kidnap! Kidnap! That's all I ever hear about!

ROBERT: But, Hannah, I didn't know if I would live or die.

HANNAH: I wish you'd never even been kidnapped.

JOANNE: Well, what about Wilbur?

WILBUR: Leave me out of this.

JOANNE: Wilbur, you could be kidnapped.

WILBUR: I know, I know. It just hasn't happened yet, that's all.

HANNAH: Listen, Joanne. Count your blessings. It's not that great a thing. If they live,
they never stop talking about it.

ROBERT: But the publicity!—I sign newspapers all the time!

JOANNE: I'm just saying that Robert's not the only one worth kidnapping.

HANNAH: Joanne, no one's saying that.

AMA: Yes. We all desire Wilbur to be kidnapped also.

POPO: And Robert. Again. This time, longer.

JOANNE: I mean, Wilbur has a lot of assets.

ROBERT: Wilbur, maybe next time you can get kidnapped.

WILBUR: Never mind, honey.

JOANNE: You do.

WILBUR: I can defend myself.

ROBERT: But it takes more than assets to be kidnapped. You have to be cosmopolitan.

HANNAH: Hey, wait. What kind of example are we setting for Di-gou?

ROBERT: See? That's why I'm talking about it. To show Di-gou the greatness of
America. I'm just an immigrant, Di-gou, an FOB—but in America, I get kidnapped.

HANNAH: I mean, a Christian example.

DI-GOU: Oh, do not worry about me. This is all very fascinating.

JOANNE: [*To* ROBERT] So, you think you're cosmopolitan, huh?

ROBERT: I am. Before they let me loose, those kidnappers—they respected me.

JOANNE: They probably let you go because they couldn't stand to have you in
their car.

POPO: Probably you sing to them.

ROBERT: No. They said, "We've been kidnapping a long time, but—"

JOANNE: Because we can't stand to have you in our house! [*Pause*]

ROBERT: [*To* JOANNE] Now what kind of example are you setting for Di-gou?

WILBUR: Joanne, just shut up, okay?

HANNAH: [*To* DI-GOU] It's not always like this.

JOANNE: [*To* WILBUR] You never let me talk! You even let him [*Refers to* ROBERT] talk,
but you never let me talk!

AMA: [*To* JOANNE] He [*Refers to* WILBUR] cannot deprive you of right to speak. Look.
No gun.

ROBERT: Joanne, I have to tell this because Di-gou is here.

DI-GOU: Me?

JOANNE: [*To* ROBERT] You tell it to waiters!

ROBERT: Joanne, I want him [*Refers to* DI-GOU] to understand America. The American Dream. From rags to kidnap victim.

JOANNE: [*To* ROBERT] Well, I don't like you making Di-gou think that Wilbur's a bum.

WILBUR: [*To* JOANNE] Dear, he doesn't think that.

JOANNE: [*To* DI-GOU] You see, don't you, Di-gou? This house. Wilbur bought this.

DI-GOU: It is a palace.

JOANNE: It's larger than Robert's.

HANNAH: Joanne, how can you sink to my husband's level?

ROBERT: My house would be larger, but we had to pay the ransom.

POPO: Waste of money.

JOANNE: Look, all of you always put down Wilbur. Well, look at what he's done.

WILBUR: [*To* JOANNE] Just shut up, all right?

JOANNE: [*To* WILBUR] Well, if you're not going to say it.

WILBUR: I don't need you to be my PR firm.

ROBERT: [*To anybody*] He doesn't have a PR firm. We do. Tops firm.

JOANNE: [*To* WILBUR] Let me say my mind!

WILBUR: There's nothing in your mind worth saying.

JOANNE: What?

WILBUR: Face it, honey, you're boring.

AMA: [*To* WILBUR] At least she does not torture!

WILBUR: Please! No more talking about torture, all right?

AMA: All right. I will be quiet. No need to torture me.

POPO: [*To* DI-GOU] This small family disagreement.

JOANNE: So I'm boring, huh?

WILBUR: [*To* JOANNE] Look, let's not do this here.

POPO: [*To* DI-GOU] But power of God will overcome this.

JOANNE: I'm boring—that's what you're saying?

HANNAH: Joanne! Not in front of Di-gou!

JOANNE: [*To* DI-GOU] All right. You're objective. Who do you think is more boring?

DI-GOU: Well, I can hardly—

WILBUR: Please, Joanne.

POPO: [*To* DI-GOU] Do you understand how power of God will overcome this?

JOANNE: He [*Refers to* WILBUR] spends all his time with machines, and he calls me boring!

AMA: Di-gou, see the trials of this world?

WILBUR: [*To* JOANNE] Honey, I'm sorry, all right?

JOANNE: Sure, you're sorry.

AMA: [*To* DI-GOU] Argument, fight, no-good husbands.

WILBUR: "No-good husbands"?

[ROBERT, *in disgust exits into the house.*]

AMA: [*To* DI-GOU] Turn your eyes from this. [POPO *and* AMA *turn* DI-GOU'S *eyes from the fight.*]

JOANNE: [*To* WILBUR] She's [*Refers to* AMA] right, you know.

WILBUR: All right, honey, let's discuss this later.

JOANNE: Later! Oh, right.

[WILBUR *runs off into the house;* JOANNE *yells after him.*]

JOANNE: When we're with *your* family, that's when you want to talk about my denting the Ferrari.

HANNAH: Joanne! Don't be so boring!

JOANNE: [*To* HANNAH] With *our* family, it's "later."

AMA: [*To* DI-GOU] Look up to God!

[POPO *and* AMA *force* DI-GOU *to look up.*]

DI-GOU: Please! [DI-GOU *breaks away from the sisters' grip, but they knock him down.*]

POPO: Now—is time to join family in Heaven.

AMA: Time for you to return to God.

HANNAH: [*To* JOANNE] Look—they're converting Di-gou.

POPO: Return. Join us for eternity.

AMA: Pray now.

[POPO *and* AMA *try to guide* DI-GOU *to the neon cross.*]

DI-GOU: Where are we going?

AMA: He will wash you in blood of the lamb.

POPO: Like when you are a child. Now! You bow down!

HANNAH: Ask God for His forgiveness.

JOANNE: You won't regret it, Di-gou.

DI-GOU: Do you mind? [*He breaks away.*]

POPO: Why will you not accept Him?

AMA: There is no good reason.

DI-GOU: I want to take responsibility for my own life.

POPO: You cannot!

AMA: Satan is rule your life now.

DI-GOU: I am serving the people.

AMA: You are not.

POPO: You serve them, they all die, go to Hell. So what?

DI-GOU: How can you abandon China for this Western religion?

AMA: It is not.

POPO: God is God of all people.

DI-GOU: There is no God!

[*Pause*]

AMA: There is too much Communist demon in him. We must cast out demon.

POPO: Now, tie him on table.

DI-GOU: This is ridiculous. Stop this.

[*The women grab* DI-GOU, *tie him on the table.*]

POPO: We have too much love to allow demon to live.

DI-GOU: What?

POPO: [*To* JOANNE *and* HANNAH, *who are hesitating*] Now!

DI-GOU: You can't—!

POPO: Now! Or demon will escape!

AMA: We must kill demon.

POPO: Shoot him!

AMA: Kill for good.

POPO: Make demon into *jok!*[1]

DI-GOU: This is barbaric! You live with the barbarians, you become one yourself!

POPO: Di-gou, if we do not punish your body, demon will never leave.

AMA: Then you will return to China.

POPO: And you will die.

AMA: Go to Hell.

POPO: And it will be too late.

DI-GOU: I never expected Chinese children to tie down their elders. [DI-GOU *is now securely tied to the table.*]

HANNAH: All right. We're ready.

POPO: Now   you give your testimony.

DI-GOU: I'll just lie here and listen, thank you.

AMA: You tell of God's mercies to you.

JOANNE: How He let you out of China.

AMA: Where you are torture.

JOANNE: Whipped.

POPO: After thirty year, He let you out. Praise Him!

DI-GOU: I will never do such a thing!

HANNAH: If you wait too long, He'll lose patience.

POPO: Now—tell of your trip with See-goh-poh.

POPO: The trip which begin your faith.

DI-GOU: I was only eight years old. I don't remember.

POPO: Tell how many were convert on her tour.

HANNAH: Tell them, Di-gou.

DI-GOU: I cannot.

JOANNE: Why? Just tell the truth.

POPO: Tell how you saw the miracle of a great evangelist, great servant of God.

HANNAH: Tell them before they lose their patience.

DI-GOU: I'm sorry. I will not speak.

---

[1] A Chinese rice porridge. [Author's note]

POPO: Then we are sorry, Di-gou, but we must punish your body. Punish to drive out the demon and make you speak.

HANNAH: Don't make them do this, Di-gou.

AMA: If you will not speak See-goh-poh's stories in language you know, we will punish you until you speak in tongue of fire. [AMA *hits* DI-GOU *with an electrical cord, using it like a whip.*]

JOANNE: Please, Di-gou!

HANNAH: Tell them!

AMA: Our Lord was beat, nails drive through His body, for our sin. Your body must suffer until you speak the truth. [AMA *hits him.*]

HANNAH: Tell them, See-goh-poh was a great evangelist.

AMA: You were on her evangelism tour—we were not—you must remember her converts, her miracle. [*Hit*]

JOANNE: Just tell them and they'll let you go!

AMA: Think of See-goh-poh! She is sit! [*Hit*] Sit beside God. He is praising her! Praise her for her work in China.

[CHESTER *enters the tennis court; he looks into the sunroom and sees* AMA *hit* DI-GOU.]

AMA: She is watching you!

[*Hit.* CHESTER *tries to get into the sunroom, but the glass door is locked. He bangs on it, but everyone inside stands shocked at* AMA's *ritual, and no one notices him. He exits off the tennis court, running.*]

AMA: Praying for you! Want you to tell her story! [*Hit*]

AMA: We will keep you in float. Float for one second between life and death. Float until you lose will to hold to either—hold to anything at all.

[AMA *quickly slips the cord around* DI-GOU's *neck, begins pulling on it.* JOANNE *and* HANNAH *run to get* AMA *off of* DI-GOU. CHESTER *enters from the house, with* JENNY *close behind him. He pulls* AMA *off of* DI-GOU.]

CHESTER: Ama! Stop it!

[DI-GOU *suddenly breaks out of his bonds and rises up on the table. He grabs* CHESTER. *The barbecue bursts into flames.* DI-GOU, *holding on to* CHESTER, *begins speaking in tongues.*]

AMA: [*Looking up from the ground*] He is speaking in tongues! He has returned!

[*Everyone falls to their knees.*]

[*As* DI-GOU's *tongues continue,* CHESTER *is suddenly filled with words, and begins interpreting* DI-GOU's *babbling.*]

CHESTER: Di-gou at eight goes with See-goh-poh on her first evangelism tour. Di-gou and See-goh-poh traveling through the summer heat to a small village in Fukien. Sleeping in the straw next to See-goh-poh. Hearing a sound. A human sound. A cry in my sleep. Looking up and seeing a fire. A fire and See-goh-poh. See-goh-poh is naked. Naked and screaming. Screaming with legs spread so far apart. So far that a mouth opens up. A mouth between her legs. A mouth that is throwing up blood, spitting out blood. More and more blood. See-goh-poh's hands making a baby out of the blood. See-goh-poh hits the blood baby. Hits the baby and the baby cries. Watching the baby at See-goh-poh's breast. Hearing the sucking.

[AMA *and* POPO *spring up.*]

POPO: Such a thing never happened!
AMA: See-goh-poh never did this!
POPO: This is not tongues. This is not God. This is demon!
CHESTER: Sucking. Praying. Sucking. Squeezing. Crying.
AMA: He is possess by demon!
CHESTER: Biting. Blood. Milk.
POPO: Both have the demon!
CHESTER: Blood and milk. Blood and milk running down.
AMA: [*To the other women*] You pray.
CHESTER: Running down, further and further down.
POPO: We must cast out the demon!

[DI-GOU'*s tongues slowly become English, first overlapping, then overtaking* CHESTER'*s translation.* CHESTER *becomes silent and exhausted, drops to the ground.*]

CHESTER *and* DI-GOU: Down. Down and into the fire. The fire down there. The fire down there.

[DI-GOU *breaks the last of his bonds, gets off the table.*]

DI-GOU: [*To the sisters*] Your stories are dead now that you know the truth.
AMA: We have faith. We know our true family stories.
DI-GOU: You do not know your past.
AMA: Are you willing to match your stories against ours?

[DI-GOU *indicates his willingness to face* AMA, *and the two begin a ritualistic battle.* POPO *supports* AMA *by speaking in tongues.* AMA *and* DI-GOU *square off in seated positions, facing one another.*]

AMA: We will begin. How many rooms in our house in Amoy?
DI-GOU: Eighteen. How many bedrooms?
AMA: Ten. What year was it built?
DI-GOU: 1893. What year was the nineteenth room added?
AMA: 1923.

DI-GOU: On whose instructions?

AMA: See-goh-poh.

DI-GOU: What year did See-goh-poh die?

AMA: 1945. What disease?

DI-GOU: Malaria. How many teeth was she missing?

AMA: Three.

DI-GOU: What villages were on See-goh-poh's evangelism tour? [*Silence*] Do you know?

AMA: She preached to all villages in Fukien.

DI-GOU: Name one. [*Silence*] Do you know? Your stories don't know. It never happened.

AMA: It did! What year was she baptized? [*Silence*] What year was she baptized?

DI-GOU: She was never baptized.

AMA: You see? You don't remember.

DI-GOU: Never baptized.

AMA: It was 1921. Your stories do not remember.

DI-GOU: Who was converted on her evangelism tour?

AMA: Perhaps five hundred or more.

DI-GOU: Who? Name one. [*Silence*]

AMA: It is not important.

DI-GOU: You see? It never happened.

AMA: It did.

DI-GOU: You do not remember. You do not know the past. See-goh-poh never preached.

AMA: How can you say this?

DI-GOU: She traveled.

AMA: To preach.

DI-GOU: To travel.

AMA: She visited many—

DI-GOU: I was there! She was thrown out—thrown out on her evangelism tour when she tried to preach. [*Silence*]

AMA: It does not matter.

DI-GOU: You forced her to invent the stories.

AMA: We demand nothing!

DI-GOU: You expected! Expected her to convert all Amoy!

AMA: She did!

DI-GOU: Expected many miracles.

AMA: She did! She was a great—

DI-GOU: Expected her not to have a baby.

AMA: She had no husband. She had no baby. This is demon talk. Demon talk and lie.

DI-GOU: She turned away from God.

AMA: We will never believe this!

DI-GOU: On her tours she could both please you and see China.

[POPO's *tongues become weaker; she starts to falter.*]

AMA: See-goh-poh was a great—

DI-GOU: Only on her tours could she see both China and her baby.

AMA: She was a great . . . a great evangelist . . . many . . .

DI-GOU: Where is she buried?

AMA: . . . many miracle . . .

DI-GOU: She is not buried within the walls of the church in Amoy.

AMA: . . . many miracle a great evangelist . . .

[POPO *collapses.*]

DI-GOU: In her last moment, See-goh-poh wanted to be buried in Chinese soil, not Christian soil. You don't know. You were in the Philippines. [*Pause*] I come to bring you back to China. Come, sisters. To the soil you've forsaken with ways born of memories, of stories that never happened. Come, sisters. The stories written on your face are the ones you must believe.

[AMA *rises from her chair.*]

AMA: We will never believe this! [*She collapses back into her chair, closes her eyes.*]

[*Silence*]

DI-GOU: Sisters? [*Silence*] Sisters!

[JENNY, CHESTER, JOANNE, HANNAH, *and* DI-GOU *stare at the two inert forms.*]

CHESTER: Jenny! Jenny!

[JENNY *goes to* CHESTER's *side.*]

JOANNE: Hannah? Hannah—come here.

[HANNAH *does not move.*]

HANNAH: I see.

JOANNE: No! Come here!

HANNAH: I know, Joanne. I see.

DI-GOU: Once again. Once again my pleas are useless. But now—this is the last time. I have given all I own.

[POPO *and* AMA *have died.* DI-GOU *picks up his suitcase and the Chinese toys, heads for the door.*]

JOANNE: [*To* DI-GOU] Are you leaving?

DI-GOU: Now that my sisters have gone, I learn. No one leaves America. And I desire only to drive an American car—very fast—down an American freeway. [DI-GOU *exits.*]

JOANNE: [*Yelling after him*] This is our home, not yours! Why didn't you stay in China! This is not your family!

[JENNY *starts to break away from* CHESTER, *but he hangs on to her.* JOANNE *turns, sees the figures of* AMA *and* POPO.]

JOANNE: Wilbur! Wilbur, come here!

JENNY: [*To* CHESTER] Let go of me! Get away! [*She breaks away from* CHESTER.] I don't understand this, but whatever it is, it's ugly and it's awful and it causes people to die. It causes people to die and I don't want to have anything to do with it.

[JENNY *runs out onto the tennis court and away. On her way, she passes* ROBERT, *who has entered onto the court.* ROBERT *walks into the sunroom. Silence.*]

ROBERT: What's wrong with her? She acts like someone just died. [*Silence. He pulls up a chair next to* CHESTER.] Let's chit-chat, okay?

CHESTER: Sure, Dad.

ROBERT: So, how's Dorrie? [*Silence*] How much they paying you in Boston? [*Silence*] Got any new newspaper clippings?

[*Silence*]

[CHESTER *gets up, picks up his suitcase, walks onto the tennis court, and shuts the glass doors.*]

[AMA *and* POPO *lie in the center of the room.* JOANNE *and* HANNAH *stare at them.* ROBERT *sits, staring off into space.*]

[CHESTER *turns around, looks through the glass door onto the scene.*]

[*The* LIGHTS BEGIN TO DIM *until there is a single spotlight on* CHESTER'*s face, standing where* DI-GOU *stood at the beginning of the play.*]

[*The shape of* CHESTER'*s face begins to change.*]

Curtain

QUESTIONS

1. What are some of the actions and rituals in Act I that demonstrate we are in the home of a typical American family?

2. What are the major differences in values, beliefs, attitudes, and language among the three generations of the family as they are shown in Act I? How do these differences create conflict among the various characters?

3. What is the importance to Ama and Popo of See-goh-poh? Contrast their attitude about religion with Di-gou's.

4. What irony is there in Robert's dropping the tray of *guo-tieh* to demonstrate how much abundance there is in the United States? What other ironies does the author suggest through action or dialogue that reflect on the American Dream?

5. In Act I, what similarity does Chester find between himself and Di-gou? How does this similarity foreshadow what occurs in Act II?

6. What is ironic about Robert having been kidnapped? How does his kidnapping reflect the irony of American life, particularly as it applies to achieving affluence in America?

7. What is the significance of Chester's interpreting Di-gou when the latter begins to "speak in tongues"?

8. What do you believe to be the cause of the simultaneous deaths of Ama and Popo?

C h i l d r e n & F a m i l i e s

D r a m a

TOPICS FOR WRITING

1. Drama often involves the transformation of a character from one set of circumstances or beliefs to another. Write an essay explaining the transformation of Walter Younger.

2. Write an essay wherein you argue for or against the proposition that the issues presented in *A Raisin in the Sun* are as pertinent today as they were in 1959, when the play was produced.

3. *A Raisin in the Sun* and *Family Devotions* portray families that have had as their goals the American Dream. Compare and contrast the impact of the American Dream on the behaviors, attitudes, and emotional life of several major characters from each play.

4. *A Raisin in the Sun* and *Soul Gone Home* depict the injuries perpetrated upon African Americans by our society. Select a central character from each play, and discuss what the particular injury is to each.

5. In *A Raisin in the Sun*, Walter makes an anguished decision as to whether to move into an all-white neighborhood. Given the context of the play and the time it was written (1959), argue for or against the thesis that Walter made the right decision.

6. It is often said in drama that the choices a character makes reveal the personality of that character. Select one character from either *A Raisin in the Sun* or *Family Devotions*, and trace the choices that he or she makes in the course of the play. Explain how these actions elucidate the personality of the character you have selected.

7. Write a dialogue between two people who have a major conflict over an ethical issue such as abortion, homelessness, unemployment, or public assistance. Through their argument, we should be able to discern the personality of each person.

8. As a research project, study the life of Lorraine Hansberry, and write an essay wherein you discuss the major influences that contributed to her themes in *A Raisin in the Sun*.

Women

&

Men

"Dancing Lesson" by Raphael Soyer. 1926. Oil on canvas. Courtesy, The Renee and Chaim Gross Foundation. Photo, Jonathan Morris-Ebbs.

INTRODUCTION

What does it mean to be a woman? What does it mean to be a man? What relationships exist between men and women? Humankind has been asking these questions throughout the history of literature. Issues centering on women and men often were central themes of ancient myths, whether arising from traditional European culture, Oriental cultures, or the early cultures of Africa or North America. Until modern times, the roles of women and men were fairly differentiated as to functions, responsibilities, and activities. In the cave paintings of Lascaux in France and Altamira in Spain, which date back approximately 30,000 years, the hunters appear to be male; we may presume that women had gender-defined tasks of their own. Although there were exceptions in isolated societies and regions, men have traditionally wielded the power in matters of state, politics, and law. However, owing to evolutionary trends in society, particularly during the eighteenth and nineteenth centuries, the philosophy and enforcement of unequal status for the sexes have slowly been changing. Thinkers such as John Stuart Mill and Mary Wollstonecraft reflected on and affected their time by advocating more equitable relations between men and women. In the past 200 years, women's fight for equality has increased dramatically, and today we see women in public- and private-sector positions that could not have been imagined in previous eras—although most would argue that there are vast areas where the philosophy of gender equality has yet to emerge.

In complementary fashion, men too have been affected by the changing roles of the sexes. At one time, being a man meant you were expected to fulfill certain obligations and perform certain tasks as far as work, family, and society were concerned. Nowadays, men are redefining their duties as husbands, fathers, sons, workers, employers, or employees. In this last decade of the twentieth century, men find themselves constantly reassessing their roles, not always confident as to what are appropriate changes and modifications. In any time of flux, boundaries are not well drawn; appropriate actions are often determined through trial and error. The stories, poems, and plays in this section reflect the many facets of gender-related issues that face individuals, couples, families, and society as a whole.

Take, for example, two of the short stories from this section: "Astronomer's Wife" and "A Respectable Woman," written by Kay Boyle and Kate Chopin, respectively. Each portrays a woman awakening to the realization that her home life—particularly her relationship with her husband—is less than satisfactory. We see both women protagonists grapple with the dawning awareness that they are attracted to a man other than their husband. While in a more conservative era such thoughts might have been considered immoral, or even taboo, both of these stories acknowledge them and demonstrate how the characters confront their feelings. While these stories were written over a half-century ago, they foretell thoughts and emotions that today we consider so commonplace they are the subject of popular novels, films, and television programs.

Margaret Atwood, in her poem "Against Still Life," takes this theme of dissatisfaction a step further. The narrator ponders her environment, finding it cold and mechanistic. Similarly, Anne Sexton celebrates what she sees as the unique power and contribution of women poets, explaining in her poem "The Black Art" that women's creativity differs from men's, and suggesting that it is more mystical and profound. Many of the poets in this section explore the issues of what it means to be a modern woman. They confront such central issues as relationships, gender identity, social causes, and parenthood. We see unveiled before us the way women perceive themselves, as well as the way men perceive them.

Other works in this section reflect the changing nature of manhood. The stereotypical male—the steady, reliable, nearly machinelike provider who has reigned in many cultures—is shown to have given way to a more varied creature with a range of feelings, behaviors, and attitudes. Must men be self-assured, confident, "tough," and stoic? If we examine the way the narrator is depicted in T. S. Eliot's "The Love Song of J. Alfred Prufrock," the answer must be a resounding no! In this rather long poem, considered by many critics to be a milestone in twentieth-century poetry (if not in the entire history of poetic art), we peer into the psyche of a man who has many doubts, insecurities, and confusions. Rather than a typical love poem in which we might expect strong emotional expression, "Prufrock" presents a wan, meandering, passive individual who feels tossed about by his environment, unsure of how he should react to the personages and events around him.

In great contrast to J. Alfred Prufrock is the narrator of the Walt Whitman poem, "I Saw in Louisiana a Live-Oak Growing." Unlike the unhinged hero of the Eliot poem, Whitman portrays a man with powerfully rooted feelings and urges, an individual who implicitly compares himself to a tree that dominates the landscape. In the image of the tree we may infer the poet's projection of his own power, sexual energy, and sensuality. Written in the nineteenth century, at a time when such subject matter was not encouraged by society, the poem also demonstrates the traditional role of the poet, which is to uncover and reveal important areas of life that go unmentioned by the majority, who are ruled by standards, tastes, and mores that dictate what is appropriate.

Before proceeding to the literary works themselves, note that the selections here span time and place, genre and culture. Some, like John Donne's "The Bait" and William Shakespeare's *Othello*, were written hundreds of years ago while others, like Rita Dove's "Adolescence—II," are contemporary, composed by vital writers who have their creative fingers on the pulse of society. Style also figures as an important variable among the works presented here. "The Blue Jar" by Isak Dinesen has the mark of a fairy tale; "Leda and the Swan" by William Butler Yeats presents a rendition of an ancient Greek myth. On the other hand, works like "The Found Boat" by

Alice Munro or "The Wedding" by June Jordan are realistic portraits of people we can easily imagine meeting in our everyday lives. Also represented are perspectives on men's and women's lives from the Middle East, China, Eastern and Western Europe, and Latin America—demonstrating that the basic issues and themes of sex and gender apparently are universal ones. The result is the recognition that we are more alike than not.

Fiction

Kay Boyle

ASTRONOMER'S WIFE

There is an evil moment on awakening when all things seem to pause. But for women, they only falter and may be set in action by a single move: a lifted hand and the pendulum will swing, or the voice raised and through every room the pulse takes up its beating. The astronomer's wife felt the interval gaping and at once filled it to the brim. She fetched up her gentle voice and sent it warily down the stairs for coffee, swung her feet out upon the oval mat, and hailed the morning with her bare arms' quivering flesh drawn taut in rhythmic exercise: left, left, left my wife and fourteen children, right, right, right in the middle of the dusty road.

The day would proceed from this, beat by beat, without reflection, like every other day. The astronomer was still asleep, or feigning it, and she, once out of bed, had come into her own possession. Although scarcely ever out of sight of the impenetrable silence of his brow, she would be absent from him all the day in being clean, busy, kind. He was a man of other things, a dreamer. At times he lay still for hours, at others he sat upon the roof behind his telescope, or wandered down the pathway to the road and out across the mountains. This day, like any other, would go on from the removal of the spot left there from dinner on the astronomer's vest to the severe thrashing of the mayonnaise for lunch. That man might be each time the new arching wave, and woman the undertow that sucked him back, were things she had been told by his silence were so.

In spite of the earliness of the hour, the girl had heard her mistress's voice and was

189

coming up the stairs. At the threshold of the bedroom she paused, and said: "Madame, the plumber is here."

The astronomer's wife put on her white and scarlet smock very quickly and buttoned it at the neck. Then she stepped carefully around the motionless spread of water in the hall.

"Tell him to come right up," she said. She laid her hands on the bannisters and stood looking down the wooden stairway. "Ah, I am Mrs. Ames," she said softly as she saw him mounting. "I am Mrs. Ames," she said softly, softly down the flight of stairs. "I am Mrs. Ames," spoken soft as a willow weeping. "The professor is still sleeping. Just step this way."

The plumber himself looked up and saw Mrs. Ames with her voice hushed, speaking to him. She was a youngish woman, but this she had forgotten. The mystery and silence of her husband's mind lay like a chiding finger on her lips. Her eyes were gray, for the light had been extinguished in them. The strange dim halo of her yellow hair was still uncombed and sideways on her head.

For all of his heavy boots, the plumber quieted the sound of his feet, and together they went down the hall, picking their way around the still lake of water that spread as far as the landing and lay docile there. The plumber was a tough, hardy man; but he took off his hat when he spoke to her and looked her fully, almost insolently in the eye.

"Does it come from the wash-basin," he said, "or from the other . . . ?"

"Oh, from the other," said Mrs. Ames without hesitation.

In this place the villas were scattered out few and primitive, and although beauty lay without there was no reflection of her face within. Here all was awkward and unfit; a sense of wrestling with uncouth forces gave everything an austere countenance. Even the plumber, dealing as does a woman with matters under hand, was grave and stately. The mountains round about seemed to have cast them into the shadow of great dignity.

Mrs. Ames began speaking of their arrival that summer in the little villa, mourning each event as it followed on the other.

"Then, just before going to bed last night," she said, "I noticed something was unusual."

The plumber cast down a folded square of sack-cloth on the brimming floor and laid his leather apron on it. Then he stepped boldly onto the heart of the island it shaped and looked long into the overflowing bowl.

"The water should be stopped from the meter in the garden," he said at last.

"Oh, I did that," said Mrs. Ames, "the very first thing last night. I turned it off at once, in my nightgown, as soon as I saw what was happening. But all this had already run in."

The plumber looked for a moment at her red kid slippers. She was standing just at the edge of the clear, pure-seeming tide.

"It's no doubt the soil lines," he said severely. "It may be that something has stopped them, but my opinion is that the water seals aren't working. That's the trouble often enough in such cases. If you had a valve you wouldn't be caught like this."

Mrs. Ames did not know how to meet this rebuke. She stood, swaying a little, looking into the plumber's blue relentless eye.

"I'm sorry—I'm sorry that my husband," she said, "is still—resting and cannot go into this with you. I'm sure it must be very interesting. . . ."

"You'll probably have to have the traps sealed," said the plumber grimly, and at the sound of this Mrs. Ames' hand flew in dismay to the side of her face. The plumber made no move, but the set of his mouth as he looked at her seemed to soften. "Anyway, I'll have a look from the garden end," he said.

"Oh, do," said the astronomer's wife in relief. Here was a man who spoke of action and object as simply as women did! But however hushed her voice had been, it carried clearly to Professor Ames who lay, dreaming and solitary, upon his bed. He heard their footsteps come down the hall, pause, and skip across the pool of overflow.

"Katherine!" said the astronomer in a ringing tone. "There's a problem worthy of your mettle!"

Mrs. Ames did not turn her head, but led the plumber swiftly down the stairs. When the sun in the garden struck her face, he saw there was a wave of color in it, but this may have been anything but shame.

"You see how it is," said the plumber, as if leading her mind away. "The drains run from these houses right down the hill, big enough for a man to stand upright in them, and clean as a whistle too." There they stood in the garden with the vegetation flowering in disorder all about. The plumber looked at the astronomer's wife. "They come out at the torrent on the other side of the forest beyond there," he said.

But the words the astronomer had spoken still sounded in her in despair. The mind of man, she knew, made steep and sprightly flights, pursued illusion, took foothold in the nameless things that cannot pass between the thumb and finger. But whenever the astronomer gave voice to the thoughts that soared within him, she returned in gratitude to the long expanses of his silence. Desert-like they stretched behind and before the articulation of his scorn.

Life, life is an open sea, she sought to explain it in sorrow, and to survive women cling to the floating débris on the tide. But the plumber had suddenly fallen upon his knees in the grass and had crooked his fingers through the ring of the drains' trap-door. When she looked down she saw that he was looking up into her face, and she saw too that his hair was as light as gold.

"Perhaps Mr. Ames," he said rather bitterly, "would like to come down with me and have a look around?"

"Down?" said Mrs. Ames in wonder.

"Into the drains," said the plumber brutally. "They're a study for a man who likes to know what's what."

"Oh, Mr. Ames," said Mrs. Ames in confusion. "He's still—still in bed, you see."

The plumber lifted his strong, weathered face and looked curiously at her. Surely it seemed to him strange for a man to linger in bed, with the sun pouring yellow as wine all over the place. The astronomer's wife saw his lean cheeks, his high, rugged bones, and the deep seams in his brow. His flesh was as firm and clean as wood, stained richly tan with the climate's rigor. His fingers were blunt, but comprehensible to her, gripped in the ring and holding the iron door wide. The backs of his hands were bound round and round with ripe blue veins of blood.

"At any rate," said the astronomer's wife, and the thought of it moved her lips to smile a little, "Mr. Ames would never go down there alive. He likes going up," she said. And she, in her turn, pointed, but impudently, towards the heavens. "On the roof. Or on the mountains. He's been up on the tops of them many times."

"It's a matter of habit," said the plumber, and suddenly he went down the trap, Mrs. Ames saw a bright little piece of his hair still shining, like a star, long after the rest of him had gone. Out of the depths, his voice, hollow and dark with foreboding, returned to her. "I think something has stopped the elbow," was what he said.

This was speech that touched her flesh and bone and made her wonder. When her husband spoke of height, having no sense of it, she could not picture it nor hear. Depth or magic passed her by unless a name was given. But madness in a daily shape, as elbow stopped, she saw clearly and well. She sat down on the grasses, bewildered that it should be a man who had spoken to her so.

She saw the weeds springing up, and she did not move to tear them up from life. She sat powerless, her senses veiled, with no action taking shape beneath her hands. In this way some men sat for hours on end, she knew, tracking a single thought back to its origin. The mind of man could balance and divide, weed out, destroy. She sat on the full, burdened grasses, seeking to think, and dimly waiting for the plumber to return.

Whereas her husband had always gone up, as the dead go, she knew now that there were others who went down, like the corporeal being of the dead. That men were then divided into two bodies now seemed clear to Mrs. Ames. This knowledge stunned her with its simplicity and took the uneasy motion from her limbs. She could not stir, but sat facing the mountains' rocky flanks, and harking in silence to lucidity. Her husband was the mind, this other man the meat, of all mankind.

After a little, the plumber emerged from the earth: first the light top of his head, then the burnt brow, and then the blue eyes fringed with whitest lash. He braced his thick hands flat on the pavings of the garden-path and swung himself completely from the pit.

"It's the soil lines," he said pleasantly. "The gases," he said as he looked down upon her lifted face, "are backing up the drains."

"What in the world are we going to do?" said the astronomer's wife softly. There was a young and strange delight in putting questions to which true answers would be given. Everything the astronomer had ever said to her was a continuous query to which there could be no response.

"Ah, come, now," said the plumber, looking down and smiling. "There's a remedy for every ill, you know. Sometimes it may be that," he said as if speaking to a child, "or sometimes the other thing. But there's always a help for everything a-miss."

Things come out of herbs and make you young again, he might have been saying to her; or the first good rain will quench any drought; or time of itself will put a broken bone together.

"I'm going to follow the ground pipe out right to the torrent," the plumber was saying. "The trouble's between here and there and I'll find it on the way. There's nothing at all that can't be done over for the caring," he was saying, and his eyes were fastened on her face in insolence, or gentleness, or love.

The astronomer's wife stood up, fixed a pin in her hair, and turned around towards the kitchen. Even while she was calling the servant's name, the plumber began speaking again.

"I once had a cow that lost her cud," the plumber was saying. The girl came out on the kitchen-step and Mrs. Ames stood smiling at her in the sun.

"The trouble is very serious, very serious," she said across the garden. "When Mr. Ames gets up, please tell him I've gone down."

She pointed briefly to the open door in the pathway, and the plumber hoisted his kit on his arm and put out his hand to help her down.

"But I made her another in no time," he was saying, "out of flowers and things and what-not."

"Oh," said the astronomer's wife in wonder as she stepped into the heart of the earth. She took his arm, knowing that what he said was true.

QUESTIONS

1. When do we get the first inkling of Mrs. Ames's feelings toward her husband? What are they?
2. What significance does water have as a symbol in the story? Does this symbol go through various transformations, and if so, what are they?
3. Is the astronomer portrayed sympathetically or unsympathetically? Explain.
4. What types of observations does Mrs. Ames make about the plumber? How are they similar to what the plumber notices about Mrs. Ames?
5. How are images of height and depth used in the story? How do they contribute to the story's theme?

Anton Chekhov

THE LADY WITH THE PET DOG

I

A new person, it was said, had appeared on the esplanade: a lady with a pet dog. Dmitry Dmitrich Gurov, who had spent a fortnight at Yalta and had got used to the place, had also begun to take an interest in new arrivals. As he sat in Vernet's confectionery shop, he saw, walking on the esplanade, a fair-haired young woman of medium height, wearing a beret; a white Pomeranian was trotting behind her.

And afterwards he met her in the public garden and in the square several times a day. She walked alone, always wearing the same beret and always with the white dog; no one knew who she was and everyone called her simply "the lady with the pet dog."

"If she is here alone without husband or friends," Gurov reflected, "it wouldn't be a bad thing to make her acquaintance."

He was under forty, but he already had a daughter twelve years old, and two sons at school. They had found a wife for him when he was very young, a student in his second year, and by now she seemed half as old again as he. She was a tall, erect woman with dark eyebrows, stately and dignified and, as she said of herself, intellectual. She read a great deal, used simplified spelling in her letters, called her husband, not Dmitry, but Dimitry, while he privately considered her of limited intelligence, narrow-minded, dowdy, was afraid of her, and did not like to be at home. He had begun being unfaithful to her long ago—had been unfaithful to her often and, probably for that reason, almost always spoke ill of women, and when they were talked of in his presence used to call them "the inferior race."

It seemed to him that he had been sufficiently tutored by bitter experience to call them what he pleased, and yet he could not have lived without "the inferior race" for two days together. In the company of men he was bored and ill at ease, he was chilly and uncommunicative with them; but when he was among women he felt free, and knew what to speak to them about and how to comport himself; and even to be silent with them was no strain on him. In his appearance, in his character, in his whole makeup there was something attractive and elusive that disposed women in his favor and allured them. He knew that, and some force seemed to draw him to them, too.

Oft-repeated and really bitter experience had taught him long ago that with decent people—particularly Moscow people—who are irresolute and slow to move, every affair which at first seems a light and charming adventure inevitably grows into a whole problem of extreme complexity, and in the end a painful situation is created. But at every new meeting with an interesting woman this lesson of experience seemed to slip from his memory, and he was eager for life, and everything seemed so simple and diverting.

One evening while he was dining in the public garden the lady in the beret walked up without haste to take the next table. Her expression, her gait, her dress, and the way she did her hair told him that she belonged to the upper class, that she was married, that she was in Yalta for the first time and alone, and that she was bored there. The stories told of the immorality in Yalta are to a great extent untrue; he despised them, and knew that such stories were made up for the most part by persons who would have been glad to sin themselves if they had had the chance; but when the lady sat down at the next table three paces from him, he recalled these stories of easy conquests, of trips to the mountains, and the tempting thought of a swift, fleeting liaison, a romance with an unknown woman of whose very name he was ignorant suddenly took hold of him.

He beckoned invitingly to the Pomeranian, and when the dog approached him, shook his finger at it. The Pomeranian growled; Gurov threatened it again.

The lady glanced at him and at once dropped her eyes.

"He doesn't bite," she said and blushed.

"May I give him a bone?" he asked; and when she nodded he inquired affably, "Have you been in Yalta long?"

"About five days."

"And I am dragging out the second week here."

There was a short silence.

"Time passes quickly, and yet it is so dull here!" she said, not looking at him.

"It's only the fashion to say it's dull here. A provincial will live in Belyov or Zhizdra and not be bored, but when he comes here it's 'Oh, the dullness! Oh, the dust!' One would think he came from Granada."

She laughed. Then both continued eating in silence, like strangers, but after dinner they walked together and there sprang up between them the light banter of people who are free and contented, to whom it does not matter where they go or what they talk about. They walked and talked of the strange light on the sea: the water was a soft, warm, lilac color, and there was a golden band of moonlight upon it. They talked of how sultry it was after a hot day. Gurov told her that he was a native of Moscow, that he had studied languages and literature at the university, but had a post in a bank; that at one time he had trained to become an opera singer but had given it up, that he owned two houses in Moscow. And he learned from her that she had grown up in Petersburg, but had lived in S—— since her marriage two years previously, that she was going to stay in Yalta for about another month, and that her husband, who needed a rest, too, might perhaps come to fetch her. She was not certain whether her husband was a member of a Government Board or served on a Zemstvo Council,[1] and this amused her. And Gurov learned too that her name was Anna Sergeyevna.

Afterwards in his room at the hotel he thought about her—and was certain that he would meet her the next day. It was bound to happen. Getting into bed he recalled that she had been a schoolgirl only recently, doing lessons like his own daughter; he thought how much timidity and angularity there was still in her laugh and her manner of talking with a stranger. It must have been the first time in her life that she was alone in a setting in which she was followed, looked at, and spoken to for one secret purpose alone, which she could hardly fail to guess. He thought of her slim, delicate throat, her lovely gray eyes.

"There's something pathetic about her, though," he thought, and dropped off.

II

A week had passed since they had struck up an acquaintance. It was a holiday. It was close indoors, while in the street the wind whirled the dust about and blew people's hats off. One was thirsty all day, and Gurov often went into the restaurant and offered Anna Sergeyevna a soft drink or ice cream. One did not know what to do with oneself.

In the evening when the wind had abated they went out on the pier to watch the steamer come in. There were a great many people walking about the dock; they had come to welcome someone and they were carrying bunches of flowers. And two peculiarities of a festive Yalta crowd stood out: the elderly ladies were dressed like young ones and there were many generals.

Owing to the choppy sea, the steamer arrived late, after sunset, and it was a long time

---

[1] *Zemstvo Council*—county council.

tacking about before it put in at the pier. Anna Sergeyevna peered at the steamer and the passengers through her lorgnette as though looking for acquaintances, and whenever she turned to Gurov her eyes were shining. She talked a great deal and asked questions jerkily, forgetting the next moment what she had asked; then she lost her lorgnette in the crush.

The festive crowd began to disperse; it was now too dark to see people's faces; there was no wind any more, but Gurov and Anna Sergeyevna still stood as though waiting to see someone else come off the steamer. Anna Sergeyevna was silent now, and sniffed her flowers without looking at Gurov.

"The weather has improved this evening," he said. "Where shall we go now? Shall we drive somewhere?"

She did not reply.

Then he looked at her intently, and suddenly embraced her and kissed her on the lips, and the moist fragrance of her flowers enveloped him; and at once he looked round him anxiously, wondering if anyone had seen them.

"Let us go to your place," he said softly. And they walked off together rapidly.

The air in her room was close and there was the smell of the perfume she had bought at the Japanese shop. Looking at her, Gurov thought: "What encounters life offers!" From the past he preserved the memory of carefree, good-natured women whom love made gay and who were grateful to him for the happiness he gave them, however brief it might be; and of women like his wife who loved without sincerity, with too many words, affectedly, hysterically, with an expression that it was not love or passion that engaged them but something more significant; and of two or three others, very beautiful, frigid women, across whose faces would suddenly flit a rapacious expression—an obstinate desire to take from life more than it could give, and these were women no longer young, capricious, unreflecting, domineering, unintelligent, and when Gurov grew cold to them their beauty aroused his hatred, and the lace on their lingerie seemed to him to resemble scales.

But here there was the timidity, the angularity of inexperienced youth, a feeling of awkwardness; and there was a sense of embarrassment, as though someone had suddenly knocked at the door. Anna Sergeyevna, "the lady with the pet dog," treated what had happened in a peculiar way, very seriously, as though it were her fall—so it seemed, and this was odd and inappropriate. Her features drooped and faded, and her long hair hung down sadly on either side of her face; she grew pensive and her dejected pose was that of a Magdalene in a picture by an old master.

"It's not right," she said. "You don't respect me now, you first of all."

There was a watermelon on the table. Gurov cut himself a slice and began eating it without haste. They were silent for at least half an hour.

There was something touching about Anna Sergeyevna; she had the purity of a well-bred, naive woman who has seen little of life. The single candle burning on the table barely illumined her face, yet it was clear that she was unhappy.

"Why should I stop respecting you, darling?" asked Gurov. "You don't know what you're saying."

"God forgive me," she said, and her eyes filled with tears. "It's terrible."

"It's as though you were trying to exonerate yourself."

"How can I exonerate myself? No. I am a bad, low woman; I despise myself and I have no thought of exonerating myself. It's not my husband but myself I have deceived. And not only just now; I have been deceiving myself for a long time. My husband may be a good, honest man, but he is a flunkey! I don't know what he does, what his work is, but I know he is a flunkey! I was twenty when I married him. I was tormented by curiosity; I wanted something better. 'There must be a different sort of life,' I said to myself. I wanted to live! To live, to live! Curiosity kept eating at me—you don't understand it, but I swear to God I could no longer control myself; something was going on in me; I could not be held back. I told my husband I was ill, and came here. And here I have been walking about as though in a daze, as though I were mad; and now I have become a vulgar, vile woman whom anyone may despise."

Gurov was already bored with her; he was irritated by her naive tone, by her repentance, so unexpected and so out of place, but for the tears in her eyes he might have thought she was joking or play-acting.

"I don't understand, my dear," he said softly. "What do you want?"

She hid her face on his breast and pressed close to him.

"Believe me, believe me, I beg you," she said, "I love honesty and purity, and sin is loathsome to me; I don't know what I'm doing. Simple people say, 'The Evil One has led me astray.' And I may say of myself now that the Evil One has led me astray."

"Quiet, quiet," he murmured.

He looked into her fixed, frightened eyes, kissed her, spoke to her softly and affectionately, and by degrees she calmed down, and her gaiety returned; both began laughing.

Afterwards when they went out there was not a soul on the esplanade. The town with its cypresses looked quite dead, but the sea was still sounding as it broke upon the beach; a single launch was rocking on the waves and on it a lantern was blinking sleepily.

They found a cab and drove to Oreanda.

"I found out your surname in the hall just now: it was written on the board—von Dideritz," said Gurov. "Is your husband German?"

"No; I believe his grandfather was German, but he is Greek Orthodox himself."

At Oreanda they sat on a bench not far from the church, looked down at the sea, and were silent. Yalta was barely visible through the morning mist; white clouds rested motionlessly on the mountaintops. The leaves did not stir on the trees, cicadas twanged, and the monotonous muffled sound of the sea that rose from below spoke of the peace, the eternal sleep awaiting us. So it rumbled below when there was no Yalta, no Oreanda here; so it rumbles now, and it will rumble as indifferently and as hollowly when we are no more. And in this constancy, in this complete indifference to the life and death of each of us, there lies, perhaps, a pledge of our eternal salvation, of the unceasing advance of life upon earth, of unceasing movement towards perfection. Sitting beside a young woman who in the dawn seemed so lovely, Gurov, soothed and spellbound by these magical surroundings—the sea, the mountains, the clouds, the wide sky—thought how everything is really beautiful in this world when one reflects: everything except what we think or do ourselves when we forget the higher aims of life and our own human dignity.

A man strolled up to them—probably a guard—looked at them and walked away.

And this detail, too, seemed so mysterious and beautiful. They saw a steamer arrive from Feodosia, its lights extinguished in the glow of dawn.

"There is dew on the grass," said Anna Sergeyevna, after a silence.

"Yes, it's time to go home."

They returned to the city.

Then they met every day at twelve o'clock on the esplanade, lunched and dined together, took walks, admired the sea. She complained that she slept badly, that she had palpitations, asked the same questions, troubled now by jealousy and now by the fear that he did not respect her sufficiently. And often in the square or the public garden, when there was no one near them, he suddenly drew her to him and kissed her passionately. Complete idleness, these kisses in broad daylight exchanged furtively in dread of someone's seeing them, the heat, the smell of the sea, and the continual flitting before his eyes of idle, well-dressed, well-fed people, worked a complete change in him; he kept telling Anna Sergeyevna how beautiful she was, how seductive, was urgently passionate; he would not move a step away from her, while she was often pensive and continually pressed him to confess that he did not respect her, did not love her in the least, and saw in her nothing but a common woman. Almost every evening rather late they drove somewhere out of town, to Oreanda or to the waterfall; and the excursion was always a success, the scenery invariably impressed them as beautiful and magnificent.

They were expecting her husband, but a letter came from him saying that he had eye-trouble, and begging his wife to return home as soon as possible. Anna Sergeyevna made haste to go.

"It's a good thing I am leaving," she said to Gurov. "It's the hand of Fate!"

She took a carriage to the railway station, and he went with her. They were driving the whole day. When she had taken her place in the express, and when the second bell had rung, she said, "Let me look at you once more—let me look at you again. Like this."

She was not crying but was so sad that she seemed ill and her face was quivering.

"I shall be thinking of you—remembering you," she said. "God bless you; be happy. Don't remember evil against me. We are parting forever—it has to be, for we ought never to have met. Well, God bless you."

The train moved off rapidly, its lights soon vanished, and a minute later there was no sound of it, as though everything had conspired to end as quickly as possible that sweet trance, that madness. Left alone on the platform, and gazing into the dark distance, Gurov listened to the twang of the grasshoppers and the hum of the telegraph wires, feeling as though he had just waked up. And he reflected, musing, that there had now been another episode or adventure in his life, and it, too, was at an end, and nothing was left of it but a memory. He was moved, sad, and slightly remorseful: this young woman whom he would never meet again had not been happy with him; he had been warm and affectionate with her, but yet in his manner, his tone, and his caresses there had been a shade of light irony, the slightly coarse arrogance of a happy male who was, besides, almost twice her age. She had constantly called him kind, exceptional, high-minded; obviously he had seemed to her different from what he really was, so he had involuntarily deceived her.

Here at the station there was already a scent of autumn in the air; it was a chilly evening.

"It is time for me to go north, too," thought Gurov as he left the platform. "High time!"

III

At home in Moscow the winter routine was already established; the stoves were heated, and in the morning it was still dark when the children were having breakfast and getting ready for school, and the nurse would light the lamp for a short time. There were frosts already. When the first snow falls, on the first day the sleighs are out, it is pleasant to see the white earth, the white roofs; one draws easy, delicious breaths, and the season brings back the days of one's youth. The old limes and birches, white with hoar-frost, have a good-natured look; they are closer to one's heart than cypresses and palms, and near them one no longer wants to think of mountains and the sea.

Gurov, a native of Moscow, arrived there on a fine frosty day, and when he put on his fur coat and warm gloves and took a walk along Petrovka, and when on Saturday night he heard the bells ringing, his recent trip and the places he had visited lost all charm for him. Little by little he became immersed in Moscow life, greedily read three newspapers a day, and declared that he did not read the Moscow papers on principle. He already felt a longing for restaurants, clubs, formal dinners, anniversary celebrations, and it flattered him to entertain distinguished lawyers and actors, and to play cards with a professor at the physicians' club. He could eat a whole portion of meat stewed with pickled cabbage and served in a pan, Moscow style.

A month or so would pass and the image of Anna Sergeyevna, it seemed to him, would become misty in his memory, and only from time to time he would dream of her with her touching smile as he dreamed of others. But more than a month went by, winter came into its own, and everything was still clear in his memory as though he had parted from Anna Sergeyevna only yesterday. And his memories glowed more and more vividly. When in the evening stillness the voices of his children preparing their lessons reached his study, or when he listened to a song or to an organ playing in a restaurant, or when the storm howled in the chimney, suddenly everything would rise up in his memory; what had happened on the pier and the early morning with the mist on the mountains, and the steamer coming from Feodosia, and the kisses. He would pace about his room a long time, remembering and smiling; then his memories passed into reveries, and in his imagination the past would mingle with what was to come. He did not dream of Anna Sergeyevna, but she followed him about everywhere and watched him. When he shut his eyes he saw her before him as though she were there in the flesh, and she seemed to him lovelier, younger, tenderer than she had been, and he imagined himself a finer man than he had been in Yalta. Of evenings she peered out at him from the bookcase, from the fireplace, from the corner—he heard her breathing, the caressing rustle of her clothes. In the street he followed the women with his eyes, looking for someone who resembled her.

Already he was tormented by a strong desire to share his memories with someone. But in his home it was impossible to talk of his love, and he had no one to talk to outside;

certainly he could not confide in his tenants or anyone at the bank. And what was there to talk about? He hadn't loved her then, had he? Had there been anything beautiful, poetical, edifying, or simply interesting in his relations with Anna Sergeyevna? And he was forced to talk vaguely of love, of women, and no one guessed what he meant; only his wife would twitch her black eyebrows and say, "The part of a philanderer does not suit you at all, Dimitry."

One evening, coming out of the physicians' club with an official with whom he had been playing cards, he could not resist saying:

"If you only knew what a fascinating woman I became acquainted with at Yalta!"

The official got into his sledge and was driving away, but turned suddenly and shouted:

"Dmitry Dmitrich!"

"What is it?"

"You were right this evening; the sturgeon was a bit high."

These words, so commonplace, for some reason moved Gurov to indignation, and struck him as degrading and unclean. What savage manners, what mugs! What stupid nights, what dull, humdrum days! Frenzied gambling, gluttony, drunkenness, continual talk always about the same thing! Futile pursuits and conversations always about the same topics take up the better part of one's time, the better part of one's strength, and in the end there is left a life clipped and wingless, an absurd mess, and there is no escaping or getting away from it—just as though one were in a madhouse or a prison.

Gurov, boiling with indignation, did not sleep all night. And he had a headache all the next day. And the following nights too he slept badly; he sat up in bed, thinking, or paced up and down his room. He was fed up with his children, fed up with the bank; he had no desire to go anywhere or to talk of anything.

In December during the holidays he prepared to take a trip and told his wife he was going to Petersburg to do what he could for a young friend—and he set off for S——. What for? He did not know, himself. He wanted to see Anna Sergeyevna and talk with her, to arrange a rendezvous if possible.

He arrived at S—— in the morning, and at the hotel took the best room, in which the floor was covered with gray army cloth, and on the table there was an inkstand, gray with dust and topped by a figure on horseback, its hat in its raised hand and its head broken off. The porter gave him the necessary information: von Dideritz lived in a house of his own on Staro-Goncharnaya Street, not far from the hotel: he was rich and lived well and kept his own horses; everyone in the town knew him. The porter pronounced the name: "Dridiritz."

Without haste Gurov made his way to Staro-Goncharnaya Street and found the house. Directly opposite the house stretched a long gray fence studded with nails.

"A fence like that would make one run away," thought Gurov, looking now at the fence, now at the windows of the house.

He reflected: this was a holiday, and the husband was apt to be at home. And in any case, it would be tactless to go into the house and disturb her. If he were to send her a note, it might fall into her husband's hands, and that might spoil everything. The best thing was to rely on chance. And he kept walking up and down the street and along the fence, waiting for the chance. He saw a beggar go in at the gate and heard the dogs attack him; then an hour later he heard a piano, and the sound came to him faintly and indistinctly. Probably it was Anna Sergeyevna playing. The front door opened suddenly, and an old woman came out, followed by the familiar white Pomeranian. Gurov was on the point of calling to the dog, but his heart began beating violently, and in his excitement he could not remember the Pomeranian's name.

He kept walking up and down, and hated the gray fence more and more, and by now the thought irritably that Anna Sergeyevna had forgotten him, and was perhaps already diverting herself with another man, and that that was very natural in a young woman who from morning till night had to look at that damn fence. He went back to his hotel room and sat on the couch for a long while, not knowing what to do, then he had dinner and a long nap.

"How stupid and annoying all this is!" he thought when he woke and looked at the dark windows: it was already evening. "Here I've had a good sleep for some reason. What am I going to do at night?"

He sat on the bed, which was covered with a cheap gray blanket of the kind seen in hospitals, and he twitted himself in his vexation:

"So there's your lady with the pet dog. There's your adventure. A nice place to cool your heels in."

That morning at the station a playbill in large letters had caught his eye. *The Geisha* was to be given for the first time. He thought of this and drove to the theater.

"It's quite possible that she goes to first nights," he thought.

The theater was full. As in all provincial theaters, there was a haze above the chandelier, the gallery was noisy and restless; in the front row, before the beginning of the performance the local dandies were standing with their hands clasped behind their backs; in the Governor's box the Governor's daughter, wearing a boa, occupied the front seat, while the Governor himself hid modestly behind the portiere and only his hands were visible; the curtain swayed; the orchestra was a long time tuning up. While the audience was coming in and taking their seats, Gurov scanned the faces eagerly.

Anna Sergeyevna, too, came in. She sat down in the third row, and when Gurov looked at her his heart contracted, and he understood clearly that in the whole world there was no human being so near, so precious, and so important to him; she, this little, undistinguished woman, lost in a provincial crowd, with a vulgar lorgnette in her hand, filled his whole life now, was his sorrow and his joy, the only happiness that he now desired for himself, and to the sounds of the bad orchestra, of the miserable local violins, he thought how lovely she was. He thought and dreamed.

A young man with small side-whiskers, very tall and stooped, came in with Anna Sergeyevna and sat down beside her; he nodded his head at every step and seemed to be bowing continually. Probably this was the husband whom at Yalta, in an access of bitter feeling, she had called a flunkey. And there really was in his lanky figure, his side-whiskers, his small bald patch, something of a flunkey's retiring manner; his smile was mawkish, and in his buttonhole there was an academic badge like a waiter's number.

During the first intermission the husband went out to have a smoke; she remained in her seat. Gurov, who was also sitting in the orchestra, went up to her and said in a shaky voice, with a forced smile:

"Good evening!"

She glanced at him and turned pale, then looked at him again in horror, unable to believe her eyes, and gripped the fan and the lorgnette tightly together in her hands, evidently trying to keep herself from fainting. Both were silent. She was sitting, he was standing, frightened by her distress and not daring to take a seat beside her. The violins and the flute that were being tuned up sang out. He suddenly felt frightened: it seemed as if all the people in the boxes were looking at them. She got up and went hurriedly to the exit; he followed her, and both of them walked blindly along the corridors and up and down stairs, and figures in the uniforms prescribed for magistrates, teachers, and officials of the Department of Crown Lands, all wearing badges, flitted before their eyes, as did also ladies, and fur coats on hangers; they were conscious of drafts and the smell of stale tobacco. And Gurov, whose heart was beating violently, thought:

"Oh, Lord! Why are these people here and this orchestra!"

And at that instant he suddenly recalled how when he had seen Anna Sergeyevna off at the station he had said to himself that all was over between them and that they would never meet again. But how distant the end still was!

On the narrow, gloomy staircase over which it said "To the Amphitheatre," she stopped.

"How you frightened me!" she said, breathing hard, still pale and stunned. "Oh, how you frightened me! I am barely alive. Why did you come? Why?"

"But do understand, Anna, do understand—" he said hurriedly, under his breath. "I implore you, do understand—"

She looked at him with fear, with entreaty, with love; she looked at him intently, to keep his features more distinctly in her memory.

"I suffer so," she went on, not listening to him. "All this time I have been thinking of nothing but you; I live only by the thought of you. And I wanted to forget, to forget; but why, oh, why have you come?"

On the landing above them two high school boys were looking down and smoking, but it was all the same to Gurov; he drew Anna Sergeyevna to him and began kissing her face and hands.

"What are you doing, what are you doing!" she was saying in horror, pushing him away. "We have lost our senses. Go away today; go away at once—I conjure you by all that is sacred, I implore you—People are coming this way!"

Someone was walking up the stairs.

"You must leave," Anna Sergeyevna went on in a whisper. "Do you hear, Dmitry Dmitrich? I will come and see you in Moscow. I have never been happy; I am unhappy now, and I never, never shall be happy, never! So don't make me suffer still more! I swear I'll come to Moscow. But now let us part. My dear, good, precious one, let us part!"

She pressed his hand and walked rapidly downstairs, turning to look round at him, and from her eyes he could see that she really was unhappy. Gurov stood for a while, listening, then when all grew quiet, he found his coat and left the theater.

IV

And Anna Sergeyevna began coming to see him in Moscow. Once every two or three months she left S—— telling her husband that she was going to consult a doctor about a woman's ailment from which she was suffering—and her husband did and did not believe her. When she arrived in Moscow she would stop at the Slavyansky Bazar Hotel, and at once send a man in a red cap to Gurov. Gurov came to see her, and no one in Moscow knew of it.

Once he was going to see her in this way on a winter morning (the messenger had come the evening before and not found him in). With him walked his daughter, whom he wanted to take to school; it was on the way. Snow was coming down in big wet flakes.

"It's three degrees above zero,[2] and yet it's snowing," Gurov was saying to his daughter. "But this temperature prevails only on the surface of the earth; in the upper layers of the atmosphere there is quite a different temperature."

"And why doesn't it thunder in winter, papa?"

He explained that, too. He talked, thinking all the while that he was on his way to a rendezvous, and no living soul knew of it, and probably no one would ever know. He had two lives, an open one, seen and known by all who needed to know it, full of conventional truth and conventional falsehood, exactly like the lives of his friends and acquaintances; and another life that went on in secret. And through some strange, perhaps accidental, combination of circumstances, everything that was of interest and importance to him, everything that was essential to him, everything about which he felt sincerely and did not deceive himself, everything that constituted the core of his life, was going on concealed from others; while all that was false, the shell in which he hid to cover the truth—his work at the bank, for instance, his discussions at the club, his references to the "inferior race," his appearances at anniversary celebrations with his wife—all that went on in the open. Judging others by himself, he did not believe what he saw, and always fancied that every man led his real, most interesting life under cover of secrecy as under cover of night. The personal life of every individual is based on secrecy, and perhaps it is partly for that reason that civilized man is so nervously anxious that personal privacy should be respected.

Having taken his daughter to school, Gurov went on to the Slavyansky Bazar Hotel. He took off his fur coat in the lobby, went upstairs, and knocked gently at the door. Anna Sergeyevna, wearing his favorite gray dress, exhausted by the journey and by waiting, had been expecting him since the previous evening. She was pale, and looked at him without a smile, and he had hardly entered when she flung herself on his breast. That kiss was a long, lingering one, as though they had not seen one another for two years.

"Well, darling, how are you getting on there?" he asked. "What news?"

"Wait; I'll tell you in a moment—I can't speak."

She could not speak; she was crying. She turned away from him, and pressed her handkerchief to her eyes.

"Let her have her cry; meanwhile I'll sit down," he thought, and he seated himself in an armchair.

Then he rang and ordered tea, and while he was having his tea she remained standing at the window with her back to him. She was crying out of sheer agitation, in the sorrowful consciousness that their life was so sad; that they could only see each other in secret and had to hide from people like thieves! Was it not a broken life?

"Come, stop now, dear!" he said.

---

[2]*three degrees above zero*—Celsius—about thirty-seven degrees Fahrenheit

It was plain to him that this love of theirs would not be over soon, that the end of it was not in sight. Anna Sergeyevna was growing more and more attached to him. She adored him, and it was unthinkable to tell her that their love was bound to come to an end some day; besides, she would not have believed it!

He went up to her and took her by the shoulders, to fondle her and say something diverting, and at that moment he caught sight of himself in the mirror.

His hair was already beginning to turn gray. And it seemed odd to him that he had grown so much older in the last few years, and lost his looks. The shoulders on which his hands rested were warm and heaving. He felt compassion for this life, still so warm and lovely, but probably already about to begin to fade and wither like his own. Why did she love him so much? He always seemed to women different from what he was, and they loved in him not himself, but the man whom their imagination created and whom they had been eagerly seeking all their lives; and afterwards, when they saw their mistake, they loved him nevertheless. And not one of them had been happy with him. In the past he had met women, come together with them, parted from them, but he had never once loved; it was anything you please, but not love. And only now when his head was gray he had fallen in love, really, truly—for the first time in his life.

Anna Sergeyevna and he loved each other as people do who are very close and intimate, like man and wife, like tender friends; it seemed to them that Fate itself had meant them for one another, and they could not understand why he had a wife and she a husband; and it was as though they were a pair of migratory birds, male and female, caught and forced to live in different cages. They forgave each other what they were ashamed of in their past, they forgave everything in the present, and felt that this love of theirs had altered them both.

Formerly in moments of sadness he had soothed himself with whatever logical arguments came into his head, but now he no longer cared for logic; he felt profound compassion, he wanted to be sincere and tender.

"Give it up now, my darling," he said. "You've had your cry; that's enough. Let us have a talk now, we'll think up something."

Then they spent a long time taking counsel together, they talked of how to avoid the necessity for secrecy, for deception, for living in different cities, and not seeing one another for long stretches of time. How could they free themselves from these intolerable fetters?

"How? How?" he asked, clutching his head. "How?"

And it seemed as though in a little while the solution would be found, and then a new and glorious life would begin; and it was clear to both of them that the end was still far off, and that what was to be most complicated and difficult for them was only just beginning.

Translated by Avrahm Yarmolinsky

QUESTIONS

1. In what ways are Gurov and Anna Sergeyevna unfulfilled when they first meet?
2. What attracts Gurov to Anna Sergeyevna?

3. Does the story end on an optimistic note, a pessimistic one, or a combination of the two? Explain.
4. What is Gurov's general attitude toward women? Does it change or remain the same during the course of the story?
5. Compare the love affair described in the story with one of your own or with a friend's that you have personal knowledge of.
6. It is often said that Chekhov's work foreshadowed the emotional complexity of much twentieth-century writing. Do his characters have the conflicts we find in today's men and women? Explain.

Kate Chopin

A RESPECTABLE WOMAN

Mrs. Baroda was a little provoked to learn that her husband expected his friend, Gouvernail, up to spend a week or two on the plantation.

They had entertained a good deal during the winter; much of the time had also been passed in New Orleans in various forms of mild dissipation. She was looking forward to a period of unbroken rest, now, and undisturbed tête-a-tête with her husband, when he informed her that Gouvernail was coming up to stay a week or two.

This was a man she had heard much of but never seen. He had been her husband's college friend; was now a journalist, and in no sense a society man or "a man about town," which were, perhaps, some of the reasons she had never met him. But she had unconsciously formed an image of him in her mind. She pictured him tall, slim, cynical; with eye-glasses, and his hands in his pockets; and she did not like him. Gouvernail was slim enough, but he wasn't very tall nor very cynical; neither did he wear eye-glasses nor carry his hands in his pockets. And she rather liked him when he first presented himself.

But why she liked him she could not explain satisfactorily to herself when she partly attempted to do so. She could discover in him none of those brilliant and promising traits which Gaston, her husband, had often assured her that he possessed. On the contrary, he sat rather mute and receptive before her chatty eagerness to make him feel at home and in face of Gaston's frank and wordy hospitality. His manner was as courteous toward her as the most exacting woman could require; but he made no direct appeal to her approval or even esteem.

Once settled at the plantation he seemed to like to sit upon the wide portico in the shade of one of the big Corinthian pillars, smoking his cigar lazily and listening attentively to Gaston's experience as a sugar planter.

"This is what I call living," he would utter with deep satisfaction, as the air that swept across the sugar field caressed him with its warm and scented velvety touch. It pleased him also to get on familiar terms with the big dogs that came about him, rubbing themselves sociably against his legs. He did not care to fish, and displayed no eagerness to go out and kill grosbecs when Gaston proposed doing so.

Gouvernail's personality puzzled Mrs. Baroda, but she liked him. Indeed, he was a lovable, inoffensive fellow. After a few days, when she could understand him no better than at first, she gave over being puzzled and remained piqued. In this mood she left her husband and her guest, for the most part, alone together. Then finding that Gouvernail took no manner of exception to her action, she imposed her society upon him, accompanying him in his idle strolls to the mill and walks along the batture. She persistently sought to penetrate the reserve in which he had unconsciously enveloped himself.

"When is he going—your friend?" she one day asked her husband. "For my part, he tires me frightfully."

"Not for a week yet, dear. I can't understand; he gives you no trouble."

"No. I should like him better if he did; if he were more like others, and I had to plan somewhat for his comfort and enjoyment."

Gaston took his wife's pretty face between his hands and looked tenderly and laughingly into her troubled eyes. They were making a bit of toilet sociably together in Mrs. Baroda's dressing-room.

"You are full of surprises, ma belle," he said to her. "Even I can never count upon how you are going to act under given conditions." He kissed her and turned to fasten his cravat before the mirror.

"Here you are," he went on, "taking poor Gouvernail seriously and making a commotion over him, the last thing he would desire or expect."

"Commotion!" she hotly resented. "Nonsense! How can you say such a thing? Commotion, indeed! But, you know, you said he was clever."

"So he is. But the poor fellow is run down by overwork now. That's why I asked him here to take a rest."

"You used to say he was a man of ideas," she retorted, unconciliated. "I expected him to be interesting, at least. I'm going to the city in the morning to have my spring gowns fitted. Let me know when Mr. Gouvernail is gone; I shall be at my Aunt Octavie's."

That night she went and sat alone upon a bench that stood beneath a live oak tree at the edge of the gravel walk.

She had never known her thoughts or her intentions to be so confused. She could gather nothing from them but the feeling of a distinct necessity to quit her home in the morning.

Mrs. Baroda heard footsteps crunching the gravel; but could discern in the darkness only the approaching red point of a lighted cigar. She knew it was Gouvernail, for her husband did not smoke. She hoped to remain unnoticed, but her white gown revealed her to him. He threw away his cigar and seated himself upon the bench beside her; without a suspicion that she might object to his presence.

"Your husband told me to bring this to you, Mrs. Baroda," he said, handing her a filmy, white scarf with which she sometimes enveloped her head and shoulders. She accepted the scarf from him with a murmur of thanks, and let it lie in her lap.

He made some commonplace observation upon the baneful effect of the night air at that season. Then as his gaze reached out into the darkness, he murmured, half to himself:

"'Night of south winds—night of the large few stars!
Still nodding night——'"

She made no reply to this apostrophe to the night, which indeed, was not addressed to her.

Gouvernail was in no sense a diffident man, for he was not a self-conscious one. His periods of reserve were not constitutional, but the result of moods. Sitting there beside Mrs. Baroda, his silence melted for the time.

He talked freely and intimately in a low, hesitating drawl that was not unpleasant to hear. He talked of the old college days when he and Gaston had been a good deal to each other; of the days of keen and blind ambitions and large intentions. Now there was left with him, at least, a philosophic acquiescence to the existing order—only a desire to be permitted to exist, with now and then a little whiff of genuine life, such as he was breathing now.

Her mind only vaguely grasped what he was saying. Her physical being was for the moment predominant. She was not thinking of his words, only drinking in the tones of his voice. She wanted to reach out her hand in the darkness and touch him with the sensitive tips of her fingers upon the face or the lips. She wanted to draw close to him and whisper against his cheek—she did not care what—as she might have done if she had not been a respectable woman.

The stronger the impulse grew to bring herself near him, the further, in fact, did she draw away from him. As soon as she could do so without an appearance of too great rudeness, she rose and left him there alone.

Before she reached the house, Gouvernail had lighted a fresh cigar and ended his apostrophe to the night.

Mrs. Baroda was greatly tempted that night to tell her husband—who was also her friend—of this folly that had seized her. But she did not yield to the temptation. Beside being a respectable woman she was a very sensible one; and she knew there are some battles in life which a human being must fight alone.

When Gaston arose in the morning, his wife had already departed. She had taken an early morning train to the city. She did not return till Gouvernail was gone from under her roof.

There was some talk of having him back during the summer that followed. That is, Gaston greatly desired it; but this desire yielded to his wife's strenuous opposition.

However, before the year ended, she proposed, wholly from herself, to have Gouvernail visit them again. Her husband was surprised and delighted with the suggestion coming from her.

"I am glad, chère amie, to know that you have finally overcome your dislike for him; truly he did not deserve it."

"Oh," she told him, laughingly, after pressing a long, tender kiss upon his lips, "I have overcome everything! you will see. This time I shall be very nice to him."

QUESTIONS

1. Of Mrs. Baroda's feelings toward Gouvernail, the author states, "But why she liked him she could not explain satisfactorily to herself when she partly attempted to do so." At what point do Mrs. Baroda's feelings toward Gouvernail change? What causes this change?

2. The mood of the story is sedate, understated, and enigmatic. How does the physical description of the setting complement this mood?

3. How does the title of the story prove to be an ironic one?

4. Compare and contrast the attraction of Mrs. Ames to the plumber in "Astronomer's Wife" with that of Mrs. Baroda to Gouvernail.

5. Kate Chopin is often viewed as an early feminist writer. From what you know of feminism, explain what themes in the story support this characterization.

Isak Dinesen

THE BLUE JAR

There was once an immensely rich old Englishman who had been a courtier and a councillor to the Queen and who now, in his old age, cared for nothing but collecting ancient blue china. To that end he travelled to Persia, Japan, and China, and he was everywhere accompanied by his daughter, the Lady Helena. It happened, as they sailed in the Chinese Sea, that the ship caught fire on a still night, and everybody went into the lifeboats and left her. In the dark and the confusion the old peer was separated from his daughter. Lady Helena got up on deck late, and found the ship quite deserted. In the last moment a young English sailor carried her down into a lifeboat that had been forgotten. To the two fugitives it seemed as if fire was following them from all sides, for the phosphorescence played in the dark sea, and, as they looked up, a falling star ran across the sky, as if it was going to drop into the boat. They sailed for nine days, till they were picked up by a Dutch merchantman, and came home to England.

The old lord had believed his daughter to be dead. He now wept with joy, and at once took her off to a fashionable watering-place so that she might recover from the hardships she had gone through. And as he thought it must be unpleasant to her that a young sailor, who made his bread in the merchant service, should tell the world that he had sailed for nine days alone with a peer's daughter, he paid the boy a fine sum, and made him promise to go shipping in the other hemisphere and never come back. "For what," said the old nobleman, "would be the good of that?"

When Lady Helena recovered, and they gave her the news of the Court and of her family, and in the end also told her how the young sailor had been sent away never to come back, they found that her mind had suffered from her trials, and that she cared for nothing in all the world. She would not go back to her father's castle in its park, nor go to Court, nor travel to any gay town of the continent. The only thing which she now wanted to do was to go, like her father before her, to collect rare blue china. So she began to sail, from one country to the other, and her father went with her.

In her search she told the people, with whom she dealt, that she was looking for a particular blue color, and would pay any price for it. But although she bought many hundred blue jars and bowls, she would always after a time put them aside and say: "Alas, alas, it is not the right blue." Her father, when they had sailed for many years, suggested to her that perhaps the color which she sought did not exist. "O God, Papa," said she, "how can you speak so wickedly? Surely there must be some of it left from the time when all the world was blue."

Her two old aunts in England implored her to come back, still to make a great match. But she answered them: "Nay, I have got to sail. For you must know, dear aunts, that it is all nonsense when learned people tell you that the seas have got a bottom to them. On the contrary, the water, which is the noblest of the elements, does, of course, go all through the earth, so that our planet really floats in the ether, like a soapbubble. And there, on the other hemisphere, a ship sails, with which I have got to keep pace. We two are like the reflection of one another, in the deep sea, and the ship of which I speak is always exactly beneath my own ship, upon the opposite side of the globe. You have never seen a big fish swimming underneath a boat, following it like a dark-blue shade in the water. But in that way this ship goes, like the shadow of my ship, and I draw it to and fro wherever I go, as the moon draws the tides, all through the bulk of the earth. If I stopped sailing, what would these poor sailors who make their bread in the merchant service do? But I shall tell you a secret," she said. "In the end my ship will go down, to the center of the globe, and at the very same hour the other ship will sink as well—for people call it sinking, although I can assure you that there is no up and down in the sea—and there, in the midst of the world, we two shall meet."

Many years passed, the old lord died, and Lady Helena became old and deaf, but she still sailed. Then it happened, after the plunder of the summer palace of the Emperor of China, that a merchant brought her a very old blue jar. The moment she set eyes on it she gave a terrible shriek. "There it is!" she cried. "I have found it at last. This is the true blue. Oh, how light it makes one. Oh, it is as fresh as a breeze, as deep as a deep secret, as full as I say not what." With trembling hands she held the jar to her bosom, and sat for six hours sunk in contemplation of it. Then she said to her doctor and her lady-companion: "Now I can die. And when I am dead you will cut out my heart and lay it in the blue jar. For then everything will be as it was then. All shall be blue round me, and in the midst of the blue world my heart will be innocent and free, and will beat gently, like a wake that sings, like the drops that fall from an oar blade." A little later she asked them: "Is it not a sweet thing to think that, if only you have patience, all that has ever been, will come back to you?" Shortly afterwards the old lady died.

QUESTIONS

1. What stylistic conventions does the author use to signal that this story has similarities to a fairy tale?

2. Does the lack of description of the young sailor help or hinder our sympathizing with the loss felt by Lady Helena?
3. What social strictures exist in the story that doom the relationship between Lady Helena and the sailor?
4. How does the direct, spare diction of the story contribute to its emotional tenor?
5. Does this story seem hopelessly outdated given contemporary mores, or does it carry a relevant message about romantic relationships today? Explain.

Louise Erdrich

SNARES

It began after church with Margaret and her small granddaughter, Lulu, and was not to end until the long days of Lent and a hard-packed snow. There were factions on the reservation, a treaty settlement in the Agent's hands. There were Chippewa who signed their names in the year 1924, and there were Chippewa who saw the cash offered as a flimsy bait. I was one and Fleur Pillager, Lulu's mother, was another who would not lift her hand to sign. It was said that all the power to witch, harm, or cure lay in Fleur, the lone survivor of the old Pillager clan. But as much as people feared Fleur, they listened to Margaret Kashpaw. She was the ringleader of the holdouts, a fierce, one-minded widow with a vinegar tongue.

Margaret Kashpaw had knots of muscles in her arms. Her braids were thin, gray as iron, and usually tied strictly behind her back so they wouldn't swing. She was plump as a basket below and tough as roots on top. Her face was gnarled around a beautiful sharp nose. Two shell earrings caught the light and flashed whenever she turned her head. She had become increasingly religious in the years after her loss, and finally succeeded in dragging me to the Benediction Mass, where I was greeted by Father Damien, from whom I occasionally won small sums at dice.

"Grandfather Nanapush," he smiled, "at last."

"These benches are a hardship for an old man," I complained. "If you spread them with soft pine-needle cushions I'd have come before."

Father Damien stared thoughtfully at the rough pews, folded his hands inside the sleeves of his robe.

"You must think of their unyielding surfaces as helpful," he offered. "God sometimes enters the soul through the humblest parts of our anatomies, if they are sensitized to suffering."

"A god who enters through the rear door," I countered, "is no better than a thief."

Father Damien was used to me, and smiled as he walked to the altar. I adjusted my old bones, longing for some relief, trying not to rustle for fear of Margaret's jabbing elbow. The time was long. Lulu probed all my pockets with her fingers until she found a piece of hard candy. I felt no great presence in this cold place and decided, as my back end ached and my shoulders stiffened, that our original gods were better, the Chippewa characters who were not exactly perfect but at least did not require sitting on hard boards.

When Mass was over and the smell of incense was thick in all our clothes, Margaret, Lulu, and I went out into the starry cold, the snow and stubble fields, and began the long walk to our homes. It was dusk. On either side of us the heavy trees stood motionless and blue. Our footsteps squeaked against the dry snow, the only sound to hear. We spoke very little, and even Lulu ceased her singing when the moon rose to half, poised like a balanced cup. We knew the very moment someone else stepped upon the road.

We had turned a bend and the footfalls came unevenly, just out of sight. There were two men, one mixed-blood or white, from the drop of his hard boot soles, and the other one quiet, an Indian. Not long and I heard them talking close behind us. From the rough, quick tension of the Indian's language, I recognized Lazarre. And the mixed-blood must be Clarence Morrissey. The two had signed the treaty and spoke in its favor to anyone they could collar at the store. They even came to people's houses to beg and argue that this was our one chance, our good chance, that the government would withdraw the offer. But wherever Margaret was, she slapped down their words like mosquitoes and said the only thing that lasts life to life is land. Money burns like tinder, flows like water. And as for promises, the wind is steadier. It is no wonder that, because she spoke so well, Lazarre and Clarence Morrissey wished to silence her. I sensed their bad intent as they passed us, an unpleasant edge of excitement in their looks and greetings.

They went on, disappeared in the dark brush.

"Margaret," I said, "we are going to cut back." My house was close, but Margaret kept walking forward as if she hadn't heard.

I took her arm, caught the little girl close, and started to turn, but Margaret would have none of this and called me a coward. She grabbed the girl to her. Lulu, who did not mind getting tossed between us, laughed, tucked her hand into her grandma's pocket, and never missed a step. Two years ago she had tired of being carried, got up, walked. She had the balance of a little mink. She was slippery and clever, too, which was good because when the men jumped from the darkest area of brush and grappled with us half a mile on, Lulu slipped free and scrambled into the trees.

They were occupied with Margaret and me, at any rate. We were old enough to snap in two, our limbs dry as dead branches, but we fought as though our enemies were the Nadouissouix kidnappers of our childhood. Margaret uttered a war cry that had not been heard for fifty years, and bit Lazarre's hand to the bone, giving a wound which would later prove the death of him. As for Clarence, he had all he could do to wrestle me to the ground and knock me half unconscious. When he'd accomplished that, he tied me and tossed me into a wheelbarrow, which was hidden near the road for the purpose of lugging us to the Morrissey barn.

I came to my senses trussed to a manger, sitting on a bale. Margaret was roped to another bale across from me, staring straight forward in a rage, a line of froth caught between her lips. On either side of her, shaggy cows chewed and shifted their thumping hooves. I rose and staggered, the weight of the manger on my back. I planned on Margaret biting through my ropes with her strong teeth, but then the two men entered.

I'm a talker, a fast-mouth who can't keep his thoughts straight, but lets fly with words and marvels at what he hears from his own mouth. I'm a smart one. I always was a devil for convincing women. And I wasn't too bad a shot, in other ways, at convincing men. But I had never been tied up before.

"Booshoo," I said. "Children, let us loose, your game is too rough!"

They stood between us, puffed with their secrets.

"Empty old windbag," said Clarence.

"I have a bargain for you," I said, looking for an opening. "Let us go and we won't tell Pukwan." Edgar Pukwan was the tribal police. "Boys get drunk sometimes and don't know what they're doing."

Lazarre laughed once, hard and loud. "We're not drunk," he said. "Just wanting what's coming to us, some justice, money out of it."

"Kill us," said Margaret. "We won't sign."

"Wait," I said. "My cousin Pukwan will find you boys, and have no mercy. Let us go. I'll sign and get it over with, and I'll persuade the old widow."

I signaled Margaret to keep her mouth shut. She blew air into her cheeks. Clarence looked expectantly at Lazarre, as if the show were over, but Lazarre folded his arms and was convinced of nothing.

"You lie when it suits, skinny old dog," he said, wiping at his lips as if in hunger. "It's her we want, anyway. We'll shame her so she shuts her mouth."

"Easy enough," I said, smooth, "now that you've got her tied. She's plump and good looking. Eyes like a doe! But you forget that we're together, almost man and wife."

This wasn't true at all, and Margaret's face went rigid with tumbling fury and confusion. I kept talking.

"So of course if you do what you're thinking of doing you'll have to kill me afterward, and that will make my cousin Pukwan twice as angry, since I owe him a fat payment for a gun which he lent me and I never returned. All the same," I went on—their heads were spinning—"I'll forget you bad boys ever considered such a crime, something so terrible that Father Damien would nail you on boards just like in the example on the wall in church."

"Quit jabbering." Lazarre stopped me in a deadly voice.

It was throwing pebbles in a dry lake. My words left no ripple. I saw in his eyes that he intended us great harm. I saw his greed. It was like watching an ugly design of bruises come clear for a moment and reconstructing the evil blows that made them.

I played my last card.

"Whatever you do to Margaret you are doing to the Pillager woman!" I dropped my voice. "The witch, Fleur Pillager, is her own son's wife."

Clarence was too young to be frightened, but his mouth hung in interested puzzlement. My words had a different effect on Lazarre, as a sudden light shone, a consequence he hadn't considered.

I cried out, seeing this, "Don't you know she can think about you hard enough to stop your heart?" Lazarre was still deciding. He raised his fist and swung it casually and tapped my face. It was worse not to be hit full on.

"Come near!" crooned Margaret in the old language. "Let me teach you how to die."

But she was trapped like a fox. Her earrings glinted and spun as she hissed her death song over and over, which signaled something to Lazarre, for he shook himself angrily and drew a razor from his jacket. He stropped it with fast, vicious movements while Margaret sang shriller, so full of hate that the ropes should have burned, shriveled, fallen from her body. My struggle set the manger cracking against the barn walls and further confused the cows, who bumped each other and complained. At a sign from Lazarre, Clarence sighed, rose, and smashed me. The last I saw before I blacked out, through the tiny closing pinhole of light, was Lazarre approaching Margaret with the blade.

When I woke, minutes later, it was to worse shock. For Lazarre had sliced Margaret's long braids off and was now, carefully, shaving her scalp. He started almost tenderly at the wide part, and then pulled the edge down each side of her skull. He did a clean job. He shed not one drop of her blood.

And I could not even speak to curse them. For pressing my jaw down, thick above my tongue, her braids, never cut in this life till now, were tied to silence me. Powerless, I tasted their flat, animal perfume.

It wasn't much later, or else it was forever, that we walked out into the night again. Speechless, we made our way in fierce pain down the road. I was damaged in spirit, more so than Margaret. For now she tucked her shawl over her naked head and forgot her own bad treatment. She called out in dread each foot of the way, for Lulu. But the smart, bold girl had hidden till all was clear and then run to Margaret's house. We opened the door and found her sitting by the stove in a litter of scorched matches and kindling. She had not the skill to start a fire, but she was dry-eyed. Though very cold, she was alert and then captured with wonder when Margaret slipped off her shawl.

"Where is your hair?" she asked.

I took my hand from my pocket. "Here's what's left of it. I grabbed this when they cut me loose." I was shamed by how pitiful I had been, relieved when Margaret snatched the thin gray braids from me and coiled them round her fist.

"I knew you would save them, clever man!" There was satisfaction in her voice.

I set the fire blazing. It was strange how generous this woman was to me, never blaming me or mentioning my failure. Margaret stowed her braids inside a birchbark box and merely instructed me to lay it in her grave, when that time occurred. Then she came near the stove with a broken mirror from beside her washstand and looked at her own image.

"My," she pondered, "my." She put the mirror down. "I'll take a knife to them."

And I was thinking too. I was thinking I would have to kill them.

But how does an aching and half-starved grandfather attack a young, well-fed Morrissey and a tall, sly Lazarre? Later, I rolled up in blankets in the corner by Margaret's stove, and I put my mind to this question throughout that night until, exhausted, I slept. And I thought of it first thing next morning, too, and still nothing came. It was only after we had some hot *gaulette* and walked Lulu back to her mother that an idea began to grow.

Fleur let us in, hugged Lulu into her arms, and looked at Margaret, who took off her scarf and stood bald, face burning again with smoldered fire. She told Fleur all of what happened, sparing no detail. The two women's eyes held, but Fleur said nothing. She put Lulu down, smoothed the front of her calico shirt, flipped her heavy braids over her shoulders, tapped one finger on her perfect lips. And then, calm, she went to the washstand and scraped the edge of her hunting knife keen as glass. Margaret and Lulu and I watched as Fleur cut her braids off, shaved her own head, and folded the hair into a quilled skin pouch. Then she went out, hunting, and didn't bother to wait for night to cover her tracks.

I would have to go out hunting too.

I had no gun, but anyway that was a white man's revenge. I knew how to wound with barbs of words, but had never wielded a skinning knife against a human, much less two young men. Whomever I missed would kill me, and I did not want to die by their lowly hands.

In fact, I didn't think that after Margaret's interesting kindness I wanted to leave this life at all. Her head, smooth as an egg, was ridged delicately with bone, and gleamed as if it had been buffed with a flannel cloth. Maybe it was the strangeness that attracted me. She looked forbidding, but the absence of hair also set off her eyes, so black and full of lights. She reminded me of that queen from England, of a water snake or a shrewd young bird. The earrings, which seemed part of her, mirrored her moods like water, and when they were still rounds of green lights against her throat I seemed, again, to taste her smooth, smoky braids in my mouth.

I had better things to do than fight. So I decided to accomplish revenge as quickly as possible. I was a talker who used my brains as my weapon. When I hunted, I preferred to let my game catch itself.

Snares demand clever fingers and a scheming mind, and snares had never failed me. Snares are quiet, and best of all snares are slow. I wanted to give Lazarre and Morrissey time to consider why they had to strangle. I thought hard. One- or two-foot deadfalls are required beneath a snare so that a man can't put his hand up and loosen the knot. The snares I had in mind also required something stronger than a cord, which could be broken, and finer than a rope, which even Lazarre might see and avoid. I pondered this closely, yet even so I might never have found the solution had I not gone to Mass with Margaret and grown curious about the workings of Father Damien's pride and joy, the piano in the back of the church, the instrument whose keys he breathed on, polished, then played after services, and sometimes alone. I had noticed that his hands usually stayed near the middle of the keyboard, so I took the wires from either end.

In the meantime, I was not the only one concerned with punishing Lazarre and Clarence Morrissey. Fleur was seen in town. Her thick skirts brushed the snow into clouds behind her. Though it was cold she left her head bare so everyone could see the frigid sun glare off her skull. The light reflected in the eyes of Lazarre and Clarence, who were standing at the door of the pool hall. They dropped their cue sticks in the slush and ran back to Morrissey land. Fleur walked the four streets, once in each direction, then followed.

The two men told of her visit, how she passed through the Morrissey house touching here, touching there, sprinkling powders that ignited and stank on the hot stove. How

Clarence swayed on his feet, blinked hard, and chewed his fingers. How Fleur stepped up to him, drew her knife. He smiled foolishly and asked her for supper. She reached forward and trimmed off a hank of his hair. Then she stalked from the house, leaving a taste of cold wind, and then chased Lazarre to the barn.

She made a black silhouette against the light from the door. Lazarre pressed against the wood of the walls, watching, hypnotized by the sight of Fleur's head and the quiet blade. He did not defend himself when she approached, reached for him, gently and efficiently cut bits of his hair, held his hands, one at a time, and trimmed the nails. She waved the razor-edged knife before his eyes and swept a few eyelashes into a white square of flour sacking that she then carefully folded into her blouse.

For days after, Lazarre babbled and wept. Fleur was murdering him by use of bad medicine, he said. He showed his hand, the bite that Margaret had dealt him, and the dark streak from the wound, along his wrist and inching up his arm. He even used that bound hand to scratch his name from the treaty, but it did no good.

I figured that the two men were doomed at least three ways now. Margaret won the debate with her Catholic training and decided to damn her soul by taking up the ax, since no one else had destroyed her enemies. I begged her to wait for another week, all during which it snowed and thawed and snowed again. It took me that long to arrange the snare to my satisfaction, near Lazarre's shack, on a path both men took to town.

I set it out one morning before anyone stirred, and watched from an old pine twisted along the ground. I waited while the smoke rose in a silky feather from the tiny tin spout on Lazarre's roof. I had to sit half a day before Lazarre came outside, and even then it was just for wood, nowhere near the path. I had a hard time to keep my blood flowing, my stomach still. I ate a handful of dry berries Margaret had given me, and a bit of pounded meat. I doled it to myself and waited until finally Clarence showed. He walked the trail like a blind ghost and stepped straight into my noose.

It was perfect, or would have been if I had made the deadfall two inches wider, for in falling Clarence somehow managed to spread his legs and straddle the deep hole I'd cut. It had been invisible, covered with snow, and yet in one foot-pedaling instant, the certain knowledge of its construction sprang into Clarence's brain and told his legs to reach for the sides. I don't know how he did it, but there he was poised. I waited, did not show myself. The noose jerked enough to cut slightly into the fool's neck, a too-snug fit. He was spread-eagled and on tiptoe, his arms straight out. If he twitched a finger, lost the least control, even tried to yell, one foot would go, the noose constrict.

But Clarence did not move. I could see from behind my branches that he didn't even dare to change the expression on his face. His mouth stayed frozen in shock. Only his eyes shifted, darted fiercely and wildly, side to side, showing all the agitation he must not release, searching desperately for a means of escape. They focused only when I finally stepped toward him, quiet, from the pine.

We were in full view of Lazarre's house, face to face. I stood before the boy. Just a touch, a sudden kick, perhaps no more than a word, was all that it would take. But I looked into his eyes and saw the knowledge of his situation. Pity entered me. Even for Margaret's shame, I couldn't do the thing I might have done.

I turned away and left Morrissey still balanced on the ledge of snow.

• • •

What money I did have, I took to the trading store next day. I bought the best bonnet on the reservation. It was black as a coal scuttle, large, and shaped the same.

"It sets off my doe eyes," Margaret said and stared me down.

She wore it every day, and always to Mass. Not long before Lent and voices could be heard: "There goes Old Lady Coalbucket." Nonetheless, she was proud, and softening day by day, I could tell. By the time we got our foreheads crossed with ashes, she consented to be married.

"I hear you're thinking of exchanging the vows," said Father Damien as I shook his hand on our way out the door.

"I'm having relations with Margaret already," I told him, "that's the way we do things."

This had happened to him before, so he was not even stumped as to what remedy he should use.

"Make a confession, at any rate," he said, motioning us back into the church.

So I stepped into the little box and knelt. Father Damien slid aside the shadowy door. I told him what I had been doing with Margaret and he stopped me partway through.

"No more details. Pray to Our Lady."

"There is one more thing."

"Yes?"

"Clarence Morrissey, he wears a scarf to church around his neck each week. I snared him like a rabbit."

Father Damien let the silence fill him.

"And the last thing," I went on. "I stole the wire from your piano."

The silence spilled over into my stall, and I was held in its grip until the priest spoke.

"Discord is hateful to God. You have offended his ear." Almost as an afterthought, Damien added, "And his commandment. The violence among you must cease."

"You can have the wire back," I said. I had used only one long strand. I also agreed that I would never use my snares on humans, an easy promise. Lazarre was already caught.

Just two days later, while Margaret and I stood with Lulu and her mother inside the trading store, Lazarre entered, gesturing, his eyes rolled to the skull. He stretched forth his arm and pointed along its deepest black vein and dropped his jaw wide. Then he stepped backward into a row of traps that the trader had set to show us how they worked. Fleur's eye lit, her white scarf caught the sun as she turned. All the whispers were true. Fleur had scratched Lazarre's figure into a piece of birchbark, drawn his insides, and rubbed a bit of rouge up his arm until the red stain reached his heart. There was no sound as he fell, no cry, no word, and the traps of all types that clattered down around his body jumped and met for a long time, snapping air.

QUESTIONS

1. How would you summarize Grandfather Nanapush's personality? What aspects of his personality do you ascribe to his cultural heritage as a Native American?

2. This story is filled with figurative language. Identify at least five metaphors and similes. What qualities do they have in common? How do they reflect the ethnic culture and life-style of the characters?
3. What elements of the story appear fantastic or magical? How do they contribute to the mood of the story? How do they effect the story's outcome?
4. What is Grandfather Nanapush's reaction to Margaret's having her head shaven? What does this reveal about his personality? How does he respond to this event?
5. What are the figurative and literal "snares" that are described or implied in the story? How do they relate to the story's theme?

William Faulkner

A ROSE FOR EMILY

I

When Miss Emily Grierson died, our whole town went to her funeral: the men through a sort of respectful affection for a fallen monument, the women mostly out of curiosity to see the inside of her house, which no one save an old manservant—a combined gardener and cook—had seen in at least ten years.

It was a big, squarish frame house that had once been white, decorated with cupolas and spires and scrolled balconies in the heavily lightsome style of the seventies, set on what had once been our most select street. But garages and cotton gins had encroached and obliterated even the august names of that neighborhood; only Miss Emily's house was left, lifting its stubborn and coquettish decay above the cotton wagons and the gasoline pumps—an eyesore among eyesores. And now Miss Emily had gone to join the representatives of those august names where they lay in the cedar-bemused cemetery among the ranked and anonymous graves of Union and Confederate soldiers who fell at the battle of Jefferson.

Alive, Miss Emily had been a tradition, a duty, and a care; a sort of hereditary obligation upon the town, dating from that day in 1894 when Colonel Sartoris, the mayor—he who fathered the edict that no Negro woman should appear on the streets without an apron—remitted her taxes, the dispensation dating from the death of her father on into perpetuity. Not that Miss Emily would have accepted charity. Colonel Sartoris invented an involved tale to the effect that Miss Emily's father had loaned money to the town, which the town, as a matter of business, preferred this way of repaying. Only a man of Colonel Sartoris' generation and thought could have invented it, and only a woman could have believed it.

When the next generation, with its more modern ideas, became mayors and aldermen, this arrangement created some little dissatisfaction. On the first of the year they mailed her a tax notice. February came, and there was no reply. They wrote her a

formal letter, asking her to call at the sheriff's office at her convenience. A week later
the mayor wrote her himself, offering to call or to send his car for her, and received in
reply a note on paper of an archaic shape, in a thin, flowing calligraphy in faded ink,
to the effect that she no longer went out at all. The tax notice was also enclosed, without
comment.

They called a special meeting of the Board of Aldermen. A deputation waited upon
her, knocked at the door through which no visitor had passed since she ceased giving
china-painting lessons eight or ten years earlier. They were admitted by the old Negro
into a dim hall from which a stairway mounted into still more shadow. It smelled of dust
and disuse—a close, dank smell. The Negro led them into the parlor. It was furnished
in heavy, leather-covered furniture. When the Negro opened the blinds of one window,
they could see that the leather was cracked; and when they sat down, a faint dust rose
sluggishly about their thighs, spinning with slow motes in the single sunray. On a
tarnished gilt easel before the fireplace stood a crayon portrait of Miss Emily's father.

They rose when she entered—a small, fat woman in black, with a thin gold chain
descending to her waist and vanishing into her belt, leaning on an ebony cane with a
tarnished gold head. Her skeleton was small and spare; perhaps that was why what
would have been merely plumpness in another was obesity in her. She looked bloated,
like a body long submerged in motionless water, and of that pallid hue. Her eyes, lost
in the fatty ridges of her face, looked like two small pieces of coal pressed into a lump
of dough as they moved from one face to another while the visitors stated their errand.

She did not ask them to sit. She just stood in the door and listened quietly until the
spokesman came to a stumbling halt. Then they could hear the invisible watch ticking
at the end of the gold chain.

Her voice was dry and cold. "I have no taxes in Jefferson. Colonel Sartoris explained
it to me. Perhaps one of you can gain access to the city records and satisfy yourselves."

"But we have. We are the city authorities, Miss Emily. Didn't you get a notice from
the sheriff, signed by him?"

"I received a paper, yes," Miss Emily said. "Perhaps he considers himself the sheriff
. . . I have no taxes in Jefferson."

"But there is nothing on the books to show that, you see. We must go by the—"

"See Colonel Sartoris. I have no taxes in Jefferson."

"But, Miss Emily—"

"See Colonel Sartoris." (Colonel Sartoris had been dead almost ten years.) "I have
no taxes in Jefferson. Tobe!" The Negro appeared. "Show these gentlemen out."

II

So she vanquished them, horse and foot, just as she had vanquished their fathers thirty
years before about the smell. That was two years after her father's death and a short
time after her sweetheart—the one we believed would marry her—had deserted her.
After her father's death she went out very little; after her sweetheart went away, people
hardly saw her at all. A few of the ladies had the temerity to call, but were not received,
and the only sign of life about the place was the Negro man—a young man then—
going in and out with a market basket.

"Just as if a man—any man—could keep a kitchen properly," the ladies said; so they were not surprised when the smell developed. It was another link between the gross, teeming world and the high and mighty Griersons.

A neighbor, a woman, complained to the mayor, Judge Stevens, eighty years old. "But what will you have me do about it, madam?" he said.

"Why, send her word to stop it," the woman said. "Isn't there a law?"

"I'm sure that won't be necessary," Judge Stevens said. "It's probably just a snake or a rat that nigger of hers killed in the yard. I'll speak to him about it."

The next day he received two more complaints, one from a man who came in diffident deprecation. "We really must do something about it, Judge. I'd be the last one in the world to bother Miss Emily, but we've got to do something." That night the Board of Aldermen met—three graybeards and one younger man, a member of the rising generation.

"It's simple enough," he said. "Send her word to have her place cleaned up. Give her a certain time to do it in, and if she don't . . . ."

"Dammit, sir," Judge Stevens said, "will you accuse a lady to her face of smelling bad?"

So the next night, after midnight, four men crossed Miss Emily's lawn and slunk about the house like burglars, sniffing along the base of the brickwork and at the cellar openings while one of them performed a regular sowing motion with his hand out of a sack slung from his shoulder. They broke open the cellar door and sprinkled lime there, and in all the outbuildings. As they recrossed the lawn, a window that had been dark was lighted and Miss Emily sat in it, the light behind her, and her upright torso motionless as that of an idol. They crept quietly across the lawn and into the shadow of the locusts that lined the street. After a week or two the smell went away.

That was when people had begun to feel really sorry for her. People in our town, remembering how old lady Wyatt, her great-aunt, had gone completely crazy at last, believed that the Griersons held themselves a little too high for what they really were. None of the young men were quite good enough for Miss Emily and such. We had long thought of them as a tableau, Miss Emily a slender figure in white in the background, her father a spraddled silhouette in the foreground, his back to her and clutching a horsewhip, the two of them framed by the back-flung front door. So when she got to be thirty and was still single, we were not pleased exactly, but vindicated; even with insanity in the family she wouldn't have turned down all of her chances if they had really materialized.

When her father died, it got about that the house was all that was left to her; and in a way, people were glad. At last they could pity Miss Emily. Being left alone, and a pauper, she had become humanized. Now she too would know the old thrill and the old despair of a penny more or less.

The day after his death all the ladies prepared to call at the house and offer condolence and aid, as is our custom. Miss Emily met them at the door, dressed as usual and with no trace of grief on her face. She told them that her father was not dead. She did that for three days, with the ministers calling on her, and the doctors, trying to persuade her to let them dispose of the body. Just as they were about to resort to law and force, she broke down, and they buried her father quickly.

We did not say she was crazy then. We believed she had to do that. We remembered all the young men her father had driven away, and we knew that with nothing left, she would have to cling to that which had robbed her, as people will.

III

She was sick for a long time. When we saw her again, her hair was cut short, making her look like a girl, with a vague resemblance to those angels in colored church windows—sort of tragic and serene.

The town had just let the contracts for paving the sidewalks, and in the summer after her father's death they began the work. The construction company came with niggers and mules and machinery, and a foreman named Homer Barron, a Yankee—a big, dark, ready man, with a big voice and eyes lighter than his face. The little boys would follow in groups to hear him cuss the niggers, and the niggers singing in time to the rise and fall of picks. Pretty soon he knew everybody in town. Whenever you heard a lot of laughing anywhere about the square, Homer Barron would be in the center of the group. Presently we began to see him and Miss Emily on Sunday afternoons driving in the yellow-wheeled buggy and the matched team of bays from the livery stable.

At first we were glad that Miss Emily would have an interest, because the ladies all said. "Of course a Grierson would not think seriously of a Northerner, a day laborer." But there were still others, older people, who said that even grief could not cause a real lady to forget *noblesse oblige*—without calling it *noblesse oblige*. They just said, "Poor Emily. Her kinsfolk should come to her." She had some kin in Alabama; but years ago her father had fallen out with them over the estate of old lady Wyatt, the crazy woman, and there was no communication between the two families. They had not even been represented at the funeral.

And as soon as the old people said, "Poor Emily," the whispering began. "Do you suppose it's really so?" they said to one another. "Of course it is. What else could . . ." This behind their hands; rustling of craned silk and satin behind jalousies closed upon the sun of Sunday afternoon as the thin, swift clop-clop-clop of the matched team passed: "Poor Emily."

She carried her head high enough—even when we believed that she was fallen. It was as if she demanded more than ever the recognition of her dignity as the last Grierson; as if it had wanted that touch of earthiness to reaffirm her imperviousness. Like when she bought the rat poison, the arsenic. That was over a year after they had begun to say "Poor Emily," and while the two female cousins were visiting her.

"I want some poison," she said to the druggist. She was over thirty then, still a slight woman, though thinner than usual, with cold, haughty black eyes in a face the flesh of which was strained across the temples and about the eyesockets as you imagine a lighthouse-keeper's face ought to look. "I want some poison," she said.

"Yes, Miss Emily. What kind? For rats and such? I'd recom—"

"I want the best you have. I don't care what kind."

The druggist named several. "They'll kill anything up to an elephant. But what you want is—"

"Arsenic," Miss Emily said. "Is that a good one?"

"Is . . . arsenic? Yes, ma'am. But what you want—"

"I want arsenic."

The druggist looked down at her. She looked back at him, erect, her face like a strained flag. "Why, of course," the druggist said. "If that's what you want. But the law requires you to tell what you are going to use it for."

Miss Emily just stared at him, her head tilted back in order to look him eye for eye, until he looked away and went and got the arsenic and wrapped it up. The Negro delivery boy brought her the package; the druggist didn't come back. When she opened the package at home there was written on the box, under the skull and bones: "For rats."

IV

So the next day we all said, "She will kill herself"; and we said it would be the best thing. When she had first begun to be seen with Homer Barron, we had said, "She will marry him." Then we said, "She will persuade him yet," because Homer himself had remarked—he liked men, and it was known that he drank with the younger men in the Elks' Club—that he was not a marrying man. Later we said, "Poor Emily" behind the jalousies as they passed on Sunday afternoon in the glittering buggy, Miss Emily with her head high and Homer Barron with his hat cocked and a cigar in his teeth, reins and whip in a yellow glove.

Then some of the ladies began to say that it was a disgrace to the town and a bad example to the young people. The men did not want to interfere, but at last the ladies forced the Baptist minister—Miss Emily's people were Episcopal—to call upon her. He would never divulge what happened during that interview, but he refused to go back again. The next Sunday they again drove about the streets, and the following day the minister's wife wrote to Miss Emily's relations in Alabama.

So she had blood-kin under her roof again and we sat back to watch developments. At first nothing happened. Then we were sure that they were to be married. We learned that Miss Emily had been to the jeweler's and ordered a man's toilet set in silver, with the letters H. B. on each piece. Two days later we learned that she had bought a complete outfit of men's clothing, including a nightshirt, and we said, "They are married." We were really glad. We were glad because the two female cousins were even more Grierson than Miss Emily had ever been.

So we were not surprised when Homer Barron—the streets had been finished some time since—was gone. We were a little disappointed that there was not a public blowing-off, but we believed that he had gone on to prepare for Miss Emily's coming, or to give her a chance to get rid of the cousins. (By that time it was a cabal, and we were all Miss Emily's allies to help circumvent the cousins.) Sure enough, after another week they departed. And, as we had expected all along, within three days Homer Barron was back in town. A neighbor saw the Negro man admit him at the kitchen door at dusk one evening.

And that was the last we saw of Homer Barron. And of Miss Emily for some time. The Negro man went in and out with the market basket, but the front door remained closed. Now and then we would see her at a window for a moment, as the men did that night when they sprinkled the lime, but for almost six months she did not appear on the streets. Then we knew that this was to be expected too; as if that quality of her father which had thwarted her woman's life so many times had been too virulent and too furious to die.

When we next saw Miss Emily, she had grown fat and her hair was turning gray. During the next few years it grew grayer and grayer until it attained an even pepper-and-salt iron-gray, when it ceased turning. Up to the day of her death at seventy-four it was still that vigorous iron-gray, like the hair of an active man.

From that time on her front door remained closed, save for a period of six or seven years, when she was about forty, during which she gave lessons in china-painting. She fitted up a studio in one of the downstairs rooms, where the daughters and granddaughters of Colonel Sartoris' contemporaries were sent to her with the same regularity and in the same spirit that they were sent to church on Sundays with a twenty-five-cent piece for the collection plate. Meanwhile her taxes had been remitted.

Then the newer generation became the backbone and the spirit of the town, and the painting pupils grew up and fell away and did not send their children to her with boxes of color and tedious brushes and pictures cut from the ladies' magazines. The front door closed upon the last one and remained closed for good. When the town got free postal delivery, Miss Emily alone refused to let them fasten the metal numbers above her door and attach a mailbox to it. She would not listen to them.

Daily, monthly, yearly we watched the Negro grow grayer and more stooped, going in and out with the market basket. Each December we sent her a tax notice, which would be returned by the post office a week later, unclaimed. Now and then we would see her in one of the downstairs windows—she had evidently shut up the top floor of the house—like the carven torso of an idol in a niche, looking or not looking at us, we could never tell which. Thus she passed from generation to generation—dear, inescapable, impervious, tranquil, and perverse.

And so she died. Fell ill in the house filled with dust and shadows, with only a doddering Negro man to wait on her. We did not even know she was sick; we had long since given up trying to get any information from the Negro. He talked to no one, probably not even to her, for his voice had grown harsh and rusty, as if from disuse.

She died in one of the downstairs rooms, in a heavy walnut bed with a curtain, her gray head propped on a pillow yellow and moldy with age and lack of sunlight.

V

The Negro met the first of the ladies at the front door and let them in, with their hushed, sibilant voices and their quick, curious glances, and then he disappeared. He walked right through the house and out the back and was not seen again.

The two female cousins came at once. They held the funeral on the second day, with the town coming to look at Miss Emily beneath a mass of bought flowers, with the crayon face of her father musing profoundly above the bier and the ladies sibilant and macabre; and the very old men—some in their brushed Confederate uniforms—on the porch and the lawn, talking of Miss Emily as if she had been a contemporary of theirs, believing that they had danced with her and courted her perhaps, confusing time with its mathematical progression, as the old do, to whom all the past is not a diminishing road but, instead, a huge meadow which no winter ever quite touches, divided from them now by the narrow bottle-neck of the most recent decade of years.

Already we knew that there was one room in that region above stairs which no one had seen in forty years, and which would have to be forced. They waited until Miss Emily was decently in the ground before they opened it.

The violence of breaking down the door seemed to fill this room with pervading dust. A thin, acrid pall as of the tomb seemed to lie everywhere upon this room decked and furnished as for a bridal: upon the valance curtains of faded rose color, upon the rose-shaded lights, upon the dressing table, upon the delicate array of crystal and the man's toilet things backed with tarnished silver, silver so tarnished that the monogram was obscured. Among them lay a collar and tie, as if they had just been removed, which, lifted, left upon the surface a pale crescent in the dust. Upon a chair hung the suit, carefully folded; beneath it the two mute shoes and the discarded socks.

The man himself lay in the bed.

For a long while we just stood there, looking down at the profound and fleshless grin. The body had apparently once lain in the attitude of an embrace, but now the long sleep that outlasts love, that conquers even the grimace of love, had cuckolded him. What was left of him, rotted beneath what was left of the nightshirt, had become inextricable from the bed in which he lay; and upon him and upon the pillow beside him lay that even coating of the patient and biding dust.

Then we noticed that in the second pillow was the indentation of a head. One of us lifted something from it, and leaning forward, that faint and invisible dust dry and acrid in the nostrils, we saw a long strand of iron-gray hair.

QUESTIONS

1. In the first line of the story, Emily is referred to as a "fallen monument." In what sense is she a monument? What, if anything, in Faulkner's description suggests this image?
2. Miss Emily's father has a prominent place in her home as well as in the story. What is his significance both when he is alive and after he has died?
3. Who is found dead at the end of the story? Why was he murdered? What suggestions of or references to death occur before the end of the story?
4. How do the people in the town look upon Emily? What is the cause of their attitude toward her?

Yussef Idriss

A HOUSE OF FLESH

The ring beside the lamp . . . silence hangs heavy, ears grow blind. Fingers move
stealthily, in silence grasp the ring and put out the light. Darkness reigns and
in darkness eyes grow blind. The woman, her three daughters, and their house,
a mere room.

The beginning is silence. The widow is tall, fair-skinned, willowy, about thirty-five. Her daughters are also tall and full-bodied. They continue to wear their long black mourning dresses. The youngest is sixteen, the eldest in her twenties, all three unattractive, having inherited the father's dark, badly proportioned body, corpulent and flabby; retaining their mother's build. The room, in spite of its size, holds them during the daytime. Despite its extreme poverty, the room is neatly arranged in an intimate, cozy atmosphere which reflects a feminine touch. When night falls, their bodies are scattered all over the room. Huge piles of warm throbbing flesh, sprawled on the single bed or on the couch: breathing, heaving, deeply insomniac.

Silence has hovered over the home since the man's death two years ago after a long illness. The mourning period was over, but the habits of those in mourning remained, most predominantly the habit of silence. It was in fact a silence of waiting, for the girls were growing older and the period of waiting was weighing upon them. No suitors were knocking on their doors. What man would dare to knock on the door of poor unattractive girls, particularly if they happened to be fatherless? But hope still lived of course (wine can remain in the barrels until the right buyer comes along), and each girl believed her luck would change. (No matter how poor one may be, there will always be someone else yet poorer, and if ugliness prevails there will always be someone even uglier . . . and dreams are fulfilled if one has enough patience. . . .)

That silence was occasionally interrupted by the sound of a voice reciting the Koran, a voice rising monotonously, emotionless. A recitation by a *muqri*.[1] The *muqri* is blind, but the prayers are for the soul of the deceased, always delivered at the same time. Every Friday afternoon, he comes poking his stick at their door. He abandons himself to the extended hand that leads him inside. There he sits cross-legged on the mat and recites. When it is over, he gropes for his sandals and pronounces a greeting that no one bothers to reciprocate, and then leaves. Out of habit he comes, out of habit he recites, and out of habit he leaves. No one notices him any more.

Forever this silence . . . even when the Friday afternoon recitation disturbs it. It is as if silence is broken only with silence. Waiting is forever, like hope, little hope but constant hope, for there is hope for every insignificant being, there is somewhere one who is even more insignificant. And they do not aspire to much, no, they do not aspire.

Silence persisted until something happened, until one Friday when the *muqri* did not show up. Every agreement comes to an end, no matter how long it has lasted, and it seemed this agreement had come to its end. Only then did the widow and her daughters

---

[1] *muqri*—reader of Koranic verses.

realize that not only was he the sole male voice that broke their silence once a week, but also that he was the only man who ever knocked at their door. Other things began to dawn upon them. True, he was as poor as they were, but his outfits were always clean, his sandals always shone, his headdress was wrapped meticulously (putting to shame any man with eyes), and above all, his voice was strong, deep and melodious. The proposition hovered in the air: why not renew the agreement, and why not summon him immediately? Could he be busy elsewhere? They could wait, for waiting was an old game they were very good at.

Evening was drawing to its end, and he recited as if for the first time. Then the proposition came up: why shouldn't one of them marry a man whose voice would fill the house?

He was a bachelor with a sprouting moustache, a young man. Words generate words, and he too was looking for the right woman. The girls confer about the matter and the mother scans their faces trying to figure who the lucky one would be. But their faces evade her searching looks and seem to say: Is this how we are to be rewarded for our long wait? Shall we break our fast with a blind man? For they still dreamt of suitors, and suitors are usually young men with eyes. Poor things, they have yet to know the world of men. Impossible for them to perceive at this stage in their lives that a man is not to be judged by sight alone.

"Mother, you marry him . . . marry him."

"Me? What shame, what will people say!"

"Let them say what they will, no matter what. It will be better than living in a house without a man, the resounding voice of a man."

"Do you want me to marry before you? Never . . ."

"Wouldn't it be better if you marry before us, so that our house becomes a treading ground for men? Then we can marry after you."

"Marry him, mother. O marry him . . ."

And she married him . . . and one more breath was added to the air and their income grew just a little bit more, and a much greater problem arose. True, they survived their first night, but they didn't dare come close to each other, even inadvertently. The girls were sleeping, or pretending to do so, but the mother could feel pairs of searching beams inspecting the space that lay between them, searching lights of human eyes, prospecting antennas. The girls are old enough to understand, and the room is suddenly transformed into sentient throbbing presences, vibrating in the light of day.

One by one, each left the house when morning set in, only to return by sunset, hesitant, embarrassed. Dragging their feet, they came back to a house filled with laughter, occasionally interrupted by faint noises of a woman. It must be the mother laughing, and the dignified *muqri* they had known was now laughing too. Their mother greeted them, bareheaded, hair wet and with a comb in hand, still laughing. They looked at her face and realized that it had been for all those years like an unlit lamp in whose corners spiders and cobwebs had taken refuge. Now suddenly that face had burst into light, electrified, glistening tearful eyes, with laughter lodged there instead. The silence dissipated completely. Suppertime bustled with loud voices, jokes, highlighted by the *muqri's* imitation of Umm Kulthum and Abd al-Wahab in his gushing, whining, beautiful voice.

Well done, mother. Soon this gaiety and laughter will draw more men to the house, for the presence of men attracts other men.

Be confident, girls. Soon men will be coming and suitors will make their calls. But in fact what was preoccupying her was that young man, not the suitors. True, he was blind, but how often are we blinded ourselves from seeing others, just because they happen to be blind? Yes, she was seeing this healthy young man. His overflowing vitality had made up for those years of sickness, impotence, and early old age.

The silence was gone, never to return, and the beat of life was there to stay. The man is her legal husband; she married him according to the law of God and his Prophet, and according to his Sunna.[2] No, nothing will make her feel ashamed, for all that she does is legitimate, even when she makes no effort to hide or keep the secret, or when night creeps up and they are all huddled together, and the power of the body and soul takes over, even with the girls there aware and awake in their observation posts, fighting to control sighs and groans.

Her mornings were spent washing clothes in rich people's homes, and his days were whiled away by reciting the Quran in homes of the poor.

At the beginning, he didn't return home for a break during the day, but as his nights grew longer, he started coming home to rest his exhausted body, to regain strength for the night to come.

And once, after they had had their fill of the night, and the night had had its fill of them, he suddenly asked her what had been the matter with her during the lunch hour. Why was it that she was now so voluble and eager to talk, but then had adopted total silence? Why was she now wearing his cherished ring, the ring that was all he had given her in form of dowry, gift, wedding band? Why hadn't she been wearing it during the lunch hour?

She could have torn herself away distraught, screaming. She could have lost her senses. He could have gotten himself killed. For there could be but one meaning to what he was saying, a horrible, atrocious meaning. A choking sob kept everything back. She held her breath and kept her peace. With her ears, which she transformed into noses, eyes, and other organs of sense, she strained her every fibre to find out who the culprit was. For some reason she was positive it was the middle one, because in her eyes had grown a certain daring look that only a bullet could check. But she listened. The breathing of the three grew louder, deeper and feverish, flaming hot, hesitant and intermittent, growling in youthful dreams which would be sinful to interrupt!

Heavings turn into burning flames, into lava vomited by thirsty lands. The knots in her throat deepen and choke her. There are hungry breaths. With all her straining she cannot differentiate between one vibrant, hot pile of flesh and another. All are hungry. All groan and scream. And the groans are not just groans. They are pleas, supplications perhaps, perhaps something more.

She has totally immersed herself in her second legitimate right, and forgotten all about her first legitimate duty, her girls. Patience has become myrrh. Even the mirage of suitors is no more. Suddenly, as if bitten, as though awakened to a secret call, the girls

[2] Sunna—traditional teachings of Islam, according to the Prophet.

are hungry. The food is forbidden, but hunger is yet more sinful. There exists nothing more sinful than this hunger. How well she has known it. And how well it has known her, freed her spirit, searched her bones. She has known it. Now that she has had her fill, it is impossible for her to forget.

Hungry ones! She who took the bread from her own mouth to feed them, she whose only preoccupation was to feed them even if she were to go hungry, she the mother—has she forgotten?

And no matter how insistent his demands, her pain was changed into silence. The mother became silent, and from that moment onwards, silence never left her. At breakfast, just as she had thought, the middle girl was silent and was to remain silent from then onwards. At suppertime, the young man was gay and jovial, blind and happy, singing and laughing, with only the youngest and eldest tuning in.

Patience is tried and its bitterness becomes a sickness and no one comes knocking on their door. One day the eldest looks at the mother's ring and expresses her admiration, and the mother's heart sinks; and its beating grows louder when the daughter begs to wear the ring just for the day. In silence the mother takes it off her finger, and in silence the girl slips it onto her own.

And that evening the eldest girl keeps silent, refusing to utter a word.

And the blind man is singing and laughing boisterously with only the youngest tuning in.

With unrewarded patience, and luck that has never turned with her worrying, the youngest grows older, and asks for her turn in the ring game, and in silence her turn comes.

The ring lies beside the lamp and silence sets in and ears become blind, and in silence the finger whose turn comes gropes stealthily for the ring and turns off the light.

Darkness prevails, and in darkness eyes grow blind. Only the blind young man remains happy. Yet behind his loudness and happiness he is tormented by this silence, he is tortured by uncertainty. At the beginning he would say to himself, it must be a woman's nature to be ever-changing. One time she is fresh as the morning dew, at another time she is worn out, exhausted like swampy waters. At times satiny like rose leaves, at others prickly like cacti. True, the ring is always there, but each time the finger it encircles seems to be different. He was almost positive that they knew for sure. So why doesn't silence speak, why doesn't it speak? The mere thought made him choke on his bread. And from that moment on, he never uttered a word. He lived in fear of the violation of that collapse. This time the silence was different, respected by all. A conscious silence, not caused by poverty, nor patience, nor despair, but the most profound kind of silence, the most binding of all, a silence implemented without formal agreement. The widow and her three daughters, and the house which was a room. This was a new kind of silence. The blind reciter brought along this silence, with silence convincing himself that his companion in bed was always his legitimate wife, bearer of his ring, ever changing, unpredictable. Young and old, silken soft or callous and scaly, sometimes fat, at other times thin, whatever, this really was her business. Actually, all this was the business of those with sight and their sole responsibility.

For *they* alone possess the grace of certainty; *they* are capable of discernment; but the most *he* can know is doubt, doubt that can be removed only through the blessing of sight. So long as he is deprived of it, he will be denied certainty, for he is the one who is blind and there is no shame for the blind.

Or is there shame for the blind?

Translated by Mona Mikhail

QUESTIONS

1. What transformations does the household undergo after the mother remarries? How do the daughters respond after this marriage?
2. How is blindness central to the plot and theme of the story? What are the different ways the author uses blindness in conveying the physical and emotional life of the characters?
3. What is the significance of the continual reference to silence? How does the import of silence change during the course of the story?
4. Explain the significance of the title.

Alice Munro

THE FOUND BOAT

At the end of Bell Street, McKay Street, Mayo Street, there was the Flood. It was the Wawanash River, which every spring overflowed its banks. Some springs, say one in every five, it covered the roads on that side of town and washed over the fields, creating a shallow choppy lake. Light reflected off the water made everything bright and cold, as it is in a lakeside town, and woke or revived in people certain vague hopes of disaster. Mostly during the late afternoon and early evening, there were people straggling out to look at it, and discuss whether it was still rising, and whether this time it might invade the town. In general, those under fifteen and over sixty-five were most certain that it would.

Eva and Carol rode out on their bicycles. They left the road—it was the end of Mayo Street, past any houses—and rode right into a field, over a wire fence entirely flattened by the weight of the winter's snow. They coasted a little way before the long grass stopped them, then left their bicycles lying down and went to the water.

"We have to find a log and ride on it," Eva said.

"Jesus, we'll freeze our legs off."

"Jesus, we'll freeze our legs off!" said one of the boys who were there too at the water's edge. He spoke in a sour whine, the way boys imitated girls although it was nothing like the way girls talked. These boys—there were three of them—were all in the same class as Eva and Carol at school and were known to them by name (their names being Frank, Bud and Clayton), but Eva and Carol, who had seen and recognized them from the road, had not spoken to them or looked at them or, even yet, given any sign of knowing they were there. The boys seemed to be trying to make a raft, from lumber they had salvaged from the water.

Eva and Carol took off their shoes and socks and waded in. The water was so cold it sent pain up their legs, like blue electric sparks shooting through their veins, but they went on, pulling their skirts high, tight behind and bunched so they could hold them in front.

"Look at the fat-assed ducks in wading."

"Fat-assed fucks."

Eva and Carol, of course, gave no sign of hearing this. They laid hold of a log and climbed on, taking a couple of boards floating in the water for paddles. There were always things floating around in the Flood—branches, fence-rails, logs, road signs, old lumber; sometimes boilers, washtubs, pots and pans, or even a car seat or stuffed chair, as if somewhere the Flood had got into a dump.

They paddled away from shore, heading out into the cold lake. The water was perfectly clear, they could see the brown grass swimming along the bottom. Suppose it was the sea, thought Eva. She thought of drowned cities and countries. Atlantis. Suppose they were riding in a Viking boat—Viking boats on the Atlantic were more frail and narrow than this log on the Flood—and they had miles of clear sea beneath them, then a spired city, intact as a jewel irretrievable on the ocean floor.

"This is a Viking boat," she said. "I am the carving on the front." She stuck her chest out and stretched her neck, trying to make a curve, and she made a face, putting out her tongue. Then she turned and for the first time took notice of the boys.

"Hey, you sucks!" she yelled at them. "You'd be scared to come out here, this water is ten feet deep!"

"Liar," they answered without interest, and she was.

They steered the log around a row of trees, avoiding floating barbed wire, and got into a little bay created by a natural hollow of the land. Where the bay was now, there would be a pond full of frogs later in the spring, and by the middle of summer there would be no water visible at all, just a low tangle of reeds and bushes, green, to show that mud was still wet around their roots. Larger bushes, willows, grew around the steep bank of this pond and were still partly out of the water. Eva and Carol let the log ride in. They saw a place where something was caught.

It was a boat, or part of one. An old rowboat with most of one side ripped out, the board that had been the seat just dangling. It was pushed up among the branches, lying on what would have been its side, if it had a side, the prow caught high.

Their idea came to them without consultation, at the same time:

"You guys! Hey, you guys!"

"We found you a boat!"

"Stop building your stupid raft and come and look at the boat!"

What surprised them in the first place was that the boys really did come, scrambling overland, half running, half sliding down the bank, wanting to see.

"Hey, where?"

"Where is it, I don't see no boat."

What surprised them in the second place was that when the boys did actually see what boat was meant, this old flood-smashed wreck held up in the branches, they did not understand that they had been fooled, that a joke had been played on them. They did not show a moment's disappointment, but seemed as pleased at the discovery as if the boat had been whole and new. They were already barefoot, because they had been wading in the water to get lumber, and they waded in here without a stop, surrounding the boat and appraising it and paying no attention even of an insulting kind to Eva and Carol who bobbed up and down on their log. Eva and Carol had to call to them.

"How do you think you're going to get it off?"

"It won't float anyway."

"What makes you think it will float?"

"It'll sink. Glub-blub-blub, you'll all be drownded."

The boys did not answer, because they were too busy walking around the boat, pulling at it in a testing way to see how it could be got off with the least possible damage. Frank, who was the most literate, talkative and inept of the three, began referring to the boat as *she*, an affectation which Eva and Carol acknowledged with fish-mouths of contempt.

"She's caught two places. You got to be careful not to tear a hole in her bottom. She's heavier than you'd think."

It was Clayton who climbed up and freed the boat, and Bud, a tall fat boy, who got the weight of it on his back to turn it into the water so that they could half float, half carry it to shore. All this took some time. Eva and Carol abandoned their log and waded out of the water. They walked overland to get their shoes and socks and bicycles. They did not need to come back this way but they came. They stood at the top of the hill, leaning on their bicycles. They did not go on home, but they did not sit down and frankly watch, either. They stood more or less facing each other, but glancing down at the water and at the boys struggling with the boat, as if they had just halted for a moment out of curiosity, and staying longer than they intended, to see what came of this unpromising project.

About nine o'clock, or when it was nearly dark—dark to people inside the houses, but not quite dark outside—they all returned to town, going along Mayo Street in a sort of procession. Frank and Bud and Clayton came carrying the boat, upside-down, and Eva and Carol walked behind, wheeling their bicycles. The boys' heads were almost hidden in the darkness of the overturned boat, with its smell of soaked wood, cold swampy water. The girls could look ahead and see the street lights in their tin reflectors, a necklace of lights climbing Mayo Street, reaching all the way up to the standpipe. They turned onto Burns Street heading for Clayton's house, the nearest house belonging to any of them. This was not the way home for Eva or for Carol either, but they followed along. The boys were perhaps too busy carrying the boat to tell them to go away. Some younger children were still out playing, playing hopscotch on the sidewalk though they could hardly see. At this time of year the bare sidewalk was still such a novelty and delight. These children cleared out of the way and watched the boat go by with unwilling respect; they shouted questions after it, wanting to know where it came from and what was going to be done with it. No one answered them. Eva and Carol as well as the boys refused to answer or even look at them.

The five of them entered Clayton's yard. The boys shifted weight, as if they were going to put the boat down.

"You better take it round to the back where nobody can see it," Carol said. That was the first thing any of them had said since they came into town.

The boys said nothing but went on, following a mud path between Clayton's house and a leaning board fence. They let the boat down in the back yard.

"It's a stolen boat, you know," said Eva, mainly for the effect. "It must've belonged to somebody. You stole it."

"You was the ones who stole it then," Bud said, short of breath. "It was you seen it first."

"It was you took it."

"It was all of us then. If one of us gets in trouble then all of us does."

"Are you going to tell anybody on them?" said Carol as she and Eva rode home, along the streets which were dark between the lights now and potholed from winter.

"It's up to you. I won't if you won't."

"I won't if you won't."

They rode in silence, relinquishing something, but not discontented.

The board fence in Clayton's back yard had every so often a post which supported it, or tried to, and it was on these posts that Eva and Carol spent several evenings sitting, jauntily but not very comfortably. Or else they just leaned against the fence while the boys worked on the boat. During the first couple of evenings neighborhood children attracted by the sound of hammering tried to get into the yard to see what was going on, but Eva and Carol blocked their way.

"Who said you could come in here?"

"Just us can come in this yard."

These evenings were getting longer, the air milder. Skipping was starting on the sidewalks. Further along the street there was a row of hard maples that had been tapped. Children drank the sap as fast as it could drip into the buckets. The old man and woman who owned the trees, and who hoped to make syrup, came running out of the house making noises as if they were trying to scare away crows. Finally, every spring, the old man would come out on his porch and fire his shotgun into the air, and then the thieving would stop.

None of those working on the boat bothered about stealing sap, though all had done so last year.

The lumber to repair the boat was picked up here and there, along back lanes. At this time of year things were lying around—old boards and branches, sodden mitts, spoons flung out with the dishwater, lids of pudding pots that had been set in the snow to cool, all the debris that can sift through and survive winter. The tools came from Clayton's cellar—left over, presumably, from the time when his father was alive—and though they had nobody to advise them the boys seemed to figure out more or less the manner in which boats are built, or rebuilt. Frank was the one who showed up with diagrams from books and *Popular Mechanics* magazines. Clayton looked at these diagrams and listened to Frank read the instructions and then went ahead and decided in his own way what was to be done. Bud was best at sawing. Eva and Carol watched everything from the fence and offered criticism and thought up names. The names for the boat that they thought of were: Water Lily, Sea Horse, Flood Queen, and Caro-Eve, after them because they had found it. The boys did not say which, if any, of these names they found satisfactory.

The boat had to be tarred. Clayton heated up a pot of tar on the kitchen stove and brought it out and painted slowly, his thorough way, sitting astride the overturned boat. The other boys were sawing a board to make a new seat. As Clayton worked, the tar cooled and thickened so that finally he could not move the brush any more. He turned to Eva and held out the pot and said, "You can go in and heat this on the stove."

Eva took the pot and went up the back steps. The kitchen seemed black after outside, but it must be light enough to see in, because there was Clayton's mother standing at the ironing board, ironing. She did that for a living, took in wash and ironing.

"Please may I put the tar pot on the stove?" said Eva, who had been brought up to talk politely to parents, even wash-and-iron ladies, and who for some reason especially wanted to make a good impression on Clayton's mother.

"You'll have to poke up the fire then," said Clayton's mother, as if she doubted whether Eva would know how to do that. But Eva could see now, and she picked up the lid with the stove-lifter, and took the poker and poked up a flame. She stirred the tar as it softened. She felt privileged. Then and later. Before she went to sleep a picture of Clayton came to her mind; she saw him sitting astride the boat, tarpainting, with such concentration, delicacy, absorption. She thought of him speaking to her, out of his isolation, in such an ordinary peaceful taking-for-granted voice.

On the twenty-fourth of May, a school holiday in the middle of the week, the boat was carried out of town, a long way now, off the road over fields and fences that had been repaired, to where the river flowed between its normal banks. Eva and Carol, as well as the boys, took turns carrying it. It was launched in the water from a cow-trampled spot between willow bushes that were fresh out in leaf. The boys went first. They yelled with triumph when the boat did float, when it rode amazingly down the river current. The boat was painted black, and green inside, with yellow seats, and a strip of yellow all the way around the outside. There was no name on it, after all. The boys could not imagine that it needed any name to keep it separate from the other boats in the world.

Eva and Carol ran along the bank, carrying bags full of peanut butter-and-jam sandwiches, pickles, bananas, chocolate cake, potato chips, graham crackers stuck together with corn syrup and five bottles of pop to be cooled in the river water. The bottles bumped against their legs. They yelled for a turn.

"If they don't let us they're bastards," Carol said, and they yelled together, "We found it! We found it!"

The boys did not answer, but after a while they brought the boat in, and Carol and Eva came crashing, panting down the bank.

"Does it leak?"

"It don't leak yet."

"We forgot a bailing can," wailed Carol, but nevertheless she got in, with Eva, and Frank pushed them off, crying, "Here's to a Watery Grave!"

And the thing about being in a boat was that it was not solidly bobbing, like a log, but was cupped in the water, so that riding in it was not like being on something in the water, but like being in the water itself. Soon they were all going out in the boat in mixed-up turns, two boys and a girl, two girls and a boy, a girl and a boy, until things were so confused it was impossible to tell whose turn came next, and nobody cared anyway. They went down the river—those who weren't riding, running along the bank to keep up. They passed under two bridges, one iron, one cement. Once they saw a big carp just resting, it seemed to smile at them, in the bridge-shaded water. They did not know how far they had gone on the river, but things had changed—the water had got shallower, and the land flatter. Across an open field they saw a building that looked like a house, abandoned. They dragged the boat up on the bank and tied it and set out across the field.

"That's the old station," Frank said. "That's Pedder Station." The others had heard this name but he was the one who knew, because his father was the station agent in town. He said that this was a station on a branch line that had been torn up, and that there had been a sawmill here, but a long time ago.

Inside the station it was dark, cool. All the windows were broken. Glass lay in shards and in fairly big pieces on the floor. They walked around finding the larger pieces of glass and tramping on them, smashing them, it was like cracking ice on puddles. Some partitions were still in place, you could see where the ticket window had been. There was a bench lying on its side. People had been here, it looked as if people came here all the time, though it was so far from anywhere. Beer bottles and pop bottles were lying around, also cigarette packages, gum and candy wrappers, the paper from a loaf of bread. The walls were covered with dim and fresh pencil and chalk writings and carved with knives.

I LOVE RONNIE COLES
I WANT TO FUCK
KILROY WAS HERE
RONNIE COLES IS AN ASS-HOLE
WHAT ARE YOU DOING HERE?
WAITING FOR A TRAIN
DAWNA   MARY-LOU   BARBARA   JOANNE

It was exciting to be inside this large, dark, empty place, with the loud noise of breaking glass and their voices ringing back from the underside of the roof. They tipped the old beer bottles against their mouths. That reminded them that they were hungry and thirsty and they cleared a place in the middle of the floor and sat down and ate the lunch. They drank the pop just as it was, lukewarm. They ate everything there was and licked the smears of peanut butter and jam off the bread-paper in which the sandwiches had been wrapped.

They played Truth or Dare.

"I dare you to write on the wall, I am a Stupid Ass, and sign your name."

"Tell the truth—what is the worst lie you ever told?"

"Did you ever wet the bed?"

"Did you ever dream you were walking down the street without any clothes on?"

"I dare you to go outside and pee on the railway sign."

It was Frank who had to do that. They could not see him, even his back, but they knew he did it, they heard the hissing sound of his pee. They all sat still, amazed, unable to think of what the next dare would be.

"I dare everybody," said Frank from the doorway, "I dare—Everybody."

"What?"

"Take off all our clothes."

Eva and Carol screamed.

"Anybody who won't do it has to walk—has to *crawl*—around this floor on their hands and knees."

They were all quiet, till Eva said, almost complacently, "What first?"

"Shoes and socks."

"Then we have to go outside, there's too much glass here."

They pulled off their shoes and socks in the doorway, in the sudden blinding sun. The field before them was bright as water. They ran across where the tracks used to go.

"That's enough, that's enough," said Carol. "Watch out for thistles!"

"Tops! Everybody take off their tops!"

"I won't! We won't, will we, Eva?"

But Eva was whirling round and round in the sun where the track used to be. "I don't care, I don't care! Truth or Dare! Truth or Dare!"

She unbuttoned her blouse as she whirled, as if she didn't know what her hand was doing, she flung it off.

Carol took off hers. "I wouldn't have done it, if you hadn't!"

"Bottoms!"

Nobody said a word this time, they all bent and stripped themselves. Eva, naked first, started running across the field, and then all the others ran, all five of them running bare through the knee-high hot grass, running towards the river. Not caring now about being caught but in fact leaping and yelling to call attention to themselves, if there was anybody to hear or see. They felt as if they were going to jump off a cliff and fly. They felt that something was happening to them different from anything that had happened before, and it had to do with the boat, the water, the sunlight, the dark ruined station, and each other. They thought of each other now hardly as names or people, but as echoing shrieks, reflections, all bold and white and loud and scandalous, and as fast as arrows. They went running without a break into the cold water and when it came almost to the tops of their legs they fell on it and swam. It stopped their noise. Silence, amazement, came over them in a rush. They dipped and floated and separated, sleek as mink.

Eva stood up in the water her hair dripping, water running down her face. She was waist deep. She stood on smooth stones, her feet fairly wide apart, water flowing between her legs. About a yard away from her Clayton also stood up, and they were blinking the water out of their eyes, looking at each other. Eva did not turn or try to hide; she was quivering from the cold of the water, but also with pride, shame, boldness, and exhilaration.

Clayton shook his head violently, as if he wanted to bang something out of it, then bent over and took a mouthful of river water. He stood up with his cheeks full and made a tight hole of his mouth and shot the water at her as if it was coming out of a hose, hitting her exactly, first one breast and then the other. Water from his mouth ran down her body. He hooted to see it, a loud self-conscious sound that nobody would have expected, from him. The others looked up from wherever they were in the water and closed in to see.

Eva crouched down and slid into the water, letting her head go right under. She swam, and when she let her head out downstream, Carol was coming after her and the boys were already on the bank, already running into the grass, showing their skinny backs, their white, flat buttocks. They were laughing and saying things to each other but she couldn't hear, for the water in her ears.

"What did he do?" said Carol.

"Nothing."

They crept in to shore. "Let's stay in the bushes till they go," said Eva. "I hate them anyway. I really do. Don't you hate them?"

"Sure," said Carol, and they waited, not very long, until they heard the boys still noisy and excited coming down to the place a bit upriver where they had left the boat. They heard them jump in and start rowing.

"They've got all the hard part, going back," said Eva, hugging herself and shivering violently. "Who cares? Anyway. It never was our boat."

"What if they tell?" said Carol.

"We'll say it's all a lie."

Eva hadn't thought of this solution until she said it, but as soon as she did she felt almost light-hearted again. The ease and scornfulness of it did make them both giggle, and slapping themselves and splashing out of the water they set about developing one of those fits of laughter in which, as soon as one showed signs of exhaustion, the other would snort and start up again, and they would make helpless—soon genuinely helpless—faces at each other and bend over and grab themselves as if they had the worst pain.

QUESTIONS

1. What impact does the found boat have upon the lives of the boys? Of the girls? What impact does it have on the relationship between them?
2. What activities do the boys perform that are traditionally masculine? What activities do the girls perform that are traditionally feminine?
3. Examine the way the author escalates the action in the story. What incidents, in particular, lead up to the final scene?
4. Compare and contrast the mood and tone the author uses in describing the town, and the mood and tone she uses in describing the actions of the girls and boys. What is the relationship between them?

Isaac Bashevis Singer

GIMPEL THE FOOL

I

I am Gimpel the fool. I don't think myself a fool. On the contrary. But that's what folks call me. They gave me the name while I was still in school. I had seven names in all: imbecile, donkey, flax-head, dope, glump, ninny, and fool. The last name stuck. What did my foolishness consist of? I was easy to take in. They said, "Gimpel, you know the rabbi's wife has been brought to childbed?" So I skipped school. Well, it turned out to be a lie. How was I supposed to know? She hadn't had a big belly. But I never looked at her belly. Was that really so foolish? The gang laughed and hee-hawed, stomped and danced and chanted a good-night prayer. And instead of the raisins they give when a woman's lying in, they stuffed my hand full of goat turds. I was no weakling. If I slapped someone he'd see all the way to Cracow. But I'm really not a slugger by nature. I think to myself, Let it pass. So they take advantage of me.

I was coming home from school and heard a dog barking. I'm not afraid of dogs, but of course I never want to start up with them. One of them may be mad, and if he bites there's not a Tartar in the world who can help you. So I made tracks. Then I looked around and saw the whole market place wild with laughter. It was no dog at all but Wolf-Leib the thief. How was I supposed to know it was he? It sounded like a howling bitch.

When the pranksters and leg-pullers found that I was easy to fool, every one of them tried his luck with me. "Gimpel, the Czar is coming to Frampol; Gimpel, the moon fell down in Turbeen; Gimpel, little Hodel Furpiece found a treasure behind the bath-house." And I like a *golem* believed everyone. In the first place, everything is possible, as it is written in the Wisdom of the Fathers, I've forgotten just how. Second, I had to believe when the whole town came down on me! If I ever dared to say, "Ah, you're kidding!" there was trouble. People got angry. "What do you mean! You want to call everyone a liar?" What was I to do? I believed them, and I hope at least that did them some good.

I was an orphan. My grandfather who brought me up was already bent toward the grave. So they turned me over to a baker, and what a time they gave me there! Every woman or girl who came to bake a pan of cookies or dry a batch of noodles had to fool me at least once. "Gimpel, there's a fair in heaven; Gimpel, the rabbi gave birth to a calf in the seventh month; Gimpel, a cow flew over the roof and laid brass eggs." A student from the *yeshiva* came once to buy a roll, and he said, "You, Gimpel, while you stand here scraping with your baker's shovel the Messiah has come. The dead have arisen." "What do you mean?" I said. "I heard no one blowing the ram's horn!" He said, "Are you deaf?" And all began to cry, "We heard it, we heard!" Then in came Reitze the candle-dipper and called out in her hoarse voice, "Gimpel, your father and mother have stood up from the grave. They're looking for you."

To tell the truth, I knew very well that nothing of the sort had happened, but all the same, as folks were talking, I threw on my wool vest and went out. Maybe something had happened. What did I stand to lose by looking? Well, what a cat music went up! And then I took a vow to believe nothing more. But that was no go either. They confused me so that I didn't know the big end from the small.

I went to the rabbi to get some advice. He said, "It is written, better to be a fool all your days than for one hour to be evil. You are not a fool. They are the fools. For he who causes his neighbor to feel shame loses Paradise himself." Nevertheless the rabbi's daughter took me in. As I left the rabbinical court she said, "Have you kissed the wall yet?" I said, "No; what for?" She answered, "It's a law; you've got to do it after every visit." Well, there didn't seem to be any harm in it. And she burst out laughing. It was a fine trick. She put one over on me, all right.

I wanted to go off to another town, but then everyone got busy matchmaking, and they were after me so they nearly tore my coat tails off. They talked at me and talked until I got water on the ear. She was no chaste maiden, but they told me she was virgin pure. She had a limp, and they said it was deliberate, from coyness. She had a bastard, and they told me the child was her little brother. I cried, "You're wasting your time. I'll never marry that whore." But they said indignantly, "What a way to talk! Aren't you ashamed of yourself? We can take you to the rabbi and have you fined for giving her a bad name." I saw then that I wouldn't escape them so easily and I thought, They're set on making me their butt. But when you're married the husband's the master, and if that's all right with her it's agreeable to me too. Besides, you can't pass through life unscathed, nor expect to.

I went to her clay house, which was built on the sand, and the whole gang, hollering and chorusing, came after me. They acted like bearbaiters. When we came to the well they stopped all the same. They were afraid to start anything with Elka. Her mouth would open as if it were on a hinge, and she had a fierce tongue. I entered the house. Lines were strung from wall to wall and clothes were drying. Barefoot she stood by the tub, doing the wash. She was dressed in a worn hand-me-down gown of plush. She had her hair put up in braids and pinned across her head. It took my breath away, almost the reek of it all.

Evidently she knew who I was. She took a look at me and said, "Look who's here! He's come, the drip. Grab a seat."

I told her all; I denied nothing. "Tell me the truth," I said, "are you really a virgin, and is that mischievous Yechiel actually your little brother? Don't be deceitful with me, for I'm an orphan."

"I'm an orphan myself," she answered, "and whoever tries to twist you up, may the end of his nose take a twist. But don't let them think they can take advantage of me. I want a dowry of fifty guilders, and let them take up a collection besides. Otherwise they can kiss my you-know-what." She was very plain-spoken. I said, "Don't bargain with me. Either a flat 'yes' or a flat 'no'—go back where you came from."

I thought, No bread will ever be baked from *this* dough. But ours is not a poor town. They consented to everything and proceeded with the wedding. It so happened that there was a dysentery epidemic at the time. The ceremony was held at the cemetery gates, near the little corpse-washing hut. The fellows got drunk. While the marriage contract was being drawn up I heard the most pious high rabbi ask, "Is the bride a widow or a divorced woman?" And the sexton's wife answered for her, "Both a widow and divorced." It was a black moment for me. But what was I to do, run away from under the marriage canopy?

There was singing and dancing. An old granny danced opposite me, hugging a braided white *chalah*. The master of revels made a "God 'a mercy" in memory of the bride's parents. The schoolboys threw burrs, as on *Tishe b' Av* fast day. There were a lot of gifts after the sermon: a noodle board, a kneading trough, a bucket, brooms, ladles, household articles galore. Then I took a look and saw two strapping young men carrying a crib. "What do we need this for?" I asked. So they said, "Don't rack your brains about it. It's all right, it'll come in handy." I realized I was going to be rooked. Take it another way though, what did I stand to lose? I reflected, I'll see what comes of it. A whole town can't go altogether crazy.

II

At night I came where my wife lay, but she wouldn't let me in. "Say, look here, is this what they married us for?" I said. And she said, "My monthly has come." "But yesterday they took you to the ritual bath, and that's afterward, isn't it supposed to be?" "Today isn't yesterday," said she, "and yesterday's not today. You can beat it if you don't like it." In short, I waited.

Not four months later she was in childbed. The townsfolk hid their laughter with their knuckles. But what could I do? She suffered intolerable pains and clawed at the walls. "Gimpel," she cried, "I'm going. Forgive me!" The house filled with women. They were boiling pans of water. The screams rose to the welkin.

The thing to do was to go to the House of Prayer to repeat Psalms, and that was what I did.

The townsfolk liked that, all right. I stood in a corner saying Psalms and prayers, and they shook their heads at me. "Pray, pray!" they told me. "Prayer never made any woman pregnant." One of the congregation put a straw to my mouth and said, "Hay for the cows." There was something to that too, by God!

She gave birth to a boy. Friday at the synagogue the sexton stood up before the Ark, pounded on the reading table, and announced, "The wealthy Reb Gimpel invites the congregation to a feast in honor of the birth of a son." The whole House of Prayer rang with laughter. My face was flaming. But there was nothing I could do. After all, I *was* the one responsible for the circumcision honors and rituals.

Half the town came running. You couldn't wedge another soul in. Women brought peppered chick-peas, and there was a keg of beer from the tavern. I ate and drank as much as anyone, and they all congratulated me. Then there was a circumcision, and I named the boy after my father, may he rest in peace. When all were gone and I was left with my wife alone, she thrust her head through the bed-curtain and called me to her.

"Gimpel," said she, "why are you silent? Has your ship gone and sunk?"

"What shall I say?" I answered. "A fine thing you've done to me! If my mother had known of it she'd have died a second time."

She said, "Are you crazy, or what?"

"How can you make such a fool," I said, "of one who should be the lord and master?"

"What's the matter with you?" she said. "What have you taken it into your head to imagine?"

I saw that I must speak bluntly and openly. "Do you think this is the way to use an orphan?" I said. "You have borne a bastard."

She answered, "Drive this foolishness out of your head. The child is yours."

"How can he be mine?" I argued. "He was born seventeen weeks after the wedding."

She told me then that he was premature. I said, "Isn't he a little too premature?" She said she had had a grandmother who carried just as short a time and she resembled this grandmother of hers as one drop of water does another. She swore to it with such oaths that you would have believed a peasant at the fair if he had used them. To tell the plain truth, I didn't believe her; but when I talked it over the next day with the schoolmaster he told me that the very same thing had happened to Adam and Eve. Two they went up to bed, and four they descended.

"There isn't a woman in the world who is not the granddaughter of Eve," he said.

That was how it was—they argued me dumb. But then, who really knows how such things happen?

I began to forget my sorrow. I loved the child madly, and he loved me too. As soon as he saw me he'd wave his little hands and want me to pick him up, and when he was colicky I was the only one who could pacify him. I bought him a little bone teething ring and a little gilded cap. He was forever catching the evil eye from someone, and then I had to run to get one of those abracadabras for him that would get him out of it. I worked like an ox. You know how expenses go up when there's an infant in the house. I don't want to lie about it; I didn't dislike Elka either, for that matter. She swore at me and cursed, and I couldn't get enough of her. What strength she had! One of her looks could rob you of the power of speech. And her orations! Pitch and sulphur, that's what they were full of, and yet somehow also full of charm. I adored her every word. She gave me bloody wounds though.

In the evening I brought her a white loaf as well as a dark one, and also poppyseed rolls I baked myself. I thieved because of her and swiped everything I could lay hands on, macaroons, raisins, almonds, cakes. I hope I may be forgiven for stealing from the Saturday pots the women left to warm in the baker's oven. I would take out scraps of meat, a chunk of pudding, a chicken leg or head, a piece of tripe, whatever I could nip quickly. She ate and became fat and handsome.

I had to sleep away from home all during the week, at the bakery. On Friday nights when I got home she always made an excuse of some sort. Either she had heartburn, or a stitch in the side, or hiccups, or headaches. You know what women's excuses are. I had a bitter time of it. It was rough. To add to it, this little brother of hers, the bastard, was growing bigger. He'd put lumps on me, and when I wanted to hit back she'd open her mouth and curse so powerfully I saw a green haze floating before my eyes. Ten times a day she threatened to divorce me. Another man in my place would have taken French leave and disappeared. But I'm the type that bears it and says nothing. What's one to do? Shoulders are from God, and burdens too.

One night there was a calamity in the bakery; the oven burst, and we almost had a fire. There was nothing to do but go home, so I went home. Let me, I thought, also taste the joy of sleeping in bed in midweek. I didn't want to wake the sleeping mite and tiptoed into the house. Coming in, it seemed to me that I heard not the snoring of one but, as it were, a double snore, one a thin enough snore and the other like the snoring of a slaughtered ox. Oh, I didn't like that! I didn't like it at all. I went up to the bed, and things suddenly turned black. Next to Elka lay a man's form. Another in my place would have made an uproar, and enough noise to rouse the whole town, but the thought occurred to me that I might wake the child. A little thing like that—why frighten a little swallow like that, I thought. All right then, I went back to the bakery and stretched out on a sack of flour, and till morning I never shut an eye. I shivered as if I had had malaria. "Enough of being a donkey," I said to myself. "Gimpel isn't going to be a sucker all his life. There's a limit even to the foolishness of a fool like Gimpel."

In the morning I went to the rabbi to get advice, and it made a great commotion in the town. They sent the beadle for Elka right away. She came, carrying the child. And what do you think she did? She denied it, denied everything, bone and stone! "He's out of his head," she said. "I know nothing of dreams or divinations." They yelled at her, warned her, hammered on the table, but she stuck to her guns: it was a false accusation, she said.

The butchers and the horse-traders took her part. One of the lads from the slaughter-house came by and said to me, "We've got our eye on you, you're a marked man." Meanwhile the child started to bear down and soiled itself. In the rabbinical court there was an Ark of the Covenant, and they couldn't allow that, so they sent Elka away.

I said to the rabbi, "What shall I do?"

"You must divorce her at once," said he.

"And what if she refuses?" I asked.

He said, "You must serve the divorce, that's all you'll have to do."

I said, "Well, all right, Rabbi. Let me think about it."

"There's nothing to think about," said he. "You mustn't remain under the same roof with her."

"And if I want to see the child?" I asked.

"Let her go, the harlot," said he, "and her brood of bastards with her."

The verdict he gave was that I mustn't even cross her threshold—never again, as long as I should live.

During the day it didn't bother me so much. I thought, It was bound to happen, the abscess had to burst. But at night when I stretched out upon the sacks I felt it all very bitterly. A longing took me, for her and for the child. I wanted to be angry, but that's my misfortune exactly, I don't have it in me to be really angry. In the first place—this was how my thoughts went—there's bound to be a slip sometimes. You can't live without errors. Probably that lad who was with her led her on and gave her presents and what not, and women are often long on hair and short on sense, and so he got around her. And then since she denies it so, maybe I was only seeing things? Hallucinations do happen. You see a figure or a mannikin or something, but when you come up closer it's nothing, there's not a thing there. And if that's so, I'm doing her an injustice.

And when I got so far in my thoughts I started to weep. I sobbed so that I wet the flour where I lay. In the morning I went to the rabbi and told him that I had made a mistake. The rabbi wrote on with his quill, and he said that if that were so he would have to reconsider the whole case. Until he had finished I wasn't to go near my wife, but I might send her bread and money by messenger.

III

Nine months passed before all the rabbis could come to an agreement. Letters went back and forth. I hadn't realized that there could be so much erudition about a matter like this.

Meantime Elka gave birth to still another child, a girl this time. On the Sabbath I went to the synagogue and invoked a blessing on her. They called me up to the Torah, and I named the child for my mother-in-law, may she rest in peace. The louts and loudmouths of the town who came into the bakery gave me a going over. All Frampol refreshed its spirits because of my trouble and grief. However, I resolved that I would always believe what I was told. What's the good of *not* believing? Today it's your wife you don't believe; tomorrow it's God Himself you won't take stock in.

By an apprentice who was her neighbor I sent her daily a corn or a wheat loaf, or a piece of pastry, rolls or bagels, or, when I got the chance, a slab of pudding, a slice of honeycake, or wedding strudel—whatever came my way. The apprentice was a goodhearted lad, and more than once he added something on his own. He had formerly annoyed me a lot, plucking my nose and digging me in the ribs, but when he started to be a visitor to my house he became kind and friendly. "Hey, you, Gimpel," he said to me, "you have a very decent little wife and two fine kids. You don't deserve them."

"But the things people say about her," I said.

"Well, they have long tongues," he said, "and nothing to do with them but babble. Ignore it as you ignore the cold of last winter."

One day the rabbi sent for me and said, "Are you certain, Gimpel, that you were wrong about your wife?"

I said, "I'm certain."

"Why, but look here! You yourself saw it."

"It must have been a shadow," I said.

"The shadow of what?"

"Just of one of the beams, I think."

"You can go home then. You owe thanks to the Yanover rabbi. He found an obscure reference in Maimonides that favored you."

I seized the rabbi's hand and kissed it.

I wanted to run home immediately. It's no small thing to be separated for so long a time from wife and child. Then I reflected, I'd better go back to work now, and go home in the evening. I said nothing to anyone, although as far as my heart was concerned it was like one of the Holy Days. The women teased and twitted me as they did every day, but my thought was, Go on, with your loose talk. The truth is out, like the oil upon the water. Maimonides says it's right, and therefore it is right!

At night, when I had covered the dough to let it rise, I took my share of bread and a little sack of flour and started homeward. The moon was full and the stars were glistening, something to terrify the soul. I hurried onward, and before me darted a long shadow. It was winter, and a fresh snow had fallen. I had a mind to sing, but it was growing late and I didn't want to wake the householders. Then I felt like whistling, but remembered that you don't whistle at night because it brings the demons out. So I was silent and walked as fast as I could.

Dogs in the Christian yards barked at me when I passed, but I thought, Bark your teeth out! What are you but mere dogs? Whereas I am a man, the husband of a fine wife, the father of promising children.

As I approached the house my heart started to pound as though it were the heart of a criminal. I felt no fear, but my heart went thump! thump! Well, no drawing back. I quietly lifted the latch and went in. Elka was asleep. I looked at the infant's cradle. The shutter was closed, but the moon forced its way through the cracks. I saw the newborn child's face and loved it as soon as I saw it—immediately—each tiny bone.

Then I came nearer to the bed. And what did I see but the apprentice lying there beside Elka. The moon went out all at once. It was utterly black, and I trembled. My teeth chattered. The bread fell from my hands and my wife waked and said, "Who is that, ah?"

I muttered, "It's me."

"Gimpel?" she asked. "How come you're here? I thought it was forbidden."

"The rabbi said," I answered and shook as with a fever.

"Listen to me, Gimpel," she said, "go out to the shed and see if the goat's all right. It seems she's been sick." I have forgotten to say that we had a goat. When I heard she was unwell I went into the yard. The nannygoat was a good little creature. I had a nearly human feeling for her.

With hesitant steps I went up to the shed and opened the door. The goat stood there on her four feet. I felt her everywhere, drew her by the arms, examined her udders, and found nothing wrong. She had probably eaten too much bark. "Good night, little goat," I said. "Keep well." And the little beast answered with a "Maa" as though to thank me for the good will.

I went back. The apprentice had vanished.

"Where," I asked, "is the lad?"

"What lad?" my wife answered.

"What do you mean?" I said. "The apprentice. You were sleeping with him."

"The things I have dreamed this night and the night before," she said, "may they come true and lay you low, body and soul! An evil spirit has taken root in you and dazzles your sight." She screamed out, "You hateful creature! You moon calf! You spook! You uncouth man! Get out, or I'll scream all Frampol out of bed!"

Before I could move, her brother sprang out from behind the oven and struck me a blow on the back of the head. I thought he had broken my neck. I felt that something about me was deeply wrong, and I said, "Don't make a scandal. All that's needed now is that people should accuse me of raising spooks and *dybbuks.*" For that was what she had meant. "No one will touch bread of my baking."

In short, I somehow calmed her.

"Well," she said, "that's enough. Lie down, and be shattered by wheels."

Next morning I called the apprentice aside. "Listen here, brother!" I said. And so on and so forth. "What do you say?" He stared at me as though I had dropped from the roof or something.

"I swear," he said, "you'd better go to an herb doctor or some healer. I'm afraid you have a screw loose, but I'll hush it up for you." And that's how the thing stood.

To make a long story short, I lived twenty years with my wife. She bore me six children, four daughters and two sons. All kinds of things happened, but I neither saw nor heard. I believed, and that's all. The rabbi recently said to me, "Belief in itself is beneficial. It is written that a good man lives by his faith."

Suddenly my wife took sick. It began with a trifle, a little growth upon the breast. But she evidently was not destined to live long; she had no years. I spent a fortune on her. I have forgotten to say that by this time I had a bakery of my own and in Frampol was considered to be something of a rich man. Daily the healer came, and every witch doctor in the neighborhood was brought. They decided to use leeches, and after that to try cupping. They even called a doctor from Lublin, but it was too late. Before she died she called me to her bed and said, "Forgive me, Gimpel."

I said, "What is there to forgive? You have been a good and faithful wife."

"Woe, Gimpel!" she said. "It was ugly how I deceived you all these years. I want to go clean to my Maker, and so I have to tell you that the children are not yours."

If I had been clouted on the head with a piece of wood it couldn't have bewildered me more.

"Whose are they?" I asked.

"I don't know," she said, "there were a lot. . . . But they're not yours." And as she spoke she tossed her head to the side, her eyes turned glassy, and it was all up with Elka. On her whitened lips there remained a smile.

I imagined that, dead as she was, she was saying, "I deceived Gimpel. That was the meaning of my brief life."

IV

One night, when the period of mourning was done, as I lay dreaming on the flour sacks, there came the Spirit of Evil himself and said to me, "Gimpel, why do you sleep?"

I said, "What should I be doing? Eating *kreplach?*"

"The whole world deceives you," he said, "and you ought to deceive the world in your turn."

"How can I deceive all the world?" I asked him.

He answered, "You might accumulate a bucket of urine every day and at night pour it into the dough. Let the sages of Frampol eat filth."

"What about judgment in the world to come?" I said.

"There is no world to come," he said. "They've sold you a bill of goods and talked you into believing you carried a cat in your belly. What nonsense!"

"Well then," I said, "and is there a God?"

He answered, "There is no God either."

"What," I said, "*is* there, then?"

"A thick mire."

He stood before my eyes with a goatish beard and horns, longtoothed, and with a tail. Hearing such words, I wanted to snatch him by the tail, but I tumbled from the flour sacks and nearly broke a rib. Then it happened that I had to answer the call of nature, and, passing, I saw the risen bread, which seemed to say to me, "Do it!" In brief, I let myself be persuaded.

At dawn the apprentice came. We kneaded the dough, scattered caraway seeds on it, and set it to bake. Then the apprentice went away, and I was left sitting in the little trench by the oven, on a pile of rags. Well, Gimpel, I thought, you've revenged yourself on them for all the shame they've put on you. Outside the frost glittered, but it was warm beside the oven. The flames heated my face. I bent my head and fell into a doze.

I saw in a dream, at once, Elka in her shroud. She called to me, "What have you done, Gimpel?"

I said to her, "It's all your fault," and started to cry.

"You fool!" she said. "You fool! Because I was false is everything false too? I never deceived anyone but myself. I'm paying for it all, Gimpel. They spare you nothing here."

I looked at her face. It was black. I was startled and waked, and remained sitting dumb. I sensed that everything hung in the balance. A false step now and I'd lose Eternal Life. But God gave me His help. I seized the long shovel and took out the loaves, carried them into the yard, and started to dig a hole in the frozen earth.

My apprentice came back as I was doing it. "What are you doing, boss?" he said, and grew pale as a corpse.

"I know what I'm doing," I said, and I buried it all before his very eyes.

Then I went home, took my hoard from its hiding place, and divided it among the children. "I saw your mother tonight," I said. "She's turning black, poor thing."

They were so astounded they couldn't speak a word.

"Be well," I said, "and forget that such a one as Gimpel ever existed." I put on my short coat, a pair of boots, took the bag that held my prayer shawl in one hand, my stick in the other, and kissed the *mezzuzah*. When people saw me in the street they were greatly surprised.

"Where are you going?" they said.

I answered, "Into the world." And so I departed from Frampol.

I wandered over the land, and good people did not neglect me. After many years I became old and white; I heard a great deal, many lies and falsehoods, but the longer I lived the more I understood that there were really no lies. Whatever doesn't really happen is dreamed at night. It happens to one if it doesn't happen to another, tomorrow if not today, or a century hence if not next year. What difference can it make? Often I heard tales of which I said, "Now this is a thing that cannot happen." But before a year had elapsed I heard that it actually had come to pass somewhere.

Going from place to place, eating at strange tables, it often happens that I spin yarns—improbable things that could never have happened—about devils, magicians, windmills, and the like. The children run after me, calling, "Grandfather, tell us a story." Sometimes they ask for particular stories, and I try to please them. A fat young boy once said to me, "Grandfather, it's the same story you told us before." The little rogue, he was right.

So it is with dreams too. It is many years since I left Frampol, but as soon as I shut my eyes I am there again. And whom do you think I see? Elka. She is standing by the washtub, as at our first encounter, but her face is shining and her eyes as radiant as the eyes of a saint, and she speaks outlandish words to me, strange things. When I wake I have forgotten it all. But while the dream lasts I am comforted. She answers all my queries, and what comes out is that all is right. I weep and implore, "Let me be with you." And she consoles me and tells me to be patient. The time is nearer than it is far. Sometimes she strokes and kisses me and weeps upon my face. When I awaken I feel her lips and taste the salt of her tears.

No doubt the world is entirely an imaginary world, but it is only once removed from the true world. At the door of the hovel where I lie, there stands the plank on which the dead are taken away. The gravedigger Jew has his spade ready. The grave waits and the worms are hungry; the shrouds are prepared—I carry them in my beggar's sack. Another *shnorrer* is waiting to inherit my bed of straw. When the time comes I will go joyfully. Whatever may be there, it will be real, without complication, without ridicule, without deception. God be praised: there even Gimpel cannot be deceived.

Translated by Saul Bellow

QUESTIONS

1. Gimpel is portrayed in three separate stages of his life. In what way does he remain a "fool" throughout? How does the nature of his foolishness transform during these stages?
2. How is Gimpel's character tested when the Spirit of Evil tries to persuade him to urinate into the dough? What lesson does he learn from this incident?
3. The author's style is sometimes referred to as magical realism. What aspects of this story seem to corroborate this?

Alice Walker
ROSELILY

Dearly Beloved,

She dreams; dragging herself across the world. A small girl in her mother's white robe and veil, knee raised waist high through a bowl of quicksand soup. The man who stands beside her is against this standing on the front porch of her house, being married to the sound of cars whizzing by on highway 61.

we are gathered here

Like cotton to be weighed. Her fingers at the last minute busily removing dry leaves and twigs. Aware it is a superficial sweep. She knows he blames Mississippi for the respectful way the men turn their heads up in the yard, the women stand waiting and knowledge-able, their children held from mischief by teachings from the wrong God. He glares beyond them to the occupants of the cars, white faces glued to promises beyond a country wedding, noses thrust forward like dogs on a track. For him they usurp the wedding.

in the sight of God

Yes, open house. That is what country black folks like. She dreams she does not already have three children. A squeeze around the flowers in her hands chokes off three and four and five years of breath. Instantly she is ashamed and frightened in her superstition. She looks for the first time at the preacher, forces humility into her eyes, as if she believes he is, in fact, a man of God. She can imagine God, a small black boy, timidly pulling the preacher's coattail.

to join this man and this woman

She thinks of ropes, chains, handcuffs, his religion. His place of worship. Where she will be required to sit apart with covered head. In Chicago, a word she hears when thinking of smoke, from his description of what a cinder was, which they never had in Panther Burn. She sees hovering over the heads of the clean neighbors in her front yard black specks falling, clinging, from the sky. But in Chicago. Respect, a chance to build. Her children at last from underneath the detrimental wheel. A chance to be on top. What a relief, she thinks. What a vision, a view, from up so high.

in holy matrimony.

Her fourth child she gave away to the child's father who had some money. Certainly a good job. Had gone to Harvard. Was a good man but weak because good language meant so much to him he could not live with Roselily. Could not abide TV in the living room, five beds in three rooms, no Bach except from four to six on Sunday afternoons. No chess at all. She does not forget to worry about her son among his father's people. She wonders if the New England climate will agree with him. If he will ever come down to Mississippi, as his father did, to try to right the country's wrongs. She wonders if he will be stronger than his father. His father cried off and on throughout her pregnancy. Went to skin and bones. Suffered nightmares, retching and falling out of bed. Tried to kill himself. Later told his wife he found the right baby through friends. Vouched for the sterling qualities that would make up his character.

It is not her nature to blame. Still, she is not entirely thankful. She supposes New England, the North, to be quite different from what she knows. It seems right somehow to her that people who move there to live return home completely changed. She thinks of the air, the smoke, the cinders. Imagines cinders big as hailstones; heavy, weighing on the people. Wonders how this pressure finds its way into the veins, roping the springs of laughter.

if there's anybody here that knows a reason why

But of course they know no reason why beyond what they daily have come to know. She thinks of the man who will be her husband, feels shut away from him because of the stiff severity of his plain black suit. His religion. A lifetime of black and white. Of veils. Covered head. It is as if her children are already gone from her. Not dead, but exalted on a pedestal, a stalk that has no roots. She wonders how to make new roots. It is beyond her. She wonders what one does with memories in a brand-new life. This had seemed easy, until she thought of it. "The reasons why . . . the people who" . . . she thinks, and does not wonder where the thought is from.

these two should not be joined

She thinks of her mother, who is dead. Dead, but still her mother. Joined. This is confusing. Of her father. A gray old man who sold wild mink, rabbit, fox skins to Sears, Roebuck. He stands in the yard, like a man waiting for a train. Her young sisters stand behind her in smooth green dresses, with flowers in their hands and hair. They giggle, she feels, at the absurdity of the wedding. They are ready for something new. She thinks the man beside her should marry one of them. She feels old. Yoked. An arm seems to reach out from behind her and snatch her backward. She thinks of cemeteries and the long sleep of grandparents mingling in the dirt. She believes that she believes in ghosts. In the soil giving back what it takes.

together,

In the city. He sees her in a new way. This she knows, and is grateful. But is it new enough? She cannot always be a bride and virgin, wearing robes and veil. Even now her body itches to be free of satin and voile, organdy and lily of the valley. Memories crash against her. Memories of being bare to the sun. She wonders what it will be like.

Not to have to go to a job. Not to work in a sewing plant. Not to worry about learning to sew straight seams in workingmen's overalls, jeans, and dress pants. Her place will be in the home, he has said, repeatedly, promising her rest she had prayed for. But now she wonders. When she is rested, what will she do? They will make babies—she thinks practically about her fine brown body, his strong black one. They will be inevitable. Her hands will be full. Full of what? Babies. She is not comforted.

let him speak

She wishes she had asked him to explain more of what he meant. But she was impatient. Impatient to be done with sewing. With doing everything for three children, alone. Impatient to leave the girls she had known since childhood, their children growing up, their husbands hanging around her, already old, seedy. Nothing about them that she wanted, or needed. The fathers of her children driving by, waving, not waving; reminders of times she would just as soon forget. Impatient to see the South Side, where they would live and build and be respectable and respected and free. Her husband would free her. A romantic hush. Proposal. Promises. A new life! Respectable, reclaimed, renewed. Free! In robe and veil.

or forever hold

She does not even know if she loves him. She loves his sobriety. His refusal to sing just because he knows the tune. She loves his pride. His blackness and his gray car. She loves his understanding of her *condition*. She thinks she loves the effort he will make to redo her into what he truly wants. His love of her makes her completely conscious of how unloved she was before. This is something; though it makes her unbearably sad. Melancholy. She blinks her eyes. Remembers she is finally being married, like other girls. Like other girls, women? Something strains upward behind her eyes. She thinks of the something as a rat trapped, cornered, scurrying to and fro in her head, peering through the windows of her eyes. She wants to live for once. But doesn't know quite what that means. Wonders if she has ever done it. If she ever will. The preacher is odious to her. She wants to strike him out of the way, out of her light, with the back of her hand. It seems to her he has always been standing in front of her, barring her way.

his peace.

The rest she does not hear. She feels a kiss, passionate, rousing, within the general pandemonium. Cars drive up blowing their horns. Firecrackers go off. Dogs come from under the house and begin to yelp and bark. Her husband's hand is like the clasp of an iron gate. People congratulate. Her children press against her. They look with awe and distaste mixed with hope at their new father. He stands curiously apart, in spite of the people crowding about to grasp his free hand. He smiles at them all but his eyes are as if turned inward. He knows they cannot understand that he is not a Christian. He will not explain himself. He feels different, he looks it. The old women thought he was like one of their sons except that he had somehow got away from them. Still a son, not a son. Changed.

She thinks how it will be later in the night in the silvery gray car. How they will spin through the darkness of Mississippi and in the morning be in Chicago, Illinois. She thinks of Lincoln, the president. That is all she knows about the place. She feels ignorant, *wrong,* backward. She presses her worried fingers into his palm. He is standing in front of her. In the crush of well-wishing people, he does not look back.

QUESTIONS

1. What is the effect of dividing the story between the italicized words of the minister and the "inner thoughts" of Roselily? How does each complement the other?
2. What attitudes and emotions does Roselily seem to display toward her husband-to-be? What seems to be her main motivation in marrying him?
3. Compare and contrast Roselily and her future husband in terms of their values, temperament, attitude, and demeanor.
4. How would you characterize the story's diction? What does it reveal about Roselily's social class and family background?
5. Alice Walker is noted for her particular sensitivity to the struggles of black women in America. How does this story bear this out?

W o m e n & M e n

Fiction

TOPICS FOR WRITING

1. Compare and contrast two married couples you know. Include a description of their attitudes, behaviors, roles, and communication styles.
2. Narrate a social event such as a wedding, party, festival, or holiday that you attended, and contrast the ways that selected men and women behaved that demonstrate typical or atypical sex roles.
3. Reread "The Blue Jar." Write a brief fable or fairy tale illuminating one aspect of relationships between men and women.
4. As an exercise in evaluation, write an essay on a story in this section that you like or dislike or feel is a success or failure. Support your position with critical reasons and evidence.
5. In a single extended paragraph, try to summarize what Alice Munro is saying in "The Found Boat."
6. Select the male or female character you found most intriguing in these stories, and write an essay describing what it was about that person that impressed you.
7. In "Astronomer's Wife," "The Lady with the Pet Dog," "A Rose for Emily," and "Roselily," women are depicted in unsatisfying relationships. Select two of these stories and compare and contrast the reasons for their dissatisfaction.
8. Alice Walker's story "Roselily" is an unconventional narrative. Write an essay in which you describe several ways she breaks convention.
9. Argue for or against the proposition that men and women would be much more alike if it weren't for the sex-role differentiations that society and culture impose on them. Refer to specific stories to support your contentions.
10. For a critical study, do biographic research into the life of Louise Erdrich, and show how her true life cultural heritage is reflected in the characters, setting, and theme of her story "Snares." As an alternative, select the same assignment for Isaac Bashevis Singer and his story "Gimpel the Fool," or Yussef Idriss and his story "A House of Flesh."

Poetry

Anna Akhmatova

LOT'S WIFE

The just man followed then his angel guide
Where he strode on the black highway, hulking and bright;
But a wild grief in his wife's bosom cried,
Look back, it is not too late for a last sight

Of the red towers of your native Sodom, the square   5
Where once you sang, the gardens you shall mourn,
And the tall house with empty windows where
You loved your husband and your babes were born.

She turned, and looking on the bitter view
Her eyes were welded shut by mortal pain;   10
Into transparent salt her body grew,
And her quick feet were rooted in the plain.

Who would waste tears upon her? Is she not
The least of our losses, this unhappy wife?
Yet in my heart she will not be forgot   15
Who, for a single glance, gave up her life.

Translated by Richard Wilbur

251

Al-Tutili

SEVILLE

I was bored with old Seville
And Seville was bored with me;
Had the city shared my skill
To invent abusive rhyme,
Rivals in invective, we   5
Would have had a lovely time.

So at last my weary heart
Could endure no more, and cried
It was time that we should part:
Water is much more purified   10
Than the dribble of a pool.

Translated by A. J. Arberry

QUESTIONS

1. Why does the poet want to leave Seville?
2. What can we infer about the personality of the poet?
3. When the poet says "Seville was bored with me," to what or whom is he referring? The city itself? Residents of the city? City life in general?
4. Al-Tutili was a Moorish poet who wrote sometime between A.D. 632–1050, in the southern Spanish city of Seville, then famous for its beauty and its arts. Poets competed with each other in poetry contests. This poem is called a *Zajal.* Discuss the rhyme scheme and compare or contrast it with the sonnet.

Paula Gunn Allen

WOMANWORK

some make potteries
some weave and spin
remember
the Woman/celebrate
webs and making   5
out of own flesh

earth
bowl and urn
to hold water
and ground corn   10
balanced on heads
and springs lifted
and rivers in our eyes
brown hands shaping
earth into earth   15
food for bodies
water for fields
they use old pots
broken   bits
fragments   20   to make new
castaway   mixed with clay
                                   it makes strong   25
                                   bowls, jars
                                   new
                                   She
                                   brought
                                   light   30
                                   we remember this
                                   as we make
                                   the water bowl
                                   broken
                                   marks the grandmother's grave   35
                                   so she will shape water
                                   for bowls
                                   for food growing
                                   for bodies
                                   eating   40
                                   at drink
                                   thank Her

Yehuda Amichai

THE SWEET BREAKDOWN
OF ABIGAIL

We hit her with little blows
like an egg for peeling.

Desperate, perfume-blows
She hits back at the world.

With pointed gigglings she takes revenge   5
For all that sadness.

And with hasty fallings-in-love,
Like hiccups of emotion.

Terrorist of sweetness
She fills bombs   10
With despair and cinnamon, cloves and love-splinters.

At night when she tears her jewelry
Off herself
There's great danger she won't know the limit
And will go on tearing and slashing away   15
All of her life.

Translated by Ted Hughes

Maya Angelou

TO A HUSBAND

Your voice at times a fist
    Tight in your throat
Jabs ceaselessly at phantoms
    In the room,
Your hand a carved and   5
    skimming boat
Goes down the Nile
    To point out Pharaoh's tomb.

You're Africa to me
    At brightest dawn.   10
The Congo's green and
    Copper's brackish hue,
A continent to build
    With Black Man's brawn.
I sit at home and see it all   15
    Through you.

Margaret Atwood

AGAINST STILL LIFE

Orange in the middle of a table:

It isn't enough
to walk around it
at a distance, saying
it's an orange: 5
nothing to do
with us, nothing
else: leave it alone

I want to pick it up
in my hand   10
I want to peel the
skin off; I want
more to be said to me
than just Orange:
want to be told   15
everything it has to say

And you, sitting across
the table, at a distance, with
your smile contained, and like the orange
in the sun; silent: 20

Your silence
isn't enough for me
now, no matter with what
contentment you fold
your hands together; I want   25
anything you can say
in the sunlight:

stories of your various
childhoods, aimless journeyings,
your loves; your articulate   30
skeleton; your posturings; your lies.

These orange silences
(sunlight and hidden smile)
make me want to
wrench you into saying: 35

now I'd crack your skull
like a walnut, split it like a pumpkin
to make you talk, or get
a look inside

But quietly: 40
if I take the orange
with care enough and hold it
gently

I may find
an egg   45
a sun
an orange moon
perhaps a skull; centre
of all energy
resting in my hand   50

can change it to
whatever I desire
it to be

and you, man, orange afternoon
lover, wherever   55
you sit across from me
(tables, trains, buses)

if I watch
quietly enough
and long enough   60

at last, you will say
(maybe without speaking)

(there are mountains
inside your skull
garden and chaos, ocean   65
and hurricane; certain
corners of rooms, portraits
of great-grandmothers, curtains
of a particular shade;
your deserts; your private   70
dinosaurs; the first
woman)

all I need to know:
tell me
everything   75
just as it was
from the beginning.

QUESTIONS

1. The poet does not seem satisfied with the man. What does she want that is not being fulfilled?
2. How is the man similar to the orange? What action would the poet do to both? What is the symbolic significance of this action?
3. The poet uses unusual imagery in describing what is inside the man's skull. What do the various images suggest?
4. What does the title of the poem signify or suggest?

Ingeborg Bachmann

THE GREAT FREIGHT

The great freight of the summer has been loaded.
The sun ship in the harbour waits the tide,
if behind you the seagull dives and cries.
The great freight of the summer has been loaded.

The sun-ship in the harbour waits the tide.   5
The unmasked smile of the lemurs treads
on the lips of the figureheads.
The sun-ship in the harbour waits the tide.

If behind you the seagull dives and cries,
from the west comes the order to sink from sight.   10
You will drown with open eyes in light,
if behind you the seagull dives and cries.

Translated by Bill Crisman

Aphra Behn

THE DEFIANCE

By Heaven 'tis false, I am not vain;
    And rather would the subject be
Of your indifference, or disdain,
    Than wit or raillery.

Take back the trifling praise you give,   5
    And pass it on some other fool,
Who may the injuring wit believe,
    That turns her into ridicule.

Tell her, she's witty, fair, and gay,
    With all the charms that can subdue: 10
Perhaps she'll credit what you say;
    But curse me if I do.

If your diversion you design,
    On my good-nature you have prest:
Or if you do intend it mine,   15
    You have mistook the jest.

Louise Bogan

CASSANDRA

To me, one silly task is like another.
I bare the shambling tricks of lust and pride.
This flesh will never give a child its mother,—
Song, like a wing, tears through my breast, my side,
And madness chooses out my voice again,   5
Again. I am the chosen no hand saves:
The shrieking heaven lifted over men,
Not the dumb earth, wherein they set their graves.

William Stanley Braithwaite

THE WATCHERS

Two women on the lone wet strand
  (The wind's out with a will to roam)
The waves wage war on rocks and sand,
  (And a ship is long due home.)

The sea sprays in the women's eyes—   5
  (Hearts can writhe like the sea's wild foam)
Lower descend the tempestuous skies,
  (For the wind's out with a will to roam.)

"O daughter, thine eyes be better than mine,"
  (The waves ascend high as yonder dome)   10
"North or south is there never a sign?"
  (And a ship is long due home.)

They watched there all the long night through—
  (The wind's out with a will to roam)
Wind and rain and sorrow for two,—   15
  (And heaven on the long reach home.)

Gwendolyn Brooks

THE BEAN EATERS

They eat beans mostly, this old yellow pair.
Dinner is a casual affair.
Plain chipware on a plain and creaking wood,
Tin flatware.

Two who are Mostly Good.   5
Two who have lived their day,
But keep on putting on their clothes
And putting things away.

And remembering . . .
Remembering, with twinklings and twinges,   10
As they lean over the beans in their rented back room that
            is full of beads and receipts and dolls and cloths,
            tobacco crumbs, vases and fringes.

Elizabeth Barrett Browning

IF THOU MUST LOVE ME,
LET IT BE FOR NAUGHT

If thou must love me, let it be for naught
Except for love's sake only. Do not say
"I love her for her smile—her look—her way
Of speaking gently—for a trick of thought
That falls in well with mine, and certes brought   5
A sense of pleasant ease on such a day"—
For these things in themselves, Belovéd, may
Be changed, or change for thee—and love, so wrought,
May be unwrought so. Neither love me for
Thine own dear pity's wiping my cheeks dry—   10
A creature might forget to weep, who bore
Thy comfort long, and lose thy love thereby!
But love me for love's sake, that evermore
Thou mayst love on, through love's eternity.

QUESTIONS

1. How does the speaker distinguish permanent love from temporary love?
2. How would you characterize the poet's diction? What words in particular are representative of this diction?
3. How reasonable or impossible is it to love the way the poet suggests one should love?

Robert Browning

MY LAST DUCHESS

Ferrara

That's my last Duchess painted on the wall,
Looking as if she were alive. I call
That piece a wonder, now: Frà Pandolf's hands
Worked busily a day, and there she stands.
Will't please you sit and look at her? I said   5
"Frà Pandolf" by design, for never read
Strangers like you that pictured countenance,
The depth and passion of its earnest glance,
But to myself they turned (since none puts by
The curtain I have drawn for you, but I)   10
And seemed as they would ask me, if they durst,
How such a glance came there; so, not the first
Are you to turn and ask thus Sir, 'twas not
Her husband's presence only, called that spot
Of joy into the Duchess' cheek: perhaps   15
Frà Pandolf chanced to say "Her mantle laps
Over my lady's wrist too much," or "Paint
Must never hope to reproduce the faint
Half-flush that dies along her throat": such stuff
Was courtesy, she thought, and cause enough   20
For calling up that spot of joy. She had
A heart—how shall I say?—too soon made glad,
Too easily impressed; she liked whate'er
She looked on, and her looks went everywhere.
Sir, 'twas all one! My favor at her breast,   25
The dropping of the daylight in the West,
The bough of cherries some officious fool
Broke in the orchard for her, the white mule
She rode with round the terrace—all and each
Would draw from her alike the approving speech,   30
Or blush, at least. She thanked men—good! but thanked
Somehow—I know not how—as if she ranked
My gift of a nine-hundred-years-old name
With anybody's gift. Who'd stoop to blame
This sort of trifling? Even had you skill   35
In speech—(which I have not)—to make your will
Quite clear to such an one, and say, "Just this
Or that in you disgusts me; here you miss,

Or there exceed the mark"—and if she let
Herself be lessoned so, nor plainly set   40
Her wits to yours, forsooth, and made excuse
—E'en then would be some stooping; and I choose
Never to stoop. Oh sir, she smiled, no doubt,
Whene'er I passed her; but who passed without
Much the same smile? This grew; I gave commands;   45
Then all smiles stopped together. There she stands
As if alive. Will't please you rise? We'll meet
The company below, then. I repeat,
The Count your master's known munificence
Is ample warrant that no just pretense   50
Of mine for dowry will be disallowed;
Though his fair daughter's self, as I avowed
At starting, is my object. Nay, we'll go
Together down, sir. Notice Neptune, though,
Taming a sea horse, thought a rarity,   55
Which Claus of Innsbruck cast in bronze for me!

George Gordon, Lord Byron

SHE WALKS IN BEAUTY

1

She walks in Beauty, like the night
  Of cloudless climes and starry skies;
And all that's best of dark and bright
  Meet in her aspect and her eyes:
Thus mellowed to that tender light   5
  Which Heaven to gaudy day denies.

2

One shade the more, one ray the less,
  Had half impaired the nameless grace
Which waves in every raven tress,
  Or softly lightens o'er her face;   10
Where thoughts serenely sweet express
  How pure, how dear their dwelling-place.

3

And on that cheek, and o'er that brow,
　So soft, so calm, yet eloquent,
The smiles that win, the tints that glow,　　　　　　15
　But tell of days in goodness spent,
A mind at peace with all below,
　A heart whose love is innocent!

So Chongju

POETICS

The sea women of Cheju
　diving for abalone deep in the sea
leave the very best of the shells they find
　stuck to the rocks deep down
in the water, to pluck and gather　　　　　　5
　the day their loves return.
The very best shellfish
　of poems too:
　　　　　　Leave them there!
What empty, aimless wandering　　　　　　10
　if every last one is gathered up.
Longing for the sea, just leave it there,
　this being a poet.
　　　　　　Translated by D. R. McCann

QUESTIONS

1. What is the central analogy the poet makes in the poem? Is it an apt analogy? Explain.
2. The poet says to leave one's best poems "there." Where is there?
3. What danger does the poet foresee in expressing all of oneself and holding nothing back?

Emily Dickinson

SHE ROSE TO
HIS REQUIREMENT

She rose to his Requirement—dropt
The Playthings of Her Life
To take the honorable Work
Of Woman, and of Wife—

If ought She missed in Her new Day,   5
Of Amplitude, or Awe—
Or first Prospective—Or the Gold
In using, wear away,

It lay unmentioned—as the Sea
Develop Pearl, and Weed,   10
But only to Himself—be known
The Fathoms they abide—

WILD NIGHTS—
WILD NIGHTS!

Wild Nights—Wild Nights!
Were I with thee
Wild Nights should be
Our Luxury!

Futile—the Winds—   5
To a Heart in port—
Done with the Compass—
Done with the Chart!

Rowing in Eden—
Ah, the Sea!
Might I but moor—Tonight—   10
In Thee!

John Donne

THE BAIT

Come, live with me, and be my love,
And we will some new pleasures prove,
Of golden sands, and crystal brooks,
With silken lines, and silver hooks.

There will the river whisp'ring run,   5
Warm'd by thy eyes more than the sun;
And there the enamoured fish will stay,
Begging themselves they may betray.

When thou wilt swim in that live bath,
Each fish, which every channel hath,   10
Most amorously to thee will swim,
Gladder to catch thee, than thou him.

If thou, to be so seen, beest loath
By sun or moon, thou dark'nest both;
And if mine eyes have leave to see,   15
I need not their light, having thee.

Let others freeze with angling reeds,
And cut their legs with shells and weeds,
Or treacherously poor fish beset
With strangling snares or windowy net;   20

Let coarse bold hands, from slimy nest,
The bedded fish in banks outwrest;
Or curious traitors, sleave-silk flies,
Bewitch poor fishes' wand'ring eyes.

For thee, thou need'st no such deceit,   25
For thou thyself art thine own bait;
That fish, that is not catch'd thereby,
Is wiser far, alas, than I.

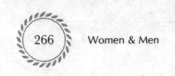

Rita Dove

ADOLESCENCE—II

Although it is night, I sit in the bathroom, waiting.
Sweat prickles behind my knees, the baby-breasts are alert.
Venetian blinds slice up the moon; the tiles quiver in pale strips.

Then they come, the three seal men with eyes as round
As dinner plates and eyelashes like sharpened tines.   5
They bring the scent of licorice. One sits in the washbowl,

One on the bathtub edge; one leans against the door.
"Can you feel it yet?" they whisper.
I don't know what to say, again. They chuckle,

Patting their sleek bodies with their hands.   10
"Well, maybe next time." And they rise,
Glittering like pools of ink under moonlight,

And vanish. I clutch at the ragged holes
They leave behind, here at the edge of darkness.
Night rests like a ball of fur on my tongue.   15

QUESTIONS

1. What aspect or aspects of adolescent experience is the poet suggesting? What clues
   are provided that helped you reach your conclusion?
2. Study the many images of water in the poem. What might these images symbolize?
3. Examine the way the men are described. What do they mean by "Can you feel it
   yet?" How does their presence make the narrator feel?

Alan Dugan

LOVE SONG:
I AND THOU

Nothing is plumb, level or square:
   the studs are bowed, the joists
are shaky by nature, no piece fits
   any other piece without a gap
or pinch, and bent nails   5
   dance all over the surfacing
like maggots. By Christ
   I am no carpenter. I built
the roof for myself, the walls
   for myself, the floors   10
for myself, and got
   hung up in it myself. I
danced with a purple thumb
   at this house-warming, drunk
with my prime whiskey: rage.   15
   Oh I spat rage's nails
into the frame-up of my work:
   it held. It settled plumb,
level, solid, square and true
   for that great moment. Then   20
it screamed and went on through,
   skewing as wrong the other way.
God damned it. This is hell,
   but I planned it, I sawed it,
I nailed it, and I   25
   will live in it until it kills me.
I can nail my left palm
   to the left-hand cross-piece but
I can't do everything myself.
   I need a hand to nail the right,   30
a help, a love, a you, a wife.

T. S. Eliot

THE LOVE SONG OF J. ALFRED PRUFROCK

S'io credessi che mia risposta fosse
a persona che mai tornasse al mondo,
questa fiamma staria senza più scosse.
Ma per ció che giammai di questo fondo
non tornó vivo alcun, s'i'odo il vero,
senza tema d'infamia ti rispondo. *

Let us go then, you and I,
When the evening is spread out against the sky
Like a patient etherised upon a table;
Let us go, through certain half-deserted streets,
The muttering retreats   5
Of restless nights in one-night cheap hotels
And sawdust restaurants with oyster-shells:
Streets that follow like a tedious argument
Of insidious intent
To lead you to an overwhelming question . . .   10
Oh, do not ask, 'What is it?'
Let us go and make our visit.

In the room the women come and go
Talking of Michelangelo.

The yellow fog that rubs its back upon the window-panes,   15
The yellow smoke that rubs its muzzle on the window-panes,
Licked its tongue into the corners of the evening,
Lingered upon the pools that stand in drains,
Let fall upon its back the soot that falls from chimneys,
Slipped by the terrace, made a sudden leap,   20
And seeing that it was a soft October night,
Curled once about the house, and fell asleep.

And indeed there will be time
For the yellow smoke that slides along the street
Rubbing its back upon the window-panes;   25
There will be time, there will be time

---

*Epigraph: "If I thought my answer were to one who would never return to the world, this flame would shake
no more; but since no one did ever return alive from this depth, if what I hear be true, without fear of infamy
I answer you." (Inferno 27:61–66)

To prepare a face to meet the faces that you meet;
There will be time to murder and create,
And time for all the works and days of hands
That lift and drop a question on your plate;   30
Time for you and time for me,
And time yet for a hundred indecisions,
And for a hundred visions and revisions,
Before the taking of a toast and tea.

In the room the women come and go   35
Talking of Michelangelo.

And indeed there will be time
To wonder, 'Do I dare?' and, 'Do I dare?'
Time to turn back and descend the stair,
With a bald spot in the middle of my hair—   40
(They will say: 'How his hair is growing thin!')
My morning coat, my collar mounting firmly to the chin,
My necktie rich and modest, but asserted by a simple pin—
(They will say: "But how his arms and legs are thin!')
Do I dare   45
Disturb the universe?
In a minute there is time
For decisions and revisions which a minute will reverse.

For I have known them all already, known them all—
Have known the evenings, mornings, afternoons,   50
I have measured out my life with coffee spoons;
I know the voices dying with a dying fall
Beneath the music from a farther room.
    So how should I presume?

And I have known the eyes already, known them all—   55
The eyes that fix you in a formulated phrase,
And when I am formulated, sprawling on a pin,
When I am pinned and wriggling on the wall,
Then how should I begin
To spit out all the butt-ends of my days and ways?   60
    And how should I presume?

And I have known the arms already, known them all—
Arms that are braceleted and white and bare
(But in the lamplight, downed with light brown hair!)
Is it perfume from a dress   65
That makes me so digress?

Arms that lie along a table, or wrap about a shawl.
  And should I then presume?
  And how should I begin?

    . . . . .

Shall I say, I have gone at dusk through narrow streets   70
And watched the smoke that rises from the pipes
Of lonely men in shirt-sleeves, leaning out of windows? . . .
I should have been a pair of ragged claws
Scuttling across the floors of silent seas.

    . . . . .

And the afternoon, the evening, sleeps so peacefully!   75
Smoothed by long fingers,
Asleep . . . tired . . . or it malingers,
Stretched on the floor, here beside you and me.
Should I, after tea and cakes and ices,
Have the strength to force the moment to its crisis?   80
But though I have wept and fasted, wept and prayed,
Though I have seen my head (grown slightly bald) brought in upon a platter,
I am no prophet—and here's no great matter;
I have seen the moment of my greatness flicker,
And I have seen the eternal Footman hold my coat, and snicker,   85
And in short, I was afraid.

And would it have been worth it, after all,
After the cups, the marmalade, the tea,
Among the porcelain, among some talk of you and me,
Would it have been worth while,   90
To have bitten off the matter with a smile,
To have squeezed the universe into a ball
To roll it towards some overwhelming question,
To say: 'I am Lazarus, come from the dead,
Come back to tell you all, I shall tell you all'—   95
If one, settling a pillow by her head,
  Should say: 'That is not what I meant at all.
  That is not it, at all.'
And would it have been worth it, after all,
Would it have been worth while,   100
After the sunsets and the dooryards and the sprinkled streets,
After the novels, after the teacups, after the skirts that trail along the floor—
And this, and so much more?—
It is impossible to say just what I mean!
But as if a magic lantern threw the nerves in patterns on a screen: 105
Would it have been worth while
If one, settling a pillow or throwing off a shawl,

And turning toward the window, should say:
  'That is not it at all,
  That is not what I meant, at all.'   110
   . . . . .

No! I am not Prince Hamlet, nor was meant to be;
Am an attendant lord, one that will do
To swell a progress, start a scene or two,
Advise the prince; no doubt, an easy tool,
Deferential, glad to be of use,   115
Politic, cautious, and meticulous;
Full of high sentence, but a bit obtuse;
At times, indeed, almost ridiculous —
Almost, at times, the Fool.

I grow old . . . I grow old . . .   120
I shall wear the bottoms of my trousers rolled.

Shall I part my hair behind? Do I dare to eat a peach?
I shall wear white flannel trousers, and walk upon the beach.
I have heard the mermaids singing, each to each.

I do not think that they will sing to me.   125

I have seen them riding seaward on the waves
Combing the white hair of the waves blown back
When the wind blows the water white and black.

We have lingered in the chambers of the sea
By sea-girls wreathed with seaweed red and brown   130
Till human voices wake us, and we drown.

QUESTIONS

1. What is the irony in the title? What seems to be the narrator's attitude toward love?
2. What emotional tone pervades the poem? What are some salient images that reflect this tone?
3. What type of man is the narrator? What is his outlook on his own life? What clues do we get from the line "I am not Prince Hamlet, nor was meant to be"? What is the narrator's outlook on human existence in general?
4. There are two sections of the poem that employ animal imagery. What kind of animals are being suggested? What is the effect of using these two images?
5. At the time of its publication, this poem caused quite a stir in the literary world, owing to the way the narrator depicts and evaluates his life. Why might this be?

Forūgh Farrokhzād

BORN AGAIN

One dark word is all I am
uttering you again and again
until you wake where you blossom forever

In this word I breathed you, breathed
and in this word bound you   5
to trees, water, flame

Life may be
a street she walks down every long day, a basket in her hand
Life may be
the rope over the limb he hangs himself with   10
Life may be a child home from school

Life may be lighting a cigarette in the languid pause of lovemaking

Or the pedestrian's void gaze
as he tips his hat to another's
void smile, saying, Good morning   15

Life may be that sealed moment
when my gaze disintegrates in the lens of your eyes
and I know myself
sensing the moon in me, and joined to darkness

In a room measured by solitude   20
my heart
measured by love
finds ordinary excuses for its happiness
the lovely lapse of flowers vased
the sapling you set in our yard   25
the canaries' cantilena
their singing fills the window

Ah . . .
This has fallen to me
This has fallen to me   30
This to me
A sky a curtain shrouds

The descent of a broken stair
Marriage to exile and rot
My lot pacing the sad gardens of memory   35
Dying sorrowing, a voice saying to me:
I love
your hands

In the garden I plant my hands
I know I shall grow, I know, I know   40
swallows will lay their eggs
in the nest of my inkstained fingers
twin pairs of bright cherries
will be my earrings
and dahlia petals dress my fingernails   45

There's a certain lane where
boys with the same tousled hair, thin necks and scrawny legs
who loved me once still
recall the simple smile of a girl
swept away one night by the wind   50

A certain lane my heart stole
from my childhood's quarter

A body wanders time's arid trajectory
If only that body could make that barren path conceive it
A body conscious of an image   55
Emerging from the festal mirror

And that's how
one dies
how one lingers on

No diver will ever fetch a pearl from the well a brooklet drowns in   60

I
know a sad little nymph
who lives in the sea
and plays the wooden flute of her heart
tenderly, tenderly   65
sad little nymph
dying at night of a kiss
and by a kiss reborn each day

Translated by Jascha Kessler with Amin Banani

Joy Harjo

FISHING

This is the longest day of the year, on the Illinois River or a similar river in
the same place. Cicadas are part of the song as they praise their invisible
ancestors while fish blinking back the relentless sun in Oklahoma circle in
the muggy river of life. They dare the fisher to come and get them. Fish too
anticipate the game of fishing. Their ancestors perfected the moves, sent   5
down stories that appear as electrical impulse when sunlight hits water.
The hook carries great symbology in the coming of age, and is crucial to
the making of warriors. The greatest warriors are those who dangle a
human for hours on a string, break sacred water for the profanity of air
then snap fiercely back into pearly molecules that describe fishness. They   10
smell me as I walk the banks with fishing pole, nightcrawlers and a
promise I made to that old friend Louis to fish with him this summer. This
is the only place I can keep that promise, inside a poem as familiar to him
as the banks of his favorite fishing place. I try not to let the fish see me see
them as they look for his tracks on the soft earth made of fossils and ashes.   15
I hear the burble of fish talk: When is that old Creek coming back? He
was the one we loved to tease most, we liked his songs and once in awhile
he gave us a good run. Last night I dreamed I tried to die, I was going to
look for Louis. It was rather comical. I worked hard to muster my last
breath, then lay down in the summer, along the banks of the last mythic   20
river, my pole and tackle box next to me. What I thought was my last
breath floated off as a cloud making an umbrella of grief over my relatives.
How embarrassing when the next breath came, and then the next. I reeled
in one after another, as if I'd caught a bucket of suckers instead of bass. I
guess it wasn't my time, I explained, and went fishing anyway as a liar   25
and I know most fishers to be liars most of the time. Even Louis when it
came to fishing, or even dying. The leap between the sacred and profane is
as thin as a fishing line, and is part of the mystery on this river of life, as is
the way our people continue to make warriors in the strangest of times. I
save this part of the poem for the fish camp next to the oldest spirits whose   30
dogs bark to greet visitors. It's near Louis's favorite spot where the wisest
and fattest fish laze. I'll meet him there.

Seamus Heaney

SUNLIGHT

There was a sunlit absence.
The helmeted pump in the yard
heated its iron,
water honeyed

in the slung bucket   5
and the sun stood
like a griddle cooling
against the wall

of each long afternoon.
So, her hands scuffled   10
over the bakeboard,
the reddening stove

sent its plaque of heat
against her where she stood
in a floury apron   15
by the window.

Now she dusts the board
with a goose's wing,
now sits, broad-lapped,
with whitened nails   20

and measling shins:
here is a space
again, the scone rising
to the tick of two clocks.

And here is love   25
like a tinsmith's scoop
sunk past its gleam
in the meal-bin.

Robert Herrick

TO THE VIRGINS,
TO MAKE MUCH OF TIME

Gather ye rosebuds while ye may,
    Old Time is still a-flying;
And this same flower that smiles today
    Tomorrow will be dying.

The glorious lamp of heaven, the Sun,   5
    The higher he's a-getting,
The sooner will his race be run,
    And nearer he's to setting.

That age is best which is the first,
    When youth and blood are warmer;   10
But being spent, the worse, and worst
    Times still succeed the former.

Then be not coy, but use your time;
    And while ye may, go marry;
For having lost but once your prime,   15
    You may forever tarry.

QUESTIONS

1. What is the theme of the poem? Is it as apt today as it was when the poet wrote it in the seventeenth century?
2. What words and syntax indicate that the poem is not contemporary?
3. Read the poem aloud several times. How does the author use sound to enhance the effect of the poem? What is the effect of rhyme on the poem?

Henry Howard

TO HIS LADY

Set me whereas the sun doth parch the green,
  Or where his beams may not dissolve the ice,
In temperate heat, where he is felt and seen,
  With proud people, in presence sad and wise;
Set me in base, or yet in high degree,   5
  In the long night, or in the shortest day,
In clear weather, or where mists thickest be,
  In lofty youth, or when my hairs be gray;
Set me in earth, in heaven, or yet in hell,
  In hill, in dale, or in the foaming flood,   10
Thrall, or at large, alive whereso I dwell,
  Sick, or in health, in ill fame, or in good;
    Yours will I be, and with that only thought
    Comfort myself when that my hap is nought.

Ben Jonson

TO CELIA

Come my *Celia,* let us prove,
While we may, the sports of love;
Time will not be ours, for ever:
He, at length, our good will sever.
Spend not then his gifts in vain.   5
Sunnes, that set, may rise again:
But if once we lose this light,
'Tis, with us, perpetual night.
Why should we defer our joys?
Fame, and rumor are but toys.   10
Cannot we delude the eyes
Of a few poor houshold spys?
Or his easier ears beguile,
So removed by our wile?

June Jordan

THE WEDDING

Tyrone married her this afternoon
not smiling as he took the aisle
and her slightly rough hand.
Dizzella listened to the minister
staring at his wrist and twice   5
forgetting her name:
Do you promise to obey?
Will you honor humility and love
as poor as you are?
Tyrone stood small but next   10
to her person
trembling. Tyrone stood
straight and bony
black alone with one key
in his pocket.   15
By marrying today
they made themselves a man
and woman
answered friends or unknown
curious about the Cadillacs   20
displayed in front of Beaulah Baptist.
Beaulah Baptist
life in general
indifferent
barely known   25

QUESTIONS

1. How would you characterize the mood of the wedding day? What images, in
   particular, suggest this mood?
2. What is the significance of the "one key" in Tyrone's pocket?
3. What is the poet implying about the effect of poverty on the emotional life of the
   bride and groom? Of "life in general" in Beaulah Baptist Church?

Maxine Kumin

TOGETHER

The water closing
over us and the
going down is all.
Gills are given.
We convert in a   5
town of broken hulls
and green doubloons.
O you dead pirates
hear us! There is
no salvage. All   10
you know is the color
of warm caramel. All
is salt. See how
our eyes have migrated
to the uphill side?   15
Now we are new round
mouths and no spines
letting the water cover.
It happens over
and over, me in   20
your body and you
in mine.

Denise Levertov

ABOUT MARRIAGE

Don't lock me in wedlock, I want
marriage, an
encounter—

I told you about the
green light of   5
May

  (a veil of quiet befallen
  the downtown park,
  late

Saturday after   10
noon, long
shadows and cool

air, scent of
new grass,
fresh leaves,   15

blossom on the threshold of
abundance

and the birds I met there,
birds of passage breaking their journey,
three birds each of a different species: 20

the azalea-breasted with round poll, dark,
the brindled, merry, mousegliding one,
and the smallest, golden as gorse and wearing
a black Venetian mask

and with them the three douce hen-birds   25
feathered in tender, lively brown—

I stood
a half-hour under the enchantment,
no-one passed near,
the birds saw me and   30

let me be
near them.)

It's not
irrelevant:
I would be   35
met

and meet you
so,
in a green

airy space, not   40
locked in.

THE ACHE OF MARRIAGE

The ache of marriage:

thigh and tongue, beloved,
are heavy with it,
it throbs in the teeth

We look for communion   5
and are turned away, beloved,
each and each

It is leviathan and we
in its belly
looking for joy, some joy   10
not to be known outside it

two by two in the ark of
the ache of it.

Shirley Geok-lin Lim

AH MAH

Grandmother was smaller
than me at eight. Had she
been child forever?

Helpless, hopeless, chin sharp
as a knuckle, fan face   5
hardly half-opened, not a scrap

of fat anywhere: she tottered
in black silk, leaning on
handmaids, on two tortured

fins. At sixty, his sons all   10
married, grandfather bought her,
Soochow flower song girl.

Every bone in her feet
had been broken, bound tighter
than any neighbor's sweet   15

daughter's. Ten toes and instep
curled inwards, yellow petals
of chrysanthemum, wrapped

in gold cloth. He bought the young
face, small knobby breasts   20
he swore he'd not dress in sarong

of maternity. Each night
he held her feet in his palms,
like lotus in the tight

hollows of celestial lakes.   25
In his calloused flesh, her
weightless soles, cool and slack,

clenched in his stranger's fever.

QUESTIONS

1. The poet provides a physical description of her grandmother as well as clues to her personality and emotional life. How are all these elements similar?
2. What aspects of the poem suggest the cultural milieu of the couple? What tone does the poet seem to adopt in describing this milieu? Which words suggest it and why?
3. What is the grandmother's relationship to the world she lives in? To her husband, in particular?

Amy Lowell
THE TAXI

When I go away from you
The world beats dead
Like a slackened drum.
I call out for you against the jutted stars
And shout into the ridges of the wind.   5
Streets coming fast,
One after the other,
Wedge you away from me,
And the lamps of the city prick my eyes
So that I can no longer see your face.   10
Why should I leave you,
To wound myself upon the sharp edges of the night?

Andrew Marvell
TO HIS COY MISTRESS

Had we but world enough, and time,
This coyness, lady, were no crime.
We would sit down, and think which way
To walk, and pass our long love's day.
Thou by the Indian Ganges' side   5
Should'st rubies find: I by the tide
Of Humber would complain. I would
Love you ten years before the Flood,
And you should, if you please, refuse
Till the conversion of the Jews,   10
My vegetable love should grow
Vaster than empires, and more slow,
An hundred years should go to praise
Thine eyes, and on thy forehead gaze:
Two hundred to adore each breast: 15
But thirty thousand to the rest;
An age at least to every part,
And the last age should show your heart.

For, lady, you deserve this state,
Nor would I love at lower rate.   20
    But at my back I always hear
Time's wingèd chariot hurrying near;
And yonder all before us lie
Deserts of vast eternity.
Thy beauty shall no more be found,   25
Nor in thy marble vault shall sound
My echoing song; then worms shall try
That long preserved virginity,
And your quaint honor turn to dust,
And into ashes all my lust.   30
The grave's a fine and private place,
But none, I think, do there embrace.
    Now therefore, while the youthful hue
Sits on thy skin like morning dew,
And while thy willing soul transpires   35
At every pore with instant fires,
Now let us sport us while we may;
And now, like am'rous birds of prey,
Rather at once our time devour,
Than languish in his slow-chapped power.   40
Let us roll all our strength, and all
Our sweetness, up into one ball;
And tear our pleasures with rough strife
Thorough the iron gates of life.
Thus, though we cannot make our sun   45
Stand still, yet we will make him run.

Annette M'Baye

SILHOUETTE

for Henriette Bathily

Behind, sun, before, shadow!
A watergourd on a stately head,
A breast, a strip of loincloth fluttering,
Two feet that erase the pattern on the sand.
                    Translated by Kathleen Weaver

Josephine Miles

HOUSEWIFE

Occasional mornings when an early fog
Not yet dispersed stands in every yard
And drips and undiscloses, she is severely
Put to the task of herself.

Usually here we have view window dawns,   5
The whole East Bay at least some spaces into the room,
Puffing the curtains, and then she is out
In the submetropolitan stir.

But when the fog at the glass pauses and closes
She is put to ponder   10
A life-line, how it chooses to run obscurely
In her hand, before her.

QUESTIONS

1. How does the title provide us with a clue to the woman's life? Would your response
   to and interpretation of the poem have been different had there been no title?
2. What is the effect of the fog on the woman? What does it reveal about the woman's
   own conception of her role in life?
3. What does the poet mean by "Put to the task of herself"? What is the woman "put
   to ponder"? How are these two lines related?
4. Compare and contrast the description of the fog and its effect on the woman with
   the description and effect of the fog in "The Love Song of J. Alfred Prufrock."

Nancy Morejón

CENTRAL PARK
SOME PEOPLE (3 P.M.)

he who crosses a park in great and flourishing Havana
amidst a flood of blinding white light
a white and blinding light
which would have driven that Van Gogh's sunflower mad

that blinding white light   5
which fills the Chinese eyes of the Chinese street photographers
he who crosses a park and doesn't understand
that blinding white light that almost repeats itself
he who is at a loss at that time of day
takes all kinds of roundabout and unnecessary   10
sojourns around Havana's Central Park
he who crosses a park strewn with sacred trees
who walks through it with open yet closed eyes
loving the Revolution's impact on the eyes
the impact he felt in his eyes and waist   15
he who is sustained by that light might know about the night and the wine

because in parks and in this one so central the one in Havana
old men sit on benches
light cigars look at each other
and talk about the Revolution and Fidel   20
the old men who now remain on the benches
and are forever basking in the sun
it is a secret to no one
there go two men and an old worn-out briefcase
a fat bloated hand a shout wearing a grey hat   25
the old men meet next to the statue
of the Apostle Martí in 1966 in December of 1966
the year nearly over and waiting for
'the anniversary of freedom and paying tribute to the martyrs'
yes for all the men of the people who died and their blood   30
to bask in the afternoon sun in Havana Cuba free territory of America
he who crosses the park this world the womb of the Revolution in this
    manner

must sigh and walk slowly and breathe
and step lightly and sigh and breathe and walk slowly   35
and forfeit his whole life
rabidly
        compañeros

                                        Translated by Sylvia Carranza

Papyrus Harris 500

BEGINNING OF THE SONGS OF DELIGHT

1

Portulaca: apportioned to you is my heart,
I do for you what it desires,
When I am in your arms.
My longing for you is my eye-paint,
When I see you my eyes shine;   5
I press close to you to look at you,
Beloved of men, who rules my heart!
O happiness of this hour,
Let the hour go on forever!
Since I have lain with you,   10
You raised up my heart;
Be it sad or gay,
Do not leave me!

2

Saam-plants here summon us,
I am your sister, your best one;   15
I belong to you like this plot of ground
That I planted with flowers
And sweet-smelling herbs.
Sweet is its stream,
Dug by your hand,   20
Refreshing in the northwind.
A lovely place to wander in,
Your hand in my hand.
My body thrives, my heart exults
At our walking together;   25
Hearing your voice is pomegranate wine,
I live by hearing it.
Each look with which you look at me
Sustains me more than food and drink.

Pepi I Pyramid Texts

UTTERANCE 446

Sarcophagus Chamber, West Wall

The sky-goddess protects the king

O Osiris Pepi,
Nut, your mother, spreads herself above you,
She conceals you from all evil,
Nut protects you from all evil,
You, the greatest of her children!

Octavio Paz

ENGAGED

Stretched out on the grass
a boy and a girl.
Sucking their oranges, giving their kisses
like waves exchanging foam.

Stretched out on the beach   5
a boy and a girl.
Sucking their limes, giving their kisses,
like clouds exchanging foam.

Stretched out underground
a boy and a girl.   10
Saying nothing, never kissing,
giving silence for silence.

Translated by Muriel Rukeyser

QUESTIONS

1. Compare and contrast the first two stanzas with the last. Do they conflict or complement or both? Explain.

2. What is suggested by the word *underground?*
3. Many phrases and words are repeated in the poem. How can you tie this use of repetition to the title?

Katherine Philips

AGAINST LOVE

Hence, Cupid! with your cheating toys,
Your real Griefs, and painted Joys,
Your Pleasure which itself destroys.
Lovers like men in fevers burn and rave,
And only what will injure them do crave.   5
Men's weakness makes Love so severe,
They give him power by their fear,
And make the shackles which they wear.
    Who to another does his heart submit;
    Makes his own Idol, and then worships it.   10
Him whose heart is all his own,
Peace and liberty does crown;
He apprehends no killing frown.
    He feels no raptures which are joys diseas'd,
    And is not much transported, but still pleas'd.   15

Sylvia Plath

THE APPLICANT

First, are you our sort of a person?
Do you wear
A glass eye, false teeth or a crutch,
A brace or a hook,
Rubber breasts or a rubber crotch,   5

Stitches to show something's missing? No, no? Then
How can we give you a thing?
Stop crying.

Open your hand.
Empty? Empty. Here is a hand   10

To fill it and willing
To bring teacups and roll away headaches
And do whatever you tell it.
Will you marry it?
It is guaranteed   15

To thumb shut your eyes at the end
And dissolve of sorrow.
We make new stock from the salt.
I notice you are stark naked.
How about this suit—   20

Black and stiff, but not a bad fit.
Will you marry it?
It is waterproof, shatterproof, proof
Against fire and bombs through the roof.
Believe me, they'll bury you in it.   25

Now your head, excuse me, is empty.
I have the ticket for that.
Come here, sweetie, out of the closet.
Well, what do you think of *that?*
Naked as paper to start   30

But in twenty-five years she'll be silver,
In fifty, gold.
A living doll, everywhere you look.
It can sew, it can cook,
It can talk, talk, talk.   35

It works, there is nothing wrong with it.
You have a hole, it's a poultice.
You have an eye, it's an image.
My boy, it's your last resort.
Will you marry it, marry it, marry it.   40

Ezra Pound

A VIRGINAL

No, no! Go from me. I have left her lately.
I will not spoil my sheath with lesser brightness,
For my surrounding air hath a new lightness;
Slight are her arms, yet they have bound me straitly
And left me cloaked as with a gauze of aether;   5
As with sweet leaves; as with subtle clearness.
Oh, I have picked up magic in her nearness
To sheathe me half in half the things that sheathe her.
No, no! Go from me. I have still the flavour,
Soft as spring wind that's come from birchen bowers.   10
Green come the shoots, aye April in the branches,
As winter's wound with her sleight hand she staunches,
Hath of the trees a likeness of the savour;
As white their bark, so white this lady's hours.

THE RIVER-MERCHANT'S WIFE: A LETTER

While my hair was still cut straight across my forehead
I played about the front gate, pulling flowers.
You came by on bamboo stilts, playing horse,
You walked about my seat, playing with blue plums.
And we went on living in the village of Chokan: 5
Two small people, without dislike or suspicion.

At fourteen I married My Lord you.
I never laughed, being bashful.
Lowering my head, I looked at the wall.
Called to, a thousand times, I never looked back.   10

At fifteen I stopped scowling,
I desired my dust to be mingled with yours
For ever and for ever and for ever.
Why should I climb the look out?
At sixteen you departed,   15
You went into far Ku-to-yen, by the river of swirling eddies,
And you have been gone five months.
The monkeys make sorrowful noise overhead.

You dragged your feet when you went out.
By the gate now, the moss is grown, the different mosses,   20
Too deep to clear them away!
The leaves fall early this autumn, in wind.
The paired butterflies are already yellow with August
Over the grass in the West garden;
They hurt me. I grow older.   25
If you are coming down through the narrows of the river Kiang,
Please let me know beforehand,
And I will come out to meet you
                        As far as Cho-fu-Sa.

QUESTIONS

1. What emotional transformation does the narrator of the poem undergo during the course of the poem?
2. Why does the narrator call her husband "My Lord you"? What does it reveal about their relationship?
3. What is the tone of the poem? What particular words and images contribute to the tone? Does the tone change during the poem or does it remain constant throughout? Explain.
4. What does the line "Why should I climb the look out" mean? Is it meant to be taken literally, figuratively, or both?

Ibn Quzman

THE RADISH

The radish is a good
And doubtless wholesome food,
But proves, to vex the eater,
A powerful repeater.

This only fault I find: 5
What should be left behind
Comes issuing instead
Right from the eater's head!

Adrienne Rich
I COME HOME FROM YOU

I come home from you through the early light of spring
flashing off ordinary walls, the Pez Dorado,
the Discount Wares, the shoe-store. . . . I'm lugging my sack
of groceries, I dash for the elevator
where a man, taut, elderly, carefully composed   5
lets the door almost close on me.—*For god's sake hold it!*
I croak at him.—*Hysterical,*—he breathes my way.
I let myself into the kitchen, unload my bundles,
make coffee, open the window, put on Nina Simone
singing *Here comes the sun.* . . . I open the mail,   10
drinking delicious coffee, delicious music,
my body still both light and heavy with you. The mail
lets fall, a Xerox of something written by a man
aged 27, a hostage, tortured in prison:
My genitals have been the object of such a sadistic display   15
they keep me constantly awake with the pain . . .
Do whatever you can to survive.
You know, I think that men love wars . . .
And my incurable anger, my unmendable wounds
break open further with tears, I am crying helplessly,   20
And they still control the world, and you are not in my arms.

AUGUST

Two horses in yellow light
eating windfall apples under a tree

as summer tears apart   milkweeds stagger
and grasses grow more ragged

They say there are ions in the sun   5
neutralizing magnetic fields on earth

Some way to explain
what this week has been, and the one before it!

If I am flesh sunning on rock
if I am brain burning in fluorescent light   10

if I am dream like a wire with fire
throbbing along it

if I am death to man
I have to know it

His mind is too simple, I cannot go on   15
sharing his nightmares

My own are becoming clearer, they open
into prehistory

which looks like a village lit with blood
where all the fathers are crying: *My son is mine!*   20

Theodore Roethke

I KNEW A WOMAN

I knew a woman, lovely in her bones,
When small birds sighed, she would sigh back at them;
Ah, when she moved, she moved more ways than one:
The shapes a bright container can contain!
Of her choice virtues only gods should speak,   5
Or English poets who grew up on Greek
(I'd have them sing in chorus, cheek to cheek).

How well her wishes went! She stroked my chin,
She taught me Turn, and Counter-turn, and Stand;
She taught me Touch, that undulant white skin;   10
I nibbled meekly from her proffered hand;
She was the sickle; I, poor I, the rake,
Coming behind her for her pretty sake;
(But what prodigious mowing we did make).

Love likes a gander, and adores a goose: 15
Her full lips pursed, the errant note to seize;
She played it quick, she played it light and loose;
My eyes, they dazzled at her flowing knees;

Her several parts could keep a pure repose,
Or one hip quiver with a mobile nose   20
(She moved in circles, and those circles moved).

Let seed be grass, and grass turn into hay:
I'm martyr to a motion not my own;
What's freedom for? To know eternity.
I swear she cast a shadow white as stone.   25
But who would count eternity in days?
These old bones live to learn her wanton ways:
(I measure time by how a body sways).

Anne Sexton

THE BLACK ART

A woman who writes feels too much,
those trances and portents!
As if cycles and children and islands
weren't enough; as if mourners and gossips
and vegetables were never enough.   5
She thinks she can warn the stars.
A writer is essentially a spy.
Dear love, I am that girl.

A man who writes knows too much,
such spells and fetiches!   10
As if erections and congresses and products
weren't enough; as if machines and galleons
and wars were never enough.
With used furniture he makes a tree.
A writer is essentially a crook.   15
Dear love, you are that man.

Never loving ourselves,
hating even our shoes and our hats,
we love each other, *precious, precious.*
Our hands are light blue and gentle.   20
Our eyes are full of terrible confessions.

But when we marry,
the children leave in disgust
There is too much food and no one left over
to eat up all the weird abundance.   25

QUESTIONS

1. According to the poet, what is the primary difference between a female poet and a male poet? Between men and women in general?
2. To whom does the line "Never loving ourselves" refer?
3. Why do "the children leave in disgust"? What is the "food" in the last sentence?
4. What seems to be the poet's general view of marriage?

William Shakespeare

LET ME NOT TO THE MARRIAGE OF TRUE MINDS

Let me not to the marriage of true minds
Admit impediments. Love is not love
Which alters when it alteration finds,
Or bends with the remover to remove:
O, no; it is an ever-fixèd mark,   5
That looks on tempests and is never shaken:
It is the star to every wandering bark,
Whose worth's unknown, although his height be taken.
Love's not Time's fool, though rosy lips and cheeks
Within his bending sickle's compass come;   10
Love alters not with his brief hours and weeks,
But bears it out even to the edge of doom.
    If this be error and upon me proved,
    I never writ, nor no man ever loved.

SHALL I COMPARE THEE TO A SUMMER'S DAY?

Shall I compare thee to a summer's day?
Thou art more lovely and more temperate,
Rough winds do shake the darling buds of May,
And summer's lease hath all too short a date.
Sometime too hot the eye of heaven shines,   5
And often is his gold complexion dimm'd;
And every fair from fair sometime declines,
By chance, or nature's changing course, untrimm'd;
But thy eternal summer shall not fade
Nor lose possession of that fair thou ow'st,   10
Nor shall Death brag thou wand'rest in his shade
When in eternal lines to time thou grow'st.
   So long as men can breathe or eyes can see,
   So long lives this, and this gives life to thee.

Sir Philip Sidney

WITH HOW SAD STEPS, O MOON

With how sad steps, O Moon, thou climb'st the skies,
How silently, and with how wan a face!
What! may it be that even in heav'nly place
That busy archer his sharp arrows tries?
Sure, if that long-with-love-acquainted eyes   5
Can judge of love, thou feel'st a lover's case.
I read it in thy looks; thy languisht grace
To me, that feel the like, thy state descries.
Then, ev'n of fellowship, O Moon, tell me,
Is constant love deem'd there but want of wit?   10
Are beauties there as proud as here they be?
Do they above love to be lov'd, and yet
Those lovers scorn whom that love doth possess?
Do they call virtue there ungratefulness?

Mohan Singh

EVENING

The sun horse panting and snorting
Reaches the shores of evening
Kicking his hoofs and flicking red dust
His vermilion mane wet with perspiration
He throws red foam from his mouth   5

The mellow-colored Evening comes
And places her hand between his pricked ears
Her long fingers
Feel the hot breath from his nostrils
And take off the bridle from his mouth   10

The restive animal
Tamed and quietened
Walks behind the Evening slowly
And goes into the stable of darkness

Translated by Balwant Gargi

QUESTIONS

1. Images of redness occur three times in the first stanza. What mood do they create?
    What is the effect of their contrast with the "mellow-colored Evening" that occurs
    in the first line of the second stanza?
2. How is evening personified? Why does the poet capitalize the word?
3. What progression in mood occurs from the first to the final stanza? What progression
    in time occurs?

Cathy Song

PICTURE BRIDE

She was a year younger
than I,
twenty-three when she left Korea.
Did she simply close
the door of her father's house   5

and walk away. And
was it a long way
through the tailor shops of Pusan
to the wharf where the boat
waited to take her to an island   10
whose name she had
only recently learned,
on whose shore
a man waited,
turning her photograph   15
to the light when the lanterns
in the camp outside
Waialua Sugar Mill were lit
and the inside of his room
grew luminous   20
from the wings of moths
migrating out of the cane stalks?
What things did my grandmother
take with her? And when
she arrived to look   25
into the face of the stranger
who was her husband,
thirteen years older than she,
did she politely untie
the silk bow of her jacket,   30
her tent-shaped dress
filling with the dry wind
that blew from the surrounding fields
where the men were burning the cane?

Mohamud S. Togane

ARFAYE

A man without a nickname is like a goat without horns.
a Somali proverb

Arfaye: the sweet-smelling one,
fattest Somali in the city of Mogadishu,
city without deodorants.
Everybody knows his nickname and the irony
that sweetens the truth. Nobody knows his real name.   5

I can see him now in my mind's eye
in the middle of Main Street
in the frying sun
melting away
about to drown in his sweaty khaki uniform   10
flinging sweat away from his eyes
trying to direct a traffic of stubborn donkeys,
skittish camels (impatient drivers poking their behinds)
hauling grass and milk;
donkey-carts driven by heedless drivers   15
who claim the city belongs to their tribe and donkeys;
goats, sheep, and cattle on their way to the slaughter-house;
jay walkers, paraplegic beggars scuttling on all fours
(an American nicknamed them spidermen);
beeping Fiats and thunder-farting ancient trucks without mufflers. 20
Out of this medley sometimes a relief would appear:
quivering ripe breasts of a careless bushwoman
or some undulating steatopygous behind
then Arfaye would pause, tilt his head in worshipful wonder,
flash a smile, and throw darts of desire.   25

Diane Wakoski

TO AN AUTOCRAT

Today you told me
you kicked the first lady
you lived with
out
because she washed her underwear,   5
blue silky things,
and hung them in the bathroom to dry.

A few days ago
you told me
another girl got kicked out   10
for mentioning
grandchildren.

These anecdotes
about taboos

begin to extend from telephone calls   15
to toothbrushing
and leave me trembling
as I suppose you think a lady should
afraid to make any independent move.
There is no doubt   20
you possess this house
and everything in it.
You can move me out or in
at will;
have done so to prove your power.   25
My only weapon
is logic
which salts you like a withering garden snail.
                                            Because
it is you   30
who give me lectures
about the hang-ups of marriage,
and of people wanting to possess each other.
Save your stories for men,
I ought to tell you,   35
because any woman who buys them
is a guerrilla fighter who believes you've been master
of your house too long.
When you move all us silly ones
with our dripping underwear out   40
and install this one liberated lady with her fine panties
and spider-web bras,
her short icy slips,
and satin garters that draw your eyes up her legs
like filings following a magnet,   45
and you never see a vestige of how she launders them,
and she follows all your rules
and makes no demands,
while we poor offenders are always needing things
and trying to live our own lives too,   50
then,
sir,
I tremble for you
for real.
Will she cut your throat one night as you sleep   55
or take off your balls?
Will she steal you blind
and leave with your stockbroker
or debilitate you with your own weaknesses

and jump in to mastery after   60
she's spoiled you for anything but drink and talk?
She is your fate,
anyway,
if you don't realize
that living together   65
is what makes us human and decent.
We give in to others' needs, their rights,
making a fair division of privileges
and chores.
Our dog finds a long beam of sunshine   70
coming in an afternoon window
and she stretches her doberman body
to fit it.
   She follows the sunshine around the house
from morning to late afternoon,   75
stretching or curling into the patterns it makes
on the floor.
She is not perfect,
but she fits
the hours of the day.   80
    She understands
living/
  loving what you have,
making
the fit.   85

Margaret Walker

POPPA CHICKEN

Poppa was a sugah daddy
Pimping in his prime;
All the gals for miles around
Walked to Poppa's time.

Poppa Chicken owned the town,   5
Give his women hell;
All the gals on Poppa's time
Said that he was swell.

Poppa's face was long and black;
Poppa's grin was broad.   10
When Poppa Chicken walked the streets
The gals cried Lawdy! Lawd!

Poppa Chicken made his gals
Toe his special line:
"Treat 'em rough and make 'em say   15
Poppa Chicken's fine!"

Poppa Chicken toted guns;
Poppa wore a knife.
One night Poppa shot a guy
Threat'ning Poppa's life.   20

Poppa done his time in jail
Though he got off light;
Bought his pardon in a year;
Come back out in might.

Poppa walked the streets this time,   25
Gals around his neck.
And everybody said the jail
Hurt him nary speck.

Poppa smoked his long cigars—
Special Poppa brands   30
Rocks all glist'ning in his tie;
On his long black hands.

Poppa lived without a fear;
Walked without a rod.
Poppa cussed the coppers out;   35
Talked like he was God.

Poppa met a pretty gal;
Heard her name was Rose;
Took one look at her and soon
Bought her pretty clothes.   40

One night she was in his arms,
In walked her man Joe,
All he done was look and say,
"Poppa's got to go."

Poppa Chicken still is hot   45
Though he's old and gray,
Walking round here with his gals
Pimping every day.

Walt Whitman

I SAW IN LOUISIANA
A LIVE-OAK GROWING

I saw in Louisiana a live-oak growing,
All alone stood it and the moss hung down from the branches,
Without any companion it grew there uttering joyous leaves of dark green,
And its look, rude, unbending, lusty, made me think of myself,
But I wonder'd how it could utter joyous leaves standing alone there without
  its friend near, for I knew I could not,   5
And I broke off a twig with a certain number of leaves upon it, and twined
  around it a little moss,
And brought it away, and I have placed it in sight in my room,
It is not needed to remind me as of my own dear friends,
(For I believe lately I think of little else than of them,)
Yet it remains to me a curious token, it makes me think of manly love;   10
For all that, and though the live-oak glistens there in Louisiana solitary in a
  wide flat space,
Uttering joyous leaves all its life without a friend a lover near,
I know very well I could not.

QUESTIONS

1. The poet compares himself to the tree. In what ways are they similar? In what ways
   are they distinct?
2. What methods does the poet use to personify the tree? What might be the reason for
   this personification?
3. What sexual allusions are included in the poem? What does the poet mean by
   "manly love"?
4. The term *celebratory* is often used in describing Walt Whitman's poetry. What and
   how is the poet celebrating in this poem?

Sir Thomas Wyatt

THEY FLEE FROM ME

They flee from me, that sometime did me seek,
With naked foot stalking in my chamber.
I have seen them, gentle, tame, and meek,
That now are wild, and do not remember
That sometime they put themselves in danger   5
To take bread at my hand; and now they range,
Busily seeking with a continual change.

Thankéd be fortune it hath been otherwise,
Twenty times better; but once in special,
In thin array, after a pleasant guise,   10
When her loose gown from her shoulders did fall,
And she me caught in her arms long and small,
And therewithall sweetly did me kiss
And softly said, "Dear heart, how like you this?"

It was no dream, I lay broad waking.   15
But all is turned, thorough my gentleness,
Into a strange fashion of forsaking;
And I have leave to go, of her goodness,
And she also to use newfangleness.
But since that I so kindely am servéd,   20
I fain would know what she hath deservéd.

William Butler Yeats

LEDA AND THE SWAN

A sudden blow; the great wings beating still
Above the staggering girl, her thighs caressed
By the dark webs, her nape caught in his bill,
He holds her helpless breast upon his breast.

How can those terrified vague fingers push   5
The feathered glory from her loosening thighs?

And how can body, laid in that white rush,
But feel the strange heart beating where it lies?

A shudder in the loins engenders there
The broken wall, the burning roof and tower   10
And Agamemnon dead.
                 Being so caught up,
So mastered by the brute blood of the air,
Did she put on his knowledge with his power
Before the indifferent beak could let her drop?   15

W o m e n & M e n

P o e t r y

TOPICS FOR WRITING

1. Write an imaginary first-person narrative about marriage. Select a narrator who is your opposite gender. Thus, if you are a male, write from the perspective of a female, and vice-versa.

2. Describe a relationship between two people you know that displays a broad range of emotions—the broader the better.

3. Describe a person in your life for whom your feelings changed radically over the course of your relationship. What was the cause of the original attraction? Why did the feelings change? What was the result?

4. Jordan's "The Wedding," Levertov's "The Ache of Marriage," and Sexton's "The Black Art" describe paradoxes of marriage from a woman's perspective. Compare and contrast the ways these three poets view marriage.

5. Both "Ah Mah" by Lim and "The River-Merchant's Wife: A Letter" by Pound describe Chinese marriages. Compare and contrast the relationships described in each.

6. Animal imagery abounds in Dove's "Adolescence—II" and Singh's "Evening." Select one of these poems, then analyze and interpret the use and meaning of this imagery.

7. Write a classification essay that explains the main types of relationships explored by the poets in this section. Use at least one example to illustrate each of your categories.

8. An honest relationship cannot escape moments of intense conflict. Argue for or against this proposition.

9. Based on your understanding and appreciation of the poems in this section, argue for or against the proposition that reading poetry enables one to understand love in ways that other forms of writing cannot. Refer to specific poems to support your ideas.

10. Myth plays a crucial role in the subject and imagery of Yeats's "Leda and the Swan." As a research project, study the source of the myth, and write an essay explaining how the poem reflects and expresses the substance of the myth.

Drama

Susan Glaspell

SUPPRESSED DESIRES

A Comedy in Two Episodes

In Collaboration with George Cram Cook

CHARACTERS

HENRIETTA BREWSTER
STEPHEN BREWSTER
MABEL

Scene—A Studio Apartment

SCENE I

A studio apartment in an upper story, Washington Square South. Through an immense north window in the back wall appear tree tops and the upper part of the Washington Arch. Beyond it you look up Fifth Avenue. Near the window is a big table, loaded at one end with serious-looking books and austere scientific periodicals. At the other end are architect's drawings, blue prints, dividing compasses, square, ruler, etc. At the left is a door leading to the rest of the apartment; at the right the outer door. A breakfast table is set for three, but only two are seated at it—HENRIETTA *and* STEPHEN BREWSTER. *As the curtains withdraw* STEVE *pushes back his coffee cup and sits dejected.*

HENRIETTA: It isn't the coffee, Steve dear. There's nothing the matter with the coffee. There's something the matter with *you.*

STEVE [*doggedly*]: There may be something the matter with my stomach.

HENRIETTA [*scornfully*]: Your stomach! The trouble is not with your stomach but in your subconscious mind.

STEVE: Subconscious piffle! [*Takes morning paper and tries to read.*]

HENRIETTA: Steve, you never used to be so disagreeable. You certainly have got some sort of a complex. You're all inhibited. You're no longer open to new ideas. You won't listen to a word about psychoanalysis.

STEVE: A word! I've listened to volumes!

HENRIETTA: You've ceased to be creative in architecture—your work isn't going well. You're not sleeping well—.

STEVE: How can I sleep, Henrietta, when you're always waking me up to find out what I'm dreaming?

HENRIETTA: But dreams are so important, Steve. If you'd tell yours to Dr. Russell he'd find out exactly what's wrong with you.

STEVE: There's nothing wrong with me.

HENRIETTA: You don't even talk as well as you used to.

STEVE: Talk? I can't say a thing without you looking at me in that dark fashion you have when you're on the trail of a complex.

HENRIETTA: This very irritability indicates that you're suffering from some suppressed desire.

STEVE: I'm suffering from a suppressed desire for a little peace.

HENRIETTA: Dr. Russell is doing simply wonderful things with nervous cases. Won't you go to him, Steve?

STEVE [*slamming down his newspaper*]: No, Henrietta, I won't!

HENRIETTA: But Stephen—!

STEVE: Tst! I hear Mabel coming. Let's not be at each other's throats the first day of her visit. [*He takes out cigarettes.* MABEL *comes in from door left, the side opposite* STEVE, *so that he is facing her. She is wearing a rather fussy negligee in contrast to* HENRIETTA, *who wears "radical" clothes.* MABEL *is what is called plump.*]

MABEL: Good morning.

HENRIETTA: Oh, here you are, little sister.

STEVE: Good morning, Mabel.

[MABEL *nods to him and turns, her face lighting up, to* HENRIETTA.]

HENRIETTA [*giving* MABEL *a hug as she leans against her*]: It's so good to have you here. I was going to let you sleep, thinking you'd be tired after the long trip. Sit down. There'll be fresh toast in a minute and [*rising*] will you have—

MABEL: Oh, I ought to have told you, Henrietta. Don't get anything for me. I'm not eating breakfast.

HENRIETTA [*at first in mere surprise*]: Not eating breakfast? [*She sits down, then leans toward* MABEL *who is seated now, and scrutinizes her.*]

STEVE [*half to himself*]: The psychoanalytical look!

HENRIETTA: Mabel, why are you not eating breakfast?

MABEL [*a little startled*]: Why, no particular reason. I just don't care much for breakfast, and they say it keeps down—[*A hand on her hip—the gesture of one who is "reducing"*] that is, it's a good thing to go without it.

HENRIETTA: Don't you sleep well? Did you sleep well last night?

MABEL: Oh, yes, I slept all right. Yes, I slept fine last night, only [*laughing*] I did have the funniest dream!

STEVE: S-h! S-t!

HENRIETTA [*moving closer*]: And what did you dream, Mabel?

STEVE: Look-a-here, Mabel, I feel it's my duty to put you on. Don't tell Henrietta your dreams. If you do she'll find out that you have an underground desire to kill your father and marry your mother—

HENRIETTA: Don't be absurd, Stephen Brewster. [*Sweetly to* MABEL] What was your dream, dear?

MABEL [*laughing*]: Well, I dreamed I was a hen.

HENRIETTA: A hen?

MABEL: Yes; and I was pushing along through a crowd as fast as I could, but being a hen I couldn't walk very fast—it was like having a tight skirt, you know; and there was some sort of creature in a blue cap—you know how mixed up dreams are—and it kept shouting after me, "Step, Hen! Step, Hen!" until I got all excited and just couldn't move at all.

HENRIETTA [*resting chin in palm and peering*]: You say you became much excited?

MABEL [*laughing*]: Oh, yes; I was in a terrible state.

HENRIETTA [*leaning back, murmurs*]: This is significant.

STEVE: She dreams she's a hen. She is told to step lively. She becomes violently agitated. What can it mean?

HENRIETTA [*turning impatiently from him*]: Mabel, do you know anything about psycho-analysis?

MABEL [*feebly*]: Oh—not much. No—I— [*Brightening*] It's something about the war, isn't it?

STEVE: Not that kind of war.

MABEL [*abashed*]: I thought it might be the name of a new explosive.

STEVE: It *is*.

MABEL [*apologetically to* HENRIETTA, *who is frowning*]: You see, Henrietta, I—we do not live in touch with intellectual things, as you do. Bob being a dentist—somehow our friends—

STEVE [*softly*]: Oh, to be a dentist! [*Goes to window and stands looking out.*]

HENRIETTA: Don't you see anything more of that editorial writer—what was his name?

MABEL: Lyman Eggleston?

HENRIETTA: Yes, Eggleston. He was in touch with things. Don't you see him?

MABEL: Yes, I see him once in a while. Bob doesn't like him very well.

HENRIETTA: Your husband does not like Lyman Eggleston? [*Mysteriously*] Mabel, are you perfectly happy with your husband?

STEVE [*sharply*]: Oh, come now, Henrietta—that's going a little strong!

HENRIETTA: Are you perfectly happy with him, Mabel?

[STEVE *goes to work-table.*]

MABEL: Why—yes—I guess so. Why—of course I am!

HENRIETTA: Are you happy? Or do you only think you are? Or do you only think you *ought* to be?

MABEL: Why, Henrietta, I don't know what you mean!

STEVE [*seizes stack of books and magazines and dumps them on the breakfast table*]: This is what she means, Mabel. Psychoanalysis. My work-table groans with it. Books by Freud, the new Messiah; books by Jung, the new St. Paul; the Psychoanalytical Review— back numbers two-fifty per.

MABEL: But what's it all about?

STEVE: All about your sub-un-non-conscious mind and desires you know not of. They may be doing you a great deal of harm. You may go crazy with them. Oh, yes! People are doing it right and left. Your dreaming you're a hen— [*Shakes his head darkly.*]

HENRIETTA: Any fool can ridicule anything.

MABEL [*hastily, to avert a quarrel*]: But what do you say it is, Henrietta?

STEVE [*looking at his watch*]: Oh, if Henrietta's going to start that! [*During* HENRIETTA'S *next speech settles himself at work-table and sharpens a lead pencil.*]

HENRIETTA: It's like this, Mabel. You want something. You think you can't have it. You think it's wrong. So you try to think you don't want it. Your mind protects you—avoids pain—by refusing to think the forbidden thing. But it's there just the same. It stays there shut up in your unconscious mind, and it festers.

STEVE: Sort of an ingrowing mental toenail.

HENRIETTA: Precisely. The forbidden impulse is there full of energy which has simply got to do something. It breaks into your consciousness in disguise, masks itself in dreams, makes all sorts of trouble. In extreme cases it drives you insane.

MABEL [*with a gesture of horror*]: Oh!

HENRIETTA [*reassuring*]: But psychoanalysis has found out how to save us from that. It brings into consciousness the suppressed desire that was making all the trouble. Psychoanalysis is simply the latest scientific method of preventing and curing in- sanity.

STEVE [*from his table*]: It is also the latest scientific method of separating families.

HENRIETTA [*mildly*]: Families that ought to be separated.

STEVE: The Dwights, for instance. You must have met them, Mabel, when you were here before. Helen was living, apparently, in peace and happiness with good old Joe. Well—she went to this psychoanalyzer—she was "psyched," and biff!—bang!— home she comes with an unsuppressed desire to leave her husband. [*He starts work, drawing lines on a drawing board with a T-square.*]

MABEL: How terrible! Yes, I remember Helen Dwight. But—but did she have such a desire?

STEVE: First she'd known of it.

MABEL: And she *left* him?

HENRIETTA [*coolly*]: Yes, she did.

MABEL: Wasn't he good to her?

HENRIETTA: Why, yes, good enough.

MABEL: Wasn't he kind to her?

HENRIETTA: Oh, yes—kind to her.

MABEL: And she left her good, kind husband—!

HENRIETTA: Oh, Mabel! "Left her good, kind husband!" How naïve—forgive me, dear, but how bourgeois you are! She came to know herself. And she had the courage!

MABEL: I may be very naïve and—bourgeois—but I don't see the good of a new science that breaks up homes.

[STEVE *applauds*.]

STEVE: In enlightening Mabel, we mustn't neglect to mention the case of Art Holden's private secretary, Mary Snow, who has just been informed of her suppressed desire for her employer.

MABEL: Why, I think it is terrible, Henrietta! It would be better if we didn't know such things about ourselves.

HENRIETTA: No, Mabel, that is the old way.

MABEL: But—but her employer? Is he married?

STEVE [*grunts*]: Wife and four children.

MABEL: Well, then, what good does it do the girl to be told she has a desire for him? There's nothing can be done about it.

HENRIETTA: Old institutions will have to be reshaped so that something can be done in such cases. It happens, Mabel, that this suppressed desire was on the point of landing Mary Snow in the insane asylum. Are you so tight-minded that you'd rather have her in the insane asylum than break the conventions?

MABEL: But—but have people always had these awful suppressed desires?

HENRIETTA: Always.

STEVE: But they've just been discovered.

HENRIETTA: The harm they do has just been discovered. And free, sane people must face the fact that they have to be dealt with.

MABEL [*stoutly*]: I don't believe they have them in Chicago.

HENRIETTA [*business of giving* MABEL *up*]: People "have them" wherever the living Libido—the center of the soul's energy—is in conflict with petrified moral codes. That means everywhere in civilization. Psychoanalysis—

STEVE: Good God! I've got the roof in the cellar!

HENRIETTA: The roof in the cellar!

STEVE [*holding plan at arm's length*]: That's what psychoanalysis does!

HENRIETTA: That's what psychoanalysis could *un*-do. Is it any wonder I'm concerned about Steve? He dreamed the other night that the walls of his room melted away and he found himself alone in a forest. Don't you see how significant it is for an architect to have *walls* slip away from him? It symbolizes his loss of grip in his work. There's some suppressed desire—

STEVE [*hurling his ruined plan viciously to the floor*]: Suppressed hell!

HENRIETTA: You speak more truly than you know. It is through suppressions that hells are formed in us.

MABEL [*looking at* STEVE, *who is tearing his hair*]: Don't you think it would be a good thing, Henrietta, if we went somewhere else? [*They rise and begin to pick up the dishes.* MABEL *drops a plate which breaks.* HENRIETTA *draws up short and looks at her—the psychoanalytic look*] I'm sorry, Henrietta. One of the Spode plates, too. [*Surprised and resentful as* HENRIETTA *continues to peer at her*] Don't take it so to heart, Henrietta.

HENRIETTA: I can't help taking it to heart.

MABEL: I'll get you another. [*Pause. More sharply as* HENRIETTA *does not answer*] I said I'll get you another plate, Henrietta.

HENRIETTA: It's not the plate.

MABEL: For heaven's sake, what is it then?

HENRIETTA: It's the significant little false movement that made you drop it.

MABEL: Well, I suppose everyone makes a false movement once in a while.

HENRIETTA: Yes, Mabel, but these false movements all mean something.

MABEL [*about to cry*]: I don't think that's very nice! It was just because I happened to think of that Mabel Snow you were talking about—

HENRIETTA: *Mabel* Snow!

MABEL: Snow—Snow—well, what was her name, then?

HENRIETTA: Her name is Mary. You substituted *your own* name for hers.

MABEL: Well, *Mary* Snow, then; *Mary* Snow. I never heard her name but once. I don't see anything to make such a fuss about.

HENRIETTA [*gently*]: Mabel dear— mistakes like that in names—

MABEL [*desperately*]: They don't mean something, too, do they?

HENRIETTA [*gently*]: I am sorry, dear, but they do.

MABEL: But I'm always doing that!

HENRIETTA [*after a start of horror*]: My poor little sister, tell me about it.

MABEL: About what?

HENRIETTA: About your not being happy. About your longing for another sort of life.

MABEL: But I *don't.*

HENRIETTA: Ah, I understand these things, dear. You feel Bob is limiting you to a life in which you do not feel free—

MABEL: Henrietta! When did I ever say such a thing?

HENRIETTA: You said you are not in touch with things intellectual. You showed your feeling that it is Bob's profession—that has engendered a resentment which has colored your whole life with him.

MABEL: Why—Henrietta!

HENRIETTA: Don't be afraid of me, little sister. There's nothing can shock me or turn me from you. I am not like that. I wanted you to come for this visit because I had a feeling that you needed more from life than you were getting. No one of these things I have seen would excite my suspicion. It's the combination. You don't eat breakfast [*enumerating on her fingers*]; you make false moves; you substitute your own name for the name of another *whose love is misdirected*. You're nervous; you *look* queer; in your eyes there's a frightened look that is most unlike you. And this dream. A *hen*. Come with me this afternoon to Dr. Russell! Your whole life may be at stake, Mabel.

MABEL [*gasping*]: Henrietta, I—you—you always were the smartest in the family, and all that, but—this is terrible! I don't think we *ought* to think such things. [*Brightening*] Why, I'll tell you why I dreamed I was a hen. It was because last night, telling about that time in Chicago, you said I was as mad as a wet hen.

HENRIETTA [*superior*]: Did you dream you were a *wet* hen?

MABEL [*forced to admit it*]: No.

HENRIETTA: No. You dreamed you were a *dry* hen. And why, being a hen, were you urged to step?

MABEL: Maybe it's because when I am getting on a street car it always irritates me to have them call "Step lively."

HENRIETTA: No, Mabel, that is only a child's view of it—if you will forgive me. You see merely the elements used in the dream. You do not see into the dream; you do not see its meaning. This dream of the hen—

STEVE: Hen—hen—wet hen—dry hen—mad hen! [*Jumps up in a rage*] Let me out of this!

HENRIETTA [*hastily picking up dishes, speaks soothingly*]: Just a minute, dear, and we'll have things so you can work in quiet. Mabel and I are going to sit in my room. [*She goes out left, carrying dishes.*]

STEVE [*seizing hat and coat from an alcove near the outside door*]: I'm going to be psychoana-lyzed. I'm going now! I'm going straight to that infallible doctor of hers—that priest of this new religion. If he's got honesty enough to tell Henrietta there's nothing the matter with my unconscious mind, perhaps I can be let alone about it, and then I *will* be all right. [*From the door in a low voice*] Don't tell Henrietta I'm going. It might take weeks, and I couldn't stand all the talk. [*He hurries out.*]

HENRIETTA [*returning*]: Where's Steve? Gone? [*With a hopeless gesture*] You see how impatient he is—how unlike himself! I tell you, Mabel, I'm nearly distracted about Steve.

MABEL: I think he's a little distracted, too.

HENRIETTA: Well, if he's gone—you might as well stay here. I have a committee meeting at the bookshop, and will have to leave you to yourself for an hour or two. [*As she puts her hat on, taking it from the alcove where* STEVE *found his, her eye, lighting up almost carnivorously, falls on an enormous volume on the floor beside the work-table. The book has been half hidden by the wastebasket. She picks it up and carries it around the table toward* MABEL] Here, dear, is one of the simplest statements of psychoanalysis. You just read this and then we can talk more intelligently. [MABEL *takes volume and staggers back under its weight to chair rear center,* HENRIETTA *goes to outer door, stops and asks abruptly*] How old is Lyman Eggleston?

MABEL [*promptly*]: He isn't forty yet. Why, what made you ask that, Henrietta? [*As she turns her head to look at* HENRIETTA *her hands move toward the upper corners of the book balanced on her knees.*]

HENRIETTA: Oh, nothing. Au revoir. [*She goes out.* MABEL *stares at the ceiling. The book slides to the floor. She starts; looks at the book, then at the broken plate on the table*] The plate!

The book! [*She lifts her eyes, leans forward, elbow on knee, chin on knuckles and plaintively queries*] Am I unhappy?

SCENE II

Two weeks later. The stage is as in Scene I, except that the breakfast table has been removed. During the first few minutes the dusk of a winter afternoon deepens. Out of the darkness spring rows of double street-lights almost meeting in the distance. HENRIETTA *is at the psychoanalytical end of* STEVE.'s *work-table, surrounded by open books and periodicals, writing.* STEVE *enters briskly.*

STEVE: What are you doing, my dear?

HENRIETTA: My paper for the Liberal Club.

STEVE: Your paper on—?

HENRIETTA: On a subject which does not have your sympathy.

STEVE: Oh, I'm not sure I'm wholly out of sympathy with psychoanalysis, Henrietta. You worked it so hard. I couldn't even take a bath without its meaning something.

HENRIETTA [*loftily*]: I talked it because I knew you needed it.

STEVE: You haven't said much about it these last two weeks. Uh—your faith in it hasn't weakened any?

HENRIETTA: Weakened? It's grown stronger with each new thing I've come to know. And Mabel. She is with Dr. Russell now. Dr. Russell is wonderful! From what Mabel tells me I believe his analysis is going to prove that I was right. Today I discovered a remarkable confirmation of my theory in the hen-dream.

STEVE: What is your theory?

HENRIETTA: Well, you know about Lyman Eggleston. I've wondered about him. I've never seen him, but I know he's less bourgeois than Mabel's other friends—more intellectual—and [*significantly*] she doesn't see much of him because Bob doesn't like him.

STEVE: But what's the confirmation?

HENRIETTA: Today I noticed the first syllable of his name.

STEVE: Ly?

HENRIETTA: No—egg.

STEVE: Egg?

HENRIETTA [*patiently*]: Mabel dreamed she was a *hen*. [STEVE *laughs*] You wouldn't laugh if you knew how important names are in interpreting dreams. Freud is full of just such cases in which a whole hidden complex is revealed by a single significant syllable—like this egg.

STEVE: Doesn't the traditional relation of hen and egg suggest rather a maternal feeling?

HENRIETTA: There is something maternal in Mabel's love, of course, but that's only one element.

STEVE: Well, suppose Mabel hasn't a suppressed desire to be this gentleman's mother, but his beloved. What's to be done about it? What about Bob? Don't you think it's going to be a little rough on him?

HENRIETTA: That can't be helped. Bob, like everyone else, must face the facts of life. If Dr. Russell should arrive independently at this same interpretation I shall not hesitate to advise Mabel to leave her present husband.

STEVE: Um—hum! [*The lights go up on Fifth Avenue.* STEVE *goes to the window and looks out*] How long is it we've lived here, Henrietta?

HENRIETTA: Why, this is the third year, Steve.

STEVE: I—we—one would miss this view if one went away, wouldn't one?

HENRIETTA: How strangely you speak! Oh, Stephen, I *wish* you'd go to Dr. Russell. Don't think my fears have abated because I've been able to restrain myself. I had to on account of Mabel. But now, dear—won't you go?

STEVE: I— [*He breaks off, turns on the light, then comes and sits beside* HENRIETTA] How long have we been married, Henrietta?

HENRIETTA: Stephen, I don't understand you! You *must* go to Dr. Russell.

STEVE: I have gone.

HENRIETTA: You—what?

STEVE [*jauntily*]: Yes, Henrietta, I've been psyched.

HENRIETTA: You went to Dr. Russell?

STEVE: The same.

HENRIETTA: And what did he say?

STEVE: He said—I—I was a little surprised by what he said, Henrietta.

HENRIETTA [*breathlessly*]: Of course—one can so seldom anticipate. But tell me— your dream, Stephen? It means—?

STEVE: It means—I was considerably surprised by what it means.

HENRIETTA: *Don't* be so exasperating!

STEVE: It means—you really want to know, Henrietta?

HENRIETTA: Stephen, you'll drive me mad!

STEVE: He said—of course he may be wrong in what he said.

HENRIETTA: He *isn't* wrong. *Tell* me!

STEVE: He said my dream of the walls receding and leaving me alone in a forest indicates a suppressed desire—

HENRIETTA: Yes—yes!

STEVE: To be freed from—

HENRIETTA: Yes—freed from—?

STEVE: Marriage.

HENRIETTA [*crumples. Stares*]: Marriage!

STEVE: He—he may be mistaken, you know.

HENRIETTA: *May* be mistaken?

STEVE: I—well, of course, I hadn't taken any stock in it myself. It was only your great confidence—

HENRIETTA: Stephen, are you telling me that Dr. Russell—Dr. A. E. Russell—told you this? [STEVE *nods*] Told you you have a suppressed desire to separate from *me?*

STEVE: That's what he said.

HENRIETTA: Did he know who you were?

STEVE: Yes.

HENRIETTA: That you were married to me?

STEVE: Yes, he knew that.

HENRIETTA: And he told you to leave me?

STEVE: It seems he must be wrong, Henrietta.

HENRIETTA [*rising*]: And I've sent him more patients—! [*Catches herself and resumes coldly*] What reason did he give for this analysis?

STEVE: He says the confining walls are a symbol of my feeling about marriage and that their fading away is a wish-fulfillment.

HENRIETTA [*gulping*]: Well, is it? Do you want our marriage to end?

STEVE: It was a great surprise to me that I did. You see I hadn't known what was in my unconscious mind.

HENRIETTA [*flaming*]: What did you tell Dr. Russell about me to make him think you weren't happy?

STEVE: I never told him a thing, Henrietta. He got it all from his confounded clever inferences. I—I tried to refute them, but he said that was only part of my self-protective lying.

HENRIETTA: And that's why you were so—happy—when you came in just now!

STEVE: Why, Henrietta, how can you say such a thing? I was *sad*. Didn't I speak sadly of—of the view? Didn't I ask how long we had been married?

HENRIETTA [*rising*]: Stephen Brewster, have you no sense of the seriousness of this? Dr. Russell doesn't know what our marriage has been. You do. You should have laughed him down! Confined—in life with me? Did you tell him that I *believe* in freedom?

STEVE: I very emphatically told him that his results were a great surprise to me.

HENRIETTA: But you accepted them.

STEVE: Oh, not at all. I merely couldn't refute his arguments. I'm not a psychologist. I came home to talk it over with you. You being a disciple of psychoanalysis—

HENRIETTA: If you are going, I wish you would go tonight!

STEVE: Oh, my dear! I—surely I couldn't do that! Think of my feelings. And my laundry hasn't come home.

HENRIETTA: I ask you to go tonight. Some women would falter at this, Steve, but I am not such a woman. I leave you free. I do not repudiate psychoanalysis; I say again that it has done great things. It has also made mistakes, of course. But since you accept this analysis— [*She sits down and pretends to begin work*] I have to finish this paper. I wish you would leave me.

STEVE [*scratches his head, goes to the inner door*]: I'm sorry, Henrietta, about my unconscious mind. [*Alone*, HENRIETTA's *face betrays her outraged state of mind—disconcerted, resentful, trying to pull herself together. She attains an air of bravely bearing an outrageous thing.—The outer door opens and* MABEL *enters in great excitement.*]

MABEL [*breathless*]: Henrietta, I'm so glad you're here. And alone? [*Looks toward the inner door*] Are you alone, Henrietta?

HENRIETTA [*with reproving dignity*]: Very much so.

MABEL [*rushing to her*]: Henrietta, he's found it!

HENRIETTA [*aloof*]: Who has found what?

MABEL: Who has found what? Dr. Russell has found my suppressed desire!

HENRIETTA: That is interesting.

MABEL: He finished with me today—he got hold of my complex—in the most amazing way! But, oh, Henrietta—it is so terrible!

HENRIETTA: Do calm yourself, Mabel. Surely there's no occasion for all this agitation.

MABEL: But there is! And when you think of the lives that are affected—the readjust-
ments that must be made in order to bring the suppressed hell out of me and save
me from the insane asylum—!

HENRIETTA: The insane asylum!

MABEL: You said that's where these complexes brought people!

HENRIETTA: What did the doctor tell you, Mabel?

MABEL: Oh, I don't know how I can tell you—it is so awful—so unbelievable.

HENRIETTA: I rather have my hand in at hearing the unbelievable.

MABEL: Henrietta, who would ever have thought it? How can it be true? But the
doctor is perfectly certain that I have a suppressed desire for— [*Looks at* HENRIETTA,
is unable to continue.]

HENRIETTA: Oh, go on, Mabel. I'm not unprepared for what you have to say.

MABEL: Not unprepared? You mean you have suspected it?

HENRIETTA: From the first. It's been my theory all along.

MABEL: But, Henrietta, I didn't know myself that I had this secret desire for Stephen.

HENRIETTA [*jumps up*]: Stephen!

MABEL: My brother-in-law! My own sister's husband!

HENRIETTA: *You* have a suppressed desire for *Stephen!*

MABEL: Oh, Henrietta, aren't these unconscious selves terrible? They seem so unlike *us!*

HENRIETTA: What insane thing are you driving at?

MABEL [*blubbering*]: Henrietta, don't you use that word to me. I don't *want* to go to the
insane asylum.

HENRIETTA: What did Dr. Russell say?

MABEL: Well, you see—oh, it's the strangest thing! But you know the voice in my
dream that called "Step, Hen!" Dr. Russell found out today that when I was a little
girl I had a story-book in words of one syllable and I read the name Stephen wrong.
I used to read it S-t-e-p, step, h-e-n, hen. [*Dramatically*] Step Hen is Stephen. [*Enter*
STEPHEN, *his head bent over a time-table*] Stephen is Step Hen!

STEVE: I? Step Hen?

MABEL [*triumphantly*]: S-t-e-p, step, H-e-n, hen, Stephen!

HENRIETTA [*exploding*]: Well, what if Stephen is Step Hen? [*Scornfully*] Step Hen! Step
Hen! For that ridiculous coincidence—

MABEL: Coincidence! But it's childish to look at the mere elements of a dream. You
have to look *into* it—you have to see what it *means!*

HENRIETTA: On account of that trivial, meaningless play on syllables—on that flimsy
basis—you are ready— [*Wails*] O-h!

STEVE: What on earth's the matter? What has happened? Suppose I *am* Step Hen?
What about it? What does it mean?

MABEL [*crying*]: It means—that I—have a suppressed desire for *you!*

STEVE: For me! The deuce you have! [*Feebly*] What—er—makes you think so?

MABEL: Dr. Russell has worked it out scientifically.

HENRIETTA: Yes. Through the amazing discovery that Step Hen equals Stephen!

MABEL [*tearfully*]: Oh, that isn't all—that isn't near all. Henrietta won't give me a chance to tell it. She'd rather I'd go to the insane asylum than be unconventional.

HENRIETTA: We'll all go there if you can't control yourself. We are still waiting for some rational report.

MABEL [*drying her eyes*]: Oh, there's such a lot about names. [*With some pride*] I don't see how I ever did it. It all works in together. I dreamed I was a hen because that's the first syllable of Henrietta's name, and when I dreamed I was a hen, I was putting myself in Henrietta's place.

HENRIETTA: With Stephen?

MABEL: With Stephen.

HENRIETTA [*outraged*]: Oh! [*Turns in rage upon* STEPHEN, *who is fanning himself with the time-table*] What are you doing with that time-table?

STEVE: Why—I thought—you were so keen to have me go tonight—I thought I'd just take a run up to Canada, and join Billy—a little shooting— but—

MABEL: But there's more about the names.

HENRIETTA: Mabel, have you thought of Bob—dear old Bob—your good, kind husband?

MABEL: Oh, Henrietta, "my good, kind husband!"

HENRIETTA: Think of him, Mabel, out there alone in Chicago, working his head off, fixing people's *teeth*—for you!

MABEL: Yes, but think of the living Libido—in conflict with petrified moral codes! And think of the perfectly wonderful way the names all prove it. Dr. Russell said he's never seen anything more convincing. Just look at Stephen's last name—Brewster. I dream I'm a hen, and the name Brewster—you have to say its first letter by itself—and then the hen, that's me, she says to him: "Stephen, Be Rooster!"

[HENRIETTA *and* STEPHEN *collapse into the nearest chairs.*]

MABEL: I think it's perfectly wonderful! Why, if it wasn't for psychoanalysis you'd never find out how wonderful your own mind is!

STEVE [*begins to chuckle*]: Be Rooster! Stephen, Be Rooster!

HENRIETTA: You think it's funny, do you?

STEVE: Well, what's to be done about it? Does Mabel have to go away with me?

HENRIETTA: Do you want Mabel to go away with you?

STEVE: Well, but Mabel herself—her complex, her suppressed desire—!

HENRIETTA [*going to her*]: Mabel, are you going to insist on going away with Stephen?

MABEL: I'd rather go with Stephen than go to the insane asylum!

HENRIETTA: For heaven's sake, Mabel, drop that insane asylum! If you *did* have a suppressed desire for Stephen hidden away in you—God knows it isn't hidden now. Dr. Russell has brought it into your consciousness—with a vengeance. That's all that's necessary to break up a complex. Psychoanalysis doesn't say you have to *gratify* every suppressed desire.

STEVE [*softly*]: Unless it's for Lyman Eggleston.

HENRIETTA [*turning on him*]: Well, if it comes to that, Stephen Brewster, I'd like to know why that interpretation of mine isn't as good as this one? Step, Hen!

STEVE: But Be Rooster! [*He pauses, chuckling to himself*] Step-Hen B-rooster. And *Hen*-rietta. Pshaw, my dear, Doc Russell's got you beat a mile! [*He turns away and chuckles*] Be rooster!

MABEL: What has Lyman Eggleston got to do with it?

STEVE: According to Henrietta, you, the hen, have a suppressed desire for *Eggleston*, the egg.

MABEL: Henrietta, I think that's indecent of you! He is bald as an egg and little and fat—the idea of you thinking such a thing of me!

HENRIETTA: Well, Bob isn't little and bald and fat! Why don't you stick to your own husband? [*To* STEPHEN] What if Dr. Russell's interpretation has got mine "beat a mile"? [*Resentful look at him*] It would only mean that Mabel doesn't want Eggleston and does want you. Does that mean she has to have you?

MABEL: But you said Mabel Snow—

HENRIETTA: *Mary* Snow! You're not as much like her as you think—substituting your name for hers! The cases are entirely different. Oh, I wouldn't have *believed* this of you, Mabel. [*Beginning to cry*] I brought you here for a pleasant visit—thought you needed brightening *up*—wanted to be *nice* to you—and now you—my husband— you insist— [*In fumbling her way to her chair she brushes to the floor some sheets from the psychoanalytical table.*]

STEVE [*with solicitude*]: Careful, dear. Your paper on psychoanalysis! [*Gathers up sheets and offers them to her.*]

HENRIETTA: I don't want my paper on psychoanalysis! I'm sick of psychoanalysis!

STEVE [*eagerly*]: Do you mean that, Henrietta?

HENRIETTA: Why shouldn't I mean it? Look at all I've done for psychoanalysis— and— [*Raising a tear-stained face*] what has psychoanalysis done for me?

STEVE: Do you mean, Henrietta, that you're going to stop *talking* psychoanalysis?

HENRIETTA: Why shouldn't I stop talking it? Haven't I seen what it does to people? Mabel has gone crazy about psychoanalysis!

[*At the word "crazy" with a moan* MABEL *sinks to chair and buries her face in her hands.*]

STEVE [*solemnly*]: Do you swear never to wake me up in the night to find out what I'm dreaming?

HENRIETTA: Dream what you please—I don't care what you're dreaming.

STEVE: Will you clear off my work-table so the Journal of Morbid Psychology doesn't stare me in the face when I'm trying to plan a house?

HENRIETTA [*pushing a stack of periodicals off the table*]: I'll *burn* the Journal of Morbid Psychology!

STEVE: My dear Henrietta, if you're going to separate from psychoanalysis, there's no reason why I should separate from *you*.

[*They embrace ardently.* MABEL *lifts her head and looks at them woefully.*]

MABEL [*jumping up and going toward them*]: But what about me? What am I to do with my suppressed desire?

STEVE [*with one arm still around* HENRIETTA, *gives* MABEL *a brotherly hug*]: Mabel, you just keep right on suppressing it!

Curtain

QUESTIONS

1. Compare the tone used in describing the setting of the play with the tone of the dialogue. How does the contrast between the two set the stage for the play's humor?
2. Henrietta initiates all the conflict in Scene I. What is the source of this conflict?
3. There is a reversal of action in Scene II. How does the author create this reversal? Does the action escalate in Scene II. If so, how?
4. Does the dialogue of the play appear natural or artificial? Explain your answer.
5. What is the author satirizing in the play?

Estela Portillo

DAY OF THE SWALLOWS

──────── **CAST OF CHARACTERS** ────────

ALYSEA	EDUARDO
CLEMENCIA	CLARA
JOSEFA	DON MIGUEL ESQUINAS
TOMÁS	FATHER PRADO

The tierra del Lago de San Lorenzo *is within memory of mountain sweet pine. There the maguey thickens with the ferocity of the sun. The desert yawns, drinking the sun in madness. The village of Lago de San Lorenzo is a stepchild of the Esquinas hacienda, both a frugal mother and a demanding father. Two hundred years before, the Esquinas family had settled in the town on a Spanish grant of fifty thousand acres. The Indians were pushed out farther into the desert. Gradually they returned, building the barrio around the hacienda, depending on it for a livilihood. The greedy vitality of the hacienda owners, the gachupins, was a wonder to the Indian. The bearded gachupins with their arrogance became the masters. Or did they? As the barrio clustered itself around the hacienda, time and desert life, symbiotic with the Indian, conquered the conquerors.*

The Indian, with his own distinct vision of the universe, endures, unchanged, stoic, accepting of a stunted existence. The tempo of life in the village remains unbroken, woven out of myth, ritual, and the instinctive tenacity for survival. The Esquinas hacienda is the fiber upon which existence hangs. The church is the fluid hope, dissolving human suffering into enthralling and refreshing faith.

All things happen on the day of San Lorenzo. The town is invaded by swallows flying north. On this fiesta day, a good Catholic is honored by the church. He or she leads a procession to the church for a general blessing of the people and the animals of the village. But the most important ritual of the Day of San Lorenzo is the bathing of the virgins in the lake. The church bells toll eleven in the sun. The lake becomes a sacred temple where the young girls of the village bathe and wash their hair in spring water to insure a future marriage "made in heaven." No one has seen a "marriage made in heaven," but each girl secretly hugs the hope that hers will be the one. Here the young women dig their feet in the mud with lyrical intimacy, eyes burning, heart beating, the smell of pine heavy in their nostrils as they trace mountain against sky. All the women of the village have shared in this experience except one—Josefa. Yet, hers is the only house built close to the edge of the lake, some distance from the barrio.

ACT I

SCENE I

JOSEFA's *sitting room: it is an unusually beautiful room, very feminine and done in good taste. The profusion of lace everywhere gives the room a delicate, ephemeral appearance. The lace pieces are lovely: needlepoint, hairpin, limerick, the work of patience and love. Upstage left is a large bay window; from it, one can view a large tree with a bird house of unusual size and shape, an orb that can accommodate a great number of birds. The room faces south, so it is flooded with light. There is almost a melting of light into lace, a peaceful serenity. To the right is a door leading to the kitchen; there is another door leading to a bedroom. Downstage left is a door leading to the outside.*

When the curtain rises, ALYSEA *is sitting on the floor. It is before dawn, but a minute or so after the curtain rises, light begins to fill the room.* ALYSEA *is cleaning the sitting room carpet, an unusual task for this hour. Next to her is a pail. She uses a piece of cloth with quick frantic movements, rinses, and continues the rubbing of the carpet. After a while, she looks at the cloth in her hand almost in a trance, then with a growing horror. She drops it, raising herself to her knees, she stares at it, then covers her face with her hands. She sits back on the floor leaning her head against a chair, looking helpless and lost. She is sobbing quietly. After a while, she stares at the new streaming light from the window, feeling its warmth as a comfort. The sound of a milk bell interrupts the silence. When she hears it, she jumps up, looks desperately about the room, wipes the traces of tears from her eyes and goes to the window and looks out.*

ALYSEA: If I'm not at the door to pay her, she'll come right in.

[*She looks around the room one more time. She notices the long kitchen knife with traces of blood on it on a small side table next to the couch. She picks it up with the cleaning cloth gingerly, wraps the knife inside the cloth, and puts it in a drawer (side table). During this interval,* CLEMENCIA's *noisy arrival is heard.* CLEMENCIA *is an older barrio woman who has been delivering milk for many years. From the kitchen comes the sound of the door opening, the tugging of a milk can, the pouring of milk. Sighs and ejaculations about hard work are heard.* CLEMENCIA *comes into the sitting room.*]

CLEMENCIA: Ah, there you are. My centavos were not on the kitchen table. Hombre—do I have to beg for my money?

ALYSEA: I'm sorry. I just didn't get around to it.

CLEMENCIA [*staring at* ALYSEA]: You look terrible. What is the matter? Have you been up all night?

ALYSEA [*smooths hair and looks at her hands guiltily*]: We—I stayed up late. I was trying to learn a new lace pattern.

CLEMENCIA: Josefa, eh? She teaches you well, eh?

ALYSEA: Oh, yes, yes.

CLEMENCIA: And you try to please her, eh?

ALYSEA: I try.

CLEMENCIA: You do. You do. She likes you very much. She tells everybody what a fine girl you are. [*She catches* ALYSEA *looking at her hands.*] What's the matter with your hands?

ALYSEA: Hands? Oh, nothing. Nothing.

CLEMENCIA: Of course nothing! You are young. Look at mine. Rheumatism—eaten up by life. Oh, well, pain comes with age, eh?

ALYSEA: I suppose. [*She goes to the table drawer and takes out a money box. She takes out a set of keys from her apron pocket and opens it.*] Here's your money. [*Counts it out.*] Cinco—seis—siete pesos.

CLEMENCIA: Gracias. [*Peers into* ALYSEA's *face.*] You look bad. Sleep some. You can rest in this house.

ALYSEA: I will.

CLEMENCIA: You are a lucky girl. You have a good guardian angel. Aren't you glad Josefa brought you here to live with her? You are one lucky girl.

ALYSEA: She has been very kind.

CLEMENCIA: She is loved by all. A fine woman. Mañana will be her day. Ah! She will lead the procession to the church. A day to honor Josefa. She was chosen for her goodness.

ALYSEA: Tomorrow?

CLEMENCIA: You have forgotten! What is the matter with you? San Lorenzo's day. The procession to the church.

ALYSEA: Of course. How silly of me. I—I'm not myself today.

CLEMENCIA: No you're not. You need rest and some of my good milk. [*Looks around the room.*] Nice—nice. May I sit down for a minute. I started delivering two hours ago. The chill of the desert is in my bones. [*She sits without waiting for an answer.*] Isn't it different living in this beautiful house instead of that hovel you were born in—what town was that?

ALYSEA: Moteca, south of San Miguel.

CLEMENCIA: Tch, tch, tch, tch—that's a poor town. My brother's family almost died of starvation there. But you were in the city when Josefa found you, eh? Oh, that

Josefa! All her life, she goes around with—that walking stick of hers—always she goes like an avenging angel. [*Looks at* ALYSEA *who is still standing.*] Sit down. Sit down. [CLEMENCIA *stands up suddenly.*] An avenging angel, that Josefa! [*Pretends to pound away with a walking stick.*] Take that! and that! She beats those devils. The man who tried to hurt you. And that old drunk buzzard, David's father, when he was beating the poor child to death. [*At the mention of* DAVID's *name,* ALYSEA *puts her hands to her temples. She is trembling.*] You *are* sick.

ALYSEA: No. I'm alright.

CLEMENCIA: She saved you. You are very lucky. You make beautiful lace like Josefa. She teaches you well. Everything she does, she does beautiful.

ALYSEA [*rises and goes to window*]: Appearances. They are very funny—aren't they? Tomorrow the church will honor Josefa. How very funny! [*She begins to laugh, but the laughter becomes a desperate sobbing.*] Oh, God!

CLEMENCIA: You must have a fever. [*Goes to* ALYSEA *and touches her forehead.*] No—but something's wrong with you. Where is Josefa?

[JOSEFA *enters. She is a tall, regal woman about thirty-five. Her bones are Indian, her coloring Aryan. She wears her hair severely back. Her movements are graceful. The cuffs and collar of her dress are of exquisite lace. She walks up to* ALYSEA *and puts her arms around her.*]

JOSEFA: Shhhhh, stop crying. [*Goes to* CLEMENCIA.] I don't often see you in my sitting room. Alysea doesn't seem to be feeling well.

CLEMENCIA: Stayed up all night, she says.

JOSEFA: Oh?

CLEMENCIA: You must make her rest.

JOSEFA: Of course.

CLEMENCIA: Well, I must be going. I'm late on my rounds. [*She sighs.*] I wish I could stay here.

JOSEFA: My home is your home.

CLEMENCIA: You are an angel.

JOSEFA: You have your money?

CLEMENCIA: Oh, yes, gracias. Now, you make her rest.

JOSEFA: I shall. Goodbye.

[JOSEFA *escorts* CLEMENCIA *to the door.* CLEMENCIA *takes one anxious look at* ALYSEA *again before she leaves.*]

CLEMENCIA: She's coming down with something.

JOSEFA: I'll take good care of her.

CLEMENCIA: Oh, you will. You will. [*Exits.*]

[JOSEFA *turns to* ALYSEA.]

JOSEFA: She's right, you know. You should rest [ALYSEA, *still in the midst of great distress, shakes her head.*] Is it wise. . . .

ALYSEA: Wise! The way you word it—wise!

JOSEFA: Very well, I'll put it another way. Must you break down now? It's such a beautiful day. We must be faithful to loveliness.

ALYSEA: How can you say that? How can you justify in that way?

JOSEFA: There are things we must do to keep our sanity, to make each moment clear. [*Pause, voice becomes lighter.*] Any sign of the swallows? Look at the tree. Oh, I love that tree.

ALYSEA: Have you gone mad? Last night. . . .

[ALYSEA *is overwhelmed with the memory; she runs out of the room.* JOSEFA *looks for a moment after her, then she touches the lace curtains.*]

JOSEFA: We pattern our lives for rare, beautiful moments like this lace—little bits and pieces come together. My life—this lace—a crystal thing of light. She must understand. Alysea must understand—she must!

[*There is a knock at the door. She hesitates before opening. Then, she decides to do so. It is* TOMÁS, *her shiftless uncle.*]

TOMÁS: Josefa, buenos días. I thought you might be at the hacienda—ha, ha, ha. Not today?

JOSEFA: What are you doing here?

TOMÁS: The pump. . . .

JOSEFA: You fixed that already. I've told you not to come around here at this time of day.

TOMÁS: The pump, I tell you. I have to hone the cylinder. What do women know about this?

JOSEFA: I've warned you about bothering Alysea.

TOMÁS: She say that?

JOSEFA: I know you.

TOMÁS: You think bad. Woman like you always think bad of Tomás. Not good. My wife say, "Go, help Josefa. We need provisions." I come.

JOSEFA: Take whatever you need for your family.

TOMÁS: My family thanks you. Can you spare a few centavos for me?

JOSEFA: Go help yourself to beans and rice. There's apples for the children.

TOMÁS: Beans and rice—beans and rice—who can get happy on beans and rice? A few centavos? Just one bottle?

JOSEFA: Go get your provisions.

TOMÁS: No bottle for me. But you get lots of bottles for your friend, Clara.

JOSEFA: Mind your tongue.

TOMÁS: Does Don Miguel Esquinas know you buy liquor for his wife? [*Notices the pail. Peers into it.*] It's blood. Blood?

JOSEFA: Go to the kitchen and get your rice and beans. [TOMÁS *is still staring into the pail.*] Did you hear me?

TOMÁS: Rice and beans—rice and beans. Yes, yes, Doña Perfecta—Doña Perfecta—so charitable—ha, ha, ha. . . .

JOSEFA: I'm not in the mood for your sarcasm.

TOMÁS: Queen of the world. No liquor for Tomás. Lots of liquor for la Doña Esquinas. Queen of the world. Is that blood in the pail?

JOSEFA: I do not have to satisfy your curiosity.

TOMÁS: Cálmate, cálmate. [*Walks out with his eyes on the pail.*]

[JOSEFA *turns her back to him. He shrugs and leaves through the kitchen door. His grumbling is heard as he helps himself to the food.* JOSEFA *stares at the contents of the pail. She looks away and touches her temple with her fingertips. Crosses over to a rocking chair, sits, and leans back, closes her eyes and grips the arms of the chair.*]

JOSEFA: I will not fall again, that cold, blinding misery. No, no—it can't crumble—this world I put together with such care. Alysea must understand. Fires, fires winding up my soul. Last night can be forgotten. Last night can be forgiven.

[*She rises and walks to the window and stands absorbing the light; one can sense an obvious union between the light and* JOSEFA.]

JOSEFA [*softly*]: How moist your lips, my light. Through me, through me—you live. Oh, you shape my soul with such care. I am . . . air . . . and you, my spirits—the moon's cold fire, the pulsing heat of sun. [*She comes back from the intimacy and looks at the bird house.*] They will come, my swallows. They will come after the desert flight.

[*As she looks at the tree,* TOMÁS *comes through the patio outside the window. He has a sack over his shoulder.* JOSEFA *is oblivious of him until he calls out.*]

TOMÁS: Josefa, casting your spell, so early? You can't scare me, querida. I know you. I know many things. You burn inside.

[JOSEFA *stares at him unbelievingly as if his intrusion were a blasphemy. She turns away from the window.*]

TOMÁS: Hey, Josefa, why you run away? The great Doña Perfecta runs from her sweet, loving uncle. That's funny, ha, ha, ha, ha.

JOSEFA [*ominous tone*]: Go home, Tomás, go home.

[*She closes the window and walks to an unfinished damask close to the window. She sits down, unhooks the needle, and begins to work on it. Her concentration becomes a fiery intensity; this is obvious in her finger movements.* ALYSEA *comes into the room. She is now composed and refreshed. She has on a pretty dress. She sees the pail, hesitates, then forces herself to remove it, taking it into the kitchen. All this time* JOSEFA *remains absorbed in the damask.* ALYSEA *returns.* JOSEFA *looks up.*]

JOSEFA: You look so nice. For Eduardo, I suppose?

ALYSEA: He likes this dress. Did I hear someone?

JOSEFA: Tomás, sneaking around.

ALYSEA: Oh, no!

JOSEFA: Stop that! He's gone. Do you want Eduardo to see you this way? Now smile and go make some coffee. This morning I want him to have some with us before you go off on your walk.

ALYSEA: He'd like that. He's asked about you.

JOSEFA: Oh? He's a familiar face around the hacienda. Don Miguel has often said Eduardo is the most efficient foreman he has ever had. Such a handsome young man. [ALYSEA *begins to cry softly again.*] I told you to stop that. Everything's going to be alright. I promise. Last night doesn't matter.

ALYSEA: It was so horrible, so horrible. . . .

JOSEFA: Compose yourself. Last night could not be helped.

[ALYSEA *shudders in her lostness.* JOSEFA *goes to her and takes the girl's face in her hands.*]

JOSEFA: You are so dear to me, so dear. You know that. [*She strokes* ALYSEA's *hair.*] Your hair, your beautiful hair. I want so much to make you happy.

[ALYSEA *breaks away from her.*]

ALYSEA [*bitterly*]: Happy?

JOSEFA: Eduardo will be here any moment now. Go make that coffee. Suddenly I'm hungry. Bring some scones too.

ALYSEA: The lace. . . .

JOSEFA: Let that wait.

ALYSEA: It must make the morning express to the capital.

JOSEFA: Let it wait. There'll be time. Now go make that coffee.

ALYSEA: I don't think I can face Eduardo this morning.

JOSEFA: Yes, you will. And you will behave as if nothing happened. You owe me that. Do you hear? David is alright. I took him to the hospital; they took good care of him.

ALYSEA: What did you tell them?

JOSEFA: Someone had broken into the house, a criminal.

ALYSEA: We are the criminals. We did it.

JOSEFA: For the last time, control yourself. You did nothing. I did it. I did it, do you hear? You did nothing. I take full responsibility, and I hope you have enough sense not to become hysterical. Now, promise me. Promise.

ALYSEA: I—I promise.

JOSEFA: Thank you. We must be careful. Even with Eduardo.

ALYSEA: I'll get the coffee.

[ALYSEA *exits into kitchen.* JOSEFA *walks around the room at random, picks up a book, turns its pages, reads aloud.*]

JOSEFA: "El hombre toma, toma y hierre, la flor desnuda temblorosa. . . ." David? Little David? Will you forgive?

[Crosses to workbasket, picks up piece of lace, traces pattern.]

JOSEFA: I saw such terror in your eyes, David . . . such terror. But this piece of lace, my lace is beauty, light, all the good things. . . .

[Exits to bedroom, clutching piece of lace. ALYSEA returns, crosses to window, looks out. Knock on door: ALYSEA opens it to EDUARDO.]

EDUARDO: Ready?

ALYSEA: Come in.

EDUARDO: Our walk. . . .

ALYSEA: She wants to meet you.

EDUARDO: Your pagan goddess?

ALYSEA: She'll hear you.

EDUARDO: Have you told her about us?

ALYSEA: Not yet.

EDUARDO: Woman, we're leaving tonight! You haven't told her?

ALYSEA: It's hard. She's done so much for me. Brought me to this house, this room.

EDUARDO: This is her room, you said—fragile, full of light—like her.

ALYSEA: Very much so. Isn't it beautiful?

EDUARDO: Something you might see in a dream, an uncomfortable dream.

ALYSEA: Yes, yes . . . you're right! So right. I've never looked at it that way before. All that's happened. Can I blame it on a dream?

EDUARDO: Blame what? What's happened?

ALYSEA: I do want to go with you.

EDUARDO: Then, let's go—now. We can pack two horses, take the trail, find a clear field, build a cabin, plant seed, make babies. . . .

ALYSEA: Be serious. . . .

EDUARDO: I've never been more serious. There's nothing to stop us. Father Prado can marry us tonight. . . .

ALYSEA: I can't marry you.

EDUARDO: You're going to—this very night.

ALYSEA: Find a clear field, build a cabin . . . how wonderful it sounds. In pine country?

EDUARDO: Yes, in pine country.

ALYSEA: I was born in a dirty little village called Moteca. All I remember as a child was starving. When I was fourteen they came to the village. . . .

EDUARDO: Who came?

ALYSEA: Two big women dressed in satin. You can't imagine how beautiful they seemed to me who was dressed in rags. They came from the city, looking for seamstresses, they said. I could sew.

EDUARDO: You went with them to the city at fourteen?

ALYSEA: Two other girls who went with me were only twelve. I can still remember the women's body sweat, their dirty satin dresses. They took us to a house that smelled of whiskey, rotten food and cheap perfume.

EDUARDO: Your eyes—so full of pain.

ALYSEA: I want you to know how Josefa saved me.

EDUARDO: Saved you?

ALYSEA: Women with faces of cruel men told us there would be customers. We knew then we had been tricked. The twelve year olds trembled with terror, whimpering as they were led out to where men waited. I ran and tried to hide under some sordid limp dresses. But the women found me. They had a huge man who dragged me out, down some stairs, a hallway. I broke free and found my way to the street. But the man caught up with me, twisted my arm behind my back and started to shove me back into the house. The man was swearing and laughing like an animal, and the filth that came from his mouth . . . then, out of the darkness, Josefa appeared—with that walking stick of hers. She raised it over her head and beat the man, over and over again, until he lay so still, so still. She took my hand and led me away—to this place, this haven. . . .

EDUARDO: The open sky, the warm stars, the mountain top will be our haven.

ALYSEA: Oh, I want to belong to you so much. . . .

EDUARDO: And I, to you. . . . Something is the matter with you. I can feel it. What's wrong?

ALYSEA: That uncomfortable dream you sensed—no, no—much more horrible than just a dream—a nightmare, more. . . .

[JOSEFA *enters, composed, calmed.*]

JOSEFA: There you are [*to* ALYSEA]. What on earth is the matter child?

EDUARDO: Something about a nightmare.

ALYSEA: It's nothing—nothing. I'll get some coffee [*exits to kitchen*].

JOSEFA: She's been so nervous lately. Sometimes I fear I ask too much of her. I have so many orders for my lace. It's turning into a big enterprise. We've been working our fingers to the bone. . . .

EDUARDO: Ah, yes! I've heard about your beautiful lace.

JOSEFA: And where are you going for your walk?

EDUARDO: To a place where the pines blot out all the world. To a place where she believes everything I tell her.

JOSEFA: How clever of you. Are you not afraid to take walks into forbidden country?

EDUARDO: Forbidden by whom? It's beautiful country.

JOSEFA: You're not from around here, are you? The village people—all good Catholics—believe that the old pagan gods roam the area along the lake to its very source where pine country swallows up the desert.

EDUARDO: Funny—when Alysea talks about the things you do, the ways you weave your magic—I called you a pagan goddess. Now you tell me gods roam the hills—more than coincidence. But this room, your room, is too ordered to be pagan.

JOSEFA: The order of women—but have you seen my garden?

EDUARDO: Ah! that is another thing. It is wild, profuse, and all the colors of the world.

JOSEFA: You are so nice. How easily you feel what others feel. My flowers—they open to the sun and close to darkness. Then there are my night blooms, wanting from the moon, mysterious, strange, giving out the scents that excite passions. . . .

EDUARDO: You are a poet.

JOSEFA: Am I? I believe you to be a poet too. A dangerous poet, though.

[ALYSEA *comes in with coffee tray, places on coffee table.* JOSEFA *begins to serve.* ALYSEA *offers some scones to* EDUARDO.]

ALYSEA: Have one. I made them from an old recipe—Josefa's.

EDUARDO [*takes one*]: Very, very good. There is no end to your talents, Josefa.

ALYSEA: I'll leave you two for a while. I must mail this lace off with the morning express.

JOSEFA: Have some coffee with us, child.

ALYSEA: I don't feel like coffee this morning.

EDUARDO: Are you alright? You look a little pale. Have you been crying?

ALYSEA: No, no—some speck got in my eye . . . I'll be back soon. [ALYSEA *exits.*]

EDUARDO: She'll be alright, I suppose.

JOSEFA: Yes. I suspect she wants us to get to know each other.

EDUARDO: Every person in the village has given me a glowing picture of you. A saint, they call you. A giving, loving woman. . . .

JOSEFA: Stop! I am none of those things. The Josefa they talk about is a myth—like the old gods.

EDUARDO: When Alysea came in, you called me a dangerous poet. What do you mean?

JOSEFA: Gentlemen, men who feel what others feel, who have an eye for beauty can be dangerous—to women. It's so easy to fall in love with them.

EDUARDO: You flatter me.

JOSEFA: Am I not right? Don't women fall in love with you too easily?

EDUARDO: I . . . I. . . .

JOSEFA: Am I embarrassing you?

EDUARDO: I never thought you and I would be talking of such things.

JOSEFA: You forget, I am Clara's friend and her confidant.

EDUARDO: Of course. She has told you everything. I love Clara.

JOSEFA: Love or loved?

EDUARDO: Both, I suppose. It's not the first passion we felt some time ago. It's something deeper, something I cannot explain.

JOSEFA: You are dangerous. With one breath you tell me you love Clara, with the next one you'll tell me you love Alysea.

EDUARDO: You know!

JOSEFA: You come around too often, those walks of yours.

EDUARDO: What can I say?

JOSEFA: Explain it to me—this loving two women.

EDUARDO: I do not love Clara the way I love Alysea. I've asked her to be my wife.

JOSEFA: Alysea—to be your wife? Have you told her about Clara?

EDUARDO: No.

JOSEFA: How convenient.

EDUARDO: Alysea does not want to leave you. She thinks she owes you too much.

JOSEFA: It's called loyalty. Something that perhaps you owe to Clara?

[ALYSEA *returns.*]

ALYSEA: Have you two been getting along?

JOSEFA: Marvelously.

ALYSEA: Have you told him about the duendes?

JOSEFA: Really, child.

EDUARDO: Oh, you must. That's all she talks about—the mystery of your energy.

JOSEFA: It is something beyond reason.

EDUARDO: Tell me.

JOSEFA: You know the lake just beyond my property—that runs all the way to pine country.

EDUARDO: That's all I hear in the village from the young girls. Tomorrow, isn't it?—when all the girls in the village will bathe in its waters at high noon?

JOSEFA: A hopeless ritual. Poor girls! It is believed that if you bathe in the lake at high noon on San Lorenzo's day, you will find the perfect love to marry.

EDUARDO: All girls like to dream.

JOSEFA: Ah! but the reality. In this village what can they expect? Some callous Indian boy, someone who'll kiss them hotly on the lips behind some bush. Hot breath, awkward hands—and foolishly they call it love, and marry—their fate? A slavish existence. Soon they're milked dry of beauty, youth, and they call that a perfect marriage planned in Heaven.

EDUARDO: You never bathed in the lake—as a young girl—at midday—on San Lorenzo's day?

JOSEFA: Never! I was aware of the trap early in life. My desire was of a purer grain.

EDUARDO: Your desire?

JOSEFA: A pouring of self.

ALYSEA: Doesn't she say wonderful things? I don't understand them all, but they are mysterious.

JOSEFA: All alone, while the villagers were celebrating San Lorenzo's Day at night, I went to the lake. It was forbidden at night, old beliefs in roaming pagan gods. But I wanted that—the green gods of the pines, the source of the lake—and the moon— Ah! the moon.

EDUARDO: You are bewitched. . . .

ALYSEA: Tell him—tell him about the moon.

JOSEFA: One night, I went, on the saint's day. I remember the distant barrio lanterns, mixed with the laughing of happy people and the music . . . guitars. The darkness was moist, an orange moon filled the sky, and its light seemed to pour into me. I felt a green desire, a glorious longing—a suffering, a music, a stillness sung in me. I reached the lake to see it shimmer, tremble in the moonlight. I looked up and the moon was even larger than before. I felt the beginning of some strange fear. I ran and ran towards the pines. I looked around to see the moon following me. Suddenly I was in an open field and I dared not look at the moon again. I sat down to catch my breath, and I felt the moon pouring a passionate warmth, like blood syrup, into me. I lay down on the grass, face down. So still I lay. But my senses told me I must turn around. I did, with my eyes still closed. I felt the moon take me in its arms. I opened my eyes and saw the moon—like a sea around me. No fear anymore—just a joy, open and free.

ALYSEA: She mated with the moon.

EDUARDO: My reason tells me it could not be. But looking at you, Josefa, I have to believe.

JOSEFA: The light was me. I was to bear the children of light—the moon, the burning lake, spirits—all regenerating themselves in me—shaping my soul.

[*The harsh voice of* TOMÁS *outside the window suddenly breaks the spell.*]

TOMÁS: Josefa! Mujer!

EDUARDO: Who in the Devil . . .

ALYSEA [*in a frightened voice*]: Tomás.

[JOSEFA *crosses to window.*]

JOSEFA: Stop all that shouting! What do you want?

TOMÁS: Very strange. I found David's horse.

JOSEFA: Where?

TOMÁS: Running in the pasture, wearing a broken bridle.

JOSEFA: Are you sure it's David's horse?

TOMÁS: Of course, woman.

EDUARDO: Can I be of any help?

JOSEFA: Thank you, no. He can handle it [*to* TOMÁS]. Take him back to the stable.

TOMÁS: Sí, querida.

[*At the mention of* DAVID, ALYSEA *becomes frightened, sits in utter helplessness, begins to cry.* JOSEFA *remains calm, begins to pick up cups, napkins, etc. Goes to* EDUARDO, *takes his hand, leads him to* ALYSEA.]

JOSEFA: Take her for a walk.

EDUARDO: What is wrong, my love?

[TOMÁS *comes in through kitchen door.*]

TOMÁS: That's a bad sign. Something frightened the poor horse and he broke free.

JOSEFA: Nonsense. Take him back to the hacienda.

EDUARDO [*steering* ALYSEA *towards door.*]: I'm taking you to a very special place, where we can trace the path of the swallows. Now smile. [ALYSEA *smiles half-heartedly and leans against him for safety.*]

JOSEFA: Off with you two. Now go and enjoy yourselves.

[EDUARDO *and* ALYSEA *exit.* TOMÁS *looks after them shaking his head.*]

TOMÁS: She's in bad shape—bad. I heard you had an intruder last night   ha, ha, ha. And that terrible thing that happened to that little urchin you adopted. Poor little David. Who do you suppose did that terrible thing to him? That girl—she's afraid—like you're afraid.

JOSEFA: What?

TOMÁS: This morning, why didn't you admit that was blood in the pail? David's blood, yes? No, not a word—why?

JOSEFA: Why should I tell you anything.

TOMÁS: Your smart uncle does not believe all that talk about an intruder.

JOSEFA: I don't care what you believe.

TOMÁS: Poor little boy, poor little boy—all that blood—ha, ha, ha. All those times you have saved the poor, innocent, helpless ones, you never say anything. Smart, smart. The barrio always puts the story together—in your favor—making you out an angel. You are clever.

JOSEFA: Don't be ridiculous.

TOMÁS: People have no idea how clever you really are, Doña Perfecta. You saved Alysea from the whore house, eh? You had to cripple a man for life to do it, to be sure. You wouldn't stop beating him. But nobody remembers that. You saved David from a drunken father. Now, where was it that you beat David's father? Ah, yes, as the story goes. Ah, yes, some isolated road. The drunken old man was beating the boy without mercy. Then you came, the avenging angel, and returned the favor. Oh, how conveniently you forgot to tell anyone that the old man had been left on the road until—how many days later? Of course no one cared. The old man was the villain. You are the angel.

JOSEFA: You have an evil twisted mind.

TOMÁS: Perhaps you'll get your hands on me too, eh? Ha, ha, ha.

JOSEFA: Hadn't you better see about that horse?

TOMÁS: That girl is breaking apart. You better watch out. But look at you, such pious silence. You are the dangerous one alright.

JOSEFA: All your garbage, is it leading up to some form of blackmail?

TOMÁS: After all, I'm on your side, querida. You should be—grateful. We have the same blood running through our veins, verdad?

JOSEFA: Get out of here and look after that horse.

TOMÁS: A little money.

JOSEFA: Get out.

TOMÁS: You're made of stone, mujer.

JOSEFA: You have tried my patience long enough. Stop wasting my time. Now go.

TOMÁS: You can spare a few pesos.

[JOSEFA *looks at him contemptuously, then walks out into the kitchen without another word.* TOMÁS *scratches his head and looks around the room.*]

TOMÁS: Stupid woman. I'll break her yet. I know they keep money somewhere in this room.

[*He begins to search. Comes to the table drawer, opens it. He finds the box, pries open the lock, takes the money. He suddenly sees the knife. He picks it up, stares at it, then leaves the room with it.*]

ACT II

SCENE I

Later the same morning. EDUARDO *and* ALYSEA *are back from their walk. They come into the room laughing.*

EDUARDO: No more sadness. You promised.

ALYSEA: No more sadness. Come in. Stay a while.

EDUARDO: I must get back to the hacienda. If we're leaving tonight. . . .

ALYSEA: Leaving tonight. I can hardly believe it. I feel as if I were somebody new.

EDUARDO: You are my love.

ALYSEA: Your love. . . .

EDUARDO: Is something the matter?

ALYSEA: I don't know what you mean.

EDUARDO: You—tightened up.

ALYSEA: I have a hundred things to do myself before we leave tonight. Flowers! I must cut fresh flowers. She loves them so—on the table over there.

EDUARDO: You cannot bear to leave her, can you?

ALYSEA: Oh, I want to leave—I want to leave. You don't know how much. Thank you. Thank you for saving me.

EDUARDO: Saving you? From this—this dream of a woman's world?

ALYSEA: Go now. Go do what you have to do. I must cut those flowers.

[ALYSEA *leaves him, goes to garden. He shrugs and turns to leave. The front door opens. It is* CLARA ESQUINAS. *She carries a knitting bag.*]

EDUARDO: Clara.

CLARA: I didn't. . . .

EDUARDO: Expect to find me here?

CLARA: I don't see why not. She's going with you, isn't she?

EDUARDO: Yes. We're going to be married.

CLARA: She's very lucky.

EDUARDO: I asked you to leave your husband and marry me once, remember? You never could. Clara, this is awkward.

CLARA: No reason to feel that way. Just because you've been my lover. . . .

EDUARDO: It's awkward for you too.

CLARA: Ask me again.

EDUARDO: What?

CLARA: Ask me again—to go with you—to leave my husband. Yes, yes, yes, I'll go anywhere in the world with you.

EDUARDO: It's too late, Clara. We're not good for each other.

CLARA: Why? Because I'm too old? Because I drink? Because my husband would go after us? No . . . no, he doesn't care. He only loves himself, poor man. And I am just a pitiful, ageing woman . . . How easily you forgot me after all we've been to each other. But then, you *are* so young. There are no more Springs for me!

EDUARDO: I'll always love you, Clara, for being Clara, but. . . .

CLARA: Don't worry, I won't embarrass you. See? I'm wiping away all traces of my tears.

EDUARDO: Lovely, lovely Clara. If only I had reached the core of whatever is free in you. . . .

CLARA: Free?

EDUARDO: Goodbye, Clara.

[CLARA *turns away from him. After he leaves, she opens the knitting bag, searches for a cigarette, lights it with trembling hands. Then she takes out a small flask and drinks.* ALYSEA *returns from the garden, her arms full of flowers.*]

ALYSEA: Doña Clara.

CLARA: I came for my dress. Did Josefa finish my dress?

ALYSEA: Yes. I'll get it [*goes behind a screen, comes back with a simple gown, hands it to* CLARA]. She finished it a few days ago.

CLARA: How simple, how bare.

ALYSEA: There's a reason.

CLARA: I'll try it on [*goes behind screen*]. I saw Eduardo at the door.

ALYSEA: Oh. . . .

CLARA: Has he told you about me?

ALYSEA: About you?

CLARA: Never mind. He's in love with you, isn't he?

ALYSEA: Yes.

CLARA: And you're going away with him.

ALYSEA: He told you that? He shouldn't have. I haven't told Josefa.

CLARA: I won't mention anything to her.

ALYSEA: Thank you. It must come from me. She's been so kind.

CLARA: It'll break her heart. She's so fond of you [*comes back from behind the screen*]. Well, how does it look?

ALYSEA: You look beautiful.

CLARA [*pulls* ALYSEA *to her side, both facing a mirror*]: Look at you! How young you are. How very, very young. Would you believe that all you have now, I had, once?

ALYSEA: You're very beautiful.

CLARA: The skin, the hair, the bloom of youth, the firm, firm skin. See the lines around my eyes. And this pallor. Time is so unkind.

ALYSEA: I see a lovely face.

CLARA: How kind you are. Things do not fall easily in place for me nowadays. All will fall into place for you. Make the most of it. Before you realize it, one day you'll wake up, and youth will be gone, love will be gone, all good things like that. I'm embarrassing you, aren't I. . . .

ALYSEA: I don't know what to say. You are Doña Esquinas. You have everything.

CLARA: Go with him gladly, Alysea. Hold him, keep him, love him, be young and beautiful for him.

ALYSEA: Yes, I can do that.

CLARA: Don't look at me so strangely. I'm alright. The dress! Something's missing, don't you think?

ALYSEA: Josefa made a shawl to go with it.

CLARA: A shawl!

ALYSEA: I'll go find it.

[ALYSEA *goes to bedroom.* CLARA *watches her leave, takes flask from knitting bag, drinks.*]

CLARA [*crosses to mirror*]: He did love me. Oh, Angels in Heaven, I still love him so. The feel of his arms, the smell of his skin, his lovely, lovely hands. I mustn't . . . I mustn't.

[ALYSEA *returns with shawl.*]

ALYSEA: May I?

CLARA: Of course. [ALYSEA *places the shawl over one shoulder and adjusts it to* CLARA's *waist.*]

ALYSEA: The design is Andalusian.

CLARA: The design—it's so fragile. Where on earth did she find the design to copy?

ALYSEA: It's her design.

CLARA: Her design? Of course. She's so clever. It's almost unearthly.

ALYSEA: It came to her in a dream.

CLARA: I believe it. So delicate, the filigree of angels. . . .

ALYSEA: Her duendes, she said.

CLARA: Of course—her duendes. She's so lucky. Everything she touches becomes a miracle. If I know Josefa, the design means something.

ALYSEA: Here, let me unpin it so you can hold it up to the light [*unpins shawl*].

CLARA [*holds it up to light*]: I can't seem to make it out. . . .

ALYSEA [*tracing design with finger*]: See? A transparent mountain.

CLARA: Yes, yes, I see it.

ALYSEA: The mountain of sighs.

CLARA: The mountains of Andalusia. The caves where the gypsies live, starving sometimes, dying from the cold. People so much like the earth. A dream, you say?

ALYSEA: Yes. She was overwhelmed by depression in her dream—then, all of a sudden, from the core of the mountain, a spiral of light began to grow. Fireflies!

CLARA: Fireflies! How lovely. I see the spiral, the fireflies. . . . Oh, why can't I belong to Josefa's universe? I need some wondrous sustenance to fill my soul. But the mistress of the great Esquinas Hacienda is trapped and cannot escape. There I go again, saying things you cannot understand.

[JOSEFA *enters, crosses to them.*]

JOSEFA: A dream, Clara.
CLARA: Alysea told me about it.
JOSEFA: I have some combs for your hair. Alysea, will you please get them?

[ALYSEA *exits to bedroom for combs.*]

CLARA [*places shawl back around shoulder, holds it at her waist*]: I believe this is the way you want it.
JOSEFA: You've been drinking.
CLARA: Yes, I have. Don't preach. Drink is my faithful companion.
JOSEFA: You promised me you wouldn't drink unless you felt that desperation. . . .
CLARA: I'm desperate from sunup to sundown these days.
JOSEFA: I will not let you have any more liquor. I don't see how I weakened. . . .
CLARA: You supply me with liquor because you cannot stand my misery.
JOSEFA: I don't understand your misery.
CLARA: How can you? You are the Priestess of Light. Isn't that what you told me?
JOSEFA: You must find your own light, dear Clara. I hate to see you suffer so.
CLARA: Don't bother with me. I'm hopeless.
JOSEFA: You have to commit yourself to something, something other than a man.
CLARA: That's you. Not me. To be desired by a man—what else can a woman be upon the earth?
JOSEFA: I refuse to listen to such gibberish. You cannot have him back. I'm afraid he wants Alysea.
CLARA: I'm a coward. My husband calls me a coward because I drink. He thinks I'm greedy, vain. . . .
JOSEFA: How well he describes himself. I know the unhappiness he has caused you. Don't stay with him.
CLARA: Underneath it all, he really loves me, you know. Don Miguel Esquinas with his two hundred year old pride, loves me in his cruel way, his killing way. . . . [*begins to weep softly*].
JOSEFA: Leave him.
CLARA: I can't. I can't. He wasn't like that in the beginning, you know. But I was young and fresh. Then, we discovered I could have no children, and time went on, day after day, after day . . . Time is the villain, Josefa, not men.
JOSEFA: All they do is take and destroy. Haven't you already learned that yet?
CLARA: You're wrong. A woman was made to be loved by a man. To love a man is enough for a woman. But they don't let us love them.
JOSEFA: I wish I knew how to help free you.
CLARA: Free me? [*Laughs.*]

JOSEFA: That drink is making you hysterical.

CLARA: No. No. How can you understand? What do you know of loneliness?

JOSEFA: Loneliness? The mists full of pain when we stumble and fall and loneliness stretches out tearing at your heart. Then—chaos. But you save yourself. Do you hear me, save yourself!

CLARA: Did you?

JOSEFA: Yes! When you win the struggle, something emerges from inside, something that is solely yours and, then, there is no more emptiness.

[ALYSEA *returns with combs, hands them to* JOSEFA.]

JOSEFA: Here [*places them in* CLARA's *hair*], they're perfect.

CLARA: You have transformed me.

JOSEFA: A gypsy queen. Gypsy queens are free because they know the secrets of the earth.

ALYSEA: Look! [*Points to window, runs to it.*] They're coming! The swallows are coming! The sky is full of them.

[JOSEFA *and* CLARA *join her.*]

JOSEFA: They'll come in droves now. My birdhouse will be full by tomorrow.

CLARA: At noon tomorrow, all the village girls will be at the lake, bathing in the midday sun, dreaming of the perfect marriage made in heaven.

JOSEFA: Look at the lake. It shimmers with love. See—the light on the water is singing. I can feel the music in my skin.

CLARA: I can't see what you see or feel what you feel.

ALYSEA: Only Josefa.

JOSEFA: Water—fire—breathing pines. A temple waits.

SCENE II

Early afternoon of the same day. JOSEFA *enters from the outside. She is carrying an injured swallow. She cradles it gently as she examines it.*

JOSEFA: You poor little thing. Your wing is broken.

[ALYSEA *comes through the kitchen door.*]

JOSEFA: Look, he fell from the tree. I found it in the garden, a soft piece of life, fluttering. So small, so helpless. I think it's thirsty. Get an eye-dropper. Hurry.

[ALYSEA *goes back in the kitchen.* JOSEFA *sits in her rocking chair, placing the bird gently on her lap.* ALYSEA *comes back with a cup and a dropper. She sits on the floor next to* JOSEFA *and watches her feed the bird water.*]

JOSEFA: He has life, this one.

ALYSEA: Just a baby. Let's set the wing—some twigs and thread.

[ALYSEA *leaves again.* JOSEFA *continues feeding the bird.*]

JOSEFA: You'll be alright, little one. Here you can rest in the warmth of the sun. You must have been born near here. But your mother, she must have come from the long winter, stopping in low, wet lands, cutting the cold winds. Oh, the world is harsh! harsh! But something inside her, inside you flies to the sun. Now you are safe, safe. . . .

[ALYSEA *comes back. Together they set the wing.* ALYSEA *is absorbed in what she is doing.* JOSEFA *reaches out and strokes her hair.* ALYSEA *looks up and smiles, then finishes the setting of the wing.*]

ALYSEA: There.

JOSEFA: Let's put it back in the birdhouse.

[*They take the bird and place it carefully in the birdhouse.*]

JOSEFA: There are so many of them now. The pines near the lake must be full of them too. [*Looks at* ALYSEA.] It's been such a beautiful year, hasn't it?

ALYSEA: No.

JOSEFA: Alysea! How can you say that? We have shared so much. [*She reaches out and strokes* ALYSEA'*s hair.* ALYSEA *breaks away from her.*] What's the matter?

ALYSEA: I cannot blame you. I was a part of all that's happened.

JOSEFA: We have been so happy.

ALYSEA: I'm so miserable. I can't tell Eduardo what's between you and me.

JOSEFA: You make it sound so ugly.

ALYSEA: Isn't it?

JOSEFA: Ugly? Alysea, we share days of work; we share laughter, dreams. That is far from ugly.

ALYSEA: That's not what I'm talking about. You easily choose to forget, don't you?

JOSEFA: I suppose I do. You should try to forget.

ALYSEA: I can't! I can't! Eduardo loves me. I love him—but I feel so guilty, so unclean.

JOSEFA: I suffer the same guilt.

ALYSEA: Then why, why did you demand. . . .

JOSEFA: Demand . . . force you? Is that what you're saying?

ALYSEA: I'm sorry. We're both to blame. You've been so good to me. I can't refuse you anything.

JOSEFA: Terror and darkness overwhelms the soul—sometimes; that's why I've created a world of light, a sanctuary. Most of the time we are happy with ourselves—aren't we?

ALYSEA: Oh, yes, Josefa, of course, except . . . [*covers face with hands*] last night was one of terror and of darkness. Aren't you afraid?

JOSEFA: Afraid?

ALYSEA: Yes, afraid.

JOSEFA: I cannot afford to be afraid.

ALYSEA: Oh, my God, what we've become.

JOSEFA: We are the same, no different.

ALYSEA: The same? After what we did last night. What happened here last night was the most gross of violences. I'll show you! [*Crosses to table drawer to get the hidden knife. The drawer's empty.*] The knife! The knife! It's gone, Josefa, gone. [*Searches frantically. Stares unbelievingly.*] The money box—it's gone too. Do you suppose it was. . . .

JOSEFA: Tomás, of course—that lying, filthy thief.

ALYSEA: He'll, he'll. . . .

JOSEFA: He'll do nothing. I'll take care of him.

ALYSEA: What are we going to do—what are we going to do? He took it. He knows.

[ALYSEA *collapses in a chair; she's crying hysterically. The voice of* TOMÁS *is heard outside the window. He is singing a popular love song.* JOSEFA *goes to the window and calls out.*]

JOSEFA: Tomás, come in here. Tomás!

ALYSEA: Don't. I—I can't face him. What are we going to do?

[TOMÁS *comes through the kitchen door, still singing. He looks at* JOSEFA *and then at the terrified* ALYSEA.]

TOMÁS: Did you call me, querida? [*He strokes* JOSEFA's *arm. She breaks away.*]

JOSEFA: Keep your hands off me.

TOMÁS: Ha, ha, ha—Doña Perfecta. [*Looks at* ALYSEA.] What's the matter with you? As if I didn't know. . . .

[ALYSEA *covers her face.*]

TOMÁS: Don't cry, pretty one, Tomás is on your side. [*He flops on the sofa, spreads out his arms and looks around.*] I think I'll move in here with you two. I need a little elegance in my life. And, both of you need a man—eh? Ha, ha, ha. . . .

JOSEFA: You've been drinking.

TOMÁS: Of course I've been drinking, preciosa. You can afford it.

JOSEFA: You bought that liquor with the money you stole from this house.

TOMÁS: Yes, and I took the knife too. The knife! Doesn't that frighten you, dear niece? Look at her! What are you going to do about her?

[ALYSEA *is crying in total despair.* JOSEFA *goes to her.*]

JOSEFA: Hush, child. Go pack David's things. Remember—he needs them in the hospital. Don't cry any more. Now, go and pack.

[ALYSEA *tries to contain herself, then goes into the bedroom to pack.*]

TOMÁS: David, poor little David—ha, ha, ha.

JOSEFA: Have you ever done anything kind in your life?

TOMÁS: Why me? You are the angel of mercy.

JOSEFA: What do you intend to do?

TOMÁS: What I said—move in. And you will give me money now and then. I know about you and her. No more crumbs for me chula. I call the play.

JOSEFA: You're lying—bluffing—as usual.

TOMÁS: Am I?

[*There is a knock at the door. With great alacrity,* TOMÁS *goes to open it. It is* DON MIGUEL ESQUINAS.]

TOMÁS: Ah, Don Miguel. Come in. Come in.

[DON MIGUEL *brushes past* TOMÁS *contemptuously.* TOMÁS *bows with mock humility. He faces* JOSEFA.]

DON MIGUEL: You know what you've done?

JOSEFA: What I've done?

DON MIGUEL: Don't play the innocent with me. It's all your fault.

JOSEFA: Oh, my God, something's happened to Clara. Tell me. I must go to her. [*She starts towards the door.* DON MIGUEL *stops her.*]

DON MIGUEL: You'll never see her again.

JOSEFA: What do you mean? Where is she?

DON MIGUEL: When I hired you to be her companion, I expected you to follow my orders. I told you you must keep her away from liquor. That was your job.

JOSEFA: She is my friend.

DON MIGUEL: Your friend! You destroyed her—with all your lies and your liquor.

JOSEFA: At first, I tried—I tried to keep her from the liquor, but she suffered so. I didn't have the heart.

DON MIGUEL: How dare you take matters into your own hands! You were paid to stop her from drinking. Now she's beyond help. You know how I found her this afternoon? She was walking out into the desert—naked. Do you understand. She was irrational. I took her back to the house and she became a mad woman—throwing things—hallucinating, screaming about your spirits. She claimed they had no faces. Then she broke loose again and ran towards the lake. Not a stitch of clothing on her. I'll be the laughing stock. . . .

JOSEFA: That's all that matters to you, isn't it?

DON MIGUEL: Of course it matters to me. Do you think I deserve an alcoholic for a wife?

JOSEFA: She became that because of you.

DON MIGUEL: How dare you! You fed her the liquor! You fed her the lies!

JOSEFA: How easy it is to blame me. You just can't see, can you?

DON MIGUEL: What do you mean? She had everything. She was the wife of Don Miguel Esquinas. There was nothing she did not have.

JOSEFA: Except you.

DON MIGUEL: You stupid woman! I married her.

JOSEFA: She wanted you to love her.

DON MIGUEL: Love her? You women are insane with your disgusting sentimentality.

JOSEFA: She knew all about your women.

DON MIGUEL: That is a man's right. How dare you!

JOSEFA: She wanted a baby. How many times did she beg you for a baby?

DON MIGUEL: She couldn't have any.

JOSEFA: She begged you to let her adopt a baby.

DON MIGUEL: We settled that long ago. It was past and forgotten.

JOSEFA: It was never forgotten. She was so lonely, so lonely. She cried every night for the baby she did not have.

DON MIGUEL: Tears of a drunken woman. Adopt a baby? A baby not of the Esquinas blood? Never! An heir not of my blood? Absurd!

JOSEFA: Which of your bastards are you going to choose as your heir?

DON MIGUEL: How dare you, you, you, peasant! You'll never see her again.

JOSEFA: I'm going to her right now.

DON MIGUEL: She's gone, do you hear? Gone. A doctor and a nurse have taken her to the sanitorium. This time for good. I shall sign permanent commitment papers.

JOSEFA: You can't do that to her! You mustn't!

DON MIGUEL: I have. The matter is closed. I only came here to tell you not to show your face around the hacienda again.

[*She turns her back to him. He stands watching her for a second, then turns to leave.* TOMÁS *follows him to the door, still assuming a pose of mock humility.*]

TOMÁS: It's terrible what my niece has done. Terrible!

[DON MIGUEL *ignores him and leaves. When he is gone,* TOMÁS *turns to* JOSEFA.]

TOMÁS: Tch—tch—tch—Doña Perfecta is not perfecta, eh?

JOSEFA: She wanted so much to believe in my spirits. My poor darling . . . so lost— so lost.

TOMÁS [*grabs her arm angrily*]: Did you hear me? You are not perfect, are you? You're going to listen to me from now on.

[JOSEFA *does not move, waits for him to let go of her arm. He does. She turns away from him with contempt.*]

JOSEFA: Leave me. I do not feel well.

TOMÁS: None of your tricks, do you hear? I know about you and the girl. I put two and two together. You see, I saw the both of you, last San Lorenzo's day. I left the fiesta in town early and walked towards the lake to sober up. It was you and she—you came out of the lake and ran after her towards the pines. Kind of blurred in my mind—the drink. But I remember now.

JOSEFA: Drunken hallucinations.

TOMÁS: La reina del barrio—ha, ha, ha. You're nothing but a . . .

JOSEFA: If you have nothing else to threaten me with . . . [*She walks away from him with disdain.*]

TOMÁS: You don't fool me, reina del barrio. Look at you—pretending to be so superior. You're afraid of me.

[JOSEFA *turns abruptly and faces him haughtily. They stand in silent defiance then* TOMÁS *falters. He turns away and leaves.* JOSEFA *looks after him.* ALYSEA *comes from the bedroom wearing traveling clothes.*]

JOSEFA: He's gone. He won't do anything. I'll see to it. Do you have all the things David will need?

ALYSEA: Yes, I think so.

[JOSEFA *goes to her and strokes her cheek.*]

JOSEFA: The ride will do you good. When you come back from the hospital, we'll have supper here. We'll plan. No one, nothing can defeat us. Trust me.

ALYSEA [*breaking away from* JOSEFA]: I'm not coming back.

JOSEFA: Not coming back?

ALYSEA: Eduardo and I made plans to leave tonight. We're going to be married.

JOSEFA: Indeed. So you've made a choice. You've chosen to become a sacrifice.

ALYSEA: I do not see it that way. I love him and he loves me.

JOSEFA: How long will your precious Eduardo love you? Don Miguel was here. Clara drank herself insane. You know why? Because Eduardo left her. Promised to love her forever. He was her lover until you came along. Of course he betrayed her. What do you think he'll do to you?

ALYSEA: He loves me. I know he loves me.

JOSEFA: All your pain is still to come. Haven't I taught you anything?

ALYSEA: Oh, you taught me beautiful things, a wonder in believing—but it's all fallen apart, Josefa. David's eyes. I remember his eyes so full of terror. His eyes told me you and I were all the terror in the world.

JOSEFA: How wrong you are. The terror's out there—wherever you're going with Eduardo.

ALYSEA: The violence—the useless violence.

JOSEFA: No. One time does not erase the beauty of our days. Each day was radiant and resplendent—we created with our hearts, our hands, our minds—it was all ours. And, out of those days flowed freedom, beauty, meaning. You know that's true.

ALYSEA: Yes. It's true. That's why I can't understand. . . .

[JOSEFA *walks to the window and reaches into the birdhouse, finding the injured bird. She picks it up, fondles it, holds it against her cheek.*]

JOSEFA: Remember how he came—all broken?

ALYSEA: I came to you the same way.

JOSEFA: You came to my sanctuary, my world. The birds come here for the same reason. [*She remembers something painful, goes to the rocking chair, places the bird on her lap and strokes it gently.*]

JOSEFA: When I was seven, the swallows came as they do each year. My mother had been dead one season. The birds came one hot dry dawn and continued all day. I had walked to the edge of the desert that still hotter afternoon. Boys were catching birds, stoning them, killing them, laughing about it with a fearful joy. It was like a bad dream. The sand was a sea of dead birds. I ran towards the boys and hit them with my fists. I screamed, "Stop, stop." They laughed at me. Then for a joke, they threw me to the ground and held me down, the burning sand against my back. In spite of my terror, I opened my eyes to see a big, burly boy take a knife. In his hand he held a trembling little swallow. He cut the bird, oh, God! [JOSEFA *strokes the bird, shakes her head, closes eyes, pausing.*] I saw the bird's insides and something spilled into my face, ran into my mouth—warm—warm—salt warm. Was it tears? Was it blood? [*Stands, goes to window, caresses bird, places it in the birdhouse. The rosary bell begins to toll.* JOSEFA *looks out at sunset.*] Alysea, look! the lake is screaming with life—Oh, such colors. Stay with me. Stay with me.

ALYSEA: No. I don't belong here. The lace, the light, the garden, the peace are all yours. You were so kind and I—I could not refuse you anything. I felt in time that the Alysea with you was someone else, not me.

JOSEFA: I've never loved anyone the way I love you.

ALYSEA: No. No. never again. I was meant to love Eduardo. I know I owe you so much. But it's not the same. I can't stay here.

[ALYSEA *turns and goes into bedroom.* JOSEFA *starts to follow, then changes her mind. She sits and begins to work on the unfinished damask. She unhooks the needle and works with great concentration. After a minute or so,* ALYSEA *returns with a suitcase.* JOSEFA *does not look up, although she is aware that* ALYSEA *has come into the room.* ALYSEA *crosses behind* JOSEFA *and looks at the damask.*]

JOSEFA: What do you think?

ALYSEA: It's very beautiful.

JOSEFA: I think the design should have a name. Some nights ago I had a most vivid dream—swallows flying into tall, flowing, golden grain, and the earth was moist-sweet. And, I could hear the rustle of their wings whispering the honey language of the sun, and I, without body, was the vibration of the light in harmony with wings, with flowing grain and with—with the passionate breathing of the earth. I started working on this design—how many weeks ago. . . . Well, that doesn't matter. But look at it. It's as if my fingers knew with celestial precision the contents of that dream before I dreamt it. Look at the design.

ALYSEA [*looking intently at the design*]: I see the grain, the outline of a swallow's wing, yes. There it is.

JOSEFA: And here, the gold thread. That is I—disembodied—free—elemental. Oh, I know it!

ALYSEA: What's this up here—see? The zigzag. It looks like lightning piercing the sky. See.

JOSEFA: No. I do not see lightning. Perhaps, the traces of sweet, sweet rain.

ALYSEA: Of course, gentle Josefa, you can't see the lightning, can you? But I see it, clearly. How strange! Beauty and terror so well intermingled. Lovely Josefa. I shall remember you and all the beauty of this place. Goodbye, sweet lady of light.

[JOSEFA *does not respond. She is absorbed with the design, tracing it meticulously with her fingers, perhaps her own way of not hearing the goodbye.* ALYSEA *picks up the suitcase, hesitates and turns to look at* JOSEFA *once more, then she goes to the door.*]

JOSEFA: Alysea.

ALYSEA: Yes?

JOSEFA: Stop by the rectory on your way to town—will you? I won't be going to rosary services tonight. Please ask Father Prado, if at all possible, to come and see me after service tonight.

ALYSEA: Of course. [ALYSEA *stands for a moment looking at* JOSEFA, *then departs.* JOSEFA *continues putting the final stitches on the damask.*]

JOSEFA: There. It's finished. My spirits have spoken.

[*She stands, rubs the back of her neck, breathes deeply. She goes to the window. It has turned dark, though the moon flows golden into the room. She looks out to the lake.*]

JOSEFA: My lover! You look like morning crystal in the water. So still, so deep. I ache for you so! Only you, you—can console me, love me, fulfill me. Only you can take me in your arms and make me whole. You beckon me so shamelessly.

ACT III

SCENE I

Late the same evening. There's a knock at the door. JOSEFA, *sitting by the light of the moon streaming through the window, rises, goes to the door. It is Father Prado.*

JOSEFA: Father, I've been waiting for you. Thank you for coming. Wait, let me turn on a light. I was sitting in the dark, thinking. [*She turns on a lamp. She leads him to the couch.*] I know I asked you to come at such a late hour.

FATHER PRADO: The hour does not matter. I'm glad to be here. Señora Escobar led the rosary since you weren't there. She always throws in some extra "Hail, Marys." Now we can talk over the plans.

JOSEFA: Plans?

FATHER PRADO: For the procession tomorrow. Isn't that why you asked me to come?

JOSEFA: I had forgotten about the procession. How terrible of me.

FATHER PRADO: You simply cannot do that, my child. You would disappoint many people. They want to honor you. They love and respect you very much.

JOSEFA: I do not deserve it.

FATHER PRADO: You? with your splendid nature, your spiritual strength. You, who have done so much for so many? You must give them a chance to repay. Give them their day.

JOSEFA: Their day.

FATHER PRADO: I shall be here early in the morning. Three rings of the church bell will summon the people to congregate by the fountain in the town square. That fountain—it was full of swallows this morning. They're here.

JOSEFA: I know. My birdhouse is full.

FATHER PRADO: Well, everything is ready. The ladies have laid out the fine embroidered altar linens you sent, made by your lovely little hands, and the surplices for the altar boys—how can I thank you? It is your way, your way. I get the feeling you are not looking forward to tomorrow.

JOSEFA: Oh Father, so many things have happened.

FATHER PRADO: Of course, of course—I understand. Terrible, terrible things.

JOSEFA: You know about Clara?

FATHER PRADO: May God help her, give her strength.

JOSEFA: Don Miguel doesn't want her back.

FATHER PRADO: He's been very patient for some years now. She's had the drinking problem for a long time.

JOSEFA: Patient! He wasn't patient; he simply ignored her—left her alone in the hacienda for months at a time. Father—sometimes, sometimes I would let her drink because I couldn't stand her anguish. It was so—so empty—like a deep, dark chasm—and she kept falling down, down, down, never coming to the bottom. She couldn't help herself. At least—at least—when she drank she pretended gaiety. It gave her some kind of strength. Nothing else seemed to help.

FATHER PRADO: Did you pray with her?

JOSEFA: Pray? No we never did.

FATHER PRADO: Then you must pray for her now.

JOSEFA: Oh Father, I'm so confused. I—I. . . . Alysea has left me. She's going to marry Eduardo. I shall never see her again.

FATHER PRADO: She's not that way. She loves you too much and is very grateful for all you did for her. She told me that before she left. She'll come back. And you should be happy for her and Eduardo.

JOSEFA: Happy?

FATHER PRADO: You look so pale. Are you feeling alright?

JOSEFA: David . . .

FATHER PRADO: I'm so sorry, my dear. I didn't want to speak of it because I thought it might upset you. A tragedy! No one but a deranged person could have done that to the poor, defenseless child.

JOSEFA: Father!

FATHER PRADO: Yes, my child. . . .

JOSEFA: I want confession now.

FATHER PRADO: Here?

JOSEFA: Please, Father.

FATHER PRADO: Of course, if that's what you want.

[He comes to her; she falls on her knees before him.]

FATHER PRADO: What is wrong?

JOSEFA: Forgive me, Father, for I have sinned—I have sinned—I have sinned.

FATHER PRADO: Tell me, my daughter.

JOSEFA: I'm so lost.

FATHER PRADO: All of us are, at one time or another.

JOSEFA: I am guilty of grievious sins—beyond forgiveness.

FATHER PRADO: God forgives all. His mercy is boundless.

JOSEFA: Love takes with soundless force, shapes and forms we cannot control.

FATHER PRADO: What do you mean?

JOSEFA: There was no intruder. It was I who hurt David.

FATHER PRADO: I can't believe. . . .

JOSEFA: I did it.

FATHER PRADO: Why?

JOSEFA: He saw something he was not meant to see—between Alysea and me.

FATHER PRADO: What could have been so terrible for you to hurt the child? You love David.

JOSEFA: I don't have the right to say that. What is love?

FATHER PRADO: Tell me, tell me what happened.

JOSEFA: It began a year ago.

FATHER PRADO: A year ago?

JOSEFA: Yes. Please hear me out. I don't want to excuse the things I've done. I know now that somehow I seem to hurt all the people I profess to love. Why?

FATHER PRADO: Tomorrow the people of this town are honoring you because you care for others. You are generous and kind.

JOSEFA: There's another side. The things I do for people, the miracles I create with my hands—the lace, my garden—are the deeds of Josefa, High Priestess of the Moon. Don't look at me that way—let me explain. Los duendes, my spirits, have given me certain energies, creative energies.

FATHER PRADO: You speak in riddles, my child. I know you to be most devout. Why do you talk such nonsense? You, a good Christian.

JOSEFA: I lived alone for a long time, Father—a recluse, you might say. Even when I am with people, I am still alone—because I'm different—almost as if I belong to another world. The world of the elements—sun, earth, rain, vegetation, light— mostly light. A year ago I convinced Alysea not to bathe in the lake with the barrio girls. Theirs was a hopeless dream. I told her that if there were any spirits in the lake, they belonged to the night and the moon. My energies had always been spiritual. I lived a life, a good life, thinking this was enough. I took Alysea to the lake at night, a year ago, to bathe by moonlight—to feel the spirits, to feel as one with the pines, the moon, the water. She was caught up in my magic.

FATHER PRADO: This is all news to me—as if another person were telling me all this.

JOSEFA: I kept my body mute, physical desire, for worthier things.

FATHER PRADO: You never married.

JOSEFA: No. I took care of my mother who was an invalid, until she died. I never knew my father. He deserted my mother before I was born. It was enough for me to devote my life to caring for my mother. But many times I was overwhelmed by loneliness, a lostness, until my spirits came. Then came Alysea and little David.

FATHER PRADO: You said you took Alysea to bathe in the lake at night. . . .

JOSEFA: Oh, yes . . . Forgive me. I seem to ramble so.

FATHER PRADO: Did something happen?

JOSEFA: The water had a bright warmth, as if the moon had melted into the ripples. My body became alive with a silver desire. I could not help it. There was a fire in me, lapping, wanting. I think Alysea sensed it. She left the water and started running, away from me perhaps. I became a creature I had never known before. I followed and and caught up with her. I gently held her in my arms and found her lips.

FATHER PRADO: And found her lips?

JOSEFA: Alysea became my lover that one time—a year ago. After that I felt such guilt and disgust for myself. I didn't talk about it to Alysea. I was too ashamed.

FATHER PRADO: We have all transgressed—in one way or another. The body has needs.

JOSEFA: Not my body—not my body—I told myself after it happened. It had all been some temporary madness—or have I been mad all along?

FATHER PRADO: Of course not.

JOSEFA: But, Father, it came over me again last night. That bestial desire came over me again. Against Alysea's wish I begin to caress her. Out of gratitude for what I've done for her, she refuses me nothing. David came into the room. Oh, his eyes! His eyes . . . was it only fear I saw in his eyes? His eyes were my eyes—I was looking at myself . . . Slime, smut, maggots, mire. A fury took my heart. All I could think of was—He'll tell people—he'll tell the world. I took a kitchen knife—wanting to silence him—I tried to cut his tongue. . . .

FATHER PRADO: The ways of the Devil! You were mad. I believe it.

JOSEFA: I came to my senses and saw the horror of what I was doing. I dropped the knife—but I had already wounded him. . . . I did not cut off his tongue, did I? Oh, my God. . . . I didn't—did I? The nurses—what did they say? A wound, only a wound. I remember slashing once, and then the child broke free, and I grew cold—cold with my sin—oh, the heinous Josefa. Don't you see. Look, I'll show you. [*Looks for finished damask, finds it, holds it up to him.*] See, Father? Lightning-terror. Alysea pointed it out to me, and I never knew, or would believe. I am the lightning piercing . . . I am beauty and terror intermingled. It shouldn't be—it shouldn't be . . . but it is . . . and I must separate the two. I must! I must!

FATHER: Put your trust in Christ. Follow his way. Be true to your Faith. . . .

JOSEFA: That won't work, Father. I have to separate the two.

FATHER: Your life is far from tragic. You are greatly beloved in this pueblo. I have always admired. . . . Well, that was the Josefa as seen by those who could not see.

JOSEFA: I could not see! But now I do. The Josefa of the world is empty, confined. She strikes out in terror without forethought. But the me that the spirits created! Oh, I am the light that is the fallen flame of sunset; I am my night blooms that open to the moon; I am the delicate, intricate design of my lace—belonging to something other than the world. Not the world. This body that I wear holds all my passions—yes. I am a woman of hungry passions. If I had had a husband, a lover—long before this—I would cling to the world, celebrate my body and desire. But, it was never so. My spirits took my passions, shaped them into light—That is the Josefa you admire, Father—not the one that is alien to the world.

FATHER: You are of the world. That is the reality. You are wanted in the world. Your spirit belongs to God—not to any duendes. Oh, my child, I forgive your sins. You are absolved. Kneel and pray an act of contrition. Truly repent and feel your God.

[JOSEFA *kneels and prays the act of contrition, a comforting outlet of emotion. When she finishes,* FATHER PRADO *helps her to her feet and holds her for a moment.*]

FATHER: Don't despair, my child. Don't despair. You are exhausted. Tomorrow is an important day for you. Sleep, rest. I'll take my leave now. Goodnight, my child.

[JOSEFA *accompanies him to the door. She looks around the room with fond memories, touches curtains, lace, flowers, then goes to the window.*]

JOSEFA: You are trembling, my waters, silver, deep, and the moon is waiting. I must take a stroll to the lake—I must have comfort from my spirits. Surely they know I must find the spiral of my origin. They must take me to my origin. . . .

SCENE II

Two weeks later. The birdhouse is empty now. The room is unseemly bright. CLEMENCIA *is busily dusting. Knock at the door.* CLEMENCIA *opens it.*

CLEMENCIA: Don Eduardo—Alysea—Ah, back from your honeymoon. Come in, come in. Here, I am—in Josefa's house.

EDUARDO: So you are. How do you like it here?

CLEMENCIA: It's a beautiful house. So peaceful. Such light!

ALYSEA: It's unusually bright, isn't it?

CLEMENCIA: And the garden—all in bloom. Poor Josefa. . . .

EDUARDO: Any news?

ALYSEA: We just came in from town. We heard about Josefa disappearing.

CLEMENCIA: No one knows where she is—where she went. Some believe this. Others believe that. No one knows.

EDUARDO: People in the pueblo told us they dragged the lake looking for her body. They found no trace.

ALYSEA: My poor darling Josefa.

CLEMENCIA: I know what a loss it must be to you and little David. But Father Prado has a will—she left this house to David, and I am to stay here and take care of him. Imagine me living here—no more delivering milk, getting up at the break of dawn— not that I wanted Josefa to disappear. We all love her too much. Sad—sad. The whole town sits in the evenings wondering, believing this and that—superstitions. I myself wonder if they are only superstitions.

ALYSEA: What are they saying?

CLEMENCIA: Well—some believe she went for a walk at night—into forbidden country, up in the pines where the ancient gods live—and they kept her as one of their own. Others believe she was kidnapped by the intruders who hurt David.

ALYSEA: How is David?

CLEMENCIA: Coming home tonight. I'm going to cook his favorite dinner.

ALYSEA: Chicken caldo with fresh corn.

CLEMENCIA: That's what he said.

ALYSEA: Thank God—he can talk.

CLEMENCIA: A mile a minute—that child! He still does not know about Josefa. Stay for supper. He would love to see you.

EDUARDO: Thank you, but that will be impossible. We are on our way to Guadala-jara. We just stopped by—or at least—Alysea wanted to see the house one last time. She says something was telling her to come.

CLEMENCIA: She wanted to say goodbye to the beautiful house where she was so happy—isn't that it, Alysea?

ALYSEA: I suppose. . . .

CLEMENCIA: You will love Guadalajara. It is paradise.

EDUARDO: Not exactly—but I do have a job waiting for me there.

CLEMENCIA: Two young people—their whole life before them—Ah! that's good. Josefa would be so happy for you. I'm sorry you had to come back to such sad news. This pueblo—I don't know what is happening.

ALYSEA: The birds are gone—that's one thing that happened. Come and look, Eduardo. The bird house is empty. Oh, no—look, not our little bird. It had a broken wing and Josefa and I mended it. It's still here—the only one. When did they leave?

CLEMENCIA: Three days ago. One of the omens. . . .

EDUARDO: What do you mean—omen?

CLEMENCIA: There have been many since Josefa disappeared. Everyone believes it's because she disappeared. You know that when the birds leave every year, they follow a straight path north. Not this time. At dawn—they took off—towards the lake and they circled the lake for hours, some coming down to rest on the reeds, to fly low on the water. The whole town went out to look. Finally, when the sun was in the West, they flew off following the path north. Very strange. Why did they do such a thing?

EDUARDO: You said "omens." Have there been others?

CLEMENCIA: Oh, yes. Two days after she disappeared, the sky up in the pine woods was filled with millions of fireflies. It looked as if the stars had come down to dance among the pines. It was so beautiful to see.

ALYSEA: A happy omen. I believe that.

CLEMENCIA: Then there was the moon. The night after she disappeared, when the moon came out—it was red, blood red—then it seemed to come down low, very low. When we looked out into the lake—the moon seemed to have turned to silver—then it seemed to fall into the lake—yes fall into the water. The world was dark for a few seconds. Then the moon appeared among the trees—yellow and bright. Those who saw it thought it was the end of the world.

ALYSEA: Josefa. . . .

CLEMENCIA: What?

ALYSEA: Oh, nothing, nothing . . . were there any other strange things that happened?

CLEMENCIA: In this very house. The first few days, everybody was looking for Josefa.

When she wasn't found, Father Prado asked me to come and water her garden. You know it's the only beautiful garden in the whole town. Well, I noticed that all the night flowers, those strange ones that give off that strong fragrance, they were all dead—all of them. The stalks brown—also the leaves. The day the moon fell into the lake, I came to dig them out to clean up a bit. Alysea, you will not believe this—neither did my eyes at the time—the flowers had come to life again. I went to the garden at night—they were opened. They were beautiful. They were dancing in the night breeze—and the fragrance was so strong, some one from the village told me they could smell it in the town. What do you think of that?

EDUARDO: Strange, indeed! But, I suppose, in one way or another, it can all be explained.

CLEMENCIA: Well, I certainly cannot explain any of it. Oh, look at the time. I must go to el mercado to get the things for David's supper. Now you stay here and enjoy the house one last time, though I hope you will come back and visit. You will, won't you?

EDUARDO: Oh, certainly we shall.

ALYSEA: I'll always come back.

CLEMENCIA: Well—I must be off. [*Exits.*]

EDUARDO: You think she's here, don't you?

ALYSEA: Oh, yes—she is!

EDUARDO: You are the most superstitious one of all.

ALYSEA: No—it's not superstition. It's more than that. Josefa believed that we humans know so little of ourselves. Creation—that that was the wonder—the mystery—the awe. No, superstitions—most of them come from fear. This has something to do with beauty, with things eternal and unexplained.

EDUARDO: You really loved her, didn't you?

ALYSEA: I still do. [*Goes to window, then looks around the room.*] Josefa, you're here. I sense you. I know you're here. . . .

EDUARDO: It must be catching. I have this strange feeling. Is it the light in this room? It is unearthly. . . .

ALYSEA: The light, the flowers, the lake, the moon, and the history of what she has become is in this. [*She picks up a piece of Josefa's lace.*] See how intricate, how fragile. Little bits and pieces coming together—a crystal thing of light—beautiful Josefa— we love you—we'll always love you.

Curtain

QUESTIONS

1. Describe the tone of the prologue. How does it prefigure the mood of the action?
2. Josefa's house seems to be shrouded in mystery. What sort of mysteries exist that are hinted at, but not explained?
3. When Josefa and Eduardo have their first dialogue in Act I, each seems to have a different concept of love. What are they?
4. Toward the end of Act I, Josefa remarks that the swallows "have a long, lonely

flight." What does she mean in light of the fact that they arrive in droves? What might the swallows symbolize?

5. Who are the magicians that Josefa refers to?

6. In Act II, Josefa tells the injured bird that they "share so much." What do they share?

7. In Act II, Alysea decides to leave the house. What might she gain by leaving? What might she lose?

8. What is the significance of the unfinished damask? Why does Josefa consider naming it "Swallow Song"?

9. In Act III, why does Josefa refer to the house as an "oasis in the desert"?

10. Josefa and Father Prado argue over the significance of the ritual. What is each one's point of view about it?

11. Why has Josefa cut off David's tongue?

12. Josefa claims she has a desire to create beauty. What sort of beauty is she referring to? What is the purpose of creating such beauty?

William Shakespeare

THE TRAGEDY OF OTHELLO, THE MOOR OF VENICE

--- **CHARACTERS** ---

OTHELLO, the Moor
BRABANTIO, (a Venetian senator), father to Desdemona
CASSIO, an honorable lieutenant (to Othello)
IAGO (Othello's ancient), a villain
RODERIGO, a gulled gentleman
DUKE OF VENICE
SENATORS (of Venice)
MONTANO, governor of Cyprus
LODOVICO AND GRATIANO (kinsmen to Brabantio), two noble Venetians
SAILORS
CLOWN
DESDEMONA, wife to Othello
EMILIA, wife to Iago
BIANCA, a courtesan
MESSENGER, HERALD, OFFICERS, VENETIAN GENTLEMEN, MUSICIANS, ATTENDANTS

Scene: Venice and Cyprus

ACT I

SCENE I

[*Enter* RODERIGO *and* IAGO.]

RODERIGO:
  Tush, never tell me! I take it much unkindly
  That thou, Iago, who has had my purse
  As if the strings were thine, shouldst know of this.   3
IAGO:
  'Sblood, but you'll not hear me!   4
  If ever I did dream of such a matter,
  Abhor me.
RODERIGO:
  Thou told'st me thou didst hold him in thy hate.
IAGO:
  Despise me if I do not. Three great ones of the city,
  In personal suit to make me his lieutenant,
  Off-capped to him; and, by the faith of man,   10
  I know my price; I am worth no worse a place.
  But he, as loving his own pride and purposes,
  Evades them with a bombast circumstance.   13
  Horribly stuffed with epithets of war;
  [And, in conclusion,]
  Nonsuits my mediators; for, "Certes," says he,   16
  "I have already chose my officer."
  And what was he?
  Forsooth, a great arithmetician,   19
  One Michael Cassio, a Florentine
  (A fellow almost damned in a fair wife)   21
  That never set a squadron in the field,
  Nor the division of a battle knows
  More than a spinster; unless the bookish theoric,
  Wherein the tongued consuls can propose
  As masterly as he. Mere prattle without practice
  Is all his soldiership. But he, sir, had th' election;
  And I (of whom his eyes had seen the proof
  At Rhodes, at Cyprus, and on other grounds
  Christian and heathen) must be belee'd and calmed   30

Scene i A street in Venice   **3** *this* i.e. Desdemona's elopement   **4** *'Sblood* by God's blood   **10** *him* i.e.
Othello   **13** *a bombast circumstance* pompous circumlocutions   **16** *Nonsuits* rejects   **19** *arithmetician* theoreti-
cian   **21** *almost . . . wife* (an obscure allusion: Cassio is unmarried, but see IV,i, 123)   **30** *belee'd and calmed*
left in the lurch

By debitor and creditor; this counter-caster,   31
He, in good time, must his lieutenant be,
And I—God bless the mark!—his Moorship's ancient.   33
RODERIGO:
By heaven, I rather would have been his hangman.
IAGO:
Why, there's no remedy; 'tis the curse of service.
Preferment goes by letter and affection,   36
And not by old gradation, where each second
Stood heir to th'first. Now, sir, be judge yourself,
Whether I in any just term am affined   39
To love the Moor.
RODERIGO: I would not follow him then.
IAGO:
O, sir, content you;
I follow him to serve my turn upon him.
We cannot all be masters, nor all masters
Cannot be truly followed. You shall mark
Many a duteous and knee-crooking knave
That, doting on his own obsequious bondage,
Wears out his time, much like his master's ass,
For naught but provender; and when he's old, cashiered.   48
Whip me such honest knaves! Others there are
Who, trimmed in forms and visages of duty,   50
Keep yet their hearts attending on themselves;
And, throwing but shows of service on their lords,
Do well thrive by them, and when they have lined their coats,
Do themselves homage. These fellows have some soul;
And such a one do I profess myself. For, sir,
It is as sure as you are Roderigo,
Were I the Moor, I would not be Iago.
In following him, I follow but myself;
Heaven is my judge, not I for love and duty,
But seeming so, for my peculiar end;
For when my outward action doth demonstrate
The native act and figure of my heart   62
In compliment extern, 'tis not long after   63
But I will wear my heart upon my sleeve
For daws to peck at; I am not what I am.

---

31 *counter-caster* bookkeeper **33** *ancient* ensign **36** *affection* favoritism **39** *affined* obliged **48** *cashiered* turned off **50** *trimmed* dressed up **62** *The . . . heart* what I really believe and intend **63** *compliment extern* outward appearance

RODERIGO:
    What a full fortune does the thick-lips owe   66
    If he can carry't thus!
IAGO: Call up her father,
    Rouse him. Make after him, poison his delight,
    Proclaim him in the streets. Incense her kinsmen,
    And though he in a fertile climate dwell,
    Plague him with flies; though that his joy be joy,
    Yet throw such changes of vexation on't
    As it may lose some color.
RODERIGO:
    Here is her father's house. I'll call aloud.
IAGO:
    Do, with like timorous accent and dire yell   75
    As when, by night and negligence, the fire
    Is spied in populous cities.
RODERIGO:
    What, ho, Brabantio! Signior Brabantio, ho!
IAGO:
    Awake! What, ho, Brabantio! Thieves! thieves! thieves!
    Look to your house, your daughter, and your bags!
    Thieves! thieves!   81

[BRABANTIO *at a window.*]

BRABANTIO [*above*]:
    What is the reason of this terrible summons?
    What is the matter there?
RODERIGO:
    Signior, is all your family within?
IAGO:
    Are your doors locked?
BRABANTIO: Why, wherefore ask you this?
IAGO:
    Zounds, sir, y' are robbed! For shame, put on your gown!
    Your heart is burst; you have lost half your soul.
    Even now, now, very now, an old black ram
    Is tupping your white ewe. Arise, arise!
    Awake the snorting citizens with the bell,   90
    Or else the devil will make a grandsire of you.
    Arise, I say!

---

66 *thick-lips* (Elizabethans made no clear distinction between Moors and Negroes); *owe* own   **75** *timorous* terrifying   **81 s.d.** *Brabantio at a window* (added from quarto)   **90** *snorting* snoring

BRABANTIO: What, have you lost your wits?

RODERIGO:

Most reverend signior, do you know my voice?

BRABANTIO:

Not I. What are you?

RODERIGO:

My name is Roderigo.

BRABANTIO: The worser welcome!

I have charged thee not to haunt about my doors.

In honest plainness thou hast heard me say

My daughter is not for thee; and now, in madness,

Being full of supper and distemp'ring draughts,

Upon malicious knavery dost thou come

To start my quiet.

RODERIGO:

Sir, sir, sir—

BRABANTIO: But thou must needs be sure

My spirit and my place have in them power

To make this bitter to thee.

RODERIGO: Patience, good sir.

BRABANTIO:

What tell'st thou me of robbing? This is Venice;

My house is not a grange.   106

RODERIGO: Most grave Brabantio,

In simple and pure soul I come to you.

IAGO: Zounds, sir, you are one of those that will not serve God if the devil

bid you. Because we come to do you service, and you think we are

ruffians, you'll have your daughter covered with a Barbary horse; you'll

have your nephews neigh to you; you'll have coursers for cousins, and   112

gennets for germans.   113

BRABANTIO:

What profane wretch art thou?

IAGO: I am one, sir, that comes to tell you your daughter and the Moor are

now making the beast with two backs.

BRABANTIO:

Thou art a villain.

IAGO: You are—a senator.

BRABANTIO:

This thou shalt answer. I know thee, Roderigo.

RODERIGO:

Sir, I will answer anything. But I beseech you,

If't be your pleasure and most wise consent,

106 *grange* isolated farmhouse   **112** *nephews* i.e. grandsons   **113** *gennets for germans* Spanish horses for near kinsmen

As partly I find it is, that your fair daughter,
At this odd-even and dull watch o' the' night, 123
Transported, with no worse nor better guard
But with a knave of common hire, a gondolier,
To the gross clasps of a lascivious Moor—
If this be known to you, and your allowance, 127
We then have done you bold and saucy wrongs;
But if you know not this, my manners tell me
We have your wrong rebuke. Do not believe
That, from the sense of all civility, 131
I thus would play and trifle with your reverence.
Your daughter, if you have not given her leave,
I say again, hath made a gross revolt,
Tying her duty, beauty, wit, and fortunes
In an extravagant and wheeling stranger 136
Of here and everywhere. Straight satisfy yourself.
If she be in her chamber, or your house,
Let loose on me the justice of the state
For thus deluding you.
BRABANTIO: Strike on the tinder, ho!
Give me a taper! Call up all my people!
This accident is not unlike my dream. 143
Belief of it oppresses me already
Light, I say! light!   [*Exit (above)*.]
IAGO: Farewell, for I must leave you.
It seems not meet, nor wholesome to my place,
To be produced—as, if I stay, I shall—
Against the Moor. For I do know the state,
However, this may gall him with some check, 149
Cannot with safety cast him; for he's embarked 150
With such loud reason to the Cyprus wars,
Which even now stand in act, that for their souls 152
Another of his fathom they have none 153
To lead their business; in which regard,
Though I do hate him as I do hell-pains,
Yet, for necessity of present life,
I must show out a flag and sign of love,
Which is indeed but sign. That you shall surely find him,
Lead to the Sagittary the raised search; 159
And there will I be with him. So farewell.   [*Exit.*] 160

---

123 *odd-even* between night and morning **127** *allowance* approval **131** *from the sense* in violation **136** *extravagant and wheeling* expatriate and roving **143** *accident* occurrence **149** *check* reprimand **150** *cast* discharge **152** *stand in act* are going on **153** *fathom* capacity **159** *Sagittary* an inn **160 s.d.** *nightgown* dressing gown

[*Enter (below)* BRABANTIO *in his nightgown, and servants with torches.*]

BRABANTIO:
It is too true an evil. Gone she is;
And what's to come of my despisèd time
Is naught but bitterness. Now, Roderigo,
Where didst thou see her?—O unhappy girl!—
With the Moor, say'st thou?—Who would be a father?—
How didst thou know 'twas she?—O, she deceives me
Past thought!—What said she to you?—Get moe tapers!   167
Raise all my kindred!—Are they married, think you?

RODERIGO:
Truly I think they are.

BRABANTIO:
O heaven! How got she out? O treason of the blood!
Fathers, from hence trust not your daughters' minds
By what you see them act. Is there not charms
By which the property of youth and maidhood   173
May be abused? Have you not read, Roderigo,
Of some such thing?

RODERIGO: Yes, sir, I have indeed.

BRABANTIO:
Call up my brother.—O, would you had had her!—
Some one way, some another.—Do you know
Where we may apprehend her and the Moor?

RODERIGO:
I think I can discover him, if you please
To get good guard and go along with me.

BRABANTIO:
Pray you lead on. At every house I'll call;
I may command at most.—Get weapons, ho!
And raise some special officers of night.—
On, good Roderigo; I'll deserve your pains.   [*Exeunt.*]   185

SCENE II

[*Enter* OTHELLO, IAGO, *and attendants with torches.*]

IAGO:
Though in the trade of war I have slain men,
Yet do I hold it very stuff o' th' conscience

167 *moe* more 173 *property* nature 185 *deserve* show gratitude for
Scene ii Before the lodgings of Othello

To do no contrived murther. I lack iniquity
Sometimes to do me service. Nine or ten times
I had thought t' have yerked him here under the ribs.   5
OTHELLO:
   'Tis better as it is.
IAGO: Nay, but he prated,
And spoke such scurvy and provoking terms
Against your honor
That with the little godliness I have
I did full hard forbear him. But I pray you, sir,
Are you fast married? Be assured of this,   11
That the magnifico is much beloved,   12
And hath in his effect a voice potential   13
As double as the Duke's. He will divorce you,   14
Or put upon you what restraint and grievance
The law, with all his might to enforce it on,
Will give him cable.
OTHELLO: Let him do his spite.
My services which I have done the signiory   18
Shall out-tongue his complaints. 'Tis yet to know—   19
Which, when I know that boasting is an honor,
I shall promulgate—I fetch my life and being
From men of royal siege; and my demerits   22
May speak unbonneted to as proud a fortune   23
As this that I have reached. For know, Iago,
But that I love the gentle Desdemona,
I would not my unhousèd free condition   26
Put into circumscription and confine
For the sea's worth. But look, what lights come yond?
IAGO:
Those are the raisèd father and his friends.
You were best go in.
OTHELLO: Not I; I must be found.
My parts, my title, and my perfect soul   31
Shall manifest me rightly. Is it they?
IAGO:
By Janus, I think no.

[*Enter* CASSIO, *with torches, officers.*]

---

5 *yerked* stabbed   **11** *fast* securely   **12** *magnifico* grandee (Brabantio)   **13** *potential* powerful   **14** *double* doubly influential   **18** *signiory* Venetian government   **19** *yet to know* still not generally known   **22** *siege* rank; *demerits* deserts   **23-24** *May speak . . . reached* are equal, I modestly assert, to those of Desdemona's family   **26** *unhoused* unrestrained   **31** *perfect soul* stainless conscience

OTHELLO:
  The servants of the Duke, and my lieutenant.
  The goodness of the night upon you, friends!
  What is the news?
CASSIO: The Duke does greet you, general;
  And he requires your haste-post-haste appearance
  Even on the instant.
OTHELLO: What's the matter, think you?
CASSIO:
  Something from Cyprus, as I may divine.
  It is a business of some heat. The galleys
  Have sent a dozen sequent messengers   41
  This very night at one another's heels,
  And many of the consuls, raised and met,
  Are at the Duke's already. You have been hotly called for;
  When, being not at your lodging to be found,
  The Senate hath sent about three several quests
  To search you out.
OTHELLO: 'Tis well I am found by you.
  I will but spend a word here in the house,
  And go with you.   [*Exit.*]
CASSIO: Ancient, what makes he here?
IAGO:
  Faith, he to-night hath boarded a land carack.   50
  If it prove lawful prize, he's made for ever.
CASSIO:
  I do not understand.
IAGO: He's married.
CASSIO: To who?

[*Enter* OTHELLO.]

IAGO:
  Marry, to—Come, captain, will you go?
OTHELLO: Have with you.
CASSIO:
  Here comes another troop to seek for you.

[*Enter* BRABANTIO, RODERIGO, *and others with lights and weapons.*]

IAGO:
  It is Brabantio. General, be advised.
  He comes to bad intent.

41 *sequent* consecutive   **50** *carack* treasure ship

OTHELLO: Holla! stand there!
RODERIGO:
  Signior, it is the Moor.
BRABANTIO: Down with him, thief!

[They draw on both sides.]

IAGO:
  You, Roderigo! Come, sir, I am for you.
OTHELLO:
  Keep up your bright swords, for the dew will rust them.   59
  Good signior, you shall more command with years
  Than with your weapons.
BRABANTIO:
  O thou foul thief, where hast thou stowed my daughter?
  Damned as thou art, thou hast enchanted her!
  For I'll refer me to all things of sense,
  If she in chains of magic were not bound,
  Whether a maid so tender, fair, and happy,
  So opposite to marriage that she shunned
  The wealthy curlèd darlings of our nation,
  Would ever have, t'incur a general mock,
  Run from her guardage to the sooty bosom
  Of such a thing as thou—to fear, not to delight.
  Judge me the world if 'tis not gross in sense   72
  That thou hast practiced on her with foul charms,
  Abused her delicate youth with drugs or minerals
  That weaken motion. I'll have't disputed on;   75
  'Tis probable, and palpable to thinking.
  I therefore apprehend and do attach thee   77
  For an abuser of the world, a practicer
  Of arts inhibited and out of warrant.
  Lay hold upon him. If he do resist,
  Subdue him at his peril.
OTHELLO: Hold your hands,
  Both you of my inclining and the rest.
  Were it my cue to fight, I should have known it
  Without a prompter. Where will you that I go
  To answer this your charge?
BRABANTIO: To prison, till fit time
  Of law and course of direct session   86
  Call thee to answer.

---

59 *Keep up* i.e. sheath **72** *gross in sense* obvious **75** *motion* perception **77** *attach* arrest **86** *direct session*
regular trial

OTHELLO: What if I do obey?
  How may the Duke be therewith satisfied,
  Whose messengers are here about my side
  Upon some present business of the state
  To bring me to him?
OFFICER: 'Tis true, most worthy signior.
  The Duke's in council, and your noble self
  I am sure is sent for.
BRABANTIO: How? The Duke in council?
  In this time of the night? Bring him away.
  Mine's not an idle cause. The Duke himself,   95
  Or any of my brothers of state,
  Cannot but feel this wrong as 'twere their own;
  For if such actions may have passage free,
  Bondslaves and pagans shall our statesmen be.   [*Exeunt.*]

SCENE III

[*Enter* DUKE *and senators, set at a table, with lights and attendants.*]

DUKE:
  There is no composition in these news   1
  That gives them credit.
1 SENATOR: Indeed they are disporportioned.
  My letters say a hundred and seven galleys.
DUKE:
  And mine a hundred forty.
2 SENATOR: And mine two hundred.
  But though they jump not on a just account—   5
  As in these cases where the aim reports   6
  'Tis oft with difference—yet do they all confirm
  A Turkish fleet, and bearing up to Cyprus.
DUKE:
  Nay, it is possible enough to judgement.
  I do not so secure me in the error   10
  But the main article I do approve   11
  In fearful sense.
SAILOR [*within*]: What, ho! what, ho! what, ho!
OFFICER:
  A messenger from the galleys.

---

95 *idle* trifling
Scene iii The Venetian Senate Chamber   **1** *composition* consistency   **5** *jump* agree   **6** *aim* conjecture
10 *so secure me* take such comfort   **11** *article* substance; *approve* accept

[*Enter* SAILOR]

DUKE: Now, what's the business?
SAILOR:
  The Turkish preparation makes for Rhodes.
  So was I bid report here to the state
  By Signior Angelo.
DUKE:
  How say you by this change?
1 SENATOR: This cannot be

  By no assay of reason. 'Tis a pageant   18
  To keep us in false gaze. When we consider   19
  Th'importancy of Cyprus to the Turk,
  And let ourselves again but understand
  That, as it more concerns the Turk than Rhodes,
  So may he with more facile question bear it,   23
  For that it stands not in such warlike brace,   24
  But altogether lacks th' abilities
  That Rhodes is dressed in—if we make thought of this,
  We must not think the Turk is so unskillful
  To leave that latest which concerns him first,
  Neglecting an attempt of ease and gain
  To wake and wage a danger profitless.   30
DUKE:
  Nay, in all confidence, he's not for Rhodes.
OFFICER:
  Here is more news.

[*Enter a messenger.*]

MESSENGER:
  The Ottomites, reverend and gracious,
  Steering with due course toward the isle of Rhodes,
  Have there injointed them with an after fleet.
1 SENATOR:
  Ay, so I thought. How many, as you guess?
MESSENGER:
  Of thirty sail; and now they do restem   37
  Their backward course, bearing with frank appearance
  Their purposes toward Cyprus. Signior Montano,
  Your trusty and most valiant servitor,

---

18 *assay* test   **19** *in false gaze* looking the wrong way   **23** *with . . . bear* more easily capture   **24** *brace* posture of defense   **30** *wake and wage* rouse and risk   **37** *restem* steer again

With his free duty recommends you thus,
And prays you to believe him.
DUKE:
'Tis certain then for Cyprus.
Marcus Luccicos, is not he in town?   44
1 SENATOR:
He's now in Florence.
DUKE:
Write from us to him; post, post-haste dispatch.
1 SENATOR:
Here comes Brabantio and the valiant Moor.

[*Enter* BRABANTIO, OTHELLO, CASSIO, IAGO, RODERIGO, *and officers.*]

DUKE:
Valiant Othello, we must straight employ you
Against the general enemy Ottoman.
[*To* BRABANTIO]
I did not see you. Welcome, gentle signior.
We lacked your counsel and your help to-night.
BRABANTIO:
So did I yours. Good your grace, pardon me.
Neither my place, nor aught I heard of business,
Hath raised me from my bed; nor doth the general care
Take hold on me; for my particular grief
Is of so floodgate and o'erbearing nature   56
That it engluts and swallows other sorrows,   57
And it is still itself.
DUKE: Why, what's the matter?
BRABANTIO:
My daughter! O, my daughter!
ALL: Dead?
BRABANTIO: Ay, to me.
She is abused, stol'n from me, and corrupted
By spells and medicines bought of mountebanks;
For nature so prepost'rously to err,
Being not deficient, blind, or lame of sense,   63
Sans witchcraft could not.
DUKE:
Who'er he be that in this foul proceeding
Hath thus beguiled your daughter of herself,
And you of her, the bloody book of law

44 *Marcus Luccicos* (presumably a Venetian envoy) **56** *floodgate* torrential **57** *engluts* devours **63** *deficient* feeble-minded

You shall yourself read in the bitter letter
After your own sense; yea, though our proper son   69
Stood in your action.   70
BRABANTIO: Humbly I thank your grace.
Here is the man—this Moor, whom now, it seems,
Your special mandate for the state affairs
Hath hither brought.
ALL: We are very sorry for't.
DUKE [*to* OTHELLO]:
What, in your own part, can you say to this?
BRABANTIO:
Nothing, but this is so.
OTHELLO:
Most potent, grave, and reverend signiors,
My very noble, and approved good masters,   77
That I have ta'en away this old man's daughter,
It is most true; true I have married her.
The very head and front of my offending
Hath this extent, no more. Rude am I in my speech,   81
And little blessed with the soft phrase of peace;
For since these arms of mine had seven years' pith   83
Till now some nine moons wasted, they have used
Their dearest action in the tented field;
And little of this great world can I speak
More than pertains to feats of broil and battle;
And therefore little shall I grace my cause
In speaking for myself. Yet, by your gracious patience,
I will a round unvarnished tale deliver   90
Of my whole course of love—what drugs, what charms,
What conjuration, and what mighty magic
(For such proceeding am I charged withal)
I won his daughter.
BRABANTIO: A maiden never bold;
Of spirit so still and quiet that her motion   95
Blushed at herself; and she—in spite of nature,
Of years, of country, credit, everything—
To fall in love with what she feared to look on!
It is a judgment maimed and most imperfect
That will confess perfection so could err
Against all rules of nature, and must be driven
To find out practices of cunning hell   102

---

69 *our proper* my own   **70** *stood in your action* were accused by you   **77** *approved* tested by experience
81 *rude* unpolished   **83** *pith* strength   **90** *round* plain   **95–96** *her motion Blushed* her own emotions caused
her to blush   **102** *practices* plots

Why this should be. I therefore vouch again	103
That with some mixtures pow'rful o'er the blood,	104
Or with some dram, conjured to this effect,	
He wrought upon her.	

DUKE: To vouch this is no proof,
Without more certain and more overt test
Than these thin habits and poor likelihoods   108
Of modern seeming do prefer against him.   109

1 SENATOR:
But, Othello, speak.
Did you by indirect and forcèd courses   111
Subdue and poison this young maid's affections?
Or came it by request, and such fair question   113
As soul to soul affordeth?

OTHELLO: I do beseech you,
Send for the lady to the Sagittary
And let her speak of me before her father.
If you do find me foul in her report,
The trust, the office, I do hold of you
Not only take away, but let your sentence
Even fall upon my life.

DUKE: Fetch Desdemona hither.

OTHELLO:
Ancient, conduct them; you best know the place.

                            [*Exit* IAGO, *with two or three attendants.*]

And still she come, as truly as to heaven
I do confess the vices of my blood,
So justly to your grave ears I'll present
How I did thrive in this fair lady's love,
And she in mine.

DUKE:
Say it, Othello.

OTHELLO:
Her father loved me, oft invited me;
Still questioned me the story of my life   129
From year to year—the battles, sieges, fortunes
That I have passed.
I ran it through, even from my boyish days
To th' very moment that he bade me tell it.
Wherein I spoke of most disastrous chances,
Of moving accidents by flood and field;
Of hairbreadth scapes i' th' imminent deadly breach;

---

103 *vouch* assert   **104** *blood* passions   **108** *thin habits* slight appearances   **109** *modern seeming* everyday supposition   **111** *forced* violent   **113** *question* conversation   **129** *Still* continually

Of being taken by the insolent foe
And sold to slavery; of my redemption thence
And portance in my travels' history;   139
Wherin of anters vast and deserts idle,   140
Rough quarries, rocks, and hills whose heads touch heaven,
It was my hint to speak—such was the process;   142
And of the Cannibals that each other eat,
The Anthropophagi, and men whose heads   144
Do grow beneath their shoulders. This to hear
Would Desdemona seriously incline;
But still the house affairs would draw her thence;
Which ever as she could with haste dispatch,
She'd come again, and with a greedy ear
Devour up my discourse. Which I observing,
Took once a pliant hour, and found good means   151
To draw from her a prayer of earnest heart
That I would all my pilgrimage dilate,   153
Whereof by parcels she had something heard,   154
But not intentively. I did consent,   155
And often did beguile her of her tears
When I did speak of some distressful stroke
That my youth suffered. My story being done,
She gave me for my pains a world of sighs.
She swore, i' faith, 'twas strange, 'twas passing strange;
'Twas pitiful, 'twas wondrous pitiful.
She wished she had not heard it; yet she wished
That heaven had made her such a man. She thanked me;
And bade me, if I had a friend that loved her,
I should but teach him how to tell my story,
And that would woo her. Upon this hint I spake.   166
She loved me for the dangers I had passed,
And I loved her that she did pity them.
This only is the witchcraft I have used.
Here comes the lady. Let her witness it.

[*Enter* DESDEMONA, IAGO, *attendants.*]

DUKE:
I think this tale would win my daughter too.
Good Brabantio,
Take up this mangled matter at the best.

---

139 *portance* behavior **140** *anters* caves **142** *hint* occasion **144** *Anthropophagi* man-eaters **151** *pliant* propitious **153** *dilate* recount in full **154** *parcels* portions **155** *intentively* with full attention **166** *hint* opportunity

Men do their broken weapons rather use
Than their bare hands.

BRABANTIO: I pray you hear her speak.
If she confess that she was half the wooer,
Destruction on my head if my bad blame
Light on the man! Come hither, gentle mistress.
Do you perceive in all this noble company
Where most you owe obedience?

DESDEMONA: My noble father,
I do perceive here a divided duty.
To you I am bound for life and education;   182
My life and education both do learn me
How to respect you: you are the lord of duty;
I am hitherto your daughter. But here's my husband;
And so much duty as my mother showed
To you, preferring you before her father,
So much I challenge that I may profess   188
Due to the Moor my lord.

BRABANTIO: God be with you! I have done.
Please it your grace, on to the state affairs.
I had rather to adopt a child than get it.   191
Come hither, Moor.
I here do give thee that with all my heart
Which, but thou hast already, with all my heart
I would keep from thee. For your sake, jewel,   195
I am glad at soul I have no other child;
For thy escape would teach me tyranny,   197
To hang clogs on them. I have done, my lord.

DUKE:
Let me speak like yourself and lay a sentence   199
Which, as a grise or step, may help these lovers   200
Into your favor.
When remedies are past, the griefs are ended
By seeing the worst, which late on hopes depended.
To mourn a mischief that is past and gone
Is the next way to draw new mischief on.
What cannot be preserved when fortune takes,
Patience her injury a mock'ry makes.
The robbed that smiles steals something from the thief;
He robs himself that spends a bootless grief.

BRABANTIO:
So let the Turk of Cyprus us beguile: 210
We lose it not so long as we can smile.

---

182 *education* upbringing   **188** *challenge* claim the right   **191** *get* beget   **195** *For your sake* because of you
197 *escape* escapade   **199** *like yourself* as you should; *sentence* maxim   **200** *grise* step

He bears the sentence well that nothing bears
But the free comfort which from thence he hears;
But he bears both the sentence and the sorrow
That to pay grief must of poor patience borrow.
These sentences, to sugar, or to gall,
Being strong on both sides, are equivocal.
But words are words. I never yet did hear
That the bruised heart was piercèd through the ear.
I humbly beseech you, now to the affairs of state.
DUKE: The Turk with a most mighty preparation makes
  for Cyprus. Othello, the fortitude of the place is best   222
  known to you; and though we have there a substitute
  of most allowed sufficiency, yet opinion, a more sover-   224
  eign mistress of effects, throws a more safer voice on you.
  You must therefore be content to slubber the gloss of   226
  your new fortunes with this more stubborn and
  boist'rous expedition.
OTHELLO:
  The tyrant custom, most grave senators,
  Hath made the flinty and steel couch of war
  My thrice-driven bed of down. I do agnize   231
  A natural and prompt alacrity
  I find in hardness; and do undertake
  These present wars against the Ottomites.
  Most humbly, therefore, bending to your state,
  I crave fit disposition for my wife,
  Due reference of place, and exhibition,   237
  With such accommodation and besort   238
  As levels with her breeding.   239
DUKE: If you please,
  Be't at her father's.
BRABANTIO: I will not have it so.
OTHELLO:
  Nor I.
DESDEMONA: Nor I. I would not there reside,
  To put my father in impatient thoughts
  By being in his eye. Most gracious Duke,
  To my unfolding lend your prosperous ear,   244
  And let me find a charter in your voice,
  T' assist my simpleness.   246
DUKE:
  What would you, Desdemona?

---

222 *fortitude* fortification   **224** *allowed* acknowledged; *opinion* public opinion   **226** *slubber* sully   **231–33** *ag-nize . . . hardness* recognize in myself a natural and easy response to hardship   **237** *exhibition* allowance of money   **238** *besort* suitable company   **239** *levels* corresponds   **244** *prosperous* favorable   **246** *simpleness* lack of skill

DESDEMONA:

That I did love the Moor to live with him,
My downright violence, and storm of fortunes,
May trumpet to the world. My heart's subdued
Even to the very quality of my lord.
I saw Othello's visage in his mind,
And to his honors and his valiant parts
Did I my soul and fortunes consecrate.
So that, dear lords, if I be left behind,
A moth of peace, and he go to the war,
The rites for which I love him are bereft me,
And I a heavy interim shall support
By his dear absence. Let me go with him.

OTHELLO:

Let her have your voice.
Vouch with me, heaven, I therefore beg it not
To please the palate of my appetite,
Not to comply with heat—the young affects   263
In me defunct—and proper satisfaction;
But to be free and bounteous to her mind;
And heaven defend your good souls that you think
I will your serious and great business scant
When she is with me. No, when light-winged toys
Of feathered Cupid seel with wanton dullness   269
My speculative and officed instruments,   270
That my disports corrupt and taint my business,   271
Let housewives make a skillet of my helm,
And all indign and base adversities   273
Make head against my estimation!   274

DUKE:

Be it as you shall privately determine,
Either for her stay or going. Th' affair cries haste,
And speed must answer it.

1 SENATOR:

You must away to-night.

OTHELLO: With all my heart.

DUKE:

At nine i' th' morning here we'll meet again.
Othello, leave some officer behind,
And he shall our commission bring to you,
With such things else of quality and respect
As doth import you.   283

---

263 *heat* passions; *young affects* tendencies of youth   **269** *seel* blind   **270** *My . . . instruments* my perceptive and responsible faculties   **271** *That* so that   **273** *indign* unworthy   **274** *estimation* reputation   **283** *import* concern

OTHELLO: So please your grace, my ancient;
   A man he is of honesty and trust.
   To his conveyance I assign my wife,
   With what else needful your good grace shall think
   To be sent after me.
DUKE: Let it be so.
   Good night to every one.
   [*To* BRABANTIO]   And, noble signior,
   If virtue no delighted beauty lack,   289
   Your son-in-law is far more fair than black.
1 SENATOR:
   Adieu, brave Moor. Use Desdemona well.
BRABANTIO:
   Look to her, Moor, if thou hast eyes to see:
   She has deceived her father, and may thee.
                            [*Exeunt* DUKE, *senators, officers, etc.*]
OTHELLO:
   My life upon her faith!—Honest Iago,
   My Desdemona must I leave to thee.
   I prithee let thy wife attend on her,
   And bring them after in the best advantage.   297
   Come, Desdemona. I have but an hour
   Of love, of worldly matters and direction,
   To spend with thee. We must obey the time.
                          [*Exit* MOOR *and* DESDEMONA.]
RODERIGO: Iago,—
IAGO: What say'st thou, noble heart?
RODERIGO: What will I do, think'st thou?
IAGO: Why, go to bed and sleep.
RODERIGO: I will incontinently drown myself.   305
IAGO: If thou dost, I shall never love thee after. Why, thou silly gentleman!
RODERIGO: It is silliness to live when to live is torment; and then have we a
   prescription to die when death is our physician.
IAGO: O villainous! I have looked upon the world for four times seven
   years; and since I could distinguish betwixt a benefit and an injury, I
   never found man that knew how to love himself. Ere I would say I would
   drown myself for the love of a guinea hen, I would change my humanity
   with a baboon.
RODERIGO: What should I do? I confess it is my shame to be so fond, but it
   is not in my virtue to amend it.
IAGO: Virtue? a fig! 'Tis in ourselves that we are thus or,
   thus. Our bodies are our gardens, to the which our wills
   are gardeners; so that if we will plant nettles or sow

289 *delighted* delightful   **297** *in the best advantage* at the best opportunity   **305** *incontinently* forthwith

lettuce, set hyssop and weed up thyme, supply it with
one gender of herbs or distract it with many—either to   320
have it sterile with idleness or manured with industry—
why, the power and corrigible authority of this lies in   322
our wills. If the balance of our lives had not one scale
of reason to poise another of sensuality, the blood and   324
baseness of our natures would conduct us to most
preposterous conclusions. But we have reason to cool our
raging motions, our carnal stings, our unbitted lusts;   327
whereof I take this that you call love to be a sect or scion.   328

RODERIGO: It cannot be.

IAGO: It is merely a lust of the blood and a permission of
the will. Come, be a man! Drown thyself? Drown cats
and blind puppies! I have professed me thy friend, and I
confess me knit to thy deserving with cables of perdurable
toughness. I could never better stead thee than now. Put
money in thy purse. Follow thou the wars; defeat thy   335
favor with an usurped beard. I say, put money in thy
purse. It cannot be that Desdemona should long continue her love to the Moor—put money in thy purse—nor
he his to her. It was a violent commencement in her, and
thou shalt see an answerable sequestration—put but   340
money in thy purse. These Moors are changeable in their
wills—fill thy purse with money. The food that to him
now is as luscious as locusts shall be to him shortly as bitter as coloquintida. She must change for youth: when she   344
is sated with his body, she will find the error of her choice.
She must have change, she must. Therefore put money
in thy purse. If thou wilt needs damn thyself, do it a more
delicate way than drowning. Make all the money thou   348
canst. If sanctimony and a frail vow betwixt an erring   349
barbarian and a supersubtle Venetian be not too hard for
my wits and all the tribe of hell, thou shalt enjoy her.
Therefore make money. A pox of drowning thyself! 'Tis
clean out of the way. Seek thou rather to be hanged in
compassing thy joy than to be drowned and go without
her.

RODERIGO: Wilt thou be fast to my hopes, if I depend on
the issue?

---

320 *gender* species   **322** *corrigible authority* corrective power   **324** *poise* counterbalance   **324–25** *blood and
baseness* animal instincts   **327** *motions* appetites; *unbitted* uncontrolled   **328** *sect or scion* offshoot, cutting
335–36 *defeat thy favor* spoil thy appearance   **340** *sequestration* estrangement   **344** *coloquintida* a medicine
348 *Make* raise   **349** *erring* wandering

IAGO: Thou art sure of me. Go, make money. I have told,
    thee often, and I retell thee again and again, I hate the
    Moor. My cause is hearted; thine hath no less reason.   360
    Let us be conjunctive in our revenge against him. If
    thou canst cuckold him, thou dost thyself a pleasure, me
    a sport. There are many events in the womb of time,
    which will be delivered. Traverse, go, provide thy   364
    money! We will have more of this to-morrow. Adieu.
RODERIGO: Where shall we meet i' th' morning?
IAGO: At my lodging.
RODERIGO: I'll be with thee betimes.
IAGO: Go to, farewell.—Do you hear, Roderigo?
RODERIGO: What say you?
IAGO: No more of drowning, do you hear?
RODERIGO: I am changed.
IAGO: Go to, farewell. Put money enough in your purse.
RODERIGO: I'll sell all my land.   [*Exit.*]
IAGO:
    Thus do I ever make my fool my purse;
    For I mine own gained knowledge should profane
    If I would time expend with such a snipe   377
    But for my sport and profit. I hate the Moor;
    And it is thought abroad that 'twixt my sheets
    H'as done my office. I know not if't be true;
    But I, for mere suspicion in that kind,
    Will do as if for surety. He holds me well;   382
    The better shall my purpose work on him.
    Cassio's a proper man. Let me see now:
    To get his place, and to plume up my will   385
    In double knavery—How, how?—Let's see:—
    After some time, to abuse Othello's ears
    That he is too familiar with his wife.
    He hath a person and a smooth dispose   389
    To be suspected—framed to make women false.
    The Moor is of a free and open nature   391
    That thinks men honest that but seem to be so;
    And will as tenderly be led by th' nose
    As asses are.
    I have't! It is engend'red! Hell and night
    Must bring this monstrous birth to the world's light.

                            [*Exit.*]

---

360 *My cause is hearted* my heart is in it **364** *Traverse* forward march **377** *snipe* fool **382** *well* in high regard **385** *plume up* gratify **389** *dispose* manner **391** *free* frank

ACT II

SCENE I

[Enter MONTANO *and two gentlemen.]*

MONTANO:
  What from the cape can you discern at sea?
1 GENTLEMAN:
  Nothing at all: it is a high-wrought flood.
  I cannot 'twixt the heaven and the main
  Descry a sail.
MONTANO:
  Methinks the wind hath spoke aloud at land;
  A fuller blast ne'er shook our battlements.
  If it hath ruffianed so upon the sea,
  What ribs of oak, when mountains melt on them,
  Can hold the mortise? What shall we hear of this?   9
2 GENTLEMAN:
  A segregation of the Turkish fleet.   10
  For do but stand upon the foaming shore,
  The chidden billow seems to pelt the clouds;
  The wind-shaked surge, with high and monstrous mane,
  Seems to cast water on the burning Bear
  And quench the Guards of th' ever-fixèd pole.   15
  I never did like molestation view   16
  On the enchafèd flood.
MONTANO: If that the Turkish fleet
  Be not ensheltered and embayed, they are drowned;
  It is impossible to bear it out.

[Enter a third gentleman.]

3 GENTLEMAN:
  News, lads! Our wars are done.
  The desperate tempest hath so banged the Turks
  That their designment halts. A noble ship of Venice   22
  Hath seen a grievous wrack and sufferance   23
  On most part of their fleet.
MONTANO:
  How? Is this true?

Scene i An open place in Cyprus, near the harbor   **9** *hold the mortise* hold their joints together   **10** *segregation* scattering   **15** *Guards* stars near the North Star; *pole* polestar   **16** *molestation* tumult   **22** *desegment halts* plan is crippled   **23** *sufferance* disaster

3 GENTLEMAN: The ship is here put in,
   A Veronesa; Michael Cassio,   26
   Lieutenant to the warlike Moor Othello,
   Is come on shore; the Moor himself at sea,
   And is in full commission here for Cyprus.
MONTANO:
   I am glad on't. 'Tis a worthy governor.
3 GENTLEMAN:
   But this same Cassio, though he speak of comfort
   Touching the Turkish loss, yet he looks sadly
   And prays the Moor be safe, for they were parted
   With foul and violent tempest.
MONTANO: Pray heaven he be;
   For I have served him, and the man commands
   Like a full soldier. Let's to the seaside, ho!
   As well to see the vessel that's come in
   As to throw out our eyes for brave Othello,
   Even till we make the main and th' aerial blue
   An indistinct regard.   40
3 GENTLEMAN: Come, let's do so;
   For every minute is expectancy
   Of more arrivance.

   [*Enter* CASSIO.]

CASSIO:
   Thanks, you the valiant of this warlike isle,
   That so approve the Moor! O, let the heavens
   Give him defense against the elements,
   For I have lost him on a dangerous sea!
MONTANO:
   Is he well shipped?
CASSIO:
   His bark is stoutly timbered, and his pilot
   Of very expert and approved allowance;
   Therefore my hopes, not surfeited to death,   50
   Stand in bold cure.   51
   [*Within.*] A sail, a sail, a sail!

   [*Enter a messenger.*]

CASSIO:
   What noise?

26 *Veronesa* ship furnished by Verona   40 *An indistinct regard* indistinguishable   50 *surfeited to death* over indulged   51 *in bold cure* a good chance of fulfillment

1 GENTLEMAN:
  The town is empty; on the brow o' th' sea
  Stand ranks of people, and they cry "A sail!"
CASSIO:
  My hopes do shape him for the governor.

[*A shot.*]

2 GENTLEMAN:
  They do discharge their shot of courtesy:
  Our friends at least.
CASSIO: I pray you, sir, go forth
  And give us truth who 'tis that is arrived.
2 GENTLEMAN:
  I shall.   [*Exit.*]
MONTANO:
  But, good lieutenant, is your general wived?
CASSIO:
  Most fortunately. He hath achieved a maid
  That paragons description and wild fame;   62
  One that excels the quirks of blazoning pens,   63
  And in th' essential vesture of creation   64
  Does tire the ingener.

[*Enter second gentleman.*]

                    How now? Who has put in?
2 GENTLEMAN:
  'Tis one Iago, ancient to the general.
CASSIO:
  H'as had most favorable and happy speed:
  Tempests themselves, high seas, and howling winds,
  The guttered rocks and congregated sands,   69
  Traitors ensteeped to clog the guiltless keel,   70
  As having sense of beauty, do omit
  Their mortal natures, letting go safely by   72
  The divine Desdemona.
MONTANO: What is she?
CASSIO:
  She that I spake of, our great captain's captain,
  Left in the conduct of the bold Iago,
  Whose footing here anticipates our thoughts   76
  A se'nnight's speed. Great Jove, Othello guard,   77

---

62 *paragons* surpasses **63** *quirks* ingenuities; *blazoning* describing **64–65** *And . . . ingener* merely to describe her as God made her exhausts her praiser **69** *guttered* jagged **70** *ensteeped* submerged **72** *mortal* deadly **76** *footing* landing **77** *sen'night's* week's

And swell his sail with thine own pow'rful breath,
That he may bless this bay with his tall ship,
Make love's quick pants in Desdemona's arms,
Give renewed fire to our extincted spirits,
And bring all Cyprus comfort!

[*Enter* DESDEMONA, IAGO, RODERIGO, *and* EMILIA *with attendants.*]

                    O, behold!
The riches of the ship is come on shore!
You men of Cyprus, let her have your knees.   84
Hail to thee, lady! and the grace of heaven,
Before, behind thee, and on every hand,
Enwheel thee round!
DESDEMONA: I thank you, valiant Cassio.
What tidings can you tell me of my lord?
CASSIO:
He is not yet arrived; nor know I aught
But that he's well and will be shortly here.
DESDEMONA:
O but I fear! How lost you company?
CASSIO:
The great contention of the sea and skies
Parted our fellowship.
[*Within.*]   A sail, a sail! [*A shot.*]
                    But hark. A sail!
2 GENTLEMAN:
They give their greeting to the citadel;
This likewise is a friend.
CASSIO: See for the news.

                                        [*Exit gentleman.*]

Good ancient, you are welcome.
[*To* EMILIA.]   Welcome, mistress.—
Let it not gall your patience, good Iago,
That I extend my manners. 'Tis my breeding
That gives me this bold show of courtesy.   99

[*Kisses* EMILIA.]

IAGO:
Sir, would she give you so much of her lips
As of her tongue she oft bestows on me,
You would have enough.
DESDEMONA: Alas, she has no speech!

---

84 *knees* i.e. kneeling   **99 s.d.** *Kisses* EMILIA (kissing was a common Elizabethan form of social courtesy)

IAGO:

> In faith, too much.
> I find it still when I have list to sleep.
> Marry, before your ladyship, I grant,
> She puts her tongue a little in her heart
> And chides with thinking.

EMILIA:

> You have little cause to say so.

IAGO:

> Come on, come on! You are pictures out of doors,
> Bells in your parlors, wildcats in your kitchens,
> Saints in your injuries, devils being offended,
> Players in your housewifery, and housewives in your   112
> beds.

DESDEMONA:

> O, fie upon thee, slanderer!

IAGO:

> Nay, it is true, or else I am a Turk:
> You rise to play, and go to bed to work.

EMILIA:

> You shall not write my praise.

IAGO: No, let me not.

DESDEMONA:

> What wouldst thou write of me, if thou shouldst praise me?

IAGO:

> O gentle lady, do not put me to't,
> For I am nothing if not critical.

DESDEMONA:

> Come on, assay.—There's one gone to the harbor?   120

IAGO:

> Ay, madam.

DESDEMONA:

> I am not merry; but I do beguile
> The thing I am by seeming otherwise.—
> Come, how wouldst thou praise me?

IAGO:

> I am about it; but indeed my invention
> Comes from my pate as birdlime does from frieze—   126
> It plucks out brains and all. But my Muse labors,
> And thus she is delivered:
> If she be fair and wise, fairness and wit—
> The one's for use, the other useth it.

---

112 *housewifery* housekeeping; *housewives* hussies   **120** *assay* try   **126** *birdlime* a sticky paste; *frieze* rough cloth

DESDEMONA:

    Well praised! How if she be black and witty? 131

IAGO:

    If she be black, and thereto have a wit,

    She'll find a white that shall her blackness fit.

DESDEMONA:

    Worse and worse!

EMILIA:

    How if fair and foolish?

IAGO:

    She never yet was foolish that was fair,

    For even her folly helped her to an heir. 137

DESDEMONA: These are old fond paradoxes to make fools 138

    laugh i' th' alehouse. What miserable praise hast thou

    for her that's foul and foolish? 140

IAGO:

    There's none so foul, and foolish thereunto,

    But does foul pranks which fair and wise ones do.

DESDEMONA: O heavy ignorance! Thou praisest the worst best. But what

    praise couldst thou bestow on a deserving woman indeed—one that in

    the authority of her merit did justly put on the vouch of very malice 145

    itself?

IAGO:

    She that was ever fair, and never proud;

    Had tongue at will, and yet was never loud;

    Never lacked gold, and yet went never gay;

    Fled from her wish, and yet said "Now I may";

    She that, being ang'red, her revenge being nigh,

    Bade her wrong stay, and her displeasure fly;

    She that in wisdom never was so frail

    To change the cod's head for the salmon's tail; 154

    She that could think, and ne'er disclose her mind;

    See suitors following, and not look behind:

    She was a wight (if ever such wight were)—

DESDEMONA: To do what?

IAGO:

    To suckle fools and chronicle small beer. 159

DESDEMONA: O most lame and impotent conclusion! Do not learn of him,

    Emilia, though he be thy husband. How say you, Cassio? Is he not a

    most profane and liberal counsellor? 162

---

131 *black* brunette **137** *folly* wantonness **138** *fond* foolish **140** *foul* ugly **145** *put on the vouch* compel the approval **154** *To . . . tail* i.e. to exchange the good for poor but expensive **159** *chronicle small beer* keep petty household accounts **162** *profane and liberal* worldly and licentious

CASSIO: He speaks home, madam. You may relish him more in the soldier   163
than in the scholar.

IAGO [*aside*]: He takes her by the palm. Ay, well said, whisper! With as little
a web as this will I ensnare as great a fly as Cassio. Ay, smile upon her,
do! I will gyve thee in thine own courtship.—You say true; 'tis so,   167
indeed!—If such tricks as these strip you out of your lieutenantry, it
had been better you had not kissed your three fingers so oft—which
now again you are most apt to play the sir in. Very good! well kissed! an   170
excellent courtesy! 'Tis so, indeed. Yet again your fingers to your lips?
Would they were clyster pipes for your sake! [*Trumpet within.*] The   172
Moor! I know his trumpet.

CASSIO: 'Tis truly so.

DESDEMONA: Let's meet him and receive him.

CASSIO: Lo, where he comes.

[*Enter* OTHELLO *and attendants.*]

OTHELLO:
O my fair warrior!

DESDEMONA: My dear Othello!

OTHELLO:
It gives me wonder great as my content
To see you here before me. O my soul's joy!
If after every tempest come such calms,
May the winds blow till they have wakened death!
And let the laboring bark climb hills of seas
Olympus-high, and duck again as low
As hell's from heaven! If it were now to die,
'Twere now to be most happy; for I fear   185
My soul hath her content so absolute
That not another comfort like to this
Succeeds in unknown fate.

DESDEMONA: The heavens forbid
But that our loves and comforts should increase
Even as our days do grow.

OTHELLO: Amen to that, sweet powers!
I cannot speak enough of this content;
It stops me here; it is too much of joy.
And this, and this, the greatest discords be
[*They kiss.*]
That e'er our hearts shall make!

---

163 *home* bluntly   **167** *gyve . . . courtship* manacle you by your courtly manners   **170** *sir* courtly gentleman
172 *clyster pipes* syringes   **185** *happy* fortunate

IAGO [*aside*]:   O, you are well tuned now!
  But I'll set down the pegs that make this music,   195
  As honest as I am.
OTHELLO: Come, let us to the castle.
  News, friends! Our wars are done; the Turks are drowned.
  How does my old acquaintance of this isle?—
  Honey, you shall be well desired in Cyprus;   199
  I have found great love amongst them. O my sweet,
  I prattle out of fashion, and I dote
  In mine own comforts. I prithee, good Iago,
  Go to the bay and disembark my coffers.
  Bring thou the master to the citadel;   204
  He is a good one, and his worthiness
  Does challenge much respect.—Come, Desdemona,   206
  Once more well met at Cyprus.
                   [*Exit* OTHELLO *(with all but* IAGO *and* RODERIGO.*)*]
IAGO [*to an attendant, who goes out*]: Do thou meet me presently at the
  harbor. [*to* RODERIGO] Come hither. If you be'st valiant (as they say base
  men being in love have then a nobility in their natures more than is
  native to them), list me. The lieutenant to-night watches on the court of   211
  guard. First, I must tell thee this: Desdemona is directly in love with
  him.
RODERIGO: With him? Why, 'tis not possible.
IAGO: Lay thy finger thus, and let thy soul be instructed. Mark me with   215
  what violence she first loved the Moor, but for bragging and telling her
  fantastical lies; and will she love him still for prating? Let not thy
  discreet heart think it. Her eye must be fed; and what delight shall she
  have to look on the devil? When the blood is made dull with the act of
  sport, there should be, again to inflame it and to give satiety a fresh
  appetite, loveliness in favor, sympathy in years, manners, and beauties;
  all which the Moor is defective in. Now for want of these required
  conveniences, her delicate tenderness will find itself abused, begin to   223
  heave the gorge, disrelish and abhor the Moor. Very nature will instruct   224
  her in it and compel her to some second choice. Now sir, this
  granted—as it is a most pregnant and unforced position—who stands   226
  so eminent in the degree of this fortune as Cassio does? A knave very
  voluble; no further conscionable than in putting on the mere form of   228
  civil and humane seeming for the better compassing of his salt and   229
  most hidden loose affection? Why, none! why, none! A slipper and   230

---

195 *set down* loosen   **199** *well desired* warmly welcomed   **204** *master* ship captain   **206** *challenge* deserve
211–12 *court of guard* headquarters   **215** *thus* i.e. on your lips   **223** *conveniences* compatibilities   **224** *heave the gorge* be nauseated   **226** *pregnant* evident   **228** *conscionable* conscientious   **229** *humane* polite; *salt* lecherous
230 *slipper* slippery

subtle knave; a finder-out of occasions; that has an eye can stamp and counterfeit advantages, though true advantage never present itself; a devilish knave! Besides, the knave is handsome, young, and hath all those requisites in him that folly and green minds look after. A pestilent complete knave! and the woman hath found him already.

RODERIGO: I cannot believe that in her; she's full of most blessed condition.   236

IAGO: Blessed fig's-end! The wine she drinks is made of grapes. If she had been blessed, she would never have loved the Moor. Blessed pudding! Didst thou not see her paddle with the palm of his hand? Didst not mark that?

RODERIGO: Yes, that I did; but that was but courtesy.

IAGO: Lechery, by this hand! an index and obscure prologue to the history of lust and foul thoughts. They met so near with their lips that their breaths embraced together. Villainous thoughts, Roderigo! When these mutualities so marshal the way, hard at hand comes the master and   245
main exercise, th' incorporate conclusion. Pish! But, sir, be you ruled by   246
me: I have brought you from Venice. Watch you to-night; for the command, I'll lay't upon you. Cassio knows you not. I'll not be far from you: do you find some occasion to anger Cassio, either by speaking too loud, or tainting his discipline, or from what other course you please   250
which the time shall more favorably minister.

RODERIGO: Well.

IAGO: Sir, he's rash and very sudden in choler, and haply with his   253
truncheon may strike at you. Provoke him that he may; for even out of that will I cause these of Cyprus to mutiny; whose qualification shall   255
come into no true taste again but by the displanting of Cassio. So shall   256
you have a shorter journey to your desires by the means I shall then have to prefer them; and the impediment most profitably removed   258
without the which there were no expectation of our prosperity.

RODERIGO: I will do this if you can bring it to any opportunity.

IAGO: I warrant thee. Meet me by and by at the citadel; I must fetch his necessaries ashore. Farewell.

RODERIGO: Adieu.   [*Exit.*]

IAGO:
That Cassio loves her, I do well believe't;
That she loves him, 'tis apt and of great credit.   265
The Moor, howbeit that I endure him not,
Is of a constant, loving, noble nature,
And I dare think he'll prove to Desdemona

---

236 *condition* character **245** *mutualities* exchanges **246** *incorporate* carnal **250** *tainting* discrediting **253** *sudden in choler* violent in anger **255** *qualification* appeasement **256** *true taste* satisfactory state **258** *prefer* advance **265** *apt* probable

A most dear husband. Now I do love her too;
Not out of absolute lust, though peradventure
I stand accountant for as great a sin,   271
But partly led to diet my revenge,   272
For that I do suspect the lusty Moor
Hath leaped into my seat; the thought whereof
Doth, like a poisonous mineral, gnaw my inwards;
And nothing can or shall content my soul
Till I am evened with him, wife for wife;
Of failing so, yet that I put the Moor
At least into a jealousy so strong
That judgment cannot cure. Which think to do,
If this poor trash of Venice, whom I trash   281
For his quick hunting, stand the putting on,   282
I'll have our Michael Cassio on the hip,   283
Abuse him to the Moor in the rank garb   284
(For I fear Cassio with my nightcap too),
Make the Moor thank me, love me, and reward me
For making him egregiously an ass
And practicing upon his peace and quiet   288
Even to madness. 'Tis here, but yet confused:
Knavery's plain face is never seen till used.   [*Exit.*]

SCENE II

[*Enter* OTHELLO'*s herald, with a proclamation.*]

HERALD: It is Othello's pleasure, our noble and valiant general, that, upon
certain tidings now arrived, importing the mere perdition of the   2
Turkish fleet, every man put himself into triumph; some to dance, some
to make bonfires, each man to what sport and revels his addiction leads
him. For, besides these beneficial news, it is the celebration of his
nuptial. So much was his pleasure should be proclaimed. All offices are   6
open, and there is full liberty of feasting from the present hour of five
till the bell have told eleven. Heaven bless the isle of Cyprus and our
noble general Othello!

                                                                 [*Exit.*]

---

271 *accountant* accountable   **272** *diet* feed   **281** *I trash* I weight down (in order to keep under control)
282 *For* in order to develop; *stand the putting on* responds to my inciting   **283** *on the hip* at my mercy
284 *rank garb* gross manner   **288** *practicing upon* plotting against
Scene ii A street in Cyprus   **2** *mere perdition* complete destruction   **6** *offices* kitchens and storerooms

SCENE III

[Enter OTHELLO, DESDEMONA, CASSIO, *and attendants.]*

OTHELLO:
Good Michael, look you to the guard to-night.
Let's teach ourselves that honorable stop,
Not to outsport discretion.
CASSIO:
Iago hath direction what to do;
But not withstanding, with my personal eye
Will I look to't.
OTHELLO: Iago is most honest.
Michael, good night. To-morrow with your earliest
Let me have speech with you.
[To DESDEMONA*]*   Come, my dear love.
The purchase made, the fruits are to ensue;
That profit's yet to come 'tween me and you.—
Good night.

[Exit OTHELLO *with* DESDEMONA *and attendants.]*
[Enter IAGO.*]*

CASSIO: Welcome, Iago. We must to the watch.
IAGO: Not this hour, lieutenant; 'tis not yet ten o' th' clock. Our general cast   13
    us thus early for the love of his Desdemona; who let us not therefore
    blame. He hath not yet made wanton the night with her, and she is
    sport for Jove.
CASSIO: She's a most exquisite lady.
IAGO: And, I'll warrant her, full of game.
CASSIO: Indeed, she's a most fresh and delicate creature.
IAGO: What an eye she has! Methinks it sounds a parley to provocation.
CASSIO: An inviting eye; and yet methinks right modest:
IAGO: And when she speaks, is it not an alarum to love?
CASSIO: She is indeed perfection.
IAGO: Well, happiness to their sheets! Come, lieutenant, I have a stoup of   24
    wine, and here without are a brace of Cyprus gallants that would fain
    have a measure to the health of black Othello.
CASSIO: Not to-night, good Iago. I have very poor and unhappy brains for
    drinking; I could well wish courtesy would invent some other custom of
    entertainment.
IAGO: O, they are our friends. But one cup! I'll drink for you.

Scene iii The Cyprian castle   **13** *cast* dismissed   **24** *stoup* two-quart tankard

CASSIO: I have drunk but one cup to-night, and that was craftily qualified
    too; and behold what innovation it makes here. I am unfortunate in the   32
    infirmity and dare not task my weakness with any more.
IAGO: What, man! 'Tis a night of revels: the gallants desire it.
CASSIO: Where are they?
IAGO: Here at the door; I pray you call them in.
CASSIO: I'll do't, but it dislikes me.   [*Exit.*]
IAGO:
    If I can fasten but one cup upon him
    With that which he hath drunk to-night already,
    He'll be as full of quarrel and offense
    As my young mistress' dog. Now my sick fool Roderigo,
    Whom love hath turned almost the wrong side out,
    To Desdemona hath to-night caroused
    Potations pottle-deep; and he's to watch.   44
    Three lads of Cyprus—noble swelling spirits,
    That hold their honors in a wary distance,   46
    The very elements of this warlike isle—   47
    Have I to-night flustered with flowing cups,
    And they watch too. Now, 'mongst this flock of drunkards
    Am I to put our Cassio in some action
    That may offend the isle.

[*Enter* CASSIO, MONTANO, *and gentleman servants following with wine.*]

                    But here they come.
    If consequence do but approve my dream,
    My boat sails freely, both with wind and stream.
CASSIO: 'Fore God, they have given me a rouse already.   54
MONTANO: Good faith, a little one; not past a pint, as I
    am a soldier.
IAGO: Some wine, ho!
    [*Sings.*]   And let me the canakin clink, clink;
                   And let me the canakin clink.
                   A soldier's a man;
                   A life's but a span,
                   Why then, let a soldier drink.
    Some wine boys!
CASSIO: Fore God, an excellent song!
IAGO: I learned it in England, where indeed they are most potent in potting.
    Your Dane, your German, and your swag-bellied Hollander—Drink,
    ho!—are nothing to your English.

32 *qualified* diluted; *innovation* disturbance   **44** *pottle-deep* bottoms up   **46** *That . . . distance* very sensitive about
their honor   **47** *very elements* true representatives   **54** *rouse* bumper

CASSIO: Is your Englishman so expert in his drinking?

IAGO: Why, he drinks you with facility your Dane dead drunk; he sweats not
to overthrow your Almain; he gives your Hollander a vomit ere the next
pottle can be filled.

CASSIO: To the health of our general!

MONTANO: I am for it, lieutenant, and I'll do you justice.

IAGO: O sweet England!

> [*Sings.*]   King Stephen was a worthy peer;
> His breeches cost him but a crown;
> He held 'em sixpence all too dear,
> With that he called the tailor lown.   78
> He was a wight of high renown,
> And thou art but of low degree.
> 'Tis pride that pulls the country down;
> Then take thine auld cloak about thee.

Some wine, ho!

CASSIO: 'Fore God, this is a more exquisite song than the other.

IAGO: Will you hear 't again?

CASSIO: No, for I hold him to be unworthy of his place that does those   86
things. Well, God's above all; and there be souls must be saved, and
there be souls must not be saved.

IAGO: It's true, good lieutenant.

CASSIO: For mine own part—no offense to the general,
nor any man of quality—I hope to be saved.

IAGO: And so do I too, lieutenant.

CASSIO: Ay, but, by your leave, not before me. The lieutenant is to be saved before the ancient. Let's have no
more of this; let's to our affairs.—God forgive us our
sins!—Gentlemen, let's look to our business. Do not
think, gentlemen, I am drunk. This is my ancient; this
is my right hand, and this is my left. I am not drunk now.
I can stand well enough, and I speak well enough.

ALL: Excellent well!

CASSIO: Why, very well then. You must not think then
that I am drunk.   [*Exit.*]

MONTANO:
To th' platform, masters, Come, let's set the watch.

IAGO:
You see this fellow that is gone before.
He's a soldier fit to stand by Caesar
And give direction; and do but see his vice.
'Tis to his virtue a just equinox,   107
The one as long as th'other. 'Tis pity of him.

---

78 *lown* rascal   **86-7** *does . . . things* i.e. behaves in this fashion   **107** *just equinox* exact equivalent

I fear the trust Othello puts him in,
On some odd time of his infirmity,
Will shake this island.

MONTANO: But is he often thus?

IAGO:
'Tis evermore his prologue to his sleep:
He'll watch the horologe a double set   113
If drink rock not his cradle.

MONTANO: It were well
The general were put in mind of it.
Perhaps he sees it not, or his good nature
Prizes the virtue that appears in Cassio
And looks not on his evils. Is not this true?

[*Enter* RODERIGO.]

IAGO [*aside to him*]:
How now, Roderigo?
I pray you after the lieutenant, go!   [*Exit* RODERIGO.]

MONTANO:
And 'tis great pity that the noble Moor
Should hazard such a place as his own second
With one of an ingraft infirmity.   123
It were an honest action to say
So to the Moor.

IAGO: Not I, for this fair island!
I do love Cassio well and would do much
To cure him of this evil.

[*Within*]   Help! help!
                        But hark! What noise?

[*Enter* CASSIO, *driving in* RODERIGO.]

CASSIO:
Zounds, you rogue! you rascal!

MONTANO:
What's the matter, lieutenant?

CASSIO: A knave teach me my duty?
I'll beat the knave into a twiggen bottle.   130

RODERIGO:
Beat me?

CASSIO: Dost thou prate, rogue?
[*Strikes him.*]

113 *watch . . . set* stay awake twice around the clock   **123** *ingraft* i.e. ingrained   **130** *twiggen* wicker-covered

MONTANO: Nay, good lieutenant!
  [*Stays him.*]
  I pray you, sir, hold your hand.
CASSIO: Let me go, sir,
  Or I'll knock you o'er the mazzard.   133
MONTANO: Come, come, you're drunk!
CASSIO: Drunk?

  [*They fight.*]

IAGO [*aside to* RODERIGO]:
  Away, I say! Go out and cry a mutiny!   [*Exit* RODERIGO.]
  Nay, good lieutenant. God's will, gentlemen!
  Help, ho!—lieutenant—sir—Montano—sir—
  Help, masters!—Here's a goodly watch indeed!

  [*A bell rung.*]

  Who's that which rings the bell? Diablo, ho!
  The town will rise. God's will, lieutenant, hold!   140
  You'll be shamed for ever.

  [*Enter* OTHELLO *and gentlemen with weapons.*]

OTHELLO: What is the matter here?
MONTANO:
  Zounds, I bleed still, I am hurt to th' death.
  He dies!
OTHELLO:
  Hold for your lives!
IAGO:
  Hold, hold! Lieutenant—sir—Montano—gentlemen!
  Have you forgot all sense of place and duty?
  Hold! The general speaks to you. Hold, for shame!
OTHELLO:
  Why, how now, ho? From whence ariseth this?
  Are we turned Turks, and to ourselves do that
  Which heaven hath forbid the Ottomites?
  For Christian shame put by this barbarous brawl!
  He that stirs next to carve for his own rage   151
  Holds his soul light; he dies upon his motion.
  Silence that dreadful bell! It frights the isle
  From her propriety. What is the matter, masters?   154

133 *mazzard* head   **140** *rise* grow riotous   **151** *carve for* indulge   **154** *propriety* proper self

Honest Iago, that looks dead with grieving,
Speak. Who began this? On thy love, I charge thee.
IAGO:
I do not know. Friends, all, but now, even now,
In quarter, and in terms like bride and groom   158
Devesting them for bed; and then, but now—
As if some planet had unwitted men—
Swords out, and tilting one at other's breast
In opposition bloody. I cannot speak
Any beginning to this peevish odds,   163
And would in action glorious I had lost
Those legs that brought me to a part of it!
OTHELLO:
How comes it, Michael, you are thus forgot?
CASSIO:
I pray you pardon me; I cannot speak.
OTHELLO:
Worthy Montano, you were wont to be civil;
The gravity and stillness of your youth
The world hath noted, and your name is great
In mouths of wisest censure. What's the matter   171
That you unlace your reputation thus   172
And spend your rich opinion for the name   173
Of a night-brawler? Give me answer to it.
MONTANO:
Worthy Othello, I am hurt to danger.
Your officer, Iago, can inform you,
While I spare speech, which something now offends me,   177
Of all that I do know; nor know I aught
By me that's said or done amiss this night,
Unless self-charity be sometimes a vice,
And to defend ourselves it be a sin
When violence assails us.
OTHELLO: Now, by heaven,
My blood begins my safer guides to rule,   183
And passion, having my best judgement collied,   184
Assays to lead the way. If I once stir   185
Or do but lift this arm, the best of you
Shall sink in my rebuke. Give me to know
How this foul rout began, who set it on;
And he that is approved in this offense,   189

---

158 *quarter* friendliness **163** *peevish odds* childish quarrel **171** *censure* judgment **172** *unlace* undo
173 *rich opinion* high reputation **177** *offends* pains **183** *blood* passion **184** *collied* darkened **185** *Assays*
tries **189** *approved in* proved guilty of

Though he had twinned with me, both at a birth,
Shall lose me. What! in a town of war,
Yet wild, the people's hearts brimful of fear,
To manage private and domestic quarrel?   193
In night, and on the court and guard of safety?
'Tis monstrous. Iago, who began't?

MONTANO:
If partially affined, or leagued in office,   196
Thou dost deliver more or less than truth,
Thou art no soldier.

IAGO: Touch me not so near.
I had rather have this tongue cut from my mouth
Than it should do offense to Michael Cassio;
Yet I persuade myself, to speak the truth
Shall nothing wrong him. This it is, general.
Montano and myself being in speech,
There comes a fellow crying out for help,
And Cassio following him with determined sword
To execute upon him. Sir, this gentleman   206
Steps in to Cassio and entreats his pause.
Myself the crying fellow did pursue,
Lest by his clamor—as it so fell out—
The town might fall in fright. He, swift of foot,
Outran my purpose; and I returned then rather
For that I heard the clink and fall of swords,
And Cassio high in oath; which till to-night   213
I ne'er might say before. When I came back—
For this was brief—I found them close together
At blow and thrust, even as again they were
When you yourself did part them.
More of this matter cannot I report;
But men are men; the best sometimes forget.
Though Cassio did some little wrong to him,
As men in rage strike those that wish them best,
Yet surely Cassio I believe received
From him that fled some strange indignity,
Which patience could not pass.   224

OTHELLO: I know, Iago,
Thy honesty and love doth mince this matter,
Making it light to Cassio. Cassio, I love thee;
But never more be officer of mine.

---

193 *manage* carry on **196** *partially . . . office* prejudiced by comradeship or official relations **206** *execute* work
his will **213** *high in oath* cursing **224** *pass* pass over, ignore

[*Enter* DESDEMONA, *attended.*]

Look if my gentle love be not raised up!
I'll make thee an example.
DESDEMONA: What's the matter?
OTHELLO:
All's well now, sweeting; come away to bed.
[*To* MONTANO.]
Sir, for your hurts, myself will be your surgeon.
Lead him off.
[MONTANO *is led off.*]
Iago, look with care about the town
And silence those whom this vile brawl distracted.   234
Come, Desdemona; 'tis the soldiers' life
To have their balmy slumbers waked with strife.
                              [*Exit, with all but* IAGO *and* CASSIO.]

IAGO: What, are you hurt, lieutenant?
CASSIO: Ay, past all surgery.
IAGO: Marry, God forbid!
CASSIO: Reputation, reputation, reputation! O, I have lost my reputation! I
  have lost the immortal part of myself, and what remains is bestial. My
  reputation, Iago, my reputation!
IAGO: As I am an honest man, I thought you had received some bodily
  wound. There is more sense in that than in reputation. Reputation is an
  idle and most false imposition; oft got without merit and lost without
  deserving. You have lost no reputation at all unless you repute yourself
  such a loser. What, man! there are ways to recover the general again.   247
  You are but now cast in his mood—a punishment more in policy than in   248
  malice, even so as one would beat his offenseless dog to affright an
  imperious lion. Sue to him again, and he's yours.
CASSIO: I will rather sue to be despised than to deceive so good a
  commander with so slight, so drunken, and so indiscreet an officer.
  Drunk! and speak parrot! and squabble! swagger! swear! and discourse   253
  fustian with one's own shadow! O thou invisible spirit of wine, if thou   254
  hast no name to be known by, let us call thee devil!
IAGO: What was he that you followed with your sword? What had he done to
  you?
CASSIO: I know not.
IAGO: Is't possible?
CASSIO: I remember a mass of things, but nothing distinctly; a quarrel, but
  nothing wherefore. O God, that men should put an enemy in their

---

234 *distracted* excited   **247** *recover* regain favor with   **248** *cast in his mood* dismissed because of his anger
253 *parrot* meaningless phrases   **254** *fustian* bombastic nonsense

mouths to steal away their brains! that we should with joy, pleasance,
revel, and applause transform ourselves into beasts!   263

IAGO: Why, but you are now well enough. How came you thus recovered?

CASSIO: It hath pleased the devil drunkenness to give place to the devil
wrath. One unperfectness shows me another, to make me frankly
despise myself.

IAGO: Come, you are too severe a moraler. As the time, the place, and the
condition of this country stands, I could heartily wish this had not so
befall'n; but since it is as it is, mend it for your own good.

CASSIO: I will ask him for my place again: he shall tell me I am a drunkard!
Had I as many mouths as Hydra, such an answer would stop them all.   272
To be now a sensible man, by and by a fool, and presently a beast! O
strange! Every inordinate cup is unblest, and the ingredient is a devil.   274

IAGO: Come, come, good wine is a good familiar creature if it be well used.
Exclaim no more against it. And, good lieutenant, I think you think I
love you.

CASSIO: I have well approved it, sir. I drunk!   278

IAGO: You or any man living may be drunk at some time, man. I'll tell you
what you shall do. Our general's wife is now the general. I may say so in
this respect, for that he hath devoted and given up himself to the
contemplation, mark, and denotement of her parts and graces. Confess
yourself freely to her; importune her help to put you in your place again.
She is of so free, so kind, so apt, so blessed a disposition she holds it a   284
vice in her goodness not to do more than she is requested. This broken
joint between you and her husband entreat her to splinter; and my   286
fortunes against any lay worth naming, this crack of your love shall   287
grow stronger than it was before.

CASSIO: You advise me well.

IAGO: I protest, in the sincerity of love and honest kindness.

CASSIO: I think if freely; and betimes in the morning will I beseech the
virtuous Desdemona to undertake for me. I am desperate of my fortunes
if they check me here.

IAGO: You are in the right. Good night, lieutenant; I must to the watch.

CASSIO: Good night, honest Iago.   [*Exit* CASSIO.]

IAGO:
And what's he then that says I play the villain,
When this advice is free I give and honest,
Probal to thinking, and indeed the course   298
To win the Moor again? For 'tis most easy
Th' inclining Desdemona to subdue   300
In any honest suit; she's framed as fruitful

---

263 *applause* desire to please   272 *Hydra* monster with many heads   274 *ingredient* contents   278 *approved* proved   284 *free* bounteous   286 *splinter* bind up with splints   287 *lay* wager   298 *Probal* probable   300 *subdue* persuade

As the free elements. And then for her
To win the Moor—were't to renounce his baptism,
All seals and symbols of redeemèd sin—
His soul is so enfettered to her love
That she may make, unmake, do what she list,
Even as her appetite shall play the god
With his weak function. How am I then a villain
To counsel Cassio to this parallel course,   309
Directly to his good? Divinity of hell!   310
When devils will the blackest sins put on,   311
They do suggest at first with heavenly shows,
As I do now. For whiles this honest fool
Plies Desdemona to repair his fortunes,
And she for him pleads strongly to the Moor,
I'll pour this pestilence into his ear,
That she repeals him for her body's lust;   317
And by how much she strives to do him good,
She shall undo her credit with the Moor.
So will I turn her virtue into pitch,
And out of her own goodness make the net
That shall enmesh them all.
   [*Enter* RODERIGO.]   How, now, Roderigo?

RODERIGO: I do follow here in the chase, not like a hound that hunts, but
   one that fills up the cry. My money is almost spent; I have been to-night   324
   exceedingly well cudgelled; and I think the issue will be—I shall have so
   much experience for my pains; and so, with no money at all, and a little
   more wit, return again to Venice.

IAGO:
How poor are they that have not patience!
What wound did ever heal but by degrees?
Thou know'st we work by wit, and not by witchcraft;
And wit depends on dilatory time.
Does't not go well? Cassio hath beaten thee,
And thou by that small hurt hast cashiered Cassio.   333
Though other things grow fair against the sun,
Yet fruits that blossom first will first be ripe.
Content thyself awhile. By the mass, 'tis morning!
Pleasure and action make the hours seem short.
Retire thee; go where thou art billeted.
Away, I say! Thou shalt know more hereafter.
Nay, get thee gone!   [*Exit* RODERIGO.]
      Two things are to be done:

---

309 *parallel* corresponding   **310** *Divinity* theology   **311** *put on* incite   **317** *repeals him* seeks his recall
324 *cry* pack   **333** *cashiered Cassio* maneuvered Cassio's discharge

My wife must move for Cassio to her mistress;
I'll set her on;
Myself the while to draw the Moor apart
And bring him jump when he may Cassio find   344
Soliciting his wife. Ay, that's the way!
Dull not device by coldness and delay.   *[Exit.]*

ACT III

SCENE I

[Enter CASSIO, *with musicians and the* CLOWN.]

CASSIO:
Masters, play here, I will content your pains: 1
Something that's brief; and bid "Good morrow, general."
[They play.]
CLOWN: Why, masters, ha' your instruments been in Naples, that they speak   3
i' th' nose thus?
MUSICIAN: How, sir, how?
CLOWN: Are these, I pray you, called wind instruments?
MUSICIAN: Ay, marry, are they, sir.
CLOWN: O, thereby hangs a tail.
MUSICIAN: Whereby hangs a tale, sir?
CLOWN: Marry, sir, by many a wind instrument that I know. But, masters,
here's money for you; and general so likes your music that he desires
you, for love's sake, to make no more noise with it.
MUSICIAN: Well, sir, we will not.
CLOWN: If you have any music that may not be heard, to't again: but, as they
say, to hear music the general does not greatly care.
MUSICIAN: We have none such, sir.
CLOWN: Then put up your pipes in your bag, for I'll away.
Go, vanish into air, away!
                    [Exit MUSICIAN *(with his fellows).]*
CASSIO: Dost thou hear, my honest friend?
CLOWN: No, I hear not your honest friend. I hear you.
CASSIO: Prithee keep up thy quillets. There's a poor piece of gold for thee. If   21
the gentlewoman that attends the general's wife be stirring, tell her there's
one Cassio entreats her a little favor of speech. Wilt thou do this?
CLOWN: She is stirring sir. If she will stir hither, I shall
seem to notify unto her.

---

344 *jump* at the exact moment
Scene i Before the chamber of Othello and Desdemona   **1** *content* reward   **3** *Naples* (notorious for its association with venereal disease)   **21** *quillets* quips

CASSIO:

Do, good my friend.   [*Exit* CLOWN.]

[*Enter* IAGO.]   In happy time, Iago.   27

IAGO:

You have not been abed then?

CASSIO:

Why, no; the day had broke
Before we parted. I have made bold, Iago,
To send in to your wife: my suit to her
Is that she will to virtuous Desdemona
Procure me some access.

IAGO: I'll send her to you presently;
And I'll devise a mean to draw the Moor
Out of the way, that your converse and business
May be more free.

CASSIO:

I humbly thank you for't.   [*Exit* IAGO.]
                        I never knew
A Florentine more kind and honest.   38

[*Enter* EMILIA.]

EMILIA:

Good morrow, good lieutenant. I am sorry
For your displeasure; but all will sure be well.
The general and his wife are talking of it,
And she speaks for you stoutly. The Moor replies
That he you hurt is of great fame in Cyprus
And great affinity, and that in wholesome wisdom   44
He might not but refuse you; but he protests he loves you,
And needs no other suitor but his likings
To take the safest occasion by the front   47
To bring you in again.

CASSIO: Yet I beseech you,
If you think fit, or that it may be done,
Give me advantage of some brief discourse
With Desdemona alone.

EMILIA: Pray you come in.
I will bestow you where you shall have time
To speak your bosom freely.   53

CASSIO: I am much bound to you.

                                                        [*Exeunt.*]

27 *In happy time* well met   38 *Florentine* i.e. even a Florentine (like Cassio; Iago was a Venetian)   44 *affinity*
family connections   47 *occasion* opportunity; *front* forelock   53 *your bosom* your inmost thoughts

SCENE II

[*Enter* OTHELLO, IAGO, *and gentlemen.*]

OTHELLO:
These letters given Iago, to the pilot
And by him do my duties to the Senate.
That done, I will be walking on the works;   3
Repair there to me.
IAGO: Well, my good lord, I'll do't.
OTHELLO:
This fortification, gentlemen, shall we see't?
GENTLEMEN:
We'll wait upon your lordship.   [*Exeunt.*]

SCENE III

[*Enter* DESDEMONA, CASSIO, *and* EMILIA.]

DESDEMONA:
Be thou assured, good Cassio, I will do
All my abilities in thy behalf.
EMILIA:
Good madam, do. I warrant it grieves my husband
As if the cause were his.
DESDEMONA:
O, that's an honest fellow. Do not doubt, Cassio,
But I will have my lord and you again
As friendly as you were.
CASSIO: Bounteous madam,
Whatever shall become of Michael Cassio,
He's never anything but your true servant.
DESDEMONA:
I know't; I thank you. You do love my lord;
You have known him long; and be you well assured
He shall in strangeness stand no farther off   12
Than in a politic distance.   13
CASSIO: Ay, but, lady,
That policy may either last so long,
Or feed upon such nice and waterish diet,   15
Or breed itself so out of circumstance,

Scene ii The castle   **3** *works* fortifications
Scene iii The castle grounds   **12** *strangeness* aloofness   **13** *Than . . . distance* than wise policy requires
15 *Or . . . diet* or be continued for such slight reasons

That, I being absent, and my place supplied,
My general will forget my love and service.
DESDEMONA:
   Do not doubt that; before Emilia here   19
   I give thee warrant of thy place. Assure thee,
   If I do vow a friendship, I'll perform it
   To the last article. My lord shall never rest;
   I'll watch him tame and talk him out of patience;   23
   His bed shall seem a school, his board a shrift;   24
   I'll intermingle everything he does
   With Cassio's suit. Therefore be merry, Cassio,
   For thy solicitor shall rather die
   Than give thy cause away.

[*Enter* OTHELLO *and* IAGO *(at a distance).*]

EMILIA:
   Madam, here comes my lord.
CASSIO:
   Madam, I'll take my leave.   30
DESDEMONA:
   Why, stay, and hear me speak.
CASSIO:
   Madam, not now: I am very ill at ease,
   Unfit for mine own purposes.
DESDEMONA:
   Well, do your descretion.   [*Exit* CASSIO.]
IAGO:
   Ha! I like not that.
OTHELLO: What dost thou say?
IAGO:
   Nothing, my lord; or if—I know not what.
OTHELLO:
   Was not that Cassio parted from my wife?
IAGO:
   Cassio, my lord? No, sure, I cannot think it,
   That he would steal away so guilty-like,
   Seeing your coming.
OTHELLO: I do believe 'twas he.   40
DESDEMONA:
   How now, my lord?
   I have been talking with a suitor here,
   A man that languishes in your displeasure.

---

19 *doubt* fear   **23** *watch him tame* keep him awake until he gives in   **24** *shrift* confessional

OTHELLO:
Who is't you mean?
DESDEMONA:
Why, your lieutenant, Cassio. Good my lord,
If I have any grace or power to move you,
His present reconciliation take;   47
For if he be not one that truly loves you,
That errs in ignorance, and not in cunning,
I have no judgment in an honest face.
I prithee call him back.
OTHELLO: Went he hence now?
DESDEMONA:
Yes, faith; so humbled
That he hath left part of his grief with me
To suffer with him. Good love, call him back.
OTHELLO:
Not now, sweet Desdemon; some other time.
DESDEMONA:
But shall't be shortly?
OTHELLO: The sooner, sweet, for you.
DESDEMONA:
Shall't be to-night at supper?
OTHELLO: No, not to-night.
DESDEMONA:
To-morrow dinner then?
OTHELLO: I shall not dine at home;
I meet the captains at the citadel.
DESDEMONA:
Why, then, to-morrow night, or Tuesday morn,
On Tuesday noon or night, or Wednesday morn.
I prithee name the time, but let it not
Exceed three days. I' faith, he's penitent;
And yet his trespass, in our common reason
(Save that, they say, the wars must make examples
Out of their best), is not almost a fault   66
T'incur a private check. When shall he come?   67
Tell me, Othello. I wonder in my soul
What you could ask me that I should deny
Or stand so mamm'ring on. What? Michael Cassio,   70
That came a-wooing with you, and so many a time,
When I have spoke of you dispraisingly,

---

47 *present* immediate   **66** *not almost* hardly   **67** *a private check* even a private reprimand   **70** *mamm'ring on* hesitating about

Hath ta'en your part—to have so much to do
To bring him in? By'r Lady, I could do much—
OTHELLO:
    Prithee no more. Let him come when he will!
    I will deny thee nothing.
DESDEMONA: Why, this is not a boon;
    'Tis as I should entreat you wear your gloves,
    Or feed on nourishing dishes, or keep you warm,
    Or sue to you to do a peculiar profit
    To your own person. Nay, when I have a suit
    Wherein I mean to touch your love indeed,
    It shall be full of poise and difficult weight,
    And fearful to be granted.   83
OTHELLO: I will deny thee nothing!
    Whereon I do beseech thee grant me this,
    To leave me but a little to myself.
DESDEMONA:
    Shall I deny you? No. Farewell, my lord.
OTHELLO:
    Farewell, my Desdemon: I'll come to thee straight.
DESDEMONA:
    Emilia, come.—Be as your fancies teach you;
    Whate'er you be, I am obedient.   [*Exit (with* EMILIA).]
OTHELLO:
    Excellent wretch! Perdition catch my soul   90
    But I do love thee! and when I love thee not,
    Chaos is come again.
IAGO:
    My noble lord—
OTHELLO: What dost thou say, Iago?
IAGO:
    Did Michael Cassio, when you wooed my lady,
    Know of your love?
OTHELLO:
    He did, from first to last. Why dost thou ask?
IAGO:
    But for a satisfaction of my thought;
    No further harm.
OTHELLO: Why of thy thought, Iago?
IAGO:
    I did not think he had been acquainted with her.
OTHELLO:
    O, yes, and went between us very oft.   100

83 *fearful* dangerous   **90** *wretch* (a term of endearment)   **100** *went . . . us* (i.e. as messenger)

IAGO:
Indeed?

OTHELLO:
Indeed? Ay, indeed! Discern'st thou aught in that?
Is he not honest?

IAGO: Honest, my lord?

OTHELLO: Honest. Ay, honest.

IAGO:
My lord, for aught I know.

OTHELLO:
What dost thou think?

IAGO: Think, my lord?

OTHELLO: Think, my lord?
By heaven, he echoes me,
As if there were some monster in his thought
Too hideous to be shown. Thou dost mean something:
I heard thee say even now, thou lik'st not that,
When Cassio left my wife. What didst not like?
And when I told thee he was of my counsel
In my whole course of wooing, thou cried'st "Indeed?"
And didst contract and purse thy brow together,
As if you then hadst shut up in thy brain
Some horrible conceit. If thou dost love me,   115
Show me thy thought.

IAGO:
My lord, you know I love you.

OTHELLO: I think thou dost;
And, for I know thou'rt full of love and honesty
And weigh'st thy words before thou giv'st them breath,
Therefore these stops of thine fright me the more;
For such things in a false disloyal knave
Are tricks of custom; but in a man that's just
They are close dilations, working from the heart   123
That passion cannot rule.

IAGO: For Michael Cassio,
I dare be sworn I think that he is honest.

OTHELLO:
I think so too.

IAGO: Men should be what they seem;
Or those that be not, would they might seem none!   127

OTHELLO:
Certain, men should be what they seem.

---

115 *conceit* fancy **123–24** *close dilations* . . . *rule* secret emotions which well up in spite of restraint
127 *seem none* i.e. not pretend to be men when they are really monsters

IAGO:

Why then, I think Cassio's an honest man.

OTHELLO:

Nay, yet there's more in this.
I prithee speak to me as to thy thinkings,
As thou dost ruminate, and give thy worst of thoughts
The worst of words.

IAGO: Good my lord, pardon me:
Though I am bound to every act of duty,
I am not bound to that all slaves are free to.   135
Utter my thoughts? Why, say they are vile and false,
As where's that palace whereinto foul things
Sometimes intrude not? Who has a breast so pure
But some uncleanly apprehensions
Keep leets and law days, and in Sessions sit   140
With meditations lawful?

OTHELLO:

Thou dost conspire against thy friend, Iago,
If thou but think'st him wronged, and mak'st his ear
A stranger to thy thoughts.

IAGO: I do beseech you—
Though I perchance am vicious in my guess
(As I confess it is my nature's plague
To spy into abuses, and oft my jealousy   147
Shapes faults that are not), that your wisdom yet
From one that so imperfectly conjects   149
Would take no notice, nor build yourself a trouble
Out of his scattering and unsure observance.
It were not for your quiet nor your good,
Nor for my manhood, honesty, and wisdom,
To let you know my thoughts.

OTHELLO: What dost thou mean?

IAGO:

Good name in man and woman, dear my lord,
Is the immediate jewel of their souls.   156
Who steals my purse steals trash; 'tis something, nothing;
'Twas mine, 'tis his, and has been slave to thousands;
But he that filches from me my good name
Robs me of that which not enriches him
And makes me poor indeed.

OTHELLO:

By heaven, I'll know thy thoughts!

---

135 *bound . . . free to* bound to tell that which even slaves are allowed to keep to themselves   **140** *leets and law days* sittings of the courts   **147** *jealousy* suspicion   **149** *conjects* conjectures   **156** *immediate* nearest the heart

IAGO:

   You cannot, if my heart were in your hand;

   Nor shall not whilst 'tis in my custody.

OTHELLO:

   Ha!

IAGO: O, beware, my lord, of jealousy!

   It is the green-eyed monster, which doth mock   166

   The meat it feeds on. That cuckold lives in bliss

   Who, certain of his fate, loves not his wronger;

   But O, what damnèd minutes tells he o'er

   Who dotes, yet doubts—suspects, yet strongly loves!

OTHELLO:

   O misery!

IAGO:

   Poor and content is rich, and rich enough;

   But riches fineless is as poor as winter   173

   To him that ever fears he shall be poor.

   Good God, the souls of all my tribe defend

   From jealousy!

OTHELLO: Why, why is this?

   Think'st thou I'd make a life of jealousy,

   To follow still the changes of the moon

   With fresh suspicions? No! To be once in doubt

   Is once to be resolved. Exchange me for a goat

   When I shall turn the business of my soul

   To such exsufflicate and blown surmises,   182

   Matching this inference. 'Tis not to make me jealous

   To say my wife is fair, feeds well, loves company,

   Is free of speech, sings, plays, and dances;

   Where virtue is, these are more virtuous.

   Nor from mine own weak merits will I draw

   The smallest fear or doubt of her revolt,   188

   For she had eyes, and chose me. No, Iago;

   I'll see before I doubt; when I doubt, prove;

   And on the proof there is no more but this—

   Away at once with love or jealousy!

IAGO:

   I am glad of this; for now I shall have reason

   To show the love and duty that I bear you

   With franker spirit. Therefore, as I am bound,

   Receive it from me. I speak not yet of proof.

   Look to your wife; observe her well with Cassio;

166 *mock* play with, like a cat with a mouse   **173** *fineless* unlimited   **182** *exsufficate and blown* spat out and flyblown   **188** *revolt* unfaithfulness

Wear your eyes thus, not jealous nor secure: 198
I would not have your free and noble nature,
Out of self-bounty, be abused. Look to't.   200
I know our country disposition well:
In Venice they do let God see the pranks
They dare not show their husbands; their best conscience
Is not to leav't undone, but keep't unknown.

OTHELLO:
     Dost thou say so?

IAGO:
     She did deceive her father, marrying you;
     And when she seemed to shake and fear your looks,
     She loved them most.

OTHELLO: And so she did.

IAGO: Why, go to then!
     She that, so young, could give out such a seeming
     To seel her father's eyes up close as oak—   210
     He thought 'twas witchcraft—but I am much to blame.
     I humbly do beseech you of your pardon
     For too much loving you.

OTHELLO: I am bound to thee for ever.

IAGO:
     I see this hath a little dashed your spirits.

OTHELLO:
     Not a jot, not a jot.

IAGO: I' faith, I fear it has.
     I hope you will consider what is spoke
     Comes from my love. But I do see y' are moved.
     I am to pray you not to strain my speech
     To grosser issues nor to larger reach   219
     Than to suspicion.

OTHELLO:
     I will not.

IAGO: Should you do so, my lord,
     My speech should fall into such vile success   222
     As my thoughts aim not at. Cassio's my worthy friend—
     My lord, I see y' are moved.

OTHELLO: No, not much moved:
     I do not think but Desdemona's honest.   225

IAGO:
     Long live she so! and long live you to think so!

---

198 *secure* overconfident   **200** *self-bounty* natural goodness   **210** *seel* close; *oak* oak grain   **219** *To grosser issues* to mean something more monstrous   **222** *vile success* evil outcome   **225** *honest* chaste

OTHELLO:
And yet, how nature erring from itself—
IAGO:
Ay, there's the point! as (to be bold with you)
Not to affect many proposèd matches
Of her own clime, complexion, and degree,
Whereto we see in all things nature tends—
Foh! one may smell in such a will most rank,
Foul disproportions, thoughts unnatural—
But pardon me—I do not in position   234
Distinctly speak of her; though I may fear
Her will, recoiling to her better judgment,   236
May fall to match you with her country forms,   237
And happily repent.   238
OTHELLO: Farewell, farewell!
If more thou dost perceive, let me know more.
Set on thy wife to observe. Leave me, Iago.
IAGO:
My lord, I take my leave.   [*Going.*]
OTHELLO:
Why did I marry? This honest creature doubtless
Sees and knows more, much more, than he unfolds.
IAGO [*returns*]:
My lord, I would I might entreat your honor
To scan this thing no further: leave it to time.
Although 'tis fit that Cassio have his place,
For sure he fills it up with great ability,
Yet, if you please to hold him off awhile,
You shall by that perceive him and his means.
Note if your lady strain his entertainment   250
With any strong or vehement importunity;
Much will be seen in that. In the mean time
Let me be thought too busy in my fears   253
(As worthy cause I have to fear I am)
And hold her free, I do beseech your honor.   255
OTHELLO:
Fear not my government.   256
IAGO:
I once more take my leave.   [*Exit.*]
OTHELLO:
This fellow's of exceeding honesty,
And knows all qualities, with a learned spirit   259

234 *position* definite assertion   **236** *recoiling* reverting   **237** *fall to match* happen to compare   **238** *happily* haply, perhaps   **250** *strain his entertainment* urge his recall   **253** *busy* meddlesome   **255** *hold her free* consider her guiltless   **256** *government* self-control   **259** *qualities* natures   **259–60** *learned spirit* Of mind informed about

Of human dealings. If I do prove her haggard,   260
Though that her jesses were my dear heartstrings,   261
I'd whistle her off and let her down the wind   262
To prey at fortune. Haply, for I am black
And have not those soft parts of conversation   264
That chamberers have, or for I am declined   265
Into the vale of years—yet that's not much—
She's gone. I am abused, and my relief
Must be to loathe her. O curse of marriage,
That we can call these delicate creatures ours,
And not their appetites! I had rather be a toad
And live upon the vapor of a dungeon
Than keep a corner in the thing I love
For others' uses. Yet 'tis the plague of great ones;   273
Prerogatived are they less than the base.   274
'Tis destiny unshunnable, like death.
Even then this forkèd plague is fated to us   276
When we do quicken. Look where she comes.   277

[Enter DESDEMONA and EMILIA.]

If she be false, O, then heaven mocks itself!
I'll not believe't.
DESDEMONA: How now, my dear Othello?
Your dinner, and the generous islanders   280
By you invited, do attend your presence.
OTHELLO:
I am to blame.
DESDEMONA: Why do you speak so faintly?
Are you not well?
OTHELLO:
I have a pain upon my forehead, here.
DESDEMONA:
Faith, that's with watching; 'twill away again.   285
Let me but bind it hard, within this hour
It will be well.
OTHELLO: Your napkin is too little;   287
[He pushes the handkerchief from him, and it falls unnoticed.]
Let it alone. Come, I'll go in with you.   288
DESDEMONA:
I am very sorry that you are not well.   [Exit (with OTHELLO).]

260 *haggard* a wild hawk   261 *jesses* thongs for controlling a hawk   262–63 *whistle . . . fortune* turn her out and let her take care of herself   264 *soft . . . conversation* ingratiating manners   265 *chamberers* courtiers   273 *great ones* prominent men   274 *Prerogatived* privileged   276 *forkèd plague* i.e. horns of a cuckold   277 *do quicken* are born   280 *generous* noble   285 *watching* working late   287 *napkin* handkerchief   288 *it* i.e. his forehead

EMILIA:
   I am glad I have found this napkin;
   This was her first remembrance from the Moor,
   My wayward husband hath a hundred times
   Wooed me to steal it; but she so loves the token
   (For he conjured her she should ever keep it)
   That she reserves it evermore about her
   To kiss and talk to. I'll have the work ta'en out   296
   And give't Iago.
   What he will do with it heaven knows, not I;
   I nothing but to please his fantasy.   299

   [*Enter* IAGO.]

IAGO:
   How now? What do you here alone?
EMILIA:
   Do not you chide; I have a thing for you.
IAGO:
   A thing for me? It is a common thing—
EMILIA: Ha?
IAGO:
   To have a foolish wife.
EMILIA:
   O, is that all? What will you give me now
   For that same handkerchief?
IAGO: What handkerchief?
EMILIA:
   What handkerchief!
   Why, that the Moor first gave to Desdemona;
   That which so often you did bid me steal.
IAGO:
   Hast stol'n it from her?
EMILIA:
   No, faith; she let it drop by negligence,
   And to th' advantage, I, being here, took't up.   312
   Look, here it is.
IAGO: A good wench! Give it me.
EMILIA:
   What will you do with't, that you have been so earnest
   To have me filch it?
IAGO: Why, what is that to you?
   [*Snatches it.*]

296 *work ta'en out* pattern copied   **299** *fantasy* whim   **312** *to th' advantage* opportunely

EMILIA:

    If it be not for some purpose of import, 316

    Give't me again. Poor lady, she'll run mad

    When she shall lack it.

IAGO:

    Be not acknown on't; I have use for it. 319

    Go, leave me.   [*Exit* EMILIA.]

    I will in Cassio's lodgings lose this napkin

    And let him find it. Trifles light as air

    Are to the jealous confirmations strong

    As proofs of holy writ. This may do something.

    The Moor already changes with my poison:

    Dangerous conceits are in their natures poisons, 326

    Which at the first are scarce found to distaste,

    But with a little act upon the blood

    Burn like the mines of sulphur.

    [*Enter* OTHELLO.]   I did say so.

    Look where he comes! Not poppy nor mandragora, 330

    Nor all the drowsy syrups of the world,

    Shall ever med'cine thee to that sweet sleep

    Which thou owedst yesterday.

OTHELLO: Ha! ha! false to me?

IAGO:

    Why, how now, general? No more of that!

OTHELLO:

    Avaunt! be gone! Thou hast set me on the rack.

    I swear 'tis better to be much abused

    Than but to know't a little.

IAGO: How now, my lord?

OTHELLO:

    What sense had I of her stol'n hours of lust?

    I saw't not, thought it not, it harmed not me;

    I slept the next night well, fed well, was free and merry; 340

    I found not Cassio's kisses on her lips.

    He that is robbed, not wanting what is stol'n, 342

    Let him not know't, and he's not robbed at all.

IAGO:

    I am sorry to hear this.

OTHELLO:

    I had been happy if the general camp,

    Pioners and all, had tasted her sweet body, 346

    So I had nothing known. O, now for ever

---

316 *import* importance   **319** *Be . . . on't* do not acknowledge it   **326** *conceits* ideas   **330** *mandragora* a narcotic
340 *free* carefree   **342** *wanting* missing   **346** *Pioners* sappers, laborers

Farewell the tranquil mind! farewell content!
Farewell the plumèd troop, and the big wars   349
That make ambition virtue! O, farewell!
Farewell the neighing steed and the shrill trump,
The spirit-stirring drum, th' ear-piercing fife,
The royal banner, and all quality,
Pride, pomp, and circumstance of glorious war!   354
And O you mortal engines whose rude throats   355
Th' immortal Jove's dread clamors counterfeit,   356
Farewell! Othello's occupation's gone!

IAGO:
Is't possible, my lord?

OTHELLO:
Villain, be sure thou prove my love a whore!
Be sure of it; give me the ocular proof;
Or, by the worth of mine eternal soul,
Thou hadst been better have been born a dog
Than answer my waked wrath!

IAGO: Is't come to this?

OTHELLO:
Make me to see't; or at the least so prove it
That the probation bear no hinge nor loop   365
To hang a doubt on—or woe upon thy life!

IAGO:
My noble lord—

OTHELLO:
If thou dost slander her and torture me,
Never pray more; abandon all remorse;
On horror's head horrors accumulate;
Do deeds to make heaven weep, all earth amazed;
For nothing canst thou to damnation add
Greater than that.

IAGO: O grace! O heaven forgive me!
Are you a man? Have you a soul or sense?—
God b' wi' you! take mine office. O wretched fool,
That liv'st to make thine honesty a vice!
O monstrous would! Take note, take note, O world,
To be direct and honest is not safe.
I thank you for this profit; and from hence   379
I'll love no friend, sith love breeds such offense.

OTHELLO:
Nay stay. Thou shouldst be honest.

---

349 *big* stately   **354** *circumstance* pageantry   **355** *mortal engines* deadly artillery   **356** *counterfeit* imitate
365 *probation* proof   **379** *profit* profitable lesson

IAGO:

    I should be wise; for honesty's a fool

    And loses that it works for.

OTHELLO: By the world,

    I think my wife be honest, and think she is not;

    I think that thou art just, and think thou art not.

    I'll have some proof. Her name, that was as fresh

    As Dian's visage, is now begrimed and black

    As mine own face. If there be cords, or knives,

    Poison, or fire, or suffocating streams,

    I'll not endure it. Would I were satisfied!   390

IAGO:

    I see, sir, you are eaten up with passion:

    I do repent me that I put it to you.

    You would be satisfied?

OTHELLO: Would? Nay, I will.

IAGO:

    And may; but how? how satisfied, my lord?

    Would you, the supervisor, grossly gape on?   395

    Behold her topped?

OTHELLO: Death and damnation! O!

IAGO:

    It were a tedious difficulty, I think,

    To bring them to that prospect. Damn them then,

    If ever mortal eyes do see them bolster   399

    More than their own! What then? How then?

    What shall I say? Where's satisfaction?

    It is impossible you should see this,

    Were they as prime as goats, as hot as monkeys,   403

    As salt as wolves in pride, and fools as gross   404

    As ignorance made drunk. But yet, I say,

    If imputation and strong circumstances

    Which lead directly to the door of truth

    Will give you satisfaction, you may have't.

OTHELLO:

    Give me a living reason she's disloyal.

IAGO:

    I do not like the office.   410

    But sith I am ent'red in this cause so far,

    Pricked to't by foolish honesty and love,

    I will go on. I lay with Cassio lately,

    And being troubled with a raging tooth,

---

390 *satisfied* completely informed **395** *supervisor* spectator **399** *bolster* lie together **403** *prime* lustful
404 *salt* lecherous; *pride* heat

I could not sleep.
There are a kind of men so loose of soul
That in their sleeps will mutter their affairs.
One of this kind is Cassio.
In sleep I heard him say, "Sweet Desdemona,
Let us be wary, let us hide our loves!"   420
And then, sir, would he gripe and wring my hand,
Cry "O sweet creature!" and then kiss me hard,
As if he plucked up kisses by the roots
That grew upon my lips; then laid his leg
Over my thigh, and sighed, and kissed, and then
Cried "Cursèd fate that gave thee to the Moor!"

OTHELLO:
O monstrous! monstrous!

IAGO: Nay, this was but his dream.

OTHELLO:
But this denoted a foregone conclusion: 428
'Tis a shrewd doubt, though it be but a dream.   429

IAGO:
And this may help to thicken other proofs
That do demonstrate thinly.

OTHELLO: I'll tear her all to pieces!

IAGO:
Nay, but be wise. Yet we see nothing done;
She may be honest yet. Tell me but this—
Have you not sometimes seen a handkerchief
Spotted with strawberries in your wife's hand?

OTHELLO:
I gave her such a one; 'twas my first gift.

IAGO:
I know not that; but such a handkerchief—
I am sure it was your wife's—did I to-day
See Cassio wipe his beard with.

OTHELLO: If it be that—

IAGO:
If it be that, or any that was hers,   440
It speaks against her with the other proofs.

OTHELLO:
O, that the slave had forty thousand lives!
One is too poor, too weak for my revenge.
Now do I see 'tis true. Look here, Iago:
All my fond love thus do I blow to heaven.
'Tis gone.

428 *foregone conclusion* previous experience   **429** *a shrewd doubt* cursedly suspicious

Arise, black vengeance, from the hollow hell!
Yield up, O love, thy crown and hearted throne
To tyrannous hate! Swell, bosom, with thy fraught,   449
For 'tis of aspics' tongues!   450
IAGO: Yet be content.
OTHELLO:
O, blood, blood, blood!
IAGO:
Patience, I say. Your mind perhaps may change.
OTHELLO:
Never, Iago. Like to the Pontic sea,   453
Whose icy current and compulsive course
Ne'er feels retiring ebb, but keeps due on
To the Propontic and the Hellespont,
Even so my bloody thoughts, with violent pace,
Shall ne'er look back, ne'er ebb to humble love,
Till that a capable and wide revenge   459
Swallow them up.
[He kneels.]   Now, by yond marble heaven,
In the due reverence of a sacred vow
I here engage my words.
IAGO: Do not rise yet.

[IAGO kneels.]

Witness, you ever-burning lights above,
You elements that clip us round about,   464
Witness that here Iago doth give up
The execution of his wit, hands, heart   466
To wronged Othello's service! Let him command,
And to obey shall be in me remorse,   468
What bloody business ever.
[They rise.]
OTHELLO: I greet thy love,
Not with vain thanks but with acceptance bounteous,
And will upon the instant put thee to't.
Within these three days let me hear thee say
That Cassio's not alive.
IAGO:
My friend is dead; 'tis done at your request
But let her live.

449 *fraught* burden   450 *aspics* deadly poisonous snakes   453 *Pontic sea* Black Sea   459 *capable* all-embracing   464 *clip* encompass   466 *execution* activities; *wit* mind   468 *remorse* pity

OTHELLO:
  Damn her, lewd minx! O, damn her! damn her!
  Come, go with me apart. I will withdraw
  To furnish me with some swift means of death
  For the fair devil. Now art thou my lieutenant.
IAGO:
  I am your own for ever.   [*Exeunt.*]

SCENE IV

  [*Enter* DESDEMONA, EMILIA, *and* CLOWN.]

DESDEMONA: Do you know, sirrah, where Lieutenant Cassio lies?   2
CLOWN: I dare not say he lies anywhere.
DESDEMONA: Why, man?
CLOWN: He's a soldier, and for me to say a soldier lies is
  stabbing.
DESDEMONA: Go to. Where lodges he?
CLOWN: To tell you where he lodges is to tell you where I lie.
DESDEMONA: Can anything be made of this?
CLOWN: I know not where he lodges; and for me to devise
  a lodging, and say he lies here or he lies there, were to
  lie in mine own throat.
DESDEMONA: Can you enquire him out, and be edified by
  report?
CLOWN: I will catechize the world for him; that is, make
  questions, and by them answer.
DESDEMONA: Seek him, bid him come hither. Tell him I
  have moved my lord on his behalf and hope all will be   19
  well.
CLOWN: To do this is within the compass of man's wit,
  and therefore I'll attempt the doing of it.   [*Exit.*]
DESDEMONA:
  Where should I lose that handkerchief, Emilia?
EMILIA:
  I know not, madam.
DESDEMONA:
  Believe me, I had rather have lost my purse
  Full of crusadoes; and but my noble Moor   26
  Is true of mind, and made of no such baseness
  As jealous creatures are, it were enough
  To put him to ill thinking.
EMILIA: Is he not jealous?

Scene iv The environs of the castle   **2** *lies* lives, lodges   **19** *moved* made proposals   **26** *crusadoes* Portuguese
gold coins

DESDEMONA:
Who? he? I think the sun where he was born
Drew all such humors from him.   31

[*Enter* OTHELLO.]

EMILIA: Look where he comes.
DESDEMONA:
I will not leave him now till Cassio
Be called to him.—How is't with you, my lord?
OTHELLO:
Well, my good lady. [*aside*] O, hardness to dissemble!—
How do you, Desdemona?
DESDEMONA: Well, my good lord.
OTHELLO:
Give me your hand. This hand is moist, my lady.
DESDEMONA:
It yet hath felt no age nor known no sorrow.
OTHELLO:
This argues fruitfulness and liberal heart.
Hot, hot, and moist. This hand of yours requires
A sequester from liberty, fasting and prayer,   40
Much castigation, exercise devout;
For here's a young and sweating devil here
That commonly rebels. 'Tis a good hand,
A frank one.
DESDEMONA: You may, indeed, say so;
For 'twas that hand that gave away my heart.
OTHELLO:
A liberal hand! The hearts of old gave hands;
But our new heraldry is hands, not hearts.   47
DESDEMONA:
I cannot speak of this. Come now, your promise!
OTHELLO:
What promise, chuck?
DESDEMONA:
I have sent to bid Cassio come speak with you.
OTHELLO:
I have a salt and sorry rheum offends me.   51
Lend me thy handkerchief.
DESDEMONA: Here, my lord.
OTHELLO:
That which I gave you.

31 *humors* inclinations   **40** *sequester* removal   **47** *heraldry* heraldic symbolism   **51** *salt . . . rheum* distressing
head-cold

DESDEMONA: I have it not about me.
OTHELLO:
  Not?
DESDEMONA: No, faith, my lord.
OTHELLO: That's a fault.
  That handkerchief
  Did an Egyptian to my mother give.   56
  She was a charmer, and could almost read   57
  The thoughts of people. She told her, while she kept it,
  'Twould make her amiable and subdue my father   59
  Entirely to her love; but if she lost it
  Or made a gift of it, my father's eye
  Should hold her loathèd, and his spirits should hunt
  After new fancies. She, dying, gave it me,
  And bid me, when my fate would have me wive,
  To give it her. I did so; and take heed on't;
  Make it a darling like your precious eye.
  To lose't or give't away were such perdition   67
  As nothing else could match.
DESDEMONA: Is't possible?
OTHELLO:
  'Tis true. There's magic in the web of it.
  A sibyl that had numb'red in the world
  The sun to course two hundred compasses,   71
  In her prophetic fury sewed the work;
  The worms were hallowed that did breed the silk;
  And it was dyed in mummy which the skillful   74
  Conserved of maiden's hearts.
DESDEMONA: I' faith? Is't true?
OTHELLO:
  Most veritable. Therefore look to't well.
DESDEMONA:
  Then would to God that I had never seen't!
OTHELLO: Ha! Wherefore?
DESDEMONA:
  Why do you speak so startingly and rash?
OTHELLO:
  Is't lost? Is't gone? Speak, is it out o' th' way?
DESDEMONA: Heaven bless us!
OTHELLO: Say you?
DESDEMONA:
  It is not lost. But what an if it were?

---

56 *Egyptian* gypsy **57** *charmer* sorceress **59** *amiable* lovable **67** *perdition* disaster **71** *compasses* annual rounds **74** *mummy* a drug made from mummies

OTHELLO: How?

DESDEMONA:

  I say it is not lost.

OTHELLO: Fetch't, let me see't!

DESDEMONA:

  Why, so I can, sir; but I will not now.

  This is a trick to put me from my suit: 87

  Pray you let Cassio be received again.

OTHELLO:

  Fetch me the handkerchief! My mind misgives.

DESDEMONA:

  Come, come!

  You'll never meet a more sufficient man.

OTHELLO:

  The handkerchief!

DESDEMONA: I pray talk me of Cassio.

OTHELLO:

  The handkerchief!

DESDEMONA: A man that all his time   93

  Hath founded his good fortunes on your love,

  Shared dangers with you—

OTHELLO:

  The handkerchief!

DESDEMONA:

  I' faith, you are to blame.

OTHELLO: Zounds!   [*Exit* OTHELLO.]

EMILIA: Is not this man jealous?

DESDEMONA:

  I ne'er saw this before.

  Sure there's some wonder in this handkerchief;

  I am most unhappy in the loss of it.

EMILIA:

  'Tis not a year or two shows us a man.

  They are all but stomachs, and we all but food;

  They eat us hungerly, and when they are full,

  They belch us.

[*Enter* IAGO *and* CASSIO.]

              Look you—Cassio and my husband!

IAGO:

  There is no other way; 'tis she must do't.

  And lo the happiness! Go and importune her.   108

87 *put* divert   **93** *all . . . time* during his whole career   **108** *happiness* good luck

DESDEMONA:

How now, good Cassio? What's the news with you?

CASSIO:

Madam, my former suit. I do beseech you
That by your virtuous means I may again
Exist, and be a member of his love
Whom I with all the office of my heart
Entirely honor. I would not be delayed.
If my offense be of such mortal kind
That neither service past, nor present sorrows,
Nor purposed merit in futurity,
Can ransom me into his love again,
But to know so must be my benefit.
So shall I clothe me in a forced content,
And shut myself up in some other course,   121
To fortune's alms.

DESDEMONA: Alas, thrice-gentle Cassio!
My advocation is not now in tune.   123
My lord is not my lord; nor should I know him,
Were he in favor as in humor altered.   125
So help me every spirit sanctified
As I have spoken for you all my best
And stood within the blank of his displeasure   128
For my free speech! You must awhile be patient.
What I can do I will; and more I will
Than for myself I dare. Let that suffice you.

IAGO:

Is my lord angry?

EMILIA: He went hence but now,
And certainly in strange unquietness.

IAGO:

Can he be angry? I have seen the cannon
When it hath blown his ranks into the air
And, like the devil, from his very arm
Puffed his own brother—and is he angry?
Something of moment then. I will go meet him.
There's matter in't indeed if he be angry.

DESDEMONA:

I prithee do so.   [*Exit* IAGO.]
                  Something sure of state,   140
Either from Venice or some unhatched practice   141
Made demonstrable here in Cyprus to him,
Hath puddled his clear spirit; and in such cases   143

---

121 *shut myself up in* confine myself to   **123** *advocation* advocacy   **125** *favor* appearance   **128** *blank* bull's-eye
of the target   **140** *state* public affairs   **141** *unhatched practice* budding plot   **143** *puddled* muddied

Men's natures wrangle with inferior things,
Though great ones are their object. 'Tis even so;
For let our finger ache, and it endues   146
Our other, healthful members even to a sense
Of pain. Nay, we must think men are not gods,
Nor of them look for such observancy
As fits the bridal. Beshrew me much, Emilia,
I was, unhandsome warrior as I am,   151
Arraigning his unkindness with my soul;   152
But now I find I had suborned the witness,
And he's indicted falsely.

EMILIA:
Pray heaven it be state matters, as you think,
And no conception nor no jealous toy   156
Concerning you.

DESDEMONA:
Alas the day! I never gave him cause.

EMILIA:
But jealous souls will not be answered so;
They are not ever jealous for the cause,
But jealous for they're jealous. 'Tis a monster
Begot upon itself, born on itself.   162

DESDEMONA:
Heaven keep that monster from Othello's mind!

EMILIA: Lady, amen.

DESDEMONA:
I will go seek him. Cassio, walk here about:
If I do find him fit, I'll move your suit
And seek to effect it to my uttermost.

CASSIO:
I humbly thank your ladyship.

> [*Exeunt* DESDEMONA *and* EMILIA.]

[*Enter* BIANCA.]

BIANCA:
Save you, friend Cassio!

CASSIO: What make you from home?
How is't with you, my most fair Bianca?
I' faith, sweet love, I was coming to your house.

BIANCA:
And I was going to your lodging, Cassio.
What, keep a week away? seven days and nights?

---

146 *endues* brings   **151** *unhandsome warrior* inadequate soldier   **152** *Arraigning . . . soul* indicting his unkindness
before the bar of my soul   **156** *toy* fancy   **162** *Begot . . . itself* self-engendered

Eightscore eight hours? and lovers' absent hours,
More tedious than the dial eightscore times?   175
O weary reck'ning!
CASSIO: Pardon me, Bianca:
I have this while with leaden thoughts been pressed;
But I shall in a more continuate time   178
Strike off this score of absence. Sweet Bianca,
[*Gives her* DESDEMONA'*s handkerchief.*]
Take me this work out.   180
BIANCA: O Cassio, whence came this?
This is some token from a newer friend.
To the felt absence now I feel a cause.
Is't come to this? Well, well.
CASSIO: Go to, woman!
Throw your vile guesses in the devil's teeth,
From whence you have them. You are jealous now
That this is from some mistress, some remembrance.
No, by my faith, Bianca.
BIANCA: Why, whose is it?
CASSIO:
I know not, sweet; I found it in my chamber.
I like the work well; ere it be demanded,   189
As like enough it will, I'd have it copied.
Take it and do't, and leave me for this time.
BIANCA:
Leave you? Wherefore?
CASSIO:
I do attend here on the general
And think it no addition, nor my wish,
To have him see me womaned.
BIANCA: Why, I pray you?
CASSIO:
Not that I love you not.
BIANCA: But that you do not love me!
I pray you bring me on the way a little,
And say if I shall see you soon at night.
CASSIO:
'Tis but a little way that I can bring you,
For I attend here; but I'll see you soon.
BIANCA:
'Tis very good. I must be circumstanced.   [*Exeunt.*]   201

---

175 *dial* clock   **178** *continuate* uninterrupted   **180** *Take . . . out* copy this embroidery for me   **189** *work* needlework   **201** *circumstanced* governed by circumstances

ACT IV

SCENE I

[*Enter* OTHELLO *and* IAGO.]

IAGO:
  Will you think so?
OTHELLO: Think so, Iago?
IAGO: What,
  To kiss in private?
OTHELLO: An unauthorized kiss.
IAGO:
  Or to be naked with her friend in bed
  An hour or more, not meaning any harm?
OTHELLO:
  Naked in bed, Iago, and not mean harm?
  It is hypocrisy against the devil.   6
  They that mean virtuously, and yet do so,
  The devil their virtue tempts, and they tempt heaven.
IAGO:
  So they do nothing, 'tis a venial slip.
  But if I give my wife a handkerchief—
OTHELLO:
  What then?
IAGO:
  Why, then 'tis hers, my lord; and being hers,
  She may, I think, bestow't on any man.
OTHELLO:
  She is protectress of her honor too;
  May she give that?
IAGO:
  Her honor is an essence that's not seen;
  They have it very oft that have it not.
  But for the handkerchief—
OTHELLO:
  By heaven, I would most gladly have forgot it!
  Thou said'st—O, it comes o'er my memory
  As doth the raven o'er the infected house,   21
  Boding to all!—he had my handkerchief.
IAGO:
  Ay, what of that?

Scene i The environs of the castle   **6** *hyprocrisy . . . devil* i.e. feigned sin instead of feigned virtue
21 *infected* plague-stricken

OTHELLO: That's not so good now.

IAGO: What
If I had said I had seen him do you wrong?
Or heard him say—as knaves be such abroad
Who having, by their own importunate suit,
Or voluntary dotage of some mistress,
Convincèd or supplied them, cannot choose   28
But they must blab—

OTHELLO: Hath he said anything?

IAGO:
He hath, my lord; but be you well assured,
No more than he'll unswear.

OTHELLO: What hath he said?

IAGO:
Faith, that he did—I know not what he did.

OTHELLO: What? what?

IAGO:
Lie—

OTHELLO: With her?

IAGO: With her, on her; what you will.

OTHELLO: Lie with her? lie on her?—We say lie on her when they belie
her.—Lie with her! Zounds, that's fulsome.—Handkerchief—
confessions—handkerchief!—To confess, and be hanged for his
labor—first to be hanged, and then to confess! I tremble at it. Nature   38
would not invest herself in such shadowing passion without some
instruction. It is not words that shakes me thus.—Pish! Noses, ears,
and lips? Is't possible?—Confess?—Handkerchief?—O devil!

[*Falls in a trance.*]

IAGO: Work on,
My med'cine, work! Thus credulous fools are caught,
And many worthy and chaste dames even thus,
All guiltless, meet reproach.—What, ho! my lord!
My lord, I say! Othello!
[*Enter* CASSIO.]   How now, Cassio?

CASSIO:
What's the matter?

IAGO:
My lord is fall'n into an epilepsy.
This is his second fit; he had one yesterday.

CASSIO:
Rub him about the temples.

---

28 *Convincèd or supplied* overcome or gratified   **38–40** *Nature . . . instruction* my natural faculties would not be
so overcome by passion without reason

IAGO: No, forbear.
  The lethargy must have his quiet course.   51
  If not, he foams at mouth, and by and by
  Breaks out to savage madness. Look, he stirs.
  Do you withdraw yourself a little while.
  He will recover straight. When he is gone,
  I would on great occasion speak with you.   [*Exit* CASSIO.]
  How is it, general? Have you not hurt your head?
OTHELLO:
  Dost thou mock me?
IAGO: I mock you? No, by heaven.
  Would you would bear your fortune like a man!
OTHELLO:
  A hornèd man's a monster and a beast.   60
IAGO:
  There's many a beast then in a populous city,
  And many a civil monster.
OTHELLO:
  Did he confess it?
IAGO: Good sir, be a man.
  Think every bearded fellow that's but yoked
  May draw with you. There's millions now alive
  That nightly lie in those unproper beds   66
  Which they dare swear peculiar: your case is better.   67
  O, 'tis the spite of hell, the fiend's arch-mock,
  To lip a wanton in a secure couch,   69
  And to suppose her chaste! No, let me know,
  And knowing what I am, I know what she shall be.
OTHELLO:
  O, thou art wise! 'Tis certain.
IAGO: Stand you awhile apart;
  Confine yourself but in a patient list.   73
  Whilst you were here, o'erwhelmèd with your grief—
  A passion most unsuiting such a man—
  Cassio came hither. I shifted him away
  And laid good'scuse upon your ecstasy;   77
  Bade him anon return, and he speak with me;
  The which he promised. Do but encave yourself   79
  And mark the fleers, the gibes, and notable scorns
  That dwell in every region of his face;
  For I will make him tell the tale anew—
  Where, how, how oft, how long ago, and when

---

51 *lethargy* coma   **60** *hornèd man* cuckold   **66** *unproper* not exclusively their own   **67** *peculiar* exclusively their own   **69** *secure* free from fear of rivalry   **73** *in a patient list* within the limits of self-control   **77** *ecstasy* trance **79** *encave* conceal

He hath, and is again to cope your wife.   84
I say, but mark his gesture. Marry, patience!
Or I shall say y'are all in all in spleen,   86
And nothing of a man.
OTHELLO: Dost thou hear, Iago?
I will be found most cunning in my patience;
But—dost thou hear?—most bloody.
IAGO: That's not amiss;
But yet keep time in all. Will you withdraw?
[OTHELLO *retires*.]
Now will I question Cassio of Bianca,
A huswife that by selling her desires   92
Buys herself bread and clothes. It is a creature
That dotes on Cassio, as 'tis the strumpet's plague
To beguile many and be beguiled by one.
He, when he hears of her, cannot refrain
From the excess of laughter. Here he comes.

[*Enter* CASSIO.]

As he shall smile, Othello shall go mad;
And his unbookish jealousy must conster   99
Poor Cassio's smiles, gestures, and light behavior
Quite in the wrong. How do you now, lieutenant?
CASSIO:
The worser that you give me the addition   102
Whose want even kills me.
IAGO:
Ply Desdemona well, and you are sure on't.
Now, if this suit lay in Bianca's power,
How quickly should you speed!
CASSIO: Alas, poor caitiff!   106
OTHELLO:
Look how he laughs already!
IAGO:
I never knew a woman love man so.
CASSIO:
Alas, poor rogue! I think, i' faith, she loves me.
OTHELLO:
Now he denies it faintly, and laughs it out.
IAGO:
Do you hear, Cassio?

84 *cope* meet   **86** *all in all in spleen* wholly overcome by your passion   **92** *huswif* hussy   **99** *unbookish* unin-
structed; *conster* construe, interpret   **102** *addition* title   **106** *caitiff* wretch

OTHELLO: Now he importunes him
   To tell it o'er. Go to! Well said, well said!
IAGO:
   She gives it out that you shall marry her.
   Do you intend it?
CASSIO: Ha, ha, ha!
OTHELLO:
   Do you triumph, Roman? Do you triumph?
CASSIO: I marry her? What, a customer? Prithee bear some charity to my   117
   wit; do not think it so unwholesome. Ha, ha, ha!
OTHELLO: So, so, so, so! They laugh that win!
IAGO:
   Faith, the cry goes that you shall marry her.
CASSIO: Prithee say true.
IAGO: I am a very villain else.
OTHELLO: Have you scored me? Well.   123
CASSIO: This is the monkey's own giving out. She is persuaded I will marry
   her out of her own love and flattery, not out of my promise.
OTHELLO: Iago beckons me; now he begins the story.   126
CASSIO: She was here even now; she haunts me in every place. I was t' other
   day talking on the sea bank with certain Venetians, and thither comes
   the bauble, and, by this hand, she falls me thus about my neck—   129
OTHELLO: Crying "O dear Cassio!" as it were. His gesture imports it.
CASSIO: So hangs, and lolls, and weeps upon me; so shakes and pulls me!
   Ha, ha, ha!
OTHELLO: Now he tells how she plucked him to my chamber. O, I see that
   nose of yours, but not that dog I shall throw it to.
CASSIO: Well, I must leave her company.

[*Enter* BIANCA.]

IAGO: Before me! Look where she comes.
CASSIO: 'Tis such another fitchew! marry, a perfumed one. What do you   137
   mean by this haunting of me?
BIANCA: Let the devil and his dam haunt you! What did you mean by that
   same handkerchief you gave me even now? I was a fine fool to take it. I
   must take out the whole work? A likely piece of work that you should
   find it in your chamber and know not who left it there! This is some
   minx's token, and I must take out the work? There! Give it your
   hobby-horse. Wheresoever you had it, I'll take out no work on't.   144
CASSIO: How now, my sweet Bianca? How now? how now?
OTHELLO: By heaven, that should be my handkerchief!

---

117 *customer* prostitute **123** *scored me* settled my account (?) **126** *beckons* signals **129** *bauble* plaything
137 *fitchew* polecat (slang for whore) **144** *hobby-horse* harlot

BIANCA: An you'll come to supper to-night, you may; an you will not, come
    when you are next prepared for.   [*Exit.*]

IAGO: After her, after her!

CASSIO: Faith, I must; she'll rail in the street else.

IAGO: Will you sup there?

CASSIO: Yes, I intend so.

IAGO: Well, I may chance to see you; for I would very fain
    speak with you.

CASSIO: Prithee come. Will you?

IAGO: Go to! say no more.   [*Exit* CASSIO.]

OTHELLO [*comes forward*]: How shall I murder him, Iago?

IAGO: Did you perceive how he laughed at his vice?   158

OTHELLO: O Iago!

IAGO: And did you see the handkerchief?

OTHELLO: Was that mine?

IAGO: Yours, by this hand! And to see how he prizes the foolish woman your   162
    wife! She gave it him, and he hath giv'n it his whore.

OTHELLO: I would have him nine years a-killing!—A fine woman! a fair
    woman! a sweet woman!

IAGO: Nay, you must forget that.

OTHELLO: Ay, let her rot, and perish, and be damned to-night; for she shall
    not live. No, my heart is turned to stone; I strike it, and it hurts my
    hand. O, the world hath not a sweeter creature! She might lie by an
    emperor's side and command him tasks.

IAGO: Nay, that's not your way.

OTHELLO: Hang her! I do but say what she is. So delicate with her needle! an
    admirable musician! O, she will sing the savageness out of a bear! Of so
    high and plenteous wit and invention—   174

IAGO: She's the worse for all this.

OTHELLO: O, a thousand thousand times! And then, of so gentle a condition!   176

IAGO: Ay, too gentle.

OTHELLO: Nay, that's certain. But yet the pity of it, Iago! O Iago, the pity of
    it, Iago!

IAGO: If you are so fond over her iniquity, give her patent to offend; for if it   180
    touch not you, it comes near nobody.

OTHELLO: I will chop her into messes! Cuckold me!

IAGO: O, 'tis foul in her.

OTHELLO: With mine officer!

IAGO: That's fouler.

OTHELLO: Get me some poison, Iago, this night. I'll not
    expostulate with her, lest her body and beauty un-   187
    provide my mind again. This night, Iago!

---

158 *vice* i.e. vicious conduct **162** *prizes* values **174** *invention* imagination **176** *condition* disposition
180 *patent* license **187–88** *unprovide* disarm

IAGO: Do it not with poison. Strangle her in her bed, even
    the bed she hath contaminated.

OTHELLO: Good, good! The justice of it pleases. Very good!

IAGO: And for Cassio, let me be his undertaker: you shall hear more by   192
    midnight.

OTHELLO:
    Excellent good!
    [*A trumpet.*]   What trumpet is that same?

IAGO:
    I warrant something from Venice.

[*Enter* LODOVICO, DESDEMONA, *and attendants.*]

                    'Tis Lodovico.
    This comes from the Duke; and see, your wife is with him.

LODOVICO:
    God save you, worthy general!

OTHELLO: With all my heart, sir.

LODOVICO:
    The Duke and senators of Venice greet you.
    [*Gives him a letter.*]

OTHELLO:
    I kiss the instrument of their pleasures.
    [*Opens the letter and reads.*]

DESDEMONA:
    And what's the news, good cousin Lodovico?

IAGO:
    I am very glad to see you, signior.
    Welcome to Cyprus.

LODOVICO:
    I thank you. How does Lieutenant Cassio?

IAGO: Lives, sir.

DESDEMONA:
    Cousin, there's fall'n between him and my lord
    An unkind breach; but you shall make all well.

OTHELLO: Are you sure of that?

DESDEMONA: My lord?

OTHELLO [*reads*]: "This fail you not to do, as you will—"

LODOVICO:
    He did not call; he's busy in the paper.
    Is there division 'twixt thy lord and Cassio?

DESDEMONA:
    A most unhappy one. I would do much
    T'atone them, for the love I bear to Cassio?   212

192 *be his undertaker* undertake to deal with him   **212** *atone* reconcile

OTHELLO:
  Fire and brimstone!
DESDEMONA: My lord?
OTHELLO: Are you wise?
DESDEMONA:
  What, is he angry?
LODOVICO: May be the letter moved him;
  For, as I think, they do command him home,
  Deputing Cassio in his government.
DESDEMONA:
  By my troth, I am glad on't.
OTHELLO: Indeed?
DESDEMONA: My lord?
OTHELLO:
  I am glad to see you mad.   218
DESDEMONA: Why, sweet Othello—
OTHELLO: Devil!
  [*Strikes her.*]
DESDEMONA: I have not deserved this.
LODOVICO:
  My lord, this would not be believed in Venice,
  Though I should swear I saw't. 'Tis very much.
  Make her amends; she weeps.
OTHELLO: O devil, devil!
  If that the earth could teem with woman's tears,   224
  Each drop she falls would prove a crocodile.   225
  Out of my sight!
DESDEMONA: I will not stay to offend you.   [*Going.*]
LODOVICO:
  Truly, an obedient lady.
  I do beseech your lordship call her back.
OTHELLO:
  Mistress!
DESDEMONA: My lord?
OTHELLO: What would you with her, sir?
LODOVICO:
  Who? I, my lord?
OTHELLO:
  Ay! You did wish that I would make her turn.
  Sir, she can turn, and turn, and yet go on
  And turn again; and she can weep, sir, weep;
  And she's obedient; as you say, obedient,
  Very obedient.—Proceed you in your tears.—

218 *mad* i.e. waggish   **224** *teem* breed   **225** *crocodile* (crocodiles were supposed to shed hypocritical tears to lure men to destruction)

Concerning this, sir—O well-painted passion!—   236
I am commanded home.—Get you away;
I'll send for you anon.—Sir, I obey the mandate
And will return to Venice.—Hence, avaunt!   [*Exit* DESDEMONA.]
Cassio shall have my place. And, sir, to-night
I do entreat that we may sup together.
You are welcome, sir, to Cyprus.—Goats and monkeys!   [*Exit.*]

LODOVICO:
Is this the noble Moor whom our full Senate
Call all in all sufficient? Is this the nature
Whom passion could not shake? whose solid virtue
The shot of accident nor dart of chance
Could neither graze nor pierce?

IAGO: He is much changed.

LODOVICO:
Are his wits safe? Is he not light of brain?

IAGO:
He's that he is; I may not breath my censure.
What he might be—if what he might he is not—
I would to heaven he were!

LODOVICO: What, strike his wife?

IAGO:
Faith, that was not so well; yet would I knew
That stroke would prove the worst!

LODOVICO: Is it his usc?   253
Or did the letters work upon his blood
And new-create this fault?

IAGO: Alas, alas!
It is not honesty in me to speak.
What I have seen and known. You shall observe him,
And his own courses will denote him so
That I may save my speech. Do but go after
And mark how he continues.

LODOVICO:
I am sorry that I am deceived in him.   [*Exeunt.*]

SCENE II

[*Enter* OTHELLO *and* EMILIA.]

OTHELLO:
You have seen nothing then?

236 *passion* grief   **253** *use* custom
Scene ii Within the castle

EMILIA:

Nor ever heard, nor ever did suspect.

OTHELLO:

Yes, you have seen Cassio and she together.

EMILIA:

But then I saw no harm, and then I heard

Each syllable that breath made up between them.

OTHELLO:

What, did they never whisper?

EMILIA: Never, my lord.

OTHELLO:

Nor send you out o' th' way?

EMILIA: Never.

OTHELLO:

To fetch her fan, her gloves, her mask, nor nothing?

EMILIA: Never, my lord.

OTHELLO: That's strange.

EMILIA:

I durst, my lord, to wager she is honest,

Lay down my soul as stake. If you think other,

Remove your thought; it doth abuse your bosom.   14

If any wretch have put this in your head,

Let heaven requite it with the serpent's curse!   16

For if she be not honest, chaste, and true,

There's no man happy; the purest of their wives

Is foul as slander.

OTHELLO: Bid her come hither. Go.   [*Exit* EMILIA.]

She says enough; yet she's a simple bawd

That cannot say as much. This is a subtle whore,

A closet lock and key of villanous secrets;

And yet she'll kneel and pray; I have seen her do't.

[*Enter* DESDEMONA *and* EMILIA.]

DESDEMONA:

My lord, what is you will?

OTHELLO: Pray, chuck, come hither.

DESDEMONA:

What is your pleasure?

OTHELLO: Let me see your eyes.

Look in my face.

DESDEMONA: What horrible fancy's this?

14 *abuse . . . bosom* deceive your heart   **16** *serpent's curse* (cf. Genesis iii, 14)

OTHELLO [*to* EMILIA]:
   Some of your function, mistress.
   Leave procreants alone and shut the door;   28
   Cough or cry hem if anybody come.
   Your mystery, your mystery! Nay, dispatch!   [*Exit* EMILIA.]   30
DESDEMONA:
   Upon my knees, what doth your speech import?
   I understand a fury in your words,
   (But not the words.)
OTHELLO:
   Why, what art thou?
DESDEMONA: Your wife, my lord; your true
   And loyal wife.
OTHELLO: Come, swear it, damn thyself;
   Lest, being like one of heaven, the devils themselves   36
   Should fear to seize thee. Therefore be double-damned—
   Swear thou art honest.   38
DESDEMONA: Heaven doth truly know it.
OTHELLO:
   Heaven truly knows that thou art false as hell.
DESDEMONA:
   To whom, my lord? With whom? How am I false?
OTHELLO:
   Ah, Desdemona! away! away! away!
DESDEMONA:
   Alas the heavy day! Why do you weep?
   Am I the motive of these tears, my lord?
   If haply you my father do suspect
   An instrument of this your calling back,   45
   Lay not your blame on me. If you have lost him,
   Why, I have lost him too.
OTHELLO: Had it pleased heaven
   To try me with affliction, had they rained
   All kinds of sores and shames on my bare head,
   Steeped me in poverty to the very lips,
   Given to captivity me and my utmost hopes,
   I should have found in some place of my soul
   A drop of patience. But, alas, to make me
   A fixèd figure for the time of scorn   54
   To point his slow unmoving finger at!
   Yet could I bear that too; well, very well.
   But there where I have garnered up my heart,

---

28 *procreants* mating couples   **30** *mystery* trade, occupation   **36** *being . . . heaven* looking like an angel
38 *honest* chaste   **45** *An instrument* to be the cause   **54** *time of scorn* scornful world

Where either I must live or bear no life,
The fountain from the which my current runs
Or else dries up—to be discarded thence,
Or keep it as a cistern for fouls toads
To knot and gender in—turn thy complexion there,   62
Patience, thou young and rose-lipped cherubin!
Ay, there look grim as hell!

DESDEMONA:
I hope my noble lord esteems me honest.

OTHELLO:
O, ay; as summer flies are in the shambles,   66
That quicken even with blowing. O thou weed,   67
Who art so lovely fair, and smell'st so sweet,
That the sense aches at thee, would thou hadst ne'er
    been born!

DESDEMONA:
Alas, what ignorant sin have I committed?

OTHELLO:
Was this fair paper, this most goodly book,
Made to write "whore" upon? What committed?
Committed? O thou public commoner!   73
I should make very forges of my cheeks
That would to cinders burn up modesty,
Did I but speak thy deeds. What committed?
Heaven stops the nose at it, and the moon winks;   77
The bawdy wind, that kisses all it meets,
Is hushed within the hollow mine of earth
And will not hear it. What committed?
Impudent strumpet!

DESDEMONA: By heaven, you do me wrong!

OTHELLO:
Are not you a strumpet?

DESDEMONA: No, as I am a Christian!
If to preserve this vessel for my lord
From any other foul unlawful touch
Be not to be a strumpet, I am none.

OTHELLO:
What, not a whore?

DESDEMONA: No, as I shall be saved!

OTHELLO: Is't possible?

DESDEMONA:
O, heaven forgive us!

62 *turn thy complexion there* change thy color at that point   **66** *shambles* slaughterhouse   **67** *quicken* come to life
73 *commoner* harlot   **77** *winks* closes her eyes

OTHELLO: I cry you mercy then.   88
    I took you for that cunning whore of Venice
    That married with Othello.—[*calling*] You, mistress,
    That have the office opposite to Saint Peter
    And keep the gate of hell!
    [*Enter* EMILIA.]   You, you, ay, you!
    We have done our course; there's money for your pains:
    I pray you turn the key, and keep our counsel.   [*Exit.*]
EMILIA:
    Alas, what does this gentleman conceive?
    How do you, madam? How do you, my good lady?
DESDEMONA: Faith, half asleep.   97
EMILIA:
    Good madam, what's the matter with my lord?
DESDEMONA: With who?
EMILIA: Why, with my lord, madam.
DESDEMONA:
    Who is thy lord?
EMILIA: He that is yours, sweet lady.
DESDEMONA:
    I have none. Do not talk to me, Emilia.
    I cannot weep; nor answers have I none
    But what should go by water. Prithee to-night
    Lay on my bed my wedding sheets, remember;
    And call thy husband hither.
EMILIA: Here's a change indeed!   [*Exit.*]
DESDEMONA:
    'Tis meet I should be used so, very meet.
    How have I been behaved, that he might stick
    The small'st opinion on my least misuse?   109

[*Enter* IAGO *and* EMILIA.]

IAGO:
    What is your pleasure, madam? How is't with you?
DESDEMONA:
    I cannot tell. Those that do teach young babes
    Do it with gentle means and easy tasks:
    He might have chid me so; for, in good faith,
    I am a child to chiding.
IAGO: What is the matter, lady?

88 *cry you mercy* beg your pardon   **97** *half asleep* i.e. stunned   **109** *small'st opinion* least suspicion; *least misuse* slightest misconduct

EMILIA:
    Alas, Iago, my lord hath so bewhored her,
    Thrown such despite and heavy terms upon her
    As true hearts cannot bear.
DESDEMONA:
    Am I that name, Iago?
IAGO: What name, fair lady?
DESDEMONA:
    Such as she said my lord did say I was.
EMILIA:
    He called her whore. A beggar in his drink
    Could not have laid such terms upon his callet.   121
IAGO:
    Why did he so?
DESDEMONA:
    I do not know; I am sure I am none such.
IAGO:
    Do not weep, do not weep. Alas the day!
EMILIA:
    Hath she forsook so many noble matches,
    Her father and her country, and her friends,
    To be called whore? Would it not make one weep?
DESDEMONA:
    It is my wretched fortune.
IAGO: Beshrew him for't!
    How comes this trick upon him?   129
DESDEMONA: Nay, heaven doth know.
EMILIA:
    I will be hanged if some eternal villain,
    Some busy and insinuating rogue,
    Some cogging, cozening slave, to get some office,   132
    Have not devised this slander. I'll be hanged else.
IAGO:
    Fie, there is no such man! It is impossible.
DESDEMONA:
    If any such there be, heaven pardon him!
EMILIA:
    A halter pardon him! and hell gnaw his bones!
    Why should he call her whore? Who keeps her company?
    What place? what time? what form? what likelihood?
    The Moor's abused by some most villainous knave,

121 *callet* whore   **129** *trick* freakish behavior   **132** *cogging, cozening* cheating, defrauding

Some base notorious knave, some scurvy fellow.
O heaven, that such companions thou'dst unfold, 141
And put in every honest hand a whip
To lash the rascals naked through the world
Even from the east to th' west!

IAGO: Speak within door. 144

EMILIA:

O, fie upon them! Some such squire he was
That turned your wit the seamy side without
And made you to suspect me with the Moor.

IAGO:

You are a fool. Go to.

DESDEMONA: Alas, Iago,
What shall I do to win my lord again?
Good friend, go to him; for, by this light of heaven,
I know not how I lost him. Here I kneel:
If e'er my will did trespass 'gainst his love
Either in discourse of thought or actual deed, 153
Or that mine eyes, mine ears, or any sense
Delighted them in any other form,
Or that I do not yet, and ever did,
And ever will (though he do shake me off
To beggarly divorcement) love him dearly,
Comfort forswear me! Unkindness may do much; 159
And his unkindness may defeat my life, 160
But never taint my love. I cannot say "whore."
It does abhor me now I speak the word;
To do the act that might the addition earn
Not the world's mass of vanity could make me.

IAGO:

I pray you be content. 'Tis but his humor.
The business of the state does him offense,
And he does chide with you.

DESDEMONA:

If 'twere no other

IAGO: 'Tis but so, I warrant.

[*Trumpets within.*]

Hark how these instruments summon you to supper.
The messengers of Venice stay the meat:
Go in, and weep not. All things shall be well.

[*Exeunt* DESDEMONA *and* EMILIA.]

---

141 *companions* rogues; *unfold* expose   **144** *within door* with restraint   **153** *discourse* course   **159** *Comfort forswear* happiness forsake   **160** *defeat* destroy

[*Enter* RODERIGO.]

How now, Roderigo?

RODERIGO: I do not find that thou deal'st justly with me.

IAGO: What in the contrary?

RODERIGO: Every day thou daff'st me with some device, Iago, and rather, as   175
  it seems to me now, keep'st from me all conveniency than suppliest me   176
  with the least advantage of hope. I will indeed no longer endure it; nor
  am I yet persuaded to put up in peace what already I have foolishly
  suffered.

IAGO: Will you hear me, Roderigo?

RODERIGO: Faith, I have heard too much; for your words and performances
  are no kin together.

IAGO: You charge me most unjustly.

RODERIGO: With naught but truth. I have wasted myself out of my means.
  The jewels you have had from me to deliver to Desdemona would half
  have corrupted a votarist. You have told me she hath received them, and   186
  returned me expectations and comforts of sudden respect and   187
  acquaintance; but I find none.

IAGO: Well, go to; very well.

RODERIGO: Very well! go to! I cannot go to, man; nor 'tis not very well. By
  this hand, I say 'tis very scurvy, and begin to find myself fopped in it.   191

IAGO: Very well.

RODERIGO: I tell you 'tis not very well. I will make myself known to
  Desdemona. If she will return me my jewels, I will give over my suit and
  repent my unlawful solicitation; if not, assure yourself I will seek
  satisfaction of you.

IAGO: You have said now.

RODERIGO: Ay, and said nothing but what I protest intendment of doing.

IAGO: Why, now I see there's mettle in thee; and even from this instant do
  build on thee a better opinion than ever before. Give me thy hand,
  Roderigo. Thou hast taken against me a most just exception; but yet I
  protest I have dealt most directly in thy affair.   202

RODERIGO: It hath not appeared.

IAGO: I grant indeed it hath not appeared, and your suspicion is not
  without wit and judgment. But, Roderigo, if thou hast that in thee
  indeed which I have greater reason to believe now than ever, I mean
  purpose, courage, and valor, this night show it. If thou the next night
  following enjoy not Desdemona, take me from this world with treachery
  and devise engines for my life.   209

RODERIGO: Well, what is it? Is it within reason and compass?

---

175 *thou . . . device* you put me off with some trick   **176** *conveniency* favorable opportunities   **186** *votarist* nun
187 *sudden respect* immediate notice   **191** *fopped* duped   **202** *directly* straightforwardly   **209** *engines for* plots
against

IAGO: Sir, there is especial commission come from Venice to depute Cassio in Othello's place.

RODERIGO: Is that true? Why, then Othello and Desdemona return again to Venice.

IAGO: O, no; he goes into Mauritania and takes away with him the fair Desdemona, unless his abode be lingered here by some accident; 216
wherein none can be so determinate as the removing of Cassio. 217

RODERIGO: How do you mean removing of him?

IAGO: Why, by making him uncapable of Othello's place—knocking out his brains.

RODERIGO: And that you would have me to do?

IAGO: Ay, if you dare do yourself a profit and a right. He sups to-night with a harlotry, and thither will I go to him. He knows not yet of his honorable fortune. If you will watch his going thence, which I will fashion to fall out between twelve and one, you may take him at your pleasure. I will be near to second your attempt, and he shall fall between us. Come, stand not amazed at it, but go along with me. I will show you such a necessity in his death that you shall think yourself bound to put it on him. It is now high supper time, and the night grows to waste. About it!

RODERIGO: I will hear further reason for this.

IAGO: And you shall be satisfied. [Exeunt.]

SCENE III

[Enter OTHELLO, LODOVICO, DESDEMONA, EMILIA, and attendants.]

LODOVICO:
I do beseech you, sir, trouble yourself no further.

OTHELLO:
O, pardon me; 'twill do me good to walk.

LODOVICO:
Madam, good night, I humbly thank your ladyship.

DESDEMONA:
Your honor is most welcome.

OTHELLO: Will you walk, sir?
O, Desdemona—

DESDEMONA: My lord?

OTHELLO: Get you to bed on th' instant; I will be returned forthwith. Dismiss your attendant there. Look't be done.

DESDEMONA: I will, my lord.

[Exit OTHELLO, with LODOVICO and attendants.]

216 abode . . . here stay here be extended   217 determinate effective
Scene iii Within the castle

EMILIA: How goes it now? He looks gentler than he did.

DESDEMONA:

He says he will return incontinent.   11

He hath commanded me to go to bed,

And bade me to dismiss you.

EMILIA: Dismiss me?

DESDEMONA:

It was his bidding; therefore, good Emilia,

Give me my nightly wearing, and adieu.

We must not now displease him.

EMILIA: I would you had never seen him!

DESDEMONA:

So would not I. My love doth so approve him

That even his stubbornness, his checks, his frowns—   19

Prithee unpin me—have grace and favor in them.

EMILIA: I have laid those sheets you bade me on the bed.

DESDEMONA:

All's one. Good faith, how foolish our minds!

If I do die before thee, prithee shroud me

In one of those same sheets.

EMILIA: Come, come! You talk.

DESDEMONA:

My mother had a maid called Barbary.

She was in love; and he she loved proved mad   26

And did forsake her. She had a song of "Willow";

An old thing 'twas; but it expressed her fortune,

And she died singing it. That song to-night

Will not go from my mind; I have much to do

But to go hang my head all at one side

And sing it like poor Barbary. Prithee dispatch.

EMILIA:

Shall I go fetch your nightgown?   33

DESDEMONA: No, unpin me here.

This Lodovico is a proper man.

EMILIA: A very handsome man.

DESDEMONA: He speaks well.

EMILIA: I know a lady in Venice would have walked bare-

foot to Palestine for a touch of his nether lip.

DESDEMONA [sings]:

"The poor soul sat sighing by a sycamore tree,

    Sing all a green willow;

Her hand on her bosom, her head on her knee,

    Sing willow, willow, willow.

11 *incontinent* at once   **19** *stubbornness* roughness; *checks* rebukes   **26** *mad* wild, faithless   **33** *nightgown* dressing gown

The fresh streams ran by her and murmured her moans;
   Sing willow, willow, willow;
Her salt tears fell from her, and soft'ned the stones"—
Lay by these.
   "Sing willow, willow, willow"—
Prithee hie thee; he'll come anon.   48
   "Sing all a green willow must be my garland.
   Let nobody blame him; his scorn I approve"—
Nay, that's not next. Hark! who is't that knocks?
EMILIA: It's the wind.
DESDEMONA [*sings*]:
   "I called my love false love; but what said he then?
   Sing willow, willow, willow:
If I court moe women, you'll couch with moe men."
So, get thee gone; good night. Mine eyes do itch.
Doth that bode weeping?
EMILIA: 'Tis neither here nor there.
DESDEMONA:
   I have heard it said so. O, these men, these men!
   Dost thou in conscience think—tell me, Emilia—
   That there be women do abuse their husbands   60
   In such gross kind?
EMILIA: There be some such, no question.
DESDEMONA:
   Wouldst thou do such a deed for all the world?
EMILIA:
   Why, would not you?
DESDEMONA: No, by this heavenly light!
EMILIA:
   Nor I neither by this heavenly light.
   I might do't as well i' th' dark.
DESDEMONA:
   Wouldst thou do such as deed for all the world?
EMILIA: The world's a huge thing; it is a great price for a small vice.
DESDEMONA:
   In troth, I think thou wouldst not.
EMILIA: In troth, I think I should; and undo't when I had done it. Marry, I
   would not do such a thing for a joint-ring, nor for measures of lawn,   70
   nor for gowns, petticoats, nor caps, nor any petty exhibition; but, for all   71
   the whole world—'Ud's pity! who would not make her husband a
   cuckold to make him a monarch? I should venture purgatory for't.
DESDEMONA:
   Beshrew me if I would do such a wrong
   For the whole world.

---

48 *hie thee* hurry   **70** *joint-ring* ring made in separable halves   **71** *exhibition* gift

EMILIA: Why, the wrong is but a wrong i' th' world; and having the world for
    your labor, 'tis a wrong in your own world, and you might quickly make
    it right.

DESDEMONA: I do not think there is any such woman.

EMILIA: Yes, a dozen; and as many to th' vantage as would store the world   80
    they played for.
    But I do think it is their husbands' faults
    If wives do fall. Say that they slack their duties
    And pour our treasures into foreign laps;
    Or else break out in peevish jealousies,   85
    Throwing restraint upon us; or say they strike us,
    Or scant our former having in despite—   87
    Why, we have galls; and though we have some grace,   88
    Yet have we some revenge. Let husbands know
    Their wives have sense like them. They see, and smell,
    And have their palates both for sweet and sour,
    As husbands have. What is it that they do
    When they change us for others? Is it sport?
    I think it is. And doth affection breed it?
    I think it doth. Is't frailty that thus errs?
    It is so too. And have not we affections,
    Desires for sport, and frailty, as men have?
    Then let them use us well; else let them know,
    The ills we do, their ills instruct us so.

DESDEMONA:
    Good night, good night. God me such usage send,   100
    Not to pick from bad, but by bad mend!   [*Exeunt.*]

ACT V

SCENE I

[*Enter* IAGO *and* RODERIGO.]

IAGO:
    Here, stand behind this bulk; straight will he come.   1
    Wear thy good rapier bare, and put it home.
    Quick, quick! Fear nothing; I'll be at thy elbow.
    It makes us, or it mars us—think on that,
    And fix most firm thy resolution.

80 *to th' vantage* besides; *store* populate   **85** *peevish* senseless   **87** *having* allowance   **88** *galls* spirits to resent
100 *usage* habits
Scene i A street in Cyprus   **1** *bulk* projecting shop-front

RODERIGO:
Be near at hand; I may miscarry in't.
IAGO:
Here, at thy hand. Be bold, and take thy stand.
[*Stands aside.*]
RODERIGO:
I have no great devotion to the deed,
And yet he hath given me satisfying reasons.
'Tis but a man gone. Forth my sword! He dies!
IAGO:
I have rubbed this young quat almost to the sense, 11
And he grows angry. Now whether he kill Cassio,
Or Cassio him, or each do kill the other,
Every way makes by gain. Live Roderigo,
He calls me to a restitution large
Of gold and jewels that I bobbed from him 16
As gifts to Desdemona.
It must not be. If Cassio do remain,
He hath a daily beauty in his life.
That makes me ugly; and besides, the Moor
May unfold me to him; there stand I in much peril.
No, he must die. Be't so! I hear him coming.

[*Enter* CASSIO.]

RODERIGO:
I know his gait. 'Tis he. Villain, thou diest!
[*Makes a pass at* CASSIO.]
CASSIO:
That thrust had been mine enemy indeed
But that my coat is better than thou know'st. 25
I will make proof of thine.
[*Draws, and wounds* RODERIGO.]
RODERIGO: O, I am slain!
                    [IAGO *darts from concealment behind* CASSIO,
                    wounds him in the leg, and exits.]

CASSIO:
I am maimed for ever. Help, ho! Murder! murder!
[*Falls.*]

[*Enter* OTHELLO.]

OTHELLO:
The voice of Cassio. Iago keeps his word.

11 *quat* pimple; *sense* quick   16 *bobbed* swindled   25 *coat* under-shirt of mail

RODERIGO:
  O, villain that I am!
OTHELLO: It is even so.
CASSIO:
  O, help, ho! light! a surgeon!
OTHELLO:
  'Tis he. O brave Iago, honest and just,
  That hast such noble sense of thy friend's wrong!
  Thou teachest me. Minion, your dear lies dead,   33
  And your unblest fate hies. Strumpet, I come.   34
  Forth of my heart those charms, thine eyes, are blotted.
  Thy bed, lust-stained, shall with lust's blood be spotted.

                                        [*Exit* OTHELLO.]

  [*Enter* LODOVICO *and* GRATIANO.]

CASSIO:
  What, ho? No watch? No passage? Murder! murder!   37
GRATIANO:
  'Tis some mischance. The cry is very direful.
CASSIO: O, help!
LODOVICO: Hark!
RODERIGO: O wretched villain!
LODOVICO:
  Two or three groan. It is a heavy night.   42
  These may be counterfeits. Let's think't unsafe
  To come in to the cry without more help.
RODERIGO:
  Nobody come? Then shall I bleed to death.
LODOVICO: Hark!

  [*Enter* IAGO, *with a light.*]

GRATIANO:
  Here's one comes in his shirt, with light and weapons.
IAGO:
  Who's there? Whose noise is this that cries on murder?   48
LODOVICO:
  We do not know.
IAGO: Did not you hear a cry?
CASSIO:
  Here, here! For heaven's sake, help me!

33 *Minion* mistress   34 *hies* hurries on   37 *passage* passers-by   42 *heavy* cloudy, dark   48 *cries on* raises the
cry of

IAGO: What's the matter?

GRATIANO:

This is Othello's ancient, as I take it.

LODOVICO:

The same indeed, a very valiant fellow.

IAGO:

What are you here that cry so grievously?

CASSIO:

Iago? O, I am spoiled, undone by villains!
Give me some help.

IAGO:

O me, lieutenant! What villains have done this?

CASSIO:

I think that one of them is hereabout
And cannot make away.   58

IAGO: O treacherous villains!
[*To* LODOVICO *and* GRATIANO.]
What are you there? Come in, and give some help.

RODERIGO:

O, help me here!

CASSIO:

That's one of them.

IAGO: O mur'drous slave! O villain!
[*Stabs* RODERIGO.]

RODERIGO:

O damned Iago! O inhuman dog!

IAGO:

Kill men i' th' dark?—Where be these bloody thieves?—
How silent is this town!—Ho! murder! murder!—
What may you be? Are you of good or evil?

LODOVICO:

As you shall prove us, praise us.

IAGO: Signior Lodovico?

LODOVICO: He, sir.

IAGO:

I cry you mercy. Here's Cassio hurt by villains.

GRATIANO: Cassio?

IAGO: How is't, brother?

CASSIO:

My leg is cut in two.

IAGO: Marry, heaven forbid!   72
Light, gentleman. I'll bind it with my shirt.

58 *make* get   **72** *Marry* (from By Mary)

[*Enter* BIANCA.]

BIANCA:
  What is the matter, ho? Who is't that cried?
IAGO:
  Who is't that cried?
BIANCA:
  O my dear Cassio! my sweet Cassio!
  O Cassio, Cassio, Cassio!
IAGO:
  O notable strumpet!—Cassio, may you suspect
  Who they should be that have thus mangled you?
CASSIO: No.
GRATIANO: I am sorry to find you thus. I have been to seek you.
IAGO:
  Lend me a garter. So. O for a chair   82
  To bear him easily hence!
BIANCA:
  Alas, he faints! O Cassio, Cassio, Cassio!
IAGO:
  Gentlemen all, I do suspect this trash
  To be a party in this injury.—
  Patience awhile, good Cassio.—Come, come!
  Lend me a light. Know we this face or no?
  Alas, my friend and my dear countryman
  Roderigo? No.—Yes, sure.—O heaven, Roderigo!
GRATIANO: What, of Venice?
IAGO:
  Even he, sir. Did you know him?
GRATIANO: Know him? Ay.
IAGO:
  Signior Gratiano? I cry your gentle pardon.
  These bloody accidents must excuse my manners
  That so neglected you.
GRATIANO: I am glad to see you.
IAGO:
  How do you, Cassio?—O, a chair, a chair!
GRATIANO: Roderigo?
IAGO:
  He, he, 'tis he!
  [*A chair brought in.*] O, that's well said; the chair.   98
  Some good man bear him carefully from hence.

82 *chair* litter 98 *well said* well done

I'll fetch the general's surgeon.
[*To* BIANCA]   For you, mistress,
Save you your labor.—He that lies slain here, Cassio,
Was my dear friend. What malice was between you?
CASSIO:
    None in the world; nor do I know the man.
IAGO [*to* BIANCA]:
    What, look you pale?—O, bear him out o' th' air.
    [CASSIO *and* RODERIGO *are borne off.*]
    Stay you, good gentlemen.—Look you pale, mistress?—
    Do you perceive the gastness of her eye?—   106
    Nay, if you stare, we shall hear more anon.
    Behold her well; I pray you look upon her.
    Do you see, gentlemen? Nay, guiltiness will speak,
    Though tongues were out of use.

    [*Enter* EMILIA.]

EMILIA:
    'Las, what's the matter? What's the matter, husband?
IAGO:
    Cassio hath here been set on in the dark
    By Roderigo, and fellows that are scaped.
    He's almost slain, and Roderigo dead.
EMILIA:
    Alas, good gentleman! alas, good Cassio!
IAGO:
    This is the fruits of whoring. Prithee, Emilia,
    Go know of Cassio where he supped to-night.
    [*To* BIANCA.]
    What, do you shake at that?
BIANCA:
    He supped at my house; but I therefore shake not.
IAGO:
    O, did he so? I charge you go with me.
EMILIA:
    Fie, fie upon thee, strumpet!
BIANCA:
    I am no strumpet, but of life as honest   122
    As you that thus abuse me.
EMILIA: As I? Foh! fie upon thee!

106 *gastness* terror   **122** *honest* chaste

IAGO:

   Kind gentlemen, let's go see poor Cassio dressed.

   [*To* BIANCA.]

   Come, mistress, you must tell's another tale.

   Emilia, run you to the citadel

   And tell my lord and lady what hath happed.

[Exit EMILIA.]

   Will you go on afore?   [*Exeunt (all but* IAGO*).*]

                This is the night

   That either makes me or fordoes me quite.   [*Exit.*]   129

SCENE II

   [DESDEMONA *asleep in her bed. Enter* OTHELLO *with a light.*]

OTHELLO:

   It is the cause, it is the cause, my soul.   1

   Let me not name it to you, you chaste stars!

   It is the cause. Yet I'll not shed her blood,

   Nor scar that whiter skin of hers than snow,

   And smooth as monumental alabaster.

   Yet she must die, else she'll betray more men.

   Put out the light, and then put out the light.

   If I quench thee, thou flaming minister,   8

   I can again thy former light restore,

   Should I repent me; but once put out thy light,

   Thou cunning'st pattern of excelling nature,

   I know not where is that Promethean heat   12

   That can thy light relume. When I have plucked the rose,   13

   I cannot give it vital growth again;

   It needs must wither. I'll smell thee on the tree.

   [*He kisses her.*]

   O balmy breath, that dost almost persuade

   Justice to break her sword! One more, one more!

   Be thus when thou art dead, and I will kill thee,

   And love thee after. One more, and that's the last!

   So sweet was ne'er so fatal. I must weep,

   But they are cruel tears. This sorrow's heavenly;

   It strikes where it doth love. She wakes.

DESDEMONA:

   Who's there? Othello?

---

129 *fordoes* destroys

Scene ii A bedchamber in the castle   **1** *cause* cause of justice   **8** *minister* servant   **12** *Promethean heat* divine fire   **13** *relume* relight

OTHELLO: Ay, Desdemona.

DESDEMONA:
Will you come to bed, my lord?

OTHELLO:
Have you prayed to-night, Desdemona?

DESDEMONA: Ay, my lord.

OTHELLO:
If you bethink yourself of any crime   26
Unreconciled as yet to heaven and grace,
Solicit for it straight.

DESDEMONA:
Alack, my lord, what may you mean by that?

OTHELLO:
Well, do it, and be brief; I will walk by.
I would not kill thy unpreparèd spirit.
No, heaven forfend! I would not kill thy soul.   32

DESDEMONA:
Talk you of killing?

OTHELLO: Ay, I do.

DESDEMONA: Then heaven
Have mercy on me!

OTHELLO: Amen, with all my heart!

DESDEMONA:
If you say so, I hope you will not kill me.

OTHELLO: Hum!

DESDEMONA:
And yet I fear you; for you're fatal then
When your eyes roll so. Why I should fear I know not,
Since guiltiness I know not; but yet I feel I fear.

OTHELLO:
Think on thy sins.

DESDEMONA: They are loves I bear to you.

OTHELLO:
Ay, and for that thou diest.

DESDEMONA:
That death's unnatural that kills for loving.
Alas, why gnaw you so your nether lip?
Some bloody passion shakes your very frame.
These are portents; but yet I hope, I hope,   45
They do not point on me.

OTHELLO: Peace and be still!

DESDEMONA:
I will so. What's the matter?

26 *crime* sin   **32** *forfend* forbid   **45** *portents* signs of impending violence

OTHELLO:
  That handkerchief which I so loved and gave thee
  Thou gav'st to Cassio.
DESDEMONA: No, by my life and soul!
  Send for the man and ask him.
OTHELLO: Sweet soul, take heed,
  Take heed of perjury; thou art on thy deathbed.
DESDEMONA:
  Ay, but not yet to die.
OTHELLO: Yes, presently.   52
  Therefore confess thee freely of thy sin;
  For to deny each article with oath
  Cannot remove nor choke that strong conception   55
  That I do groan withal. Thou art to die.
DESDEMONA:
  Then Lord have mercy on me!
OTHELLO: I say amen.
DESDEMONA:
  And have you mercy too! I never did
  Offend you in my life; never loved Cassio   59
  But with such general warranty of heaven
  As I might love. I never gave him token.
OTHELLO:
  By heaven, I saw my handkerchief in's hand!
  O perjured woman! thou dost stone my heart,   63
  And mak'st me call what I intend to do
  A murder, which I thought a sacrifice.
  I saw the handkerchief.
DESDEMONA: He found it then.
  I never gave it him. Send for him hither.
  Let him confess a truth.
OTHELLO: He hath confessed.
DESDEMONA:
  What, my lord?
OTHELLO:
  That he hath used thee.
DESDEMONA: How? unlawfully?
OTHELLO: Ay.
DESDEMONA:
  He will not say so.
OTHELLO: No, his mouth is stopped.
  Honest Iago hath ta'en order for't.   72

---

52 *presently* at once **55** *conception* belief **59** *Offend* wrong **63** *stone my heart* turn my heart to stone
72 *ta'en order* taken measures

DESDEMONA:

O, my fear interprets. What, is he dead?

OTHELLO:

Had all his hairs been lives, my great revenge

Had stomach for them all.

DESDEMONA:

Alas, he is betrayed, and I undone!

OTHELLO:

Out, strumpet! Weep'st thou for him to my face?

DESDEMONA:

O, banish me, my lord, but kill me not!

OTHELLO:

Down, strumpet!

DESDEMONA:

Kill me to-morrow; let me live to-night!   80

OTHELLO:

Nay, if you strive—

DESDEMONA:

But half an hour!

OTHELLO: Being done, there is no pause.

DESDEMONA:

But while I say on prayer!

OTHELLO: It is too late.

[*Smothers her.*]

DESDEMONA: O Lord, Lord, Lord!

[EMILIA *at the door.*]

EMILIA [*calls within*]:

My lord, my lord! What, ho! my lord, my lord!

OTHELLO:

What noise is this? Not dead? not yet quite dead?

I that am cruel am yet merciful;

I would not have thee linger in thy pain.

So, so.

EMILIA [*within*]:

What, ho! my lord, my lord!

OTHELLO: Who's there?

EMILIA [*within*]:

O, good my lord, I would speak a word with you!

OTHELLO:

Yes, 'tis Emilia.—By and by.—She's dead.—   92

'Tis like she comes to speak of Cassio's death.

92 *By and by* just a moment (addressed to Emilia)

The noise was here. Ha! no more moving?
Still as the grave.—Shall she come in? Were't good?—
I think she stirs again. No.—What's best to do?
If she come in, she'll sure speak to my wife.
My wife! my wife! what wife! I have no wife.
O, insupportable! O heavy hour!
Methinks it should be now a huge eclipse
Of sun and moon, and that th'affrighted globe
Should yawn at yawn at alteration.   102

EMILIA [within]:   I do beseech you
    That I may speak with you, O good my lord!

OTHELLO:
    I had forgot thee. O, come in, Emilia.
    Soft, by and by.—Let me the curtains draw.—
    [Closes the bed-curtains.]
    Where art thou?
    [Opens the door.]

    [Enter EMILIA.]

                    What's the matter with thee now?

EMILIA:
    O my good lord, yonder's foul murder done!

OTHELLO: What? Now?

EMILIA: But now, my lord.

OTHELLO:
    It is the very error of the moon.   110
    She comes more nearer earth than she was wont
    And makes men mad.

EMILIA:
    Cassio, my lord, hath killed a young Venetian
    Called Roderigo.

OTHELLO: Roderigo killed?
    And Cassio killed?

EMILIA: No, Cassio is not killed.

OTHELLO:
    Not Cassio killed? Then murder's out of tune,
    And sweet revenge grows harsh

DESDEMONA:
    O, falsely, falsely murdered!

EMILIA: O Lord! what cry is that?

OTHELLO: That? What?

102 *yawn* open, as in an earthquake   110 *error* straying off course

EMILIA:

Out and alas! that was my lady's voice.

Help! help, ho! help! O lady, speak again!

Sweet Desdemona! O sweet mistress, speak!

DESDEMONA:

A guiltless death I die.

EMILIA:

O, who hath done this deed?

DESDEMONA:

Nobody—I myself. Farewell.

Commend me to my kind lord. O, farewell!   126

[*She dies.*]

OTHELLO:

Why, how should she be murd'red?

EMILIA: Alas, who knows?

OTHELLO:

You heard her say herself, it was not I.

EMILIA:

She said so. I must needs report the truth.

OTHELLO:

She's like a liar gone to burning hell!

'Twas I that killed her.

EMILIA: O, the more angel she,

And you the blacker devil!

OTHELLO:

She turned to folly, and she was a whore.

EMILIA:

Thou dost belie her, and thou art a devil.

OTHELLO:

She was false as water.   135

EMILIA: Thou art rash as fire to say

That she was false. O, she was heavenly true!

OTHELLO:

Cassio did top her. Ask thy husband else.

O, I were damned beneath all depth in hell

But that I did proceed upon just grounds

To this extremity. Thy husband knew it all.

EMILIA: My husband?

OTHELLO: Thy husband.

EMILIA:

That she was false to wedlock?

126 *Commend* remember **135** *water* (which is yielding)

OTHELLO:
Ay, with Cassio. Nay, had she been true,
If heaven would make me such another world
Of one entire and perfect chrysolite,   146
I'd not have sold her for it.

EMILIA:
My husband?

OTHELLO: Ay, 'twas he that told me first.
An honest man he is, and hates the slime
That sticks on filthy deeds.

EMILIA: My husband?

OTHELLO:
What needs this iterance, woman? I say thy husband.   151

EMILIA:
O mistress, villainy hath made mocks with love!
My husband say that she was false?

OTHELLO: He, woman.
I say, thy husband. Dost understand the word?
My friend, thy husband; honest, honest Iago.

EMILIA:
If he say so, may his pernicious soul
Rot half a grain a day! he lies to th' heart.
She was too fond of her most filthy bargain.

OTHELLO: Ha!

EMILIA: Do thy worst.
This deed of thine is no more worthy heaven
Than thou wast worthy her.

OTHELLO: Peace, you were best.

EMILIA:
Thou hast not half the power to do me harm
As I have to be hurt. O gull! O dolt!   164
As ignorant as dirt! thou hast done a deed—
I care not for thy sword; I'll make thee known,
Though I lost twenty lives. Help! help! Ho! help!
The Moor hath killed my mistress! Murder! murder!

[*Enter* MONTANO, GRATIANO, IAGO, *and others.*]

MONTANO:
What is the matter? How now, general?

EMILIA:
O, are you come, Iago? You have done well,   170
That men must lay their murders on your neck.

146 *chrysolite* (precious topaz)   151 *iterance* repetition   164 *to be hurt* to endure hurt

GRATIANO:

　What is the matter?

EMILIA:

　Disprove this villain, if thou be'st a man.

　He says thou told'st him that his wife was false.

　I know thou didst not; thou'rt not such a villain.

　Speak, for my heart is full.

IAGO:

　I told him what I thought, and told no more

　Than what he found himself was apt and true.

EMILIA:

　But did you ever tell him she was false?

IAGO: I did.

EMILIA:

　You told a lie, an odious damnèd lie!

　Upon my soul, a lie! a wicked lie!

　She false with Cassio? Did you say with Cassio?

IAGO:

　With Cassio, mistress. Go to, charm your tongue.　　　　　　184

EMILIA:

　I will not charm my tongue; I am bound to speak:

　My mistress here lies murdered in her bed—

ALL:

　O heavens forfend!

EMILIA:

　And your reports have set the murder on.

OTHELLO:

　Nay, stare not, masters. It is true indeed.

GRATIANO:

　'Tis a strange truth.　　　　　　　　　　　　　　　190

MONTANO:

　O monstrous act!

EMILIA:　　　　　　　　Villainy, villainy, villainy!

　I think upon't—I think I smell't!—O villainy!

　I thought so then.—I'll kill myself for grief.—

　O villainy, villainy!

IAGO:

　What, are you mad? I charge you get you home.

EMILIA:

　Good gentlemen, let me have leave to speak.

　'Tis proper I obey him, but not now.

　Perchance, Iago, I will ne'er go home.

184 *charm* cast a spell on

OTHELLO:
  O! O! O!

[Falls on the bed.]

EMILIA: Nay, lay thee down and roar!
  For thou hast killed the sweetest innocent
  That e'er lift up eye.
OTHELLO: O, she was foul!
  [Rises.]
  I scarce did know you, uncle. There lies your niece,
  Whose breath, indeed, these hands have newly stopped.
  I know this act shows horrible and grim.   204
GRATIANO:
  Poor Desdemona! I am glad thy father's dead.
  Thy match was mortal to him, and pure grief
  Shore his old thread in twain. Did he live now,
  This sight would make him do a desperate turn;   208
  Yea, curse his better angel from his side,
  And fall to reprobation.   210
OTHELLO:
  'Tis pitiful; but yet Iago knows
  That she with Cassio hath the act of shame
  A thousand times committed. Cassio confessed it;
  And she did gratify his amorous works   214
  With that recognizance and pledge of love   215
  Which I first gave her. I saw it in his hand.
  It was a handkerchief, an antique token
  My father gave my mother.
EMILIA:
  O God! O heavenly God!
IAGO:
  Zounds, hold your peace!
EMILIA: 'Twill out, 'twill out! I peace?
  No, I will speak as liberal as the north,   221
  Let heaven and men and devils, let them all,
  All, all, cry shame against me, yet I'll speak.
IAGO:
  Be wise, and get you home.
EMILIA: I will not.
  [IAGO draws and threatens EMILIA.]

204 *shows* appears **208** *turn* act **210** *reprobation* rejection by God, damnation **214** *gratify* reward
215 *recognizance* token **221** *liberal as the north* unchecked as the north wind blows

GRATIANO: Fie!
   Your sword upon a woman?
EMILIA:
   O thou dull Moor, that handkerchief thou speak'st of
   I found by fortune, and did give my husband;
   For often with a solemn earnestness—
   More than indeed belonged to such a trifle—
   He begged of me to steal't.
IAGO: Villainous whore!
EMILIA:
   She give it Cassio? No, alas, I found it,
   And I did give't my husband.
IAGO: Filth, thou liest!
EMILIA:
   By heaven, I do not, I do not, gentlemen.
   O murd'rous coxcomb! what should such a fool
   Do with so good a wife?
OTHELLO: Are there no stones in heaven   235
   But what serves for the thunder? Precious villain!

[*The* MOOR *runs at* IAGO, *but is disarmed by* MONTANO. IAGO *kills his wife.*]

GRATIANO:
   The woman falls. Sure he hath killed his wife.
EMILIA:
   Ay, ay. O, lay me by my mistress' side.   [*Exit* IAGO.]
GRATIANO:
   He's gone, but his wife's killed.
MONTANO:
   'Tis a notorious villain. Take you this weapon,   240
   Which I have here recovered from the Moor.
   Come, guard the door without. Let him not pass,
   But kill him rather. I'll after that same villain,
   For 'tis a damnèd slave.
                 [*Exit* MONTANO, *with all but* OTHELLO *and* EMILIA.]
OTHELLO: I am not valiant neither;
   But every puny whipster gets my sword.   245
   But why should honor outlive honesty?
   Let it go all.
EMILIA: What did thy song bode, lady?
   Hark, canst thou hear me? I will play the swan,
   And die in music. [*Sings.*] "Willow, willow, willow."

235 *stones* bolts like those used for thunderbolts   **240** *notorious* notable   **245** *puny whipster* top-whipping boy

Moor, she was chaste. She loved thee, cruel Moor:
So come my soul to bliss as I speak true.
So speaking as I think, alas, I die.

[*She dies.*]

OTHELLO:
I have another weapon in this chamber;
It is a sword of Spain, the ice brook's temper.   254
O, here it is.—Uncle, I must come forth.
GRATIANO [*within*]:
If thou attempt it, it will cost thee dear.
Thou hast no weapon, and perforce must suffer.
OTHELLO:
Look in upon me then and speak with me,
Or, naked as I am, I will assault thee.   259

[*Enter* GRATIANO.]

GRATIANO:
What is the matter?
OTHELLO: Behold, I have a weapon;
A better never did itself sustain
Upon a soldier's thigh. I have seen the day
That with this little arm and this good sword
I have made my way through more impediments
Than twenty times your stop. But O vain boast!   265
Who can control his fate? 'Tis not so now.
Be not afraid, though you do see me weaponed.
Here is my journey's end, here is my butt,   268
And very seamark of my utmost sail: 269
Do you go back dismayed? 'Tis a lost fear.   270
Man but a rush against Othello's breast,   271
And he retires. Where should Othello go?
Now, how dost thou look now? O ill-starred wench!
Pale as thys mock! When we shall meet at compt,   274
This look of thine will hurl my soul from heaven,
And fiends will snatch at it. Cold, cold, my girl?
Even like thy chastity.
O cursèd, cursèd slave! Whip me, ye devils,
From the possession of this heavenly sight!

---

254 *ice brook's* i.e. a Spanish blade, tempered in cold running water   **259** *naked* disarmed   **265** *stop* power
to stop   **268** *butt* limit   **269** *seamark* beacon, destination   **270** *lost* wasted   **271** *Man but a rush* wield only
a reed   **274** *compt* final accounting, Last Judgment

Blow me about in winds! roast me in sulphur!
Wash me in steep-down gulfs of liquid fire!
Oh Desdemon! dead Desdemon! dead! Oh! Oh!

[*Enter* LODOVICO, MONTANO, IAGO *(as prisoner), and officers;* CASSIO *in a chair.*]

LODOVICO:
Where is this rash and most unfortunate man?
OTHELLO:
That's he that was Othello. Here I am.
LODOVICO:
Where is that viper? Bring the villain forth.
OTHELLO:
I look down towards his feet—but that's a fable.   286
If that thou be'st a devil, I cannot kill thee.
[*Wounds* IAGO.]
LODOVICO:
Wrench his sword from him.
[OTHELLO *is disarmed.*]
IAGO: I bleed, sir, but not killed.
OTHELLO:
I am not sorry neither. I'd have thee live;
For in my sense, 'tis happiness to die.
LODOVICO:
O thou Othello that wert once so good,
Fall'n in the practice of a damnèd slave,   292
What shall be said to thee?
OTHELLO: Why, anything:
An honorable murderer, if you will;
For naught did I in hate, but all in honor.
LODOVICO:
This wretch hath part confessed his villainy.
Did you and he consent in Cassio's death?   297
OTHELLO: Ay.
CASSIO:
Dear general, I never gave you cause.
OTHELLO:
I do believe it, and I ask your pardon.
Will you, I pray, demand that demi-devil
Why he hath thus ensnared my soul and body?
IAGO:
Demand me nothing. What you know, you know.
From this time forth I never will speak word.

286 *I . . . feet* i.e. to see if they are cloven, like the Devil's   **292** *practice* plot   **297** *consent in* agree upon

LODOVICO:
　What, not to pray?
GRATIANO:　　　　　Torments will ope your lips.
OTHELLO:
　Well, thou dost best.
LODOVICO:
　Sir, you shall understand what hath befall'n,
　Which, as I think, you know not. Here is a letter
　Found in the pocket of the slain Roderigo;
　And here another. The one of them imports　　　　　　310
　The death of Cassio to be undertook
　By Roderigo.
OTHELLO:
　O villain!
CASSIO:　　Most heathenish and most gross!
LODOVICO:
　Now here's another discontented paper
　Found in his pocket too; and this, it seems,
　Roderigo meant t' have sent this damnèd villain;
　But that, belike, Iago in the nick　　　　　　　　　　317
　Came in and satisfied him.
OTHELLO:　　　　　　O thou pernicious caitiff!—
　How came you, Cassio, by that handkerchief
　That was my wife's?
CASSIO:　　　　　　I found it in my chamber;
　And he himself confessed but even now
　That there he dropped it for a special purpose
　Which wrought to his desire.
OTHELLO:　　　　　　O fool! fool! fool!
CASSIO:
　There is besides in Roderigo's letter,
　How he upbraids Iago that he made him
　Brave me upon the watch; whereon it came
　That I was cast; and even but now he spake,　　　　　327
　After long seeming dead—Iago hurt him,
　Iago set him on.
LODOVICO:
　You must forsake this room and go with us.
　Your power and your command is taken off,
　And Cassio rules Cyprus. For this slave,
　If there by any cunning cruelty
　That can torment him much and hold him long,

317 *nick* nick of time　**327** *cast* dismissed

It shall be his. You shall close prisoner rest
Till that the nature of your fault be known
To the Venetian state. Come, bring away.
OTHELLO:
Soft you! a word or two before you go.
I have done the state some service, and they know't.
No more of that. I pray you, in your letters,
When you shall these unlucky deeds relate,   341
Speak of me as I am. Nothing extenuate,
Nor set down aught in malice. Then must you speak
Of one that loved not wisely, but too well;
Of one not easily jealous, but, being wrought,
Perplexed in the extreme; of one whose hand,   346
Like the base Judean, threw a pearl away   347
Richer than all his tribe; of one whose subdued eyes,   348
Albeit unusèd to the melting mood,
Drop tears as fast as the Arabian trees
Their med'cinable gum. Set you down this.
And say besides that in Aleppo once,
Where a malignant and a turbaned Turk
Beat a Venetian and traduced the state,
I took by th' throat the circumcisèd dog
And smote him—thus.

[*He stabs himself.*]

LODOVICO:
O bloody period!   357
GRATIANO: All that's spoke is marred.
OTHELLO:
I kissed thee ere I killed thee. No way but this,
Killing myself, to die upon a kiss.

[*He falls upon the bed and dies.*]

CASSIO:
This did I fear, but thought he had no weapon;
For he was great of heart.
LODOVICO [*to* IAGO]:   O Spartan dog,
More fell than anguish, hunger, or the sea!   362
Look on the tragic loading of this bed.

341 *unlucky* fatal **346** *Perplexed* distracted **347** *Judean* Judas Iscariot (?) (quarto reads "Indian")
348 *subdued* i.e. conquered by grief **357** *period* ending **362** *fell* cruel

This is thy work. The object poisons sight;
Let it be hid. Gratiano, keep the house,   365
And seize upon the fortunes of the Moor,   366
For they succeed on you. To you, lord governor,
Remains the censure of this hellish villain,   368
The time, the place, the torture. O, enforce it!
Myself will straight aboard, and to the state
This heavy act with heavy heart relate.   [*Exeunt.*]

QUESTIONS

Act I

1. All three scenes in Act I are set in Venice. What do we learn about the Venetian state from these scenes? What elements make up the "world" of each scene? What, especially, does the Venetian senate symbolize in terms of values?

2. We get three distinct impressions of Iago as we move through each scene in Act I. What is he like in each? Point carefully to his key speeches to support your character analysis. What composite picture of his character is formed by the end of Act I?

3. It has been noted that Othello is a dignified, noble, and heroic figure. How does this impression emerge in Act I? In this context, examine one of Othello's greatest speeches, in which he recapitulates his life (scene iii, lines 128–170). Analyze the diction, images, and tone. Comment on Othello's growing love for Desdemona, culminating in the lines, "She loved me for the dangers I had passed/And I loved her that she did pity them."

4. Why does Shakespeare delay the entrance of Desdemona until the third scene? How does she complement Othello in her speech and behavior? How does she begin to contrast with Iago?

Act II

5. Act II opens on Cyprus, a shift in setting that Samuel Johnson objected to: "Had the scene [the play] opened in Cyprus and the preceeding incidents been occasionally related, there had been wanting to a drama of the most exact and scrupulous regularity." What is the critic objecting to here? Do you agree or disagree with Dr. Johnson's complaint? Explain.

6. Note that Venice, Cyprus, and the lands beyond the sea's horizon (symbolized in part by the invading Turkish fleet) seem to represent three different "worlds" in terms of values and levels of civilization. How does Shakespeare characterize each of these worlds? What is Othello's relationship to them?

7. Images of a turbulent sea—that "high-wrought flood," as Shakespeare describes it at the start of Act II—dominate the first scene. How does this sea imagery influence action, mood, and theme? For instance, why does Shakespeare contrive a triple

---

365 *Let it be hid* i.e. draw the bed curtains   **366** *seize upon* take legal possession of   **368** *censure* judicial
sentence

landing? What does nature symbolize in the first scene? How does nature's "tempest" reflect the tempests brewing between various characters?

8. What is Iago's conception of women, love, and sexuality in Act II?

9. Analyze the dramatic effectiveness of Othello's reunion with Desdemona (with Iago looking on) in scene i, lines 178–207.

10. Of what new element in Othello's character do we learn from his speech in scene iii, lines 182–195?

11. Explain how Iago begins to succeed in his dark plans in the third scene of Act II. What is the significance of the fact that Othello charges that people are beginning to act like Turks (see lines 147–156)? How does the looming tragedy expand when Iago, toward the end of the act (see lines 296–322) likens himself to the devil, declaring of Desdemona, "So will I turn her virtue into pitch,/And out of her own goodness make the net/That shall enmesh them all"?

Act III

12. Why does Cassio bring musicians to play beneath Othello's window in the first scene? What is the function of this relatively lighthearted interlude? How does this action benefit Iago's ends?

13. What is Othello's state of mind in his soliloquy beginning, "This fellow's of exceeding honesty" (lines 258–277)? Why is this an unusual speech for him?

14. Contrast the relationship between Iago and Emilia in the third scene with that between Othello and Desdemona.

15. Trace the changes in the three meetings between Othello and Desdemona in Act III.

16. Explain the progression and complication of the tragic action in *Othello* through the first three acts of the play. Has the action moved too fast? Explain.

Act IV

17. How does Iago's language change at the start of Act IV? What does this change in the tone of his language tell us about the progression of the conflict?

18. What new trick does Iago devise to advance Othello's jealousy in the first scene? Why does Othello fall for such an obvious deception?

19. Analyze Desdemona's character during the episode in the second scene in which Othello accuses her of being a whore. Why can't Othello perceive her essential goodness and innocence?

20. The second scene concludes with a confrontation between Roderigo and Iago. Summarize this scene and explain its importance in the advancement of the tragedy. Does Iago betray his true motives at this point or not? Explain.

21. Compare and contrast the minds of Desdemona and Emilia in the third scene. Why is Desdemona so passive?

Act V

22. Compare and contrast the two scenes in this act.

23. Divide the second scene into three parts, corresponding to the major stages of the action. What happens in each episode?

24. Analyze Othello's first speech at the start of the second scene. Why must he kill Desdemona quickly, rather than listening to her pleas?
25. Describe the importance of Emilia in Act V, after Desdemona has been killed.
26. How does Othello regain some of his lost stature and heroic character at the end of the play?
27. In what way is order restored at the end of the tragedy?

W o m e n & M e n

D r a m a

TOPICS FOR WRITING

1. Select a central conflict between men and women, and write a short dialogue between two characters whereby this conflict is confronted.
2. Describe a woman you know who has balanced a family life and a professional life. How was she able to achieve this balance? How does she maintain it?
3. Analyze the character of Josefa in *Day of the Swallows*. Include the function she serves in the play, her relationship to other characters, her internal conflict, and the conflicts she creates among the other characters.
4. Compare and contrast the diction and tone of *Othello* with that of *Day of the Swallows*. Include in your analysis such issues as whether one is more "formal" than the other, more "serious" than the other, and more "realistic" than the other.
5. Select one of the characters from either *Day of the Swallows* or *Othello*. Write a character study describing the individual's personality, conflicts, values, attitudes, and so on.
6. Describe the different ways the author employs humor in *Suppressed Desires*. How does the humor shed a unique light on the subject of the play?
7. There are certain irreconcilable differences between the attitudes and beliefs of men and women that will always exist. Argue for or against this proposition.
8. In *Day of the Swallows*, the character Josefa states that beauty and terror are closely allied. Argue for or against the proposition that with love, comes both beauty and terror.
9. As a research project, study the history of racism and anti-Semitism in England during the period that Shakespeare wrote his plays. Write an essay connecting your findings to *Othello* and any other relevant plays by Shakespeare—for example, *The Merchant of Venice*.
10. Estela Portillo [Tremblay] is a Mexican-American (Chicana) writer. As a research project, review the history of this particular ethnic literature, and demonstrate how Portillo fits within its domain in terms of theme and style.

Caste

Class

"Interior with Housemaid" by Vanessa Bell. 1939. Copyright Williamson Art Gallery and Museum, Birkenhead, Merseyside.

INTRODUCTION

All men and women are created equal. Or are they? If you visited the maternity ward of a typical hospital, you would see rows of newborns in their tiny cribs. Special cases such as premature babies or infants with special needs and handicaps are given exceptional attention. But even among the healthy ones—seemingly receiving (in an ideal environment, of course) equal care—there will result very different lives and life-styles. Why, if this seeming equality exists in a neonatal care unit of a hospital, would some of these babies grow up to be rich, some poor, some oppressors, some oppressed? Why would some become powerful political and business leaders while others resign themselves to an underpaid, exploitative job, where they will toil unknown except for a few friends or relatives? Why will one person grow up to grace the cover of *Time* magazine while another will only have a subscription?

The literary works in this section deal with the complex issues of caste and social class. Some societies, such as the one in India, maintain informal yet rigid and complex caste systems that have a strong influence on people's opportunities in life, although programs similar to affirmative action in the United States are being instituted. In South Africa, while acknowledged by the government and slowly weakening owing to world pressure, there is still a particularly insidious caste system based solely on ethnicity. In fact, we can view a snapshot of life under this system in Nadine Gordimer's short story, "The Train from Rhodesia." Living in the United States provides many of us with first-hand knowledge of a caste system that, despite gains owing to civil rights activists and legal precedence, remains intact, as the inequality of salaries, health care, and housing among whites, blacks, and Hispanics indicates.

We should not get the impression that inequality or differentiation among groups within a society is solely the result of race or ethnicity. Other factors also influence one's lot in life. For example, young people are more or less likely to achieve the approximate level of affluence as their parents. Of course, there are exceptions to this; many wealthy and influential people have grown up in humble surroundings. Such is the philosophy behind the American Dream.

Nevertheless, the position of our parents in society has a significant effect regarding what schools we attend, what professional level we rise to, what type of friendships we develop, who we live with, and where we live. As an extension of our family, we must also take into account the type of community we reside in, which usually reflects the economic and social level of our family. Growing up in an affluent community where the role models are in professional or managerial classes certainly has a bearing on our

465

sense of where we fit in the world and what our potential is. Similarly, if we live in a working-class or impoverished neighborhood, where adults lack the social and economic power found in more prosperous areas, we may very well feel that our opportunities are limited or circumscribed.

However, we must be careful not to categorize or stereotype people of the same race or ethnicity. Many people have the mistaken belief that individuals in groups other than the one they belong to are more or less the same. But as three of the short stories in this section reveal, differences exist within all groups of people, and conflicts common to one group will most likely be common to all.

For example, in Gloria Naylor's short story "Kiswana Browne," a young single black woman is paid a visit by her mother, and their time together is spent arguing over such issues as life-style, politics, work, and relationships. Slowly, over the course of the conversation, they find certain things in common, and their appreciation for one another is reaffirmed. Nonetheless, the intergenerational conflict common to many mothers and daughters is portrayed as vividly here as in any contemporary story about identity and maturation.

In "Hindus" by Bharati Mukherjee, we are shown the world of Indian expatriates living in New York City. While there are certain similarities in attitude among the characters we encounter, we discover that each has a unique personality, each has differing views about the newly adopted culture, and each has personal conflicts common to members of any group.

Issues of race and caste enter Richard Wright's "The Man Who Was Almost a Man," but at the same time we see members of a black family as fully drawn characters with separate values and needs. Dave, the teenager upon whom the story focuses, experiences issues of autonomy, identity, and liberation as many adolescents do. While his quest to become a "man" is set against the backdrop of a racist caste-driven American society, he shows the conflicts, determination, and self-discovery that render him a thoroughly three-dimensional character who makes his own decision regarding independence from his family and community.

Of course, social class is not necessarily correlated with race or ethnic background. Many Americans with European roots live in humble surroundings, work at blue-collar or middle-class jobs, and struggle to make ends meet. The capacity of the writer—as one who gives voice to people whose emotional and psychological lives remain hidden from public view—has grown over the past century, and several of the works in this section fulfill this role. For example, Flick Webb, who is the subject of John Updike's poem "Ex-Basketball Player," was a star basketball player in high school, admired by the entire county. But his glory days are long gone and he works in a gas station, eking out a living, his time in the spotlight only a memory. Why has Flick ended up at the lower end of the economic ladder? Is it because he "never learned a trade" as the poet states? Perhaps. But this portrait of Flick never quite explains why he spends his workdays fixing flats and pumping gas. Thus, we see that individual factors may contribute to one's class—factors that are subtle, mysterious, and not as obvious as they might seem at first glance.

James Wright also looks at Middle America in his poem "Autumn Begins in Martins Ferry, Ohio." And what he sees are local factory workers watching a local high school football game. But Wright peers beneath the veneer of this typical weekend event to show the irony of people caught in the confines of a daily struggle, even in a moment's respite.

As these examples have attempted to show, issues of caste and class are universal and most likely have existed since humans formed societies. The ubiquitous dilemma of interclass and intraclass conflict is perhaps most apparent in a work in this section that bears a structural resemblance to the fable. (Fables often depict less specifically drawn characters and have strong moral messages. In fact, because the characters seem to represent aspects of society, the moral message comes across strongly.) In Edgar Allan Poe's "The Masque of the Red Death," we are introduced to an odd imaginary country where the privileged class attempts to shield itself from harsh reality. But, like any social group that tries to insulate itself, its very estrangement leads to its destruction.

Thus, race, ethnicity, class, family, and individual temperament all play a part in how we are socially and economically positioned. While some us "rise above" such chance circumstances, these factors often assert themselves throughout our lives, subtly molding us from within.

F i c t i o n

Arna Bontemps

A SUMMER TRAGEDY

Old Jeff Patton, the black share farmer, fumbled with his bow tie. His fingers trembled and the high stiff collar pinched his throat. A fellow loses his hand for such vanities after thirty or forty years of simple life. Once a year, or maybe twice if there's a wedding among his kinfolks, he may spruce up; but generally fancy clothes do nothing but adorn the wall of the big room and feed the moths. That had been Jeff Patton's experience. He had not worn his stiff-bosomed shirt more than a dozen times in all his married life. His swallow-tailed coat lay on the bed beside him, freshly brushed and pressed, but it was as full of holes as the overalls in which he worked on weekdays. The moths had used it badly. Jeff twisted his mouth into a hideous toothless grimace as he contended with the obstinate bow. He stamped his good foot and decided to give up the struggle.

"Jennie," he called.

"What's that, Jeff?" His wife's shrunken voice came out of the adjoining room like an echo. It was hardly bigger than a whisper.

"I reckon you'll have to he'p me wid this heah bow tie, baby," he said meekly. "Dog if I can hitch it up."

Her answer was not strong enough to reach him, but presently the old woman came to the door, feeling her way with a stick. She had a wasted, dead-leaf appearance. Her body, as scrawny and gnarled as a string bean, seemed less than nothing in the ocean of frayed and faded petticoats that surrounded her. These hung an inch or two above the tops of her heavy unlaced shoes and showed little grotesque piles where the stockings had fallen down from her negligible legs.

"You oughta could do a heap mo' wid a thing like that'n me—beingst as you got yo' good sight."

"Looks like I oughta could," he admitted. "But ma fingers is gone democrat on me. I get all mixed up in the looking glass an' can't tell wicha way to twist the devilish thing."

Jennie sat on the side of the bed and old Jeff Patton got down on one knee while she tied the bow knot. It was a slow and painful ordeal for each of them in this position. Jeff's bones cracked, his knee ached, and it was only after a half dozen attempts that Jennie worked a semblance of a bow into the tie.

"I got to dress maself now," the old woman whispered. "These is ma old shoes an' stockings, and I ain't so much as unwrapped ma dress."

"Well, don't worry 'bout me no mo', baby," Jeff said. "That 'bout finishes me. All I gotta do now is slip on that old coat 'n ves' an' I'll be fixed to leave."

Jennie disappeared again through the dim passage into the shed room. Being blind was no handicap to her in that black hole. Jeff heard the cane placed against the wall beside the door and knew that his wife was on easy ground. He put on his coat, took a battered top hat from the bedpost and hobbled to the front door. He was ready to travel. As soon as Jennie could get on her Sunday shoes and her old black silk dress, they would start.

Outside the tiny log house, the day was warm and mellow with sunshine. A host of wasps were humming with busy excitement in the trunk of a dead sycamore. Gray squirrels were searching through the grass for hickory nuts and blue jays were in the trees, hopping from branch to branch. Pine woods stretched away to the left like a black sea. Among them were scattered scores of log houses like Jeff's, houses of black share farmers. Cows and pigs wandered freely among the trees. There was no danger of loss. Each farmer knew his own stock and knew his neighbor's as well as he knew his neighbor's children.

Down the slope to the right were the cultivated acres on which the colored folks worked. They extended to the river, more than two miles away, and they were today green with the unmade cotton crop. A tiny thread of a road, which passed directly in front of Jeff's place, ran through these green fields like a pencil mark.

Jeff, standing outside the door, with his absurd hat in his left hand, surveyed the wide scene tenderly. He had been forty-five years on these acres. He loved them with the unexplained affection that others have for the countries to which they belong.

The sun was hot on his head, his collar still pinched his throat, and the Sunday clothes were intolerably hot. Jeff transferred the hat to his right hand and began fanning with it. Suddenly the whisper that was Jennie's voice came out of the shed room.

"You can bring the car round front whilst you's waitin'," it said feebly. There was a tired pause; then it added, "I'll soon be fixed to go."

"A'right, baby," Jeff answered. "I'll get it in a minute."

But he didn't move. A thought struck him that made his mouth fall open. The mention of the car brought to his mind, with new intensity, the trip he and Jennie were about to take. Fear came into his eyes; excitement took his breath. Lord, Jesus!

"Jeff . . . O Jeff," the old woman's whisper called.

He awakened with a jolt. "Hunh, baby?"

"What you doin'?"

"Nuthin. Jes studyin'. I jes been turnin' things round'n round in ma mind."

"You could be gettin' the car," she said.

"Oh yes, right away, baby."

He started round to the shed, limping heavily on his bad leg. There were three frizzly chickens in the yard. All his other chickens had been killed or stolen recently. But the frizzly chickens had been saved somehow. That was fortunate indeed, for these curious creatures had a way of devouring "Poison" from the yard and in that way protecting against conjure and black luck and spells. But even the frizzly chickens seemed now to be in a stupor. Jeff thought they had some ailment; he expected all three of them to die shortly.

The shed in which the old T-model Ford stood was only a grass roof held up by four corner poles. It had been built by tremulous hands at a time when the little rattletrap car had been regarded as a peculiar treasure. And, miraculously, despite wind and downpour it still stood.

Jeff adjusted the crank and put his weight upon it. The engine came to life with a sputter and bang that rattled the old car from radiator to taillight. Jeff hopped into the seat and put his foot on the accelerator. The sputtering and banging increased. The rattling became more violent. That was good. It was good banging, good sputtering and rattling, and it meant that the aged car was still in running condition. She could be depended on for this trip.

Again Jeff's thought halted as if paralyzed. The suggestion of the trip fell into the machinery of his mind like a wrench. He felt dazed and weak. He swung the car out into the yard, made a half turn and drove around to the front door. When he took his hands off the wheel, he noticed that he was trembling violently. He cut off the motor and climbed to the ground to wait for Jennie.

A few minutes later she was at the window, her voice rattling against the pane like a broken shutter.

"I'm ready, Jeff."

He did not answer, but limped into the house and took her by the arm. He led her slowly through the big room, down the step and across the yard.

"You reckon I'd oughta lock the do'?" he asked softly.

They stopped and Jennie weighed the question. Finally she shook her head.

"Ne' mind the do'," she said. "I don't see no cause to lock up things."

"You right," Jeff agreed. "No cause to lock up."

Jeff opened the door and helped his wife into the car. A quick shudder passed over him. Jesus! Again he trembled.

"How come you shaking so?" Jennie whispered.

"I don't know," he said.

"You mus' be scairt, Jeff."

"No, baby, I ain't scairt."

He slammed the door after her and went around to crank up again. The motor started easily. Jeff wished that it had not been so responsive. He would have liked a few more minutes in which to turn things around in his head. As it was, with Jennie chiding him about being afraid, he had to keep going. He swung the car into the little pencil-mark road and started off toward the river, driving very slowly, very cautiously.

Chugging across the green countryside, the small battered Ford seemed tiny indeed. Jeff felt a familiar excitement, a thrill, as they came down the first slope to the immense levels on which the cotton was growing. He could not help reflecting that the crops were good. He knew what that meant, too; he had made forty-five of them with his own hands. It was true that he had worn out nearly a dozen mules, but that was the fault of old man Stevenson, the owner of the land. Major Stevenson had the odd notion that one mule was all a share farmer needed to work a thirty-acre plot. It was an expensive notion, the way it killed mules from overwork, but the old man held to it. Jeff thought it killed a good many share farmers as well as mules, but he had no sympathy for them. He had always been strong, and he had been taught to have no patience with weakness in men. Women or children might be tolerated if they were puny, but a weak man was a curse. Of course, his own children—

Jeff's thought halted there. He and Jennie never mentioned their dead children any more. And naturally he did not wish to dwell upon them in his mind. Before he knew it, some remark would slip out of his mouth and that would make Jennie feel blue. Perhaps she would cry. A woman like Jennie could not easily throw off the grief that comes from losing five grown children within two years. Even Jeff was still staggered by the blow. His memory had not been much good recently. He frequently talked to himself. And, although he had kept it a secret, he knew that his courage had left him. He was terrified by the least unfamiliar sound at night. He was reluctant to venture far from home in the daytime. And that habit of trembling when he felt fearful was now far beyond his control. Sometimes he became afraid and trembled without knowing what had frightened him. The feeling would just come over him like a chill.

The car rattled slowly over the dusty road. Jennie sat erect and silent, with a little absurd hat pinned to her hair. Her useless eyes seemed very large, very white in their deep sockets. Suddenly Jeff heard her voice, and he inclined his head to catch the words.

"Is we passed Delia Moore's house yet?" she asked.

"Not yet," he said.

"You must be drivin' mighty slow, Jeff."

"We might just as well take our time, baby."

There was a pause. A little puff of steam was coming out of the radiator of the car. Heat wavered above the hood. Delia Moore's house was nearly half a mile away. After a moment Jennie spoke again.

"You ain't really scairt, is you, Jeff?"

"Nah, baby, I ain't scairt."

"You know how we agreed—we gotta keep on goin'."

Jewels of perspiration appeared on Jeff's forehead. His eyes rounded, blinked, becamed fixed on the road.

"I don't know," he said with a shiver. "I reckon it's the only thing to do."

"Hm."

A flock of guinea fowls, pecking in the road, were scattered by the passing car. Some of them took to their wings; others hid under bushes. A blue jay, swaying on a leafy twig, was annoying a roadside squirrel. Jeff held an even speed till he came near Delia's place. Then he slowed down noticeably.

Delia's house was really no house at all, but an abandoned store building converted into a dwelling. It sat near a crossroads, beneath a single black cedar tree. There Delia, a cattish old creature of Jennie's age, lived alone. She had been there more years than anybody could remember, and long ago had won the disfavor of such women as Jennie. For in her young days Delia had been gayer, yellower and saucier than seemed proper in those parts. Her ways with menfolks had been dark and suspicious. And the fact that she had had as many husbands as children did not help her reputation.

"Yonder's old Delia," Jeff said as they passed.

"What she doin'?"

"Jes sittin' in the do'," he said.

"She see us?"

"Hm," Jeff said. "Musta did."

That relieved Jennie. It strengthened her to know that her old enemy had seen her pass in her best clothes. That would give the old she-devil something to chew her gums and fret about, Jennie thought. Wouldn't she have a fit if she didn't find out? Old evil Delia! This would be just the thing for her. It would pay her back for being so evil. It would also pay her, Jennie thought, for the way she used to grin at Jeff—long ago when her teeth were good.

The road became smooth and red, and Jeff could tell by the smell of the air that they were nearing the river. He could see the rise where the road turned and ran along parallel to the stream. The car chugged on monotonously. After a long silent spell, Jennie leaned against Jeff and spoke.

"How many bale o' cotton you think we got standin'?" she said.

Jeff wrinkled his forehead as he calculated.

" 'Bout twenty-five, I reckon."

"How many you make las' year?"

"Twenty-eight," he said. "How come you ask that?"

"I's jes thinkin'," Jennie said quietly.

"It don't make a speck o' difference though," Jeff reflected. "If we get much or if we get little, we still gonna be in debt to old man Stevenson when he gets through counting up agin us. It's took us a long time to learn that."

Jennie was not listening to these words. She had fallen into a trance-like meditation. Her lips twitched. She chewed her gums and rubbed her gnarled hands nervously. Suddenly she leaned forward, buried her face in the nervous hands and burst into tears. She cried aloud in a dry cracked voice that suggested the rattle of fodder on dead stalks. She cried aloud like a child, for she had never learned to suppress a genuine sob. Her slight old frame shook heavily and seemed hardly able to sustain such violent grief.

"What's the matter, baby?" Jeff asked awkwardly. "Why you cryin' like all that?"

"I's jes thinkin'," she said.

"So you the one what's scairt now, hunh?"

"I ain't scairt, Jeff. I's jes thinkin' 'bout leavin' eve'thing like this—eve'thing we been used to. It's right sad-like."

Jeff did not answer, and presently Jennie buried her face again and cried.

The sun was almost overhead. It beat down furiously on the dusty wagon-path road, on the parched roadside grass and the tiny battered car. Jeff's hands, gripping the wheel, became wet with perspiration; his forehead sparkled. Jeff's lips parted. His mouth shaped a hideous grimace. His face suggested the face of a man being burned. But the torture passed and his expression softened again.

"You mustn't cry, baby," he said to his wife. "We gotta be strong. We can't break down."

Jennie waited a few seconds, then said, "You reckon we oughta do it, Jeff? You reckon we oughta go 'head an' do it, really?"

Jeff's voice choked; his eyes blurred. He was terrified to hear Jennie say the thing that had been in his mind all morning. She had egged him on when he had wanted more than anything in the world to wait, to reconsider, to think things over a little longer. Now she was getting cold feet. Actually there was no need of thinking the question through again. It would only end in making the same painful decision once more. Jeff knew that. There was no need of fooling around longer.

"We jes as well to do like we planned," he said. "They ain't nothin' else for us now—it's the bes' thing."

Jeff thought of the handicaps, the near impossibility, of making another crop with his leg bothering him more and more each week. Then there was always the chance that he would have another stroke, like the one that had made him lame. Another one might kill him. The least it could do would be to leave him helpless. Jeff gasped—Lord, Jesus! He could not bear to think of being helpless, like a baby, on Jennie's hands. Frail, blind Jennie.

The little pounding motor of the car worked harder and harder. The puff of steam from the cracked radiator became larger. Jeff realized that they were climbing a little rise. A moment later the road turned abruptly and he looked down upon the face of the river.

"Jeff."

"Hunh?"

"Is that the water I hear?"

"Hm. Tha's it."

"Well, which way you goin' now?"

"Down this-a way," he said. "The road runs 'long 'side o' the water a lil piece."

She waited a while calmly. Then she said, "Drive faster."

"A'right, baby," Jeff said.

The water roared in the bed of the river. It was fifty or sixty feet below the level of the road. Between the road and the water there was a long smooth slope, sharply inclined. The slope was dry, the clay hardened by prolonged summer heat. The water below, roaring in a narrow channel, was noisy and wild.

"Jeff."

"Hunh?"

"How far you goin'?"

"Jes a lil piece down the road."

"You ain't scairt, is you, Jeff?"

"Nah, baby," he said trembling. "I ain't scairt."

"Remember how we planned it, Jeff. We gotta do it like we said. Brave-like."

"Hm."

Jeff's brain darkened. Things suddenly seemed unreal, like figures in a dream. Thoughts swam in his mind foolishly, hysterically, like little blind fish in a pool within a dense cave. They rushed, crossed one another, jostled, collided, retreated and rushed again. Jeff soon became dizzy. He shuddered violently and turned to his wife.

"Jennie, I can't do it. I can't." His voice broke pitifully.

She did not appear to be listening. All the grief had gone from her face. She sat erect, her unseeing eyes wide open, strained and frightful. Her glossy black skin had become dull. She seemed as thin, as sharp and bony, as a starved bird. Now, having suffered and endured the sadness of tearing herself away from beloved things, she showed no anguish. She was absorbed with her own thoughts, and she didn't even hear Jeff's voice shouting in her ear.

Jeff said nothing more. For an instant there was light in his cavernous brain. The great chamber was, for less than a second, peopled by characters he knew and loved. They were simple, healthy creatures, and they behaved in a manner that he could understand. They had quality. But since he had already taken leave of them long ago, the remembrance did not break his heart again. Young Jeff Patton was among them, the Jeff Patton of fifty years ago who went down to New Orleans with a crowd of country boys to the Mardi Gras doings. The gay young crowd, boys with candy-striped shirts and rouged-brown girls in noisy silks, was like a picture in his head. Yet it did not make him sad. On that very trip Slim Burns had killed Joe Beasley—the crowd had been broken up. Since then Jeff Patton's world had been the Greenbriar Plantation. If there had been other Mardi Gras carnivals, he had not heard of them. Since then there had been no time; the years had fallen on him like waves. Now he was old, worn out. Another paralytic stroke (like the one he had already suffered) would put him on his back for keeps. In that condition, with a frail blind woman to look after him, he would be worse off than if he were dead.

Suddenly Jeff's hands became steady. He actually felt brave. He slowed down the motor of the car and carefully pulled off the road. Below, the water of the stream boomed, a soft thunder in the deep channel. Jeff ran the car onto the clay slope, pointed it directly toward the stream and put his foot heavily on the accelerator. The little car leaped furiously down the steep incline toward the water. The movement was nearly as swift and direct as a fall. The two old black folks, sitting quietly side by side, showed no excitement. In another instant the car hit the water and dropped immediately out of sight.

A little later it lodged in the mud of a shallow place. One wheel of the crushed and upturned little Ford became visible above the rushing water.

QUESTIONS

1. Images of paralysis, decay, and deterioration abound in the story. Locate them. How do they help set the tone and mood of the story?
2. The author says that Jeff had "no patience with weakness in men." Why is this an ironic statement? What other ironies exist in the story? How do they help build the story's tension?

3. Where in the story is the suicide foreshadowed? How does Bontemps hint at the purpose of the trip?
4. How would you characterize Jeff Patton's personality? How would you characterize Jennie's?

Nadine Gordimer

THE TRAIN FROM RHODESIA

The train came out of the red horizon and bore down toward them over the single straight track.

The stationmaster came out of his little brick station with its pointed chalet roof, feeling the creases in his serge uniform in his legs as well. A stir of preparedness rippled through the squatting native vendors waiting in the dust; the face of a carved wooden animal, eternally surprised, stuck out of a sack. The stationmaster's barefoot children wandered over. From the gray mud huts with the untidy heads that stood within a decorated mud wall, chickens, and dogs with their skin stretched like parchment over their bones, followed the piccanins down to the track. The flushed and perspiring west cast a reflection, faint, without heat, upon the station, upon the tin shed marked "Goods," upon the walled kraal, upon the gray tin house of the stationmaster and upon the sand, that lapped all around, from sky to sky, cast little rhythmical cups of shadow, so that the sand became the sea, and closed over the children's black feet softly and without imprint.

The stationmaster's wife sat behind the mesh of her verandah. Above her head the hunk of a sheep's carcass moved slightly, dangling in a current of air.

They waited.

The train called out, along the sky; but there was no answer; and the cry hung on: I'm coming . . . I'm coming. . . .

The engine flared out now, big, whisking a dwindling body behind it; the track flared out to let it in.

Creaking, jerking, jostling, gasping, the train filled the station.

Here, let me see that one—the young woman curved her body further out of the corridor window. Missus? smiled the old boy, looking at the creatures he held in his hand. From a piece of string on his gray finger hung a tiny woven basket; he lifted it, questioning. No, no, she urged, leaning down toward him, across the height of the train, toward the man in the piece of old rug; that one, that one, her hand commanded. It was a lion, carved out of soft dry wood that looked like spongecake; heraldic, black and white, with impressionistic detail burnt in. The old man held it up to her still smiling, not from the heart, but at the customer. Between its Vandyke teeth, in the mouth opened in an endless roar too terrible to be heard, it had a black tongue. Look, said the young husband, if you don't mind! And round the neck of the thing, a piece of fur (rat? rabbit? meerkat?); a real mane, majestic, telling you somehow that the artist had delight in the lion.

All up and down the length of the train in the dust the artists sprang, walking bent, like performing animals, the better to exhibit the fantasy held toward the faces on the train. Buck, startled and stiff, staring with round black and white eyes. More lions, standing erect, grappling with strange, thin, elongated warriors who clutched spears and showed no fear in their slits of eyes. How much, they asked from the train, how much?

Give me penny, said the little ones with nothing to sell. The dogs went and sat, quite still, under the dining car, where the train breathed out the smell of meat, cooking with onion.

A man passed beneath the arch of reaching arms meeting gray-black and white in the exchange of money for the staring wooden eyes, the stiff wooden legs sticking up in the air; went along under the voices and the bargaining, interrogating the wheels. Past the dogs; glancing up at the dining car where he could stare at the faces, behind glass, drinking beer, two by two, on either side of a uniform railway vase with its pale dead flower. Right to the end, to the guard's van, where the stationmaster's children had just collected their mother's two loaves of bread; to the engine itself, where the stationmaster and the driver stood talking against the steaming complaint of the resting beast.

The man called out to them, something loud and joking. They turned to laugh, in a twirl of steam. The two children careered over the sand, clutching the bread, and burst through the iron gate and up the path through the garden in which nothing grew.

Passengers drew themselves in at the corridor windows and turned into compartments to fetch money, to call someone to look. Those sitting inside looked up: suddenly different, caged faces, boxed in, cut off, after the contact of outside. There was an orange a piccanin would like. . . . What about that chocolate? It wasn't very nice. . . .

A young girl had collected a handful of the hard kind, that no one liked, out of the chocolate box, and was throwing them to the dogs, over at the dining car. But the hens darted in, and swallowed the chocolates, incredibly quick and accurate, before they had even dropped in the dust, and the dogs, a little bewildered, looked up with their brown eyes, not expecting anything.

—No, leave it, said the girl, don't take it. . . .

Too expensive, too much, she shook her head and raised her voice to the old boy, giving up the lion. He held it up where she had handed it to him. No, she said, shaking her head. Three-and-six? insisted her husband, loudly. Yes baas! laughed the boy. *Three-and-six?*—the young man was incredulous. Oh leave it—she said. The young man stopped. Don't you want it? he said, keeping his face closed to the boy. No, never mind, she said, leave it. The old native kept his head on one side, looking at them sideways, holding the lion. Three-and-six, he murmured, as old people repeat things to themselves.

The young woman drew her head in. She went into the coupé and sat down. Out of the window, on the other side, there was nothing; sand and bush; a thorn tree. Back through the open doorway, past the figure of her husband in the corridor, there was the station, the voices, wooden animals waving, running feet. Her eye followed the funny little valance of scrolled wood that outlined the chalet roof of the station; she thought of the lion and smiled. That bit of fur round the neck. But the wooden buck, the hippos, the elephants, the baskets that already bulked out of their brown paper under the seat and on the luggage rack! How will they look at home? Where will you put them? What will they mean away from the places you found them? Away from the unreality of the last few weeks? The man outside. But he is not part of the unreality; he is for good now. Odd . . . somewhere there was an idea that he, that living with him, was part of the holiday, the strange places.

Outside, a bell rang. The stationmaster was leaning against the end of the train, green flag rolled in readiness. A few men who had got down to stretch their legs sprang on to the train, clinging to the observation platforms, or perhaps merely standing on the iron step, holding the rail; but on the train, safe from the one dusty platform, the one tin house, the empty sand.

There was a grunt. The train jerked. Through the glass the beer drinkers looked out, as if they could not see beyond it. Behind the fly-screen, the stationmaster's wife sat facing back at them beneath the darkening hunk of meat.

There was a shout. The flag drooped out. Joints not yet coordinated, the segmented body of the train heaved and bumped back against itself. It began to move; slowly the scrolled chalet moved past it, the yells of the natives, running alongside, jetted up into the air, fell back at different levels. Staring wooden faces waved drunkenly, there, then gone, questioning for the last time at the windows. Here, one-and-six baas!—As one automatically opens a hand to catch a thrown ball, a man fumbled wildly down his pocket, brought up the shilling and sixpence and threw them out; the old native, gasping, his skinny toes splaying the sand, flung the lion.

The piccanins were waving, the dogs stood, tails uncertain, watching the train go: past the mud huts, where a woman turned to look, up from the smoke of the fire, her hand pausing on her hip.

The stationmaster went slowly in under the chalet.

The old native stood, breath blowing out the skin between his ribs, feet tense, balanced in the sand, smiling and shaking his head. In his opened palm, held in the attitude of receiving, was the retrieved shilling and sixpence.

The blind end of the train was being pulled helplessly out of the station.

The young man swung in from the corridor, breathless. He was shaking his head with laughter and triumph. Here! he said. And waggled the lion at her. One-and-six!

What? she said.

He laughed. I was arguing with him for fun, bargaining—when the train had pulled out already, he came tearing after. . . . One-and-six Baas! So there's your lion.

She was holding it away from her, the head with the open jaws, the pointed teeth, the black tongue, the wonderful ruff of fur facing her. She was looking at it with an expression of not seeing, of seeing something different. Her face was drawn up, wryly, like the face of a discomforted child. Her mouth lifted nervously at the corner. Very slowly, cautious, she lifted her finger and touched the mane, where it was joined to the wood.

But how could you, she said. He was shocked by the dismay of her face.

Good Lord, he said, what's the matter?

If you wanted the thing, she said, her voice rising and breaking with the shrill impotence of anger, why didn't you buy it in the first place? If you wanted it, why didn't you pay for it? Why didn't you take it decently, when he offered it? Why did you have to wait for him to run after the train with it, and give him one-and-six? One-and-six!

She was pushing it at him, trying to force him to take it. He stood astonished, his hands hanging at his sides.

But you wanted it! You liked it so much?

—It's a beautiful piece of work, she said fiercely, as if to protect it from him.

You liked it so much! You said yourself it was too expensive—

Oh *you*—she said, hopeless and furious. *You.* . . . She threw the lion on to the seat.

He stood looking at her.

She sat down again in the corner and, her face slumped in her hand, stared out of the window. Everything was turning round inside her. One-and-six. One-and-six. One-and-six for the wood and the carving and the sinews of the legs and the switch of the tail. The mouth open like that and the teeth. The black tongue, rolling, like a wave. The mane round the neck. To give one-and-six for that. The heat of shame mounted through her legs and body and sounded in her ears like the sound of sand pouring. Pouring, pouring. She sat there, sick. A weariness, a tastelessness, the discovery of a void made her hands slacken their grip, atrophy emptily, as if the hour was not worth their grasp. She was feeling like this again. She had thought it was something to do with singleness, with being alone and belonging too much to oneself.

She sat there not wanting to move or speak, or to look at anything, even; so that the mood should be associated with nothing, no object, word or sight that might recur and so recall the feeling again. . . . Smuts blew in grittily, settled on her hands. Her back remained at exactly the same angle, turned against the young man sitting with his hands drooping between his sprawled legs, and the lion, fallen on its side in the corner.

The train had cast the station like a skin. It called out to the sky, I'm coming, I'm coming; and again, there was no answer.

QUESTIONS

1. What type of imagery does Gordimer use to describe the train itself? What does this imagery suggest about the train?
2. How do the people on the train contrast with the people who live in the town? How do the people from the town modify their behavior when in the presence of those on the train? What political and social statements is Gordimer making by showing us this contrast? Does the author seem to favor one group over the other? If so, why?
3. The man with the carved wooden animal is referred to as an "old boy" in the story. Why?

4. What is the source of the conflict the young woman feels after the young man purchases the carved animal? Why and how has her attitude changed toward the animal during the course of the story?
5. Nadine Gordimer has been an outspoken critic of her government's policy of apartheid. What implicit criticisms of this cruel system exist in the story?

Bharati Mukherjee

HINDUS

I ran into Pat at Sotheby's on a Friday morning two years ago. Derek and I had gone to view the Fraser Collection of Islamic miniatures at the York Avenue galleries. It bothered Derek that I knew so little about my heritage. Islam is nothing more than a marauder's faith to me, but the Mogul emperors stayed a long time in the green delta of the Ganges, flattening and reflattening a fort in the village where I was born, and forcing my priestly ancestors to prove themselves brave. Evidence on that score is still inconclusive. That village is now in Bangladesh.

Derek was a filmmaker, lightly employed at that time. We had been married three hundred and thirty-one days.

"So," Pat said, in his flashy, plummy, drawn-out intonation, "you finally made it to the States!"

It was one of those early November mornings when the woodsy smell of overheated bodies in cloth coats clogged the public stairwells. Everywhere around me I detected the plaintive signs of over-preparedness.

"Whatever are you doing here?" He engulfed me in a swirl of Liberty scarf and cashmere lapels.

"Trying to get the woman there to sell me the right catalog," I said.

The woman, a very young thing with slippery skin, ate a lusty Granny Smith apple and ignored the dark, hesitant miniature-lovers hanging about like bats in daytime.

"They have more class in London," Pat said.

"I wouldn't know. I haven't been back since that unfortunate year at Roedean."

"It was always New York you wanted," Pat laughed. "Don't say I didn't warn you. The world is full of empty promises."

I didn't remember his having warned me about life and the inevitability of grief. It was entirely possible that he had—he had always been given to clowning pronouncements—but I had not seen him in nine years and in Calcutta he had never really broken through the fortifications of my shyness.

"Come have a drink with me," Pat said.

It was my turn to laugh. "You must meet Derek," I said.

Derek had learned a great deal about India. He could reel off statistics of Panchayati

Raj and the electrification of villages and the introduction of mass media, though he reserved his love for birds migrating through the wintry deserts of Jaisalmer. Knowledge of India made Derek more sympathetic than bitter, a common trait of decent outsiders. He was charmed by Pat's heedless, old-world insularity.

"Is this the lucky man?" he said to Derek. He did not hold out his hand. He waved us outside; a taxi magically appeared. "Come have a drink with me tomorrow. At my place."

He gave Derek his card. It was big and would not fit into a wallet made to hold Visa and American Express. Derek read it with his usual curiosity.

H.R.H. Maharajah Patwant Singh
of
Gotlah
Purveyor and Exporter

He tucked the card in the pocket of his raincoat. "I'll be shooting in Toronto tomorrow," he said, "but I'm sure Leela would like to keep it."

There was, in the retention of those final "h's"—even Indian maps and newspapers now referred to Gotla and to maharajas, and I had dropped the old "Leelah" in my first month in America—something of the reclusive mountebank. "I'm going to the Patels for dinner tomorrow," I said, afraid that Pat would misread the signs of healthy unpossessiveness in our marriage.

"Come for a drink before. What's the matter, Leela? Turning a prude in your old age?" To Derek he explained, "I used to rock her on my knee when she was four. She was gorgeous then, but I am no lecher."

It is true that I was very pretty at four and that Pat spent a lot of time in our house fondling us children. He brought us imported chocolates in beautiful tins and made a show of giving me the biggest. In my family, in every generation, one infant seems destined to be the repository of the family's comeliness. In my generation, I inherited the looks, like an heirloom, to keep in good condition and pass on to the next. Beauty teaches humility and responsibility in the culture I came from. By marrying well, I could have seen to the education of my poorer cousins.

Pat was in a third floor sublet in Gramercy Park South. A West Indian doorman with pendulous cheeks and an unbuttoned jacket let me into the building. He didn't give me a chance to say where I was going as I moved toward the elevator.

"The Maharaja is third floor, to the right. All the way down."

I had misunderstood the invitation. It was not to be an hour of wit and nostalgia among exotic knick-knacks squirreled into New York from the Gotla Palace. I counted thirty guests in the first quarter hour of my short stay. Plump young men in tight-fitting suits scuttled from living room to kitchen, balancing overfull glasses of gin and tonic. The women were mostly blondes, with luridly mascaraed, brooding eyes, blonde the way South Americans are blonde, with deep residual shading. I tried to edge into a group of three women. One of them said, "I thought India was spellbinding. Naresh's partner managed to get us into the Lake Palace Hotel."

"I don't think I could take the poverty," said her friend, as I retreated.

The living room walls were hung with prints of British East India Company officials at work and play, the vestibule with mirror-images of Hindu gods and goddesses.

"Take my advice," a Gujarati man said to Pat in the dim and plantless kitchen. "Get out of diamonds—emeralds *won't* bottom out. These days it *has* to be rubies and emeralds."

In my six years in Manhattan I had not entered a kitchen without plants. There was not even a straggly avocado pushing its nervous way out of a shrivelling seed.

I moved back into the living room where the smell of stale turmeric hung like yellow fog from the ceiling. A man rose from the brocade-covered cushions of a banquette near me and plumped them, smiling, to make room for me.

"You're Pat's niece, no?" The man was francophone, a Lebanese. "Pat has such pretty nieces. You have just come from Bombay? I love Bombay. Personally, Bombay to me is like a jewel. Like Paris, like Beirut before, now like Bombay. You agree?"

I disclaimed all kinship to H.R.H. I was a Bengali Brahmin; maharajas—not to put too sharp a point on it—were frankly beneath me, by at least one caste, though some of them, like Pat, would dispute it. Before my marriage to Derek no one in my family since our initial eruption from Vishnu's knee had broken caste etiquette. I disclaimed any recent connection with India. "I haven't been home in ages," I told the Lebanese. "I am an American citizen."

"I too am. I am American," he practically squealed. He rinsed his glass with a bit of gin still left in the bottom, as though he were trying to dislodge lemon pulp stuck and drying on its sides. "You want to have dinner with me tonight, yes? I know Lebanese places, secret and intimate. Food and ambiance very romantic."

"She's going to the Patels." It was Pat. The Gujarati with advice on emeralds was still lodged in the kitchen, huddling with a stocky blonde in a fuschia silk sari.

"Oh, the Patels," said the Lebanese. "You did not say. Super guy, no? He's doing all right for himself. Not as well as me, of course. I own ten stores and he only has four."

Why, I often asked myself, was Derek never around to share these intimacies? Derek would have drawn out the suave, French-speaking, soulful side of this Seventh Avenue *shmattiste*.

It shouldn't have surprised me that the Lebanese man in the ruffled shirt should have known Mohan and Motibehn Patel. For immigrants in similar trades, Manhattan is still a village. Mohan had been in the States for eighteen years and last year had become a citizen. They'd been fortunate in having only sons, now at Cal Tech and Cornell; with daughters there would have been pressure on them to return to India for a proper, arranged marriage.

"Is he still in Queens?"

"No," I told him. "They've moved to a biggish old place on Central Park West."

"Very foolish move," said the Lebanese. "They will only spend their money now." He seemed genuinely appalled.

Pat looked at me surprised. "I can't believe it," he exclaimed. "Leela Lahiri actually going crosstown at night by herself. I remember when your Daddy wouldn't let you walk the two blocks from school to the house without that armed Nepali, what was his name, dogging your steps."

"Gulseng," I said. "He was run over by a lorry three years ago. I think his name was really something-or-other-Rana, but he never corrected us."

"Short, nasty and brutal," said Pat. "They don't come that polite and loyal these days. Just as likely to slit your throat as anyone else, these days."

The Lebanese, sensing the end of brave New World overtures, the gathering of the darknesses we shared, drifted away.

"The country's changed totally, you know," Pat continued. "Crude rustic types have taken over. The *dhotiwallahs*, you know what I mean, they would wrap themselves in loincloths if it got them more votes. No integrity, no finesse. The country's gone to the dogs, I tell you."

"That whole life's outmoded, Pat. Obsolete. All over the world."

"They tried to put me in jail," he said. His face was small with bitterness and alarm. "They didn't like my politics, I tell you. Those Communists back home arrested me and threw me in jail. Me. Like a common criminal."

"On what charges?"

"Smuggling. For selling family heirlooms to Americans who understand them. No one at home understands their value. Here, I can sell off a little Pahari painting for ten thousand dollars. Americans understand our things better than we do ourselves. India wants me to starve in my overgrown palace."

"Did you really spend a night in jail?" I couldn't believe that modernization had finally come to India and that even there, no one was immune from consequences.

"Three nights!" he fumed. "Like a common *dacoit*. The country has no respect anymore. The country has nothing. It has driven us abroad with whatever assets we could salvage."

"You did well, I take it." I did not share his perspective; I did not feel my country owed me anything. Comfort, perhaps, when I was there; a different comfort when I left it. India teaches her children: you have seen the worst. Now go out and don't be afraid.

"I have nothing," he spat. "They've stripped me of everything. At night I hear the jackals singing in the courtyard of my palace."

But he had recovered by the time I left for the crosstown cab ride to the Patels. I saw him sitting on the banquette where not too long before the Lebanese had invited me to share an evening of unwholesomeness. On his knee he balanced, a tall, silver-haired woman who looked like Candice Bergen. She wore a pink cashmere sweater which she must have put through the washing machine. Creases, like worms, curled around her sweatered bosom.

I didn't see Pat for another two years. In those two years I did see a man who claimed to have bounced the real Candice Bergen on his knee. He had been a juggler at one time, had worked with Edgar Bergen on some vaudeville act and could still pull off card tricks and walk on his hands up and down my dining table. I kept the dining table when Derek and I split last May. He went back to Canada which we both realized too late he should never have left and the table was too massive to move out of our West 11th Street place and into his downtown Toronto, chic renovated apartment. The ex-juggler is my boss at a publishing house. My job is menial but I have a soothing title. I am called an Administrative Assistant.

In the two years I have tried to treat the city not as an island of dark immigrants but as a vast sea in which new Americans like myself could disappear and resurface at will. I did not avoid Indians, but without Derek's urging for me to be proud of my heritage, I did not seek them out. The Patels did invite me to large dinners where all the guests seemed to know with the first flick of their eyes in my direction that I had married a white man and was now separated, and there our friendships hit rock. I was a curiosity, a novel and daring element in the community; everyone knew my name. After a while I began to say I was busy to Motibehn Patel.

Pat came to the office with my boss, Bill Haines, the other day. "I wanted you to meet one of our new authors, Leela," Bill said.

"Leela, *dar-ling*!" Pat cried. His voice was shrill with enthusiasm, and he pressed me histrionically against his Burberry raincoat. I could feel a button tap my collarbone. "It's been years! Where have you been hiding your gorgeous self?"

"I didn't realize you two knew each other," Bill said.

All Indians in America, I could have told him, constitute a village.

"Her father bailed me out when the Indian government sought to persecute me," he said with a pout. "If it hadn't been for courageous friends like her daddy, I and my poor subjects might just as well have kicked the bucket."

"She's told me nothing about India," said Bill Haines. "No accent, Western clothes—"

"Yes, a shame, that. By the way, Leela, I just found a picture of Lahiri-*sahab* on an elephant when I was going through my official papers for Bill. If you come over for drinks—after getting out of those ridiculous clothes, I must insist—I can give it to you. Lahiri-*sahab* looks like Ernest Hemingway in that photo. You tell him I said he looks like Hemingway."

"Daddy's in Ranikhet this month," I said. "He's been bedridden for a while. Arthritis. He's just beginning to move around a bit again."

"I have hundreds of good anecdotes, Bill, about her Daddy and me doing *shikar* in the Sundarban forest. Absolutely *huge* Bengal tigers. I want to balance the politics—which as you rightly say are central—with some stirring bits about what it was like in the good old days."

"What are you writing?" I asked.

"I thought you'd never ask, my dear. My memoirs. At night I leave a Sony by my bed. Night is the best time for remembering. I hear the old sounds and voices. You remember, Leela, how the palace ballroom used to hum with dancing feet on my birthdays?"

"*Memoirs of a Modern Maharajah*," Bill Haines said.

"I seem to remember the singing of jackals," I said, not unkindly, though he chose to ignore it.

"Writing is what keeps me from going through death's gate. There are nights . . ." He didn't finish. His posture had stiffened with self-regard; he communicated great oceans of anguish. He'd probably do well. It was what people wanted to hear.

"The indignities," he said suddenly. "The atrocities." He stared straight ahead, at a watercooler. "The nights in jail, the hyenas sniffing outside your barred window. I will never forget their smell, never! It is the smell of death, Leela. The new powers-that-be are peasants. Peasants! They cannot know, they cannot suspect how they have made me suffer. The country is in the hands of tyrannical peasants!"

"Look, Pat," Bill Haines said, leading the writer toward his office, "I have to see Bob Savage, the sub-rights man one floor down. Make yourself at home. Just pull down any book you want to read. I'll be back in a minute."

"Don't worry about me. I shall be all right, Bill. I have my Sony in my pocket. I shall just sit in a corner beside the daughter of my oldest friend, this child I used to bounce on my knee, and I shall let my mind skip into the nooks and crannies of Gotlah Palace. Did I tell you, when I was a young lad my mother kept pet crocs? Big, huge gents and ladies with ugly jaws full of nasty teeth. They were her pets. She gave them names and fed them chickens every day. Come to me, Padma. Come to me, Prem."

"It'll be dynamite," Bill Haines said. "The whole project's dynamite." He pressed my hand as he eased his stubby, muscular body past the stack of dossiers on my desk. "And *you'll* be a godsend in developing this project."

"And what's with you?" Pat asked me. I could tell he already knew the essentials.

"Nothing much." But he wasn't listening anyway.

"You remember the thief my security men caught in the early days of your father's setting up a factory in my hills? You remember how the mob got excited and poured acid on his face?"

I remembered. Was the Sony recording it? Was the memory an illustration of swift and righteous justice in a collapsed Himalayan princely state, or was it the savage and disproportionate fury of a people resisting change?

"Yes, certainly I do. Can I get you a cup of coffee? Or tea?" That, of course, was an important part of my job.

"No thanks," he said with a flutter of his wrinkled hands. "I have given up all stimulants. I've even given up bed-tea. It interferes with my writing. Writing is everything to me nowadays. It has been my nirvana."

"The book sounds dynamite," I assured him. An Indian woman is brought up to please. No matter how passionately we link bodies with our new countries, we never escape the early days.

Pat dropped his voice, and, stooping conspiratorially, said to me in Hindi, "There's one big favor you can do for me, though. Bill has spoken of a chap I should be knowing. Who is this Edgar Bergen?"

"I think he was the father of a movie actress," I said. I, too, had gone through the same contortion of recognition with Bill Haines. Fortunately, like most Americans, he could not conceive of a world in which Edgar Bergen had no currency. Again in Hindi, Pat asked me for directions to the facilities, and this time I could give a full response. He left his rolled-slim umbrella propped against my desk and walked toward the fountain.

"Is he really a maharaja?" Lisa leaned over from her desk to ask me. She is from Rhode Island. Brown hasn't cured her of responding too enthusiastically to each call or visit from a literary personage. "He's terrific. So suave and distinguished! Have you known him from way back when?"

"Yes," I said, all the way from when.

"I had no idea you spoke Hindu. It's eerie to think you can speak such a hard language. I'm having trouble enough with French. I keep forgetting that you haven't lived here always."

I keep forgetting it too. I was about to correct her silly mistake—I'd learned from Derek to be easily incensed over ignorant confusions between Hindi and Hindu—but then I thought, why bother? Maybe she's right. That slight undetectable error, call it an accent, isn't part of language at all. I speak Hindu. No matter what language I speak it will come out slightly foreign, no matter how perfectly I mouth it. There's a whole world of us now, speaking Hindu.

The manuscript of *Memoirs* was not dynamite, but I stayed up all night to finish it. In spite of the arch locutions and the aggrieved posture that Pat had stubbornly clung to, I knew I was reading about myself, blind and groping conquistador who had come to the New World too late.

QUESTIONS

1. Compare and contrast the attitude the narrator has toward India with that of Pat. How do they differ? How are they alike?
2. How would you characterize the narrator's personality and values?
3. The story is divided into two parts. What is the purpose of this division? What changes has the narrator undergone during the time dividing them? What changes has Pat undergone?
4. In the last line of the story, the narrator says she is a "blind and groping conquistador who had come to the New World too late." What does she mean by this? What behaviors or actions does she show in the story that reflect this description?

Gloria Naylor

KISWANA BROWNE

From the window of her sixth-floor studio apartment, Kiswana could see over the wall at the end of the street to the busy avenue that lay just north of Brewster Place. The late-afternoon shoppers looked like brightly clad marionettes as they moved between the congested traffic, clutching their packages against their bodies to guard them from sudden bursts of the cold autumn wind. A portly mailman had abandoned his cart and was bumping into indignant window-shoppers as he puffed behind the cap that the wind had snatched from his head. Kiswana leaned over to see if he was going to be successful, but the edge of the building cut him off from her view.

A pigeon swept across her window, and she marveled at its liquid movements in the air waves. She placed her dreams on the back of the bird and fantasized that it would glide forever in transparent silver circles until it ascended to the center of the universe and was swallowed up. But the wind died down, and she watched with a sigh as the bird beat its wings in awkward, frantic movements to land on the corroded top of a fire escape on the opposite building. This brought her back to earth.

Humph, it's probably sitting over there crapping on those folks' fire escape, she thought. Now, that's a safety hazard. . . . And her mind was busy again, creating flames and smoke and frustrated tenants whose escape was being hindered because they were slipping and sliding in pigeon shit. She watched their cussing, haphazard descent on the fire escapes until they had all reached the bottom. They were milling around, oblivious to their burning apartments, angrily planning to march on the mayor's office about the pigeons. She materialized placards and banners for them, and they had just reached the corner, boldly sidestepping fire hoses and broken glass, when they all vanished.

A tall copper-skinned woman had met this phantom parade at the corner, and they had dissolved in front of her long, confident strides. She plowed through the remains of their faded mists, unconscious of the lingering wisps of their presence on her leather bag and black fur-trimmed coat. It took a few seconds for this transfer from one realm to another to reach Kiswana, but then suddenly she recognized the woman.

"Oh, God, it's Mama!" She looked down guiltily at the forgotten newspaper in her lap and hurriedly circled random job advertisements.

By this time Mrs. Browne had reached the front of Kiswana's building and was checking the house number against a piece of paper in her hand. Before she went into the building she stood at the bottom of the stoop and carefully inspected the condition of the street and the adjoining property. Kiswana watched this meticulous inventory with growing annoyance but she involuntarily followed her mother's slowly rotating head, forcing herself to see her new neighborhood through the older woman's eyes. The brightness of the unclouded sky seemed to join forces with her mother as it highlighted every broken stoop railing and missing brick. The afternoon sun glittered and cascaded across even the tiniest fragments of broken bottle, and at that very moment the wind chose to rise up again, sending unswept grime flying into the air, as a stray tin can left by careless garbage collectors went rolling noisily down the center of the street.

Kiswana noticed with relief that at least Ben wasn't sitting in his usual place on the old garbage can pushed against the far wall. He was just a harmless old wino, but Kiswana knew her mother only needed one wino or one teenager with a reefer within a twenty-block radius to decide that her daughter was living in a building seething with dope factories and hang-outs for derelicts. If she had seen Ben, nothing would have made her believe that practically every apartment contained a family, a Bible, and a dream that one day enough could be scraped from those meager Friday night paychecks to make Brewster Place a distant memory.

As she watched her mother's head disappear into the building, Kiswana gave silent thanks that the elevator was broken. That would give her at least five minutes' grace to straighten up the apartment. She rushed to the sofa bed and hastily closed it without smoothing the rumpled sheets and blanket or removing her nightgown. She felt that somehow the tangled bedcovers would give away the fact that she had not slept alone last night. She silently apologized to Abshu's memory as she heartlessly crushed his spirit between the steel springs of the couch. Lord, that man was sweet. Her toes curled involuntarily at the passing thought of his full lips moving slowly over her instep. Abshu was a foot man, and he always started his lovemaking from the bottom up. For that reason Kiswana changed the color of the polish on her toenails every week. During the course of their relationship she had gone from shades of red to brown and was now into the purples. I'm gonna have to start mixing them soon, she thought aloud as she turned from the couch and raced into the bathroom to remove any traces of Abshu from there. She took up his shaving cream and razor and threw them into the bottom drawer of her dresser beside her diaphragm. Mama wouldn't dare pry into my drawers right in front of me, she thought as she slammed the drawer shut. Well, at least not the *bottom* drawer. She may come up with some sham excuse for opening the top drawer, but never the bottom one.

When she heard the first two short raps on the door, her eyes took a final flight over the small apartment, desperately seeking out any slight misdemeanor that might have to be defended. Well, there was nothing she could do about the crack in the wall over that table. She had been after the landlord to fix it for two months now. And there had been no time to sweep the rug, and everyone knew that off-gray always looked dirtier than it really was. And it was just too damn bad about the kitchen. How was she expected to be out job-hunting every day and still have time to keep a kitchen that looked like her mother's, who didn't even work and still had someone come in twice a month for general cleaning. And besides . . .

Her imaginary argument was abruptly interrupted by a second series of knocks, accompanied by a penetrating, "Melanie, Melanie, are you there?"

Kiswana strode toward the door. She's starting before she even gets in here. She knows that's not my name anymore.

She swung the door open to face her slightly flushed mother. "Oh, hi, Mama. You know, I thought I heard a knock, but I figured it was for the people next door, since no one hardly ever calls me Melanie." Score one for me, she thought.

"Well, it's awfully strange you can forget a name you answered to for twenty-three years," Mrs. Browne said, as she moved past Kiswana into the apartment. "My, that was a long climb. How long has your elevator been out? Honey, how do you manage with your laundry and groceries up all those steps? But I guess you're young, and it wouldn't bother you as much as it does me." This long string of questions told Kiswana that her mother had no intentions of beginning her visit with another argument about her new African name.

"You know I would have called before I came, but you don't have a phone yet. I didn't want you to feel that I was snooping. As a matter of fact, I didn't expect to find you home at all. I thought you'd be out looking for a job." Mrs. Browne had mentally covered the entire apartment while she was talking and taking off her coat.

"Well, I got up late this morning. I thought I'd buy the afternoon paper and start early tomorrow."

"That sounds like a good idea." Her mother moved toward the window and picked up the discarded paper and glanced over the hurriedly circled ads. "Since when do you have experience as a fork-lift operator?"

Kiswana caught her breath and silently cursed herself for her stupidity. "Oh, my hand slipped—I meant to circle file clerk." She quickly took the paper before her mother could see that she had also marked cutlery salesman and chauffeur.

"You're sure you weren't sitting here moping and daydreaming again?" Amber specks of laughter flashed in the corner of Mrs. Browne's eyes.

Kiswana threw her shoulders back and unsuccessfully tried to disguise her embarrassment with indignation.

"Oh, God, Mama! I haven't done that in years—it's for kids. When are you going to realize that I'm a woman now?" She sought desperately for some womanly thing to do and settled for throwing herself on the couch and crossing her legs in what she hoped looked like a nonchalant arc.

"Please, have a seat," she said, attempting the same tones and gestures she'd seen Bette Davis use on the late movies.

Mrs. Browne, lowering her eyes to hide her amusement, accepted the invitation and sat at the window, also crossing her legs. Kiswana saw immediately how it should have been done. Her celluloid poise clashed loudly against her mother's quiet dignity, and she quickly uncrossed her legs. Mrs. Browne turned her head toward the window and pretended not to notice.

"At least you have a halfway decent view from here. I was wondering what lay beyond that dreadful wall—it's the boulevard. Honey, did you know that you can see the trees in Linden Hills from here?"

Kiswana knew that very well, because there were many lonely days that she would sit in her gray apartment and stare at those trees and think of home, but she would rather have choked than admit that to her mother.

"Oh, really, I never noticed. So how is Daddy and things at home?"

"Just fine. We're thinking of redoing one of the extra bedrooms since you children have moved out, but Wilson insists that he can manage all that work alone. I told him that he doesn't really have the proper time or energy for all that. As it is, when he gets home from the office, he's so tired he can hardly move. But you know you can't tell your father anything. Whenever he starts complaining about how stubborn you are, I tell him the child came by it honestly. Oh, and your brother was by yesterday," she added, as if it had just occurred to her.

So that's it, thought Kiswana. That's why she's here.

Kiswana's brother, Wilson, had been to visit her two days ago, and she had borrowed twenty dollars from him to get her winter coat out of layaway. That son-of-a-bitch probably ran straight to Mama—and after he swore he wouldn't say anything. I should have known, he was always a snotty-nosed sneak, she thought.

"Was he?" she said aloud. "He came by to see me, too, earlier this week. And I borrowed some money from him because my unemployment checks hadn't cleared in the bank, but now they have and everything's just fine." There, I'll beat you to that one.

"Oh, I didn't know that," Mrs. Browne lied. "He never mentioned you. He had just heard that Beverly was expecting again, and he rushed over to tell us."

Damn. Kiswana could have strangled herself.

"So she's knocked up again, huh?" she said irritably.

Her mother started. "Why do you always have to be so crude?"

"Personally, I don't see how she can sleep with Willie. He's such a dishrag."

Kiswana still resented the stance her brother had taken in college. When everyone at school was discovering their blackness and protesting on campus, Wilson never took part; he had even refused to wear an Afro. This had outraged Kiswana because, unlike her, he was dark-skinned and had the type of hair that was thick and kinky enough for a good "Fro." Kiswana had still insisted on cutting her own hair, but it was so thin and fine-textured, it refused to thicken even after she washed it. So she had to brush it up and spray it with lacquer to keep it from lying flat. She never forgave Wilson for telling her that she didn't look African, she looked like an electrocuted chicken.

"Now that's some way to talk. I don't know why you have an attitude against your brother. He never gave me a restless night's sleep, and now he's settled with a family and a good job."

"He's an assistant to an assistant junior partner in a law firm. What's the big deal about that?"

"The job has a future, Melanie. And at least he finished school and went on for his law degree."

"In other words, not like me, huh?"

"Don't put words into my mouth, young lady. I'm perfectly capable of saying what I mean."

Amen, thought Kiswana.

"And I don't know why you've been trying to start up with me from the moment I walked in. I didn't come here to fight with you. This is your first place away from home, and I just wanted to see how you were living and if you're doing all right. And I must say, you've fixed this apartment up very nicely."

"Really, Mama?" She found herself softening in the light of her mother's approval.

"Well, considering what you had to work with." This time she scanned the apartment openly.

"Look, I know it's not Linden Hills, but a lot can be done with it. As soon as they come and paint, I'm going to hang my Ashanti print over the couch. And I thought a big Boston Fern would go well in that corner, what do you think?"

"That would be fine, baby. You always had a good eye for balance."

Kiswana was beginning to relax. There was little she did that attracted her mother's approval. It was like a rare bird, and she had to tread carefully around it lest it fly away.

"Are you going to leave that statue out like that?"

"Why, what's wrong with it? Would it look better somewhere else?"

There was a small wooden reproduction of a Yoruba goddess with large protruding breasts on the coffee table.

"Well," Mrs. Browne was beginning to blush, "it's just that it's a bit suggestive, don't you think? Since you live alone now, and I know you'll be having male friends stop by, you wouldn't want to be giving them any ideas. I mean, uh, you know, there's no point in putting yourself in any unpleasant situations because they may get the wrong impressions and uh, you know, I mean, well . . ." Mrs. Browne stammered on miserably.

Kiswana loved it when her mother tried to talk about sex. It was the only time she was at a loss for words.

"Don't worry, Mama." Kiswana smiled. "That wouldn't bother the type of men I date. Now maybe if it had big feet . . ." And she got hysterical, thinking of Abshu.

Her mother looked at her sharply. "What sort of gibberish is that about feet? I'm being serious, Melanie."

"I'm sorry, Mama." She sobered up. "I'll put it away in the closet," she said, knowing that she wouldn't.

"Good," Mrs. Browne said, knowing that she wouldn't either. "I guess you think I'm too picky, but we worry about you over here. And you refuse to put in a phone so we can call and see about you."

"I haven't refused, Mama. They want seventy-five dollars for a deposit, and I can't swing that right now."

"Melanie, I can give you the money."

"I don't want you to be giving me money—I've told you that before. Please, let me make it by myself."

"Well, let me lend it to you, then."

"No!"

"Oh, so you can borrow money from your brother, but not from me."

Kiswana turned her head from the hurt in her mother's eyes. "Mama, when I borrow from Willie, he makes me pay him back. You never let me pay you back," she said into her hands.

"I don't care. I still think it's downright selfish of you to be sitting over here with no phone, and sometimes we don't hear from you in two weeks—anything could happen—especially living among these people."

Kiswana snapped her head up. "What do you mean, *these people*. They're my people and yours, too, Mama—we're all black. But maybe you've forgotten that over in Linden Hills."

"That's not what I'm talking about, and you know it. These streets—this building—it's so shabby and rundown. Honey, you don't have to live like this."

"Well, this is how poor people live."

"Melanie, you're not poor."

"No, Mama, *you're* not poor. And what you have and I have are two totally different things. I don't have a husband in real estate with a five-figure income and a home in Linden Hills—*you* do. What I have is a weekly unemployment check and an overdrawn checking account at United Federal. So this studio on Brewster is all I can afford."

"Well, you could afford a lot better," Mrs. Browne snapped, "if you hadn't dropped out of college and had to resort to these dead-end clerical jobs."

"Uh-huh, I knew you'd get around to that before long." Kiswana could feel the rings of anger begin to tighten around her lower backbone, and they sent her forward onto the couch. "You'll never understand, will you? Those bourgie schools were counterrevolutionary. My place was in the streets with my people, fighting for equality and a better community."

"Counterrevolutionary!" Mrs. Browne was raising her voice. "Where's your revolution now, Melanie? Where are all those black revolutionaries who were shouting and demonstrating and kicking up a lot of dust with you on that campus? Huh?

They're sitting in wood-paneled offices with their degrees in mahogany frames, and they won't even drive their cars past this street because the city doesn't fix potholes in this part of town."

"Mama," she said, shaking her head slowly in disbelief, "how can you—a black woman—sit there and tell me that what we fought for during the Movement wasn't important just because some people sold out?"

"Melanie, I'm not saying it wasn't important. It was damned important to stand up and say that you were proud of what you were and to get the vote and other social opportunities for every person in this country who had it due. But you kids thought you were going to turn the world upside down, and it just wasn't so. When all the smoke had cleared, you found yourself with a fistful of new federal laws and a country still full of obstacles for black people to fight their way over—just because they're black. There was no revolution, Melanie, and there will be no revolution."

"So what am I supposed to do, huh? Just throw up my hands and not care about what happens to my people? I'm not supposed to keep fighting to make things better?"

"Of course, you can. But you're going to have to fight within the system, because it and these so-called 'bourgie' schools are going to be here for a long time. And that means that you get smart like a lot of your old friends and get an important job where you can have some influence. You don't have to sell out, as you say, and work for some corporation, but you could become an assemblywoman or a civil liberties lawyer or open a freedom school in this very neighborhood. That way you could really help the community. But what help are you going to be to these people on Brewster while you're living hand-to-mouth on file-clerk jobs waiting for a revolution? You're wasting your talents, child."

"Well, I don't think they're being wasted. At least I'm here in day-to-day contact with the problems of my people. What good would I be after four or five years of a lot of white brainwashing in some phony, prestige institution, huh? I'd be like you and Daddy and those other educated blacks sitting over there in Linden Hills with a terminal case of middle-class amnesia."

"You don't have to live in a slum to be concerned about social conditions, Melanie. Your father and I have been charter members of the NAACP for the last twenty-five years."

"Oh, God!" Kiswana threw her head back in exaggerated disgust. "That's being concerned? That middle-of-the-road, Uncle Tom dumping ground for black Republicans!"

"You can sneer all you want, young lady, but that organization has been working for black people since the turn of the century, and it's still working for them. Where are all those radical groups of yours that were going to put a Cadillac in every garage and Dick Gregory in the White House? I'll tell you where."

I knew you would, Kiswana thought angrily.

"They burned themselves out because they wanted too much too fast. Their goals weren't grounded in reality. And that's always been your problem."

"What do you mean, my problem? I know exactly what I'm about."

"No, you don't. You constantly live in a fantasy world—always going to extremes—turning butterflies into eagles, and life isn't about that. It's accepting what is and working from that. Lord, I remember how worried you had me, putting all that lacquered hair spray on your head. I thought you were going to get lung cancer—trying to be what you're not."

Kiswana jumped up from the couch. "Oh, God, I can't take this anymore. Trying to be something I'm not—trying to be something I'm not, Mama! Trying to be proud of my heritage and the fact that I was of African descent. If that's being what I'm not, then I say fine. But I'd rather be dead than be like you—a white man's nigger who's ashamed of being black!"

Kiswana saw streaks of gold and ebony light follow her mother's flying body out of the chair. She was swung around by the shoulders and made to face the deadly stillness in the angry woman's eyes. She was too stunned to cry out from the pain of the long fingernails that dug into her shoulders, and she was brought so close to her mother's face that she saw her reflection, distorted and wavering, in the tears that stood in the older woman's eyes. And she listened in that stillness to a story she had heard from a child.

"My grandmother," Mrs. Browne began slowly in a whisper, "was a full-blooded Iroquois, and my grandfather a free black from a long line of journeymen who had lived in Connecticut since the establishment of the colonies. And my father was a Bajan who came to this country as a cabin boy on a merchant mariner."

"I know all that," Kiswana said, trying to keep her lips from trembling.

"Then, know this." And the nails dug deeper into her flesh. "I am alive because of the blood of proud people who never scraped or begged or apologized for what they were. They lived asking only one thing of this world—to be allowed to be. And I learned through the blood of these people that black isn't beautiful and it isn't ugly—black is! It's not kinky hair and it's not straight hair—it just is.

"It broke my heart when you changed your name. I gave you my grandmother's name, a woman who bore nine children and educated them all, who held off six white men with a shotgun when they tried to drag one of her sons to jail for 'not knowing his place.' Yet you needed to reach into an African dictionary to find a name to make you proud.

"When I brought my babies home from the hospital, my ebony son and my golden daughter, I swore before whatever gods would listen—those of my mother's people or those of my father's people—that I would use everything I had and could ever get to see that my children were prepared to meet this world on its own terms, so that no one could sell them short and make them ashamed of what they were or how they looked—whatever they were or however they looked. And Melanie, that's not being white or red or black—that's being a mother."

Kiswana followed her reflection in the two single tears that moved down her mother's cheeks until it blended with them into the woman's copper skin. There was nothing and then so much that she wanted to say, but her throat kept closing up every time she tried to speak. She kept her head down and her eyes closed, and thought, Oh, God, just let me die. How can I face her now?

Mrs. Browne lifted Kiswana's chin gently. "And the one lesson I wanted you to learn is not to be afraid to face anyone, not even a crafty old lady like me who can outtalk you." And she smiled and winked.

"Oh, Mama, I . . ." and she hugged the woman tightly.

"Yeah, baby." Mrs. Browne patted her back. "I know."

She kissed Kiswana on the forehead and cleared her throat. "Well, now, I better be moving on. It's getting late, there's dinner to be made, and I have to get off my feet—these new shoes are killing me."

Kiswana looked down at the beige leather pumps. "Those are really classy. They're English, aren't they?"

"Yes, but, Lord, do they cut me right across the instep." She removed the shoe and sat on the couch to massage her foot.

Bright red nail polish glared at Kiswana through the stockings. "Since when do you polish your toenails?" she gasped. "You never did that before."

"Well . . ." Mrs. Browne shrugged her shoulders, "your father sort of talked me into it, and, uh, you know, he likes it and all, so I thought, uh, you know, why not, so . . ." And she gave Kiswana an embarrassed smile.

I'll be damned, the young woman thought, feeling her whole face tingle. Daddy's into feet! And she looked at the blushing woman on her couch and suddenly realized that her mother had trod through the same universe that she herself was now traveling. Kiswana was breaking no new trails and would eventually end up just two feet away on that couch. She stared at the woman she had been and was to become.

"But I'll never be a Republican," she caught herself saying aloud.

"What are you mumbling about, Melanie?" Mrs. Browne slipped on her shoe and got up from the couch.

She went to get her mother's coat. "Nothing, Mama. It's really nice of you to come by. You should do it more often."

"Well, since it's not Sunday, I guess you're allowed at least one lie."

They both laughed.

After Kiswana had closed the door and turned around, she spotted an envelope sticking between the cushions of her couch. She went over and opened it up; there was seventy-five dollars in it.

"Oh, Mama, darn it!" She rushed to the window and started to call to the woman, who had just emerged from the building, but she suddenly changed her mind and sat down in the chair with a long sigh that caught in the upward draft of the autumn wind and disappeared over the top of the building.

QUESTIONS

1. What kind of neighborhood does Kiswana live in? How does it compare to the neighborhood her parents live in?
2. Mrs. Browne tells Kiswana, "You constantly live in a dream world." Is this true? Support your view.
3. Is Kiswana rebelling against her family? If so, how? Why does her mother think she is rebelling?
4. What are the major conflicts between Kiswana and her mother? Are they resolved by the end of the story? Explain.

Edgar Allan Poe

THE MASQUE OF
THE RED DEATH

The "Red Death" has long devastated the country. No pestilence had ever been so fatal, or so hideous. Blood was its Avatar and its seal—the redness and the horror of blood. There were sharp pains, and sudden dizziness, and then profuse bleeding at the pores, with dissolution. The scarlet stains upon the body and especially upon the face of the victim, were the pest ban which shut him out from the aid and from the sympathy of his fellow-men. And the whole seizure, progress and termination of the disease, were the incidents of half an hour.

But the Prince Prospero was happy and dauntless and sagacious. When his dominions were half depopulated, he summoned to his presence a thousand hale and light-hearted friends from among the knights and dames of his court, and with these retired to the deep seclusion of one of his castellated abbeys. This was an extensive and magnificent structure, the creation of the prince's own eccentric yet august taste. A strong and lofty wall girdled it in. This wall had gates of iron. The courtiers, having entered, brought furnaces and massy hammers and welded the bolts. They resolved to leave means neither of ingress or egress to the sudden impulses of despair or of frenzy from within. The abbey was amply provisioned. With such precautions the courtiers might bid defiance to contagion. The external world could take care of itself. In the meantime it was folly to grieve, or to think. The prince had provided all the appliances of pleasure. There were buffoons, there were improvisatori, there were ballet-dancers, there were musicians, there was Beauty, there was wine. All these and security were within. Without was the "Red Death."

It was toward the close of the fifth or sixth month of his seclusion, and while the pestilence raged most furiously abroad, that the Prince Prospero entertained his thousand friends at a masked ball of the most unusual magnificence.

It was a voluptuous scene, that masquerade. But first let me tell of the rooms in which it was held. There were seven—an imperial suite. In many palaces, however, such suites form a long and straight vista, while the folding doors slide back nearly to the walls on either hand, so that the view of the whole extent is scarcely impeded. Here the case was very different; as might have been expected from the duke's love of the *bizarre*. The apartments were so irregularly disposed that the vision embraced but little more than one at a time. There was a sharp turn at every twenty or thirty yards, and at each turn a novel effect. To the right and left, in the middle of each wall, a tall and narrow Gothic window looked out upon a closed corridor which pursued the windings of the suite. These windows were of stained glass whose color varied in accordance with the prevailing hue of the decorations of the chamber into which it opened. That at the eastern extremity was hung, for example, in blue—and vividly blue were its windows. The second chamber was purple in its ornaments and tapestries, and here the panes were purple. The third was green throughout, and so were the casements. The fourth was furnished and lighted with orange—the fifth with white—the sixth with violet. The seventh apartment was closely shrouded in black velvet tapestries that hung all over the ceiling and down the walls, falling in heavy folds upon a carpet of the same material and hue. But in this chamber only, the color of the windows failed to correspond with the decorations. The panes here were scarlet—a deep blood color. Now in no one of the seven apartments was there any lamp or candelabrum, amid the profusion of golden ornaments that lay scattered to and fro or depended from the roof. There was no light of any kind emanating from lamp or candle within the suite of chambers. But in the corridors that followed the suite, there stood, opposite to each window, a heavy tripod, bearing a brazier of fire that projected its rays through the tinted glass and so glaringly illumined the room. And thus were produced a multitude of gaudy and fantastic appearances. But in the western or black chamber the effect of the fire-light that streamed upon the dark hangings through the blood-tinted panes, was ghastly in the extreme, and produced so wild a look upon the countenances of those who entered, that there were few of the company bold enough to set foot within its precincts at all.

It was in this apartment, also, that there stood against the western wall, a gigantic clock of ebony. Its pendulum swung to and fro with a dull, heavy, monotonous clang; and when the minute-hand made the circuit of the face, and the hour was to be stricken, there came from the brazen lungs of the clock a sound which was clear and loud and deep and exceedingly musical, but of so peculiar a note and emphasis that, at each lapse of an hour, the musicians of the orchestra were constrained to pause, momentarily, in their performance, to hearken to the sound; and thus the waltzers perforce ceased their evolutions; and there was a brief disconcert of the whole gay company; and, while the chimes of the clock yet rang, it was observed that the giddiest grew pale, and the more aged and sedate passed their hands over their brows as if in confused reverie or meditation. But when the echoes had fully ceased, a light laughter at once pervaded the assembly; the musicians looked at each other and smiled as if at their own nervousness and folly, and made whispering vows, each to the other, that the next chiming of the clock should produce in them no similar emotion; and then, after the lapse of sixty minutes, (which embrace three thousand and six hundred seconds of the Time that flies), there came yet another chiming of the clock, and then were the same disconcert and tremulousness and meditation as before.

But, in spite of these things, it was a gay and magnificent revel. The tastes of the duke were peculiar. He had a fine eye for colors and effects. He disregarded the *decora* of mere fashion. His plans were bold and fiery, and his conceptions glowed with barbaric lustre. There are some who would have thought him mad. His followers felt that he was not. It was necessary to hear and see and touch him to be *sure* that he was not.

He had directed, in great part, the moveable embellishments of the seven chambers, upon occasion of this great *fête;* and it was his own guiding taste which had given character to the masqueraders. Be sure they were grotesque. There were much glare and glitter and piquancy and phantasm—much of what has been since seen in "Hernani." There were arabesque figures with unsuited limbs and appointments. There were delirious fancies such as the madman fashions. There was much of the beautiful, much of the woman, much of the *bizarre*, something of the terrible, and not a little of that which might have excited disgust. To and fro in the seven chambers there stalked, in fact, a multitude of dreams. And these—the dreams—writhed in and about, taking hue from the rooms, and causing the wild music of the orchestra to seem as the echo of their steps. And, anon, there strikes the ebony clock which stands in the hall of the velvet. And then, for a moment, all is still, and all is silent save the voice of the clock. The dreams are stiff-frozen as they stand. But the echoes of the chime die away—they have endured but an instant—and a light, half-subdued laughter floats after them as they depart. And now again the music swells, and the dreams live, and writhe to and fro more merrily than ever, taking hue from the many-tinted windows through which stream the rays from the tripods. But to the chamber which lies most westwardly of the seven, there are now none of the maskers who venture; for the night is waning away; and there flows a ruddier light through the blood-colored panes; and the blackness of the sable drapery appals; and to him whose foot falls upon the sable carpet, there comes from the near clock of ebony a muffled peal more solemnly emphatic than any which reaches *their* ears who indulge in the more remote gaieties of the other apartments.

But these other apartments were densely crowded, and in them beat feverishly the heart of life. And the revel went whirlingly on, until at length there commenced the sounding of midnight upon the clock. And then the music ceased, as I have told; and the evolutions of the waltzers were quieted; and there was an uneasy cessation of all things as before. But now there were twelve strokes to be sounded by the bell of the clock; and thus it happened, perhaps, that more of thought crept, with more of time, into the meditations of the thoughtful among those who revelled. And thus, too, it happened, perhaps, that before the last echoes of the last chime had utterly sunk into silence, there were many individuals in the crowd who had found leisure to become aware of the presence of a masked figure which had arrested the attention of no single individual before. And the rumor of this new presence having spread itself whisperingly around, there arose at length from the whole company a buzz, or murmur, expressive of disapprobation and surprise—then, finally, of terror, of horror, and of disgust.

In an assembly of phantasms such as I have painted, it may well be supposed that no ordinary appearance could have excited such sensation. In truth the masquerade license of the night was nearly unlimited; but the figure in question had out-Heroded Herod, and gone beyond the bounds of even the prince's indefinite decorum. There are chords in the hearts of the most reckless which cannot be touched without emotion. Even with the utterly lost, to whom life and death are equally jests, there are matters of which no jest can be made. The whole company, indeed, seemed now deeply to feel that in the costume and bearing of the stranger neither wit nor propriety existed. The figure was tall and gaunt, and shrouded from head to foot in the habiliments of the grave. The mask which concealed the visage was made so nearly to resemble the countenance of a stiffened corpse that the closest scrutiny must have had difficulty in detecting the cheat. And yet all this might have been endured, if not approved, by the mad revellers around. But the mummer had gone so far as to assume the type of the Red Death. His vesture was dabbled in *blood*—and his broad brow, with all the features of the face, was besprinkled with the scarlet horror.

When the eyes of Prince Prospero fell upon this spectral image (which with a slow and solemn movement, as if more fully to sustain its *rôle*, stalked to and fro among the waltzers) he was seen to be convulsed, in the first moment with a strong shudder either of terror or distaste; but, in the next, his brow reddened with rage.

"Who dares?" he demanded hoarsely of the courtiers who stood near him—"who dares insult us with this blasphemous mockery? Seize him and unmask him—that we may know whom we have to hang at sunrise, from the battlements!"

It was in the eastern or blue chamber in which stood the Prince Prospero as he uttered these words. They rang throughout the seven rooms loudly and clearly—for the prince was a bold and robust man, and the music had become hushed at the waving of his hand.

It was in the blue room where stood the prince, with a group of pale courtiers by his side. At first, as he spoke, there was a slight rushing movement of this group in the direction of the intruder, who at the moment was also near at hand, and now, with deliberate and stately step, made closer approach to the speaker. But from a certain nameless awe with which the mad assumptions of the mummer had inspired the whole party, there were found none who put forth hand to seize him; so that, unimpeded, he passed within a yard of the prince's person; and, while the vast assembly, as if with one impulse, shrank from the centres of the rooms to the walls, he made his way uninterruptedly, but with the same solemn and measured step which had distinguished him from the first, through the blue chamber to the purple—through the purple to the green—through the green to the orange—through this again to the white—and even thence to the violet, ere a decided movement had been made to arrest him. It was then, however, that the Prince Prospero, maddening with rage and the shame of his own momentary cowardice, rushed hurriedly through the six chambers, while none followed him on account of a deadly terror that had seized upon all. He bore aloft a drawn dagger, and had approached, in rapid impetuosity, to within three or four feet of the retreating figure, when the latter, having attained the extremity of the velvet apartment, turned suddenly and confronted his pursuer. There was a sharp cry—and the dagger dropped gleaming upon the sable carpet, upon which, instantly afterwards fell prostrate in death the Prince Prospero. Then, summoning the wild courage of despair, a throng of the revellers at once threw themselves into the black apartment, and, seizing the mummer, whose tall figure stood erect and motionless within the shadow of the ebony clock, gasped in unutterable horror at finding the grave-cerements and corpselike mask which they handled with so violent a rudeness, untenanted by any tangible form.

And now was acknowledged the presence of the Red Death. He had come like a thief in the night. And one by one dropped the revellers in the blood-bedewed halls of their revel, and died each in the despairing posture of his fall. And the life of the ebony clock went out with that of the last of the gay. And the flames of the tripods expired. And Darkness and Decay and the Red Death held illimitable dominion over all.

QUESTIONS

1. How does Poe's syntax and word choice determine the diction of the story? How would you characterize the diction? How does it help create the atmosphere of the story?
2. The author spends a lot of time describing the physical details of the Prince's domain. What do they suggest about the Prince's life-style and personality? What is the quality of his surroundings?

3. Poe describes the clock in great detail. What might the clock symbolize and foreshadow?
4. At what point in the story does the tone shift? How does the author create tension
   once the mummer in red reveals himself?

James Thurber

THE CATBIRD SEAT

Mr. Martin bought the pack of Camels on Monday night in the most crowded cigar
store on Broadway. It was theater time and seven or eight men were buying cigarettes.
The clerk didn't even glance at Mr. Martin, who put the pack in his overcoat pocket
and went out. If any of the staff at F & S had seen him buy the cigarettes, they would
have been astonished, for it was generally known that Mr. Martin did not smoke, and
never had. No one saw him.

It was just a week to the day since Mr. Martin had decided to rub out Mrs. Ulgine
Barrows. The term "rub out" pleased him because it suggested nothing more than the
correction of an error—in this case an error of Mr. Fitweiler. Mr. Martin had spent
each night of the past week working out his plan and examining it. As he walked home
now he went over it again. For the hundredth time he resented the element of impreci-
sion, the margin of guesswork that entered into the business. The project as he had
worked it out was casual and bold, the risks were considerable. Something might go
wrong anywhere along the line. And therein lay the cunning of his scheme. No one
would ever see in it the cautious, painstaking hand of Erwin Martin, head of the filing
department at F & S, of whom Mr. Fitweiler had once said, "Man is fallible but Martin
isn't." No one would see his hand, that is, unless it were caught in the act.

Sitting in his apartment, drinking a glass of milk, Mr. Martin reviewed his case
against Mrs. Ulgine Barrows, as he had every night for seven nights. He began at the
beginning. Her quacking voice and braying laugh had first profaned the halls of F & S
on March 7, 1941 (Mr. Martin had a head for dates). Old Roberts, the personnel chief,
had introduced her as the newly appointed special adviser to the president of the firm,
Mr. Fitweiler. The woman had appalled Mr. Martin instantly, but he hadn't shown it.
He had given her his dry hand, a look of studious concentration, and a faint smile.
"Well," she had said, looking at the papers on his desk, "are you lifting the oxcart out
of the ditch?" As Mr. Martin recalled that moment, over his milk, he squirmed slightly.
He must keep his mind on her crimes as a special adviser, not on her peccadillos as a
personality. This he found difficult to do, in spite of entering an objection and sustaining
it. The faults of the woman as a woman kept chattering on in his mind like an unruly
witness. She had, for almost two years now, baited him. In the halls, in the elevator, even
in his own office, into which she romped now and then like a circus horse, she was
constantly shouting these silly questions at him. "Are you lifting the oxcart out of the

ditch? Are you tearing up the pea patch? Are you hollering down the rain barrel? Are you scraping around the bottom of the pickle barrel? Are you sitting in the catbird seat?"

It was Joey Hart, one of Mr. Martin's two assistants, who had explained what the gibberish meant. "She must be a Dodger fan," he had said. "Red Barber announces the Dodger games over the radio and he uses those expressions—picked 'em up down South." Joey had gone on to explain one or two. "Tearing up the pea patch" meant going on a rampage; "sitting in the catbird seat" meant sitting pretty, like a batter with three balls and no strikes on him. Mr. Martin dismissed all this with an effort. It had been annoying, it had driven him near to distraction, but he was too solid a man to be moved to murder by anything so childish. It was fortunate, he reflected as he passed on to the important charges against Mrs. Barrows, that he had stood up under it so well. He had maintained always an outward appearance of polite tolerance. "Why, I even believe you like the woman," Miss Paird, his other assistant, had once said to him. He had simply smiled.

A gavel rapped in Mr. Martin's mind and the case proper was resumed. Mrs. Ulgine Barrows stood charged with willful, blatant, and persistent attempts to destroy the efficiency and system of F & S. It was competent, material, and relevant to review her advent and rise to power. Mr. Martin had got the story from Miss Paird, who seemed always able to find things out. According to her, Mrs. Barrows had met Mr. Fitweiler at a party, where she had rescued him from the embraces of a powerfully built drunken man who had mistaken the president of F & S for a famous retired Middle Western football coach. She had led him to a sofa and somehow worked upon him a monstrous magic. The aging gentleman had jumped to the conclusion there and then that this was a woman of singular attainments, equipped to bring out the best in him and in the firm. A week later he had introduced her into F & S as his special adviser. On that day confusion got its foot in the door. After Miss Tyson, Mr. Brundage, and Mr. Bartlett had been fired and Mr. Munson had taken his hat and stalked out, mailing his resignation later, old Roberts had been emboldened to speak to Mr. Fitweiler. He mentioned that Mr. Munson's department had been "a little disrupted" and hadn't they perhaps better resume the old system there? Mr. Fitweiler had said certainly not. He had the greatest faith in Mrs. Barrows' ideas. "They require a little seasoning, a little seasoning, is all," he had added. Mr. Roberts had given it up. Mr. Martin reviewed in detail all the changes wrought by Mrs. Barrows. She had begun chipping at the cornices of the firm's edifice and now she was swinging at the foundation stones with a pickaxe.

Mr. Martin came now, in his summing up, to the afternoon of Monday, November 2, 1942—just one week ago. On that day, at 3 P.M., Mrs. Barrows had bounced into his office. "Boo!" she had yelled. "Are you scraping around the bottom of the pickle barrel?" Mr. Martin had looked at her from under his green eyeshade, saying nothing. She had begun to wander about the office, taking it in with her great, popping eyes. "Do you really need *all* these filing cabinets?" she had demanded suddenly. Mr. Martin's heart had jumped. "Each of these files," he had said, keeping his voice even, "plays an indispensable part in the system of F & S." She had brayed at him, "Well, don't tear up the pea patch!" and gone to the door. From there she had bawled, "But you sure have got a lot of fine scrap in here!" Mr. Martin could no longer doubt that the finger was on his beloved department. Her pickaxe was on the upswing, poised for the first blow. It had not come yet; he had received no blue memo from the enchanted Mr. Fitweiler bearing nonsensical instructions deriving from the obscene woman. But there was no doubt in Mr. Martin's mind that one would be forthcoming. He must act quickly. Already a precious week had gone by. Mr. Martin stood up in his living room, still holding his milk glass. "Gentlemen of the jury," he said to himself, "I demand the death penalty for this horrible person."

The next day Mr. Martin followed his routine, as usual. He polished his glasses more often and once sharpened an already sharp pencil, but not even Miss Paird noticed. Only once did he catch sight of his victim; she swept past him in the hall with a patronizing "Hi!" At five-thirty he walked home, as usual, and had a glass of milk, as usual. He had never drunk anything stronger in his life—unless you could count ginger ale. The late Sam Schlosser, the S of F & S, had praised Mr. Martin at a staff meeting several years before for his temperate habits. "Our most efficient worker neither drinks nor smokes," he had said. "The results speak for themselves." Mr. Fitweiler had sat by, nodding approval.

Mr. Martin was still thinking about that red-letter day as he walked over to the Schrafft's on Fifth Avenue near Forty-sixth Street. He got there, as he always did, at eight o'clock. He finished his dinner and the financial page of the *Sun* at a quarter to nine, as he always did. It was his custom after dinner to take a walk. This time he walked down Fifth Avenue at a casual pace. His gloved hands felt moist and warm, his forehead cold. He transferred the Camels from his overcoat to a jacket pocket. He wondered, as he did so, if they did not represent an unnecessary note of strain. Mrs. Barrows smoked only Luckies. It was his idea to puff a few puffs on a Camel (after the rubbing-out), stub it out in the ashtray holding her lipstick-stained Luckies, and thus drag a small red herring across the trail. Perhaps it was not a good idea. It would take time. He might even choke, too loudly.

Mr. Martin had never seen the house on West Twelfth Street where Mrs. Barrows lived, but he had a clear enough picture of it. Fortunately, she had bragged to everybody about her ducky first-floor apartment in the perfectly darling three-story red-brick. There would be no doorman or other attendants; just the tenants of the second and third floors. As he walked along, Mr. Martin realized that he would get there before nine-thirty. He had considered walking north on Fifth Avenue from Schrafft's to a point from which it would take him until ten o'clock to reach the house. At that hour people were less likely to be coming in or going out. But the procedure would have made an awkward loop in the straight thread of his casualness, and he had abandoned it. It was impossible to figure when people would be entering or leaving the house, anyway. There was a great risk at any hour. If he ran into anybody, he would simply have to place the rubbing-out of Ulgine Barrows in the inactive file forever. The same thing would hold true if there were someone in her apartment. In that case he would just say that he had been passing by, recognized her charming house, and thought to drop in.

It was eighteen minutes after nine when Mr. Martin turned into Twelfth Street. A man passed him, and a man and a woman, talking. There was no one within fifty paces when he came to the house, halfway down the block. He was up the steps and in the small vestibule in no time, pressing the bell under the card that said "Mrs. Ulgine Barrows." When the clicking in the lock started, he jumped forward against the door.

He got inside fast, closing the door behind him. A bulb in a lantern hung from the hall ceiling on a chain seemed to give a monstrously bright light. There was nobody on the stair, which went up ahead of him along the left wall. A door opened down the hall in the wall on the right. He went toward it swiftly, on tiptoe.

"Well, for God's sake, look who's here!" bawled Mrs. Barrows, and her braying laugh rang out like the report of a shotgun. He pushed past her like a football tackle, bumping her. "Hey, quit shoving!" she said, closing the door behind them. They were in her living room, which seemed to Mr. Martin to be lighted by a hundred lamps. "What's after you?" she said. "You're as jumpy as a goat." He found he was unable to speak. His heart was wheezing in his throat. "I—yes," he finally brought out. She was jabbering and laughing as she started to help him off with his coat. "No, no," he said. "I'll put it here." He took it off and put it on a chair near the door. "Your hat and gloves, too," she said. "You're in a lady's house." He put his hat on top of the coat. Mrs. Barrows seemed larger than he had thought. He kept his gloves on. "I was passing by," he said. "I recognized—is there anyone here?" She laughed louder than ever. "No," she said, "we're all alone. You're as white as a sheet, you funny man. Whatever *has* come over you? I'll mix you a toddy." She started toward a door across the room. "Scotch-and-soda be all right? But say, you don't drink, do you?" She turned and gave him her amused look. Mr. Martin pulled himself together. "Scotch-and-soda will be all right," he heard himself say. He could hear her laughing in the kitchen.

Mr. Martin looked quickly around the living room for the weapon. He had counted on finding one there. There were andirons and a poker and something in a corner that looked like an Indian club. None of them would do. It couldn't be that way. He began to pace around. He came to a desk. On it lay a metal paper knife with an ornate handle. Would it be sharp enough? He reached for it and knocked over a small brass jar. Stamps spilled out of it and it fell to the floor with a clatter. "Hey," Mrs. Barrows yelled from the kitchen, "are you tearing up the pea patch?" Mr. Martin gave a strange laugh. Picking up the knife, he tried its point against his left wrist. It was blunt. It wouldn't do.

When Mrs. Barrows reappeared, carrying two highballs, Mr. Martin, standing there with his gloves on, became acutely conscious of the fantasy he had wrought. Cigarettes in his pocket, a drink prepared for him—it was all too grossly improbable. It was more than that; it was impossible. Somewhere in the back of his mind a vague idea stirred, sprouted. "For heaven's sake, take off those gloves," said Mrs. Barrows. "I always wear them in the house," said Mr. Martin. The idea began to bloom, strange and wonderful. She put the glasses on a coffee table in front of a sofa and sat on the sofa. "Come over here, you odd little man," she said. Mr. Martin went over and sat beside her. It was difficult getting a cigarette out of the pack of Camels, but he managed it. She held a match for him, laughing. "Well," she said, handing him his drink, "this is perfectly marvelous. You with a drink and a cigarette."

Mr. Martin puffed, not too awkwardly, and took a gulp of the highball. "I drink and smoke all the time," he said. He clinked his glass against hers. "Here's nuts to that old windbag, Fitweiler," he said, and gulped again. The stuff tasted awful, but he made no grimace. "Really, Mr. Martin," she said, her voice and posture changing, "you are insulting our employer." Mrs. Barrows was now all special adviser to the president. "I am preparing a bomb," said Mr. Martin, "which will blow the old goat higher than hell." He had only had a little of the drink, which was not strong. It couldn't be that. "Do you take dope or something?" Mrs. Barrows asked coldly. "Heroin," said Mr. Martin. "I'll be coked to the gills when I bump that old buzzard off." "Mr. Martin!" she shouted, getting to her feet. "That will be all of that. You must go at once." Mr. Martin took another swallow of his drink. He tapped his cigarette out in the ashtray and put the pack of Camels on the coffee table. Then he got up. She stood glaring at him. He walked over and put on his hat and coat. "Not a word about this," he said, and laid an index finger against his lips. All Mrs. Barrows could bring out was "Really!" Mr. Martin put his hand on the doorknob. "I'm sitting in the catbird seat," he said. He stuck his tongue out at her and left. Nobody saw him go.

Mr. Martin got to his apartment, walking, well before eleven. No one saw him go in. He had two glasses of milk after brushing his teeth, and he felt elated. It wasn't tipsiness, because he hadn't been tipsy. Anyway, the walk had worn off all effects of the whiskey. He got in bed and read a magazine for a while. He was asleep before midnight.

Mr. Martin got to the office at eight-thirty the next morning, as usual. At a quarter to nine, Ulgine Barrows, who had never before arrived at work before ten, swept into his office. "I'm reporting to Mr. Fitweiler now!" she shouted. "If he turns you over to the police, it's no more than you deserve!" Mr. Martin gave her a look of shocked surprise. "I beg your pardon?" he said. Mrs. Barrows snorted and bounced out of the room, leaving Miss Paird and Joey staring after her. "What's the matter with that old devil now?" asked Miss Paird. "I have no idea," said Mr. Martin, resuming his work. The other two looked at him and then at each other. Miss Paird got up and went out. She walked slowly past the closed door of Mr. Fitweiler's office. Mrs Barrows was yelling inside, but she was not braying. Miss Paird could not hear what the woman was saying. She went back to her desk.

Forty-five minutes later, Mrs. Barrows left the president's office and went into her own, shutting the door. It wasn't until half an hour later that Mr. Fitweiler sent for Mr. Martin. The head of the filing department, neat, quiet, attentive, stood in front of the old man's desk. Mr. Fitweiler was pale and nervous. He took his glasses off and twiddled them. He made a small, bruffing sound in his throat. "Martin," he said, "you have been with us more than twenty years." "Twenty-two, sir," said Mr. Martin. "In that time," pursued the president, "your work and your—uh—manner have been exemplary." "I trust so, sir," said Mr. Martin. "I have understood, Martin," said Mr. Fitweiler, "that you have never taken a drink or smoked." "That is correct, sir," said Mr. Martin. "Ah, yes." Mr. Fitweiler polished his glasses. "You may describe what you did after leaving the office yesterday, Martin," he said. Mr. Martin allowed less than a second for his bewildered pause. "Certainly, sir," he said. "I walked home. Then I went to Schrafft's for dinner. Afterward I walked home again. I went to bed early, sir, and read a magazine for a while. I was asleep before eleven." "Ah, yes," said Mr. Fitweiler again. He was silent for a moment, searching for the proper words to say to the head of the filing department. "Mrs. Barrows," he said finally, "Mrs. Barrows has worked hard, Martin, very hard. It grieves me to report that she has suffered a severe breakdown. It has taken the form of a persecution complex accompanied by distressing hallucinations." "I am very sorry, sir," said Mr. Martin. "Mrs. Barrows is under the delusion," continued Mr. Fitweiler, "that you visited her last evening and behaved yourself in an—uh—unseemly manner." He raised his hand to silence Mr. Martin's little pained outcry. "It is the nature of these psychological diseases," Mr. Fitweiler said, "to fix upon the least likely and most innocent party as the—uh—source of persecution. These matters are not for the lay mind to grasp, Martin. I've just had my psychiatrist, Dr. Fitch, on the phone. He would not, of course, commit himself, but I suggested to Mrs. Barrows, when she had completed her—uh—story to me this morning, that she visit Dr. Fitch, for I suspected a condition at once. She flew, I regret to say, into a rage, and demanded— uh—requested that I call you on the carpet. You may not know, Martin, but Mrs. Barrows had planned a reorganization of your department—subject to my approval, of course, subject to my approval. This brought you, rather than anyone else, to her mind—but again that is a phenomenon for Dr. Fitch and not for us. So, Martin, I am afraid Mrs. Barrows' usefulness here is at an end." "I am dreadfully sorry, sir," said Mr. Martin.

It was at this point that the door to the office blew open with the suddenness of a gas-main explosion and Mrs. Barrows catapulted through it. "Is the little rat denying it?" she screamed. "He can't get away with that!" Mr. Martin got up and moved discreetly to a point beside Mr. Fitweiler's chair. "You drank and smoked at my apartment," she bawled at Mr. Martin, "and you know it! You called Mr. Fitweiler an old windbag and said you were going to blow him up when you got coked to the gills on your heroin!" She stopped yelling to catch her breath and a new glint came into her popping eyes. "If you weren't such a drab, ordinary little man," she said, "I'd think you'd planned it all. Sticking your tongue out, saying you were sitting in the catbird seat, because you thought no one would believe me when I told it! My God, it's really too perfect!" She brayed loudly and hysterically, and the fury was on her again. She glared at Mr. Fitweiler. "Can't you see how he has tricked us, you old fool? Can't you see his little game?" But Mr. Fitweiler had been surreptitiously pressing all the buttons under the top of his desk and employees of F & S began pouring into the room. "Stockton," said Mr. Fitweiler, "you and Fishbein will take Mrs. Barrows to her home. Mrs. Powell, you will go with them." Stockton, who had played a little football in high school, blocked Mrs. Barrows as she made for Mr. Martin. It took him and Fishbein together to force her out of the door into the hall, crowded with stenographers and office boys. She was still screaming imprecations at Mr. Martin, tangled and contradictory imprecations. The hubbub finally died out down the corridor.

"I regret that this has happened," said Mr. Fitweiler. "I shall ask you to dismiss it from your mind, Martin." "Yes, sir," said Mr. Martin, anticipating his chief's "That will be all" by moving to the door. "I will dismiss it." He went out and shut the door, and his step was light and quick in the hall. When he entered his department he had slowed down to his customary gait, and he walked quietly across the room to the W20 file, wearing a look of studious concentration.

QUESTIONS

1. When did you first realize the story was comic? What devices does Thurber use to maintain the comic aspect of the story?

2. What are some of the things about Mrs. Barrows that irritate Mr. Martin? How does Martin express this irritation?

3. Thurber is satirizing an aspect of modern life. What aspect is it? Which character or characters seem to embody it the most, and why?

4. The success of the story's conclusion resides in its irony. How does Thurber effectively create this irony?

Eudora Welty

A WORN PATH

It was December—a bright frozen day in the early morning. Far out in the country there was an old Negro woman with her head tied in a red rag, coming along a path through the pinewoods. Her name was Phoenix Jackson. She was very old and small and she walked slowly in the dark pine shadows, moving a little from side to side in her steps, with the balanced heaviness and lightness of a pendulum in a grandfather clock. She carried a thin, small cane made from an umbrella, and with this she kept tapping the frozen earth in front of her. This made a grave and persistent noise in the still air, that seemed meditative like the chirping of a solitary little bird.

She wore a dark striped dress reaching down to her shoe tops, and an equally long apron of bleached sugar sacks, with a full pocket: all neat and tidy, but every time she took a step she might have fallen over her shoe-laces, which dragged from her unlaced shoes. She looked straight ahead. Her eyes were blue with age. Her skin had a pattern all its own of numberless branching wrinkles and as though a whole little tree stood in the middle of her forehead, but a golden color ran underneath, and the two knobs of her cheeks were illuminated by a yellow burning under the dark. Under the red rag her hair came down on her neck in the frailest of ringlets, still black, and with an odor like copper.

Now and then there was a quivering in the thicket. Old Phoenix said, "Out of my way, all you foxes, owls, beetles, jack rabbits, coons, and wild animals! . . . Keep out from under these feet, little bob-whites. . . . Keep the big wild hogs out of my path. Don't let none of those come running my direction. I got a long way." Under her small black-freckled hand her cane, limber as a buggy whip, would switch at the brush as if to rouse up any hiding things.

On she went. The woods were deep and still. The sun made the pine needles almost too bright to look at, up where the wind rocked. The cones dropped as light as feathers. Down in the hollow was the mourning dove—it was not too late for him.

The path ran up a hill. "Seem like there is chains about my feet, time I get this far," she said, in the voice of argument old people keep to use with themselves. "Something always takes a hold of me on this hill—pleads I should stay."

After she got to the top she turned and gave a full, severe look behind her where she had come. "Up through pines," she said at length. "Now down through oaks."

Her eyes opened their widest, and she started down gently. But before she got to the bottom of the hill a bush caught her dress.

Her fingers were busy and intent, but her skirts were full and long, so that before she could pull them free in one place they were caught in another. It was not possible to allow the dress to tear. "I in the thorny bush," she said. "Thorns, you doing your appointed work. Never want to let folks pass—no sir. Old eyes thought you was a pretty little *green* bush."

Finally, trembling all over, she stood free, and after a moment dared to stoop for her cane.

"Sun so high!" she cried, leaning back and looking, while the thick tears went over her eyes. "The time getting all gone here."

At the foot of this hill was a place where a log was laid across the creek.

"Now comes the trial," said Phoenix.

Putting her right foot out, she mounted the log and shut her eyes. Lifting her skirt, levelling her cane fiercely before her, like a festival figure in some parade, she began to march across. Then she opened her eyes and she was safe on the other side.

"I wasn't as old as I thought," she said.

But she sat down to rest. She spread her skirts on the bank around her and folded her hands over her knees. Up above her was a tree in a pearly cloud of mistletoe. She did not dare to close her eyes, and when a little boy brought her a little plate with a slice of marble-cake on it she spoke to him. "That would be acceptable," she said. But when she went to take it there was just her own hand in the air.

So she left that tree, and had to go through a barbed-wire fence. There she had to creep and crawl, spreading her knees and stretching her fingers like a baby trying to climb the steps. But she talked loudly to herself: she could not let her dress be torn now, so late in the day, and she could not pay for having her arm or her leg sawed off if she got caught fast where she was.

At last she was safe through the fence and risen up out in the clearing. Big dead trees, like black men with one arm, were standing in the purple stalks of the withered cotton field. There sat a buzzard.

"Who you watching?"

In the furrow she made her way along.

"Glad this not the season for bulls," she said, looking sideways, "and the good Lord made his snakes to curl up and sleep in the winter. A pleasure I don't see no two-headed snake coming around that tree, where it come once. It took a while to get by him, back in the summer."

She passed through the old cotton and went into a field of dead corn. It whispered and shook and was taller than her head. "Through the maze now," she said, for there was no path.

Then there was something tall, black, and skinny there, moving before her.

At first she took it for a man. It could have been a man dancing in the field. But she stood still and listened, and it did not make a sound. It was as silent as a ghost.

"Ghost," she said sharply, "who be you the ghost of? For I have heard of nary death close by."

But there was no answer—only the ragged dancing in the wind.

She shut her eyes, reached out her hand, and touched a sleeve. She found a coat and inside that an emptiness, cold as ice.

"You scarecrow," she said. Her face lighted. "I ought to be shut up for good," she said with laughter. "My senses is gone. I too old. I the oldest people I ever know. Dance, old scarecrow," she said, "while I dancing with you."

She kicked her foot over the furrow, and with mouth drawn down, shook her head once or twice in a little strutting way. Some husks blew down and whirled in streamers about her skirts.

Then she went on, parting her way from side to side with the cane, through the whispering field. At last she came to the end, to a wagon track where the silver grass blew between the red ruts. The quail were walking around like pullets, seeming all dainty and unseen.

"Walk pretty," she said. "This the easy place. This the easy going."

She followed the track, swaying through the quiet bare fields, through the little strings of tree silver in their dead leaves, past cabins silver from weather, with the doors and windows boarded shut, all like old women under a spell sitting there. "I walking in their sleep," she said, nodding her head vigorously.

In a ravine she went where a spring was silently flowing through a hollow log. Old Phoenix bent and drank. "Sweet-gum makes the water sweet," she said, and drank more. "Nobody know who made this well, for it was here when I was born."

The track crossed a swampy part where the moss hung as white as lace from every limb. "Sleep on, alligators, and blow your bubbles." Then the track went into the road.

Deep, deep the road went down between the high green-colored banks. Overhead the live-oaks met, and it was as dark as a cave.

A black dog with a lolling tongue came up out of the weeds by the ditch. She was meditating, and not ready, and when he came at her she only hit him a little with her cane. Over she went in the ditch, like a little puff of milk-weed.

Down there, her senses drifted away. A dream visited her, and she reached her hand up, but nothing reached down and gave her a pull. So she lay there and presently went to talking. "Old woman," she said to herself, "that black dog come up out of the weeds to stall you off, and now there he sitting on his fine tail, smiling at you."

A white man finally came along and found her—a hunter, a young man, with his dog on a chain.

"Well, Granny!" he laughed. "What are you doing there?"

"Lying on my back like a June-bug waiting to be turned over, mister," she said, reaching up her hand.

He lifted her up, gave her a swing in the air, and set her down, "Anything broken, Granny?"

"No sir, them old dead weeds is springy enough," said Phoenix, when she had got her breath. "I thank you for your trouble."

"Where do you live, Granny?" he asked, while the two dogs were growling at each other.

"Away back yonder, sir, behind the ridge. You can't even see it from here."

"On your way home?"

"No, sir, I going to town."

"Why, that's too far! That's as far as I walk when I come out myself, and I get something for my trouble." He patted the stuffed bag he carried, and there hung down a little closed claw. It was one of the bob-whites, with its beak hooked bitterly to show it was dead. "Now you go on home, Granny!"

"I bound to go to town, mister," said Phoenix. "The time come around."

He gave another laugh, filling the whole landscape. "I know you old colored people! Wouldn't miss going to town to see Santa Claus!"

But something held Old Phoenix very still. The deep lines in her face went into a fierce and different radiation. Without warning, she had seen with her own eyes a flashing nickel fall out of the man's pocket onto the ground.

"How old are you, Granny?" he was saying.

"There is no telling, mister," she said, "no telling."

Then she gave a little cry and clapped her hands and said, "Git on away from here, dog! Look! Look at that dog!" She laughed as if in admiration. "He ain't scared of nobody. He a big black dog." She whispered, "Sic him!"

"Watch me get rid of that cur," said the man. "Sic him, Pete! Sic him!"

Phoenix heard the dogs fighting, and heard the man running and throwing sticks. She even heard a gunshot. But she was slowly bending forward by that time, further and further forward, the lids stretched down over her eyes, as if she were doing this in her sleep. Her chin was lowered almost to her knees. The yellow palm of her hand came out from the fold of her apron. Her fingers slid down and along the ground under the piece of money with the grace and care they would have in lifting an egg from under a sitting hen. The she slowly straightened up, she stood erect, and the nickel was in her apron pocket. A bird flew by. Her lips moved. "God watching me the whole time. I come to stealing."

The man came back, and his own dog panted about them. "Well, I scared him off that time," he said, and then he laughed and lifted his gun and pointed it at Phoenix.

She stood straight and faced him.

"Doesn't the gun scare you?" he said, still pointing it.

"No, sir, I seen plenty go off closer by, in my day, and for less than what I done," she said, holding utterly still.

He smiled, and shouldered the gun. "Well, Granny," he said, "you must be a hundred years old, and scared of nothing. I'd give you a dime if I had any money with me. But you take my advice and stay home, and nothing will happen to you."

"I bound to go on my way, mister," said Phoenix. She inclined her head in the red rag. Then they went in different directions, but she could hear the gun shooting again and again over the hill.

She walked on. The shadows hung from the oak trees to the road like curtains. Then she smelled wood-smoke, and smelled the river, and she saw a steeple and the cabins on their steep steps. Dozens of little black children whirled around her. There ahead was Natchez shining. Bells were ringing. She walked on.

In the paved city it was Christmas time. There were red and green electric lights strung and crisscrossed everywhere, and all turned on in the daytime. Old Phoenix would have been lost if she had not distrusted her eyesight and depended on her feet to know where to take her.

She paused quietly on the sidewalk where people were passing by. A lady came along in the crowd, carrying an armful of red-, green-, and silver-wrapped presents; she gave off perfume like the red roses in hot summer, and Phoenix stopped her.

"Please, missy, will you lace up my shoe?" She held up her foot.

"What do you want, Grandma?"

"See my shoe," said Phoenix. "Do all right for out in the country, but wouldn't look right to go in a big building."

"Stand still then, Grandma," said the lady. She put her packages down on the sidewalk beside her and laced and tied both shoes tightly.

"Can't lace 'em with a cane," said Phoenix. "Thank you, missy. I doesn't mind asking a nice lady to tie up my shoe, when I gets out on the street."

Moving slowly and from side to side, she went into the big building and into a tower of steps, where she walked up and around and around until her feet knew to stop.

She entered a door, and there she saw nailed up on the wall the document that had been stamped with the gold seal and framed in the gold frame, which matched the dream that was hung up in her head.

"Here I be," she said. There was a fixed and ceremonial stiffness over her body.

"A charity case, I suppose," said an attendant who sat at the desk before her.

But Phoenix only looked above her head. There was sweat on her face, the wrinkles in her skin shone like a bright net.

"Speak up, Grandma," the woman said. "What's your name? We must have your history, you know. Have you been here before? What seems to be the trouble with you?"

Old Phoenix only gave a twitch to her face as if a fly were bothering her.

"Are you deaf?" cried the attendant.

But then the nurse came in.

"Oh, that's just old Aunt Phoenix," she said. "She doesn't come for herself—she has a little grandson. She makes these trips just as regular as clockwork. She lives away back off the Old Natchez Trace." She bent down. "Well, Aunt Phoenix, why don't you just take a seat? We won't keep you standing after your long trip." She pointed.

The old woman sat down, bolt upright in the chair.

"Now, how is the boy?" asked the nurse.

Old Phoenix did not speak.

"I said, how is the boy?"

But Phoenix only waited and stared straight ahead, her face very solemn and withdrawn into rigidity.

"Is his throat any better?" asked the nurse. "Aunt Phoenix, don't you hear me? Is your grandson's throat any better since the last time you came for the medicine?"

With her hands on her knees, the old woman waited, silent, erect and motionless, just as if she were in armour.

"You mustn't take up our time this way, Aunt Phoenix," the nurse said. "Tell us quickly about your grandson, and get it over with. He isn't dead, is he?"

At last there came a flicker and then a flame of comprehension across her face, and she spoke.

"My grandson. It was my memory had left me. There I sat and forgot why I made my long trip."

"Forgot?" The nurse frowned. "After you came so far?"

Then Phoenix was like an old woman begging a dignified forgiveness for waking up frightened in the night. "I never did go to school, I was too old at the Surrender," she said in a soft voice. "I'm an old woman without an education. It was my memory fail me. My little grandson, he is just the same, and I forgot it in the coming."

"Throat never heals, does it?" said the nurse, speaking in a loud, sure voice to Old Phoenix. By now she had a card with something written on it, a little list. "Yes. Swallowed lye. When was it—January—two-three years ago—"

Phoenix spoke unasked now. "No, missy, he not dead, he just the same. Every little while his throat begin to close up again, and he not able to swallow. He not get his breath. He not able to help himself. So the time come around, and I go on another trip for the soothing medicine."

"All right. The doctor said as long as you came to get it, you could have it," said the nurse. "But it's an obstinate case."

"My little grandson, he sit up there in the house all wrapped up, waiting by himself," Phoenix went on. "We is the only two left in the world. He suffer and it don't seem to put him back at all. He got a sweet look. He going to last. He wear a little patch quilt and peep out holding his mouth open like a little bird. I remembers so plain now. I not going to forget him again, no, the whole enduring time. I could tell him from all the others in creation."

"All right." The nurse was trying to hush her now. She brought her a bottle of medicine. "Charity," she said, making a check mark in a book.

Old Phoenix held the bottle close to her eyes and then carefully put it into her pocket.

"I thank you," she said.

"It's Christmas time, Grandma," said the attendant. "Could I give you a few pennies out of my purse?"

"Five pennies is a nickel," said Phoenix stiffly.

"Here's a nickel," said the attendant.

Phoenix rose carefully and held out her hand. She received the nickel and then fished the other nickel out of her pocket and laid it beside the new one. She stared at her palm closely, with her head on one side.

Then she gave a tap with her cane on the floor.

"This is what come to me to do," she said. "I going to the store and buy my child a little windmill they sells, made out of paper. He going to find it hard to believe there such a thing in the world. I'll march myself back where he waiting, holding it straight up in this hand."

She lifted her free hand, gave a little nod, turned round, and walked out of the doctor's office. Then her slow step began on the stairs, going down.

QUESTIONS

1. What can you infer about Phoenix Jackson from her speech? From her dress? From her behavior toward others?

2. What type of character does Phoenix Jackson have? How did you reach your opinion? Why does she steal the hunter's nickel and get the other at the clinic?
3. What is the mood of the story? What is Phoenix Jackson's mood as she journeys to the clinic? What significance is there in her fantasy life and her forgetfulness? What do they demonstrate about her resolve?
4. Phoenix Jackson must overcome many obstacles on her journey. Do these obstacles have anything in common? Is there anything similar in the way Phoenix Jackson overcomes these obstacles?

John A. Williams

SON IN THE AFTERNOON

It was hot. I tend to be a bitch when it's hot. I goosed the little Ford over Sepulveda Boulevard toward Santa Monica until I got stuck in the traffic that pours from L.A. into the surrounding towns. I'd had a very lousy day at the studio.

I was—still am—a writer and this studio had hired me to check scripts and films with Negroes in them to make sure the Negro moviegoer wouldn't be offended. The signs were already clear that one day the whole of American industry would be racing pell-mell to get a Negro, showcase a spade. I was kind of a pioneer. I'm a *Negro* writer, you see. The day had been tough because of a couple of verbs—slink and walk. One of those Hollywood hippies had done a script calling for a Negro waiter to slink away from the table where a dinner party was glaring at him. I said the waiter should walk, not slink, because later on he becomes a hero. The Hollywood hippie, who understood it all because he had some colored friends, said that it was essential to the plot that the waiter slink. I said you don't slink one minute and become a hero the next; there has to be some consistency. The Negro actor I was standing up for said nothing either way. He had played Uncle Tom roles so long that he had become Uncle Tom. But the director agreed with me.

Anyway . . . . hear me out now. I was on my way to Santa Monica to pick up my mother, Nora. It was a long haul for such a hot day. I had planned a quiet evening: a nice shower, fresh clothes, and then I would have dinner at the Watkins and talk with some of the musicians on the scene for a quick taste before they cut to their gigs. After, I was going to the Pigalle down on Figueroa and catch Earl Grant at the organ, and still later, if nothing exciting happened, I'd pick up Scottie and make it to the Lighthouse on the Beach or to the Strollers and listen to some of the white boys play. I liked the long drive, especially while listening to Sleepy Stein's show on the radio. Later, much later of course, it would be home, back to Watts.

So you see, this picking up Nora was a little inconvenient. My mother was a maid for the Couchmans. Ronald Couchman was an architect, a good one I understood from

Nora who has a fine sense for this sort of thing; you don't work in some hundred-odd houses during your life without getting some idea of the way a house should be laid out. Couchman's wife, Kay, was a playgirl who drove a white Jaguar from one party to another. My mother didn't like her too much; she didn't seem to care much for her son, Ronald, junior. There's something wrong with a parent who can't really love her own child, Nora thought. The Couchmans lived in a real fine residential section, of course. A number of actors lived nearby, character actors, not really big stars.

Somehow it is very funny. I mean that the maids and butlers knew everything about these people, and these people knew nothing at all about the help. Through Nora and her friends I knew who was laying whose wife; who had money and who *really* had money; I knew about the wild parties hours before the police, and who smoked marijuana, when, and where they got it.

To get to Couchman's driveway I had to go three blocks up one side of a palm-planted center strip and back down the other. The driveway bent gently, then swept back out of sight of the main road. The house, sheltered by slim palms, looked like a transplanted New England Colonial. I parked and walked to the kitchen door, skirting the growling Great Dane who was tied to a tree. That was the route to the kitchen door.

I don't like kitchen doors. Entering people's houses by them, I mean. I'd done this thing most of my life when I called at places where Nora worked to pick up the patched or worn sheets or the half-eaten roasts, the battered, tarnished silver—the fringe benefits of a housemaid. As a teen-ager I'd told Nora I was through with that crap; I was not going through anyone's kitchen door. She only laughed and said I'd learn. One day soon after, I called for her and without knocking walked right through the front door of this house and right on through the living room. I was almost out of the room when I saw feet behind the couch. I leaned over and there was Mr. Jorgensen and his wife making out like crazy. I guess they thought Nora had gone and it must have hit them sort of suddenly and they went at it like the hell-bomb was due to drop any minute. I've been that way too, mostly in the spring. Of course, when Mr. Jorgensen looked over his shoulder and saw me, you know what happened. I was thrown out and Nora right behind me. It was the middle of winter, the old man was sick and the coal bill three months overdue. Nora was right about those kitchen doors: I learned.

My mother saw me before I could ring the bell. She opened the door. "Hello," she said. She was breathing hard, like she'd been running or something. "Come in and sit down. I don't know *where* that Kay is. Little Ronald is sick and she's probably out gettin' drunk again." She left me then and trotted back through the house, I guess to be with Ronnie. I hated the combination of her white nylon uniform, her dark brown face and the wide streaks of gray in her hair. Nora had married this guy from Texas a few years after the old man had died. He was all right. He made out okay. Nora didn't have to work, but she just couldn't be still; she always had to be doing something. I suggested she quit work, but I had as much luck as her husband. I used to tease her about liking to be around those white folks. It would have been good for her to take an extended trip around the country visiting my brothers and sisters. Once she got to Philadelphia, she could go right out to the cemetery and sit awhile with the old man.

I walked through the Couchman home. I liked the library. I thought if I knew Couchman I'd like him. The room made me feel like that. I left it and went into the big living room. You could tell that Couchman had let his wife do that. Everything in it was fast, dart-like, with no sense of ease. But on the walls were several of Couchman's conceptions of buildings and homes. I guess he was a disciple of Wright. My mother walked rapidly through the room without looking at me and said, "Just be patient, Wendell. She should be here real soon."

"Yeah," I said, "with a snootful." I had turned back to the drawings when Ronnie scampered into the room, his face twisted with rage.

"Nora!" he tried to roar, perhaps the way he'd seen the parents of some of his friends roar at their maids. I'm quite sure Kay didn't shout at Nora, and I don't think Couchman would. But then no one shouts at Nora. "Nora, you come right back here this minute!" the little bastard shouted and stamped and pointed to a spot on the floor where Nora was supposed to come to roost. I have a nasty temper. Sometimes it lies dormant for ages and at other times, like when the weather is hot and nothing seems to be going right, it's bubbling and ready to explode. "Don't talk to *my* mother like that, you little—!" I said sharply, breaking off just before I cursed. I wanted him to be large enough for me to strike. "How'd you like for me to talk to *your* mother like that?"

The nine-year-old looked up at me in surprise and confusion. He hadn't expected me to say anything. I was just another piece of furniture. Tears rose in his eyes and spilled out onto his pale cheeks. He put his hands behind him, twisted them. He moved backwards, away from me. He looked at my mother with a "Nora, come help me" look. And sure enough, there was Nora, speeding back across the room, gathering the kid in her arms, tucking his robe together. I was too angry to feel hatred for myself.

Ronnie was the Couchman's only kid. Nora loved him. I suppose that was the trouble. Couchman was gone ten, twelve hours a day. Kay didn't stay around the house any longer than she had to. So Ronnie had only my mother. I think kids should have someone to love, and Nora wasn't a bad sort. But somehow when the six of us, her own children, were growing up we never had her. She was gone, out scuffling to get those crumbs to put into our mouths and shoes for our feet and praying for something to happen so that all the space in between would be taken care of. Nora's affection for us took the form of rushing out into the morning's five o'clock blackness to wake some silly bitch and get her coffee; took form in her trudging five miles home every night instead of taking the streetcar to save money to buy tablets for us, to use at school, we said. But the truth was that all of us liked to draw and we went through a writing tablet in a couple of hours every day. Can you imagine? There's not a goddamn artist among us. We never had the physical affection, the pat on the head, the quick, smiling kiss, the "gimmee a hug" routine. All of this Ronnie was getting.

Now he buried his little blond head in Nora's breast and sobbed. "There, there now," Nora said. "Don't you cry, Ronnie. Ol' Wendell is just jealous, and he hasn't much sense either. He didn't mean nuthin'."

I left the room. Nora had hit it of course, hit it and passed on. I looked back. It didn't look so incongruous, the white and black together, I mean. Ronnie was still sobbing. His head bobbed gently on Nora's shoulder. The only time I ever got that close to her was when she trapped me with a bearhug so she could whale the daylights out of me after I put a snowball through Mrs. Grant's window. I walked outside and lit a cigarette. When Ronnie was in the hospital the month before, Nora got me to run her way over to Hollywood every night to see him. I didn't like that worth a damn. All right, I'll admit it: it did upset me. All that affection I didn't get nor my brothers and sisters going to that little white boy who, without a doubt, when away from her called her the names he'd learned from adults. Can you imagine a nine-year-old kid calling Nora a "girl," "our girl?" I spat at the Great Dane. He snarled and then. I bounced a rock off his fanny. "Lay down, you bastard," I muttered. It was a good thing he was tied up.

I heard the low cough of the Jaguar slapping against the road. The car was throttled down, and with a muted roar it swung into the driveway. The woman aimed it for me. I was evil enough not to move. I was tired of playing with these people. At the last moment, grinning, she swung the wheel over and braked. She bounded out of the car like a tennis player vaulting over a net.

"Hi," she said, tugging at her shorts.

"Hello."

"You're Nora's boy?"

"I'm Nora's son." Hell, I was as old as she was; besides, I can't stand "boy."

"Nora tells us you're working in Hollywood. Like it?"

"It's all right."

"You must be pretty talented."

We stood looking at each other while the dog whined for her attention. Kay had a nice body and it was well tanned. She was high, boy, was she high. Looking at her, I could feel myself going into my sexy bastard routine; sometimes I can swing it great. Maybe it all had to do with the business inside. Kay took off her sunglasses and took a good look at me. "Do you have a cigarette?"

I gave her one and lit it. "Nice tan," I said. Most white people I know think it's a great big deal if a Negro compliments them on their tans. It's a large laugh. You have all this volleyball about color and come summer you can't hold the white folks back from the beaches, anyplace where they can get some sun. And of course the blacker they get, the more pleased they are. Crazy. If there is ever a Negro revolt, it will come during the summer and Negroes will descend upon the beaches around the nation and paralyze the country. You can't conceal cattle prods and bombs and pistols and police dogs when you're showing your birthday suit to the sun.

"You like it?" she asked. She was pleased. She placed her arm next to mine. "Almost the same color," she said.

"Ronnie isn't feeling well," I said.

"Oh, the poor kid. I'm so glad we have Nora. She's such a charm. I'll run right in and look at him. Do have a drink in the bar. Fix me one too, will you?" Kay skipped inside and I went to the bar and poured out two strong drinks. I made hers stronger than mine. She was back soon. "Nora was trying to put him to sleep and she made me stay out." She giggled. She quickly tossed off her drink. "Another, please?" While I was fixing her drink she was saying how amazing it was for Nora to have such a talented son. What she was really saying was that it was amazing for a servant to have a son who was not also a servant. "Anything can happen in a democracy," I said. "Servants' sons drink with madames and so on."

"Oh, Nora isn't a servant," Kay said. "She's part of the family."

Yeah, I thought. Where and how many times had I heard *that* before?

In the ensuing silence, she started to admire her tan again. "You think it's pretty good, do you? You don't know how hard I worked to get it." I moved close to her and held her arm. I placed my other arm around her. She pretended not to see or feel it, but she wasn't trying to get away either. In fact she was pressing closer and the register in my brain that tells me at the precise moment when I'm in, went off. Kay was very high. I put both arms around her and she put both hers around me. When I kissed her, she responded completely.

"Mom!"

"Ronnie, come back to bed," I heard Nora shout from the other room. We could hear Ronnie running over the rug in the outer room. Kay tried to get away from me, push me to one side, because we could tell that Ronnie knew where to look for his Mom: he was running right for the bar, where we were. "Oh, please," she said, "don't let him see us." I wouldn't let her push me away. "Stop!" she hissed. "He'll see us!" We stopped struggling just for an instant, and we listened to the echoes of the word *see*. She gritted her teeth and renewed her efforts to get away.

Me? I had the scene laid right out. The kid breaks into the room, see, and sees his mother in this real wriggly clinch with this colored guy who's just shouted at him, see, and no matter how his mother explains it away, the kid has the image—the colored guy and his mother—for the rest of his life, see?

That's the way it happened. The kid's mother hissed under her breath, *"You're crazy!"* and she looked at me as though she were seeing me or something about me for the very first time. I'd released her as soon as Ronnie, romping into the bar, saw us and came to a full, open-mouthed halt. Kay went to him. He looked first at me, then at his mother. Kay turned to me, but she couldn't speak.

Outside in the living room my mother called, "Wendell, where are you? We can go now."

I started to move past Kay and Ronnie. I felt many things, but I made myself think mostly, *There you little bastard, there.*

My mother thrust her face inside the door and said, "Good-bye, Mrs. Couchman. See you tomorrow. 'Bye, Ronnie."

"Yes," Kay said, sort of stunned. "Tomorrow." She was reaching for Ronnie's hand as we left, but the kid was slapping her hand away. I hurried quickly after Nora, hating the long drive back to Watts.

QUESTIONS

1. What kind of man is the narrator? What different emotions does he display during the story? How do his race and race relations affect his point of view?
2. What does the narrator feel about Ronnie? What injustice exists in the way the narrator's mother treats her own son in comparison to the way she treats Ronnie?
3. What is the effect of telling the story in the first person? How would it have been different had it been told in the third person or from the viewpoint of one of the other characters?
4. At the end of the story, the narrator says "I felt many things." What might some of these things be?

Richard Wright

THE MAN WHO WAS ALMOST A MAN

Dave struck out across the fields, looking homeward through paling light. Whut's the use talkin wid 'em niggers in the field? Anyhow, his mother was putting supper on the table. Them niggers can't understan nothing. One of these days he was going to get a gun and practice shooting, then they couldn't talk to him as though he were a little boy. He slowed, looking at the ground. Shucks, Ah ain scareda them even ef they are biggern me! Aw, ah know whut Ahma do. Ahm going by ol Joe's sto n git that Sears Roebuck catlog n look at them guns. Mebbe Ma will lemme buy one when she gits mah pay from ol man Hawkins. Ahma beg her t gimme some money. Ahm ol ernough to hava gun. Ahm seventeen. Almost a man. He strode, feeling his long loose-jointed limbs. Shucks, a man oughta hava little gun aftah he done worked hard all day.

He came in sight of Joe's store. A yellow lantern glowed on the front porch. He mounted steps and went through the screen door, hearing it bang behind him. There was a strong smell of coal oil and mackerel fish. He felt very confident until he saw fat Joe walk in through the rear door, then his courage began to ooze.

"Howdy, Dave! Whutcha want?"

"How yuh, Mistah Joe? Aw, Ah don wanna buy nothing. Ah jus wanted t see ef yuhd lemme look at tha catlog erwhile."

"Sure! You wanna see it here?"

"Nawsuh, Ah wans t take it home wid me. Ah'll bring it back termorrow when Ah come in from the fiels."

"You plannin on buying something?"

"Yessuh."

"Your ma lettin you have your own money now?"

"Shucks. Mistah Joe, Ahm gittin t be a man like anybody else!"

Joe laughed and wiped his greasy white face with a red bandanna.

"Whut you plannin on buyin?"

Dave looked at the floor, scratched his head, scratched his thigh, and smiled. Then he looked up shyly.

"Ah'll tell yuh, Mistah Joe, ef yuh promise yuh won't tell."

"I promise."

"Waal, Ahma buy a gun."

"A gun? Whut you want with a gun?"

"Ah wanna keep it."

"You ain't nothing but a boy. You don't need a gun."

"Aw, lemme have the catlog, Mistah Joe. Ah'll bring it back."

Joe walked through the rear door. Dave was elated. He looked around at barrels of sugar and flour. He heard Joe coming back. He craned his neck to see if he was bringing the book. Yeah, he's got it. Gawddog, he's got it!

"Here, but be sure you bring it back. It's the only one I got."

"Sho, Mistah Joe."

"Say, if you wanna buy a gun, why don't you buy one from me? I gotta gun to sell."

"Will it shoot?"

"Sure it'll shoot."

"Whut kind is it?"

"Oh, it's kinda old . . . a left-handed Wheeler. A pistol. A big one."

"Is it got bullets in it?"

"It's loaded."

"Kin Ah see it?"

"Where's your money?"

"Whut yuh wan fer it?"

"I'll let you have it for two dollars."

"Just two dollahs? Shucks, Ah could buy tha when Ah git mah pay."

"I'll have it here when you want it."

"Awright, suh. Ah be in fer it."

He went through the door, hearing it slam again behind him. Ahma git some money from Ma n buy me a gun! Only two dollahs! He tucked the thick catalogue under his arm and hurried.

"Where yuh been, boy?" His mother held a steaming dish of black-eyed peas.

"Aw, Ma, ah jus stopped down the road to talk wid the boys."

"Yuh know bettah t keep suppah waitin."

He sat down, resting the catalogue on the edge of the table.

"Yuh git up from there and git to the well n wash yosef! Ah ain feedin no hogs in mah house!"

She grabbed his shoulder and pushed him. He stumbled out of the room, then came back to get the catalogue.

"Whut this?"

"Aw, Ma, it's jusa catlog."

"Who yuh git it from?"

"From Joe, down at the sto."

"Waal, thas good. We kin use it in the outhouse."

"Naw, Ma." He grabbed for it. "Gimme ma catlog, Ma."

She held onto it and glared at him.

"Quit hollerin at me! Whut's wrong wid yuh? Yuh crazy?"

"But Ma, please. It ain mine! It's Joe's! He tol me to bring it back t im termorrow."

She gave up the book. He stumbled down the back steps, hugging the thick book under his arm. When he had splashed water on his face and hands, he groped back to the kitchen and fumbled in a corner for the towel. He bumped into a chair; it clattered to the floor. The catalogue sprawled at his feet. When he had dried his eyes he snatched up the book and held it again under his arm. His mother stood watching him.

"Now, ef yuh gonna act a fool over that ol book, Ah'll take it n burn it up."

"Naw, Ma, please."

"Waal, set down n be still!"

He sat down and drew the oil lamp close. He thumbed page after page, unaware of the food his mother set on the table. His father came in. Then his small brother.

"Whutcha got there, Dave?" his father asked.

"Jusa catlog," he answered, not looking up.

"Yeah, here they is!" His eyes glowed at blue-and-black revolvers. He glanced up, feeling sudden guilt. His father was watching him. He eased the book under the table and rested it on his knees. After the blessing was asked, he ate. He scooped up peas and swallowed fat meat without chewing. Buttermilk helped to wash it down. He did not want to mention money before his father. He would do much better by cornering his mother when she was alone. He looked at his father uneasily out of the edge of his eye.

"Boy, how come yuh don quit foolin wid tha book n eat yo suppah?"

"Yessuh."

"How you n old man Hawkins gitten erlong?"

"Suh?"

"Can't yuh hear? Why don yuh lissen? As ast yu how wuz yuh n ol man Hawkins gittin erlong?"

"Oh, swell, Pa. Ah plows mo lan than anybody over there."

"Waal, yuh oughta keep yo mind on whut yuh doin."

"Yessuh."

He poured his plate full of molasses and sopped it up slowly with a chunk of cornbread. When his father and brother had left the kitchen, he still sat and looked again at the guns in the catalogue, longing to muster courage enough to present his case to his mother. Lawd, ef Ah only had tha pretty one! He could almost feel the slickness of the weapon with his fingers. If he had a gun like that he would polish it and keep it shining so it would never rust. N Ah'd keep it loaded, by Gawd!

"Ma?" His voice was hesitant.

"Hunh?"

"Ol man Hawkins give yuh mah money yit?"

"Yeah, but ain no usa yuh thinking bout throwin nona it erway. Ahme keeping tha money sos yuh kin have cloes t go to school this winter."

He rose and went to her side with the open catalogue in his palms. She was washing dishes, her head bent low over a pan. Shyly he raised the book. When he spoke, his voice was husky, faint.

"Ma, Gawd knows Ah wans one of these."

"One of whut?" she asked, not raising her eyes.

"One of these," he said again, not daring even to point. She glanced up at the page, then at him with wide eyes.

"Nigger, is yuh gone plumb crazy?"

"Aw, Ma—"

"Git outta here! Don yuh talk to me bout no gun! Yuh a fool!"

"Ma, Ah kin buy one fer two dollahs."

"Not ef Ah knows it, yuh ain!"

"But yuh promised me one—"

"Ah don care whut Ah promised! Yuh ain nothing but a boy yit!"

"Ma, ef yuh lemme buy one Ah'll *never* ast yuh fer nothing no mo."

"Ah tol yuh t git outta here! Yuh ain gonna toucha penny of tha money fer no gun! Thas how come Ah has Mistah Hawkins t pay yo wages t me, cause Ah knows yuh ain got no sense."

"But, Ma, we needa gun. Pa ain got no gun. We needa gun in the house. Yuh kin never tell whut might happen."

"Now don yuh try to maka fool outta me, boy! Ef we did hava gun, yuh wouldn't have it!"

He laid the catalogue down and slipped his arm around her waist.

"Aw, Ma, Ah done worked hard alla summer n ain ast yuh fer nothin, is Ah, now?"

"Thas whut yuh spose t do!"

"But Ma, Ah wans a gun. Yuh kin lemme have two dollahs outta mah money. Please, Ma. I kin give it to Pa . . . Please, Ma! Ah loves yuh, Ma."

When she spoke her voice came soft and low.

"Whut yu wan wida gun, Dave? Yuh don need no gun. Yuh'll git in trouble. N ef yo pa jus thought Ah let yuh have money to buy a gun he'd hava fit."

"I'll hide it, Ma. It ain but two dollahs."

"Lawd, chil, whut's wrong wid yuh?"

"Ain nothin wrong, Ma. Ahm almos a man now. Ah wans a gun."

"Who gonna sell yuh a gun?"

"Ol Joe at the sto."

"N it don cos but two dollahs?"

"Thas all, Ma. Jus two dollahs. Please, Ma."

She was stacking the plates away; her hands moved slowly, reflectively. Dave kept an anxious silence. Finally, she turned to him.

"Ah'll let yuh git tha gun ef yuh promise me one thing."

"Whut's tha, Ma?"

"Yuh bring it straight back t me, yuh hear? It be fer Pa."

"Yessum! Lemme go now, Ma."

She stooped, turned slightly to one side, raised the hem of her dress, rolled down the top of her stocking, and came up with a slender wad of bills.

"Here," she said. "Lawd knows yuh don need no gun. But yer pa does. Yuh bring it right back to me, yuh hear? Ahma put it up. Now ef yuh don, Ahma have yuh pa lick yuh so hard yuh won fergit it."

"Yessum."

He took the money, ran down the steps, and across the yard.

"Dave! Yuuuuuh Daaaaave!"

He heard, but he was not going to stop now. "Naw, Lawd!"

The first movement he made the following morning was to reach under his pillow for the gun. In the gray light of dawn he held it loosely, feeling a sense of power. Could kill a man with a gun like this. Kill anybody, black or white. And if he were holding his gun in his hand, nobody could run over him; they would have to respect him. It was a big gun, with a long barrel and a heavy handle. He raised and lowered it in his hand, marveling at its weight.

He had not come straight home with it as his mother had asked; instead he had stayed out in the fields, holding the weapon in his hand, aiming it now and then at some imaginary foe. But he had not fired it; he had been afraid that his father might hear. Also he was not sure he knew how to fire it.

To avoid surrendering the pistol he had not come into the house until he knew that they were all asleep. When his mother had tiptoed to his bedside late that night and demanded the gun, he had first played possum; then he had told her that the gun was hidden outdoors, that he would bring it to her in the morning. Now he lay turning it slowly in his hands. He broke it, took out the cartridges, felt them, and then put them back.

He slid out of bed, got a long strip of old flannel from a trunk, wrapped the gun in it, and tied it to his naked thigh while it was still loaded. He did not go in to breakfast. Even though it was not yet daylight, he started for Jim Hawkins' plantation. Just as the sun was rising he reached the barns where the mules and plows were kept.

"Hey! That you, Dave?"

He turned. Jim Hawkins stood eying him suspiciously.

"What're yuh doing here so early?"

"Ah didn't know Ah wuz gittin up so early, Mistah Hawkins. Ah wuz fixin t hitch up ol Jenny n take her t the fiels."

"Good. Since you're so early, how about plowing that stretch down by the woods?"

"Suits me, Mistah Hawkins."

"O.K. Go to it!"

He hitched Jenny to a plow and started across the fields. Hot dog! This was just what he wanted. If he could get down by the woods, he could shoot his gun and nobody would hear. He walked behind the plow, hearing the traces creaking, feeling the gun tied tight to his thigh.

When he reached the woods, he plowed two whole rows before he decided to take out the gun. Finally, he stopped, looked in all directions, then untied the gun and held it in his hand. He turned to the mule and smiled.

"Know whut this is, Jenny? Naw, yuh wouldn know! Yuhs jusa ol mule! Anyhow, this is a gun, n it kin shoot, by Gawd!"

He held the gun at arm's length. Whut t hell, Ahma shoot this thing! He looked at Jenny again.

"Lissen here, Jenny! When Ah pull this ol trigger, Ah don wan yuh t run n acka fool now!"

Jenny stood with head down, her short ears pricked straight. Dave walked off about twenty feet, held the gun far out from him at arm's length, and turned his head. Hell, he told himself, Ah ain afraid. The gun felt loose in his fingers; he waved it wildly for a moment. Then he shut his eyes and tightened his forefinger. Bloom! A report half deafened him and he thought his right hand was torn from his arm. He heard Jenny whinnying and galloping over the field, and he found himself on his knees, squeezing his fingers hard between his legs. His hand was numb; he jammed it into his mouth, trying to warm it, trying to stop the pain. The gun lay at his feet. He did not quite know what had happened. He stood up and stared at the gun as though it were a living thing. He gritted his teeth and kicked the gun. Yuh almos broke mah arm! He turned to look for Jenny; she was far over the fields, tossing her head and kicking wildly.

"Hol on there, ol mule!"

When he caught up with her she stood trembling, walling her big white eyes at him. The plow was far away; the traces had broken. Then Dave stopped short, looking, not believing. Jenny was bleeding. Her left side was red and wet with blood. He went closer.

Lawd, have mercy! Wondah did Ah shoot this mule? He grabbed for Jenny's mane. She flinched, snorted, whirled, tossing her head.

"Hol on now! Hol on."

Then he saw the hole in Jenny's side, right between the ribs. It was round, wet, red. A crimson stream streaked down the front leg, flowing fast, Good Gawd! Ah wuzn't shootin at tha mule. He felt panic. He knew he had to stop that blood, or Jenny would bleed to death. He had never seen so much blood in all his life. He chased the mule for half a mile, trying to catch her. Finally she stopped, breathing hard, stumpy tail half arched. He caught her mane and led her back to where the plow and gun lay. Then he stooped and grabbed handfuls of damp black earth and tried to plug the bullet hole. Jenny shuddered, whinnied, and broke from him.

"Hol on! Hol on now!"

He tried to plug it again, but blood came anyhow. His fingers were hot and sticky. He rubbed dirt into his palms, trying to dry them. Then again he attempted to plug the bullet hole, but Jenny shied away, kicking her heels high. He stood helpless. He had to do something. He ran at Jenny; she dodged him. He watched a red stream of blood flow down Jenny's leg and form a bright pool at her feet.

"Jenny . . . . Jenny," he called weakly.

His lips trembled. She's bleeding t death! He looked in the direction of home, wanting to go back, wanting to get help. But he saw the pistol lying in the damp black clay. He had a queer feeling that if he only did something, this would not be; Jenny would not be there bleeding to death.

When he went to her this time, she did not move. She stood with sleepy, dreamy eyes; and when he touched her she gave a low-pitched whinny and knelt to the ground, her front knees slopping in blood.

"Jenny . . . Jenny . . ." he whispered.

For a long time she held her neck erect; then her head sank, slowly. Her ribs swelled with a mighty heave and she went over.

Dave's stomach felt empty, very empty. He picked up the gun and held it gingerly between his thumb and forefinger. He buried it at the foot of a tree. He took a stick and tried to cover the pool of blood with dirt—but what was the use? There was Jenny lying with her mouth open and her eyes walled and glassy. He could not tell Jim Hawkins he had shot his mule. But he had to tell something. Yeah, Ah'll tell en Jenny started gittin wil n fell on the joint of the plow. . . . But that would hardly happen to a mule. He walked across the field slowly, head down.

It was sunset. Two of Jim Hawkins' men were over near the edge of the woods digging a hole in which to bury Jenny. Dave was surrounded by a knot of people, all of whom were looking down at the dead mule.

"I don't see how in the world it happened," said Jim Hawkins for the tenth time.

The crowd parted and Dave's mother, father, and small brother pushed into the center.

"Where Dave?" his mother called.

"There he is," said Jim Hawkins.

His mother grabbed him.

"What happened, Dave? Whut yuh done?"

"Nothin."

"C mon, boy, talk," his father said.

Dave took a deep breath and told the story he knew nobody believed.

"Waal," he drawled. "Ah brung ol Jenny down here sos Ah could do mah plowin. Ah plowed bout two rows, just like yuh see." He stopped and pointed at the long rows of upturned earth. "Then somethin musta been wrong wid ol Jenny. She wouldn ack right a-tall. She started snortin n kickin her heels. Ah tried t hol her, but she pulled erway, rearin n goin in. Then when the point of the plow was stickin up in the air, she swung erroun n twisted herself back on it . . . She stuck herself n started t bleed. N fo Ah could do anything, she wuz dead."

"Did you ever hear of anything like that in all your life?" asked Jim Hawkins.

There were white and black standing in the crowd. They murmured. Dave's mother came close to him and looked hard into his face. "Tell the truth, Dave," she said.

"Looks like a bullet hole to me," said one man.

"Dave, whut yuh do wid the gun?" his mother asked.

The crowd surged in, looking at him. He jammed his hands into his pockets, shook his head slowly from left to right, and backed away. His eyes were wide and painful.

"Did he hava gun?" asked Jim Hawkins.

"By Gawd, Ah tol yuh that wuz a gun wound," said a man, slapping his thigh.

His father caught his shoulders and shook him till his teeth rattled.

"Tell whut happened, yuh rascal! Tell whut . . ."

Dave looked at Jenny's stiff legs and began to cry.

"Whut yuh do wid tha gun?" his mother asked.

"Whut wuz he doin wida gun?" his father asked.

"Come on and tell the truth." said Hawkins. "Ain't nobody going to hurt you . . ."

His mother crowded close to him.

"Did yuh shoot tha mule, Dave?"

Dave cried, seeing blurred white and black faces.

"Ahh ddinn gggo tt sshooot hher . . . Ah ssswear ffo Gawd Ahh ddin. . . . Ah wuz a-tryin t sssee ef the old gggun would sshoot—"

"Where yuh git the gun from?" his father asked.

"Ah got it from Joe, at the sto."

"Where yuh git the money?"

"Ma give it t me."

"He kept worryin me, Bob. Ah had t. Ah tol im t bring the gun right back t me . . . It was fer yuh, the gun."

"But how yuh happen to shoot that mule?" asked Jim Hawkins.

"Ah wuzn shootin at the mule, Mistah Hawkins. The gun jumped when Ah pulled the trigger . . . N fo Ah knowed anythin Jenny was there a-bleedin."

Somebody in the crowd laughed. Jim Hawkins walked close to Dave and looked into his face.

"Well, looks like you have bought you a mule, Dave."

"Ah swear fo Gawd, Ah didn go t kill the mule, Mistah Hawkins!"

"But you killed her!"

All the crowd was laughing now. They stood on tiptoe and poked heads over one another's shoulders.

"Well, boy, look like yuh done bought a dead mule! Hahaha!"

"Ain tha ershame."

"Hohohohoho."

Dave stood, head down, twisting his feet in the dirt.

"Well, you needn't worry about it, Bob," said Jim Hawkins to Dave's father. "Just let the boy keep on working and pay me two dollars a month."

"Whut yuh wan fer yo mule, Mistah Hawkins?"

Jim Hawkins screwed up his eyes.

"Fifty dollars."

"Whut yuh do wid tha gun?" Dave's father demanded.

Dave said nothing.

"Yuh wan me t take a tree n beat yuh till yuh talk!"

"Nawsuh!"

"Whut yuh do wid it?"

"Ah throwed it erway."

"Where?"

"Ah . . . Ah throwed it in the creek."

"Waal, c mon home. N firs thing in the mawnin git to tha creek n fin tha gun."

"Yessuh."

"What yuh pay fer it?"

"Two dollahs."

"Take tha gun n git yo money back n carry it t Mistah Hawkins, yuh hear? N don fergit Ahma lam you black bottom good fer this! Now march yosef on home, suh!"

Dave turned and walked slowly. He heard people laughing. Dave glared, his eyes welling with tears. Hot anger bubbled in him. Then he swallowed and stumbled on.

That night Dave did not sleep. He was glad that he had gotten out of killing the mule so easily, but he was hurt. Something hot seemed to turn over inside him each time he remembered how they laughed. He tossed on his bed, feeling his hard pillow. N Pa says he's gonna beat me . . . He remembered other beatings, and his back quivered. Naw, naw, Ah sho don wan im t beat me tha way no mo. Dam em all! Nobody ever gave him anything. All he did was work. They treat me like a mule, n then they beat me. He gritted his teeth. N Ma had t tell on me.

Well, if he had to, he would take old man Hawkins that two dollars. But that meant selling the gun. And he wanted to keep that gun. Fifty dollars for a dead mule.

He turned over, thinking how he had fired the gun. He had an itch to fire it again. Ef other men kin shoota gun, by Gawd, Ah kin! He was still, listening. Mebbe they all sleepin now. The house was still. He heard the soft breathing of his brother. Yes, now! He would go down and get that gun and see if he could fire it! He eased out of bed and slipped into overalls.

The moon was bright. He ran almost all the way to the edge of the woods. He stumbled over the ground, looking for the spot where he had buried the gun. Yeah, here it is. Like a hungry dog scratching for a bone, he pawed it up. He puffed is black cheeks and blew dirt from the trigger and barrel. He broke it and found four cartridges unshot.

He looked around; the fields were filled with silence and moonlight. He clutched the gun stiff and hard in his fingers. But, as soon as he wanted to pull the trigger, he shut his eyes and turned his head. Naw, Ah can't shoot wid mah eyes closed n mah head turned. With effort he held his eyes open; then he squeezed. *Blooooom!* He was stiff, not breathing. The gun was still in his hands. Dammit, he'd done it. He fired again. *Blooooom!* He smiled. *Bloooom! Bloooom! Click, click.* There! It was empty. If anybody could shoot a gun, he could. He put the gun into his hip pocket and started across the fields.

When he reached the top of a ridge he stood straight and proud in the moonlight, looking at Jim Hawkins' big white house, feeling the gun sagging in his pocket. Lawd, ef Ah had just one mo bullet Ah'd taka shot at tha house. Ah'd like t scare ol man Hawkins jusa little . . . Jusa enough t let im know Dave Saunders is a man.

To his left the road curved, running to the tracks of the Illinois Central. He jerked his head, listening. From far off came a faint *hoooof-hoooof; hoooof-hoooof; hoooof-hoooof.* . . . He stood rigid. Two dollahs a mont. Les see now . . . Tha means it'll take bout two years. Shucks! Ah'll be dam!

He started down the road, toward the tracks. Yeah, here she comes! He stood beside the track and held himself stiffly. Here she comes, erroun the ben . . . C mon, yuh slow poke! C mon! He had his hand on his gun; something quivered in his stomach. Then the train thundered past, the gray and brown box cars rumbling and clinking. He gripped the gun tightly; then he jerked his hand out of his pocket. Ah betcha Bill wouldn't do it! Ah betcha . . . The cars slid past, steel grinding upon steel. Ahm ridin yuh ternight, so hep me Gawd! He was hot all over. He hesitated just a moment; then he grabbed, pulled atop of a car, and lay flat. He felt his pocket; the gun was still there. Ahead the long rails were glinting in the moonlight, stretching away, away to some- where, somewhere where he could be a man . . .

QUESTIONS

1. Why does Dave want to buy a gun? Do you feel he is justified in his desire?
2. Critics have said Richard Wright has a good ear for dialogue. Does this story confirm this view? Explain.
3. How much of Dave's desire to become more manly is a result of being a typical adolescent? How much can be attributed to his race and class?
4. Why does Dave leave town at the end of the story? Is this an act of courage or cowardice? Does it make him more of a "man" or less of one?

Caste & Class

Fiction

TOPICS FOR WRITING

1. Many stories in this section depict the individual victimized by race, class, or both. Write a first-person narrative describing a time when you were victimized owing to your race, class, gender, or anything else that prejudiced people against you.
2. Select the character you admire most from among the stories you have read in this section. Explain what qualities you admire about that character, and why those qualities are particularly important to you.
3. Describe the evolution in self-awareness of Dave in "The Man Who Was Almost a Man."
4. Many of the characters in these stories learn to compromise their ambitions and impulses because of their circumstances. Select any two stories and compare and contrast the way the major characters employ the strategy of compromise in their dealings with others.
5. Both the character Kiswana Browne in the story by Gloria Naylor and the narrator in "Son in the Afternoon" by John A. Williams defy the status quo inherent in their social circumstances. Write a paper in which you discuss what the status quo is that they are rebelling against, and their method of rebellion.
6. Blaming society for one's own struggles is just an excuse. It is up to the individual to rise above one's circumstances. Argue for or against the proposition.
7. The tragedy of James and Jessie Patton would not occur today because equality among the races has greatly advanced since the time in which "A Summer Tragedy" was written. Argue for or against this proposition.
8. As a research project, select one of the stories in this section and another story by the same author. Compare and contrast each story for style, theme, and setting.
9. Satire is a means writers have used to reveal some of the more absurd aspects of our social life. Write a research paper wherein you define and describe the elements of satire. Then use "The Catbird Seat" as an example to elucidate your research.

525

P o e t r y

Maya Angelou

SOUTHEAST ARKANASIA

After Eli Whitney's gin
brought to generations' end
bartered flesh and broken bones
Did it cleanse you of your sin
    Did you ponder?   5

Now, when farmers bury wheat
and the cow men dump the sweet
butter down on Davy Jones
Does it sanctify your street
    Do you wonder?   10

Or is guilt your nightly mare
bucking wake your evenings' share
of the stilled repair of groans
and the absence of despair
        over yonder?   15

Margaret Atwood

THE CITY PLANNERS

Cruising these residential Sunday
streets in dry August sunlight:
what offends us is
the sanities:
the houses in pedantic rows, the planted   5
sanitary trees, assert
levelness of surface like a rebuke
to the dent in our car door.
No shouting here, or
shatter of glass; nothing more abrupt   10
than the rational whine of a power mower
cutting a straight swath in the discouraged grass.

But though the driveways neatly
sidestep hysteria
by being even, the roofs all display   15
the same slant of avoidance to the hot sky,
certain things:
the smell of spilled oil a faint

sickness lingering in the garages,
a splash of paint on brick surprising as a bruise,   20
a plastic hose poised in a vicious
coil; even the too-fixed stare of the wide windows

give momentary access to
the landscape behind or under
the future cracks in the plaster   25

when the houses, capsized, will slide
obliquely into the clay seas, gradual as glaciers
that right now nobody notices.

That is where the City Planners
with the insane faces of political conspirators   30
are scattered over unsurveyed
territories, concealed from each other,
each in his own private blizzard;

guessing directions, they sketch
transitory lines rigid as wooden borders   35
on a wall in the white vanishing air

tracing the panic of suburb
order in a bland madness of snows.

QUESTIONS

1. How does Atwood use imagery and tone to establish the sense of place?
2. What is the theme of the poem? How does the form of the poem reflect its theme?
3. Atwood describes both the surface features of the town and what is "below the surface." How does the juxtaposition of these two aspects create psychological tension in the poem?
4. Atwood is often called a feminist writer. What in this poem reveals that aspect of her ideology?

Elizabeth Bishop

FILLING STATION

Oh, but it is dirty!
—this little filling station,
oil-soaked, oil-permeated
to a disturbing, over-all
black translucency.   5
Be careful with that match!

Father wears a dirty,
oil-soaked monkey suit
that cuts him under the arms,
and several quick and saucy   10
and greasy sons assist him
(it's a family filling station),
all quite thoroughly dirty.

Do they live in the station?
It has a cement porch   15

behind the pumps, and on it
a set of crushed and grease-
impregnated wickerwork;
on the wicker sofa
a dirty dog, quite comfy.   20

Some comic books provide
the only note of color—
of certain color. They lie
upon a big dim doily
draping a taboret   25
(part of the set), beside
a big hirsute begonia.

Why the extraneous plant?
Why the taboret?
Why, oh why, the doily?   30
(Embroidered in daisy stitch
with marguerites, I think,
and heavy with gray crochet.)

Somebody embroidered the doily.
Somebody waters the plant,   35
or oils it, maybe. Somebody
arranges the rows of cans
so that they softly say:
ESSO—SO—SO—SO
to high-strung automobiles.   40
Somebody loves us all.

William Blake

LONDON

I wander thro' each charter'd street,
Near where the charter'd Thames does flow,
And mark in every face I meet
Marks of weakness, marks of woe.

In every cry of every Man,   5
In every Infant's cry of fear,

In every voice, in every ban,
The mind-forg'd manacles I hear.

How the Chimney-sweeper's cry   10
Every black'ning Church appalls;
And the hapless Soldier's sigh
Runs in blood down Palace walls.

But most thro' midnight streets I hear
How the youthful Harlot's curse
Blasts the new born Infant's tear,   15
And blights with plagues the Marriage hearse.

Gwendolyn Brooks

WE REAL COOL

The Pool Players.
Seven at the Golden Shovel.

We real cool. We
Left school. We

Lurk late. We   5
Strike straight. We

Sing sin. We
Thin gin. We

Jazz June. We
Die soon.   10

Sterling A. Brown

SOUTHERN ROAD

Swing dat hammer—hunh—
Steady, bo';
Swing dat hammer—hunh—
Steady, bo';
Ain't no rush, bcbby,   5
Long ways to go.

Burner tore his—hunh—
Black heart away;
Burner tore his—hunh—
Black heart away;   10
Got me life, bebby,
An' a day.

Gal's on Fifth Street—hunh—
Son done gone;
Gal's on Fifth Street—hunh—   15
Son done gone;
Wife's in de ward, bebby,
Babe's not bo'n.

My ole man died—hunh—
Cussin' me;   20
My ole man died—hunh—
Cussin' me;
Ole lady rocks, bebby,
Huh misery.

Doubleshackled—hunh—   25
Guard behin';
Doubleshackled—hunh—
Guard behin';
Ball an' chain, bebby,
On my min'.   30

White man tells me—hunh—
Damn yo' soul;
White man tells me—hunh—
Damn yo' soul;

Got no need, bebby,   35
To be tole.

Chain gang nevah—hunh—
Let me go;
Chain gang nevah—hunh—
Let me go;   40
Po' los' boy, bebby,
Evahmo'. . . .

QUESTIONS

1. What is the function of repetition in "Southern Road"?
2. Is this a song or poem or both? Should it be read or sung? What elements in it contribute to your definition?
3. What is the speaker of the poem protesting? What does he forecast for his future?

Lorna Dee Cervantes

REFUGEE SHIP

Like wet cornstarch, I slide
past my grandmother's eyes. Bible
at her side, she removes her glasses.
The pudding thickens.

Mama raised me without language.   5
I'm orphaned from my Spanish name.
The words are foreign, stumbling
on my tongue. I see in the mirror
my reflection: bronzed skin, black hair.

I feel I am a captive   10
aboard the refugee ship.
The ship that will never dock.
El barco que nunca atraca.

Judith Ortiz Cofer

WHAT THE GYPSY SAID TO HER CHILDREN

We are like the dead
invisible to those who do not
want to see,
and color is our only protection against
the killing silence of their eyes,   5
the crimson of our tents pitched
like a scream
in the fields of our foes,
the amber warmth of our fires
where we gather to lift our voices   10
in the purple lament of our songs,
And beyond the scope of their senses
where all colors blend into one
we will build our cities of light,
we will carve them   15
out of the granite of their hatred,
with our own brown hands.

Countee Cullen

INCIDENT

(For Eric Walrond)

Once riding in old Baltimore,
  Heart-filled, head-filled with glee,
I saw a Baltimorean
  Keep looking straight at me.

Now I was eight and very small,   5
  And he was no whit bigger,
And so I smiled, but he poked out
  His tongue, and called me, "Nigger."

I saw the whole of Baltimore
    From May until December;   10
Of all the things that happened there
    That's all that I remember.

Gisele Fong

CORROSION

Ashamed of you
    woman pushing her way rudely to the snowpeas
    Loud restaurants and the slurpings, accents,
        the strange animal parts
        that show up in your soup   5
    Old man sitting on a corner
        slowly rocking, slowly rocking,
        ranting of old days,
        as the pigeons
            clutter   10
        by his feet
You are not a part of me.

I am
    a normal teenager
    eat pizza, go roller skating, listen to top 40   15
    flirt with boys, go to the beach;
    fit in.

"Are you Chinese, Japanese, Korean, Filipino, Hawaiian?
    Do you eat lice . . . Do you know Bruce?
    Oh AAAAH So, Sukiyaki!   20
        Sahlee, Chalee!"
You are not a part of me.

Immigrant, sweatshop woman,
    kung fu man, laundry worker,
    Chinese waiter, computer nerd.   25
You are not a part of me.

Eyes, tongue,
  leg, breast,
    heart
You are not a part of me.   30

Carolyn Forché

DULCIMER MAKER

Calf-deep in spruce dust
wood curls off his knife
blade wet bare bulb light.

The finish of his hands
shows oil, grain, knots   5
where his growth scarred him.

Planing black oak
thin to flow sounds.
Tones of wind filling
bottle lips.   10

It is his work tying strings
across fresh-cut pine.

He sings into wood, listens:
tree rings, water!

The wood drinks his cloth,   15
its roots going to the depths of him,
spreading.

He wants to build a lute for music
carved on Sumerian stones, a music
no one has heard for three thousand years.   20

For this he will work
the oldest wood he can find.
It will not be as far away,
as unfamiliar.

Robert Frost

MENDING WALL

Something there is that doesn't love a wall,
That sends the frozen-ground-swell under it,
And spills the upper boulders in the sun;
And makes gaps even two can pass abreast.
The work of hunters is another thing: 5
I have come after them and made repair
Where they have left not one stone on a stone,
But they would have the rabbit out of hiding,
To please the yelping dogs. The gaps I mean,
No one has seen them made or heard them made,   10
But at spring mending-time we find them there.
I let my neighbor know beyond the hill;
And on a day we meet to walk the line
And set the wall between us once again.
We keep the wall between us as we go.   15
To each the boulders that have fallen to each.
And some are loaves and some so nearly balls
We have to use a spell to make them balance:
'Stay where you are until our backs are turned!'
We wear our fingers rough with handling them.   20
Oh, just another kind of outdoor game,
One on a side. It comes to little more:
There where it is we do not need the wall:
He is all pine and I am apple orchard.
My apple trees will never get across   25
And eat the cones under his pines, I tell him.
He only says, 'Good fences make good neighbors.'
Spring is the mischief in me, and I wonder
If I could put a notion in his head:
'*Why* do they make good neighbors? Isn't it   30
Where there are cows? But here there are no cows.
Before I built a wall I'd ask to know
What I was walling in or walling out,
And to whom I was like to give offense.
Something there is that doesn't love a wall,   35
That wants it down.' I could say 'Elves' to him,
But it's not elves exactly, and I'd rather
He said it for himself. I see him there
Bringing a stone grasped firmly by the top
In each hand, like an old-stone savage armed.   40

He moves in darkness as it seems to me,
Not of woods only and the shade of trees.
He will not go behind his father's saying,
And he likes having thought of it so well
He says again, 'Good fences make good neighbors.'   45

Thom Gunn

ON THE MOVE

'Man, you gotta Go!

The blue jay scuffling in the bushes follows
Some hidden purpose, and the gust of birds
That spurts across the field, the wheeling swallows,
Have nested in the trees and undergrowth.
Seeking their instinct, or their poise, or both.   5
One moves with an uncertain violence
Under the dust thrown by a baffled sense
Or the dull-thunder of approximate words.

On motorcycles, up the road, they come:
Small, black, as flies hanging in heat, the Boys,   10
Until the distance throws them forth, their hum
Bulges to thunder held by calf and thigh.
In goggles, donned impersonality,
In gleaming jackets trophied with the dust,
They strap in doubt—by hiding it, robust—   15
And almost hear a meaning in their noise.

Exact conclusion of their hardiness
Has no shape yet, but from known whereabouts
They ride, direction where the tires press.
They scare a flight of birds across the field: 20
Much that is natural, to the will must yield.
Men manufacture both machine and soul,
And use what they imperfectly control
To dare a future from the taken routes.

It is a part solution, after all.   25
One is not necessarily discord

On earth; or damned because, half animal,
One lacks direct instinct, because one wakes
Afloat on movement that divides and breaks.
One joins the movement in a valueless world,   30
Choosing it, till, both hurler and the hurled,
One moves as well, always toward, toward.

A minute holds them, who have come to go:
The self-defined, astride the created will
They burst away; the towns they travel through   35
Are home for neither bird nor holiness,
For birds and saints complete their purposes.
At worst, one is in motion; and at best,
Reaching no absolute, in which to rest,
One is always nearer by not keeping still.   40

QUESTIONS

1. What is the primary difference between nature and human purpose as presented in the poem? What evidence do you have for your view?
2. Examine the way assonance (the repetition of vowel sounds) is used in stanza 1. Which words contain this device? What is its effect?
3. The poet says "men manufacture both machine and soul." What does this portend for the way humans encounter and deal with their experience?

Joy Harjo

I GIVE YOU BACK

I release you, my beautiful and terrible
fear. I release you. You were my beloved
and hated twin, but now, I don't know you
as myself. I release you with all the
pain I would know at the death of   5
my daughters.

You are not my blood anymore.

I give you back to the white soldiers
who burned down my home, beheaded my children,

raped and sodomized my brothers and sisters.   10
I give you back to those who stole the
food from our plates when we were starving.

I release you, fear, because you hold
these scenes in front of me and I was born
with eyes that can never close.   15

I release you, fear, so you can no longer
keep me naked and frozen in the winter,
or smothered under blankets in the summer.

I release you
I release you   20
I release you
I release you

I am not afraid to be angry.
I am not afraid to rejoice.
I am not afraid to be black.   25
I am not afraid to be white.
I am not afraid to be hungry.
I am not afraid to be full.
I am not afraid to be hated.
I am not afraid to be loved.   30

to be loved, to be loved, fear.

Oh, you have choked me, but I gave you the leash.
You have gutted me but I gave you the knife.
You have devoured me, but I laid myself across the fire.
You held my mother down and raped her,   35
                    but I gave you the heated thing.

I take myself back, fear.
You are not my shadow any longer.
I won't hold you in my hands.
You can't live in my eyes, my ears, my voice   40
my belly, or in my heart my heart
my heart my heart

But come here, fear
I am alive and you are so afraid
                    of dying.   45

Langston Hughes

EVENIN' AIR BLUES

Folks, I come up North
Cause they told me de North was fine.
I come up North
Cause they told me de North was fine.
Been up here six months—   5
I'm about to lose my mind.

This mornin' for breakfast
I chawed de mornin' air.
This mornin' for breakfast
Chawed de mornin' air.   10
But this evenin' for supper,
I got evenin' air to spare.

Believe I'll do a little dancin'
Just to drive my blues away—
A little dancin'   15
To drive my blues away,
Cause when I'm dancin'
De blues forgets to stay.

But if you was to ask me
How de blues they come to be,   20
Says if you was to ask me
How de blues they come to be—
You wouldn't need to ask me:
Just look at me and see!

THE NEGRO SPEAKS
OF RIVERS

I've known rivers:
I've known rivers ancient as the world and older than the flow of human
   blood in human veins.

My soul has grown deep like the rivers.

I bathed in the Euphrates when dawns were young.   5
I built my hut near the Congo and it lulled me to sleep.
I looked upon the Nile and raised the pyramids above it.
I heard the singing of the Mississippi when Abe Lincoln went down to New
    Orleans, and I've seen its muddy bosom turn all golden in the sunset.

I've known rivers: 10
Ancient, dusky rivers.

My soul has grown deep like the rivers.

SHARE-CROPPERS

Just a herd of Negroes
Driven to the field,
Plowing, planting, hoeing,
To make the cotton yield.

When the cotton's picked   5
And the work is done
Boss man takes the money
And we get none,

Leaves us hungry, ragged
As we were before.   10
Year by year goes by
And we are nothing more

Than a herd of Negroes
Driven to the field—
Plowing life away   15
To make the cotton yield.

VAGABONDS

We are the desperate
Who do not care,
The hungry
Who have nowhere

To eat,   5
No place to sleep,
The tearless
Who cannot
Weep.

Lawson Fusao Inada

NIGHTSONG IN ASIAN AMERICA

**For the living memory of
John Okada, pioneer, novelist:
No-No Boy, 1957**

The sky fits perfectly on all matter.
Nothing is jagged enough: volcanic
mass of the Cascades; structures of Seattle.

To come upon disaster at Cottage Grove—
the smashed front end of a Chevrolet,   5
occupants and lights strewn in order . . .

Which is why the moon hides
half of itself over Roseburg, or beacons
seek and find in the cracks of cliffs.

Napa tsukemono in the back seat   10
spreads its lovely, abundant musk

Everything we eat needs rice.
These supplies must reach the people.

Philip Levine

SPRING IN THE OLD WORLD

In the central terminal rain pouring
through the broken glass on the trains below,
loading and unloading. Above the gray dome
the great sky twisting in from the North Sea.
Cold, wet, wondering, I stood in the corner.   5
A dark boy walked in off the streets, a shepherd
born of shepherds. At 14 come to Tetuan
for work, then to Ceuta, Algeciras, Amsterdam.
His robes black now with rain, he cracks
sunflower seeds between his teeth, *pipas*   10
he calls them, and spits the shells and laughs.
In the lower Atlas the hills are green
where his brothers and he raced
through the long grass and wildflowers,
shouting to the air, their skirts   15
flared out around them, open and burning.

QUESTIONS

1. What irony exists in the title?
2. In what two continents does the action described in the poem take place?
3. How does the poet create mood and atmosphere in describing the train terminal?
   How are they contrasted in the final five lines of the poem?

Shirley Geok-lin Lim

MODERN SECRETS

Last night I dreamt in Chinese.
Eating Yankee shredded wheat
I said it in English
To a friend who answered

In monosyllables: 5
All of which I understood.

The dream shrank to its fiction.
I had understood its end
Many years ago. The sallow child
Ate rice from its ricebowl   10
And hides still in the cupboard
With the china and tea-leaves.

Claude McKay

OUTCAST

For the dim regions whence my fathers came
My spirit, bondaged by the body, longs.
Words felt, but never heard, my lips would frame;
My soul would sing forgotten jungle songs.
I would go back to darkness and to peace,   5
But the great western world holds me in fee,
And I may never hope for full release
While to its alien gods I bend my knee.
Something in me is lost, forever lost,
Some vital thing has gone out of my heart,   10
And I must walk the way of life a ghost
Among the sons of earth, a thing apart.

For I was born, far from my native clime,
Under the white man's menace, out of time.

Marianne Moore

THE STEEPLE-JACK

Revised, 1961

Dürer[1] would have seen a reason for living
    in a town like this, with eight stranded whales
to look at; with the sweet sea air coming into your house
on a fine day, from water etched
    with waves as formal as the scales   5
on a fish.

One by one in two's and three's, the seagulls keep
    flying back and forth over the town clock,
or sailing around the lighthouse without moving their wings—
rising steadily with a slight   10
    quiver of the body—or flock
mewing where

a sea the purple of the peacock's neck is
    paled to greenish azure as Dürer changed
the pine green of the Tyrol to peacock blue and guinea   15
gray. You can see a twenty-five-
    pound lobster; and fish nest arranged
to dry. The

whirlwind fife-and-drum of the storm bends the salt
    marsh grass, disturbs stars in the sky and the   20
star on the steeple; it is a privilege to see so
much confusion. Disguised by what
    might seem the opposite, the sea-
side flowers and

trees are favored by the fog so that you have   25
    the tropics at first hand: the trumpet vine,
foxglove, giant snapdragon, a salpiglossis that has
spots and stripes; morning-glories, gourds,
    or moon-vines trained on fishing twine
at the back door: 30

cattails, flags, blueberries and spiderwort,
    striped grass, lichens, sunflowers, asters, daisies—

[1]Albrecht Dürer (1471–1528), German artist.

yellow and crab-claw ragged sailors with green bracts—toad-plant,
petunias, ferns; pink lilies, blue
    ones, tigers; poppies; black sweet-peas.   35
The climate

is not right for the banyan, frangipani, or
    jack-fruit trees; or for exotic serpent
life. Ring lizard and snakeskin for the foot, if you see fit;
but here they've cats, not cobras, to   40
    keep down the rats. The diffident
little newt[2]

with white pin-dots on black horizontal spaced-
    out bands lives here; yet there is nothing that
ambition can buy or take away. The college student   45
named Ambrose sits on the hillside
    with his not-native books and hat
and sees boats

at sea progress white and rigid as if in
    a groove. Liking an elegance of which   50
the source is not bravado, he knows by heart the antique
sugar-bowl shaped summerhouse of
    interlacing slats, and the pitch
of the church

spire, not true, from which a man in scarlet lets   55
    down a rope as a spider spins a thread;
he might be part of a novel, but on the sidewalk a
sign says C. J. Poole, Steeple Jack,[3]
    in black and white; and one in red
and white says   60

Danger. The church portico has four fluted
    columns, each a single piece of stone, made
modester by whitewash. This would be a fit haven for
waifs, children, animals, prisoners,
    and presidents who have repaid   65
sin-driven

[2] Small salamander.
[3] Moore identifies him as the steeple-jack "who removed the Lafayette Avenue Presbyterian Church steeple at the time the 8th Avenue Independent Subway on Lafayette Avenue was being completed, threatening the foundation and other stonework of the church."

senators by not thinking about them. The
 place has a schoolhouse, a post-office in a
store, fish-houses, hen-houses, a three-masted schooner on
the stocks. The hero, the student,   70
 the steeple jack, each in his way,
is at home.

It could not be dangerous to be living
 in a town like this, of simple people,
who have a steeple-jack placing danger signs by the church   75
while he is gilding the solid-
 pointed star, which on a steeple
stands for hope.

Pat Mora

ELENA

My Spanish isn't enough.
I remember how I'd smile
listening to my little ones,
understanding every word they'd say,
their jokes, their songs, their plots.   5
   Vamos a pedirle dulces a mamá. Vamos.
But that was in Mexico.
Now my children go to American high schools.
They speak English. At night they sit around
the kitchen table, laugh with one another.   10
I stand by the stove and feel dumb, alone.
I bought a book to learn English.
My husband frowned, drank more beer.
My oldest said, *"Mamá,* he doesn't want you
to be smarter than he is." I'm forty,   15
embarrassed at mispronouncing words,
embarrassed at the laughter of my children,
the grocer, the mailman. Sometimes I take
my English book and lock myself in the bathroom,
say the thick words softly,   20
for if I stop trying, I will be deaf
when my children need my help.

QUESTIONS

1. What are the main problems the narrator has developed after having moved to the United States? How does she try to rectify them? How successful is she?
2. What does the narrator fear when she says "I will be deaf when my children need my help"?
3. The narrator contends that she does not speak English well. Does the way she uses English in the poem reinforce this or refute it?

Carlos Nejar

OIL LAMPS

Jesualdo Monte,
when you are free
there will be no bundle
on your back.

Today you rip away   5
the paper wrap
that set the fence on fire
around your master's land.

When you are free
there will be no bundle   10
on your back.
No more stables
no more ration cards
no more laughing whips
that punish your belly   15
that punish your dreams.

When you are free
there will be no bundle
on your back.

Alexander Pushkin

A SOWER WENT OUT
TO SOW HIS SEED

The seeds of freedom freely sowing
I rose betimes, before the sun.
In faith and innocence unknowing
I plied the furrows, one by one.
The fruits I sowed were never tasted,   5
My labour lost, my fervour wasted.
For strength expended—nothing won!

Graze on, ye peaceful sheep and cattle.
The call of honour cannot grip
Or charm you into freedom's battle.   10
For you—the knife, the shearer's clip!
Your heritage—the herdsman's rattle,
The yoke, the chain, the drover's whip!

            Interpreted by Henry Jones

QUESTIONS

1. What is the speaker's attitude toward work? What is the fruit of his labor?
2. Compare and contrast the lives of the farm animals as the speaker describes them with the life of the worker. How are they similar? How are they different?
3. Does the poem have a metaphoric quality, does it refer to only the narrator, or both? Explain your view.

Edward Arlington Robinson

RICHARD CORY

Whenever Richard Cory went down town,
We people on the pavement looked at him:
He was a gentleman from sole to crown,
Clean favored, and imperially slim.

And he was always quietly arrayed,   5
And he was always human when he talked;

But still he fluttered pulses when he said,
'Good-morning,' and he glittered when he walked.

And he was rich—yes, richer than a king—
And admirably schooled in every grace: 10
In fine, we thought that he was everything
To make us wish that we were in his place.

So on we worked, and waited for the light,
And went without the meat, and cursed the bread;
And Richard Cory, one calm summer night,   15
Went home and put a bullet through his head.

Carl Sandburg

WORKING GIRLS

The working girls in the morning are going to work—long lines
    of them afoot amid the downtown stores and factories,
    thousands with little brick-shaped lunches wrapped in
    newspapers under their arms.
Each morning as I move through this river of young-woman life I   5
    feel a wonder about where it is all going, so many with a
    peach bloom of young years on them and laughter of red lips
    and memories in their eyes of dances the night before and
    plays and walks.
Green and grey streams run side by side in a river and so here are   10
    always the others, those who have been over the way, the
    women who know each one the end of life's gamble for her,
    the meaning and the clue, the how and the why of the
    dances and the arms that passed around their waists and the
    fingers that played in their hair.   15
Faces go by written over: "I know it all, I know where the bloom
    and the laughter go and I have memories," and the feet of
    these move slower and they have wisdom where the others
    have beauty.
So the green and the grey move in the early morning on the   20
    downtown streets.

Percy Bysshe Shelley

SONG

To the Men of England

I

Men of England, wherefore plough
For the lords who lay ye low?
Wherefore weave with toil and care
The rich robes your tyrants wear?

II

Wherefore feed, and clothe, and save,   5
From the cradle to the grave,
Those ungrateful drones who would
Drain your sweat—nay, drink your blood?

III

Wherefore, Bees of England, forge
Many a weapon, chain, and scourge,   10
That these stingless drones may spoil
The forced produce of your toil?

IV

Have ye leisure, comfort, calm,
Shelter, food, love's gentle balm?
Or what is it ye buy so dear   15
With your pain and with your fear?

V

The seed ye sow, another reaps;
The wealth ye find, another keeps;
The robes ye weave, another wears;
The arms ye forge, another bears.   20

VI

Sow seed,—but let no tyrant reap;
End wealth,—let no impostor heap;

Weave robes,—let not the idle wear;
Forge arms,—in your defence to bear.

VII

Shrink to your cellars, holes, and cells;   25
In halls ye deck, another dwells.
Why shake the chains ye wrought? Ye see
The steel ye tempered glance on ye.

VIII

With plough and spade, and hoe and loom,
Trace your grave, and build your tomb,   30
And weave your winding-sheet, till fair
England be your sepulchre.

W. D. (William Dewitt) Snodgrass

THE CAMPUS ON THE HILL

Up the reputable walks of old established trees
They stalk, children of the *nouveaux riches;* chimes
Of the tall Clock Tower drench their heads in blessing:
"I don't wanna play at your house;
I don't like you any more."   5
My house stands opposite, on the other hill,
Among meadows, with the orchard fences down and falling;
Deer come almost to the door.
You cannot see it, even in this clearest morning.
White birds hang in the air between   10
Over the garbage landfill and those homes thereto adjacent,
Hovering slowly, turning, settling down
Like the flakes sifting imperceptibly onto the little town
In a waterball of glass.
And yet, this morning, beyond this quiet scene,   15
The floating birds, the backyards of the poor,
Beyond the shopping plaza, the dead canal, the hillside lying tilted in the air,
Tomorrow has broken out today:
Riot in Algeria, in Cyprus, in Alabama;

Aged in wrong, the empires are declining,   20
And China gathers, soundlessly, like evidence.
What shall I say to the young on such a morning?—
Mind is the one salvation?—also grammar?—
No; my little ones lean not toward revolt. They
Are the Whites, the vaguely furiously driven, who resist   25
Their souls with such passivity
As would make Quakers swear. All day, dear Lord, all day
They wear their godhead lightly.
They look out from their hill and say,
To themselves, "We have nowhere to go but down;   30
The great destination is to stay."
Surely the nations will be reasonable;
They look at the world—don't they?—the world's way?
The clock just now has nothing more to say.

QUESTIONS

1. What is the narrator's profession? What is his attitude toward this profession in the poem?
2. To which social class does the narrator belong? To what other social classes does he refer, and where in the poem does he refer to them?
3. Compare and contrast the attitude of the affluent children with the poor children.
4. What function does the clock play in the poem? What does it symbolize for the wealthy? For the poor?

Gary Soto

DAYBREAK

In this moment when the light starts up
In the east and rubs
The horizon until it catches fire,

We enter the fields to hoe,
Row after row, among the small flags of onion,   5
Waving off the dragonflies
That ladder the air.

And tears the onions raise
Do not begin in your eyes but in ours,
In the salt blown   10
From one blister into another;

They begin in knowing
You will never waken to bear
The hour timed to a heart beat,
The wind pressing us closer to the ground.   15

When the season ends,
And the onions are unplugged from their sleep,
We won't forget what you failed to see,
And nothing will heal
Under the rain's broken fingers.   20

Wole Soyinka

TELEPHONE CONVERSATION

The price seemed reasonable, location
Indifferent. The landlady swore she lived
Off premises. Nothing remained
But self-confession. 'Madam,' I warned,
'I hate a wasted journey—I am African.'   5
Silence. Silenced transmission of
Pressurized good-breeding. Voice, when it came,
Lipstick coated, long gold-rolled
Cigarette-holder pipped. Caught I was, foully.
'HOW DARK?' . . . I had not misheard. . . . 'ARE YOU LIGHT   10
OR VERY DARK?' Button B. Button A. Stench
Of rancid breath of public hide-and-speak.
Red booth. Red pillar-box. Red double-tiered
Omnibus squelching tar. It *was* real! Shamed
By ill-mannered silence, surrender   15
Pushed dumbfoundment to beg simplification.
Considerate she was, varying the emphasis—

'ARE YOU DARK? OR VERY LIGHT?' Revelation came.
'You mean—like plain or milk chocolate?'
Her assent was clinical, crushing in its light   20
Impersonality. Rapidly, wave-length adjusted,
I chose. 'West African sepia'—and as afterthought,
'Down in my passport.' Silence for spectroscopic
Flight of fancy, till truthfulness changed her accent
Hard on the mouthpiece. 'WHAT'S THAT?' conceding   25
'DON'T KNOW WHAT THAT IS.' 'Like brunette.'
'THAT'S DARK, ISN'T IT?' 'Not altogether.
Facially, I am brunette, but madam, you should see
The rest of me. Palm of my hand, soles of my feet
Are a peroxide blonde. Friction, caused—   30
Foolishly madam—by sitting down, has turned
My bottom raven black—One moment madam!'—sensing
Her receiver rearing on the thunderclap
About my ears—'Madam,' I pleaded, 'wouldn't you rather
See for yourself?'   35

Stephen Spender

AN ELEMENTARY SCHOOL CLASSROOM IN A SLUM

Far far from gusty waves, these children's faces.
Like rootless weeds the torn hair round their paleness.
The tall girl with her weighed-down head. The paper-
seeming boy with rat's eyes. The stunted unlucky heir
Of twisted bones, reciting a father's gnarled disease,   5
His lesson from his desk. At back of the dim class,
One unnoted, sweet and young: his eyes live in a dream
Of squirrels' game, in tree room, other than this.

On sour cream walls, donations. Shakespeare's head
Cloudless at dawn, civilized dome riding all cities.   10
Belled, flowery, Tyrolese valley. Open-handed map
Awarding the world its world. And yet, for these
Children, these windows, not this world, are world,
Where all their future's painted with a fog,

A narrow street sealed in with a lead sky,   15
Far far from rivers, capes, and stars of words.

Surely Shakespeare is wicked, the map a bad example
With ships and sun and love tempting them to steal—
For lives that slyly turn in their cramped holes
From fog to endless night? On their slag heap, these children   20
Wear skins peeped through by bones and spectacles of steel
With mended glass, like bottle bits on stones.
All of their time and space are foggy slum
So blot their maps with slums as big as doom.

Unless, governor, teacher, inspector, visitor,   25
This map becomes their window and these windows
That open on their lives like crouching tombs
Break, O break open, till they break the town
And show the children to the fields and all their world
Azure on their sands, to let their tongues   30
Run naked into books, the white and green leaves open
The history theirs whose language is the sun.

Jonathan Swift

A DESCRIPTION
OF A CITY SHOWER

    Careful observers may foretell the hour
(By sure prognostics) when to dread a shower:
While rain depends, the pensive cat gives o'er
Her frolics, and pursues her tail no more.
Returning home at night, you'll find the sink   5
Strike your offended sense with double stink.
If you be wise, then go not far to dine;
You'll spend in coach hire more than save in wine.
A coming shower your shooting corns presage,
Old aches throb, your hollow tooth will rage.   10
Sauntering in coffeehouse is Dulman seen;
He damns the climate and complains of spleen.
    Meanwhile the South, rising with dabbled wings,
A sable cloud athwart the welkin flings,

That swilled more liquor than it could contain,   15
And, like a drunkard, gives it up again.
Brisk Susan whips her linen from the rope,
While the first drizzling shower is borne aslope:
Such is that sprinkling which some careless quean
Flirts on you from her mop, but not so clean: 20
You fly, invoke the gods; then turning, stop
To rail; she singing, still whirls on her mop.
Not yet the dust had shunned the unequal strife,
But, aided by the wind, fought still for life,
And wafted with its foe by violent gust,   25
Twas doubtful which was rain and which was dust.
Ah! where must needy poet seek for aid,
When dust and rain at once his coat invade?
Sole coat, where dust cemented by the rain
Erects the nap, and leaves a mingled stain.   30
    Now in contiguous drops the flood comes down,
Threatening with deluge this devoted town.
To shops in crowds the daggled females fly,
Pretend to cheapen goods, but nothing buy.
The Templar spruce, while every spout's abroach,   35
Stays till 'tis fair, yet seems to call a coach.
The tucked-up sempstress walks with hasty strides,
While streams run down her oiled umbrella's sides.
Here various kinds, by various fortunes led,
Commence acquaintance underneath a shed.   40
Triumphant Tories and desponding Whigs
Forget their feuds, and join to save their wigs.
Boxed in a chair the beau impatient sits,
While spouts run clattering o'er the roof by fits,
And ever and anon with frightful din   45
The leather sounds, he trembles from within.
So when Troy chairmen bore the wooden steed,
Pregnant with Greeks impatient to be freed
(Those bully Greeks, who, as the moderns do,
Instead of paying chairmen, run them through),   50
Laocoön struck the outside with his spear,
And each imprisoned hero quaked for fear.
    Now from all parts the swelling kennels flow,
And bear their trophies with them as they go:
Filth of all hues and odors seem to tell   55
What street they sailed from, by their sight and smell.
They, as each torrent drives with rapid force,
From Smithfield or St. Pulchre's shape their course,
And in huge confluence joined at Snow Hill ridge,

Fall from the conduit prone to Holborn Bridge.   60
Sweepings from butchers' stalls, dung, guts, and blood,
Drowned puppies, stinking sprats, all drenched in mud,
Dead cats, and turnip tops, come tumbling down the flood.

John Updike

EX-BASKETBALL PLAYER

Pearl Avenue runs past the high-school lot,
Bends with the trolley tracks, and stops, cut off
Before it has a chance to go two blocks,
At Colonel McComsky Plaza. Berth's Garage
Is on the corner facing west, and there,   5
Most days, you'll find Flick Webb, who helps Berth out.

Flick stands tall among the idiot pumps—
Five on a side, the old bubble-head style,
Their rubber elbows hanging loose and low.
One's nostrils are two S's, and his eyes   10
An E and O. And one is squat, without
A head at all—more of a football type.

Once Flick played for the high-school team, the Wizards.
He was good: in fact, the best. In '46
He bucketed three hundred ninety points,   15
A county record still. The ball loved Flick.
I saw him rack up thirty-eight or forty
In one home game. His hands were like wild birds.

He never learned a trade, he just sells gas,
Checks oil, and changes flats. Once in a while,   20
As a gag, he dribbles an inner tube,
But most of us remember anyway.
His hands are fine and nervous on the lug wrench.
It makes no difference to the lug wrench, though.

Off work, he hangs around Mae's luncheonette.   25
Grease-gray and kind of coiled, he plays pinball,

Smokes thin cigars, and nurses lemon phosphates.
Flick seldom says a word to Mae, just nods
Beyond her face toward bright applauding tiers
Of Necco Wafers, Nibs, and Juju Beads.   30

QUESTIONS

1. Describe the poet's use of personification in describing the gas station.
2. What metaphors and similes does the poet use to describe Flick?
3. What are Flick Webb's temperament and attitude? What in the poem provides a clue to them?
4. What analogy does the poet make in the last stanza? What does this analogy reveal about Flick's present life?
5. Some critics have drawn comparisons between the setting of this poem and Flick's life. How might this comparison be apt?

David Wagoner

A VALEDICTORY
TO STANDARD OIL
OF INDIANA

In the darkness east of Chicago, the sky burns over the plumbers'
    nightmares
Red and blue, and my hometown lies there loaded with gasoline.
Registers ring like gas-pumps, pumps like pinballs, pinballs like broken alarm
    clocks,
And it's time for morning, but nothing's going to work.
From cat-cracker to candle-shop, from grease-works along the pipeline,   5
Over storage tanks like kings on a checkerboard ready to jump the county,
The word goes out: With refined regrets
We suggest you sleep all day in your houses shaped like lunch buckets
And don't show up at the automated gates.
Something else will tap the gauges without yawning   10
And check the valves at the feet of the cooling-towers without complaining.
Standard Oil is canning my high school classmates
And the ones who fell out of junior high or slipped in the grades.

What should they do, gassed up in their Tempests and Comets, raring to go
Somewhere with their wives scowling in front and kids stuffed in the back,   15
Past drive-ins jammed like car-lots, trying to find the beaches
But blocked by freights for hours, stopped dead in their tracks
Where the rails, as thick as thieves along the lakefront,
Lower their crossing gates to shut the frontier? What can they think about
As they stare at the sides of boxcars for a sign,   20
And Lake Michigan drains slowly into Lake Huron,
The mills level the Dunes, and the eels go sailing through the trout,
And mosquitoes inherit the evening, while toads no bigger than horseflies
Hop crazily after them over the lawns and sidewalks, and the rainbows fall
Flat in the oil they came from? There are two towns now,   25
One dark, one going to be dark, divided by cyclone fences:
One pampered and cared for like pillboxes and cathedrals,
The other vanishing overnight in the dumps and swamps like a struck
    sideshow.
As the Laureate of the Class of '44—which doesn't know it has one—
I offer this poem, not from hustings or barricades   30
Or the rickety stage where George Rogers Clark stood glued to the wall,
But from another way out, like Barnum's "This Way to the Egress,"
Which moved the suckers when they'd seen enough. Get out of town.

Chad Walsh

PORT AUTHORITY
TERMINAL:
9 A.M. MONDAY

From buses beached like an invasion fleet
They fill the waiting room with striding feet.

Their faces, white, and void of hate or pity,
Move on tall bodies toward the conquered city.

Among the lesser breeds of black and brown   5
They board their taxis with an absent frown,

Each to his concrete citadel,
To rule the city and to buy and sell.

At five o'clock they ride the buses back,
Leaving their Irish to guard the brown and black.   10

At six a drink, at seven dinner's served.
At ten or twelve, depressed, undressed, unnerved,

They mount their wives, dismount, they doze and dream
Apocalyptic Negroes in a stream

Of moving torches, marching from the slums,   15
Beating a band of garbage pails for drums,

Marching, with school-age children in their arms,
Advancing on the suburbs and the farms,

To integrate the schools and burn the houses . . .
The normal morning comes, the clock arouses   20

Junior and senior executive alike.
Back on the bus, and down the usual pike.

From buses beached like an invasion fleet
They fill the waiting room with striding feet.

James Welch

THE ONLY BAR IN DIXON

These Indians once imitated life.
Whatever made them warm
they called wine, song or sleep,
a lucky number on the tribal roll.

Now the stores have gone the gray   5
of this November sky. Cars
whistle by, chrome wind, knowing
something lethal in the dust.

A man could build a reputation here.
Take that redhead at the bar—   10

she knows we're thugs, killers
on a fishing trip with luck.

No luck. No room for those
sensitive enough to know they're beat.
Even the Flathead turns away,   15
A river thick with bodies,

Indians on their way to Canada.
Take the redhead—yours for just a word,
a promise that the wind will warm
and all the saints come back for laughs.   20

Phillis Wheatley

TO THE RIGHT HONORABLE WILLIAM, EARL OF DARTMOUTH

Hail, happy day, when, smiling like the morn,
Fair Freedom rose New England to adorn:
The northern clime beneath her genial ray,
Dartmouth, congratulates thy blissful sway:
Elate with hope her race no longer mourns,   5
Each soul expands, each grateful bosom burns,
While in thine hand with pleasure we behold
The silken reins, and Freedom's charms unfold.
Long lost to realms beneath the northern skies
She shines supreme, while hated faction dies: 10
Soon as appear'd the Goddess long desir'd,
Sick as the view, she languish'd and expir'd;
Thus from the splendors of the morning light
The owl in sadness seeks the caves of night.

  No more America in mournful strain   15
Of wrongs, and grievance unredress'd complain,
No longer shalt thou dread the iron chain,
Which wanton Tyranny with lawless hand
Had made, and which it meant t' enslave the land.

Should you, my lord, while you peruse my song,   20
Wonder from whence my love of Freedom sprung,
Whence flow these wishes for the common good,
By feeling hearts alone best understood,
I, young in life, by seeming cruel fate
Was snatch'd from Afric's fancy'd happy seat: 25
What pangs excruciating must molest,
What sorrows labour in my parent's breast!
Steel'd was the soul and by no misery mov'd
That from a father seiz'd his babe belov'd.
Such, such my case. And can I then but pray   30
Others may never feel tyrannic sway?
    For favours past, great Sir, our thanks are due,
And thee we ask thy favours to renew,
Since in thy pow'r, as in thy will before,
To sooth the griefs, which thou did'st once deplore.   35
May heav'nly grace the sacred sanction give
To all thy works, and thou for ever live
Not only on the wings of fleeting Fame,
Though praise immortal crowns the patriot's name,
But to conduct to heav'n's refulgent fane,   40
May fiery courses sweep th' ethereal plain,
And bear thee upwards to that blest abode,
Where, like prophet, thou shalt find thy God.

QUESTIONS

1. What central metaphor does the poet use to describe the idea of freedom?
2. Describe the diction in the poem. What words and phrases contribute to the diction? Which words seem archaic or out of fashion?
3. What was the narrator's personal experience? What seems to be her attitude regarding this experience?

Walt Whitman

I HEAR AMERICA SINGING

I hear America singing, the varied carols I hear,
Those of mechanics, each one singing his as it should be blithe
    and strong,
The carpenter singing his as he measures his plank or beam,
The mason singing his as he makes ready for work, or leaves off   5
    work,
The boatman singing what belongs to him in his boat, the deck-
    hand singing on the steamboat deck,
The shoemaker singing as he sits on his bench, the hatter singing
    as he stands,   10
The wood-cutter's song, the ploughboy's on his way in the
    morning, or at noon intermission or at sundown,
The delicious singing of the mother, or of the young wife at work,
    or of the girl sewing or washing,
Each singing what belongs to him or her and to none else,   15
The day what belongs to the day—at night the party of young
    fellows, robust, friendly,
Singing with open mouths their strong melodious songs.

James Wright

AUTUMN BEGINS IN MARTINS FERRY, OHIO

In the Shreve High football stadium,
I think of Polacks nursing long beers in Tiltonsville,
And gray faces of Negroes in the blast furnace at Benwood,
And the ruptured night watchman of Wheeling Steel,
Dreaming of heroes.   5

All the proud fathers are ashamed to go home.
Their women cluck like starved pullets,
Dying for love.

Therefore,
Their sons grow suicidally beautiful   10
At the beginning of October,
And gallop terribly against each other's bodies.

QUESTIONS

1. To which economic class does the poet refer in paragraph 1?
2. Why are the "proud fathers . . . ashamed to go home"?
3. What does the phrase "Their sons grow suicidally beautiful" mean? What is the
   psychological relationship between the sons and their fathers?
4. James Wright's father was a coal miner, and his youth was spent in a blue-collar
   environment in the Midwest. How does the poem demonstrate his knowledge of this
   aspect of America?

Mitsuye Yamada

DESERT RUN

I

I return to the desert
where criminals
were abandoned to wander
away to their deaths
where scorpions   5
spiders
snakes
lizards
and rats
live in outcast harmony   10
where the sculptor's wreck
was reclaimed
by the gentle drifting sands.

We approach the dunes while
the insistent flies bother our ears   15
the sound of crunching gravel under

our shoes cracks the desolate stillness
and opens our way.

Everything is done in silence here:
the wind fingers fluted stripes   20
over mounds and mounds of sand
the swinging grasses sweep
patterns on the slopes
the sidewinder passes out of sight.
I was too young to hear silence before.   25

II

I spent 547 sulking days here
in my own dreams
there was not much to marvel at
I thought
only miles of sagebrush and   30
lifeless sand.

I watched the most beautiful
sunsets in the world and saw nothing
forty years ago
I wrote my will here   35
my fingers moved slowly in the
hot sand the texture of whole wheat flour
three words: I died here
the winds filed them away.

I am back to claim my body   40
my carcass lies
between the spiny branches
of two creosote bushes
it looks strangely like a small calf
left to graze and die   45
half of its bones are gone
after all these years

but no matter
I am satisfied
I take a dry stick   50
and give myself
a ritual burial.

III

Like the bull snakes brought
into this desert by the soldiers
we were transported here   55
to drive away rattlers
in your nightmares
we were part of some one's plan
to spirit away spies
in your peripheral vision.   60

My skin turned pink brown
in the bright desert light
I slithered in the matching sand
doing what you put me here to do
we were predators at your service   65
I put your mind at ease.

I am that odd creature
the female bull snake
I flick my tongue in your face
an image trapped in your mirror.   70
You will use me or
you will honor me in a shrine
to keep me pure.

IV

At night the outerstellar darkness
above is only an arm's length away   75
I am pressed by the silence around me
the stars are bold as big as quarters
against the velvet blue sky
their beams search for the marrow
of my bones   80
I shiver as I stumble my way to
the outhouse.

In the morning we find
kangaroo rats
have built mounds of messy homes   85
out of dry sticks and leavings
behind our wagon
They have accepted our alien presence.

The night creatures keep a discreet   90
distance.

V

The desert is the lungs of the world.
This land of sudden lizards and nappy ants
is only useful when not used
We must leave before we feel we can   95
change it.

When we leave the dirt roads
my body is thankful for the
paved ride the rest of the way
home.
Rows of yucca trees with spiked crowns   100
wave stiffly at us
Some watch us arms akimbo.

I cannot stay in the desert
where you will have me nor
will I be brought back in a cage   105
to grace your need for exotica.
I write these words at night
for I am still a night creature
but I will not keep a discreet distance
If you must fit me to your needs   110
I will die
and so will you.

Al Young

A POEM FOR
WILLARD MOTLEY

Sometimes at the mouth of this river,
from the far right side of my brain,
I fish all night
in Mexican remembrance
of you, Willard Motley; your elegant   5

hoodlums, your cinematic wops
trapped by themselves between midnight and dawn inside air bubbles
no fish could ever fill
with sly, spicy cartoon talk.   10
I don't suppose you had to be
womanless or manless to cast
such virulent lines into the mouths
of your violent, somnolent characters,
but I'd be willing to bet   15
a Kentucky Derby to a Frank Yerby
that fearlessness helped.

Your forget-me-not bohemian ways
live on in the slow memory
of someone who only heard   20
about your private, festive outbursts
in a sea-surrounded salt & tequila land
the abrupt & unnameable color
of the fathomless dreams of our race.
And so sometimes at the muddy banks   25
of these waters I stand & unreel
my own knotted lines; a knucklehead
shadowed in silver light & weary
as Bogart of knocking at doors.

Again & again I picture John Derek,   30
the way he was: your first-born
prettyboy screen-heroic victim
whose latest wife Bo played Jane
to a Tarzan I couldn't even stick
around the theater long enough to see.   35
My eyes were too lidded with sad, rusting
ironies to stay open in the heavy-colored
dark. Somehow I couldn't stop
thinking about Fred Astaire,
that agile, singing step-dancer   40
the whole world loved up there.
After all the riches Negroes paved
his way with, how could he go &
marry that frisky young jockey
of a wife who openly championed the KKK?   45

It's a very old story, you know;
washed out, wish-defying; so fishy

& predictable you could chart it
on a graph. What waters were you
treading when you realized no man could   50
write your epitaph? What Chicago,
what Sicily possessed you at that point?

Bernice Zamora

NOTES FROM A
CHICANA "COED"

for P.H.

To cry that the *gabacho*
is our oppressor is to shout
in abstraction, *carnal*.
He no more oppresses us
than you do now as you tell me   5
"It's the gringo who oppresses you, Babe."
You cry "The gringo is our oppressor!"
to the tune of $20,000 to $30,000
a year, brother, and I wake up
alone each morning and ask,   10
"Can I feed my children today?"

To make the day easier
I write poems about
pájaros, mariposas,
and the fragrance   15
of perfume I
smell on your collar;
you're quick to point out
that I must write
about social reality,   20
about "the gringo who
oppresses you, Babe."
And so I write about
how I worked in beet fields
as a child, about how I   25
worked as a waitress

eight hours at night to
get through high school,
about working as a
seamstress, typist, and field clerk   30
to get through college, and
about how, in graduate school
I held two jobs, seven days
a week, still alone, still asking,
"Can I feed my children today?"   35

To give meaning to my life
you make love to me in alleys,
in back seats of borrowed Vegas,
in six-dollar motel rooms
after which you talk about   40
your five children and your wife
who writes poems at home
about *pájaros, mariposas,*
and the fragrance of perfume
she smells on your collar.   45
Then you tell me how you
bear the brunt of the
gringo's oppression for me,
and how you would go
to prison for me, because   50
"The gringo is oppressing you, Babe!"

And when I mention
your G.I. Bill, your
Ford Fellowship, your
working wife, your   55
three *gabacha guisás*
when you ask me to
write your thesis,
you're quick to shout,
"Don't give me that   60
Women's Lib trip, *mujer,*
that only divides us,
and we have to work
together for the *movimiento;*
the *gabacho* is oppressing us!"   65

Oye carnal, you may as well
tell me that moon water
cures constipation, that

penguin soup prevents *crudas,*
or that the Arctic Ocean is *menudo,*   70
because we both learned in the barrios,
man, that pigeon shit slides easier.

Still, because of the *gabacho,*
I must write poems about
pájaros, mariposas, and the fragrance   75
of oppressing perfume I smell somewhere.

Cyn. Zarco

ASPARAGUS

There's a washcloth
with a picture of asparagus
in my bathroom.

Did you know
that Pilipinos were picked   5
to grow asparagus in the West
because they were short
and built closer to the ground?

I'm 5'3". I don't use
that washcloth anymore.   10

C a s t e & C l a s s

P o e t r y

TOPICS FOR WRITING

1. Compare and contrast two regions, neighborhoods, or cities you have lived in or visited that differ in economic and/or social class.
2. Narrate an incident you witnessed that demonstrates a gross injustice. Explain the circumstances, the people involved, and the cause of the injustice.
3. Compare and contrast "Share-Croppers" by Langston Hughes and "Working Girls" by Carl Sandburg. Discuss how each poem describes the effects of work on its respective subjects.
4. Many of the poems in this section describe the effects of place on the economic, social, and psychological health of its citizens. Select three of your favorite poems in this section, and write an essay discussing in detail how each poet establishes and conveys the complex relationship between the individual and his or her environment.
5. Select a poem with a strict rhyme scheme and meter, such as "London" by William Blake, and compare and contrast its structure to a poem with a freer structure, such as "A Valedictory to Standard Oil of Indiana" by David Wagoner. Discuss the influence of the presence or absence of these two traditional poetic devices.
6. Classify the types of discrimination found in poetry presented in this section. Be sure to refer to specific poems to illustrate your key divisions.
7. Argue for or against the proposition that poetry can be an effective way to communicate the injustices that occur owing to class, race, or gender.
8. In order to understand the exploitation of one group by another, it is necessary for one to have experienced such exploitation first-hand. Argue for or against this proposition, selecting poems from this section that support your position.
9. As a research project, study the life of one of the better-known poets in this section, and discuss how the poet's own experience had an impact on his or her selection of subject matter.
10. Many of the poems in this section describe a particular geographic locale. Select one of them such as London, the Midwest, Chicago, and write a research paper exploring the ways several poets have described and depicted that particular place.

573

Drama

Brigid Brophy

THE WASTE DISPOSAL UNIT

CHARACTERS

The Waste Disposal Unit was first presented by B.B.C. Radio, Great
Britain, on April 9, 1964, with the following cast:

HOMER KNOCKERBICKER   Harry Towb
VIRGIL KNOCKERBICKER   Ronald Wilson
MERRY KNOCKERBICKER   Mavis Villiers
LIA-PIA   Nicolette Bernard
ANGELO LUMACA   John Baddeley
MRS. VAN DEN MOST   Mavis Villiers

(*Note:* The roles of MERRY and her mother, MRS. VAN DEN MOST, are
performed by the same actress.)

Scene: The salone *of a palazzo in northern Italy. The time is the present.*

The salone of a palazzo in northern Italy.

*The room is marbled and splendid, but the splendour is of a cool and echoing kind because the place
is simply not furnished at all, apart from a crate of Coca-Cola bottles—some full, some already
used—that has been nakedly dumped in the middle of the intricately patterned floor.*

574

Luckily there are two marble windowseats beneath the tall uncurtained windows.

On one of these VIRGIL KNOCKERBICKER *is lying reading a small black-bound notebook which is propped up on his humped knees. He is dressed in black himself— cashmere sweater, narrow trousers, black plimsolls; his soft dark hair is cropped to the point of seeming a mere continuance of the pile on his jumper. In his black costume and his complete absorption in his small volume, he resembles—no doubt on purpose—the young Lord Hamlet.*

HOMER KNOCKERBICKER, *a slightly older and considerably plumper American is walking echoingly up and down the room. He is as worried and hot as Virgil is cool and controlled—this despite the fact that his clothing, unlike Virgil's, is designed for coolness rather than picturesque effect. His light-coloured, loose cotton suit and his transparent nylon-seersucker shirt are already crumpled, though the day (some of whose brilliance spills in through the windows) is not yet far advanced. In patches, his shirt is already even more translucent than the manufacturer intended, where his sweat has affected it as grease affects paper. From time to time he takes a vast handkerchief from his breast pocket and uses it to wipe his spectacles.*

Doors to left and right of the salone *lead out to the rest of the* palazzo.

Through the window there are summer country Italian sounds: chickens, occasional cicadas, lambrettas.

HOMER: Virgil?

VIRGIL [*without looking up from his reading*]: Homer?

HOMER: Virgil, you planning on lying around all day today, the way you did yesterday?

VIRGIL: Mm-hm. [VIRGIL *thinks he has now disposed of the subject.*]

HOMER: This heat's murder. Merry says it isn't any worse than Southern California, but I tell her it is, it carries a higher degree of humidity. Southern California, you get the ocean. [*After a pause.*] Gee, it's hot. It's hot as hell.

VIRGIL: Maybe you should relax more.

HOMER: I guess one in the family is enough.

VIRGIL: One what?

HOMER: O, you know. You know what I mean, Virgil. It's hot enough so it even mists up my lenses. You're lucky you don't have to wear glasses. This heat, you wouldn't be able to see to write.

VIRGIL: I'm not writing. I'm reading back what I already did.

HOMER: That reminds me, sometime I got to talk with you—you want a drink, Virgil?

VIRGIL: Mm-hm. Whisky sour.

HOMER: I didn't mean hard liquor.

VIRGIL: O. No thanks.

HOMER: I wish we had a water cooler in this place. Guess I'll have myself a Coke. I wonder if Merry could use a Coke. You think Merry could use a Coke, Virgil?

[HOMER *alludes to the door at the left.*]

VIRGIL: How would I know? Go on in and ask her.

HOMER: O, I can't go in there right now. She isn't through fixing her face.

VIRGIL: O. Well yell.

HOMER [*as he helps himself to a bottle of Coca-Cola and removes the cap*]: What?

VIRGIL: Yell. Ask her through the bedroom door.

HOMER: Yeh, I might *do* that. [*He drinks deep, directly from the bottle.*] I might *do* that. Sure.

VIRGIL: Well go ahead.

HOMER: Sure.

MERRY [*offstage, calling cooingly in a pretty, tinkling voice*]: Ho-mer!

HOMER [*calling hastily back, towards the door at the left*]: I'll be right in, honey. I just grabbed myself a Coke. I just gotta find some place to put it down. [*He crams it into the crate and runs over to the door at the left; but as his hand turns the knob:*]

MERRY: O, don't come *in*, Homer.

[HOMER *shuts the door hastily.*]

HOMER: I certainly am sorry, Merry.

MERRY: Why, that's perfectly all right, Homer, think no more of it. Homer?

HOMER: Yes, Merry?

MERRY: Would you take a look round the *palazzo* see if I left my Kleenex some place.

HOMER: Sure, Merry. [HOMER *returns to the middle of the room.*] I don't see too well, my lenses got misted up again. [*Calling:*] I don't see them any place, honey, but I'll keep right on searching. Virgil, you seen them?

VIRGIL: See what?

HOMER: Merry's Kleenex.

VIRGIL: Sure. [VIRGIL *pulls out a box from behind his back.*]

HOMER: Now why in the world would you want to do that?

VIRGIL: This window-seat isn't too soft, Homer.

HOMER: If you wouldn't lie around all day—

VIRGIL: Don't you want them?

HOMER: What?

VIRGIL: Merry's Kleenex.

HOMER: Wait a moment, can't you, I got to wipe off these lenses again.

VIRGIL: Don't *you* get steamed up, too.

HOMER: I'm not getting steamed up, but you don't seem to understand, I got to get those Kleenex to Merry. Give here. [*He takes the box from* VIRGIL.] Why, Virgil, you crushed in one whole side of the pack. I don't know how Merry's going to—

VIRGIL: Yeh, well, these sharp-angled packs aren't really any more comfortable than marble. I guess I really took Merry's Kleenex more as a kind of talisman. You know, like a chicken sits on a china egg. To inspire my work.

HOMER: Now that's something I have to talk with you about, Virgil. I'll just go give these to Merry. I'll be right back. [*Approaching the door at the left and calling:*] Merry! I found them, honey. But I'm afraid the pack didn't stand up too well—

MERRY: Now isn't that just too bad of me, Homer. I was just going to call out I didn't need them any more.

HOMER: O.

MERRY: Homer, don't be sore. I found another pack right in here.

HOMER: O, I'm not sore, Merry. I'm certainly glad you found another pack. That's swell. You through yet, honey?

MERRY: Not yet, Homer.

HOMER: O. O.K.

VIRGIL [*as, without looking away from his book, he reaches a hand out towards the Kleenex*]: Give here.

HOMER: What?

VIRGIL: If Merry doesn't want them, I may as well sit on them a while longer. You never know what might hatch. I'll take a look round later, see if I can find a pack that isn't crushed. You don't have any scatter cushions round the place, Homer, I guess you don't have the domesticated touch, but you have to hand it to Merry, she certainly does have scatter Kleenex.

HOMER: Now see here, Virgil—

MERRY [*offstage*]: I don't hear you too well but you boys sound to be having a lot of fun out there. I'll be right along.

HOMER: That's swell, honey.

VIRGIL: I don't figure how it takes a woman that long to make up like she was twenty-five when she *is* twenty-five.

HOMER: Now wait a moment, Virgil—

VIRGIL: Mm-hm?

HOMER: Merry's a lovely person.

VIRGIL: Sure. Sure, Homer. Merry's just great. She's great material.

HOMER: What do you mean, "material"?

VIRGIL: You know how it is, Homer. I guess I have a professional attitude, that's all. I'm certainly glad you married Merry.

HOMER [*not sure whether to be angered*]: I don't know just how you mean that, Virgil. Do you mean you're glad on account of your work?

VIRGIL: O, I don't separate my work from my life.

HOMER: Now that's something we have to talk about. I'll just have myself that Coke. . . .

VIRGIL: In fact, I don't separate my work from *your* life.

[HOMER *puts the bottle abruptly back into the crate, and prepares to be angry.*]

HOMER: I didn't hear you too well, Virgil, I was kind of swallowing, but did you say my life or my wife?

VIRGIL: O, I wouldn't dare—

HOMER: Let's leave Merry out of this, Virgil. I want to talk with you.

VIRGIL: Mm-hm?

HOMER: Don't you ever look up from that book?

VIRGIL: I'm told I have very remarkable concentration.

HOMER: I guess you wouldn't break your concentration no matter what happened.

VIRGIL: Nothing does happen.

HOMER: Maybe not, but most of the time it sounds like it did. Know what I think, Virgil? I think Italy's the noisiest country I was ever in.

VIRGIL: It's no worse than Southern California.

HOMER: It is *so* worse than Southern California. Out here you got the cicadas. If it isn't the cicadas, it's the lambrettas. If it isn't the lambrettas, it's the doves. If it isn't the doves, it's those goddam chickens out there in the yard.

VIRGIL: I don't mind the chickens in the *yard* too much.

HOMER: Now see h—

VIRGIL: Cool off, Homer.

HOMER: How can I cool off, this heat? We ought to have drapes at those windows, cut out the sun, but I don't know the Italian for drapes, anyway Merry likes looking out the window. . . . I'm worried, Virgil. I don't know how Merry's going to take this kind of climatic conditions.

VIRGIL: Relax, Homer. Merry doesn't feel it at all.

HOMER: You don't know how Merry feels. Merry is a very delicate character. I don't see how I can ask Merry to live in a climate like this.

VIRGIL: You didn't ask her. It was Merry's idea.

HOMER: You know what I *mean*, Virgil. You know how it is. A guy has to look out for his wife, he has to make provision. If I'd have known there wouldn't even have been a shower in this *palazzo*—

VIRGIL: You had one fixed.

HOMER: Sure I had one fixed, and I'm going to have plenty else fixed, I'm going to make this old *palazzo* like so it won't know itself. . . . But Merry's a very sensitive person. She's delicate, Virgil, even though she doesn't make any song and dance—

MERRY [*calling musically from the next room*]: Ho-mer!

HOMER: Yes, honey?

MERRY: Could you step in here for a moment, Homer?

HOMER: Sure, Merry. I'll be right in. You through now? [*A bell rings loudly.*]

HOMER: I'll get it. [*He stops making towards the door at the left, and sets out for the door at the right; checks himself; executes a step-dance of hesitation; and finally calls, in a despairing flurry, towards the door on the left:*] I'll be right back, Merry. I just got to go see to the front door bell.

VIRGIL: Let Lia-Pia get it.

HOMER: How can I let Lia-Pia get it? She doesn't speak English.

VIRGIL: So she doesn't speak English. Maybe it was an Italian dropped by.

HOMER: Are you crazy? How would an Italian drop by?

VIRGIL: Well, we're in Italy.

HOMER: Sure, I *know* we're in Italy, but—

MERRY: Ho-mer! Would you step along to the front door. The bell just rang.

HOMER: Sure, Merry, sure. I'll get it.

[*As* HOMER *leaves by the door at the right,* MERRY *trips in by the door at the left. She tiptoes on her sneakers across the room, comes up behind* VIRGIL *as he reads, and places her hands as a blindfold over his eyes.*]

MERRY: Morning, Virgil. Guess who?

VIRGIL [*sourly*]: Merry.

MERRY [*releasing his eyes*]: You're a good guesser, Virgil.

VIRGIL [*craning round and looking at her*]: Mm-hm, Merry. Just like I thought. Morning, Merry. You look cute.

MERRY [*dropping him a mock curtsey*]: Why, thank you, Virgil.

VIRGIL [*looking her up and down*]: Sure, cute. Little pony tail, all done up in a tartan bow, and those long white kneehose, and your Bermuda shorts, and that cute little—what you call it?

MERRY: Shirtwaister?

VIRGIL: Sure, shirtwaister. O, you look cute, Merry. You look like all the college girls in Southern California rolled into one.

MERRY: Why, Virgil, that's the darlingest thing you ever said to me, I guess you must be becoming a better integrated personality. I'm going to give you a little kiss on your brow, just for saying that. [*She bends over and neatly deposits the kiss.*]

VIRGIL: O, don't take any account of me, Merry, I'm just apple-polishing. There's something I want you to tell me.

MERRY: Well, I'll certainly tell you anything I can, Virgil, but Homer says you already know 'most everything. I'm going to just curl up alongside of you on this lovely *Renaissance* window-seat, and then you can ask me anything you want. [*Doing so.*] I guess wherever I am I find myself some corner I can curl up in. There now, Virgil. What's your problem? You know, Virgil, Homer has a very, very high regard for your intellectual integrity.

VIRGIL: Now how would he be able to judge, I wonder?

MERRY: Now, Virgil, Homer's—

VIRGIL: O sure, Homer's a lovely person.

MERRY [*subsiding*]: I'm certainly glad you appreciate it. Now what is it I can tell you?

VIRGIL: Why don't you let your husband in your bedroom, Merry?

MERRY [*rising in fury*]: Virgil Knockerbicker, how can you make such an absolutely awful insinuation? If you dare imply for one moment—

VIRGIL: Merry, I only asked—

MERRY: Virgil Knockerbicker, I'm going right back in the bou*doir* until Homer returns. [*She turns her back on* VIRGIL.]

VIRGIL: Merry, what did I do?

MERRY [*swinging on him*]: What did you *do!* You were insinuating that my relationship with Homer is not perfectly adjusted on the physical side.

VIRGIL: Merry, I only—

MERRY: You as good as called me a frigid wife!

VIRGIL: Merry, I—

MERRY [*stamping*]: I do so let him in my bedroom!

VIRGIL: He told me a while back he couldn't go in there.

MERRY [*losing all her anger, now the trouble is explained*]: O sure, but that was in the morning.

VIRGIL: What's the difference?

MERRY: Virgil, you certainly seem a little naïve for your age. Homer comes in my room nights—*of* course—and then he always goes away while it's still dark. He promised me that's how it would always be, and I know Homer won't break his promise. Then mornings he doesn't come in again before I got my face fixed.

VIRGIL: Is it that important he shouldn't see you without you got your face fixed?

MERRY: Well maybe it isn't that important right now, Virgil, but it will be. And the way Homer is, it could do a lot of damage to his feelings if I suddenly had to ask him to quit coming in when I got to be of age when it would matter. Right after Homer became my beau, I figured I ought to start right in planning for the future. It was our wedding night I asked him to give me this promise. That way I know he'll never break it.

VIRGIL [*laying his book down on his knees and surrendering himself to musing in wonder on* MERRY*'s revelation*]: And you feel you couldn't possibly let him in till you're through fixing your face?

MERRY [*with quiet resolution*]: No, I couldn't do that, Virgil. I just couldn't *do* that. [*Dreamily*] You see, Virgil, I have something I want to preserve.

VIRGIL: Your face?

MERRY [*gently*]: No, Virgil, something intangible, something that's been kind of entrusted to me. I don't know that you can understand very well, Virgil. Although you and I are pretty much of an age, I guess a woman matures faster than a man. I doubt that you have achieved sufficient maturation yet to understand. But what I feel is—well, I guess I feel that romance is a very wonderful and a very fragile thing. [*She lets these words hang like a beautiful sunset in the air for a moment. Then she trips to the door at the right.*]

MERRY: I guess I'll just go along and see who it was dropped by. Maybe I can help Homer some. [*Opening the door and pausing.*] Well . . . I'm glad you talked with me about this, Virgil. I'm not going to tell Homer we talked about it, because I believe that even within the marital framework there ought to be areas of privacy. If you have some more problems, Virgil, I hope you will talk with me about them. I have a personal conviction that relationships can only achieve a completely adjusted orientation if problems are brought right out in the open. And I sincerely hope we can all three pass a wonderful vacation in this lovely old *palazzo*.

[MERRY *leaves by the door at the right.* LIA-PIA *shuffles in by the door at the left. She is a dear old thing in a black overall and lopsided bedroom slippers. She is ushering in a smartly dressed young Italian.*]

LIA-PIA [*clucking comfortingly, like a dove*]: Si accomodi, signore, si accomodi, si accomodi.

[LIA-PIA *shuffles out, leaving the visitor, as he thinks, alone. He deposits his smart, speckled-leather briefcase against his side of the Coca-Cola crate, settles the sit of his perfectly pressed suit, puts one foot up on the side of the crate and bends to pull up one of his quite unsagging thin-nylon socks.*]

VIRGIL [*picking up his book to resume reading and speaking without looking at the stranger*]: I don't know why the old thing told you to accommodate yourself. I don't see where you can.

THE VISITOR [*whirling round in surprise*]: Ah, scusi, non avevo visto—

VIRGIL: O.K. maybe I *am* insignificant. You could sit on the Coca-Cola crate but I doubt that it's comfortable.

THE ITALIAN: Please, it is no matter. I am come to work, not sit. You are Mr. Knockerbicker?

VIRGIL: Mm-hm.

ANGELO: I am the man who is come to fix the—

VIRGIL: O, then I'm not the Mr. Knockerbicker you want. The Mr. Knockerbicker you want, the Mr. Knockerbicker who counts, will be along presently. Pardon me if I catch up on some reading while you wait. [*He begins to do so.*]

ANGELO: Please? The Mr. Knockerbicker who counts?

VIRGIL: Sure, who counts out the dough. I'm just the kid brother. The Mr. Knocker-bicker who counts went to meet you, and the Mrs. Knockerbicker who counts went right after him, but the way this palace is constructed, if you miss somebody the first time round, you have to go through the whole tour of the building before you get back where you started. I guess the *Renaissance* just wasn't *onto* the principle of the corridor.

ANGELO [*with a self-introductory bow*]: Lumaca, Angelo.

VIRGIL [*with an inclination of his head, sidelong, over his book*]: Knockerbicker, Virgil.

ANGELO: You are reading?

VIRGIL [*continuing to do so*]: Mm-hm.

ANGELO: I, too, read very often. It is being very hot. I take off my coat. This is not a nuisance?

VIRGIL [*without attending*]: Go right ahead.

[ANGELO *takes off coat, folds it inside out, removes his wallet, hangs his coat on a knob of the shutters at the window not occupied by* VIRGIL *and returns to talk to* VIRGIL.]

ANGELO: Ah, that is better. You are not being too hot, dressed all in black?

VIRGIL: Black is the coolest colour there is. And I am one of the coolest characters there is.

ANGELO: I am sorry. I have been bad to ask that question.

VIRGIL: How so?

ANGELO: Probably you are wearing the black because you are being bereaved.

VIRGIL: No, I wasn't bereaved recently, but now you come to mention it I'm prepared.

ANGELO: You are reading a book which is interesting?

VIRGIL [*still reading*]: Enthralling.

ANGELO: Love story, police story, espionage, *Reader's Digest*, Science Fiction?

VIRGIL: Poetry.

ANGELO: Ah, I, too, am loving poetry. Even though I am being an engineer, I am loving poetry. You know what I am thinking, Mr. Knockerbicker junior? I am thinking in life today there is not being enough poetry. I am loving beauty in all its forms. I love poetry, music, paintings—I am loving all the arts. And you know why, Mr. Knockerbicker junior? Because they are so beautiful. To me, they are so beautiful. I am loving all the beautiful things—including the women, yes?

VIRGIL [*without interest*]: That so?

ANGELO: I think you are feeling the same, eh, Mr. Knockerbicker junior?

VIRGIL: Mm-hm. [*As an afterthought.*] All except the women.

ANGELO [*astounded*]: How is this? You are not loving the women?

VIRGIL [*without emphasis*]: I'm homosexual.

ANGELO [*completely taken aback*]: O. [*After a pause of swallowing the information.*] I am begging your pardon.

VIRGIL [*without looking up*]: Don't mention it. [*Musing.*] What a *peculiar* conversation.

ANGELO: Mr. Knockerbicker junior, this poem you read, who is the author?

[VIRGIL *reads to the end of the page before replying.*]

VIRGIL: I am.

[ANGELO *laughs politely.* VIRGIL *continues to read.*]

ANGELO: You are meaning this is true? Really you have written a poem?

VIRGIL: Am writing. I didn't finish it yet.

ANGELO: And you are beginning it when?

VIRGIL: When I was ten.

ANGELO: You are writing since you have been ten one poem? So many years, one poem?

VIRGIL: I'm not that old.

ANGELO: No, but—

VIRGIL: I guess it was the romantic movement spread the idea a poem has to be a lyric.

ANGELO: Without the lyric feeling, where is the poetry?

VIRGIL: Before romanticism was invented, there were plenty of long poems. My namesake Virgil, who was born not too far from here, wrote an extremely long poem. My brother's namesake wrote two of them. Dante and Milton also wrote long poems, but as my parents didn't have any more sons they are not commemorated in our family.

ANGELO: Dante, Milton, that was long ago. Modern life moves with more pace, Mr. Knockerbicker junior. How did you find rhymes for a long poem? It is difficult, yes?

VIRGIL: I don't use rhyme.

ANGELO: Without the rhyme, how is it poetry? You are writing the blank verses?

VIRGIL: I don't use meter.

ANGELO: What can it be like, your poem?

VIRGIL: My poem is kind of an American Song of Songs.

ANGELO: But without the rhyme, without the meter, where is the poetry?

VIRGIL: The poetry is in the subject.

ANGELO: Mr. Knockerbicker junior, what *is* the subject of your poem?

VIRGIL: The subject of my poem is the American Woman.

ANGELO: Ah, now I am understanding. The American Woman, she is poetry herself.

VIRGIL [*prosaically agreeing*]: Yes, I include her among the ideas which have a sufficient poetic content in themselves, along with the collision of planets and the copulation of dinosaurs.

ANGELO [*overwhelmed*]: You must be a very poetical person, Mr. Knockerbicker junior.

VIRGIL: Fortunately I don't have to reply to that compliment because I hear the other

Mr. Knockerbicker on his way back. He has a very weighty tread. Come to think of it, Homer must weigh all of a hundred and sixty.

[HOMER *comes worriedly through the door at the left.*]

VIRGIL: Meet Mr. Homer Knockerbicker. Homer, meet Mr. Angelo Lumaca.

HOMER [*politely, but too distractedly worried to pay attention*]: Mr. Lumaca.

ANGELO: Call me Angelo.

HOMER: Sure. [*Worry bursting out of him.*] Virgil, did you see Merry any place? Lia-Pia was saying something about the *signora*, but I didn't follow her too well—

VIRGIL: Merry went right after you. She'll be back. [*Virgil resumes his reading.*]

HOMER: I certainly hope she will. This *palazzo*. . . . . [*Sighs, and wipes his spectacles.*] A person as delicate as Merry could easily get lost in a *palazzo* like this. Pardon me, Angelo, I'm sorry I had to keep you waiting, I got snarled up with the hired help, she only speaks Italian, I didn't get what she was trying to tell me. . . .

[MERRY *comes through the door at the left.*]

MERRY: O, Homer, there you are. I was— [*Stopping and dimpling prettily*] Why, I didn't know we had company.

HOMER: Honey, I'd like to have you meet Mr. Angelo Lumaca.

ANGELO: Call me please Angelo.

MERRY: Angelo? Why, that must mean angel. That's a perfectly darling name. I'd certainly feel very privileged to call you by a name like that. Welcome to our *palazzo*, Angelo. I certainly never thought I'd be welcoming a real Italian to a real Italian *palazzo*.

ANGELO: Welcome to Italy, Mrs. Knockerbicker. [*He kisses her hand.*]

MERRY [*delighted*]: You certainly have *palazzo* manners.

VIRGIL: Now she'll want us all to kiss her hand every morning. It'll become a ritual, like the breakfast food.

HOMER: Now see here, Virgil—

MERRY: Now, Homer, quit picking on Virgil. You know he can't help himself.

ANGELO [*conversationally, trying to help them steer past a family row*]: You hired this *palazzo*, Mr. Knockerbicker?

HOMER [*distractedly*]: What? O yeh, sure. For our vacation.

ANGELO: You have a very old *palazzo* here, Mr. Knockerbicker. *Cinquecento.*

VIRGIL: And boy is it hideous.

MERRY [*deeply reproachful*]: Why, Virgil, how can you *say* such a thing?

ANGELO: O, no, Mr. Knockerbicker junior, you must be mistaken. This *palazzo* is very old, it is of the *rinascimento*, you understand? of the sixteenth century. So it *cannot* be hideous.

MERRY: O, don't take any account of Virgil. Have you looked out the window, Angelo? We have a real Italian yard out there, a *giardino.*

ANGELO: La signora parla italiano!

MERRY [*almost ecstatic with pleasure*]: O, no, not really, just a word or two I picked up from the hired help, but I certainly hope to learn a lot more. Yes, we have a real Italian *giardino,* and real Italian doves and real Italian chickens. I didn't learn the Italian for doves and chickens yet. But I get a big thrill just from watching those chickens and knowing every one of them is a real Italian chicken.

ANGELO [*with a glance through the window*]: You have twenty, thirty hens out there and only two cocks. Nice life for the cocks, eh?

VIRGIL: If you like responsibility.

HOMER [*belatedly understanding some at least of* ANGELO's *remark*]: O, you mean roosters.

ANGELO: Please?

VIRGIL: Somebody sold you English English instead of American English, Angelo. In the United States we have to call them roosters, because American women have such effortlessly sexual trains of thought.

MERRY [*very rappingly*]: Virgil, will you please be quiet?

HOMER: What'd he say, Merry? I didn't get it.

MERRY: Don't let's any of us pay any attention to Virgil. He certainly has some anti-social compulsions this morning. But I'm not going to let anything spoil this wonderful place. D'you know, Angelo, living here, I can just imagine I'm back in those old days, with knights and cardinals and poison and frescoes and illuminated manuscripts. . . . O, I was just wild to get here. Last fall, I said to Mr. Knockerbicker "Homer, if it's the last thing you ever do for me, take me to Italy."

HOMER [*worrying*]: Yeh, I know, honey, but in those days they didn't have too good a concept of hygiene, and an old place like this . . .

MERRY: Homer, quit worrying. We're making out fine.

HOMER: So far honey. Knock on wood. [*Casting about anxiously.*] Where *is* some wood? Hell, this *palazzo's* all marble.

VIRGIL: There's the Coca-Cola crate.

HOMER: O, sure. [*He knocks on it.*] Thanks, Virgil.

MERRY: Now, Homer, quit fussing. What *could* happen?

HOMER [*putting an arm round her, drawing her convulsively to him and drooling a little over her hair*]: You're a brave little person, Merry. D'you know, Angelo, when we came here, they didn't even have a *shower* in this *palazzo,* only a tub.

MERRY: Relax, Homer, will you. You'll get yourself a duodenal. Just relax, and let the lovely Italian culture just seep into you.

HOMER: Maybe I'll get around to that, baby, when I got this place fixed so it's good enough for you.

MERRY: O, you take marvellous care of me, Homer. D'you know, Angelo, Homer had a shower fitted.

HOMER: Yeh, I had this shower fitted, and I installed another icebox—

MERRY: Why, yes, Angelo, Homer had a complete kitchen installed right here [*She points to the door at the right.*] —it's right through there just next door to the living room, so we don't have to have our food cooked by the hired help any more—

HOMER: When we first came, the hired help wanted to cook everything, but she was operating under pretty primitive conditions—

MERRY: O, it wasn't just the con*di*tions, Homer dear, it was the calories. I don't know, Angelo, if you ever saw a breakdown of the calorific content of olive oil, but believe you me it would horrify you. Well, the first thing Homer did, he imported a stock of low-calory cooking medium from the States, and then he fixed up this little kitchen right out there—

HOMER: Yeh, well, we have this kitchen, but there are some gadgets I wasn't yet able to find in Italy, and some we have that I imported but they're not yet operational—

ANGELO [*excitedly trying to get a word in*]: But, Mr. Knockerbicker, listen, *please*. This is why I am here.

HOMER: Why you are—I don't get it. Pardon me a moment, Angelo, I have to wipe off my lenses again. [*He does so.*]

ANGELO [*pleadingly*]: *Please*, Mr. Knockerbicker. I am the man who has come to fix the waste disposal unit!

HOMER [*amazed*]: No-o-o? [*Putting on his now wiped spectacles and stepping forward.*] Well, how do you like that? Hullo there again.

ANGELO: Hullo.

HOMER: Hi.

ANGELO: Ciao.

HOMER [*laughing*]: We-ell. I guess that just about takes care of it. You know, I guess I thought that as you aren't an American you wouldn't know how to fix a waste disposal unit.

ANGELO: I am the accredited Italian agent. I have here my card. [*He proffers it, then reads it aloud.*] You see. I am the accredited agent of the Atlantic Seaboard Waste Disposal Unit Corporation of New York, NY, USA.

HOMER: Well, what do you know? Isn't that swell, Merry? Now we can have that waste disposal unit operational.

ANGELO [*with self-assurance*]: You certainly can, Mr. Knockerbicker.

MERRY [*graciously social*]: Homer, would you take Angelo through there and show him where it has to be connected?

HOMER [*happily*]: I sure will. [*He ushers* ANGELO *across the room and opens the door at the right for him.*] Right through here, Angelo.

ANGELO [*pausing at the door to make a declaration*]: You are going to enjoy this waste disposal unit, Mrs. Knockerbicker. [*Reciting.*] This is the finest waste disposal unit on the market, a triumph of American technical know-how. This unit will dispose of *anything*. Say goodbye forever to malodorous, unhygienic, germ-breeding, squelchy bundles. The Atlantic Seaboard waste disposal unit takes over. Soggy, crunchy, pulpy, bony, mushy, spiny—it's all one to the Atlantic Seaboard waste disposal unit.

VIRGIL: The guy certainly is accredited.

MERRY [*on a sudden thought*]: Say, Homer, ask him if he ever fixed one before.

HOMER: You got something there, Merry. They told me this was the first they imported into Italy. Say, Angelo, did you ever fix one before?

ANGELO [*pained, and holding up his hand like a traffic policeman*]: Mr. Knockerbicker. Mrs. Knockerbicker. Please. I am the accredited agent. I fix it.

[HOMER *and* ANGELO *go through the door at the right.* MERRY, *swinging her pony tail, trips her way to the unoccupied window-seat, perches one urchin knee on it and looks out of the window.* VIRGIL *reads for a moment, then without looking up:*]

VIRGIL: You mad at me, Merry?

MERRY: Why, no, Virgil. I guess I maybe would be, if I didn't know you had problems.

VIRGIL: I got problems O.K. How'm I going to end this poem?

MERRY: Maybe it'd help you feel less mixed-up, Virgil, if you kind of explained your problem to me.

VIRGIL: I guess it's easier for composers. They just come back to the key note, and it sounds swell.

MERRY: And you want kind of a key note for your poem?

VIRGIL: It's not that simple. I need a climax—something terrible and tragic: and then a resolution: and then some kind of final chorus, to round the thing off.

MERRY: I'll keep it in mind, Virgil. Maybe I'll come up with something we can kick around together.

[HOMER *returns, much less worried than usual.*]

HOMER: He's making out fine in there. We'll soon have that unit operational. [*Going up to her and giving her a squeeze.*] And how're *you* making out, Merry? [*He places an infatuated kiss on top of her head.*] Still looking out that window?

MERRY: O, I'm as happy as I can be just so I can watch those romantic old doves and those quaint little old chickens.

HOMER [*sifting her pony tail through his fingers*]: You're just a lovely little person, Merry. You're just so satisfied with the simple things in life.

MERRY [*suddenly freezing with horror as she gazes through the window*]: Homer!

HOMER: Why, Merry! Hey, Merry! Merry, what's your problem? Merry, look at me! Virgil! She's gone quite rigid, like she was in shock. I guess I ought to pat her cheeks. Hey, Merry, Merry! [HOMER *nervously pats her cheeks.*]

MERRY: Homer, I been watching those roosters—

HOMER: Sure, Merry, I know it—

MERRY: Homer, *one of those roosters is a degenerate.*

HOMER [*agonisedly, very gently*]: My poor little Merry, my poor little Merry, why did you have to be born so sensitive? Now, listen, Merry, you quit thinking of it right now. You start right in thinking about something beautiful. You start thinking about music or lovely old paintings or beautiful literature. . . .

VIRGIL: Why don't you tell her go take a look at the waste disposal unit?

HOMER: Why, Merry, you hear what Virgil said? I think that's a swell idea. Come along now. [*He leads her across the room to the door at the right.*] If there's one thing that ought to take your mind off all the ugly, unclean things that happen in this world, it's that waste disposal unit. [*Opening the door for her.*] You go right on in there, Merry, and see how the project's making out. [HOMER *tenderly closes the door after Merry and then marches back across the room.*]

HOMER: Now what're we going to do?

VIRGIL: I don't know why, but that question always panics me. Do about what, anyway?

HOMER: That rooster, of course. I can't ask Merry to share the premises with a rooster that's a degenerate.

VIRGIL: I don't see why it's any worse than asking her to share them with a brother-in-law that's a degenerate.

HOMER [*angrily*]: Will you quit talking that way? You'd be a perfectly healthful American boy, if you'd only try.

VIRGIL: I guess that's what's unhealthful about me. I can't even try to try.

HOMER: Why not, for pity's sakes? Don't I have enough on my mind as it is?

VIRGIL: Maybe I'm afraid it would spoil my work.

HOMER: Now that's another thing. I keep trying to get round to talking with you about that. How much longer is your work going to take?

VIRGIL: I can't say. I'm kind of held up for a climax.

[HOMER *deliberates, then:*]

HOMER: You know, Virgil, I sometimes get to wondering if you wrote anything at all.

VIRGIL [*deliberates, then deciding to take up the challenge*]: O.K. I'll read it to you.

HOMER: Right now?

VIRGIL: Mm-hm.

HOMER: But you didn't finish it yet.

VIRGIL: I'll read it as far as I went. Maybe you'll come up with something for the ending.

HOMER: I don't think I have any talent.

VIRGIL: Then sit down, brother, and listen to mine.

HOMER: How can I sit, there's no place to—I guess I can stand. It won't take that long, will it?

VIRGIL: Why didn't you hire some furnishings for this *palazzo?*

HOMER: That's a very selfish request, Virgil. You're the one that sits around all day. Maybe I'll hire some furnishings when I get round to it, but the first problem is to make the basic living conditions fit for Merry.

VIRGIL: O.K. brother, you stand. But don't move around any, you could distract me.

HOMER: O.K. O.K. Quit stalling, Virgil. Shoot.

VIRGIL [*turns back to the beginning of his book, clears his throat, then breaks off for a preliminary*]: Say, Homer. I hope you know this isn't going to be poetry like you mean poetry. It's more like—did you ever read any Chinese poetry?

HOMER: Sure, I guess I read some Chinese poetry some place, some magazine or something. In English.

VIRGIL: O, my poetry's in English, too. I just wanted you to know the opening sequences are modelled on Chinese poetry.

HOMER: Virgil, do you figure you can sell this? Is there a market for it? I don't know that the Chinese market's too easy to break into. I don't know, but it could even be that poetry is scheduled.

VIRGIL: Scheduled?

HOMER: Schedule of prohibited exports. I mean, if you're thinking of *Red* China.

VIRGIL: Brother!

HOMER: O.K. O.K., I didn't say a thing, go right ahead.

VIRGIL [*announcing*]: Section One. [*Reading:*]

> The American Woman
> Is strange, terrible and beautiful,
> Like fruits from the sea.
> There is nothing she would not ask her husband to do for her.
> For this reason
> She appears to be the most independent woman in the world,
> Just as aristocrats are said to be "of independent means"
> When in fact they are supported by slave labour.

[*There is a pause.*]

HOMER: Is that all?

VIRGIL: That's all of Section One.

HOMER: Maybe I'll get to see more in it when I become better accustomed to it.

VIRGIL [*reading*]:

> Section Two.
> The American Woman has grown
> Like a cactus
> In a place where there is no water.
> The American Woman would rather be a lovely person
> Than be herself.
> The American Woman would rather be a lovely, warm, genuine, sincere person
> Than simply be.

[VIRGIL *leaves a brief pause.*]

HOMER: Say, Virgil, do you think Merry's making out O.K. in there? Suppose this guy Angelo makes a pass at her?

VIRGIL: Homer, quit worrying and concentrate. Merry can handle it.

HOMER: I doubt that she can. That guy's a Latin, he's hot-blooded—

VIRGIL: You don't seem too well acquainted with Latin mores. If he does make a pass, he'll just pinch her fanny. That's the climactic act for Latins. Merry'll just think a mosquito got her.

HOMER: I don't know that she—

VIRGIL: Of *course* she can handle it, Homer, she'll handle it with a flit gun. Now can I read the third *canto?*

HOMER: Third what? Sounds like you were going horseback riding.

VIRGIL: Homer, you're not *that* illiterate. Or maybe you meant it as a gag. The third *canto* is freer and more rhapsodic in style.

HOMER: O.K. O.K. I guess we'll get to hear of it if Merry has problems.

VIRGIL [*reading*]: There is only one American Woman but she has two faces: one young, one old.

When she is young, she is younger than you would have thought possible. When she is old, she is older than the rocks she has persuaded her husband to buy for her.

The young American Woman is like an ad in a magazine of a glass of milk fresh from the icebox. She looks thirst quenching. But when you taste her, she tastes of wood-pulp.

The young American Woman is a wax apple. She is flawless. But she has no sap. Except her husband.

When you have talked with her a little while, you realise she was not begotten by sexual intercourse. Therefore:

When she grows old, she becomes a goddess. I love her best when she is old. For then she commands me more.

[*Aside*] You know, I really mean that, Homer. I'm determined to live to be a very old man, because I want to see Merry grow old. [*Resuming:*]

I followed the American goddess
Through the beautiful shrines of Europe.
I shadowed her through the Louvre,
I nearly caught up with her in the Rue de la Paix;
I watched her buying leather goods from a tiny but very expensive basement shop
    in Florence;
I dodged between her and the sunlight in Roman colonnades;
I glimpsed her in Castile;
When I stood in the Parthenon she was there.
She loves all that is old and said to be beautiful.
She has no taste.
But she has attended many seminars on good taste.

The old American Woman
Is all locust and no wild honey.
She is dry and mottled, like peanut brittle.
If you held her and bent her, she would snap.
But you do not lay hands on a cult object.
The strands of her hair are one with the spun gold she wears at her wrists and
    neck;
Her eyes are one with the topazes she wears on her knucklebones;
The skin of her forearms is one with the alligator hide that makes her purse.
I followed the tinkle of her charms on her charm bracelet
And the tinkle of her beaten metal hair.
I followed the clacking of her heels
And the clacking of her voice,
Which is an almost perfect imitation of the human voice.
I followed. I am unnatural; I am perverse.

The American Woman is more strange and more bizarre
Than the art of the mummy-maker.
And she is more old.
Organic in form, she is not created by life,
But is slowly deposited, like a tree of crystals
Imitating a baroque pearl.
The American Woman is a wax avocado pear
From a desert under the sea

[ANGELO *bursts in from the door at the right and flings himself, across the doorway, into the posture of the blinded Oedipus.*]

ANGELO [*sobbing and groaning*]: O no no no no no no no no. Orrore! [*He falls silent; his groans are quietly reiterated by a soft mechanical chug-chug from the next room. For a second everyone is too shocked to show reaction. Then* HOMER *dashes across the room towards* ANGELO, *who compassionately bars the way.*]

HOMER [*trying desperately to get past*]: What happened? What happened to Merry? Let me in there, Angelo, I got to get in there and see what happened to Merry.

ANGELO: Non c'è niente da vedere.

HOMER [*distractedly over his shoulder*]: What'd he say, Virgil?

VIRGIL [*threnodically*]: He says there is nothing to see.

HOMER [*in a groan of horror*]: What?

ANGELO [*pleading distressfully*]: Mr. Knockerbicker, I *tell* her not to lean over it and peer down it, but she wants to check I fixed it right—

HOMER [*beside himself*]: Can't you reverse the machinery or something? [*Bursting past* ANGELO.] Let me *in* there—

ANGELO [*appealing to Virgil*]: Mr. Knockerbicker junior, *you* are understanding, are you not? I *did* fix it right. If only she had believed me. Of *course* I reverse the machinery, but this is a very efficient unit. In thirty seconds, everything is—you understand, Mr. Knockerbicker junior?—*everything* . . .

[*The noise of the machinery is switched off.* HOMER *plods brokenly back into the* salone.]

HOMER: My little Merry! My little Merry! She was such a dainty little person, the last thing she would have wanted was to get mixed up with the garbage.

[*There is a moment's respectful silence.*]

Virgil, I know you will never forget that just before—why, it could even have been at the very moment—[HOMER *nearly breaks down.*] Well, anyhow, that you were just saying you wanted to live to see what a lovely lovely old lady Merry was going to grow into.

[LIA-PIA *shuffles unperturbedly into the room by the door at the left. She is followed by* MRS. VAN DEN MOST—*an older Merry and taken, of course, by the same actress.*]

LIA-PIA: Signori, ho incontrato queste signore davanti alla casa, non so cosa vuole. . . .

[LIA-PIA *shuffles out by the route she came, closing the door behind her.*]

HOMER [*horrified to reeling point*]: Mrs. van den *Most!*

MRS. VAN DEN MOST [*waggishly reproachful*]: Now, Homer. You know I asked you to call me something more intimate, such as Mom, because I think it will be so lovely for Merry to feel her family has been really integrated into her marriage.

HOMER: I didn't know—

MRS. VAN DEN MOST [*wagging a waggish finger at him*]: I know it, Homer, you didn't even know I was in Europe. Well, I figured I'd just hop over and see how you were taking care of my little girl. [HOMER *hides his face, and groans.*] I was counting on giving you a real surprise, and I must say you certainly seem to have gotten one. I wasn't even going to ring the doorbell, I was just snooping around outside, when your lovely old Italian hired help came out to feed your chickens. Those certainly are lovely chickens, Homer, I can just guess how Merry loves those chickens. And your lovely old Italian hired help brought me right along in. [*Noticing, with displeasure.*] O. Virgil's here. Hi, Virgil. I certainly hope you're beginning to get a hold on those problems of yours. [*Noticing, with pleasure.*] Why, we have company, I didn't notice.

VIRGIL: This is Signor Angelo Lumaca.

MRS. VAN DEN MOST: Why, you must be an Italian! I just love Italians, I love your *Renaissance*, I feel sure you must be a very good friend of my little girl, because she just loves your *Renaissance* too. Now where *is* my little girl? No, don't tell me. I can guess. Merry always takes such good care of her husband, Signor Lumaca, she's a real homebody, I don't have to ask where she is. I feel positive she's right along in the kitchen. Homer just loves her homebody ways, don't you, Homer? Right from the start, that girl loved to be in the kitchen. She has such a happy temperament, she makes everyone happy. Well, I should know. Right from the start she made *me* happy. Why, d'you know, Signor Lumaca, that little girl was toilet-trained before she was one year old. It was on account of she had such a happy temperament I persuaded Mr. van den Most to let me call her Merry. Lots of folks, when they first meet her, they think she's called Mary—Maria, as you would say it, Signor Lumaca—but no, her name is really Merry, M-E-double-R-Y, because, I always tell them, she *is*. Now where *is* the kitchen? No, naughty me, I don't need to ask. I didn't pass it on my way along, so I guess it must be right through here. [*She opens the door at the right.*] I'll just go give Merry a little surprise. [*Calling:*] Merry! Merry dear! [*Popping her head back into the* salone] I didn't find Merry yet, Homer, but I saw you had a waste disposal unit installed. Now that's very thoughtful of you, Homer, I'm sure Merry appreciates that. I wouldn't have thought you could obtain one over here. Well, I guess you imported it, but I reckon it was quite a problem for you getting it operational. I wonder if you got it fixed right. I'll just go take a quick look.

[MRS. VAN DEN MOST *hurries out. At once, the machinery noise begins again.*]

ANGELO [*lunging after her*]: No! Mrs. van den Most, no! Come back! No!

HOMER [*dashing across the room*]: Stop her, Angelo! I'm coming! Stop her!

[ANGELO *and* HOMER *sprint through the door at the right. Even* VIRGIL *is sufficiently anxious to discard his book, rises from the window-seat, and stands tense while he awaits the outcome.*]

[*The noise of the W.D.U. rises to a climax, and stops.* HOMER *and* ANGELO *return to the* salone.]

ANGELO [*with an explanatory, proving-his-point gesture*]: You see, Mr. Knockerbicker—

HOMER: Virgil—

VIRGIL [*incredulously*]: No?

HOMER: ⎫
ANGELO: ⎬ *Yes.*

HOMER [*with deep, plodding philosophy*]: The way I look at it, God proposes—

VIRGIL: And the Atlantic Seaboard waste disposal unit disposes.

HOMER [*with not altogether reluctant resignation*]: Well, everything has come to an end—

VIRGIL [*rising to exultation*]: And the Atlantic Seaboard waste disposal unit is the American male's best friend.

HOMER ⎫
VIRGIL ⎬ [*beginning a stomping dance with one another*]:

> Soggy crunchy
> Pulpy bony
> Mushy spiny

VIRGIL: Mottled shiny

HOMER: ⎫
VIRGIL: ⎬ Pulpy bony

ANGELO [*trying a last plea*]: Signori Knockerbicker, *please*—

VIRGIL [*stomping gaily*]: How're you feeling now, brother?

HOMER [*likewise*]: How'm I feeling now? [*As in a college cry*] M-E-double-R-Y.

HOMER ⎫
VIRGIL ⎬ [*in a shout in unison*]: Merry!

VIRGIL: Say goodbye forever to squelchy bundles!

ANGELO [*giving up restraint and joining the dance with a wild, free-lance fling, as he sings in a bold tenor*]: La donna è mobile! La donna è mobile!

HOMER ⎫
VIRGIL ⎬ [*stomping and chanting*]:
ANGELO ⎭

> Soggy crunchy
> Honeybunchy
> Sodden dry
> Sweetiepie
> Say goodbye

Mushy spiny
Dainty tiny
Lovely happy
Minced-up pappy
Very merry

ANGELO [*floating his tenor above the stomp*]: La donna è mobile.
VIRGIL [*basso profondo*]: E disponibile!

[*There is a general, happy, panting collapse onto the floor.*]

VIRGIL [*happily*]: Angelo, did it take but *everything?*
ANGELO [*with happy assurance*]: Every single thing, Mr. Knockerbicker junior.
HOMER: Even the second time round?
ANGELO: Second time round was even more efficient, Mr. Knockerbicker. That machine likes something tough to bite on.
VIRGIL [*solemnly*]: Angelo, Homer, I guess we have witnessed the ultimate triumph of American technology.

Curtain

QUESTIONS

1. What class and culture is the playwright satirizing?
2. The playwright mentions that Virgil has spent ten years writing his poem. What does she mean to imply about his personality?
3. The Knockerbickers display a great deal of concern about propriety. What are some of the more absurd anxieties about doing things the "proper" way?
4. Why does the family appear so happy at the end of the play, despite the fact that Merry has disappeared down the waste disposal unit? What aspect of bourgeois life is the author commenting on?

August Wilson

MA RAINEY'S BLACK BOTTOM

A Play in Two Acts

They tore the railroad down
so the Sunshine Special can't run
I'm going away baby
build me a railroad of my own
—Blind Lemon Jefferson

For my mother

CHARACTERS

Ma Rainey's Black Bottom opened on April 6, 1984, at the Yale Repertory Theater in New Haven, Connecticut, with the following cast:

STURDYVANT   Richard M. Davidson
IRVIN   Lou Criscuolo
CUTLER   Joe Seneca
TOLEDO   Robert Judd
SLOW DRAG   Leonard Jackson
LEVEE   Charles S. Dutton
MA RAINEY   Theresa Merritt
POLICEMAN   David Wayne Nelson
DUSSIE MAE   Sharon Mitchell
SYLVESTER   Steven R. Blye

Director: Lloyd Richards
Settings: Charles Henry McClennahan
Costumes: Daphne Pascucci
Lighting: Peter Maradudin
Music Director: Dwight Andrews

THE SETTING

There are two playing areas: what is called the "band room," and the recording studio. The band room is at stage left and is in the basement of the building. It is entered through a door up left. There are benches and chairs scattered about, a piano, a row of lockers, and miscellaneous paraphernalia stacked in a corner and long since forgotten. A mirror hangs on a wall with various posters.

The studio is upstairs at stage right, and resembles a recording studio of the late 1920's. The entrance is from a hall on the right wall. A small control booth is at the rear and its access is gained by means of a spiral staircase. Against one wall there is a line of chairs, and a horn through which the control room communicates with the performers. A door in the rear wall allows access to the band room.

THE PLAY

It is early March in Chicago, 1927. There is a bit of a chill in the air. Winter has broken but the wind coming off the lake does not carry the promise of spring. The people of the city are bundled and brisk in their defense against such misfortunes as the weather, and the business of the city proceeds largely undisturbed.

Chicago in 1927 is a rough city, a bruising city, a city of millionaires and derelicts, gangsters and roughhouse dandies, whores and Irish grandmothers who move through its streets fingering long black rosaries. Somewhere a man is wrestling with the taste of a woman in his cheek. Somewhere a dog is barking. Somewhere the moon has fallen through a window and broken into thirty pieces of silver.

It is one o'clock in the afternoon. Secretaries are returning from their lunch, the noon Mass at St. Anthony's is over, and the priest is mumbling over his vestments while the altar boys practice their Latin. The procession of cattle cars through the stockyards continues unabated. The busboys in Mac's Place are cleaning away the last of the corned beef and cabbage, and on the city's Southside, sleepy-eyed negroes move lazily toward their small cold-water flats and rented rooms to await the onslaught of night, which will find them crowded in the bars and juke joints both dazed and dazzling in their rapport with life. It is with these negroes that our concern lies most heavily: their values, their attitudes, and particularly their music.

It is hard to define this music. Suffice it to say that it is music that breathes and touches. That connects. *That is in itself a way of being, separate and distinct from any other. This music is called blues. Whether this music came from Alabama or Mississippi or other parts of the South doesn't matter anymore. The men and women who make this music have learned it from the narrow crooked streets of East St. Louis, or the streets of the city's Southside, and the Alabama or Mississippi roots have been strangled by the northern manners and customs of free men of definite and sincere worth, men for whom this music often lies at the forefront of their conscience and concerns. Thus they are laid open to be consumed by it; its warmth and redress, its braggadocio and roughly poignant comments, its vision and prayer, which would instruct and allow them to reconnect, to reassemble and gird up for the next battle in which they would be both victim and the ten thousand slain.*

ACT ONE

The lights come up in the studio. IRVIN *enters, carrying a microphone. He is a tall, fleshy man who prides himself on his knowledge of blacks and his ability to deal with them. He hooks up the microphone, blows into it, taps it, etc. He crosses over to the piano, opens it, and fingers a few keys.* STURDYVANT *is visible in the control booth. Preoccupied with money, he is insensitive to black performers and prefers to deal with them at arm's length. He puts on a pair of earphones.*

STURDYVANT [*over speaker*]: Irv . . . let's crack that mike, huh? Let's do a check on it.

IRVIN [*crosses to mike, speaks into it*]: Testing . . . one . . . two . . . three . . .

[*There is a loud feedback.* STURDYVANT *fiddles with the dials.*]

Testing . . . one . . . two . . . three . . . testing. How's that, Mel?

[STURDYVANT *doesn't respond.*]

Testing . . . one . . . two . . .

STURDYVANT [*taking off earphones*]: Okay . . . that checks. We got a good reading.

[*Pause.*]

You got that list, Irv?

IRVIN: Yeah . . . yeah, I got it. Don't worry about nothing.

STURDYVANT: Listen, Irv . . . you keep her in line, okay? I'm holding you responsible for her . . . If she starts any of her . . .

IRVIN: Mel, what's with the goddamn horn? You wanna talk to me . . . okay! I can't talk to you over the goddamn horn . . . Christ!

STURDYVANT: I'm not putting up with any shenanigans. You hear, Irv?

[IRVIN *crosses over to the piano and mindlessly runs his fingers over the keys.*]

I'm just not gonna stand for it. I want you to keep her in line. Irv?

[STURDYVANT *enters from the control booth.*]

Listen, Irv . . . you're her manager . . . she's your responsibility . . .

IRVIN: Okay, okay, Mel . . . let me handle it.

STURDYVANT: She's your responsibility. I'm not putting up with any Royal Highness . . . Queen of the Blues bullshit!

IRVIN: Mother of the Blues, Mel. Mother of the Blues.

STURDYVANT: I don't care what she calls herself. I'm not putting up with it. I just want to get her in here . . . record those songs on that list . . . and get her out. Just like clockwork, huh?

IRVIN: Like clockwork, Mel. You just stay out of the way and let me handle it.

STURDYVANT: Yeah . . . yeah . . . you handled it last time. Remember? She marches in here like she owns the damn place . . . doesn't like the songs we picked out . . . says her throat is sore . . . doesn't want to do more than one take . . .

IRVIN: Okay . . . okay . . . I was here! I know all about it.

STURDYVANT: Complains about the building being cold . . . and then . . . trips over the mike wire and threatens to sue me. That's taking care of it?

IRVIN: I've got it all worked out this time. I talked with her last night. Her throat is fine . . . We went over the songs together . . . I got everything straight, Mel.

STURDYVANT: Irv, that horn player . . . the one who gave me those songs . . . is he gonna be here today? Good. I want to hear more of that sound. Times are changing. This is a tricky business now. We've got to jazz it up . . . put in something different. You know, something wild . . . with a lot of rhythm.

[*Pause.*]

You know what we put out last time, Irv? We put out garbage last time. It was garbage. I don't even know why I bother with this anymore.

IRVIN: You did all right last time, Mel. Not as good as you did before, but you did all right.

STURDYVANT: You know how many records we sold in New York? You wanna see the sheet? And you know what's in New York, Irv? Harlem. Harlem's in New York, Irv.

IRVIN: Okay, so they didn't sell in New York. But look at Memphis . . . Birmingham . . . Atlanta. Christ, you made a bundle.

STURDYVANT: It's not the money, Irv. You know I couldn't sleep last night? This business is bad for my nerves. My wife is after me to slow down and take a vacation. Two more years and I'm gonna get out . . . get into something respectable. Textiles. That's a respectable business. You know what you could do with a shipload of textiles from Ireland?

[*A buzzer is heard offstage.*]

IRVIN: Why don't you go upstairs and let me handle it, Mel?

STURDYVANT: Remember . . . you're responsible for her.

[STURDYVANT *exits to the control booth.* IRVIN *crosses to get the door.* CUTLER, SLOW DRAG, *and* TOLEDO *enter.* CUTLER *is in his mid-fifties, as are most of the others. He plays guitar and trombone and is the leader of the group, possibly because he is the most sensible. His playing is solid and almost totally unembellished. His understanding of his music is limited to the chord he is playing at the time he is playing it. He has all the qualities of a loner except the introspection.* SLOW DRAG, *the bass player, is perhaps the one most bored by life. He resembles* CUTLER, *but lacks* CUTLER'*s energy. He is deceptively intelligent, though, as his name implies, he appears to be slow. He is a rather large man with a wicked smile. Innate African rhythms underlie everything he plays, and he plays with an ease that is at times startling.* TOLEDO *is the piano player. In control of his instrument, he understands and recognizes that its limitations are an extension of himself. He is the only one in the group who can read. He is self-taught but misunderstands and misapplies his knowledge, though he is quick to penetrate to the core of a situation and his insights are thought-provoking. All of the men are dressed in a style of clothing befitting the members of a successful band of the era.*]

IRVIN: How you boys doing, Cutler? Come on in.
[*Pause.*]
Where's Ma? Is she with you?

CUTLER: I don't know, Mr. Irvin. She told us to be here at one o'clock. That's all I know.

IRVIN: Where's . . . huh . . . the horn player? Is he coming with Ma?

CUTLER: Levee's supposed to be here same as we is. I reckon he'll be here in a minute. I can't rightly say.

IRVIN: Well, come on . . . I'll show you to the band room, let you get set up and rehearsed. You boys hungry? I'll call over to the deli and get some sandwiches. Get you fed and ready to make some music. Cutler . . . here's the list of songs we're gonna record.

STURDYVANT [*over speaker*]: Irvin, what's happening? Where's Ma?

IRVIN: Everything under control, Mel. I got it under control.

STURDYVANT: Where's Ma? How come she isn't with the band?

IRVIN: She'll be here in a minute, Mel. Let me get these fellows down to the band room, huh?

[*They exit the studio. The lights go down in the studio and up in the band room.* IRVIN *opens the door and allows them to pass as they enter.*]

You boys go ahead and rehearse. I'll let you know when Ma comes.

[IRVIN *exits.* CUTLER *hands* TOLEDO *the list of songs.*]

CUTLER: What we got here, Toledo?

TOLEDO [*reading*]: We got . . . "Prove It on Me" . . . "Hear Me Talking to You" . . . "Ma Rainey's Black Bottom" . . . and "Moonshine Blues."

CUTLER: Where Mr. Irvin go? Them ain't the songs Ma told me.

SLOW DRAG: I wouldn't worry about it if I were you, Cutler. They'll get it straightened out. Ma will get it straightened out.

CUTLER: I just don't want no trouble about these songs, that's all. Ma ain't told me them songs. She told me something else.

SLOW DRAG: What she tell you?

CUTLER: This "Moonshine Blues" wasn't in it. That's one of Bessie's songs.

TOLEDO: Slow Drag's right . . . I wouldn't worry about it. Let them straighten it up.

CUTLER: Levee know what time he supposed to be here?

SLOW DRAG: Levee gone out to spend your four dollars. He left the hotel this morning talking about he was gonna go buy some shoes. Say it's the first time he ever beat you shooting craps.

CUTLER: Do he know what time he supposed to be here? That's what I wanna know. I ain't thinking about no four dollars.

SLOW DRAG: Levee sure was thinking about it. That four dollars liked to burn a hole in his pocket.

CUTLER: Well, he's supposed to be here at one o'clock. That's what time Ma said. That nigger get out in the streets with that four dollars and ain't no telling when he's liable to show. You ought to have seen him at the club last night, Toledo. Trying to talk to some gal Ma had with her.

TOLEDO: You ain't got to tell me. I know how Levee do.

[*Buzzer is heard offstage.*]

SLOW DRAG: Levee tried to talk to that gal and got his feelings hurt. She didn't want no part of him. She told Levee he'd have to turn his money green before he could talk with her.

CUTLER: She out for what she can get. Anybody could see that.

SLOW DRAG: That's why Levee run out to buy some shoes. He's looking to make an impression on that gal.

CUTLER: What the hell she gonna do with his shoes? She can't do nothing with the nigger's shoes.

[SLOW DRAG *takes out a pint bottle and drinks.*]

TOLEDO: Let me hit that, Slow Drag.

SLOW DRAG [*handing him the bottle*]: This some of that good Chicago bourbon!

[*The door opens and* LEVEE *enters, carrying a shoe box. In his early thirties,* LEVEE *is younger than the other men. His flamboyance is sometimes subtle and sneaks up on you. His temper is rakish and bright. He lacks fuel for himself and is somewhat of a buffoon. But it is an intelligent buffoonery, clearly calculated to shift control of the situation to where he can grasp it. He plays trumpet. His voice is strident and totally dependent on his manipulation of breath. He plays wrong notes frequently. He often gets his skill and talent confused with each other.*]

CUTLER: Levee . . . where Mr. Irvin go?

LEVEE: Hell, I don't know. I ain't none of his keeper.

SLOW DRAG: What you got there, Levee?

LEVEE: Look here, Cutler . . . I got me some shoes!

CUTLER: Nigger, I ain't studying you.

[LEVEE *takes the shoes out of the box and starts to put them on.*]

TOLEDO: How much you pay for something like that, Levee?

LEVEE: Eleven dollars. Four dollars of it belong to Cutler.

SLOW DRAG: Levee say if it wasn't for Cutler . . . he wouldn't have no new shoes.

CUTLER: I ain't thinking about Levee or his shoes. Come on . . . let's get ready to rehearse.

SLOW DRAG: I'm with you on that score, Cutler. I wanna get out of here. I don't want to be around here all night. When it comes time to go up there and record them songs . . . I just wanna go up there and do it. Last time it took us all day and half the night.

TOLEDO: Ain't but four songs on the list. Last time we recorded six songs.

SLOW DRAG: It felt like it was sixteen!

LEVEE [*finishes with his shoes*]: Yeah! Now I'm ready! I can play some good music now! [*He goes to put up his old shoes and looks around the room.*]

Damn! They done changed things around. Don't never leave well enough alone.

TOLEDO: Everything changing all the time. Even the air you breathing change. You got, monoxide, hydrogen . . . changing all the time. Skin changing . . . different molecules and everything.

LEVEE: Nigger, what is you talking about? I'm talking about the room. I ain't talking about no skin and air. I'm talking about something I can see! Last time the band room was upstairs. This time it's downstairs. Next time it be over there. I'm talking about what I can see. I ain't talking about no molecules or nothing.

TOLEDO: Hell, I know what you talking about. I just said everything changin'. I know what you talking about, but you don't know what I'm talking about.

LEVEE: That door! Nigger, you see that door? That's what I'm talking about. That door wasn't there before.

CUTLER: Levee, you wouldn't know your right from your left. This is where they used to keep the recording horns and things . . . and damn if that door wasn't there. How in hell else you gonna get in here? Now, if you talking about they done switched rooms, you right. But don't go telling me that damn door wasn't there!

SLOW DRAG: Damn the door and let's get set up. I wanna get out of here.

LEVEE: Toledo started all that about the door. I'm just saying that things change.

TOLEDO: What the hell you think I was saying? Things change. The air and everything. Now you gonna say you was saying it. You gonna fit two propositions on the same track . . . run them into each other, and because they crash, you gonna say it's the same train.

LEVEE: Now this nigger talking about trains! We done went from the air to the skin to the door . . . and now trains. Toledo, I'd just like to be inside your head for five minutes. Just to see how you think. You done got more shit piled up and mixed up in there than the devil got sinners. You been reading too many goddamn books.

TOLEDO: What you care about how much I read? I'm gonna ignore you 'cause you ignorant.

[LEVEE *takes off his coat and hangs it in the locker.*]

SLOW DRAG: Come on, let's rehearse the music.

LEVEE: You ain't gotta rehearse that . . . ain't nothing but old jug-band music. They need one of them jug bands for this.

SLOW DRAG: Don't make me no difference. Long as we get paid.

LEVEE: That ain't what I'm talking about, nigger. I'm talking about art!

SLOW DRAG: What's drawing got to do with it?

LEVEE: Where you get this nigger from, Cutler? He sound like one of them Alabama niggers.

CUTLER: Slow Drag's all right. It's you talking all that weird shit about art. Just play the piece, nigger. You wanna be one of them . . . what you call . . . virtuoso or something, you in the wrong place. You ain't no Buddy Bolden or King Oliver . . . you just an old trumpet player come a dime a dozen. Talking about art.

LEVEE: What is you? I don't see your name in lights.

CUTLER: I just play the piece. Whatever they want. I don't go talking about art and criticizing other people's music.

LEVEE: I ain't like you, Cutler. I got talent! Me and this horn . . . we's tight. If my daddy knowed I was gonna turn out like this, he would've named me Gabriel. I'm gonna get me a band and make me some records. I done give Mr. Sturdyvant some of my songs I wrote and he say he's gonna let me record them when I get my band together.

[*Takes some papers out of his pocket.*]

I just gotta finish the last part of this song. And Mr. Sturdyvant want me to write another part to this song.

SLOW DRAG: How you learn to write music, Levee?

LEVEE: I just picked it up . . . like you pick up anything. Miss Eula used to play the piano . . . she learned me a lot. I knows how to play *real* music . . . not this old jug-band shit. I got style!

TOLEDO: Everybody got style. Style ain't nothing but keeping the same idea from beginning to end. Everybody got it.

LEVEE: But everybody can't play like I do. Everybody can't have their own band.

CUTLER: Well, until you get your own band where you can play what you want, you just play the piece and stop complaining. I told you when you came on here, this ain't none of them hot bands. This is an accompaniment band. You play Ma's music when you here.

LEVEE: I got sense enough to know that. Hell, I can look at you all and see what kind of band it is. I can look at Toledo and see what kind of band it is.

TOLEDO: Toledo ain't said nothing to you now. Don't let Toledo get started. You can't even spell music, much less play it.

LEVEE: What you talking about? I can spell music. I got a dollar say I can spell it! Put your dollar up. Where your dollar?

[TOLEDO *waves him away.*]

Now come on. Put your dollar up. Talking about I can't spell music.

[LEVEE *peels a dollar off his roll and slams it down on the bench beside* TOLEDO.]

TOLEDO: All right, I'm gonna show you. Cutler. Slow Drag. You hear this? The nigger betting me a dollar he can spell music. I don't want no shit now!

[TOLEDO *lays a dollar down beside* LEVEE'S.]

All right. Go ahead. Spell it.

LEVEE: It's a bet then. Talking about I can't spell music.

TOLEDO: Go ahead, then. Spell it. Music. Spell it.

LEVEE: I can spell it, nigger! M-U-S-I-K. There!

[*He reaches for the money.*]

TOLEDO: Naw! Naw! Leave that money alone! You ain't spelled it.

LEVEE: What you mean I ain't spelled it? I said M-U-S-I-K!

TOLEDO: That ain't how you spell it! That ain't how you spell it! It's M-U-S-I-*C!* C, nigger. Not K! C! M-U-S-I-C!

LEVEE: What you mean, C? Who say it's C?

TOLEDO: Cutler. Slow Drag. Tell this fool.

[*They look at each other and then away.*]

Well, I'll be a monkey's uncle!

[TOLEDO *picks up the money and hands* LEVEE *his dollar back.*]

Here's your dollar back, Levee. I done won it, you understand. I done won the dollar. But if don't nobody know but me, how am I gonna prove it to you?

LEVEE: You just mad 'cause I spelled it.

TOLEDO: Spelled what! M-U-S-I-K don't spell nothing. I just wish there was some way I could show you the right and wrong of it. How you gonna know something if the other fellow don't know if you're right or not? Now I can't even be sure that I'm spelling it right.

LEVEE: That's what I'm talking about. You don't know it. Talking about C. You ought to give me that dollar I won from you.

TOLEDO: All right. All right. I'm gonna show you how ridiculous you sound. You know the Lord's Prayer?

LEVEE: Why? You wanna bet a dollar on that?

TOLEDO: Just answer the question. Do you know the Lord's Prayer or don't you?

LEVEE: Yeah, I know it. What of it?

TOLEDO: Cutler?

CUTLER: What you Cutlering me for? I ain't got nothing to do with it.

TOLEDO: I just want to show the man how ridiculous he is.

CUTLER: Both of you all sound like damn fools. Arguing about something silly. Yeah, I know the Lord's Prayer. My daddy was a deacon in the church. Come asking me if I know the Lord's Prayer. Yeah, I know it.

TOLEDO: Slow Drag?

SLOW DRAG: Yeah.

TOLEDO: All right. Now I'm gonna tell you a story to show just how ridiculous he sound. There was these two fellows, see. So, the one of them go up to this church and commence to taking up the church learning. The other fellow see him out on the road and he say, "I done heard you taking up the church learning," say, "Is you learning anything up there?" The other one say, "Yeah, I done take up the church learning and I's learning all kinds of things about the Bible and what it say and all. Why you be asking?" The other one say, "Well, do you know the Lord's Prayer?" And he say, "Why, sure I know the Lord's Prayer, I'm taking up learning at the church ain't I? I know the Lord's Prayer backwards and forewards." And the other fellow says, "I bet you five dollars you don't know the Lord's Prayer, 'cause I don't think you knows it. I think you be going up to the church 'cause the Widow Jenkins be going up there and you just wanna be sitting in the same room with her when she cross them big, fine, pretty legs she got." And the other one say, "Well, I'm gonna prove you wrong and I'm gonna bet you that five dollars." So he say, "Well, go on and say it then." So he commenced to saying the Lord's Prayer. He say, "Now I lay me down to sleep, I pray the Lord my soul to keep." The other one say, "Here's your five dollars. I didn't think you knew it."

[*They all laugh.*]

Now, that's just how ridiculous Levee sound. Only 'cause I knowed how to spell music, I still got my dollar.

LEVEE: That don't prove nothing. What's that supposed to prove?

[TOLEDO *takes a newspaper out of his back pocket and begins to read.*]

TOLEDO: I'm through with it.

SLOW DRAG: Is you all gonna rehearse this music or ain't you?

[CUTLER *takes out some papers and starts to roll a reefer.*]

LEVEE: How many times you done played them songs? What you gotta rehearse for?

SLOW DRAG: This a recording session. I wanna get it right the first time and get on out of here.

CUTLER: Slow Drag's right. Let's go on and rehearse and get it over with.

LEVEE: You all go and rehearse, then. I got to finish this song for Mr. Sturdyvant.

CUTLER: Come on, Levee . . . I don't want no shit now. You rehearse like everybody else. You in the band like everybody else. Mr. Sturdyvant just gonna have to wait. You got to do that on your own time. This is the band's time.

LEVEE: Well, what is you doing? You sitting there rolling a reefer talking about let's rehearse. Toledo reading a newspaper. Hell, I'm ready if you wanna rehearse. I just say there ain't no point in it. Ma ain't here. What's the point in it?

CUTLER: Nigger, why you gotta complain all the time?

TOLEDO: Levee would complain if a gal ain't laid across his bed just right.

CUTLER: That's what I know. That's why I try to tell him just play the music and forget about it. It ain't no big thing.

TOLEDO: Levee ain't got an eye for that. He wants to tie on to some abstract component and sit down on the elemental.

LEVEE: This is get-on-Levee time, huh? Levee ain't said nothing except this some old jug-band music.

TOLEDO: Under the right circumstances you'd play anything. If you know music, then you play it. Straight on or off to the side. Ain't nothing abstract about it.

LEVEE: Toledo, you sound like you got a mouth full of marbles. You the only cracker-talking nigger I know.

TOLEDO: You ought to have learned yourself to read . . . then you'd understand the basic understanding of everything.

SLOW DRAG: Both of you all gonna drive me crazy with that philosophy bullshit. Cutler, give me a reefer.

CUTLER: Ain't you got some reefer? Where's your reefer? Why you all the time asking me?

SLOW DRAG: Cutler, how long I done known you? How long we been together? Twenty-two years. We been doing this together for twenty-two years. All up and down the back roads, the side roads, the front roads . . . We done played the juke joints, the whorehouses, the barn dances, and city sit-downs . . . I done lied for you and lied with you . . . We done laughed together, fought together, slept in the same bed together, done sucked on the same titty . . . and now you don't wanna give me no reefer.

CUTLER: You see this nigger trying to talk me out of my reefer, Toledo? Running all that about how long he done knowed me and how we done sucked on the same titty. Nigger, you *still* ain't getting none of my reefer!

TOLEDO: That's African.

SLOW DRAG: What? What you talking about? What's African?

LEVEE: I know he ain't talking about me. You don't see me running around in no jungle with no bone between my nose.

TOLEDO: Levee, you worse than ignorant. You ignorant without a premise.

[*Pauses.*]

Now, what I was saying is what Slow Drag was doing is African. That's what you call an African conceptualization. That's when you name the gods or call on the ancestors to achieve whatever your desires are.

SLOW DRAG: Nigger, I ain't no African! I ain't doing no African nothing!

TOLEDO: Naming all those things you and Cutler done together is like trying to solicit some reefer based on a bond of kinship. That's African. An ancestral retention. Only you forgot the name of the gods.

SLOW DRAG: I ain't forgot nothing. I was telling the nigger how cheap he is. Don't come talking that African nonsense to me.

TOLEDO: You just like Levee. No eye for taking an abstract and fixing it to a specific. There's so much that goes on around you and you can't even see it.

CUTLER: Wait a minute . . . wait a minute. Toledo, now when this nigger . . . when an African do all them things you say and name all the gods and whatnot . . . then what happens?

TOLEDO: Depends on if the gods is sympathetic with his cause for which he is calling them with the right names. Then his success comes with the right proportion of his naming. That's the way that go.

CUTLER: [*Taking out a reefer.*] Here, Slow Drag. Here's a reefer. You done talked yourself up on that one.

SLOW DRAG: Thank you. You ought to have done that in the first place and saved me all the aggravation.

CUTLER: What I wants to know is . . . what's the same titty we done sucked on. That's what I want to know.

SLOW DRAG: Oh, I just threw that in there to make it sound good.

[*They all laugh.*]

CUTLER: Nigger, you ain't right.

SLOW DRAG: I knows it.

CUTLER: Well, come on . . . let's get it rehearsed. Time's wasting.
[*The musicians pick up their instruments.*]
Let's do it. "Ma Rainey's Black Bottom." One . . . two . . . You know what to do.

[*They begin to play.* LEVEE *is playing something different. He stops.*]

LEVEE: Naw! Naw! We ain't doing it that way.
[TOLEDO *stops playing, then* SLOW DRAG.]
We doing my version. It say so right there on that piece of paper you got. Ask Toledo. That's what Mr. Irvin told me . . . say it's on the list he gave you.

CUTLER: Let me worry about what's on the list and what ain't on the list. How you gonna tell me what's on the list?

LEVEE: 'Cause I know what Mr. Irvin told me! Ask Toledo!

CUTLER: Let me worry about what's on the list. You just play the song I say.

LEVEE: What kind of sense it make to rehearse the wrong version of the song? That's what I wanna know. Why you wanna rehearse that version.

SLOW DRAG: You supposed to rehearse what you gonna play. That's the way they taught me. Now, *whatever* version we gonna play . . . let's go on and rehearse it.

LEVEE: That's what I'm trying to tell the man.

CUTLER: You trying to tell me what we is and ain't gonna play. And that ain't none of your business. Your business is to play what I say.

LEVEE: Oh, I see now. You done got jealous cause Mr. Irvin using my version. You done got jealous cause I proved I know something about music.

CUTLER: What the hell . . . nigger, you talk like a fool! What the hell I got to be jealous of you about? The day I get jealous of you I may as well lay down and die.

TOLEDO: Levee started all that 'cause he too lazy to rehearse.

[*To* LEVEE.]

You ought to just go on and play the song . . . What difference does it make?

LEVEE: Where's the paper? Look at the paper! Get the paper and look at it! See what it say. Gonna tell me I'm too lazy to rehearse.

CUTLER: We ain't talking about the paper. We talking about you understanding where you fit in when you around here. You just play what I say.

LEVEE: Look . . . I don't care what you play! All right? It don't matter to me. Mr. Irvin gonna straighten it up! I don't care what you play.

CUTLER: Thank you.

[*Pauses.*]

Let's play this "Hear Me Talking to You" till we find out what's happening with the "Black Bottom." Slow Drag, you sing Ma's part.

[*Pauses.*]

"Hear Me Talking to You." Let's do it. One . . . Two . . . You know what to do.

[*They play.*]

SLOW DRAG [*singing*]:

> Rambling man makes no change in me
> I'm gonna ramble back to my used-to-be
> Ah, you hear me talking to you
> I don't bite my tongue
> You wants to be my man
> You got to fetch it with you when you come.
>
> Eve and Adam in the garden taking a chance
> Adam didn't take time to get his pants
> Ah, you hear me talking to you
> I don't bite my tongue
> You wants to be my man
> You got to fetch it with you when you come.
>
> Our old cat swallowed a ball of yarn
> When the kittens were born they had sweaters on

Ah, you hear me talking to you
I don't bite my tongue
You wants to be my man
You got to fetch it with you when you come.

[IRVIN *enters. The musicians stop playing.*]

IRVIN: Any of you boys know what's keeping Ma?
CUTLER: Can't say, Mr. Irvin. She'll be along directly, I reckon. I talked to her this morning, she say she'll be here in time to rehearse.
IRVIN: Well, you boys go ahead.

[*He starts to exit.*]

CUTLER: Mr. Irvin, about these songs . . . Levee say . . .
IRVIN: Whatever's on the list, Cutler. You got that list I gave you?
CUTLER: Yessir, I got it right here.
IRVIN: Whatever's on there. Whatever that says.
CUTLER: I'm asking about this "Black Bottom" piece . . . Levee say . . .
IRVIN: Oh, it's on the list. "Ma Rainey's Black Bottom" on the list.
CUTLER: I know it's on the list. I wanna know what version. We got two versions of that song.
IRVIN: Oh. Levee's arrangement. We're using Levee's arrangement.
CUTLER: Ok. I got that straight. Now, this "Moonshine Blues" . . .
IRVIN: We'll work it out with Ma, Cutler. Just rehearse whatever's on the list and use Levee's arrangement on that "Black Bottom" piece.

[*He exits.*]

LEVEE: See, I told you! It don't mean nothing when I say it. You got to wait for Mr. Irvin to say it. Well, I told you the way it is.
CUTLER: Levee, the sooner you understand it ain't what you say, or what Mr. Irvin say . . . it's what Ma say that counts.
SLOW DRAG: Don't nobody say when it come to Ma. She's gonna do what she wants to do. Ma says what happens with her.
LEVEE: Hell, the man's the one putting out the record! He's gonna put out what he wanna put out!
SLOW DRAG: He's gonna put out what Ma want him to put out.
LEVEE: You heard what the man told you . . . "Ma Rainey's Black Bottom," Levee's arrangement. There you go! That's what he told you.
SLOW DRAG: What you gonna do, Cutler?
CUTLER: Ma ain't told me what version. Let's go on and play it Levee's way.
TOLEDO: See, now . . . I'll tell you something. As long as the colored man look to white folks to put the crown on what he say . . . as long as he looks to white folks

for approval . . . then he ain't never gonna find out who he is and what he's about. He's just gonna be about what white folks want him to be about. That's one sure thing.

LEVEE: I'm just trying to show Cutler where he's wrong.

CUTLER: Cutler don't need you to show him nothing.

SLOW DRAG: [*irritated*] Come on, let's get this shit rehearsed! You all can bicker afterward!

CUTLER: Levee's confused about who the boss is. He don't know Ma's the boss.

LEVEE: Ma's the boss on the road! We at a recording session. Mr. Sturdyvant and Mr. Irvin say what's gonna be here! We's in Chicago, we ain't in Memphis! I don't know why you all wanna pick me about it, shit! I'm with Slow Drag . . . Let's go on and get it rehearsed.

CUTLER: All right. All right. I know how to solve this. "Ma Rainey's Black Bottom." Levee's version. Let's do it. Come on.

TOLEDO: How that first part go again, Levee?

LEVEE: It go like this.

[*He plays.*]

That's to get the people's attention to the song. That's when you and Slow Drag come in with the rhythm part. Me and Cutler play on the breaks.

[*Becoming animated.*]

Now we gonna dance it . . . but we ain't gonna countrify it. This ain't no barn dance. We gonna play it like . . .

CUTLER: The man ask you how the first part go. He don't wanna hear all that. Just tell him how the piece go.

TOLEDO: I got it. I got it. Let's go. I know how to do it.

CUTLER: "Ma Rainey's Black Bottom." One . . . two . . . You know what to do.

[*They begin to play.* LEVEE *stops.*]

LEVEE: You all got to keep up now. You playing in the wrong time. Ma come in over the top. She got to find her own way in.

CUTLER: Nigger, will you let us play this song? When you get your own band . . . then you tell them that nonsense. We know how to play the piece. I was playing music before you was born. Gonna tell me how to play . . . All right. Let's try it again.

SLOW DRAG: Cutler, wait till I fix this. This string started to unravel.

[*Playfully.*]

And you know I want to play Levee's music right.

LEVEE: If you was any kind of musician, you'd take care of your instrument. Keep it in tip-top order. If you was any kind of musician, I'd let you be in my band.

SLOW DRAG: Shhheeeeet!

[*He crosses to get his string and steps on* LEVEE's *shoes.*]

LEVEE: Damn, Slow Drag! Watch them big-ass shoes you got.

SLOW DRAG: Boy, ain't nobody done nothing to you.

LEVEE: You done stepped on my shoes.

SLOW DRAG: Move them the hell out the way, then. You was in my way . . . I wasn't in your way.

[CUTLER *lights up another reefer.* SLOW DRAG *rummages around in his belongings for a string.* LEVEE *takes out a rag and begins to shine his shoes.*]

You can shine these when you get done, Levee.

CUTLER: If I had them shoes Levee got, I could buy me a whole suit of clothes.

LEVEE: What kind of difference it make what kind of shoes I got? Ain't nothing wrong with having nice shoes. I ain't said nothing about your shoes. Why you wanna talk about me and my Florsheims?

CUTLER: Any man who takes a whole week's pay and puts it on some shoes—you understand what I mean, what you walk around on the ground with—is a fool! And I don't mind telling you.

LEVEE [*irritated*]: What difference it make to you, Cutler?

SLOW DRAG: The man ain't said nothing about your shoes. Ain't nothing wrong with having nice shoes. Look at Toledo.

TOLEDO: What about Toledo?

SLOW DRAG: I said ain't nothing wrong with having nice shoes.

LEVEE: Nigger got them clodhoppers! Old brogans! He ain't nothing but a share-cropper.

TOLEDO: You can make all the fun you want. It don't mean nothing. I'm satisfied with them and that's what counts.

LEVEE: Nigger, why don't you get some decent shoes? Got nerve to put on a suit and tie with them farming boots.

CUTLER: What you just tell me? It don't make no difference about the man's shoes. That's what you told me.

LEVEE: Aw, hell, I don't care what the nigger wear. I'll be honest with you. I don't care if he went barefoot.

[SLOW DRAG *has put his string on the bass and is tuning it.*]

Play something for me, Slow Drag.

[SLOW DRAG *plays.*]

A man got to have some shoes to dance like this! You can't dance like this with them clodhoppers Toledo got.

[LEVEE *sings.*]

> Hello Central give me Doctor Jazz
> He's got just what I need I'll say he has
> When the world goes wrong and I have got the blues
> He's the man who makes me get on my dancing shoes.

TOLEDO: That's the trouble with colored folks . . . always wanna have a good time. Good times done got more niggers killed than God got ways to count. What the hell having a good time mean? That's what I wanna know.

LEVEE: Hell, nigger . . . it don't need explaining. Ain't you never had no good time before?

TOLEDO: The more niggers get killed having a good time, the more good times niggers wanna have.

[SLOW DRAG *stops playing.*]

There's more to life than having a good time. If there ain't, then this is a piss-poor life we're having . . . if that's all there is to be got out of it.

SLOW DRAG: Toledo, just 'cause you like to read them books and study and whatnot . . . that's your good time. People get other things they likes to do to have a good time. Ain't no need you picking them about it.

CUTLER: Niggers been having a good time before you was born, and they gonna keep having a good time after you gone.

TOLEDO: Yeah, but what else they gonna do? Ain't nobody talking about making the lot of the colored man better for him here in America.

LEVEE: Now you gonna be Booker T. Washington.

TOLEDO: Everybody worried about having a good time. Ain't nobody thinking about what kind of world they gonna leave their youngens. "Just give me the good time, that's all I want." It just makes me sick.

SLOW DRAG: Well, the colored man's gonna be all right. He got through slavery, and he'll get through whatever else the white man put on him. I ain't worried about that. Good times is what makes life worth living. Now, you take the white man . . . The white man don't know how to have a good time. That's why he's troubled all the time. He don't know how to have a good time. He don't know how to laugh at life.

LEVEE: That's what the problem is with Toledo . . . reading all them books and things. He done got to the point where he forgot how to laugh and have a good time. Just like the white man.

TOLEDO: I know how to have a good time as well as the next man. I said, there's got to be more to life than having a good time. I said the colored man ought to be doing more than just trying to have a good time all the time.

LEVEE: Well, what is you doing, nigger? Talking all them highfalutin ideas about making a better world for the colored man. What is you doing to make it better? You playing the music and looking for your next piece of pussy same as we is. What is you doing? That's what I wanna know. Tell him, Cutler.

CUTLER: You all leave Cutler out of this. Cutler ain't got nothing to do with it.

TOLEDO: Levee, you just about the most ignorant nigger I know. Sometimes I wonder why I ever bother to try and talk with you.

LEVEE: Well, what is you doing? Talking that shit to me about I'm ignorant! What is you doing? You just a whole lot of mouth. A great big windbag. Thinking you smarter than everybody else. What is you doing, huh?

TOLEDO: It ain't just me, fool! It's everybody! What you think . . . I'm gonna solve the colored man's problems by myself? I said, we. You understand that? We. That's every living colored man in the world got to do his share. Got to do his part. I ain't talking about what I'm gonna do . . . or what you or Cutler or Slow Drag or anybody else. I'm talking about all of us together. What all of us is gonna do. That's what I'm talking about, nigger!

LEVEE: Well, why didn't you say that, then?

CUTLER: Toledo, I don't know why you waste your time on this fool.

TOLEDO: That's what I'm trying to figure out.

LEVEE: Now there go Cutler with his shit. Calling me a fool. You wasn't even in the conversation. Now you gonna take sides and call me a fool.

CUTLER: Hell, I was listening to the man. I got sense enough to know what he was saying. I could tell it straight back to you.

LEVEE: Well, you go on with it. But I'll tell you this . . . I ain't gonna be too many more of your fools. I'll tell you that. Now you put that in your pipe and smoke it.

CUTLER: Boy, ain't nobody studying you. Telling me what to put in my pipe. Who's you to tell me what to do?

LEVEE: All right, I ain't nobody. Don't pay me no mind. I ain't nobody.

TOLEDO: Levee, you ain't nothing but the devil.

LEVEE: There you go! That's who I am. I'm the devil. I ain't nothing but the devil.

CUTLER: I can see that. That's something you know about. You know all about the devil.

LEVEE: I ain't saying what I know. I know plenty. What you know about the devil? Telling me what I know. What you know?

SLOW DRAG: I know a man sold his soul to the devil.

LEVEE: There you go! That's the only thing I ask about the devil . . . to see him coming so I can sell him this one I got. 'Cause if there's a god up there, he done went to sleep.

SLOW DRAG: Sold his soul to the devil himself. Name of Eliza Cottor. Lived in Tuscaloosa County, Alabama. The devil came by and he done upped and sold him his soul.

CUTLER: How you know the man done sold his soul to the devil, nigger? You talking that old-woman foolishness.

SLOW DRAG: Everybody know. It wasn't no secret. He went around working for the devil and everybody knowed it. Carried him a bag . . . one of them carpetbags. Folks say he carried the devil's papers and whatnot where he put your fingerprint on the paper with blood.

LEVEE: Where he at now? That's what I want to know. He can put my whole handprint if he want to!

CUTLER: That's the damnedest thing I ever heard! Folks kill me with that talk.

TOLEDO: Oh, that's real enough, all right. Some folks go arm in arm with the devil, shoulder to shoulder, and talk to him all the time. That's real, ain't nothing wrong in believing that.

SLOW DRAG: That's what I'm saying. Eliza Cotter is one of them. All right. The man living up in an old shack on Ben Foster's place, shoeing mules and horses, making them charms and things in secret. He done hooked up with the devil, showed up one day all fancied out with just the finest clothes you ever seen on a colored man . . . dressed just like one of them crackers . . . and carrying this bag with them papers and things. All right. Had a pocketful of money, just living the life of a rich man. Ain't done no more work or nothing. Just had him a string of women he run around with and throw his money away on. Bought him a big fine house . . . Well, it wasn't all that big, but it did have one of them white picket fences around it. Used to hire a man once a week just to paint that fence. Messed around there and one of the fellows of them gals he was messing with got fixed on him wrong and Eliza killed him. And he laughed about it. Sheriff come and arrest him, and then let him go. And he went around in that town laughing about killing this fellow. Trial come up, and the judge cut him loose. He must have been in converse with the devil too . . . 'cause he cut him loose and give him a bottle of whiskey! Folks ask what done happened to make him change, and he'd tell them straight out he done sold his soul to the devil and ask them if they wanted to sell theirs 'cause he could arrange it for them. Preacher see him coming, used to cross on the other side of the road. He'd just stand there and laugh at the preacher and call him a fool to his face.

CUTLER: Well, whatever happened to this fellow? What come of him? A man who, as you say, done sold his soul to the devil is bound to come to a bad end.

TOLEDO: I don't know about that. The devil's strong. The devil ain't no pushover.

SLOW DRAG: Oh, the devil had him under his wing, all right. Took good care of him. He ain't wanted for nothing.

CUTLER: What happened to him? That's what I want to know.

SLOW DRAG: Last I heard, he headed north with that bag of his, handing out hundred-dollar bills on the spot to whoever wanted to sign on with the devil. That's what I hear tell of him.

CUTLER: That's a bunch of fool talk. I don't know how you fix your mouth to tell that story. I don't believe that.

SLOW DRAG: I ain't asking you to believe it. I'm just telling you the facts of it.

LEVEE: I sure wish I knew where he went. He wouldn't have to convince me long. Hell, I'd even help him sign people up.

CUTLER: Nigger, God's gonna strike you down with that blasphemy you talking.

LEVEE: Oh, shit! God don't mean nothing to me. Let him strike me! Here I am, standing right here. What you talking about he's gonna strike me? Here I am! Let him strike me! I ain't scared of him. Talking that stuff to me.

CUTLER: All right. You gonna be sorry. You gonna fix yourself to have bad luck. Ain't nothing gonna work for you.

[*Buzzer sounds offstage.*]

LEVEE: Bad luck? What I care about some bad luck? You talking simple. I ain't knowed nothing but bad luck all my life. Couldn't get no worse. What the hell I care about some bad luck? Hell, I eat it everyday for breakfast! You dumber than I thought you was . . . talking about bad luck.

CUTLER: All right, nigger, you'll see! Can't tell a fool nothing. You'll see!

IRVIN [IRVIN *enters the studio, checks his watch, and calls down the stairs.*]: Cutler . . . you boys' sandwiches are up here . . . Cutler?

CUTLER: Yessir, Mr. Irvin . . . be right there.

TOLEDO: I'll walk up there and get them.

[TOLEDO *exits. The lights go down in the band room and up in the studio.* IRVIN *paces back and forth in an agitated manner.* STURDYVANT *enters.*]

STURDYVANT: Irv, what's happening? Is she here yet? Was that her?

IRVIN: It's the sandwiches, Mel. I told you . . . I'll let you know when she comes, huh?

STURDYVANT: What's keeping her? Do you know what time it is? Have you looked at the clock? You told me she'd be here. You told me you'd take care of it.

IRVIN: Mel, for Chrissakes! What do you want from me? What do you want me to do?

STURDYVANT: Look what time it is, Irv. You told me she'd be here.

IRVIN: She'll be here, okay? I don't know what's keeping her. You know they're always late, Mel.

STURDYVANT: You should have went by the hotel and made sure she was on time. You should have taken care of this. That's what you told me, huh? "I'll take care of it."

IRVIN: Okay! Okay! I didn't go by the hotel! What do you want me to do? She'll be here, okay? The band's here . . . she'll be here.

STURDYVANT: Okay, Irv. I'll take your word. But if she doesn't come . . . if she doesn't come . . .

[STURDYVANT *exits to the control booth as* TOLEDO *enters.*]

TOLEDO: Mr. Irvin . . . I come up to get the sandwiches.

IRVIN: Say . . . uh . . . look . . . one o'clock, right? She said one o'clock.

TOLEDO: That's what time she told us. Say be here at one o'clock.

IRVIN: Do you know what's keeping her? Do you know why she ain't here?

TOLEDO: I can't say, Mr. Irvin. Told us one o'clock.

[*The buzzer sounds.* IRVIN *goes to the door. There is a flurry of commotion as* MA RAINEY *enters, followed closely by the* POLICEMAN, DUSSIE MAE, *and* SYLVESTER. MA RAINEY *is a short, heavy woman. She is dressed in a full-length fur coat with matching hat, an emerald-green dress, and several strands of pearls of varying lengths. Her hair is secured by a headband that matches her dress. Her manner is simple and direct, and she carries herself in a royal fashion.* DUSSIE MAE *is a young, dark-skinned woman whose greatest asset is the sensual energy which seems to flow from her. She is dressed in a fur jacket and a tight-fitting canary-yellow dress.* SYLVESTER *is an Arkansas country boy, the size of a fullback. He wears a new suit and coat, in which he is obviously uncomfortable. Most of the time, he stutters when he speaks.*]

MA RAINEY: Irvin . . . you better tell this man who I am! You better get him straight!

IRVIN: Ma, do you know what time it is? Do you have any idea? We've been waiting . . .

DUSSIE MAE [*to* SYLVESTER]: If you was watching where you was going . . .

SYLVESTER: I was watching . . . What you mean?

IRVIN [*notices* POLICEMAN]: What's going on here? Officer, what's the matter?

MA RAINEY: Tell the man who he's messing with!

POLICEMAN: Do you know this lady?

MA RAINEY: Just tell the man who I am! That's all you gotta do.

POLICEMAN: Lady, will you let me talk, huh?

MA RAINEY: Tell the man who I am!

IRVIN: Wait a minute . . . wait a minute! Let me handle it. Ma, will you let me handle it?

MA RAINEY: Tell him who he's messing with!

IRVIN: Okay! Okay! Give me a chance! Officer, this is one of our recording artists . . . Ma Rainey.

MA RAINEY: Madame Rainey! Get it straight! Madame Rainey! Talking about taking me to jail!

IRVIN: Look, Ma . . . give me a chance, okay? Here . . . sit down. I'll take care of it. Officer, what's the problem?

DUSSIE MAE [to SYLVESTER]: It's all your fault.

SYLVESTER: I ain't done nothing . . . Ask Ma.

POLICEMAN: Well . . . when I walked up on the incident . . .

DUSSIE MAE: Sylvester wrecked Ma's car.

SYLVESTER: I d-d-did not! The m-m-man ran into me!

POLICEMAN [to IRVIN.]: Look, buddy . . . if you want it in a nutshell, we got her charged with assault and battery.

MA RAINEY: Assault and what for what!

DUSSIE MAE: See . . . we was trying to get a cab . . . and so Ma . . .

MA RAINEY: Wait a minute! I'll tell you if you wanna know what happened. [She points to SYLVESTER.]

Now, that's Sylvester. That's my nephew. He was driving my car . . .

POLICEMAN: Lady, we don't know whose car he was driving.

MA RAINEY: That's my car!

DUSSIE MAE and SYLVESTER: That's Ma's car!

MA RAINEY: What you mean you don't know whose car it is? I bought and paid for that car.

POLICEMAN: That's what you say, lady . . . We still gotta check.

[To IRVIN.]

They hit a car on Market Street. The guy said the kid ran a stoplight.

SYLVESTER: What you mean? The man c-c-come around the corner and hit m-m-me!

POLICEMAN: While I was calling a paddy wagon to haul them to the station, they try to hop into a parked cab. The cabbie said he was waiting on a fare . . .

MA RAINEY: The man was just sitting there. Wasn't waiting for nobody. I don't know why he wanna tell that lie.

POLICEMAN: Look, lady . . . will you let me tell the story?

MA RAINEY: Go ahead and tell it then. But tell it right!

POLICEMAN: Like I say . . . she tries to get in this cab. The cabbie's waiting on a fare. She starts creating a disturbance. The cabbie gets out to try and explain the situation to her . . . and she knocks him down.

DUSSIE MAE: She ain't hit him! He just fell!

SYLVESTER: He just s-s-s-slipped!

POLICEMAN: He claims she knocked him down. We got her charged with assault and battery.

MA RAINEY: If that don't beat all to hell. I ain't touched the man! The man was trying to reach around me to keep his car door closed. I opened the door and it hit him and he fell down. I ain't touched the man!

IRVIN: Okay. Okay . . . I got it straight now, Ma. You didn't touch him. All right? Officer, can I see you for a minute?

DUSSIE MAE: Ma was just trying to open the door.

SYLVESTER: He j-j-just got in t-t-the way!

MA RAINEY: Said he wasn't gonna haul no colored folks . . . if you want to know the truth of it.

IRVIN: Okay, Ma . . . I got it straight now. Officer?

[IRVIN *pulls the* POLICEMAN *off to the side.*]

MA RAINEY [*noticing* TOLEDO]: Toledo, Cutler and everybody here?

TOLEDO: Yeah, they down in the band room. What happened to your car?

STURDYVANT [*entering*]: Irv, what's the problem? What's going on? Officer . . .

IRVIN: Mel, let me take care of it. I can handle it.

STURDYVANT: What's happening? What the hell's going on?

IRVIN: Let me handle it, Mel, huh?

[STURDYVANT *crosses over to* MA RAINEY.]

STURDYVANT: What's going on, Ma. What'd you do?

MA RAINEY: Sturdyvant, get on away from me! That's the last thing I need . . . to go through some of your shit!

IRVIN: Mel, I'll take care of it. I'll explain it all to you. Let me handle it, huh?

[STURDYVANT *reluctantly returns to the control booth.*]

POLICEMAN: Look, buddy, like I say . . . we got her charged with assault and battery . . . and the kid with threatening the cabbie.

SYLVESTER: I ain't done n-n-nothing!

MA RAINEY: You leave the boy out of it. He ain't done nothing. What's he supposed to have done?

POLICEMAN: He threatened the cabbie, lady! You just can't go around threatening people.

SYLVESTER: I ain't done nothing to him! He's the one talking about he g-g-gonna get a b-b-baseball bat on me! I just told him what I'd do with it. But I ain't done nothing 'cause he didn't get the b-b-bat!

IRVIN [*pulling the* POLICEMAN *aside*]: Officer . . . look here . . .

POLICEMAN: We was on our way down to the precinct . . . but I figured I'd do you a favor and bring her by here. I mean, if she's as important as she says she is . . .

IRVIN [*slides a bill from his pocket*]: Look, Officer . . . I'm Madame Rainey's manager . . . It's good to meet you.

[*He shakes the* POLICEMAN's *hand and passes him the bill.*]

As soon as we're finished with the recording session, I'll personally stop by the precinct house and straighten up this misunderstanding.

POLICEMAN: Well . . . I guess that's all right. As long as someone is responsible for them.

[*He pockets the bill and winks at* IRVIN.]

No need to come down . . . I'll take care of it myself. Of course, we wouldn't want nothing like this to happen again.

IRVIN: Don't worry, Officer . . . I'll take care of everything. Thanks for your help.

[IRVIN *escorts the* POLICEMAN *to the door and returns. He crosses over to* MA RAINEY.]

Here, Ma . . . let me take your coat.

[*To* SYLVESTER.]

I don't believe I know you.

MA RAINEY: That's my nephew, Sylvester.

IRVIN: I'm very pleased to meet you. Here . . . you can give me your coat.

MA RAINEY: That there is Dussie Mae.

IRVIN: Hello . . .

[DUSSIE MAE *hands* IRVIN *her coat.*]

Listen, Ma, just sit there and relax. The boys are in the band room rehearsing. You just sit and relax a minute.

MA RAINEY: I ain't for no sitting. I ain't never heard of such. Talking about taking me to jail. Irvin, call down there and see about my car.

IRVIN: Okay, Ma . . . I'll take care of it. You just relax.

[IRVIN *exits with the coats.*]

MA RAINEY: Why you all keep it so cold in here? Sturdyvant try and pinch every penny he can. You all wanna make some records, you better put some heat on in here or give me back my coat.

IRVIN [*entering*]: We got the heat turned up, Ma. It's warming up. It'll be warm in a minute.

DUSSIE MAE [*whispering to* MA RAINEY]: Where's the bathroom?

MA RAINEY: It's in the back. Down the hall next to Sturdyvant's office. Come on, I'll show you where it is. Irvin, call down there and see about my car. I want my car fixed today.

IRVIN: I'll take care of everything, Ma.

[*He notices* TOLEDO.]

Say . . . uh . . . uh . . .

TOLEDO: Toledo.

IRVIN: Yeah . . . Toledo. I got the sandwiches, you can take down to the rest of the boys. We'll be ready to go in a minute. Give you boys a chance to eat and then we'll be ready to go.

[IRVIN *and* TOLEDO *exit. The lights go down in the studio and come up in the band room.*]

LEVEE: Slow Drag, you ever been to New Orleans?

SLOW DRAG: What's in New Orleans that I want?

LEVEE: How you call yourself a musician and ain't never been to New Orleans.

SLOW DRAG: You ever been to Fat Back, Arkansas?

[*Pauses.*]

All right, then. Ain't never been nothing in New Orleans that I couldn't get in Fat Back.

LEVEE: That's why you backwards. You just an old country boy talking about Fat Back, Arkansas, and New Orleans in the same breath.

CUTLER: I been to New Orleans. What about it?

LEVEE: You ever been to Lula White's?

CUTLER: Lula White's? I ain't never heard of it.

LEVEE: Man, they got some gals in there just won't wait! I seen a man get killed in there once. Got drunk and grabbed one of the gals wrong . . . I don't know what the matter of it was. But he grabbed her and she stuck a knife in him all the way up to the hilt. He ain't even fell. He just stood there and choked on his own blood. I was just asking Slow Drag 'cause I was gonna take him to Lula White's when we get down to New Orleans and show him a good time. Introduce him to one of them gals I know down there.

CUTLER: Slow Drag don't need you to find him no pussy. He can take care of his own self. Fact is . . . you better watch your gal when Slow Drag's around. They don't call him Slow Drag for nothing.

[*He laughs.*]

Tell him how you got your name Slow Drag.

SLOW DRAG: I ain't thinking about Levee.

CUTLER: Slow Drag break a woman's back when he dance. They had this contest one time in this little town called Bolingbroke about a hundred miles outside of Macon. We was playing for this dance and they was giving twenty dollars to the best slow draggers. Slow Drag looked over the competition, got down off the bandstand, grabbed hold of one of them gals, and stuck to her like a fly to jelly. Like wood to glue. Man had that gal whooping and hollering so . . . everybody stopped to watch. This fellow come in . . . this gal's fellow . . . and pulled a knife a foot long on Slow Drag. 'Member that, Slow Drag?

SLOW DRAG: Boy that mama was hot! The front of her dress was wet as a dishrag!

LEVEE: So what happened? What the man do?

CUTLER: Slow Drag ain't missed a stroke. The gal, she just look at her man with that sweet dizzy look in her eye. She ain't about to stop! Folks was clearing out, ducking and hiding under tables, figuring there's gonna be a fight. Slow Drag just looked over the gal's shoulder at the man and said, "Mister, if you'd quit hollering and wait a minute . . . you'll see I'm doing you a favor. I'm helping this gal win ten dollars so she can buy you a gold watch." The man just stood there and looked at him, all the while stroking that knife. Told Slow Drag, say, "All right, then, nigger. You just better make damn sure you win." That's when folks started calling him Slow Drag. The women got to hanging around him so bad after that, them fellows in that town ran us out of there.

[TOLEDO *enters, carrying a small cardboard box with the sandwiches.*]

LEVEE: Yeah . . . well, them gals in Lula White's will put a harness on his ass.

TOLEDO: Ma's up there. Some kind of commotion with the police.

CUTLER: Police? What the police up there for?

TOLEDO: I couldn't get it straight. Something about her car. They gone now . . . she's all right. Mr. Irvin sent some sandwiches.

[LEVEE *springs across the room.*]

LEVEE: Yeah, all right. What we got here?

[*He takes two sandwiches out of the box.*]

TOLEDO: What you doing grabbing two? There ain't but five in there . . . How you figure you get two?

LEVEE: 'Cause I grabbed them first. There's enough for everybody . . . What you talking about? It ain't like I'm taking food out of nobody's mouth.

CUTLER: That's all right. He can have mine too. I don't want none.

[LEVEE *starts toward the box to get another sandwich.*]

TOLEDO: Nigger, you better get out of here. Slow Drag, you want this?

SLOW DRAG: Naw, you can have it.

TOLEDO: With Levee around, you don't have to worry about no leftovers. I can see that.

LEVEE: What's the matter with you? Ain't you eating two sandwiches? Then why you wanna talk about me? Talking about there won't be no leftovers with Levee around. Look at your own self before you look at me.

TOLEDO: That's what you is. That's what we all is. A leftover from history. You see now, I'll show you.

LEVEE: Aw, shit . . . I done got the nigger started now.

TOLEDO: Now, I'm gonna show you how this goes . . . where you just a leftover from history. Everybody come from different places in Africa, right? Come from different tribes and things. Soonawhile they began to make one big stew. You had the carrots, the peas, and potatoes and whatnot over here. And over there you had the meat, the nuts, the okra, corn . . . and then you mix it up and let it cook right through to get the flavors flowing together . . . then you got one thing. You got a stew.

Now you take and eat the stew. You take and make your history with that stew. All right. Now it's over. Your history's over and you done ate the stew. But you look around and you see some carrots over here, some potatoes over there. That stew's still there. You done made your history and it's still there. You can't eat it all. So what you got? You got some leftovers. That's what it is. You got leftovers and you can't do nothing with it. You already making you another history . . . cooking you another meal, and you don't need them leftovers no more. What to do?

See, we's the leftovers. The colored man is the leftovers. Now, what's the colored man gonna do with himself? That's what we waiting to find out. But first we gotta know we the leftovers. Now, who knows that? You find me a nigger that knows that and I'll turn any whichaway you want me to. I'll bend over for you. You ain't gonna find that. And that's what the problem is. The problem ain't with the white man. The white man knows you just a leftover. 'Cause he the one who done the eating and he know what he done ate. But we don't know that we been took and made history out of. Done went and filled the white man's belly and now he's full and tired and wants you to get out the way and let him be by himself. Now, I know what I'm talking about. And if you wanna find out, you just ask Mr. Irvin what he had for supper yesterday. And if he's an honest white man . . . which is asking for a whole heap of a lot . . . he'll tell you he done ate your black ass and if you please I'm full up with you . . . so go on and get off the plate and let me eat something else.

SLOW DRAG: What that mean? What's eating got to do with how the white man treat you? He don't treat you no different according to what he ate.

TOLEDO: I ain't said it had nothing to do with how he treat you.

CUTLER: The man's trying to tell you something, fool!

SLOW DRAG: What he trying to tell me? Ain't you here. Why you say he was trying to tell *me* something? Wasn't he trying to tell you too?

LEVEE: He was trying all right. He was trying a whole heap. I'll say that for him. But trying ain't worth a damn. I got lost right there trying to figure out who puts nuts in their stew.

SLOW DRAG: I knowed that before. My grandpappy used to put nuts in his stew. He and my grandmama both. That ain't nothing new.

TOLEDO: They put nuts in their stew all over Africa. But the stew they eat, and the stew your grandpappy made, and all the stew that you and me eat, and the stew Mr. Irvin eats . . . ain't in no way the same stew. That's the way that go. I'm through with it. That's the last you know me to ever try and explain something to you.

CUTLER [*after a pause*]: Well, time's getting along . . . Come on, let's finish rehearsing.

LEVEE [*stretching out on a bench*]: I don't feel like rehearsing. I ain't nothing but a leftover. You go and rehearse with Toledo . . . He's gonna teach you how to make a stew.

SLOW DRAG: Cutler, what you gonna do? I don't want to be around here all day.

LEVEE: I know my part. You all go on and rehearse your part. You all need some rehearsal.

CUTLER: Come on, Levee, get up off your ass and rehearse the songs.

LEVEE: I already know them songs . . . What I wanna rehearse them for?

SLOW DRAG: You in the band, ain't you? You supposed to rehearse when the band rehearse.

TOLEDO: Levee think he the king of the barnyard. He thinks he's the only rooster know how to crow.

LEVEE: All right! All right! Come on, I'm gonna show you I know them songs. Come on, let's rehearse. I bet you the first one mess be Toledo. Come on . . . I wanna see if he know how to crow.

CUTLER: "Ma Rainey's Black Bottom," Levee's version. Let's do it.

[*They begin to rehearse. The lights go down in the band room and up in the studio.* MA RAINEY *sits and takes off her shoe, rubs her feet.* DUSSIE MAE *wanders about looking at the studio.* SYLVESTER *is over by the piano.*]

MA RAINEY [*singing to herself*]:

> Oh, Lord, these dogs of mine
> They sure do worry me all the time
> The reason why I don't know
> Lord, I beg to be excused
> I can't wear me no sharp-toed shoes.
> I went for a walk
> I stopped to talk
> Oh, how my corns did bark.

DUSSIE MAE: It feels kinda spooky in here. I ain't never been in no recording studio before. Where's the band at?

MA RAINEY: They off somewhere rehearsing. I don't know where Irvin went to. All this hurry up and he goes off back there with Sturdyvant. I know he better come on 'cause Ma ain't gonna be waiting. Come here . . . let me see that dress.

[DUSSIE MAE *crosses over.* MA RAINEY *tugs at the dress around the waist, appraising the fit.*]

That dress looks nice. I'm gonna take you tomorrow and get you some more things before I take you down to Memphis. They got clothes up here you can't get in Memphis. I want you to look nice for me. If you gonna travel with the show you got to look nice.

DUSSIE MAE: I need me some more shoes. These hurt my feet.

MA RAINEY: You get you some shoes that fit your feet. Don't you be messing around with no shoes that pinch your feet. Ma know something about bad feet. Hand me my slippers out my bag over yonder.

[DUSSIE MAE *brings the slippers.*]

DUSSIE MAE: I just want to get a pair of them yellow ones. About a half-size bigger.

MA RAINEY: We'll get you whatever you need. Sylvester, too . . . I'm gonna get him some more clothes. Sylvester, tuck your clothes in. Straighten them up and look nice. Look like a gentleman.

DUSSIE MAE: Look at Sylvester with that hat on.

MA RAINEY: Sylvester, take your hat off inside. Act like your mama taught you something. I know she taught you better than that.

[SYLVESTER *bangs on the piano.*]

Come on over here and leave that piano alone.

SYLVESTER: I ain't d-d-doing nothing to the p-p-piano. I'm just l-l-looking at it.

MA RAINEY: Well. Come on over here and sit down. As soon as Mr. Irvin comes back, I'll have him take you down and introduce you to the band.

[SYLVESTER *comes over.*]

He's gonna take you down there and introduce you in a minute . . . have Cutler show you how your part go. And when you get your money, you gonna send some of it home to your mamma. Let her know you doing all right. Make her feel good to know you doing all right in the world.

[DUSSIE MAE *wanders about the studio and opens the door leading to the band room. The strains of* LEVEE'*s version of "Ma Rainey's Black Bottom" can be heard.* IRVIN *enters.*]

IRVIN: Ma, I called down to the garage and checked on your car. It's just a scratch. They'll have it ready for you this afternoon. They're gonna send it over with one of their fellows.

MA RAINEY: They better have my car fixed right too. I ain't going for that. Brand-new car . . . they better fix it like new.

IRVIN: It was just a scratch on the fender, Ma . . . They'll take care of it . . . don't worry . . . they'll have it like new.

MA RAINEY: Irvin, what is that I hear? What is that the band's rehearsing? I know they ain't rehearsing Levee's "Black Bottom." I know I ain't hearing that?

IRVIN: Ma, listen . . . that's what I wanted to talk to you about. Levee's version of that song . . . it's got a nice arrangement . . . a nice horn intro . . . It really picks it up . . .

MA RAINEY: I ain't studying Levee nothing. I know what he done to that song and I don't like to sing it that way. I'm doing it the old way. That's why I brought my nephew to do the voice intro.

IRVIN: Ma, that's what the people want now. They want something they can dance to. Times are changing. Levee's arrangement gives the people what they want. It gets them excited . . . makes them forget about their troubles.

MA RAINEY: I don't care what you say, Irvin. Levee ain't messing up my song. If he got what the people want, let him take it somewhere else. I'm singing Ma Rainey's song. I ain't singing Levee's song. Now that's all there is to it. Carry my nephew on down there and introduce him to the band. I promised my sister I'd look out for him and he's gonna do the voice intro on the song my way.

IRVIN: Ma, we just figured that . . .

MA RAINEY: Who's this "we"? What you mean "we"? I ain't studying Levee nothing. Come talking this "we" stuff. Who's "we"?

IRVIN: Me and Sturdyvant. We decided that it would . . .

MA RAINEY: You decided, huh? I'm just a bump on the log. I'm gonna go which ever way the river drift. Is that it? You and Sturdyvant decided.

IRVIN: Ma, it was just that we thought it would be better.

MA RAINEY: I ain't got good sense. I don't know nothing about music. I don't know what's a good song and what ain't. You know more about my fans than I do.

IRVIN: It's not that, Ma. It would just be easier to do. It's more what the people want.

MA RAINEY: I'm gonna tell you something, Irvin . . . and you go on up there and tell Sturdyvant. What you all say don't count with me. You understand? Ma listens to her heart. Ma listens to the voice inside her. That's what counts with Ma. Now, you carry my nephew on down there . . . tell Cutler he's gonna do the voice intro on that

"Black Bottom" song and that Levee ain't messing up my song with none of his music shit. Now, if that don't set right with you and Sturdyvant . . . then I can carry my black bottom on back down South to my tour, 'cause I don't like it up here no ways.

IRVIN: Okay, Ma . . . I don't care. I just thought . . .

MA RAINEY: Damn what you thought! What you look like telling me how to sing my song? This Levee and Sturdyvant nonsense . . . I ain't going for it! Sylvester, go on down there and introduce yourself. I'm through playing with Irvin.

SYLVESTER: Which way you go? Where they at?

MA RAINEY: Here . . . I'll carry you down there myself.

DUSSIE MAE: Can I go? I wanna see the band.

MA RAINEY: You stay your behind up here. Ain't no cause in you being down there. Come on, Sylvester.

IRVIN: Okay, Ma. Have it your way. We'll be ready to go in fifteen minutes.

MA RAINEY: We'll be ready to go when Madame says we're ready. That's the way it goes around here.

[MA RAINEY *and* SYLVESTER *exit. The lights go down in the studio and up in the band room.* MA RAINEY *enters with* SYLVESTER.]

Cutler, this here is my nephew Sylvester. He's gonna do that voice intro on the "Black Bottom" song using the old version.

LEVEE: What you talking about? Mr. Irvin say he's using my version. What you talking about?

MA RAINEY: Levee, I ain't studying you or Mr. Irvin. Cutler, get him straightened out on how to do his part. I ain't thinking about Levee. These folks done messed with the wrong person this day. Sylvester, Cutler gonna teach you your part. You go ahead and get it straight. Don't worry about what nobody else say.

[MA RAINEY *exits.*]

CUTLER: Well, come on in, boy. I'm Cutler. You got Slow Drag . . . Levee . . . and that's Toledo over there. Sylvester, huh?

SYLVESTER: Sylvester Brown.

LEVEE: I done wrote a version of that song what picks it up and sets it down in the people's lap! Now she come talking this! You don't need that old circus bullshit! I know what I'm talking about. You gonna mess up the song Cutler and you know it.

CUTLER: I ain't gonna mess up nothing. Ma say . . .

LEVEE: I don't care what Ma say! I'm talking about what the intro gonna do to the song. The peoples in the North ain't gonna buy all that tent-show nonsense. They wanna hear some music!

CUTLER: Nigger, I done told you time and again . . . you just in the band. You plays the piece . . . whatever they want! Ma says what to play! Not you! You ain't here to be doing no creating, Your job is to play whatever Ma says!

LEVEE: I might not play nothing! I might quit!

CUTLER: Nigger, don't nobody care if you quit. Whose heart you gonna break?

TOLEDO: Levee ain't gonna quit. He got to make some money to keep him in shoe polish.

LEVEE: I done told you all . . . you all don't know me. You don't know what I'll do.

CUTLER: I don't think nobody too much give a damn! Sylvester, here's the way your part go. The band plays the intro . . . I'll tell you where to come in. The band plays the intro and then you say, "All right, boys, you done seen the rest . . . Now I'm gonna show you the best. Ma Rainey's gonna show you her black bottom." You got that?

[SYLVESTER *nods.*]

Let me hear you say it one time.

SYLVESTER: "All right, boys, you done s-s-seen the rest n-n-now I'm gonna show you the best. M-m-m-m-m-m-ma Rainey's gonna s-s-show you her black b-b-bottom."

LEVEE: What kind of . . . All right, Cutler! Let me see you fix that! You straighten that out! You hear that shit, Slow Drag? How in the hell the boy gonna do the part and he can't even talk!

SYLVESTER: W-w-w-who's you to tell me what to do, nigger! This ain't your band! Ma tell me to d-d-do it and I'm gonna do it. You can go to hell, n-n-n-nigger!

LEVEE: B-b-b-boy, ain't nobody studying you. You go on and fix that one, Cutler. You fix that one and I'll . . . I'll shine your shoes for you. You go on and fix that one!

TOLEDO: You say you Ma's nephew, huh?

SYLVESTER: Yeah. So w-w-what that mean?

TOLEDO: Oh, I ain't meant nothing . . . I was just asking.

SLOW DRAG: Well, come on and let's rehearse so the boy can get it right.

LEVEE: I ain't rehearsing nothing! You just wait till I get my band. I'm gonna record that song and show you how it supposed to go!

CUTLER: We can do it without Levee. Let him sit on over there. Sylvester, you remember your part?

SYLVESTER: I remember it pretty g-g-g-good.

CUTLER: Well, come on, let's do it, then.

[*The band begins to play.* LEVEE *sits and pouts.* STURDYVANT *enters the band room.*]

STURDYVANT: Good . . . you boys are rehearsing, I see.

LEVEE [*jumping up*]: Yessir! We rehearsing, We know them songs real good.

STURDYVANT: Good! Say, Levee, did you finish that song?

LEVEE: Yessir, Mr. Sturdyvant. I got it right here. I wrote that other part just like you say. It go like:

> You can shake it, you can break it
> You can dance at any hall
> You can slide across the floor
> You'll never have to stall
> My jelly, my roll,
> Sweet Mama, don't you let it fall.

Then I put that part in there for the people to dance, like you say, for them to forget about their troubles.

STURDYVANT: Good! Good! I'll just take this. I wanna see you about your songs as soon as I get the chance.

LEVEE: Yessir! As soon as you get the chance, Mr. Sturdyvant.

[STURDYVANT *exits*.]

CUTLER: You hear, Levee? You hear this nigger? "Yessuh, we's rehearsing, boss."

SLOW DRAG: I heard him. Seen him too. Shuffling them feet.

TOLEDO: Aw, Levee can't help it none. He's like all of us. Spooked up with the white man.

LEVEE: I'm spooked up with him, all right. You let one of them crackers fix on me wrong. I'll show you how spooked up I am with him.

TOLEDO: That's the trouble of it. You wouldn't know if he was fixed on you wrong or not. You so spooked up by him you ain't had the time to study him.

LEVEE: I studies the white man. I got him studied good. The first time one fixes on me wrong, I'm gonna let him know just how much I studied. Come telling me I'm spooked up with the white man. You let one of them mess with me, I'll show you how spooked up I am.

CUTLER: You talking out your hat. The man come in here, call you a boy, tell you to get up off your ass and rehearse, and you ain't had nothing to say to him, except "Yessir!"

LEVEE: I can say "yessir" to whoever I please. What you got to do with it? I know how to handle white folks. I been handling them for thirty-two years, and now you gonna tell me how to do it. Just 'cause I say "yessir" don't mean I'm spooked up with him. I know what I'm doing. Let me handle him my way.

CUTLER: Well, go on and handle it, then.

LEVEE: Toledo, you always messing with somebody! Always agitating somebody with that old philosophy bullshit you be talking. You stay out of my way about what I do and say. I'm my own person. Just let me alone.

TOLEDO: You right, Levee. I apologize. It ain't none of my business that you spooked up by the white man.

LEVEE: All right! See! That's the shit I'm talking about. You all back up and leave Levee alone.

SLOW DRAG: Aw, Levee, we was all just having fun. Toledo ain't said nothing about you he ain't said about me. You just taking it all wrong.

TOLEDO: I ain't meant nothing by it Levee.

[*Pauses.*]

Cutler, you ready to rehearse?

LEVEE: Levee got to be Levee! And he don't need nobody messing with him about the white man—cause you don't know nothing about me. You don't know Levee. You don't know nothing about what kind of blood I got! What kind of heart I got beating here!

[*He pounds his chest.*]

I was eight years old when I watched a gang of white mens come into my daddy's house and have to do with my mama any way they wanted.

[*Pauses.*]

We was living in Jefferson County, about eighty miles outside of Natchez. My daddy's name was Memphis . . . Memphis Lee Green . . . had him near fifty acres of good farming land. I'm talking about good land! Grow anything you want! He done gone off of shares and bought this land from Mr. Hallie's widow woman after he done passed on. Folks called him an uppity nigger 'cause he done saved and borrowed to where he could buy this land and be independent.

[*Pauses.*]

It was coming on planting time and my daddy went into Natchez to get him some seed and fertilizer. Called me, say, "Levee you the man of the house now. Take care of your mama while I'm gone." I wasn't but a little boy, eight years old.

[*Pauses.*]

My mama was frying up some chicken when them mens come in that house. Must have been eight or nine of them. She standing there frying that chicken and them mens come and took hold of her just like you take hold of a mule and make him do what you want.

[*Pauses.*]

There was my mama with a gang of white mens. She tried to fight them off, but I could see where it wasn't gonna do her any good, I didn't know what they were doing to her . . . but I figured whatever it was they may as well do to me too. My daddy had a knife that he kept around there for hunting and working and whatnot. I knew where he kept it and I went and got it.

I'm gonna show you how spooked up I was by the white man. I tried my damndest to cut one of them's throat! I hit him on the shoulder with it. He reached back and grabbed hold of that knife and whacked me across the chest with it.

[LEVEE *raises his shirt to show a long ugly scar.*]

That's what made them stop. They was scared I was gonna bleed to death. My mama wrapped a sheet around me and carried me two miles down to the Furlow place and they drove me up to Doc Albans. He was waiting on a calf to be born, and say he ain't had time to see me. They carried me up to Miss Etta, the midwife, and she fixed me up.

My daddy came back and acted like he done accepted the facts of what happened. But he got the names of them mens from mama. He found out who they was and then we announced we was moving out of that county. Said good-bye to everybody . . . all the neighbors. My daddy went and smiled in the face of one of them crackers who had been with my mama. Smiled in his face and sold him our land. We moved over with relations in Caldwell. He got us settled in and then he took off one day. I ain't never seen him since. He sneaked back, hiding up in the woods, laying to get them eight or nine men.

[*Pauses.*]

He got four of them before they got him. They tracked him down in the woods. Caught up with him and hung him and set him afire.

[*Pauses.*]

My daddy wasn't spooked up by the white man. Nosir! And that taught me how to handle them. I seen my daddy go up and grin in this cracker's face . . . smile in his face and sell him his land. All the while he's planning how he's gonna get him and what he's gonna do to him. That taught me how to handle them. So you all just back up and leave Levee alone about the white man. I can smile and say yessir to whoever I please. I got time coming to me. You all just leave Levee alone about the white man.

[*There is a long pause.* SLOW DRAG *begins playing on the bass and sings.*]

SLOW DRAG [*singing*]:

> If I had my way
> If I had my way
> If I had my way
> I would tear this old building down.

ACT TWO

The lights come up in the studio. The musicians are setting up their instruments. MA RAINEY *walks about shoeless, singing softly to herself.* LEVEE *stands near* DUSSIE MAE, *who hikes up her dress and crosses her leg.* CUTLER *speaks to* IRVIN *off to the side.*

CUTLER: Mr. Irvin, I don't know what you gonna do. I ain't got nothing to do with it, but the boy can't do the part. He stutters. He can't get it right. He stutters right through it every time.

IRVIN: Christ! Okay. We'll . . . Shit! We'll just do it like we planned. We'll do Levee's version. I'll handle it, Cutler. Come on, let's go. I'll think of something.

[*He exits to the control booth.*]

MA RAINEY [*calling* CUTLER *over*]: Levee's got his eyes in the wrong place. You better school him, Cutler.

CUTLER: Come on, Levee . . . let's get ready to play! Get your mind on your work!

IRVIN [*over speaker*]: Okay, boys, we're gonna do "Moonshine Blues" first. "Moonshine Blues," Ma.

MA RAINEY: I ain't doing no "Moonshine" nothing. I'm doing the "Black Bottom" first. Come on, Sylvester.
[*To* IRVIN.]
Where's Sylvester's mike? You need a mike for Sylvester. Irvin . . . get him a mike.

IRVIN: Uh . . . Ma, the boys say he can't do it. We'll have to do Levee's version.

MA RAINEY: What you mean he can't do it? Who say he can't do it? What boys say he can't do it?

IRVIN: The band, Ma . . . the boys in the band.

MA RAINEY: What band? The band work for me! I say what goes! Cutler, what's he talking about? Levee, this some of your shit?

IRVIN: He stutters, Ma. They say he stutters.

MA RAINEY: I don't care if he do. I promised the boy he could do the part . . . and he's gonna do it! That's all there is to it. He don't stutter all the time. Get a microphone down here for him.

IRVIN: Ma, we don't have time. We can't . . .

MA RAINEY: If you wanna make a record, you gonna find time. I ain't playing with you, Irvin. I can walk out of here and go back to my tour. I got plenty fans. I don't need to go through all of this. Just go and get the boy a microphone.

[IRVIN *and* STURDYVANT *consult in the booth,* IRVIN *exits.*]

STURDYVANT: All right, Ma . . . we'll get him a microphone. But if he messes up . . . He's only getting one chance . . . The cost . . .

MA RAINEY: Damn the cost. You always talking about the cost. I make more money for this outfit than anybody else you got put together. If he messes up he'll just do it till he gets it right. Levee, I know you had something to do with this. You better watch yourself.

LEVEE: It was Cutler!

SYLVESTER: It was you! You the only one m-m-mad about it.

LEVEE: The boy stutter. He can't do the part. Everybody see that. I don't know why you want the boy to do the part no ways.

MA RAINEY: Well, can or can't . . . he's gonna do it! You ain't got nothing to do with it!

LEVEE: I don't care what you do! He can sing the whole goddamned song for all I care!

MA RAINEY: Well, all right. Thank you.

[IRVIN *enters with a microphone and hooks it up. He exits to the control booth.*]

MA RAINEY: Come on, Sylvester. You just stand here and hold your hands like I told you. Just remember the words and say them . . . That's all there is to it. Don't worry about messing up. If you mess up, we'll do it again. Now, let me hear you say it. Play for him, Cutler.

CUTLER: One . . . two . . . you know what to do.

[*The band begins to play and* SYLVESTER *curls his fingers and claps his hands together in front of his chest, pulling in opposite directions as he says his lines.*]

SYLVESTER: "All right, boys, you d-d-done s-s-seen the best . . .
[LEVEE *stops playing.*]
Now I'm g-g-g-gonna show you the rest . . . Ma R-r-rainey's gonna show you her b-b-b-black b-b-b-bottom."

[*The rest of the band stops playing.*]

MA RAINEY: That's all right. That's real good. You take your time, you'll get it right.

STURDYVANT [*over speaker*]: Listen, Ma . . . now, when you come in, don't wait so long to come in. Don't take so long on the intro, huh?

MA RAINEY: Sturdyvant, don't you go trying to tell me how to sing. You just take care of that up there and let me take care of this down here. Where's my Coke?

IRVIN: Okay, Ma. We're all set up to go up here. "Ma Rainey's Black Bottom," boys.

MA RAINEY: Where's my Coke? I need a Coke. You ain't got no Coke down here? Where's my Coke?

IRVIN: What's the matter, Ma? What's . . .

MA RAINEY: Where's my Coke? I need a Coca-Cola.

IRVIN: Uh . . . Ma, look, I forgot the Coke, huh? Let's do it without it, huh? Just this one song. What say, boys?

MA RAINEY: Damn what the band say! You know I don't sing nothing without my Coca-Cola!

STURDYVANT: We don't have any, Ma. There's no Coca-Cola here. We're all set up and we'll just go ahead and . . .

MA RAINEY: You supposed to have Coca-Cola. Irvin knew that. I ain't singing nothing without my Coca-Cola!

[*She walks away from the mike, singing to herself.* STURDYVANT *enters from the control booth.*]

STURDYVANT: Now, just a minute here, Ma. You come in an hour late . . . we're way behind schedule as it is . . . the band is set up and ready to go . . . I'm burning my lights . . . I've turned up the heat . . . We're ready to make a record and what? You decide you want a Coca-Cola?

MA RAINEY: Sturdyvant, get out of my face.

[IRVIN *enters.*]

Irvin . . . I told you keep him away from me.

IRVIN: Mel, I'll handle it.

STURDYVANT: I'm tired of her nonsense, Irv. I'm not gonna put up with this!

IRVIN: Let me handle it, Mel. I know how to handle her.

[IRVIN *to* MA RAINEY.]

Look, Ma . . . I'll call down to the deli and get you a Coke. But let's get started, huh? Sylvester's standing there ready to go . . . the band's set up . . . let's do this one song, huh?

MA RAINEY: If you too cheap to buy me a Coke, I'll buy my own. Slow Drag! Sylvester, go with Slow Drag and get me a Coca-Cola.

[SLOW DRAG *comes over.*]

Slow Drag, walk down to that store on the corner and get me three bottles of Coca-Cola. Get out my face, Irvin. You all just wait until I get my Coke. It ain't gonna kill you.

IRVIN: Okay, Ma. Get your Coke, for Chrissakes! Get your coke!

[IRVIN *and* STURDYVANT *exit into the hallway followed by* SLOW DRAG *and* SYLVESTER. TOLEDO, CUTLER *and* LEVEE *head for the band room.*]

MA RAINEY: Cutler, come here a minute. I want to talk to you.

[CUTLER *crosses over somewhat reluctantly.*]

What's all this about "the boys in the band say"? I tells you what to do. I says what the matter is with the band. I say who can and can't do what.

CUTLER: We just say 'cause the boy stutter . . .

MA RAINEY: I know he stutters. Don't you think I know he stutters? This is what's gonna help him.

CUTLER: Well, how can he do the part if he stutters? You want him to stutter through it? We just thought it be easier to go on and let Levee do it like we planned.

MA RAINEY: I don't care if he stutters or not! He's doing the part and I don't wanna hear any more of this shit about what the band says. And I want you to find somebody to replace Levee when we get to Memphis. Levee ain't nothing but trouble.

CUTLER: Levee's all right. He plays good music when he puts his mind to it. He knows how to write music too.

MA RAINEY: I don't care what he know. He ain't nothing but bad news. Find somebody else. I know it was his idea about who to say who can do what.

[DUSSIE MAE *wanders over to where they are sitting.*]

Dussie Mae, go sit your behind down somewhere and quit flaunting yourself around.

DUSSIE MAE: I ain't doing nothing.

MA RAINEY: Well, just go on somewhere and stay out of the way.

CUTLER: I been meaning to ask you, Ma . . . about these songs. This "Moonshine Blues" . . . that's one of them songs Bessie Smith sang, I believes.

MA RAINEY: Bessie what? Ain't nobody thinking about Bessie. I taught Bessie. She ain't doing nothing but imitating me. What I care about Bessie? I don't care if she sell a million records. She got her people and I got mine. I don't care what nobody else do. Ma was the *first* and don't you forget it!

CUTLER: Ain't nobody said nothing about that. I just said that's the same song she sang.

MA RAINEY: I been doing this a long time. Ever since I was a little girl. I don't care what nobody else do. That's what gets me so mad with Irvin. White folks try to be put out with you all the time. Too cheap to buy me a Coca-Cola. I lets them know it, though. Ma don't stand for no shit. Wanna take my voice and trap it in them fancy boxes with all them buttons and dials . . . and then too cheap to buy me a Coca-Cola. And it don't cost but a nickle a bottle.

CUTLER: I knows what you mean about that.

MA RAINEY: They don't care nothing about me. All they want is my voice. Well, I done learned that, and they gonna treat me like I want to be treated no matter how much it hurt them. They back there now calling me all kinds of names . . . calling me everything but a child of god. But they can't do nothing else. They ain't got what they wanted yet. As soon as they get my voice down on them recording machines, then it's just like if I'd be some whore and they roll over and put their pants on. Ain't got no use for me then. I know what I'm talking about. You watch. Irvin right there with the rest of them. He don't care nothing about me either. He's been my manager for six years, always talking about sticking together, and the only time he had me in his house was to sing for some of his friends.

CUTLER: I know how they do.

MA RAINEY: If you colored and can make them some money, then you all right with them. Otherwise, you just a dog in the alley. I done made this company more money from my records than all the other recording artists they got put together. And they wanna balk about how much this session is costing them.

CUTLER: I don't see where it's costing them all what they say.

MA RAINEY: It ain't! I don't pay that kind of talk to mind.

[*The lights go down on the studio and come up on the band room.* TOLEDO *sits reading a newspaper.* LEVEE *sings and hums his song.*]

LEVEE [*singing*]:

> You can shake it, you can break it
> You can dance at any hall
> You can slide across the floor
> You'll never have to stall
> My jelly, my roll,
> Sweet Mama, don't you let it fall.

Wait till Sturdyvant hear me play that! I'm talking about some real music, Toledo! I'm talking about *real* music!

[*The door opens and* DUSSIE MAE *enters.*]

Hey, mama! Come on in.

DUSSIE MAE: Oh, hi! I just wanted to see what it looks like down here.

LEVEE: Well, come on in . . . I don't bite.

DUSSIE MAE: I didn't know you could really write music. I thought you was just jiving me at the club last night.

LEVEE: Naw, baby . . . I knows how to write music. I done give Mr. Sturdyvant some of my songs and he says he's gonna let me record them. Ask Toledo. I'm gonna have my own band! Toledo, ain't I give Mr. Sturdyvant some of my songs I wrote?

TOLEDO: Don't get Toledo mixed up in nothing.

[*He exits.*]

DUSSIE MAE: You gonna get your own band sure enough?

LEVEE: That's right! Levee Green and his Footstompers.

DUSSIE MAE: That's real nice.

LEVEE: That's what I was trying to tell you last night. A man what's gonna get his own band need to have a woman like you.

DUSSIE MAE: A woman like me wants somebody to bring it and put it in my hand. I don't need nobody wanna get something for nothing and leave me standing in my door.

LEVEE: That ain't Levee's style, sugar. I got more style than that. I knows how to treat a woman. Buy her presents and things . . . treat her like she wants to be treated.

DUSSIE MAE: That's what they all say . . . till it come time to be buying the presents.

LEVEE: When we get down to Memphis, I'm gonna show you what I'm talking about. I'm gonna take you out and show you a good time. Show you Levee knows how to treat a woman.

DUSSIE MAE: When you getting your own band?

LEVEE [*moves closer to slip his arm around her*]: Soon as Mr. Sturdyvant say. I done got my fellows already picked out. Getting me some good fellows know how to play real sweet music.

DUSSIE MAE [*moves away*]: Go on now, I don't go for all that pawing and stuff. When you get your own band, maybe we can see about this stuff you talking.

LEVEE [*moving toward her*]: I just wanna show you I know what the women like. They don't call me Sweet Lemonade for nothing.

[LEVEE *takes her in his arms and attempts to kiss her.*]

DUSSIE MAE: Stop it now. Somebody's gonna come in here.

LEVEE: Naw they ain't. Look here, sugar . . . what I wanna know is . . . can I introduce my red rooster to your brown hen?

DUSSIE MAE: You get your band, then we'll see if that rooster know how to crow.

[*He grinds up against her and feels her buttocks.*]

LEVEE: Now I know why my grandpappy sat on the back porch with his straight razor when grandma hung out the wash.

DUSSIE MAE: Nigger, you crazy!

LEVEE: I bet you sound like the midnight train from Alabama when it crosses the Maxon-Dixon line.

DUSSIE MAE: How's you get so crazy?

LEVEE: It's women like you . . . drives me that way.

[*He moves to kiss her as the lights go down in the band room and up in the studio.* MA RAINEY *sits with* CUTLER *and* TOLEDO.]

MA RAINEY: It sure done got quiet in here. I never could stand no silence. I always got to have some music going on in my head somewhere. It keeps things balanced. Music will do that. It fills things up. The more music you got in the world, the fuller it is.

CUTLER: I can agree with that. I got to have my music too.

MA RAINEY: White folks don't understand about the blues. They hear it come out, but they don't know how it got there. They don't understand that's life's way of talking. You don't sing to feel better. You sing 'cause that's a way of understanding life.

CUTLER: That's right. You get that understanding and you done got a grip on life to where you can hold your head up and go on to see what else life got to offer.

MA RAINEY: The blues help you get out of bed in the morning. You get up knowing you ain't alone. There's something else in the world. Something's been added by that song. This be an empty world without the blues. I take that emptiness and try to fill it up with something.

TOLEDO: You fill it up with something the people can't be without, Ma. That's why they call you the Mother of the Blues. You fill up that emptiness in a way ain't nobody ever thought of doing before. And now they can't be without it.

MA RAINEY: I ain't started the blues way of singing. The blues always been here.

CUTLER: In the church sometimes you find that way of singing. They got blues in the church.

MA RAINEY: They say I started it . . . but I didn't. I just helped it out. Filled up that empty space a little bit. That's all. But if they wanna call me the Mother of the Blues, that's all right with me. It don't hurt none.

[SLOW DRAG *and* SYLVESTER *enter with the Cokes.*]

It sure took you long enough. That store ain't but on the corner.

SLOW DRAG: That one was closed. We had to find another one.

MA RAINEY: Sylvester, go and find Mr. Irvin and tell him we ready to go.

[SYLVESTER *exits. The lights in the band room come up while the lights in the studio stay on.* LEVEE *and* DUSSIE MAE *are kissing.* SLOW DRAG *enters. They break their embrace.* DUSSIE MAE *straightens up her clothes.*]

SLOW DRAG: Cold out. I just wanted to warm up with a little sip.

[*He goes to his locker, takes out his bottle and drinks.*]

Ma got her Coke, Levee. We about ready to start.

[SLOW DRAG *exits.* LEVEE *attempts to kiss* DUSSIE MAE *again.*]

DUSSIE MAE: No . . . Come on! I got to go. You gonna get me in trouble.

[*She pulls away and exits up the stairs.* LEVEE *watches after her.*]

LEVEE: Good God! Happy birthday to the lady with the cakes!

[*The lights go down in the band room and come up in the studio.* MA RAINEY *drinks her Coke.* LEVEE *enters from the band room. The musicians take their places.* SYLVESTER *stands by his mike.* IRVIN *and* STURDYVANT *look on from the control booth.*]

IRVIN: We're all set up here, Ma. We're all set to go. You ready down there?

MA RAINEY: Sylvester you just remember your part and say it. That's all there is to it.

[*To* IRVIN.]

Yeah, we ready.

IRVIN: Okay, boys. "Ma Rainey's Black Bottom". Take one.

CUTLER: One . . . two . . . You know what to do.

[*The band plays.*]

SYLVESTER: All right, boys, you d-d-d-done s-s-seen the rest. . . .
IRVIN: Hold it!
> [*The band stops.* STURDYVANT *changes the recording disk and nods to* IRVIN.]
> Okay. Take two.
CUTLER: One . . . two . . . You know what to do.

[*The band plays.*]

SYLVESTER: All right, boys, you done seen the rest . . . now I'm gonna show you the
best. Ma Rainey's g-g-g-gonna s-s-show you her b-b-black bottom.
IRVIN: Hold it! Hold it!
> [*The band stops.* STURDYVANT *changes the recording disk.*]
> Okay. Take Three. Ma, let's do it without the intro, huh? No voice intro . . . you
> just come in singing.
MA RAINEY: Irvin, I done told you . . . the boy's gonna do the part. He don't stutter
all the time. Just give him a chance. Sylvester, hold your hands like I told you and
just relax. Just relax and concentrate.
IRVIN: All right. Take three.
CUTLER: One . . . Two . . . You know what to do.

[*The band plays.*]

SYLVESTER: All right, boys, you done seen the rest . . . now, I'm gonna show you the
best. Ma Rainey's gonna show you her black bottom."
MA RAINEY [*singing*]:

> Way down south in Alabamy
> I got a friend they call dancing Sammy
> Who's crazy about all the latest dances
> Black Bottom stomping, two babies prancing
>
> The other night at a swell affair
> As soon as the boys found out that I was there
> They said, come on, Ma, let's go to the cabaret.
> When I got there, you ought to hear them say,
>
> I want to see the dance you call the black bottom
> I want to learn that dance
> I want to see the dance you call your big black bottom
> It'll put you in a trance.
>
> All the boys in the neighborhood
> They say your black bottom is really good
> Come on and show me your black bottom
> I want to learn that dance

I want to see the dance you call the black bottom
I want to learn that dance
Come on and show the dance you call your big black bottom
It puts you in a trance.

Early last morning about the break of day
Grandpa told my grandma, I heard him say,
Get up and show your old man your black bottom
I want to learn that dance

[*Instrumental break.*]

I done showed you all my black bottom
You ought to learn that dance.

IRVIN: Okay, that's good, Ma. That sounded great! Good job, boys!

MA RAINEY [*to* SYLVESTER]: See! I told you. I knew you could do it. You just have to put your mind to it. Didn't he do good, Cutler? Sound real good. I told him he could do it.

CUTLER: He sure did. He did better than I thought he was gonna do.

IRVIN [*entering to remove* SYLVESTER'*s mike*]: Okay, boys . . . Ma . . . let's do "Moonshine Blues" next, huh? "Moonshine Blues," boys.

STURDYVANT [*over speaker*]: Irv! Something's wrong down there. We don't have it right.

IRVIN: What? What's the matter Mel . . .

STURDYVANT: We don't have it right. Something happened. We don't have the goddamn song recorded!

IRVIN: What's the matter? Mel, what happened? You sure you don't have nothing?

STURDYVANT: Check that mike, huh, Irv. It's the kid's mike. Something's wrong with the mike. We've got everything all screwed up here.

IRVIN: Christ almighty! Ma, we got to do it again. We don't have it. We didn't record the song.

MA RAINEY: What you mean you didn't record it? What was you and Sturdyvant doing up there?

IRVIN [*following the mike wire*]: Here . . . Levee must have kicked the plug out.

LEVEE: I ain't done nothing! I ain't kicked nothing!

SLOW DRAG: If Levee had his mind on what he's doing . . .

MA RAINEY: Levee, if it ain't one thing, it's another. You better straighten yourself up!

LEVEE: Hell . . . it ain't my fault. I ain't done nothing!

STURDYVANT: What's the matter with that mike, Irv? What's the problem?

IRVIN: It's the cord, Mel. The cord's all chewed up. We need another cord.

MA RAINEY: This is the most disorganized . . . Irvin, I'm going home! Come on. Come on, Dussie.

[MA RAINEY *walks past* STURDYVANT *as he enters from the control booth. She exits offstage to get her coat.*]

STURDYVANT [*to* IRVIN]: Where's she going?

IRVIN: She said she's going home.

STURDYVANT: Irvin, you get her! If she walks out of here . . .

[MA RAINEY *enters carrying her and* DUSSIE MAE*'s coat.*]

MA RAINEY: Come on, Sylvester.

IRVIN [*helping her with her coat*]: Ma . . . Ma . . . listen. Fifteen minutes! All I ask is fifteen minutes!

MA RAINEY: Come on, Sylvester, get your coat.

STURDYVANT: Ma, if you walk out of this studio . . .

IRVIN: Fifteen minutes, Ma!

STURDYVANT: You'll be through . . . washed up! If you walk out on me . . .

IRVIN: Mel, for Chrissakes, shut up and let me handle it!

[*He goes after* MA RAINEY, *who has started for the door.*]

Ma, listen. These records are gonna be hits! They're gonna sell like crazy! Hell, even Sylvester will be a star. Fifteen minutes. That's all, I'm asking! Fifteen minutes.

MA RAINEY [*crosses to a chair and sits with her coat on*]: Fifteen minutes! You hear me, Irvin? Fifteen minutes . . . and then I'm gonna take my black bottom on back down to Georgia. Fifteen minutes. Then Madame Rainey is leaving!

IRVIN [*kisses her*]: All right, Ma . . . fifteen minutes. I promise.

[*To the band.*]

You boys go ahead and take a break. Fifteen minutes and we'll be ready to go.

CUTLER: Slow Drag, you got any of that bourbon left?

SLOW DRAG: Yeah, there's some down there.

CUTLER: I could use a little nip.

[CUTLER *and* SLOW DRAG *exit to the band room, followed by* LEVEE *and* TOLEDO. *The lights go down in the studio and up in the band room.*]

SLOW DRAG: Don't make me no difference if she leave or not. I was kinda hoping she would leave.

CUTLER: I'm like Mr. Irvin . . . After all this time we done put in here, it's best to go ahead and get something out of it.

TOLEDO: Ma gonna do what she wanna do, that's for sure. If I was Mr. Irvin, I'd best go on and get them cords and things hooked up right. And I wouldn't take no longer than fifteen minutes doing it.

CUTLER: If Levee had his mind on his work, we wouldn't be in this fix. We'd be up there finishing up. Now we got to go back and see if that boy get that part right. Ain't no telling if he ever get that right again in his life.

LEVEE: Hey, Levee ain't done nothing!

SLOW DRAG: Levee up there got one eye on the gal and the other on his trumpet.

CUTLER: Nigger, don't you know that's Ma's gal?

LEVEE: I don't care whose gal it is. I ain't done nothing to her. I just talk to her like I talk to anybody else.

CUTLER: Well, that being Ma's gal, and that being that boy's gal, is one and two different things. The boy is liable to kill you . . . but you' ass gonna be out there scraping the concrete looking for a job if you messing with Ma's gal.

LEVEE: How am I messing with her? I ain't done nothing to the gal. I just asked her her name. Now, if you telling me I can't do that, then Ma will just have to go to hell.

CUTLER: All I can do is warn you.

SLOW DRAG: Let him hang himself, Cutler. Let him string his neck out.

LEVEE: I ain't done nothing to the gal! You all talk like I done went and done something to her. Leave me go with my business.

CUTLER: I'm through with it. Try and talk to a fool . . .

TOLEDO: Some mens got it worse than others . . . this foolishness I'm talking about. Some mens is excited to be fools. That excitement is something else. I know about it. I done experienced it. It makes you feel good to be a fool. But it don't last long. It's over in a minute. Then you got to tend with the consequences. You got to tend with what comes after. That's when you wish you had learned something about it.

LEVEE: That's the best sense you made all day. Talking about being a fool. That's the only sensible thing you said today. Admitting you was a fool.

TOLEDO: I admits it, all right. Ain't nothing wrong with it. I done been a little bit of everything.

LEVEE: Now you're talking. You's as big a fool as they make.

TOLEDO: Gonna be a bit more things before I'm finished with it. Gonna be foolish again. But I ain't never been the same fool twice. I might be a different kind of fool, but I ain't gonna be the same fool twice. That's where we parts ways.

SLOW DRAG: Toledo, you done been a fool about a woman?

TOLEDO: Sure. Sure I have. Same as everybody.

SLOW DRAG: Hell, I ain't never seen you mess with no woman. I thought them books was your woman.

TOLEDO: Sure I messed with them. Done messed with a whole heap of them. And gonna mess with some more. But I ain't gonna be no fool about them. What you think? I done come in the world full-grown, with my head in a book? I done been young. Married. Got kids. I done been around and I done loved women to where you shake in your shoes just at the sight of them. Feel it all up and down your spine.

SLOW DRAG: I didn't know you was married.

TOLEDO: Sure. Legally. I been married legally. Got the papers and all. I done been through life. Made my marks. Followed some signs on the road. Ignored some others. I done been all through it. I touched and been touched by it. But I ain't never been the same fool twice. That's what I can say.

LEVEE: But you been a fool. That's what counts. Talking about I'm a fool for asking the gal her name and here you is one yourself.

TOLEDO: Now, I married a woman. A good woman. To this day I can't say she wasn't a good woman. I can't say nothing bad about her. I married that woman with all the good graces and intentions of being hooked up and bound to her for the rest of my life. I was looking for her to put me in my grave. But, you see . . . it ain't all the time what you' intentions and wishes are. She went out and joined the church. All right. There ain't nothing wrong with that. A good Christian woman going to church and wanna do right by her god. There ain't nothing wrong with that. But she got up there, got to seeing them good Christian mens and wondering why I ain't like that. Soon she figure she got a heathen on her hands. She figured she couldn't live like that. The church was more important than I was. So she left. Packed up one day and moved out. To this day I ain't never said another word to her. Come home one day and my house was empty! And I sat down and figured out that I was a fool not to see that she needed something that I wasn't giving her. Else she wouldn't have been up there at the church in the first place. I ain't blaming her. I just said it wasn't gonna happen to me again. So, yeah, Toledo been a fool about a woman. That's part of making life.

CUTLER: Well, yeah, I been a fool too. Everybody done been a fool once or twice. But, you see, Toledo, what you call a fool and what I call a fool is two different things. I can't see where you was being a fool for that. You ain't done nothing foolish. You can't help what happened, and I wouldn't call you a fool for it. A fool is responsible for what happens to him. A fool cause it to happen. Like Levee . . . if he keeps messing with Ma's gal and his feet be out there scraping the ground. That's a fool.

LEVEE: Ain't nothing gonna happen to Levee. Levee ain't gonna let nothing happen to him. Now, I'm gonna say it again. I asked the gal her name. That's all I done. And if that's being a fool, then you looking at the biggest fool in the world . . . 'cause I sure as hell asked her.

SLOW DRAG: You just better not let Ma see you ask her. That's what the man's trying to tell you.

LEVEE: I don't need nobody to tell me nothing.

CUTLER: Well, Toledo, all I gots to say is that from the looks of it . . . from your story . . . I don't think life did you fair.

TOLEDO: Oh, life is fair. It's just in the taking what it gives you.

LEVEE: Life ain't shit. You can put it in a paper bag and carry it around with you. It ain't got no balls. Now, death . . . death got some style! Death will kick your ass and make you wish you never been born! That's how bad death is! But you can rule over life. Life ain't nothing.

TOLEDO: Cutler, how's your brother doing?

CUTLER: Who, Nevada? Oh, he's doing all right. Staying in St. Louis. Got a bunch of kids, last I heard.

TOLEDO: Me and him was all right with each other. Done a lot of farming together down in Plattsville.

CUTLER: Yeah, I know you all was tight. He in St. Louis now. Running an elevator, last I hear about it.

SLOW DRAG: That's better than stepping in muleshit.

TOLEDO: Oh, I don't know now. I liked farming. Get out there in the sun . . . smell that dirt. Be out there by yourself . . . nice and peaceful. Yeah, farming was all right by me. Sometimes I think I'd like to get me a little old place . . . but I done got too old to be following behind one of them balky mules now.

LEVEE: Nigger talking about life is fair. And ain't got a pot to piss in.

TOLEDO: See, now, I'm gonna tell you something. A nigger gonna be dissatisfied no matter what. Give a nigger some bread and butter . . . and he'll cry 'cause he ain't got no jelly. Give him some jelly, and he'll cry 'cause he ain't got no knife to put it on with. If there's one thing I done learned in this life, it's that you can't satisfy a nigger no matter what you do. A nigger's gonna make his own dissatisfaction.

LEVEE: Niggers got a right to be dissatisfied. Is you gonna be satisfied with a bone somebody done throwed you when you see them eating the whole hog?

TOLEDO: You lucky they let you be an entertainer. They ain't got to accept your way of entertaining. You lucky and don't even know it. You's entertaining and the rest of the people is hauling wood. That's the only kind of job for the colored man.

SLOW DRAG: Ain't nothing wrong with hauling wood. I done hauled plenty wood. My daddy used to haul wood. Ain't nothing wrong with that. That's honest work.

LEVEE: That ain't what I'm talking about. I ain't talking about hauling no wood. I'm talking about being satisfied with a bone somebody done throwed you. That's what's the matter with you all. You satisfied sitting in one place. You got to move on down the road from where you sitting . . . and all the time you got to keep an eye out for that devil who's looking to buy up souls. And hope you get lucky and find him!

CUTLER: I done told you about that blasphemy. Taking about selling your soul to the devil.

TOLEDO: We done the same thing, Cutler. There ain't no difference. We done sold Africa for the price of tomatoes. We done sold ourselves to the white man in order to be like him. Look at the way you dressed . . . That ain't African. That's the white man. We trying to be just like him. We done sold who we are in order to become someone else. We's imitation white men.

CUTLER: What else we gonna be, living over here?

LEVEE: I'm Levee. Just me. I ain't no imitation nothing!

SLOW DRAG: You can't change who you are by how you dress. That's what I got to say.

TOLEDO: It ain't all how you dress. It's how you act, how you see the world. It's how you follow life.

LEVEE: It don't matter what you talking about. I ain't no imitation white man. And I don't want to be no white man. As soon as I get my band together and make them records like Mr. Sturdyvant done told me I can make, I'm gonna be like Ma and tell the white man just what he can do. Ma tell Mr. Irvin she gonna leave . . . and Mr. Irvin get down on his knees and beg her to stay! That's the way I'm gonna be! Make the white man respect me!

CUTLER: The white man don't care nothing about Ma. The colored folks made Ma a star. White folks don't care nothing about who she is . . . what kind of music she make.

SLOW DRAG: That's the truth about that. You let her go down to one of them white-folks hotels and see how big she is.

CUTLER: Hell, she ain't got to do that. She can't even get a cab up here in the North. I'm gonna tell you something. Reverend Gates . . . you know Reverend Gates? . . . Slow Drag know who I'm talking about. Reverend Gates . . . now I'm gonna show you how this go where the white man don't care a thing about who you is. Reverend

Gates was coming from Tallahassee to Atlanta, going to see his sister, who was sick at that time with the consumption. The train come up through Thomasville, then past Moultrie, and stopped in this little town called Sigsbee . . .

LEVEE: You can stop telling that right there! That train don't stop in Sigsbee. I know what train you talking about. That train got four stops before it reach Macon to go on to Atlanta. One in Thomasville, one in Moultrie, one in Cordele . . . and it stop in Centerville.

CUTLER: Nigger, I know what I'm talking about. You gonna tell me where the train stop?

LEVEE: Hell, yeah, if you talking about it stop in Sigsbee. I'm gonna tell you the truth.

CUTLER: I'm talking about *this* train! I don't know what train you been riding. I'm talking about *this* train!

LEVEE: Ain't but one train. Ain't but one train come out of Tallahassee heading north to Atlanta, and it don't stop at Sigsbee. Tell him, Toledo . . . that train don't stop at Sigsbee. The only train that stops at Sigsbee is the Yazoo Delta, and you have to transfer at Moultrie to get it!

CUTLER: Well, hell, maybe that what he done! I don't know. I'm just telling you the man got off the train at Sigsbee . . .

LEVEE: All right . . . you telling it. Tell it your way. Just make up anything.

SLOW DRAG: Levee, leave the man alone and let him finish.

CUTLER: I ain't paying Levee no never mind.

LEVEE: Go on and tell it your way.

CUTLER: Anyway . . . Reverend Gates got off this train in Sigsbee. The train done stopped there and he figured he'd get off and check the schedule to be sure he arrive in time for somebody to pick him up. All right. While he's there checking the schedule, it come upon him that he had to go to the bathroom. Now, they ain't had no colored rest rooms at the station. The only colored rest room is an outhouse they got sitting way back two hundred yards or so from the station. All right. He in the outhouse and the train go off and leave him there. He don't know nothing about this town. Ain't never been there before—in fact, ain't never even heard of it before.

LEVEE: I heard of it! I know just where it's at . . . and he ain't got off no train coming out of Tallahassee in Sigsbee!

CUTLER: The man standing there, trying to figure out what he's gonna do . . . where this train done left him in this strange town. It started getting dark. He see where the sun's getting low in the sky and he's trying to figure out what he's gonna do, when he noticed a couple of white fellows standing across the street from this station. Just standing there, watching him. And then two or three more come up and joined the other one. He look around, ain't seen no colored folks nowhere. He didn't know what was getting in these here fellows' minds, so he commence to walking. He ain't knowed where he was going. He just walking down the railroad tracks when he hear them call him. "Hey, nigger!" See, just like that. "Hey, nigger!" He kept on walking. They called him some more and he just keep walking. Just going down the tracks. And then he heard a gunshot where somebody done fired a gun in the air. He stopped then, you know.

TOLEDO: You don't even have to tell me no more. I know the facts of it. I done heard the same story a hundred times. It happened to me too. Same thing.

CUTLER: Naw, I'm gonna show you how the white folks don't care nothing about who or what you is. They crowded around him. These gang of mens made a circle around him. Now, he's standing there, you understand . . . got his cross around his neck like them preachers wear. Had his little Bible with him what he carry all the time. So they crowd on around him and one of them ask who he is. He told them he was Reverend Gates and that he was going to see his sister who was sick and the train left without him. And they said, "Yeah, nigger . . . but can you dance?" He looked at them and commenced to dancing. One of them reached up and tore his cross off his neck. Said he was committing a heresy by dancing with a cross and Bible. Took his Bible and tore it up and had him dancing till they got tired of watching him.

SLOW DRAG: White folks ain't never had no respect for the colored minister.

CUTLER: That's the only way he got out of there alive . . . was to dance. Ain't even had no respect for a man of God! Wanna make him into a clown. Reverend Gates sat right in my house and told me that story from his own mouth. So . . . the white folks don't care nothing about Ma Rainey. She's just another nigger who they can use to make some money.

LEVEE: What I wants to know is . . . if he's a man of God, then where the hell was God when all of this was going on? Why wasn't God looking out for him. Why didn't God strike down them crackers with some of this lightning you talk about to me?

CUTLER: Levee, you gonna burn in hell.

LEVEE: What I care about burning in hell? You talk like a fool . . . burning in hell. Why didn't God strike some of them crackers down? Tell me that! That's the question! Don't come telling me this burning-in-hell shit! He a man of God . . . why didn't God strike some of them crackers down? I'll tell you why! I'll tell you the truth! It's sitting out there as plain as day! 'Cause he a white man's God. That's why! God ain't never listened to no nigger's prayers. God take a nigger's prayers and throw them in the garbage. God don't pay niggers no mind. In fact . . . God hate niggers! Hate them with all the fury in his heart. Jesus don't love you, nigger! Jesus hate your black ass! Come talking that shit to me. Talking about burning in hell! God can kiss my ass.

[CUTLER *can stand no more. He jumps up and punches* LEVEE *in the mouth. The force of the blow knocks* LEVEE *down and* CUTLER *jumps on him.*]

CUTLER: You worthless . . . That's my God! That's my God! That's my God! You wanna blaspheme my God!

[TOLEDO *and* SLOW DRAG *grab* CUTLER *and try to pull him off* LEVEE.]

SLOW DRAG: Come on, Cutler . . . let it go! It don't mean nothing!

[CUTLER *has* LEVEE *down on the floor and pounds on him with a fury.*]

CUTLER: Wanna blaspheme my God! You worthless . . . talking about my God!

[TOLEDO *and* SLOW DRAG *succeed in pulling* CUTLER *off* LEVEE, *who is bleeding at the nose and mouth.*]

LEVEE: Naw, let him go! Let him go!
[*He pulls out a knife.*]
That's your God, huh? That's your God, huh? Is that right? Your God, huh? All right. I'm gonna give your God a chance. I'm gonna give your God a chance. I'm gonna give him a chance to save your black ass.

[LEVEE *circles* CUTLER *with the knife.* CUTLER *picks up a chair to protect himself.*]

TOLEDO: Come on, Levee . . . put the knife up!
LEVEE: Stay out of this, Toledo!
TOLEDO: That ain't no way to solve nothing.

[LEVEE *alternately swipes at* CUTLER *during the following.*]

LEVEE: I'm calling Cutler's God! I'm talking to Cutler's God! You hear me? Cutler's God! I'm calling Cutler's God. Come on and save this nigger! Strike me down before I cut his throat!
SLOW DRAG: Watch him, Cutler! Put that knife up, Levee!
LEVEE [*to* CUTLER]: I'm calling your God! I'm gonna give him a chance to save you! I'm calling your God! We gonna find out whose God he is!
CUTLER: You gonna burn in hell, nigger!
LEVEE: Cutler's God! Come on and save this nigger! Come on and save him like you did my mama! Save him like you did my mama! I heard her when she called you! I heard her when she said, "Lord, have mercy! Jesus, help me! Please, God, have mercy on me, Lord Jesus, help me!" And did you turn your back? Did you turn your back, motherfucker? Did you turn your back?
[LEVEE *becomes so caught up in his dialogue with God that he forgets about* CUTLER *and begins to stab upward in the air, trying to reach God.*]
Come on! Come on and turn your back on me! Turn your back on me! Come on! Where is you? Come on and turn your back on me! Turn your back on me, motherfucker! I'll cut your heart out! Come on, turn your back on me! Come on! What's the matter? Where is you? Come on and turn your back on me! Come on, what you scared of? Turn your back on me! Come on! Coward, motherfucker!
[LEVEE *folds his knife and stands triumphantly.*]
Your God ain't shit, Cutler.

[*The lights fade to black.*]

MA RAINEY [*singing*]:

> Ah, you hear me talking to you
> I don't bite my tongue

You wants to be my man
You got to fetch it with you when you come.

[*Lights come up in the studio. The last bars of the last song of the session are dying out.*]

IRVIN [*over speaker*]: Good! Wonderful! We have that, boys. Good session. That's great, Ma. We've got ourselves some winners.

TOLEDO: Well, I'm glad that's over.

MA RAINEY: Slow Drag, where you learn to play the bass at? You had it singing! I heard you! Had that bass jumping all over the place.

SLOW DRAG: I was following Toledo. Nigger got them long fingers striding all over the piano. I was trying to keep up with him.

TOLEDO: That's what you supposed to do, ain't it? Play the music. Ain't nothing abstract about it.

MA RAINEY: Cutler, you hear Slow Drag on that bass? He make it do what he want it to do! Spank it just like you spank a baby.

CUTLER: Don't be telling him that. Nigger's head get so big his hat won't fit him.

SLOW DRAG: If Cutler tune that guitar up, we would really have something!

CUTLER: You wouldn't know what a tuned-up guitar sounded like if you heard one.

TOLEDO: Cutler was talking. I heard him moaning. He was all up in it.

MA RAINEY: Levee . . . what is that you doing? Why you playing all them notes? You play ten notes for every one you supposed to play. It don't call for that.

LEVEE: You supposed to improvise on the theme. That's what I was doing.

MA RAINEY: You supposed to play the song the way I sing it. The way everybody else play it. You ain't supposed to go off by yourself and play what you want.

LEVEE: I was playing the song. I was playing it the way I felt it.

MA RAINEY: I couldn't keep up with what was going on. I'm trying to sing the song and you up there messing up my ear. That's what you was doing. Call yourself playing music.

LEVEE: Hey . . . I know what I'm doing. I know what I'm doing, all right. I know how to play music. You all back up and leave me alone about my music.

CUTLER: I done told you . . . it ain't about *your* music. It's about *Ma's* music.

MA RAINEY: That's all right, Cutler. I done told you what to do.

LEVEE: I don't care what you do. You supposed to improvise on the theme. Not play note for note the same thing over and over again.

MA RAINEY: You just better watch yourself. You hear me?

LEVEE: What I care what you or Cutler do? Come telling me to watch myself. What's that supposed to mean?

MA RAINEY: All right . . . you gonna find out what it means.

LEVEE: Go ahead and fire me. I don't care. I'm gonna get my own band anyway.

MA RAINEY: You keep messing with me.

LEVEE: Ain't nobody studying you. You ain't gonna do nothing to me. Ain't nobody gonna do nothing to Levee.

MA RAINEY: All right, nigger . . . you fired!

LEVEE: You think I care about being fired? I don't care nothing about that. You doing me a favor.

MA RAINEY: Cutler, Levee's out! He don't play in my band no more.

LEVEE: I'm fired . . . Good! Best thing that ever happened to me. I don't need this shit!

[LEVEE *exits to the band room.* IRVIN *enters from the control booth.*]

MA RAINEY: Cutler, I'll see you back at the hotel.

IRVIN: Okay, boys . . . you can pack up. I'll get your money for you.

CUTLER: That's cash money, Mr. Irvin. I don't want no check.

IRVIN: I'll see what I can do. I can't promise you nothing.

CUTLER: As long as it ain't no check. I ain't got no use for a check.

IRVIN: I'll see what I can do, Cutler.

[CUTLER, TOLEDO, *and* SLOW DRAG *exit to the band room.*]

Oh, Ma, listen . . . I talked to Sturdyvant, and he said . . . Now, I tried to talk him out of it . . . He said the best he can do is to take twenty-five dollars of your money and give it to Sylvester.

MA RAINEY: Take what and do what? If I wanted the boy to have twenty-five dollars of my money, I'd give it to him. He supposed to get his own money. He supposed to get paid like everybody else.

IRVIN: Ma, I talked to him . . . He said . . .

MA RAINEY: Go talk to him again! Tell him if he don't pay that boy, he'll never make another record of mine again. Tell him that. You supposed to be my manager. All this talk about sticking together. Start sticking! Go on up there and get that boy his money!

IRVIN: Okay, Ma . . . I'll talk to him again. I'll see what I can do.

MA RAINEY: Ain't no see about it! You bring that boy's money back here!

[IRVIN *exits. The lights stay on in the studio and come up in the band room. The men have their instruments packed and sit waiting for* IRVIN *to come and pay them.* SLOW DRAG *has a pack of cards.*]

SLOW DRAG: Come on, Levee, let me show you a card trick.

LEVEE: I don't want to see no card trick. What you wanna show me for? Why you wanna bother me with that?

SLOW DRAG: I was just trying to be nice.

LEVEE: I don't need you to be nice to me. What I need you to be nice to me for? I ain't gonna be nice to you. I ain't even gonna let you be in my band no more.

SLOW DRAG: Toledo, let me show you a card trick.

CUTLER: I just hope Mr. Irvin don't bring no check down here. What the hell I'm gonna do with a check?

SLOW DRAG: All right now . . . pick a card. Any card . . . go on . . . take any of them. I'm gonna show you something.

TOLEDO: I agrees with you, Cutler. I don't want no check either.

CUTLER: It don't make no sense to give a nigger a check.

SLOW DRAG: Okay, now. Remember your card. Remember which one you got. Now
. . . put it back in the deck. Anywhere you want. I'm gonna show you something.
[TOLEDO *puts the card in the deck*.]
You remember your card? All right. Now I'm gonna shuffle the deck. Now . . . I'm
gonna show you what card you picked. Don't say nothing now. I'm gonna tell you
what card you picked.

CUTLER: Slow Drag, that trick is as old as my mama.

SLOW DRAG: Naw, naw . . . wait a minute! I'm gonna show him his card . . . There
it go! The six of diamonds. Ain't that your card? Ain't that it?

TOLEDO: Yeah, that's it . . . the six of diamonds.

SLOW DRAG: Told you! Told you I'd show him what it was!

[*The lights fade in the band room and come up full on the studio*. STURDYVANT *enters with* IRVIN.]

STURDYVANT: Ma, is there something wrong? Is there a problem?

MA RAINEY: Sturdyvant, I want you to pay that boy his money.

STURDYVANT: Sure, Ma. I got it right here. Two hundred for you and twenty-five for
the kid, right?
[STURDYVANT *hands the money to* IRVIN, *who hands it to* MA RAINEY *and* SYLVESTER.]
Irvin misunderstood me. It was all a mistake. Irv made a mistake.

MA RAINEY: A mistake, huh?

IRVIN: Sure, Ma. I made a mistake. He's paid, right? I straightened it out.

MA RAINEY: The only mistake was when you found out I hadn't signed the release
forms. That was the mistake. Come on, Sylvester.

[*She starts to exit*.]

STURDYVANT: Hey, Ma . . . come on, sign the forms, huh?

IRVIN: Ma . . . come on now.

MA RAINEY: Get your coat, Sylvester. Irvin, where's my car?

IRVIN: It's right out front, Ma. Here . . . I got the keys right here. Come on, sign the
forms, huh?

MA RAINEY: Irvin, give me my car keys!

IRVIN: Sure, Ma . . . just sign the forms, huh?

[*He gives her the keys, expecting a trade-off*.]

MA RAINEY: Send them to my address and I'll get around to them.

IRVIN: Come on, Ma . . . I took care of everything, right? I straightened everything out.

MA RAINEY: Give me the pen, Irvin.
[*She signs the forms*.]
You tell Sturdyvant . . . one more mistake like that and I can make my records
someplace else.
[*She turns to exit*.]
Sylvester, straighten up your clothes. Come on, Dussie Mae.

[*She exits, followed by* DUSSIE MAE *and* SYLVESTER. *The lights go down in the studio and come up on the band room.*]

CUTLER: I know what's keeping him so long. He up there writing out checks. You watch. I ain't gonna stand for it. He ain't gonna bring me no check down here. If he do, he's gonna take it right back upstairs and get some cash.

TOLEDO: Don't get yourself all worked up about it. Wait and see. Think positive.

CUTLER: I am thinking positive. He positively gonna give me some cash. Man give me a check last time . . . you remember . . . we went all over Chicago trying to get it cashed. See a nigger with a check, the first thing they think is he done stole it someplace.

LEVEE: I ain't had no trouble cashing mine.

CUTLER: I don't visit no whorehouses.

LEVEE: You don't know about my business. So don't start nothing. I'm tired of you as it is. I ain't but two seconds off your ass no way.

TOLEDO: Don't you all start nothing now.

CUTLER: What the hell I care what you tired of. I wasn't even talking to you. I was talking to this man right here.

[IRVIN *and* STURDYVANT *enter.*]

IRVIN: Okay boys. Mr. Sturdyvant has your pay.

CUTLER: As long as it's cash money, Mr. Sturdyvant. 'Cause I have too much trouble trying to cash a check.

STURDYVANT: Oh, yes . . . I'm aware of that. Mr. Irvin told me you boys prefer cash, and that's what I have for you.

[*He starts handing out the money.*]

That was a good session you boys put in . . . That's twenty-five for you. Yessir, you boys really know your business and we are going to . . . Twenty-five for you . . . We are going to get you back in here real soon . . . twenty-five . . . and have another session so you can make some more money . . . and twenty-five for you. Okay, thank you, boys. You can get your things together and Mr. Irvin will make sure you find your way out.

IRVIN: I'll be out front when you get your things together, Cutler.

[IRVIN *exits.* STURDYVANT *starts to follow.*]

LEVEE: Mr. Sturdyvant, sir. About them songs I give you? . . .

STURDYVANT: Oh, yes, . . . uh . . . Levee. About them songs you gave me. I've thought about it and I just don't think the people will buy them. They're not the type of songs we're looking for.

LEVEE: Mr. Sturdyvant, sir . . . I done got my band picked out and they's real good fellows. They knows how to play real good. I know if the peoples hear the music, they'll buy it.

STURDYVANT: Well, Levee, I'll be fair with you . . . but they're just not the right songs.

LEVEE: Mr. Sturdyvant, you got to understand about that music. That music is what the people is looking for. They's tired of jug-band music. They wants something that excites them. Something with some fire to it.

STURDYVANT: Okay, Levee. I'll tell you what I'll do. I'll give you five dollars a piece for them. Now that's the best I can do.

LEVEE: I don't want no five dollars, Mr. Sturdyvant. I wants to record them songs, like you say.

STURDYVANT: Well, Levee, like I say . . . they just aren't the kind of songs we're looking for.

LEVEE: Mr. Sturdyvant, you asked me to write them songs. Now, why didn't you tell me that before when I first give them to you? You told me you was gonna let me record them. What's the difference between then and now?

STURDYVANT: Well, look . . . I'll pay you for your trouble . . .

LEVEE: What's the difference, Mr. Sturdyvant? That's what I wanna know.

STURDYVANT: I had my fellows play your songs, and when I heard them, they just didn't sound like the kind of songs I'm looking for right now.

LEVEE: You got to hear *me* play them, Mr. Sturdyvant! You ain't heard *me* play them. That's what's gonna make them sound right.

STURDYVANT: Well, Levee, I don't doubt that really. It's just that . . . well, I don't think they'd sell like Ma's records. But I'll take them off your hands for you.

LEVEE: The people's tired of jug-band music, Mr. Sturdyvant. They wants something that's gonna excite them! They wants something with some fire! I don't know what fellows you had playing them songs . . . but if I could play them! I'd set them down in the people's lap! Now you told me I could record them songs!

STURDYVANT: Well, there's nothing I can do about that. Like I say, it's five dollars a piece. That's what I'll give you. I'm doing you a favor. Now, if you write any more, I'll help you out and take them off your hands. The price is five dollars apiece. Just like now.

[*He attempts to hand* LEVEE *the money, finally shoves it in* LEVEE's *coat pocket and is gone in a flash.* LEVEE *follows him to the door and it slams in his face. He takes the money from his pocket, balls it up and throws it on the floor. The other musicians silently gather up their belongings.* TOLEDO *walks past* LEVEE *and steps on his shoe.*]

LEVEE: Hey! Watch it . . . Shit Toledo! You stepped on my shoe!

TOLEDO: Excuse me there, Levee.

LEVEE: Look at that! Look at that! Nigger, you stepped on my shoe. What you do that for?

TOLEDO: I said I'm sorry.

LEVEE: Nigger gonna step on my goddamn shoe! You done fucked up my shoe! Look at that! Look at what you done to my shoe, nigger! I ain't stepped on your shoe! What you wanna step on my shoe for?

CUTLER: The man said he's sorry.

LEVEE: Sorry! How the hell he gonna be sorry after he gone ruint my shoe? Come talking about sorry!

[*Turns his attention back to* TOLEDO.]

Nigger, you stepped on my shoe! You know that!
[LEVEE *snatches his shoe off his foot and holds it up for* TOLEDO *to see.*]
See what you done done?
TOLEDO: What you want me to do about it? It's done now. I said excuse me.
LEVEE: Wanna go and fuck up my shoe like that. I ain't done nothing to your shoe.
Look at this!

[TOLEDO *turns and continues to gather up his things.* LEVEE *spins him around by his shoulder.*]

LEVEE: Naw . . . naw . . . look what you done!
[*He shoves the shoe in* TOLEDO's *face.*]
Look at that! That's my shoe! Look at that! You did it! You did it! You fucked up
my shoe! You stepped on my shoe with them raggedy-ass clodhoppers!
TOLEDO: Nigger, ain't nobody studying you and your shoe! I said excuse me. If you
can't accept that, then the hell with it. What you want me to do?

[LEVEE *is in a near rage, breathing hard. He is trying to get a grip on himself, as even he senses,
or perhaps only he senses, he is about to lose control. He looks around, uncertain of what to do.*
TOLEDO *has gone back to packing, as have* CUTLER *and* SLOW DRAG. *They purposefully avoid
looking at* LEVEE *in hopes he'll calm down if he doesn't have an audience. All the weight in the world
suddenly falls on* LEVEE *and he rushes at* TOLEDO *with his knife in his hand.*]

LEVEE: Nigger, you stepped on my shoe!
[*He plunges the knife into* TOLEDO's *back up to the hilt.* TOLEDO *lets out a sound of surprise and
agony.* CUTLER *and* SLOW DRAG *freeze.* TOLEDO *falls backward with* LEVEE, *his hand still on
the knife, holding him up.* LEVEE *is suddenly faced with the realization of what he has done. He
shoves* TOLEDO *forward and takes a step back.* TOLEDO *slumps to the floor.*]
He . . . he stepped on my shoe. He did. Honest, Cutler, he stepped on my shoe. What
he do that for? Toledo, what you do that for? Cutler, help me. He stepped on my
shoe, Cutler.
[*He turns his attention to* TOLEDO.]
Toledo! Toledo, get up.
[*He crosses to* TOLEDO *and tries to pick him up.*]
It's okay, Toledo. Come on . . . I'll help you. Come on, stand up now. Levee'll
help you.
[TOLEDO *is limp and heavy and awkward. He slumps back to the floor.* LEVEE *gets mad at him.*]
Don't look at me like that! Toledo! Nigger, don't look at me like that! I'm warning
you, nigger! Close your eyes! Don't you look at me like that! [*He turns to* CUTLER.]
Tell him to close his eyes. Cutler. Tell him don't look at me like that.
CUTLER: Slow Drag, get Mr. Irvin down here.

[*The sound of a trumpet is heard,* LEVEE's *trumpet, a muted trumpet struggling for the highest of
possibilities and blowing pain and warning.*]

Black out

QUESTIONS

1. How does the prologue reveal the social milieu of the play and its characters?
2. What distinguishes Toledo from his two colleagues, Cutler and Slow Drag? When he says of them in Act I, "you forgot the name of the gods," what does he mean? Why does Toledo call Levee the devil? What does Toledo believe to be the chief shortcoming of African-Americans in the United States?
3. Why does Sturdyvant want to use Levee's renditions of the blues songs? Why do the other musicians resist playing them?
4. Describe the relationships among the members of the band, Ma Rainey, and the two recording producers—Sturdyvant and Irvin—in Act I.
5. In Act II, Ma Rainey describes what "White Folks" want from her. What do they want?
6. In Act II, Ma Rainey says "You sing 'cause that's a way of understanding life." What type of singing is she referring to? What does she mean by this?
7. In Act II, Toledo and Levee have an argument over "life." What does each feel about life in general? How do they differ?
8. Cutler says that whites "wanna make him [the black man] a clown." What does he mean? What special relevance does it have to the lives of Ma Rainey and the musicians?
9. Why does Levee stab Toledo?

Caste & Class

Drama

TOPICS FOR WRITING

1. Using your personal experience and/or observations, write an essay describing the day-to-day life of people living in an ethnic, racial, or religious neighborhood. What delineates their lives? What types of work, recreation, and cultural activities distinguish them?

2. Write about a personal experience when you felt out of place owing to your social, economic, ethnic, or racial class. How did you feel? How did others make you feel different or isolated? What strategy did you use to address the situation?

3. Compare and contrast the use of comedy in *The Waste Disposal Unit* and *Ma Rainey's Black Bottom*.

4. Write an essay describing the values of the Knockerbickers in *The Waste Disposal Unit*. How does the playwright reveal these values?

5. In one way or another, all the black characters in *Ma Rainey's Black Bottom* have been oppressed by white society. Select any two of the characters, and compare and contrast their oppression and how they address it, based upon what they say and do during the play.

6. Argue for or against the proposition that so long as there are separate economic classes in the United States, there will always be conflict among them.

7. Owing to the success of black musicians like Michael Jackson and Paula Abdul in contemporary America, the exploitation as described in *Ma Rainey's Black Bottom* is not relevant to understanding the black experience today. Argue for or against this proposition.

8. Read another of August Wilson's plays, and compare and contrast its themes and style with those of *Ma Rainey's Black Bottom*.

War

&

Peace

"War Dance and Gathering Scene" by Earnest Spybuck. National Museum of the American Indian. M. R. Harrington Collection 2/5614.

INTRODUCTION

Not surprisingly, the first examples of written literature in the world have had as a prominent part of their subject matter depictions and explorations of war and peace. Ancient Greece, Scandinavia, Africa, the Far East, the Middle East, and the Indian subcontinent all have classic works that show the significance of war in the life of society and its effects on the average citizen, on kings and queens and other royalty, on the military, and even on the gods.

Today, our literature seems replete with this topic. Just check the bestseller lists, film schedules, or your TV program guide, and there is sure to be some novel, film, or television show set during wartime or during a period that foreshadows armed conflict or shows its aftermath. Besides fiction and film, other forms of art and communication express the horrors of war as well; for example, the famous painting "Guernica" by Pablo Picasso depicts in expressionist style the ruthless bombing of the town of that name during the Spanish Civil War. In fact, two of the poems in this section, Babette Deutsch's "Disasters of War" and Lawrence Ferlinghetti's "In Goya's Greatest Scenes" both make reference to paintings that depict the anguish of battle.

Even themes set during times of peace or truce explore subjects such as espionage, political repression, and subversion, and so are closely related to the themes of war. In them, one can find conflict, disorder, high stakes, and violence. For example, in the story "Civil Peace" by the African writer Chinua Achebe, the main character, Jonathan Iwegbu, lives at a time when no official battles are being waged. Nevertheless, his life is filled with uncertainty and confusion, with the threat of violent death always close by owing to looters, corruption, and general social confusion. In the story "The South" by Argentine writer Jorge Luis Borges, we see portrayed one Johannes Dahlmann. He is not a member of any standing armed force, and in fact leads a fairly mundane and routine life. Yet circumstances arise whereby he is face-to-face with an armed man against whom he must summon personal courage and patriotic pride to meet the threat of death. In Bobbie Ann Mason's "Big Bertha Stories," the leading character, a Vietnam veteran, bears the psychological scars of war years after it has ended, demonstrating the profound effect war can have not only on those who have experienced it but on those close to the individual, such as friends, family, and acquaintances.

There is a flip side to issues of war and peace that is often overlooked, but which is also addressed in the fiction and poetry in this section. That is the sin of omission rather than commission. In other words, some of the works show individuals who are not willing to challenge the status quo—who in effect choose not to struggle against the threat of war or tyranny. In "The Censors" by Luisa Valenzuela, the character Juan seems an amiable fellow, and we see him portrayed within a society seemingly at peace; but beneath the façade of affability there lurks an oppressive government that prevents its citizens from expressing themselves freely. But Juan, rather than challenge this threat to freedom, passively and willingly becomes part of it, thereby doomed to aid in upholding the general repression. And so strong is the grip of tyranny over the people, they are not even aware of their oppression—a society reminiscent of that depicted in the classic novel *1984* by George Orwell. Or, we may wonder, is the story meant to be an allegory that depicts societies in general?

Two other works in this section portray the unknowing, unthinking, or conforming individual. Auden's "The Unknown Citizen" satirizes the "model citizen" who does whatever he is called upon to do. He has the "right" attitude toward all things political and social, and dies unaware that his duty as a citizen should be to consider, reflect upon, or even challenge what is expected of him by society. A similar persona can be found in e. e. cummings's "next to of course god." In this satirical poem, the narrator mindlessly praises patriotism, loyalty, and duty while demonstrating that he hasn't an inkling as to what these abstractions are.

Such themes aside, however—for good or ill—the things about war that seem to intrigue many of us are the violence, the heightened intensity of life that permeates it, and the extraordinary extremes of human behavior and action that characterize it. "Patriotism" by the Japanese writer Yukio Mishima—who committed *sanpuku,* a form of ritual suicide—describes in minute and meticulous detail the process by which a Japanese officer and his wife prepare and carry out their suicides. The story is at times gory, and some may even find it repulsive, but its attention to detail provides an intimate account of another culture's view of violence and mutilation far different from that which most of us know. Wilfred Owen's two poems "Dulce et Decorum Est" and "Anthem for Doomed Youth" as well as Randall Jarrell's "The Death of the Ball Turret Gunner" also provide a grisly picture of the immediacy of and potential violence and death of war—in these cases, amid actual combat. Their goal, however, is not to tantalize and thrill, as are the motives of so many current movies, but to serve as antiwar statements by destroying the illusion many unknowing individuals have about the so-called glory and excitement of war.

Yet despite the horror, uncertainty, and confusion that many of the works in this section portray, there is room for some humor. Perhaps it is the very absurdity of war that has inspired writers to treat it thus. *Lysistrata,* by the classic Greek comedic writer Aristophanes, is an early example of applying raillery and wit to the theme of war. Lysistrata and her female cohorts come up with a practical and manageable plan to end war. They will refuse to have sex with their husbands unless they pledge to throw down their arms and swear to eschew war forever. While the idea might be satiric, it demonstrates the power of creative writers to look on a topic in a unique way; they provide food for thought that age-old problems might be solved if only we worked harder to find original solutions.

Fiction

Chinua Achebe

CIVIL PEACE

Jonathan Iwegbu counted himself extra-ordinarily lucky. "Happy survival!" meant so much more to him than just a current fashion of greeting old friends in the first hazy days of peace. It went deep to his heart. He had come out of the war with five inestimable blessings—his head, his wife Maria's head and the heads of three out of their four children. As a bonus he also had his old bicycle—a miracle too but naturally not to be compared to the safety of five human heads.

The bicycle had a little history of its own. One day at the height of the war it was commandeered "for urgent military action." Hard as its loss would have been to him he would still have let it go without a thought had he not had some doubts about the genuineness of the officer. It wasn't his disreputable rags, nor the toes peeping out of one blue and one brown canvas shoes, nor yet the two stars of his rank done obviously in a hurry in biro, that troubled Jonathan; many good and heroic soldiers looked the same or worse. It was rather a certain lack of grip and firmness in his manner. So Jonathan, suspecting he might be amenable to influence, rummaged in his raffia bag and produced the two pounds with which he had been going to buy firewood which his wife, Maria, retailed to camp officials for extra stock-fish and corn meal, and got his bicycle back. That night he buried it in the little clearing in the bush where the dead of the camp, including his own youngest son, were buried. When he dug it up again a year later after the surrender all it needed was a little palm-oil greasing. "Nothing puzzles God," he said in wonder.

He put it to immediate use as a taxi and accumulated a small pile of Biafran money ferrying camp officials and their families across the four-mile stretch to the nearest tarred road. His standard charge per trip was six pounds and those who had the money were only glad to be rid of some of it in this way. At the end of a fortnight he had made a small fortune of one hundred and fifteen pounds.

Then he made the journey to Enugu and found another miracle waiting for him. It was unbelievable. He rubbed his eyes and looked again and it was still standing there before him. But, needless to say, even that monumental blessing must be accounted also totally inferior to the five heads in the family. This newest miracle was his little house in Ogui Overside. Indeed nothing puzzles God! Only two houses away a huge concrete edifice some wealthy contractor had put up just before the war was a mountain of rubble. And here was Jonathan's little zinc house of no regrets built with mud blocks quite intact! Of course the doors and windows were missing and five sheets off the roof. But what was that? And anyhow he had returned to Enugu early enough to pick up bits of old zinc and wood and soggy sheets of cardboard lying around the neighbourhood before thousands more came out of their forest holes looking for the same things. He got a destitute carpenter with one old hammer, a blunt plane and a few bent and rusty nails in his tool bag to turn this assortment of wood, paper and metal into door and window shutters for five Nigerian shillings or fifty Biafran pounds. He paid the pounds, and moved in with his overjoyed family carrying five heads on their shoulders.

His children picked mangoes near the military cemetery and sold them to soldiers' wives for a few pennies—real pennies this time—and his wife started making breakfast akara balls for neighbours in a hurry to start life again. With his family earnings he took his bicycle to the villages around and bought fresh palm-wine which he mixed generously in his rooms with the water which had recently started running again in the public tap down the road, and opened up a bar for soldiers and other lucky people with good money.

At first he went daily, then every other day and finally once a week, to the offices of the Coal Corporation where he used to be a miner, to find out what was what. The only thing he did find out in the end was that that little house of his was even a greater blessing than he had thought. Some of his fellow ex-miners who had nowhere to return at the end of the day's waiting just slept outside the doors of the offices and cooked what meal they could scrounge together in Bournvita tins. As the weeks lengthened and still nobody could say what was what Jonathan discontinued his weekly visits altogether and faced his palm-wine bar.

But nothing puzzles God. Came the day of the windfall when after five days of endless scuffles in queues and counter-queues in the sun outside the Treasury he had twenty pounds counted into his palms as ex-gratia award for the rebel money he had turned in. It was like Christmas for him and for many others like him when the payments began. They called it (since few could manage its proper official name) *egg-rasher.*

As soon as the pound notes were placed in his palm Jonathan simply closed it tight over them and buried fist and money inside his trouser pocket. He had to be extra careful because he had seen a man a couple of days earlier collapse into near-madness in an instant before that oceanic crowd because no sooner had he got his twenty pounds than some heartless ruffian picked it off him. Though it was not right that a man in such an extremity of agony should be blamed yet many in the queues that day were able to remark quietly on the victim's carelessness, especially after he pulled out the innards of his pocket and revealed a hole in it big enough to pass a thief's head. But of course he had insisted that the money had been in the other pocket, pulling it out too to show its comparative wholeness. So one had to be careful.

Jonathan soon transferred the money to his left hand and pocket so as to leave his right free for shaking hands should the need arise, though by fixing his gaze at such an elevation as to miss all approaching human faces he made sure that the need did not arise, until he got home.

He was normally a heavy sleeper but that night he heard all the neighbourhood noises die down one after another. Even the night watchman who knocked the hour on some metal somewhere in the distance had fallen silent after knocking one o'clock. That must have been the last thought in Jonathan's mind before he was finally carried away himself. He couldn't have been gone for long, though, when he was violently awakened again.

"Who is knocking?" whispered his wife lying beside him on the floor.

"I don't know," he whispered back breathlessly.

The second time the knocking came it was so loud and imperious that the rickety old door could have fallen down.

"Who is knocking?" he asked them, his voice parched and trembling.

"Na tief-man and him people," came the cool reply. "Make you hopen de door." This was followed by the heaviest knocking of all.

Maria was the first to raise the alarm, then he followed and all their children.

"Police-o! Thieves-o! Neighbours-o! Police-o! We are lost! We are dead! Neighbours, are you asleep? Wake up! Police-o!"

This went on for a long time and then stopped suddenly. Perhaps they had scared the thief away. There was total silence. But only for a short while.

"You done finish?" asked the voice outside. "Make we help you small. Oya, every-body!"

"Police-o! Tief-man-o! Neighbours-o! we done loss-o! Police-o! . . ."

There were at least five other voices besides the leader's.

Jonathan and his family were now completely paralysed by terror. Maria and the children sobbed inaudibly like lost souls. Jonathan groaned continuously.

The silence that followed the thieves' alarm vibrated horribly. Jonathan all but begged their leader to speak again and be done with it.

"My frien," said he at long last, "we don try our best for call dem but I tink say dem all done sleep-o . . . So wetin we go do now? Sometaim you wan call soja? Or you wan make we call dem for you? Soja better pass police. No be so?"

"Na so!" replied his men. Jonathan thought he heard even more voices now than before and groaned heavily. His legs were sagging under him and his throat felt like sand-paper.

"My frien, why you no de talk again. I de ask you say you wan make we call soja?"

"No."

"Awrighto. Now make we talk business. We no be bad tief. We no like for make trouble. Trouble done finish. War done finish and all the katakata wey de for inside. No Civil War again. This time na Civil Peace. No be so?"

"Na so!" answered the horrible chorus.

"What do you want from me? I am a poor man. Everything I had went with this war. Why do you come to me? You know people who have money. We . . ."

"Awright! We know say you no get plenty money. But we sef no get even anini. So derefore make you open dis window and give us one hundred pound and we go commot. Orderwise we de come for inside now to show you guitar-boy like dis . . ."

A volley of automatic fire rang through the sky. Maria and the children began to weep aloud again.

"Ah, missisi de cry again. No need for dat. We done talk say we na good tief. We just take our small money and go nwayorly. No molest. Abi we de molest?"

"At all!" sang the chorus.

"My friends," began Jonathan hoarsely. "I hear what you say and I thank you. If I had one hundred pounds . . ."

"Lookia my frien, no be play we come play for your house. If we make mistake and step for inside you no go like am-o. So derefore . . ."

"To God who made me; if you come inside and find one hundred pounds, take it and shoot me and shoot my wife and children. I swear to God. The only money I have in this life is this twenty-pounds *egg-rasher* they gave me today . . ."

"OK. Time de go. Make you open dis window and bring the twenty pound. We go manage am like dat."

There were now loud murmurs of dissent among the chorus: "Na lie de man de lie; e get plenty money . . . Make we go inside and search properly well . . . Wetin be twenty pound? . . ."

"Shurrup!" rang the leader's voice like a lone shot in the sky and silenced the murmuring at once. "Are you dere? Bring the money quick!"

"I am coming," said Jonathan fumbling in the darkness with the key of the small wooden box he kept by his side on the mat.

At the first sign of light as neighbours and others assembled to commiserate with him he was already strapping his five-gallon demijohn to his bicycle carrier and his wife, sweating in the open fire, was turning over akara balls in a wide clay bowl of boiling oil. In the corner his eldest son was rinsing out dregs of yesterday's palm wine from old beer bottles.

"I count it as nothing," he told his sympathizers, his eyes on the rope he was tying. "What is *egg-rasher*? Did I depend on it last week? Or is it greater than other things that went with the war? I say, let *egg-rasher* perish in the flames! Let it go where everything else has gone. Nothing puzzles God."

QUESTIONS

1. What is Jonathan Iwegbu's general attitude toward life? How would you characterize his personality? What aspects of the story lead you to your views?
2. What type of country does Jonathan Iwegbu live in? How would you characterize it economically, politically, geographically, and socially?

3. Why don't the thieves merely enter Iwegbu's house rather than negotiate with him? What tactics does he use to keep them at bay?
4. Does Iwegbu's character undergo a transformation during the course of the story, or does he maintain the same outlook on life? Explain your view.

Isaac Babel

MY FIRST GOOSE

Savitsky, Commander of the VI Division, rose when he saw me, and I wondered at the beauty of his giant's body. He rose, the purple of his riding-breeches and the crimson of his little tilted cap and the decorations stuck on his chest cleaving the hut as a standard cleaves the sky. A smell of scent and sickly sweet freshness of soap emanated from him. His long legs were like girls sheathed to the neck in shining riding-boots.

He smiled at me, struck his riding-whip on the table, and drew toward him an order that the Chief of Staff had just finished dictating. It was an order for Ivan Chesnokov to advance on Chugunov-Dobryvodka with the regiment entrusted to him, to make contact with the enemy and destroy the same.

"For which destruction," the Commander began to write, smearing the whole sheet, "I make this same Chesnokov entirely responsible, up to and including the supreme penalty, and will if necessary strike him down on the spot; which you, Chesnokov, who have been working with me at the front for some months now, cannot doubt."

The Commander signed the order with a flourish, tossed it to his orderlies, and turned upon me grey eyes that danced with merriment.

I handed him a paper with my appointment to the Staff of the Division.

"Put it down in the Order of the Day," said the Commander. "Put him down for every satisfaction save the front one. Can you read and write?"

"Yes, I can read and write," I replied, envying the flower and iron of that youthfulness. "I graduated in law from St. Petersburg University."

"Oh, are you one of those grinds?" he laughed. "Specs on your nose, too! What a nasty little object! They've sent you along without making any inquiries; and this is a hot place for specs. Think you'll get on with us?"

"I'll get on all right," I answered, and went off to the village with the quartermaster to find a billet for the night.

The quartermaster carried my trunk on his shoulder. Before us stretched the village street. The dying sun, round and yellow as a pumpkin, was giving up its roseate ghost to the skies.

We went up to a hut painted over with garlands. The quartermaster stopped, and said suddenly, with a guilty smile:

"Nuisance with specs. Can't do anything to stop it, either. Not a life for the brainy type here. But you go and mess up a lady, and a good lady too, and you'll have the boys patting you on the back."

He hesitated, my little trunk on his shoulder; then he came quite close to me, only to dart away again despairingly and run to the nearest yard. Cossacks were sitting there, shaving one another.

"Here, you soldiers," said the quartermaster, setting my little trunk down on the ground. "Comrade Savitsky's orders are that you're to take this chap in your billets, so no nonsense about it, because the chap's been through a lot in the learning line."

The quartermaster, purple in the face, left us without looking back. I raised my hand to my cap and saluted the Cossacks. A lad with long straight flaxen hair and the handsome face of the Ryazan Cossacks went over to my little trunk and tossed it out at the gate. Then he turned his back on me and with remarkable skill emitted a series of shameful noises.

"To your guns—number double-zero!" an older Cossack shouted at him, and burst out laughing. "Running fire!"

His guileless art exhausted, the lad made off. Then, crawling over the ground, I began to gather together the manuscripts and tattered garments that had fallen out of the trunk. I gathered them up and carried them to the other end of the yard. Near the hut, on a brick stove, stood a cauldron in which pork was cooking. The steam that rose from it was like the far-off smoke of home in the village, and it mingled hunger with desperate loneliness in my head. Then I covered my little broken trunk with hay, turning it into a pillow, and lay down on the ground to read in *Pravda* Lenin's speech at the Second Congress of the Comintern. The sun fell upon me from behind the toothed hillocks, the Cossacks trod on my feet, the lad made fun of me untiringly, the beloved lines came toward me along a thorny path and could not reach me. Then I put aside the paper and went out to the landlady, who was spinning on the porch.

"Landlady," I said, "I've got to eat."

The old woman raised to me the diffused whites of her purblind eyes and lowered them again.

"Comrade," she said, after a pause, "what with all this going on, I want to go and hang myself."

"Christ!" I muttered, and pushed the old woman in the chest with my fist. "You don't suppose I'm going to go into explanations with you, do you?"

And turning around I saw somebody's sword lying within reach. A severe-looking goose was waddling about the yard, inoffensively preening its feathers. I overtook it and pressed it to the ground. Its head cracked beneath my boot, cracked and emptied itself. The white neck lay stretched out in the dung, the wings twitched.

"Christ!" I said, digging into the goose with my sword. "Go and cook it for me, landlady."

Her blind eyes and glasses glistening, the old woman picked up the slaughtered bird, wrapped it in her apron, and started to bear it off toward the kitchen.

"Comrade," she said to me, after a while. "I want to go and hang myself." And she closed the door behind her.

The Cossacks in the yard were already sitting around their cauldron. They sat motionless, stiff as heathen priests at a sacrifice, and had not looked at the goose.

"The lad's all right," one of them said, winking and scooping up the cabbage soup with his spoon.

The Cossacks commenced their supper with all the elegance and restraint of peasants who respect one another. And I wiped the sword with sand, went out at the gate, and came in again, depressed. Already the moon hung above the yard like a cheap earring.

"Hey, you," suddenly said Surovkov, an older Cossack. "Sit down and feed with us till your goose is done."

He produced a spare spoon from his boot and handed it to me. We supped up the cabbage soup they had made, and ate the pork.

"What's in the newspaper?" asked the flaxen-haired lad, making room for me.

"Lenin writes in the paper," I said, pulling out *Pravda*. "Lenin writes that there's a shortage of everything."

And loudly, like a triumphant man hard of hearing, I read Lenin's speech out to the Cossacks.

Evening wrapped about me the quickening moisture of its twilight sheets; evening laid a mother's hand upon my burning forehead. I read on and rejoiced, spying out exultingly the secret curve of Lenin's straight line.

"Truth tickles everyone's nostrils," said Surovkov, when I had come to the end. "The question is, how's it to be pulled from the heap. But he goes and strikes at it straight off like a hen pecking at a grain!"

This remark about Lenin was made by Surovkov, platoon commander of the Staff Squadron; after which we lay down to sleep in the hayloft. We slept, all six of us, beneath a wooden roof that let in the stars, warming one another, our legs intermingled. I dreamed: and in my dreams saw women. But my heart, stained with bloodshed, grated and brimmed over.

Translated by Walter Morison

QUESTIONS

1. What is the significance of the title?
2. What sort of transformation does the narrator go through during the course of the story? What is the cause of this transformation? What is the narrator's attitude toward the transformation?
3. How does the narrator's ability to read give him power?
4. Why and how has he earned the respect of the Cossacks?

Jorge Luis Borges

THE SOUTH

The man who landed in Buenos Aires in 1871 bore the name of Johannes Dahlmann and he was a minister in the Evangelical Church. In 1939, one of his grandchildren, Juan Dahlmann, was secretary of a municipal library on Calle Córdoba, and he considered himself profoundly Argentinian. His maternal grandfather had been that Francisco Flores, of the Second Line-Infantry Division, who had died on the frontier of Buenos Aires, run through with a lance by Indians from Catriel; in the discord inherent between his two lines of descent, Juan Dahlmann (perhaps driven to it by his Germanic blood) chose the line represented by his romantic ancestor, his ancestor of the romantic death. An old sword, a leather frame containing the daguerreotype of a blank-faced man with a beard, the dash and grace of certain music, the familiar strophes of *Martin Fierro*, the passing years, boredom and solitude, all went to foster this voluntary, but never ostentatious nationalism. At the cost of numerous small privations, Dahlmann had managed to save the empty shell of a ranch in the South which had belonged to the Flores family: he continually recalled the image of the balsamic eucalyptus trees and the great rose-colored house which had once been crimson. His duties, perhaps even indolence, kept him in the city. Summer after summer he contented himself with the abstract idea of possession and with the certitude that his ranch was waiting for him on a precise site in the middle of the plain. Late in February, 1939, something happened to him.

Blind to all fault, destiny can be ruthless at one's slightest distraction. Dahlmann had succeeded in acquiring, on that very afternoon, an imperfect copy of Weil's edition of *The Thousand and One Nights*. Avid to examine this find, he did not wait for the elevator but hurried up the stairs. In the obscurity, something brushed by his forehead: a bat, a bird? On the face of the woman who opened the door to him he saw horror engraved, and the hand he wiped across his face came away red with blood. The edge of a recently painted door which someone had forgotten to close had caused this wound. Dahlmann was able to fall asleep, but from the moment he awoke at dawn the savor of all things was atrociously poignant. Fever wasted him and the pictures in *The Thousand and One Nights* served to illustrate nightmares. Friends and relatives paid him visits and, with exaggerated smiles, assured him that they thought he looked fine. Dahlmann listened to them with a kind of feeble stupor and he marveled at their not knowing that he was in hell. A week, eight days passed, and they were like eight centuries. One afternoon, the usual doctor appeared, accompanied by a new doctor, and they carried him off to a sanitarium on the Calle Ecuador, for it was necessary to X-ray him. Dahlmann, in the hackney coach which bore them away, thought that he would, at last, be able to sleep in a room different from his own. He felt happy and communicative. When he arrived at his destination, they undressed him, shaved his head, bound him with metal fastenings to a stretcher; they shone bright lights on him until he was blind and dizzy, auscultated him, and a masked man stuck a needle into his arm. He awoke with a feeling of nausea, covered with a bandage, in a cell with something of a well about it; in the days and nights which followed the operation he came to realize that he had merely been, up until then, in a suburb of hell. Ice in his mouth did not leave the least trace of freshness. During these days Dahlmann hated himself in minute detail; he hated his identity, his bodily necessities, his humiliation, the beard which bristled upon his face. He stoically endured the curative measures, which were painful, but when the surgeon told him he had been on the point of death from septicemia, Dahlmann dissolved in tears of self-pity for his fate. Physical wretchedness and the incessant anticipation of horrible nights had not allowed him time to think of anything so abstract as death. On another day, the surgeon told him he was healing and that, very soon, he would be able to go to his ranch for convalescence. Incredibly enough, the promised day arrived.

Reality favors symmetries and slight anachronisms: Dahlmann had arrived at the sanitarium in a hackney coach and now a hackney coach was to take him to the Constitución station. The first fresh tang of autumn, after the summer's oppressiveness, seemed like a symbol in nature of his rescue and release from fever and death. The city, at seven in the morning, had not lost that air of an old house lent it by the night; the streets seemed like long vestibules, the plazas were like patios. Dahlmann recognized the city with joy on the edge of vertigo: a second before his eyes registered the phenomena themselves, he recalled the corners, the billboards, the modest variety of Buenos Aires. In the yellow light of the new day, all things returned to him.

Every Argentine knows that the South begins at the other side of Rivadavia. Dahlmann was in the habit of saying that this was no mere convention, that whoever crosses this street enters a more ancient and sterner world. From inside the carriage he sought out, among the new buildings, the iron grille window, the brass knocker, the arched door, the entranceway, the intimate patio.

At the railroad station he noted that he still had thirty minutes. He quickly recalled that in a café on the Calle Brazil (a few dozen feet from Yrigoyen's house) there was an enormous cat which allowed itself to be caressed as if it were a disdainful divinity. He entered the café. There was the cat, asleep. He ordered a cup of coffee, slowly stirred the sugar, sipped it (this pleasure had been denied him in the clinic), and thought, as he smoothed the cat's black coat, that this contact was an illusion and that the two beings, man and cat, were as good as separated by a glass, for man lives in time, in succession, while the magical animal lives in the present, in the eternity of the instant.

Along the next to the last platform the train lay waiting. Dahlmann walked through the coaches until he found one almost empty. He arranged his baggage in the network rack. When the train started off, he took down his valise and extracted, after some hesitation, the first volume of *The Thousand and One Nights*. To travel with this book, which was so much a part of the history of his ill-fortune, was a kind of affirmation that his ill-fortune had been annulled; it was a joyous and secret defiance of the frustrated forces of evil.

Along both sides of the train the city dissipated into suburbs; this sight, and then a view of the gardens and villas, delayed the beginning of his reading. The truth was that Dahlmann read very little. The magnetized mountain and the genie who swore to kill his benefactor are—who would deny it?—marvelous, but not so much more than the morning itself and the mere fact of being. The joy of life distracted him from paying attention to Scheherazade and her superfluous miracles. Dahlmann closed his book and allowed himself to live.

Lunch—the bouillon served in shining metal bowls, as in the remote summers of childhood—was one more peaceful and rewarding delight.

Tomorrow I'll wake up at the ranch, he thought, and it was as if he was two men at a time: the man who traveled through the autumn day and across the geography of the fatherland, the other one, locked up in a sanitarium and subject to methodical servitude. He saw unplastered brick houses, long and angled, timelessly watching the trains go by; he saw horsemen along the dirt roads; he saw gullies and lagoons and ranches; he saw great luminous clouds that resembled marble; and all these things were accidental, casual, like dreams of the plain. He also thought he recognized trees and crop fields; but he would not have been able to name them, for his actual knowledge of the countryside was quite inferior to his nostalgic and literary knowledge.

From time to time he slept, and his dreams were animated by the impetus of the train. The intolerable white sun of high noon had already become the yellow sun which precedes nightfall, and it would not be long before it would turn red. The railroad car was now also different; it was not the same as the one which had quit the station siding at Constitución; the plain and the hours had transfigured it. Outside, the moving shadow of the railroad car stretched toward the horizon. The elemental earth was not perturbed either by settlements or other signs of humanity. The country was vast but at the same time intimate and, in some measure, secret. The limitless country sometimes contained only a solitary bull. The solitude was perfect, perhaps hostile, and it might have occurred to Dahlmann that he was traveling into the past and not merely south. He was distracted from these considerations by the railroad inspector who, on reading his ticket, advised him that the train would not let him off at the regular station but at another: an earlier stop, one scarcely known to Dahlmann. (The man added an explanation which Dahlmann did not attempt to understand, and which he hardly heard, for the mechanism of events did not concern him.)

The train laboriously ground to a halt, practically in the middle of the plain. The station lay on the other side of the tracks; it was not much more than a siding and a shed. There was no means of conveyance to be seen, but the station chief supposed that the traveler might secure a vehicle from a general store and inn to be found some ten or twelve blocks away.

Dahlmann accepted the walk as a small adventure. The sun had already disappeared from view, but a final splendor exalted the vivid and silent plain, before the night erased its color. Less to avoid fatigue than to draw out his enjoyment of these sights, Dahlmann walked slowly, breathing in the odor of clover with sumptuous joy.

The general store at one time had been painted a deep scarlet, but the years had tempered this violent color for its own good. Something in its poor architecture recalled a steel engraving, perhaps one from an old edition of *Paul et Virginie*. A number of horses were hitched up to the paling. Once inside, Dahlmann thought he recognized the shopkeeper. Then he realized that he had been deceived by the man's resemblance to one of the male nurses in the sanitarium. When the shopkeeper heard Dahlmann's request, he said he would have the shay made up. In order to add one more event to that day and to kill time, Dahlmann decided to eat at the general store.

Some country louts, to whom Dahlmann did not at first pay any attention, were eating and drinking at one of the tables. On the floor, and hanging on to the bar, squatted an old man, immobile as an object. His years had reduced and polished him as water does a stone or the generations of men do a sentence. He was dark, dried up, diminutive, and seemed outside time, situated in eternity. Dahlmann noted with satisfaction the kerchief, the thick poncho, the long *chiripá*, and the colt boots, and told himself, as he recalled futile discussions with people from the Northern counties or from the province of Entre Rios, that gauchos like this no longer existed outside the South.

Dahlmann sat down next to the window. The darkness began overcoming the plain, but the odor and sound of the earth penetrated the iron bars of the window. The shop owner brought him sardines, followed by some roast meat. Dahlmann washed the meal down with several glasses of red wine. Idling, he relished the tart savor of the wine, and let his gaze, now grown somewhat drowsy, wander over the shop. A kerosene lamp hung from a beam. There were three customers at the other table: two of them appeared to be farm workers; the third man, whose features hinted at Chinese blood, was drinking with his hat on. Of a sudden, Dahlmann felt something brush lightly against his face. Next to the heavy glass of turbid wine, upon one of the stripes in the tablecloth, lay a spit ball of breadcrumb. That was all: but someone had thrown it there.

The men at the other table seemed totally cut off from him. Perplexed, Dahlmann decided that nothing had happened, and he opened the volume of *The Thousand and One Nights,* by way of suppressing reality. After a few moments another little ball landed on his table, and now the *peones* laughed outright. Dahlmann said to himself that he was not frightened, but he reasoned that it would be a major blunder if he, a convalescent, were to allow himself to be dragged by strangers into some chaotic quarrel. He determined to leave, and had already gotten to his feet when the owner came up and exhorted him in an alarmed voice:

"*Señor* Dahlmann, don't pay any attention to those lads; they're half high."

Dahlmann was not surprised to learn that the other man, now, knew his name. But he felt that these conciliatory words served only to aggravate the situation. Previously to this moment, the *peones'* provocation was directed against an unknown face, against no one in particular, almost against no one at all. Now it was an attack against him, against his name, and his neighbors knew it. Dahlmann pushed the owner aside, confronted the *peones,* and demanded to know what they wanted of him.

The tough with the Chinese look staggered heavily to his feet. Almost in Juan Dahlmann's face he shouted insults, as if he had been a long way off. His game was to exaggerate his drunkenness, and this extravagance constituted a ferocious mockery. Between curses and obscenities, he threw a long knife into the air, followed it with his eyes, caught and juggled it, and challenged Dahlmann to a knife fight. The owner objected in a tremulous voice, pointing out that Dahlmann was unarmed. At this point, something unforeseeable occurred.

From a corner of the room, the old ecstatic gaucho—in whom Dahlmann saw a summary and cipher of the South (his South)—threw him a naked dagger, which landed at his feet. It was as if the South had resolved that Dahlmann should accept the duel. Dahlmann bent over to pick up the dagger, and felt two things. The first, that this almost instinctive act bound him to fight. The second, that the weapon, in his torpid hand, was no defense at all, but would merely serve to justify his murder. He had once played with a poniard, like all men, but his idea of fencing and knife-play did not go further than the notion that all strokes should be directed upward, with the cutting edge held inward. *They would not have allowed such things to happen to me in the sanitarium,* he thought.

"Let's get on our way," said the other man.

They went out and if Dahlmann was without hope, he was also without fear. As he crossed the threshold, he felt that to die in a knife fight, under the open sky, and going forward to the attack, would have been a liberation, a joy, and a festive occasion, on the first night in the sanitarium, when they stuck him with the needle. He felt that if he had been able to choose, then, or to dream his death, this would have been the death he would have chosen or dreamt.

Firmly clutching his knife, which he perhaps would not know how to wield, Dahlmann went out into the plain.

QUESTIONS

1. At the beginning of the story which one of his grandfathers does Johannes Dahlmann appear to be emulating? Explain.
2. At what point in the story does the routine of Dahlmann's life change? When do events begin to seem unreal?
3. In what ways does his reading of *The Thousand and One Nights* coincide with Dahlmann's experience?
4. Who does the "old ecstatic gaucho" who throws Dahlmann a knife resemble? What inspires Dahlmann to take up the challenge made by the drunken tough? How does this challenge transform Dahlmann's perception of himself? How can Dahlmann's evolution be considered a metaphor for a larger transformation? What is the nature of this other transformation?
5. The structure of Borges's stories often resembles the genres of fantasy, science fiction, and mystery. Which if any of these forms of writing appear to have influenced this story?

Ray Bradbury

AUGUST 2026: THERE WILL COME SOFT RAINS

In the living room the voice-clock sang, *Tick-tock, seven o'clock, time to get up, time to get up, seven o'clock!* as if it were afraid that nobody would. The morning house lay empty. The clock ticked on, repeating and repeating its sounds into the emptiness. *Seven-nine, breakfast time, seven-nine!*

In the kitchen the breakfast stove gave a hissing sigh and ejected from its warm interior eight pieces of perfectly browned toast, eight eggs sunnyside up, sixteen slices of bacon, two coffees, and two cool glasses of milk.

"Today is August 4, 2026," said a second voice from the kitchen ceiling, "in the city of Allendale, California." It repeated the date three times for memory's sake. "Today is Mr. Featherstone's birthday. Today is the anniversary of Tilita's marriage. Insurance is payable, as are the water, gas, and light bills."

Somewhere in the walls, relays clicked, memory tapes glided under electric eyes.

Eight-one, tick-tock, eight-one o'clock, off to school, off to work, run, run, eight-one! But no doors slammed, no carpets took the soft tread of rubber heels. It was raining outside. The weather box on the front door sang quietly: "Rain, rain, go away; rubbers, raincoats for today . . ." And the rain tapped on the empty house, echoing.

Outside, the garage chimed and lifted its door to reveal the waiting car. After a long wait the door swung down again.

At eight-thirty the eggs were shriveled and the toast was like stone. An aluminum wedge scraped them into the sink, where hot water whirled them down a metal throat which digested and flushed them away to the distant sea. The dirty dishes were dropped into a hot washer and emerged twinkling dry.

Nine-fifteen, sang the clock, *time to clean.*

Out of warrens in the wall, tiny robot mice darted. The rooms were acrawl with the small cleaning animals, all rubber and metal. They thudded against chairs, whirling their mustached runners, kneading the rug nap, sucking gently at hidden dust. Then, like mysterious invaders, they popped into their burrows. Their pink electric eyes faded. The house was clean.

Ten o'clock. The sun came out from behind the rain. The house stood alone in a city of rubble and ashes. This was the one house left standing. At night the ruined city gave off a radioactive glow which could be seen for miles.

Ten-fifteen. The garden sprinklers whirled up in golden founts, filling the soft morning air with scatterings of brightness. The water pelted windowpanes, running down the charred west side where the house had been burned evenly free of its white paint. The entire west face of the house was black, save for five places. Here the silhouette in paint of a man mowing a lawn. Here, as in a photograph, a woman bent to pick flowers. Still farther over, their images burned on wood in one titanic instant, a small boy, hands flung into the air higher up, the image of a thrown ball, and opposite him, a girl, hands raised to catch a ball which never came down.

The five spots of paint—the man, the woman, the children, the ball—remained. The rest was a thin charcoaled layer.

The gentle sprinkler rain filled the garden with falling light.

Until this day, how well the house had kept its peace. How carefully it had inquired, "Who goes there? What's the password?" and, getting no answer from lonely foxes and whining cats, it had shut up its windows and drawn shades in an old-maidenly preoccupation with self-protection which bordered on a mechanical paranoia.

It quivered at each sound, the house did. If a sparrow brushed a window the shade snapped up. The bird, startled, flew off! No, not even a bird must touch the house!

The house was an altar with ten thousand attendants, big, small, servicing, attending, in choirs. But the gods had gone away, and the ritual of the religion continued sense-lessly, uselessly.

Twelve noon.

A dog whined, shivering, on the front porch.

The front door recognized the dog voice and opened. The dog, once huge and fleshy, but now gone to bone and covered with sores, moved in and through the house, tracking mud. Behind it whirred angry mice, angry at having to pick up mud, angry at inconvenience.

For not a leaf fragment blew under the door but what the wall panel flipped open and the copper scrap rats flashed swiftly out. The offending dust, hair, or paper, seized in miniature steel jaws, was raced back to the burrow. There, down tubes which fed into the cellar, it was dropped into the sighing vent of an incinerator which sat like evil Baal in a dark corner.

The dog ran upstairs, hysterically yelping to each door, at last realizing, as the house realized, that only silence was here.

It sniffed the air and scratched the kitchen door. Behind the door, the stove was making pancakes which filled the house with a rich baked odor and the scent of maple syrup.

The dog frothed at the mouth, lying at the door, sniffing, its eyes turned to fire. It ran wildly in circles, biting at its tail, spun in a frenzy, and died. It lay in the parlor for an hour.

Two o'clock, sang a voice.

Delicately sensing decay at last, the regiments of mice hummed out as softly as blown gray leaves in an electrical wind.

Two-fifteen.

The dog was gone.

In the cellar, the incinerator glowed suddenly and a whirl of sparks leaped up the chimney.

Two thirty-five.

Bridge tables sprouted from patio walls. Playing cards fluttered onto pads in a shower of pips. Martinis manifested on an oaken bench with egg-salad sandwiches. Music played.

But the tables were silent and the cards untouched.

At four o'clock the tables folded like great butterflies back through the paneled walls.

Four-thirty.

The nursery walls glowed.

Animals took shape: yellow giraffes, blue lions, pink antelopes, lilac panthers cavort-ing in crystal substance. The walls were glass. They looked out upon color and fantasy. Hidden films clocked through well-oiled sprockets, and the walls lived. The nursery floor was woven to resemble a crisp, cereal meadow. Over this ran aluminum roaches and iron crickets, and in the hot still air butterflies of delicate red tissue wavered among the sharp aroma of animal spoors! There was the sound like a great matted yellow hive of bees within a dark bellows, the lazy bumble of a purring lion. And there was the patter of okapi feet and the murmur of a fresh jungle rain, like other hoofs, falling upon the summer-starched grass. Now the walls dissolved into distances of parched weed, mile on mile, and warm endless sky. The animals drew away into thorn brakes and water holes.

It was the children's hour.

Five o'clock. The bath filled with clear hot water.

Six, seven, eight o'clock. The dinner dishes manipulated like magic tricks, and in the study a *click.* In the metal stand opposite the hearth where a fire now blazed up warmly, a cigar popped out, half an inch of soft gray ash on it, smoking, waiting.

Nine o'clock. The beds warmed their hidden circuits, for nights were cool here.

Nine-five. A voice spoke from the study ceiling:

"Mrs. McClellan, which poem would you like this evening?"

The house was silent.

The voice said at last, "Since you express no preference, I shall select a poem at random." Quiet music rose to back the voice. "Sara Teasdale. As I recall, your favorite. . . ."

There will come soft rains and the smell of the ground,
And swallows circling with their shimmering sound;

And frogs in the pools singing at night,
And wild plum trees in tremulous white;

Robins will wear their feathery fire,
Whistling their whims on a low fence-wire;

And not one will know of the war, not one
Will care at last when it is done.

Not one would mind, neither bird nor tree,
If mankind perished utterly;

And Spring herself, when she woke at dawn
Would scarcely know that we were gone.

The fire burned on the stone hearth and the cigar fell away into a mound of quiet ash on its tray. The empty chairs faced each other between the silent walls, and the music played.

At ten o'clock the house began to die.

The wind blew. A falling tree bough crashed through the kitchen window. Cleaning solvent, bottled, shattered over the stove. The room was ablaze in an instant!

"Fire!" screamed a voice. The house lights flashed, water pumps shot water from the ceilings. But the solvent spread on the linoleum, licking, eating, under the kitchen door, while the voices took it up in chorus: "Fire, fire, fire!"

The house tried to save itself. Doors sprang tightly shut, but the windows were broken by the heat and the wind blew and sucked upon the fire.

The house gave ground as the fire in ten billion angry sparks moved with flaming ease from room to room and then up the stairs. While scurrying water rats squeaked from the walls, pistoled their water, and ran for more. And the wall sprays let down showers of mechanical rain.

But too late. Somewhere, sighing, a pump shrugged to a stop. The quenching rain ceased. The reserve water supply which had filled baths and washed dishes for many quiet days was gone.

The fire crackled up the stairs. It fed upon Picassos and Matisses in the upper halls, like delicacies, baking off the oily flesh, tenderly crisping the canvases into black shavings.

QUESTIONS

1. In what ways does the house resemble a contemporary affluent home in the United States? What has happened to its occupants? What is the chief irony about this home?
2. Bradbury describes the house as having an elaborate security system. What is ironic about this? What is he implying about the American value system and life-style?
3. What is the significance of the Sara Teasdale poem?

Bobbie Ann Mason

BIG BERTHA STORIES

Donald is home again, laughing and singing. He comes home from Central City, near the strip mines, only when he feels like it, like an absentee landlord checking on his property. He is always in such a good humor when he returns that Jeannette forgives him. She cooks for him—ugly, pasty things she gets with food stamps. Sometimes he brings steaks and ice cream, occasionally money. Rodney, their child, hides in the closet when he arrives, and Donald goes around the house talking loudly about the little boy named Rodney who used to live there—the one who fell into a septic tank, or the one stolen by gypsies. The stories change. Rodney usually stays in the closet until he has to pee, and then he hugs his father's knees, forgiving him, just as Jeannette does. The way Donald saunters through the door, swinging a six-pack of beer, with a big grin on his face, takes her breath away. He leans against the door facing, looking sexy in his baseball cap and his shaggy red beard and his sunglasses. He wears sunglasses to be like the Blues Brothers, but he in no way resembles either of the Blues Brothers. I should have my head examined, Jeannette thinks.

The last time Donald was home, they went to the shopping center to buy Rodney some shoes advertised on sale. They stayed at the shopping center half the afternoon, just looking around. Donald and Rodney played video games. Jeannette felt they were a normal family. Then, in the parking lot, they stopped to watch a man on a platform demonstrating snakes. Children were petting a twelve-foot python coiled around the man's shoulders. Jeannette felt faint.

"Snakes won't hurt you unless you hurt them," said Donald as Rodney stroked the snake.

"It feels like chocolate," he said.

The snake man took a tarantula from a plastic box and held it lovingly in his palm. He said, "If you drop a tarantula, it will shatter like a Christmas ornament."

"I hate this," said Jeannette.

"Let's get out of here," said Donald.

Jeannette felt her family disintegrating like a spider shattering as Donald hurried them away from the shopping center. Rodney squalled and Donald dragged him along. Jeannette wanted to stop for ice cream. She wanted them all to sit quietly together in a booth, but Donald rushed them to the car, and he drove them home in silence, his face growing grim.

"Did you have bad dreams about the snakes?" Jeannette asked Rodney the next morning at breakfast. They were eating pancakes made with generic pancake mix. Rodney slapped his fork in the pond of syrup on his pancakes. "The black racer is the farmer's friend," he said soberly, repeating a fact learned from the snake man.

"Big Bertha kept black racers," said Donald. "She trained them for the 500." Donald doesn't tell Rodney ordinary children's stories. He tells him a series of strange stories he makes up about Big Bertha. Big Bertha is what he calls the huge strip-mining machine in Muhlenberg County, but he has Rodney believing that Big Bertha is a female version of Paul Bunyan.

"Snakes don't run in the 500," said Rodney.

"This wasn't the Indy 500 or the Daytona 500—none of your well-known 500s," said Donald. "This was the Possum Trot 500, and it was a long time ago. Big Bertha started the original 500, with snakes. Black racers and blue racers mainly. Also some red-and-white-striped racers, but those are rare."

"We always ran for the hoe if we saw a black racer," Jeannette said, remembering her childhood in the country.

In a way, Donald's absences are a fine arrangement, even considerate. He is sparing them his darkest moods, when he can't cope with his memories of Vietnam. Vietnam had never seemed such a meaningful fact until a couple of years ago, when he grew depressed and moody, and then he started going away to Central City. He frightened Jeannette, and she always said the wrong thing in her efforts to soothe him. If the welfare people find out he is spending occasional weekends at home, and even bringing some money, they will cut off her assistance. She applied for welfare because she can't depend on him to send money, but she knows he blames her for losing faith in him. He isn't really working regularly at the strip mines. He is mostly just hanging around there, watching the land being scraped away, trees coming down, bushes flung in the air. Sometimes he operates a steam shovel, and when he comes home his clothes are filled with the clay and it is caked on his shoes. The clay is the color of butterscotch pudding.

At first, he tried to explain to Jeannette. He said, "If we could have had tanks over there as big as Big Bertha, we wouldn't have lost the war. Strip mining is just like what we were doing over there. We were stripping off the top. The topsoil is like the culture and the people, the best part of the land and the country. America was just stripping off the top, the best. We ruined it. Here, at least the coal companies have to plant vetch and loblolly pines and all kinds of trees and bushes. If we'd done that in Vietnam, maybe we'd have left that country in better shape."

"Wasn't Vietnam a long time ago?" Jeannette asked.

She didn't want to hear about Vietnam. She thought it was unhealthy to dwell on it so much. He should live in the present. Her mother is afraid Donald will do something violent, because she once read in the newspaper that a veteran in Louisville held his little girl hostage in their apartment until he had a shootout with the police and was killed. But Jeannette can't imagine Donald doing anything so extreme. When she first met him, several years ago, at her parents' pit-barbecue luncheonette, where she was working then, he had a good job at a lumberyard and he dressed nicely. He took her out to eat at a fancy restaurant. They got plastered and ended up in a motel in Tupelo, Mississippi, on Elvis Presley Boulevard. Back then, he talked nostalgically about his year in Vietnam, about how beautiful it was, how different the people were. He could never seem to explain what he meant. "They're just different," he said.

They went riding around in a yellow 1957 Chevy convertible. He drives too fast now, but he didn't then, maybe because he was so protective of the car. It was a classic. He sold it three years ago and made a good profit. About the time he sold the Chevy, his moods began changing, his even-tempered nature shifting, like driving on a smooth interstate and then switching to a secondary road. He had headaches and bad dreams. But his nightmares seemed trivial. He dreamed of riding a train through the Rocky Mountains, of hijacking a plane to Cuba, of stringing up barbed wire around the house. He dreamed he lost a doll. He got drunk and rammed the car, the Chevy's successor, into a Civil War statue in front of the courthouse. When he got depressed over the meaninglessness of his job, Jeannette felt guilty about spending money on something nice for the house, and she tried to make him feel his job had meaning by reminding him that, after all, they had a child to think of. "I don't like his name," Donald said once. "What a stupid name. Rodney. I never did like it."

Rodney has dreams about Big Bertha, echoes of his father's nightmare, like TV cartoon versions of Donald's memories of the war. But Rodney loves the stories, even though they are confusing, with lots of loose ends. The latest in the Big Bertha series is "Big Bertha and the Neutron Bomb." Last week it was "Big Bertha and the MX Missile." In the new story, Big Bertha takes a trip to California to go surfing with Big Mo, her male counterpart. On the beach, corn dogs and snow cones are free and the surfboards turn into dolphins. Everyone is having fun until the neutron bomb comes. Rodney loves the part where everyone keels over dead. Donald acts it out, collapsing on the rug. All the dolphins and the surfers keel over, everyone except Big Bertha. Big Bertha is so big she is immune to the neutron bomb.

"Those stories aren't true," Jeannette tells Rodney.

Rodney staggers and falls down on the rug, his arms and legs akimbo. He gets the giggles and can't stop. When his spasms finally subside, he says, "I told Scottie Bidwell about Big Bertha and he didn't believe me."

Donald picks Rodney up under the armpits and sets him upright. "You tell Scottie Bidwell if he saw Big Bertha he would pee in his pants on the spot, he would be so impressed."

"Are you scared of Big Bertha?"

"No, I'm not. Big Bertha is just like a wonderful woman, a big fat woman who can sing the blues. Have you ever heard Big Mama Thornton?"

"No."

"Well, Big Bertha's like her, only she's the size of a tall building. She's slow as a turtle and when she crosses the road they have to reroute traffic. She's big enough to straddle a four-lane highway. She's so tall she can see all the way to Tennessee, and when she belches, there's a tornado. She's really something. She can even fly."

"She's too big to fly," Rodney says doubtfully. He makes a face like a wadded-up washrag and Donald wrestles him to the floor again.

Donald has been drinking all evening, but he isn't drunk. The ice cubes melt and he pours the drink out and refills it. He keeps on talking. Jeannette cannot remember him talking so much about the war. He is telling her about an ammunitions dump. Jeannette had the vague idea that an ammo dump is a mound of shotgun shells, heaps of cartridge casings and bomb shells, or whatever is left over, a vast waste pile from the war, but Donald says that is wrong. He has spent an hour describing it in detail, so that she will understand.

He refills the glass with ice, some 7-Up, and a shot of Jim Beam. He slams doors and drawers, looking for a compass. Jeannette can't keep track of the conversation. It doesn't matter that her hair is uncombed and her lipstick eaten away. He isn't seeing her.

"I want to draw the compound for you," he says, sitting down at the table with a sheet of Rodney's tablet paper.

Donald draws the map in red and blue ballpoint, with asterisks and technical labels that mean nothing to her. He draws some circles with the compass and measures some angles. He makes a red dot on an oblique line, a patch that leads to the ammo dump.

"That's where I was. Right there," he says. "There was a water buffalo that tripped a land mine and its horn just flew off and stuck in the wall of the barracks like a machete thrown backhanded." He puts a dot where the land mine was, and he doodles awhile with the red ballpoint pen, scribbling something on the edge of the map that looks like feathers. "The dump was here and I was there and over there was where we piled the sandbags. And here were the tanks." He draws tanks, a row of squares with handles—guns sticking out.

"Why are you going to so much trouble to tell me about a buffalo horn that got stuck in a wall?" she wants to know.

But Donald just looks at her as though she has asked something obvious.

"Maybe I *could* understand if you'd let me," she says cautiously.

"You could never understand." He draws another tank.

In bed, it is the same as it has been since he started going away to Central City—the way he claims his side of the bed, turning away from her. Tonight, she reaches for him and he lets her be close to him. She cries for a while and he lies there, waiting for her to finish, as though she were merely putting on makeup.

"Do you want me to tell you a Big Bertha story?" he asks playfully.

"You act like you're in love with Big Bertha."

He laughs, breathing on her. But he won't come closer.

"You don't care what I look like anymore," she says. "What am I supposed to think?"

"There's nobody else. There's not anybody but you."

Loving a giant machine is incomprehensible to Jeannette. There must be another woman, someone that large in his mind. Jeannette has seen the strip-mining machine. The top of the crane is visible beyond a rise along the parkway. The strip mining is kept just out of sight of travelers because it would give them a poor image of Kentucky.

For three weeks, Jeannette has been seeing a psychologist at the free mental health clinic. He's a small man from out of state. His name is Dr. Robinson, but she calls him The Rapist, because the word *therapist* can be divided into two words, *the rapist*. He doesn't think her joke is clever, and he acts as though he has heard it a thousand times before. He has a habit of saying, "Go with that feeling," the same way Bob Newhart did on his old TV show. It's probably the first lesson in the textbook, Jeannette thinks.

She told him about Donald's last days on his job at the lumberyard—how he let the stack of lumber fall deliberately and didn't know why, and about how he went away soon after that, and how the Big Bertha stories started. Dr. Robinson seems to be waiting for her to make something out of it all, but it's maddening that he won't tell her what to do. After three visits, Jeannette has grown angry with him, and now she's holding back things. She won't tell him whether Donald slept with her or not when he came home last. Let him guess, she thinks.

"Talk about yourself," he says.

"What about me?"

"You speak so vaguely about Donald that I get the feeling that you see him as somebody larger than life. I can't quite picture him. That makes me wonder what that says about you." He touches the end of his tie to his nose and sniffs it.

When Jeannette suggests that she bring Donald in, the therapist looks bored and says nothing.

"He had another nightmare when he was home last," Jeannette says. "He dreamed he was crawling through tall grass and people were after him."

"How do *you* feel about that?" The Rapist asks eagerly.

"I didn't have the nightmare," she says coldly. "Donald did. I came to you to get advice about Donald, and you're acting like I'm the one who's crazy. I'm not crazy. But I'm lonely."

Jeannette's mother, behind the counter of the luncheonette, looks lovingly at Rodney pushing buttons on the jukebox in the corner. "It's a shame about that youngun," she says tearfully. "That boy needs a daddy."

"What are you trying to tell me? That I should file for divorce and get Rodney a new daddy?"

Her mother looks hurt. "No, honey," she says. "You need to get Donald to seek the Lord. And you need to pray more. You haven't been going to church lately."

"Have some barbecue," Jeannette's father booms, as he comes in from the back kitchen. "And I want you to take a pound home with you. You've got a growing boy to feed."

"I want to take Rodney to church," Mama says. "I want to show him off, and it might do some good."

"People will think he's an orphan," Dad says.

"I don't care," Mama says. "I just love him to pieces and I want to take him to church. Do you care if I take him to church, Jeannette?"

"No. I don't care if you take him to church." She takes the pound of barbecue from her father. Grease splotches the brown wrapping paper. Dad has given them so much barbecue that Rodney is burned out on it and won't eat it anymore.

Jeannette wonders if she would file for divorce if she could get a job. It is a thought—for the child's sake, she thinks. But there aren't many jobs around. With the cost of a baby-sitter, it doesn't pay her to work. When Donald first went away, her mother kept Rodney and she had a good job, waitressing at a steak house, but the steak house burned down one night—a grease fire in the kitchen. After that, she couldn't find a steady job, and she was reluctant to ask her mother to keep Rodney again because of her bad hip. At the steak house, men gave her tips and left their telephone numbers on the bill when they paid. They tucked dollar bills and notes in the pockets of her apron. One note said, "I want to hold your muffins." They were real-estate developers and businessmen on important missions for the Tennessee Valley Authority. They were boisterous and they drank too much. They said they'd take her for a cruise on the *Delta Queen*, but she didn't believe them. She knew how expensive that was. They talked about their speedboats and invited her for rides on Lake Barkley, or for spins in their private planes. They always used the word *spin*. The idea made her dizzy. Once, Jeannette let an electronics salesman take her for a ride in his Cadillac, and they breezed down the wilderness road through the Land Between the Lakes. His car had automatic windows and a stereo system and lighted computer-screen numbers on the dash that told him how many miles to the gallon he was getting and other statistics. He said the numbers distracted him and he had almost had several wrecks. At the restaurant, he had been flamboyant, admired by his companions. Alone with Jeannette in the Cadillac, on The Trace, he was shy and awkward, and really not very interesting. The most interesting thing about him, Jeannette thought, was all the lighted numbers on his dashboard. The Cadillac had everything but video games. But she'd rather be riding around with Donald, no matter where they ended up.

While the social worker is there, filling out her report, Jeannette listens for Donald's car. When the social worker drove up, the flutter and wheeze of her car sounded like Donald's old Chevy, and for a moment Jeannette's mind lapsed back in time. Now she listens, hoping he won't drive up. The social worker is younger than Jeannette and has been to college. Her name is Miss Bailey, and she's excessively cheerful, as though in her line of work she has seen hardships that make Jeannette's troubles seem like a trip to Hawaii.

"Is your little boy still having those bad dreams?" Miss Bailey asks, looking up from her clipboard.

Jeannette nods and looks at Rodney, who has his finger in his mouth and won't speak.

"Has the cat got your tongue?" Miss Bailey asks.

"Show her your pictures, Rodney." Jeannette explains, "He won't talk about the dreams, but he draws pictures of them."

Rodney brings his tablet of pictures and flips through them silently. Miss Bailey says, "Hmm." They are stark line drawings, remarkably steady lines for his age. "What is this one?" she asks. "Let me guess. Two scoops of ice cream?"

The picture is two huge circles, filling the page, with three tiny stick people in the corner.

"These are Big Bertha's titties," says Rodney.

Miss Bailey chuckles and winks at Jeannette. "What do you like to read, hon?" she asks Rodney.

"Nothing."

"He can read," says Jeannette. "He's smart."

"Do you like to read?" Miss Bailey asks Jeannette. She glances at the pile of paperbacks on the coffee table. She is probably going to ask where Jeannette got the money for them.

"I don't read," says Jeannette. "If I read, I just go crazy."

When she told The Rapist she couldn't concentrate on anything serious, he said she read romance novels in order to escape from reality. "Reality, hell!" she had said. "Reality's my whole problem."

It's too bad Rodney's not here," Donald is saying. Rodney is in the closet again. "Santa Claus has to take back all these toys. Rodney would love this bicycle! And this Pac-Man game. Santa has to take back so many things he'll have to have a pickup truck!"

"You didn't bring him anything. You never bring him anything," says Jeannette.

He has brought doughnuts and dirty laundry. The clothes he is wearing are caked with clay. His beard is lighter from working out in the sun, and he looks his usual joyful self, the way he always is before his moods take over, like migraine headaches, which some people describe as storms.

Donald coaxes Rodney out of the closet with the doughnuts.

"Were you a good boy this week?"

"I don't know."

"I hear you went to the shopping center and showed out." It is not true that Rodney made a big scene. Jeannette has already explained that Rodney was upset because she wouldn't buy him an Atari. But she didn't blame him for crying. She was tired of being unable to buy him anything.

Rodney eats two doughnuts and Donald tells him a long, confusing story about Big Bertha and a rock-and-roll band. Rodney interrupts him with dozens of questions. In the story, the rock-and-roll band gives a concert in a place that turns out to be a toxic-waste dump and the contamination is spread all over the country. Big Bertha's solution to this problem is not at all clear. Jeannette stays in the kitchen, trying to think of something original to do with instant potatoes and leftover barbecue.

"We can't go on like this," she says that evening in bed. "We're just hurting each other. Something has to change."

He grins like a kid. "Coming home from Muhlenberg County is like R and R—rest and recreation. I explain that in case you think R and R means rock and roll. Or maybe rumps and rears. Or rust and rot." He laughs and draws a circle in the air with his cigarette.

"I'm not that dumb."

"When I leave, I go back to the mines." He sighs, as though the mines were some eternal burden.

Her mind skips ahead to the future: Donald locked away somewhere, coloring in a coloring book and making clay pots, her and Rodney in some other town, with another man—someone dull and not at all sexy. Summoning up her courage, she says, "I haven't been through what you've been through and maybe I don't have a right to say this, but sometimes I think you act superior because you went to Vietnam, like nobody can ever know what you know. Well, maybe not. But you've still got your legs, even if you don't know what to do with what's between them anymore." Bursting into tears of apology, she can't help adding, "You can't go on telling Rodney those awful stories. He has nightmares when you're gone."

Donald rises from bed and grabs Rodney's picture from the dresser, holding it as he might have held a hand grenade. "Kids betray you," he says, turning the picture in his hand.

"If you cared about him, you'd stay here." As he sets the picture down, she asks, "What can I do? How can I understand what's going on in your mind? Why do you go there? Strip mining's bad for the ecology and you don't have any business strip mining."

"My job is serious, Jeannette. I run that steam shovel and put the topsoil back on. I'm reclaiming the land." He keeps talking, in a gentler voice, about strip mining, the same old things she has heard before, comparing Big Bertha to a supertank. If only they had had Big Bertha in Vietnam. He says, "When they strip off the top, I keep looking for those tunnels where the Viet Cong hid. They had so many tunnels it was unbelievable. Imagine Mammoth Cave going all the way across Kentucky."

"Mammoth Cave's one of the natural wonders of the world," says Jeannette brightly. She is saying the wrong thing again.

At the kitchen table at 2 A.M., he's telling about C-5A's. A C-5A is so big it can carry troops and tanks and helicopters, but it's not big enough to hold Big Bertha. Nothing could hold Big Bertha. He rambles on, and when Jeannette shows him Rodney's drawings of the circles, Donald smiles. Dreamily, he begins talking about women's breasts and thighs—the large, round thighs and big round breasts of American women, contrasted with the frail, delicate beauty of the Orientals. It is like comparing oven broilers and banties, he says. Jeannette relaxes. A confession about another lover from long ago is not so hard to take. He seems stuck on the breasts and thighs of American women—insisting that she understand how small and delicate the Orientals are, but then he abruptly returns to tanks and helicopters.

"A Bell Huey Cobra—my God, what a beautiful machine. So efficient!" Donald takes the food processor blade from the drawer where Jeannette keeps it. He says, "A rotor blade from a chopper could just slice anything to bits."

"Don't do that," Jeannette says.

He is trying to spin the blade on the counter, like a top. "Here's what would happen when a chopper blade hits a power line—not many of those over there!—or a tree. Not many trees, either, come to think of it, after all the Agent Orange." He drops the blade and it glances off the open drawer and falls to the floor, spiking the vinyl.

At first, Jeannette thinks the screams are hers, but they are his. She watches him cry. She has never seen anyone cry so hard, like an intense summer thundershower. All she knows to do is shove Kleenex at him. Finally, he is able to say, "You thought I was going to hurt you. That's why I'm crying."

"Go ahead and cry," Jeannette says, holding him close.

"Don't go away."

"I'm right here. I'm not going anywhere."

In the night, she still listens, knowing his monologue is being burned like a tattoo into her brain. She will never forget it. His voice grows soft and he plays with a ballpoint pen, jabbing holes in a paper towel. Bullet holes, she thinks. His beard is like a bird's nest, woven with dark corn silks.

"This is just a story," he says. "Don't mean nothing. Just relax." She is sitting on the hard edge of the kitchen chair, her toes cold on the floor, waiting. His tears have dried up and left a slight catch in his voice.

"We were in a big camp near a village. It was pretty routine and kind of soft there for a while. Now and then we'd go into Da Nang and whoop it up. We had been in the jungle for several months, so the two months at this village was a sort of rest—an R and R almost. Don't shiver. This is just a little story. Don't mean nothing! This is nothing, compared to what I could tell you. Just listen. We lost our fear. At night there would be some incoming and we'd see these tracers in the sky, like shooting stars up close, but it was all pretty minor and we didn't take it seriously, after what we'd been through. In the village I knew this Vietnamese family—a woman and her two daughters. They sold Cokes and beer to GIs. The oldest daughter was named Phan. She could speak a little English. She was really smart. I used to go see them in their hooch in the afternoons—in the siesta time of day. It was so hot there. Phan was beautiful, like the country. The village was ratty, but the country was pretty. And she was beautiful, just like she had grown up out of the jungle, like one of those flowers that bloomed high up in the trees and freaked us out sometimes, thinking it was a sniper. She was so gentle, with these eyes shaped like peach pits, and she was no bigger than a child of maybe thirteen or fourteen. I felt funny about her size at first, but later it didn't matter. It was just some wonderful feature about her, like a woman's hair, or her breasts."

He stops and listens, the way they used to listen for crying sounds when Rodney was a baby. He says, "She'd take those big banana leaves and fan me while I lay there in the heat."

"I didn't know they had bananas over there."

"There's a lot you don't know! Listen! Phan was twenty-three, and her brothers were off fighting. I never even asked which side they were fighting on." He laughs. "She got a kick out of the word *fan*. I told her that *fan* was the same word as her name. She thought I meant her name was banana. In Vietnamese the same word can have a dozen different meanings, depending on your tone of voice. I bet you didn't know that, did you?"

"No. What happened to her?"

"I don't know."

"Is that the end of the story?"

"I don't know." Donald pauses, then goes on talking about the village, the girl, the banana leaves, talking in a monotone that is making Jeannette's flesh crawl. He could be the news radio from the next room.

"You must have really liked that place. Do you wish you could go back there to find out what happened to her?"

"It's not there anymore," he says. "It blew up."

Donald abruptly goes to the bathroom. She hears the water running, the pipes in the basement shaking.

"It was so pretty," he says when he returns. He rubs his elbow absentmindedly. "That jungle was the most beautiful place in the world. You'd have thought you were in paradise. But we blew it sky-high."

In her arms, he is shaking, like the pipes in the basement, which are still vibrating. Then the pipes let go, after a long shudder, but he continues to tremble.

They are driving to the Veterans Hospital. It was Donald's idea. She didn't have to persuade him. When she made up the bed that morning—with a finality that shocked her, as though she knew they wouldn't be in it again together—he told her it would be like R and R. Rest was what he needed. Neither of them had slept at all during the night. Jeannette felt she had to stay awake, to listen for more.

"Talk about strip mining," she says now. "That's what they'll do to your head. They'll dig out all those ugly memories, I hope. We don't need them around here." She pats his knee.

It is a cloudless day, not the setting for this sober journey. She drives and Donald goes along obediently, with the resignation of an old man being taken to a rest home. They are driving through southern Illinois, known as Little Egypt, for some obscure reason Jeannette has never understood. Donald still talks, but very quietly, without urgency. When he points out the scenery, Jeannette thinks of the early days of their marriage, when they would take a drive like this and laugh hysterically. Now Jeannette points out funny things they see. The Little Egypt Hot Dog World, Pharaoh Cleaners, Pyramid Body Shop. She is scarcely aware that she is driving, and when she sees a sign, LITTLE EGYPT STARLITE CLUB, she is confused for a moment, wondering where she has been transported.

As they part, he asks, "What will you tell Rodney if I don't come back? What if they keep me here indefinitely?"

"You're coming back. I'm telling him you're coming back soon."

"Tell him I went off with Big Bertha. Tell him she's taking me on a sea cruise, to the South Seas."

"No. You can tell him that yourself."

He starts singing "Sea Cruise." He grins at her and pokes her in the ribs.
"You're coming back," she says.

Donald writes from the VA Hospital, saying that he is making progress. They are
running tests, and he meets in a therapy group in which all the veterans trade memories.
Jeannette is no longer on welfare because she now has a job waitressing at Fred's Family
Restaurant. She waits on families, waits for Donald to come home so they can come
here and eat together like a family. The fathers look at her with downcast eyes, and the
children throw food. While Donald is gone, she rearranges the furniture. She reads
some books from the library. She does a lot of thinking. It occurs to her that even though
she loved him, she has thought of Donald primarily as a husband, a provider, someone
whose name she shared, the father of her child, someone like the fathers who come to
the Wednesday night all-you-can-eat fish fry. She hasn't thought of him as himself. She
wasn't brought up that way, to examine someone's soul. When it comes to something
deep inside, nobody will take it out and examine it, the way they will look at clothing
in a store for flaws in the manufacturing. She tries to explain all this to The Rapist, and
he says she's looking better, got sparkle in her eyes. "Big deal," says Jeannette. "Is that
all you can say?"

She takes Rodney to the shopping center, their favorite thing to do together, even
though Rodney always begs to buy something. They go to Penney's perfume counter.
There, she usually hits a sample bottle of cologne—Chantilly or Charlie or something
strong. Today she hits two or three and comes out of Penney's smelling like a flower
garden.

"You stink!" Rodney cries, wrinkling his nose like a rabbit.

"Big Bertha smells like this, only a thousand times worse, she's so big," says Jeannette
impulsively. "Didn't Daddy tell you that?"

"Daddy's a messenger from the devil."

This is an idea he must have gotten from church. Her parents have been taking him
every Sunday. When Jeannette tries to reassure him about his father, Rodney is skeptical.
"He gets that funny look on his face like he can see through me," the child says.

"Something's missing," Jeannette says, with a rush of optimism, a feeling of recognition. "Something happened to him once and took out the part that shows how much
he cares about us."

"The way we had the cat fixed?"

"I guess. Something like that." The appropriateness of his remark stuns her, as
though, in a way, her child has understood Donald all along. Rodney's pictures have
been more peaceful lately, pictures of skinny trees and airplanes flying low. This
morning he drew pictures of tall grass, with creatures hiding in it. The grass is tilted at
an angle, as though a light breeze is blowing through it.

With her paycheck, Jeannette buys Rodney a present, a miniature trampoline they
have seen advertised on television. It is called Mr. Bouncer. Rodney is thrilled about the
trampoline, and he jumps on it until his face is red. Jeannette discovers that she enjoys
it, too. She puts it out on the grass, and they take turns jumping. She has an image of
herself on the trampoline, her sailor collar flapping, at the moment when Donald
returns and sees her flying. One day a neighbor driving by slows down and calls out to
Jeannette as she is bouncing on the trampoline, "You'll tear your insides loose!"

Jeannette starts thinking about that, and the idea is so horrifying she stops jumping so much. That night, she has a nightmare about the trampoline. In her dream, she is jumping on soft moss, and then it turns into a springy pile of dead bodies.

QUESTIONS

1. Why does Donald tell his "Big Bertha stories"? What function do they serve in his life?
2. How does Jeannette think and feel about her husband? Would she have gotten divorced sooner had she been financially independent?
3. There are many references to strip-mining in the story. And Donald himself makes reference to his work stating, "I'm reclaiming the land." What symbolic significance might these references have?
4. Toward the end of the story, Jeannette says about Donald, "Something's missing. . . . Something happened to him once and took out the part that shows how much he cares about us." What is she referring to? What in Donald's behavior makes her reach this conclusion?

Yukio Mishima

PATRIOTISM

On the twenty-eighth of February, 1936 (on the third day, that is, of the February 26 Incident), Lieutenant Shinji Takeyama of the Konoe Transport Battalion—profoundly disturbed by the knowledge that his closest colleagues had been with the mutineers from the beginning, and indignant at the imminent prospect of Imperial troops attacking Imperial troops—took his officer's sword and ceremonially disemboweled himself in the eight-mat room of his private residence in the sixth block of Aoba-chō, in Yotsuya Ward. His wife, Reiko, followed him, stabbing herself to death. The lieutenant's farewell note consisted of one sentence: "Long live the Imperial Forces." His wife's, after apologies for her unfilial conduct in thus preceding her parents to the grave, concluded: "The day which, for a soldier's wife, had to come, has come. . . ." The last moments of this heroic and dedicated couple were such as to make the gods themselves weep. The lieutenant's age, it should be noted, was thirty-one, his wife's twenty-three; and it was not half a year since the celebration of their marriage.

II

Those who saw the bride and bridegroom in the commemorative photograph—perhaps no less than those actually present at the lieutenant's wedding—had exclaimed in wonder at the bearing of this handsome couple. The lieutenant, majestic in military uniform, stood protectively beside his bride, his right hand resting upon his sword, his officer's cap held at his left side. His expression was severe, and his dark brows and wide-gazing eyes well conveyed the clear integrity of youth. For the beauty of the bride in her white over-robe no comparisons were adequate. In the eyes, round beneath soft brows, the slender, finely shaped nose, and in the full lips, there was both sensuousness and refinement. One hand, emerging shyly from a sleeve of the over-robe, held a fan, and the tips of the fingers, clustering delicately, were like the bud of a moonflower.

After the suicide, people would take out this photograph and examine it, and sadly reflect that too often there was a curse on these seemingly flawless unions. Perhaps it was no more than imagination, but looking at the picture after the tragedy it almost seemed as if the two young people before the gold-lacquered screen were gazing, each with equal clarity, at the deaths which lay before them.

Thanks to the good offices of their go-between, Lieutenant General Ozeki, they had been able to set themselves up in a new home at Aoba-chō in Yotsuya. "New home" is perhaps misleading. It was an old three-room rented house backing onto a small garden. As neither the six- nor the four-and-a-half-mat room downstairs was favored by the sun, they used the upstairs eight-mat room as both bedroom and guest room. There was no maid, so Reiko was left alone to guard the house in her husband's absence.

The honeymoon trip was dispensed with on the grounds that these were times of national emergency. The two of them had spent the first night of their marriage at this house. Before going to bed, Shinji, sitting erect on the floor with his sword laid before him, had bestowed upon his wife a soldierly lecture. A woman who had become the wife of a soldier should know and resolutely accept that her husband's death might come at any moment. It could be tomorrow. It could be the day after. But, no matter when it came—he asked—was she steadfast in her resolve to accept it? Reiko rose to her feet, pulled open a drawer of the cabinet, and took out what was the most prized of her new possessions, the dagger her mother had given her. Returning to her place, she laid the dagger without a word on the mat before her, just as her husband had laid his sword. A silent understanding was achieved at once, and the lieutenant never again sought to test his wife's resolve.

In the first few months of her marriage Reiko's beauty grew daily more radiant, shining serene like the moon after rain.

As both were possessed of young, vigorous bodies, their relationship was passionate. Nor was this merely a matter of the night. On more than one occasion, returning home straight from maneuvers, and begrudging even the time it took to remove his mud-splashed uniform, the lieutenant had pushed his wife to the floor almost as soon as he had entered the house. Reiko was equally ardent in her response. For a little more or a little less than a month, from the first night of their marriage Reiko knew happiness, and the lieutenant, seeing this, was happy too.

Reiko's body was white and pure, and her swelling breasts conveyed a firm and chaste refusal; but, upon consent, those breasts were lavish with their intimate, welcoming warmth. Even in bed these two were frighteningly and awesomely serious. In the very midst of wild, intoxicating passions, their hearts were sober and serious.

By day the lieutenant would think of his wife in the brief rest periods between training; and all day long, at home, Reiko would recall the image of her husband. Even when apart, however, they had only to look at the wedding photograph for their happiness to be once more confirmed. Reiko felt not the slightest surprise that a man who had been a complete stranger until a few months ago should now have become the sun about which her whole world revolved.

All these things had a moral basis, and were in accordance with the Education Rescript's injunction that "husband and wife should be harmonious." Not once did Reiko contradict her husband, nor did the lieutenant ever find reason to scold his wife. On the god shelf below the stairway, alongside the tablet from the Great Ise Shrine, were set photographs of their Imperial Majesties, and regularly every morning, before leaving for duty, the lieutenant would stand with his wife at this hallowed place and together they would bow their heads low. The offering water was renewed each morning, and the sacred sprig of *sasaki* was always green and fresh. Their lives were lived beneath the solemn protection of the gods and were filled with an intense happiness which set every fiber in their bodies trembling.

III

Although Lord Privy Seal Saitō's house was in their neighborhood, neither of them heard any noise of gunfire on the morning of February 26. It was a bugle, sounding muster in the dim, snowy dawn, when the ten-minute tragedy had already ended, which first disrupted the lieutenant's slumbers. Leaping at once from his bed, and without speaking a word, the lieutenant donned his uniform, buckled on the sword held ready for him by his wife, and hurried swiftly out into the snowcovered streets of the still darkened morning. He did not return until the evening of the twenty-eighth.

Later, from the radio news, Reiko learned the full extent of this sudden eruption of violence. Her life throughout the subsequent two days was lived alone, in complete tranquillity, and behind locked doors.

In the lieutenant's face, as he hurried silently out into the snowy morning, Reiko had read the determination to die. If her husband did not return, her own decision was made: she too would die. Quietly she attended to the disposition of her personal possessions. She chose her sets of visiting kimonos as keepsakes for friends of her schooldays, and she wrote a name and address on the stiff paper wrapping in which each was folded. Constantly admonished by her husband never to think of the morrow, Reiko had not even kept a diary and was now denied the pleasure of assiduously rereading her record of the happiness of the past few months and consigning each page to the fire as she did so. Ranged across the top of the radio were a small china dog, a rabbit, a squirrel, a bear, and a fox. There were also a small vase and a water pitcher. These comprised Reiko's one and only collection. But it would hardly do, she imagined, to give such things as keepsakes. Nor again would it be quite proper to ask specifically for them to be included in the coffin. It seemed to Reiko, as these thoughts passed through her mind, that the expressions on the small animals' faces grew even more lost and forlorn.

Reiko took the squirrel in her hand and looked at it. And then, her thoughts turning to a realm far beyond these child-like affections, she gazed up into the distance at the great sunlike principle which her husband embodied. She was ready, and happy, to be hurtled along to her destruction in that gleaming sun chariot—but now, for these few moments of solitude, she allowed herself to luxuriate in this innocent attachment to trifles. The time when she had genuinely loved these things, however, was long past. Now she merely loved the memory of having once loved them, and their place in her heart had been filled by more intense passions, by a more frenzied happiness. . . . For Reiko had never, even to herself, thought of those soaring joys of the flesh as a mere pleasure. The February cold, and the icy touch of the china squirrel, had numbed Reiko's slender fingers; yet, even so, in her lower limbs, beneath the ordered repetition of the pattern which crossed the skirt of her trim *meisen* kimono, she could feel now, as she thought of the lieutenant's powerful arms reaching out toward her, a hot moistness of the flesh which defied the snows.

She was not in the least afraid of the death hovering in her mind. Waiting alone at home, Reiko firmly believed that everything her husband was feeling or thinking now, his anguish and distress, was leading her—just as surely as the power in his flesh—to a welcome death. She felt as if her body could melt away with ease and be transformed to the merest fraction of her husband's thought.

Listening to the frequent announcements on the radio, she heard the names of several of her husband's colleagues mentioned among those of the insurgents. This was news of death. She followed the developments closely, wondering anxiously, as the situation became daily more irrevocable, why no Imperial ordinance was sent down, and watching what had at first been taken as a movement to restore the nation's honor come gradually to be branded with the infamous name of mutiny. There was no communication from the regiment. At any moment, it seemed, fighting might commence in the city streets, where the remains of the snow still lay.

Toward sundown on the twenty-eighth Reiko was startled by a furious pounding on the front door. She hurried downstairs. As she pulled with fumbling fingers at the bolt, the shape dimly outlined beyond the frosted-glass panel made no sound, but she knew it was her husband. Reiko had never known the bolt on the sliding door to be so stiff. Still it resisted. The door just would not open.

In a moment, almost before she knew she had succeeded, the lieutenant was standing before her on the cement floor inside the porch, muffled in a khaki greatcoat, his top boots heavy with slush from the street. Closing the door behind him, he returned the bolt once more to its socket. With what significance, Reiko did not understand.

"Welcome home."

Reiko bowed deeply, but her husband made no response. As he had already unfastened his sword and was about to remove his greatcoat, Reiko moved around behind to assist. The coat, which was cold and damp and had lost the odor of horse dung it normally exuded when exposed to the sun, weighed heavily upon her arm. Draping it across a hanger, and cradling the sword and leather belt in her sleeves, she waited while her husband removed his top boots and then followed behind him into the "living room." This was the six-mat room downstairs.

Seen in the clear light from the lamp, her husband's face, covered with a heavy growth of bristle, was almost unrecognizably wasted and thin. The cheeks were hollow, their luster and resilience gone. In his normal good spirits he would have changed into old clothes as soon as he was home and have pressed her to get supper at once, but now he sat before the table still in his uniform, his head drooping dejectedly. Reiko refrained from asking whether she should prepare the supper.

After an interval the lieutenant spoke.

"I knew nothing. They hadn't asked me to join. Perhaps out of consideration, because I was newly married. Kanō, and Homma too, and Yamaguchi."

Reiko recalled momentarily the faces of high-spirited young officers, friends of her husband, who had come to the house occasionally as guests.

"There may be an Imperial ordinance sent down tomorrow. They'll be posted as rebels, I imagine. I shall be in command of a unit with orders to attack them. . . . I can't do it. It's impossible to do a thing like that."

He spoke again.

"They've taken me off guard duty, and I have permission to return home for one night. Tomorrow morning, without question, I must leave to join the attack. I can't do it, Reiko."

Reiko sat erect with lowered eyes. She understood clearly that her husband had spoken of his death. The lieutenant was resolved. Each word, being rooted in death, emerged sharply and with powerful significance against this dark, unmovable background. Although the lieutenant was speaking of his dilemma, already there was no room in his mind for vacillation.

However, there was a clarity, like the clarity of a stream fed from melting snows, in the silence which rested between them. Sitting in his own home after the long two-day ordeal, and looking across at the face of his beautiful wife, the lieutenant was for the first time experiencing true peace of mind. For he had at once known, though she said nothing, that his wife divined the resolve which lay beneath his words.

"Well, then . . ." The lieutenant's eyes opened wide. Despite his exhaustion they were strong and clear, and now for the first time they looked straight into the eyes of his wife. "To-night I shall cut my stomach."

Reiko did not flinch.

Her round eyes showed tension, as taut as the clang of a bell.

"I am ready," she said. "I ask permission to accompany you."

The lieutenant felt almost mesmerized by the strength in those eyes. His words flowed swiftly and easily, like the utterances of a man in delirium, and it was beyond his understanding how permission in a matter of such weight could be expressed so casually.

"Good. We'll go together. But I want you as a witness, first, for my own suicide. Agreed?"

When this was said a sudden release of abundant happiness welled up in both their hearts. Reiko was deeply affected by the greatness of her husband's trust in her. It was vital for the lieutenant, whatever else might happen, that there should be no irregularity in his death. For that reason there had to be a witness. The fact that he had chosen his wife for this was the first mark of his trust. The second, and even greater mark, was that though he had pledged that they should die together he did not intend to kill his wife first—he had deferred her death to a time when he would no longer be there to verify it. If the lieutenant had been a suspicious husband, he would doubtless, as in the usual suicide pact, have chosen to kill his wife first.

When Reiko said, "I ask permission to accompany you," the lieutenant felt these words to be the final fruit of the education which he had himself given his wife, starting on the first night of their marriage, and which had schooled her, when the moment came, to say what had to be said without a shadow of hesitation. This flattered the lieutenant's opinion of himself as a self-reliant man. He was not so romantic or conceited as to imagine that the words were spoken spontaneously, out of love for her husband.

With happiness welling almost too abundantly in their hearts, they could not help smiling at each other. Reiko felt as if she had returned to her wedding night.

Before her eyes was neither pain nor death. She seemed to see only a free and limitless expanse opening out into vast distances.

"The water is hot. Will you take your bath now?"

"Ah yes, of course."

"And supper . . . ?"

The words were delivered in such level, domestic tones that the lieutenant came near to thinking, for the fraction of a second, that everything had been a hallucination.

"I don't think we'll need supper. But perhaps you could warm some sake?"

"As you wish."

As Reiko rose and took a *tanzen* gown from the cabinet for after the bath, she purposely directed her husband's attention to the opened drawer. The lieutenant rose, crossed to the cabinet, and looked inside. From the ordered array of paper wrappings he read, one by one, the addresses of the keepsakes. There was no grief in the lieutenant's response to this demonstration of heroic resolve. His heart was filled with tenderness. Like a husband who is proudly shown the childish purchases of a young wife, the lieutenant, overwhelmed by affection, lovingly embraced his wife from behind and implanted a kiss upon her neck.

Reiko felt the roughness of the lieutenant's unshaven skin against her neck. This sensation, more than being just a thing of this world, was for Reiko almost the world itself, but now—with the feeling that it was soon to be lost forever—it had freshness beyond all her experience. Each moment had its own vital strength, and the senses in every corner of her body were reawakened. Accepting her husband's caresses from behind, Reiko raised herself on the tips of her toes, letting the vitality seep through her entire body.

"First the bath, and then, after some sake . . . lay out the bedding upstairs, will you?"

The lieutenant whispered the words into his wife's ear. Reiko silently nodded.

Flinging off his uniform, the lieutenant went to the bath. To faint background noises of slopping water Reiko tended the charcoal brazier in the living room and began the preparations for warming the sake.

Taking the *tanzen*, a sash, and some underclothes, she went to the bathroom to ask how the water was. In the midst of a coiling cloud of steam the lieutenant was sitting cross-legged on the floor, shaving, and she could dimly discern the rippling movements of the muscles on his damp, powerful back as they responded to the movement of his arms.

There was nothing to suggest a time of any special significance. Reiko, going busily about her tasks, was preparing side dishes from odds and ends in stock. Her hands did not tremble. If anything, she managed even more efficiently and smoothly than usual. From time to time, it is true, there was a strange throbbing deep within her breast. Like distant lightning, it had a moment of sharp intensity and then vanished without trace. Apart from that, nothing was in any way out of the ordinary.

The lieutenant, shaving in the bathroom, felt his warmed body miraculously healed at last of the desperate tiredness of the days of indecision and filled—in spite of the death which lay ahead—with pleasurable anticipation. The sound of his wife going about her work came to him faintly. A healthy physical craving, submerged for two days, reasserted itself.

The lieutenant was confident there had been no impurity in that joy they had experienced when resolving upon death. They had both sensed at that moment— though not, of course, in any clear and conscious way—that those permissible pleasures which they shared in private were once more beneath the protection of Righteousness and Divine Power, and of a complete and unassailable morality. On looking into each other's eyes and discovering there an honorable death, they had felt themselves safe once more behind steel walls which none could destroy, encased in an impenetrable armor of Beauty and Truth. Thus, so far from seeing any inconsistency or conflict between the urges of his flesh and the sincerity of his patriotism, the lieutenant was even able to regard the two as parts of the same thing.

Thrusting his face close to the dark, cracked, misted wall mirror, the lieutenant shaved himself with great care. This would be his death face. There must be no unsightly blemishes. The clean-shaven face gleamed once more with a youthful luster, seeming to brighten the darkness of the mirror. There was a certain elegance, he even felt, in the association of death with this radiantly healthy face.

Just as it looked now, this would become his death face! Already, in fact, it had half departed from the lieutenant's personal possession and had become the bust above a dead soldier's memorial. As an experiment he closed his eyes tight. Everything was wrapped in blackness, and he was no longer a living, seeing creature.

Returning from the bath, the traces of the shave glowing faintly blue beneath his smooth cheeks, he seated himself beside the now well-kindled charcoal brazier. Busy though Reiko was, he noticed, she had found time lightly to touch up her face. Her cheeks were gay and her lips moist. There was no shadow of sadness to be seen. Truly, the lieutenant felt, as he saw this mark of his young wife's passionate nature, he had chosen the wife he ought to have chosen.

As soon as the lieutenant had drained his sake cup he offered it to Reiko. Reiko had never before tasted sake, but she accepted without hesitation and sipped timidly.

"Come here," the lieutenant said.

Reiko moved to her husband's side and was embraced as she leaned backward across his lap. Her breast was in violent commotion, as if sadness, joy, and the potent sake were mingling and reacting within her. The lieutenant looked down into his wife's face. It was the last face he would see in this world, the last face he would see of his wife. The lieutenant scrutinized the face minutely, with the eyes of a traveler bidding farewell to splendid vistas which he will never revisit. It was a face he could not tire of looking at—the features regular yet not cold, the lips lightly closed with a soft strength. The lieutenant kissed those lips, unthinkingly. And suddenly, though there was not the slightest distortion of the face into the unsightliness of sobbing, he noticed that tears were welling slowly from beneath the long lashes of the closed eyes and brimming over into a glistening stream.

When, a little later, the lieutenant urged that they should move to the upstairs bedroom, his wife replied that she would follow after taking a bath. Climbing the stairs alone to the bedroom, where the air was already warmed by the gas heater, the lieutenant lay down on the bedding with arms outstretched and legs apart. Even the time at which he lay waiting for his wife to join him was no later and no earlier than usual.

He folded his hands beneath his head and gazed at the dark boards of the ceiling in the dimness beyond the range of the standard lamp. Was it death he was now waiting for? Or a wild ecstasy of the senses? The two seemed to overlap, almost as if the object of this bodily desire was death itself. But, however that might be, it was certain that never before had the lieutenant tasted such total freedom.

There was the sound of a car outside the window. He could hear the screech of its tires skidding in the snow piled at the side of the street. The sound of its horn re-echoed from near-by walls. . . . Listening to these noises he had the feeling that this house rose like a solitary island in the ocean of a society going as restlessly about its business as ever. All around, vastly and untidily, stretched the country for which he grieved. He was to give his life for it. But would that great country, with which he was prepared to remonstrate to the extent of destroying himself, take the slightest heed of his death? He did not know; and it did not matter. His was a battlefield without glory, a battlefield where none could display deeds of valor: it was the front line of the spirit.

Reiko's footsteps sounded on the stairway. The steep stairs in this old house creaked badly. There were fond memories in that creaking, and many a time, while waiting in bed, the lieutenant had listened to its welcome sound. At the thought that he would hear it no more he listened with intense concentration, striving for every corner of every moment of this precious time to be filled with the sound of those soft footfalls on the creaking stairway. The moments seemed transformed to jewels, sparkling with inner light.

Reiko wore a Nagoya sash about the waist of her *yukata,* but as the lieutenant reached toward it, its redness sobered by the dimness of the light, Reiko's hand moved to his assistance and the sash fell away, slithering swiftly to the floor. As she stood before him, still in her *yukata,* the lieutenant inserted his hands through the side slits beneath each sleeve, intending to embrace her as she was; but at the touch of his finger tips upon the warm naked flesh, and as the armpits closed gently about his hands, his whole body was suddenly aflame.

In a few moments the two lay naked before the glowing gas heater.

Neither spoke the thought, but their hearts, their bodies, and their pounding breasts blazed with the knowledge that this was the very last time. It was as if the words "The Last Time" were spelled out, in invisible brushstrokes, across every inch of their bodies.

The lieutenant drew his wife close and kissed her vehemently. As their tongues explored each other's mouths, reaching out into the smooth, moist interior, they felt as if the still-unknown agonies of death had tempered their senses to the keenness of red-hot steel. The agonies they could not yet feel, the distant pains of death, had refined their awareness of pleasure.

"This is the last time I shall see your body," said the lieutenant. "Let me look at it closely." And, tilting the shade on the lampstand to one side, he directed the rays along the full length of Reiko's outstretched form.

Reiko lay still with her eyes closed. The light from the low lamp clearly revealed the majestic sweep of her white flesh. The lieutenant, not without a touch of egocentricity, rejoiced that he would never see this beauty crumble in death.

At his leisure, the lieutenant allowed the unforgettable spectacle to engrave itself upon his mind. With one hand he fondled the hair, with the other he softly stroked the magnificent face, implanting kisses here and there where his eyes lingered. The quiet coldness of the high, tapering forehead, the closed eyes with their long lashes beneath faintly etched brows, the set of the finely shaped nose, the gleam of teeth glimpsed between full, regular lips, the soft cheeks and the small, wise chin . . . these things conjured up in the lieutenant's mind the vision of a truly radiant death face, and again and again he pressed his lips tight against the white throat—where Reiko's own hand was soon to strike—and the throat reddened faintly beneath his kisses. Returning to the mouth he laid his lips against it with the gentlest of pressures, and moved them rhythmically over Reiko's with the light rolling motion of a small boat. If he closed his eyes, the world became a rocking cradle.

Wherever the lieutenant's eyes moved his lips faithfully followed. The high, swelling breasts, surmounted by nipples like the buds of a wild cherry, hardened as the lieutenant's lips closed about them. The arms flowed smoothly downward from each side of the breast, tapering toward the wrists, yet losing nothing of their roundness or symmetry, and at their tips were those delicate fingers which had held the fan at the wedding ceremony. One by one, as the lieutenant kissed them, the fingers withdrew behind their neighbor as if in shame. . . . The natural hollow curving between the bosom and the stomach carried in its lines a suggestion not only of softness but of resilient strength, and while it gave forewarning of the rich curves spreading outward from here to the hips it had, in itself, an appearance only of restraint and proper discipline. The whiteness and richness of the stomach and hips was like milk brimming in a great bowl, and the sharply shadowed dip of the navel could have been the fresh impress of a raindrop, fallen there that very moment. Where the shadows gathered more thickly, hair clustered, gentle and sensitive, and as the agitation mounted in the now no longer passive body there hung over this region a scent like the smoldering of fragrant blossoms, growing steadily more pervasive.

At length, in a tremulous voice, Reiko spoke.

"Show me. . . . Let me look too, for the last time."

Never before had he heard from his wife's lips so strong and unequivocal a request. It was as if something which her modesty had wished to keep hidden to the end had suddenly burst its bonds of constraint. The lieutenant obediently lay back and surrendered himself to his wife. Lithely she raised her white, trembling body, and—burning with an innocent desire to return to her husband what he had done for her—placed two white fingers on the lieutenant's eyes, which gazed fixedly up at her, and gently stroked them shut.

Suddenly overwhelmed by tenderness, her cheeks flushed by a dizzying uprush of emotion, Reiko threw her arms about the lieutenant's close-cropped head. The bristly hairs rubbed painfully against her breast, the prominent nose was cold as it dug into her flesh, and his breath was hot. Relaxing her embrace, she gazed down at her husband's masculine face. The severe brows, the closed eyes, the splendid bridge of the nose, the shapely lips drawn firmly together . . . the blue, cleanshaven cheeks reflecting the light and gleaming smoothly. Reiko kissed each of these. She kissed the broad nape of the neck, the strong, erect shoulders, the powerful chest with its twin circles like shields and its russet nipples. In the armpits, deeply shadowed by the ample flesh of the shoulders and chest, a sweet and melancholy odor emanated from the growth of hair, and in the sweetness of this odor was contained, somehow, the essence of young death. The lieutenant's naked skin glowed like a field of barley, and everywhere the muscles showed in sharp relief, converging on the lower abdomen about the small, unassuming navel. Gazing at the youthful, firm stomach, modestly covered by a vigorous growth of hair, Reiko thought of it as it was soon to be, cruelly cut by the sword, and she laid her head upon it, sobbing in pity, and bathed it with kisses.

At the touch of his wife's tears upon his stomach the lieutenant felt ready to endure with courage the cruelest agonies of his suicide.

What ecstasies they experienced after these tender exchanges may well be imagined. The lieutenant raised himself and enfolded his wife in a powerful embrace, her body now limp with exhaustion after her grief and tears. Passionately they held their faces close, rubbing cheek against cheek. Reiko's body was trembling. Their breasts, moist with sweat, were tightly joined, and every inch of the young and beautiful bodies had become so much one with the other that it seemed impossible there should ever again be a separation. Reiko cried out. From the heights they plunged into the abyss, and from the abyss they took wing and soared once more to dizzying heights. The lieutenant panted like the regimental standard-bearer on a route march. . . . As one cycle ended, almost immediately a new wave of passion would be generated, and together—with no trace of fatigue—they would climb again in a single breathless movement to the very summit.

IV

When the lieutenant at last turned away, it was not from weariness. For one thing, he was anxious not to undermine the considerable strength he would need in carrying out his suicide. For another, he would have been sorry to mar the sweetness of these last memories by over indulgence.

Since the lieutenant had clearly desisted, Reiko too, with her usual compliance, followed his example. The two lay naked on their backs, with fingers interlaced, staring fixedly at the dark ceiling. The room was warm from the heater, and even when the sweat had ceased to pour from their bodies they felt no cold. Outside, in the hushed night, the sounds of passing traffic had ceased. Even the noises of the trains and streetcars around Yotsuya station did not penetrate this far. After echoing through the region bounded by the moat, they were lost in the heavily wooded park fronting the broad driveway before Akasaka Palace. It was hard to believe in the tension gripping this whole quarter, where the two factions of the bitterly divided Imperial Army now confronted each other, poised for battle.

Savoring the warmth glowing within themselves, they lay still and recalled the ecstasies they had just known. Each moment of the experience was relived. They remembered the taste of kisses which had never wearied, the touch of naked flesh, episode after episode of dizzying bliss. But already, from the dark boards of the ceiling, the face of death was peering down. These joys had been final, and their bodies would never know them again. Not that joy of this intensity—and the same thought had occurred to them both—was ever likely to be reexperienced, even if they should live on to old age.

The feel of their fingers intertwined—this too would soon be lost. Even the wood-grain patterns they now gazed at on the dark ceiling boards would be taken from them. They could feel death edging in, nearer and nearer. There could be no hesitation now. They must have the courage to reach out to death themselves, and to seize it.

"Well, let's make our preparations," said the lieutenant. The note of determination in the words was unmistakable, but at the same time Reiko had never heard her husband's voice so warm and tender.

After they had risen, a variety of tasks awaited them.

The lieutenant, who had never once before helped with the bedding, now cheerfully slid back the door of the closet, lifted the mattress across the room by himself, and stowed it away inside.

Reiko turned off the gas heater and put away the lamp standard. During the lieutenant's absence she had arranged this room carefully, sweeping and dusting it to a fresh cleanness, and now—if one over-looked the rosewood table drawn into one corner—the eight-mat room gave all the appearance of a reception room ready to welcome an important guest.

"We've seen some drinking here, haven't we? With Kanō and Homma and Noguchi . . ."

"Yes, they were great drinkers, all of them."

"We'll be meeting them before long, in the other world. They'll tease us, I imagine, when they find I've brought you with me."

Descending the stairs, the lieutenant turned to look back into this calm, clean room, now brightly illuminated by the ceiling lamp. There floated across his mind the faces of the young officers who had drunk there, and laughed, and innocently bragged. He had never dreamed then that he would one day cut open his stomach in this room.

In the two rooms downstairs husband and wife busied themselves smoothly and serenely with their respective preparations. The lieutenant went to the toilet, and then to the bathroom to wash. Meanwhile Reiko folded away her husband's padded robe, placed his uniform tunic, his trousers, and a newly cut bleached loincloth in the bathroom, and set out sheets of paper on the living-room table for the farewell notes. Then she removed the lid from the writing box and began rubbing ink from the ink tablet. She had already decided upon the wording of her own note.

Reiko's fingers pressed hard upon the cold gilt letters of the ink tablet, and the water in the shallow well at once darkened, as if a black cloud had spread across it. She stopped thinking that this repeated action, this pressure from her fingers, this rise and fall of faint sound, was all and solely for death. It was a routine domestic task, a simple paring away of time until death should finally stand before her. But somehow, in the increasingly smooth motion of the tablet rubbing on the stone, and in the scent from the thickening ink, there was unspeakable darkness.

Neat in his uniform, which he now wore next to his skin, the lieutenant emerged from the bathroom. Without a word he seated himself at the table, bolt upright, took a brush in his hand, and stared undecidedly at the paper before him.

Reiko took a white silk kimono with her and entered the bathroom. When she reappeared in the living room, clad in the white kimono and with her face lightly made up, the farewell note lay completed on the table beneath the lamp. The thick black brushstrokes said simply:

"Long Live the Imperial Forces—Army Lieutenant Takeyama Shinji."

While Reiko sat opposite him writing her own note, the lieutenant gazed in silence, intensely serious, at the controlled movement of his wife's pale fingers as they manipulated the brush.

With their respective notes in their hands—the lieutenant's sword strapped to his side, Reiko's small dagger thrust into the sash of her white kimono—the two of them stood before the god shelf and silently prayed. Then they put out all the downstairs lights. As he mounted the stairs the lieutenant turned his head and gazed back at the striking, white-clad figure of his wife, climbing behind him, with lowered eyes, from the darkness beneath.

The farewell notes were laid side by side in the alcove of the upstairs room. They wondered whether they ought not to remove the hanging scroll, but since it had been written by their go-between, Lieutenant General Ozeki, and consisted, moreover, of two Chinese characters signifying "Sincerity," they left it where it was. Even if it were to become stained with splashes of blood, they felt that the lieutenant general would understand.

The lieutenant, sitting erect with his back to the alcove, laid his sword on the floor before him.

Reiko sat facing him, a mat's width away. With the rest of her so severely white the touch of rouge on her lips seemed remarkably seductive.

Across the dividing mat they gazed intently into each other's eyes. The lieutenant's sword lay before his knees. Seeing it, Reiko recalled their first night and was overwhelmed with sadness. The lieutenant spoke, in a hoarse voice:

"As I have no second to help me I shall cut deep. It may look unpleasant, but please do not panic. Death of any sort is a fearful thing to watch. You must not be discouraged by what you see. Is that all right?"

"Yes."

Reiko nodded deeply.

Looking at the slender white figure of his wife the lieutenant experienced a bizarre excitement. What he was about to perform was an act in his public capacity as a soldier, something he had never previously shown his wife. It called for a resolution equal to the courage to enter battle; it was a death of no less degree and quality than death in the front line. It was his conduct on the battlefield that he was now to display.

Momentarily the thought led the lieutenant to a strange fantasy. A lonely death on the battlefield, a death beneath the eyes of his beautiful wife . . . in the sensation that he was now to die in these two dimensions, realizing an impossible union of them both, there was sweetness beyond words. This must be the very pinnacle of good fortune, he thought. To have every moment of his death observed by those beautiful eyes—it was like being borne to death on a gentle, fragrant breeze. There was some special favor here. He did not understand precisely what it was, but it was a domain unknown to others: a dispensation granted to no one else had been permitted to himself. In the radiant, bridelike figure of his white-robed wife the lieutenant seemed to see a vision of all those things he had loved and for which he was to lay down his life—the Imperial Household, the Nation, the Army Flag. All these, no less than the wife who sat before him, were presences observing him closely with clear and never-faltering eyes.

Reiko too was gazing intently at her husband, so soon to die, and she thought that never in this world had she seen anything so beautiful. The lieutenant always looked well in uniform, but now, as he contemplated death with severe brows and firmly closed lips, he revealed what was perhaps masculine beauty at its most superb.

"It's time to go," the lieutenant said at last.

Reiko bent her body low to the mat in a deep bow. She could not raise her face. She did not wish to spoil her make-up with tears, but the tears could not be held back.

When at length she looked up she saw hazily through the tears that her husband had wound a white bandage around the blade of his now unsheathed sword, leaving five or six inches of naked steel showing at the point.

Resting the sword in its cloth wrapping on the mat before him, the lieutenant rose from his knees, resettled himself cross-legged, and unfastened the hooks of his uniform collar. His eyes no longer saw his wife. Slowly, one by one, he undid the flat brass buttons. The dusky brown chest was revealed, and then the stomach. He unclasped his belt and undid the buttons of his trousers. The pure whiteness of the thickly coiled loincloth showed itself. The lieutenant pushed the cloth down with both hands, further to ease his stomach, and then reached for the white-bandaged blade of his sword. With his left hand he massaged his abdomen, glancing downward as he did so.

To reassure himself on the sharpness of his sword's cutting edge the lieutenant folded back the left trouser flap, exposing a little of his thigh, and lightly drew the blade across the skin. Blood welled up in the wound at once, and several streaks of red trickled downward, glistening in the strong light.

It was the first time Reiko had ever seen her husband's blood, and she felt a violent throbbing in her chest. She looked at her husband's face. The lieutenant was looking at the blood with calm appraisal. For a moment—though thinking at the same time that it was hollow comfort—Reiko experienced a sense of relief.

The lieutenant's eyes fixed his wife with an intense, hawk-like stare. Moving the sword around to his front, he raised himself slightly on his hips and let the upper half of his body lean over the sword point. That he was mustering his whole strength was apparent from the angry tension of the uniform at his shoulders. The lieutenant aimed to strike deep into the left of his stomach. His sharp cry pierced the silence of the room.

Despite the effort he had himself put into the blow, the lieutenant had the impression that someone else had struck the side of his stomach agonizingly with a thick rod of iron. For a second or so his head reeled and he had no idea what had happened. The five or six inches of naked point had vanished completely into his flesh, and the white bandage, gripped in his clenched fist, pressed directly against his stomach.

He returned to consciousness. The blade had certainly pierced the wall of the stomach, he thought. His breathing was difficult, his chest thumped violently, and in some far deep region, which he could hardly believe was a part of himself, a fearful and excruciating pain came welling up as if the ground had split open to disgorge a boiling stream of molten rock. The pain came suddenly nearer, with terrifying speed. The lieutenant bit his lower lip and stifled an instinctive moan.

Was this *seppuku?*—he was thinking. It was a sensation of utter chaos, as if the sky had fallen on his head and the world was reeling drunkenly. His will power and courage, which had seemed so robust before he made the incision, had now dwindled to something like a single hairlike thread of steel, and he was assailed by the uneasy feeling that he must advance along this thread, clinging to it with desperation. His clenched fist had grown moist. Looking down, he saw that both his hand and the cloth about the blade were drenched in blood. His loincloth too was dyed a deep red. It struck him as incredible that, amidst this terrible agony, things which could be seen could still be seen, and existing things existed still.

The moment the lieutenant thrust the sword into his left side and she saw the deathly pallor fall across his face, like an abruptly lowered curtain, Reiko had to struggle to prevent herself from rushing to his side. Whatever happened, she must watch. She must be a witness. That was the duty her husband had laid upon her. Opposite her, a mat's space away, she could clearly see her husband biting his lip to stifle the pain. The pain was there, with absolute certainty, before her eyes. And Reiko had no means of rescuing him from it.

The sweat glistened on her husband's forehead. The lieutenant closed his eyes, and then opened them again, as if experimenting. The eyes had lost their luster, and seemed innocent and empty like the eyes of a small animal.

The agony before Reiko's eyes burned as strong as the summer sun, utterly remote from the grief which seemed to be tearing herself apart within. The pain grew steadily in stature, stretching upward. Reiko felt that her husband had already become a man in a separate world, a man whose whole being had been resolved into pain, a prisoner in a cage of pain where no hand could reach out to him. But Reiko felt no pain at all. Her grief was not pain. As she thought about this, Reiko began to feel as if someone had raised a cruel wall of glass high between herself and her husband.

Ever since her marriage her husband's existence had been her own existence, and every breath of his had been a breath drawn by herself. But now, while her husband's existence in pain was a vivid reality, Reiko could find in this grief of hers no certain proof at all of her own existence.

With only his right hand on the sword the lieutenant began to cut sideways across his stomach. But as the blade became entangled with the entrails it was pushed constantly outward by their soft resilience; and the lieutenant realized that it would be necessary, as he cut, to use both hands to keep the point pressed deep into his stomach. He pulled the blade across. It did not cut as easily as he had expected. He directed the strength of his whole body into his right hand and pulled again. There was a cut of three or four inches.

The pain spread slowly outward from the inner depths until the whole stomach reverberated. It was like the wild clanging of a bell. Or like a thousand bells which jangled simultaneously at every breath he breathed and every throb of his pulse, rocking his whole being. The lieutenant could no longer stop himself from moaning. But by now the blade had cut its way through to below the navel, and when he noticed this he felt a sense of satisfaction, and a renewal of courage.

The volume of blood had steadily increased, and now it spurted from the wound as if propelled by the beat of the pulse. The mat before the lieutenant was drenched red with splattered blood, and more blood overflowed onto it from pools which gathered in the folds of the lieutenant's khaki trousers. A spot, like a bird, came flying across to Reiko and settled on the lap of her white silk kimono.

By the time the lieutenant had at last drawn the sword across to the right side of his stomach, the blade was already cutting shallow and had revealed its naked tip, slippery with blood and grease. But, suddenly stricken by a fit of vomiting, the lieutenant cried out hoarsely. The vomiting made the fierce pain fiercer still, and the stomach, which had thus far remained firm and compact, now abruptly heaved, opening wide its wound, and the entrails burst through, as if the wound too were vomiting. Seemingly ignorant of their master's suffering, the entrails gave an impression of robust health and almost disagreeable vitality as they slipped smoothly out and spilled over into the crotch. The lieutenant's head drooped, his shoulders heaved, his eyes opened to narrow slits, and a thin trickle of saliva dribbled from his mouth. The gold markings on his epaulettes caught the light and glinted.

Blood was scattered everywhere. The lieutenant was soaked in it to his knees, and he sat now in a crumpled and listless posture, one hand on the floor. A raw smell filled the room. The lieutenant, his head drooping, retched repeatedly, and the movement showed vividly in his shoulders. The blade of the sword, now pushed back by the entrails and exposed to its tip, was still in the lieutenant's right hand.

It would be difficult to imagine a more heroic sight than that of the lieutenant at this moment, as he mustered his strength and flung back his head. The movement was performed with sudden violence, and the back of his head struck with a sharp crack against the alcove pillar. Reiko had been sitting until now with her face lowered, gazing in fascination at the tide of blood advancing toward her knees, but the sound took her by surprise and she looked up.

The lieutenant's face was not the face of a living man. The eyes were hollow, the skin parched, the once so lustrous cheeks and lips the color of dried mud. The right hand alone was moving. Laboriously gripping the sword, it hovered shakily in the air like the hand of a marionette and strove to direct the point at the base of the lieutenant's throat. Reiko watched her husband make this last, most heartrending, futile exertion. Glistening with blood and grease, the point was thrust at the throat again and again. And each time it missed its aim. The strength to guide it was no longer there. The straying point struck the collar and the collar badges. Although its hooks had been unfastened, the stiff military collar had closed together again and was protecting the throat.

Reiko could bear the sight no longer. She tried to go to her husband's help, but she could not stand. She moved through the blood on her knees, and her white skirts grew deep red. Moving to the rear of her husband, she helped no more than by loosening the collar. The quivering blade at last contacted the naked flesh of the throat. At that moment Reiko's impression was that she herself had propelled her husband forward;

but that was not the case. It was a movement planned by the lieutenant himself, his last exertion of strength. Abruptly he threw his body at the blade, and the blade pierced his neck, emerging at the nape. There was a tremendous spurt of blood and the lieutenant lay still, cold blue-tinged steel protruding from his neck at the back.

V

Slowly, her socks slippery with blood, Reiko descended the stairway. The upstairs room was now completely still.

Switching on the ground-floor lights, she checked the gas jet and the main gas plug and poured water over the smoldering, half-buried charcoal in the brazier. She stood before the upright mirror in the four-and-a-half mat room and held up her skirts. The bloodstains made it seem as if a bold, vivid pattern was printed across the lower half of her white kimono. When she sat down before the mirror, she was conscious of the dampness and coldness of her husband's blood in the region of her thighs, and she shivered. Then, for a long while, she lingered over her toilet preparations. She applied the rouge generously to her cheeks, and her lips too she painted heavily. This was no longer make-up to please her husband. It was make-up for the world which she would leave behind, and there was a touch of the magnificent and the spectacular in her brushwork. When she rose, the mat before the mirror was wet with blood. Reiko was not concerned about this.

Returning from the toilet, Reiko stood finally on the cement floor of the porchway. When her husband had bolted the door here last night it had been in preparation for death. For a while she stood immersed in the consideration of a simple problem. Should she now leave the bolt drawn? If she were to lock the door, it could be that the neighbors might not notice their suicide for several days. Reiko did not relish the thought of their two corpses putrefying before discovery. After all, it seemed, it would be best to leave it open. . . . She released the bolt, and also drew open the frosted-glass door a fraction. . . . At once a chill wind blew in. There was no sign of anyone in the midnight streets, and stars glittered ice-cold through the trees in the large house opposite.

Leaving the door as it was, Reiko mounted the stairs. She had walked here and there for some time and her socks were no longer slippery. About halfway up, her nostrils were already assailed by a peculiar smell.

The lieutenant was lying on his face in a sea of blood. The point protruding from his neck seemed to have grown even more prominent than before. Reiko walked heedlessly across the blood. Sitting beside the lieutenant's corpse, she stared intently at the face, which lay on one cheek on the mat. The eyes were opened wide, as if the lieutenant's attention had been attracted by something. She raised the head, folding it in her sleeve, wiped the blood from the lips, and bestowed a last kiss.

Then she rose and took from the closet a new white blanket and a waist cord. To prevent any derangement of her skirts, she wrapped the blanket about her waist and bound it there firmly with the cord.

Reiko sat herself on a spot about one foot distant from the lieutenant's body. Drawing the dagger from her sash, she examined its dully gleaming blade intently, and held it to her tongue. The taste of the polished steel was slightly sweet.

Reiko did not linger. When she thought how the pain which had previously opened such a gulf between herself and her dying husband was now to become a part of her own experience, she saw before her only the joy of herself entering a realm her husband had already made his own. In her husband's agonized face there had been something inexplicable which she was seeing for the first time. Now she would solve that riddle. Reiko sensed that at last she too would be able to taste the true bitterness and sweetness of that great moral principle in which her husband believed. What had until now been tasted only faintly through her husband's example she was about to savor directly with her own tongue.

Reiko rested the point of the blade against the base of her throat. She thrust hard. The wound was only shallow. Her head blazed, and her hands shook uncontrollably. She gave the blade a strong pull sideways. A warm substance flooded into her mouth, and everything before her eyes reddened, in a vision of spouting blood. She gathered her strength and plunged the point of the blade deep into her throat.

Translated by Geoffrey W. Sargent

QUESTIONS

1. At the end of the story, Reiko thinks that she would be able to taste "the true bitterness and sweetness of that great moral principle in which her husband believed." What is this moral principle?
2. Compare and contrast the various attitudes the lieutenant has toward death, patriotism, and love of his wife.
3. The preparation for, implementation of, and carrying out of the lieutenant's suicide is told in great detail. What are some of the possible reasons that Mishima provided such specific particulars of the process?
4. What effect does the imminent suicide have on the couple's perceptions during their lovemaking?
5. How does the lieutenant combine patriotism and love in a unified principle?
6. Mishima was concerned that Japan would become westernized, and lose its long-standing cultural and social values. How does the story show his strong interest in the traditions of his homeland?

Luigi Pirandello
WAR

The passengers who had left Rome by the night express had had to stop until dawn at the small station of Fabriano in order to continue their journey by the small old-fashioned "local" joining the main line with Sulmona.

At dawn, in a stuffy and smoky second-class carriage in which five people had already spent the night, a bulky woman in deep mourning, was hoisted in—almost like a shapeless bundle. Behind her—puffing and moaning, followed her husband—a tiny man, thin and weakly, his face death-white, his eyes small and bright and looking shy and uneasy.

Having at last taken a seat he politely thanked the passengers who had helped his wife and who had made room for her; then he turned round to the woman trying to pull down the collar of her coat and politely inquired:

"Are you all right, dear?"

The wife, instead of answering, pulled up her collar again to her eyes, so as to hide her face.

"Nasty world," muttered the husband with a sad smile.

And he felt it his duty to explain to his traveling companions that the poor woman was to be pitied for the war was taking away from her her only son, a boy of twenty to whom both had devoted their entire life, even breaking up their home at Sulmona to follow him to Rome where he had to go as a student, then, allowing him to volunteer for war with an assurance, however, that at least for six months he would not be sent to the front and now, all of a sudden, receiving a wire saying that he was due to leave in three days' time and asking them to go and see him off.

The woman under the big coat was twisting and wriggling, at times growling like a wild animal, feeling certain that all those explanations would not have aroused even a shadow of sympathy from those people who—most likely—were in the same plight as herself. One of them, who had been listening with particular attention, said:

"You should thank God that your son is only leaving now for the front. Mine has been sent there the first day of the war. He has already come back twice wounded and been sent back again to the front."

"What about me? I have two sons and three nephews at the front," said another passenger.

"Maybe, but in our case it is our *only* son," ventured the husband.

"What difference can it make? You may spoil your only son with excessive attentions, but you cannot love him more than you would all your other children if you had any. Paternal love is not like bread that can be broken into pieces and split amongst the children in equal shares. A father gives *all* his love to each one of his children without discrimination, whether it be one or ten, and if I am suffering now for my two sons, I am not suffering half for each of them but double. . . ."

"True . . . true . . ." sighed the embarrassed husband, "but suppose (of course we all hope it will never be your case) a father has two sons at the front and he loses one of them, there is still one left to console him . . . while . . ."

"Yes," answered the other, getting cross, "a son left to console him but also a son left for whom he must survive, while in the case of the father of an only son if the son dies the father can die too and put an end to his distress. Which of the two positions is the worse? Don't you see how my case would be worse than yours?"

"Nonsense," interrupted another traveler, a fat, red-faced man with bloodshot eyes of the palest gray.

He was panting. From his bulging eyes seemed to spurt inner violence of an uncontrolled vitality which his weakened body could hardly contain.

"Nonsense," he repeated, trying to cover his mouth with his hand so as to hide the two missing front teeth. "Nonsense. Do we give life to our children for our own benefit?"

The other travelers stared at him in distress. The one who had had his son at the front since the first day of the war sighed: "You are right. Our children do not belong to us, they belong to the Country. . . ."

"Bosh," retorted the fat traveler. "Do we think of the Country when we give life to our children? Our sons are born because . . . well, because they must be born and when they come to life they take our own life with them. This is the truth. We belong to them but they never belong to us. And when they reach twenty they are exactly what we were at their age. We too had a father and mother, but there were so many other things as well . . . girls, cigarettes, illusions, new ties . . . and the Country, of course, whose call we would have answered—when we were twenty—even if father and mother had said no. Now, at our age, the love of our Country is still great, of course, but stronger than it is the love for our children. Is there any one of us here who wouldn't gladly take his son's place at the front if he could?"

There was a silence all round, everybody nodding as to approve.

"Why then," continued the fat man, "shouldn't we consider the feelings of our children when they are twenty? Isn't it natural that at their age they should consider the love for their Country (I am speaking of decent boys, of course) even greater than the love for us? Isn't it natural that it should be so, as after all they must look upon us as upon old boys who cannot move any more and must stay at home? If Country exists, if Country is a natural necessity like bread, of which each of us must eat in order not to die of hunger, somebody must go to defend it. And our sons go, when they are twenty, and they don't want tears, because if they die, they died inflamed and happy (I am speaking, of course, of decent boys). Now, if one dies young and happy, without having the ugly sides of life, the boredom of it, the pettiness, the bitterness of disillusion . . . what more can we ask for him? Everyone should stop crying: everyone should laugh, as I do . . . or at least thank God—as I do—because my son, before dying, sent me a message saying that he was dying satisfied at having ended his life in the best way he could have wished. That is why, as you see, I do not even wear mourning. . . ."

He shook his light fawn coat as to show it; his livid lip over his missing teeth was trembling, his eyes were watery and motionless and soon after he ended with a shrill laugh which might well have been a sob.

"Quite so . . . Quite so . . ." agreed the others.

The woman who, bundled in a corner under her coat, had been sitting and listening had—for the last three months—tried to find in the words of her husband and her friends something to console her in her deep sorrow, something that might show her how a mother should resign herself to send her son not even to death but to a probable danger of life. Yet not a word had she found amongst the many which had been said . . . and her grief had been greater in seeing that nobody—as she thought—could share her feelings.

But now the words of the traveler amazed and almost stunned her. She suddenly realized that it wasn't the others who were wrong and could not understand her but herself who could not rise up to the same height of those fathers and mothers willing to resign themselves, without crying, not only to the departure of their sons but even to their death.

She lifted her head, she bent over from her corner trying to listen with great attention to the details which the fat man was giving to his companions about the way his son had fallen as a hero, for his King and his Country, happy and without regrets. It seemed to her that she had stumbled into a world she had never dreamt of, a world so far unknown to her and she was so pleased to hear everyone joining in congratulating that brave father who could so stoically speak of his child's death.

Then suddenly, just as if she had heard nothing of what had been said and almost as if waking up from a dream, she turned to the old man, asking him:

"Then . . . is your son really dead?"

Everybody stared at her. The old man, too, turned to look at her, fixing his great, bulging, horribly watery light gray eyes, deep in her face. For some little time he tried to answer, but words failed him. He looked and looked at her, almost as if only then—at that silly, incongruous question—he had suddenly realized at last that his son was really dead . . . gone forever . . . forever. His face contracted, became horribly distorted, then he snatched in haste a handkerchief from his pocket and, to the amazement of everyone, broke into harrowing, heart-rending, uncontrollable sobs.

QUESTIONS

1. What point does the author make by having the traveling companions argue over whose plight is the most tragic?
2. Why does the fat man emphasize the term "decent boys" when he makes reference to soldiering and duty? What emotion is hidden behind his reasoning?
3. Why does the fat man break down and cry at the end?
4. Compare the view of patriotism voiced by the characters in this story with that of the lieutenant in "Patriotism."

Hernando Téllez

JUST LATHER, THAT'S ALL

He said nothing when he entered. I was passing the best of my razors back and forth on a strop. When I recognized him I started to tremble. But he didn't notice. Hoping to conceal my emotion, I continued sharpening the razor. I tested it on the meat of my thumb, and then held it up to the light. At that moment he took off the bullet-studded belt that his gun holster dangled from. He hung it up on a wall hook and placed his military cap over it. Then he turned to me, loosening the knot of his tie, and said, "It's hot as hell. Give me a shave." He sat in the chair.

I estimated he had a four-day beard. The four days taken up by the latest expedition in search of our troops. His face seemed reddened, burned by the sun. Carefully, I began to prepare the soap. I cut off a few slices, dropped them into the cup, mixed in a bit of warm water, and began to stir with the brush. Immediately the foam began to rise. "The other boys in the group should have this much beard, too." I continued stirring the lather.

"But we did all right, you know. We got the main ones. We brought back some dead, and we've got some others still alive. But pretty soon they'll all be dead."

"How many did you catch?" I asked.

"Fourteen. We had to go pretty deep into the woods to find them. But we'll get even. Not one of them comes out of this alive, not one."

He leaned back on the chair when he saw me with the lather-covered brush in my hand. I still had to put the sheet on him. No doubt about it, I was upset. I took a sheet out of a drawer and knotted it around my customer's neck. He wouldn't stop talking. He probably thought I was in sympathy with his party.

"The town must have learned a lesson from what we did the other day," he said.

"Yes," I replied, securing the knot at the base of his dark, sweaty neck.

"That was a fine show, eh?"

"Very good," I answered, turning back for the brush. The man closed his eyes with a gesture of fatigue and sat waiting for the cool caress of the soap. I had never had him so close to me. The day he ordered the whole town to file into the patio of the school to see the four rebels hanging there, I came face to face with him for an instant. But the sight of the mutilated bodies kept me from noticing the face of the man who had directed it all, the face I was now about to take into my hands. It was not an unpleasant face, certainly. And the beard, which made him seem a bit older than he was, didn't suit him badly at all. His name was Torres. Captain Torres. A man of imagination, because who else would have thought of hanging the naked rebels and then holding target practice on certain parts of their bodies? I began to apply the first layer of soap. With his eyes closed, he continued. "Without any effort I could go straight to sleep," he said, "but there's plenty to do this afternoon." I stopped the lathering and asked with a feigned lack of interest: "A firing squad?" "Something like that, but a little slower." I got on with the job of lathering his beard. My hands started trembling again. The man could not possibly realize it, and this was in my favor. But I would have preferred that he hadn't come. It was likely that many of our faction had seen him enter. And an enemy under one's roof imposes certain conditions. I would be obliged to shave that beard like any other one, carefully, gently, like that of any customer, taking pains to see that no single pore emitted a drop of blood. Being careful to see that the little tufts of hair did not lead the blade astray. Seeing that his skin ended up clean, soft, and healthy, so that passing the back of my hand over it I couldn't feel a hair. Yes, I was secretly a rebel, but I was also a conscientious barber, and proud of the preciseness of my profession. And this four-days' growth of beard was a fitting challenge.

I took the razor, opened up the two protective arms, exposed the blade and began the job, from one of the sideburns downward. The razor responded beautifully. His beard was inflexible and hard, not too long, but thick. Bit by bit the skin emerged. The razor rasped along, making its customary sound as fluffs of lather mixed with bits of hair gathered along the blade. I paused a moment to clean it, then took up the strop again to sharpen the razor, because I'm a barber who does things properly. The man, who had kept his eyes closed, opened them now, removed one of his hands from under the sheet, felt the spot on his face where the soap had been cleared off, and said, "Come to the school today at six o'clock." "The same thing as the other day?" I asked horrified. "It could be better," he replied. "What do you plan to do?" "I don't know yet. But we'll amuse ourselves." Once more he leaned back and closed his eyes. I approached him with the razor poised. "Do you plan to punish them all?" I ventured timidly. "All." The soap was drying on his face. I had to hurry. In the mirror I looked toward the street. It was the same as ever: the grocery store with two or three customers in it. Then I glanced at the clock: two-twenty in the afternoon. The razor continued on its downward stroke. Now from the other sideburn down. A thick, blue beard. He should have let it grow like some poets or priests do. It would suit him well. A lot of people wouldn't recognize him. Much to his benefit, I thought, as I attempted to cover the neck area smoothly. There, for sure, the razor had to be handled masterfully, since the hair, although softer, grew into little swirls. A curly beard. One of the tiny pores could be opened up and issue forth its pearl of blood. A good barber such as I prides himself on never allowing this to happen to a client. And this was a first-class client. How many of us had he ordered shot? How many of us had he ordered mutilated? It was better not to think about it. Torres did not know that I was his enemy. He did not know it nor did the rest. It was a secret shared by very few, precisely so that I could inform the revolutionaries of what Torres was doing in the town and of what he was planning each time he undertook a rebel-hunting excursion. So it was going to be very difficult to explain that I had him right in my hands and let him go peacefully—alive and shaved.

The beard was now almost completely gone. He seemed younger, less burdened by years than when he had arrived. I suppose this always happens with men who visit barber shops. Under the stroke of my razor Torres was being rejuvenated—rejuvenated because I am a good barber, the best in the town, if I may say so. A little more lather here, under his chin, on his Adam's apple, on this big vein. How hot it is getting! Torres must be sweating as much as I. But he is not afraid. He is a calm man, who is not even thinking about what he is going to do with the prisoners this afternoon. On the other hand I, with this razor in my hands, stroking and re-stroking this skin, trying to keep blood from oozing from these pores, can't even think clearly. Damn him for coming, because I'm a revolutionary and not a murderer. And how easy it would be to kill him. And he deserves it. Does he? No! What the devil! No one deserves to have someone else make the sacrifice of becoming a murderer. What do you gain by it? Nothing. Others come along and still others, and the first ones kill the second ones and they the next ones and it goes on like this until everything is a sea of blood. I could cut this throat just so, zip! zip! I wouldn't give him time to complain and since he has his eyes closed he wouldn't see the glistening knife blade or my glistening eyes. But I'm trembling like a real murderer. Out of his neck a gush of blood would spout onto the sheet, on the chair, on my hands, on the floor. I would have to close the door. And the blood would keep inching along the floor, warm, ineradicable, uncontainable, until it reached the street, like a little scarlet stream. I'm sure that one solid stroke, one deep incision, would prevent any pain. He wouldn't suffer. But what would I do with the body? Where would I hide it? I would have to flee, leaving all I have behind, and take refuge far away, far, far away. But they would follow until they found me. "Captain Torres' murderer. He slit his throat while he was shaving him—a coward." And then on the other side. "The avenger of us all. A name to remember. (And here they would mention my name.) He was the town barber. No one knew he was defending our cause."

And what of all this? Murderer or hero? My destiny depends on the edge of this blade. I can turn my hand a bit more, press a little harder on the razor, and sink it in. The skin would give way like silk, like rubber, like the strop. There is nothing more tender than human skin and blood is always there, ready to pour forth. A blade like this doesn't fail. It is my best. But I don't want to be a murderer, no sir. You came to me for a shave. And I perform my work honorably. . . . I don't want blood on my hands. Just lather, that's all. You are an executioner and I am only a barber. Each person has his own place in the scheme of things. That's right. His own place.

Now his chin had been stroked clean and smooth. The man sat up and looked into the mirror. He rubbed his hands over his skin and felt it fresh, like new.

"Thanks," he said. He went to the hanger for his belt, pistol and cap. I must have been very pale; my shirt felt soaked. Torres finished adjusting the buckle, straightened his pistol in the holster and after automatically smoothing down his hair, he put on the cap. From his pants pocket he took out several coins to pay me for my services. And he began to head toward the door. In the doorway he paused for a moment, and turning to me he said:

"They told me that you'd kill me. I came to find out. But killing isn't easy. You can take my word for it." And he headed on down the street.

Translated by Donald Yates

QUESTIONS

1. Why does the narrator repeatedly reassure himself that he is a good barber? What significance does this have to Torres's explaining at the end that "killing isn't easy"?
2. Does the author portray Torres sympathetically or unsympathetically? Explain your view.

3. The author describes in detail the process of shaving. Why do you suppose so much space is devoted to the specifics of this process?

4. We learn in the last line that Torres knew all along the barber was sympathetic to the rebel cause. Why did he risk his life merely for a shave?

Luisa Valenzuela

THE CENSORS

Poor Juan! One day they caught him with his guard down before he could even realize that what he had taken as a stroke of luck was really one of fate's dirty tricks. These things happen the minute you're careless, as one often is. Juancito let happiness—a feeling you can't trust—get the better of him when he received from a confidential source Mariana's new address in Paris and knew that she hadn't forgotten him. Without thinking twice, he sat down at his table and wrote her a letter. *The* letter that now keeps his mind off his job during the day and won't let him sleep at night (what had he scrawled, what had he put on that sheet of paper he sent to Mariana?).

Juan knows there won't be a problem with the letter's contents, that it's irreproachable, harmless. But what about the rest? He knows that they examine, sniff, feel, and read between the lines of each and every letter, and check its tiniest comma and most accidental stain. He knows that all letters pass from hand to hand and go through all sorts of tests in the huge censorship offices and that, in the end, very few continue on their way. Usually it takes months, even years, if there aren't any snags; all this time the freedom, maybe even the life, of both sender and receiver is in jeopardy. And that's why Juan's so troubled: thinking that something might happen to Mariana because of his letters. Of all people, Mariana, who must finally feel safe there where she always dreamt she'd live. But he knows that the *Censor's Secret Command* operates all over the world and cashes in on the discount in air fares; there's nothing to stop them from going as far as that hidden Paris neighborhood, kidnapping Mariana, and returning to their cozy homes, certain of having fulfilled their noble mission.

Well, you've got to beat them to the punch, do what everyone tries to do: sabotage the machinery, throw sand in its gears, get to the bottom of the problem so as to stop it.

This was Juan's sound plan when he, like many others, applied for a censor's job—not because he had a calling or needed a job: no, he applied simply to intercept his own letter, a consoling albeit unoriginal idea. He was hired immediately, for each day more and more censors are needed and no one would bother to check on his references.

Ulterior motives couldn't be overlooked by the *Censorship Division,* but they needn't be too strict with those who applied. They knew how hard it would be for the poor guys to find the letter they wanted and even if they did, what's a letter or two when the new censor would snap up so many others? That's how Juan managed to join the *Post Office's Censorship Division,* with a certain goal in mind.

The building had a festive air on the outside that contrasted with its inner staidness. Little by little, Juan was absorbed by his job, and he felt at peace since he was doing everything he could to get his letter for Mariana. He didn't even worry when, in his first month, he was sent to *Section K* where envelopes are very carefully screened for explosives.

It's true that on the third day, a fellow worker had his right hand blown off by a letter, but the division chief claimed it was sheer negligence on the victim's part. Juan and the other employees were allowed to go back to their work, though feeling less secure. After work, one of them tried to organize a strike to demand higher wages for unhealthy work, but Juan didn't join in; after thinking it over, he reported the man to his superiors and thus got promoted.

You don't form a habit by doing something once, he told himself as he left his boss's office. And when he was transferred to *Section F,* where letters are carefully checked for poison dust, he felt he had climbed a rung in the ladder.

By working hard, he quickly reached *Section E* where the job became more interesting, for he could now read and analyze the letters' contents. Here he could even hope to get hold of his letter, which, judging by the time that had elapsed, had gone through the other sections and was probably floating around in this one.

Soon his work became so absorbing that his noble mission blurred in his mind. Day after day he crossed out whole paragraphs in red ink, pitilessly chucking many letters into the censored basket. These were horrible days when he was shocked by the subtle and conniving ways employed by people to pass on subversive messages; his instincts were so sharp that he found behind a simple "the weather's unsettled" or "prices continue to soar" the wavering hand of someone secretly scheming to overthrow the Government.

His zeal brought him swift promotion. We don't know if this made him happy. Very few letters reached him in *Section B*—only a handful passed the other hurdles—so he read them over and over again, passed them under a magnifying glass, searched for microprint with an electronic microscope, and tuned his sense of smell so that he was beat by the time he made it home. He'd barely manage to warm up his soup, eat some fruit, and fall into bed, satisfied with having done his duty. Only his darling mother worried, but she couldn't get him back on the right track. She'd say, though it wasn't always true: Lola called, she's at the bar with the girls, they miss you, they're waiting for you. Or else she'd leave a bottle of red wine on the table. But Juan wouldn't overdo it: any distraction could make him lose his edge and the perfect censor had to be alert, keen, attentive, and sharp to nab cheats. He had a truly patriotic task, both self-denying and uplifting.

His basket for censored letters became the best fed as well as the most cunning basket in the whole *Censorship Division.* He was about to congratulate himself for having finally discovered his true mission, when his letter to Mariana reached his hands. Naturally, he censored it without regret. And just as naturally, he couldn't stop them from executing him the following morning, another victim of his devotion to his work.

Translated by David Unger

QUESTIONS

1. How can this story be viewed as a metaphor for the average individual's role in society?
2. The author says that Juan's idea to become a censor was an "unoriginal idea." What does this reflect about Juan's personality? What does it say about citizens in general?
3. The Censorship Department seems omnipotent and omnipresent. What agency or agencies could it symbolize in real life?
4. This story is marked by a scarcity of physical detail. Would precise detail have added to or distracted from the impact of the story?

W a r & P e a c e

F i c t i o n

TOPICS FOR WRITING

1. The lieutenant in "Patriotism" feels strong allegiance toward his country. Describe someone you know who has an equally strong sense of allegiance. What is the object of his or her loyalty? Why does this person feel loyal? How does he or she demonstrate that loyalty?

2. The barber in "Just Lather, That's All" feels conflict about what he should do with his enemy, Torres. Describe a time in your life when you were faced with a crucial decision. What was at stake? What did you do? How did you decide on your course of action?

3. Select your favorite character from among those depicted in this group of stories. Analyze his or her personality, motivations, attitudes, and actions. Explain why you find these qualities are attractive.

4. The main characters in Babel's "My First Goose" and in Borges's "The South" confront challenges to their lives and integrity. Compare and contrast the nature of these challenges. What is at stake? What actions does each character take? What is the outcome?

5. The average citizen can determine the course of his or her own life, but is powerless to influence public opinion. Argue for or against this proposition.

6. War is always the same regardless of its cultural context. Therefore, the stories in this section tend to be repetitive and too narrow in theme. Argue for or against this proposition.

7. If an individual feels that a law is unjust, it is the duty of that individual to protest that law. Argue for or against this proposition.

8. As a research project, study the roles of men and women in traditional Japanese culture. Write an essay discussing how closely the couple in the story "Patriotism" adhere to these prescribed roles.

9. The story "The Censors" by Luisa Valenzuela bears a resemblance to certain short stories by the eminent twentieth-century writer Franz Kafka. As a research project, read and select a story by the latter and compare and contrast it to "The Censors."

10. "Big Bertha Stories" by Bobbie Ann Mason focuses on the life and family of a Vietnam War veteran. Research the fiction of the highly significant Vietnam era, and write a paper in which you discuss how various authors address the effects of the war on its combatants.

Poetry

W. H. Auden

THE UNKNOWN CITIZEN

(TO JS/07/M/378

THIS MARBLE MONUMENT
IS ERECTED BY THE STATE)

He was found by the Bureau of Statistics to be
One against whom there was no official complaint,
And all the reports on his conduct agree
That, in the modern sense of an old-fashioned word, he was a saint.
For in everything he did he served the Greater Community.   5
Except for the War till the day he retired
He worked in a factory and never got fired,
But satisfied his employers, Fudge Motors Inc.
Yet he wasn't a scab or odd in his views,
For his Union reports that he paid his dues,   10
(Our report on his Union shows it was sound)
And our Social Psychology workers found
That he was popular with his mates and liked a drink.
The Press are convinced that he bought a paper every day
And that his reactions to advertisements were normal in every way.   15
Policies taken out in his name prove that he was fully insured,
And his Health-card shows he was once in hospital but left it cured.

706

Both Producers Research and High-Grade Living declare
He was fully sensible to the advantages of the Installment Plan
And had everything necessary to the Modern Man, 20
A phonograph, radio, a car and a frigidaire.
Our researchers into Public Opinion are content
That he held the proper opinions for the time of year;
When there was peace, he was for peace; when there was war, he went.
He was married and added five children to the population, 25
Which our Eugenist says was the right number for a parent of his generation,
And our teachers report that he never interfered with their education.
Was he free? Was he happy? The question is absurd:
Had anything been wrong, we should certainly have heard.

QUESTIONS

1. How would you characterize the tone and diction of the poem?
2. What specific standards and institutions of society did the citizen conform to?
3. What is the theme of the poem? How does the simple rhyme scheme of the poem contribute to its theme? In other words, how does the form support its content?
4. Many of the words in this poem are capitalized. What is the poet suggesting by this device?

Kofi Awoonor

SONG OF WAR

I shall sleep in white calico;
War has come upon the sons of men
And I shall sleep in calico;
Let the boys go forward,
Kpli and his people should go forward; 5
Let the white man's guns boom,
We are marching forward;
We all shall sleep in calico.

When we start, the ground shall shake;
The war is within our very huts; 10
Cowards should fall back
And live at home with the women;
They who go near our wives

While we are away in battle
Shall lose their calabashes when we come.   15

Where has it been heard before
That a snake has bitten a child
In front of its own mother;
The war is upon us
It is within our very huts   20
And the sons of men shall fight it
Let the white man's guns boom
And its smoke cover us
We are fighting them to die.

We shall die on the battlefield   25
We shall like death at no other place,
Our guns shall die with us
And our sharp knives shall perish with us
We shall die on the battlefield.

George Gordon, Lord Byron

ON THIS DAY I COMPLETE MY THIRTY-SIXTH YEAR

Missolonghi, Jan. 22, 1824.

'Tis time this heart should be unmoved,
    Since others it hath ceased to move:
Yet, though I cannot be beloved,
        Still let me love!

My days are in the yellow leaf;   5
    The flowers and fruits of love are gone;
The worm, the canker, and the grief
        Are mine alone!

The fire that on my bosom preys
    Is lone as some volcanic isle;   10
No torch is kindled at its blaze—
        A funeral pile.

The hope, the fear, the jealous care,
   The exalted portion of the pain
And power of love, I cannot share,   15
      But wear the chain.

But 'tis not *thus*—and 'tis not *here*—
   Such thoughts should shake my soul, nor *now*,
Where glory decks the hero's bier,
      Or binds his brow.   20

The sword, the banner, and the field,
   Glory and Greece, around me see!
The Spartan, borne upon his shield,
      Was not more free.

Awake! (not Greece—she is awake!)   25
   Awake, my spirit! Think through *whom*
Thy life-blood tracks its parent lake,
      And then strike home!

Tread those reviving passions down,
   Unworthy manhood!—unto thee   30
Indifferent should the smile or frown
      Of beauty be.

If thou regrett'st thy youth, *why live?*
   The land of honourable death
Is here:—up to the field, and give   35
      Away thy breath!

Seek out—less often sought than found—
   A soldier's grave, for thee the best;
Then look around, and choose thy ground,
      And take thy rest.   40

QUESTIONS

1. This is one of the last poems that Byron wrote. What do you find that foretells his death?
2. Why does Byron declare in the first stanza, "Still let me love"? What type of love does he have in mind? Is it the same love that animates "She Walks in Beauty"? Explain.
3. What does the "fire" in stanza 3 symbolize?

Aimé Césaire

SPIRALS

we ascend
braids of gallows birds from the cañafistulas
(the executioner must have forgotten the last grooming)
we ascend
beautiful hands hanging from ferns and waving farewells that no one hears   5
we ascend
the balisiers are breaking their hearts on the precise moment when the
    phoenix is reborn from its
         highest consuming flame
we ascend
we descend   10
the Cecropias hide their faces
and their dreams in the skeletons of their phosphorescent hands
the circles of the funnel now close faster and faster
it is the end of hell
we crawl we float   15
we coil the chasms of the earth
the resentments of men
the rancor of races tighter and tighter
and the abyssal undertows carry us back
in a tangle of lianas   20
of stars and shudders

Translated by Clayton Eshelman and Annette Smith

Stephen Crane

WAR IS KIND

Do not weep, maiden, for war is kind.
Because your lover threw wild hands toward the sky
And the affrighted steed ran on alone,
Do not weep.
War is kind.   5

    Hoarse, booming drums of the regiment
    Little souls who thirst for fight,
    These men were born to drill and die

The unexplained glory flies above them
Great is the battle-god, great, and his kingdom—   10
A field where a thousand corpses lie.

Do not weep, babe, for war is kind.
Because your father tumbled in the yellow trenches,
Raged at his breast, gulped and died,
Do not weep.   15
War is kind.

    Swift, blazing flag of the regiment
    Eagle with crest of red and gold,
    These men were born to drill and die
    Point for them the virtue of slaughter   20
    Make plain to them the excellence of killing
    And a field where a thousand corpses lie.

Mother whose heart hung humble as a button
On the bright splendid shroud of your son,
Do not weep.   25
War is kind.

QUESTIONS

1. What is the purpose of repetition in the poem?
2. What is the irony behind the title?
3. Crane refers to the soldiers as "little souls" who have "the unexplained glory" above them. How do these phrases contribute to the portrait Crane draws of the average soldier?
4. Compare and contrast the way the poet refers to men and women in the poem. How does he portray their relationships in terms of the effects of war?

e. e. cummings

NEXT TO OF COURSE GOD

"next to of course god america i
love you land of the pilgrims' and so forth oh
say can you see by the dawn's early my
country 'tis of centuries come and go

and are no more what of it we should worry   5
in every language even deafanddumb
thy sons acclaim your glorious name by gorry
by jingo by gee by gosh by gum
why talk of beauty what could be more beaut-
iful than these heroic happy dead   10
who rushed like lions to the roaring slaughter
they did not stop to think they died instead
then shall the voice of liberty be mute?"

He spoke. And drank rapidly a glass of water

Roque Dalton

LOVE POEM

Those who widened the Panama Canal
(and were on the 'silver roll' not the 'gold roll')
those who repaired the Pacific fleet
in California bases,
those who rotted in prisons in Guatemala,   5
Mexico, Honduras, Nicaragua
for stealing, smuggling, swindling,
for starving,
those always suspected of everything
("Allow me to place him in your custody   10
for suspicious loitering
aggravated by the fact of being Salvadoran")
those who pack the bars and whorehouses
in every port and capital
('The Blue Grotto,' 'The G-String,' 'Happyland')   15
The sowers of corn deep in foreign forests,
the crime barons of the scandal sheets,
those who nobody ever knows where they're from,
the best artisans in the world,
those who were riddled with bullets crossing the border,   20
those who died from malaria
or scorpion bites or swarming bees
in the hell of banana plantations,
those who got drunk and wept for the national anthem

under a Pacific cyclone or up north in the snow,　　　25
the spongers, beggers, pot-heads,
the stupid sons of whores,
those who were barely able to get back,
those who had a little more luck,
the forever undocumented,　　　30
those who do anything, sell anything, eat anything,
the first ones to pull a knife,
the wretched the most wretched of the earth,
my compatriots,
my brothers.　　　35

Translated by Richard Schaaf

Kamala Das

AN INTRODUCTION

I don't know politics but I know the names
Of those in power, and can repeat them like
Days of the week, or names of months, beginning with
Nehru.[1] I am Indian, very brown, born in
Malabar, I speak three languages, write in　　　5
Two, dream in one. Don't write in English, they said,
English is not your mother-tongue. Why not leave
Me alone, critics, friends, visiting cousins,
Every one of you? Why not let me speak in
Any language I like? The language I speak　　　10
Becomes mine, its distortions, its queernesses
All mine, mine alone. It is half English, half
Indian, funny perhaps, but it is honest,
It is as human as I am human, don't
You see? It voices my joys, my longings, my　　　15
Hopes, and it is useful to me as cawing
Is to crows or roaring to the lions, it
Is human speech, the speech of the mind that is
Here and not there, a mind that sees and hears and
Is aware. Not the deaf, blind speech　　　20
Of trees in storm or of monsoon clouds or of rain or the

---

[1] Jawaharlal Nehru (1889–1964), India's first prime minister after she gained independence.

Incoherent mutterings of the blazing
Funeral pyre. I was child, and later they
Told me I grew, for I became tall, my limbs
Swelled and one or two places sprouted hair. When   25
I asked for love, not knowing what else to ask
For, he drew a youth of sixteen into the
Bedroom and closed the door. He did not beat me
But my sad woman-body felt so beaten.
The weight of my breasts and womb crushed me. I shrank   30
Pitifully. Then . . . I wore a shirt and my
Brother's trousers, cut my hair short and ignored
My womanliness. Dress in saris,[2] be girl,
Be wife, they said. Be embroiderer, be cook,
Be a quarreller with servants. Fit in. Oh,   35
Belong, cried the categorizers. Don't sit
On walls or peep in through our lace-draped windows.
Be Amy, or be Kamala. Or, better
Still, be Madhavikutty.[3] It is time to
Choose a name, a role. Don't play pretending games.   40
Don't play at schizophrenia or be a
Nympho. Don't cry embarrassingly loud when
Jilted in love . . . I met a man, loved him. Call
Him not by any name, he is every man
Who wants a woman, just as I am every   45
Woman who seeks love. In him . . . . the hungry haste
Of rivers, in me . . . the ocean's tireless
Waiting. Who are you, I ask each and everyone,
The answer is, it is I. Anywhere and
Everywhere, I see the one who calls himself   50
I; in this world, he is tightly packed like the
Sword in its sheath. It is I who drink lonely
Drinks at twelve, midnight, in hotels of strange towns,
It is I who laugh, it is I who make love
And then feel shame, it is I who lie dying   55
With a rattle in my throat. I am sinner,
I am saint. I am the beloved and the
Betrayed. I have no joys which are not yours, no
Aches which are not yours. I too call myself I.

---

[2] Traditional dress of Indian women.
[3] "Madhavikutty is the pseudonym I use when I write stories in Malayalam, the language spoken here in
Kerala State" [Das's note].

Babette Deutsch

DISASTERS OF WAR

Streets opening like wounds: Madrid's. The thresh
Of resistance ends before a tumbled wall;
    The coward and the cursing sprawl
    Brotherly, one white heap of flesh
    Char-mouthed and boneyard black.   5
A woman, dragged off, howls—a lively sack
Of loot. An infant, fallen on its back,
Scowls from the stones at the Herodian lark.
Light is the monster fattening on this dark.

If shadow takes cadavers for her chair,   10
Where fresh fires glare life lifts a wolfish snout.
    Bruised and abused by hope, the rout,
    Turning, is gunned across the square
    And scattered. Rope, knife, lead
Slice prayer short. A lolling head   15
Grins, as with toothache. Stubbornly, the dead
Thrust forward like a beggar's senseless claw.
What is scrawled there in acid? THIS I SAW.

Beyond the Madonnas and marbles, Goya's brute
Testament pits itself against the hush   20
    Of the blond halls, the urbane crush—
    Against the slat-eyed, the astute,
    Craning, against the guard, who yawns.
And pits itself in vain: this dark, these dawns,
Vomit of an old war, things the nightmare spawns   25
Are pictures at an exhibition. We
Look, having viewed too much, and cannot see.

Rita Dove

PARSLEY*

1. The Cane Fields

There is a parrot imitating spring
in the palace, its feathers parsley green.
Out of the swamp the cane appears

to haunt us, and we cut it down. El General
searches for a word; he is all the world   5
there is. Like a parrot imitating spring,

we lie down screaming as rain punches through
and we come up green. We cannot speak an R—
out of the swamp, the cane appears

and then the mountain we call in whispers *Katalina*.   10
The children gnaw their teeth to arrowheads.
There is a parrot imitating spring.

El General has found his word: *perejil*.
Who says it, lives. He laughs, teeth shining
out of the swamp. The cane appears   15

in our dreams, lashed by wind and streaming.
And we lie down. For every drop of blood
there is a parrot imitating spring.
Out of the swamp the cane appears.

2. The Palace

The word the general's chosen is parsley.   20
It is fall, when thoughts turn
to love and death; the general thinks
of his mother, how she died in the fall
and he planted her walking cane at the grave
and it flowered, each spring stolidly forming   25
four-star blossoms. The general

*On October 2, 1957, Rafael Trujillo (1891–1961), dictator of the Dominican Republic, ordered 20,000 blacks killed because they could not pronounce the letter "r" in *perejil*, the Spanish word for parsley.

pulls on his boots, he stomps to
her room in the palace, the one without
curtains, the one with a parrot
in a brass ring. As he paces he wonders   30
Who can I kill today. And for a moment
the little knot of screams
is still. The parrot, who has traveled

all the way from Australia in an ivory
cage, is, coy as a widow, practising   35
spring. Ever since the morning
his mother collapsed in the kitchen
while baking skull-shaped candies
for the Day of the Dead, the general
has hated sweets. He orders pastries   40
brought up for the bird; they arrive
dusted with sugar on a bed of lace.
The knot in his throat starts to twitch;
he sees his boots the first day in battle
splashed with mud and urine   45
as a soldier falls at his feet amazed—
how stupid he looked!—at the sound
of artillery. *I never thought it would sing*
the soldier said, and died. Now

the general sees the fields of sugar   50
cane, lashed by rain and streaming.
He sees his mother's smile, the teeth
gnawed to arrowheads. He hears
the Haitians sing without R's
as they swing the great machetes: 55
Katalina, they sing, *Katalina,*

mi madle, mi amol en muelte. God knows
his mother was no stupid woman; she
could roll an R like a queen. Even
a parrot can roll an R! In the bare room   60
the bright feathers arch in a parody
of greenery, as the last pale crumbs
disappear under the blackened tongue. Someone

calls out his name in a voice
so like his mother's, a startled tear   65
splashes the tip of his right boot.

My mother, my love in death.
The general remembers the tiny green sprigs
men of his village wore in their capes
to honor the birth of a son. He will   70
order many, this time, to be killed

for a single, beautiful word.

Lawrence Ferlinghetti

IN GOYA'S
GREATEST SCENES

In Goya's greatest scenes we seem to see
                        the people of the world
   exactly at the moment when
    they first attained the title of
                 'suffering humanity'   5
    They writhe upon the page
             in a veritable rage
              of adversity
    Heaped up
       groaning with babies and bayonets   10
            under cement skies
   in an abstract landscape of blasted trees
    bent statues bats wings and beaks
       slippery gibbets
    cadavers and carnivorous cocks   15
    and all the final hollering monsters
    of the
         'imagination of disaster'
   they are so bloody real
       it is as if they really still existed   20

And they do

    Only the landscape is changed
They still are ranged along the roads
   plagued by legionaires
       false windmills and demented roosters   25

They are the same people
                       only further from home
     on freeways fifty lanes wide
               on a concrete continent
                   spaced with bland billboards   30
             illustrating imbecile illusions of happiness

          The scene shows fewer tumbrils
                   but more maimed citizens
                         in painted cars
             and they have strange license plates   35
    and engines
             that devour America

QUESTIONS

1. What is the central comparison that the poet is making? What details exist between the two things being compared?
2. The first stanza describes a work of visual art. What purpose might the author have for choosing to describe a work of art using words? Does the author assume the reader is familiar with the art being described?
3. Ferlinghetti's line structure is quite unusual. What is unusual about it? What do you think his purpose is in structuring the poem this way? What relationship is there between the line structure of the poem and the way the poem is intended to be read?

Anne Finch

TRAIL ALL YOUR PIKES

Trail all your pikes, dispirit every drum,
March in a slow procession from afar,
Ye silent, ye dejected, men of war.
Be still the hautboys, and the flute be dumb!
Display no more, in vain, the lofty banner;   5
For see where on the bier before ye lies
The pale, the fall'n, the untimely sacrifice
To your mistaken shrine, to your false idol Honour.

Anthony Grooms

HOMESPACE

My mother did not know me when I knocked.
She said her son was killed in the war.
It was only when I blurted my tears
That she opened the screen and fell

Into my arms. My father welcomed me as a hero.   5
They gave a cookout. No one my age came.
I made myself busy with the fire
So I wouldn't have to talk. When the fuel

Exploded on the coals, I heard screams.
In the evening the orange sun dropped   10
Into the haze of the blue ridges. August seemed cool.
Women and children laughed from the porch.

Men sat under the elms.
I watched the sky for the enemy.

Langston Hughes

HARLEM

What happens to a dream deferred?
    Does it dry up
    like a raisin in the sun?
    Or fester like a sore—
    And then run?   5

    Does it stink like rotten meat?
    Or crust and sugar over—
    like a syrupy sweet?

    Maybe it just sags
    like a heavy load.   10

    Or does it explode?

QUESTIONS

1. This poem consists of four progressively smaller stanzas. What is the effect of structuring the poem this way?
2. What is the function of the repetition in punctuation in stanzas 1 and 2? How does it contribute to the poem's effect?
3. Why do you suppose Hughes ended the poem with an italicized question?
4. If you have read Lorraine Hansberry's play *A Raisin in the Sun* (included in this anthology), discuss the implication of having taken the title from Langston Hughes's poem.

Langston Hughes

WITHOUT BENEFIT OF DECLARATION

Listen here, Joe
Don't you know
That tomorrow
You got to go
Out yonder where   5
The steel winds blow?

Listen here, kid,
It's been said
Tomorrow you'll be dead
Out there where   10
The snow is lead.

Don't ask me why.
Just go ahead and die.
Hidden from the sky
Out yonder you'll lie;   15
A medal to your family—
In exchange for
A guy.

Mama, don't cry.

Randall Jarrell

THE DEATH OF THE
BALL TURRET GUNNER

From my mother's sleep I fell into the State,
And I hunched in its belly till my wet fur froze.
Six miles from earth, loosed from its dream of life,
I woke to black flak and the nightmare fighters.
When I died they washed me out of the turret with a hose.   5

June Jordan

SAFE

The Río Escondido at night
in between
jungle growing down to the muddy
edges of deep water possibilities
    helicopter attack   5
    alligator assault
    contra confrontations
    blood sliding into the silent scenery
where I sat cold and wet
but surrounded by five   10
compañeros
in a dugout canoe

Denise Levertov

THE VICTORS

In June the bush we call
alder was heavy, listless,
its leaves studded with galls,

growing wherever we didn't
want it. We cut it   5
savagely, hunted it from the pasture, chopped it

away from the edge of the wood.
In July, still everywhere, it appeared
wearing green berries.

Anyway it must go. It takes   10
the light and air and the good of the earth
from flowers and young trees.

But now in August
its berries are red. Do the birds
eat them? Swinging   15

clusters of red, the hedges are full of them,
red-currant red, a graceful
ornament or a merry smile.

QUESTIONS

1. Who are "The Victors" referred to in the poem's title?
2. If we assume that the alders are symbols, what might they symbolize? Explain your
   view.
3. Has the speaker's attitude toward the alders changed during the course of the poem?
   If so, how?
4. Explain the meaning of the last sentence. Explain why it has such unusual syntax.

Robert Lowell

CHILDREN OF LIGHT

Our fathers wrung their bread from stocks and stones
And fenced their gardens with the Redman's bones;
Embarking from the Nether Land of Holland,
Pilgrims unhouseled by Geneva's night,
They planted here the Serpent's seeds of light;   5
And here the pivoting searchlights probe to shock
The riotous glass houses built on rock,
And candles gutter by an empty altar,
And light is where the landless blood of Cain
Is burning, burning the unburied grain.   10

Mairi Macinnes

VJ DAY

This minute you're in Japan
    Lecturing the enemy
That thirty odd years ago
    Aimed at your little ship
Rocket, torpedo and bomb.   5
    Now you confer over poetry.

Tonight I seem to hear
    Lorries whine and rumble
Over the crossing in town
    In convoy from factory,   10
And then the far-off hum
    Of raiders coming to bomb.

In fact we both got off
    With the rest of our lives.
Why do I dream of blood   15
    Instead of your nightingales?
This clearing of my sight
    Makes me grope for you in bed—

The mind so denies you're there
   While I am here; or you fought,   20
I stayed at home; or war
   Brought you the fuller peace;
Or you survive by fate,
   I only because I'm a woman.

Claude McKay

AMERICA

Although she feeds me bread of bitterness,
And sinks into my throat her tiger's tooth,
Stealiing my breath of life, I will confess
I love this cultured hell that tests my youth!
Her vigor flows like tides into my blood,   5
Giving me strength against her hate.
Her bigness sweeps my being like a flood.
Yet as a rebel fronts a king in state,
I stand within her walls with not a shred
Of terror, malice, not a word of jeer.   10
Darkly I gaze into the days ahead,
And see her might and granite wonders there,
Beneath the touch of Time's unerring hand,
Like priceless treasures sinking in the sand.

Ifeanyi Menkiti

VETERANS DAY

And because somebody
fired a gun
at somebody else
at Sarajevo;
but more because   5
of a man named Darwin,

who said his daddy
was an ape,
and proved it in a book;

therefore did the nations   10
fight amongst themselves
to decide who was fittest to survive
and killed a few million people
among whom were Africans
conscripted to serve;   15

bloodied, that is, to prove a point
concerning civilization's
monkey-mongering ways.

Janice Mirikitani

PRISONS OF SILENCE

1.

The strongest prisons are built
with walls of silence.

2.

Morning light falls between us
like a wall.
We have laid beside each other   5
as we have for years.
Before the war, when life
would clamor through our windows,
we woke joyfully to the work.

I keep those moments   10
like a living silent seed.

After day's work, I would
smell the damp soil in his hands,
his hands that felt the outlines

of my body in the velvet   15
night of summers.

I hold his warm hands to this
cold wall of flesh
as I have for years.

   3.

Jap!   20
Filthy Jap!

Who lives within me?

Abandoned homes, confiscated land,
loyalty oaths, barbed wire prisons
in a strange wasteland.   25

   Go home, Jap!
   Where is home?

A country of betrayal.
No one speaks to us.

We would not speak to each other.   30

We were accused.

Hands in our hair,
hands that spread our legs
and searched our thighs for secret weapons,
hands that knit barbed wire   35
to cripple our flight.

Giant hot hands flung me,
fluttering, speechless into
barbed wire, thorns in a broken wing.

The strongest prisons are built   40
with walls of silence.

   4.

I watched him depart that day
from the tedious wall of wire,

the humps of barracks,
handsome in his uniform.   45

I would look each day for letters
from a wall of time,
waiting for approach of my deliverance
from a wall of dust.

I do not remember   50
reading about his death
only the wall of wind
that encased me, as I turned my head.

5.

U.S. Japs hailed as heroes!

I do not know the face of this country   55
it is inhabited by strangers
who call me obscene names.

Jap. Go home.
Where is home?

I am alone wandering   60
in this desert.

Where is home?
Who lives within me?

A stranger with a knife in her tongue
and broken wing,   65
mad from separations and losses cruel
as hunger.

Walls suffocate her as a tomb,
encasing history.

6.

I have kept myself contained   70
within these walls shaped to my body
and buried my rage.
I rebuilt my life
like a wall, unquestioning.
Obeyed their laws . . . their laws.   75

7.

All persons of Japanese ancestry
  filthy jap.
Both alien and non-alien
  japs are enemy aliens.
To be incarcerated   80
  for their own good
A military necessity
  The army to handle only the japs
Where is home?
A country of betrayal.   85

8.

This wall of silence crumbles
from the bigness of their crimes.
This silent wall
crushed by living memory.

He awakens from the tomb   90
I have made for myself
and unearths my rage.

I must speak.

9.

He faces me in this small
room of myself.   95
I find the windows
where light escapes.

From this cell of history
this mute grave,
we birth our rage.   100

We heal our tongues.

We listen to ourselves

  Korematsu, Hirabayashi, Yasui.

We ignite the syllables of our names.

We give testimony.   105

We hear the bigness of our sounds freed
like many clapping hands,
thundering for reparations.

We give testimony.

Our noise is dangerous.   110

10.

We beat our hands
like wings healed.

We soar
from these walls of silence.

Pablo Neruda

THE UNITED FRUIT CO.

When the trumpet sounded, it was
all prepared on the earth,
and Jehovah parceled out the earth
to Coca-Cola, Inc., Anaconda,
Ford Motors, and other entities: 5
The Fruit Company, Inc.
reserved for itself the most succulent,
the central coast of my own land,
the delicate waist of America.
It rechristened its territories   10
as the "Banana Republics"
and over the sleeping dead,
over the restless heroes
who brought about the greatness,
the liberty and the flags,   15
it established the comic opera:
abolished the independencies,
presented crowns of Caesar,

unsheathed envy, attracted
the dictatorship of the flies,   20
Trujillo flies, Tacho flies,
Carias flies, Martinez flies,
Ubico flies, damp flies
of modest blood and marmalade,
drunken flies who zoom   25
over the ordinary graves,
circus flies, wise flies
well trained in tyranny.

Among the bloodthirsty flies
the Fruit Company lands its ships,   30
taking off the coffee and the fruit;
the treasure of our submerged
territories flows as though
on plates into the ships.

Meanwhile Indians are falling   35
into the sugared chasms
of the harbors, wrapped
for burial in the mist of the dawn:
a body rolls, a thing
that has no name, a fallen cipher,   40
a cluster of dead fruit
thrown down on the dump.
                    Translated by Robert Bly

Wilfred Owen

ANTHEM FOR DOOMED YOUTH

What passing-bells for these who die as cattle?
  Only the monstrous anger of the guns.

  Only the stuttering rifles' rapid rattle
Can patter out their hasty orisons.
No mockeries now for them; no prayers nor bells,   5
  Nor any voice of mourning save the choirs,—

The shrill, demented choirs of wailing shells;
    And bugles calling for them from sad shires.

What candles may be held to speed them all?
    Not in the hands of boys, but in their eyes   10
Shall shine the holy glimmers of good-byes.
    The pallor of girls' brows shall be their pall;
Their flowers the tenderness of patient minds,
And each slow dusk a drawing-down of blinds.

QUESTIONS

1. How would you summarize the nature of the "anthem" to which the poet is referring?
2. What appears to be the poet's attitude toward war? What evidence does he provide to support your view?
3. While the poet describes responses to the doomed soldiers, he does not depict nor describe the soldiers themselves. How does this affect the mood of the poem? How does it contribute to the theme?

Wilfred Owen

DULCE ET DECORUM EST

Bent double, like old beggars under sacks,
Knock-kneed, coughing like hags, we cursed through sludge,
Till on the haunting flares we turned our backs
And towards our distant rest began to trudge.
Men marched asleep. Many had lost their boots   5
But limped on, blood-shod. All went lame; all blind;
Drunk with fatigue; deaf even to the hoots
Of tired, outstripped Five-Nines that dropped behind.

Gas! Gas! Quick, boys!—An ecstasy of fumbling,
Fitting the clumsy helmets just in time,   10
But someone still was yelling out and stumbling
And floundʼring like a man in fire or lime . . .
Dim through the misty panes and thick green light,
As under a green sea, I saw him drowning.

In all my dreams, before my helpless sight,   15
He plunges at me, guttering, choking, drowning.

If in some smothering dreams you too could pace
Behind the wagon that we flung him in,
And watch the white eyes writhing in his face,
His hanging face, like a devil's sick of sin;   20
If you could hear, at every jolt, the blood
Come gargling from the froth-corrupted lungs
Obscene as cancer, bitter as the cud
Of vile, incurable sores on innocent tongues,—
My friend, you would not tell with such high zest   25
To children ardent for some desperate glory,
The old lie: *Dulce et decorum est*
Pro patria mori.

Rahel

TO MY COUNTRY

I haven't sung your praise,
nor glorified your name
in tales of bravery
and the spoils of war.
I only plant a tree   5
on Jordan's quiet banks.
I only wear a path
over the fields.
Surely very meagre,
Mother, I know.   10
Surely very meagre,
your daughter's offering:
Only a joyous shout
on a radiant day,
only secret weeping   15
over your barrenness.

Translated from Hebrew
by Diane Mintz

Adrienne Rich

FOR THE RECORD

The clouds and the stars didn't wage this war
the brooks gave no information
if the mountain spewed stones of fire into the river
it was not taking sides
the raindrop faintly swaying under the leaf   5
had no political opinions

and if here or there a house
filled with backed-up raw sewage
or poisoned those who lived there
with slow fumes, over years   10
the houses were not at war
nor did the tinned-up buildings

intend to refuse shelter
to homeless old women and roaming children
they had no policy to keep them roaming   15
or dying, no, the cities were not the problem
the bridges were non-partisan
the freeways burned, but not with hatred

Even the miles of barbed wire
stretched around crouching temporary huts   20
designed to keep the unwanted
at a safe distance, out of sight
even the boards that had to absorb
year upon year, so many human sounds

so many depths of vomit, tears   25
slow-soaking blood
had not offered themselves for this
The trees didn't volunteer to be cut into boards
nor the thorns for tearing flesh
Look around at all of it   30

and ask whose signature
is stamped on the orders, traced
in the corner of the building plans
Ask where the illiterate, big-bellied
women were, the drunks and crazies,   35
the ones you fear most of all: ask where you were.

QUESTIONS

1. What are some of the possible meanings of the title? Upon what in the poem do you base your view?
2. How would you summarize the mood of the poem? Which imagery contributes most to the mood? How does it contribute?
3. How many questions does the poet pose? What is the effect? What answer is implied?
4. Who does the "you" refer to in the last line? Why does the poet want the reader to "ask where you were"?

Muriel Rukeyser

THE LOST ROMANS

Where are they, not those young men, not those
            young women
Who walked among the bullet-headed Romans with their
            roads, their symmetry, their iron rule—
We know the dust and bones they are gone to, those   5
            young Romans
Who stood against the bitter imperial, their young
            green life with its poems—
Where are the poems made music against the purple
Setting their own purple up for a living sign,   10
Bright fire of some forgotten future against empire,
Their poems in the beautiful Roman tongue
Sex-songs, love-poems, freedom-songs?
Not only the young, but the old and in chains,
The slaves in their singing, the fierce northern   15
            gentle blond rhythms,
The Judean cantillations, lullabies of Carthage,
Gaul with her cries, all the young Roman rebels,
Where are their songs? Who will unlock them,
Who will find them for us, in some undiscovered   20
            painted cave
For we need you, sisters, far brothers, poems
            of our lost Rome.

Percy Bysshe Shelley
OZYMANDIAS

I met a traveler from an antique land
Who said: Two vast and trunkless legs of stone
Stand in the desert . . . Near them, on the sand,
Half sunk, a shattered visage lies, whose frown,
And wrinkled lip, and sneer of cold command,   5
Tell that its sculptor well those passions read
Which yet survive, stamped on these lifeless things,
The hand that mocked them, and the heart that fed;
And on the pedestal these words appear:
"My name is Ozymandias, king of kings: 10
Look on my works, ye Mighty, and despair!"
Nothing beside remains. Round the decay
Of that colossal wreck, boundless and bare
The lone and level sands stretch far away.

Wole Soyinka
PRISONER

Grey, to the low grass cropping
Slung, wet-lichened, wisps from such
Smoke heaviness, elusive of thin blades
Curl inward to the earth, breed
The grey hours,   5

And days, and years, for do not
The wise grey temples we shall build
To febrile years, here begin—not
In tears and ashes, but on the sad mocking
Threads, compulsive of the hour?   10

In the desert wildness, when, lone cactus,
Cannibal in his love—even amidst the
Crag and gorge, the leap and night tremors
Even as the potsherd stayed and the sandstorm
Fell—intimations came.   15

In the whorled centre of the storm, a threnody
But not from this. For that far companion,
Made sudden stranger when the wind slacked
And the centre fell, grief. And the stricken
Potsherd lay, disconsolate—intimations then   20

But not from these. He knew only
Sudden seizure. And time conquest
Bound him helpless to each grey essence.
Nothing remained if pains and longings
Once, once set the walls; Sadness   25
Closed him, rootless, lacking cause.

Melvin B. Tolson

A LEGEND OF VERSAILLES

Lloyd George and Woodrow Wilson and Clemenceau—
The Big Three: England, America, and France—
Met at Versailles. The Tiger ached to know
About the myth to end war's dominance.

"One moment, gentlemen," the Tiger said,   5
"Do you really want a lasting peace?" And then
Lloyd George assented with his shaggy head
And Woodrow Wilson, nodding, chafed his chin.

"The price of such a peace is great. We must give
Up secret cartels, spheres of power and trade;   10
Tear down our tariff walls; let lesser breeds live
As equals; scrap the empires we have made."

The gentlemen protested, "You go too far."
The Tiger shouted, "You don't mean peace, but war!"

Fadwa Tuquan

AFTER TWENTY YEARS

Here the foot prints stop;
Here the moon
Lies with the wolves, the dogs, and the stones,
Behind the rocks and the tents, behind the trees.
Here the moon   5
Sells its face every night,
For a dagger, a candle, a braid of rain.
Don't throw a stone in their fire;
Don't steal the glass rings
From the gypsies' fingers.   10
They slept, and so did the fish and the stones and the trees.

Here the foot prints stop;
Here the moon was in labour.
Gypsies!
Give her then the glass rings   15
And the blue bracelets.

Translated from Arabic, translator unknown

QUESTIONS

1. How would you characterize the mood of the poem? What images contribute to the establishment of this mood?
2. The moon is described three times. How would you characterize these descriptions? What do they have in common?
3. The exact locale of the poem is not named. What sort of place is the poet describing? What type of atmosphere does it suggest? What goes on there? Who inhabits it?
4. Why has the poet separated the poem into two stanzas? What change, if any, has occurred between the first stanza and the second? What might be the significance of the moon "in labour."

Derek Walcott

NEARING LA GUAIRA

At dead of night, the sailors sprawled on deck.
The wind shakes out its blanket overhead.
All are ribbed equally; all must shipwreck.
The breakers kiss, then bitterly separate,
There is one error flesh cannot repent   5
Nor motion drown, not while one moon makes white
The tossed sea and her sheet's dishevellment.
Like men in graves, each disappointing west,
They wait in patience for the coming east;
Farewell to that, I have made my separate peace,   10
Bitter and sleepless as the ocean's curse.
A sailor in an oil-stained vest looks down
To the sea's lace, ripped by the raging wind.
"Buenas noches, amigo, qué tal?"
"Nada, amigo, nada."   15
The stars fly from his cigarette in the wind.
A broken man, with a dead wife in mind.
"Mañana estaremos en La Guaira."
I ask him what La Guaira means, he grins,
Says it means nothing.   20

So, the next morning, nothing is green water,
Sun to the left like a starfish, the moon a washed-out shell
And on rust hills, La Guaira, strict as sorrow,
And nothing is a cornet in the plaza, nothing the Morro
Where the garbage drifts, nothing   25
The bullfight roaring for six thousand tickets,
Nothing Christ's blood forgotten
In the arena of the free cathedral.
Nothing the soldiers drilling in the square,
And the green fountain with its sacrament.   30
Señor, we have joined a different detachment.

Nothing her mouth, my east and crimson west,
Nothing our restless, separated sleep;
Nothing is bitter and is very deep.

Walt Whitman

CAVALRY CROSSING
A FORD

A line in long array, where they wind betwixt green islands;
They take a serpentine course—their arms flash in the sun—Hark to the
   musical clank;
Behold the silvery river—in it the splashing horses, loitering, stop to drink;
Behold the brown-faced men—each group, each person, a picture—the   5
   negligent rest on the saddles;
Some emerge on the opposite bank—others are just entering the
   ford—while,
Scarlet, and blue, and snowy white,
The guidon flags flutter gaily in the wind.   10

Dorothy Wordsworth

HE SAID HE HAD BEEN
A SOLDIER

He said he had been a soldier,
That his wife and children
Had died in Jamaica.
He had a beggar's wallet over his shoulders,
And a coat of shreds and patches.   5
And though his body was bent,
He was tall
And had the look of one
Used to have been upright.

I talked a while, and then   10
I gave him a piece of cold bacon
And a penny.

William Butler Yeats

EASTER, 1916

I have met them at close of day
Coming with vivid faces
From counter or desk among grey
Eighteenth-century houses.
I have passed with a nod of the head   5
Or polite meaningless words,
Or have lingered awhile and said
Polite meaningless words,
And thought before I had done
Of a mocking tale or a gibe   10
To please a companion
Around the fire at the club,
Being certain that they and I
But lived where motley is worn:
All changed, changed utterly: 15
A terrible beauty is born.

That woman's days were spent
In ignorant good-will,
Her nights in argument
Until her voice grew shrill.   20
What voice more sweet than hers
When, young and beautiful,
She rode to harriers?
This man had kept a school
And rode our wingèd horse;   25
This other his helper and friend
Was coming into his force;
He might have won fame in the end,
So sensitive his nature seemed,
So daring and sweet his thought.   30
This other man I had dreamed
A drunken, vainglorious lout.
He had done most bitter wrong
To some who are near my heart,
Yet I number him in the song;   35
He, too, has resigned his part
In the casual comedy;
He, too, has been changed in his turn,

Transformed utterly:
A terrible beauty is born.   40

Hearts with one purpose alone
Through summer and winter seem
Enchanted to a stone
To trouble the living stream.
The horse that comes from the road,   45
The rider, the birds that range
From cloud to tumbling cloud,
Minute by minute they change;
A shadow of cloud on the stream
Changes minute by minute;   50
A horse-hoof slides on the brim,
And a horse plashes within it;
The long-legged moor-hens dive,
And hens to moor-cocks call;
Minute by minute they live: 55
The stone's in the midst of all.

Too long a sacrifice
Can make a stone of the heart.
O when may it suffice?
That is Heaven's part, our part   60
To murmur name upon name,
As a mother names her child
When sleep at last has come
On limbs that had run wild.
What is it but nightfall?   65
No, no, not night but death;
Was it needless death after all?
For England may keep faith
For all that is done and said.
We know their dream; enough   70
To know they dreamed and are dead;
And what if excess of love
Bewildered them till they died?
I write it out in a verse—
MacDonagh and MacBride   75
And Connolly and Pearse
Now and in time to be,
Wherever green is worn,
Are changed, changed utterly:
A terrible beauty is born.   80

QUESTIONS

1. What is the attitude of the narrator toward the people whom he depicts in the poem? Why does he have such an attitude?
2. What purpose does the repetition of the phrase "A terrible beauty is born" have in the poem? What is the meaning of the phrase?
3. The image of a stone is mentioned several times in stanza 3. What is its purpose? What might the stone represent?
4. Yeats personally knew some of the personages in this poem. Does this show in the way he refers to them? If so, why? If not, why not?

W a r & P e a c e

P o e t r y

TOPICS FOR WRITING

1. Describe the worst conflict you ever confronted, whether it involved a family member, a social group, an armed force, or a criminal. What started the conflict? How did it progress? How was it resolved or left unresolved?

2. Interview an older member in your community who was engaged in armed conflict—for example, the Vietnam War, the Korean War, World War II, or other. Devise salient questions to ask the interviewee. Then through a process of selection, organize and write an essay describing that person's experience.

3. Irony is employed in several of the poems in this section, perhaps because official discussions of war nearly always involve elements of subterfuge, hypocrisy, and propaganda. Compare the use of irony in "The Unknown Citizen" by Auden, "War is Kind" by Crane, and "next to of course god" by cummings.

4. Wilfred Owen states in his poem "Anthem for Doomed Youth" that soldiers "die as cattle," while Derek Walcott in "Nearing La Guaira" speaks of sailors who are "like men in graves." Many poems about war and conflict contain powerful imagery. Select the poem in this section whose imagery you find particularly vivid, and discuss what about the imagery causes the poem to have such a strong impact on you.

5. In general, do men and women view war differently? Select two poems that describe war from a woman's viewpoint; then select two others that describe it from a man's viewpoint. Compare and contrast the subject matter, tone, and imagery.

6. To write about matters of war and conflict accurately, one must have had first-hand experience. Argue for or against this proposition.

7. So long as there are different cultures, different countries, and different political systems, there will always be conflict. Argue for or against this proposition.

8. Both Deutsch's "Disasters of War" and Ferlinghetti's "In Goya's Greatest Scenes" make references to the visual art of the Spanish painter Francisco Goya. After studying Goya's paintings of warfare, write an essay comparing and contrasting the way each poet incorporates images of the paintings into his or her poem.

9. The Vietnam War has inspired many stories, novels, and movies, but it has also been the subject of many poems. Research the literature of the Vietnam era, select two poets who wrote about that era, and compare and contrast their perspectives.

D r a m a

Aristophanes

LYSISTRATA

Translated by Dudley Fitts

―――――――――― **PERSONS REPRESENTED** ――――――――――

LYSISTRATA,		SPARTAN HERALD
KALONIKE,	Athenian women	SPARTAN AMBASSADOR
MYRRHINE,		A SENTRY
LAMPITO, a Spartan woman		[BABY SON OF KINESIAS
CHORUS		STRATYLLIS
COMMISSIONER		SPARTANS
KINESIAS, husband of Myrrhine		ATHENIANS]

*Scene: Athens. First, a public square; later, beneath the walls of the Akropolis;°
later, a courtyard within the Akropolis.*

Akropolis: Fortress of Athens, sacred to the goddess Athena.

PROLOGUE°

Athens; a public square; early morning; Lysistrata alone.

LYSISTRATA: If someone had invited them to a festival—
    of Bacchos,° say; or to Pan's° shrine, or to Aphrodite's°
    over at Kolias—, you couldn't get through the streets,
    what with the drums and the dancing. But now,
    not a woman in sight!

                Except—oh, yes!   5

[*Enter* KALONIKE.]

    Here's one of my neighbors, at last. Good
        morning, Kalonike.
KALONIKE: Good morning, Lysistrata.
                        Darling,
    don't frown so! You'll ruin your face!
LYSISTRATA: Never mind my face.
    Kalonike,
    the way we women behave! Really, I don't blame the men   10
    for what they say about us.
KALONIKE: No; I imagine they're right.
LYSISTRATA: For example: I call a meeting
    to think out a most important matter—and what happens?
    The women all stay in bed!
KALONIKE: Oh, they'll be along.
    It's hard to get away, you know: a husband, a cook,
    a child . . . Home life can be *so* demanding!   15
LYSISTRATA: What I have in mind is even more demanding.
KALONIKE: Tell me: what is it?
LYSISTRATA: It's big.
KALONIKE: Goodness! *How* big?
LYSISTRATA: Big enough for all of us.
KALONIKE: But we're not all here!
LYSISTRATA: We would be, if *that's* what was up!
                    No, Kalonike,   20
    this is something I've been turning over for nights,
    long sleepless nights.
KALONIKE: It must be getting worn down, then,
    if you've spent so much time on it.

Prologue: Portion of the play explaining the background and current action.   **Bacchos:** (Bacchus) God of wine and the object of wild, orgiastic ritual and celebration; also called Dionysus.   **Pan:** God of nature, forests, flocks, and shepherds, depicted as half-man and half-goat. Pan was considered playful and lecherous. **Aphrodite:** Goddess of love.

LYSISTRATA: Worn down or not,
  it comes to this: Only we women can save Greece!
KALONIKE: Only we women? Poor Greece!
LYSISTRATA: Just the same,   25
  it's up to us. First, we must liquidate
  the Peloponnesians—
KALONIKE: Fun, fun!
LYSISTRATA: —and then the Boiotians.°
KALONIKE: Oh! But not those heavenly eels!
LYSISTRATA: You needn't worry.
  I'm not talking about eels.—But here's the point:
  If we can get the women from those places—   30
  all those Boiotians and Peloponnesians—
  to join us women here, why, we can save
  all Greece!
KALONIKE: But dearest Lysistrata!
  How can women do a thing so austere, so
  political? We belong at home. Our only armor's   35
  our perfumes, our saffron dresses and
  our pretty little shoes!
LYSISTRATA: Exactly. Those
  transparent dresses, the saffron, the
    perfume, those pretty shoes—
KALONIKE: Oh?
LYSISTRATA: Not a single man would lift
  his spear—
KALONIKE: I'll send my dress to the dyer's tomorrow!   40
LYSISTRATA: —or grab a shield—
KALONIKE: The sweetest little negligee—
LYSISTRATA: —or haul out his sword.
KALONIKE: I know where
    I can buy the dreamiest sandals!
LYSISTRATA: Well, so you see. Now, shouldn't
  the women have come?
KALONIKE: Come? They should have *flown!*
LYSISTRATA: Athenians are always late.
                      But imagine!   45
  There's no one here from the South Shore, or from Salamis.
KALONIKE: Things are hard over in Salamis, I swear.
  They have to get going at dawn.
LYSISTRATA: And nobody from Acharnai.
  I thought they'd be here hours ago.

Boiotians: Crude-mannered inhabitants of Boiotia, which was noted for its seafood.

KALONIKE: Well, you'll get
that awful Theagenes woman: she'll be   50
a sheet or so in the wind.
                    But look!
Someone at last! Can you see who they are?

[*Enter* MYRRHINE *and other women.*]

LYSISTRATA: They're from Anagyros.
KALONIKE: They certainly are.
You'd know them anywhere, by the scent.
MYRRHINE: Sorry to be late, Lysistrata.
                    Oh come,   55
don't scowl so. Say something!
LYSISTRATA: My dear Myrrhine,
what is there to say? After all,
you've been pretty casual about the whole thing.
MYRRHINE: Couldn't find
my girdle in the dark, that's all.
                    But what *is*
"the whole thing"?
KALONIKE: No, we've got to wait   60
for those Boiotians and Peloponnesians.
LYSISTRATA: That's more like it.—But, look!
Here's Lampito!

[*Enter* LAMPITO *with women from Sparta.*]

LYSISTRATA: Darling Lampito,
how pretty you are today! What a nice color!
Goodness, you look as though you could strangle a bull!   65
LAMPITO: Ah think Ah could! It's the work-out
in the gym every day; and, of co'se that dance of ahs
where y' kick yo' own tail.
KALONIKE: What an adorable figure!
LAMPITO: Lawdy, when y' touch me lahk that,
Ah feel lahk a heifer at the altar!
LYSISTRATA: And this young lady?   70
Where is she from?
LAMPITO: Boiotia. Social-Register type.
LYSISTRATA: Ah. "Boiotia of the fertile plain."
KALONIKE: And if you look,
you'll find the fertile plain has just been mowed.
LYSISTRATA: And this lady?

LAMPITO: Hagh, wahd, handsome.
　　She comes from Korinth.
KALONIKE: High and wide's the word for it.
LAMPITO: Which one of you   75
　　called this heah meeting, and why?
LYSISTRATA: I did.
LAMPITO: Well, then, tell us:
　　What's up?
MYRRHINE: Yes, darling, what *is* on your mind, after all?
LYSISTRATA: I'll tell you.—But first, one little question.
MYRRHINE: Well?
LYSISTRATA: It's your husbands. Fathers of your children. Doesn't it
　　bother you
　　that they're always off with the Army? I'll stake my life,   80
　　not one of you has a man in the house this minute!
KALONIKE: Mine's been in Thrace the last five months, keeping an eye
　　on that General.
MYRRHINE: Mine's been in Pylos for seven.
LAMPITO: And mahn,
　　whenever he gets a *dis*charge, he goes raht back
　　with that li'l ole shield of his, and enlists again!   85
LYSISTRATA: And not the ghost of a lover to be found!
　　From the very day the war began—
　　　　　　　　　　　　those Milesians!
　　I could skin them alive!
　　　　　　　　—I've not seen so much, even,
　　as one of those leather consolation prizes.—
　　But there! What's important is: If I've found a way   90
　　to end the war, are you with me?
MYRRHINE: I should *say* so!
　　Even if I have to pawn my best dress and
　　drink up the proceeds.
KALONIKE: Me, too! Even if they split me
　　right up the middle, like a flounder.
LAMPITO: Ah'm shorely with you.
　　Ah'd crawl up Taygetos° on mah knees   95
　　if that'd bring peace.
LYSISTRATA: All right, then; here it is:
　　Women! Sisters!
　　If we really want our men to make peace,
　　we must be ready to give up—
MYRRHINE: Give up what?
　　Quick, tell us!

Taygetos: A mountain range.

LYSISTRATA: But *will* you?
MYRRHINE: We will, even if it kills us.   100
LYSISTRATA: Then we must give up going to bed with our men.

[*Long silence.*]

Oh? So now you're sorry? Won't look at me?
Doubtful? Pale? All teary-eyed?
                      But come: be frank with me.
Will you do it, or not? Well? Will you do it?
MYRRHINE: I couldn't. No.
Let the war go on.
KALONIKE: Nor I. Let the war go on.   105
LYSISTRATA: You, you little flounder,
ready to be split up the middle?
KALONIKE: Lysistrata, no!
I'd walk through fire for you—you *know* I would!—but don't
ask us to give up *that!* Why, there's nothing like it!
LYSISTRATA: And you?
BOIOTIAN: No. I must say *I'd* rather walk through fire.   110
LYSISTRATA: What an utterly perverted sex we women are!
No wonder poets write tragedies about us.
There's only one thing we can think of.
                            But you from Sparta:
if you stand by me, we may win yet! Will you?
It means so much!
LAMPITO: Ah sweah, it means *too* much!   115
By the Two Goddesses,° it does! Asking a girl
to sleep—Heaven knows how long!—in a great big bed
with nobody there but herself! But Ah'll stay with you!
Peace comes first!
LYSISTRATA: Spoken like a true Spartan!
KALONIKE: But if—
              oh dear!
              —if we give up what you tell us to,   120
will there *be* any peace?
LYSISTRATA: Why, mercy, of course there will!
We'll just sit snug in our very thinnest gowns,
perfumed and powdered from top to bottom, and those men
simply won't stand still! And when we say No,

Two Goddesses: A woman's oath referring to Demeter, the earth goddess, and her daughter Persephone,
who was associated with seasonal cycles of fertility.

they'll go out of their minds! And there's your peace.   125
  You can take my word for it.
LAMPITO: Ah seem to remember
  that Colonel Menelaos threw his sword away
  when he saw Helen's breast all bare.°
KALONIKE: But, goodness me!
  What if they just get up and leave us?
LYSISTRATA: In that case
  we'll have to fall back on ourselves, I suppose.   130
  But they won't.
KALONIKE: I must say that's not much help. But
  what if they drag us into the bedroom?
LYSISTRATA: Hang on to the door.
KALONIKE: What if they slap us?
LYSISTRATA: If they do, you'd better give in.
  But be sulky about it. Do I have to teach you how?
  You know there's no fun for men when they have to force you.   135
  There are millions of ways of getting them to see reason.
  Don't you worry: a man
  doesn't like it unless the girl cooperates.
KALONIKE: I suppose so. Oh, all right. We'll go along.
LAMPITO: Ah imagine us Spahtans can arrange a peace. But you   140
  Athenians! Why, you're just war-mongerers!
LYSISTRATA: Leave that to me.
  I know how to make them listen.
LAMPITO: Ah don't see how.
  After all, they've got their boats; and there's lots of money
  piled up in the Akropolis.
LYSISTRATA: The Akropolis? Darling,
  we're taking over the Akropolis today!   145
  That's the older women's job. All the rest of us
  are going to the Citadel to sacrifice—you understand me?
  And once there, we're in for good!
LAMPITO: Whee! Up the rebels!
  Ah can see you're a good strat*eeg*ist.
LYSISTRATA: Well, then, Lampito,
  what we have to do now is take a solemn oath.   150
LAMPITO: Say it. We'll sweah.
LYSISTRATA: This is it.
  —But where's our Inner Guard?

Colonel Menelaos . . . Helen's breast: Helen, wife of King Menelaos of Sparta, was abducted by Paris and taken to Troy. The incident led to the Trojan War.

—Look, Guard: you see this shield?
Put it down here. Now bring me the victim's entrails.
KALONIKE: But the oath?
LYSISTRATA: You remember how in Aischylos' *Seven*°
they killed a sheep and swore on a shield? Well, then?   155
KALONIKE: But I don't see how you can swear for peace on a shield.
LYSISTRATA: What else do you suggest?
KALONIKE: Why not a white horse?
We could swear by that.
LYSISTRATA: And where will you get a white horse?
KALONIKE: I never thought of that. *What* can we do?
LYSISTRATA: I have it!
Let's set this big black wine-bowl on the ground   160
and pour in a gallon or so of Thasian,° and swear
not to add one drop of water.
LAMPITO: Ah lahk *that* oath!
LYSISTRATA: Bring the bowl and the wine-jug.
KALONIKE: Oh, what a simply *huge* one!
LYSISTRATA: Set it down. Girls, place your hands on the gift-offering.
O Goddess of Persuasion! And thou, O Loving-cup: 165
Look upon this our sacrifice, and
be gracious!
KALONIKE: See the blood spill out. How red and pretty it is!
LAMPITO: And Ah must say it smells good.
MYRRHINE: Let me swear first!
KALONIKE: No, by Aphrodite, we'll match for it!   170
LYSISTRATA: Lampito: all of you women: come, touch the bowl,
and repeat after me—remember, this is an oath—:
I WILL HAVE NOTHING TO DO WITH MY HUSBAND OR MY
    LOVER
KALONIKE: *I will have nothing to do with my husband or my lover*
LYSISTRATA: THOUGH HE COME TO ME IN PITIABLE CONDITION 175
KALONIKE: *Though he come to me in pitiable condition*
(Oh Lysistrata! This is killing me!)
LYSISTRATA: IN MY HOUSE I WILL BE UNTOUCHABLE
KALONIKE: *In my house I will be untouchable*
LYSISTRATA: IN MY THINNEST SAFFRON SILK   180
KALONIKE: *In my thinnest saffron silk*
LYSISTRATA: AND MAKE HIM LONG FOR ME.
KALONIKE: *And make him long for me.*
LYSISTRATA: I WILL NOT GIVE MYSELF
KALONIKE: *I will not give myself*   185

Seven: Aeschylus's *Seven Against Thebes,* which deals with the war between the sons of Oedipus for the throne of Thebes.   **Thasian:** Wine from Thasos.

LYSISTRATA: AND IF HE CONSTRAINS ME

KALONIKE: *And if he constrains me*

LYSISTRATA: I WILL BE COLD AS ICE AND NEVER MOVE

KALONIKE: *I will be cold as ice and never move*

LYSISTRATA: I WILL NOT LIFT MY SLIPPERS TOWARD THE
CEILING   190

KALONIKE: *I will not lift my slippers toward the ceiling*

LYSISTRATA: OR CROUCH ON ALL FOURS LIKE THE LIONESS IN
THE CARVING

KALONIKE: *Or crouch on all fours like the lioness in the carving*

LYSISTRATA: AND IF I KEEP THIS OATH LET ME DRINK FROM
THIS BOWL

KALONIKE: *And if I keep this oath let me drink from this bowl*   195

LYSISTRATA: IF NOT, LET MY OWN BOWL BE FILLED WITH
WATER.

KALONIKE: *If not, let my own bowl be filled with water.*

LYSISTRATA: You have all sworn?

MYRRHINE: We have.

LYSISTRATA: Then thus
I sacrifice the victim.

[*Drinks largely.*]

KALONIKE: Save some for us!
Here's to you, darling, and to you, and to you!   200

[*Loud cries offstage.*]

LAMPITO: What's all *that* whoozy-goozy?

LYSISTRATA: Just what I told you.
The older women have taken the Akropolis.
Now you, Lampito,
rush back to Sparta. We'll take care of things here. Leave
these girls here for hostages.
                              The rest of you,   205
up to the Citadel: and mind you push in the bolts.

KALONIKE: But the men? Won't they be after us?

LYSISTRATA: Just you leave
the men to me. There's not fire enough in the world,
or threats either, to make me open these doors
except on my own terms.

KALONIKE: I hope not, by Aphrodite!   210
After all,
we've got a reputation for bitchiness to live up to.   [*Exeunt.°*]

Exeunt: Latin for "they go out."

PARODOS:°
CHORAL EPISODE

The hillside just under the Akropolis. Enter Chorus of Old Men with burning torches and braziers; much puffing and coughing.

KORYPHAIOS ^(man):° Forward march, Drakes, old friend: never you mind
　　that damn big log banging hell down on your back.

Strophe° 1

CHORUS ^(men): There's this to be said for longevity:
　　You see things you thought that you'd never see.
　　　　Look, Strymodoros, who would have thought it?　　　　　　　　5
　　　　We've caught it—
　　　　　　　　　　the New Femininity!
　　The wives of our bosom, our board, our bed—
　　Now, by the gods, they've gone ahead
　　And taken the Citadel (Heaven knows why!),
　　Profanèd the sacred statuar-y,　　　　　　　　　　　　　　　　10
　　　　　　　　　　And barred the doors,
　　　　　　　　　　The subversive whores!
KORYPHAIOS ^(m): Shake a leg there, Philurgos, man: The Akropolis or bust!
　　Put the kindling around here. We'll build one almighty big
　　bonfire for the whole bunch of bitches, every last one;　　　　　　15
　　and the first we fry will be old Lykon's woman.

Antistrophe° 1

CHORUS ^(m): They're not going to give me the old horse-laugh!
　　No, by Demeter, they won't pull this off!
　　　　Think of Kleomenes: even he
　　　　Didn't go free
　　　　　　　　　　till he brought me his stuff.　　　　　　　　　　20
　　A good man he was, all stinking and shaggy,
　　Bare as an eel except for the bag he
　　Covered his rear with. God, what a mess!
　　Never a bath in six years, I'd guess.
　　　　　　　　　　Pure Sparta, man!　　　　　　　　　　　　　25
　　　　　　　　　　He also ran.

Parodos: The song or ode chanted by the Chorus on their entry.　**Koryphaios:** Leader of the Chorus; also called *Choragos*. There are two Choruses and two Koryphaioi, one male and one female.　**Strophe:** Song sung by the Chorus as they danced from stage right to stage left.　**Antistrophe:** Song sung by the Chorus following the Strophe, as they danced back from stage left to stage right.

KORYPHAIOS^(m): That was a siege, friends! Seventeen ranks strong
   we slept at the Gate. And shall we not do as much
   against these women, whom God and Euripides hate?
   If we don't, I'll turn in my medals from Marathon.   30

Strophe 2

CHORUS^(m): Onward and upward! A little push,
    And we're there.
  Ouch, my shoulders! I could wish
    For a pair
  Of good strong oxen. Keep your eye   35
    On the fire there, it mustn't die.
            Akh! Akh!
  The smoke would make a cadaver cough!

Antistrophe 2

  Holy Herakles, a hot spark
    Bit my eye!   40
  Damn this hellfire, damn this work!
    So say I.
  Onward and upward just the same.
  (Laches, remember the Goddess: for shame!)
            Akh! Akh!   45
  The smoke would make a cadaver cough!
KORYPHAIOS^(m): At last (and let us give suitable thanks to God
   for his infinite mercies) I have managed to bring
  my personal flame to the common goal. It breathes, it lives.
  Now, gentlemen, let us consider. Shall we insert   50
  the torch, say, into the brazier, and thus extract
  a kindling brand? And shall we then, do you think,
  push on to the gate like valiant sheep? On the whole yes.
  But I would have you consider this, too: if they—
  I refer to the women—should refuse to open,   55
  what then? Do we set the doors afire
  and smoke them out? At ease, men. Meditate.
  Akh, the smoke! Woof! What we really need
  is the loan of a general or two from the Samos Command.°
  At least we've got this lumber off our backs.   60
  That's something. And now let's look to our fire.

Samos Command: Headquarters of the Athenian military.

O Pot, brave Brazier, touch my torch with flame!
Victory, Goddess, I invoke thy name!
Strike down these paradigms of female pride,
And we shall hang our trophies up inside.   65

[*Enter* CHORUS OF OLD WOMEN *on the walls of the Akropolis, carrying jars of water.*]

KORYPHAIOS (woman): Smoke, girls, smoke! There's smoke all over the place!
   Probably fire, too. Hurry, girls! Fire! Fire!

Strophe 1

CHORUS (women): Nikodike, run!
   Or Kalyke's done
   To a turn, and poor Kritylla's   70
   Smoked like a ham.
               Damn
   These old men! Are we too late?
   I nearly died down at the place
   Where we fill our jars:
      Slaves pushing and jostling—   75
      Such a hustling
   I never saw in all my days.

Antistrophe 1

   But here's water at last.
   Haste, sisters, haste!
   Slosh it on them, slosh it down,   80
   the silly old wrecks!
               Sex
   Almighty! What they want's
   A hot bath? Good. Send one down.
   Athena of Athens town,
      Trito-born!° Helm of Gold!   85
      Cripple the old
   Firemen! Help us help them drown!

[*The old men capture a woman,* STRATYLLIS.]

STRATYLLIS: Let me go! Let me go!
KORYPHAIOS (w):   You walking corpses,
   have you no shame?

Trito-born: Athena, goddess of wisdom, was said to have been born near Lake Tritonis, in Libya.

KORYPHAIOS ^(m):   I wouldn't have believed it!
An army of women in the Akropolis!   90
KORYPHAIOS ^(w): So we scare you, do we? Grandpa, you've seen
only our pickets yet!
KORYPHAIOS ^(m):   Hey, Phaidrias!
Help me with the necks of these jabbering hens!
KORYPHAIOS ^(w): Down with your pots, girls! We'll need both hands
if these antiques attack us!
KORYPHAIOS ^(m):   Want your face kicked in?   95
KORYPHAIOS ^(w): Want your balls chewed off?
KORYPHAIOS ^(m):   Look out! I've got a stick!
KORYPHAIOS ^(w): You lay a half-inch of your stick on Stratyllis,
and you'll never stick again!
KORYPHAIOS ^(m): Fall apart!
KORYPHAIOS ^(w):   I'll spit up your guts!
KORYPHAIOS ^(m):   Euripides! Master!
How well you knew women!
KORYPHAIOS ^(w):   Listen to him, Rhodippe,   100
up with the pots!
KORYPHAIOS ^(m):   Demolition of God,
what good are your pots?
KORYPHAIOS ^(w):   You refugee from the tomb,
what good is your fire?
KORYPHAIOS ^(m):   Good enough to make a pyre
to barbecue you!
KORYPHAIOS ^(w): We'll squizzle your kindling!
KORYPHAIOS ^(m): You think so?
KORYPHAIOS ^(w):   Yah! Just hang around a while!   105
KORYPHAIOS ^(m): Want a touch of my torch?
KORYPHAIOS ^(w):.   It needs a good soaping.
KORYPHAIOS ^(m): How about you?
KORYPHAIOS ^(w):   Soap for a senile bridegroom!
KORYPHAIOS ^(m): Senile? Hold your trap
KORYPHAIOS ^(w):   Just *you* try to hold it!
KORYPHAIOS ^(m): The yammer of women!
KORYPHAIOS ^(w):   Oh is that so?
You're not in the jury room now, you know.   110
KORYPHAIOS ^(m): Gentlemen, I beg you, burn off that woman's hair!
KORYPHAIOS ^(w): Let it come down!

[*They empty their pots on the men.*]

KORYPHAIOS ^(m): What a way to drown!
KORYPHAIOS ^(w):   Hot, hey?

KORYPHAIOS^(m):　　　　　　　　　　　　　　　Say,
enough!
KORYPHAIOS^(w): Dandruff
needs watering. I'll make you　　　　　　　　　　　　　　　　115
nice and fresh.
KORYPHAIOS^(m):　For God's sake, you,
hold off!

SCENE 1

[*Enter a Commissioner accompanied by four constables.*]

COMMISSIONER: These degenerate women! What a racket of little drums,
　　what a yapping for Adonis° on every house-top!
　　It's like the time in the Assembly when I was listening
　　to a speech—out of order, as usual—by that fool
　　Demostratos,° all about troops for Sicily,°　　　　　　　　　　5
　　that kind of nonsense—
　　　　　　　　　　　and there was his wife
　　trotting around in circles howling
　　Alas for Adonis!—
　　　　　　　　　　and Demostratos insisting
　　we must draft every last Zakynthian that can walk—
　　and his wife up there on the roof,　　　　　　　　　　　　　　10
　　drunk as an owl, yowling
　　Oh weep for Adonis!—
　　　　　　　　　　and that damned ox Demostratos
　　mooing away through the rumpus. That's what we get
　　for putting up with this wretched woman-business!
KORYPHAIOS^(m): Sir, you haven't heard the half of it. They laughed at us!　　15
　　Insulted us! They took pitchers of water
　　and nearly drowned us! We're still wringing out our clothes,
　　for all the world like unhousebroken brats.
COMMISSIONER: Serves you right, by Poseidon!
　　Whose fault is it if these women-folk of ours　　　　　　　　　20
　　get out of hand? We coddle them,
　　we teach them to be wasteful and loose. You'll see a husband
　　go into a jeweler's. "Look," he'll say,
　　"jeweler," he'll say, "you remember that gold choker
　　you made for my wife? Well, she went to a dance last night　　　25
　　and broke the clasp. Now, I've got to go to Salamis,
　　and can't be bothered. Run over to my house tonight,
　　will you, and see if you can put it together for her."

Adonis: Fertility god, loved by Aphrodite. **Demostratos:** Athenian orator and politician. **Sicily:** Reference to the Sicilian Expedition (415–413 B.C.) in which Athens was decisively defeated.

Or another one
goes to a cobbler—a good strong workman, too,   30
with an awl that was never meant for child's play. "Here,"
he'll tell him, "one of my wife's shoes is pinching
her little toe. Could you come up about noon
and stretch it out for her?"
                          Well, what do you expect?
Look at me, for example, I'm a Public Officer,   35
and it's one of my duties to pay off the sailors.
And where's the money? Up there in the Akropolis!
And those blasted women slam the door in my face!
But what are we waiting for?
                          —Look here, constable,
stop sniffing around for a tavern, and get us   40
some crowbars. We'll force their gates! As a matter of fact,
I'll do a little forcing myself.

[*Enter* LYSISTRATA, *above, with* MYRRHINE, KALONIKE, *and the* BOIOTIAN.]

LYSISTRATA: No need of forcing.
Here I am, of my own accord. And all this talk
about locked doors—! We don't need locked doors,
but just the least bit of common sense.   45
COMMISSIONER: Is that so, ma'am!
                          —Where's my constable?
                          —Constable,
arrest that woman, and tie her hands behind her.
LYSISTRATA: If he touches me, I swear by Artemis
there'll be one scamp dropped from the public pay-roll tomorrow!
COMMISSIONER: Well, constable? You're not afraid, I suppose? Grab her,   50
two of you, around the middle!
KALONIKE: No, by Pandrosos!°
Lay a hand on her, and I'll jump on you so hard
your guts will come out the back door!
COMMISSIONER: That's what *you* think!
Where's the sergeant?—Here, you: tie up that trollop first,
the one with the pretty talk!
MYRRHINE: By the Moon-Goddess,°   55
just try! They'll have to scoop you up with a spoon!
COMMISSIONER: Another one!
                          Officer, seize that woman!
                          I swear
I'll put an end to this riot!

Pandrosos: A woman's oath referring to one of the daughters of the founder of Athens.   **Moon-Goddess:**
Artemis, goddess of the hunt and of fertility, daughter of Zeus.

BOIOTIAN: By the Taurian,°
   one inch closer, you'll be one screaming bald-head!
COMMISSIONER: Lord, what a mess! And my constables seem ineffective.   60
   But—women get the best of us? By God, no!
                       —Skythians!°
   Close ranks and forward march!
LYSISTRATA: "Forward," indeed!
   By the Two Goddesses, what's the sense in *that?*
   They're up against four companies of women
   armed from top to bottom.
COMMISSIONER: Forward, my Skythians!   65
LYSISTRATA: Forward, yourselves, dear comrades!
   You grainlettucebeanseedmarket girls!
   You garlicandonionbreadbakery girls!
   Give it to 'em! Knock 'em down! Scratch 'em!
   Tell 'em what you think of 'em!

[*General melee, the* SKYTHIANS *yield.*]

                    —Ah, that's enough!   70
   Sound a retreat: good soldiers don't rob the dead.
COMMISSIONER: A nice day *this* has been for the police!
LYSISTRATA: Well, there you are.—Did you really think we women
   would be driven like slaves? Maybe now you'll admit
   that a woman knows something about spirit.
COMMISSIONER: Spirit enough,   75
   especially spirits in bottles! Dear Lord Apollo!
KORYPHAIOS (m): Your Honor, there's no use talking to them. Words
   mean nothing whatever to wild animals like these.
   Think of the sousing they gave us! and the water
   was not, I believe, of the purest.   80
KORYPHAIOS (w): You shouldn't have come after us. And if you try it again,
   you'll be one eye short!—Although, as a matter of fact,
   what I like best is just to stay at home and read,
   like a sweet little bride: never hurting a soul, no,
   never going out. But if you *must* shake hornets' nests,   85
   look out for the hornets.

Strophe 1

CHORUS (m): Of all the beasts that God hath wrought
    What monster's worse than woman?

Taurian: Reference to Artemis, who was said to have been worshiped in a cult at Taurica Chersonesos.
Skythians: Athenian archers.

Who shall encompass with his thought
   Their guile unending? No man. 90

They've seized the Heights, the Rock, the Shrine—
   But to what end? I wot not.
Sure there's some clue to their design!
   Have you the key? I thought not.
KORYPHAIOS^(m): We might question them, I suppose. But I warn you, sir, 95
don't believe anything you hear! It would be un-Athenian
not to get to the bottom of this plot.
COMMISSIONER: Very well.
My first question is this: Why, so help you God,
did you bar the gates of the Akropolis?
LYSISTRATA: Why?
   To keep the money, of course. No money, no war. 100
COMMISSIONER: You think that money's the cause of war?
LYSISTRATA: I do.
   Money brought about that Peisandros° business
and all the other attacks on the State. Well and good!
   They'll not get another cent here!
COMMISSIONER: And what will you do?
LYSISTRATA: What a question! From now on, we intend 105
to control the Treasury.
COMMISSIONER: Control the Treasury!
LYSISTRATA: Why not? Does that seem strange? After all,
we control our household budgets.
COMMISSIONER: But that's different!
LYSISTRATA: "Different"? What do you mean?
COMMISSIONER: I mean simply this:
it's the Treasury that pays for National Defense. 110
LYSISTRATA: Unnecessary. We propose to abolish war.
COMMISSIONER: Good God.—And National Security?
LYSISTRATA: Leave that to us.
COMMISSIONER: You?
LYSISTRATA: Us.
COMMISSIONER: We're done for, then!
LYSISTRATA: Never mind.
We women will save you in spite of yourselves.
COMMISSIONER: What nonsense!
LYSISTRATA: If you like. But you must accept it, like it or not. 115
COMMISSIONER: Why, this is downright subversion!
LYSISTRATA: Maybe it is.
But we're going to save you, Judge.

Peisandros: A politician who plotted against the Athenian democracy.

COMMISSIONER: I don't *want* to be saved.
LYSISTRATA: Tut. The death-wish. All the more reason.
COMMISSIONER: But the idea of women bothering
          themselves about peace and war!
LYSISTRATA: Will you listen to me?
COMMISSIONER: Yes. But be brief, or I'll——   120
LYSISTRATA: This is no time for stupid threats.
COMMISSIONER: By the gods,
     I can't stand any more!
AN OLD WOMAN: Can't stand? Well, well.
COMMISSIONER: That's enough out of you, you old buzzard!
     Now, Lysistrata: tell me what you're thinking.
LYSISTRATA: Glad to.
                    Ever since this war began   125
     We women have been watching you men, agreeing with you,
     keeping our thoughts to ourselves. That doesn't mean
     we were happy: we weren't, for we saw how things were going;
     but we'd listen to you at dinner
     arguing this way and that.
                         —Oh you, and your big   130
     Top Secrets!—
               And then we'd grin like little patriots
     (though goodness knows we didn't feel like grinning) and ask you:
     "Dear, did the Armistice come up in Assembly today?"
     And you'd say, "None of your business! Pipe down!" you'd say.
     And so we would.
AN OLD WOMAN: *I* wouldn't have, by God!   135
COMMISSIONER: You'd have taken a beating, then!
                         —Go on.
LYSISTRATA: Well, we'd be quiet. But then, you know, all at once
     you men would think up something worse than ever.
     Even *I* could see it was fatal. And, "Darling," I'd say,
     "have you gone completely mad?" And my husband would look at me   140
     and say, "Wife, you've got your weaving to attend to.
     Mind your tongue, if you don't want a slap. 'War's
     a man's affair!' "°
COMMISSIONER: Good words, and well pronounced.
LYSISTRATA: You're a fool if you think so.
                         It was hard enough
     to put up with all this banquet-hall strategy.   145
     But then we'd hear you out in the public square:
     "Nobody left for the draft-quota here in Athens?"
     you'd say; and, "No," someone else would say, "not a man!"

'War's a man's affair!': Quoted from Homer's *Iliad*, VI, 492, Hector's farewell to his wife, Andromache.

And so we women decided to rescue Greece.
  You might as well listen to us now: you'll have to, later. 150
COMMISSIONER: *You* rescue Greece? Absurd.
LYSISTRATA: You're the absurd one.
COMMISSIONER: You expect me to take orders from a woman?
    I'd die first!
LYSISTRATA: Heavens, if that's what's bothering you, take my veil,
  here, and wrap it around your poor head.
KALONIKE: Yes,
  and you can have my market-basket, too. 155
  Go home, tighten your girdle, do the washing, mind
  your beans! "War's a woman's affair!"
KORYPHAIOS (w): Ground pitchers! Close ranks!

Antistrophe

CHORUS (w): This is a dance that I know well,
  My knees shall never yield. 160
  Wobble and creak I may, but still
  I'll keep the well-fought field.
  Valor and grace march on before,
    Love prods us from behind.
  Our slogan is EXCELSIOR, 165
    Our watchword SAVE MANKIND.
KORYPHAIOS (w): Women, remember your grandmothers! Remember
  that little old mother of yours, what a stinger she was!
  On, on, never slacken. There's a strong wind astern!
LYSISTRATA: O Eros of delight! O Aphrodite! Kyprian!° 170
  If ever desire has drenched our breasts or dreamed
  in our thighs, let it work so now on the men of Hellas°
  that they shall tail us through the land, slaves, slaves
  to Woman, Breaker of Armies!
COMMISSIONER: And if we do?
LYSISTRATA: Well, for one thing, we shan't have to watch you 175
  going to market, a spear in one hand, and heaven knows
  what in the other.
KALONIKE: Nicely said, by Aphrodite!
LYSISTRATA: As things stand now, you're neither men nor women.
  Armor clanking with kitchen pans and pots—
  You sound like a pack of Korybantes!° 180
COMMISSIONER: A man must do what a man must do.

Kyprian: Reference to Aphrodite's association with Cyprus (Kyprus), a place sacred to her and a center for her worship. **Hellas:** Greece. **Korybantes:** Priestesses of Cybele, a fertility goddess, who was celebrated in frenzied rituals accompanied by the beating of cymbals.

LYSISTRATA: So I'm told.
  But to see a General, complete with Gorgon-shield,
  jingling along the dock to buy a couple of herrings!
KALONIKE: *I* saw a Captain the other day—lovely fellow he was,
  nice curly hair—sitting on his horse; and—can you believe it?— 185
  he'd just bought some soup, and was pouring it into his helmet!
  And there was a soldier from Thrace
  swishing his lance like something out of Euripides,
  and the poor fruit-store woman got so scared
  that she ran away and let him have his figs free! 190
COMMISSIONER: All this is beside the point.
                          Will you be so kind
  as to tell me how you mean to save Greece?
LYSISTRATA: Of course.
  Nothing could be simpler.
COMMISSIONER: I assure you, I'm all ears.
LYSISTRATA: Do you know anything about weaving?
  Say the yarn gets tangled: we thread it 195
  this way and that through the skein, up and down,
  until it's free. And it's like that with war.
  We'll send our envoys
  up and down, this way and that, all over Greece,
  until it's finished.
COMMISSIONER: Yarn? Thread? Skein? 200
  Are you out of your mind? I tell you,
  war is a serious business.
LYSISTRATA: So serious
  that I'd like to go on talking about weaving.
COMMISSIONER: All right. Go ahead.
LYSISTRATA: The first thing we have to do
  is to wash our yarn, get the dirt out of it. 205
  You see? Isn't there too much dirt here in Athens?
  You must wash those men away.
                          Then our spoiled wool—
  that's like your job-hunters, out for a life
  of no work and big pay. Back to the basket,
  citizens or not, allies or not, 210
  or friendly immigrants.
                          And your colonies?
  Hanks of wool lost in various places. Pull them
  together, weave them into one great whole,
  and our voters are clothed for ever.
COMMISSIONER: It would take a woman
  to reduce state questions to a matter of carding and weaving. 215

LYSISTRATA: You fool! Who were the mothers whose sons sailed off
   to fight for Athens in Sicily?
COMMISSIONER: Enough!
   I beg you, do not call back those memories.
LYSISTRATA: And then,
   instead of the love that every woman needs,
   we have only our single beds, where we can dream   220
   of our husbands off with the Army.
                   Bad enough for wives!
   But what about our girls, getting older every day,
   and older, and no kisses?
COMMISSIONER: Men get older, too.
LYSISTRATA: Not in the same sense.
               A soldier's discharged,
   and he may be bald and toothless, yet he'll find   225
   a pretty young thing to go to bed with.
                  But a woman!
   Her beauty is gone with the first gray hair.
   She can spend her time
   consulting the oracles and the fortune-tellers,
   but they'll never send her a husband.   230
COMMISSIONER: Still, if a man can rise to the occasion—
LYSISTRATA: Rise? Rise, yourself!

[Furiously]

Go invest in a coffin!
               You've money enough.
                  I'll bake you
   a cake for the Underworld.
               And here's your funeral
   wreath!

[She pours water upon him.]

MYRRHINE: And here's another!

[More water.]

KALONIKE: And here's   235
   my contribution!

[More water.]

LYSISTRATA: What are you waiting for?
   All aboard Styx Ferry!
                              Charon's° calling for you!
   It's sailing-time: don't disrupt the schedule!
COMMISSIONER: The insolence of women! And to me!
   No, by God, I'll go back to town and show   240
   the rest of the Commission what might happen
         to them.   [*Exit* COMMISSIONER.]
LYSISTRATA: Really, I suppose we should have laid out his corpse
   on the doorstep, in the usual way.
                         But never mind.
   We'll give him the rites of the dead tomorrow morning.
         [*Exit* LYSISTRATA *with* MYRRHINE *and* KALONIKE.]

PARABASIS:° CHORAL EPISODE

Ode° 1

KORYPHAIOS (m): Sons of Liberty, awake! The day of glory is at hand.
CHORUS (m): I smell tyranny afoot, I smell it rising from the land.
   I scent a trace of Hippias,° I sniff upon the breeze
   A dismal Spartan hogo that suggests King Kleisthenes.°
      Strip, strip for action, brothers!   5
      Our wives, aunts, sisters, mothers
   Have sold us out: the streets are full of godless female rages.
   Shall we stand by and let our women confiscate our wages?
                                        [Epirrhema° 1]
KORYPHAIOS (m): Gentlemen, it's a disgrace to Athens, a disgrace
   to all that Athens stands for, if we allow these grandmas   10
   to jabber about spears and shields and making friends
   with the Spartans. What's a Spartan? Give me a wild wolf
   any day. No. They want the Tyranny back, I suppose.
   Are we going to take that? No. Let us look like
   the innocent serpent, but be the flower under it,   15
   as the poet sings. And just to begin with,
   I propose to poke a number of teeth
   down the gullet of that harridan over there.

Charon: The god who ferried the souls of the newly dead across the river Styx to Hades.   **Parabasis:** Section of the play in which the author presented his own views through the Koryphaios directly to the audience. The parabasis in *Lysistrata* is shorter than those in Aristophanes' other works and unusual in that the Koryphaios does not speak directly for the author.   **Ode:** Song sung by the Chorus.   **Hippias:** An Athenian tyrant.   **Kleisthenes:** A bisexual Athenian.   **Epirrhema:** A part of the parabasis spoken by the Koryphaios following an ode delivered by his or her half of the Chorus.

Antode° 1

KORYPHAIOS^(w): Oh, is that so? When you get home, your own mamma
    won't know you!
CHORUS^(w): Who do you think we are, you senile bravos? Well, I'll show you.   20
  I bore the sacred vessels in my eighth year,° and at ten
  I was pounding out the barley for Athena Goddess;° then
    They made me Little Bear
    At the Brauronian Fair;°
  I'd held the Holy Basket° by the time I was of age,   25
  The Blessed Dry Figs had adorned my plump decolletage.

[Antepirrhema° 1]

KORYPHAIOS^(w): A "disgrace to Athens," and I, just at the moment
  I'm giving Athens the best advice she ever had?
  Don't I pay taxes to the State? Yes, I pay them
  in baby boys. And what do you contribute,   30
  you impotent horrors? Nothing but waste: all
  our Treasury,° dating back to the Persian Wars,
  gone! rifled! And not a penny out of your pockets!
  Well, then? Can you cough up an answer to that?
  Look out for your own gullet, or you'll get a crack   35
  from this old brogan that'll make your teeth see stars!

Ode 2

CHORUS^(m): Oh insolence!
  Am I unmanned?
  Incontinence!
  Shall my scarred hand
  Strike never a blow   40
  To curb this flow-
  ing female curse?

  Leipsydrion!°
  Shall I betray   45

Antode: Lyric song sung by half of the Chorus in response to the Ode sung by the other half.   **eighth year:** Young girls between the ages of seven and eleven served in the temple of Athena in the Akropolis. **pounding out the barley for Athena Goddess:** At age ten a girl could be chosen to grind the sacred grain of Athena.   **Brauronian Fair:** A ritual in the cult of Artemis, who is associated with wild beasts, in which young girls dressed up as bears and danced for the goddess.   **Holy Basket:** In one ritual to Athena, young girls carried baskets of objects sacred to the goddess.   **Antepirrhema:** The speech delivered by the second Koryphaios after the second half of the Chorus had sung an ode.   **Treasury:** Athenian politicians were raiding the funds that were collected by Athens to finance a war against Persia.   **Leipsydrion:** A place where Athenian patriots had heroically fought.

The laurels won
On that great day?
Come, shake a leg,
Shed old age, beg
The years reverse!   50

[Epirrhema 2]

KORYPHAIOS^(m): Give them an inch, and we're done for! We'll have them
  launching boats next and planning naval strategy,
  sailing down on us like so many Artemisias.
  Or maybe they have ideas about the cavalry.
  That's fair enough, women are certainly good   55
  in the saddle. Just look at Mikon's paintings,
  all those Amazons wrestling with all those men!
  On the whole, a straitjacket's their best uniform.

Antode 2

CHORUS^(w): Tangle with me,
  And you'll get cramps.
  Ferocity
  's no use now, Gramps!   60
  By the Two,
  I'll get through
  To you wrecks yet!   65

  I'll scramble your eggs,
  I'll burn your beans,
  With my two legs.
  You'll see such scenes
  As never yet   70
  Your two eyes met.
  A curse? You bet!

[Antepirrhema 2]

KORYPHAIOS^(w): If Lampito stands by me, and that delicious Theban girl,
  Ismenia—what good are *you?* You and your seven
  Resolutions! Resolutions? Rationing Boiotian eels   75
  and making our girls go without them at Hekate's° Feast!
  That was statesmanship! And we'll have to put up with it
  and all the rest of your decrepit legislation
  until some patriot—God give him strength!—
  grabs you by the neck and kicks you off the Rock.   80

Hekate: Patron of successful wars, object of a Boiotian cult (later associated with sorcery).

SCENE 2

[*Reenter* LYSISTRATA *and her lieutenants.*]

KORYPHAIOS (w) (*tragic tone*): *Great Queen, fair Architect of our emprise,*
    Why lookst thou on us with foreboding eyes?
LYSISTRATA: The behavior of these idiotic women!
    There's something about the female temperament
    that I can't bear!
KORYPHAIOS (w):   What in the world do you mean?   5
LYSISTRATA: Exactly what I say.
KORYPHAIOS (w): What dreadful thing has happened?
    Come, tell us: we're all your friends.
LYSISTRATA: It isn't easy
    to say it; yet, God knows, we can't hush it up.
KORYPHAIOS (w): Well, then? Out with it!
LYSISTRATA: To put it bluntly,
    we're dying to get laid.
KORYPHAIOS (w):   Almighty God!   10
LYSISTRATA: Why bring God into it?—No, it's just as I say.
    I can't manage them any longer: they've gone man-crazy,
    they're all trying to get out.
                      Why, look:
    one of them was sneaking out the back door
    over there by Pan's cave; another   15
    was sliding down the walls with rope and tackle;
    another was climbing aboard a sparrow, ready to take off
    for the nearest brothel—I dragged *her* back by the hair!
    They're all finding some reason to leave.
                     Look there!
    There goes another one.
                 —Just a minute, you!   20
    Where are you off to so fast?
FIRST WOMAN: I've got to get home.
    I've a lot of Milesian wool, and the worms are spoiling it.
LYSISTRATA: Oh bother you and your worms! Get back inside!
FIRST WOMAN: I'll be back right away, I swear I will.
    I just want to get it stretched out on my bed.   25
LYSISTRATA: You'll do no such thing. You'll stay right here.
FIRST WOMAN: And my wool?
    You want it ruined?
LYSISTRATA: Yes, for all I care.
SECOND WOMAN: Oh dear! My lovely new flax from Amorgos—
    I left it at home, all uncarded!

LYSISTRATA: Another one!
  And all she wants is someone to card her flax.   30
  Get back in there!
SECOND WOMAN: But I swear by the Moon-Goddess,
  the minute I get it done, I'll be back!
LYSISTRATA: I say No.
  If you, why not all the other women as well?
THIRD WOMAN: O Lady Eileithyia!° Radiant goddess! Thou
  intercessor for women in childbirth! Stay, I pray thee,   35
  oh stay this parturition. Shall I pollute
  a sacred spot?°
LYSISTRATA: And what's the matter with *you?*
THIRD WOMAN: I'm having a baby—any minute now.
LYSISTRATA: But you weren't pregnant yesterday.
THIRD WOMAN: Well, I am today.
  Let me go home for a midwife, Lysistrata: 40
  there's not much time.
LYSISTRATA: I never heard such nonsense.
  What's that bulging under your cloak?
THIRD WOMAN: A little baby boy.
LYSISTRATA: It certainly isn't. But it's something hollow,
  like a basin or—Why, it's the helmet of Athena!
  And you said you were having a baby.
THIRD WOMAN: Well, I am! So there!   45
LYSISTRATA: Then why the helmet?
THIRD WOMAN: I was afraid that my pains
  might begin here in the Akropolis; and I wanted
  to drop my chick into it, just as the dear doves do.
LYSISTRATA: Lies! Evasions!—But at least one thing's clear:
  you can't leave the place before your purification.°   50
THIRD WOMAN: But I can't stay here in the Akropolis! Last night I dreamed
  of the Snake.
FIRST WOMAN: And those horrible owls, the noise they make!
  I can't get a bit of sleep; I'm just about dead.
LYSISTRATA: You useless girls, that's enough: Let's have no more lying.
  Of course you want your men. But don't you imagine   55
  that they want you just as much? I'll give you my word,
  their nights must be pretty hard.
                         Just stick it out!
  A little patience, that's all, and our battle's won.
  I have heard an Oracle. Should you like to hear it?

Eileithyia: Goddess of childbirth.   **pollute a sacred spot:** Giving birth on the Akropolis was forbidden because it was sacred ground.   **purification:** A ritual cleansing of a woman after childbirth.

FIRST WOMAN: An Oracle? Yes, tell us!

LYSISTRATA: Here is what it says: 60
  WHEN SWALLOWS SHALL THE HOOPOE SHUN
    AND SPURN HIS HOT DESIRE,
  ZEUS WILL PERFECT WHAT THEY'VE BEGUN
    AND SET THE LOWER HIGHER.

FIRST WOMAN: Does that mean we'll be on top?   65

LYSISTRATA: BUT IF THE SWALLOWS SHALL FALL OUT
    AND TAKE THE HOOPOE'S BAIT,
  A CURSE MUST MARK THEIR HOUR OF DOUBT,
    INFAMY SEAL THEIR FATE.

THIRD WOMAN: I swear, *that* Oracle's all too clear.

FIRST WOMAN: Oh the dear gods!   70

LYSISTRATA: Let's not be downhearted, girls. Back to our places!
  The god has spoken. How can we possibly fail him?

                [*Exit* LYSISTRATA *with the dissident women.*]

CHORAL EPISODE

Strophe

CHORUS[m]: I know a little story that I learned way back in school
  Goes like this:
  Once upon a time there was a young man—and no fool—
  Named Melanion; and his
  One aversi-on was marriage. He loathed the very thought.   5
  So he ran off to the hills, and in a special grot
  Raised a dog, and spent his days
  Hunting rabbits. And it says
  That he never never never did come home.
  It might be called a refuge *from* the womb.   10
  All right,
        all right,
            all right!
  We're as bright as young Melanion, and we hate
  the very sight
  Of you women!

A MAN: How about a kiss, old lady?

A WOMAN: Here's an onion for your eye!   15

A MAN: A kick in the guts, then?

A WOMAN: Try, old bristle-tail, just try!

A MAN: Yet they say Myronides
  On hands and knees
  Looked just as shaggy fore and aft as I!   20

Antistrophe

CHORUS^(w): Well, *I* know a little story, and it's just as good as yours.
    Goes like this:
    Once there was a man named Timon—a rough diamond, of course,
    And that whiskery face of his
    Looked like murder in the shrubbery. By God, he was a son   25
    Of the Furies, let me tell you! And what did he do but run
    From the world and all its ways,
    Cursing mankind! And it says
    That his choicest execrations as of then
    Were leveled almost wholly at *old* men.   30
    All right,
          all right,
               all right!
    But there's one thing about Timon: he could always stand the sight
    of us women.
A WOMAN: How about a crack in the jaw, Pop?
A MAN: I can take it, Ma—no fear!   35
A WOMAN: How about a kick in the face?
A MAN: You'd reveal your old caboose?
A WOMAN: What I'd show,
    I'll have you know,
    Is an instrument you're too far gone to use.   40

SCENE 3

[*Reenter* LYSISTRATA.]

LYSISTRATA: Oh, quick, girls, quick! Come here!
A WOMAN: What is it?
LYSISTRATA: A man.
    A man simply bulging with love.
                    O Kyprian Queen,°
    O Paphian, O Kythereian! Hear us and aid us!
A WOMAN: Where is this enemy?
LYSISTRATA: Over there, by Demeter's shrine.
A WOMAN: Damned if he isn't. But who *is* he?
MYRRHINE: My husband.   5
    Kinesias.
LYSISTRATA: Oh then, get busy! Tease him! Undermine him!
    Wreck him! Give him everything—kissing, tickling, nudging,

---

Kyprian Queen: Aphrodite.

whatever you generally torture him with—: give him everything
except what we swore on the wine we would not give.
MYRRHINE: Trust me.
LYSISTRATA: I do. But I'll help you get him started.   10
The rest of you women, stay back.

[*Enter* KINESIAS.]

KINESIAS: Oh God! Oh my God!
   I'm stiff from lack of exercise. All I can do to stand up.
LYSISTRATA: Halt! Who are you, approaching our lines?
KINESIAS: Me? I.
LYSISTRATA: A man?
KINESIAS: You have eyes, haven't you?
LYSISTRATA: Go away.
KINESIAS: Who says so?
LYSISTRATA: Officer of the Day.
KINESIAS: Officer, I beg you,   15
   by all the gods at once, bring Myrrhine out.
LYSISTRATA: Myrrhine? And who, my good sir, are you?
KINESIAS: Kinesias. Last name's Pennison. Her husband.
LYSISTRATA: Oh, of course. I beg your pardon. We're glad to see you.
   We've heard so much about you. Dearest Myrrhine   20
   is always talking about Kinesias—never nibbles an egg
   or an apple without saying
   "Here's to Kinesias!"
KINESIAS: Do you really mean it?
LYSISTRATA: I do.
   When we're discussing men, she always says
   "Well, after all, there's nobody like Kinesias!"   25
KINESIAS: Good God.—Well, then, please send her down here.
LYSISTRATA: And what do *I* get out of it?
KINESIAS: A standing promise.
LYSISTRATA: I'll take it up with her.

                                    [*Exit* LYSISTRATA.]
KINESIAS: But be quick about it!
   Lord, what's life without a wife? Can't eat. Can't sleep.
   Every time I go home, the place is so empty, so   30
   insufferably sad. Love's killing me, Oh,
   hurry!

[*Enter* MANES, *a slave, with* KINESIAS*'s baby; the voice of* MYRRHINE *is heard offstage.*]

MYRRHINE: But of course I love him! Adore him—But no,
   he hates love. No. I won't go down.

[Enter MYRRHINE, *above.]*

KINESIAS: Myrrhine!
   Darlingest Myrrhinette! Come down quick!
MYRRHINE: Certainly not.
KINESIAS: Not? But why, Myrrhine?   35
MYRRHINE: Why? You don't need me.
KINESIAS: Need you? My God, *look* at me!
MYRRHINE: So long!

[Turns to go.]

KINESIAS: Myrrhine, Myrrhine, Myrrhine!
   If not for my sake, for our child!

[Pinches Baby.]

                          —All right, you: pipe up!
BABY: Mummie! Mummie! Mummie!
KINESIAS: You hear that?
   Pitiful, I call it. Six days now   40
   with never a bath; no food; enough to break your heart!
MYRRHINE: My darlingest child! What a father *you* acquired!
KINESIAS: At least come down for his sake.
MYRRHINE: I suppose I must.
   Oh, this mother business!   *[Exit.]*
KINESIAS: How pretty she is! And younger!
   The harder she treats me, the more bothered I get.

*[*MYRRHINE *enters, below.]*

MYRRHINE: Dearest child,   45
   you're as sweet as your father's horrid. Give me a kiss.
KINESIAS: Now don't you see how wrong it was to get involved
   in this scheming League of women? It's bad
   for us both.
MYRRHINE: Keep your hands to yourself!
KINESIAS: But our house
   going to rack and ruin?
MYRRHINE: *I* don't care.
KINESIAS: And your knitting   50
   all torn to pieces by the chickens? Don't you care?
MYRRHINE: Not at all.
KINESIAS: And our debt to Aphrodite?
   Oh, *won't* you come back?

MYRRHINE:　No.—At least, not until you men
　make a treaty and stop this war.
KINESIAS:　　　　　　　Why, I suppose
　that might be arranged.
MYRRHINE:　　　　　Oh? Well, I suppose　　　　　　55
　I might come down then. But meanwhile,
　I've sworn not to.
KINESIAS:　Don't worry.—Now let's have fun.
MYRRHINE: No! Stop it! I said no!
　　　　　　　　　—Although, of course,
　I *do* love you.
KINESIAS:　I know you do. Darling Myrrhine:
　come, shall we?
MYRRHINE: Are you out of your mind? In front of the child?　　60
KINESIAS: Take him home, Manes.

　　　　　　　　　　　[*Exit* MANES *with* BABY.]

　　　　　　　There. He's gone.

　　　　　　　　　　Come on!
　There's nothing to stop us now.
MYRRHINE:　　　　　You devil! But where?
KINESIAS: In Pan's cave. What could be snugger than that?
MYRRHINE: But my purification before I go back to the Citadel?
KINESIAS: Wash in the Klepsydra.°
MYRRHINE:　　　　　　And my oath?
KINESIAS:　　　　　　Leave the oath to me.　　　　65
　After all, I'm the man.
MYRRHINE:　　　　Well . . . if you say so.
　　　　　　　　　I'll go find a bed.
KINESIAS: Oh, bother a bed! The ground's good enough for me.
MYRRHINE: No. You're a bad man, but you deserve something better
　than dirt.

　　　　　　　　　　　　[*Exit* MYRRHINE.]

KINESIAS: What a love she is! And how thoughtful!

　[*Reenter* MYRRHINE.]

MYRRHINE:　　　　　Here's your bed.
　Now let me get my clothes off.
　　　　　　　　But, good horrors!　　　　70
　We haven't a mattress.
KINESIAS:　　　　Oh, forget the mattress!
MYRRHINE:　　　　　　　　No.
　Just lying on blankets? Too sordid.

Klepsydra: A water clock beneath the walls of the Akropolis. Kinesias's suggestion borders on blasphemy.

KINESIAS: Give me a kiss.
MYRRHINE: Just a second.   [*Exit* MYRRHINE.]
KINESIAS: I swear, I'll explode!

[*Reenter* MYRRHINE.]

MYRRHINE: Here's your mattress.
   I'll just take my dress off.
                         But look—
   where's our pillow?
KINESIAS: I don't *need* a pillow!
MYRRHINE: Well, *I* do.   75
                                        [*Exit* MYRRHINE.]

KINESIAS: I don't suppose even Herakles°
   would stand for this!

[*Reenter* MYRRHINE.]

MYRRHINE: There we are. Ups-a-daisy!
KINESIAS: So we are. Well, come to bed.
MYRRHINE: But I wonder:
   is everything ready now?
KINESIAS: I can swear to that. Come, darling!
MYRRHINE: Just getting out of my girdle.
                              But remember, now,   80
   what you promised about the treaty.
KINESIAS: Yes, yes, yes!
MYRRHINE: But no coverlet!
KINESIAS: Damn it, I'll be
   your coverlet!
MYRRHINE: Be right back.   [*Exit* MYRRHINE.]
KINESIAS: This girl and her coverlets
   will be the death of me.

[*Reenter* MYRRHINE.]

MYRRHINE: Here we are. Up you go!
KINESIAS: Up? I've been up for ages.
MYRRHINE: Some perfume?   85
KINESIAS: No, by Apollo!
MYRRHINE: Yes, by Aphrodite!
   I don't care whether you want it or not.

                                        [*Exit* MYRRHINE.]

KINESIAS: For love's sake, hurry!

Herakles: Greek hero (Hercules) known for his Twelve Labors.

[*Reenter* MYRRHINE.]

MYRRHINE: Here, in your hand. Rub it right in.
KINESIAS: Never cared for perfume.
  And this is particularly strong. Still, here goes.   90
MYRRHINE: What a nitwit I am! I brought you the Rhodian bottle.
KINESIAS: Forget it.
MYRRHINE: No trouble at all. You just wait here.

[*Exit* MYRRHINE.]

KINESIAS: God damn the man who invented perfume!

[*Reenter* MYRRHINE.]

MYRRHINE: At last! The right bottle!
KINESIAS: I've got the rightest
  bottle of all, and it's right here waiting for you.   95
  Darling, forget everything else. Do come to bed.
MYRRHINE: Just let me get my shoes off.
                 —And, by the way,
  you'll vote for the treaty?
KINESIAS: I'll think about it.

[MYRRHINE *runs away.*]

  There! That's done it! The damned woman,
  she gets me all bothered, she half kills me,   100
  and off she runs! What'll I do? Where
  can I get laid?
         —And you, little prodding pal,
  who's going to take care of *you?* No, you and I
  had better get down to old Foxdog's Nursing Clinic.
CHORUS [m]: Alas for the woes of man, alas   105
  Specifically for you.
  She's brought you to a pretty pass:
  What are you going to do?
  Split, heart! Sag, flesh! Proud spirit, crack!
  Myrrhine's got you on your back.   110
KINESIAS: The agony, the protraction!
KORYPHAIOS [m]:   Friend,
  What woman's worth a damn?
  They bitch us all, world without end.
KINESIAS: Yet they're so damned sweet, man!
KORYPHAIOS [m]: Calamitous, that's what I say.   115
  You should have learned that much today.
CHORUS [m]: O blessed Zeus, roll womankind.
  Up into one great ball;

Blast them aloft on a high wind,
  And once there, let them fall.   120
Down, down they'll come, the pretty dears,
And split themselves on our thick spears.

                                               [*Exit* KINESIAS.]

SCENE 4

[*Enter a Spartan Herald.*]

HERALD: Gentlemen, Ah beg you will be so kind
  as to direct me to the Central Committee.
  Ah have a communication.

[*Reenter* COMMISSIONER.]

COMMISSIONER: Are you a man,
  or a fertility symbol?
HERALD: Ah refuse to answer that question!
  Ah'm a certified Herald from Spahta, and Ah've come   5
  to talk about an ahmistice.
COMMISSIONER: Then why
  that spear under your cloak?
HERALD: Ah have no speah!
COMMISSIONER: You don't walk naturally, with your tunic
  poked out so. You have a tumor, maybe,
  or a hernia?
HERALD: You lost yo' mahnd, man?
COMMISSIONER: Well,   10
  something's up, I can see that. And I don't like it.
HERALD: Colonel, Ah resent this.
COMMISSIONER: So I see. But what *is* it?
HERALD: A staff
  with a message from Spahta.
COMMISSIONER: Oh, I know about those staffs.
  Well, then, man, speak out: How are things in Sparta?
HERALD: Hahd, Colonel, hahd! We're at a standstill.   15
  Cain't seem to think of anything but women.
COMMISSIONER: How curious! Tell me, do you Spartans think
  that maybe Pan's to blame?
HERALD: Pan? No, Lampito and her little naked friends.
  They won't let a man come nigh them.   20
COMMISSIONER: How are you handling it?

HERALD: Losing our mahnds,
   if y' want to know, and walking around hunched over
   lahk men carrying candles in a gale.
   The women have swohn they'll have nothing to do with us
   until we get a treaty.
COMMISSIONER: Yes. I know.   25
   It's a general uprising, sir, in all parts of Greece.
   But as for the answer—
             Sir: go back to Sparta
   and have them send us your Armistice Commission.
   I'll arrange things in Athens.
             And I may say
   that my standing is good enough to make them listen.   30
HERALD: A man after mah own haht! Seh, Ah thank you.   [*Exit* HERALD.]

CHORAL EPISODE

Strophe

CHORUS^(m): Oh these women! Where will you find
   A slavering beast that's more unkind?
     Where's a hotter fire?
   Give me a panther, any day.
   He's not so merciless as they,   5
     And panthers don't conspire.

Antistrophe

CHORUS^(w): We may be hard, you silly old ass,
   But who brought you to this stupid pass?
     You're the ones to blame.
   Fighting with us, your oldest friends,   10
   Simply to serve your selfish ends—
     Really, you have no shame!
KORYPHAIOS^(m): No, I'm through with women for ever.
KORYPHAIOS^(w): If you say so.
   Still, you might put some clothes on. You look too absurd
   standing around naked. Come, get into this cloak.   15
KORYPHAIOS^(m): Thank you; you're right. I merely took it off
   because I was in such a temper.
KORYPHAIOS^(w):   That's much better.
   Now you resemble a man again.
          Why have you been so horrid?
   And look: there's some sort of insect in your eye.
   Shall I take it out?

KORYPHAIOS^(m):   An insect, is it? So that's   20
    what's been bothering me. Lord, yes: take it out!
KORYPHAIOS^(w): You might be more polite.
                                        —But, heavens!
    What an enormous mosquito!
KORYPHAIOS^(m):   You've saved my life.
    That mosquito was drilling an artesian well
    in my left eye.
KORYPHAIOS^(w):   Let me wipe   25
    those tears away.—And now: one little kiss?
KORYPHAIOS^(m): No, no kisses.
KORYPHAIOS^(w): You're so difficult.
KORYPHAIOS^(m): You impossible women! How you do get around us!
    The poet was right: Can't live with you, or without you.
    But let's be friends.   30
    And to celebrate, you might join us in an Ode.

Strophe 1

CHORUS^(m and w): Let it never be said
    That my tongue is malicious:
    Both by word and by deed
I would set an example that's noble and gracious.   35
    We've had sorrow and care
    Till we're sick of the tune.
    Is there anyone here
    Who would like a small loan?
        My purse is crammed,
        As you'll soon find;   40
And you needn't pay me back if the Peace gets signed.

Strophe 2

    I've invited to lunch
    Some Karystian rips°—
    An esurient bunch,   45
But I've ordered a menu to water their lips.
    I can still make soup
    And slaughter a pig.
    You're all coming, I hope?
    But a bath first, I beg!   50

Karystian rips: The Karystians were allies of Athens but were scorned for their primitive ways and loose
morals.

Walk right up
As though you owned the place,
And you'll get the front door slammed to in your face.

SCENE 5

[*Enter* SPARTAN AMBASSADOR, *with entourage.*]

KORYPHAIOS^(m): The Commission has arrived from Sparta.
        How oddly they're walking!
                Gentlemen, welcome to Athens!
  How is life in Lakonia?
AMBASSADOR: Need we discuss that?
  Simply use your eyes.
CHORUS^(m):   The poor man's right:
            What a sight!
AMBASSADOR: Words fail me.   5
  But come, gentlemen, call in your Commissioners,
  and let's get down to a Peace.
CHORAGOS^(m):   The state we're in! Can't bear
  a stitch below the waist. It's a kind of pelvic
  paralysis.
COMMISSIONER: Won't somebody call
      Lysistrata?—Gentlemen,
  we're no better off than you.
AMBASSADOR: So I see.   10
A SPARTAN: Sch, do y'all feel a certain strain
  early in the morning?
AN ATHENIAN: I do, sir. It's worse than a strain.
  A few more days, and there's nothing for us but Kleisthenes,
  that broken blossom.
CHORAGOS^(m): But you'd better get dressed again.
  You know these people going around Athens with chisels,   15
  looking for statues of Hermes.°
ATHENIAN: Sir, you are right.
SPARTAN: He certainly is! Ah'll put mah own clothes back on.

[*Enter* ATHENIAN COMMISSIONERS.]

COMMISSIONER: Gentlemen from Sparta, welcome. This is a sorry business.
SPARTAN [*to one of his own group*]: Colonel, we got dressed just in time. Ah
  sweah, if they'd seen us the way we were, there'd have been a new wah   20
  between the states.

---

statues of Hermes: The usual representation of Hermes was with an erect phallus. Statues of Hermes were scattered through Athens and were attacked by vandals just before the Sicilian Expedition.

COMMISSIONER: Shall we call the meeting to order?
                            Now, Lakonians,
    what's your proposal?
AMBASSADOR: We propose to consider peace.
COMMISSIONER: Good. That's on our minds, too.
                            —Summon Lysistrata.
    We'll never get anywhere without her.
AMBASSADOR: Lysistrata?   25
    Summon Lysis-*any*body! Only, summon!
KORYPHAIOS[(m)]:   No need to summon:
    here she is, herself.

[*Enter* LYSISTRATA.]

COMMISSIONER: Lysistrata! Lion of women!
    This is your hour to be
    hard and yielding, outspoken and shy, austere and
    gentle. You see here   30
    the best brains of Hellas (confused, I admit,
    by your devious charming) met as one man
    to turn the future over to you.
LYSISTRATA: That's fair enough,
    unless you men take it into your heads
    to turn to each other instead of to us. But I'd know   35
    soon enough if you did.
                            —Where is Reconciliation?
    Go, some of you: bring her here.
                                            [*Exeunt two women.*]
                            And now, women,
    lead the Spartan delegates to me: not roughly
    or insultingly, as our men handle them, but gently,
    politely, as ladies should. Take them by the hand,   40
    or by anything else if they won't give you their hands.

[*The* SPARTANS *are escorted over.*]

There.—The Athenians next, by any convenient handle.

[*The* ATHENIANS *are escorted.*]

Stand there, please.—Now, all of you, listen to me.

[*During the following speech the two women reenter, carrying an enormous statue of a
naked girl; this is Reconciliation.*]

I'm only a woman, I know; but I've a mind,
and, I think, not a bad one: I owe it to my father   45
and to listening to the local politicians.
So much for that.
                        Now, gentlemen,
since I have you here, I intend to give you a scolding.
We are all Greeks.
Must I remind you of Thermopylai,° of Olympia,   50
of Delphoi? names deep in all our hearts?
Are they not a common heritage?
                        Yet you men
go raiding through the country from both sides,
Greek killing Greek, storming down Greek cities—
and all the time the Barbarian across the sea   55
is waiting for his chance!
                        —That's my first point.
AN ATHENIAN: Lord! I can hardly contain myself.
LYSISTRATA: As for you Spartans:
Was it so long ago that Perikleides°
came here to beg our help? I can see him still,
his gray face, his sombre gown. And what did he want?   60
An army from Athens. All Messene
was hot at your heels, and the sea-god splitting your land.
Well, Kimon and his men,
four thousand strong, marched out and saved all Sparta.
And what thanks do we get? You come back to murder us.   65
AN ATHENIAN: They're aggressors, Lysistrata!
A SPARTAN: Ah admit it.
When Ah look at those laigs, Ah sweah Ah'll aggress mahself!
LYSISTRATA: And you, Athenians: do you think you're blameless?
Remember that bad time when we were helpless,   70
and an army came from Sparta, and that was the end of the Thessalian
        menace,
the end of Hippias and his allies.
                        And that was Sparta,
and only Sparta; but for Sparta, we'd be
cringing slaves today, not free Athenians.

[*From this point, the male responses are less to* LYSISTRATA *than to the statue.*]

A SPARTAN: A well shaped speech.
AN ATHENIAN: Certainly it has its points.   75

Thermopylai: A narrow pass where, in 480 B.C., an army of three hundred Spartans held out for three days against a superior Persian force. **Perikleides:** Spartan ambassador to Athens who successfully urged Athenians to aid Sparta in quelling a rebellion.

LYSISTRATA: Why are we fighting each other? With all this history
    of favors given and taken, what stands in the way
    of making peace?
AMBASSADOR: Spahta is ready, ma'am,
    so long as we get that place back.
LYSISTRATA: What place, man?
AMBASSADOR: Ah refer to Pylos.
COMMISSIONER: Not a chance, by God!   80
LYSISTRATA: Give it to them, friend.
COMMISSIONER: But—what shall we have to bargain with?
LYSISTRATA: Demand something in exchange.
COMMISSIONER: Good idea.—Well, then:
    Cockeville first, and the Happy Hills, and the country
    between the Legs of Megara.
AMBASSADOR: Mah government objects.
LYSISTRATA: Overruled. Why fuss about a pair of legs?   85

[*General assent. The statue is removed.*]

AN ATHENIAN: I want to get out of these clothes and start my plowing.
A SPARTAN: Ah'll fertilize mahn first, by the Heavenly Twins!
LYSISTRATA: And so you shall,
    once you've made peace. If you are serious,
    go, both of you, and talk with your allies.   90
COMMISSIONER: Too much talk already. No, we'll stand together.
    We've only one end in view. All that we want
    is our women; and I speak for our allies.
AMBASSADOR: Mah government concurs.
AN ATHENIAN: So does Karystos.
LYSISTRATA: Good—But before you come inside   95
    to join your wives at supper, you must perform
    the usual lustration. Then we'll open
    our baskets for you, and all that we have is yours.
    But you must promise upright good behavior
    from this day on. Then each man home with his woman!   100
AN ATHENIAN: Let's get it over with.
A SPARTAN: Lead on. Ah follow.
AN ATHENIAN: Quick as a cat can wink!
                [*Exeunt all but the* CHORUSES.]

Antistrophe 1

CHORUS[(w)]: Embroideries and
    Twinkling ornaments and
    Pretty dresses—I hand   105

them all over to you, and with never a qualm.
    They'll be nice for your daughters
    On festival days
    When the girls bring the Goddess
    The ritual prize.   110
    Come in, one and all:
    Take what you will.
I've nothing here so tightly corked that you can't make it spill.

Antistrophe 2

    You may search my house,
    But you'll not find   115
    The least thing of use,
Unless your two eyes are keener than mine.
    Your numberless brats
    Are half starved? And your slaves?
    Courage, grandpa! I've lots   120
    Of grain left, and big loaves.
      I'll fill your guts,
      I'll go the whole hog;
But if you come too close to me, remember:
      'ware the dog!   *[Exeunt* CHORUSES.]

EXODOS°

[*A* DRUNKEN CITIZEN *enters, approaches the gate, and is halted by a sentry.*]

CITIZEN: Open. The. Door.
SENTRY: Now, friend, just shove along!
  —So you want to sit down. If it weren't such an old joke,
  I'd tickle your tail with this torch. Just the sort of gag
  this audience appreciates.
CITIZEN: I. Stay. Right. Here.
SENTRY: Get away from there, or I'll scalp you! The gentlemen from Sparta   5
  are just coming back from dinner.

[*Exit* CITIZEN; *the general company reenters; the two* CHORUSES *now represent* SPAR-TANS *and* ATHENIANS.]

A SPARTAN: Ah must say,
  Ah never tasted better grub.

Exodos: Final scene.

AN ATHENIAN: And those Lakonians!
  They're gentlemen, by the Lord! Just goes to show,
  a drink to the wise is sufficient.
COMMISSIONER: And why not?
  A sober man's an ass.   10
  Men of Athens, mark my words: the only efficient
  Ambassador's a drunk Ambassador. Is that clear?
  Look: we go to Sparta,
  and when we get there we're dead sober. The result?
  Everyone cackling at everyone else. They make speeches;   15
  and even if we understand, we get it all wrong
  when we file our reports in Athens. But today—!
  Everybody's happy. Couldn't tell the difference
  between *Drink to Me Only* and
  The Star-spangled Athens.
                  What's a few lies,   20
  washed down in good strong drink?

[*Reenter the* DRUNKEN CITIZEN.]

SENTRY: God almighty,
  he's back again!
CITIZEN: I. Resume. My. Place.
A SPARTAN [*to an Athenian*]: Ah beg yo', seh,
  take yo' instrument in yo' hand and play for us.
  Ah'm told   25
  yo' understand the in*tri*cacies of the floot?
  Ah'd lahk to execute a song and dance
  in honor of Athens,
            and, of cohse, of Spahta.
CITIZEN: Toot. On. Your. Flute.

[*The following song is a solo—an aria—accompanied by the flute. The* CHORUS OF
SPARTANS *begins a slow dance.*]

A SPARTAN: O memory,   30
  Let the Muse speak once more
  In my young voice. Sing glory.
  Sing Artemision's shore,
  Where Athens fluttered the Persians. *Alalai,*°
  Sing glory, that great   35
  Victory! Sing also
  Our Leonidas and his men,

Alalai: War cry.

Those wild boars, sweat and blood
Down in a red drench. Then, then
The barbarians broke, though they had stood   40
Numberless as the sands before!

O Artemis,
Virgin Goddess, whose darts
Flash in our forests: approve
This pact of peace and join our hearts,   45
From this day on, in love.
Huntress, descend!
LYSISTRATA: All that will come in time.
                     But now, Lakonians,
take home your wives. Athenians, take yours.
Each man be kind to his woman; and you, women   50
be equally kind. Never again, pray God,
shall we lose our way in such madness.
KORYPHAIOS (Athenian):   And now
      let's dance our joy.

[*From this point the dance becomes general.*]

CHORUS (Athenian): Dance, you Graces
                 Artemis, dance
  Dance, Phoibos,° Lord of dancing
                Dance,   55
  In a scurry of Maenads,° Lord Dionysos
           Dance, Zeus Thunderer
       Dance, Lady Hera°
  Queen of the sky
          Dance, dance, all you gods
  Dance witness everlasting of our pact
Evohi Evohe°   60
  Dance for the dearest
           the Bringer of Peace
  Deathless Aphrodite!
COMMISSIONER: Now let us have another song from Sparta.
CHORUS (Spartan): From Taygetos, from Taygetos,
  Lakonian Muse, come down.   65
  Sing to the Lord Apollo
    Who rules Amyklai Town.

Phoibos: Apollo, god of the sun.   **Maenads:** Female worshipers of Bacchus (Dionysus).   **Hera:** Wife of Zeus.   *Evohi Evohe:* "Come forth! Come forth!" An orgiastic cry associated with rituals of Bacchus.

Sing Athena of the House of Brass!°
Sing Leda's Twins,° that chivalry
    Resplendent on the shore   70
Of our Eurotas; sing the girls
    That dance along before:

Sparkling in dust their gleaming feet,
    Their hair a Bacchant fire,
And Leda's daughter, thyrsos° raised,   75
    Leads their triumphant choir.
CHORUS ^(S and A): *Evohé!*
             Evohaí!
               Evohé!
                   We pass
           Dancing
              dancing
                  to greet
Athena of the House of Brass.

QUESTIONS

1. How does Aristophanes build dramatic suspense at the beginning of the play? What characters and action account for the suspense?
2. Describe Lysistrata's personality. Does she bear any resemblance to comic characters we find today on TV or in the movies?
3. What are the main traits Aristophanes draws in depicting the women in the play? What traits does he draw in depicting the men? Which of the two sexes appears the stronger willed? How does the contrast between the two sexes create comedy?
4. There are quite a few references to sex during the play. How does Aristophanes incorporate these references into the dialogue? Into the action on stage?
5. Lysistrata has a prolonged argument with the Magistrate. Who wins the argument? Who has the better argument? Explain.

House of Brass: Temple to Athena on the Akropolis of Sparta. **Leda's Twins:** Leda, raped by Zeus, bore quadruplets, two daughters (one of whom was Helen) and two sons. **thyrsos:** A staff twined with ivy and carried by Bacchus and his followers.

Lady Gregory

THE RISING OF THE MOON

PERSONS

SERGEANT
POLICEMAN X
POLICEMAN B
A RAGGED MAN

Scene: Side of a quay in a seaport town. Some posts and chains. A large barrel. Enter three policemen. Moonlight.

[SERGEANT, *who is older than the others, crosses the stage to right and looks down steps. The others put down a pastepot and unroll a bundle of placards.*]

POLICEMAN B: I think this would be a good place to put up a notice.

[*He points to barrel.*]

POLICEMAN X: Better ask him. [*Calls to* SERGEANT.] Will this be a good place for a placard?

[*No answer.*]

POLICEMAN B: Will we put up a notice here on the barrel?

[*No answer.*]

SERGEANT: There's a flight of steps here that leads to the water. This is a place that should be minded well. If he got down here, his friends might have a boat to meet him; they might send it in here from outside.
POLICEMAN B: Would the barrel be a good place to put a notice up?
SERGEANT: It might; you can put it there.

[*They paste the notice up.*]

SERGEANT [*reading it*]: Dark hair—dark eyes, smooth face, height five feet five— there's not much to take hold of in that—It's a pity I had no chance of seeing him before he broke out of gaol. They say he's a wonder, that it's he makes all the plans for the whole organization. There isn't another man in Ireland would have broken gaol the way he did. He must have some friends among the gaolers.

POLICEMAN B: A hundred pounds is little enough for the Government to offer for him. You may be sure any man in the force that takes him will get promotion.

SERGEANT: I'll mind this place myself. I wouldn't wonder at all if he came this way. He might come slipping along there [*points to side of quay*], and his friends might be waiting for him there [*points down steps*], and once he got away it's little chance we'd have of finding him; it's maybe under a load of kelp he'd be in a fishing boat, and not one to help a married man that wants it to the reward.

POLICEMAN X: And if we get him itself, nothing but abuse on our heads for it from the people, land maybe from our own relations.

SERGEANT: Well, we have to do our duty in the force. Haven't we the whole country depending on us to keep law and order? It's those that are down would be up and those that are up would be down, if it wasn't for us. Well, hurry on, you have plenty of other places to placard yet, and come back here then to me. You can take the lantern. Don't be too long now. It's very lonesome here with nothing but the moon.

POLICEMAN B: It's a pity we can't stop with you. The Government should have brought more police into the town, with *him* in gaol, and at assize[1] time too. Well, good luck to your watch.

[*They go out.*]

SERGEANT [*walks up and down once or twice and looks at placard*]: A hundred pounds and promotion sure. There must be a great deal of spending in a hundred pounds. It's a pity some honest man not to be better of that.

[A RAGGED MAN *appears at left and tries to slip past.* SERGEANT *suddenly turns.*]

SERGEANT: Where are you going?

MAN: I'm a poor ballad-singer, your honor. I thought to sell some of these [*holds out bundle of ballads*] to the sailors. [*He goes on.*]

SERGEANT: Stop! Didn't I tell you to stop? You can't go on there.

MAN: Oh, very well. It's a hard thing to be poor. All the world's against the poor!

SERGEANT: Who are you?

MAN: You'd be as wise as myself if I told you, but I don't mind. I'm one Jimmy Walsh, a ballad-singer.

SERGEANT: Jimmy Walsh? I don't know that name.

MAN: Ah, sure, they know it well enough in Ennis. Were you ever in Ennis, sergeant?

SERGEANT: What brought you here?

MAN: Sure, it's to the assizes I came, thinking I might make a few shillings here or there. It's in the one train with the judges I came.

SERGEANT: Well, if you came so far, you may as well go farther, for you'll walk out of this.

MAN: I will, I will; I'll just go on where I was going. [*Goes toward steps.*]

---

[1] Periodical legal proceedings.

SERGEANT: Come back from those steps; no one has leave to pass down them to-night.

MAN: I'll just sit on the top of the steps till I see will some sailor buy a ballad off me that would give me my supper. They do be late going back to the ship. It's often I saw them in Cork carried down the quay in a hand-cart.

SERGEANT: Move on, I tell you. I won't have any one lingering about the quay to-night.

MAN: Well, I'll go. It's the poor have the hard life! Maybe yourself might like one, sergeant. Here's a good sheet now. [*Turns one over.*] "Content and a pipe"—that's not much. "The Peeler and the goat"—you wouldn't like that. "Johnny Hart"—that's a lovely song.

SERGEANT: Move on.

MAN: Ah, wait till you hear it. [*Sings.*]

> There was a rich farmer's daughter lived near the town of Ross;
> She courted a Highland soldier, his name was Johnny Hart;
> Says the mother to her daughter, "I'll go distracted mad
> If you marry that Highland soldier dressed up in Highland plaid."

SERGEANT: Stop that noise.

[MAN *wraps up his ballads and shuffles towards the steps.*]

SERGEANT: Where are you going?

MAN: Sure you told me to be going, and I am going.

SERGEANT: Don't be a fool. I didn't tell you to go that way; I told you to go back to the town.

MAN: Back to the town, is it?

SERGEANT [*taking him by the shoulder and shoving him before him*]: Here, I'll show you the way. Be off with you. What are you stopping for?

MAN [*who has been keeping his eye on the notice, points to it*]: I think I know what you're waiting for, sergeant.

SERGEANT: What's that to you?

MAN: And I know well the man you're waiting for—I know him well—I'll be going. [*He shuffles on.*]

SERGEANT: You know him? Come back here. What sort is he?

MAN: Come back is it, sergeant? Do you want to have me killed?

SERGEANT: Why do you say that?

MAN: Never mind. I'm going. I wouldn't be in your shoes if the reward was ten times as much. [*Goes on off stage to left.*] Not if it was ten times as much.

SERGEANT [*rushing after him*]: Come back here, come back. [*Drags him back.*] What sort is he? Where did you see him?

MAN: I saw him in my own place, in the County Clare. I tell you you wouldn't like to be looking at him. You'd be afraid to be in the one place with him. There isn't a weapon he doesn't know the use of, and as to strength, his muscles are as hard as that board. [*Slaps barrel.*]

SERGEANT: Is he as bad as that?

MAN: He is then.

SERGEANT: Do you tell me so?

MAN: There was a poor man in our place, a sergeant from Bally-vaughan.—It was with a lump of stone he did it.

SERGEANT: I never heard of that.

MAN: And you wouldn't, sergeant. It's not everything that happens gets into the papers. And there was a policeman in plain clothes, too . . . It is in Limerick he was. . . . It was after the time of the attack on the police barrack in Kilmallock. . . . Moonlight . . . just like this . . . waterside. . . . Nothing was known for certain.

SERGEANT: Do you say so? It's a terrible county to belong to.

MAN: That's so, indeed! You might be standing there, looking out that way, thinking you saw him coming up this side of the quay [*points*], and he might be coming up this other side [*points*], and he'd be on you before you knew where you were.

SERGEANT: It's a whole troop of police they ought to put here to stop a man like that.

MAN: But if you'd like me to stop with you, I could be looking down this side. I could be sitting up here on this barrel.

SERGEANT: And you know him well, too?

MAN: I'd know him a mile off, sergeant.

SERGEANT: But you wouldn't want to share the reward?

MAN: Is it a poor man like me, that has to be going the roads and singing in fairs, to have the name on him that he took a reward? but you don't want me. I'll be safer in the town.

SERGEANT: Well, you can stop.

MAN [*getting up on barrel*]: All right, sergeant, I wonder, now, you're tired out, sergeant, walking up and down the way you are.

SERGEANT: If I'm tired I'm used to it.

MAN: You might have hard work before you to-night yet. Take it easy while you can. There's plenty of room up here on the barrel, and you see farther when you're higher up.

SERGEANT: Maybe so. [*Gets up beside him on barrel, facing right.*]

[*They sit back to back, looking different ways.*]

You made me feel a bit queer with the way you talked.

MAN: Give me a match, sergeant [*he gives it and* MAN *lights pipe*]; take a draw yourself? It'll quiet you. Wait now till I give you a light, but you needn't turn round. Don't take your eye off the quay for the life of you.

SERGEANT: Never fear, I won't. [*Lights pipe.*]

[*They both smoke.*]

Indeed it's a hard thing to be in the force, out at night and no thanks for it, for all the danger we're in. And it's little we get but abuse from the people, and no choice but to obey our orders, and never asked when a man is sent into danger, if you are a married man with a family.

MAN [*sings*]:

> As through the hills I walked to view the hills and shamrock plain,
> I stood awhile where nature smiles to view the rocks and streams,
> On a matron fair I fixed my eyes beneath a fertile vale,
> And she sang her song it was on the wrong of poor old Granuaile.

SERGEANT: Stop that; that's no song to be singing in these times.

MAN: Ah, sergeant, I was only singing to keep my heart up. It sinks when I think of him. To think of us two sitting here, and he creeping up the quay, maybe, to get to us.

SERGEANT: Are you keeping a good lookout?

MAN: I am; and for no reward too. Amn't I the fool man? But when I saw a man in trouble, I never could help trying to get him out of it. What's that? Did something hit me? [*Rubs his heart.*]

SERGEANT [*patting him on the shoulder*]: You will get your reward in heaven.

MAN: I know that, I know that, sergeant, but life is precious.

SERGEANT: Well, you can sing if it gives you more courage.

MAN [*sings*]:

> Her head was bare, her hands and feet with iron bands were bound,
> Her pensive strain and plaintive wail mingles with the evening gale,
> And the song she sang with mournful air, I am old Granuaile.
> Her lips so sweet that monarchs kissed . . .

SERGEANT: That's not it. . . . "Her gown she wore was stained with gore." . . . That's it—you missed that.

MAN: You're right, sergeant, so it is; I missed it. [*Repeats line.*] But to think of a man like you knowing a song like that.

SERGEANT: There's many a thing a man might know and might not have any wish for.

MAN: Now, I daresay, sergeant, in your youth, you used to be sitting up on a wall, the way you are sitting up on this barrel now, and the other lads beside you, and you singing "Granuaile"? . . .

SERGEANT: I did then.

MAN: And the "Shan Van Vocht"?[2] . . .

SERGEANT: I did then.

---

[2]Song of a poor old woman, personification of Ireland, foretelling the coming of the French to aid Irish rebellion; the Shan Van Vocht personification of Ireland also informs Yeats's *Cathleen Ni Houlihan*.

MAN: And the "Green on the Cape?"

SERGEANT: That was one of them.

MAN: And maybe the man you are watching for to-night used to be sitting on the wall, when he was young, and singing those same songs. . . . It's a queer world. . . .

SERGEANT: Whisht! . . . I think I see something coming. . . . It's only a dog.

MAN: And isn't it a queer world? . . . Maybe it's one of the boys you used to be singing with that time you will be arresting to-day or to-morrow, and sending into the dock. . . .

SERGEANT: That's true indeed.

MAN: And maybe one night, after you had been singing, if the other boys had told you some plan they had, some plan to free the country, you might have joined with them . . . and maybe it is you might be in trouble now.

SERGEANT: Well, who knows but I might? I had a great spirit in those days.

MAN: It's a queer world, sergeant, and it's little any mother knows when she sees her child creeping on the floor what might happen to it before it has gone through its life, or who will be who in the end.

SERGEANT: That's a queer thought now, and a true thought. Wait now till I think it out. . . . If it wasn't for the sense I have, and for my wife and family, and for me joining the force the time I did, it might be myself now would be after breaking gaol and hiding in the dark, and it might be him that's hiding in the dark and that got out of gaol would be sitting up here where I am on this barrel. . . . And it might be myself would be creeping up trying to make my escape from himself, and it might be himself would be keeping the law, and myself would be breaking it, and myself would be trying to put a bullet in his head, or to take up a lump of stone the way you said he did . . . no, that myself did. . . . Oh! [*Gasps. After a pause*] What's that? [*Grasps man's arm.*]

MAN [*jumps off barrel and listens, looking out over water*]: It's nothing, sergeant.

SERGEANT: I thought it might be a boat. I had a notion there might be friends of his coming about the quays with a boat.

MAN: Sergeant, I am thinking it was with the people you were, and not with the law you were, when you were a young man.

SERGEANT: Well, if I was foolish then, that time's gone.

MAN: Maybe, sergeant, it comes into your head sometimes, in spite of your belt and your tunic, that it might have been as well for you to have followed Granuaile.

SERGEANT: It's no business of yours what I think.

MAN: Maybe, sergeant, you'll be on the side of the country yet.

SERGEANT [*gets off barrel*]: Don't talk to me like that. I have my duties and I know them. [*Looks round.*] That was a boat; I hear the oars. [*Goes to the steps and looks down.*]

MAN [*sings*]:

> O, then, tell me, Shawn O'Farrell,
>   Where the gathering is to be.
> In the old spot by the river
>   Right well known to you and me!

SERGEANT: Stop that! Stop that, I tell you!
MAN [*sings louder*]:

> One word more, for signal token,
> Whistle up the marching tune,
> With your pike upon your shoulder,
> At the Rising of the Moon.

SERGEANT: If you don't stop that, I'll arrest you.

[*A whistle from below answers, repeating the air.*]

SERGEANT: That's a signal. [*Stands between him and steps.*] You must not pass this way.
. . . Step farther back. . . . Who are you? You are no ballad-singer.
MAN: You needn't ask who I am; that placard will tell you. [*Points to placard.*]
SERGEANT: You are the man I am looking for.
MAN [*takes off hat and wig*].

[SERGEANT *seizes them.*]

I am. There's a hundred pounds on my head. There is a friend of mine below in a
boat. He knows a safe place to bring me to.
SERGEANT [*looking still at hat and wig*]: It's a pity! It's a pity. You deceived me. You
deceived me well.
MAN: I am a friend of Granuaile. There is a hundred pounds on my head.
SERGEANT: It's a pity, it's a pity!
MAN: Will you let me pass, or must I make you let me?
SERGEANT: I am in the force. I will not let you pass.
MAN: I thought to do it with my tongue. [*Puts hand in breast.*] What is that?

[*Voice of* POLICEMAN X *outside.*]

Here, this is where we left him.
SERGEANT: It's my comrades coming.
MAN: You won't betray me . . . the friend of Granuaile. [*Slips behind barrel.*]

[*Voice of* POLICEMAN B.]

That was the last of the placards.

POLICEMAN X [*as they come in*]: If he makes his escape it won't be unknown he'll
make it.

[SERGEANT *puts hat and wig behind his back.*]

POLICEMAN B: Did any one come this way?

SERGEANT [*after a pause*]: No one.

POLICEMAN B: No one at all?

SERGEANT: No one at all.

POLICEMAN B: We had no orders to go back to the station; we can stop along with you.

SERGEANT: I don't want you. There is nothing for you to do here.

POLICEMAN B: You bade us to come back here and keep watch with you.

SERGEANT: I'd sooner be alone. Would any man come this way and you making all that talk? It is better the place to be quiet.

POLICEMAN B: Well, we'll leave you the lantern anyhow.

[*Hands it to him.*]

SERGEANT: I don't want it. Bring it with you.

POLICEMAN B: You might want it. There are clouds coming up and you have the darkness of the night before you yet. I'll leave it over here on the barrel. [*Goes to barrel.*]

SERGEANT: Bring it with you I tell you. No more talk.

POLICEMAN B: Well, I thought it might be a comfort to you. I often think when I have it in my hand and can be flashing it about into every dark corner [*doing so*] that it's the same as being beside the fire at home, and the bits of bogwood blazing up now and again. [*Flashes it about, now on the barrel, now on* SERGEANT.]

SERGEANT [*furious*]: Be off the two of you, yourselves and your lantern!

[*They go out.* MAN *comes from behind barrel. He and* SERGEANT *stands looking at one another.*]

SERGEANT: What are you waiting for?

MAN: For my hat, of course, and my wig. You wouldn't wish me to get my death of cold?

[SERGEANT *gives them.*]

MAN [*going towards steps*]: Well, good-night, comrade, and thank you. You did me a good turn to-night, and I'm obliged to you. Maybe I'll be able to do as much for you when the small rise up and the big fall down . . . when we all change places at the rising [*waves his hand and disappears*] of the Moon.

SERGEANT [*turning his back to audience and reading placard*]: A hundred pounds reward! A hundred pounds! [*turns towards audience.*] I wonder, now, am I as great a fool as I think I am?

QUESTIONS

1. In this short play, time, setting, and plot are set up very quickly. How does the author achieve this? At what point are all these basic elements in place?

2. Follow the steps by which the Man changes the Sergeant's view of capturing the fugitive and collecting the reward money. What methods does he employ, in what order, and to what effect?

3. Describe the *internal* and *external* conflicts of the Sergeant. How do they complement one another?

4. Why does the fugitive sing his ballads? What is the effect of these ballads on the Sergeant?

5. A great deal of light imagery is used in the play. Find each reference to this imagery, and explain what this imagery might represent besides a pure description of the setting and action.

John A. Williams

AUGUST FORTY-FIVE
A Play in One Act

CAST

DAVID BRIGHT, Pharmacist's Mate 3rd/Class, about 20
FRANKIE, Chamorro boy, 10 or 11
DIXON, Seaman, about 20
LYONS, Cook, 3rd/Class, 30 or more
ROY, Seaman, late 20's
PERKINS, Chief Pharmacist's Mate, about 30

The action takes place during 48 hours.

SCENE I

It is the first week of August 1945, on an island in the South Pacific. It is dark; the stage is dark, and in this darkness before the curtain goes up, we hear the sound of many, many big, heavy planes. The sound builds until it is almost unbearable to hear.

Lights come up very slowly, as the sound of the planes begins to fade. We see the interior of a three-man tent, which is raised from the ground and has steps leading up into it. A table is centered. There are footlockers at the foot of each cot. Mess kits hang on nails above the cots. The sound of the planes fades altogether now, as the lights come up full on the empty tent.

DAVID BRIGHT enters. He is about 20, of average build and height. He wears green fatigue pants and a white T-shirt. He sits on his cot with a sigh and pulls from beneath it a bucket filled with soiled clothes and soapy water. He takes a handy stick and begins to push it up and down and around in the bucket, holding the latter between his legs so it will not topple.

Now, in the quietness of the camp, we hear the clattering of a typewriter, perhaps two; birds; and, from time to time, voices offstage. We will hear the typewriter throughout the day scenes, except at meal times.

Everything is white, as though the sun is taking a special vengeance on the camp. We should be made to feel uncomfortable by the suggested intensity of the sun. BRIGHT *lights a cigarette and continues to pummel the clothes, although rather absently.*

We hear a Jeep, its gears being broken down from third to second to first. BRIGHT *turns and peers in the direction of the sound, which stops abruptly.* BRIGHT *strains. We hear new voices off, hearty, brisk, perfunctory.* BRIGHT *has stopped with the clothes, absorbed by what he sees. He stands to get a better view. His body seems to slump. He slides the bucket back under the cot and lays down.*

FRANKIE, *a Chamorro boy of about 10 or 11, sneaks into the tent holding a twig.* BRIGHT*'s back is to him. He touches* BRIGHT *on the back with the twig.* BRIGHT *slaps at it, but* FRANKIE *has jerked the twig away. Stealthily, he pushes it back. This time* BRIGHT *slaps and hits the twig. He sits up quickly.* FRANKIE *dances away, laughing.*

BRIGHT: Cut the crap, Frankie. [FRANKIE *throws the twig at him. It misses.*] I'll kick your butt good, you little punk. [*Picks up the twig and throws it out of the tent. He lays down again.* FRANKIE *digs in his pocket, then makes throwing motions toward* BRIGHT.] I wish you would. I just wish you would.

FRANKIE [*disdainfully*]: Aw, shut up Bright. You no so hot.

BRIGHT [*snapping upright*]: Little bastard! You get away with murder around here, but not with me. Now you stop fuckin' around. [*Softer.*] Damned little gook.

FRANKIE [*edging toward the steps*]: Where's Lyons?

BRIGHT: He's a cook, isn't he?

FRANKIE: Yes—

BRIGHT: Then he'd be in the goddamn chowhall, wouldn't he? [FRANKIE *has opened his mouth to speak, but closes it. He has one foot on the steps as he studies* BRIGHT.] And don't go around calling your father by his last name.

FRANKIE: He's no my father yet. What I spoze call him?

BRIGHT: I don't give a damn *what* you call him. If *I* was him, I wouldn't adopt a smartass like you! I'd let you rot on this fuckin' rock, just where he found you!

FRANKIE: Bright, you mad for yesterday?

BRIGHT: You got *that* right! Damned right, I'm mad!

FRANKIE [*half-teasing*]: Why you fellas no like that name when white fellas call it you?

BRIGHT: It's not a nice name. It makes you fight. It makes you want to kill.

FRANKIE [*putting on a fake scowl*]: So you get mad, Bright? Very mad! [*Laughs tentatively.*]

BRIGHT: It's not funny, Frankie. You better try and understand that!

FRANKIE: And Lyons, him mad too?

BRIGHT [*sitting and pounding his feet to the floor.* FRANKIE *jumps*]: He should have kicked your little ass! You play bad games with him, Frank, and he loves you. [*Beat.*] You like the white fellas better than the black fellas, don't you, Frankie? [FRANKIE *edges back.*] In America, you'd be just like *us*. Shit, they already locked up 100,000 Jap Americans! You wouldn't be like *them*. They'd make you know that pretty quick, boy!

FRANKIE [*defensively*]: I not say I white!

BRIGHT [*snapping at him*]: You *act* like it!

FRANKIE [*now he is for real, a little boy*]: I—I not.

BRIGHT [*tense with anger*]: You think you're better than us already. So where do you and your people get off? Any white fellas offer to adopt your skinny little ass like Lyons, and take you to the States? No! Those white boys are down there all the time doin' it to your women, and your women tellin' us all the time, none for us, 'cause we got *tails!* [FRANKIE *is frightened by the anger. He sidles close to the entrance of the tent.* BRIGHT *gets up and moves close to him.*] Shit, Frankie, I'm talkin to you. They didn't wanna take your ass home, DID THEY? You don't have no right to ask a man to care for you and then you up and call him a nigger! Takin' his time, money, love . . . [*Makes a sudden move toward* FRANKIE, *who leaps out of the tent.*] A little rat, that's what you are, a little, gook *rat!*

FRANKIE [*off, in a fright-filled voice that tries to be brave*]: Bright! You nigger, Bright! Nigger! [BRIGHT *starts to rush out, stops and shakes his head.*]

DIXON [*entering as* BRIGHT *backs out of the way. He is dressed like* BRIGHT, *but wears a white sailor cap unfolded down on his head. A bag is slung over one shoulder; he holds a stick with a nail in it in the other hand*]: What's all this nigger shit, Doc? Where's Frankie runnin' to?

BRIGHT: Aw, that kid pisses me off. Shouldn't have popped my cork like *that*, though. Did I hear you cats playin' ball a while ago?

DIXON [*sitting on a cot*]: Yeh. Got fifteen points, man. Hittin from all over, like Sidat-Singh [*demonstrating*] bip! bop!

BRIGHT [*also sitting*]: Planes out again today, huh?

DIXON: Whoooeee, man. Sure wouldn't wanna be no Jap this mornin'! They got B-29s, B-24s, and I thought I saw some B-17s. They flyin' everything. They droppin' some powerful shit these days, Doc. This sumbitch spozed to be over soon. Home alive in '45!

BRIGHT: Sure you don't mean chow line till '49? Hey, them Marines still over there in the C.O.'s office?

DIXON: Yeah, Doc. You saw them cats roll in here, too? Now what's *that* all about? I hope we ain't in for another push, man. I mean that Peliliu was enough for *me*. I ain't never seen so many dead people in my life, Jim.

BRIGHT [*staring out*]: Those First Marines *loves* this 27th Special. You cats really humped that ammo into Peliliu. Lift them shells, tote them rounds.

DIXON [*proudly*]: We got a Presidential Unit Citation, too, Jim, for that shit.

BRIGHT: Sure did. Washburne didn't. Malone didn't get it. Jefferson didn't get it. Vann didn't get it—

DIXON [*interrupting*]: I *know* that, Doc. [*Beats.*] Yeah, they dead, all right. And now, down by the beach, they got shit stacked *up*, Jim! Jeeps, Recons, trucks, tires, ambulances, rations, ammo—where the sumbitches goin *this* time?

BRIGHT [*teasing*]: Aw, man, you know. Ja-*pan.*

DIXON [*scornfully*]: You fulla shit, Doc.

BRIGHT: What else they got to in*vade*, Dixon?

DIXON [*upset*]: Aw, man! You don't know what you're talkin' about.

BRIGHT [*rubbing it in*]: The other day I was over in Agaña trying to find a girl, and I came up by COMSOPAC and saw more brass than I've ever seen on this rock or any other rock. Enough gold braid to make Fort Knox look like a Salvation Army collection plate! Man, these white folks gonna kick the shit outa them Japs!

DIXON: Yeah? How come you think you know so much?

BRIGHT [*calmly*]: I feel it right in my bones, Dixon.

DIXON [*rising, troubled*]: I got to go. I don't think the cat'sll wanna hear this shit when they come in from the docks for lunch! [*Exits.*]

LYONS [*off*]: Hiya, Dixon?

DIXON [*off*]: What say, Lyons! What's for lunch?

LYONS [*off*]: Pussy!

DIXON [*off*]: Hot or cold?

LYONS [*off*]: Seen Frankie?

DIXON [*off*]: He was around not too long ago, man.

LYONS [*Enters. He's chubby, wearing soiled white pants and T-shirt and a towel around his neck*]: Hey ole buddy.

BRIGHT [*studying him*]: Lyons, I don't understand how come you don't lose some weight in that kitchen. If it's 200 degrees out here, it's got to be 300 in there—[*Breaks off at the sound of loud voices from the C.O.'s office. Both stare off until we hear the Jeep starting up and driving away. Both sit down. They are pensive.*] Seen Frankie, Doc?

BRIGHT: He was here. Went off somewhere in the boondocks.

LYONS [*removes his shoes, folds himself down on his cot sighing with pleasure*]: After that business yesterday, I wanted to see him. Explain things to him. I guess he'll be around for evening chow. Seem okay?

BRIGHT [*starts to say something, changes his mind*]: Yeah, he's okay. Any word on what the Marines wanted?

LYONS: Not yet, but if there's any scuttlebutt, we'll hear it soon enough.

BRIGHT: Fuckin' Marines. Act like they found a home with this outfit.

LYONS: Another push, you think?

BRIGHT: Yeah. Japan. That's what I told Dixon.

LYONS [*sitting up, quick*]: What? Why you say that?

BRIGHT: I was only kidding then. But, I been thinkin', Lyons. There ain't no place left to go.

LYONS [*laying down again*]: You right, Doc. Don't look good. Don't look good at all. If we do go, I guess Frankie could wait here. Maybe I should try to get him sent to my wife. What'd you do, Doc?

BRIGHT [*with infinite weariness*]: You gotta get the papers cleared before you do anything, Lyons. That can take a lotta time. Look how long it's takin' already. [*Beats.*] Those goddamn Marines, man. They worry me. I wish the sumbitches'd never come. They so goddamn bad. Shit. They die just like anyone else, hollerin' and screamin' for Momma and morphine. Them Japs don't read no English. They don't know the Marines is supposed to be bad.

LYONS: Remember the Japs callin' and askin' us what we were doin' there? Now them cats spoke *good* English, Doc. Made sense, too. [*Beats.*] I wish it was over. Been out here two years and ain't met more than four-five decent white men. Twenty-four months. Still a cook third class.

BRIGHT: You know they ain't about to give us too many promotions, man. Shit. I been a pecker-checker, chancre mechanic for two years, too. I ain't gonna make it to pharmacists mate deuce. I'ma develop an illness, some mysterious jungle shit.

LYONS [*alarmed*]: Don't you go fuckin' up, now, Doc. It's a sometime proposition with those white boys in the sick bay. They just lookin' to finish sick call.

BRIGHT: Don't worry, Lyons. They'd never believe me.

LYONS [*satisfied*]: Now that's more like it! [*Beats.*] Got a letter from my ole lady today. Thinks Frankie's a good-lookin' little cat. Sent her those pictures you took.

BRIGHT: You think he'll really like it back there?

LYONS: Detroit? Sure.

BRIGHT [*bitterly*]: Yeah, sure. What're a few race riots.

LYONS: Things've changed, Doc. Anyway, the word is that once you get the papers moving, it shouldn't take long.

BRIGHT: White guy said that?

LYONS: Yeah.

BRIGHT [*taking a magazine from under his pillow and opening it*]: Great.

LYONS: My wife says she's starting to buy things already. [*Laughs.*] They may be too small or too big!

BRIGHT [*monotone, skimming*]: Ain't that the truth.

LYONS: I guess I could send him on ahead. Let him get used to things back there. [*Sits up.*] Oh, I know he's got a nasty, wild mouth, Doc. All this GI shit been rubbin' off on him after he lost his folks except for that slick ole uncle. It's been hard on him.

BRIGHT: Yeah, I guess so.

LYONS [*fixing a gaze on* BRIGHT]: You don't like him much, do you Doc?

BRIGHT [*still skimming*]: I like him fine, Lyons, no shit.

LYONS: Naw you don't.

BRIGHT [*now looking up*]: He's all right, man. Honest. If you wanna adopt him, more power to you.

LYONS: He'll be all right. I can raise him right.

BRIGHT [*suddenly, as though making a decision*]: Lyons.

LYONS: Huh?

BRIGHT [*hesitates*]: What's for chow?

LYONS [*wiping his face with the towel*]: Shit on shingles.

BRIGHT [*distastefully*]: Christ!

LYONS [*mockingly*]: Chicken on Sunday!

BRIGHT [*as* LYONS *laughs*]: Aw, man. We have chicken *every* Sunday. It's a wonder we don't have a fuckin' ice cream parlor, too.

LYONS [*stretching*]: I got to get back. Trucks should be on the way. [*Sits up. Stares off and smiles.*] How do Miz Camel?

BRIGHT [*sitting up quickly*]: Say, Camel. You folks g'one be down by the stream tonight?

CAMEL [*off, sweetly*]: Hello, Lyons. Hello, Doc. You know we at the stream *every* night. Come on down.

LYONS [*giggling; falls back onto his cot*]: That faggot's somethin' else!

BRIGHT [*staring after* CAMEL]: I swear, man, that cat is startin' to look good to me, what with these goddamn crackers lockin' up *all* the pussy. They better get me off this rock, quick!

LYONS [*standing again*]: Doc, you know you done already been down there!

BRIGHT [*laying down again*]: Not yet, but the Shadow knows—I might! Dick's gettin' hard as times in '32.

LYONS [*exiting*]: See ya.

[BRIGHT *lies, hands over his eyes. Loud laughter makes him sit up again and he looks off.*]

BRIGHT [*cupping his hands around his mouth*]: You guys take your salt pills?

VOICE [*off*]: Yeah, Doc. You see those Marines?

BRIGHT: Fuck a Marine! [*As he pulls out his bucket of wash again, we hear the sound of many heavy trucks approaching camp. They stop. Off, we also hear many voices.* ROY, *a big, husky man in his late twenties, a cap pulled down over his eyes, enters and snatches his mess kit.*]

ROY: Say, Doc.

BRIGHT [*getting his kit, too*]: I'll go with you. The Marines were here this morning.

ROY: What for?

BRIGHT [*stabbing him in the chest with his finger*]: You.

Lights

SCENE II

Forty-eight hours later. We hear no planes. BRIGHT *is sitting on his cot pummeling his clothes.* DIXON *enters.*

DIXON [*sitting*]: Doc, you got it made. Mornin' sick call and evenin' sick call and sacktime in between.

BRIGHT: You got yourself a pretty good hustle, too, Dixon.

DIXON: Say, Doc, you got any of those morphine things?

BRIGHT: Syrettes?

DIXON: Yeah, that's the stuff. Gimmee a couple of those, will ya?

BRIGHT [*snorting*]: For *what?* You ain't got no battle wound.

DIXON: I got a bad toothache, Doc.

BRIGHT: So how come you didn't make sick call?

DIXON: Sell 'em to me.

BRIGHT: Get 'em from McElhenny.

DIXON: Aw, man. You know that cracker wouldn't give me anything without a lot of who-struck-john, and then pass me on to the doctor. That's a brutal sumbitch, Jim. Cats come in from the docks, their backs messed up and he give 'em a prostate massage, man. What's a finger up your ass got to do with a broke back, is what I want to know.

BRIGHT: Don't ask me. Besides some of the cats must like it—they're on sick call for the same thing every week. Anyway, man, I can't just give the shit out. The doctor keeps a check. Regulations. What're you, some kind of addick?

DIXON: Who? Me? [*Beats.*] How about some of that 190 proof alcohol you corpsmen got? You know, the shit you drink with Coke and then you can't smoke for five hours 'cause it'll blow you up?

BRIGHT: Man, can't you see I'm busy?

DIXON [*running out of hope*]: Got an extra beer?

BRIGHT [*bitingly*]: How about two atabrine tablets, two APCs, two sulfathiazole tablets, two sulfanilamide tablets, and two sulfadiazine tablets, swallowed down with a glass of potassium permanganate instead?

DIXON [*hopefully*]: Will that get me high?

BRIGHT [*disgusted*]: No, but they'll put you outa your misery. [*Both turn at the sound of trucks.*] What's that?

DIXON: A travelin' whorehouse—I hope.

BRIGHT [*tensing*]: Fuckin' Marine trucks, Dixon.

DIXON: Kiss my wrist!

BRIGHT: It's your ass they want.

DIXON: I want it, too.

CAMEL [*off, sweetly*]: Dixon! Ho, Dixon!

DIXON [*flattens on the deck*]: Lookin' for men to unload those trucks. Me, I have just gone on sick leave.

CAMEL [*off*]: Cleaning detail on the double! On the double! Dixon, Baker, Robertson, Shorter! On the double, now!

DIXON [*mimicking*]: Cleaning detail on the double now!

BRIGHT [*still looking off*]: They got some people now. Big ole sarge with a checklist.

MARINE SGT.'S VOICE [*very loud*]: 'kay you men. Five hundred helmets, and they ain't to piss in.

CAMEL [*also off*]: We know what they're for.

SGT.: Oh, you does, does you?

DIXON: He's *great* big, right?

BRIGHT: Sure is. Looks like a house with legs.

DIXON: Pot belly.

BRIGHT: Sure 'nuff. Cat looks pregnant.

DIXON: Gotta a four-five on his hip.

BRIGHT: You ain't lyin', man.

DIXON: I'ma kick that sumbitch's ass!

BRIGHT: Hummmm. When you gonna kick his ass, Dixon?

DIXON: Not right now.

SGT.:

> Five hundred pairs of fatigues.
> Five hundred pairs of flesh-outs.
> Five thousand boxes rations.
> Five hundred M-1s.
> Fifty thousand rounds .30 caliber ammo.
> Five hundred battle packs.
> One hundred twenty crosses.
> Twenty-five Stars of David—y'all got some Jews in this outfit? [*Laughs.*]

DIXON [*muttering*]: Yo momma, you cracker sumbitch. Doc, why they issue all that new shit to die in?

SGT.: Five hundred ampules, cholera vaccine. [*Voice fades.*]

DIXON: I guess you were right, Doc.

BRIGHT: I'd rather be wrong, man.

DIXON [*vehemently*]: Shit! Last time we got new stuff—shit! This ain't got nothin' to do with me, man.

BRIGHT: Eat your own shit. They'll give a Section Eight.

DIXON: Ain't my style, Doc.

BRIGHT: Blow off a toe.

DIXON [*crouching now, peering off, too*]: I need my toes for dancin'.

BRIGHT: AWOL.

DIXON: On this rock? You crazy?

BRIGHT: Then shut the fuck up! [LYONS *enters.*] Hi, man.

LYONS [*as before, sweating and wiping*]: Whaddaya say. You cats seen Frankie this mornin'?

BRIGHT: No.

DIXON: Looks to me like you don't have no time to be worryin' about no Frankie, man.

LYONS [*snapping*]: Dixon, how come you ain't down there helpin' to unload? Ain't you on the cleaning detail?

DIXON: I had to have a special conference with Doc here.

LYONS: Conference my ass!

DIXON: Another fuckin' push! Shit!

LYONS [*laying down*]: You don't have to worry about that, Dixon. They just got a new secret weapon, a gun.

BRIGHT [*turning from watching action, off*]: Another one?

LYONS: All the battlewagons been fitted with this gun and when one of them special shells lands, nothin'll grow for a thousand years.

BRIGHT: People, too, I guess, huh?

LYONS: Especially people.

DIXON: Aw, bullshit, Lyons. Last secret weapon we heard about was this phosphorous bomb. Remember one got stuck in the bomb-bay of a B-29 and that gunner had to free it? Burned that cracker from his toenails to his eyebrows.

BRIGHT: Well, they gave him some medals.

DIXON: Yeah. Let's see how they work in place of his dick. They always comin' up with some secret weapon that turns out to be as great as a box of K-rations.

BRIGHT [*disgusted*]: If they *had* somethin', they'd a used it, right? Don't make sense, they just now discoverin' somethin', right?

LYONS: I don't understand how come Frankie ain't been around in two days.

BRIGHT: Frankie was doin' all right before we got here, and he's probably doin' all right now, and will do all right when we—

LYONS: What?

BRIGHT [*a glance at* DIXON]: Nothin'. He's all right.

LYONS [*huffily*]: Oh, he's comin' home with me, all right, Doc. Don't you worry none about that!

BRIGHT: Sure, I'm hip.

DIXON [*rising now*]: They're almost done. Time to lend a hand. See you cats. [*Exits.*]

LYONS: Doc, I'm worried about Frankie.

BRIGHT: You *sure* you want to adopt that kid, Lyons?

LYONS: Yeah, I'm sure! You youngbloods don't take me serious. I want him. He wants me. He was livin' like an animal when we found him back up in the hills. He's come a long way since then.

BRIGHT: Yeah.

LYONS: It was *us* comin' damn near 15,000 miles and some of us didn't know diddley about no fuckin' Japan until Pearl Harbor. We was . . . liberators. So here's this kid. Ain't got nobody but this slick old, toothless uncle who'd rather not be bothered with him. I can't have no kids, Doc. So there's Frankie, and we hit it off right away. It made me feel good when he needed me, made me feel important. I thought a lot about the adoption, man. You can't hardly get Negro kids in adoption agencies, 'cause colored folks don't give 'em away. I hope that never changes. I can do things for the kid, Doc. I can love him. I do love him.

BRIGHT: Love's a two-way street, man. Do you really *know* this kid? What happens if those crackers start snatching Negroes again in Detroit? Back there, he ain't gonna be white and not quite black. Somethin' in between. And, maybe, just maybe, man, he'll decide that he wants to stay here. Nother thing: we go on another push you know there isn't anything for sure except bein' black. Maybe your wife wouldn't wanna be bothered if you weren't around. . . .

LYONS [*sitting up, shaking these things off*]: I'ma go to his uncle's.

BRIGHT: You haven't been listenin' to me.

LYONS: Wanna come?

BRIGHT: Naw.

LYONS [*standing, briskly*]: Gotta go. The guys'll be in for noon chow direckly. You chowin' down?

BRIGHT [*as LYONS exits*]: I'm not hungry. [*Lies down as if very weary and draws up his knees and closes his eyes. Lights dim. And dim again. And a third time, to denote the passage of time and late afternoon. Now we hear the trucks grinding up to the camp again, and the voices of many men. It is now about 5:30.* BRIGHT *is still asleep as* ROY, *a worried look on his face, enters carrying new equipment: fatigues, shoes, rifle, pack and helmet. He throws it all on his cot and looks at the sleeping* BRIGHT *with disgust.*]

ROY: Bright! Wake the fuck up, Doc. [*Kicks the legs of the cot.*] Doc!

BRIGHT [*bolting upright*]: What! What! Aw, shit, Roy. Don't do that, man. What time's it?

ROY [*full head of anger*]: Looka that shit! (Points to the gear.) *Lookatit!* They just gave us this crap. A *push*, we're goin' on another fuckin *push!* [*Strips to his shorts and grabs a towel. Pauses in the door.*] And you layin' there sleepin'!

BRIGHT [*as ROY exits*]: What you want me to do, call Nimitz or Truman? [*Calling after.*] How long you guys been in?

[BRIGHT *stands and stretches. Goes to* ROY'*s cot and distastefully looks at the gear.*]

CHIEF PERKINS [*entering with a can of beer he gives to* BRIGHT. *The* CHIEF *is white, wears his cap tough-guy style, on the side of his head*]: Gettin' a little sacktime, eh, Bright?

BRIGHT: Hi, Chief. Heh, heh. Thanks for the beer. Damn! Ice cold, too.

CHIEF: Yeah, we got some ice from the kitchen. [*Sits.*] We gotta start cholera innocula-tions tomorrow.

BRIGHT: Where we goin' Chief?

CHIEF: Japan. Honshu. I heard it at the Fleet Hospital today.

BRIGHT: Okay, where's Honshu?

CHIEF [*drinking from his own can*]: That's where Tokyo is.

BRIGHT: Yep, that's just where it'd be all right.

CHIEF: I want you to skip sick call tonight and check out the kits against this list. [*Removes paper from his pocket and hands it over.*] Also, we need some stretcher-bearers. At least fifty. Dardano is stenciling the helmets now.

BRIGHT [*quickly*]: Tell 'im not to stencil mine. I'll take it the way it is.

CHIEF: Geneva convention. Big white circle, red cross in the middle. You know that. Make sure there're plenty of ABDs, extras, all the sulfas, morphine syrettes, and tags. The doctor will have cleared the morphine by the time you're ready.

BRIGHT: Who else is workin' on that detail, Chief?

CHIEF: Nobody. [*Stands.*] Beats the docks, don't it? [*Exits.*]

ROY [*storming in*]: What the fuck's he doin' here? [*Puts on fresh clothes from his footlocker.*]

BRIGHT: Announcing our destination—TO-KEE-YO!

ROY: Straight shit?

BRIGHT: That's what the man said. Tokyo on the island of Honshu.

ROY: Let's chow down, Doc. [*They take their mess kits and exit, meeting* LYONS, *who rushes in.*] Say, Lyons?

LYONS [*wiping off, pulling out fresh clothes*]: How you doin' man? Doc?

BRIGHT: What's the rush?

LYONS [*still dressing*]: Got a ride out to Frankie's uncle's house.

BRIGHT: Didn't you hear the news?

LYONS [*as they finish the exit*]: Why you think I'm rushin'? [*Finishes and exits.*]

DIXON [*off, but near the tent*]: Camel! Camel! Wait up. [*Beats. His voice is low, secretive.*] Goin' to chow?

CAMEL [*his voice is normal, sweet*]: No.

DIXON: What're you gonna do?

CAMEL: Why, nothing. Why do I have to *do* anything?

DIXON: Wanna go for a walk?

CAMEL: With who?

DIXON: With me, who do you think?

CAMEL [*after a pause*]: No, thank you.

DIXON [*surprised*]: Why not?

CAMEL: I don't want to.

DIXON [*incredulous*]: You sure?

CAMEL [*laughing ribbons of sweet laughter*]: Of course, I'm sure.

DIXON [*indignant, loud*]: You damned faggot, runnin' around here shakin' your skinny ass, you ain't— [CAMEL'*s laughter interrupts and overrides* DIXON'*s rantings. It quickly grows darker.*]

SCENE III

It is two hours later. The darkness has a silvery quality to it. The tent is empty, but all around we hear the voices of the men in the camp, singing, yelling at cards or craps, just plain talking. The PA system goes on. Perry Como sings "Dream"; Woody Herman's "Herd" blasts through "Caldonia" and "Lemon Drop"; Duke Ellington does "I'm Beginning to See the Light," and "Sentimental Lady." From time to time we hear the DJ through the following:

ROY [*entering with* BRIGHT, *who is carrying his new gear, including the stenciled helmet and M-1 carbine. He dumps it all on his cot*]: Doc, you know you ain't supposed to have no weapon.

BRIGHT [*muttering*]: Suppose my ass. [*Hefts the carbine.*] Had one of these on Peliliu. Look, Roy, I wanna be ready in case one of them jumps in my hole. I can't say to the cat, "Look here, Jim. You can't shoot me. *I'm* a pharmacist's mate, a corpsman, a medic, and I'm here on an errand of mercy."

ROY [*laughing*]: You ain't supposed to be in no hole, Doc. You *spozed* to be out there helpin' us. If we need it.

BRIGHT: An' you're gonna need it! Here come a buncha crackers walkin' through your hometown, shootin' down your kids, your ole lady, blowin' up your house— [*Beats.*] Is that how come you don't wanna be a stretcher-bearer?

ROY [*after beats*]: The war's got to be close to over. I just don't want my ass shot on a hummer, an' I mean a hummer! Look how they fucked over you with that medal you was supposed to get after Peliliu. They don't give a shit 'bout what you done, we done. I don't want to be involved in no heroics. Every man save his own ass best way he can.

BRIGHT [*patiently*]: Once you on the beach, Roy, you could get it any whichaway. Spoze that happened to you and you were layin' out there with a hole in your ass. Would you want me or stretcher-bearers to try to get to you or just leave you whinin' and cryin'? Ain't talkin' about no heroics, man; I'm talkin about obligation.

ROY [*sullenly*]: What do you think?

BRIGHT: Well, that's all there is, man. Nobody lookin' to be a hero. You think the Chief, McElhenny, Dardano, or them others gonna look after us better than we look out for our own? You gonna work with me, Roy?

ROY: Ah, shit, I guess so. We gonna have to wear those helmets?

BRIGHT [*sharing a confidence*]: Nothin' to it. Take some mud and smear it over that white circle and the red cross. Same with the arm band. Just put some goddamn mud on 'em.

ROY: Okay, man. I got the message. You goin' to the movie?

BRIGHT: I gotta get back over to the sick bay. [*There is a sudden break in the background sounds of music and voices, and we hear the DJ talking, though we cannot yet understand him, hurriedly, excitedly. A shout goes up. There are running footsteps. Voices are louder. The music resumes.*]

ROY [*as* BRIGHT *hesitates*]: What's goin' on? [*Shouts out of the entrance.*] What's goin' on?

DIXON [*flying through the entrance*]: You hear *that* shit? They dropped an atom bomb on Hiroshima.

BRIGHT [*as they huddle*]: What kinda bomb is that?

DIXON: Brighter than a hundred suns, they said. Killed every swingin' dick for miles around.

ROY [*walking around the tent, slamming his fist into his hand*]: Oh, yeah! Oh, yeah! Surrender, you bastards! Surrender!

DIXON [*excitedly*]: That's what they tole those suckers. Surrender or we'll drop another one. Oh, man, let this shit be *over!*

CAMEL [*off*]: The C.O.'s called off everything for tomorrow, work, shots . . .

DIXON [*smiling out at him*]: No shit, Camel. We *got* to celebrate! [*Sidles out of the tent.*]

[*There is another break in the music and noise. The DJ's voice, louder now, echoing through the camp, says "the bomb was released at 8:15 this morning by crews of the Pacific Strategic Air Command. President Truman has urged the Japanese government to accept his demand for unconditional surrender. We will broadcast the latest bulletins as they come in and now back to . . ." There is more music. Within the camp, the sounds of exuberance move to a higher pitch.* ROY *goes into his footlocker and brings out a bottle.*]

ROY [*breaking the seal and taking a swallow*]: Dunbar's Canadian! [*Passes it to* BRIGHT, *then gets up and starts dancing to the music.* BRIGHT *passes it back as* LYONS *comes up the steps, his face set.*] Hi, Lyons! Looks like this shit is about over! [*Passes him the bottle.*] Drink up! [LYONS *refuses with a shake of his head.* ROY *stops dancing, looks from* LYONS *to* BRIGHT.]

LYONS: Doc?

BRIGHT: Yeah, man, what's up?

LYONS [*in a monotone*]: Step outside.

ROY: What's wrong, Lyons?

BRIGHT: You serious?

LYONS: Yeah, come *on!*

ROY [*menacingly*]: Hey!

BRIGHT [*placatingly*]: Listen, Lyons.

LYONS: You gonna fight or not?

ROY [*flexing every muscle*]: What's this all about?

BRIGHT [*standing*]: Frankie, I guess.

ROY [*restraining* BRIGHT]: So, what about Frankie?

BRIGHT: Lyons, tell him.

LYONS [*rocking on the balls of his feet*]: He's not coming home with me. This fuckin' Bright here. After what he told the kid, Frankie said he didn't want to be like *us*, didn't want to be treated the way we're treated here—

ROY [*a harsh laugh*]: Man, you're lucky.

LYONS [*without heat*]: Shut up, Roy. [BRIGHT *starts through the entrance.* LYONS *starts to follow, but* ROY *grabs his arm.*]

BRIGHT: Let him go, Roy.

ROY: No. What'd you say, Doc?

BRIGHT: I just told him the way it was for us; how it'd be for him, and that he was treating Lyons like shit.

ROY: There ain't a sumbitch in this outfit that wouldn't agree with that, Lyons. Man, the kid was rotten. He laughed at you. He was making a fool of you. You'd a got him back there—maybe—and he'd a walked away from you in a minute. Don't you dig, man? Frankie and the rest of these Chamorros, do not dig black people! The crackers got to them. Shit, they half black themselves—

LYONS [*tearing loose*]: C'mon, Doc, les go!

ROY [*thrusting himself between them as they start out*]: Oh, no! Not over that kid. Some pussy, maybe, but not Frankie. We been together for two years, man don't that count for somethin'? We've seen a whole lotta Frankies, from the Solomons all the way up here, now ain't we? *Ain't* we, Lyons? Lotas black kids down there, New Guinea, Guadalcanal . . . *Melanesians*, remember? [*Softer.*] Didn't want to adopt any of them, hey, ole buddy? That's America you wanted to take that boy to, where the school-books are poisoned. We all hoped you'd wake up, man. Doc did you a favor. He loves you more than you love yourself. *Now*, if you still wanna fight, you're gonna have to whip me first, and you know there ain't a sumbitch in this outfit that can whip me.

BRIGHT [*as* LYONS *wrenches away and throws himself down on his cot*]: Lyons? Lyons, listen, man. You just picked the wrong kid at the wrong time in the wrong war. It ain't nothin'. [*Takes the bottle from* ROY, *passes it to* LYONS. *This time he accepts, takes a deep breath and nods.*] All right man?

LYONS [*voice shaky*]: I *know* you cats are right. But it—hurts.

ROY: The whole fuckin' war hurts, Lyons. But Doc wouldn't bullshit you. None of us would. [*Takes the bottle, drinks, sighs. Peers out.*] Well, looks like this shit is just about over.

LYONS [*climbs slowly to his feet*]: Yeah, it does. I think I'll take a walk. See what's goin' on.

BRIGHT: I'll come with you.

ROY: Me, too. [*They start out with the bottle.* BRIGHT *pauses to look around the tent.*]

BRIGHT: You wrong, Roy. I think this shit's just starting.

Slow lights as they exit.

QUESTIONS

1. What mood is established in the opening description? What images in particular set this mood?
2. How would you characterize Bright? What are his attitudes, values, beliefs?
3. What are the reasons the black land-based sailors feel hostility toward the whites? What irony is there in the fact that they are participating in a war fought against Orientals?
4. What does Roy mean when he tells Lyons "that's America you wanted to take that boy to, where the schoolbooks are poisoned"? In the last line of the play, Bright says, "You wrong, Roy. I think this shit's just starting." What is he referring to?

War & Peace

Drama

TOPICS FOR WRITING

1. Lysistrata chooses to enact a plan to end war; the Sergeant decides to let the Irish Revolutionary go free. Select a time in your life when you were faced with a moral issue that would have an impact on others. Describe how you dealt with the issue and how you resolved it.
2. To study dramatic form, select one of the short stories in this section and adapt it as a play.
3. Write an essay analyzing the reasons for anger among the black soldiers toward the white soldiers and white society in general in *August Forty-Five*. Quote directly from the characters' dialogue to support your points.
4. The Irish Revolutionary subtly persuades the Sergeant not to arrest him. Write an essay describing the various methods used by the fugitive in achieving his goal.
5. There are methods for achieving world peace that no one has attempted to implement. Argue for or against this position by enumerating the methods and explaining how they might be realized.
6. Understanding among races has progressed so that today in any given environment—for example, school, the armed forces, corporations, social gathering places—separation among races is a rarity and certainly not like the environment depicted in *August Forty-Five*. Agree or disagree.
7. As a research project, study the genre of Greek classic comedy. Write an essay describing how Aristophanes' *Lysistrata* conforms to the conventions of this form.
8. Both "Easter 1916" and *The Rising of the Moon* concern the Irish independence movement. Research the literature written about that movement and select two plays, two poems, or two short stories to compare and contrast in terms of theme or character.
9. Compare and contrast the attitude toward war and army life among the land-based sailors in *August Forty-Five* with that of soldiers from a play about the Vietnam War. Find the latter through library research and with assistance from your instructor.

Faith

Doubt

"I Baptize Thee" by William H. Johnson. c. 1940. National Museum of American Art, Washington, D.C./Art Resource, N.Y. (1967.59.977)

INTRODUCTION

To "have faith" has several connotations. Taken in its more religious aspect, faith usually signifies belief in a metaphysical being or spirit without the necessity for empirical proof. Having religious faith means trusting that something exists apart from the mundane world, without benefit of evidence. All religions are based on faith, and could not exist without it. But there are other forms of faith that, although perhaps less global, are nevertheless essential for our day-to-day existence. For example, most of us have faith in our doctor, the local police officer, the fire fighter; we must have faith that the mode of transportation we take to school or work will be reliable; we need to have faith that our efforts today will pay off tomorrow. While these convictions may not be religious in nature, this form of faith also requires trust without certainty. So whether one adheres to the teachings of an organized religion—either strictly or casually—or whether one is an atheist or agnostic, faith is essential to our lives.

It is most likely true, however, that all of us have experienced doubt at one time or another. We may have doubted the existence of God; doubted the wisdom of our parents or teachers; doubted the reliability of a tool or technological device; and doubted ourselves. Healthy doubt is probably necessary for our well-being as well. If we were absolutely sure of our convictions, we would be rigid, unflinching individuals who could not be open to change or growth. Finding a balance between the two, then, is essential if we are to live reasonably healthy lives. Miguel de Unamuno, the Spanish writer and philosopher, wrote: "To doubt is to have faith." Perhaps he meant that to believe in something blindly, without ever questioning our convictions, makes us unthinking, unfeeling automatons, and therefore would make our faith rather insipid and pointless.

This idea is addressed comically in Philip Roth's story "The Conversion of the Jews." In it, the young man Ozzie questions his rabbi, who is the religious leader of the community. Ozzie's skepticism is quite logical. If, as the rabbi says, God can do anything, then Ozzie reasons he can arrange a virgin birth. The rabbi, acting in accordance with his faith, claims God cannot perform such a miracle. This argument leads to a hilarious confrontation between Ozzie and the rabbi that raises important questions concerning the relationship of doubt and faith. In a darker mode, the Colombian writer Gabriel García Márquez presents the story of a rather pathetic-looking angel (at least he appears to be an angel) in "A Very Old Man with Enormous Wings." No one in the small town where this angel lands feels comfortable with him although

813

he bears some resemblance to a heavenly being. Not only that, a child in the village is miraculously cured of an illness when the winged man arrives. Nevertheless, the townspeople are skeptical, not knowing what to make of this odd creature in their midst. Perhaps Márquez is implying that one should not have stereotypical visions of what is holy and sent by God. If the villagers in the Márquez story appear closeminded, those in Shirley Jackson's story "The Lottery" are positively pathological in their adherence to faith and tradition. Jackson paints a morbid picture of a place where blind allegiance to ritual supercedes any form of independent thought. In this biting allegory, the local tradition of stoning to death a member of the community is performed without questioning. The mere fact that it has been done in the past is reason enough to continue the rite in the present.

These stories deal with either an individual's or a group's response to a form of longstanding, traditional faith. However, just as valid and relevant is a faith in everyday things. Take the poem "Preface to a Twenty Volume Suicide Note" by Amiri Baraka, whose narrator amidst the precariousness of his life finds profound meaning in peeking into his daughter's room where she is kneeling and praying. Or take as another example the narrator in Raymond Carver's short story "Cathedral." He is a skeptical, sardonic man who seems to carry a certain resentment toward life. Yet this cynical attitude is changed one night when a blind man—a friend of his wife—visits the household. Through the narrator's simple act of helping the blind man trace the form of a cathedral onto a piece of paper, a communion is formed that changes the attitude of this doubtful, pessimistic man through the influence of the positive and hopeful sightless one.

Somewhere between traditional images of faith and doubt and everyday expressions of these phenomena lies a twilight region where individuals have personal, singular visions that can be described and defined as religious, although one would be hardpressed to find such images in conventional iconography or sacred texts. Perhaps this is due to the modern world's general crisis in faith, when issues of right and wrong are not as clearcut as they once were. René Depestre describes such an experience in his poem "Nothingness." The narrator refers to his heart being replaced, and in its stead "A hard little pebble shines in the sun." We can only infer from this image that he is expressing the anguish of doubt and confusion. But even this poem's imagery of a crisis of faith is conventional compared to the situation as described in Jayne Cortez's "Making It." What the latter describes is the world of the urban ghetto with its "eye droppers" (a common tool of drug addicts) and "pills." When the narrator says "I know they want me to make it/but i'm not in a hurry," she may be implying that drug addiction is simultaneously a heaven and hell—a state probably inconceivable to earlier writers.

To round out our discussion of this section of the book, a brief look at Louise Erdrich's poem "The Strange People" is apt, for here we see the issue of spirituality—not in the Judeo-Christian model which most in the West are familiar with—but through the eyes of a Native American whose tradition of religious practice and beliefs are quite different. Erdrich allows us to enter the psyche of one who has grown up in a culture of animism, which has, as part of its doctrine, the view that all living things are imbued with spirit. In this poem, the narrator speaks through the persona of a doe who is being tracked by a hunter, and describes the symbiotic spiritual relationship between the two. While this poem may be outside the purview of what we ordinarily think of as the spiritual, it opens up a sanctified world that we may never have been exposed to. And like all good literature, it broadens our understanding of ourselves through the imagination and experience of another.

Raymond Carver
CATHEDRAL

This blind man, an old friend of my wife's, he was on his way to spend the night. His wife had died. So he was visiting the dead wife's relatives in Connecticut. He called my wife from his in-laws'. Arrangements were made. He would come by train, a five-hour trip, and my wife would meet him at the station. She hadn't seen him since she worked for him one summer in Seattle ten years ago. But she and the blind man had kept in touch. They made tapes and mailed them back and forth. I wasn't enthusiastic about his visit. He was no one I knew. And his being blind bothered me. My idea of blindness came from the movies. In the movies, the blind moved slowly and never laughed. Sometimes they were led by seeing-eye dogs. A blind man in my house was not something I looked forward to.

That summer in Seattle she had needed a job. She didn't have any money. The man she was going to marry at the end of the summer was in officers' training school. He didn't have any money, either. But she was in love with the guy, and he was in love with her, etc. She'd seen something in the paper: HELP WANTED—*Reading to Blind Man,* and a telephone number. She phoned and went over, was hired on the spot. She'd worked with this blind man all summer. She read stuff to him, case studies, reports, that sort of thing. She helped him organize his little office in the county social-service department. They'd become good friends, my wife and the blind man. How do I know these things? She told me. And she told me something else. On her last day in the office, the blind man asked if he could touch her face. She agreed to this. She told me he touched his fingers to every part of her face, her nose—even her neck! She never forgot it. She even tried to write a poem about it. She was always trying to write a poem. She wrote a poem or two every year, usually after something really important had happened to her.

When we first started going out together, she showed me the poem. In the poem, she recalled his fingers and the way they had moved around over her face. In the poem, she talked about what she had felt at the time, about what went through her mind when the blind man touched her nose and lips. I can remember I didn't think much of the poem. Of course, I didn't tell her that. Maybe I just don't understand poetry. I admit it's not the first thing I reach for when I pick up something to read.

Anyway, this man who'd first enjoyed her favors, the officer-to-be, he'd been her childhood sweetheart. So okay. I'm saying that at the end of the summer she let the blind man run his hands over her face, said goodbye to him, married her childhood etc., who was now a commissioned officer, and she moved away from Seattle. But they'd kept in touch, she and the blind man. She made the first contact after a year or so. She called him up one night from an Air Force base in Alabama. She wanted to talk. They talked. He asked her to send him a tape and tell him about her life. She did this. She sent the tape. On the tape, she told the blind man about her husband and about their life together in the military. She told the blind man she loved her husband but she didn't like it where they lived and she didn't like it that he was a part of the military-industrial thing. She told the blind man she'd written a poem and he was in it. She told him that she was writing a poem about what it was like to be an Air Force officer's wife. The poem wasn't finished yet. She was still writing it. The blind man made a tape. He sent her the tape. She made a tape. This went on for years. My wife's officer was posted to one base and then another. She sent tapes from Moody AFB, McGuire, McConnell, and finally Travis, near Sacramento, where one night she got to feeling lonely and cut off from people she kept losing in that moving-around life. She got to feeling she couldn't go it another step. She went in and swallowed all the pills and capsules in the medicine chest and washed them down with a bottle of gin. Then she got into a hot bath and passed out.

But instead of dying, she got sick. She threw up. Her officer—why should he have a name? he was the childhood sweetheart, and what more does he want?—came home from somewhere, found her, and called the ambulance. In time, she put it all on a tape and sent the tape to the blind man. Over the years, she put all kinds of stuff on tapes and sent the tapes off lickety-split. Next to writing a poem every year, I think it was her chief means of recreation. On one tape, she told the blind man she'd decided to live away from her officer for a time. On another tape, she told him about her divorce. She and I began going out, and of course she told her blind man about it. She told him everything, or so it seemed to me. Once she asked me if I'd like to hear the latest tape from the blind man. This was a year ago. I was on the tape, she said. So I said okay, I'd listen to it. I got us drinks and we settled down in the living room. We made ready to listen. First she inserted the tape into the player and adjusted a couple of dials. Then she pushed a lever. The tape squeaked and someone began to talk in this loud voice. She lowered the volume. After a few minutes of harmless chitchat, I heard my own name in the mouth of this stranger, this blind man I didn't even know! And then this:

"From all you've said about him, I can only conclude—" But we were interrupted, a knock at the door, something, and we didn't ever get back to the tape. Maybe it was just as well. I'd heard all I wanted to.

Now this same blind man was coming to sleep in my house.

"Maybe I could take him bowling," I said to my wife. She was at the draining board doing scalloped potatoes. She put down the knife she was using and turned around.

"If you love me," she said, "you can do this for me. If you don't love me, okay. But if you had a friend, any friend, and the friend came to visit, I'd make him feel comfortable." She wiped her hands with the dish towel.

"I don't have any blind friends," I said.

"You don't have *any* friends," she said. "Period. Besides," she said, "goddamn it, his wife's just died! Don't you understand that? The man's lost his wife!"

I didn't answer. She'd told me a little about the blind man's wife. Her name was Beulah. Beulah! That's a name for a colored woman.

"Was his wife a Negro?" I asked.

"Are you crazy?" my wife said. "Have you just flipped or something?" She picked up a potato. I saw it hit the floor, then roll under the stove. "What's wrong with you?" she said. "Are you drunk?"

"I'm just asking," I said.

Right then my wife filled me in with more detail than I cared to know. I made a drink and sat at the kitchen table to listen. Pieces of the story began to fall into place.

Beulah had gone to work for the blind man the summer after my wife had stopped working for him. Pretty soon Beulah and the blind man had themselves a church wedding. It was a little wedding—who'd want to go to such a wedding in the first place?—just the two of them, plus the minister and the minister's wife. But it was a church wedding just the same. It was what Beulah had wanted, he'd said. But even then Beulah must have been carrying the cancer in her glands. After they had been inseparable for eight years—my wife's word, *inseparable*—Beaulah's health went into a rapid decline. She died in a Seattle hospital room, the blind man sitting beside the bed and holding on to her hand. They'd married, lived and worked together, slept together— had sex, sure—and then the blind man had to bury her. All this without his having ever seen what the goddamned woman looked like. It was beyond my understanding. Hearing this, I felt sorry for the blind man for a little bit. And then I found myself thinking what a pitiful life this woman must have led. Imagine a woman who could never see herself as she was seen in the eyes of her loved one. A woman who could go on day after day and never receive the smallest compliment from her beloved. A woman whose husband could never read the expression on her face, be it misery or something better. Someone who could wear makeup or not—what difference to him? She could, if she wanted, wear green eyeshadow around one eye, a straight pin in her nostril, yellow slacks and purple shoes, no matter. And then to slip off into death, the blind man's hand on her hand, his blind eyes streaming tears—I'm imagining now—her last thought maybe this: that he never even knew what she looked like, and she on an express to the grave. Robert was left with a small insurance policy and half of a twenty-peso Mexican coin. The other half of the coin went into the box with her. Pathetic.

So when the time rolled around, my wife went to the depot to pick him up. With nothing to do but wait—sure, I blamed him for that—I was having a drink and watching the TV when I heard the car pull into the drive. I got up from the sofa with my drink and went to the window to have a look.

I saw my wife laughing as she parked the car. I saw her get out of the car and shut the door. She was still wearing a smile. Just amazing. She went around to the other side of the car to where the blind man was already starting to get out. This blind man, feature this, he was wearing a full beard! A beard on a blind man! Too much, I say. The blind man reached into the back seat and dragged out a suitcase. My wife took his arm, shut the car door, and, talking all the way, moved him down the drive and then up the steps to the front porch. I turned off the TV. I finished my drink, rinsed the glass, dried my hands. Then I went to the door.

My wife said, "I want you to meet Robert. Robert, this is my husband. I've told you all about him." She was beaming. She had this blind man by his coat sleeve.

The blind man let go of his suitcase and up came his hand. I took it. He squeezed hard, held my hand, and then he let it go.

"I feel like we've already met," he boomed.

"Likewise," I said. I didn't know what else to say. Then I said. "Welcome. I've heard a lot about you." We began to move then, a little group, from the porch into the living room, my wife guiding him by the arm. The blind man was carrying his suitcase in his other hand. My wife said things like, "To your left here, Robert. That's right. Now watch it, there's a chair. That's it. Sit down right here. This is the sofa. We just bought this sofa two weeks ago."

I started to say something about the old sofa. I'd liked that old sofa. But I didn't say anything. Then I wanted to say something else, small-talk, about the scenic ride along the Hudson. How going *to* New York, you should sit on the right-hand side of the train, and coming *from* New York, the left-hand side.

"Did you have a good train ride?" I said, "Which side of the train did you sit on, by the way?"

"What a question, which side!" my wife said. "What's it matter which side?" she said.

"I just asked," I said.

"Right side," the blind man said. "I hadn't been on a train in nearly forty years. Not since I was a kid. With my folks. That's been a long time. I'd nearly forgotten the sensation. I have winter in my beard now," he said. "So I've been told, anyway. Do I look distinguished, my dear?" the blind man said to my wife.

"You look distinguished, Robert," she said. "Robert," she said. "Robert, it's just so good to see you."

My wife finally took her eyes off the blind man and looked at me. I had the feeling she didn't like what she saw. I shrugged.

I've never met, or personally known, anyone who was blind. This blind man was late forties, a heavy-set, balding man with stooped shoulders, as if he carried a great weight there. He wore brown slacks, brown shoes, a light-brown shirt, a tie, a sports coat. Spiffy. He also had this full beard. But he didn't use a cane and he didn't wear dark glasses. I'd always thought dark glasses were a must for the blind. Fact was, I wished he had a pair. At first glance, his eyes looked like anyone else's eyes. But if you looked close, there was something different about them. Too much white in the iris, for one thing, and the pupils seemed to move round in the sockets without his knowing it or being able to stop it. Creepy. As I stared at his face, I saw the left pupil turn in toward his nose while the other made an effort to keep in one place. But it was only an effort, for that eye was on the roam without knowing it or wanting it to be.

I said, "Let me get you a drink. What's your pleasure? We have a little of everything. It's one of our pastimes."

"Bub, I'm a Scotch man myself," he said fast enough in this big voice.

"Right," I said. Bub! "Sure you are. I knew it."

He let his fingers touch his suitcase, which was sitting alongside the sofa. He was taking his bearings. I didn't blame him for that.

"I'll move that up to your room," my wife said.

"No, that's fine," the blind man said loudly. "It can go up when I go up."

"A little water with the Scotch?" I said.

"Very little," he said.

"I knew it," I said.

He said, "Just a tad. The Irish actor, Barry Fitzgerald? I'm like that fellow. When I drink water, Fitzgerald said, I drink water. When I drink whiskey, I drink whiskey." My wife laughed. The blind man brought his hand up under his beard. He lifted his beard slowly and let it drop.

I did the drinks, three big glasses of Scotch with a splash of water in each. Then we made ourselves comfortable and talked about Robert's travels. First the long flight from the West Coast to Connecticut, we covered that. Then from Connecticut up here by train. We had another drink concerning that leg of the trip.

I remembered having read somewhere that the blind didn't smoke because, as speculation had it, they couldn't see the smoke they exhaled. I thought I knew that much and that much only about blind people. But this blind man smoked his cigarette down to the nubbin and then lit another one. This blind man filled his ashtray and my wife emptied it.

When we sat down at the table for dinner, we had another drink. My wife heaped Robert's plate with cube steak, scalloped potatoes, green beans. I buttered him up two slices of bread. I said, "Here's bread and butter for you." I swallowed some of my drink. "Now let us pray," I said, and the blind man lowered his head. My wife looked at me, her mouth agape. "Pray the phone won't ring and the food doesn't get cold," I said.

We dug in. We ate everything there was to eat on the table. We ate like there was no tomorrow. We didn't talk. We ate. We scarfed. We grazed that table. We were into serious eating. The blind man had right away located his foods, he knew just where everything was on his plate. I watched with admiration as he used his knife and fork on the meat. He'd cut two pieces of meat, fork the meat into his mouth, and then go all out for the scalloped potatoes, the beans next, and then he'd tear off a hunk of buttered bread and eat that. He'd follow this up with a big drink of milk. It didn't seem to bother him to use his fingers once in a while, either.

We finished everything, including half a strawberry pie. For a few moments, we sat as if stunned. Sweat beaded on our faces. Finally, we got up from the table and left the dirty plates. We didn't look back. We took ourselves into the living room and sank into our places again. Robert and my wife sat on the sofa. I took the big chair. We had us two or three more drinks while they talked about the major things that had come to pass for them in the past ten years. For the most part, I just listened. Now and then I joined in. I didn't want him to think I'd left the room, and I didn't want her to think I was feeling left out. They talked of things that had happened to them—to them!—these past ten years. I waited in vain to hear my name on my wife's sweet lips: "And then my dear husband came into my life"—something like that. But I heard nothing of the sort. More talk of Robert. Robert had done a little of everything, it seemed, a regular blind jack-of-all trades. But most recently he and his wife had had an Amway distributorship, from which, I gathered, they'd earned their living, such as it was. The blind man was also a ham radio operator. He talked in his loud voice about conversations he'd had with fellow operators in Guam, in the Philippines, in Alaska, and even in Tahiti. He said he'd have a lot of friends there if he ever wanted to go visit those places. From time to time, he'd turn his blind face toward me, put his hand under his beard, ask me something. How long had I been in my present position? (Three years.) Did I like my work? (I didn't.) Was I going to stay with it? (What were the options?) Finally, when I thought he was beginning to run down, I got up and turned on the TV.

My wife looked at me with irritation. She was heading toward a boil. Then she looked at the blind man and said, "Robert, do you have a TV?"

The blind man said, "My dear, I have two TVs. I have a color set and a black-and-white thing, an old relic. It's funny, but if I turn the TV on, and I'm always turning it on, I turn on the color set. It's funny, don't you think?"

I didn't know what to say to that. I had absolutely nothing to say to that. No opinion. So I watched the news program and tried to listen to what the announcer was saying.

"This is a color TV," the blind man said. "Don't ask me how, but I can tell."

"We traded up a while ago," I said.

The blind man had another taste of his drink. He lifted his beard, sniffed it, and let it fall. He leaned forward on the sofa. He positioned his ashtray on the coffee table, then put the lighter to his cigarette. He leaned back on the sofa and crossed his legs at the ankles.

My wife covered her mouth, and then she yawned. She stretched. She said, "I think I'll go upstairs and put on my robe. I think I'll change into something else. Robert, you make yourself comfortable," she said.

"I'm comfortable," the blind man said.

"I want you to feel comfortable in this house," she said.

"I am comfortable," the blind man said.

After she'd left the room, he and I listened to the weather report and then to the sports roundup. By that time, she'd been gone so long I didn't know if she was going to come back. I thought she might have gone to bed. I wished she'd come back downstairs. I didn't want to be left alone with a blind man. I asked him if he wanted another drink, and he said sure. Then I asked if he wanted to smoke some dope with me. I said I'd just rolled a number. I hadn't, but I planned to do so in about two shakes.

"I'll try some with you," he said.

"Damn right," I said. "That's the stuff."

I got our drinks and sat down on the sofa with him. Then I rolled us two fat numbers. I lit one and passed it. I brought it to his fingers. He took it and inhaled.

"Hold it as long as you can," I said. I could tell he didn't know the first thing.

My wife came back downstairs wearing her pink robe and her pink slippers.

"What do I smell?" she said.

"We thought we'd have us some cannabis," I said.

My wife gave me a savage look. Then she looked at the blind man and said, "Robert, I didn't know you smoked."

He said, "I do now, my dear. There's a first time for everything. But I don't feel anything yet."

"This stuff is pretty mellow," I said. "This stuff is mild. It's dope you can reason with," I said. "It doesn't mess you up."

"Not much it doesn't, bub," he said, and laughed.

My wife sat on the sofa between the blind man and me. I passed her the number. She took it and toked and then passed it back to me. "Which way is this going?" she said. Then she said, "I shouldn't be smoking this. I can hardly keep my eyes open as it is. That dinner did me in. I shouldn't have eaten so much."

"It was the strawberry pie," the blind man said. "That's what did it," he said, and he laughed his big laugh. Then he shook his head.

"There's more strawberry pie," I said.

"Do you want some more, Robert?" my wife said.

"Maybe in a little while," he said.

We gave our attention to the TV. My wife yawned again. She said, "Your bed is made up when you feel like going to bed, Robert. I know you must have had a long day. When you're ready to go to bed, say so." She pulled his arm. "Robert?"

He came to and said, "I've had a real nice time. This beats tapes, doesn't it?"

I said, "Coming at you," and I put the number between his fingers. He inhaled, held the smoke, and then let it go. It was like he'd been doing it since he was nine years old.

"Thanks, bub," he said. "But I think this is all for me. I think I'm beginning to feel it," he said. He held the burning roach out for my wife.

"Same here," she said. "Ditto. Me, too." She took the roach and passed it to me. "I may just sit here for a while between you two guys with my eyes closed. But don't let me bother you, okay? Either one of you. If it bothers you, say so. Otherwise, I may just sit here with my eyes closed until you're ready to go to bed," she said. "Your bed's made up, Robert, when you're ready. It's right next to our room at the top of the stairs. We'll show you up when you're ready. You wake me up now, you guys, if I fall asleep." She said that and then she closed her eyes and went to sleep.

The news program ended. I got up and changed the channel. I sat back down on the sofa. I wished my wife hadn't pooped out. Her head lay across the back of the sofa, her mouth open. She'd turned so that her robe had slipped away from her legs, exposing a juicy thigh. I reached to draw her robe back over her, and it was then that I glanced at the blind man. What the hell! I flipped the robe open again.

"You say when you want some strawberry pie," I said.

"I will," he said.

I said, "Are you tired? Do you want me to take you up to your bed? Are you ready to hit the hay?"

"Not yet," he said. "No, I'll stay up with you, bub. If that's all right. I'll stay up until you're ready to turn in. We haven't had a chance to talk. Know what I mean? I feel like me and her monopolized the evening." He lifted his beard and he let it fall. He picked up his cigarettes and his lighter.

"That's all right," I said. Then I said, "I'm glad for the company."

And I guess I was. Every night I smoked dope and stayed up as long as I could before I fell asleep. My wife and I hardly ever went to bed at the same time. When I did go to sleep, I had these dreams. Sometimes I'd wake up from one of them, my heart going crazy.

Something about the church and the Middle Ages was on the TV. Not your run-of-the-mill TV fare. I wanted to watch something else. I turned to the other channels. But there was nothing on them, either. So I turned back to the first channel and apologized.

"Bub, it's all right," the blind man said. "It's fine with me. Whatever you want to watch is okay. I'm always learning something. Learning never ends. It won't hurt me to learn something tonight. I got ears," he said.

We didn't say anything for a time. He was leaning forward with his head turned at me, his right ear aimed in the direction of the set. Very disconcerting. Now and then his eyelids drooped and then they snapped open again. Now and then he put his fingers into his beard and tugged, like he was thinking about something he was hearing on the television.

On the screen, a group of men wearing cowls was being set upon and tormented by men dressed in skeleton costumes and men dressed as devils. The men dressed as devils wore devil masks, horns, and long tails. This pageant was part of a procession. The Englishman who was narrating the thing said it took place in Spain once a year. I tried to explain to the blind man what was happening.

"Skeletons," he said. "I know about skeletons," he said, and he nodded.

The TV showed this one cathedral. Then there was a long, slow look at another one. Finally, the picture switched to the famous one in Paris, with its flying buttresses and its spires reaching up to the clouds. The camera pulled away to show the whole of the cathedral rising above the skyline.

There were times when the Englishman who was telling the thing would shut up, would simply let the camera move around over the cathedrals. Or else the camera would tour the countryside, men in fields walking behind oxen. I waited as long as I could. Then I felt I had to say something. I said, "They're showing the outside of this cathedral now. Gargoyles. Little statues carved to look like monsters. Now I guess they're in Italy. Yeah, they're in Italy. There's paintings on the walls of this one church."

"Are those fresco paintings, bub?" he asked, and he sipped from his drink.

I reached for my glass. But it was empty. I tried to remember what I could remember. "You're asking me are those frescoes?" I said. "That's a good question. I don't know."

The camera moved to a cathedral outside Lisbon. The differences in the Portuguese cathedral compared with the French and Italian were not that great. But they were there. Mostly the interior stuff. Then something occurred to me, and I said, "Something has occurred to me. Do you have any idea what a cathedral is? What they look like, that is? Do you follow me? If somebody says cathedral to you, do you have any notion what they're talking about? Do you know the difference between that and a Baptist church, say?"

He let the smoke dribble from his mouth. "I know they took hundreds of workers fifty or a hundred years to build," he said. "I just heard the man say that, of course. I know generations of the same families worked on a cathedral. I heard him say that, too. The men who began their life's work on them, they never lived to see the completion of their work. In that wise, bub, they're no different from the rest of us, right?" He laughed. Then his eyelids drooped again. His head nodded. He seemed to be snoozing. Maybe he was imagining himself in Portugal. The TV was showing another cathedral now. This one was in Germany. The Englishman's voice droned on. "Cathedrals," the blind man said. He sat up and rolled his head back and forth. "If you want the truth, bub, that's about all I know. What I just said. What I heard him say. But maybe you could describe one to me? I wish you'd do it. I'd like that. If you want to know, I really don't have a good idea."

I stared hard at the shot of the cathedral on the TV. How could I even begin to describe it? But say my life depended on it. Say my life was being threatened by an insane guy who said I had to do it or else.

I stared some more at the cathedral before the picture flipped off into the countryside. There was no use. I turned to the blind man and said, "To begin with, they're very tall." I was looking around the room for clues. "They reach way up. Up and up. Toward the sky. They're so big, some of them, they have to have these supports. To help hold them up, so to speak. These supports are called buttresses. They remind me of viaducts, for some reason. But maybe you don't know viaducts, either? Sometimes the cathedrals have devils and such carved into the front. Sometimes lords and ladies. Don't ask me why this is," I said.

He was nodding. The whole upper part of his body seemed to be moving back and forth.

"I'm not doing so good, am I?" I said.

He stopped nodding and leaned forward on the edge of the sofa. As he listened to me, he was running his fingers through his beard. I wasn't getting through to him, I could see that. But he waited for me to go on just the same. He nodded, like he was trying to encourage me. I tried to think what else to say. "They're really big," I said. "They're massive. They're built of stone. Marble, too, sometimes. In those olden days, when they built cathedrals, men wanted to be close to God. In those olden days, God was an important part of everyone's life. You could tell this from their cathedral-building. I'm sorry," I said, "but it looks like that's the best I can do for you. I'm just no good at it."

"That's all right, bub," the blind man said. "Hey, listen. I hope you don't mind my asking you. Can I ask you something? Let me ask you a simple question, yes or no. I'm just curious and there's no offense. You're my host. But let me ask if you are in any way religious? You don't mind my asking?"

I shook my head. He couldn't see that, though. A wink is the same as a nod to a blind man. "I guess I don't believe in it. In anything. Sometimes it's hard. You know what I'm saying?"

"Sure, I do," he said.

"Right," I said.

The Englishman was still holding forth. My wife sighed in her sleep. She drew a long breath and went on with her sleeping.

"You'll have to forgive me," I said. "But I can't tell you what a cathedral looks like. It just isn't in me to do it. I can't do any more than I've done."

The blind man sat very still, his head down, as he listened to me.

I said, "The truth is, cathedrals don't mean anything special to me. Nothing. Cathedrals. They're something to look at on late-night TV. That's all they are."

It was then that the blind man cleared his throat. He brought something up. He took a handkerchief from his back pocket. Then he said. "I get it, bub. It's okay. It happens. Don't worry about it," he said. "Hey, listen to me. Will you do me a favor? I got an idea. Why don't you find us some heavy paper? And a pen. We'll do something. We'll draw one together. Get us a pen and some heavy paper. Go on, bub, get the stuff," he said.

So I went upstairs. My legs felt like they didn't have any strength in them. They felt like they did after I'd done some running. In my wife's room, I looked around. I found some ballpoints in a little basket on her table. And then I tried to think where to look for the kind of paper he was talking about.

Downstairs, in the kitchen, I found a shopping bag with onion skins in the bottom of the bag. I emptied the bag and shook it. I brought it into the living room and sat down with it near his legs. I moved some things, smoothed the wrinkles from the bag, spread it out on the coffee table.

The blind man got down from the sofa and sat next to me on the carpet.

He ran his fingers over the paper. He went up and down the sides of the paper. The edges, even the edges. He fingered the corners.

"All right," he said. "All right, let's do her."

He found my hand, the hand with the pen. He closed his hand over my hand. "Go ahead, bub, draw," he said. "Draw. You'll see. I'll follow along with you. It'll be okay. Just begin now like I'm telling you. You'll see. Draw," the blind man said.

So I began. First I drew a box that looked like a house. It could have been the house I lived in. Then I put a roof on it. At either end of the roof, I drew spires. Crazy.

"Swell," he said. "Terrific. You're doing fine," he said. "Never thought anything like this could happen in your lifetime, did you, bub? Well, it's a strange life, we all know that. Go on now. Keep it up."

I put in windows with arches. I drew flying buttresses. I hung great doors. I couldn't stop. The TV station went off the air. I put down the pen and closed and opened my fingers. The blind man felt around over the paper. He moved the tips of his fingers over the paper, all over what I had drawn, and he nodded.

"Doing fine," the blind man said.

I took up the pen again, and he found my hand. I kept at it. I'm no artist. But I kept drawing just the same.

My wife opened up her eyes and gazed at us. She sat up on the sofa, her robe hanging open. She said, "What are you doing? Tell me, I want to know."

I didn't answer her.

The blind man said, "We're drawing a cathedral. Me and him are working on it. Press hard," he said to me. "That's right. That's good," he said. "Sure. You got it, bub. I can tell. You didn't think you could. But you can, can't you? You're cooking with gas now. You know what I'm saying? We're going to really have us something here in a minute. How's the old arm?" he said. "Put some people in there now. What's a cathedral without people?"

My wife said, "What's going on? Robert, what are you doing? What's going on?"

"It's all right," he said to her. "Close your eyes now," the blind man said to me.

I did it. I closed them just like he said.

"Are they closed?" he said. "Don't fudge."

"They're closed," I said.

"Keep them that way," he said. He said, "Don't stop now. Draw."

So we kept on with it. His fingers rode my fingers as my hand went over the paper. It was like nothing else in my life up to now.

Then he said, "I think that's it. I think you got it," he said. "Take a look. What do you think?"

But I had my eyes closed. I thought I'd keep them that way for a little longer. I thought it was something I ought to do.

"Well?" he said. "Are you looking?"

My eyes were still closed. I was in my house. I knew that. But I didn't feel like I was inside anything.

"It's really something," I said.

QUESTIONS

1. What is the narrator's initial attitude toward the blind man? Is his attitude based on observation, jealousy, prejudice, or a combination of these? Explain.
2. What type of personality does the narrator have? What about what he says and thinks leads you to your conclusion?
3. The blind man says while they're preparing to watch educational television that "Learning never ends. It won't hurt me to learn something tonight. I got ears." How does this remark reflect the personality of the blind man in general? How does it complement the narrator's general attitude about learning? What irony, if any, is there in their viewpoints?
4. Why do you suppose the wife enjoys the company of the blind man?
5. What insight does the husband have at the end of the story? What instigates this insight? How does it make him change as a person?
6. Carver has often been said to write about the "voiceless" people of America. What do you suppose this means? How does this story demonstrate this quality in his writing?

Gabriel García Márquez

A VERY OLD MAN WITH ENORMOUS WINGS
A Tale for Children

On the third day of rain they had killed so many crabs inside the house that Pelayo had to cross his drenched courtyard and throw them into the sea, because the newborn child had a temperature all night and they thought it was due to the stench. The world had been sad since Tuesday. Sea and sky were a single ash-gray thing and the sands of the beach, which on March nights glimmered like powdered light, had become a stew of mud and rotten shellfish. The light was so weak at noon that when Pelayo was coming back to the house after throwing away the crabs, it was hard for him to see what it was that was moving and groaning in the rear of the courtyard. He had to go very close to see that it was an old man, a very old man, lying face down in the mud, who, in spite of his tremendous efforts, couldn't get up, impeded by his enormous wings.

Frightened by that nightmare, Pelayo ran to get Elisenda, his wife, who was putting compresses on the sick child, and he took her to the rear of the courtyard. They both looked at the fallen body with mute stupor. He was dressed like a ragpicker. There were only a few faded hairs left on his bald skull and very few teeth in his mouth, and his pitiful condition of a drenched great-grandfather had taken away any sense of grandeur he might have had. His huge buzzard wings, dirty and half-plucked, were forever entangled in the mud. They looked at him so long and so closely that Pelayo and Elisenda very soon overcame their surprise and in the end found him familiar. Then they dared speak to him, and he answered in an incomprehensible dialect with a strong sailor's voice. That was how they skipped over the inconvenience of the wings and quite intelligently concluded that he was a lonely castaway from some foreign ship wrecked by the storm. And yet, they called in a neighbor woman who knew everything about life and death to see him, and all she needed was one look to show them their mistake.

"He's an angel," she told them. "He must have been coming for the child, but the poor fellow is so old that the rain knocked him down."

On the following day everyone knew that a flesh-and-blood angel was held captive in Pelayo's house. Against the judgment of the wise neighbor woman, for whom angels in those times were the fugitive survivors of a celestial conspiracy, they did not have the heart to club him to death. Pelayo watched over him all afternoon from the kitchen, armed with his bailiff's club, and before going to bed he dragged him out of the mud and locked him up with the hens in the wire chicken coop. In the middle of the night, when the rain stopped, Pelayo and Elisenda were still killing crabs. A short time afterward the child woke up without a fever and with a desire to eat. Then they felt magnanimous and decided to put the angel on a raft with fresh water and provisions for three days and leave him to his fate on the high seas. But when they went out into the courtyard with the first light of dawn, they found the whole neighborhood in front of the chicken coop having fun with the angel, without the slightest reverence, tossing him things to eat through the openings in the wire as if he weren't a supernatural creature but a circus animal.

Father Gonzaga arrived before seven o'clock, alarmed at the strange news. By that time onlookers less frivolous than those at dawn had already arrived and they were making all kinds of conjectures concerning the captive's future. The simplest among them thought that he should be named mayor of the world. Others of sterner mind felt that he should be promoted to the rank of five-star general in order to win all wars. Some visionaries hoped that he could be put to stud in order to implant on earth a race of winged wise men who could take charge of the universe. But Father Gonzaga, before becoming a priest, had been a robust woodcutter. Standing by the wire, he reviewed his catechism in an instant and asked them to open the door so that he could take a close look at that pitiful man who looked more like a huge decrepit hen among the fascinated chickens. He was lying in a corner drying his open wings in the sunlight among the fruit peels and breakfast leftovers that the early risers had thrown him. Alien to the impertinences of the world, he only lifted his antiquarian eyes and murmured something in his dialect when Father Gonzaga went into the chicken coop and said good morning to him in Latin. The parish priest had his first suspicion of an imposter when he saw that he did not understand the language of God or know how to greet His ministers. Then he noticed that seen close up he was much too human: he had an unbearable smell of the outdoors, the back side of his wings was strewn with parasites and his main feathers had been mistreated by terrestrial winds, and nothing about him measured up to the proud dignity of angels. Then he came out of the chicken coop and in a brief sermon warned the curious against the risks of being ingenuous. He reminded them that the devil had the bad habit of making use of carnival tricks in order to confuse the unwary. He argued that if wings were not the essential element in determining the difference between a hawk and an airplane, they were even less so in the recognition of angels. Nevertheless, he promised to write a letter to his bishop so that the latter would write to his primate so that the latter would write to the Supreme Pontiff in order to get the final verdict from the highest courts.

His prudence fell on sterile hearts. The news of the captive angel spread with such rapidity that after a few hours the courtyard had the bustle of a marketplace and they had to call in troops with fixed bayonets to disperse the mob that was about to knock the house down. Elisenda, her spine all twisted from sweeping up so much marketplace trash, then got the idea of fencing in the yard and charging five cents admission to see the angel.

The curious came from far away. A traveling carnival arrived with a flying acrobat who buzzed over the crowd several times, but no one paid any attention to him because his wings were not those of an angel but, rather, those of a sidereal bat. The most unfortunate invalids on earth came in search of health: a poor woman who since childhood had been counting her heartbeats and had run out of numbers; a Portuguese man who couldn't sleep because the noise of the stars disturbed him; a sleepwalker who got up at night to undo the things he had done while awake; and many others with less serious ailments. In the midst of that shipwreck disorder that made the earth tremble,

Pelayo and Elisenda were happy with fatigue, for in less than a week they had crammed their rooms with money and the line of pilgrims waiting their turn to enter still reached beyond the horizon.

The angel was the only one who took no part in his own act. He spent his time trying to get comfortable in his borrowed nest, befuddled by the hellish heat of the oil lamps and sacramental candles that had been placed along the wire. At first they tried to make him eat some mothballs, which, according to the wisdom of the wise neighbor woman, were the food prescribed for angels. But he turned them down, just as he turned down the papal lunches that the penitents brought him, and they never found out whether it was because he was an angel or because he was an old man that in the end he ate nothing but eggplant mush. His only supernatural virtue seemed to be patience. Especially during the first days, when the hens pecked at him, searching for the stellar parasites that proliferated in his wings, and the cripples pulled out feathers to touch their defective parts with, and even the most merciful threw stones at him, trying to get him to rise so they could see him standing. The only time they succeeded in arousing him was when they burned his side with an iron for branding steers, for he had been motionless for so many hours that they thought he was dead. He awoke with a start, ranting in his hermetic language and with tears in his eyes, and he flapped his wings a couple of times, which brought on a whirlwind of chicken dung and lunar dust and a gale of panic that did not seem to be of this world. Although many thought that his reaction had been one not of rage but of pain, from then on they were careful not to annoy him, because the majority understood that his passivity was not that of a hero taking his ease but that of a cataclysm in repose.

Father Gonzaga held back the crowd's frivolity with formulas of maidservant inspiration while awaiting the arrival of a final judgment on the nature of the captive. But the mail from Rome showed no sense of urgency. They spent their time finding out if the prisoner had a navel, if his dialect had any connection with Aramaic, how many times he could fit on the head of a pin, or whether he wasn't just a Norwegian with wings. Those meager letters might have come and gone until the end of time if a providential event had not put an end to the priest's tribulations.

It so happened that during those days, among so many other carnival attractions, there arrived in town the traveling show of the woman who had been changed into a spider for having disobeyed her parents. The admission to see her was not only less than the admission to see the angel, but people were permitted to ask her all manner of questions about her absurd state and to examine her up and down so that no one would ever doubt the truth of her horror. She was a frightful tarantula the size of a ram and with the head of a sad maiden. What was most heart-rending, however, was not her outlandish shape but the sincere affliction with which she recounted the details of her misfortune. While still practically a child she had sneaked out of her parents' house to go to a dance, and while she was coming back through the woods after having danced all night without permission, a fearful thunderclap rent the sky in two and through the crack came the lightning bolt of brimstone that changed her into a spider. Her only nourishment came from the meatballs that charitable souls chose to toss into her mouth. A spectacle like that, full of so much human truth and with such a fearful lesson, was bound to defeat without even trying that of a haughty angel who scarcely deigned to look at mortals. Besides, the few miracles attributed to the angel showed a certain mental disorder, like the blind man who didn't recover his sight but grew three new teeth, or the paralytic who didn't get to walk but almost won the lottery, and the leper whose sores sprouted sunflowers. Those consolation miracles, which were more like mocking fun, had already ruined the angel's reputation when the woman who had been changed into a spider finally crushed him completely. That was how Father Gonzaga was cured forever of his insomnia and Pelayo's courtyard went back to being as empty as during the time it had rained for three days and crabs walked through the bedrooms.

The owners of the house had no reason to lament. With the money they saved they built a two-story mansion with balconies and gardens and high netting so that crabs wouldn't get in during the winter, and with iron bars on the windows so that angels wouldn't get in. Pelayo also set up a rabbit warren close to town and gave up his job as bailiff for good, and Elisenda bought some satin pumps with high heels and many dresses of iridescent silk, the kind worn on Sunday by the most desirable women in those times. The chicken coop was the only thing that didn't receive any attention. If they washed it down with creolin and burned tears of myrrh inside it every so often, it was not in homage to the angel but to drive away the dungheap stench that still hung everywhere like a ghost and was turning the new house into an old one. At first, when the child learned to walk, they were careful that he not get too close to the chicken coop. But then they began to lose their fears and got used to the smell, and before the child got his second teeth he'd gone inside the chicken coop to play, where the wires were falling apart. The angel was no less standoffish with him than with other mortals, but he tolerated the most ingenious infamies with the patience of a dog who had no illusions. They both came down with chicken pox at the same time. The doctor who took care of the child couldn't resist the temptation to listen to the angel's heart, and he found so much whistling in the heart and so many sounds in his kidneys that it seemed impossible for him to be alive. What surprised him most, however, was the logic of his wings. They seemed so natural on that completely human organism that he couldn't understand why other men didn't have them too.

When the child began school it had been some time since the sun and rain had caused the collapse of the chicken coop. The angel went dragging himself about here and there like a stray dying man. They would drive him out of the bedroom with a broom and a moment later find him in the kitchen. He seemed to be in so many places at the same time that they grew to think that he'd been duplicated, that he was reproducing himself all through the house, and the exasperated and unhinged Elisenda shouted that it was awful living in that hell full of angels. He could scarcely eat and his antiquarian eyes had also become so foggy that he went about bumping into posts. All he had left were the bare cannulae of his last feathers. Pelayo threw a blanket over him and extended him the charity of letting him sleep in the shed, and only then did they notice that he had a temperature at night, and was delirious with the tongue twisters of an old Norwegian. That was one of the few times they became alarmed, for they thought he was going to die and not even the wise neighbor woman had been able to tell them what to do with dead angels.

And yet he not only survived his worst winter, but seemed improved with the first sunny days. He remained motionless for several days in the farthest corner of the courtyard, where no one would see him, and at the beginning of December some large, stiff feathers began to grow on his wings, the feathers of a scarecrow, which looked more like another misfortune of decrepitude. But he must have known the reason for those changes, for he was quite careful that no one should notice them, that no one should hear the sea chanteys that he sometimes sang under the stars. One morning Elisenda was cutting some bunches of onions for lunch when a wind that seemed to come from the high seas blew into the kitchen. Then she went to the window and caught the angel in his first attempts at flight. They were so clumsy that his fingernails opened a furrow in the vegetable patch and he was on the point of knocking the shed down with the ungainly flapping that slipped on the light and couldn't get a grip on the air. But he did manage to gain altitude. Elisenda let out a sigh of relief, for herself and for him, when she saw him pass over the last houses, holding himself up in some way with the risky flapping of a senile vulture. She kept watching him even when she was through cutting the onions and she kept on watching until it was no longer possible for her to see him, because then he was no longer an annoyance in her life but an imaginary dot on the horizon of the sea.

Translated by Gregory Rabassa

QUESTIONS

1. Is there any indication in the story of why the angel has come to earth? What do think is the purpose of his mission?
2. What is the general attitude of the townspeople when the man with enormous wings lands? Why do they have this attitude?
3. What is the attitude of the church in Rome toward the angel? Compare and contrast it with the attitude of the town.
4. How would you characterize the faith of Pelayo and Elisenda? What actions do they take that demonstrate the nature of their faith?

Nathaniel Hawthorne

YOUNG GOODMAN BROWN

Young Goodman Brown came forth at sunset into the street at Salem village; but put his head back, after crossing the threshold, to exchange a parting kiss with his young wife. And Faith, as the wife was aptly named, thrust her own pretty head into the street, letting the wind play with the pink ribbons of her cap while she called to Goodman Brown.

"Dearest heart," whispered she, softly and rather sadly, when her lips were close to his ear, "prithee put off your journey until sunrise and sleep in your own bed to-night. A lone woman is troubled with such dreams and such thoughts that she's afeared of herself sometimes. Pray tarry with me this night, dear husband, of all nights in the year."

"My love and my Faith," replied young Goodman Brown, "of all nights in the year, this one night must I tarry away from thee. My journey, as thou callest it, forth and back again, must needs be done 'twixt now and sunrise. What, my sweet, pretty wife, dost thou doubt me already, and we but three months married?"

"Then God bless you!" said Faith, with the pink ribbons; "and may you find all well when you come back."

"Amen!" cried Goodman Brown. "Say thy prayers, dear Faith, and go to bed at dusk, and no harm will come to thee."

So they parted; and the young man pursued his way until, being about to turn the corner by the meeting-house, he looked back and saw the head of Faith still peeping after him with a melancholy air, in spite of her pink ribbons.

"Poor little Faith!" thought he, for his heart smote him. "What a wretch am I to leave her on such an errand! She talks of dreams, too. Methought as she spoke there was trouble in her face, as if a dream had warned her what work is to be done to-night. But no, no; 't would kill her to think it. Well, she's a blessed angel on earth; and after this one night I'll cling to her skirts and follow her to heaven."

With this excellent resolve for the future, Goodman Brown felt himself justified in making more haste on his present evil purpose. He had taken a dreary road, darkened by all the gloomiest trees of the forest, which barely stood aside to let the narrow path creep through, and closed immediately behind. It was all as lonely as could be; and there is this peculiarity in such a solitude, that the traveller knows not who may be concealed by the innumerable trunks and the thick boughs overhead; so that with lonely footsteps he may yet be passing through an unseen multitude.

"There may be a devilish Indian behind every tree," said Goodman Brown to himself; and he glanced fearfully behind him as he added, "What if the devil himself should be at my very elbow!"

His head being turned back, he passed a crook of the road, and, looking forward again, beheld the figure of a man, in grave and decent attire, seated at the foot of an old tree. He arose at Goodman Brown's approach and walked onward side by side with him.

"You are late, Goodman Brown," said he. "The clock of the Old South was striking as I came through Boston, and that is full fifteen minutes agone."

"Faith kept me back a while," replied the young man, with a tremor in his voice, caused by the sudden appearance of his companion, though not wholly unexpected.

It was now deep dusk in the forest, and deepest in that part of it where these two were journeying. As nearly as could be discerned, the second traveller was about fifty years old, apparently in the same rank of life as Goodman Brown, and bearing a considerable resemblance to him, though perhaps more in expression than features. Still they might have been taken for father and son. And yet, though the elder person was as simply clad as the younger, and as simple in manner too, he had an indescribable air of one who knew the world, and who would not have felt abashed at the governor's dinner table or in King William's court, were it possible that his affairs should call him thither. But the only thing about him that could be fixed upon as remarkable was his staff, which bore the likeness of a great black snake, so curiously wrought that it might almost be seen to twist and wriggle itself like a living serpent. This, of course, must have been an ocular deception, assisted by the uncertain light.

"Come, Goodman Brown," cried his fellow-traveler, "this is a dull pace for the beginning of a journey. Take my staff, if you are so soon weary."

"Friend," said the other, exchanging his slow pace for a full stop, "having kept covenant by meeting thee here, it is my purpose now to return whence I came. I have scruples touching the matter thou wot'st of."

"Sayest thou so?" replied he of the serpent, smiling apart. "Let us walk on, neverthe-less, reasoning as we go; and if I convince thee not thou shalt turn back. We are but a little way in the forest yet."

"Too far! too far!" exclaimed the goodman, unconsciously resuming his walk. "My father never went into the woods on such an errand, nor his father before him. We have been a race of honest men and good Christians since the days of the martyrs; and shall I be the first of the name of Brown that ever took this path and kept"—

"Such company, thou wouldst say," observed the elder person, interpreting his pause. "Well said, Goodman Brown! I have been as well acquainted with your family as with ever a one among the Puritans; and that's no trifle to say. I helped your grandfather, the constable, when he lashed the Quaker woman so smartly through the streets of Salem; and it was I that brought your father a pitchpine knot, kindled at my own hearth, to set fire to an Indian village, in King Philip's war. They were my good friends, both; and many a pleasant walk have we had along this path, and returned merrily after midnight. I would fain be friends with you for their sake."

"If it be as thou sayest," replied Goodman Brown, "I marvel they never spoke of these matters; or, verily, I marvel not, seeing that the least rumor of the sort would have driven them from New England. We are a people of prayer, and good works to boot, and abide no such wickedness."

"Wickedness or not," said the traveller with the twisted staff, "I have a very general acquaintance here in New England. The deacons of many a church have drunk the communion wine with me; the selectmen of divers towns make me their chairman; and a majority of the Great and General Court are firm supporters of my interest. The governor and I, too—But these are state secrets."

"Can this be so?" cried Goodman Brown, with a stare of amazement at his undis-turbed companion. "Howbeit, I have nothing to do with the governor and council; they have their own ways, and are no rule for a simple husbandman like me. But, were I to go on with thee, how should I meet the eye of that good old man, our minister, at Salem village? Oh, his voice would make me tremble both Sabbath day and lecture day."

Thus far the elder traveller had listened with due gravity; but now burst into a fit of irrepressible mirth, shaking himself so violently that his snake-like staff actually seemed to wriggle in sympathy.

"Ha! ha! ha!" shouted he again and again; then composing himself, "Well, go on, Goodman Brown, go on; but, prithee, don't kill me with laughing."

"Well, then, to end the matter at once," said Goodman Brown, considerably nettled, "there is my wife, Faith. It would break her dear little heart; and I'd rather break my own."

"Nay, if that be the case," answered the other, "e'en go thy ways, Goodman Brown. I would not for twenty old women like the one hobbling before us that Faith should come to any harm."

As he spoke he pointed his staff at a female figure on the path, in whom Goodman Brown recognized a very pious and exemplary dame, who had taught him his catechism in youth, and was still his moral and spiritual adviser, jointly with the minister and Deacon Gookin.

"A marvel, truly, that Goody Cloyse should be so far in the wilderness at nightfall," said he. "But with your leave, friend, I shall take a cut through the woods until we have left this Christian woman behind. Being a stranger to you, she might ask whom I was consorting with and whither I was going."

"Be it so," said his fellow-traveller. "Betake you the woods, and let me keep the path."

Accordingly the young man turned aside; but took care to watch his companion, who advanced softly along the road until he had come within a staff's length of the old dame. She, meanwhile, was making the best of her way, with singular speed for so aged a woman, and mumbling some indistinct words—a prayer, doubtless—as she went. The traveller put forth his staff and touched her withered neck with what seemed the serpent's tail.

"The devil!" screamed the pious old lady.

"Then Goody Cloyse knows her old friend?" observed the traveller, confronting her and leaning on his writhing stick.

"Ah, forsooth, and is it your worship indeed?" cried the good dame. "Yea, truly is it, and in the very image of my old gossip, Goodman Brown, the grandfather of the silly fellow that now is. But—would your worship believe it?—my broomstick hath strangely disappeared, stolen, as I suspect, by that unhanged witch, Goody Cory, and that, too, when I was all anointed with the juice of smallage, and cinquefoil, and wolf's bane"—

"Mingled with fine wheat and the fat of a new-born babe," said the shape of old Goodman Brown.

"Ah, your worship knows the recipe," cried the old lady, cackling aloud. "So, as I was saying, being all ready for the meeting, and no horse to ride on, I made up my mind to foot it; for they tell me there is a nice young man to be taken into communion to-night. But now your good worship will lend me your arm, and we shall be there in a twinkling."

"That can hardly be," answered her friend. "I may not spare you my arm, Goody Cloyse; but here is my staff, if you will."

So saying, he threw it down at her feet, where, perhaps, it assumed life, being one of the rods which its owner had formerly lent to the Egyptian magi. Of this fact, however, Goodman Brown could not take cognizance. He had cast up his eyes in astonishment, and, looking down again, beheld neither Goody Cloyse nor the serpentine staff, but this fellow-traveller alone, who waited for him as calmly as if nothing had happened.

"That old woman taught me my catechism," said the young man; and there was a world of meaning in this simple comment.

They continued to walk onward, while the elder traveller exhorted his companion to make good speed and persevere in the path, discoursing so aptly that his arguments seemed rather to spring up in the bosom of his auditor than to be suggested by himself. As they went, he plucked a branch of maple to serve for a walking stick, and began to strip it of the twigs and little boughs, which were wet with evening dew. The moment his fingers touched them they became strangely withered and dried up as with a week's sunshine. Thus the pair proceeded, at a good free pace, until suddenly, in a gloomy hollow of the road, Goodman Brown sat himself down on the stump of a tree and refused to go any farther.

"Friend," said he, stubbornly, "my mind is made up. Not another step will I budge on this errand. What if a wretched old woman do choose to go to the devil when I thought she was going to heaven: is that any reason why I should quit my dear Faith and go after her?"

"You will think better of this by and by," said his acquaintance, composedly. "Sit here and rest yourself a while; and when you feel like moving again, there is my staff to help you along."

Without more words, he threw his companion the maple stick, and was as speedily out of sight as if he had vanished into the deepening gloom. The young man sat a few moments by the roadside, applauding himself greatly, and thinking with how clear a conscience he should meet the minister in his morning walk, nor shrink from the eye of good old Deacon Gookin. And what calm sleep would be his that very night, which was to have been spent so wickedly, but so purely and sweetly now, in the arms of Faith! Amidst these pleasant and praiseworthy meditations, Goodman Brown heard the tramp of horses along the road, and deemed it advisable to conceal himself within the verge of the forest, conscious of the guilty purpose that had brought him thither, though now so happily turned from it.

On came the hoof tramps and the voices of the riders, two grave old voices, conversing soberly as they drew near. These mingled sounds appeared to pass along the road, within a few yards of the young man's hiding-place; but, owing doubtless to the depth of the gloom at that particular spot, neither the travellers nor their steeds were visible. Though their figures brushed the small boughs by the wayside, it could not be seen that they intercepted, even for a moment, the faint gleam from the strip of bright sky athwart which they must have passed. Goodman Brown alternately crouched and stood on tiptoe, pulling aside the branches and thrusting forth his head as far as he durst without discerning so much as a shadow. It vexed him the more, because he could have sworn, were such a thing possible, that he recognized the voices of the minister and Deacon Gookin, jogging along quietly, as they were wont to do, when bound to some ordination of ecclesiastical council. While yet within hearing, one of the riders stopped to pluck a switch.

"Of the two, reverend sir," said the voice like the deacon's, "I had rather miss an ordination dinner than to-night's meeting. They tell me that some of our community are to be here from Falmouth and beyond, and others from Connecticut and Rhode Island, besides several of the Indian powwows, who, after their fashion, know almost as much deviltry as the best of us. Moreover, there is a goodly young woman to be taken into communion."

"Mighty well, Deacon Gookin!" replied the solemn old tones of the minister. "Spur up, or we shall be late. Nothing can be done, you know, until I get on the ground."

The hoofs clattered again; and the voices, talking so strangely in the empty air, passed on through the forest, where no church had ever been gathered or solitary Christian prayed. Whither, then, could these holy men be journeying so deep into the heathen wilderness? Young Goodman Brown caught hold of a tree for support, being ready to sink down on the ground, faint and overburdened with the heavy sickness of his heart. He looked up to the sky, doubting whether there really was a heaven above him. Yet there was the blue arch, and the stars brightening it.

"With heaven above and Faith below, I will yet stand firm against the devil!" cried Goodman Brown.

While he still gazed upward into the deep arch of the firmament and had lifted his hands to pray, a cloud, though no wind was stirring, hurried across the zenith and hid the brightening stars. The blue sky was still visible, except directly overhead, where this black mass of cloud was sweeping swiftly northward. Aloft in the air, as if from the depths of the cloud, came a confused and doubtful sound of voices. Once the listener fancied that he could distinguish the accents of towns-people of his own, men and women, both pious and ungodly, many of whom he had met at the communion table, and had seen others rioting at the tavern. The next moment, so indistinct were the sounds, he doubted whether he had heard aught but the murmur of the old forest, whispering without a wind. Then came a stronger swell of those familiar tones, heard daily in the sunshine at Salem village, but never until now from a cloud of night. There was one voice, of a young woman, uttering lamentations, yet with an uncertain sorrow, and entreating for some favor, which, perhaps, it would grieve her to obtain; and all the unseen multitude, both saints and sinners, seemed to encourage her onward.

"Faith!" shouted Goodman Brown, in a voice of agony and desperation; and the echoes of the forest mocked him, crying, "Faith! Faith!" as if bewildered wretches were seeking her all through the wilderness.

The cry of grief, rage, and terror was yet piercing the night, when the unhappy husband held his breath for a response. There was a scream, drowned immediately in a louder murmur of voices, fading into far-off laughter, as the dark cloud swept away, leaving the clear and silent sky above Goodman Brown. But something fluttered lightly down through the air and caught on the branch of a tree. The young man seized it, and beheld a pink ribbon.

"My Faith is gone!" cried he, after one stupefied moment. "There is no good on earth; and sin is but a name. Come, devil; for to thee is this world given."

And, maddened with despair, so that he laughed loud and long, did Goodman Brown grasp his staff and set forth again, at such a rate that he seemed to fly along the forest path rather than to walk or run. The road grew wilder and drearier and more faintly traced, and vanished at length, leaving him in the heart of the dark wilderness, still rushing onward with the instinct that guides mortal man to evil. The whole forest was peopled with frightful sounds—the creaking of the trees, the howling of wild beasts, and the yell of Indians; while sometimes the wind tolled like a distant church bell, and sometimes gave a broad roar around the traveller, as if all Nature were laughing him to scorn. But he was himself the chief horror of the scene, and shrank not from its other horrors.

"Ha! ha! ha!" roared Goodman Brown when the wind laughed at him. "Let us hear which will laugh loudest. Think not to frighten me with your deviltry. Come witch, come wizard, come Indian powwow, come devil himself, and here comes Goodman Brown. You may as well fear him as he fear you."

In truth, all through the haunted forest there could be nothing more frightful than the figure of Goodman Brown. On he flew among the black pines, brandishing his staff with frenzied gestures, now giving vent to an inspiration of horrid blasphemy, and now shouting forth such laughter as set all the echoes of the forest laughing like demons around him. The fiend in his own shape is less hideous than when he rages in the breast of man. Thus sped the demoniac on his course, until, quivering among the trees, he saw a red light before him, as when the felled trunks and branches of a clearing have been set on fire, and throw up their lurid blaze against the sky, at the hour of midnight. He paused, in a lull of the tempest that had driven him onward, and heard the swell of what seemed a hymn, rolling solemnly from a distance with the weight of many voices. He knew the tune; it was a familiar one in the choir of the village meeting-house. The verse died heavily away, and was lengthened by a chorus, not of human voices, but of all the sounds of the benighted wilderness pealing in awful harmony together. Goodman Brown cried out, and his cry was lost to his own ear by its unison with the cry of the desert.

In the interval of silence he stole forward until the light glared full upon his eyes. At one extremity of an open space, hemmed in by the dark wall of the forest, arose a rock, bearing some rude, natural resemblance either to an altar or a pulpit, and surrounded by four blazing pines, their tops aflame, their stems untouched, like candles at an evening meeting. The mass of foliage that had overgrown the summit of the rock was all on fire, blazing high into the night and fitfully illuminating the whole field. Each pendent twig and leafy festoon was in a blaze. As the red light arose and fell, a numerous congregation alternately shone forth, then disappeared in shadow, and again grew, as it were, out of the darkness, peopling the heart of the solitary woods at once.

"A grave and dark-clad company," quoth Goodman Brown.

In truth they were such. Among them, quivering to and fro between gloom and splendor, appeared faces that would be seen next day at the council board of the province, and others which, Sabbath after Sabbath, looked devoutly heavenward, and benignantly over the crowded pews, from the holiest pulpits in the land. Some affirm that the lady of the governor was there. At least there were high dames well known to her, and wives of honored husbands, and widows, a great multitude, and ancient maidens, all of excellent repute, and fair young girls, who trembled lest their mothers should espy them. Either the sudden gleams of light flashing over the obscure field bedazzled Goodman Brown, or he recognized a score of the church members of Salem village famous for their especial sanctity. Good old Deacon Gookin had arrived, and waited at the skirts of that venerable saint, his revered pastor. But irreverently consort-ing with these grave, reputable, and pious people, these elders of the church, these chaste dames and dewy virgins, there were men of dissolute lives and women of spotted fame, wretches given over to all mean and filthy vice, and suspected even of horrid crimes. It was strange to see that the good shrank not from the wicked, nor were the sinners abashed by the saints. Scattered also among their pale-faced enemies were the Indian priests, or powwows, who had often scared their native forest with more hideous incantations than any known to English witchcraft.

"But where is Faith?" thought Goodman Brown; and, as hope came into his heart, he trembled.

Another verse of the hymn arose, a slow and mournful strain, such as the pious love, but joined to words which expressed all that our nature can conceive of sin, and darkly hinted at far more. Unfathomable to mere mortals is the lore of fiends. Verse after verse was sung; and still the chorus of the desert swelled between like the deepest tone of a mighty organ; and with the final peal of that dreadful anthem there came a sound, as if the roaring wind, the rushing streams, the howling beasts, and every other voice of the unconcerted wilderness were mingling and according with the voice of guilty man in homage to the prince of all. The four blazing pines threw up a loftier flame, and obscurely discovered shapes and visages of horror on the smoke wreaths above the impious assembly. At the same moment the fire on the rock shot redly forth and formed a glowing arch above its base, where now appeared a figure. With reverence be it spoken, the figure bore no slight similitude, both in garb and manner, to some grave divine of the New England churches.

"Bring forth the converts!" cried a voice that echoed through the field and rolled into the forest.

At the word, Goodman Brown stepped forth from the shadow of the trees and approached the congregation, with whom he felt a loathful brotherhood by the sympathy of all that was wicked in his heart. He could have well-nigh sworn that the shape of his own dead father beckoned him to advance, looking downward from a smoke wreath, while a woman, with dim features of despair, threw out her hand to warn him back. Was it his mother? But he had no power to retreat one step, nor to resist, even in thought, when the minister and good old Deacon Gookin seized his arms and led him to the blazing rock. Thither came also the slender form of a veiled female, led between Goody Cloyse, that pious teacher of the catechism, and Martha Carrier, who had received the devil's promise to be queen of hell. A rampant hag was she. And there stood the proselytes beneath the canopy of fire.

"Welcome, my children," said the dark figure, "to the communion of your race. Ye have found thus young your nature and your destiny. My children, look behind you!"

They turned; and flashing forth, as it were, in a sheet of flame, the fiend worshippers were seen; the smile of welcome gleamed darkly on every visage.

"There," resumed the sable form, "are all whom ye have reverenced from youth. Ye deemed them holier than yourselves, and shrank from your own sin, contrasting it with their lives of righteousness and prayerful aspirations heavenward. Yet here are they all in my worshipping assembly. This night it shall be granted you to know their secret deeds: how hoary-bearded elders of the church have whispered wanton words to the young maids of their households; how many a woman, eager for widows' weeds, has given her husband a drink at bedtime and let him sleep his last sleep in her bosom; how beardless youths have made haste to inherit their fathers' wealth; and how fair damsels—blush not, sweet ones—have dug little graves in the garden, and bidden me, the sole guest, to an infant's funeral. By the sympathy of your human hearts for sin ye shall scent out all the places—whether in church, bed-chamber, street, field, or forest— where crime has been committed, and shall exult to behold the whole earth one stain of guilt, one mighty blood spot. Far more than this. I shall be yours to penetrate, in every bosom, the deep mystery of sin, the fountain of all wicked arts, and which inexhaustibly supplies more evil impulses than human power—than my power at its utmost—can make manifest in deeds. And now, my children, look upon each other."

They did so; and, by the blaze of the hell-kindled torches, the wretched man beheld his Faith, and the wife her husband, trembling before that unhallowed altar.

"Lo, there ye stand, my children," said the figure, in a deep and solemn tone, almost sad with its despairing awfulness, as if his once angelic nature could yet mourn for our miserable race. "Depending upon one another's hearts, ye had still hoped that virtue were not at all a dream. Now are ye undeceived. Evil is the nature of mankind. Evil must be your only happiness. Welcome again, my children, to the communion of your race."

"Welcome," repeated the fiend worshippers, in one cry of despair and triumph.

And there they stood, the only pair, as it seemed, who were yet hesitating on the verge of wickedness in this dark world. A basin was hollowed, naturally, in the rock. Did it contain water, reddened by the lurid light? or was it blood? or, perchance, a liquid flame? Herein did the shape of evil dip his hand and prepare to lay the mark of baptism upon their foreheads, that they might be partakers of the mystery of sin, more conscious of the secret guilt of others, both in deed and thought, than they could now be of their own. The husband cast one look at his pale wife, and Faith at him. What polluted wretches would the next glance show them to each other, shuddering alike at what they disclosed and what they saw!

"Faith! Faith!" cried the husband, "look up to heaven, and resist the wicked one."

Whether Faith obeyed he knew not. Hardly had he spoken when he found himself amid calm night and solitude, listening to a roar of the wind which died heavily away through the forest. He staggered against the rock, and felt it chill and damp; while a hanging twig, that had been all on fire, besprinkled his cheek with the coldest dew.

The next morning young Goodman Brown came slowly into the street of Salem village, staring around him like a bewildered man. The good old minister was taking a walk along the graveyard to get an appetite for breakfast and meditate his sermon, and bestowed a blessing, as he passed, on Goodman Brown. He shrank from the venerable saint as if to avoid an anathema. Old Deacon Gookin was at domestic worship, and the holy words of his prayer were heard through the open window. "What God doth the wizard pray to?" quoth Goodman Brown. Goody Cloyse, that excellent old Christian, stood in the early sunshine at her own lattice, catechizing a little girl who had brought her a pint of morning's milk. Goodman Brown snatched away the child as from the grasp of the fiend himself. Turning the corner by the meeting-house, he spied the head of Faith, with the pink ribbons, gazing anxiously forth, and bursting into such joy at sight of him that she skipped along the street and almost kissed her husband before the whole village. But Goodman Brown looked sternly and sadly into her face, and passed on without a greeting.

Had Goodman Brown fallen asleep in the forest and only dreamed a wild dream of a witch-meeting?

Be it so if you will; but, alas! it was a dream of evil omen for young Goodman Brown. A stern, a sad, a darkly meditative, a distrustful, if not a desperate man did he become from the night of that fearful dream. On the Sabbath day, when the congregation were singing a holy psalm, he could not listen because an anthem of sin rushed loudly upon his ear and drowned all the blessed strain. When the minister spoke from the pulpit, with power and fervid eloquence, and with his hand on the open Bible, of the sacred truths of our religion, and of saint-like lives and triumphant deaths, and of future bliss or misery unutterable, then did Goodman Brown turn pale, dreading lest the roof should thunder down upon the gray blasphemer and his hearers. Often, awaking suddenly at midnight, he shrank from the bosom of Faith, and at morning or eventide, when the family knelt down at prayer, he scowled, and muttered to himself, and gazed sternly at his wife, and turned away. And when he had lived long, and was borne to his grave, a hoary corpse, followed by Faith, an aged woman, and children and grandchildren, a goodly procession, besides neighbors not a few, they carved no hopeful verse upon his tombstone; for his dying hour was gloom.

QUESTIONS

1. How would you characterize the story's diction? What particular words or phrases exemplify the diction?
2. Goodman Brown tells the man with the staff that he does not want to journey with him through the forest, yet he does so anyway. Explain this seeming paradox.
3. Is the witches' meeting a dream or reality? Does it matter to the theme of the story? Explain.
4. Why does Goodman Brown have a negative response to his wife when he sees her in the village? Why has Goodman Brown's life become gloomy and dismal at the end of the story?

Ernest Hemingway

A CLEAN, WELL-LIGHTED PLACE

It was late and everyone had left the café except an old man who sat in the shadow the leaves of the tree made against the electric light. In the day time the street was dusty, but at night the dew settled the dust and the old man liked to sit late because he was deaf and now at night it was quiet and he felt the difference. The two waiters inside the café knew that the old man was a little drunk, and while he was a good client they knew that if he became too drunk he would leave without paying, so they kept watch on him.

"Last week he tried to commit suicide," one waiter said.

"Why?"

"He was in despair."

"What about?"

"Nothing."

"How do you know it was nothing?"

"He has plenty of money."

They sat together at a table that was close against the wall near the door of the café and looked at the terrace where the tables were all empty except where the old man sat in the shadow of the leaves of the tree that moved slightly in the wind. A girl and a soldier went by in the street. The street light shone on the brass number on his collar. The girl wore no head covering and hurried beside him.

"The guard will pick him up," one waiter said.

"What does it matter if he gets what he's after?"

"He had better get off the street now. The guard will get him. They went by five minutes ago."

The old man sitting in the shadow rapped on his saucer with his glass. The younger waiter went over to him.

"What do you want?"

The old man looked at him. "Another brandy," he said.

"You'll be drunk," the waiter said. The old man looked at him. The waiter went away.

"He'll stay all night," he said to his colleague. "I'm sleepy now. I never get into bed before three o'clock. He should have killed himself last week."

The waiter took the brandy bottle and another saucer from the counter inside the café and marched out to the old man's table. He put down the saucer and poured the glass full of brandy.

"You should have killed yourself last week," he said to the deaf man. The old man motioned with his finger. "A little more," he said. The waiter poured on into the glass so that the brandy slopped over and ran down the stem into the top saucer of the pile. "Thank you," the old man said. The waiter took the bottle back inside the café. He sat down at the table with his colleague again.

"He's drunk now," he said.

"He's drunk every night."

"What did he want to kill himself for?"

"How should I know."

"How did he do it?"

"He hung himself with a rope."

"Who cut him down?"

"His niece."

"Why did they do it?"

"Fear for his soul."

"How much money has he got?"

"He's got plenty."

"He must be eighty years old."

"Anyway I should say he was eighty."

"I wish he would go home. I never get to bed before three o'clock. What kind of hour is that to go to bed?"

"He stays up because he likes it."

"He's lonely. I'm not lonely. I have a wife waiting in bed for me."

"He had a wife once too."

"A wife would be no good to him now."

"You can't tell. He might be better with a wife."

"His niece looks after him. You said she cut him down."

"I know."

"I wouldn't want to be that old. An old man is a nasty thing."

"Not always. This old man is clean. He drinks without spilling. Even now, drunk. Look at him."

"I don't want to look at him. I wish he would go home. He has no regard for those who must work."

The old man looked from his glass across the square, then over at the waiters.

"Another brandy," he said, pointing to his glass. The waiter who was in hurry came over.

"Finished," he said, speaking with that omission of syntax stupid people employ when talking to drunken people or foreigners. "No more tonight. Close now."

"Another," said the old man.

"No. Finished." The waiter wiped the edge of the table with a towel and shook his head.

The old man stood up, slowly counted the saucers, took a leather coin purse from his pocket and paid for the drinks, leaving half a peseta tip.

The waiter watched him go down the street, a very old man walking unsteadily but with dignity.

"Why didn't you let him stay and drink?" the unhurried waiter asked. They were putting up the shutters. "It is not half-past two."

"I want to go home to bed."

"What is an hour?"

"More to me than to him."

"An hour is the same."

"You talk like an old man yourself. He can buy a bottle and drink at home."

"It's not the same."

"No, it is not," agreed the waiter with a wife. He did not wish to be unjust. He was only in a hurry.

"And you? You have no fear of going home before your usual hour?"

"Are you trying to insult me?"

"No, hombre, only to make a joke."

"No," the waiter who was in a hurry said, rising from pulling down the metal shutters. "I have confidence. I am all confidence."

"You have youth, confidence, and a job," the older waiter said. "You have everything."

"And what do you lack?"

"Everything but work."

"You have everything I have."

"No. I have never had confidence and I am not young."

"Come on. Stop talking nonsense and lock up."

"I am of those who like to stay late at the café," the older waiter said. "With all those who do not want to go to bed. With all those who need a light for the night."

"I want to go home and into bed."

"We are of two different kinds," the older waiter said. He was now dressed to go home. "It is not only a question of youth and confidence although those things are very beautiful. Each night I am reluctant to close up because there may be some one who needs the café."

"Hombre, there are bodegas open all night long."

"You do not understand. This is a clean and pleasant café. It is well lighted. The light is very good and also, now, there are shadows of the leaves."

"Good night," said the younger waiter.

"Good night," the other said. Turning off the electric light he continued the conversation with himself. It is the light of course but it is necessary that the place be clean and pleasant. You do not want music. Certainly you do not want music. Nor can you stand before a bar with dignity although that is all that is provided for these hours. What did he fear? It was not fear or dread. It was a nothing that he knew too well. It was all a nothing and a man was nothing too. It was only that and light was all it needed and a certain cleanness and order. Some lived in it and never felt it but he knew it all was nada y pues nada y nada y pues nada. Our nada who art in nada, nada be thy name thy kingdom nada thy will be nada in nada as it is in nada. Give us this nada our daily nada and nada us our nada as we nada our nadas and nada us not into nada but deliver us from nada; pues nada. Hail nothing full of nothing, nothing is with thee. He smiled and stood before a bar with a shining steam pressure coffee machine.

"What's yours?" asked the barman.

"Nada."

"Otro loco mas," said the barman and turned away.

"A little cup," said the waiter.

The barman poured it for him.

"The light is very bright and pleasant but the bar is unpolished," the waiter said.

The barman looked at him but did not answer. It was too late at night for conversation.

"You want another copita?" the barman asked.

"No, thank you," said the waiter and went out. He disliked bars and bodegas. A clean, well-lighted café was a very different thing. Now, without thinking further, he would go home to his room. He would lie in the bed and finally, with daylight, he would go to sleep. After all, he said to himself, it is probably only insomnia. Many must have it.

QUESTIONS

1. How do the older and younger waiter differ? What is each one's attitude toward the old man?
2. Light imagery abounds in this story. At one point, the older waiter says to himself, "It is the light of course but it is necessary that the place be clean and pleasant." Why does he focus so intently on the "atmosphere" of the café?
3. What is the significance of the waiter's prayer? Why is the prayer full of negativity?
4. It seems that the deaf old man and the older waiter have a similar negative attitude toward life. What do they have in common that may have caused this attitude? What might be the key to their both finding happiness?
5. Hemingway is known for his sparse, laconic style and his ability to say much with few words. Does this story bear out this observation? Explain.

Langston Hughes

ON THE ROAD

He was not interested in the snow. When he got off the freight, one early evening during the depression, Sargeant never even noticed the snow. But he must have felt it seeping down his neck, cold, wet, sopping in his shoes. But if you had asked him, he wouldn't have known it was snowing. Sargeant didn't see the snow, not even under the bright lights of the main street, falling white and flaky against the night. He was too hungry, too sleepy, too tired.

The Reverend Mr. Dorset, however, saw the snow when he switched on his porch light, opened the front door of his parsonage, and found standing there before him a big black man with snow on his face, a human piece of night with snow on his face—obviously unemployed.

Said the Reverend Mr. Dorset before Sargeant even realized he'd opened his mouth: "I'm sorry. No! Go right on down this street four blocks and turn to your left, walk up seven and you'll see the Relief Shelter. I'm sorry. No!" He shut the door.

Sargeant wanted to tell the holy man that he had already been to the Relief Shelter, been to hundreds of relief shelters during the depression years, the beds were always gone and supper was over, the place was full, and they drew the color line anyhow. But the minister said, "No," and shut the door. Evidently he didn't want to hear about it. And he *had* a door to shut.

The big black man turned away. And even yet he didn't see the snow, walking right into it. Maybe he sensed it, cold, wet, sticking to his jaws, wet on his black hands, sopping in his shoes. He stopped and stood on the sidewalk hunched over—hungry, sleepy, cold—looking up and down. Then he looked right where he was—in front of a church. Of course! A church! Sure, right next to a parsonage, certainly a church.

It had *two* doors.

Broad white steps in the night all snowy white. Two high arched doors with slender stone pillars on either side. And way up, a round lacy window with a stone crucifix in the middle and Christ on the crucifix in stone. All this was pale in the street lights, solid and stony pale in the snow.

Sargeant blinked. When he looked up, the snow fell into his eyes. For the first time that night he *saw* the snow. He shook his head. He shook the snow from his coat sleeves, felt hungry, felt lost, felt not lost, felt cold. He walked up the steps of the church. He knocked at the door. No answer. He tried the handle. Locked. He put his shoulder against the door and his long black body slanted like a ramrod. He pushed. With loud rhythmic grunts, like the grunts in a chain-gang song, he pushed against the door.

"I'm tired . . . Huh! . . . Hongry . . . Uh! . . . I'm sleepy . . . Huh! I'm cold . . . I got to sleep somewheres," Sargeant said. "This here is a church, ain't it? Well, uh!"

He pushed against the door.

Suddenly, with an undue cracking and screaking, the door began to give way to the tall black Negro who pushed ferociously against it.

By now two or three white people had stopped in the street, and Sargeant was vaguely aware of some of them yelling at him concerning the door. Three or four more came running, yelling at him.

"Hey!" they said. "Hey!"

"Uh-huh," answered the big tall Negro, "I know it's a white folks' church, but I got to sleep somewhere." He gave another lunge at the door. "Huh!"

And the door broke open.

But just when the door gave way, two white cops arrived in a car, ran up the steps with their clubs, and grabbed Sargeant. But Sargeant for once had no intention of being pulled or pushed away from the door.

Sargeant grabbed, but not for anything so weak as a broken door. He grabbed for one of the tall stone pillars beside the door, grabbed at it and caught it. And held it. The cops pulled and Sargeant pulled. Most of the people in the street got behind the cops and helped them pull.

"A big black unemployed Negro holding onto our church!" thought the people. "The idea!"

The cops began to beat Sargeant over the head, and nobody protested. But he held on.

And then the church fell down.

Gradually, the big stone front of the church fell down, the walls and the rafters, the crucifix and the Christ. Then the whole thing fell down, covering the cops and the people with bricks and stones and debris. The whole church fell down in the snow.

Sargeant got out from under the church and went walking on up the street with the stone pillar on his shoulder. He was under the impression that he had buried the parsonage and the Reverend Mr. Dorset who said, "No!" So he laughed, and threw the pillar six blocks up the street and went on.

Sargeant thought he was alone, but listening to the *crunch, crunch, crunch* on the snow of his own footsteps, he heard other footsteps, too, doubling his own. He looked around, and there was Christ walking along beside him, the same Christ that had been on the cross on the church—still stone with a rough stone surface, walking along beside him just like he was broken off the cross when the church fell down.

"Well, I'll be dogged," said Sargeant. "This here's the first time I ever seed you off the cross."

"Yes," said Christ, crunching his feet in the snow. "You had to pull the church down to get me off the cross."

"You glad?" said Sargeant.

"I sure am," said Christ.

They both laughed.

"I'm a hell of a fellow, ain't I?" said Sargeant. "Done pulled the church down!"

"You did a good job," said Christ. "They have kept me nailed on a cross for nearly two thousand years."

"Whee-ee-e!" said Sargeant. "I know you are glad to get off."

"I sure am," said Christ.

They walked on in the snow. Sargeant looked at the man of stone.

"And you have been up there two thousand years?"

"I sure have," Christ said.

"Well, if I had a little cash," said Sargeant, "I'd show you around a bit."

"I been around," said Christ.

"Yeah, but that was a long time ago."

"All the same," said Christ, "I've been around."

They walked on in the snow until they came to the railroad yards. Sargeant was tired, sweating and tired.

"Where you goin'?" Sargeant said, stopping by the tracks. He looked at Christ. Sargeant said, "I'm just a bum on the road. How about you? Where you goin'?"

"God knows," Christ said, "but I'm leavin' here."

They saw the red and green lights of the railroad yard half veiled by the snow that fell out of the night. Away down the track they saw a fire in a hobo jungle.

"I can go there and sleep," Sargeant said.

"You can?"

"Sure," said Sargeant. "That place ain't got no doors."

Outside the town, along the tracks, there were barren trees and bushes below the embankment, snow-gray in the dark. And down among the trees and bushes there were makeshift houses made out of boxes and tin and old pieces of wood and canvas. You couldn't see them in the dark, but you knew they were there if you'd ever been on the road, if you had ever lived with the homeless and hungry in a depression.

"I'm side-tracking," Sargeant said. "I'm tired."

"I'm gonna make it on to Kansas City," said Christ.

"O.K.," Sargeant said. "So long!"

He went down into the hobo jungle and found himself a place to sleep. He never did see Christ no more. About 6:00 A.M. a freight came by. Sargeant scrambled out of the jungle with a dozen or so more hobos and ran along the track, grabbing at the freight. It was dawn, early dawn, cold and gray.

"Wonder where Christ is by now?" Sargeant thought. "He musta gone on way on down the road. He didn't sleep in this jungle."

Sargeant grabbed the train and started to pull himself up into a moving coal car, over the edge of a wheeling coal car. But strangely enough, the car was full of cops. The nearest cop rapped Sargeant soundly across the knuckles with his night stick. Wham! Rapped his big black hands for clinging to the top of the car. Wham! But Sargeant did not turn loose. He clung on and tried to pull himself into the car. He hollered at the top of his voice, "Damn it, lemme in this car!"

"Shut up," barked the cop. "You crazy coon!" He rapped Sargeant across the knuckles and punched him in the stomach. "You ain't out in no jungle now. This ain't no train. You in jail."

Wham! across his bare black fingers clinging to the bars of his cell. Wham! between the steel bars low down against his shins.

Suddenly Sargeant realized that he really was in jail. He wasn't on no train. The blood of the night before had dried on his face, his head hurt terribly, and a cop outside in the corridor was hitting him across the knuckles for holding onto the door, yelling and shaking the cell door.

"They musta took me to jail for breaking down the door last night," Sargeant thought, "that church door."

Sargeant went over and sat on a wooden bench against the cold stone wall. He was emptier than ever. His clothes were wet, clammy cold wet, and shoes sloppy with snow water. It was just about dawn. There he was, locked up behind a cell door, nursing his bruised fingers.

The bruised fingers were his, but not the *door*.

Not the *club*, but the fingers.

"You wait," mumbled Sargeant, black against the jail wall. "I'm gonna break down this door, too."

"Shut up—or I'll paste you one," said the cop.

"I'm gonna break down this door," yelled Sargeant as he stood up in his cell.

Then he must have been talking to himself because he said, "I wonder where Christ's gone? I wonder if he's gone to Kansas City?"

QUESTIONS

1. The narrator refers to the Reverend as a "holy man." What is the irony behind this title?
2. At what point in the story is it first apparent that the author is not writing a realistic story?
3. Christ says to Sargeant, "You had to pull the church down to get me off the cross." What comment is the author making about organized religion?
4. What similarities exist between the life of Christ and that of Sargeant?

Shirley Jackson

THE LOTTERY

The morning of June 27th was clear and sunny, with the fresh warmth of a full-summer day; the flowers were blossoming profusely and the grass was richly green. The people of the village began to gather in the square, between the post office and the bank, around ten o'clock; in some towns there were so many people that the lottery took two days and had to be started on June 26th, but in this village, where there were only about three hundred people, the whole lottery took less than two hours, so it could begin at ten o'clock in the morning and still be through in time to allow the villagers to get home for noon dinner.

The children assembled first, of course. School was recently over for the summer, and the feeling of liberty sat uneasily on most of them; they tended to gather together quietly for a while before they broke into boisterous play, and their talk was still of the classroom and the teacher, of books and reprimands. Bobby Martin had already stuffed his pockets full of stones, and the other boys soon followed his example, selecting the smoothest and roundest stones; Bobby and Harry Jones and Dickie Delacroix—the villagers pronounced this name "Dellacroy"—eventually made a great pile of stones in one corner of the square and guarded it against the raids of the other boys. The girls stood aside, talking among themselves, looking over their shoulders at the boys, and the very small children rolled in the dust or clung to the hands of their older brothers or sisters.

Soon the men began to gather, surveying their own children, speaking of planting and rain, tractors and taxes. They stood together, away from the pile of stones in the corner, and their jokes were quiet and they smiled rather than laughed. The women, wearing faded house dresses and sweaters, came shortly after their menfolk. They greeted one another and exchanged bits of gossip as they went to join their husbands. Soon the women, standing by their husbands, began to call to their children, and the children came reluctantly, having to be called four or five times. Bobby Martin ducked under his mother's grasping hand and ran, laughing, back to the pile of stones. His father spoke up sharply, and Bobby came quickly and took his place between his father and his oldest brother.

The lottery was conducted—as were the square dances, the teenage club, the Halloween program—by Mr. Summers, who had time and energy to devote to civic activities. He was a round-faced, jovial man and he ran the coal business, and people were sorry for him, because he had no children and his wife was a scold. When he arrived in the square, carrying the black wooden box, there was a murmur of conversation among the villagers, and he waved and called, "Little late today, folks." The postmaster, Mr. Graves, followed him, carrying a three-legged stool, and the stool was put in the center of the square and Mr. Summers set the black box down on it. The villagers kept their distance, leaving a space between themselves and the stool, and when Mr. Summers said, "Some of you fellows want to give me a hand?" there was a hesitation before two men, Mr. Martin and his oldest son, Baxter, came forward to hold the box steady on the stool while Mr. Summers stirred up the papers inside it.

The original paraphernalia for the lottery had been lost long ago, and the black box now resting on the stool had been put into use even before Old Man Warner, the oldest man in town, was born. Mr. Summers spoke frequently to the villagers about making a new box, but no one liked to upset even as much tradition as was represented by the black box. There was a story that the present box had been made with some pieces of the box that had preceded it, the one that had been constructed when the first people settled down to make a village here. Every year, after the lottery, Mr, Summers began talking again about a new box, but every year the subject was allowed to fade off without anything's being done. The black box grew shabbier each year; by now it was no longer completely black but splintered badly along one side to show the original wood color, and in some places faded or stained.

Mr. Martin and his oldest son, Baxter, held the black box securely on the stool until Mr. Summers had stirred the papers thoroughly with his hand. Because so much of the ritual had been forgotten or discarded, Mr. Summers had been successful in having slips of paper substituted for the chips of wood that had been used for generations. Chips of wood, Mr. Summers had argued, had been all very well when the village was tiny, but now that the population was more than three hundred and likely to keep on growing, it was necessary to use something that would fit more easily into the black box. The night before the lottery, Mr. Summers and Mr. Graves made up the slips of paper and put them in the box, and it was then taken to the safe of Mr. Summers' coal company and locked up until Mr. Summers was ready to take it to the square next morning. The rest of the year, the box was put away, sometimes one place, sometimes another; it had spent one year in Mr. Graves's barn and another year underfoot in the post office, and sometimes it was set on a shelf in the Martin grocery and left there.

There was a great deal of fussing to be done before Mr. Summers declared the lottery open. There were the lists to make up—of heads of families, heads of households in each family, members of each household in each family. There was the proper swearing-in of Mr. Summers by the postmaster, as the official of the lottery; at one time, some people remembered, there had been a recital of some sort, performed by the official of the lottery, a perfunctory, tuneless chant that had been rattled off duly each year; some people believed that the official of the lottery used to stand just so when he said or sang it, others believed that he was supposed to walk among the people, but years and years ago this part of the ritual had been allowed to lapse. There had been, also, a ritual salute, which the official of the lottery had had to use in addressing each person who came up to draw from the box, but this also had changed with time, until now it was felt necessary only for the official to speak to each person approaching. Mr. Summers was very good at all this; in his clean white shirt and blue jeans, with one hand resting carelessly on the black box, he seemed very proper and important as he talked interminably to Mr. Graves and the Martins.

Just as Mr. Summers finally left off talking and turned to the assembled villagers, Mrs. Hutchinson came hurriedly along the path to the square, her sweater thrown over her shoulders, and slid into place in the back of the crowd. "Clean forgot what day it was," she said to Mrs. Delacroix, who stood next to her, and they both laughed softly. "Thought my old man was out back stacking wood," Mrs. Hutchinson went on, "and then I looked out the window and the kids was gone, and then I remembered it was the twenty-seventh and came a-running." She dried her hands on her apron, and Mrs. Delacroix said, "You're in time, though. They're still talking away up there."

Mrs. Hutchinson craned her neck to see through the crowd and found her husband and children standing near the front. She tapped Mrs. Delacroix on the arm as a farewell and began to make her way through the crowd. The people separated good-humoredly to let her through; two or three people said, in voices just loud enough to be heard across the crowd, "Here comes your Missus, Hutchinson," and "Bill, she made it after all." Mrs. Hutchinson reached her husband, and Mr. Summers, who had been waiting, said cheerfully, "Thought we were going to have to get on without you, Tessie." Mrs. Hutchinson said, grinning, "Wouldn't have me leave m'dishes in the sink, now, would you, Joe?," and soft laughter ran through the crowd as the people stirred back into position after Mrs. Hutchinson's arrival.

"Well, now," Mr. Summers said soberly, "guess we better get started, get this over with, so's we can go back to work. Anybody ain't here?"

"Dunbar," several people said. "Dunbar, Dunbar."

Mr. Summers consulted his list. "Clyde Dunbar," he said. "That's right. He's broke his leg, hasn't he? Who's drawing for him?"

"Me, I guess," a woman said, and Mr. Summers turned to look at her. "Wife draws for her husband," Mr. Summers said. "Don't you have a grown boy to do it for you, Janey?" Although Mr. Summers and everyone else in the village knew the answer perfectly well, it was the business of the official of the lottery to ask such questions formally. Mr. Summers waited with an expression of polite interest while Mrs. Dunbar answered.

"Horace's not but sixteen yet," Mrs. Dunbar said regretfully. "Guess I gotta fill in for the old man this year."

"Right," Mr. Summers said. He made a note on the list he was holding. Then he asked, "Watson boy drawing this year?"

A tall boy in the crowd raised his hand. "Here," he said. "I'm drawing for m'mother and me." He blinked his eyes nervously and ducked his head as several voices in the crowd said things like "Good fellow, Jack," and "Glad to see your mother's got a man to do it."

"Well," Mr. Summers said, "guess that's everyone. Old Man Warner make it?"

"Here," a voice said, and Mr. Summers nodded.

A sudden hush fell on the crowd as Mr. Summers cleared his throat and looked at the list. "All ready?" he called. "Now, I'll read the names—heads of families first—and the men come up and take a paper out of the box. Keep the paper folded in your hand without looking at it until everyone has had a turn. Everything clear?"

The people had done it so many times that they only half listened to the directions; most of them were quiet, wetting their lips, not looking around. Then Mr. Summers raised one hand high and said, "Adams." A man disengaged himself from the crowd and came forward. "Hi, Steve," Mr. Summers said, and Mr. Adams said, "Hi, Joe." They grinned at one another humorlessly and nervously. Then Mr. Adams reached into the black box and took out a folded paper. He held it firmly by one corner as he turned and went hastily back to his place in the crowd, where he stood a little apart from his family, not looking down at his hand.

"Allen," Mr. Summers said. "Anderson. . . . Bentham."

"Seems like there's no time at all between lotteries any more," Mrs. Delacroix said to Mrs. Graves in the back row. "Seems like we got through with the last one only last week."

"Time sure goes fast," Mrs. Graves said.

"Clark. . . . Delacroix."

"There goes my old man," Mrs. Delacroix said. She held her breath while her husband went forward.

"Dunbar," Mr. Summers said, and Mrs. Dunbar went steadily to the box while one of the women said, "Go on, Janey," and another said, "There she goes."

"We're next," Mrs. Graves said. She watched while Mr. Graves came around from the side of the box, greeted Mr. Summers gravely, and selected a slip of paper from the box. By now, all through the crowd there were men holding the small folded papers in their large hands, turning them over and over nervously. Mrs. Dunbar and her two sons stood together, Mrs. Dunbar holding the slip of paper.

"Harburt. . . . Hutchinson."

"Get up there, Bill," Mrs. Hutchinson said, and the people near her laughed.

"Jones."

"They do say," Mr. Adams said to Old Man Warner, who stood next to him, "that over in the north village they're talking of giving up the lottery."

Old Man Warner snorted. "Pack of crazy fools," he said. "Listening to the young folks, nothing's good enough for *them*. Next thing you know, they'll be wanting to go back to living in caves, nobody work any more, live *that* way for a while. Used to be a saying about 'Lottery in June, corn be heavy soon.' First thing you know, we'd all be eating stewed chickweed and acorns. There's *always* been a lottery," he added petulantly. "Bad enough to see young Joe Summers up there joking with everybody."

"Some places have already quit lotteries," Mrs. Adams said.

"Nothing but trouble in *that,*" Old Man Warner said stoutly. "Pack of young fools."

"Martin." And Bobby Martin watched his father go forward. "Overdyke. . . . Percy."

"I wish they'd hurry," Mrs. Dunbar said to her older son. "I wish they'd hurry."

"They're almost through," her son said.

"You get ready to run tell Dad," Mrs. Dunbar said.

Mr. Summers called his own name and then stepped forward precisely and selected a slip from the box. Then he called, "Warner."

"Seventy-seventh year I been in the lottery," Old Man Warner said as he went through the crowd. "Seventy-seventh time."

"Watson." The tall boy came awkwardly through the crowd. Someone said, "Don't be nervous, Jack," and Mr. Summers said, "Take your time, son."

"Zanini."

After that, there was a long pause, a breathless pause, until Mr. Summers, holding his slip of paper in the air, said, "All right, fellows." For a minute, no one moved, and then all the slips of paper were opened. Suddenly, all the women began to speak at once, saying, "Who is it?," "Who's got it?," "Is it the Dunbars?," "Is it the Watsons?" Then the voices began to say, "It's Hutchinson. It's Bill," "Bill Hutchinson's got it."

"Go tell your father," Mrs. Dunbar said to her older son.

People began to look around to see the Hutchinsons. Bill Hutchinson was standing quiet staring down at the paper in his hand. Suddenly, Tessie Hutchinson shouted to Mr. Summers, "You didn't give him time enough to take any paper he wanted. I saw you. It wasn't fair."

"Be a good sport, Tessie," Mrs. Delacroix called, and Mrs. Graves said, "All of us took the same chance."

"Shut up, Tessie," Bill Hutchinson said.

"Well, everyone," Mr. Summers said, "that was done pretty fast, and now we've got to be hurrying a little more to get done in time." He consulted his next list. "Bill," he said, "You draw for the Hutchinson family. You got any other households in the Hutchinsons?"

"There's Don and Eva," Mrs. Hutchinson yelled. "Make *them* take their chance!"

"Daughters draw with their husbands' families, Tessie," Mr. Summers said gently. "You know that as well as anyone else."

"It wasn't *fair*," Tessie said.

"I guess not, Joe," Bill Hutchinson said regretfully. "My daughter draws with her husband's family, that's only fair. And I've got no other family except the kids."

"Then, as far as drawing for families is concerned, it's you," Mr. Summers said in explanation, "and as far as drawing for households is concerned, that's you, too. Right?"

"Right," Bill Hutchinson said.

"How many kids, Bill?" Mr. Summers asked formally.

"Three," Bill Hutchinson said. "There's Bill, Jr., and Nancy, and little Dave, and Tessie and me."

"All right, then," Mr. Summers said. "Harry, you got their tickets back?"

Mr. Graves nodded and held up the slips of paper. "Put them in the box, then," Mr. Summers directed. "Take Bill's and put it in."

"I think we ought to start over," Mrs. Hutchinson said, as quietly as she could. "I tell you it wasn't *fair*. You didn't give him time enough to choose. *Every*body saw that."

Mr. Graves had selected the five slips and put them in the box, and dropped all the papers but those onto the ground, where the breeze caught them and lifted them off.

"Listen, everybody," Mrs. Hutchinson was saying to the people around her.

"Ready, Bill?" Mr. Summers asked, and Bill Hutchinson, with one quick glance around at his wife and children, nodded.

"Remember," Mr. Summers said, "take the slips and keep them folded until each person has taken one. Harry, you help little Dave." Mr. Graves took the hand of the little boy, who came willingly with him up to the box. "Take a paper out of the box, Davy," Mr. Summers said. Davy put his hand into the box and laughed. "Take just *one* paper," Mr. Summers said. "Harry, you hold it for him." Mr. Graves took the child's hand and removed the folded paper from the tight fist and held it while little Dave stood next to him and looked up at him wonderingly.

"Nancy next," Mr. Summers said. Nancy was twelve, and her school friends breathed heavily as she went forward, switching her skirt, and took a slip daintily from the box. "Bill, Jr.," Mr. Summers said, and Billy, his face red and his feet over-large, nearly knocked the box over as he got a paper out. "Tessie," Mr. Summers said. She hesitated for a minute, looking around defiantly, and then set her lips and went up to the box. She snatched a paper out and held it behind her.

"Bill," Mr. Summers said, and Bill Hutchinson reached into the box and felt around, bringing his hand out at last with the slip of paper in it.

The crowd was quiet. A girl whispered, "I hope it's not Nancy," and the sound of the whisper reached the edges of the crowd.

"It's not the way it used to be," Old Man Warner said clearly. "People ain't the way they used to be."

"All right," Mr. Summers said. "Open the papers. Harry, you open little Dave's."

Mr. Graves opened the slip of paper and there was a general sigh through the crowd as he held it up and everyone could see that it was blank. Nancy and Bill, Jr., opened theirs at the same time, and both beamed and laughed, turning around to the crowd and holding their slips of paper above their heads.

"Tessie," Mr. Summers said. There was a pause, and then Mr. Summers looked at Bill Hutchinson, and Bill unfolded his paper and showed it. It was blank.

"It's Tessie," Mr. Summers said, and his voice was hushed. "Show us her paper, Bill."

Bill Hutchinson went over to his wife and forced the slip of paper out of her hand. It had a black spot on it, the black spot Mr. Summers had made the night before with the heavy pencil in the coal-company office. Bill Hutchinson held it up, and there was a stir in the crowd.

"All right, folks," Mr. Summers said. "Let's finish quickly."

Although the villagers had forgotten the ritual and lost the original black box, they still remembered to use stones. The pile of stones the boys had made earlier was ready; there were stones on the ground with the blowing scraps of paper that had come out of the box. Mrs. Delacroix selected a stone so large she had to pick it up with both hands and turned to Mrs. Dunbar. "Come on," she said. "Hurry up."

Mrs. Dunbar had small stones in both hands, and she said, gasping for breath, "I can't run at all. You'll have to go ahead and I'll catch up with you."

The children had stones already, and someone gave little Davy Hutchinson a few pebbles.

Tessie Hutchinson was in the center of a cleared space by now, and she held her hands out desperately as the villagers moved in on her. "It isn't fair," she said. A stone hit her on the side of the head.

Old Man Warner was saying, "Come on, come on, everyone." Steve Adams was in the front of the crowd of villagers, with Mrs. Graves beside him.

"It isn't fair, it isn't right," Mrs. Hutchinson screamed, and then they were upon her.

QUESTIONS

1. We never learn where the town is located nor its name. Why has Jackson left out these seemingly significant details?
2. What signs are there that the town is preparing for a stoning? What do the characters say that indicate they are preparing for it?

3. Explain the role of mass psychology in the decision of the townspeople to participate in the stoning. Explain the role of tradition in the same decision.
4. What is the theme of the story? What true event or events can you think of that mirror the central action of the story?

Franz Kafka

A HUNGER ARTIST

During these last decades the interest in professional fasting has markedly diminished. It used to pay very well to stage such great performances under one's own management, but today that is quite impossible. We live in a different world now. At one time the whole town took a lively interest in the hunger artist; from day to day of his fast the excitement mounted; everybody wanted to see him at least once a day; there were people who bought season tickets for the last few days and sat from morning till night in front of his small barred cage; even in the nighttime there were visiting hours, when the whole effect was heightened by torch flares; on fine days the cage was set out in the open air, and then it was the children's special treat to see the hunger artist; for their elders he was often just a joke that happened to be in fashion, but the children stood open-mouthed, holding each other's hands for greater security, marveling at him as he sat there pallid in black tights, with his ribs sticking out so prominently, not even on a seat but down among straw on the ground, sometimes giving a courteous nod, answering questions with a constrained smile, or perhaps stretching an arm through the bars so that one might feel how thin it was, and then again withdrawing deep into himself, paying no attention to anyone or anything, not even to the all-important striking of the clock that was the only piece of furniture in his cage, but merely staring into vacancy with half shut eyes, now and then taking a sip from a tiny glass of water to moisten his lips.

Besides casual onlookers there were also relays of permanent watchers selected by the public, usually butchers, strangely enough, and it was their task to watch the hunger artist day and night, three of them at a time, in case he should have some secret recourse to nourishment. This was nothing but a formality, instituted to reassure the masses, for the initiates knew well enough that during his fast the artist would never in any circumstances, not even under forcible compulsion, swallow the smallest morsel of food; the honor of his profession forbade it. Not every watcher, of course, was capable of understanding this, there were often groups of night watchers who were very lax in carrying out their duties and deliberately huddled together in a retired corner to play cards with great absorption, obviously intending to give the hunger artist the chance of a little refreshment, which they supposed he could draw from some private hoard. Nothing annoyed the artist more than such watchers; they made him miserable; they made his fast seem unendurable; sometimes he mastered his feebleness sufficiently to sing during their watch for as long as he could keep going, to show them how unjust their suspicions were. But that was of little use; they only wondered at his cleverness in being able to fill his mouth even while singing. Much more to his taste were the watchers who sat close up to the bars, who were not content with the dim night lighting of the hall but focused him in the full glare of the electric pocket torch given them by the impresario. The harsh light did not trouble him at all, in any case he could never sleep properly, and he could always drowse a little, whatever the light, at any hour, even when the hall was thronged with noisy onlookers. He was quite happy at the prospect of spending a sleepless night with such watchers; he was ready to exchange jokes with them, to tell them stories out of his nomadic life, anything at all to keep them awake and demonstrate to them again that he had no eatables in his cage and that he was fasting as not one of them could fast. But his happiest moment was when the morning came and an enormous breakfast was brought them, at his expense, on which they flung themselves with the keen appetite of healthy men after a weary night of wakefulness. Of course there were people who argued that this breakfast was an unfair attempt to bribe the watchers, but that was going rather too far, and when they were invited to take on a night's vigil without a breakfast, merely for the sake of the cause, they made themselves scarce, although they stuck stubbornly to their suspicions.

Such suspicions, anyhow, were a necessary accompaniment to the profession of fasting. No one could possibly watch the hunger artist continuously, day and night, and so no one could produce first-hand evidence that the fast had really been rigorous and continuous; only the artist himself could know that, he was therefore bound to be the sole completely satisfied spectator of his own fast. Yet for other reasons he was never satisfied; it was not perhaps mere fasting that had brought him to such skeleton thinness that many people had regretfully to keep away from his exhibitions, because the sight of him was too much for them, perhaps it was dissatisfaction with himself that had worn him down. For he alone knew, what no other initiate knew, how easy it was to fast. It was the easiest thing in the world. He made no secret of this, yet people did not believe him; at the best they set him down as modest, most of them, however, thought he was out for publicity or else was some kind of cheat who found it easy to fast because he had discovered a way of making it easy, and then had the impudence to admit the fact, more or less. He had to put up with all that, and in the course of time had got used to it, but his inner dissatisfaction always rankled, and never yet, after any term of fasting—this must be granted to his credit—had he left the cage of his own free will. The longest period of fasting was fixed by his impresario at forty days, beyond that term he was not allowed to go, not even in great cities, and there was good reason for it, too. Experience had proved that for about forty days the interest of the public could be stimulated by a steadily increasing pressure of advertisement, but after that the town began to lose interest, sympathetic support began notably to fall off; there were of course local variations as between one town and another or one country and another, but as a general rule forty days marked the limit. So on the fortieth day the flower-bedecked cage was opened, enthusiastic spectators filled the hall, a military band played, two doctors entered the cage to measure the results of the fast, which were announced through a megaphone, and finally two young ladies appeared, blissful at having been selected for

the honor, to help the hunger artist down the few steps leading to a small table on which
was spread a carefully chosen invalid repast. And at this very moment the artist always
turned stubborn. True, he would entrust his bony arms to the outstretched helping
hands of the ladies bending over him, but stand up he would not. Why stop fasting at
this particular moment, after forty days of it? He had held out for a long time, an
illimitably long time; why stop now, when he was in his best fasting form, or rather, not
yet quite in his best fasting form? Why should he be cheated of the fame he would get
for fasting longer, for being not only the record hunger artist of all time, which
presumably he was already, but for beating his own record by a performance beyond
human imagination, since he felt that there were no limits to his capacity for fasting?
His public pretended to admire him so much, why should it have so little patience with
him; if he could endure fasting longer, why shouldn't the public endure it? Besides, he
was tired, he was comfortable sitting in the straw, and now he was supposed to lift
himself to his full height and go down to a meal the very thought of which gave him
a nausea that only the presence of the ladies kept him from betraying, and even that
with an effort. And he looked up into the eyes of the ladies who were apparently so
friendly and in reality so cruel, and shook his head, which felt too heavy on its
strengthless neck. But then there happened yet again what always happened. The
impresario came forward, without a word—for the band made speech impossible—
lifted his arms in the air above the artist, as if inviting Heaven to look down upon its
creature here in the straw, this suffering martyr, which indeed he was, although in quite
another sense; grasped him round the emaciated waist, with exaggerated caution, so
that the frail condition he was in might be appreciated; and committed him to the care
of the blenching ladies, not without secretly giving him a shaking so that his legs and
body tottered and swayed. The artist now submitted completely; his head lolled on his
breast as if it had landed there by chance; his body was hollowed out; his legs in a spasm
of self-preservation clung close to each other at the knees, yet scraped on the ground
as if it were not really solid ground, as if they were only trying to find solid ground; and
the whole weight of his body, a feather-weight after all, relapsed onto one of the ladies,
who, looking round for help and panting a little—this post of honor was not at all what
she had expected it to be—first stretched her neck as far as she could to keep her face
at least free from contact with the artist, when finding this impossible, and her more
fortunate companion not coming to her aid but merely holding extended on her own
trembling hand the little bunch of knucklebones that was the artist's, to the great delight
of the spectators burst into tears and had to be replaced by an attendant who had long
been stationed in readiness. Then came the food, a little of which the impresario
managed to get between the artist's lips, while he sat in a kind of half-fainting trance,
to the accompaniment of cheerful patter designed to distract the public's attention from
the artist's condition; after that, a toast was drunk to the public, supposedly prompted
by a whisper from the artist in the impresario's ear; the band confirmed it with a mighty
flourish, the spectators melted away, and no one had any cause to be dissatisfied with
the proceedings, no one except the hunger artist himself, he only, as always.

So he lived for many years, with small regular intervals of recuperation, in visible
glory, honored by the world, yet in spite of that troubled in spirit, and all the more
troubled because no one would take his trouble seriously. What comfort could he

possibly need? What more could he possibly wish for? And if some good-natured person, feeling sorry for him, tried to console him by pointing out that his melancholy was probably caused by fasting, it could happen, especially when he had been fasting for some time, that he reacted with an outburst of fury and to the general alarm began to shake the bars of his cage like a wild animal. Yet the impresario had a way of punishing these outbreaks which he rather enjoyed putting into operation. He would apologize publicly for the artist's behavior, which was only to be excused, he admitted, because of the irritability caused by fasting; a condition hardly to be understood by well-fed people; then by natural transition he went on to mention the artist's equally incomprehensible boast that he could fast for much longer than he was doing; he praised the high ambition, the good will, the great self-denial undoubtedly implicit in such a statement; and then quite simply countered it by bringing out photographs, which were also on sale to the public, showing the artist on the fortieth day of a fast lying in bed almost dead from exhaustion. This perversion of the truth, familiar to the artist though it was, always unnerved him afresh and proved too much for him. What was a consequence of the premature ending of his fast was here presented as the cause of it! To fight against this lack of understanding, against a whole world of nonunderstanding, was impossible. Time and again in good faith he stood by the bars listening to the impresario, but as soon as the photographs appeared he always let go and sank with a groan back on to his straw, and the reassured public could once more come close and gaze at him.

A few years later when the witnesses of such scenes called them to mind, they often failed to understand themselves at all. For meanwhile the aforementioned change in public interest had set in; it seemed to happen almost overnight; there may have been profound causes for it, but who was going to bother about that; at any rate the pampered hunger artist suddenly found himself deserted one fine day by the amusement seekers, who went streaming past him to other more favored attractions. For the last time the impresario hurried him over half Europe to discover whether the old interest might still survive here and there; all in vain; everywhere, as if by secret agreement, a positive revulsion from professional fasting was in evidence. Of course it could not really have sprung up so suddenly as all that, and many premonitory symptoms which had not been sufficiently remarked or suppressed during the rush and glitter of success now came retrospectively to mind, but it was now too late to take any countermeasures. Fasting would surely come into fashion again at some future date, yet that was no comfort for those living in the present. What, then, was the hunger artist to do? He had been applauded by thousands in his time and could hardly come down to showing himself in a street booth at village fairs, and as for adopting another profession, he was not only too old for that but too fanatically devoted to fasting. So he took leave of the impresario, his partner in an unparalleled career, and hired himself to a large circus; in order to spare his own feelings he avoided reading the conditions of his contract.

A large circus with its enormous traffic in replacing and recruiting men, animals and apparatus can always find a use for people at any time, even for a hunger artist, provided of course that he does not ask too much, and in this particular case anyhow it was not only the artist who was taken on but his famous and long-known name as well, indeed considering the peculiar nature of his performance, which was not impaired by advancing age, it could not be objected that here was an artist past his prime, no longer at the height of his professional skill, seeking a refuge in some quiet corner of a circus; on the contrary, the hunger artist averred that he could fast as well as ever, which was entirely credible, he even alleged that if he were allowed to fast as he liked, and this was at once promised him without more ado, he could astound the world by establishing a record never yet achieved, a statement which certainly provoked a smile among the other professionals, since it left out of account the change in public opinion, which the hunger artist in his zeal conveniently forgot.

He had not, however, actually lost his sense of the real situation and took it as a matter of course that he and his cage should be stationed, not in the middle of the ring as a main attraction, but outside, near the animal cages, on a site that was after all easily accessible. Large and gaily painted placards made a frame for the cage and announced what was to be seen inside it. When the public came thronging out in the intervals to see the animals, they could hardly avoid passing the hunger artist's cage and stopping there for a moment, perhaps they might even have stayed longer had not those pressing behind them in the narrow gangway, who did not understand why they should be held up on their way toward the excitements of the menagerie, made it impossible for anyone to stand gazing quietly for any length of time. And that was the reason why the hunger artist, who had of course been looking forward to these visiting hours as the main achievement of his life, began instead to shrink from them. At first he could hardly wait for the intervals; it was exhilarating to watch the crowds come streaming his way, until only too soon—not even the most obstinate self-deception, clung to almost consciously, could hold out against the fact—the conviction was borne in upon him that these people, most of them, to judge from their actions, again and again, without exception, were all on their way to the menagerie. And the first sight of them from the distance remained the best. For when they reached his cage he was at once deafened by the storm of shouting and abuse that arose from the two contending factions, which renewed themselves continuously, of those who wanted to stop and stare at him—he soon began to dislike them more than the others—not out of real interest but only out of obstinate self-assertiveness, and those who wanted to go straight on to the animals. When the first great rush was past, the stragglers came along, and these, whom nothing could have prevented from stopping to look at him as long as they had breath, raced past with long strides, hardly even glancing at him, in their haste to get to the menagerie in time. And all too rarely did it happen that he had a stroke of luck, when some father of a family fetched up before him with his children, pointed a finger at the hunger artist and explained at length what the phenomenon meant, telling stories of earlier years when he himself had watched similar but much more thrilling performances, and the children, still rather uncomprehending, since neither inside nor outside school had they been sufficiently prepared for this lesson—what did they care about fasting?—yet showed by the brightness of their intent eyes that new and better times might be coming. Perhaps, said the hunger artist to himself many a time, things would be a little better if his cage were set not quite so near the menagerie. That made it too easy for people to make their choice, to say nothing of what he suffered from the stench of the menagerie, the animals' restlessness by night, the carrying past of raw lumps of flesh for the beasts of prey, the roaring at feeding times, which depressed him continually. But he did not dare to lodge a complaint with the management; after all, he had the animals to thank for the troops of people who passed his cage, among whom there might always be one here and there to take an interest in him, and who could tell where they might seclude him if he called attention to his existence and thereby to the fact that, strictly speaking, he was only an impediment on the way to the menagerie.

A small impediment, to be sure, one that grew steadily less. People grew familiar with the strange idea that they could be expected, in times like these, to take an interest in a hunger artist, and with this familiarity the verdict went out against him. He might fast as much as he could, and he did so; but nothing could save him now, people passed him by. Just try to explain to anyone the art of fasting! Anyone who has no feeling for it cannot be made to understand it. The fine placards grew dirty and illegible, they were torn down; the little notice board telling the number of fast days achieved, which at first was changed carefully every day, had long stayed at the same figure, for after the first few weeks even this small task seemed pointless to the staff; and so the artist simply fasted on and on, as he had once dreamed of doing, and it was no trouble to him, just as he had always foretold, but no one counted the days, no one, not even the artist himself, knew what records he was already breaking, and his heart grew heavy. And when once in a time some leisurely passer-by stopped, made merry over the old figure on the board and spoke of swindling, that was in its way the stupidest lie ever invented by indifference and inborn malice, since it was not the hunger artist who was cheating; he was working honestly, but the world was cheating him of his reward.

Many more days went by, however, and that too came to an end. An overseer's eye fell on the cage one day and he asked the attendants why this perfectly good cage should be left standing there unused with dirty straw inside it; nobody knew, until one man, helped out by the notice board, remembered about the hunger artist. They poked into the straw with sticks and found him in it. "Are you still fasting?" asked the overseer. "When on earth do you mean to stop?" "Forgive me, everybody," whispered the hunger artist; only the overseer, who had his ear to the bars, understood him. "Of course," said the overseer, and tapped his forehead with a finger to let the attendants know what state the man was in, "we forgive you." "I always wanted you to admire my fasting," said the hunger artist. "We do admire it," said the overseer, affably. "But you shouldn't admire it," said the hunger artist. "Well, then we don't admire it," said the overseer, "but why shouldn't we admire it?" "Because I have to fast, I can't help it," said the hunger artist. "What a fellow you are," said the overseer, "and why can't you help it?" "Because," said the hunger artist, lifting his head a little and speaking, with his lips pursed, as if for a kiss, right into the overseer's ear, so that no syllable might be lost, "because I couldn't find the food I liked. If I had found it, believe me, I should have made no fuss and stuffed myself like you or anyone else." These were his last words, but in his dimming eyes remained the firm though no longer proud persuasion that he was still continuing to fast.

"Well, clear this out now!" said the overseer, and they buried the hunger artist, straw and all. Into the cage they put a young panther. Even the most insensitive felt it refreshing to see this wild creature leaping around the cage that had so long been dreary. The panther was all right. The food he liked was brought him without hesitation by the attendants; he seemed not even to miss his freedom; his noble body, furnished almost to the bursting point with all that it needed, seemed to carry freedom around with it too; somewhere in his jaws it seemed to lurk; and the joy of life streamed with such ardent passion from his throat that for the onlookers it was not easy to stand the shock of it. But they braced themselves, crowded round the cage, and did not want ever to move away.

QUESTIONS

1. What figure or figures in real life could the Hunger Artist represent? What aspect of society might the impresario represent?
2. Why doesn't the public take the Hunger Artist seriously in spite of his suffering? Why does the public grow weary of the Hunger Artist and refuse to pay to observe him?
3. At the end of the story, the Hunger Artist claims he never ate "because I couldn't find the food I liked." What does he mean by this?
4. Compare and contrast the public's attitude toward the panther and the Hunger Artist.

Flannery O'Connor

A GOOD MAN
IS HARD TO FIND

The grandmother didn't want to go to Florida. She wanted to visit some of her connections in east Tennessee and she was seizing every chance to change Bailey's mind. Bailey was the son she lived with, her only boy. He was sitting on the edge of his chair at the table, bent over the orange sports section of the *Journal*. "Now look here, Bailey," she said, "see here, read this," and she stood with one hand on her thin hip and the other rattling the newspaper at his bald head. "Here this fellow that calls himself The Misfit is aloose from the Federal Pen and headed toward Florida and you read here what it says he did to these people. Just you read it. I wouldn't take my children in any direction with a criminal like that aloose in it. I couldn't answer to my conscience if I did."

Bailey didn't look up from his reading so she wheeled around then and faced the children's mother; a young mother in slacks, whose face was as broad and innocent as a cabbage and was tied around with a green headkerchief that had two points on the top like rabbit's ears. She was sitting on the sofa, feeding the baby his apricots out of a jar. "The children have been to Florida before," the old lady said. "You all ought to take them somewhere else for a change so they would see different parts of the world and be broad. They never have been to east Tennessee."

The children's mother didn't seem to hear her, but the eight-year-old boy, John Wesley, a stocky child with glasses, said, "If you don't want to go to Florida, why dontcha stay at home?" He and the little girl, June Star, were reading the funny papers on the floor.

"She wouldn't stay at home to be queen for a day," June Star said without raising her yellow head.

"Yes, and what would you do if this fellow, The Misfit, caught you?" the grandmother asked.

"I'd smack his face," John Wesley said.

"She wouldn't stay at home for a million bucks," June Star said. "Afraid she'd miss something. She has to go everywhere we go."

"All right, Miss," the grandmother said. "Just remember that the next time you want me to curl your hair."

June Star said her hair was naturally curly.

The next morning the grandmother was the first one in the car, ready to go. She had her big black valise that looked like the head of a hippopotamus in one corner, and underneath it she was hiding a basket with Pitty Sing, the cat, in it. She didn't intend for the cat to be left alone in the house for three days because he would miss her too much and she was afraid he might brush against one of the gas burners and accidentally asphyxiate himself. Her son, Bailey, didn't like to arrive at a motel with a cat.

She sat in the middle of the back seat with John Wesley and June Star on either side of her. Bailey and the children's mother and the baby sat in the front and they left Atlanta at eight forty-five with the mileage on the car at 55890. The grandmother wrote this down because she thought it would be interesting to say how many miles they had been when they got back. It took them twenty minutes to reach the outskirts of the city.

The old lady settled herself comfortably, removing her white cotton gloves and putting them up with her purse on the shelf in front of the back window. The children's mother still had on slacks and still had her head tied up in a green kerchief, but the grandmother had on a navy blue straw sailor hat with a bunch of white violets on the brim and a navy blue dress with a small white dot in the print. Her collar and cuffs were white organdy trimmed with lace and at her neckline she had pinned a purple spray of cloth violets containing a sachet. In case of an accident, anyone seeing her dead on the highway would know at once that she was a lady.

She said she thought it was going to be a good day for driving, neither too hot nor too cold, and she cautioned Bailey that the speed limit was fifty-five miles an hour and that the patrolmen hid themselves behind bill-boards and small clumps of trees and sped out after you before you had a chance to slow down. She pointed out interesting details of the scenery: Stone Mountain, the blue granite that in some places came up to both sides of the highway; the brilliant red clay banks slightly streaked with purple; and the various crops that made rows of green lack-work on the ground. The trees were full of silver-white sunlights and the meanest of them sparkled. The children were reading comic magazines and their mother had gone back to sleep.

"Let's go through Georgia fast so we won't have to look at it much," John Wesley said.

"If I were a little boy," said the grandmother, "I wouldn't talk about my native state that way. Tennessee has the mountains and Georgia has the hills."

"Tennessee is just a hillbilly dumping ground," John Wesley said, "and Georgia is a lousy state too."

"You said it," June Star said.

"In my time," said the grandmother, folding her thin veined fingers, "children were more respectful of their native states and their parents and everything else. People did right then. Oh look at the cute little pickaninny!" she said and pointed to a Negro child standing in the door of a shack. "Wouldn't that make a picture, now?" she asked and they all turned and looked at the little Negro out of the back window. He waved.

"He didn't have any britches on," June Star said.

"He probably didn't have any," the grandmother explained. "Little niggers in the country don't have things like we do. If I could paint, I'd paint that picture," she said.

The children exchanged comic books.

The grandmother offered to hold the baby and the children's mother passed him over the front seat to her. She set him on her knee and bounced him and told him about the things they were passing. She rolled her eyes and screwed up her mouth and stuck her leathery thin face into his smooth bland one. Occasionally he gave her a faraway smile. They passed a large cotton field with five or six graves fenced in the middle of it, like a small island. "Look at the graveyard!" the grandmother said, pointing it out. "That was the old family burying ground. That belonged to the plantation."

"Where's the plantation?" John Wesley asked.

"Gone With the Wind," said the grandmother. "Ha. Ha."

When the children finished all the comic books they had brought, they opened the lunch and ate it. The grandmother ate a peanut butter sandwich and an olive and would not let the children throw the box and the paper napkins out the window. When there was nothing else to do they played a game by choosing a cloud and making the other two guess what shape it suggested. John Wesley took one the shape of a cow and June Star guessed a cow and John Wesley said, no, an automobile, and June Star said he didn't play fair, and they began to slap each other over the grandmother.

The grandmother said she would tell them a story if they would keep quiet. When she told a story, she rolled her eyes and waved her head and was very dramatic. She said once when she was a maiden lady she had been courted by a Mr. Edgar Atkins Teagarden from Jasper, Georgia. She said he was a very good-looking man and a gentleman and that he brought her a watermelon every Saturday afternoon with his initials cut in it, E. A. T. Well, one Saturday, she said, Mr. Teagarden brought the watermelon and there was nobody at home and he left it on the front porch and returned in his buggy to Jasper, but she never got the watermelon, she said, because a nigger boy ate it when he saw the initials, E. A. T.! This story tickled John Wesley's funny bone and he giggled and giggled but June Star didn't think it was any good. She said she wouldn't marry a man that just brought her a watermelon on Saturday. The grandmother said she would have done well to marry Mr. Teagarden because he was a gentleman and had bought Coca-Cola stock when it first came out and that he had died only a few years ago, a very wealthy man.

They stopped at The Tower for barbecued sandwiches. The Tower was a part-stucco and part-wood filling station and dance hall set in a clearing outside of Timothy. A fat man named Red Sammy Butts ran it and there were signs stuck here and there on the building and for miles up and down the highway saying, TRY RED SAMMY'S FAMOUS BARBECUE. NONE LIKE FAMOUS RED SAMMY'S! RED SAM! THE FAT BOY WITH THE HAPPY LAUGH. A VETERAN! RED SAMMY'S YOUR MAN!

Red Sammy was lying on the bare ground outside The Tower with his head under a truck while a gray monkey about a foot high, chained to a small chinaberry tree, chattered nearby. The monkey sprang back into the tree and got on the highest limb as soon as he saw the children jump out of the car and run toward him.

Inside, The Tower was a long dark room with a counter at one end and tables at the other and dancing space in the middle. They all sat down at a broad table next to the nickelodeon and Red Sam's wife, a tall burnt-brown woman with hair and eyes lighter than her skin, came and took their order. The children's mother put a dime in the machine and played "The Tennessee Waltz," and the grandmother said that tune always made her want to dance. She asked Bailey if he would like to dance but he only glared at her. He didn't have a naturally sunny disposition like she did and trips made him nervous. The grandmother's brown eyes were very bright. She swayed her head from side to side and pretended she was dancing in her chair. June Star said play something she could tap to so the children's mother put in another dime and played a fast number and June Star stepped out onto the dance floor and did her tap routine.

"Ain't she cute?" Red Sam's wife said, leaning over the counter. "Would you like to come be my little girl?"

"No, I certainly wouldn't," June Star said. "I wouldn't live in a broken-down place like this for a million bucks!" and she ran back to the table.

"Ain't she cute?" the woman repeated, stretching her mouth politely.

"Aren't you ashamed?" hissed the grandmother.

Red Sam came in and told his wife to quit lounging on the counter and hurry up with these people's order. His khaki trousers reached just to his hip bones and his stomach hung over them like a sack of meal swaying under his shirt. He came over and sat down at a table nearby and let out a combination sigh and yodel. "You can't win," he said. "You can't win," and he wiped his sweating red face off with a gray handkerchief. "These days you don't know who to trust," he said. "Ain't that the truth?"

"People are certainly not nice like they used to be," said the grandmother.

"Two fellers come in here last week," Red Sammy said, "driving a Chrysler. It was an old beat-up car but it was a good one and these boys looked all right to me. Said they worked at the mill and you know I let them fellers charge the gas they bought? Now why did I do that?"

"Because you're a good man!" the grandmother said at once.

"Yes'm, I suppose so," Red Sam said as if he were struck with this answer.

His wife brought the orders, carrying the five plates all at once without a tray, two in each hand and one balanced on her arm. "It isn't a soul in this green world of God's that you can trust," she said. "And I don't count nobody out of that, not nobody," she repeated, looking at Red Sammy.

"Did you read about that criminal, The Misfit, that's escaped?" asked the grandmother.

"I wouldn't be a bit surprised if he didn't attack this place right here," said the woman. "If he hears about it being here, I wouldn't be none surprised to see him. If he hears it's two cent in the cash register, I wouldn't be a tall surprised if he. . . ."

"That'll do," Red Sam said. "Go bring these people their Co'-Colas," and the woman went off to get the rest of the order.

"A good man is hard to find," Red Sammy said. "Everything is getting terrible. I remember the day you could go off and leave your screen door unlatched. Not no more."

He and the grandmother discussed better times. The old lady said that in her opinion Europe was entirely to blame for the way things were now. She said the way Europe acted you would think we were made of money and Red Sam said it was no use talking about it, she was exactly right. The children ran outside into the white sunlight and looked at the monkey in the lacy chinaberry tree. He was busy catching fleas on himself and biting each one carefully between his teeth as if it were a delicacy.

They drove off again into the hot afternoon. The grandmother took cat naps and woke up every few minutes with her own snoring. Outside of Toombsboro she woke up and recalled an old plantation that she had visited in this neighborhood once when she was a young lady. She said the house had six white columns across the front and that there was an avenue of oaks leading up to it and two little wooden trellis arbors on either side in front where you sat down with your suitor after a stroll in the garden. She recalled exactly which road to turn off to get to it. She knew that Bailey would not be willing to lose any time looking at an old house, but the more she talked about it, the more she wanted to see it once again and find out if the little twin arbors were still standing. "There was a secret panel in this house," she said craftily, not telling the truth but wishing that she were, "and the story went that all the family silver was hidden in it when Sherman came through but it was never found. . . ."

"Hey!" John Wesley said. "Let's go see it! We'll find it! We'll poke all the wood work and find it! Who lives there? Where do you turn off at? Hey Pop, can't we turn off there?"

"We never have seen a house with a secret panel!" June Star shrieked. "Let's go to the house with the secret panel! Hey, Pop, can't we go see the house with the secret panel!"

"It's not far from here, I know," the grandmother said. "It wouldn't take over twenty minutes."

Bailey was looking straight ahead. His jaw was as rigid as a horseshoe. "No," he said.

The children began to yell and scream that they wanted to see the house with the secret panel. John Wesley kicked the back of the front seat and June Star hung over her mother's shoulder and whined desperately into her ear that they never had any fun even on their vacation, that they could never do what THEY wanted to do. The baby began to scream and John Wesley kicked the back of the seat so hard that his father could feel the blows in his kidney.

"All right!" he shouted and drew the car to a stop at the side of the road. "Will you all shut up? Will you all just shut up for one second? If you don't shut up, we won't go anywhere."

"It would be very educational for them," the grandmother murmured.

"All right," Bailey said, "but get this. This is the only time we're going to stop for anything like this. This is the one and only time."

"The dirt road that you have to turn down is about a mile back," the grandmother directed. "I marked it when we passed."

"A dirt road," Bailey groaned.

After they had turned around and were headed toward the dirt road, the grandmother recalled other points about the house, the beautiful glass over the front doorway and the candle lamp in the hall. John Wesley said that the secret panel was probably in the fireplace.

"You can't go inside this house," Bailey said. "You don't know who lives there."

"While you all talk to the people in front, I'll run around behind and get in a window," John Wesley suggested.

"We'll all stay in the car," his mother said.

They turned onto the dirt road and the car raced roughly along in a swirl of pink dust. The grandmother recalled the times when there were no paved roads and thirty miles was a day's journey. The dirt road was hilly and there were sudden washes in it and sharp curves on dangerous embankments. All at once they would be on a hill, looking down over the blue tops of trees for miles around, then the next minute, they would be in a red depression with the dust-coated trees looking down on them.

"This place had better turn up in a minute," Bailey said, "or I'm going to turn around."

The road looked as if no one had traveled on it in months.

"It's not much farther," the grandmother said and just as she said it, a horrible thought came to her. The thought was so embarrassing that she turned red in the face and her eyes dilated and her feet jumped up, upsetting her valise in the corner. The instant the valise moved, the newspaper top she had the basket under it rose with a snarl and Pitty Sing, the cat, sprang onto Bailey's shoulder.

The children were thrown to the floor and their mother, clutching the baby, was thrown out the door onto the ground; the old lady was thrown into the front seat. The car turned over once and landed right-side-up in a gulch on the side of the road. Bailey remained in the driver's seat with the cat—gray-striped with a broad white face and an orange nose—clinging to his neck like a caterpillar.

As soon as the children saw they could move their arms and legs, they scrambled out of the car, shouting, "We've had an ACCIDENT!" The grandmother was curled up under the dashboard, hoping she was injured so that Bailey's wrath would not come down on her all at once. The horrible thought she had had before the accident was that the house she had remembered so vividly was not in Georgia but in Tennessee.

Bailey removed the cat from his neck with both hands and flung it out the window against the side of a pine tree. Then he got out of the car and started looking for the children's mother. She was sitting against the side of the red gutted ditch, holding the screaming baby, but she only had a cut down her face and a broken shoulder. "We've had an ACCIDENT" the children screamed in a frenzy of delight.

"But nobody's killed," June Star said with disappointment as the grandmother limped out of the car, her hat still pinned to her head but the broken front brim standing up at a jaunty angle and the violet spray hanging off the side. They all sat down in the ditch, except the children, to recover from the shock. They were all shaking.

"Maybe a car will come along," said the children's mother hoarsely.

"I believe I have injured an organ," said the grandmother, pressing her side, but no one answered her. Bailey's teeth were clattering. He had on a yellow sport shirt with bright blue parrots designed in it and his face was as yellow as the shirt. The grandmother decided that she would not mention that the house was in Tennessee.

The road was about ten feet above and they could see only the tops of the trees on the other side of it. Behind the ditch they were sitting in there were more woods, tall and dark and deep. In a few minutes they saw a car some distance away on top of a hill, coming slowly as if the occupants were watching them. The grandmother stood up and waved both arms dramatically to attract their attention. The car continued to come on slowly, disappeared around a bend and appeared again, moving even slower, on top of the hill they had gone over. It was a big black battered hearselike automobile. There were three men in it.

It came to a stop just over them and for some minutes, the driver looked down with a steady expressionless gaze to where they were sitting, and didn't speak. Then he turned his head and muttered something to the other two and they got out. One was a fat boy in black trousers and a red sweat shirt with a silver stallion embossed on the front of it. He moved around on the right side of them and stood staring, his mouth partly open in a kind of loose grin. The other had on khaki pants and a blue striped coat and a gray hat pulled down very low, hiding most of his face. He came around slowly on the left side. Neither spoke.

The driver got out of the car and stood by the side of it, looking down at them. He was an older man than the other two. His hair was just beginning to gray and he wore silver-rimmed spectacles that gave him a scholarly look. He had a long creased face and didn't have on any shirt or undershirt. He had on blue jeans that were too tight for him and was holding a black hat and a gun. The two boys also had guns.

"We've had an ACCIDENT!" the children screamed.

The grandmother had the peculiar feeling that the bespectacled man was someone she knew. His face was as familiar to her as if she had known him all her life but she could not recall who he was. He moved away from the car and began to come down the embankment, placing his feet carefully so that he wouldn't slip. He had on tan and white shoes and no socks, and his ankles were red and thin. "Good afternoon," he said. "I see you all had you a little spill."

"We turned over twice!" said the grandmother.

"Oncet," he corrected. "We see it happen. Try their car and see will it run, Hiram," he said quietly to the boy with the gray hat.

"What you got that gun for?" John Wesley asked. "Whatcha gonna do with that gun?"

"Lady," the man said to the children's mother, "would you mind calling them children to sit down by you? Children make me nervous. I want all you all to sit down right together there where you're at."

"What are you telling us what to do for?" June Star asked.

Behind them the line of woods gaped like a dark open mouth. "Come here," said their mother.

"Look here now," Bailey began suddenly, "we're in a predicament! We're in. . . ."

The grandmother shrieked. She scrambled to her feet and stood staring.

"You're The Misfit!" she said. "I recognized you at once!"

"Yes'm," the man said, smiling slightly as if he were pleased in spite of himself to be known, "but it would have been better for all of you, lady, if you hadn't of reckernized me."

Bailey turned his head sharply and said something to his mother that shocked even the children. The old lady began to cry and The Misfit reddened.

"Lady," he said, "don't you get upset. Sometimes a man says things he don't mean. I don't reckon he meant to talk to you thataway."

"You wouldn't shoot a lady, would you?" the grandmother said and removed a clean handkerchief from her cuff and began to slap at her eyes with it.

The Misfit pointed the toe of his shoe into the ground and made a little hole and then covered it up again. "I would hate to have to," he said.

"Listen," the grandmother almost screamed, "I know you're a good man. You don't look a bit like you have common blood. I know you must come from nice people!"

"Yes mam," he said, "finest people in the world." When he smiled he showed a row of strong white teeth. "God never made a finer woman than my mother and my daddy's heart was pure gold," he said. The boy with the red sweat shirt had come around behind them and was standing with his gun at his hip. The Misfit squatted down on the ground. "Watch them children, Bobby Lee," he said. "You know they make me nervous." He looked at the six of them huddled together in front of him and he seemed to be embarrassed as if he couldn't think of anything to say. "Ain't a cloud in the sky," he remarked, looking up at it. "Don't see no sun but don't see no cloud neither."

"Yes, it's a beautiful day," said the grandmother. "Listen," she said, "you shouldn't call yourself The Misfit because I know you're a good man at heart. I can just look at you and tell."

"Hush!" Bailey yelled. "Hush! Everybody shut up and let me handle this!" He was squatting in the position of a runner about to sprint forward but he didn't move.

"I pre-chate that, lady," The Misfit said and drew a little circle in the ground with the butt of his gun.

"It'll take a half a hour to fix this here car," Hiram called, looking over the raised hood of it.

"Well, first you and Bobby Lee get him and that little boy to step over yonder with you," The Misfit said, pointing to Bailey and John Wesley. "The boys want to ask you something," he said to Bailey. "Would you mind stepping back in them woods there with them?"

"Listen," Bailey began, "we're in a terrible predicament! Nobody realizes what this is," and his voice cracked. His eyes were as blue and intense as the parrots in his shirt and he remained perfectly still.

The grandmother reached up to adjust her hat brim as if she were going to the woods with him but it came off in her hand. She stood staring at it and after a second she let it fall on the ground. Hiram pulled Bailey up by the arm as if he were assisting an old man. John Wesley caught hold of his father's hand and Bobby Lee followed. They went off toward the woods and just as they reached the dark edge, Bailey turned and supporting himself against a gray naked pine trunk, he shouted, "I'll be back in a minute, Mamma, wait on me!"

"Come back this instant!" his mother shrilled but they all disappeared into the woods.

"Bailey Boy!" the grandmother called in a tragic voice but she found she was looking at The Misfit squatting on the ground in front of her. "I just know you're a good man," she said desperately. "You're not a bit common!"

"Nome, I ain't a good man," The Misfit said after a second as if he had considered her statement carefully, "but I ain't the worst in the world neither. My daddy said I was a different breed of dog from my brothers and sisters. 'You know,' Daddy said, 'it's some that can live their whole life out without asking about it and it's others has to know why it is, and this boy is one of the latters. He's going to be into everything!' " He put on his black hat and looked up suddenly and then away deep into the woods as if he were embarrassed again. "I'm sorry, I don't have on a shirt before you ladies," he said, hunching his shoulders slightly. "We buried our clothes that we had on when we escaped and we're just making do until we can get better. We borrowed these from some folks we met," he explained.

"That's perfectly all right," the grandmother said. "Maybe Bailey has an extra shirt in his suitcase."

"I'll look and see terrectly," The Misfit said.

"Where are they taking him?" the children's mother screamed.

"Daddy was a card himself," The Misfit said. "You couldn't put anything over on him. He never got in trouble with the Authorities though. Just had the knack of handling them."

"You could be honest too if you'd only try," said the grandmother. "Think how wonderful it would be to settle down and live a comfortable life and not have to think about somebody chasing you all the time."

The Misfit kept scratching in the ground with the butt of his gun as if he were thinking about it. "Yes'm, somebody is always after you," he murmured.

The grandmother noticed how thin his shoulder blades were just behind his hat because she was standing up looking down on him. "Do you ever pray?" she asked.

He shook his head. All she saw was the black hat wiggle between his shoulder blades. "Nome," he said.

There was a pistol shot from the woods, followed closely by another. Then silence. The old lady's head jerked around. She could hear the wind move through the tree tops like a long satisfied insuck of breath. "Bailey Boy!" she called.

"I was a gospel singer for a while," The Misfit said. "I been most everything. Been in the arm service, both land and sea, at home and abroad, been twict married, been an undertaker, been with the railroads, plowed Mother Earth, been in a tornado, seen a man burnt alive oncet," and he looked up at the children's mother and the little girl who were sitting close together, their faces white and their eyes glass; "I even seen a woman flogged," he said.

"Pray, pray," the grandmother began, "pray, pray. . . ."

"I never was a bad boy that I remember of," The Misfit said in an almost dreamy voice, "but somewheres along the line I done something wrong and got sent to the penitentiary. I was buried alive," and he looked up and held her attention to him by a steady stare.

"That's when you should have started to pray," she said. "What did you do to get sent to the penitentiary that first time?"

"Turn to the right, it was a wall," The Misfit said, looking up again at the cloudless sky. "Turn to the left, it was a wall. Look up it was a ceiling, look down it was a floor. I forget what I done, lady. I set there and set there, trying to remember what it was I done and I ain't recalled it to this day. Oncet in a while, I would think it was coming to me, but it never come."

"Maybe they put you in by mistake," the old lady said vaguely.

"Nome," he said. "It wasn't no mistake. They had the papers on me."

"You must have stolen something," she said.

The Misfit sneered slightly. "Nobody had nothing I wanted," he said. "It was a head-doctor at the penitentiary said what I had done was kill my daddy but I known that for a lie. My daddy died in nineteen ought nineteen of the epidemic flu and I never had a thing to do with it. He was buried in the Mount Hopewell Baptist churchyard and you can go there and see for yourself."

"If you would pray," the old lady said, "Jesus would help you."

"That's right," The Misfit said.

"Well then, why don't you pray?" she asked trembling with delight suddenly.

"I don't want no hep," he said. "I'm doing all right by myself."

Bobby Lee and Hiram came ambling back from the woods. Bobby Lee was dragging a yellow shirt with bright blue parrots in it.

"Throw me that shirt, Bobby Lee," The Misfit said. The shirt came flying at him and landed on his shoulder and he put it on. The grandmother couldn't name what the shirt reminded her of. "No, lady," The Misfit said while he was buttoning it up, "I found out the crime don't matter. You can do one thing or you can do another, kill a man or take a tire off his car, because sooner or later you're going to forget what it was you done and just be punished for it."

The children's mother had begun to make heaving noises as if she couldn't get her breath. "Lady," he asked, "would you and that little girl like to step off yonder with Bobby Lee and Hiram and join your husband?"

"Yes, thank you," the mother said faintly. Her left arm dangled helplessly and she was holding the baby, who had gone to sleep, in the other. "Hep that lady up, Hiram," The Misfit said as she struggled to climb out of the ditch, "and Bobby Lee, you hold onto that little girl's hand."

"I don't want to hold hands with him," June Star said. "He reminds me of a pig."

The fat boy blushed and laughed and caught her by the arm and pulled her off into the woods after Hiram and her mother.

Alone with The Misfit, the grandmother found that she had lost her voice. There was not a cloud in the sky nor any sun. There was nothing around her but woods. She wanted to tell him that he must pray. She opened and closed her mouth several times before anything came out. Finally she found herself saying, "Jesus, Jesus," meaning, Jesus will help you, but the way she was saying it, it sounded as if she might be cursing.

"Yes'm," The Misfit said as if he agreed. "Jesus thrown everything off balance. It was the same case with Him as with me except He hadn't committed any crime and they could prove I had committed one because they had the papers on me. Of course," he said, "they never shown me my papers. That's why I sign myself now. I said long ago, you get you a signature and sign everything you do and keep a copy of it. Then you'll know what you done and you can hold up the crime to the punishment and see do they match and in the end you'll have something to prove you ain't been treated right. I call myself The Misfit," he said, "because I can't make what all I done wrong fit what all I gone through in punishment."

There was a piercing scream from the woods, followed closely by a pistol report. "Does it seem right to you, lady, that one is punished a heap and another ain't punished at all?"

"Jesus!" the old lady cried. "You've got good blood! I know you wouldn't shoot a lady! I know you come from nice people! Pray! Jesus, you ought not to shoot a lady. I'll give you all the money I've got!"

"Lady," The Misfit said, looking beyond her far into the woods, "there never was a body that give the undertaker a tip."

There were two more pistol reports and the grandmother raised her head like a parched old turkey hen crying for water and called, "Bailey Boy, Baily Boy!" as if her heart would break.

"Jesus was the only One that ever raised the dead," The Misfit continued, "and He shouldn't have done it. He thrown everything off balance. If He did what He said, then it's nothing for you to do but throw away everything and follow Him, and if He didn't then it's nothing for you to do but enjoy the few minutes you got left the best way you can—by killing somebody or burning down his house or doing some other meanness to him. No pleasure but meanness," he said and his voice had become almost a snarl.

"Maybe He didn't raise the dead," the old lady mumbled, not knowing what she was saying and feeling so dizzy that she sank down in the ditch with her legs twisted under her.

"I wasn't there so I can't say He didn't," The Misfit said. "I wisht I had of been there," he said, hitting the ground with his fist. "It ain't right I wasn't there because if I had of been there I would of known. Listen lady," he said in a high voice, "if I had of been there I would of known and I wouldn't be like I am now." His voice seemed about to crack and the grandmother's head cleared for an instant. She saw the man's face twisted close to her own as if he were going to cry and she murmured. "Why, you're one of my babies. You're one of my own children!" She reached out and touched him on the shoulder. The Misfit sprang back as if a snake had bitten him and shot her three times through the chest. Then he put his gun down on the ground and took off his glasses and began to clean them.

Hiram and Bobby Lee returned from the woods and stood over the ditch, looking down at the grandmother who half sat and half lay in a puddle of blood with her legs crossed under her like a child's and her face smiling up at the cloudless sky.

Without his glasses, The Misfit's eyes were red-rimmed and pale and defenseless-looking. "Take her off and throw her where you thrown the others," he said, picking up the cat that was rubbing itself against his leg.

"She was a talker, wasn't she?" Bobby Lee said, sliding down the ditch with a yodel.

"She would of been a good woman," The Misfit said, "if it had been somebody there to shoot her every minute of her life."

"Some fun!" Bobby Lee said.

"Shut up, Bobby Lee," The Misfit said. "It's no real pleasure in life."

QUESTIONS

1. How would you characterize the grandmother? What can you discern about her personality when she expresses her concern about her personal appearance should she die along the highway?
2. Explain the foreshadowing that indicates there may be a tragic end to the story.
3. Explain why The Misfit says, "She would of been a good woman . . . if it had been somebody there to shoot her every minute of her life."
4. Is the grandmother's praise of The Misfit sincere or merely an attempt to save her own life, or both?
5. Why does The Misfit have such a negative view of life? Based on his experience growing up, is his view justified?

Philip Roth

THE CONVERSION
OF THE JEWS

You're a real one for opening your mouth in the first place," Itzie said. "What do you open your mouth all the time for?"

"I didn't bring it up, Itz, I didn't," Ozzie said.

"What do you care about Jesus Christ for anyway?"

"I didn't bring up Jesus Christ. He did. I didn't even know what he was talking about. Jesus is historical, he kept saying. Jesus is historical." Ozzie mimicked the monumental voice of Rabbi Binder.

"Jesus was a person that lived like you and me," Ozzie continued. "That's what Binder said—"

"Yeah? . . . So what! What do I give two cents whether he lived or not. And what do you gotta open your mouth!" Itzie Lieberman favored closed-mouthedness, especially when it came to Ozzie Freedman's questions. Mrs. Freedman had to see Rabbi Binder twice before about Ozzie's questions and this Wednesday at four-thirty would be the third time. Itzie preferred to keep *his* mother in the kitchen; he settled for behind-the-back subtleties such as gestures, faces, snarls and other less delicate barnyard noises.

"He was a real person, Jesus, but he wasn't like God, and we don't believe he is God." Slowly, Ozzie was explaining Rabbi Binder's position to Itzie, who had been absent from Hebrew School the previous afternoon.

"The Catholics," Itzie said helpfully, "they believe in Jesus Christ, that he's God." Itzie Lieberman used "the Catholics" in its broadest sense—to include the Protestants.

Ozzie received Itzie's remark with a tiny head bob, as though it were a footnote, and went on. "His mother was Mary, and his father probably was Joseph," Ozzie said. "But the New Testament says his real father was God."

"His *real* father?"

"Yeah," Ozzie said, "that's the big thing, his father's supposed to be God."

"Bull."

"That's what Rabbi Binder says, that it's impossible—"

"Sure it's impossible. That stuff's all bull. To have a baby you gotta get laid," Itzie theologized. "Mary hadda get laid."

"That's what Binder says: 'The only way a woman can have a baby is to have intercourse with a man.' "

"He said *that*, Ozz?" For a moment it appeared that Itzie had put the theological question aside. "He said that, intercourse?" A little curled smile shaped itself in the lower half of Itzie's face like a pink mustache. "What you guys do, Ozz, you laugh or something?"

"I raised my hand."

"Yeah? Whatja say?"

"That's when I asked the question."

Itzie's face lit up. "Whatja ask about—intercourse?"

"No, I asked the question about God, how if He could create the heaven and earth in six days, and make all the animals and the fish and the light in six days—the light especially, that's what always gets me, that He could make the light. Making fish and animals, that's pretty good—"

"That's damn good." Itzie's appreciation was honest but unimaginative: it was as though God had just pitched a one-hitter.

"But making light . . . I mean when you think about it, it's really something," Ozzie said. "Anyway, I asked Binder if He could make all that in six days, and He could *pick* the six days he wanted right out of nowhere, why couldn't He let a woman have a baby without having intercourse."

"You said intercourse, Ozz, to Binder?"

"Yeah."

"Right in class?"

"Yeah."

Itzie smacked the side of his head.

"I mean, no kidding around," Ozzie said, "that'd really be nothing. After all that other stuff, that'd practically be nothing."

Itzie considered a moment. "What'd Binder say?"

"He started all over again explaining how Jesus was historical and how he lived like you and me but he wasn't God. So I said I under*stood* that. What I wanted to know was different."

What Ozzie wanted to know was always different. The first time he had wanted to know how Rabbi Binder could call the Jews "The Chosen People" if the Declaration of Independence claimed all men to be created equal. Rabbi Binder tried to distinguish for him between political equality and spiritual legitimacy, but what Ozzie wanted to know, he insisted vehemently, was different. That was the first time his mother had to come.

Then there was the plane crash. Fifty-eight people had been killed in a plane crash at La Guardia. In studying a casualty list in the newspaper his mother had discovered among the list of those dead eight Jewish names (his grandmother had nine but she counted Miller as a Jewish name); because of the eight she said the plane crash was "a tragedy." During free-discussion time on Wednesday Ozzie had brought to Rabbi Binder's attention this matter of "some of his relations" always picking out the Jewish names. Rabbi Binder had begun to explain cultural unity and some other things when Ozzie stood up at his seat and said that what he wanted to know was different. Rabbi Binder insisted that he sit down and it was then that Ozzie shouted that he wished all fifty-eight were Jews. That was the second time his mother came.

"And he kept explaining about Jesus being historical, and so I kept asking him. No kidding, Itz, he was trying to make me look stupid."

"So what he finally do?"

"Finally he starts screaming that I was deliberately simple-minded and a wise guy, and that my mother had to come, and this was the last time. And that I'd never get bar-mitzvahed if he could help it. Then, Itz, then he starts talking in that voice like a statue, real slow and deep, and he says that I better think over what I said about the Lord. He told me to go to his office and think it over." Ozzie leaned his body towards Itzie. "Itz, I thought it over for a solid hour, and now I'm convinced God could do it."

Ozzie had planned to confess his latest transgression to his mother as soon as she came home from work. But it was a Friday night in November and already dark, and when Mrs. Freedman came through the door she tossed off her coat, kissed Ozzie quickly on the face, and went to the kitchen table to light the three yellow candles, two for the Sabbath and one for Ozzie's father.

When his mother lit the candles she would move her two arms slowly towards her, dragging them through the air, as though persuading people whose minds were half made up. And her eyes would get glassy with tears. Even when his father was alive Ozzie remembered that her eyes had gotten glassy, so it didn't have anything to do with his dying. It had something to do with lighting the candles.

As she touched the flaming match to the unlit wick of a Sabbath candle, the phone rang, and Ozzie, standing only a foot from it, plucked it off the receiver and held it muffled to his chest. When his mother lit candles Ozzie felt there should be no noise; even breathing, if you could manage it, should be softened. Ozzie pressed the phone to his breast and watched his mother dragging whatever she was dragging, and he felt his own eyes get glassy. His mother was a round, tired, gray-haired penguin of a woman whose gray skin had begun to feel the tug of gravity and the weight of her own history. Even when she was dressed up she didn't look like a chosen person. But when she lit candles she looked like something better; like a woman who knew momentarily that God could do anything.

After a few mysterious minutes she was finished. Ozzie hung up the phone and walked to the kitchen table where she was beginning to lay the two places for the four-course Sabbath meal. He told her that she would have to see Rabbi Binder next Wednesday at four-thirty, and then he told her why. For the first time in their life together she hit Ozzie across the face with her hand.

All through the chopped liver and chicken soup part of the dinner Ozzie cried; he didn't have any appetite for the rest.

On Wednesday, in the largest of the three basement classrooms of the synagogue, Rabbi Marvin Binder, a tall, handsome, broad-shouldered man of thirty with thick strong-fibered black hair, removed his watch from his pocket and saw that it was four o'clock. At the rear of the room Yakov Blotnik, the seventy-one-year-old custodian, slowly polished the large window, mumbling to himself, unaware that it was four o'clock or six o'clock, Monday or Wednesday. To most of the students Yakov Blotnik's mumbling, along with his brown curly beard, scythe nose, and two heel-trailing black cats, made of him an object of wonder, a foreigner, a relic, towards whom they were alternately fearful and disrespectful. To Ozzie the mumbling had always seemed a monotonous, curious prayer; what made it curious was that old Blotnik had been mumbling so steadily for so many years, Ozzie suspected he had memorized the prayers and forgotten all about God.

"It is now free-discussion time," Rabbi Binder said. "Feel free to talk about any Jewish matter at all—religion, family, politics, sports—"

There was silence. It was a gusty, clouded November afternoon and it did not seem as though there ever was or could be a thing called baseball. So nobody this week said a word about that hero from the past, Hank Greenberg—which limited free discussion considerably.

And the soul-battering Ozzie Freedman had just received from Rabbi Binder had imposed its limitation. When it was Ozzie's turn to read aloud from the Hebrew book the rabbi had asked him petulantly why he didn't read more rapidly. He was showing no progress. Ozzie said he could read faster but that if he did he was sure not to understand what he was reading. Nevertheless, at the rabbi's repeated suggestion Ozzie tried, and showed a great talent, but in the midst of a long passage he stopped short and said he didn't understand a word he was reading, and started in again at a drag-footed pace. Then came the soul-battering.

Consequently when free-discussion time rolled around none of the students felt too free. The rabbi's invitation was answered only by the mumbling of feeble old Blotnik.

"Isn't there anything at all you would like to discuss?" Rabbi Binder asked again, looking at his watch. "No questions or comments?"

There was a small grumble from the third row. The rabbi requested that Ozzie rise and give the rest of the class the advantage of his thought.

Ozzie rose. "I forget it now," he said, and sat down in his place.

Rabbi Binder advanced a seat towards Ozzie and poised himself on the edge of the desk. It was Itzie's desk and the rabbi's frame only a dagger's-length away from his face snapped him to sitting attention.

"Stand up again, Oscar," Rabbi Binder said calmly, "and try to assemble your thoughts."

Ozzie stood up. All his classmates turned in their seats and watched as he gave an unconvincing scratch to his forehead.

"I can't assemble any," he announced, and plunked himself down.

"Stand up!" Rabbi Binder advanced from Itzie's desk to the one directly in front of Ozzie; when the rabbinical back was turned Itzie gave it five-fingers off the tip of his nose, causing a small titter in the room. Rabbi Binder was too absorbed in squelching Ozzie's nonsense once and for all to bother with titters. "Stand up, Oscar. What's your question about?"

Ozzie pulled a word out of the air. It was the handiest word. "Religion."

"Oh, now you remember?"

"Yes."

"What is it?"

Trapped, Ozzie blurted the first thing that came to him. "Why can't He make anything He wants to make!"

As Rabbi Binder prepared an answer, a final answer, Itzie, ten feet behind him, raised one finger on his left hand, gestured it meaningfully towards the rabbi's back, and brought the house down.

Binder twisted quickly to see what had happened and in the midst of the commotion Ozzie shouted into the rabbi's back what he couldn't have shouted to his face. It was a loud, toneless sound that had the timbre of something stored inside for about six days.

"You don't know! You don't know anything about God!"

The rabbi spun back towards Ozzie. "What?"

"You don't know—you don't—"

"Apologize, Oscar, apologize!" It was a threat.

"You don't—"

Rabbi Binder's hand flicked out at Ozzie's cheek. Perhaps it had only been meant to clamp the boy's mouth shut, but Ozzie ducked and the palm caught him squarely on the nose.

The blood came in a short, red spurt on to Ozzie's shirt front.

The next moment was all confusion. Ozzie screamed, "You bastard, you bastard!" and broke for the classroom door. Rabbi Binder lurched a step backwards, as though his own blood had started flowing violently in the opposite direction, then gave a clumsy lurch forward and bolted out the door after Ozzie. The class followed after the rabbi's huge blue-suited back, and before old Blotnik could turn from his window, the room was empty and everyone was headed full speed up the three flights leading to the roof.

If one should compare the light of day to the life of man: sunrise to birth; sunset—the dropping down over the edge—to death; then as Ozzie Freedman wiggled through the trapdoor of the synagogue roof, his feet kicking backwards bronco-style at Rabbi Binder's outstretched arms—at that moment the day was fifty years old. As a rule, fifty or fifty-five reflects accurately the age of late afternoons in November, for it is in that month, during those hours, that one's awareness of light seems no longer a matter of seeing, but of hearing: light begins clicking away. In fact, as Ozzie locked shut the trapdoor in the rabbi's face, the sharp click of the bolt into the lock might momentarily have been mistaken for the sound of the heavier gray that had just throbbed through the sky.

With all his weight Ozzie kneeled on the locked door; any instant he was certain that Rabbi Binder's shoulder would fling it open, splintering the wood into shrapnel and catapulting his body into the sky. But the door did not move and below him he heard only the rumble of feet, first loud then dim, like thunder rolling away.

A question shot through his brain. "Can this be *me?*" For a thirteen-year-old who had just labeled his religious leader a bastard, twice, it was not an improper question. Louder and louder the question came to him—"Is it me? Is it me?"—until he discovered himself no longer kneeling, but racing crazily towards the edge of the roof, his eyes crying, his throat screaming, and his arms flying everywhichway as though not his own.

"Is it me? Is it me Me ME ME ME! It has to be me—but is it!"

It is the question a thief must ask himself the night he jimmies open his first window, and it is said to be the question with which bridegrooms quiz themselves before the altar.

In the few wild seconds it took Ozzie's body to propel him to the edge of the roof, his self-examination began to grow fuzzy. Gazing down at the street, he became confused as to the problem beneath the question: was it, is-it-me-who-called-Binder-a-bastard? or, is-it-me-prancing-around-on-the-roof? However, the scene below settled all, for there is an instant in any action when whether it is you or somebody else is academic. The thief crams the money in his pockets and scoots out the window. The bridegroom signs the hotel register for two. And the boy on the roof finds a streetful of people gaping at him, necks stretched backwards, faces up, as though he were the ceiling of the Hayden Planetarium. Suddenly you know it's you.

"Oscar! Oscar Freedman!" A voice rose from the center of the crowd, a voice that, could it have been seen, would have looked like the writing on scroll. "Oscar Freedman, get down from there. Immediately!" Rabbi Binder was pointing one arm stiffly up at him; and at the end of that arm, one finger aimed menacingly. It was the attitude of a dictator, but one—the eyes confessed all—whose personal valet had spit neatly in his face.

Ozzie didn't answer. Only for a blink's length did he look towards Rabbi Binder. Instead his eyes began to fit together the world beneath him, to sort out people from places, friends from enemies, participants from spectators. In little jagged starlike clusters his friends stood around Rabbi Binder, who was still pointing. The topmost point on a star compounded not of angels but of five adolescent boys was Itzie. What a world it was, with those stars below, Rabbi Binder below . . . Ozzie, who a moment earlier hadn't been able to control his own body, started to feel the meaning of the word control: he felt Peace and he felt Power.

"Oscar Freedman, I'll give you three to come down."

Few dictators give their subjects three to do anything; but, as always, Rabbi Binder only looked dictatorial.

"Are you ready, Oscar?"

Ozzie nodded his head yes, although he had no intention in the world—the lower one of the celestial one he'd just entered—of coming down even if Rabbi Binder should give him a million.

"All right then," said Rabbi Binder. He ran a hand through his black Samson hair as though it were the gesture prescribed for uttering the first digit. Then, with his other hand cutting a circle out of the small piece of sky around him, he spoke. "One!"

There was no thunder. On the contrary, at that moment, as though "one" was the cue for which he had been waiting, the world's least thunderous person appeared on the synagogue steps. He did not so much come out the synagogue door as lean out, onto the darkening air. He clutched at the doorknob with one hand and looked up at the roof.

"Oy!"

Yakov Blotnik's old mind hobbled slowly, as if on crutches, and though he couldn't decide precisely what the boy was doing on the roof, he knew it wasn't good—that is, it wasn't-good-for-the-Jews. For Yakov Blotnik life had fractionated itself simply: things were either good-for-the-Jews or no-good-for-the-Jews.

He smacked his free hand to his in-sucked cheek, gently. "Oy, Gut!" And then quickly as he was able, he jacked down his head and surveyed the street. There was Rabbi Binder (like a man at an auction with only three dollars in his pocket, he had just delivered a shaky "Two!"); there were the students, and that was all. So far it-wasn't-so-bad-for-the-Jews. But the boy had to come down immediately, before anybody saw. The problem: how to get the boy off the roof?

Anybody who has ever had a cat on the roof knows how to get him down. You call the fire department. Or first you call the operator and you ask her for the fire department. And the next thing there is great jamming of brakes and clanging of bells and shouting of instructions. And then the cat is off the roof. You do the same thing to get a boy off the roof.

That is, you do the same thing if you are Yakov Blotnik and you once had a cat on the roof.

When the engines, all four of them, arrived, Rabbi Binder had four times given Ozzie the count of three. The big hook-and-ladder swung around the corner and one of the firemen leaped from it, plunging headlong towards the yellow fire hydrant in front of the synagogue. With a huge wrench he began to unscrew the top nozzle. Rabbi Binder raced over to him and pulled at his shoulder.

"There's no fire . . ."

The fireman mumbled back over his shoulder and, heatedly, continued working at the nozzle.

"But there's no fire, there's no fire . . ." Binder shouted. When the fireman mumbled again, the rabbi grasped his face with both his hands and pointed it up at the roof.

To Ozzie it looked as though Rabbi Binder was trying to tug the fireman's head out of his body, like a cork from a bottle. He had to giggle at the picture they made: it was a family portrait—rabbi in black skullcap, fireman in red fire hat, and the little yellow hydrant squatting beside like a kid brother, bareheaded. From the edge of the roof Ozzie waved at the portrait, a one-handed, flapping, mocking wave; in doing it his right foot slipped from under him. Rabbi Binder covered his eyes with his hands.

Firemen work fast. Before Ozzie had even regained his balance, a big, round, yellowed net was being held on the synagogue lawn. The firemen who held it looked up at Ozzie with stern, feelingless faces.

One of the firemen turned his head towards Rabbi Binder. "What, is the kid nuts or something?"

Rabbi Binder unpeeled his hands from his eyes, slowly, painfully, as if they were tape. Then he checked: nothing on the sidewalk, no dents in the net.

"Is he gonna jump, or what?" the fireman shouted.

In a voice not at all like a statue, Rabbi Binder finally answered. "Yes, Yes, I think so . . . He's been threatening to . . ."

Threatening to? Why, the reason he was on the roof, Ozzie remembered, was to get away; he hadn't even thought about jumping. He had just run to get away, and the truth was that he hadn't really headed for the roof as much as he'd been chased there.

"What's his name, the kid?"

"Freedman," Rabbi Binder answered. "Oscar Freedman."

The fireman looked up at Ozzie. "What is it with you, Oscar? You gonna jump, or what?"

Ozzie did not answer. Frankly, the question had just arisen.

"Look, Oscar, if you're gonna jump, jump—and if you're not gonna jump, don't jump. But don't waste our time, willya?"

Ozzie looked at the fireman and then at Rabbi Binder. He wanted to see Rabbi Binder cover his eyes one more time.

"I'm going to jump."

And then he scampered around the edge of the roof to the corner, where there was no net below, and he flapped his arms at his sides, swishing the air and smacking his palms to his trousers on the downbeat. He began screaming like some kind of engine, "Wheeeee . . . wheeeeee," and leaning way out over the edge with the upper half of his body. The firemen whipped around to cover the ground with the net. Rabbi Binder mumbled a few words to Somebody and covered his eyes. Everything happened quickly, jerkily, as in a silent movie. The crowd, which had arrived with the fire engines, gave out a long, Fourth-of-July fireworks oooh-aahhh. In the excitement no one had paid the crowd much heed, except, of course, Yakov Blotnik, who swung from the doorknob counting heads. "Fier und tsvansik . . . finf und tsvantsik . . . Oy, Gut!" It wasn't like this with the cat.

Rabbi Binder pecked through his fingers, checked the sidewalk and net. Empty. But there was Ozzie racing to the other corner. The firemen raced with him but were unable to keep up. Whenever Ozzie wanted to he might jump and splatter himself upon the sidewalk, and by the time the firemen scooted to the spot all they could do with their net would be to cover the mess.

"Wheeeee . . . wheeeee . . ."

"Hey, Oscar," the winded fireman yelled, "What the hell is this, a game or something?"

"Wheeeee . . . wheeeee . . ."

"Hey, Oscar—"

But he was off now to the other corner, flapping his wings fiercely. Rabbi Binder couldn't take it any longer—the fire engines from nowhere, the screaming suicidal boy, the net. He fell to his knees, exhausted, and with his hands curled together in front of his chest like a little dome, he pleaded, "Oscar, stop it, Oscar. Don't jump, Oscar. Please come down . . . Please don't jump."

And further back in the crowd a single voice, a single young voice, shouted a lone word to the boy on the roof.

"Jump!"

It was Itzie. Ozzie momentarily stopped flapping.

"Go ahead, Ozz—jump!" Itzie broke off his point of the star and courageously, with the inspiration not of a wise-guy but of a disciple, stood alone. "Jump, Ozz, jump!"

Still on his knees, his hands still curled, Rabbi Binder twisted his body back. He looked at Itzie, then, agonizingly, back to Ozzie.

"Oscar, Don't jump! Please, Don't Jump . . . please please . . ."

"Jump!" This time it wasn't Itzie but another point of the star. By the time Mrs. Freedman arrived to keep her four-thirty appointment with Rabbi Binder, the whole little upside down heaven was shouting and pleading for Ozzie to jump, and Rabbi Binder no longer was pleading with him not to jump, but was crying into the dome of his hands.

Understandably Mrs. Freedman couldn't figure out what her son was doing on the roof. So she asked.

"Ozzie, my Ozzie, what are you doing? My Ozzie, what is it?"

Ozzie stopped wheeeeeing and slowed his arms down to a cruising flap, the kind birds use in soft winds, but he did not answer. He stood against the low, clouded, darkening sky—light clicked down swiftly now, as on a small gear—flapping softly and gazing down at the small bundle of a woman who was his mother.

"What are you doing, Ozzie?" She turned towards the kneeling Rabbi Binder and rushed so close that only a paper-thickness of dusk lay between her stomach and his shoulders.

"What is my baby doing?"

Rabbi Binder gaped up at her but he too was mute. All that moved was the dome of his hands; it shook back and forth like a weak pulse.

"Rabbi, get him down! He'll kill himself. Get him down, my only baby . . ."

"I can't," Rabbi Binder said, "I can't . . ." and he turned his handsome head towards the crowd of boys behind him. "It's them. Listen to them."

And for the first time Mrs. Freedman saw the crowd of boys, and she heard what they were yelling.

"He's doing it for them. He won't listen to me. It's them." Rabbi Binder spoke like one in a trance.

"For them?"

"Yes."

"Why for them?"

"They want him to . . ."

Mrs. Freedman raised her two arms upward as though she were conducting the sky. "For them he's doing it!" And then in a gesture older than pyramids, older than prophets and floods, her arms came slapping down to her sides. "A martyr I have. Look!" She tilted her head to the roof. Ozzie was still flapping softly. "My martyr."

"Oscar, come down, *please*," Rabbi Binder groaned.

In a startlingly even voice Mrs. Freedman called to the boy on the roof. "Ozzie, come down, Ozzie. Don't be a martyr, my baby."

As though it were a litany, Rabbi Binder repeated her words. "Don't be a martyr, my baby. Don't be a martyr."

"Gawhead, Ozz—*be* a Martin!" It was Itzie. "Be a Martin, be a Martin," and all the voices joined in singing for Martindom, whatever *it* was. "Be a Martin, be a Martin . . ."

Somehow when you're on a roof the darker it gets the less you can hear. All Ozzie knew was that two groups wanted two new things: his friends were spirited and musical about what they wanted; his mother and the rabbi were even-toned, chanting, about what they didn't want. The rabbi's voice was without tears now and so was his mother's.

The big net stared up at Ozzie like a sightless eye. The big, clouded sky pushed down. From beneath it looked like a gray corrugated board. Suddenly, looking up into that unsympathetic sky, Ozzie realized all the strangeness of what these people, his friends, were asking: they wanted him to jump, to kill himself; they were singing about it now—it made them that happy. And there was an even greater strangeness: Rabbi Binder was on his knees, trembling. If there was a question to be asked now it was not "Is it me?" but rather "Is it us? . . . Is it us?"

Being on the roof, it turned out, was a serious thing. If he jumped would the singing become dancing? Would it? What would jumping stop? Yearningly, Ozzie wished he could rip open the sky, plunge his hands through, and pull out the sun; and on the sun, like a coin, would be stamped JUMP or DON'T JUMP.

Ozzie's knees rocked and sagged a little under him as though they were setting him for a dive. His arms tightened, stiffened, froze, from shoulders to fingernails. He felt as if each part of his body were going to vote as to whether he should kill himself or not—and each part as though it were independent of *him*.

The light took an unexpected click down and the new darkness, like a gag, hushed the friends singing for this and the mother and rabbi chanting for that.

Ozzie stopped counting votes, and in a curiously high voice, like one who wasn't prepared for speech, he spoke.

"Mamma?"

"Yes, Oscar."

"Mamma, get down on your knees, like Rabbi Binder."

"Oscar—"

"Get down on your knees," he said, "or I'll jump."

Ozzie heard a whimper, then a quick rustling, and when he looked down where his mother had stood he saw the top of a head and beneath that a circle of dress. She was kneeling beside Rabbi Binder.

He spoke again. "Everybody kneel." There was the sound of everybody kneeling.

Ozzie looked around. With one hand he pointed towards the synagogue entrance. "Make *him* kneel."

There was a noise, not of kneeling, but of body-and-cloth stretching. Ozzie could hear Rabbi Binder saying in a gruff whisper, ". . . or he'll *kill* himself," and when next he looked there was Yakov Blotnik off the doorknob and for the first time in his life upon his knees in the Gentile posture of prayer.

As for the firemen—it is not as difficult as one might imagine to hold a net taut while you are kneeling.

Ozzie looked around again; and then he called to Rabbi Binder.

"Rabbi?"

"Yes, Oscar."

"Rabbi Binder, do you believe in God?"

"Yes."

"Do you believe God can do Anything?" Ozzie leaned his head out into the darkness. "Anything?"

"Oscar, I think—"

"Tell me you believe God can do Anything."

There was a second's hesitation. Then: "God can do Anything."

"Tell me you believe God can make a child without intercourse."

"He can."

"Tell me!"

"God," Rabbi Binder admitted, "can make a child without intercourse."

"Mamma, you tell me."

"God can make a child without intercourse," his mother said.

"Make *him* tell me." There was no doubt who *him* was.

In a few moments Ozzie heard an old comical voice say something to the increasing darkness about God.

Next, Ozzie made everybody say it. And then he made them all say they believed in Jesus Christ—first one at a time, then all together.

When the catechizing was through it was the beginning of evening. From the street it sounded as if the boy on the roof might have sighed.

"Ozzie?" A woman's voice dared to speak. "You'll come down now?"

There was no answer, but the woman waited, and when a voice finally did speak it was thin and crying, and exhausted as that of an old man who has just finished pulling the bells.

"Mamma, don't you see—you shouldn't hit me. He shouldn't hit me. You shouldn't hit me about God, Mamma. You should never hit anybody about God—"

"Ozzie, please come down now."

"Promise me, promise me you'll never hit anybody about God."

He had asked only his mother, but for some reason everyone kneeling in the street promised he would never hit anybody about God.

Once again there was silence.

"I can come down now, Mamma," the boy on the roof finally said. He turned his head both ways as though checking the traffic lights. "Now I can come down . . ."

And he did, right into the center of the yellow net that glowed in the evening's edge like an overgrown halo.

QUESTIONS

1. Compare and contrast Ozzie's personality with that of Itzie. How are their personalities reflected in the way they interact with the rabbi?
2. Who seems to present the better argument concerning the possibility of the virgin birth, Ozzie or the rabbi? Explain your view.

3. When Ozzie scampers through the trapdoor of the synagogue roof, he repeatedly asks, "Is it me?" What is the significance of his question?
4. When Ozzie is on the roof, Itzie tells him to jump. Why?
5. In the end, who has the greater faith, Ozzie's pals or the rabbi? Explain your view.

Leslie Marmon Silko

THE MAN TO SEND RAIN CLOUDS

ONE

They found him under a big cottonwood tree. His Levi jacket and pants were faded light blue so that he had been easy to find. The big cottonwood tree stood apart from a small grove of winterbare cottonwoods which grew in the wide, sandy arroyo. He had been dead for a day or more, and the sheep had wandered and scattered up and down the arroyo. Leon and his brother-in-law, Ken, gathered the sheep and left them in the pen at the sheep camp before they returned to the cottonwood tree. Leon waited under the tree while Ken drove the truck through the deep sand to the edge of the arroyo. He squinted up at the sun and unzipped his jacket—it sure was hot for this time of year. But high and northwest the blue mountains were still deep in snow. Ken came sliding down the low, crumbling bank about fifty yards down, and he was bringing the red blanket.

Before they wrapped the old man, Leon took a piece of string out of his pocket and tied a small gray feather in the old man's long white hair. Ken gave him the paint. Across the brown wrinkled forehead he drew a streak of white, and along the high cheekbones he drew a strip of blue paint. He paused and watched Ken throw pinches of corn meal and pollen into the wind that fluttered the small gray feather. Then Leon painted with yellow under the old man's broad nose; and finally, when he had painted green across the chin, he smiled.

"Send us rain clouds, Grandfather." They laid the bundle in the back of the pickup and covered it with a heavy tarp before they started back to the pueblo.

They turned off the highway onto the sandy pueblo road. Not long after they passed the store and post office they saw Father Paul's car coming toward them. When he recognized their faces he slowed his car and waved for them to stop. The young priest rolled down the car window.

"Did you find old Teofilo?" he asked loudly.

Leon stopped the truck. "Good morning, Father. We were just out to the sheep camp. Everything is O.K. now."

"Thank God for that. Teofilo is a very old man. You really shouldn't allow him to stay at the sheep camp alone."

"No, he won't do that any more now."

"Well, I'm glad you understand. I hope I'll be seeing you at Mass this week—we missed you last Sunday. See if you can get old Teofilo to come with you." The priest smiled and waved at them as they drove away.

TWO

Louise and Teresa were waiting. The table was set for lunch, and the coffee was boiling on the black iron stove. Leon looked at Louise and then at Teresa.

"We found him under a cottonwood tree in the big arroyo near sheep camp. I guess he sat down to rest in the shade and never got up again." Leon walked toward the old man's bed. The red plaid shawl had been shaken and spread carefully over the bed, and a new brown flannel shirt and pair of stiff new Levis were arranged neatly beside the pillow. Louise held the screen door open while Leon and Ken carried in the red blanket. He looked small and shriveled, and after they dressed him in the new shirt and pants he seemed more shrunken.

It was noontime now because the church bells rang the Angelus. They ate the beans with hot bread, and nobody said anything until after Teresa poured the coffee.

Ken stood up and put on his jacket. "I'll see about the gravediggers. Only the top layer of soil is frozen. I think it can be ready before dark."

Leon nodded his head and finished his coffee. After Ken had been gone for a while, the neighbors and clanspeople came quietly to embrace Teofilo's family and to leave food on the table because the gravediggers would come to eat when they were finished.

THREE

The sky in the west was full of pale-yellow light. Louise stood outside with her hands in the pockets of Leon's green army jacket that was too big for her. The funeral was over, and the old men had taken their candles and medicine bags and were gone. She waited until the body was laid into the pickup before she said anything to Leon. She touched his arm, and he noticed that her hands were still dusty from the corn meal that she had sprinkled around the old man. When she spoke, Leon could not hear her.

"What did you say? I didn't hear you."

"I said that I had been thinking about something."

"About what?"

"About the priest sprinkling holy water for Grandpa. So he won't be thirsty."

Leon stared at the new moccasins that Teofilo had made for the ceremonial dances in the summer. They were nearly hidden by the red blanket. It was getting colder, and the wind pushed gray dust down the narrow pueblo road. The sun was approaching the long mesa where it disappeared during the winter. Louise stood there shivering and watching his face. Then he zipped up his jacket and opened the truck door. "I'll see if he's there."

FOUR

Ken stopped the pickup at the church, and Leon got out; and then Ken drove down the hill to the graveyard where people were waiting. Leon knocked at the old carved door with its symbols of the Lamb. While he waited he looked up at the twin bells from the king of Spain with the last sunlight pouring around them in their tower.

The priest opened the door and smiled when he saw who it was. "Come in! What brings you here this evening?"

The priest walked toward the kitchen, and Leon stood with his cap in his hand, playing with the earflaps and examining the living room—the brown sofa, the green armchair, and the brass lamp that hung down from the ceiling by links of chain. The priest dragged a chair out of the kitchen and offered it to Leon.

"No thank you, Father. I only came to ask you if you would bring your holy water to the graveyard."

The priest turned away from Leon and looked out the window at the patio full of shadows and the dining-room windows of the nuns' cloister across the patio. The curtains were heavy, and the light from within faintly penetrated; it was impossible to see the nuns inside eating supper. "Why didn't you tell me he was dead? I could have brought the Last Rites anyway."

Leon smiled. "It wasn't necessary, Father."

The priest stared down at his scuffed brown loafers and the worn hem of his cassock. "For a Christian burial it was necessary."

His voice was distant, and Leon thought that his blue eyes looked tired.

"It's O.K. Father, we just want him to have plenty of water."

The priest sank down into the green chair and picked up a glossy missionary magazine. He turned the colored pages full of lepers and pagans without looking at them.

"You know I can't do that, Leon. There should have been the Last Rites and a funeral Mass at the very least."

Leon put on his green cap and pulled the flaps down over his ears. "It's getting late, Father. I've got to go."

When Leon opened the door Father Paul stood up and said, "Wait." He left the room and came back wearing a long brown overcoat. He followed Leon out the door and across the dim churchyard to the adobe steps in front of the church. They both stooped to fit through the low adobe entrance. And when they started down the hill to the graveyard only half of the sun was visible above the mesa.

The priest approached the grave slowly, wondering how they had managed to dig into the frozen ground; and then he remembered that this was New Mexico, and saw the pile of cold loose sand beside the hole. The people stood close to each other with little clouds of steam puffing from their faces. The priest looked at them and saw a pile of jackets, gloves, and scarves in the yellow, dry tumbleweeds that grew in the graveyard. He looked at the red blanket, not sure that Teofilo was so small, wondering if it wasn't some perverse Indian trick—something they did in March to ensure a good harvest—wondering if maybe old Teofilo was actually at sheep camp corralling the sheep for the night. But there he was, facing into a cold dry wind and squinting at the last sunlight, ready to bury a red wool blanket while the faces of his parishioners were in shadow with the last warmth of the sun on their backs.

His fingers were stiff, and it took him a long time to twist the lid off the holy water. Drops of water fell on the red blanket and soaked into dark icy spots. He sprinkled the grave and the water disappeared almost before it touched the dim, cold sand; it reminded him of something—he tried to remember what it was, because he thought if he could remember he might understand this. He sprinkled more water; he shook the container until it was empty, and the water fell through the light from sundown like August rain that fell while the sun was still shining, almost evaporating before it touched the wilted squash flowers.

The wind pulled at the priest's brown Franciscan robe and swirled away the corn meal and pollen that had been sprinkled on the blanket. They lowered the bundle into the ground, and they didn't bother to untie the stiff pieces of new rope that were tied around the ends of the blanket. The sun was gone, and over on the highway the eastbound lane was full of headlights. The priest walked away slowly. Leon watched him climb the hill, and when he had disappeared within the tall, thick walls, Leon turned to look up at the high blue mountains in the deep snow that reflected a faint red light from the west. He felt good because it was finished, and he was happy about the sprinkling of the holy water; now the old man could send them big thunderclouds for sure.

QUESTIONS

1. There appears to be quite a cross-cultural mixture of daily life and religious tradition. What elements in the story demonstrate this blend of cultures?

2. Although the entire story is rather short, it is divided into even shorter sections. How do these sections function in the story? How does this structural element contribute to the pacing and action of the story?

3. Leon and the priest have different perspectives concerning the use of the holy water for Teofilo's burial. Explain each one's view of the role of the holy water. How are their attitudes reconciled?

4. How can the conflict and resolution in this story be viewed as a metaphor for social and cultural life in America?

Faith & Doubt

Fiction

TOPICS FOR WRITING

1. Describe a time or event in your life when your own beliefs were contrary to those of a group to which you belonged. How did you demonstrate your independence of thought? How did others react? What was the outcome?

2. Describe a religious, philosophical, or moral leader whom you admire. The person does not necessarily have to be identified with a particular faith, but rather with a particular point of view. Explain what it is you admire about that person's views, actions, and/or life-style.

3. The main characters in "A Very Old Man with Enormous Wings" and in "A Hunger Artist" are seen as outcasts in their respective communities. Compare and contrast the way society views these isolated individuals, how it behaves toward them, and how they respond, in turn, to the attention brought upon them.

4. Explore the narrator's character in "Cathedral" by discussing the transformation he goes through in terms of his attitude, opinion, and disposition as a result of meeting the blind man.

5. Write an essay wherein you discuss the effect of tradition and ritual as it influences the townspeople in "The Lottery."

6. Both Hughes and Roth use comic strategies to make certain points about organized religion. Compare and contrast "On the Road" and "The Conversion of the Jews," explaining carefully the comic techniques that the authors employ and the intended purpose or effect.

7. In the story "The Conversion of the Jews," Ozzie challenges the authority of the rabbi, who is the spiritual leader of his community. Argue for or against the proposition that it is the individual's right to dispute the authority of a religious leader, even if that leader is respected or revered.

8. In the story "On the Road," the narrator finds himself faced with some religious characters who do not act particularly humane or altruistic. Argue for or against the proposition that it is the individual's character that determines his or her spirituality rather than the particular religion he or she belongs to.

9. Select your favorite story from among this grouping, and do biographical research on the religious views of the author. Then read two other stories by the same author, and show how the author's faith (or lack thereof) influences the choices his or her characters make.

10. Research the concept of literary genre. Selecting one of the stories in this section, discuss how it meets the criteria of either a fairy tale, allegory, or myth.

Poetry

Matthew Arnold

DOVER BEACH

The sea is calm tonight,
The tide is full, the moon lies fair
Upon the straits; on the French coast the light
Gleams and is gone; the cliffs of England stand,
Glimmering and vast, out in the tranquil bay.   5
Come to the window, sweet is the night-air!
Only, from the long line of spray
Where the sea meets the moon-blanched land,
Listen! you hear the grating roar
Of pebbles which the waves draw back, and fling,   10
At their return, up the high strand,
Begin, and cease, and then again begin,
With tremulous cadence slow, and bring
The eternal note of sadness in.

Sophocles long ago   15
Heard it on the Aegean, and it brought
Into his mind the turbid ebb and flow
Of human misery; we

Find also in the sound a thought,
Hearing it by this distant northern sea.   20

The Sea of Faith
Was once, too, at the full, and round earth's shore
Lay like the folds of a bright girdle furled.
But now I only hear
Its melancholy, long, withdrawing roar,   25
Retreating, to the breath
Of the night-wind, down the vast edges drear
And naked shingles of the world.

Ah, love, let us be true
To one another! for the world, which seems   30
To lie before us like a land of dreams,
So various, so beautiful, so new,
Hath really neither joy, nor love, nor light,
Nor certitude, nor peace, nor help for pain;
And we are here as on a darkling plain   35
Swept with confused alarms of struggle and flight,
Where ignorant armies clash by night.

QUESTIONS

1. What does the "eternal note of sadness" mentioned in the first stanza refer to? What does the reference to Sophocles imply?
2. What is the general mood of the poem? How do the rhythm and sound of the poem merge to create this mood? At what point does the general mood of the poem change? What does it change to?
3. To whom may Arnold refer when he states "Ah, love" in the final stanza? A real person? An imagined one? Or something else?

Amiri Baraka

PREFACE TO A TWENTY VOLUME SUICIDE NOTE

Lately, I've become accustomed to the way
The ground opens up and envelops me
Each time I go out to walk the dog,
Or the broad edged silly music the wind
Makes when I run for a bus—   5

Things have come to that.

And now, each night I count the stars,
And each night I get the same number.
And when they will not come to be counted
I count the holes they leave.   10

Nobody sings anymore.

And then last night, I tiptoed up
To my daughter's room and heard her
Talking to someone, and when I opened
The door, there was no one there . . .   15
Only she on her knees,
Peeking into her own clasped hands.

William Blake

THE LAMB

Little Lamb, who made thee?
Dost thou know who made thee?
Gave thee life & bid thee feed,
By the stream & o'er the mead;
Gave thee clothing of delight,   5
Softest clothing wooly bright;
Gave thee such a tender voice,
Making all the vales rejoice!

Little Lamb who made thee?
Dost thou know who made thee?   10
Little Lamb I'll tell thee,
Little Lamb I'll tell thee!
He is calléd by thy name,
For he calls himself a Lamb:
He is meek & he is mild,   15
He became a little child:
I a child & thou a lamb,
We are calléd by his name.
Little Lamb God bless thee.
Little Lamb God bless thee.   20

THE TYGER

Tyger! Tyger! burning bright
In the forests of the night,
What immortal hand or eye
Could frame thy fearful symmetry?

In what distant deeps or skies   5
Burnt the fire of thine eyes?
On what wings dare he aspire?
What the hand, dare seize the fire?

And what shoulder, & what art,
Could twist the sinews of thy heart?   10
And when thy heart began to beat,
What dread hand? & what dread feet?

What the hammer? what the chain?
In what furnace was thy brain?
What the anvil? what dread grasp   15
Dare its deadly terrors clasp?

When the stars threw down their spears,
And water'd heaven with their tears,
Did he smile his work to see?
Did he who made the Lamb make thee?   20

Tyger! Tyger! burning bright
In the forests of the night,

What immortal hand or eye
Dare frame thy fearful symmetry?

Gwendolyn Brooks

HUNCHBACK GIRL: SHE THINKS OF HEAVEN

My Father, it is surely a blue place
And straight. Right. Regular. Where I shall find
No need for scholarly nonchalance or looks
A little to the left or guards upon the
Heart to halt love that runs without crookedness   5
Along its crooked corridors. My Father,
It is a planned place surely. Out of coils,
Unscrewed, released, no more to be marvelous,
I shall walk straightly through most proper halls
Proper myself, princess of properness.   10

QUESTIONS

1. How does the title make certain words in the poem suggest double meanings? Which words are these?
2. The poet uses assonance (repetition of vowel sound) and alliteration (repetition of consonants) in the poem. How does the rhythm these devices create add to the poem's theme and tone?
3. To whom is the poem's narrator speaking?
4. What does the narrator wish for?

Elizabeth Barrett Browning

CONSOLATION

All are not taken; there are left behind
Living Belovéds, tender looks to bring
And make the daylight still a happy thing,
And tender voices, to make soft the wind.
But if it were not so—if I could find   5
No love in all the world for comforting,
Nor any path but hollowly did ring
Where "dust to dust" the love from life disjoined,
And if, before those sepulchers unmoving
I stood alone (as some forsaken lamb   10
Goes bleating up the moors in weary dearth),
Crying, "Where are ye, O my loved and loving?"—
I know a Voice would sound, "Daughter, I AM.
Can I suffice for HEAVEN and not for earth?"

Jayne Cortez

MAKING IT

I know they want me to make it
to enter eye droppers and invade pills
turn around or get shot
I know they wanna vaccinate me with
the fear of myself   5
so i'll pull down my face and nod
I know they want me to make it
but i'm not in a hurry

Victor Hernandez Cruz

FROM THE SECRETS II

This morning I move like the river
moves
Science in your eyes
Say the music elevates
passed clouds   5
Some tall legs
Encircle the river
Heads bob to the ticking
of the solar calender
Do you remember   10
the fourth floor of the pyramids
The hilarious perfume of your
feathers
The soft music of the sea flute
This morning I move like the river   15
moves
In and out of rooms like the warm
wind passing through

Countee Cullen

YET DO I MARVEL

I doubt not God is good, well-meaning, kind,
And did He stoop to quibble could tell why
The little buried mole continues blind,
Why flesh that mirrors Him must some day die,
Make plain the reason tortured Tantalus   5
Is baited by the fickle fruit, declare
If merely brute caprice dooms Sisyphus
To struggle up a never-ending stair.
Inscrutable His ways are, and immune
To catechism by a mind too strewn   10
With petty cares to slightly understand
What awful brain compels His awful hand.
Yet do I marvel at this curious thing:
To make a poet black, and bid him sing!

René Depestre

NOTHINGNESS

My heart
  is slowly
    sinking inside me
I feel it
  down in my belly   5
Wiggling around
    like a little
      dog
Now at last
  it has come to rest   10
    on my knee
And in its place
    emptied
      and gaping
A hard little pebble shines in the sun   15
   Translated by Norman R. Shapiro

QUESTIONS

1. What is the relationship between the line structure of the poem and its meaning?
2. How does the title of the poem affect your understanding of it? How would your view of the poem have been altered if there had been no title at all?
3. What experience is the poet describing?
4. Does the poem end on a positive note, a negative one, both, or neither?

Emily Dickinson

A LIGHT EXISTS IN SPRING

A Light exists in Spring
Not present on the Year
At any other period—
When March is scarcely here

A Color stands abroad   5
On Solitary Fields

That Science cannot overtake
But Human Nature feels.

It waits upon the Lawn,
It shows the furthest Tree   10
Upon the furthest Slope you know
It almost speaks to you.

Then as Horizons step
Or Noons report away
Without the Formula of sound   15
It passes and we stay—

A quality of loss
Affecting our Content
As Trade had suddenly encroached
Upon a Sacrament.   20

BECAUSE I COULD NOT
STOP FOR DEATH

Because I could not stop for Death—
He kindly stopped for me—

The Carriage held but just Ourselves—
And Immortality.

We slowly drove—He knew no haste   5
And I had put away
My labor and my leisure too,
For His Civility—

We passed the School, where Children strove
At Recess—in the Ring—   10
We passed the Fields of Gazing Grain—
We passed the Setting Sun—

Or rather—He passed Us—
The Dews drew quivering and chill—
For only Gossamer, my Gown—   15
My Tippet—only Tulle—

We paused before a House that seemed
A Swelling of the Ground—
The Roof was scarcely visible—
The Cornice—in the Ground—   20

Since then—'tis Centuries—and yet
Feels shorter than the Day
I first surmised the Horses' Heads
Were toward Eternity—

THERE'S A CERTAIN
SLANT OF LIGHT

There's a certain slant of light,
On winter afternoons,
That oppresses, like the weight
Of cathedral tunes.

Heavenly hurt it gives us;   5
We can find no scar,
But internal difference
Where the meanings are.

None may teach it anything,
'Tis the seal, despair,—   10
An imperial affliction
Sent us of the air.

When it comes, the landscape listens,
Shadows hold their breath;
When it goes, 'tis like the distance   15
On the look of death.

John Donne

HOLY SONNET 7

At the round earth's imagined corners, blow
Your trumpets, angels; and arise, arise
From death, you numberless infinities
Of souls, and to your scattered bodies go;
All whom the flood did, and fire shall, o'erthrow,   5
All whom war, dearth, age, agues, tyrannies,
Despair, law, chance hath slain, and you whose eyes
Shall behold God, and never taste death's woe.
But let them sleep, Lord, and me mourn a space;
For, if above all these, my sins abound,   10
'Tis late to ask abundance of Thy grace
When we are there. Here on this lowly ground,
Teach me how to repent; for that's as good
As if Thou hadst sealed my pardon with Thy blood.

QUESTIONS

1. How does the imperative mood of the poem influence its overall effect?
2. To whom does the word *you* refer in line 7?
3. How did you respond to the unusually long series in lines 5 through 8? What might have been the poet's purpose in using this device?
4. What change in tone occurs in line 9? What is the narrator of the poem entreating God to do?

John Donne

HOLY SONNET 14

Batter my heart, three-personed God; for you
As yet but knock, breathe, shine, and seek to mend.
That I may rise and stand, o'erthrow me and bend
Your force to break, blow, burn, and make me new.
I, like an usurped town, to another due,   5
Labor to admit you, but, oh, to no end;
Reason, your viceroy in me, me should defend,

But is captived and proves weak or untrue.
Yet dearly I love you and would be lovèd fain,
But am betrothed unto your enemy: 10
Divorce me, untie or break that knot again,
Take me to you, imprison me, for I,
Except you enthrall me, never shall be free,
Nor ever chaste, except you ravish me.

Rita Dove

THE FISH IN THE STONE

The fish in the stone
would like to fall
back into the sea.

He is weary
of analysis, the small   5
predictable truths.

He is weary of waiting
in the open,
his profile stamped
by a white light.   10

In the ocean the silence
moves and moves

and so much is unnecessary!
Patient, he drifts
until the moment comes   15
to cast his
skeletal blossom.

The fish in the stone
knows to fail is
to do the living   20
a favor.

He knows why the ant
engineers a gangster's

funeral, garish
and perfectly amber.   25
He knows why the scientist
in secret delight
strokes the fern's
voluptuous braille.

Louise Erdrich

JACKLIGHT

*The same Chippewa word is used both for flirting and hunting
game, while another Chippewa word connotes both using force in
intercourse and also killing a bear with one's bare hands.*
—R. W. Dunning
*Social and Economic Change Among
the Northern Ojibwa (1959)*

We have come to the edge of the woods,
out of brown grass where we slept unseen,
out of knotted twigs, out of leaves creaked shut,
out of hiding.

At first the light wavered, glancing over us.   5
Then it clenched to a fist of light that pointed,
searched out, divided us.
Each took the beams like direct blows the heart answers.
Each of us moved forward alone.

We have come to the edge of the woods,   10
drawn out of ourselves by this night sun,
this battery of polarized acids,
that outshines the moon.

We smell them behind it
but they are faceless, invisible.   15
We smell the raw steel of their gun barrels,
mink oil on leather, their tongues of sour barley.
We smell their mothers buried chin-deep in wet dirt.
We smell their fathers with scoured knuckles,
teeth cracked from hot marrow.   20

We smell their sisters of crushed dogwood, bruised apples,
of fractured cups and concussions of burnt hooks.

We smell their breath steaming lightly behind the jacklight.
We smell the itch underneath the caked guts on their clothes.
We smell their minds like silver hammers.   25

THE STRANGE PEOPLE

*The antelope are strange people . . . they are beautiful to look at, and
yet they are tricky. We do not trust them. They appear and disappear;
they are like shadows on the plains. Because of their great beauty, young
men sometimes follow the antelope and are lost forever. Even if those
foolish ones find themselves and return, they are never again right in their
heads.*

— Pretty Shield, Medicine Woman of the Crows
transcribed and edited by Frank Linderman (1932)

All night I am the doe, breathing
his name in a frozen field,
the small mist of the word
drifting always before me.

And again he has heard it   5
and I have gone burning
to meet him, the jacklight
fills my eyes with blue fire,
the heart in my chest
explodes like a hot stone.   10

Then slung like a sack
in the back of his pickup,
I wipe the death scum
from my mouth, sit up laughing,
and shriek in my speeding grave.   15

Safely shut in the garage,
when he sharpens his knife
and thinks to have me, like that,
I come toward him,
a lean gray witch,   20
through the bullets that enter and dissolve.

I sit in his house
drinking coffee till dawn,
and leave as frost reddens on hubcaps,
crawling back into my shadowy body.   25
All day, asleep in clean grasses,
I dream of the one who could really wound me.

QUESTIONS

1. What is the purpose of the epigraph that introduces the poem? How essential is it
   for your understanding of the poem's meaning?
2. Describe the relationship between the poem's narrator and the human as it is depicted in the first two stanzas.
3. The narrator is apparently dead in stanzas 3 through 5. How then can he or she
   speak?
4. Who might be the "one who could really wound me"?

Robert Frost

ONCE BY THE PACIFIC

The shattered water made a misty din.
Great waves looked over others coming in,
And thought of doing something to the shore
That water never did to land before.
The clouds were low and hairy in the skies,   5
Like locks blown forward in the gleam of eyes.
You could not tell, and yet it looked as if
The shore was lucky in being backed by cliff,
The cliff in being backed by continent;
It looked as if a night of dark intent   10
Was coming, and not only a night, an age.
Someone had better be prepared for rage.
There would be more than ocean-water broken
Before God's last *Put out the Light* was spoken.

STOPPING BY WOODS ON A SNOWY EVENING

Whose woods these are I think I know.
His house is in the village though;
He will not see me stopping here
To watch his woods fill up with snow.

My little horse must think it queer   5
To stop without a farmhouse near
Between the woods and frozen lake
The darkest evening of the year.

He gives his harness bells a shake
To ask if there is some mistake.   10
The only other sound's the sweep
Of easy wind and downy flake.

The woods are lovely, dark and deep,
But I have promises to keep,
And miles to go before I sleep,   15
And miles to go before I sleep.

TREE AT MY WINDOW

Tree at my window, window tree,
My sash is lowered when night comes on;
But let there never be curtain drawn
Between you and me.

Vague dream-head lifted out of the ground,   5
And thing next most diffuse to cloud,
Not all your light tongues talking aloud
Could be profound.

But, tree, I have seen you taken and tossed,
And if you have seen me when I slept,   10
You have seen me when I was taken and swept
And all but lost.

That day she put our heads together,
Fate had her imagination about her,
Your head so much concerned with outer,   15
Mine with inner, weather.

QUESTIONS

1. What are the ways Frost makes use of personification in describing the tree? What relationship is established between the poet and nature through the use of this personification?
2. What does the poet mean by the metaphor "inner weather"? Where else in the poem is this weather described?
3. Compare the narrator's relationship to the tree with the narrator's relationship to the human in "The Strange People."
4. What is the theme of the poem? Which stanza, in particular, elucidates the theme?

George Herbert
CHURCH-MONUMENTS

While that my soul repairs to her devotion,
Here I intomb my flesh, that it betimes
May take acquaintance of this heap of dust;
To which the blast of death's incessant motion,
Fed with the exhalation of our crimes,   5
Drives all at last. Therefore I gladly trust

My body to this school, that it may learn
To spell his elements, and find his birth
Written in dusty heraldry and lines;
Which dissolution sure doth best discern,   10
Comparing dust with dust, and earth with earth.
These laugh at jet and marble put for signs,

To sever the good fellowship of dust,
And spoil the meeting. What shall point out them,
When they shall bow, and kneel, and fall down flat   15
To kiss those heaps, which now they have in trust?

Dear flesh, while I do pray, learn here thy stem
And true descent: that when thou shalt grow fat

And wanton in thy cravings, thou mayst know,
That flesh is but the glass, which holds the dust   20
That measures all our time; which also shall
Be crumbled into dust. Mark here below
How tame these ashes are, how free from lust,
That thou mayst fit thy self against thy fall.

Gerard Manley Hopkins
PIED BEAUTY

Glory be to God for dappled things—
　　For skies of couple-colour as a brinded cow;
　　　　For rose-moles all in stipple upon trout that swim;
Fresh-firecoal chestnut-falls; finches' wings;
　　Landscape plotted and pieced—fold, fallow, and plough;   5
　　　　And áll trádes, their gear and tackle and trim.

All things counter, original, spare, strange;
　　Whatever is fickle, freckled (who knows how?)
　　　　With swift, slow; sweet, sour; adazzle, dim;
He fathers-forth whose beauty is past change: 10
　　　　Praise him.

Ricarda Huch
DEATH SEED

　　In a field of swaying grain
　　I saw a man moving.
　　From his free hand slid seeds
　　which he sowed again.
　　Strange to me seemed a reaper   5

who blessed with new seed the same field.
Then I saw his stern face:
Behold, it was Death I had met.

Translated by Susan Strong

John Keats

TO AUTUMN

I

Season of mists and mellow fruitfulness,
   Close bosom-friend of the maturing sun;
Conspiring with him how to load and bless
   With fruit the vines that round the thatch-eves run;
To bend with apples the mossed cottage-trees,   5
   And fill all fruit with ripeness to the core;
      To swell the gourd, and plump the hazel shells
With a sweet kernel; to set budding more,
   And still more, later flowers for the bees,
   Until they think warm days will never cease,   10
      For Summer has o'er-brimmed their clammy cells.

II

Who hath not seen thee oft amid thy store?
   Sometimes whoever seeks abroad may find
Thee sitting careless on a granary floor,
   Thy hair soft-lifted by the winnowing wind;   15
Or on a half-reaped furrow sound asleep,
   Drowsed with the fume of poppies, while thy hook
      Spares the next swath and all its twinéd flowers:
And sometimes like a gleaner thou dost keep
   Steady thy laden head across a brook;   20
   Or by a cider-press, with patient look,
      Thou watchest the last oozings hours by hours.

III

Where are the songs of Spring? Ay, where are they?
   Think not of them, thou hast thy music too—
While barréd clouds bloom the soft-dying day,   25
   And touch the stubble-plains with rosy hue;

Then in a wailful choir the small gnats mourn
Among the river sallows, borne aloft
Or sinking as the light wind lives or dies;
And full-grown lambs loud bleat from hilly bourn; 30
Hedge-crickets sing; and now with treble soft
The red-breast whistles from a garden-croft;
And gathering swallows twitter in the skies.

WRITTEN IN DISGUST OF VULGAR SUPERSTITION

The church bells toll a melancholy round,
Calling the people to some other prayers,
Some other gloominess, more dreadful cares,
More hearkening to the sermon's horrid sound.
Surely the mind of man is closely bound 5
In some black spell; seeing that each one tears
Himself from fireside joys, and Lydian airs,
And converse high of those with glory crown'd.
Still, still they toll, and I should feel a damp—
A chill as from a tomb, did I not know 10
That they are going like an outburnt lamp;
That 'tis their sighing, wailing ere they go
Into oblivion;—that fresh flowers will grow,
And many glories of immortal stamp.

QUESTIONS

1. How many allusions to sadness, horror, and death can you find in the poem? How do these contribute to its tone?
2. What is the poet's attitude toward religion in the poem? What is his attitude toward religious ritual?
3. In line 2, he says the bells are "calling the people to some other prayers." What prayers are they being taken from?
4. The last two lines provide an optimistic message contrary to the rest of the poem. What is this message?

Maurice Kenny

CORN-PLANTER

I plant corn four years:
ravens steal it;
rain drowns it;
August burns it;
locusts ravage leaves.   5

I stand in a circle and throw seed.
Old men laugh because they know the wind
will carry the seed to my neighbor.

I stand in a circle on planted seed.
Moles burrow through the earth   10
and harvest my crop.

I throw seed to the wind
and wind drops it on the desert.

The eighth year I spend planting corn;
I tend my fields all season.   15
After September's harvest I take it to the market.
The people of my village are too poor to buy it.

The ninth spring I make chicken-feather headdresses,
plastic tom-toms and beaded belts.
I grow rich,   20
buy an old Ford,
drive to Chicago,
and get drunk
on Welfare checks.

Galway Kinnell

TO CHRIST OUR LORD

The legs of the elk punctured the snow's crust
And wolves floated lightfooted on the land
Hunting Christmas elk living and frozen;
Inside snow melted in a basin, and a woman basted
A bird spread over coals by its wings and head.   5

Snow had sealed the windows; candles lit
The Christmas meal. The Christmas grace chilled
The cooked bird, being long-winded and the room cold.
During the words a boy thought, is it fitting
To eat this creature killed on the wing?   10

He had killed it himself, climbing out
Alone on snowshoes in the Christmas dawn,
The fallen snow swirling and the snowfall gone,
Heard its throat scream as the gunshot scattered,
Watched it drop, and fished from the snow the dead.   15

He had not wanted to shoot. The sound
Of wings beating into the hushed air
Had stirred his love, and his fingers
Froze in his gloves, and he wondered,
Famishing, could he fire? Then he fired.   20

Now the grace praised his wicked act. At its end
The bird on the plate
Stared at his stricken appetite.
There had been nothing to do but surrender,
To kill and to eat; he ate as he had killed, with wonder.   25

At night on snowshoes on the drifting field
He wondered again, for whom had love stirred?
The stars glittered on the snow and nothing answered.
Then the Swan spread her wings, cross of the cold north,
The pattern and mirror of the acts of earth.   30

Denise Levertov

LIVING WHILE IT MAY

The young elm that must be cut
because its roots push at the house wall

taps and scrapes my window
urgently—but when I look round at it

remains still. Or if I turn by chance,   5
it seems its leaves are eyes, or the whole spray
of leaves and twigs a face flattening
its nose against the glass, breathing a cloud,

longing to see clearly my life whose term
is not yet known.   10

Czeslaw Milosz

ON PRAYER

You ask me how to pray to someone who is not.
All I know is that prayer constructs a velvet bridge
And walking it we are aloft, as on a springboard,
Above landscapes the color of ripe gold
Transformed by a magic stopping of the sun.   5
That bridge leads to the shore of Reversal
Where everything is just the opposite and the word *is*
Unveils a meaning we hardly envisioned.
Notice: I say *we;* there, every one, separately,
Feels compassion for others entangled in the flesh   10
And knows that if there is no other shore
They will walk that aerial bridge all the same.

Translated from Polish by the author

John Milton

WHEN I CONSIDER HOW MY LIGHT IS SPENT

When I consider how my light is spent
 Ere half my days, in this dark world and wide,
 And that one talent which is death to hide
 Lodged with me useless, though my soul more bent
To serve therewith my Maker, and present   5
 My true account, lest he returning chide;
 "Doth God exact day-labor, light denied?"
 I fondly ask: but Patience to prevent
That murmur, soon replies, "God doth not need
 Either man's work or his own gifts; who best   10
 Bear his mild yoke, they serve him best. His state
Is kingly. Thousands at his bidding speed
 And post o'er land and ocean without rest:
 They also serve who only stand and wait."

Nicanor Parra

PIANO SOLO

Since man's life is nothing but an action at a distance,
A bit of froth shining on the inside of a glass,
Since the trees are nothing but fluttering furniture,
Nothing but chairs and tables in perpetual motion,
Since we ourselves are nothing but beings   5
(As god himself is nothing but god)
Since we don't talk to be heard
But to make others talk
And the echo precedes the voices that raise it,
Since we haven't even the consolation of chaos   10
In a garden that yawns and fills with air,
A puzzle we have to solve before we die
So that we can be tranquilly restored to existence
After we have overdone it with women,
Since there is also a heaven in hell   15
Allow me also to do a few things:

I want to make a noise with my feet,
I want my soul to discover its body.
                    Translated by W. S. Merwin

QUESTIONS

1. This poem is replete with metaphors about life. Interpret the metaphors and explain what the poet's general view of life is.
2. According to the poet, what does a typical life lack? What negative trait do most lives have? How can a healthy balance be found?
3. What is the significance of the poem's title? What part or parts of the poem are particularly pertinent to the title?
4. The poet is also a physicist. How does this fact influence your interpretation of the poem and the images that the poet uses in the poem?

Pepi I Pyramid Texts

UTTERANCE 432
The king prays to the sky-goddess

Sarcophagus Chamber, West Wall

O Great One who became Sky,
You are strong, you are mighty,
You fill every place with your beauty,
The whole earth is beneath you, you possess it!
As you enfold earth and all things in your arms,   5
So have you taken this Pepi to you,
An indestructible star within you![1]
                    Translated by Miriam Lichtheim

---

[1] By ornamenting the ceiling of the sarcophagus chamber with stars, the chamber was made to represent the night sky; and the prayers addressed to the sky-goddess Nut ask her, as mother of the dead king, to take him in her arms and transform him into a star.

Ishmael Reed

SERMONETTE

a poet was busted by a topless judge
his friends went to morristwn nj & put
black powder on his honah's doorstep
black powder into his honah's car
black powder on his honah's briefs   5
tiny dolls into his honah's mind

by nightfall his honah could a go go no mo
his dog went crazy & ran into a crocodile
his widow fell from a wall &
hanged herself   10
his daughter was run over by a black man
cming home for the wakes the two boys
skidded into mourning
all the next of kin's teeth fell out

gimmie dat ol time   15
                    religion
it's good enough
          for me!

QUESTIONS

1. In what dialect is the poem written? What effect does the dialect have on the tone of the poem? Of what significance is the fact that the poem is written in lower-case letters?
2. What does the poet mean by "topless judge." What is the irony behind this image?
3. What has the poet actually done to the judge? Why do the series of calamities occur in the second stanza?
4. What is the significance of the title? What is the moral of this "sermonette"?

Roberto Fernandez Retamar

A MOTTO FROM POETS: LEAVE STONE

A motto from poets: leave stone
alone, it won't grow; try
trees, working their way up
and up into air.
And there they inscribe their names magnificent   5
in the sun as banners
But its rock keeps when trees
are ash, or furniture; you eat, or sleep, or lie
dead among the painted detritus of trees.
And all the time there's some stone   10
somewhere, planted, not
bigger, not
smaller, carrying still
across its livid frontage some savage
scrawl, some few letters   15
of someone long gone who,
one afternoon, graved them there,
laughing, dreaming, remembering.

Translated by Tim Reynolds

Christina Rossetti

UPHILL

Does the road wind uphill all the way?
    Yes, to the very end.
Will the day's journey take the whole long day?
    From morn to night, my friend.

But is there for the night a resting place?   5
    A roof for when the slow dark hours begin.
May not the darkness hide it from my face?
    You cannot miss that inn.

Shall I meet other wayfarers at night?
    Those who have gone before.   10

Then must I knock, or call when just in sight?
    They will not keep you standing at that door.

Shall I find comfort, travel-sore and weak?
    Of labor you shall find the sum.
Will there be beds for me and all who seek?   15
    Yea, beds for all who come.

Omar Salinas

QUETZALCOATLE

You lunged and caught fire
    flowers falling from a disenchanted
sky
You made your move
  and caught the world   5
by your nostrils
and escaped half god
        demolished

You appear in our nightmares
     sad and brave   10
your descendants
        drinking peyote

Your fingers dig into clouds
    as memory burns
and you embrace your land   15
    and disappear
        into the vapor
       of dream

Bert Schierbeek

THE BICYCLE REPAIRMAN

in his cave
dimly lit
one door open
he sits
kneels   5
and hunkers
before his umpteenth
bicycle

you say hi
he says hi   10
a twinkling in
his eyes and he sees
upon all these pedals
illuminated all over all
those legs and from the saddle   15
all those thighs those dresses
blowing up and what's under them
and he has to imagine

then he stands up
clasps the handlebar   20
can see all those hands
round the handgrip
and gives a tug

then he mumbles:
        one day   25
        at noon Mount Mola drifted
        into the mist
        and became totally invisible

Translated by Charles McHeehan

Léopold Sédar Senghor

PRAYER TO THE MASKS

Masks! O Masks!
Black mask, red mask, you white-and-black masks
Masks of the four cardinal points where the Spirit blows
I greet you in silence!
And you, not the least of all, Ancestor with the lion head.   5
You keep this place safe from women's laughter
And any wry, profane smiles
You exude the immortal air where I inhale
The breath of my Fathers.
Masks with faces without masks, stripped of every dimple   10
And every wrinkle
You created this portrait, my face leaning
On an altar of blank paper
And in your image, listen to me!
The Africa of empires is dying—it is the agony   15
Of a sorrowful princess
And Europe, too, tied to us at the navel.
Fix your steady eyes on your oppressed children
Who give their lives like the poor man his last garment.
Let us answer "present" at the rebirth of the World   20
As white flour cannot rise without the leaven.
Who else will teach rhythm to the world
Deadened by machines and cannons?
Who will sound the shout of joy at daybreak to wake
    orphans and the dead?   25
Tell me, who will bring back the memory of life
To the man of gutted hopes?
They call us men of cotton, coffee, and oil
They call us men of death.
But we are men of dance, whose feet get stronger   30
As we pound upon firm ground.

                    Translated by Melvin Dixon

QUESTIONS

1. What makes this piece a poem? What makes it a prayer?
2. What is the "place" referred to in the sixth line? Why must it be "safe from women's laughter"?
3. Who is the implied audience of this poem? Who is the stated audience of the poem? What is the significance of each to the poet?

4. What does the poet imply about the relationship between Africa and Europe? What does the poet imply concerning the difference between Africans and Europeans? What images does the poet use to illuminate these differences?
5. What does the poet predict will be the effect on the world of the liberation of Africa?

Anne Sexton

THE FURY OF FLOWERS AND WORMS

Let the flowers make a journey
on Monday so that I can see
ten daisies in a blue vase
with perhaps one red ant
crawling to the gold center.   5
A bit of the field on my table,
close to the worms
who struggle blindly,
moving deep into their slime,
moving deep into God's abdomen,   10
moving like oil through water,
sliding through the good brown.

The daisies grow wild
like popcorn.
They are God's promise to the field.   15
How happy I am, daisies, to love you.
How happy you are to be loved
and found magical, like a secret
from the sluggish field.
If all the world picked daisies   20
wars would end, the common cold would stop,
unemployment would end, the monetary market
would hold steady and no money would float.
Listen world,
if you'd just take the time to pick   25
the white fingers, the penny heart,
all would be well.
They are so unexpected.

They are as good as salt.
If someone had brought them   30

to van Gogh's room daily
his ear would have stayed on.
I would like to think that no one would die anymore
if we all believed in daisies
but the worms know better, don't they?   35
They slide into the ear of a corpse
and listen to his great sigh.

THE STARRY NIGHT

*That does not keep me from having a terrible
need of—shall I say the word—religion. Then I
go out at night to paint the stars.*
—Vincent van Gogh[1]
in a letter to his brother

The town does not exist
except where one black-haired tree slips
up like a drowned woman into the hot sky.
The town is silent. The night boils with eleven stars.
Oh starry starry night! This is how   5
I want to die.

It moves. They are all alive.
Even the moon bulges in its orange irons
to push children, like a god, from its eye.
The old unseen serpent swallows up the stars.[2]   10
Oh starry starry night! This is how
I want to die:

into that rushing beast of the night,
sucked up by that great dragon, to split
from my life with no flag,   15
no belly,
no cry.

[1] **Vincent van Gogh** Dutch painter (1853–1890); letter written September 1888
[2] The Gnostic symbol of the ouroboros, a dragon or serpent biting its own tail, describes the circumferential movement of the universe—from unity to multiplicity, and the return to unity.

Stevie Smith

THE WEAK MONK

The monk sat in his den,
He took the mighty pen
And wrote "Of God and Men."

One day the thought struck him
It was not according to Catholic doctrine;   5
His blood ran dim.

He wrote till he was ninety years old,
Then he shut the book with a clasp of gold
And buried it under the sheep fold.

He'd enjoyed it so much, he loved to plod,   10
And he thought he'd a right to expect that God
Would rescue his book alive from the sod.

Of course it rotted in the snow and rain;
No one will ever know now what he wrote of God and men.
For this the monk is to blame.   15

Edith Sodergran

HOPE

I want to forget my manners—
I couldn't care less about noble styles,
I roll up my sleeves.
The dough of poetry is rising . . .
Oh, what a sorrow—   5
I can't bake cathedrals . . .
The soaring high forms—
The goal of persistent yearning.
Child of our time—
doesn't your soul have its right shell?   10
Before I die
I'll bake a cathedral.

Translated by Jaakko A. Ahokas

Wallace Stevens

THE SNOW MAN

One must have a mind of winter
To regard the frost and the boughs
Of the pine-trees crusted with snow;

And have been cold a long time
To behold the junipers shagged with ice,   5
The spruces rough in the distant glitter

Of the January sun; and not to think
Of any misery in the sound of the wind,
In the sound of a few leaves,

Which is the sound of the land   10
Full of the same wind
That is blowing in the same bare place

For the listener, who listens in the snow,
And, nothing himself, beholds
Nothing that is not there and the nothing that is.   15

QUESTIONS

1. Who is the "snow man" referred to in the title?
2. What are the possible meanings of the phrase "one must have a mind of winter"?
3. The word *nothing* is referred to three times in the final stanza. What is the significance of each?
4. Describe the mood and tone of the poem. How do the sensory images in the poem contribute to its mood and tone? How do they reinforce the theme that is expressed in the final line?

May Swenson

HEARING THE WIND
AT NIGHT

I heard the wind coming,
transferred from tree to tree.
I heard the leaves
swish, wishing to be free

to come with the wind, yet wanting to stay   5
with the boughs like sleeves.
The wind was a green ghost.
Possessed of tearing breath

the body of each tree
whined, a whipping post,   10
then straightened and resumed
its vegetable oath.

I heard the wind going,
and it went wild.
Somewhere the forest threw itself   15
into tantrum like a child.

I heard the trees tossing
in punishment or grief,
then sighing, and soughing,
soothing themselves to sleep.   20

Sara Teasdale

BARTER

Life has loveliness to sell—
        All beautiful and splendid things,
Blue waves whitened on a cliff,
        Climbing fire that sways and sings,
And children's faces looking up   5
Holding wonder like a cup.

Life has loveliness to sell—
        Music like a curve of gold,
Scent of pine trees in the rain,
        Eyes that love you, arms that hold,
And for your spirit's still delight,
Holy thoughts that star the night.

Spend all you have for loveliness,
        Buy it and never count the cost,
For one white singing hour of peace
        Count many a year of strife well lost,
And for a breath of ecstasy
Give all you have been or could be.

William Carlos Williams

TO WAKEN AN OLD LADY

Old age is
a flight of small
cheeping birds
skimming
bare trees
above a snow glaze.
Gaining and failing
they are buffeted
by a dark wind—
But what?
On harsh weedstalks
the flock has rested,
the snow
is covered with broken
seedhusks
and the wind tempered
by a shrill
piping of plenty.

Elinor Wylie

PURITAN SONNET

Down to the Puritan marrow of my bones
There's something in this richness that I hate.
I love the look, austere, immaculate,
Of landscapes drawn in pearly monotones.
There's something in my very blood that owns   5
Bare hills, cold silver on a sky of slate,
A thread of water, churned to milky spate
Streaming through slanted pastures fenced with stones.

I love those skies, thin blue or snowy gray,
Those fields sparse-planted, rendering meager sheaves;   10
That spring, briefer than apple-blossom's breath,
Summer, so much too beautiful to stay,
Swift autumn, like a bonfire of leaves,
And sleepy winter, like the sleep of death.

QUESTIONS

1. What unifying tone is there to the images and metaphors mentioned in the poem? What colors predominate in the poem? How do the images and metaphors reflect the philosophy of Puritanism?
2. Is Wylie's depiction of the Puritan life positive, negative, both, or neither? What aspects of the poem led you to your view?
3. In part, this poem is describing a locale. Drawing on the poem itself and your knowledge of Puritanism in the United States, to which geographical area of the country could she be referring?
4. What about the sonnet form makes it a particularly suitable one for a poem about Puritanism?

Faith & Doubt

Poetry

TOPICS FOR WRITING

1. Describe a time in your life when you had a spiritual or religious experience. This time need not have been in a house of worship nor must it be associated with a particular religion or sect. What is important is that it had profound meaning to you. What were the circumstances? What did you feel? What insights did you have? Who was involved? What was the result?

2. Narrate a story—either imaginary or true, either from your own life or an acquaintance's—where the main character went through a period of doubt about something he or she had previously assumed to be sacrosanct. What caused the doubt? What was the effect of doubting on the behavior of the individual? How was the doubt resolved? Or was it left unresolved?

3. A number of the poems in this section describe aspects of spirituality in enigmatic ways—for example, Frost's "Tree at My Window," Blake's "The Tyger," and Stevens's "The Snow Man." Compare and contrast these three poems for their imagery, their depiction of the spiritual, and the relationship between the spiritual and humankind.

4. Poems in this section describe both Christian and non-Christian visions of faith and religion. Select two from each category, and compare and contrast the way spirituality, God, and humankind's relationship to God are depicted.

5. Which poems in this section describe crises of or challenges to faith? Select any two that contain these themes, and analyze the way the poet addresses his or her doubt.

6. The Spanish poet Miguel de Unamuno has stated that to have faith *is* to doubt. Write an essay supporting or rejecting this view.

7. Many of the poets in this section seem to have their own personal vision of faith and religion. Argue for or against the proposition that possessing a personal faith is far more important than adhering to the practices of an organized religion.

8. Several of the selections in this section are sonnets. Research the form, structure, and history of the sonnet. Then, selecting your two or three favorite sonnets from this section, show how they demonstrate mastery of the sonnet form.

9. Research the biographies of two of your favorite poets from this section: one Christian, the other non-Christian. Then write an essay wherein you draw parallels between the poets' own faith (or doubt) and the expression of that faith (or doubt) in the poetry.

926

Drama

Woody Allen

DEATH KNOCKS

The play takes place in the bedroom of the Nat Ackermans' two-story house, somewhere in Kew Gardens. The carpeting is wall-to-wall. There is a big double bed and a large vanity. The room is elaborately furnished and curtained, and on the walls there are several paintings and a not really attractive barometer. Soft theme music as the curtain rises. Nat Ackerman, a bald, paunchy fifty-seven-year-old dress manufacturer is lying on the bed finishing off tomorrow's Daily News. *He wears a bathrobe and slippers, and reads by a bed light clipped to the white headboard of the bed. The time is near midnight. Suddenly we hear a noise, and Nat sits up and looks at the window.*

NAT: What the hell is that?

[*Climbing awkwardly through the window is a sombre, caped figure. The intruder wears a black hood and skintight black clothes. The hood covers his head but not his face, which is middle-aged and stark white. He is something like* NAT *in appearance. He huffs audibly and then trips over the windowsill and falls into the room.*]

DEATH [*for it is no one else*]: Jesus Christ. I nearly broke my neck.
NAT [*watching with bewilderment*]: Who are you?
DEATH: Death.
NAT: Who?

DEATH: Death. Listen—can I sit down? I nearly broke my neck. I'm shaking like a leaf.

NAT: Who *are* you?

DEATH: *Death.* You got a glass of water?

NAT: Death? What do you mean, Death?

DEATH: What is wrong with you? You see the black costume and the whitened face?

NAT: Yeah.

DEATH: Is it Halloween?

NAT: No.

DEATH: Then I'm Death. Now can I get a glass of water—or a Fresca?

NAT: If this is some joke—

DEATH: What kind of joke? You're fifty-seven? Nat Ackerman? One eighteen Pacific Street? Unless I blew it—where's that call sheet? [*He fumbles through pocket, finally producing a card with an address on it. It seems to check.*]

NAT: What do you want with me?

DEATH: What do I want? What do you think I want?

NAT: You must be kidding. I'm in perfect health.

DEATH [*unimpressed*]: Uh-huh. [*Looking around.*] This is a nice place. You do it yourself?

NAT: We had a decorator, but we worked with her.

DEATH [*looking at picture on the wall*]: I love those kids with the big eyes.

NAT: I don't want to go yet.

DEATH: *You* don't want to go? Please don't start in. As it is, I'm nauseous from the climb.

NAT: What climb?

DEATH: I climbed up the drainpipe. I was trying to make a dramatic entrance. I see the big windows and you're awake reading. I figure it's worth a shot. I'll climb up and enter with a little—you know . . . [*Snaps fingers.*] Meanwhile, I get my heel caught on some vines, the drainpipe breaks, and I'm hanging by a thread. Then my cape begins to tear. Look, let's just go. It's been a rough night.

NAT: You broke my drainpipe?

DEATH: Broke. It didn't break. It's a little bent. Didn't you hear anything? I slammed into the ground.

NAT: I was reading.

DEATH: You must have really been engrossed. [*Lifting newspaper NAT was reading.*] "NAB COEDS IN POT ORGY." Can I borrow this?

NAT: I'm not finished.

DEATH: Er—I don't know how to put this to you, pal . . .

NAT: Why didn't you just ring downstairs?

DEATH: I'm telling you, I could have, but how does it look? This way I get a little drama going. Something. Did you read *Faust?*

NAT: What?

DEATH: And what if you had company? You're sitting there with important people. I'm Death—I should ring the bell and traipse right in the front? Where's your thinking?

NAT: Listen, Mister, it's very late.

DEATH: Yeah. Well, you want to go?

NAT: Go where?

DEATH: Death. It. The Thing. The Happy Hunting Grounds. [*Looking at his own knee.*] Y'know, that's a pretty bad cut. My first job, I'm liable to get gangrene yet.

NAT: Now, wait a minute. I need time. I'm not ready to go.

DEATH: I'm sorry. I can't help you. I'd like to, but it's the moment.

NAT: How can it be the moment? I just merged with Modiste Originals.

DEATH: What's the difference, a couple of bucks more or less.

NAT: Sure, what do you care? You guys probably have all your expenses paid.

DEATH: You want to come along now?

NAT [*studying him*]: I'm sorry, but I cannot believe you're Death.

DEATH: Why? What'd you expect—Rock Hudson?

NAT: No, it's not that.

DEATH: I'm sorry if I disappointed you.

NAT: Don't get upset. I don't know, I always thought you'd be . . . uh . . . taller.

DEATH: I'm five seven. It's average for my weight.

NAT: You look a little like me.

DEATH: Who should I look like? I'm your death.

NAT: Give me some time. Another day.

DEATH: I can't. What do you want me to say?

NAT: One more day. Twenty-four hours.

DEATH: What do you need it for? The radio said rain tomorrow.

NAT: Can't we work out something?

DEATH: Like what?

NAT: You play chess?

DEATH: No, I don't.

NAT: I once saw a picture of you playing chess.

DEATH: Couldn't be me, because I don't play chess. Gin rummy, maybe.

NAT: You play gin rummy?

DEATH: Do I play gin rummy? Is Paris a city?

NAT: You're good, huh?

DEATH: Very good.

NAT: I'll tell you what I'll do—

DEATH: Don't make any deals with me.

NAT: I'll play you gin rummy. If you win, I'll go immediately. If I win, give me some more time. A little bit—one more day.

DEATH: Who's got time to play gin rummy?

NAT: Come on. If you're so good.

DEATH: Although I feel like a game . . .

NAT: Come on. Be a sport. We'll shoot for a half hour.

DEATH: I really shouldn't.

NAT: I got the cards right here. Don't make a production.

DEATH: All right, come on. We'll play a little. It'll relax me.

NAT [*getting cards, pad, and pencil*]: You won't regret this.

DEATH: Don't give me a sales talk. Get the cards and give me a Fresca and put out something. For God's sake, a stranger drops in, you don't have potato chips or pretzels.

NAT: There's M&M's downstairs in a dish.

DEATH: M&M's. What if the President came? He'd get M&M's, too?

NAT: You're not the President.

DEATH: Deal.

[NAT *deals, turns up a five.*]

NAT: You want to play a tenth of a cent a point to make it interesting?

DEATH: It's not interesting enough for you?

NAT: I play better when money's at stake.

DEATH: Whatever you say, Newt.

NAT: Nat. Nat Ackerman. You don't know my name?

DEATH: Newt, Nat—I got such a headache.

NAT: You want that five?

DEATH: No.

NAT: So pick.

DEATH [*surveying his hand as he picks*]: Jesus, I got nothing here.

NAT: What's it like?

DEATH: What's what like?

[*Throughout the following, they pick and discard.*]

NAT: Death.

DEATH: What should it be like? You lay there.

NAT: Is there anything after?

DEATH: Aha, you're saving twos.

NAT: I'm asking. Is there anything after?

DEATH [*absently*]: You'll see.

NAT: Oh, then I will actually see something?

DEATH: Well, maybe I shouldn't have put it that way. Throw.

NAT: To get an answer from you is a big deal.

DEATH: I'm playing cards.

NAT: All right, play, play.

DEATH: Meanwhile, I'm giving you one card after another.

NAT: Don't look through the discards.

DEATH: I'm not looking. I'm straightening them up. What was the knock card?

NAT: Four. You ready to knock already?

DEATH: Who said I'm ready to knock? All I asked was what was the knock card.

NAT: And all I asked was is there anything for me to look forward to.

DEATH: Play.

NAT: Can't you tell me anything? Where do we go?

DEATH: We? To tell you the truth, *you* fall in a crumpled heap on the floor.

NAT: Oh, I can't wait for that! Is it going to hurt?

DEATH: Be over in a second.

NAT: Terrific. [*Sighs.*] I needed this. A man merges with Modiste Originals . . .

DEATH: How's four points?

NAT: You're knocking?

DEATH: Four points is good?

NAT: No, I got two.

DEATH: You're kidding.

NAT: No, you lose.

DEATH: Holy Christ, and I thought you were saving sixes.

NAT: No. Your deal. Twenty points and two boxes. Shoot. [*Death deals.*] I must fall on the floor, eh? I can't be standing over the sofa when it happens?

DEATH: No. Play.

NAT: Why not?

DEATH: Because you fall on the floor! Leave me alone. I'm trying to concentrate.

NAT: Why must it be on the floor? That's all I'm saying! Why can't the whole thing happen and I'll stand next to the sofa?

DEATH: I'll try my best. Now can we play?

NAT: That's all I'm saying. You remind me of Moe Lefkowitz. He's also stubborn.

DEATH: I remind him of Moe Lefkowitz. I'm one of the most terrifying figures you could possibly imagine, and him I remind of Moe Lefkowitz. What is he, a furrier?

NAT: You should be such a furrier. He's good for eighty thousand a year. Passementer-ies. He's got his own factory. Two points.

DEATH: What?

NAT: Two points. I'm knocking. What have you got?

DEATH: My hand is like a basketball score.

NAT: And it's spades.

DEATH: If you didn't talk so much.

[*They redeal and play on.*]

NAT: What'd you mean before when you said this was your first job?

DEATH: What does it sound like?

NAT: What are you telling me—that nobody ever went before?

DEATH: Sure they went. But I didn't take them.

NAT: So who did?

DEATH: Others.

NAT: There's others?

DEATH: Sure. Each one has his own personal way of going.

NAT: I never knew that.

DEATH: Why should you know? Who are you?

NAT: What do you mean who am I? Why—I'm nothing?

DEATH: Not nothing. You're a dress manufacturer. Where do you come to knowledge of the eternal mysteries?

NAT: What are you talking about? I make a beautiful dollar. I sent two kids through college. One is in advertising, the other's married. I got my own home. I drive a

Chrysler. My wife has whatever she wants. Maids, mink coat, vacations. Right now
she's at the Eden Roc. Fifty dollars a day because she wants to be near her sister. I'm
supposed to join her next week, so what do you think I am—some guy off the street?

DEATH: All right. Don't be so touchy.

NAT: Who's touchy?

DEATH: How would you like it if I got insulted quickly?

NAT: Did I insult you?

DEATH: You didn't say you were disappointed in me?

NAT: What do you expect? You want me to throw you a block party?

DEATH: I'm not talking about that. I mean me personally. I'm too short, I'm this,
I'm that.

NAT: I said you looked like me. It's like a reflection.

DEATH: All right, deal, deal.

[*They continue to play as music steals in and the lights dim until all is in total darkness. The lights
slowly come up again, and now it is later and their game is over.* NAT *tallies.*]

NAT: Sixty-eight . . . one-fifty . . . Well, you lose.

DEATH [*dejectedly looking through the deck*]: I knew I shouldn't have thrown that nine.
Damn it.

NAT: So I'll see you tomorrow.

DEATH: What do you mean you'll see me tomorrow?

NAT: I won the extra day. Leave me alone.

DEATH: You were serious?

NAT: We made a deal.

DEATH: Yeah, but—

NAT: Don't "but" me. I won twenty-four hours. Come back tomorrow.

DEATH: I didn't know we were actually playing for time.

NAT: That's too bad about you. You should pay attention.

DEATH: Where am I going to go for twenty-four hours?

NAT: What's the difference? The main thing is I won an extra day.

DEATH: What do you want me to do—walk the streets?

NAT: Check into a hotel and go to a movie. Take a *schvitz*. Don't make a federal case.

DEATH: Add the score again.

NAT: Plus you owe me twenty-eight dollars.

DEATH: *What?*

NAT: That's right, Buster. Here it is—read it.

DEATH [*going through pockets*]: I have a few singles—not twenty-eight dollars.

NAT: I'll take a check.

DEATH: From what account?

NAT: Look who I'm dealing with.

DEATH: Sue me. Where do I keep my checking account?

NAT: All right, gimme what you got and we'll call it square.

DEATH: Listen, I need that money.

NAT: Why should you need money?

DEATH: What are you talking about? You're going to the Beyond.

NAT: So?

DEATH: So—you know how far that is?

NAT: So?

DEATH: So where's gas? Where's tolls?

NAT: We're going by car!

DEATH: You'll find out. [*Agitatedly.*] Look—I'll be back tomorrow, and you'll give me a chance to win the money back. Otherwise I'm in definite trouble.

NAT: Anything you want. Double or nothing we'll play. I'm liable to win an extra week or a month. The way you play, maybe years.

DEATH: Meantime I'm stranded.

NAT: See you tomorrow.

DEATH [*being edged to the doorway*]: Where's a good hotel? What am I talking about hotel, I got no money. I'll go sit in Bickford's. [*He picks up the* News.]

NAT: Out. Out. That's my paper. [*He takes it back.*]

DEATH [*exiting*]: I couldn't just take him and go. I had to get involved in rummy.

NAT [*calling after him*]: And be careful going downstairs. On one of the steps the rug is loose.

[*And, on cue, we hear a terrific crash.* NAT *sighs, then crosses to the bedside table and makes a phone call.*]

NAT: Hello, Moe? Me. Listen, I don't know if somebody's playing a joke, or what, but Death was just here. We played a little gin . . . No, *Death.* In person. Or somebody who claims to be Death. But, Moe, he's such a *schlep!*

Curtain

QUESTIONS

1. How is humor initially established in the play? What conventions about the portrait of death has Allen broken?
2. What is Nat's attitude toward the figure he meets, claiming to be Death? How is his attitude portrayed as humorous? What does Nat's attitude toward Death reveal about his character and values?
3. Was the figure who entered Nat's home truly Death or an imposter? What are the implications in the play for either interpretation?

Samuel Beckett

KRAPP'S LAST TAPE
A Play in One Act

Krapp's Last Tape was first performed at the Royal Court Theatre in London on October 28, 1958.

It was directed by Donald McWhinnie and played by Patrick Magee.

A late evening in the future.

KRAPP's *den.*

Front centre a small table, the two drawers of which open towards audience.

Sitting at the table, facing front, i.e. across from the drawers, a wearish old man: KRAPP.

Rusty black narrow trousers too short for him. Rusty black sleeveless waistcoat, four capacious pockets. Heavy silver watch and chain. Grimy white shirt open at neck, no collar. Surprising pair of dirty white boots, size ten at least, very narrow and pointed.

White face. Purple nose. Disordered grey hair. Unshaven.

Very near-sighted (but unspectacled). Hard of hearing.

Cracked voice. Distinctive intonation.

Laborious walk.

On the table a tape-recorder with microphone and a number of cardboard boxes containing reels of recorded tapes.

Table and immediately adjacent area in strong white light. Rest of stage in darkness.

KRAPP *remains a moment motionless, heaves a great sigh, looks at his watch, fumbles in his pockets, takes out an envelope, puts it back, fumbles, takes out a small bunch of keys, raises it to his eyes, chooses a key, gets up and moves to front of table. He stoops, unlocks first drawer, peers into it, feels about inside it, takes out a reel of tape, peers at it, puts it back, locks drawer, unlocks second drawer, peers into it, feels about inside it, takes out a large banana, peers at it, locks drawer, puts keys back in his pocket. He turns, advances to edge of stage, halts, strokes banana, peels it, drops skin at his feet, puts end of banana in his mouth and remains motionless, staring vacuously before him. Finally he bites off the end, turns aside and begins pacing to and fro at edge of stage, in the light, i.e. not more than four or five paces either way, meditatively eating banana. He treads on skin, slips, nearly falls, recovers himself, stoops and peers at skin and finally pushes it, still stooping, with his foot over the edge of stage into pit. He resumes his pacing, finishes banana, returns to table, sits down, remains a moment motionless, heaves a great sigh, takes keys from his pockets, raises them to his eyes, chooses key, gets up and moves to front of table, unlocks second drawer, takes out a second large banana, peers at it, locks drawer, puts back keys in his pocket, turns, advances to edge of stage, halts, strokes banana, peels it, tosses skin into pit, puts end of banana in his mouth and remains motionless, staring vacuously before him. Finally he has an idea, puts banana in his waistcoat pocket, the end emerging, and goes with all the speed he can muster backstage into darkness. Ten seconds. Loud pop of cork. Fifteen seconds. He comes back into light carrying an old ledger and sits down at table. He lays ledger on table, wipes his mouth, wipes his hands on the front of his waistcoat, brings them smartly together and rubs them.*

KRAPP [*briskly*]: Ah! [*He bends over ledger, turns the pages, finds the entry he wants, reads.*] Box . . . three . . . spool . . . five. [*He raises his head and stares front. With relish.*] Spool! [*Pause.*] Spooool! [*Happy smile. Pause. He bends over table, starts peering and poking at the boxes.*] Box . . . thrree . . . thrree . . . four . . . two . . . [*with surprise*] nine! good God! . . . seven . . . ah! the little rascal! [*He takes up box, peers at it.*] Box thrree. [*He lays it on table, opens it and peers at spools inside.*] Spool . . . [*he peers at ledger*] . . . five . . . [*he peers at spools*] . . . five . . . five . . . ah! the little scoundrel! [*He takes out a spool, peers at it.*] Spool five. [*He lays it on table, closes box three, puts it back with the others, takes up the spool.*] Box thrree, spool five. [*He bends over the machine, looks up. With relish.*] Spooool! [*Happy smile. He bends, loads spool on machine, rubs his hands.*] Ah! [*He peers at ledger, reads entry at foot of page.*] Mother at rest at last . . . Hm . . . The black ball . . . [*He raises his head, stares blankly front. Puzzled.*] Black ball? . . . [*He peers again at ledger, reads.*] The dark nurse . . . [*He raises his head, broods, peers again at ledger, reads.*] Slight improvement in bowel condition . . . Hm . . . Memorable . . . what? [*He peers closer.*] Equinox, memorable equinox. [*He raises his head, stares blankly front. Puzzled.*] Memorable equinox? . . . [*Pause. He shrugs his shoulders, peers again at ledger, reads.*] Farewell to—[*he turns the page*]—love.

[*He raises his head, broods, bends over machine, switches on and assumes listening posture, i.e. leaning forward, elbows on table, hand cupping ear towards machine, face front.*]

TAPE [*strong voice, rather pompous, clearly* KRAPP's *at a much earlier time*]: Thirty-nine today, sound as a—[*Settling himself more comfortably he knocks one of the boxes off the table, curses, switches off, sweeps boxes and ledger violently to the ground, winds tape back to beginning, switches on, resumes posture*]: Thirty-nine today, sound as a bell, apart from my old weakness, and intellectually I have now every reason to suspect at the . . . [*hesitates*] . . . crest of the wave—or thereabouts. Celebrated the awful occasion, as in recent years, quietly at the Winehouse. Not a soul. Sat before the fire with closed eyes, separating the grain from the husks. Jotted down a few notes, on the back of an envelope. Good to be back in my den, in my old rags. Have just eaten I regret to say three bananas and only with difficulty refrained from a fourth. Fatal things for a man with my condition [*Vehemently.*] Cut 'em out! [*Pause.*] The new light above my table is a great improvement. With all this darkness round me I feel less alone. [*Pause.*] In a way. [*Pause.*] I love to get up and move about in it, then back here to . . . [*hesitates*] . . . me. [*Pause.*] Krapp.

[*Pause.*]

The grain, now what I wonder do I mean by that, I mean . . . [*hesitates*] . . . I suppose I mean those things worth having when all the dust has—when all *my* dust has settled. I close my eyes and try and imagine them.

[*Pause.* KRAPP *closes his eyes briefly.*]

Extraordinary silence this evening, I strain my ears and do not hear a sound. Old Miss McGlome always sings at this hour. But not tonight. Songs of her girlhood, she says. Hard to think of her as a girl. Wonderful woman though. Connaught, I fancy. [*Pause.*] Shall I sing when I am her age, if I ever am? No. [*Pause.*] Did I sing as a boy? No. [*Pause.*] Did I ever sing? No.

[*Pause.*]

Just been listening to an old year, passages at random. I did not check in the book, but it must be at least ten or twelve years ago. At that time I think I was still living on and off with Bianca in Kedar Street. Well out of that, Jesus yes! Hopeless business. [*Pause.*] Not much about her, apart from a tribute to her eyes. Very warm. I suddenly saw them again. [*Pause.*] Incomparable! [*Pause.*] Ah well . . . [*Pause.*] These old P.M.s are gruesome, but I often find them—[KRAPP *switches off, broods, switches on*]—a help before embarking on a new . . . [*hesitates*] . . . retrospect. Hard to believe I was ever that young whelp. The voice! Jesus! And the aspirations! [*Brief laugh in which* KRAPP *joins.*] And the resolutions! [*Brief laugh in which* KRAPP *joins.*] To drink less, in particular. [*Brief laugh of* KRAPP *alone.*] Statistics. Seventeen hundred hours, out of the preceding eight thousand odd, consumed on licensed premises alone. More than 20%, say 40% of his waking life. [*Pause.*] Plans for a less . . . [*hesitates*] . . . engrossing sexual life. Last illness of his father. Flagging pursuit of happiness. Unattainable laxation. Sneers at what he calls his youth and thanks to God that it's over. [*Pause.*] False ring there. [*Pause.*] Shadows of the opus . . . magnum. Closing with a—[*brief laugh*]—yelp to Providence. [*Prolonged laugh in which* KRAPP *joins.*] What remains of all that misery? A girl in a shabby green coat, on a railway-station platform? No?

[*Pause.*]

When I look—

[KRAPP *switches off, broods, looks at his watch, gets up, goes backstage into darkness. Ten seconds. Pop of cork. Ten seconds. Second cork. Ten seconds. Third cork. Ten seconds. Brief burst of quavering song.*]

KRAPP [*sings*]:

> Now the day is over,
> Night is drawing nigh-igh,
> Shadows—

[*Fit of coughing. He comes back into light, sits down, wipes his mouth, switches on, resumes his listening posture.*]

TAPE: —back on the year that is gone, with what I hope is perhaps a glint of the old eye to come, there is of course the house on the canal where mother lay a-dying, in the late autumn, after her long viduity [KRAPP *gives a start*], and the—[KRAPP *switches off, winds back tape a little, bends his ear closer to machine, switches on*]—a-dying, after her long viduity, and the—

[KRAPP *switches off, raises his head, stares blankly before him. His lips move in the syllables of "viduity." No sound. He gets up, goes backstage into darkness, comes back with an enormous dictionary, lays it on table, sits down and looks up the word.*]

KRAPP [*reading from dictionary*]: State—or condition of being—or remaining—a widow—or widower. [*Looks up. Puzzled.*] Being—or remaining? . . . [*Pause. He peers again at dictionary. Reading.*] "Deep weeds of viduity" . . . Also of an animal, especially a bird . . . the vidua or weaver-bird . . . Black plumage of male . . . [*He looks up. With relish.*] The vidua-bird!

[*Pause. He closes dictionary, switches on, resumes listening posture.*]

TAPE: —bench by the weir from where I could see her window. There I sat, in the biting wind, wishing she were gone. [*Pause.*] Hardly a soul, just a few regulars, nursemaids, infants, old men, dogs. I got to know them quite well—oh by appearance of course I mean! One dark young beauty I recollect particularly, all white and starch, incomparable bosom, with a big black hooded perambulator, most funereal thing. Whenever I looked in her direction she had her eyes on me. And yet when I was bold enough to speak to her—not having been introduced—she threatened to call a policeman. As if I had designs on her virtue! [*Laugh. Pause.*] The face she had! The eyes! Like . . . [*hesitates*] . . . chrysolite! [*Pause.*] Ah well . . . [*Pause.*] I was there when—[KRAPP *switches off, broods, switches on again*]—the blind went down, one of those dirty brown roller affairs, throwing a ball for a little white dog, as chance would have it. I happened to look up and there it was. All over and done with, at last. I sat on for a few moments with the ball in my hand and the dog yelping and pawing at me. [*Pause.*] Moments. Her moments, my moments. [*Pause.*] The dog's moments. [*Pause.*] In the end I held it out to him and he took it in his mouth, gently, gently. A small, old, black, hard, solid rubber ball. [*Pause.*] I shall feel it, in my hand, until my dying day. [*Pause.*] I might have kept it. [*Pause.*] But I gave it to the dog.

[*Pause.*]

Ah well . . .

[*Pause.*]

Spiritually a year of profound gloom and indigence until that memorable night in March, at the end of the jetty, in the howling wind, never to be forgotten, when suddenly I saw the whole thing. The vision, at last. This I fancy is what I have chiefly to record this evening, against the day when my work will be done and perhaps no place left in my memory, warm or cold, for the miracle that . . . [*hesitates*] . . . for the fire that set it alight. What I suddenly saw then was this, that the belief I had been going on all my life, namely— [KRAPP *switches off impatiently, winds tape forward, switches on again*]—great granite rocks the foam flying up in the light of the lighthouse and the wind-gauge spinning like a propellor, clear to me at last that the dark I have always struggled to keep under is in reality my most—[KRAPP *curses, switches off, winds tape forward, switches on again*]—unshatterable association until my dissolution of storm and night with the light of the understanding and the fire—[KRAPP *curses louder, switches off, winds tape forward, switches on again*]—my face in her breasts and my hand on her. We lay there without moving. But under us all moved, and moved us, gently, up and down, and from side to side.

[*Pause.*]

Past midnight. Never knew such silence. The earth might be uninhabited.

[*Pause.*]

Here I end—

[KRAPP *switches off, winds tape back, switches on again.*]

—upper lake, with the punt, bathed off the bank, then pushed out into the stream and drifted. She lay stretched out on the floorboards with her hands under her head and her eyes closed. Sun blazing down, bit of a breeze, water nice and lively. I noticed a scratch on her thigh and asked her how she came by it. Picking gooseberries, she said. I said again I thought it was hopeless and no good going on, and she agreed, without opening her eyes. [*Pause.*] I asked her to look at me and after a few moments—[*pause*]—after a few moments she did, but the eyes just slits, because of the glare. I bent over her to get them in the shadow and they opened. [*Pause. Low.*] Let me in. [*Pause.*] We drifted in among the flags and stuck. The way they went down, sighing, before the stem! [*Pause.*] I lay down across her with my face in her breasts and my hand on her. We lay there without moving. But under us all moved, and moved us, gently, up and down, and from side to side.

[*Pause.*]

Past midnight. Never knew—

[KRAPP *switches off, broods. Finally he fumbles in his pockets, encounters the banana, takes it out, peers at it, puts it back, fumbles, brings out the envelope, fumbles, puts back envelope, looks at his watch, gets up and goes backstage into darkness. Ten seconds. Sound of bottle against glass, then brief siphon. Ten seconds. Bottle against glass alone. Ten seconds. He comes back a little unsteadily into light, goes to front of table, takes out keys, raises them to his eyes, chooses key, unlocks first drawer, peers into it, feels about inside, takes out reel, peers at it, locks drawer, puts keys back in his pocket, goes and sits down, takes reel off machine, lays it on dictionary, loads virgin reel on machine, takes envelope from his pocket, consults back of it, lays it on table, switches on, clears his throat and begins to record.*]

KRAPP: Just been listening to that stupid bastard I took myself for thirty years ago, hard to believe I was ever as bad as that. Thank God that's all done with anyway. [*Pause.*] The eyes she had! [*Broods, realizes he is recording silence, switches off, broods. Finally.*] Everything there, everything, all the—[*Realizes this is not being recorded, switches on.*] Everything there, everything on this old muckball, all the light and dark and famine and feasting of . . . [*hesitates*] . . . the ages! [*In a shout.*] Yes! [*Pause.*] Let that go! Jesus! Take his mind off his homework! Jesus! [*Pause. Weary.*] Ah well, maybe he was right. [*Pause.*] Maybe he was right. [*Broods. Realizes. Switches off. Consults envelope.*] Pah! [*Crumples it and throws it away. Broods. Switches on.*] Nothing to say, not a squeak. What's a year now? The sour cud and the iron stool. [*Pause.*] Revelled in the word spool. [*With relish.*] Spooool! Happiest moment of the past half million. [*Pause.*] Seventeen copies sold, of which eleven at trade price to free circulating libraries beyond the seas. Getting known. [*Pause.*] One pound six and something, eight I have little doubt. [*Pause.*] Crawled out once or twice, before the summer was cold. Sat shivering in the park, drowned in dreams and burning to be gone. Not a soul. [*Pause.*] Last fancies. [*Vehemently.*] Keep 'em under! [*Pause.*] Scalded the eyes out of me reading *Effie* again, a page a day, with tears again. Effie . . . [*Pause.*] Could have been happy with her, up there on the Baltic, and the pines, and the dunes. [*Pause.*] Could I? [*Pause.*] And she? [*Pause.*] Pah! [*Pause.*] Fanny came in a couple of times. Bony old ghost of a whore. Couldn't do much, but I suppose better than a kick in the crutch. The last time wasn't so bad. How do you manage it, she said, at your age? I told her I'd been saving up for her all my life. [*Pause.*] Went to Vespers once, like when I was in short trousers. [*Pause. Sings.*]

> Now the day is over,
> Night is drawing nigh-igh,
> Shadows—[*coughing, then almost inaudible*]—of the evening
> Steal across the sky.

[*Gasping.*] Went to sleep and fell off the pew. [*Pause.*] Sometimes wondered in the night if a last effort mightn't— [*Pause.*] Ah finish your booze now and get to your bed.

Go on with this drivel in the morning. Or leave it at that. [*Pause.*] Leave it at that. [*Pause.*] Lie propped up in the dark—and wander. Be again in the dingle on a Christmas Eve, gathering holly, the red-berried. [*Pause.*] Be again on Croghan on a Sunday morning, in the haze, with the bitch, stop and listen to the bells. [*Pause.*] And so on. [*Pause.*] Be again, be again. [*Pause.*] All that old misery. [*Pause.*] Once wasn't enough for you. [*Pause.*] Lie down across her.

[*Long pause. He suddenly bends over machine, switches off, wrenches off tape, throws it away, puts on the other, winds it forward to the passage he wants, switches on, listens staring front.*]

TAPE: —gooseberries, she said. I said again I thought it was hopeless and no good going on, and she agreed, without opening her eyes. [*Pause.*] I asked her to look at me and after a few moments—[*pause*]—after a few moments she did, but the eyes just slits, because of the glare. I bent over her to get them in the shadow and they opened. [*Pause. Low.*] Let me in. [*Pause.*] We drifted in among the flags and stuck. The way they went down, sighing, before the stem! [*Pause.*] I lay down across her with my face in her breasts and my hand on her. We lay there without moving. But under us all moved, and moved us, gently, up and down, and from side to side.

[*Pause.* KRAPP's *lips move. No sound.*]

Past midnight. Never knew such silence. The earth might be uninhabited.

[*Pause.*]

Here I end this reel. Box—[*pause*]—three, spool—[*pause*]—five. [*Pause.*] Perhaps my best years are gone. When there was a chance of happiness. But I wouldn't want them back. Not with the fire in me now. No, I wouldn't want them back.

[KRAPP *motionless staring before him. The tape runs on in silence.*]

Curtain

QUESTIONS

1. What is the portrait of Krapp that Beckett gives us prior to his opening speech?
2. What is the mood of the play? How does the description of the setting contribute to this mood? What does Beckett mean by setting the play on "a late evening in the future"?
3. How many periods of Krapp's life are depicted in the play? How old is he in each of these periods? What are his overall traits, outlook, and mood in each of these periods? How are these revealed to us?
4. What is the purpose of the main action of the play (Krapp reviewing his birthday tapes)? What does it reveal about Krapp now?
5. Is Krapp happier now than before, the same, or more unhappy? Explain.

Sophocles

OEDIPUS REX

English translation by
Dudley Fitts and Robert Fitzgerald

CHARACTERS

OEDIPUS	MESSENGER
A PRIEST	SHEPHERD OF LAÏOS
CREON	SECOND MESSENGER
TEIRESIAS	CHORUS OF THEBAN ELDERS
IOCASTÊ	

SCENE   *Before the palace of* OEDIPUS, *king of Thebes. A central door and two lateral doors open onto a platform which runs the length of the façade. On the platform, right and left, are altars; and three steps lead down into the "orchestra," or chorus-ground. At the beginning of the action these steps are crowded by suppliants who have brought branches and chaplets of olive leaves and who lie in various attitudes of despair.* OEDIPUS *enters.*

PROLOGUE

OEDIPUS: My children, generations of the living
   In the line of Kadmos, nursed at his ancient hearth:
   Why have you strewn yourselves before these altars
   In supplication, with your boughs and garlands?
   The breath of incense rises from the city   5
   With a sound of prayer and lamentation.

                    Children,
   I would not have you speak through messengers,
   And therefore I have come myself to hear you—
   I, Oedipus, who bear the famous name.
   (To a Priest.) You, there, since you are eldest in the company,   10
   Speak for them all, tell me what preys upon you,
   Whether you come in dread, or crave some blessing:
   Tell me, and never doubt that I will help you
   In every way I can; I should be heartless
   Were I not moved to find you suppliant here.   15
PRIEST: Great Oedipus, O powerful King of Thebes!
   You see how all the ages of our people
   Cling to your altar steps: here are boys
   Who can barely stand alone, and here are priests
   By weight of age, as I am a priest of God,   20

And young men chosen from those yet unmarried;
As for the others, all that multitude,
They wait with olive chaplets in the squares,
At the two shrines of Pallas, and where Apollo
Speaks in the glowing embers.

                       Your own eyes   25
Must tell you: Thebes is in her extremity
And cannot lift her head from the surge of death.
A rust consumes the buds and fruits of the earth;
The herds are sick; children die unborn,
And labor is vain. The god of plague and pyre   30
Raids like detestable lightning through the city,
And all the house of Kadmos is laid waste,
All emptied, and all darkened: Death alone
Battens upon the misery of Thebes.
You are not one of the immortal gods, we know;   35
Yet we have come to you to make our prayer
As to the man of all men best in adversity
And wisest in the ways of God. You saved us
From the Sphinx, that flinty singer, and the tribute
We paid to her so long; yet you were never   40
Better informed than we, nor could we teach you:
It was some god breathed in you to set us free.

Therefore, O mighty King, we turn to you:
Find us our safety, find us a remedy,
Whether by counsel of the gods or the men.   45
A king of wisdom tested in the past
Can act in a time of troubles, and act well.
Noblest of men, restore
Life to your city! Think how all men call you
Liberator for your triumph long ago;   50
Ah, when your years of kingship are remembered,
Let them not say *We rose, but later fell*—
Keep the State from going down in the storm!
Once, years ago, with happy augury,
You brought us fortune; be the same again!   55
No man questions your power to rule the land:
But rule over men, not over a dead city!
Ships are only hulls, citadels are nothing,
When no life moves in the empty passageways.
OEDIPUS: Poor children! You may be sure I know   60
All that you longed for in your coming here.
I know that you are deathly sick; and yet,
Sick as you are, not one is as sick as I.

Each of you suffers in himself alone
His anguish, not another's; but my spirit   65
Groans for the city, for myself, for you.

I was not sleeping, you are not waking me.
No, I have been in tears for a long while
And in my restless thought walked many ways.
In all my search, I found one helpful course,   70
And that I have taken: I have sent Creon,
Son of Menoikeus, brother of the Queen,
To Delphi, Apollo's place of revelation,
To learn there, if he can,
What act or pledge of mine may save the city.   75
I have counted the days, and now, this very day,
I am troubled, for he has overstayed his time.
What is he doing? He has been gone too long.
Yet whenever he comes back, I should do ill
To scant whatever hint the god may give.   80
PRIEST: It is a timely promise. At this instant
    They tell me Creon is here.
OEDIPUS: O Lord Apollo!
    May his news be fair as his face is radiant!
PRIEST: It could not be otherwise: he is crowned with bay,
    The chaplet is thick with berries.
OEDIPUS: We shall soon know;   85
    He is near enough to hear us now.

[*Enter* CREON]

                    O Prince:
    Brother: son of Menoikeus:
    What answer do you bring us from the god?
CREON: It is favorable. I can tell you, great afflictions
    Will turn out well, if they are taken well.   90
OEDIPUS: What was the oracle? These vague words
    Leave me still hanging between hope and fear.
CREON: Is it your pleasure to hear me with all these
    Gathered around us? I am prepared to speak,
    But should we not go in?
OEDIPUS: Let them all hear it.   95
    It is for them I suffer, more than myself.
CREON: Then I will tell you what I heard at Delphi.

In plain words
The god commands us to expel from the land of Thebes

And old defilement that it seems we shelter.   100
   It is a deathly thing, beyond expiation.
   We must not let it feed upon us longer.
OEDIPUS: What defilement? How shall we rid ourselves of it?
CREON: By exile or death, blood for blood. It was
   Murder that brought the plague-wind on the city.   105
OEDIPUS: Murder of whom? Surely the god has named him?
CREON: My lord: long ago Laïos was our king,
   Before you came to govern us.
OEDIPUS: I know;
   I learned of him from others; I never saw him.
CREON: He was murdered; and Apollo commands us now   110
   To take revenge upon whoever killed him.
OEDIPUS: Upon whom? Where are they? Where shall we find a clue
   To solve that crime, after so many years?
CREON: Here in this land, he said.
                       If we make enquiry,
   We may touch things that otherwise escape us.   115
OEDIPUS: Tell me: Was Laïos murdered in his house,
   Or in the fields, or in some foreign country?
CREON: He said he planned to make a pilgrimage.
   He did not come home again.
OEDIPUS: And was there no one,
   No witness, no companion, to tell what happened?   120
CREON: They were all killed but one, and he got away
   So frightened that he could remember one thing only.
OEDIPUS: What was that one thing? One may be the key
   To everything, if we resolve to use it.
CREON: He said that a band of highwaymen attacked them,   125
   Outnumbered them, and overwhelmed the King.
OEDIPUS: Strange, that a highwayman should be so daring—
   Unless some faction here bribed him to do it.
CREON: We thought of that. But after Laïos' death
   New troubles arose and we had no avenger.   130
OEDIPUS: What troubles could prevent your hunting down the killers?
CREON: The riddling Sphinx's song
   Made us deaf to all mysteries but her own.
OEDIPUS: Then once more I must bring what is dark to light.
   It is most fitting that Apollo shows,   135
   As you do, this compunction for the dead.
   You shall see how I stand by you, as I should,
   To avenge the city and the city's god.
   And not as though it were for some distant friend,
   But for my own sake, to be rid of evil.   140
   Whoever killed King Laïos might—who knows?—

Decide at any moment to kill me as well.
By avenging the murdered king I protect myself.
Come then, my children: leave the altar steps,
Lift up your olive boughs!
                    One of you go   145
And summon the people of Kadmos to gather here.
I will do all that I can; you may tell them that.   [*Exit a* PAGE.]
So, with the help of God,
We shall be saved—or else indeed we are lost.
PRIEST: Let us rise, children. It was for this we came,   150
And now the King has promised it himself.
Phoibos has sent us an oracle; may he descend
Himself to save us and drive out the plague.

[*Exeunt* OEDIPUS *and* CREON *into the palace by the central door. The priest and the suppliants disperse right and left. After a short pause the* CHORUS *enters the orchestra.*]

PÁRODOS

Strophe 1

CHORUS: What is God singing in his profound
    Delphi of gold and shadow?
    What oracle for Thebes, the sunwhipped city?
    Fear unjoints me, the roots of my heart tremble.
    Now I remember, O Healer, your power, and wonder;   5
    Will you send doom like a sudden cloud, or weave it
    Like nightfall of the past?
    Speak, speak to us, issue of holy sound:
    Dearest to our expectancy: be tender!

Antistrophe 1

    Let me pray to Athenê, the immortal daughter of Zeus,   10
    And to Artemis her sister
    Who keeps her famous throne in the market ring,
    And to Apollo, bowman at the far butts of heaven—

    O gods, descend! Like three streams leap against
    The fires of our grief, the fires of darkness;   15
    Be swift to bring us rest!

    As in the old time from the brilliant house
    Of air you stepped to save us, come again!

Strophe 2

Now our afflictions have no end,
Now all our stricken host lies down   20
And no man fights off death with his mind;

The noble plowland bears no grain,
And groaning mothers cannot bear—
See, how our lives like birds take wing,
Like sparks that fly when a fire soars,   25
To the shore of the god of evening.

Antistrophe 2

The plague burns on, it is pitiless,
Though pallid children laden with death
Lie unwept in the stony ways,
And old gray women by every path   30
Flock to the strand about the altars

There to strike their breasts and cry
Worship of Phoibos in wailing prayers:
Be kind, God's golden child!

Strophe 3

There are no swords in this attack by fire,   35
No shields, but we are ringed with cries.
Send the besieger plunging from our homes
Into the vast sea-room of the Atlantic
Or into the waves that foam eastward of Thrace—
For the day ravages what the night spares—   40

Destroy our enemy, lord of the thunder!
Let him be riven by lightning from heaven!

Antistrophe 3

Phoibos Apollo, stretch the sun's bowstring,
That golden cord, until it sing for us,
Flashing arrows in heaven!
                    Artemis, Huntress,   45
Race with flaring lights upon our mountains!
O scarlet god, O golden-banded brow,
O Theban Bacchos in a storm of Maenads,

[*Enter* OEDIPUS, *center.*]

Whirl upon Death, that all the Undying hate!
Come with blinding cressets, come in joy!   50

SCENE I

OEDIPUS: Is this your prayer? It may be answered. Come,
 Listen to me, act as the crisis demands,
 And you shall have relief from all these evils.
 Until now I was a stranger to this tale,
 As I had been a stranger to the crime.   5
 Could I track down the murderer without a clue?
 But now, friends,
 As one who became a citizen after the murder,
 I make this proclamation to all Thebans:
 If any man knows by whose hand Laïos, son of Labdakos,   10
 Met his death, I direct that man to tell me everything,
 No matter what he fears for having so long withheld it.
 Let it stand as promised that no further trouble
 Will come to him, but he may leave the land in safety.

 Moreover: If anyone knows the murderer to be foreign,   15
 Let him not keep silent: he shall have his reward from me.
 However, if he does conceal it; if any man
 Fearing for his friend or for himself disobeys this edict,
 Hear what I propose to do:

 I solemnly forbid the people of this country,   20
 Where power and throne are mine, ever to receive that man
 Or speak to him, no matter who he is, or let him
 Join in sacrifice, lustration, or in prayer.
 I decree that he be driven from every house,

 Being, as he is, corruption itself to us: the Delphic   25
 Voice of Zeus has pronounced this revelation.
 Thus I associate myself with the oracle
 And take the side of the murdered king.

 As for the criminal, I pray to God—
 Whether it be a lurking thief, or one of a number—   30
 I pray that that man's life be consumed in evil and wretchedness.
 And as for me, this curse applies no less
 If it should turn out that the culprit is my guest here,

Sharing my hearth.
　　　　　　　You have heard the penalty.
I lay it on you now to attend to this   35
For my sake, for Apollo's, for the sick
Sterile city that heaven has abandoned.
Suppose the oracle had given you no command:
Should this defilement go uncleansed for ever?
You should have found the murderer: your king,   40
A noble king, had been destroyed!
　　　　　　　Now I,
Having the power that he held before me,
Having his bed, begetting children there
Upon his wife, as he would have, had he lived—
Their son would have been my children's brother,   45
If Laïos had had luck in fatherhood!
(But surely ill luck rushed upon his reign)—
I say I take the son's part, just as though
I were his son, to press the fight for him
And see it won! I'll find the hand that brought   50
Death to Labdakos' and Polydoros' child,
Heir of Kadmos' and Agenor's line.
And as for those who fail me,
May the gods deny them the fruit of the earth,
Fruit of the womb, and may they rot utterly!   55
Let them be wretched as we are wretched, and worse!

For you, for loyal Thebans, and for all
Who find my actions right, I pray the favor
Of justice, and of all the immortal gods.
CHORAGOS: Since I am under oath, my lord, I swear   60
　　I did not do the murder, I cannot name
　　The murderer. Might not the oracle
　　That has ordained the search tell where to find him?
OEDIPUS: An honest question. But no man in the world
　　Can make the gods do more than the gods will.   65
CHORAGOS: There is one last expedient—
OEDIPUS: 　　　　　　　　　　Tell me what it is.
　　Though it seem slight, you must not hold it back.
CHORAGOS: A lord clairvoyant to the lord Apollo,
　　As we all know, is the skilled Teiresias.
　　One might learn much about this from him, Oedipus.   70
OEDIPUS: I am not wasting time:
　　Creon spoke of this, and I have sent for him—
　　Twice, in fact; it is strange that he is not here.

CHORAGOS: The other matter—that old report—seems useless.

OEDIPUS: Tell me. I am interested in all reports.   75

CHORAGOS: The King was said to have been killed by highwaymen.

OEDIPUS: I know. But we have no witness to that.

CHORAGOS: If the killer can feel a particle of dread,
Your curse will bring him out of hiding!

OEDIPUS: No.
The man who dared that act will fear no curse.   80

[*Enter the blind seer* TEIRESIAS, *led by a page.*]

CHORAGOS: But there is one man who may detect the criminal.
This is Teiresias, this is the holy prophet
In whom, alone of all men, truth was born.

OEDIPUS: Teiresias: seer: student of mysteries,
Of all that's taught and all that no man tells,   85
Secrets of Heaven and secrets of the earth:
Blind though you are, you know the city lies
Sick with plague; and from this plague, my lord,
We find that you alone can guard or save us.

Possibly you did not hear the messengers?   90
Apollo, when we sent to him,
Sent us back word that this great pestilence
Would lift, but only if we established clearly
The identity of those who murdered Laïos.
They must be killed or exiled.
                                        Can you use   95
Birdflight or any art of divination
To purify yourself, and Thebes, and me
From this contagion? We are in your hands.
There is no fairer duty
Than that of helping others in distress.   100

TEIRESIAS: How dreadful knowledge of the truth can be
When there's no help in truth! I knew this well,
But did not act on it: else I should not have come.

OEDIPUS: What is troubling you? Why are your eyes so cold?

TEIRESIAS: Let me go home. Bear your own fate, and I'll   105
Bear mine. It is better so: trust what I say.

OEDIPUS: What you say is ungracious and unhelpful
To your native country. Do not refuse to speak.

TEIRESIAS: When it comes to speech, your own is neither temperate
Nor opportune. I wish to be more prudent.   110

OEDIPUS: In God's name, we all beg you—

TEIRESIAS: You are all ignorant.
   No; I will never tell you what I know.
   Now it is my misery; then, it would be yours.
OEDIPUS: What! You do know something, and will not tell us?
   You would betray us all and wreck the State?   115
TEIRESIAS: I do not intend to torture myself, or you.
   Why persist in asking? You will not persuade me.
OEDIPUS: What a wicked old man you are! You'd try a stone's
   Patience! Out with it! Have you no feeling at all?
TEIRESIAS: You call me unfeeling. If you could only see   120
   The nature of your own feelings . . .
OEDIPUS: Why,
   Who would not feel as I do? Who could endure
   Your arrogance toward the city?
TEIRESIAS: What does it matter!
   Whether I speak or not, it is bound to come.
OEDIPUS: Then, if "it" is bound to come, you are bound to tell me. 125
TEIRESIAS: No, I will not go on. Rage as you please.
OEDIPUS: Rage? Why not!
                  And I'll tell you what I think:
   You planned it, you had it done, you all but
   Killed him with your own hands: if you had eyes,
   I'd say the crime was yours and yours alone.   130
TEIRESIAS: So? I charge you, then.
   Abide by the proclamation you have made:
   From this day forth
   Never speak again to these men or to me;
   You yourself are the pollution of this country.   135
OEDIPUS: You dare say that! Can you possibly think you have
   Some way of going free, after such insolence?
TEIRESIAS: I have gone free. It is the truth sustains me.
OEDIPUS: Who taught you shamelessness? It was not your craft.
TEIRESIAS: You did. You made me speak. I did not want to.   140
OEDIPUS: Speak what? Let me hear it again more clearly.
TEIRESIAS: Was it not clear before? Are you tempting me?
OEDIPUS: I did not understand it. Say it again.
TEIRESIAS: I say that you are the murderer whom you seek.
OEDIPUS: Now twice you have spat out infamy. You'll pay for it!   145
TEIRESIAS: Would you care for more? Do you wish to be really angry?
OEDIPUS: Say what you will. Whatever you say is worthless.
TEIRESIAS: I say you live in hideous shame with those
   Most dear to you. You cannot see the evil.
OEDIPUS: It seems you can go on mouthing like this for ever.   150
TEIRESIAS: I can, if there is power in truth.

OEDIPUS: There is:
   But not for you, not for you,
   You sightless, witless, senseless, mad old man!
TEIRESIAS: You are the madman. There is no one here
   Who will not curse you soon, as you curse me.   155
OEDIPUS: You child of endless night! You cannot hurt me
   Or any other man who sees the sun.
TEIRESIAS: True: it is not from me your fate will come.
   That lies within Apollo's competence,
   As it is his concern.
OEDIPUS: Tell me: 160
   Are you speaking for Creon, or for yourself?
TEIRESIAS: Creon is no threat. You weave your own doom.
OEDIPUS: Wealth, power, craft of statesmanship!
   Kingly position, everywhere admired!
   What savage envy is stored up against these,   165
   If Creon, whom I trusted, Creon my friend,
   For this great office which the city once
   Put in my hands unsought—if for this power
   Creon desires in secret to destroy me!

   He has brought this decrepit fortune-teller, this   170
   Collector of dirty pennies, this prophet fraud—
   Why, he is no more clairvoyant than I am!
                       Tell us:
   Has your mystic mummery ever approached the truth?
   When that hellcat the Sphinx was performing here,
   What help were you to these people?   175
   Her magic was not for the first man who came along:
   It demanded a real exorcist. Your birds—
   What good were they? or the gods, for the matter of that?
   But I came by,
   Oedipus, the simple man, who knows nothing—   180
   I thought it out for myself, no birds helped me!
   And this is the man you think you can destroy,
   That you may be close to Creon when he's king!
   Well, you and your friend Creon, it seems to me,
   Will suffer most. If you were not an old man,   185
   You would have paid already for your plot.
CHORAGOS: We cannot see that his words or yours
   Have been spoken except in anger, Oedipus,
   And of anger we have no need. How can God's will
   Be accomplished best? That is what most concerns us.   190
TEIRESIAS: You are a king. But where argument's concerned

I am your man, as much a king as you.
I am not your servant, but Apollo's.
I have no need of Creon to speak for me.

Listen to me. You mock my blindness, do you?   195
But I say that you, with both your eyes, are blind:
You cannot see the wretchedness of your life,
Nor in whose house you live, no, nor with whom.
Who are your father and mother? Can you tell me?
You do not even know the blind wrongs   200
That you have done them, on earth and in the world below.
But the double lash of your parents' curse will whip you
Out of this land some day, with only night
Upon your precious eyes.
Your cries then—where will they not be heard?   205
What fastness of Kithairon will not echo them?
And that bridal-descant of yours—you'll know it then,
The song they sang when you came here to Thebes
And found your misguided berthing.
All this, and more, that you cannot guess at now,   210
Will bring you to yourself among your children.
Be angry, then. Curse Creon. Curse my words.
I tell you, no man that walks upon the earth
Shall be rooted out more horribly than you.
OEDIPUS: Am I to bear this from him?—Damnation   215
    Take you! Out of this place! Out of my sight!
TEIRESIAS: I would not have come at all if you had not asked me.
OEDIPUS: Could I have told that you'd talk nonsense, that
    You'd come here to make a fool of yourself, and of me?
TEIRESIAS: A fool? Your parents thought me sane enough.   220
OEDIPUS: My parents again!—Wait: who were my parents?
TEIRESIAS: This day will give you a father, and break your heart.
OEDIPUS: Your infantile riddles! Your damned abracadabra!
TEIRESIAS: You were a great man once at solving riddles.
OEDIPUS: Mock me with that if you like; you will find it true.   225
TEIRESIAS: It was true enough. It brought about your ruin.
OEDIPUS: But if it saved this town?
TEIRESIAS [to the page]: Boy, give me your hand.
OEDIPUS: Yes, boy; lead him away.
                            —While you are here
    We can do nothing. Go; leave us in peace.
TEIRESIAS: I will go when I have said what I have to say.   230
    How can you hurt me? And I tell you again:
    The man you have been looking for all this time,

The damned man, the murderer of Laïos,
That man is in Thebes. To your mind he is foreignborn,
But it will soon be shown that he is a Theban,   235
A revelation that will fail to please.
                                        A blind man,
Who has his eyes now; a penniless man, who is rich now;
And he will go tapping the strange earth with his staff;
To the children with whom he lives now he will be
Brother and father—the very same; to her   240
Who bore him, son and husband—the very same
Who came to his father's bed, wet with his father's blood.

Enough. Go think that over.
If later you find error in what I have said,
You may say that I have no skill in prophecy.   245

[*Exit* TEIRESIAS, *led by his page.* OEDIPUS *goes into the palace.*]

ODE I

Strophe 1

CHORUS: The Delphic stone of prophecies
  Remembers ancient regicide
  And a still bloody hand.
  That killer's hour of flight has come.
  He must be stronger than riderless   5
  Coursers of untiring wind,
  For the son of Zeus armed with his father's thunder
  Leaps in lightning after him;
  And the Furies follow him, the sad Furies.

Antistrophe 1

  Holy Parnossos' peak of snow   10
  Flashes and blinds that secret man,
  That all shall hunt him down:
  Though he may roam the forest shade
  Like a bull gone wild from pasture
  To rage through glooms of stone.   15
  Doom comes down on him; flight will not avail him;
  For the world's heart calls him desolate,
  And the immortal Furies follow, for ever follow.

Strophe 2

But now a wilder thing is heard
From the old man skilled at hearing Fate in the wingbeat of a bird.   20
Bewildered as a blown bird, my soul hovers and cannot find
Foothold in this debate, or any reason or rest of mind.
But no man ever brought—none can bring
Proof of strife between Thebes' royal house,
Labdakos' line, and the son of Polybos;   25
And never until now has any man brought word
Of Laïos' dark death staining Oedipus the King.

Antistrophe 2

Divine Zeus and Apollo hold
Perfect intelligence alone of all tales ever told;
And well though this diviner works, he works in his own night;   30
No man can judge that rough unknown or trust in second sight,
For wisdom changes hands among the wise.
Shall I believe my great lord criminal
At a raging word that a blind old man let fall?
I saw him, when the carrion woman faced him of old,   35
Prove his heroic mind! These evil words are lies.

SCENE II

CREON: Men of Thebes:
    I am told that heavy accusations
    Have been brought against me by King Oedipus.
    I am not the kind of man to bear this tamely.

    If in these present difficulties   5
    He holds me accountable for any harm to him
    Through anything I have said or done—why, then,
    I do not value life in this dishonor.
    It is not as though this rumor touched upon
    Some private indiscretion. The matter is grave.   10
    The fact is that I am being called disloyal
    To the State, to my fellow citizens, to my friends.
CHORAGOS: He may have spoken in anger, not from his mind.
CREON: But did you not hear him say I was the one
    Who seduced the old prophet into lying?   15
CHORAGOS: The thing was said; I do not know how seriously.

CREON: But you were watching him! Were his eyes steady?
   Did he look like a man in his right mind?
CHORAGOS: I do not know.
   I cannot judge the behavior of great men.
   But here is the King himself.

[*Enter* OEDIPUS.]

OEDIPUS: So you dared come back.   20
   Why? How brazen of you to come to my house,
   You murderer!
               Do you think I do not know
   That you plotted to kill me, plotted to steal my throne?
   Tell me, in God's name: am I coward, a fool,
   That you should dream you could accomplish this?   25
   A fool who could not see your slippery game?
   A coward, not to fight back when I saw it?
   You are the fool, Creon, are you not? hoping
   Without support or friends to get a throne?
   Thrones may be won or bought: you could do neither.   30
CREON: Now listen to me. You have talked; let me talk, too.
   You cannot judge unless you know the facts.
OEDIPUS: You speak well: there is one fact; but I find it hard
   To learn from the deadliest enemy I have.
CREON: That above all I must dispute with you.   35
OEDIPUS: That above all I will not hear you deny.
CREON: If you think there is anything good in being stubborn
   Against all reason, then I say you are wrong.
OEDIPUS: If you think a man can sin against his own kind
   And not be punished for it, I say you are mad.   40
CREON: I agree. But tell me: what have I done to you?
OEDIPUS: You advised me to send for that wizard, did you not?
CREON: I did. I should do it again.
OEDIPUS: Very well. Now tell me:
   How long has it been since Laïos—
CREON: What of Laïos?
OEDIPUS: Since he vanished in that onset by the road?   45
CREON: It was long ago, a long time.
OEDIPUS: And this prophet,
   Was he practicing here then?
CREON: He was; and with honor, as now.
OEDIPUS: Did he speak of me at that time?
CREON: He never did;
   At least, not when I was present.

OEDIPUS: But . . . the enquiry?
   I suppose you held one?
CREON: We did, but we learned nothing.   50
OEDIPUS: Why did the prophet not speak against me then?
CREON: I do not know; and I am the kind of man
   Who holds his tongue when he has no facts to go on.
OEDIPUS: There's one fact that you know, and you could tell it.
CREON: What fact is that? If I know it, you shall have it.   55
OEDIPUS: If he were not involved with you, he could not say
   That it was I who murdered Laïos.
CREON: If he says that, you are the one that knows it!—
   But now it is my turn to question you.
OEDIPUS: Put your questions. I am no murderer.   60
CREON: First, then: You married my sister?
OEDIPUS: I married your sister.
CREON: And you rule the kingdom equally with her?
OEDIPUS: Everything that she wants she has from me.
CREON: And I am the third, equal to both of you?
OEDIPUS: That is why I call you a bad friend.   65
CREON: No. Reason it out, as I have done.
   Think of this first. Would any sane man prefer
   Power, with all a king's anxieties,
   To that same power and the grace of sleep?
   Certainly not I.   70
   I have never longed for the king's power—only his rights.
   Would any wise man differ from me in this?
   As matters stand, I have my way in everything
   With your consent, and no responsibilities.
   If I were king, I should be a slave to policy.   75
   How could I desire a scepter more
   Than what is now mine—untroubled influence?
   No, I have not gone mad; I need no honors,
   Except those with the perquisites I have now.
   I am welcome everywhere; every man salutes me,   80
   And those who want your favor seek my ear,
   Since I know how to manage what they ask.
   Should I exchange this ease for that anxiety?
   Besides, no sober mind is treasonable.
   I hate anarchy   85
   And never would deal with any man who likes it.

   Test what I have said. Go to the priestess
   At Delphi, ask if I quoted her correctly.
   And as for this other thing: if I am found
   Guilty of treason with Teiresias,   90

Then sentence me to death! You have my word
It is a sentence I should cast my vote for—
But not without evidence!

          You do wrong
When you take good men for bad, bad men for good.
A true friend thrown aside—why, life itself   95
Is not more precious!

          In time you will know this well:
For time, and time alone, will show the just man,
Though scoundrels are discovered in a day.
CHORAGOS: This is well said, and a prudent man would ponder it.
Judgments too quickly formed are dangerous.   100
OEDIPUS: But is he not quick in his duplicity?
And shall I not be quick to parry him?
Would you have me stand still, hold my peace, and let
This man win everything, through my inaction?
CREON: And you want—what is it, then? To banish me?   105
OEDIPUS: No, not exile. It is your death I want,
So that all the world may see what treason means.
CREON: You will persist, then? You will not believe me?
OEDIPUS: How can I believe you?
CREON: Then you are a fool.
OEDIPUS: To save myself?
CREON: In justice, think of me.   110
OEDIPUS: You are evil incarnate.
CREON: But suppose that you are wrong?
OEDIPUS: Still I must rule.
CREON: But not if you rule badly.
OEDIPUS: O city, city!
CREON: It is my city, too!
CHORAGOS: Now, my lords, be still. I see the Queen,
Iocastê, coming from her palace chambers;   115
And it is time she came, for the sake of you both.
This dreadful quarrel can be resolved through her.

[Enter IOCASTÊ.]

IOCASTÊ: Poor foolish men, what wicked din is this?
With Thebes sick to death, is it not shameful
That you should rake some private quarrel up?   120
[To OEDIPUS.] Come into the house.
          —And you, Creon, go now:
Let us have no more of this tumult over nothing.
CREON: Nothing? No, sister: what your husband plans for me
Is one of two great evils: exile or death.

OEDIPUS: He is right.

Why, woman, I have caught him squarely   125
   Plotting against my life.
CREON: No! Let me die
   Accurst if ever I have wished you harm!
IOCASTÊ: Ah, believe it, Oedipus!
   In the name of the gods, respect this oath of his
   For my sake, for the sake of these people here!   130

Strophe 1

CHORAGOS: Open your mind to her, my lord. Be ruled by her, I beg you!
OEDIPUS: What would you have me do?
CHORAGOS: Respect Creon's word. He has never spoken like a fool,
   And now he has sworn an oath.
OEDIPUS: You know what you ask?
CHORAGOS: I do.
OEDIPUS: Speak on, then.
CHORAGOS: A friend so sworn should not be baited so,   135
   In blind malice, and without final proof.
OEDIPUS: You are aware, I hope, that what you say
   Means death for me, or exile at the least.

Strophe 2

CHORAGOS: No, I swear by Helios, first in Heaven!
   May I die friendless and accurst,   140
   The worst of deaths, if ever I meant that!
     It is the withering fields
       That hurt my sick heart:
    Must we bear all these ills,
       And now your bad blood as well?   145
OEDIPUS: Then let him go. And let me die, if I must,
   Or be driven by him in shame from the land of Thebes.
   It is your unhappiness, and not his talk,
   That touches me.
        As for him—
   Wherever he is, I will hate him as long as I live.   150
CREON: Ugly in yielding, as you were ugly in rage!
   Natures like yours chiefly torment themselves.
OEDIPUS: Can you not go? Can you not leave me?
CREON: I can.
   You do not know me; but the city knows me,
   And in its eyes I am just, if not in yours.   [*Exit* CREON.] 155

Antistrophe 1

CHORAGOS: Lady Iocastê, did you not ask the King to go to his chambers?
IOCASTÊ: First tell me what has happened.
CHORAGOS: There was suspicion without evidence; yet it rankled
   As even false charges will.
IOCASTÊ: On both sides?
CHORAGOS: On both.
IOCASTÊ: But what was said?
CHORAGOS: Oh let it rest, let it be done with!   160
   Have we not suffered enough?
OEDIPUS: You see to what your decency has brought you:
   You have made difficulties where my heart saw none.

Antistrophe 2

CHORAGOS: Oedipus, it is not once only I have told you—
   You must know I should count myself unwise   165
   To the point of madness, should I now forsake you—
      You, under whose hand,
           In the storm of another time,
      Our dear land sailed out free.
           But now stand fast at the helm!   170
IOCASTÊ: In God's name, Oedipus, inform your wife as well:
   Why are you so set in this hard anger?
OEDIPUS: I will tell you, for none of these men deserves
   My confidence as you do. It is Creon's work,
   His treachery, his plotting against me.   175
IOCASTÊ: Go on, if you can make this clear to me.
OEDIPUS: He charges me with the murder of Laïos.
IOCASTÊ: Has he some knowledge? Or does he speak from hearsay?
OEDIPUS: He would not commit himself to such a charge,
   But he has brought in that damnable soothsayer   180
   To tell his story.
IOCASTÊ: Set your mind at rest.
   If it is a question of soothsayers, I tell you
   That you will find no man whose craft gives knowledge
   Of the unknowable.
             Here is my proof:

An oracle was reported to Laïos once   185
(I will not say from Phoibos himself, but from
His appointed ministers, at any rate)
That his doom would be death at the hands of his own son—
His son, born of his flesh and of mine!

Now, you remember the story: Laïos was killed   190
By marauding strangers where three highways meet;
But his child had not been three days in this world
Before the King had pierced the baby's ankles
And left him to die on a lonely mountainside.

Thus, Apollo never caused that child   195
To kill his father, and it was not Laïos' fate
To die at the hands of his son, as he had feared.
This is what prophets and prophecies are worth!
Have no dread of them.
                    It is God himself
Who can show us what he wills, in his own way.   200

OEDIPUS: How strange a shadowy memory crossed my mind,
    Just now while you were speaking; it chilled my heart.

IOCASTÊ: What do you mean? What memory do you speak of?

OEDIPUS: If I understand you, Laïos was killed
    At a place where three roads meet.

IOCASTÊ: So it was said;   205
    We have no later story.

OEDIPUS: Where did it happen?

IOCASTÊ: Phokis, it is called: at a place where the Theban Way
    Divides into the roads towards Delphi and Daulia.

OEDIPUS: When?

IOCASTÊ: We had the news not long before you came
    And proved the right to your succession here.   210

OEDIPUS: Ah, what net has God been weaving for me?

IOCASTÊ: Oedipus! Why does this trouble you?

OEDIPUS: Do not ask me yet.
    First, tell me how Laïos looked, and tell me
    How old he was.

IOCASTÊ: He was tall, his hair just touched
    With white; his form was not unlike your own.   215

OEDIPUS: I think that I myself may be accurst
    By my own ignorant edict.

IOCASTÊ: You speak strangely.
    It makes me tremble to look at you, my King.

OEDIPUS: I am not sure that the blind man cannot see.
    But I should know better if you were to tell me—   220

IOCASTÊ: Anything—though I dread to hear you ask it.

OEDIPUS: Was the King lightly escorted, or did he ride
    With a large company, as a ruler should?

IOCASTÊ: There were five men with him in all: one was a herald;
    And a single chariot, which he was driving.   225

OEDIPUS: Alas, that makes it plain enough!

But who—

Who told you how it happened?

IOCASTÊ: A household servant,

The only one to escape.

OEDIPUS: And is he still

A servant of ours?

IOCASTÊ: No; for when he came back at last

And found you enthroned in the place of the dead king,   230

He came to me, touched my hand with his, and begged

That I would send him away to the frontier district

Where only the shepherds go—

As far away from the city as I could send him.

I granted his prayer; for although the man was a slave,   235

He had earned more than this favor at my hands.

OEDIPUS: Can he be called back quickly?

IOCASTÊ: Easily.

But why?

OEDIPUS: I have taken too much upon myself

Without enquiry; therefore I wish to consult him.

IOCASTÊ: Then he shall come.

                    But am I not one also   240

To whom you might confide these fears of yours!

OEDIPUS: That is your right; it will not be denied you,

Now least of all; for I have reached a pitch

Of wild foreboding. Is there anyone

To whom I should sooner speak?   245

Polybos of Corinth is my father.

My mother is a Dorian: Meropê.

I grew up chief among the men of Corinth

Until a strange thing happened—

Not worth my passion, it may be, but strange.   250

At a feast, a drunken man maundering in his cups

Cries out that I am not my father's son!

I contained myself that night, though I felt anger

And a sinking heart. The next day I visited

My father and mother, and questioned them. They stormed,   255

Calling it all the slanderous rant of a fool;

And this relieved me. Yet the suspicion

Remained always aching in my mind;

I knew there was talk; I could not rest;

And finally, saying nothing to my parents,   260

I went to the shrine at Delphi.

The god dismissed my question without reply;

He spoke of other things.
                    Some were clear,
Full of wretchedness, dreadful, unbearable:
As, that I should lie with my own mother, breed   265
Children from whom all men would turn their eyes;
And that I should be my father's murderer.

I heard all this, and fled. And from that day
Corinth to me was only in the stars
Descending in that quarter of the sky,   270
As I wandered farther and farther on my way
To a land where I should never see the evil
Sung by the oracle. And I came to this country
Where, so you say, King Laïos was killed.
I will tell you all that happened there, my lady.   275

There were three highways
Coming together at a place I passed;
And there a herald came towards me, and a chariot
Drawn by horses, with a man such as you describe
Seated in it. The groom leading the horses   280
Forced me off the road at his lord's command;
But as this charioteer lurched over towards me
I struck him in my rage. The old man saw me
And brought his double goad down upon my head
As I came abreast.
                    He was paid back, and more!   285
Swinging my club in this right hand I knocked him
Out of his car, and he rolled on the ground.
                              I killed him.

I killed them all.
Now if that stranger and Laïos were—kin,
Where is a man more miserable than I?   290
More hated by the gods? Citizen and alien alike
Must never shelter me or speak to me—
I must be shunned by all.
                    And I myself
Pronounced this malediction upon myself!

Think of it: I have touched you with these hands,   295
These hands that killed your husband. What defilement!

Am I all evil, then? It must be so,
Since I must flee from Thebes, yet never again

See my own countrymen, my own country,
For fear of joining my mother in marriage 300
And killing Polybos, my father.
                              Ah,
If I was created so, born to this fate,
Who could deny the savagery of God?

O holy majesty of heavenly powers!
May I never see that day! Never! 305
Rather let me vanish from the race of men
Than know the abomination destined me!
CHORAGOS: We too, my lord, have felt dismay at this.
    But there is hope: you have yet to hear the shepherd.
OEDIPUS: Indeed, I fear no other hope is left me. 310
IOCASTÊ: What do you hope from him when he comes?
OEDIPUS: This much:
    If his account of the murder tallies with yours,
    Then I am cleared.
IOCASTÊ: —What was it that I said
Of such importance?
OEDIPUS: Why, "marauders," you said,
    Killed the King, according to this man's story. 315
    If he maintains that still, if there were several,
    Clearly the guilt is not mine: I was alone.
    But if he says one man, singlehanded, did it,
    Then the evidence all points to me.
IOCASTÊ: You may be sure that he said there were several; 320
    And can he call back that story now? He cannot.
    The whole city heard it as plainly as I.
    But suppose he alters some detail of it:
    He cannot ever show that Laïos' death
    Fulfilled the oracle: for Apollo said 325
    My child was doomed to kill him; and my child—
    Poor baby!—it was my child that died first.

No. From now on, where oracles are concerned,
    I would not waste a second thought on any.
OEDIPUS: You may be right.
                    But come: let someone go 330
    For the shepherd at once. This matter must be settled.
IOCASTÊ: I will send for him.
    I would not wish to cross you in anything,
    And surely not in this.—Let us go in.

                            [Exeunt into the palace.]

ODE II

Strophe 1

CHORUS: Let me be reverent in the ways of right,
    Lowly the paths I journey on;
    Let all my words and actions keep
    The laws of the pure universe
    From highest Heaven handed down.   5
    For Heaven is their bright nurse,
    Those generations of the realms of light;
    Ah, never of mortal kind were they begot,
    Nor are they slaves of memory, lost in sleep:
    Their Father is greater than Time, and ages not.   10

Antistrophe 1

    The tyrant is a child of Pride
    Who drinks from his great sickening cup
    Recklessness and vanity,
    Until from his high crest headlong
    He plummets to the dust of hope.   15
    That strong man is not strong.
    But let no fair ambition be denied;
    May God protect the wrestler for the State
    In government, in comely policy,
    Who will fear God, and on His ordinance wait.   20

Strophe 2

    Haughtiness and the high hand of disdain
    Tempt and outrage God's holy law;
    And any mortal who dares hold
    No immortal Power in awe
    Will be caught up in a net of pain: 25
    The price for which his levity is sold.
    Let each man take due earnings, then,
    And keep his hands from holy things,
    And from blasphemy stand apart—
    Else the crackling blast of heaven   30
    Blows on his head, and on his desperate heart;
    Though fools will honor impious men,
    In their cities no tragic poet sings.

Antistrophe 2

Shall we lose faith in Delphi's obscurities,
We who have heard the world's core   35
Discredited, and the sacred wood
Of Zeus at Elis praised no more?
The deeds and the strange prophecies
Must make a pattern yet to be understood.
Zeus, if indeed you are lord of all,   40
Throned in light over night and day,
Mirror this in your endless mind:
Our masters call the oracle
Words on the wind, and the Delphic vision blind!
Their hearts no longer know Apollo,   45
And reverence for the gods has died away.

SCENE III

[*Enter* IOCASTÊ.]

IOCASTÊ: Princes of Thebes, it has occurred to me
To visit the altars of the gods, bearing
These branches as a suppliant, and this incense.
Our King is not himself: his noble soul
Is overwrought with fantasies of dread,   5
Else he would consider
The new prophecies in the light of the old.
He will listen to any voice that speaks disaster,
And my advice goes for nothing.

[*She approaches the altar, right.*]

                              To you, then, Apollo,
Lycean lord, since you are nearest, I turn in prayer.   10
Receive these offerings, and grant us deliverance
From defilement. Our hearts are heavy with fear
When we see our leader distracted, as helpless sailors
Are terrified by the confusion of their helmsman.

[*Enter* MESSENGER.]

MESSENGER: Friends, no doubt you can direct me: 15
Where shall I find the house of Oedipus,
Or, better still, where is the King himself?

CHORAGOS: It is this very place, stranger; he is inside.
  This is his wife and mother of his children.
MESSENGER: I wish her happiness in a happy house,   20
  Blest in all the fulfillment of her marriage.
IOCASTÊ: I wish as much for you: your courtesy
  Deserves a like good fortune. But now, tell me:
  Why have you come? What have you to say to us?
MESSENGER: Good news, my lady, for your house and your husband.   25
IOCASTÊ: What news? Who sent you here?
MESSENGER: I am from Corinth.
  The news I bring ought to mean joy for you,
  Though it may be you will find some grief in it.
IOCASTÊ: What is it? How can it touch us in both ways?
MESSENGER: The people of Corinth, they say,   30
  Intend to call Oedipus to be their king.
IOCASTÊ: But old Polybos—is he not reigning still?
MESSENGER: No. Death holds him in his sepulchre.
IOCASTÊ: What are you saying? Polybos is dead?
MESSENGER: If I am not telling the truth, may I die myself.   35
IOCASTÊ [to a maidservant]: Go in, go quickly; tell this to your master.

  O riddlers of God's will, where are you now!
  This was the man whom Oedipus, long ago,
  Feared so, fled so, in dread of destroying him—
  But it was another fate by which he died.   40

  [Enter OEDIPUS, center.]

OEDIPUS: Dearest Iocastê, why have you sent for me?
IOCASTÊ: Listen to what this man says, and then tell me
  What has become of the solemn prophecies.
OEDIPUS: Who is this man? What is his news for me?
IOCASTÊ: He has come from Corinth to announce your father's death!   45
OEDIPUS: Is it true, stranger? Tell me in your own words.
MESSENGER: I cannot say it more clearly: the King is dead.
OEDIPUS: Was it by treason? Or by an attack of illness?
MESSENGER: A little thing brings old men to their rest.
OEDIPUS: It was sickness, then?
MESSENGER: Yes, and his many years.   50
OEDIPUS: Ah!
  Why should a man respect the Pythian hearth, or
  Give heed to the birds that jangle above his head?
  They prophesied that I should kill Polybos,
  Kill my own father; but he is dead and buried,   55
  And I am here—I never touched him, never,

Unless he died in grief for my departure,
And thus, in a sense, through me. No. Polybos
Has packed the oracles off with him underground.
They are empty words.
IOCASTÊ: Had I not told you so? 60
OEDIPUS: You had; it was my faint heart that betrayed me.
IOCASTÊ: From now on never think of those things again.
OEDIPUS: And yet—must I not fear my mother's bed?
IOCASTÊ: Why should anyone in this world be afraid,
   Since Fate rules us and nothing can be foreseen? 65
   A man should live only for the present day.
   Have no more fear of sleeping with your mother:
   How many men, in dreams, have lain with their mothers!
   No reasonable man is troubled by such things.
OEDIPUS: That is true; only— 70
   If only my mother were not still alive!
   But she is alive. I cannot help my dread.
IOCASTÊ: Yet this news of your father's death is wonderful.
OEDIPUS: Wonderful. But I fear the living woman.
MESSENGER: Tell me, who is this woman that you fear? 75
OEDIPUS: It is Meropê, man; the wife of King Polybos.
MESSENGER: Meropê? Why should you be afraid of her?
OEDIPUS: An oracle of the gods, a dreadful saying.
MESSENGER: Can you tell me about it or are you sworn to silence?
OEDIPUS: I can tell you, and I will. 80
   Apollo said through his prophet that I was the man
   Who should marry his own mother, shed his father's blood
   With his own hands. And so, for all these years
   I have kept clear of Corinth, and no harm has come—
   Though it would have been sweet to see my parents again. 85
MESSENGER: And is this the fear that drove you out of Corinth?
OEDIPUS: Would you have me kill my father?
MESSENGER: As for that
   You must be reassured by the news I gave you.
OEDIPUS: If you could reassure me, I would reward you.
MESSENGER: I had that in mind, I will confess: I thought 90
   I could count on you when you returned to Corinth.
OEDIPUS: No: I will never go near my parents again.
MESSENGER: Ah, son, you still do not know what you are doing—
OEDIPUS: What do you mean? In the name of God tell me!
MESSENGER: —If these are your reasons for not going home. 95
OEDIPUS: I tell you, I fear the oracle may come true.
MESSENGER: And guilt may come upon you through your parents?
OEDIPUS: That is the dread that is always in my heart.
MESSENGER: Can you not see that all your fears are groundless?

OEDIPUS: How can you say that? They are my parents, surely?   100
MESSENGER: Polybos was not your father.
OEDIPUS: Not my father?
MESSENGER: No more your father than the man speaking to you.
OEDIPUS: But you are nothing to me!
MESSENGER: Neither was he.   105
OEDIPUS: Then why did he call me son?
MESSENGER: I will tell you:
   Long ago he had you from my hands, as a gift.   105
OEDIPUS: Then how could he love me so, if I was not his?
MESSENGER: He had no children, and his heart turned to you.
OEDIPUS: What of you? Did you buy me? Did you find me by chance?
MESSENGER: I came upon you in the crooked pass of Kithairon.
OEDIPUS: And what were you doing there?
MESSENGER: Tending my flocks.   110
OEDIPUS: A wandering shepherd?
MESSENGER: But your savior, son, that day.
OEDIPUS: From what did you save me?
MESSENGER: Your ankles should tell you that.
OEDIPUS: Ah, stranger, why do you speak of that childhood pain?
MESSENGER: I cut the bonds that tied your ankles together.
OEDIPUS: I have had the mark as long as I can remember.   115
MESSENGER: That was why you were given the name you bear.
OEDIPUS: God! Was it my father or my mother who did it?
   Tell me!
MESSENGER: I do not know. The man who gave you to me
   Can tell you better than I.   120
OEDIPUS: It was not you that found me, but another?
MESSENGER: It was another shepherd gave you to me.
OEDIPUS: Who was he? Can you tell me who he was?
MESSENGER: I think he was said to be one of Laïos' people.
OEDIPUS: You mean the Laïos who was king here years ago?   125
MESSENGER: Yes; King Laïos; and the man was one of his herdsmen.
OEDIPUS: Is he still alive? Can I see him?
MESSENGER: These men here
   Know best about such things.
OEDIPUS: Does anyone here
   Know this shepherd that he is talking about?
   Have you seen him in the fields, or in the town?   130
   If you have, tell me. It is time things were made plain.
CHORAGOS: I think the man he means is that same shepherd
   You have already asked to see. Iocastê perhaps
   Could tell you something.
OEDIPUS: Do you know anything
   About him, Lady? Is he the man we have summoned?   135
   Is that the man this shepherd means?

IOCASTÊ: Why think of him?
  Forget this herdsman. Forget it all.
  This talk is a waste of time.
OEDIPUS: How can you say that,
  When the clues to my true birth are in my hands?
IOCASTÊ: For God's love, let us have no more questioning!   140
  Is your life nothing to you?
  My own is pain enough for me to bear.
OEDIPUS: You need not worry. Suppose my mother a slave,
  And born of slaves: no baseness can touch you.
IOCASTÊ: Listen to me, I beg you: do not do this thing!   145
OEDIPUS: I will not listen; the truth must be made known.
IOCASTÊ: Everything that I say is for your own good!
OEDIPUS: My own good
  Snaps my patience, then: I want none of it.
IOCASTÊ: You are fatally wrong! May you never learn who you are!
OEDIPUS: Go, one of you, and bring the shepherd here.   150
  Let us leave this woman to brag of her royal name.
IOCASTÊ: Ah, miserable!
  That is the only word I have for you now.
  That is the only word I can ever have.

                                    [Exit into the palace.]

CHORAGOS: Why has she left us, Oedipus? Why has she gone   155
  In such a passion of sorrow? I fear this silence:
  Something dreadful may come of it.
OEDIPUS: Let it come!
  However base my birth, I must know about it.
  The Queen, like a woman, is perhaps ashamed
  To think of my low origin. But I   160
  Am a child of luck; I cannot be dishonored.
  Luck is my mother; the passing months, my brothers,
  Have seen me rich and poor.
                  If this is so,
  How could I wish that I were someone else?
  How could I not be glad to know my birth?   165

ODE III

Strophe

CHORUS: If ever the coming time were known
  To my heart's pondering,
  Kithairon, now by Heaven I see the torches
  At the festival of the next full moon,

And see the dance, and hear the choir sing   5
A grace to your gentle shade:
Mountain where Oedipus was found,
O mountain guard of a noble race!
May the god who heals us lend his aid,
And let that glory come to pass   10
For our king's cradling-ground.

Antistrophe

Of the nymphs that flower beyond the years,
Who bore you, royal child,
To Pan of the hills or the timberline Apollo,
Cold in delight where the upland clears,   15
Or Hermês for whom Kyllenê's heights are piled?
Or flushed as evening cloud,
Great Dionysos, roamer of mountains,
He—was it he who found you there,
And caught you up in his own proud   20
Arms from the sweet god-ravisher
Who laughed by the Muses' fountains?

SCENE IV

OEDIPUS: Sirs: though I do not know the man,
    I think I see him coming, this shepherd we want:
    He is old, like our friend here, and the men
    Bringing him seem to be servants of my house.
    But you can tell, if you have ever seen him.   5

[Enter shepherd escorted by servants.]

CHORAGOS: I know him, he was Laïos' man. You can trust him.
OEDIPUS: Tell me first, you from Corinth: is this the shepherd
    We were discussing?
MESSENGER: This is the very man.
OEDIPUS *[to shepherd]*: Come here. No, look at me. You must answer
    Everything I ask.—You belonged to Laïos?   10
SHEPHERD: Yes: born his slave, brought up in his house.
OEDIPUS: Tell me: what kind of work did you do for him?
SHEPHERD: I was a shepherd of his, most of my life.
OEDIPUS: Where mainly did you go for pasturage?
SHEPHERD: Sometimes Kithairon, sometimes the hills near-by. 15
OEDIPUS: Do you remember ever seeing this man out there?
SHEPHERD: What would he be doing there? This man?

OEDIPUS: This man standing here. Have you ever seen him before?

SHEPHERD: No. At least, not to my recollection.

MESSENGER: And that is not strange, my lord, But I'll refresh   20
His memory: he must remember when we two
Spent three whole seasons together, March to September,
On Kithairon or thereabouts. He had two flocks;
I had one. Each autumn I'd drive mine home
And he would go back with his to Laïos' sheepfold.—   25
Is this not true, just as I have described it?

SHEPHERD: True, yes; but it was all so long ago.

MESSENGER: Well, then: so you remember, back in those days
That you gave me a baby boy to bring up as my own?

SHEPHERD: What if I did? What are you trying to say?   30

MESSENGER: King Oedipus was once that little child.

SHEPHERD: Damn you, hold your tongue!

OEDIPUS: No more of that!
It is your tongue needs watching, not this man's.

SHEPHERD: My King, my Master, what is it I have done wrong?

OEDIPUS: You have not answered his question about the boy.   35

SHEPHERD: He does not know . . . He is only making trouble . . .

OEDIPUS: Come, speak plainly, or it will go hard with you.

SHEPHERD: In God's name, do not torture an old man!

OEDIPUS: Come here, one of you; bind his arms behind him.

SHEPHERD: Unhappy king! What more do you wish to learn?   40

OEDIPUS: Did you give this man the child he speaks of?

SHEPHERD: I did.
And I would to God I had died that very day.

OEDIPUS: You will die now unless you speak the truth.

SHEPHERD: Yet if I speak the truth, I am worse than dead.

OEDIPUS: Very well; since you insist upon delaying—   45

SHEPHERD: No! I have told you already that I gave him the boy.

OEDIPUS: Where did you get him? From your house?
From somewhere else?

SHEPHERD: Not from mine, no. A man gave him to me.

OEDIPUS: Is that man here? Do you know whose slave he was?

SHEPHERD: For God's love, my King, do not ask me
any more!   50

OEDIPUS: You are a dead man if I have to ask you again.

SHEPHERD: Then . . . Then the child was from the palace of Laïos.

OEDIPUS: A slave child? or a child of his own line?

SHEPHERD: Ah, I am on the brink of dreadful speech!

OEDIPUS: And I of dreadful hearing. Yet I must hear.   55

SHEPHERD: If you must be told, then . . .
They said it was Laïos' child,
But it is your wife who can tell you about that.

OEDIPUS: My wife!—Did she give it to you?

SHEPHERD: My lord, she did.
OEDIPUS: Do you know why?
SHEPHERD: I was told to get rid of it.
OEDIPUS: An unspeakable mother!
SHEPHERD: There had been prophecies . . .   60
OEDIPUS: Tell me.
SHEPHERD: It was said that the boy would kill his own father.
OEDIPUS: Then why did you give him over to this old man?
SHEPHERD: I pitied the baby, my King,
    And I thought that this man would take him far away
    To his own country.
                              He saved him—but for what a fate!   65
    For if you are what this man says you are,
    No man living is more wretched than Oedipus.
OEDIPUS: Ah God!
    It was true!
            All the prophecies!
                          —Now,
    O Light, may I look on you for the last time!   70
    I, Oedipus,
    Oedipus, damned in his birth, in his marriage damned,
    Damned in the blood he shed with his own hand!

[*He rushes into the palace.*]

ODE IV

Strophe 1

CHORUS: Alas for the seed of men.
    What measure shall I give these generations
    That breathe on the void and are void
    And exist and do not exist?

    Who bears more weight of joy   5
    Than mass of sunlight shifting in images,
    Or who shall make his thought stay on
    That down time drifts away?

    Your splendor is all fallen.

    O naked brow of wrath and tears,   10
    O change of Oedipus!
    I who saw your days call no man blest—
    Your great days like ghosts gone.

Antistrophe 1

That mind was a strong bow.
Deep, how deep you drew it then, hard archer,   15
At a dim fearful range,
And brought dear glory down!

You overcame the stranger—
The virgin with her hooking lion claws—
And though death sang, stood like a tower   20
To make pale Thebes take heart.

Fortress against our sorrow!

Divine king, giver of laws,
Majestic Oedipus!
No prince in Thebes had ever such renown,   25
No prince won such grace of power.

Strophe 2

And now of all men ever known
Most pitiful is this man's story:
His fortunes are most changed, his state
Fallen to a low slave's   30
Ground under bitter fate.

O Oedipus, most royal one!
The great door that expelled you to the light
Gave at night—ah, gave night to your glory:
As to the father, to the fathering son.   35

All understood too late,

How could that queen whom Laïos won,
The garden that he harrowed at his height,
Be silent when that act was done?

Antistrophe 2

But all eyes fail before time's eye,   40
All actions come to justice there.
Though never willed, though far down the deep past,
Your bed, your dread sirings,
Are brought to book at last.
Child by Laïos doomed to die,   45

Then doomed to lose that fortunate little death,
Would God you never took breath in this air
That with my wailing lips I take to cry:

For I weep the world's outcast.

I was blind, and now I can tell why: 50
Asleep, for you had given ease of breath
To Thebes, while the false years went by.

EXODOS

[*Enter, from the palace, second messenger.*]

SECOND MESSENGER: Elders of Thebes, most honored in this land,
    What horrors are yours to see and hear, what weight
    Of sorrow to be endured, if, true to your birth,
    You venerate the line of Labdakos!
    I think neither Istros nor Phasis, those great rivers,   5
    Could purify this place of the corruption
    It shelters now, or soon must bring to light—
    Evil not done unconsciously, but willed.

    The greatest griefs are those we cause ourselves.
CHORAGOS: Surely, friend, we have grief enough already;   10
    What new sorrow do you mean?
SECOND MESSENGER: The Queen is dead.
CHORAGOS: Iocastê? Dead? But at whose hand?
SECOND MESSENGER: Her own.
    The full horror of what happened you cannot know,
    For you did not see it; but I, who did, will tell you
    As clearly as I can how she met her death.   15

    When she had left us,
    In passionate silence, passing through the court,
    She ran to her apartment in the house,
    Her hair clutched by the fingers of both hands.
    She closed the doors behind her; then, by that bed   20
    Where long ago the fatal son was conceived—
    That son who should bring about his father's death—
    We heard her call upon Laïos, dead so many years,
    And heard her wail for the double fruit of her marriage,
    A husband by her husband, children by her child.   25

Exactly how she died I do not know:
For Oedipus burst in moaning and would not let us
Keep vigil to the end: it was by him
As he stormed about the room that our eyes were caught.
From one to another of us he went, begging a sword,   30
Cursing the wife who was not his wife, the mother
Whose womb had carried his own children and himself.
I do not know: it was none of us aided him,
But surely one of the gods was in control!
For with a dreadful cry   35
He hurled his weight, as though wrenched out of himself,
At the twin doors: the bolts gave, and he rushed in.
And there we saw her hanging, her body swaying
From the cruel cord she had noosed about her neck.
A great sob broke from him heartbreaking to hear,   40
As he loosed the rope and lowered her to the ground.
I would blot out from my mind what happened next!
For the King ripped from her gown the golden brooches
That were her ornament, and raised them, and plunged them down
Straight into his own eyeballs, crying, "No more,   45
No more shall you look on the misery about me,
The horrors of my own doing! Too long you have known
The faces of those whom I should never have seen,
Too long been blind to those for whom I was searching!
From this hour, go in darkness!" And as he spoke,   50
He struck at his eyes—not once, but many times;
And the blood spattered his beard,
Bursting from his ruined sockets like red hail.

So from the unhappiness of two this evil has sprung,
A curse on the man and woman alike. The old   55
Happiness of the house of Labdakos
Was happiness enough: where is it today?
It is all wailing and ruin, disgrace, death—all
The misery of mankind that has a name—
And it is wholly and for ever theirs.   60
CHORAGOS: Is he in agony still? Is there no rest for him?
SECOND MESSENGER: He is calling for someone to lead him to the gates
So that all the children of Kadmos may look upon
His father's murderer, his mother's—no,
I cannot say it!
        And then he will leave Thebes,   65
Self-exiled, in order that the curse
Which he himself pronounced may depart from the house.
He is weak, and there is none to lead him,

So terrible is his suffering.
                    But you will see:
Look, the doors are opening; in a moment   70
You will see a thing that would crush a heart of stone.

[*The central door is opened;* OEDIPUS, *blinded, is led in.*]

CHORAGOS: Dreadful indeed for men to see,
    Never have my own eyes
    Looked on a sight so full of fear.

    Oedipus!   75
    What madness came upon you, what daemon
    Leaped on your life with heavier
    Punishment than a mortal man can bear?
    No: I cannot even
    Look at you, poor ruined one.   80
    And I would speak, question, ponder,
    If I were able. No.
    You make me shudder.
OEDIPUS: God. God.
    Is there a sorrow greater?   85
    Where shall I find harbor in this world?
    My voice is hurled far on a dark wind.
    What has God done to me?
CHORAGOS: Too terrible to think of, or to see.

Strophe 1

OEDIPUS: O cloud of night,   90
    Never to be turned away: night coming on,
    I cannot tell how: night like a shroud!
    My fair winds brought me here.
                        Oh God. Again
    The pain of the spikes where I had sight,
    The flooding pain   95
    Of memory, never to be gouged out.
CHORAGOS: This is not strange.
    You suffer it all twice over, remorse in pain,
    Pain in remorse.

Antistrophe 1

OEDIPUS: Ah dear friend   100
    Are you faithful even yet, you alone?

Are you still standing near me, will you stay here,
Patient, to care for the blind?
                              The blind man!
Yet even blind I know who it is attends me,
By the voice's tone—   105
Though my new darkness hide the comforter.
CHORAGOS. O fearful act!
What god was it drove you to rake black
Night across your eyes?
OEDIPUS: Apollo. Apollo. Dear   110
Children, the god was Apollo.
He brought my sick, sick fate upon me.
But the blinding hand was my own!
How could I bear to see
When all my sight was horror everywhere?   115
CHORAGOS: Everywhere; that is true.
OEDIPUS: And now what is left?
Images? Love? A greeting even,
Sweet to the senses? Is there anything?
Ah, no, friends: lead me away.   120
Lead me away from Thebes.
                              Lead the great wreck
And hell of Oedipus, whom the gods hate.
CHORAGOS: Your fate is clear, you are not blind to that.
Would God you had never found it out!

Antistrophe 2

OEDIPUS: Death take the man who unbound   125
My feet on that hillside
And delivered me from death to life! What life?
If only I had died,
This weight of monstrous doom
Could not have dragged me and my darlings down.   130
CHORAGOS: I would have wished the same.
OEDIPUS: Oh never to have come here
With my father's blood upon me! Never
To have been the man they call his mother's husband!
Oh accurst! Oh child of evil,   135
To have entered that wretched bed—
                              the selfsame one!
More primal than sin itself, this fell to me.
CHORAGOS: I do not know how I can answer you.
You were better dead than alive and blind.
OEDIPUS: Do not counsel me any more. This punishment   140

That I have laid upon myself is just.
If I had eyes,
I do not know how I could bear the sight
Of my father, when I came to the house of Death,
Or my mother: for I have sinned against them both   145
So vilely that I could not make my peace
By strangling my own life.
                    Or do you think my children,
Born as they were born, would be sweet to my eyes?
Ah never, never! Nor this town with its high walls,
Nor the holy images of the gods.
                    For I,   150
Thrice miserable—Oedipus, noblest of all the line
Of Kadmos, have condemned myself to enjoy
These things no more, by my own malediction
Expelling that man whom the gods declared
To be a defilement in the house of Laïos.   155
After exposing the rankness of my own guilt,
How could I look men frankly in the eyes?
No, I swear it,
If I could have stifled my hearing at its source,
I would have done it and made all this body   160
A tight cell of misery, blank to light and sound:
So I should have been safe in a dark agony
Beyond all recollection.
                    Ah Kithairon!
Why did you shelter me? When I was cast upon you,
Why did I not die? Then I should never   165
Have shown the world my execrable birth.
Ah Polybos! Corinth, city that I believed
The ancient seat of my ancestors: how fair
I seemed, your child! And all the while this evil
Was cancerous within me!
                    For I am sick   170
In my daily life, sick in my origin.

O three roads, dark ravine, woodland and way
Where three roads met: you, drinking my father's blood,
My own blood, spilled by my own hand: can you remember
The unspeakable things I did there, and the things   175
I went on from there to do?
                    O marriage, marriage!
The act that engendered me, and again the act
Performed by the son in the same bed—
                              —Ah, the net

Of incest, mingling fathers, brothers, sons,
With brides, wives, mothers: the last evil   180
That can be known by men: no tongue can say
How evil!
            No. For the love of God, conceal me
Somewhere far from Thebes; or kill me; or hurl me
Into the sea, away from men's eyes for ever.
Come, lead me. You need not fear to touch me.   185
Of all men, I alone can bear this guilt.

[*Enter* CREON.]

CHORAGOS: We are not the ones to decide; but Creon here
    May fitly judge of what you ask. He only
    Is left to protect the city in your place.
OEDIPUS: Alas, how can I speak to him? What right have I   190
    To beg his courtesy whom I have deeply wronged?
CREON: I have not come to mock you, Oedipus,
    Or to reproach you, either.
    [*To attendants.*]   —You, standing there:
    If you have lost all respect for man's dignity,
    At least respect the flame of Lord Helios: 195
    Do not allow this pollution to show itself
    Openly here, an affront to the earth
    And Heaven's rain and the light of day. No, take him
    Into the house as quickly as you can.
    For it is proper   200
    That only the close kindred see his grief.
OEDIPUS: I pray you in God's name, since your courtesy
    Ignores my dark expectation, visiting
    With mercy this man of all men most execrable:
    Give me what I ask—for your good, not for mine.   205
CREON: And what is it that you would have me do?
OEDIPUS: Drive me out of this country as quickly as may be
    To a place where no human voice can ever greet me.
CREON: I should have done that before now—only,
    God's will had not been wholly revealed to me.   210
OEDIPUS: But his command is plain: the parricide
    Must be destroyed. I am that evil man.
CREON: That is the sense of it, yes; but as things are,
    We had best discover clearly what is to be done.
OEDIPUS: You would learn more about a man like me?   215
CREON: You are ready now to listen to the god.
OEDIPUS: I will listen. But it is to you
    That I must turn for help. I beg you, hear me.

The woman in there—
Give her whatever funeral you think proper: 220
She is your sister.
                    —But let me go, Creon!
Let me purge my father's Thebes of the pollution
Of my living here, and go out to the wild hills,
To Kithairon, that has won such fame with me,
The tomb my mother and father appointed for me,   225
And let me die there, as they willed I should.
And yet I know
Death will not ever come to me through sickness
Or in any natural way: I have been preserved
For some unthinkable fate. But let that be.   230
As for my sons, you need not care for them.
They are men, they will find some way to live.
But my poor daughters, who have shared my table,
Who never before have been parted from their father—
Take care of them, Creon; do this for me.   235
And will you let me touch them with my hands
A last time, and let us weep together?
Be kind, my lord,
Great prince, be kind!
                    Could I but touch them,
They would be mine again, as when I had my eyes.   240

[*Enter* ANTIGONÊ *and* ISMENÊ, *attended.*]

Ah, God!
Is it my dearest children I hear weeping?
Has Creon pitied me and sent my daughters?
CREON: Yes, Oedipus: I knew that they were dear to you
     In the old days, and know you must love them still.   245
OEDIPUS: May God bless you for this—and be a friendlier
     Guardian to you than he has been to me!

Children, where are you?
Come quickly to my hands: they are your brother's—
Hands that have brought your father's once clear eyes   250
To this way of seeing—
                    Ah dearest ones,
I had neither sight nor knowledge then, your father
By the woman who was the source of his own life!
And I weep for you—having no strength to see you—,
I weep for you when I think of the bitterness   255
That men will visit upon you all your lives.

What homes, what festivals can you attend
Without being forced to depart again in tears?
And when you come to marriageable age,
Where is the man, my daughters, who would dare   260
Risk the bane that lies on all my children?
Is there any evil wanting? Your father killed
His father; sowed the womb of her who bore him;
Engendered you at the fount of his own existence!
That is what they will say of you.

                             Then, whom   265
Can you ever marry? There are no bridegrooms for you,
And your lives must wither away in sterile dreaming.
O Creon, son of Menoikeus!
You are the only father my daughters have,
Since we, their parents, are both of us gone for ever.   270
They are your own blood: you will not let them
Fall into beggary and loneliness;
You will keep them from the miseries that are mine!
Take pity on them; see, they are only children,
Friendless except for you. Promise me this,   275
Great Prince, and give me your hand in token of it.

[CREON *clasps his right hand.*]

Children:
I could say much, if you could understand me,
But as it is, I have only this prayer for you:
Live where you can, be as happy as you can—   280
Happier, please God, than God has made your father!
CREON: Enough. You have wept enough. Now go within.
OEDIPUS: I must; but it is hard.
CREON: Time eases all things.
OEDIPUS: But you must promise—
CREON: Say what you desire.
OEDIPUS: Send me from Thebes!
CREON: God grant that I may!   285
OEDIPUS: But since God hates me . . .
CREON: No, he will grant your wish.
OEDIPUS: You promise?
CREON: I cannot speak beyond my knowledge.
OEDIPUS: Then lead me in.
CREON: Come now, and leave your children.
OEDIPUS: No! Do not take them from me!
CREON: Think no longer

That you are in command here, but rather think   290
How, when you were, you served your own destruction.

[Exeunt into the house all but the CHORUS; *the* CHORAGOS *chants directly to the audience.]*

CHORAGOS: Men of Thebes: look upon Oedipus.
This is the king who solved the famous riddle
And towered up, most powerful of men.
No mortal eyes but looked on him with envy,   295
Yet in the end ruin swept over him.
Let every man in mankind's frailty
Consider his last day; and let none
Presume on his good fortune until he find
Life, at his death, a memory without pain.   300

QUESTIONS

1. What kind of ruler does Oedipus seem to be when we first meet him? Why does he address his people as children?
2. What incidents have happened in this country? Why has Oedipus sent Creon to Delphi?
3. What *is* Delphi? How can it be related to a modern institution?
4. Why is revenge such a political-philosophical imperative? Which Old Testament saying supports revenge?
5. What function does the Chorus serve in the play? What is the relation of the choral odes to the scenes? How do they help to advance the plot?
6. In *Oedipus* how has kindness developed into evil, and what is the message in this development?
7. How does Oedipus's own power entrap him?
8. Explain how Sophocles has observed the unities of time, place, and action in *Oedipus.*
9. Analyze the ironic elements in the play.
10. What does Sophocles say, ultimately, about fate and human nature in this play?

F a i t h & D o u b t

D r a m a

TOPICS FOR WRITING

1. Write a 400- to 500-word personal essay wherein you describe your personal credo.
2. Write a brief monologue in which an imagined character describes his or her personal credo. (Try to make it different from your own.)
3. Describe a personal experience in which you expressed doubt about a taken-for-granted principle or rule. What were you doubting? How did you express your doubt? What was the result?
4. Write a character analysis of Nat in *Death Knocks* based on the action that occurs in the play, particularly his reaction to the character Death.
5. In *Krapp's Last Tape*, we get an inkling of Krapp during three periods of his life: as an old man, as a middle-aged man, and as a young man. Locate the sections of the play that refer to each, and compare and contrast Krapp's attitude, mood, and physical health during each period.
6. Write an essay describing the choices Oedipus is called on to make in *Oedipus Rex*, and the result of these choices.
7. Argue for or against the idea that modern dramatists like Allen and Beckett are far too bleak and pessimistic in their treatment of the theme of faith and doubt.
8. Samuel Beckett has written numerous short plays with one character. As a research project, read several of these, then select two and compare and contrast their dramatic techniques and devices, themes, and characterizations.

Biographical Profiles

Chinua Achebe (b. 1930) was born in eastern Nigeria, subsequently Biafra. His first novel, *Things Fall Apart* (1958), tracing the conflicts between European and African cultures, is a masterpiece of African fiction. Additional novels, collections of short fiction, and essays have established Achebe as a foremost contemporary writer.

Anna Akhmatova (1888–1966) is considered one of the finest modern Russian poets. She was born in Odessa and raised near St. Petersburg. Her poetry, chronicling the harsh course of Soviet history, includes *White Flock* (1917), *Collected Poems* (1963), and *The Complete Poems* (1966).

Paula Gunn Allen (b. 1939) was born in New Mexico, the daughter of Sioux-Laguna and Lebanese-Jewish parents. She received her Ph.D. from the University of New Mexico, and teaches at San Francisco State University. Her collected verse includes *Coyote's Daylight Trip* (1978).

Woody Allen (b. 1935) was born Allen Stewart Konigsberg in Brooklyn, New York. He attended New York University and City College of New York, but did not graduate. In 1964, he wrote his first screenplay, *What's New Pussycat?* Since then, he has become one of America's foremost film directors. Allen's literary collections include *Getting Even* (1971), *Without Feathers* (1975), and *Side Effects* (1980).

Al-Tutili, one of the foremost Moorish poets living in Spain, was born, lived, and died during the Age of the Caliphs (AD 632–1050). Followers of Mohammed, founder of Islam, ruled there until 1492.

Yehuda Amichai (b. 1924) was born in Germany but emigrated to Palestine with his parents when he was a child. A poet, novelist, and short story writer, he is the author of *In This Terrible Wind* (1973) and other works.

Maya Angelou (b. 1928) was born in St. Louis, Missouri, but raised in Arkansas by her grandmother, who figures prominently in her famous autobiography, *I Know Why the Caged Bird Sings* (1969). Angelou has written other books about her experience as an African-American woman. Poet, teacher, lecturer, and civil-rights leader, Angelou was selected to read one of her poems at the 1993 inauguration of President Bill Clinton.

Aristophanes   (450?–385 B.C.), generally considered the greatest classical Greek dramatic comedian, was born toward the beginning of the Age of Pericles. Nine of his plays were written during the Peloponnesian War—the struggle between Athens and Sparta that lasted from 431 to 404 B.C. This war and the conflicts it caused form a major backdrop for Aristophanes' plays, notably *The Acharians* (425 B.C.), *Peace* (421 B.C.), and *Lysistrata* (411 B.C.). Other plays include *The Wasps* (422 B.C.), *The Birds* (414 B.C.), and *The Frogs* (405 B.C.).

Matthew Arnold   (1822–1888) was born at Laleham, England, the day before Christmas. He was educated at Winchester, Rugby, and Oxford and in 1847 was secretary to the marquis of Lansdowne. Arnold published his first collection of verse, *The Strayed Pearl and Other Poems* (1849) when he was 27. His studies and teaching led him to literary criticism; in 1852 he published *Empedocles,* a poem on Wordsworth, Byron, and Goethe. His other works include *Stanzas from the Grande Chartreuse* (1855), *Merope* (1858), *Thyrsis* (1866), and *Essays in Criticism* (1865, 1888). The obligation of a critic, he wrote, is "a disinterested endeavor to learn and propagate the best that is known and thought in the world."

Margaret Eleanor Atwood   (b. 1939) studied at the University of Toronto, in her native Canada, and at Radcliffe College, in the United States (1957–1962). She has taught at Canadian universities and is the recipient of several awards for poetry, including the E. J. Pratt, the Governor's, and the President's medals. Atwood is considered to be one of the most important contemporary writers. She is also a major novelist having written *The Handmaid's Tale* (1987) and *Cat's Eye* (1989), among other works. Among her collections of published poetry Atwood includes *Double Persephone* (1961), *The Circle Game* (1967), *The Journals of Susanna Moodie* (1970), and *Power Politics* (1971).

Wystan Hugh Auden   (1907–1973) was born in England in 1907. After college at Oxford he became a member of a group of London poets that included Stephen Spender, C. Day Lewis, Louis MacNeice, and Christopher Isherwood. This was one of the most talented collections of writers in England at that time. Auden, like many other writers of the period, saw socialism as the political system that would save the world. He fought with the Republicans during the Spanish Civil War and in 1939, after his marriage to Erika Mann, emigrated to the United States and later became a citizen. Greatly influenced by W. B. Yeats and T. S. Eliot, Auden's work was first socially concerned and then more religiously concerned. He collaborated with MacNeice on *Letters from Iceland* (1937) and with Isherwood on four plays during the decade of the 1930s. A deft employer of satire, as in "The Unknown Citizen," Auden was wedged between English and American culture. His references tend to be more English, and this is true even though he lived in Greenwich Village in New York until a few years before his death. His works include *Poems* (1930), *Look, Stranger* (1936), *Spain* (1937), *The Sea and the Mirror* (1944), *For the Time Being: A Christmas Oratorio* (1944), *Selected Poetry* (1959), and *Homage to Clio* (1960).

Kofi Awoonor   (b. 1935) was born in Ghana. He was educated in Ghana, England, and the United States. One of Africa's foremost poets, he is the author of *Rediscovery* (1964), *Ride Me, Memory* (1973), and other collections. He has also written fiction, plays, and literary and political criticism.

Isaac Babel   (1894–1939?) was born in Odessa, Russia, of Jewish background. He was a soldier during World War I and later a correspondent attached to the Red Army. Two collections of his tales are *The Story of My Dove-Cote* (1925) and *Red Cavalry* (1926). He was arrested and disappeared during the Stalinist purges of the 1930s.

Ingeborg Bachmann   (1926–1973), the 1964 Buchner Prize winner, was born in Austria and studied philosophy. She traveled widely and published poetry, plays, and prose.

Amiri Baraka (b. 1934), poet, playwright, novelist, and essayist, was one of the moving forces behind the cultural explosion known as the Black Arts Movement during the 1960s. Born in Newark, New Jersey, as LeRoi Jones and educated at both Howard and Columbia universities, Baraka (the Muslim name he adopted in 1968) experienced the cultural training that was expected of both white and black intellectuals during the middle part of this century. This experience led Baraka to the realization that his own conception of who he was as a black man and who blacks as a people were within the larger white society was determined by the white man's visions of the world. His books include *Note* (1962), *Black Magic: Poetry 1961–1967* (1967), the play *Dutchman* (1967), and other works.

Samuel Beckett (1906–1989), Irish-French poet, dramatist, fiction writer, and critic, was born near Dublin. He received a B.A. degree from Trinity College, and in 1928 relocated to Paris. A major writer in the theatre of the absurd, Beckett wrote *Waiting for Godot* (1952), *Endgame* (1957), and *Krapp's Last Tape* (1959), among other plays.

Aphra Behn (1640–1689) was born in Kent, England. She spent part of her childhood in Surinam, Guiana, an experience that provided her with the background for her best-known novel, *Oroonoko* (1688). In 1666, when Behn was 26, she was sent on a mission as a spy in the Netherlands for Charles II, becoming known for her exploits as "the Incomparable." However, she fell out of royal favor, spent time in debtors' prison in London, and on her release turned to writing to earn a living. Behn wrote seventeen plays, twelve histories and novels, and poetry, and did translations.

Ulli Beier (?) A distinguished linguist, Beier was a Senior Lecturer in English Literature at the University of Papua and New Guinea when he translated, edited, and compiled the traditional poetry of Nigeria's Yoruba people during the 1960s.

John Berryman (1914–1972), born in McAlester, Oklahoma, and educated at Columbia University and Oxford, is a notable contemporary poet best known for his collections *77 Dream Songs* (1964) and *Short Poems* (1967). All of his poetry reflects psychologically intense self-reflection.

Elizabeth Bishop (1911–1979) was born in Worcester, Massachusetts, and raised by grandparents and an aunt in Nova Scotia and Boston. She graduated from Vassar in 1934 and then traveled extensively in Europe, Mexico, and finally Brazil, where she settled more or less permanently in 1951. Bishop won the Pulitzer Prize in 1956 and the National Book Award in 1970; the bulk of her verse appears in *The Complete Poems* (1969). Her friend Marianne Moore, whom she first met in 1934, once declared that Bishop was "spectacular in being unspectacular." Bishop is natural, deliberate, commonplace, modest, yet subtly contemplative in her best verse. However, she can also be, as she remarks of one of her favorite poets, George Herbert, "almost surrealistic" in her vivid descriptions of landscapes, objects, and people.

William Blake (1757–1827) was born in London, where during the course of his life he was a poet, an engraver, a painter, and a mystic whose views became recognizable in his work. Many of his works are based on a mythological structure created by Blake, one that bypasses or ignores organized religion of Blake's day. Blake illustrated many of his own works, which include *Poetical Sketches by W. B.* (1783), *Songs of Innocence* (1789), *Songs of Experience* (1794), and the "prophetical books"—*The Book of Thel* (1789), *The Marriage of Heaven and Hell* (1790), *The Gates of Paradise* (1793), *The Vision of the Daughters of Albion* (1793), and others.

Louise Bogan (1897–1970) was born in Maine and attended Boston University for one year. She lived most of her life in New York City, where she supported herself by writing stories and articles and doing translations and book reviews for *The New Republic, The Nation, The New Yorker*, and other magazines. She published her first volume of poetry in 1923. Though she wrote many things simply to pay the bills, she was a perfectionist about her poetry. She reduced the contents of her final collection, *The Blue Estuaries: Poems 1923–1968,* to only 105 poems, her lifetime's work. Often her poetry depicts the situation of women and asserts the need for a separate feminine view of the world.

Arna Wendell Bontemps   (1902–1973) was born in Alexandria, Louisiana. A courtly man, he served Fisk University in Nashville as librarian and assistant to the president for much of his life. Bontemps and Langston Hughes collaborated on many collections and other works. "He sought," says Charles Nichols, "the source and shape of his creative work in his own roots—the deep South of Louisiana and Alabama. The stark, laconic, poignant stories he wrote in the early 1930's are in the realistic mode of American regionalism." The South was the place Bontemps returned to after his graduation from Pacific Union College in 1924, and two years later he won the Alexander Pushkin Poetry Prize. He became, as well an essayist, a playwright, a short story writer, a novelist, and the author of many children's books, on some of which he collaborated with Hughes, Jack Conroy, and Countee Cullen. Bontemps was one of several writers to emerge from the Harlem Renaissance (1925–1929). Perhaps his most important novel was *Black Thunder* (1936).

Jorge Luis Borges   (1899–1986) was born in Argentina. Between 1923 and 1929 he published several volumes of poetry, which were mainly nostalgic and nationalistic (*Fervor de Buenos Aires,* 1923; *Luna de enfrente,* 1925; *Cuaderno de San Martin,* 1929). He then began writing essays on literature, metaphysics, and language. When his eyesight began to fail, he turned to writing fictional narratives, and these established his reputation. Somewhat like Kafka, Borges wove together the real and the surreal to create yet another reality. Among his better-known publications are *Historia de la infamia* (1935), *Ficciones* (1945, 1956), *El Aleph* (1949), *Other Inquisitions* (1952), and *Labyrinths, Stories and Essays* (1962).

Kay Boyle   (1903–1992) left her hometown, St. Paul, Minnesota, for study in Ohio from 1917 to 1919. She was a steady and frequent contributor to the little magazines that flourished at the close of World War I. Boyle lived in Europe, mainly France, for long periods of time, and much of her fiction is set overseas. The 1936 and 1941 winner of the O. Henry Award for short fiction, Boyle also gained great prominence as a poet. The poetic touch is easily discernible in her fiction. Her first novel, *Wedding Day,* was published in 1931 and was followed five years later by *The White Horses of Vienna and Other Stories.* These brought her considerable attention and established her as a writer who touched the world with a woman's sensibilities. *The Crazy Hunter* (1940); *American Citizen,* a poem (1944); *1939* (1948); *Generation without Farewell* (1959); *The Seagull on the Step: Three Short Novels* (1958); and *Testament for my Students,* a collection of poems (1970), are among her notable works, which also include *Thirty Stories* (1946) and *Fifty Stories* (1980).

Ray Douglas Bradbury   (b. 1920) was born in Waukegan, Illinois, a small city some 40 miles north of Chicago. He began publishing his stories in 1941, and several have been selected for the *Best American Short Stories* and *O. Henry Prize Stories* collections. Bradbury arranges his highly moralistic stories in science-fiction settings that often possess allegorical meanings for the present. He has written also for the stage, radio, and film. Among the most popular of his many works are *Dark Carnival* (1947), *The Martian Chronicles* (1950), *Fahrenheit 451* (1953), and *A Medicine for Melancholy* (1959).

Anne Bradstreet   (1612?–1672) was the first truly dedicated poet to settle in America. Bradstreet's poems were taken to London by her brother-in-law and apparently published without her consent in a volume entitled *The Tenth Muse Lately Sprung Up in America* (1650). Around 1666, Bradstreet began to revise the poems and work on others for a second edition, which she did not live to see published in 1678.

William Stanley Braithwaite   (1878–1962), born in Boston, early on became involved with literature and writing. Between 1926 and 1929 he edited eleven collections of poetry. He was himself poet, novelist, essayist, publisher, and editor. As editor of *The Poetic Journal* and *Poetry*

Review, Braithwaite published many of the contemporary imagists and Frost, Sandburg, Masters, and Lindsay—unusual for a black man and despite the racial epithets by which many of his contributors addressed him.

Gwendolyn Brooks   (b. 1917) was born in Topeka, Kansas, but was raised in Chicago's South Side. As a child, Brooks was encouraged by both of her parents to write; her mother, alluding to an earlier black American poet, predicted that she would one day be the female Paul Laurence Dunbar. Brooks attended Wilson Junior College in Chicago and published her first book of poetry, *A Street in Bronzeville,* in 1945. Her second book, *Annie Allen,* won the Pulitzer Prize in 1949, making Brooks the first black writer to win that award. Other volumes include *Bronzeville Boys and Girls* (1956), *The Bean Eaters* (1960), *In the Mecca* (1960), *Family Pictures* (1971), an autobiography, *Report from Part One* (1972); and a novel, *Maud Martha* (1953). A major poet, Brooks has been a prodigious supporter of younger artists and an inspiration for them. She has pioneered in depicting inner-city lives and in blending classical poetics with dialect and vernacular.

Bridgit Brophy   (b. 1929), English fiction writer and playwright, was born in London and attended St. Hugh's College, Oxford. Her fiction and drama examine the complex sexual relationships between people, including lesbians and bisexuals.

Sterling A. Brown   (1901–1989) was born in Washington, D.C. He received one of the best educations of the writers in the Harlem Renaissance, graduating from Williams College and earning an M.A. from Harvard University. Brown taught for many years at Howard University. His main contribution to scholarship has been his recording of the lyrics of blues and spirituals and his helping these forms earn standing as legitimate forms of artistic expression. His study of spirituals and the blues influenced his own poetry.

Elizabeth Barrett Browning   (1806–1861), born at Durham, England, received in childhood a rich, leisurely education from her brothers' tutors. She was devoted to literature, and when she was 14 her father had published her epic poem, *The Battle of Marathon.* In 1819, she apparently suffered a spinal injury that left her a semi-invalid until her marriage to Robert Browning in 1846. Elizabeth Browning enjoyed great fame for her *Sonnets from the Portuguese* (1850) and her blank-verse novel, *Aurora Leigh* (1857).

Robert Browning   (1812–1869) was born near London, of wealthy parents, and was educated at home and at the University of London. Poetry was a childhood passion, used by Browning as a therapeutic tool to rid himself of his turbulent emotions. In September 1846, he eloped to Italy with the poet Elizabeth Barrett. They were to live fairly happily together until her death fifteen years later. A fine, though often difficult, poet, he is most famous for his development, as in "My Last Duchess," of the dramatic monologue, in which he presents complex characters through their own voices.

George Gordon, Lord Byron   (1788–1824), was described by a contemporary as "mad, bad, and dangerous to know." Born of aristocratic parents with titles but little wealth, Byron grew up in poverty in the Scottish city of Aberdeen. A series of coincidences left him as the sixth Lord Byron, and he completed his education at Trinity College, Cambridge. A victim of both nature (he was born with a clubfoot) and nineteenth-century medicine, he nevertheless became a fine athlete, excelling in boxing, fencing, horse racing, and swimming. Financial difficulties and personal catastrophes plagued him most of his life, which ended with his fighting and dying in faraway Greece for the thing he loved most—freedom. Byron in his lifetime enjoyed sensational popular success as the author of such romantic narratives as *Childe Harold's Pilgrimage* (1812), *The Corsair* (1814), and the unfinished *Don Juan* (1818).

Raymond Carver   (1938–1989) grew up in a logging town in Oregon. Married and a father at 19, Carver took courses at Chico State College, in California, where he studied creative writing with writer John Gardner. Carver also studied at Humboldt State College, California, and the University of Iowa; he published six collections of short fiction, notably *What We Talk About When We Talk About Love* (1981) and *Cathedral* (1983), along with a significant body of poetry, before his death from lung cancer.

Lorna Dee Cervantes   (b. 1959) was born in San Francisco, California, of Mexican descent. She attended San Jose City College and San Francisco State University. Her first book of poems is *Emplumada* (1982).

Aimé (Fernand) Césaire   (b. 1913), long considered one of the finest modernists writing in French, was born in Martinique, West Indies. He studied at the École Normale Supérieure and the Sorbonne in Paris. Former mayor of Fort-de-France, he was also Martinique's deputy to the French National Assembly and consul general of a district in Fort-de-France. Perhaps best known for his monumental work *Notebook of a Return to the Native Land*, Césaire began his career in letters in 1946, producing voluminous works in the essay and in poetry. His volumes include *The Miracle Weapon* (*Les armes miraculeuses* 1946), *Solar Throat Slashed* (*Soleil Cou-Coupe* 1948), *Shackles* (*Ferrements* 1960), *Aimé Césaire: The Collected Poetry* (1983), and *Lost Body* (*Corps Perdu* 1949). Between 1956 and 1969, Césaire wrote four plays. He is one of the prime spokespersons of the Negritude movement, which was sparked by Langston Hughes's work during the 1920s and 1930s.

Anton Chekhov   (1860–1904), the grandson of a serf, was born in Taganrog, Russia, and studied medicine at Moscow University. He received his medical degree in 1884, the same year that his first collection of short stories was published. Chekhov wrote hundreds of stories and sketches early in his career, gaining a literary reputation and a measure of financial independence that enabled him to make writing rather than the practice of medicine his major priority. Chekhov's greatest work in both short fiction and drama came in the last years of a life drastically shortened by tuberculosis. The plays of this last period—*The Seagull* (1896), *Uncle Vanya* (1899), *The Three Sisters* (1901), and *The Cherry Orchard* (1904)—were masterpieces that established Chekhov as a great modern dramatist. Chekhov's masterpieces of short fiction are equally outstanding, a delicate mixture of comedy, pathos, and tragedy in the author's depiction of humanity.

Cho Chi-hun   (b. 1920) first published in *The Green Deer Anthology* of Korea with a group of poets, each of whom contributed fifteen poems. He is a Buddhist. The author of several books of poetry, he taught at Korea University.

So Chongju   (b. 1915) was born in North Cholla Province, Korea. In 1930 he was expelled from the high school he attended in Seoul for protesting Japan's colonial policies, but later studied at Chungan Buddhist College. He became a university teacher and has been publishing poetry—including seven collections—since 1938.

Kate Chopin   (1851–1904) was born in St. Louis, Missouri. At the age of 20, she married a man from New Orleans, and she lived there until her husband's premature death caused her to return to St. Louis and assume in 1887 a career in writing. Chopin gained a national reputation in the 1890s for her local-color tales about Louisiana. These stories were collected in *Bayou Folk* (1894) and *A Night in Acadie* (1897). In 1899, she published a novel, *The Awakening*. Termed by one critic an "American *Madame Bovary*," this novel about a passionate and independent woman was severely criticized by reviewers and even banned in Chopin's native city.

Sandra Cisneros,   Chicana feminist, poet, children's author, and short-story writer, was born in Chicago and graduated from Loyola University. She is the author of a short-story collection, *Woman Hollering Greek* (1991), and a volume of poetry, *My Wicked Wicked Ways* (1987).

Lucille Clifton   (b. 1936), African-American poet and children's writer, was born in Depew, New York, and educated at Howard University. Since 1985 she has been a professor at the University of California, Santa Cruz. Her collected poetry includes *Good Times* (1969), *Good Woman* (1987), and *Next* (1988). Her poems, typically short and graceful, focus on the African-American woman's experience.

Judith Ortiz Cofer (b. 1952) was born in Puerto Rico, and emigrated to the United States four years later. She earned her M.A. in 1977, and then attended Oxford. Her works include a play, *Latin Women Pray,* and four volumes of poetry. Her work has appeared in a variety of publications since the 1970s.

Jayne Cortez (b. 1936), an American Book Award winner in 1980, was born in Arizona and raised in California before moving to New York. Since 1969 she has published seven volumes of poetry, including *Festivals and Funerals* (1971), *Mouth on Paper* (1977), *Coagulations* (1984), and *Maintain Control* (1987).

Stephen Crane (1871–1900), born in Newark, New Jersey, and educated at Lafayette College and Syracuse University, is a pivotal figure in American fiction, poetry, and journalism—an artist who helped to shape the modern age in literature. Although he died before the age of 29, Crane did more than any other American author to assimilate the European modes of naturalism, impressionism, and sociological realism into our national literature. His novel *Maggie: A Girl of the Streets* (1893) offended the contemporary public with its harsh portrayal of slum life and of a young woman whose life ends in prostitution and death. His short novel about the Civil War, *The Red Badge of Courage* (1895), won for Crane broader and more approving recognition and today is considered a masterpiece of war fiction.

Victor Hernandez Cruz (b. 1949) was born in Aguas Buenas, Puerto Rico, and grew up in New York City. He has taught at San Francisco State University and at the University of California, Berkeley. Cruz's collections of verse include *Snaps* (1969), *Mainland* (1973), *Tropicalization* (1976), and *Red Beans* (1991). "My mind," comments Cruz, "is creole and can fuse many unlikely things together: outer variety, inner unity; we are an experiment in communications."

Countee Cullen (1903–1946) grew up in Harlem, the son of a minister. He studied at New York University and Harvard. He was 23 when he published his first volume of poetry, *Color* (1926). Like McKay, Bontemps, Hughes, and others, Cullen was involved in the Harlem Renaissance. However, his principal occupation was teaching French in the New York City schools. Cullen was also an editor of various publications. In 1927 he published *Copper Sun* and *The Ballad of the Brown Girl. The Black Christ* followed two years later. Cullen wrote two children's books and a novel, *One Way to Heaven* (1932). A year after his death a collection of selected poems was published, *On These I Stand.*

e.e. cummings (1894–1962) was an American poet, novelist, playwright, painter, and essayist. Cummings's first published work was his novel *The Enormous Room* (1922), which was considered a modern masterpiece. The plays *HIM* (1927) and *Santa Claus* (1946) came between the poetry. There were seven volumes between *Tulips and Chimneys* (1923) and *Poems 1923– 1954* (1954). Cummings, a gifted satirist, nevertheless maintained the rhythmic cadences of natural speech.

Roque Dalton (1935–1975), born in El Salvador, studied law and social science in his native country as well as in Chile and Mexico. During his studies abroad, Dalton became a Communist. As a result, he was exiled from and imprisoned in El Salvador several times. He was assassinated in May 1975. His works include *La Ventana en el Rostro* (Mexico, 1961), *El Mar* (Havana, 1962), and *Poemas Clandestinos* (1975).

Kamala Das (b. 1934), poet, short-story writer, and autobiographer, was born in Malabar, India. Urging new roles for Indian women, Das has collected her poetry in *Summer in Calcutta* (1965) and *The Old Playhouse* (1973), among other works.

René Depestre (b. 1926), born in Haiti, is a frequent contributor to *Presence Africaine* in Paris, and is considered one of the Negritude poets. Among his works are *For the Revolution, For Poetry* (1969) and *A Rainbow for the Christmas West* (1972).

Babette Deutsch   (1895–1982) was born in New York City and began publishing poetry when she was a student at Barnard College. She served as Thorstein Veblen's secretary at the New School for Social Research and married the Russian scholar Avrahm Yarmolinsky, with whom she collaborated on a number of verse translations. Deutsch wrote poetry, criticism, novels, and children's books. She is best known as a poet, a distinctive author who combines a refined intellect with emotional involvement in social and political issues. Much of her work is assembled in *Collected Poems, 1919–1962* (1963).

Emily Dickinson   (1830–1886) was born in Amherst, Massachusetts, the second child of an important local family. She attended Amherst Academy from 1840 to 1847 and spent a year at Mount Hadley Female Seminary, but ill health often forced her to interrupt her education. Aside from brief trips to Boston, Philadelphia, and Washington, Dickinson remained in Amherst all her life. She wrote poems prolifically from 1858 to 1865, but was largely uninterested in publication, arranging her poems in packets and storing them in a box—a cache that would be discovered by her sister, Lavinia, after Emily died. Only with the publication of *The Poems of Emily Dickinson* in 1955 did the bulk of her poetry—some 1,775 items—become available to readers. In much of her greatest poetry, she often deals with loneliness, loss, pain, sorrow, despair, and death. Yet Dickinson commanded many moods: she could be witty, comic, playful, irreverent. Her love lyrics are of the same order as the rest of her poetry—demanding, existing in tension with other felt emotions.

Isak Dinesen   (1985–1962) was born Karen Christentze Dinesen, near Elsinore, Denmark. In 1941 she married her cousin, Baron Boor Blixen, and went to Kenya, the source and site of her finest writing. She published her first collection of stories, *Seven Gothic Tales*, in 1934. Subsequent works include *Out of Africa* (1937), *Winter's Tales* (1942), and *Last Tales* (1957).

John Donne   (1572–1631), the first great English metaphysical poet, came from a Roman Catholic family whose ways he preferred less than those of a man about town. However, after sipping from the cup of the good life, he had a change of heart and converted to Anglicanism. He became dean of St. Paul's Cathedral in 1621. His early works were shaped by satire, irony, and eroticism and are as famous as his later poems, which, with great power and grace, express his desire for a rapprochement with God. Donne's elegies, epigrams, and devotions are an extraordinary examination of sickness and considerations of death.

Rita Dove   (b. 1952) was born in Akron, Ohio, the daughter of African-American parents who had migrated from the South. She received an M.F.A. from the writers' workshop at the University of Iowa and has been a Fulbright, Guggenheim, and National Endowment for the Humanities recipient. Her poetry collections include *The Yellow House on the Corner* (1980), *Museum* (1983), and *Thomas and Beulah* (1986).

Alan Dugan   (b. 1923), Brooklyn born, studied at Queens College of the City University of New York and Olivet College, served in the U.S. Air Force during World War II, and taught at Sarah Lawrence College. He won the Pulitzer Prize for *Poems* in 1961. His poetry is understated and ironic.

Thomas Stearns Eliot   (1888–1965) was born in St. Louis. An outstanding student, he traveled to Europe on an academic fellowship shortly before the start of World War I. He eventually settled in London, where he quickly established himself as a radically innovative poet and an influential and often acerbic critic. He counted among his friends Virginia Woolf, James Joyce, H.D., and Ezra Pound, all important figures in the literary movement known as modernism. His first volume of poetry, *Prufrock and Other Observations*, was published in 1917, but it was his long poem *The Waste Land* (1922) that established him as the leading poet writing in English between the wars, and as the most prominent spokesman for what became known as the "lost generation." He wrote comparatively little lyric poetry after World War II, but instead concentrated on verse drama and on literary and social criticism. His poetry and plays often show a courageous intelligence in confrontation with a deep, seemingly inescapable unhappiness.

Louise Erdrich (b. 1954), of Chippewa and German-American descent, grew up in North Dakota. She now lives in New Hampshire with her husband, the writer Michael Dorris. A poet, essayist, and novelist, Erdrich is the author of *Love Medicine* (1984), *The Beet Queen* (1986), *Tracks* (1988), and with Dorris, *The Crown of Columbus* (1992).

Forūgh Farrokhzād (1934–1966), Iran's foremost modern poet, was born in Teheran. She attended girls schools, but never graduated, marrying a government official at the age of 16. Her candid poetry is collected in *The Captive* (1952) and in subsequent volumes.

William Faulkner (1897–1962), 1949 winner of the Nobel Prize in literature, was born in New Albany, Mississippi. His family moved to Oxford in 1902, and Faulkner attended the University of Mississippi there. He drew extensively on his family history and the people of the region he would come to make famous in his novels as Yoknapatawpha County. The interrelated problems of race and class are recurring themes in Faulkner's work. These were, Malcolm Cowley said, "the tragic fable of Southern history." From his first novel, *Soldier's Pay* (1926), to *The Reivers* (1962), Faulkner's stories and novels, some of them difficult to comprehend at first reading, have been lyrical, interior, and brimming with characters and symbolism.

Lawrence Ferlinghetti (b. 1919) emerged first as a poet and publisher in the Beat scene of the 1950s in San Francisco. He founded City Lights Bookstore, which served as both focal point and publishing house for the movement. As a poet, playwright, novelist, and publisher, Ferlinghetti has been active in the struggle for control of our humanity within a society that seeks to make our behavior "normal." In his poem "Overheard Conversations," he defines his concept of poetry: "And still the whole idea of poetry being/to take control of life/out of the hand of/the terrible people." In his poetry Ferlinghetti often employs experimental and shocking language, but always strives to make it as accessible as possible.

Anne Finch (1661–1722) was born the daughter of a Southampton nobleman. By marriage she became the countess of Winchelsea. Her position, interests, and talent kept her in the thick of England's intellectual life, and she earned the respect and admiration of Pope and Swift, with whom she was known to banter in verse epistles. Her range is extensive, touching on the personal and public issues of her day, and some consider her a precursor of romanticism.

Gisele Fong is a third-generation Chinese American born in San Francisco, California. Her poetry has appeared in literary magazines and in the anthology *Making Face, Making Soul*.

Carolyn Forché (b. 1950), poet and political activist, was born in Detroit, Michigan. Her poetry, often reflecting political concerns, is collected in *Gathering the Tribes* (1976), which received the Yale Younger Poets award; and in *The Country Between Us* (1982).

Robert Frost (1875–1963) was born in San Francisco but moved at the age of 11 with his family to the New Hampshire farm country that would become identified with some of his finest poetry. He attended Dartmouth College briefly, leaving to assume a variety of jobs: bobbin boy in a Lawrence mill, shoemaker, newspaper editor, schoolteacher, farmer. Frost wrote poetry in his leisure hours; he published his first poem in 1894. He married in 1895, and after years of largely unsuccessful farming Frost sold his farm and moved his family to England in 1912, risking everything to become a poet. His first book, *A Boy's Will* (1913), was published in England, as well as his second, *North of Boston* (1914), which won critical acclaim. By the time Frost returned to America in 1915, he was a successful and celebrated, if somewhat embarrassed, poet. He won four Pulitzer prizes, for *New Hampshire* (1923), *Collected Poems* (1930), *A Further Range* (1936), and *A Witness Tree* (1942). A poet of the New England soil,

Frost spent the bulk of his mature career on farms in New Hampshire and Vermont, wintering later in his life at a palmetto patch he owned in Florida, and serving intermittently as poet-in-residence at Amherst, Harvard, Michigan, and Dartmouth.

Nikki Giovanni (b. 1943) was born in Nashville, Tennessee, and was raised in Ohio. She received a B.A. in history from Fisk University in 1967 and did graduate work at the University of Pennsylvania. Giovanni was witness to the crises of the 1960s and the problems of her generation. "Blacks made the sixties," she has stated, and much of her poetry from that period deals with the need for revolutionary social change. Giovanni's more recent poetry is introspective, dealing with the basic processes of life and the struggles of the individual self. One of the most popular poets today, Giovanni has published numerous volumes of verse, including *Black Judgment* (1969), *Re-Creation* (1970), *Broadside Poem of Angela Yvonne Davis* (1970), *Gemini* (1971), *My House* (1972), *The Women and the Men* (1975), *Cotton Candy on a Rainy Day* (1978), and *Sacred Cows and Other Edibles* (1988).

Susan Glaspell (1876–1948), American feminist, playwright, and fiction writer, was born in Davenport, Iowa, of Irish immigrant parents. She helped to found the Provincetown Players, writing the plays *Suppressed Desires* (1915), *Tribes* (1916), *Bernice* (1919), and *Alison's House* (1930), the latter which won a Pulitzer Prize.

Nadine Gordimer (b. 1923) was born near Johannesburg, South Africa. Growing up in South Africa, she encountered the fiction of Katherine Mansfield and she determined to become a writer. Her early stories are collected in *Face to Face* (1949) and *The Soft Voice of the Serpent* (1952). Since then, she has written short fiction and novels during a career typified by an acute social and political consciousness centered on the racial tensions in South Africa.

Lady Augusta Gregory (1852–1932), cofounder of the Abbey Theatre and a dramatist, was born in County Galway, Ireland. She wrote more than thirty plays, of which *The Workhouse Ward* (1908), *Spreading the News* (1904), and *The Rising of the Moon* (1907) are the best known.

Anthony Grooms (b. 1955) was born in Charlottesville, Virginia, and was educated at the College of William and Mary and George Mason University. Also a fiction writer, Grooms teaches at the University of Georgia. He lives in Atlanta.

Thom Gunn (b. 1929), British born, Oxbridge trained, and American experienced, has been one of the most innovative poets in both British and American letters in recent years. Speaking of the breadth of Gunn's accomplishments, Neal Corcoran has said: "Geographically he has moved from England to America, more specifically from 1950s Cambridge to 1960s San Francisco; metrically, he has moved from highly disciplined traditional forms, through syllabics to a very loose kind of free form; and thematically, he has made use of such widely varied influences as French existentialist thought and American lysergic acid. And emotionally and sexually, Gunn has moved from poems overtly addressed to women to openly frank homosexual poems. He is, altogether, a poet difficult to get clear and difficult to get whole."

Lorraine Hansberry (1930–1965) was born in Chicago, Illinois, into a middle-class African-American family. She moved to New York City in 1950 and began her career as a writer. Her major plays include *A Raisin in the Sun* (1953), which won the New York Drama Critics Award for best play; *The Sign in Sidney Brustein's Window* (1964); and the posthumous *Les Blancs* (1966).

Joy Harjo (b. 1951), a Native American poet, was born in Tulsa, Oklahoma. Her collected poetry includes *The Last Song* (1975) and *She Had Some Horses* (1983).

Nathaniel Hawthorne (1804–1869) was born in Salem, Massachusetts. Following graduation from Bowdoin College in Maine in 1825, Hawthorne returned to Salem and entered into a relatively isolated twelve-year period of writing that culminated in the publication of *Twice-Told Tales* in 1837. But it was not until 1850 that Hawthorne achieved fame with the publication of *The Scarlet Letter*. This novel, along with *The House of the Seven Gables* (1851) and his finest short fiction, centers on sin, evil, guilt, and the mysterious—almost supernatural—workings of these forces in human affairs.

Robert Hayden (1913–1980) was born and raised in the black working-class neighborhoods of Detroit. After attending Wayne State University, he became a professor of English literature at the University of Michigan. As a poet of the black experience, Hayden employed a wide variety of styles and forms—ranging from his early use of colloquial street language to his later, more stylized work with long poems—in order to explore the complexities of his own history. Among his major poetry collections are *A Ballad of Remembrance* (1962) and *Selected Poems* (1966).

Seamus Heaney (b. 1939), born and educated in Ireland, is the author of such collections of verse as *Station Island* (1984), *The Haw Lantern* (1987), and *New Selected Poems 1966–1987* (1990). He teaches at Harvard.

Ernest Miller Hemingway (1899–1961) was born in Oak Park, Illinois, and he died in Ketchum, Idaho. He was for a long time a journalist; in 1954 he won the Nobel Prize in literature. Even during his career as a novelist, story writer, and playwright, Hemingway reported from various parts of the world. It is sometimes difficult to note extreme differences between his dispatches and passages in his fiction, though he believed that the two kinds of writing were distinct. Following World War I, he lived in Europe, where he knew many writers, among them Gertrude Stein, F. Scott Fitzgerald, Wallace Stevens, Morley Callaghan, and Ezra Pound. In 1923 he published *Three Stories and Ten Poems*, which was followed the next year by a collection of stories, *In Our Time*. *The Torrents of Spring* and *The Sun Also Rises* (1926), both novels, came next. *The Sun Also Rises* established "his reputation and set him, at the age of 26, in the limelight which he both enjoyed and resented for the rest of his life," wrote critic Philip Young.

George Herbert (1593–1633), who was born into an illustrious and pious Anglo-Welsh family, was educated at Cambridge University. He was appointed reader in rhetoric in 1618 and was public orator from 1620 to 1627. Herbert was elected to Parliament in 1624, but in 1626 he debarred himself from civil service by taking minor religious orders; he was ordained a priest in 1630. A friend of John Donne and Francis Bacon, Herbert chose "to lose himself in an humble way," serving as a pious and charitable country parson. Aware early in 1633 that he was dying of consumption, Herbert readied a copy of his book, *The Temple*, for publication. The religious lyrics in this miscellany, which also includes hymns, prayers, and Church history, are varied in verse forms, but clear, concise, and natural in diction.

Robert Herrick (1591–1674) was born in London of a middle-class family. He served for ten years as an apprentice goldsmith to his uncle, Sir William Herrick. Educated at St. John's College, Cambridge, and Trinity Hall, he later accepted a clerical position and lived his life as a bachelor in Devonshire (1629–1647). In terms of his poetic style, Herrick is usually classified with the Cavaliers—poets who wrote during the reign of Charles I. Other Cavaliers included Thomas Carew, Sir John Suckling, and Richard Lovelace. Early in his career, Herrick was greatly influenced by Ben Jonson. However, poems such as "To the Virgins, to Make Much of Time" and "Delight in Disorder" reveal him to be a less didactic and more playful poet than Jonson. Herrick's major collection, *Hesperides*, was published in 1648 and contained over 1,200 sacred and secular poems.

Gerard Manley Hopkins (1844–1889) was the eldest son in a middle-class, Anglican family. His childhood was apparently uneventful, but he blossomed intellectually at Oxford, where he studied with Walter Pater and was befriended by John (later Cardinal) Newman. With Newman's sponsorship and against the wishes of his family, he converted to Catholicism in 1866. Two years later he entered the Jesuit order and, in a dramatic gesture, burned the final copy of all his early poems. At this point in his life he feared that the aesthetic and the religious might not be reconcilable. Six years later, however, with the encouragement of his prefect, he wrote a long poem to honor five nuns drowned in a shipwreck and continued to write from then on. Hopkins spent his life as a teacher and as a priest, serving many different communities, some of which were poor and isolated. He made only halfhearted attempts to have his poetry published in his lifetime.

Henry Howard   (1515–1547), son of the powerful duke of Norfolk, had a tumultuous youth, full of the customary pastimes of young aristocrats—vigorous games, traveling, and wenching. Along the way, he also acquired a first-rate education at the hands of private tutors. Fierce and absurdly proud, he almost had his right hand chopped off for striking a courtier; eventually, he was beheaded for suspicion of treason. With Thomas Wyatt, he helped establish the sonnet in English, and he was the first poet to publish in blank verse.

Ricarda Huch   (1864–1947), a historian by discipline, is considered the most important woman writer of early twentieth-century Germany. She was a literary critic as well as a novelist and essayist. Her poetry reflects her pessimistic outlook.

James Langston Hughes   (1902–1967) was born of black American and Cherokee ancestry in Joplin, Missouri, and raised in Kansas, Illinois, and Ohio. He was elected class poet in grammar school in Lincoln, Illinois, and again in high school in Ohio. Hughes attended Columbia University briefly and then roamed the world as a seaman, traveling to Africa and Europe before returning to the United States to complete his education at Lincoln University. Hughes then moved back to New York and settled in Harlem. Best known for his poetry and for his stories of Simple, Hughes also wrote journalism, opera librettos, plays and television scripts, and was a notable anthologist of black writing. His poetry reveals a keen ear for folk vernacular, and he is a major experimenter in verse technique in his use of music rhythms. It is deceptively simple and casual, but beneath the simplicity of colloquial statement there are undercurrents of humor and irony, of social criticism, and of compassion for the gallery of figures that Hughes draws. Much of Hughes's most memorable poetry deals with the history and experience of black Americans and with the struggle against hate and oppression. Among his collections of poetry are *Weary Blues* (1926), *Fine Clothes to the Jew* (1927), *The Dream Keeper* (1932), *Shakespeare in Harlem* (1942), *Fields of Wonder* (1947), *One Way Ticket* (1949), *Montage of a Dream Deferred* (1951), and *Ask Your Mama* (1961).

David Henry Hwang   (b. 1957), the son of Chinese-American immigrants, attended Stanford University, where he wrote plays as an undergraduate. Among his plays are *FOB* (1981), recipient of the Obbie Award; *Family Devotions* (1982); and *M. Butterfly* (1988), which won a Tony Award as best play.

Yussef Idriss   (b. 1927) is an Egyptian short story writer and playwright, one of the major literary figures in the Arab world. Trained as a physician, he gave up his profession in the 1970s to work as a journalist, playwright, critic, and story writer. Influenced by Gorky, Kafka, and Faulkner, Idriss combines their psychological techniques with the oral traditions of Egyptian life.

Lawson Fusao Inada   (b. 1938), born a third-generation Japanese American *(Sansei)* in Fresno, California, was once host of a radio program "Talk Story: The Written Word," in Ashland, Oregon. His work has appeared in many publications, and he is the coeditor of *AIIIEEEEE: An Anthology of Asian American Writers,* (1974). He is also the author of the poetry volume *Before the War* (1972).

Shirley Jackson   (1919–1965) was born in San Francisco and educated at Syracuse University. She married the literary critic Stanley Edgar Hyman; they lived in Bennington, Vermont, where her husband taught at Bennington College. Jackson is the heiress of Poe in her talent for tales and novels of Gothic horror. What distinguishes her from Poe is her ability to modernize Gothic conventions, locating in apparently "normal" contemporary events and situations a highly convincing realm of shock, violence, and terror. Her novels include *Life Among the Savages* (1945), *Hangsman* (1951), *The Bird's Nest* (1954), *The Haunting of Hill House* (1959), and *We Have Always Lived in the Castle* (1962). Jackson's short fiction is collected in *The Lottery* (1944) and *The Magic of Shirley Jackson* (1966).

Randall Jarrell (1914–1965) was born in Nashville, Tennessee, and received degrees in psychology and English from Vanderbilt University. During World War II, he served as an air control tower operator. Noted as much for his translations and criticism as for his poetry, Jarrell in 1956 was appointed a consultant in poetry at the Library of Congress. He also served as an editor for *The Nation, Partisan Review,* and *Yale Review.* Robert Lowell said that Jarrell was "the most heartbreaking . . . poet of his generation."

Ben Jonson (1572–1637), dramatist, poet, and literary critic, was one of the greatest writers of the English Renaissance; among his contemporaries, he was more influential than Shakespeare or Donne. Born a few months after his clergyman father's death, into impoverished circumstances, Jonson somehow managed to attend the most noted school of the period—Westminster—and to study language and literature under the famous schoolmaster William Camden. No "mouse of the scrolls," Jonson worked as a bricklayer, a soldier (he killed an enemy in single combat), and finally as an actor and playwright. Jonson's finest comedies are *Volpone* (1606) and *The Alchemist* (1610). As a poet, Jonson preferred the "plain," or "native," style. Throughout his life, he looked to the masterpieces of antiquity for inspiration. In 1616 he published his *Works,* which showed a flawless command of all the genres of the ancient world—epigram, lyric, satire, tragedy, and comedy.

June Jordan (b. 1936), poet, journalist, and novelist, was born in Harlem. She attended Barnard College and the University of Chicago and since 1975 has been a professor at the City University of New York. Committed to what she terms "the politics of survival and change," Jordan is a literary figure constantly giving poetry readings at schools and institutions around the nation, attempting to combat "the cult of negative realism" that she says affects the country's youth. Her poetry collections include *Some Changes* (1971), *New Days: Poems of Exile and Return* (1973), and *Selected Poems of June Jordan: Things That I Do in the Dark* (1977). Jordan's poems are short and structurally tight.

James Joyce (1882–1941) was born in Dublin, Ireland, a city and a country standing at the center of this literary universe. Living much of his adult life in self-imposed exile, Joyce produced a series of works in fiction, progressively more experimental in technique and vision, that established him as one of the great literary modernists of the twentieth century: *Dubliners* (1914), *A Portrait of the Artist as a Young Man* (1916), *Ulysses* (1922), and *Finnegan's Wake* (1939). Joyce was a brilliant, daring, and provocative stylist, willing to break new literary ground and to assault popular taste and conventions, notably in his treatment of human sexuality—a habit that resulted in the censorship of his masterpiece, *Ulysses,* for more than a decade.

Franz Kafka (1883–1924) was born in Prague, Czech Republic. He received a law degree from the German University in Prague in 1906 and worked subsequently in the Austrian civil service. Kafka devoted his life to writing, but at the time of his death, he directed his friend and literary executor, Max Brod, to burn all his manuscripts. Instead Brod saw Kafka's novels—*The Trial* (1925), *The Castle* (1926), and *Amerika* (1927)—and many of his short stories through production. Kafka's fiction projects a distinctive tone of the uncanny—of life and reality that tend to shift away from our ability to understand them. Typically, Kafka's protagonists embark on quests for meaning but are frustrated and ultimately alienated by the process. In many ways, Kafka's fiction captures the absurdities of modern life and the futility of seeking any lasting meaning in the twentieth century. His stories in English can be found in *The Great Wall of China* (1933), *A Franz Kafka Miscellany* (1940), *The Penal Colony* (1948), *Parables and Paradoxes* (1963), and *The Complete Stories* (1976).

Yasunari Kawabata (1899–1972), born in Osaka, became Japan's first recipient of the Nobel Prize for literature, in 1968. An orphan since infancy and a writer since high school, Kawabata was celebrated for his highly poetic short fiction and novels. His work includes *Snow Country* (1947), *Thousand Cranes* (1959), and *Palm-of-Hand Stories* (1988).

John Keats (1795–1821) was born at Finsbury, north of London, the eldest of five children. His father was killed by a fall from his horse in 1804, and when his mother remarried the same year, the children were sent to their maternal grandparents at Enfield and, later, Edmonton. In 1815, Keats went to London for medical training. He published his first poetry the following year and met many notable literary figures, including Shelley; by 1817, he had abandoned his plans for a medical career. Keats published his first collection, *Poems*, in 1817 and *Endymion* in 1818. In 1818, Keats contracted a severe sore throat during a walking tour in Scotland; he also met 18-year-old Fanny Brawne, with whom he began an affair. Keats wrote all of his major odes, including "To Autumn," in 1819; by the end of the year, his sore throat had recurred. Following hemorrhaging and an attack of blood spitting in the first half of 1820, Keats upon his doctor's advice sailed for Italy in September. *The Eve of St. Agnes and Other Poems* was published that year.

Maurice Kenny, twice nominated for the Pulitzer Prize in poetry, is the author of eighteen volumes of poetry, including *Between Two Rivers: Selected Poems, Tekonwatonti; Molly Brant, Poems of War,* and *Second Thought: A Compilation of Writings,* all published in 1992. A member of the Mohawk tribe, he is a 1984 American Book Award winner.

Jamaica Kincaid (b. 1949) was born Elaine Potter Richardson in Antigua, West Indies. Now a resident of Bennington, Vermont, she is the author of a series of fiction—*At the Bottom of the River* (1983), *Annie John* (1985), *Lucy* (1990)—exploring the impact of Caribbean culture on women's lives.

Galway Kinnell (b. 1927) was born in Providence, Rhode Island; served in the U.S. Navy during World War II; and graduated from Princeton. A poet interested in the spiritual aspects of the world, Kinnell received the Pulitzer Prize in 1983 for *Selected Poems.*

Maxine Kumin (b. 1925) was born in Philadelphia and received her B.A. and M.A. degrees from Radcliffe College. She began writing children's stories and light verse while pregnant with her third child in 1953. Since that time, she has published more than a dozen books of poetry, novels, and children's fiction. She won the Pulitzer Prize for poetry in 1973 for *Up Country* (1972). While noted for her close attention to objective details, Kumin has a talent for transforming her images into unique, sometimes grotesque statements about the processes of life.

David Herbert Lawrence (1885–1930), the son of a coalminer and a former schoolteacher, was born in Eastwood, Nottinghamshire, England. Raised in England's industrial midlands and exposed to fierce tensions within his family life, Lawrence used these twin realities to achieve his first literary recognition with *Sons and Lovers* (1913). Thereafter, his daring, inventive, and prolific literary production; his iconoclastic personal life; and his idiosyncratic search for pure alternatives to the crassness and dehumanization of English industrial and social life made Lawrence an international literary figure. Among his significant works are *The Rainbow* (1915), *Twilight in Italy* (1916), *Women in Love* (1920), *Studies in Classic American Literature* (1923), *Lady Chatterly's Lover* (1928), *The Complete Stories* (1961), and *Complete Poems* (1964).

David Leavitt (b. 1961) grew up in Palo Alto, California, where his father taught at Stanford University. He graduated from Yale University in 1983, and began publishing fiction in *The*

New Yorker, Harper's, and elsewhere. In 1989, his first collection of stories, *Family Dancing,* was nominated for the National Book Critics Circle Award. His second collection is *A Place I've Never Been* (1990).

Doris Lessing   (b. 1919) was born in Kermanshah, Iran, and moved at an early age to a large farm in Southern Rhodesia. Escaping the loneliness and isolation of African farm life, she moved to Salisbury at the age of 18, entering quickly into artistic and political life there, joining the Communist party, and marrying the first of two husbands. (Both marriages ended in divorce.) She left Africa for London in 1949, and in 1950 she published her first novel, *The Grass Is Singing.* Her fiction since then, increasingly experimental in mode, has focused on the violence and political disorders of modern life and especially on the plight of contemporary women. Lessing's novels include *A Proper Marriage* (1954), *Retreat to Innocence* (1956), *A Ripple from the Storm* (1958), *The Golden Notebook* (1962), *Briefing for a Descent into Hell* (1971), and the tetralogy *Canopus in Argos: Archives* (1981). Her stories, many of the best drawn from her African experience, have been collected in *This Was the Old Chief's Country* (1951), *The Habit of Loving* (1957), *A Man and Two Women* (1963), *African Stories* (1963), and *Stories* (1978).

Denise Levertov   (b. 1923) was born in Ilford, Essex, England, and served as a nurse during World War II. She came to the United States in 1948 after her marriage to an American, the writer Mitchell Goodman; she has been an American citizen since 1955. Levertov acknowledges, "Marrying an American and coming to live here while still young was very stimulating to me as a writer for it necessitated the finding of new rhythms in which to write, in accordance with new rhythms of life and speech." Influenced by William Carlos Williams and Wallace Stevens, and profiting from contact with other leading contemporary poets, notably Charles Olson and Robert Duncan, Levertov seeks to capture what she terms "authentic experience" in verse. She is the author of more than a dozen volumes of poetry, including *With Eyes at the Back of Our Heads* (1960), *To Stay Alive* (1971), and *Life in the Forest* (1979). Levertov's best poetry is, in the words of Kenneth Rexroth, "clear, sparse, immediate, and vibrant."

Philip Levine   (b. 1928) was born and educated in Detroit, Michigan. After graduating from Wayne State University and working a variety of jobs, he located in Fresno, California, where he taught until retirement in 1992. He has received numerous awards, including two Pulitzers. His last of several volumes of poetry is *What Work Is* (1991).

Shirley Geok-lin Lim   was born and reared in Malacca, Malaysia. She studied at Brandeis University and has taught in the United States on both the East and West coasts since 1973. Her first collection of poems, *Crossing the Peninsula* (1980), won the Commonwealth Poetry Prize, the first time ever won by a woman and an Asian. Two other volumes of poems have since followed.

Audre Lorde   (1934–1992) was born in New York City. Self-described as "black, lesbian, mother, and cancer survivor," she published more than twelve books of poetry and non-fiction before her illness overcame her. Typical of her poetry is the collection *New York Head Shop and Museum* (1975). For many years she taught English at Hunter College of the City University of New York.

Amy Lowell   (1874–1925) was born into an illustrious Boston family. As a child and young woman she often traveled to Europe, and at the age of 28, she began to write poetry. Her first volume of verse was fairly conventional, but in 1913 she met Ezra Pound and became part of the imagist movement, which she eventually dominated. She spent the last years of her life writing a biographical study of the poet John Keats. Lowell's version of imagism tempers the hard, objective, impersonal focus on a single image with a more subjective caring about the emotions of love and disappointment.

Robert Lowell   (1917–1977), described by John Berryman as "a talent whose ceiling is invisible," was one of the major innovators in contemporary American poetry. Born in Boston, the great-grandnephew of James Russell Lowell, he attended Harvard University and Kenyon College. Lowell converted to Catholicism in 1940, the same year that he married the first of his three wives, novelist Jean Stafford. (His other wives, Elizabeth Hardwick and Caroline Blackwood, were also writers.) He was a conscientious objector during World War II and served a prison term for violation of the Selective Service Act. Lowell's New England heritage, his personal experience, his Catholicism, his family, and his political and historical awareness were the forces that shaped his poetry. *Lord Weary's Castle* (1946) was awarded the Pulitzer Prize in 1947; *Life Studies* (1959), the National Book Award; *Invitations* (1961), the Bollinger Translation Prize. Each of these volumes measures Lowell's progress as an experimental poet: from formal, tightly rhymed lines; to free verse; to adaptations from poets in other languages.

Mairi MacInnes   was born in the north of England and educated in Yorkshire and at Oxford. She has worked as an advertising copywriter, editor, teacher, truck driver, and cook; and is married, with three children. She has lived in the United States for 25 years, as well as in Germany, Spain, and Mexico. MacInnes is author of *Admit One,* a novel; *Splinters,* verse; an anthology on censorship; a dictionary; and poems and articles.

Gabriel García Márquez   (b. 1928) was born in the small town of Aracataca, Colombia, near the Caribbean coastline. He was sent to school in Bogotá, and after his graduation in 1946 studied law. His first collection of stories was *Leaf Storm* (1965). His masterpiece is *One Hundred Years of Solitude* (1967); other novels include *The Autumn of the Patriarch* (1975) and *Love in the Time of Cholera* (1988). He received the Nobel Prize for literature in 1982.

Andrew Marvell   (1621–1678), the son of an Anglican clergyman, studied at Cambridge University, served as an assistant to Milton, and was a member of Parliament from 1659 until his death. He was famous in his own time as a political satirist in both prose and poetry. However, his greatest poems express diverse attitudes, ranging from seductive Cavalier lyrics, such as "To His Coy Mistress," to deeply contemplative poems.

Bobbie Ann Mason   (b. 1940) was born in Mayfield, Kentucky. Educated at the University of Kentucky and the University of Connecticut (Ph.D.), Mason has established herself as a major short story writer and novelist. She is the author of *Shiloh and Other Stories* (1962), *In Country* (1985), and *Love Life* (1990), among other works.

Annette M'Baye   (b. 1927), born in Sokhone, Senegal, has worked as a teacher in Senegal and in Paris. Active for many years in radio and journalism, she is currently with Radio Senegal and serves as editor-in-chief of *Awa: Journal of the Black Woman.*

Claude McKay   (1890–1948) was born in Jamaica, West Indies. Primarily a poet, McKay was a ranking figure of the Harlem Renaissance, which was one element of the entire post–World War I renaissance of American letters. After publishing two volumes of poetry in the West Indies, McKay came to the United States in 1912. A lukewarm supporter of the new Communist society in Russia, he was disillusioned after a visit there. Two additional volumes of verse, *Spring in New Hampshire and Other Poems* (1920) and *Harlem Shadows* (1922), preceded his popular novels, *Home to Harlem* (a best-seller, 1922), *Banjo* (1929), and *Banana Bottom* (1933).

Ifeanyi Menkiti   (b. 1940), was born in Onitsha, Nigeria, and educated at Columbia University and Pomona College. He has published in the United States and abroad in a variety of publications. His novel *Affirmations* was published in 1971, and a book of poetry, *The Jubilation of Falling Bodies,* in 1978. Menkiti's subtext in his poetry is often a recapitulation of African history. He is an English professor at Wellesley College.

Josephine Miles   (1911–1985) was born in Chicago, descended from a family which came to America aboard the *Mayflower*. Miles took an undergraduate degree at UCLA and a doctorate at the University of California, Berkeley; she joined the Berkeley faculty in 1940, becoming university professor emerita in 1978. A noted scholar, especially of the metaphysical poets,

Miles in her own finest verse is simple, factual, and incisive. Like William Carlos Williams, she seeks to render through the national vision the commonplace occurrences of American life. Much of her important work is collected in *Poems, 1930–1960*.

Czeslaw Milosz (b. 1911), Polish poet, essayist, novelist, and Nobel Prize in literature recipient, was born in Lithuania. He fought against the Nazis in World War II, then came to America. He teaches at the University of California at Berkeley. His translated poetry appears in *Bells in Winter* (1978), *Collected Poems* (1988), and other volumes.

John Milton (1608–1674) was born in London of an upper-middle-class father who was employed as a notary. He took a B.A. at Cambridge in 1629 and an M.A. in 1632. He began his literary career in earnest with the writing of *Comus* in 1634. By 1641 he was involved in the religious and political disputes that would result in the execution of King Charles I and the imposition of the Cromwell government, both of which he enthusiastically supported. His greatest work is *Paradise Lost* (1667), in which he sets out "to justify the ways of God to man." This rigorous Puritan composed the work while blind and poor.

Janice Mirikitani, as a child was interned or "camped" by the U.S. government, though she was an American, because she was of Japanese descent. She studied at UCLA and San Francisco State University. Mirikitani has been publishing for more than twenty years. Her most recent works are *Awake in the River* (1982) and *Shedding Silence* (1987).

Yukio Mishima (1925–1970), the pseudonym of Kimitare Hiraoka, was born in Tokyo, Japan. A prolific publisher of stories, novels, poems, plays, and essays, Mishima was also the leader of a right-wing political party, the Shield Society. His works include *Confessions of a Monk* (1949), *The Sailor Who Fell from Grace with the Sea* (1965), and *Death in Midsummer* (1966). Mishima committed suicide by traditional hara-kiri.

Marianne Moore (1887–1972) was born in St. Louis and educated at Bryn Mawr. After teaching at a government Indian school in Pennsylvania, she moved to New York and worked at a variety of literary jobs. Her poetry won a steady stream of awards and prizes. Though Moore's life was uncomplicated and uneventful, her poetry, while at times despairing, never expresses boredom. She lived most of her life like a "church mouse," sharing apartments with her mother. They had little money, and Moore indulged herself with two pleasures. She loved zoos and filled her poetry with exotic fauna. She was also a devotee of baseball, with its "miracles of dexterity." Moore's poetry often possesses a satiric sense of the absurd.

Patricia Mora (b. 1942) was born in El Paso, Texas, of Mexican-American ancestry. A teacher and college administrator, she has published the poetry collections *Chants* (1984) and *Borders* (1986).

Nancy Morejón (b. 1944), one of the most distinguished poets of Cuba, was born in Havana. After studies in French language and literature at the university there, she began to write poetry that, over the years, has resulted in a prodigious amount of work. She is known throughout Latin America and elsewhere.

Bharati Mukherjee (b. 1940) was born in Calcutta, India. She emigrated to Canada and then to the United States, where her short stories and novels have received critical acclaim. Her most recent novel, *Jasmine* (1991), is a brilliant portrayal of the absurdities of the immigrant experience.

Alice Munro (b. 1931) grew up on a farm in Ontario, Canada. She began publishing short stories while a student at the University of Western Ontario. Her award-winning books include *Dance of the Happy Shades* (1968), *Something I've Been Meaning to Tell You* (1974), and *The Progress of Love* (1987). Her fiction of rural life are reminiscent of the stories of Flannery O'Connor and Eudora Welty.

David Mura is a third-generation Japanese American. He is both a poet and an essayist who has published widely in *The Nation*, *The New Republic*, and *The American Poetry Review*. His poetry is collected in *After We Lost Our Way* (1989).

Rasipuraun Krishaswami Narayan   (b. 1906) was born in Madras, India, and today is India's most famous writer of fiction in English. He has published almost two dozen novels and short-story collections, including *Lawley Road* (1967) and *Under the Banyon Tree* (1985). Much of his fiction is set in the imaginary village of Malgusi.

Gloria Naylor   (b. 1950) was born in New York City. She worked as a missionary for Jehovah's Witnesses from 1968 to 1975, before studying at Brooklyn College and New York University. Her first novel, tracing the interconnected lives of African-American women— *The Women of Brewster Place,* 1982—won the American Book Award for best first novel. *Linden Hills* (1985) and *Mama Day* (1988) are two additional novels.

Carlos Nejar   (b. 1939) was born and lives in southern Brazil. Since his first book was published in 1960, he has received several major Brazilian literary awards and distinctions. His volumes of poetry include: *Sélesis* (1960), *Livro de Silbion* (1963), *Livro do Tempo* (1965), *O Campêador e o Vento* (1966), *Danações* (1969), *Ordenações* (1971), *Canga: Jesualdo Monte* (1971), and *Casa dos Arreios* (1974).

Pablo Neruda   (1904–1973), Chilean poet, essayist, short-story writer, and dramatist, is regarded as a major modern Latin American literary figure. He was honored with the Nobel Prize for Literature in 1971. His poetry, for which he is most famous, ranges from his early traditional verse to surrealism in the 1930s and to direct political poetry (Neruda was a Marxist) in later years. His principal works include *Residencia en la Tierra* (1937), *Selected Poems* (1970), and *New Poems* (1972).

Flannery O'Connor   (1925–1964) was born in Savannah, Georgia. She attended Georgia State College for Women, where her fondness for drawing cartoons and caricatures hinted at some of her future fiction methods. Awarded a fellowship to the Writers Workshop of the University of Iowa, she received an M.F.A. in creative writing in 1947. Following a brief stay in New York and Connecticut, O'Connor returned to Georgia, living on her mother's farm in Milledgeville. In 1950, she learned that she had the same disease—disseminated lupus— that had killed her father; the last fourteen years of her life involved a painful battle with that illness. O'Connor wrote two novels, *Wise Blood* (1951) and *The Violent Bear It Away* (1960). Her short stories, three of which won O. Henry first prizes, are collected in *A Good Man Is Hard to Find* (1955) and *Everything That Rises Must Converge* (1965).

Simon J. Ortiz   (b. 1941) is a member of the Acoma Pueblo in New Mexico. He received his master's degree from the University of Iowa. His book *From Sand Creek* won the Pushcart Prize in 1982.

Wilfred Owen   (1893–1918), a native of Liverpool, England, and a graduate of London University, was killed on the western front just seven days before the armistice that ended World War I. He never lived to see the publication of a projected collection of verse whose subject would be, he declared in a note, "war and the pity of war." His *Collected Poems* was published in 1920 by a friend and fellow poet, Siegfried Sassoon, whom Owen had met in a military hospital. Although he won the Military Cross, Owen once asked, "am I not myself a conscientious objector with a very seared conscience?" His most powerful poems, which were written during his thirteen months of service in France, convey Owen's opposition to war and to the false idealism spawned by it.

Grace Paley   (b. 1922) was born and raised in New York City. She taught creative writing at a number of colleges before settling in at Sarah Lawrence. Of her stories Philip Roth writes that she possesses "an understanding of loneliness, lust, selfishness, and fatigue that is splendidly comic and unladylike . . . and a style whose toughness and bumpiness arise not only out of exasperation with the language, but the daring and heart of a genuine writer of prose."

Paley's stories are collected in two volumes, *The Little Disturbances of Man* (1959) and *Enormous Changes at the Last Minute* (1975).

Nicanor Parra (b. 1914), a poet and a physicist, was born in Chile, where he was influenced by the folklore of his country. Later, he came to admire the Beat poets of the 1950s. His volumes include *Poems and Antipoems* and *Emergency Poems*.

Octavio Paz (b. 1914), Mexican poet, is concerned with the contradictions between eternal being and existence in time. He has a great lyrical gift. His masterpiece is the cyclical *Piedra de sol* (Sun Stone, 1958). His social involvement began with the Spanish Civil War. His *Laberinto de la soledad* (The Labyrinth of Solitude, 1962) examines the role of Mexico in history and the importance of its double ancestry and double heritage of civilization from the Spaniards and the Indians.

Katherine Philips (1631–1664) was the daughter of a wealthy London businessman. She was educated in Hackney, and at the age of 16 she married a prestigious man of 54. Though her husband was a strict Puritan and a supporter of Cromwell, she herself embraced more genial and open forms of religion and government. A noted translator and accomplished poet, she was widely admired throughout England as the "English Sappho" and was the founder of a literary salon that included Cowley and Vaughan. Her collected verses appeared in a pirated version in 1664.

Luigi Pirandello (1867–1936) was born in Girgenti, Italy, and was educated at Palermo, Rome, and the University of Bonn, in Germany. He was a professor of Italian literature at the Normal College for Women in Rome for approximately thirty years. Perhaps best known as a playwright, Pirandello did not begin writing for the stage until he was 46. Prior to that time, he gained a considerable reputation as a novelist and short story writer. His most famous play, *Six Characters in Search of an Author*, was published in 1921. His fiction works include *The Late Mattia Pascal* (1904) and *One, None and a Hundred Thousand* (1926). Pirandello's stories, numbering in the hundreds, have been published in English under the titles *Horse in the Moon* (1932), *Better Think Twice about It* (1935), and *The Medals and Other Stories* (1939). He was the 1934 recipient of the Nobel Prize in literature.

Sylvia Plath (1932–1963) was born in Boston, Massachusetts, and educated at Smith College and Cambridge University. At Cambridge she met and married the English poet Ted Hughes, with whom she had two children. Her style in the first and only volume of poetry that she published in her lifetime, *Colossus* (1960), is elegant and classically controlled, dominated by images and metaphors exploring the relationship between the poet and her world. Plath's later poetry, assembled notably in the posthumous volume *Ariel* (1965), reveals a preoccupation with psychic strain and death—painful warnings perhaps of her own suicide. This motif also dominates an autobiographical novel, *The Bell Jar* (1971).

Edgar Allan Poe (1809–1849), who invented the modern detective story and contributed to the early development of both short fiction and science fiction, is a unique figure in American literary history. Born Edgar Poe in Boston, he was orphaned in 1811 by the death of his mother; subsequently he was taken in by the John Allans of Richmond, Virginia, and rechristened Edgar Allan Poe. The scandal of his drinking and gambling at the University of Virginia ultimately alienated Poe from Allan and hastened his departure from college life. After a brief education at West Point, shortened again by his debauchery and gambling, Poe in 1836 married his cousin Virginia Clemm, who was then 13. Thereafter, Poe's life became a constant struggle to support his family; he wrote stories and poems and was an editor, journalist, and reviewer. His wife died in 1847. Two years later, Poe was found unconscious in a Baltimore street; he died on December 7, 1849. Poe's influence as a poet, critic, and short-story writer has been significant. His best stories—"The Fall of the House of Usher," "William Wilson," "The Purloined Letter," and "The Cask of Amontillado," among others—did much to establish that unity of effect that Poe espoused as the hallmark of modern short fiction. Poe, of course, specialized in what he termed in *Tales of the Grotesque and Arabesque* (1940) the "terrors of the soul."

Estela Portillo   (b. 1936), was born in El Paso, Texas. She has been a teacher, college administrator, theater and television director, novelist, and practicing playwright. Her works include *Day of the Swallows* (1972) and *For Juana and Other Plays* (1983).

Ezra Loomis Pound   (1885–1972) was born in Haily, Idaho, and studied at the University of Pennsylvania and Hamilton College. He moved to Europe and became a permanent resident of Italy in 1924. His first collection of poems, *A Lume Spento* (1908), was published when he was 23. Pound was drawn to medieval and Renaissance literature, translating several works from those periods. He was a forceful critic and commentator and one of the guiding lights behind the imagist movement in England and America, which involved T. E. Hulme, Hilda Doolittle, William Carlos Williams, Amy Lowell, and others. In addition to the *Cantos* (1925, 1930, 1940, 1948, and 1956), Pound produced many poetic and prose works. He was arrested and detained after World War II for collaborating with the Italian fascists.

Alexander (Sergeyevich) Pushkin   (1799–1837), a multifaceted writer, became known as the "Father of the Russian Language" because he preferred the language of the people to the French most of the Russian nobility spoke. He was the great-grandson of an African general serving under Peter the Great. Pushkin wrote *Eugene Onegin, Boris Godunov, Mozart and Salieri,* and several other works considered classics.

Ibn Quzman,   like Al-Tutili, lived out his life sometime during the Age of the Caliphs (A.D. 632–1050). While the latter indicates a world weariness in his work, Quzman displays a sharp sense of humor.

Rahel [Blaustein]   (1890–1931) emigrated to Palestine from Russia in the early 1900s. She helped to develop the *kibbutzim,* the communal agricultural settlements that flourished in modern Israel. After study in Europe, Rahel returned to Palestine and there died of tuberculosis.

Ishmael (Scott) Reed   (b. 1938), poet, novelist, filmmaker, producer, playwright, and editor, is probably foremost among those collecting and publishing multiethnic writings, largely through a variety of his own publications. Reed has published nine novels and six volumes of poems, and has been nominated for the Pulitzer Prize in both poetry and fiction.

Roberto Fernandez Retamar   (b. 1930) was born in Havana, Cuba. Retamar published his first collection, *Poetry Reunited,* in 1966; and while continuing to publish, was active in organizing the annual Cuban Premio Casa Awards that recognize writers in Spanish, Portuguese, English, and French.

Adrienne Rich   (b. 1929) was born in Baltimore, Maryland, and received her B.A. from Radcliffe College in 1951, the same year that her first book of poems, *A Change of World,* was published. She has taught at several colleges and universities, including Swarthmore, Columbia, City College of New York, and Brandeis. Rich has received numerous awards for her poetry, among them two Guggenheim Fellowships and the National Book Award for *Diving into the Wreck* (1973). Her other volumes include *The Diamond Cutters* (1955), *Snapshots of a Daughter-in-Law* (1963), *Necessities of Life* (1966), *Poems: Selected and New, 1950–1974* (1975), *Times Power* (1988), and *Atlas of the Difficult World* (1991). A determined feminist, Rich has written: "To be a woman at this time is to know extraordinary forms of anger, joy, impatience, love, and hope."

Edward Arlington Robinson   (1869–1935) was born in Head Tide and grew up in Gardiner, both barren Maine towns. He remembered his childhood as unhappy and was able to attend Harvard for only two years before the death of his father and the failure of the family business made further education impossible. He published his first volume of poetry at his own expense ($52) and soon after moved to New York to make writing his career. One of his later books of poetry came to the attention of President Theodore Roosevelt, who praised and aided Robinson. Robinson's popular reputation continued to grow during his lifetime, and today he has a firm place as a significant modern poet. Like Robert Frost, he usually writes about New England, but instead of describing a scene in nature, Robinson uses dramatic monologues to sketch New England character types: drunks, unemployed dreamers, unconventional misfits.

Theodore Roethke   (1908–1963) was born in Saginaw, Michigan, and received his education at the University of Michigan and Harvard. As a boy, Roethke worked and played around his parents' greenhouses, among the most famous in America and the center of some of his finest poems. His career began with *Open House* (1941). His second volume, *The Lost Son and Other Poems,* was published in 1948, shortly after he joined the faculty at the University of Washington. *The Waking: Poems 1933–1953* won the Pulitzer Prize in 1953, and *Words for the Wind: The Collected Verse of Theodore Roethke* (1958) won the National Book Award. In 1964 he received a second National Book Award for his posthumous volume, *The Far Field.*

Christina Rossetti   (1830–1894) was born in London, 12 years after her brother, Dante Gabriel Rossetti, the poet, painter, and founder of the Pre-Raphaelite group. Throughout her life, her two abiding loves were her brother, whom she idolized, and the Anglican Church, which she celebrated in many powerful, unself-conscious devotional poems. *Goblin Market* (1862), the first poem by any of the Pre-Raphaelites to become widely known, is an elaborate fantasy, full of images and events that suggest to many readers deep sexual repression.

Philip Roth   (b. 1933), born in Newark, New Jersey, has been called the "master of the Jewish novel of manners." His first collection of fiction, *Goodbye, Columbus* (1955), established Roth's place in American fiction. Other books include *Portnoy's Complaint* (1969), *Zukerman Bound* (1985), and the autobiographical *Patrimony* (1991).

Muriel Rukeyser   (1913–1980) was born in New York City and educated at Vassar College and Columbia University. Her *Theory of Flight* won the Yale Series of Younger Poets award in 1935. The last of twelve volumes, *Collected Poems,* was published in 1978. In both her poetry and her daily life she sought to transform the world in which she lived from one filled with violence and oppression to one in which each individual could begin to understand his or her own (potential) abilities. Much of her poetry is expressly political. Rukeyser demonstrated that poetry is the ground on which the personal and political come together to change the way we think about the world.

Luis Omar Salinas   (b. 1937) was born in Robstown, Texas, and was raised and educated in California. Among his volumes are *Crazy Gypsy, Afternoon of the Unreal,* and *Darkness Under the Elms/Walking Behind the Spanish.*

Sonia Sanchez   (b. 1934) has developed one of the most complex and yet most direct voices to come out of the black cultural revolution of the late 1960s (the Black Arts Movement). After growing up in Atlanta, Georgia, and then going on to receive a B.A. from NYU in 1955, Sanchez found that she could not reconcile the difference between her childhood upbringing as a black girl in the South and her education as an intellectual in the North. Thus she began to question (and challenge) the systems that allow such distinctions and disparities to exist. A committed activist, Sonia Sanchez uses her own voice and the voice of the American black community—with its particular idioms and diction—to evoke the personal significance of a large political situation.

Carl Sandburg   (1879–1967) was born in Illinois, the son of immigrant parents. He never finished college and spent much of his early adulthood traveling the country, supporting himself by whatever jobs came his way. At one point he hoped to attend West Point, but he failed the mathematical part of the entrance exam. His first volume of poetry, *Chicago Poems* (1914), was unorthodox in form and effusively popularistic in mood. His later volumes drew upon American folklore and insisted upon the wisdom and vocabulary of common people. He lived to be 89, and in the last decades of his life, having the air of a sage about him, he enjoyed great popular esteem. He wrote many poems in praise of Chicago.

Bert Schierbeek (b. 1918) was born in Glanerburg, The Netherlands and fought with the Dutch Resistance during the German Occupation (1940–1945). He was the lone survivor of his unit. He published a novel in 1945, which was followed by an autobiographical trilogy of poetry spanning the years 1950 through 1955. Several other works followed, including *Forment-era* (1989).

Léopold Sédar Senghor (b. 1906), poet and former President of Senegal, was born at Joal-la-Portugaise, a coastal town about sixty-five miles south of Dakar. In 1928, he left the Lycée of Dakar to study in Paris, receiving a degree from the University of Paris in 1933. In the vanguard of the Negritude movement in the arts, he published his first volume of poetry, *Chants d'Ombre* in 1945 followed by *Chants pour Naett* in 1949. A noted statesman and diplomat, Senghor became President of Senegal in 1960.

Anne Sexton (1928–1974) was born in Newton, Massachusetts. She was an indifferent student but a writer of poetry at an early age. Sexton attended Garland Junior College in Boston before eloping in the summer of 1948 with Alfred "Kayo" Sexton II. In 1953, she was hospitalized for severe depression and a suicide attempt; she subsequently began writing poetry again, on the advice of her psychiatrist. Sexton became a student of W. D. Snodgrass and Robert Lowell, and through Lowell's 1958–59 poetry seminar at Boston University she entered into a close friendship with Sylvia Plath. *To Bedlam and Part Way Back* (1960), Sexton's first poetry collection, is a confessional account of the author's confrontations with insanity and of her personal relationships with her family. In the spring of 1961, the Radcliffe Institute for Independent Study named Sexton and her friend Maxine Kumin their first scholars in poetry. Sexton's subsequent volumes, notably *All My Pretty Ones* (1962), the Pulitzer Prize-winning *Live or Die* (1966), and *Transformations* (1971), continue to trace her psychological conflicts and torments. On October 4, 1974, she had lunch with Kumin and then went home and committed suicide.

William Shakespeare (1564–1616) was born at Stratford-on-Avon, the eldest son of a prosperous English businessman who held many civic offices and of a gentlewoman whose own family, the Ardens, were relatively wealthy landowners. By 1600, at the age of 34, he was acclaimed by many as the foremost playwright of his age, the author of fourteen plays and probably the bulk of his famous sonnets (which were not published until 1609). His early plays for the group included the histories *Richard II* (1595) and *I Henry IV* (1597); the comedies *A Midsummer Night's Dream* (1595), *The Merchant of Venice* (1596), and *Much Ado about Nothing* (1598); and the tragedies *Romeo and Juliet* (1596) and *Julius Caesar* (1599). In the summer of 1599, the Lord Chamberlain's Men opened its own playhouse across the Thames in Southwick, naming it the Globe, with Shakespeare owning shares in both the company and the playhouse. *Julius Caesar* was the first play produced at the new playhouse. After 1600, Shakespeare devoted less time to acting and more to the writing of his greatest tragedies, *Hamlet* (1602), *Othello* (1604), *King Lear* (1606), *Macbeth* (1606), and *Antony and Cleopatra* (1606); and also to such "dark" comedies as *The Tempest* (1611), his last independently written play. Shakespeare's personal fortune also increased during this period. He had inherited Stratford property upon the death of his father in 1601, and he made other profitable transactions there in 1602 and 1605. In London, he continued to reside in rented lodgings. After 1608, following a year of personal upheaval that included the deaths of an illegitimate son and a younger brother, Shakespeare spent more time in Stratford. He died there on April 23, 1616, and was buried in the parish church.

Percy Bysshe Shelley (1792–1822), influenced by the credos of the Enlightenment, or the Age of Reason, revolted against his conservative upbringing. At Oxford, he wrote a pamphlet in favor of atheism and was dismissed. He first married at 19, but that marriage ended in disaster. Shelley married Mary Godwin in 1816. He was a student of Greek and spent much time in Italy, where he drowned. Shelley believed that a Platonic civilization was possible, but that men needed pushing in that direction. His works, often abstract and allegorical, were lyrical and elegiac and sometimes, as with "Ozymandias," were warnings couched in irony. Among his best-known works are "Hymn to Intellectual Beauty" (1816); "Ode to the West Wind" (1819); "To a Skylark" (1819); and *Prometheus Unbound* (1819).

Sir Philip Sidney (1554–1586) was born in Penhurst, Kent, of an aristocratic family. He attended both Oxford and Cambridge, but took no degree. He traveled to France with the English ambassador in 1572 and there witnessed the St. Bartholomew's Day Massacre, an event which turned him and his countrymen firmly toward Protestantism. Sidney became the epitome of the Elizabethan gentleman—an accomplished poet, scholar, soldier, and diplomat. Perhaps his most famous work is his *Defense of Poetry* (1595), which was published after his death from wounds received in battle. His place in English poetry has never wavered. His prose, criticism, and poetry are all considered of the highest order. Sidney's greatest achievement in poetry is the sonnet sequence *Astrophel and Stella* (1582).

Leslie Marmon Silko (b. 1948) was born in Albuquerque, New Mexico, of mixed ancestry— Laguna Pueblo, Mexican, and white. She grew up on the Laguna Pueblo reservation, where she lives today with her husband and two children. A widely published poet, novelist, and short story writer, Silko is preoccupied in her writing with the act, process, and ritual of storytelling as a way of celebrating tradition, preserving memory, and sustaining cultural continuity. "I grew up with storytelling," she writes. "My earliest memories are of my grandmother telling me stories while she watered the morning glories in her yard. Her stories were about incidents from long ago, incidents which occurred before she was born but which she told as certainly as if she had been there."

Isaac Bashevis Singer (1904–1991) was born in Radzymin, Poland, and came to the United States in 1935. He became a citizen in 1943. Singer was a journalist with the *Jewish Daily Forward*, writing first in Hebrew. Later, he said, "Hebrew was not a living language then," and he also wrote in Yiddish. A former rabbinical student, Singer injects elements of religion into much of his work. Since 1950 his work has been translated into English, in which language he gained great recognition, winning the 1979 Nobel Prize in literature. Of Singer, critic Thomas Lask wrote: "We are aware of a natural story teller who moves at his own pace, confident of his powers, fertile in invention, and able to hold the reader as long as he wishes. . . ." Singer published well over one hundred stories in collections that include *Gimpel the Fool* (1957), *The Seance* (1968), *The Spinoza of Market Street* (1961), and *The Collected Stories* (1982). His novels include *The Family Moskat* (1955) and *The Slave* (1962).

Mohan Singh (b. 1905), said to be "one of the greatest poets in the [Hindi] language," was an editor as well as a poet. Singh was strongly committed to improving life for the poor and oppressed in India.

Stevie Smith (1902–1971) was born Florence Margaret Smith in Yorkshire, England. Her nickname, "Stevie," referring to her shortness, was taken from the name of a popular jockey at the time. Until 1953, Smith worked in a London publisher's office, after which she devoted her time to writing and to broadcasts on the BBC. Known for her personal wit and charm as as well as for the wit and charm of her verse, poet and novelist Smith brought to her poetry a sense of the comic that pierced through the surface of reality. Often appearing at first irrelevant or childish because they rely on fairy tales, nursery rhymes, or childlike visions, Smith's self-illustrated poems assume a naive pose in order to probe the "agonies" of existence.

W. D. Snodgrass (b. 1926), a Pulitzer Prize-winning poet, evolved a highly personal, confessional style that allows him to express what he sees as the poet's truth of existence—that is, "what he really thinks." Snodgrass uses his personal visions to clarify the particulars of experience, which he prefers to preserve as individual moments rather than to generalize into statements of transcendental belief. Born in Williamsburg, Pennsylvania, and raised in Beavers Falls, Snodgrass attended the University of Iowa's writers' workshops after having served in the Navy during World War II. While at Iowa, he studied with poet Robert Lowell, and together they developed a new, autobiographical, introspective mode for modern poetry.

Gary Snyder (b. 1930) was born in San Francisco. In discussing Snyder's use of images culled from Buddhism, Native American folklore, experience of the wilderness, and his own social interactions, fellow poet Thom Gunn has said: "His [Snyder's] valuing of the primitive tribe and its relations to the earth is not a sentiment but a call for action. . . ." Snyder's poetry is rooted in his own widely varied experience. (Snyder has a B.A. in anthropology from Reed College; he has worked as a logger and on a Forest Service trail crew; he studied oriental languages at the University of California at Berkeley; from 1956 to 1964, he studied Buddhism in Japan; he worked on an oil tanker in the Pacific and Indian oceans before returning to Berkeley to teach.) Snyder's poems weave a fragmented web of keen observation and profound insight into a rich tapestry on which history and nature appear as two complementary pieces of the myth of humanity. This relationship underlies Snyder's poetic project because it locates poetry at the level of experience and action—at the level of change. In a 1966 *Village Voice* interview, Snyder said, "I think there's a real revolution going on somewhere below or outside the level of formal politics."

Edith Sodergran (1892–1923), a major modernist force in the literature of Sweden and Finland, was born to a wealthy Finnish-Swedish couple living in St. Petersburg, Russia. Her translated poetry, both confessional and feminist in tone, appears in *Love and Solitude* (1981) and *Complete Poems* (1984).

Cathy Song (b. 1955) was born in Hawaii and attended the University of Hawaii, Wellesley College, and Boston University. Her first collection of poetry, *Picture Bride* (1982), won the Yale Younger Poets Award. A second book of verse is *Frameless Windows, Squares of Light* (1988).

Sophocles (496?–406 B.C.) was born near Athens. His father was an arms manufacturer, and the family had status in the Athenian order of society. At 15, Sophocles was chosen to lead the paean sung by a chorus of boys in celebration of the victory over the Persians at the battle of Salamis (480 B.C.). He is believed to have been the author of about 150 plays, some of which were produced after his death, *Oedipus Rex, Electra,* and *Antigone* are his best-known works. Sophocles advanced Greek tragedy by extending dramatic action, by using three instead of two actors (later, he added a fourth), and by subordinating the chorus to the action on stage. Sophocles also improved costuming and set decorations. In his plays the action depends on motives that develop from the characters; this is true for both male and female figures.

Gary Soto (b. 1952) won the American Book Award for his reminiscence *Living Up the Street* (1985). Born of Mexican-American ancestry, Soto is a noted poet, the author of *Small Faces* (1985) and other volumes.

Wole Soyinka (b. 1934), born in Nigeria, is a noted essayist, musician, playwright, and poet. His award-winning plays have been produced throughout Africa, Europe, and America. His publications include *Five Plays* (1964) and *Ake: The Years of Childhood* (1981). He won the Nobel Prize in 1987.

Stephen Spender (1909–1990) was born in London and educated at Oxford University. As novelist, playwright, essayist, and poet, he became one of the most outspoken and concerned literary figures of our age. For most of his life he was a professor at a variety of American and

British universities, and he produced a vast body of work that attests to his concern for oppressed individuals within contemporary society. Beginning with overtly political works on the Spanish Civil War in the 1930s, Spender gradually moved toward issues of more general social concern.

Wallace Stevens (1879–1955), a major American poet, was born in Redding, Pennsylvania. He attended Harvard University and received a degree from New York University Law School. Stevens was admitted to the New York bar in 1904, and from 1916 he was associated with Hartford Accident and Indemnity Company, becoming a vice president in 1934. Few of his associates in the insurance world knew of Stevens' private penchant for jotting down poems, but he liked the blend of business and private vocations. "It gives a man character as a poet," he once observed, "to have daily contact with a job." Stevens' first book of verse, *Harmonium*, did not appear until 1923. Later volumes, including *Ideas of Order* (1935), *The Man with the Blue Guitar* (1937), *Transport to Summer* (1947), *Collected Poems* (1954), and *Opus Posthumous* (1957), secured his reputation as a "virtuoso." A poet in and of the world, singing the American landscape more persistently than any poet since Whitman, Stevens was a bold and elegant experimenter in poetics.

May Swenson (1913–1989) was born in Logan, Utah, and educated at Utah State University. She lived primarily in the New York metropolitan area after 1949, serving periodically as poet-in-residence at Purdue, the University of California at Riverside, and elsewhere. An award-winning poet and critic, Swenson was an experimental artist, seeking in her own words "to get through the curtain of things as they appear, to things as they are, and then into the larger, wilder space of things as they are becoming." She explored mysteries through riddles, and celebrated especially the sounds and colors of natural and urban landscapes, concentrating on the "thingness" (as the poet Chad Walsh observed) of the world. Her collections include *Another Animal* (1954), *A Cage of Spines* (1958), *To Mix with Time* (1963), *Half Sun Asleep* (1967), *New and Selected Things Taking Place* (1978), and *In Other Words* (1987).

Jonathan Swift (1667–1745), born in Dublin, was educated in Ireland before going to England, where he became deeply involved in politics. He also became a master of satiric prose and poetry and an important political writer for the moderate Tories. Returning to Ireland, Swift was appointed dean of St. Patrick's Cathedral in 1713 and, except for brief trips, remained in Ireland for the rest of his life. His *Tale of a Tub* and *Battle of the Books* (1704); *A Modest Proposal* (1729); and most famous work, *Gulliver's Travels* (1726), all combined to create for Swift the image of a nasty misanthrope—though he was not. In fact, he joked about the label. Swift was a true political animal, unable to refrain from the battles. Sometimes he used pen names (although most people knew they were his): "Isaac Bickerstaff," "M. B. Drapier," "Cadenus," "Presto," and "Lemuel Gulliver." Swift knew—and sometimes ridiculed—many other writers, among them Addison and Steele, Pope, Parnell, Congreve, and Gay. Swift was declared insane in 1742.

Amy Tan (b. 1952), the author of two highly acclaimed novels, *The Joy Luck Club* (1989) and *The Kitchen God's Wife* (1991), both tracing the lives of Chinese Americans, is a former business and freelance writer who was born and raised near San Francisco, California.

Sara Teasdale (1884–1933) was born in St. Louis to wealthy, middle-aged parents. She started writing poetry in high school, and her first volume of poetry was published at her parents' expense in 1907. Over the next twenty years, she became one of the most widely read poets in America, best known for her love sonnets. She won the Pulitzer Prize for poetry in 1917 for *Love Songs*.

Hernando Téllez (1908–1966) was born in Bogotá, Colombia, where for much of his life he was involved in the literary and journalistic life of the city. At 17 he joined the staff of the weekly *Mundo al Día*. Two years later, German Arciniegas started a magazine, *Universidad*, with

Téllez's help. The formation of this publication helped to draw the intellectuals of his generation into what they called *Los Nuevos* ("the New Ones"). The group succeeded the writers and journalists of an earlier generation of Colombian—more precisely, Bogotán—fiction, nonfiction, and poetry writers. Arciniegas and Alberto Lleras Camargo, who headed *El Tiempo*, which Téllez joined in 1929, were leading figures in the New Ones. Active in national politics, Téllez in 1937 was designated the consul in Marseille, France. He returned to Colombia shortly before World War II and took up the post of subdirector of another publication, *El Liberal.* He was a senator from 1944 to 1947, and in 1959 he was appointed ambassador to UNESCO in Paris. "The prose of Téllez," wrote Richard Latcham, editor of *Stories of the Hispanic American,* "is distinguished for the qualities of spiritual contention and noble power exactly synthesized and shaded." In addition to his editorial and diplomatic activities, Téllez published *Inquietud del mundo* (*The Restless of the World;* 1943); *Bagatelas* (1944); *Diario* (1946); *Luces en el bosque* (*Lights in the Woods;* 1946); *Cenizas para el viento y otras historias* (*Ashes to the Wind and Other Stories;* 1950), *Literatura* (*Literature;* 1951); *Literatura y sociedad* (1956); and *Confesión de parte* (*In the Name of Confession;* 1966).

Dylan Thomas (1914–1953) was born and received a grammar school education in Swansea, Wales. Deciding against attending a university, Thomas instead adopted the role of the bohemian poet, a role based in part on the style of Oscar Wilde. His first book of poems, *Eighteen Poems* (1934), won him the enthusiastic acclaim of London literati, especially that of the equally flamboyant Edith Sitwell. Like Sitwell, Thomas felt the need for poetry to act, to "narrate," and as a result his verbal virtuosity often produces images of darkly suggestive obscurity. This style was seen in contrast to the arid landscapes and alienated metaphors of the early modernists, of whom T. S. Eliot is the best example, and was claimed by some to be a turn toward a new romantic poetry. When this turn failed to materialize, however, Thomas remained a lone voice for unity amidst the modernists' roar of "fragmentation!" Emphasizing themes of unity within diversity, of wholeness encompassing contradiction, Thomas's poems create intricately woven webs of diverse images and metaphors.

Joyce Carol Thomas (b. 1938), born in Ponca City, Oklahoma, has been a French, Spanish, and writing teacher. A Djerassi Fellow, Thomas was also an American Book Award winner in 1982. Her writings include four volumes of poetry and five novels, plus a 1981 collection of poetry, *Black Child.*

James Thurber (1894–1961) was born in Columbus, Ohio, into a family that he claimed was "hooked on" the absurd. Some of Thurber's most humorous stories and essays retell incidents during his boyhood; it was also as a boy that an accident impaired his vision in one eye. Eventually, he would lose vision in the other and become completely blind. Before this happened, however, he studied at Ohio State University and later became a reporter and illustrator in Columbus, New York, and Paris. He was on the staff of *The New Yorker,* but left as quickly as was graciously possible. Thurber was keenly attuned to the fears and fantasies of people. "The Secret Life of Walter Mitty" was only one of many stories that explored the theme of fear and fantasy, weakness and power. Thurber's books started to come in 1929 when he wrote *Is Sex Necessary?* (with E. B. White). There followed, among others, *My Life and Hard Times* (1933), *The Middle-Aged Man on the Flying Trapeze* (1935), *The Male Animal* (a play, with Elliot Nugent, 1940), *Alarms and Diversions* (1957), and a last book of essays, *Lanterns and Lances* (1961).

Mohamud S. Togane (b. 1940), born in Somalia, came to the United States, where he studied in California, Virginia, Ohio, and then in Canada. He has been publishing since 1969. His poetry is collected in *The Bottle and the Bushman* (1989).

Melvin B. Tolson (1900–1966) was born in Moberly, Missouri. Surveying his life in an interview entitled "A Poet's Odyssey," he said: "Tennyson's protagonist says in "Ulysses," 'Much I have seen and know!' And again, 'I am a part of all that I have met. . . .'—as shoeshine boy, stevedore, soldier, janitor, packinghouse worker, cook on a railroad, waiter in a beachfront hotel, boxer, actor, football coach, director of drama, lecturer for the NAACP, organizer of sharecroppers' unions, teacher, father of Ph.D.s, poet laureate of a foreign country, painter, newspaper columnist, four-time mayor of a town, facer of mobs, I have made my way in the world since I was twelve years old." Tolson's wide experience as a black man in American culture led him to write poetry that challenged oppression wherever it occurred.

Fadwa Tuquan   (b. 1917), born into a family of Arab intellectuals and poets, was raised in the historic town of Nablus, a part of territory now held by Israel. Her poetry laments the loss of the region in 1967.

John Updike   (b. 1932) is a foremost American novelist, short story writer, poet, and critic. He was born in Pennsylvania and educated at Harvard University. His novels include *Rabbit Run* (1960) and three subsequent Rabbit sagas; his short fiction is collected in *Pigeon Feathers* (1962) and other volumes; his poetry is in such volumes as *The Carpentered Hen* (1965).

Luisa Valenzuela   (b. 1938), an Argentinean novelist and short story writer, was born in Buenos Aires; her mother was a well-known writer. She has lived in France and the United States. Valenzuela has published *Strange Things Happen Here* (1979), *The Lizard's Tale* (1983), and *Open Door* (1988). Her early fiction is aligned with the tradition of "magical realism," associated with Jorge Luis Borges and Gabriel García Márquez.

Cesar Vallejo   (1892–1938) was born in Peru and is considered one of the great poets of this century. Following the publication of his first book of poetry, *The Black Heralds*, (1923), Vallejo left for Paris, never returning to his homeland. Vallejo's verse shows a strong social consciousness and a mystical vision of humanity.

Gerald Vizenor   (b. 1934), a Native American novelist, folklorist, and poet, was born in Minneapolis, Minnesota. He teaches at the University of California at Berkeley. His books include *Poems: Born in the Wind, The Heirs of Columbus,* and *Dead Voices.*

David Wagoner   (b. 1926), raised in an Indiana suburb of Chicago and educated at both Penn State and Indiana Universities, brings to his present home in the Pacific Northwest—where he is currently a professor of English at the University of Washington at Seattle—a knowledge and experience of the diversity of the American people. Focusing his poetry on themes of human survival, of the violation of the natural world, and of the mythic reality of Native Americans, Wagoner expresses a deep concern for the problems and possibilities of the continued survival of the human race. A novelist as well as a prolific poet, he presents in his work a thoughtful and diverse perspective on modern American life.

Diane Wakoski   (b. 1937) was born in Whittier, California, and was educated at the University of California at Berkeley. A noted poet, she is the author of numerous collections, including *Inside the Blood Factory* (1968), *Motorcycle Betrayal Poems* (1971), and *Rings of Saturn* (1986).

Derek Walcott   (b. 1930) was born on the island of St. Lucia, in the Caribbean, and graduated from the University of the West Indies, in Jamaica. Although he has lived and traveled in Europe and makes the United States his home, much of his poetry is about the Caribbean. Commenting on Walcott's first volume of poetry, *Selected Poems* (1964), Robert Graves said that Walcott "handles English with a closer understanding of its inner magic than most (if not any) of his English-born contemporaries." Also the author of three plays, Walcott's poetry collections since 1964 have included *The Gulf* (1970), *Another Life* (1973), *Sea Grapes* (1976), *The Star-Apple Kingdom* (1979), and *The Fortunate Traveller* (1982). He received the Nobel Prize for literature in 1992.

Alice Walker (b. 1944) was born in Eatonton, Georgia, the eighth and youngest child of African-American sharecroppers. She attended Spelman College and Sarah Lawrence College, where she began writing poetry. Her best-known novel is *The Color Purple* (1982), which won the American Book Award and the Pulitzer Prize. Her short story collections include *In Love and Trouble* (1973) and *You Can't Keep a Good Woman Down* (1981).

Margaret Walker (b. 1915), poet and novelist, was born in Birmingham, Alabama, and educated at Northwestern University and the University of Iowa. She won the Yale Award for Younger Poets in 1942 for her volume *For My People*. Walker was then teaching at Livingston College, in North Carolina, and since that time she has held several academic posts, most recently at Jackson State University, in Mississippi. In the introduction to her prizewinning novel *Jubilee* (1966), Walker observes that hers was a "talking" family, given to anecdotes, folklore, and discussions of history, politics, and race.

Chad Walsh (b. 1914), born in South Boston, Virginia, studied at the University of Virginia and the University of Michigan. He was ordained an Episcopal priest in 1949. Walsh has taught at a number of colleges in the United States and abroad, most notably in Finland. Many of his nonfiction works have been about the interaction of modern man and modern religion. Between these he has published, among other volumes of poetry, *The Unknowing* (1964), and *Garlands for Christmas* (1965). Walsh's work is marked by a humanitarian concern and a clear vision of the problems of contemporary life. Some of his works are in traditional poetic structures into which he places contemporary themes.

James Welch (b. 1940), born in Browning, Montana, and a Native American poet, brings to his verse a knowledge of the contemporary experience of Native American life that is rarely found in American poetry. Using the images and associations that derive from his cultural knowledge, Welch focuses on providing a continuity with the physical and mythic aspects of the natural world in order to decry the way in which these aspects have been devaluated within modern society.

Eudora Welty (b. 1909) was born in Jackson, Mississippi, where she began an education that was completed at the University of Wisconsin and at Columbia University. During the Depression, she worked for the WPA as a publicist; later she became an advertising copywriter. She also wrote for radio. Welty, who has a keen eye for description, once thought about becoming a painter. Instead, she became a writer, her work first appearing in 1936; a collection of stories, *A Curtain of Green*, was published five years later. Among her novels are *Delta Wedding* (1946), *The Ponder Heart* (1954), and *The Optimist's Daughter* (1972). Though sometimes considered a Southern regionalist in the tradition of Robert Penn Warren, Faulkner, and John Crowe Ransom, Welty's main interest is in character—what the character thinks, feels, and sees; how the character adapts to the world in which she or he lives. In this sense she is closer to the Chekhovian tradition than to the American realist writers.

Phillis Wheatley (1753–1784) did not remember what part of Africa she had been taken from, nor could she recall much about her family. She arrived at the age of 7 in Boston, Massachusetts, in 1761, where John Wheatley, a minor tradesman, bought her at auction. The young girl was educated in English and Latin by her new family, and she later traveled to England with them. In 1773, her *Poems on Various Subjects, Religious and Moral* was published in England. Her fame had increased so much by 1776 that she was granted an audience by George Washington. She married John Peters in 1778; her last years were filled with poverty and illness. Wheatley's poetry is in the neoclassic tradition and typically personal in its glorification of freedom.

Walt Whitman (1819–1892) was born on Long Island, the Paumanok of his poems. He attended public schools in Brooklyn and started his career by working in rural schools, setting type, and serving as a writer for several newspapers. Whitman was editor of the influential

Brooklyn Eagle from 1846 to 1848; he used the newspaper's editorial page to espouse abolitionism, opposition to banks and to capital punishment, and endorsement of free soil—positions that probably hastened his dismissal. Subsequently Whitman spent three months on a Louisiana paper, *The Crescent,* and the impact of the South is reflected in "I Saw in Louisiana a Live-Oak Growing" and other poems. After his return to New York, he worked as a carpenter for his father, freelanced, and then served as editor of *The Brooklyn Times* from 1857 to 1859; once again he was discharged for his outspoken editorial opinions on sex, abortion, prostitution, and slavery. During the Civil War, Whitman served as a volunteer nurse for the Army in Washington, and later was given a clerkship in the Indian Department, but was fired by the secretary of the interior, who labeled *Leaves of Grass* an "indecent book." Whitman published the first edition of *Leaves of Grass,* which contained twelve untitled poems, in 1855. At the outset of this seminal book, Whitman declared his subject: "One's-self I sing, a simple separate person/Yet utter the word Democratic, the word En Masse." Frank in its subject matter and technically experimental, *Leaves of Grass* is a mystical celebration of the body and the soul, the individual and the collective, all woven into a process of regeneration that frees humanity from the absoluteness of death. From the embryonic first edition with its magnificent centerpiece, "Song of Myself," Whitman would evolve a symbolic autobiography in later, expanded editions of *Leaves of Grass.* Stricken by paralysis, Whitman spent the last nineteen years of his life in Camden, New Jersey, generally enjoying his role as "the good gray poet."

John Alfred Williams (b. 1925) was born in Mississippi and raised in Syracuse, N.Y., where, after World War II, he studied at Syracuse University. He is the author of *Sissie* (1963), *The Man Who Cried I Am* (1967), *!Click Song* (1982), and other novels and short fiction. He is a professor of English and Journalism at Rutgers University.

William Carlos Williams (1883–1963), who like his friend Wallace Stevens was both a professional man and a poet, was born in Rutherford, New Jersey. He received his medical degree from the University of Pennsylvania in 1906, and from 1910 until his retirement in 1951 he was a successful pediatrician in Rutherford. Influenced by Ezra Pound when the two were at the University of Pennsylvania, and himself a major influence on such later poets as Robert Lowell and Theodore Roethke, Williams was an advocate of American images, materials, and strategies in poetry. His books include *The Collected Later Poems* (1950), *The Collected Earlier Poems* (1951), and a magnificent five-volume philosophical poem about the American experience, *Paterson* (1946–1958). Williams was a poet of particulars, seeking to lift moments of reality from the actual world and transcribe them economically in poetry. "No ideas but in things," he declared. Taking his "things" from the native surroundings of the New Jersey landscape, Williams is unrivaled in the clarity of his images depicting parts of the world.

August Wilson (b. 1945) grew up in an impoverished family in Pittsburgh. He dropped out of school, and began writing poetry and drama. Among his celebrated plays concerned with the African-American experience are *Ma Rainey's Black Bottom* (1984), *Fences* (1987), and *Joe Turner's Come and Gone* (1988).

Dorothy Wordsworth (1771–1855), English prose writer and occasional poet, was the sister of poet William Wordsworth. Her *Journals* (1800–1803) throw light on the English Romantic Movement.

James Wright (b. 1927) was born in Martin's Ferry, Ohio, and received his B.A. from Kenyon College. After serving in the U.S. Army during the occupation of Japan, he returned to complete a Ph.D. at the University of Washington and subsequently to take up teaching at Hunter College. Speaking of his own poetry, Wright has said, "I try and say how I love my country and how I despise the way it is treated. I try to speak of the beauty and again of the ugliness in lives of the poor and neglected." Seeing poetry as a form of social concern, Wright believes that "poetry [should] say something humanly important instead of just showing off the language." As a result, Wright's poetry often expresses a directness and engagement with the external world that is reminiscent of the lucid complexities of Robert Frost, whom Wright acknowledges as one of his models.

Judith Wright   (b. 1915) was born near Armidale, New South Wales, Australia. Her parents were settlers from England and lovers of the nineteenth-century literary classics. Wright went to the University of Sydney, but found Ezra Pounds's *Guide to Kulchur* her best teacher. She spent a year in England and on the Continent, returning to Australia in 1942, during World War II. She began writing poetry and two years later moved to Brisbane to help produce the magazine *Meanjin*. Her first poems were published in 1946 in the *Sydney Bulletin,* and that same year her first collection appeared, *The Moving Image.* Between writing criticism and biography and children's books, Wright has published, among other volumes, *Woman to Man* (1949), *The Gateway* (1953), and *Collected Poems 1942–1970* (1972). *The Times Literary Supplement* said that Wright "is unquestionably the most accomplished woman poet in Australia today"—a statement laced with sexism and limitation.

Richard Wright   (1908–1960) was born on a cotton plantation near Natchez, Mississippi. Wright was 5 when his father, a mill worker, abandoned the family. His childhood, vividly recorded in his autobiography, *Black Boy* (1945), was characterized by persistent poverty, hardship, wanderings, and, following his mother's paralysis from strokes, intermittent stays in foster homes and orphanages. After working for a time in Memphis, Wright went to Chicago in 1927, joined the Communist party, and began to write, gaining his first recognition as a short story writer. In 1940, Wright published his first and most famous novel, *Native Son.* This novel is a brutal, naturalistic account of Bigger Thomas, a young black man victimized by his own blind impulses and by white society. Wright went into exile in France in 1947 and lived there until his death. His later work, still largely neglected, includes an account of his disenchantment with communism, *The God That Failed* (1950); two mildly existentialist novels, *The Outsider* (1953) and *The Long Dream* (1958); and an analysis of emerging nations in west Africa and the end of colonialism, *Black Power* (1954). Some of Wright's stories are collected in *Uncle Tom's Children* (1938) and *Eight Men* (1961). Referring to the black American experience, Wright in *12 Million Black Voices* (1941) declared, "The seasons of the plantation no longer dictate the lives of many of us."

Sir Thomas Wyatt   (1503–1542) was born in Kent and educated at Cambridge University. His life was filled with intrigues and adventures (he was even rumored to be the lover of Ann Boleyn). Before the age of 25, he had attracted the notice of Henry VIII, who used him as a deputy and an ambassador on various missions to the Continent. His Continental travels, especially his 1527 visit to Italy, bore unexpected fruit for English poetry—the sonnet. Wyatt and the hotheaded earl of Surrey, Henry Howard, introduced this verse form, which was to become one of the most important genres in the language.

Elinor Wylie   (1885–1928) was born in New Jersey and grew up in Philadelphia. She married in 1905 and later left her husband to be with Horace Wylie, whom she married soon after. Her first volume of poetry, *Nets to Catch the Wind,* was published in 1921; she published novels and poetry until her death at 43. Though she is the contemporary of T. S. Eliot and Marianne Moore, her poetry has nothing of their revolutionary "newness" of form and expression. Her best work displays a single emotion elegantly stated.

Mitsuye (May) Yamada   (b. 1923), born in Japan, came to the United States in 1926 and became a citizen in 1955. She studied at New York University, the University of Chicago, and the University of California at Irvine. She has taught at several California colleges, and has published *Camp Notes and Other Poems* (1976) and *Desert Run: Poems & Stories* (1988).

William Butler Yeats (1865–1939), the most prolific and one of the greatest modern poets, was born in Dublin, the son of the well-known painter John Butler Yeats. His Irish Protestant family moved often between London and the Irish countryside, and Yeats grew up more Irish than Protestant, a precocious youth fascinated by poetry, philosophy, politics, folklore, and the occult. He achieved early fame as a poet and wrote extraordinary poetry his entire life. In a life full of projects and accomplishments, his work in the theater and his long study of and belief in magic deserve the most attention. In 1889 he met and fell in love with the Irish radical Maud Gonne. The passion was never reciprocated. He proposed marriage to her on several occasions and at least once made the same offer to Gonne's daughter, Iseult. He finally married another woman in 1917 and, with the help of his wife, wrote *A Vision*, which presents his systematic theory of world philosophy.

Al Young (b. 1939), a 1982 American Book Award winner, is also a novelist of distinction, an editor, a musician, and a former disk jockey. His first volume of poetry was *Dancing* (1969), and was followed the next year by his first novel, *Snakes*. Since then, poetry collections and novels have come regularly, making Young one of the most productive of American writers.

Bernice Zamora (b. 1938) was born Bernice Ortiz in Pueblo, Colorado. She has a Ph.D. in English and American literature from Stanford University. Her poetry, much of it celebrating the Chicana experience, is collected in *Restless Serpents* (1976).

Cyn. Zarco (b. 1950) was born in Manila, Philippines, but now lives in California. A poet, she is the author of *Cir'cum·nav'i·ga'·tion* (1986) and other writings.

Glossary of Literary Terms

Act A major division of a play.

Affective fallacy The fallacy of wrongly evaluating a literary work by emphasizing only its emotional impact.

Allegory A narrative whose characters, symbols, and situations represent elements outside the text. For example, the character Christian in the allegory *Pilgrim's Progress* represents the Everyman who is a Christian.

Alliteration The repetition of consonant or vowel sounds at the beginning of words.

Allusion An indirect reference to some literary or historical figure or event. For example, the line in T. S. Eliot's *Love Song of J. Alfred Prufrock*, "No! I am not Prince Hamlet, nor was meant to be," is an allusion.

Ambiguity A literary device in which an author uses words with more than one meaning, deliberately leaving the reader uncertain.

Analogy A comparison of two different things on the basis of their similarity.

Anapest A metrical foot consisting of two unaccented syllables followed by an accented one ($\smile\smile\,\prime$), as in the phrase "on the ship."

Antagonist A competitor or opponent of the main character (protagonist) in a work of literature.

Antihero A protagonist in a modern literary work who has none of the noble qualities associated with a traditional hero.

Antistrophe In a Greek play, the portion of the Chorus that responds to the comments made by the first part of the Chorus, the Strophe.

Antithesis A phrase that contains words whose meanings harshly contrast with each other and are in rhetorical balance. For example, Alexander Pope's "Man proposes, God disposes" is an antithesis.

Aphorism   A terse, sharp statement of a large principle or idea. Thomas Hobbes's "The life of man, solitary, poor, nasty, brutish, and short" is an aphorism.

Apostrophe   A direct, emotional address to an absent character or quality, as it if were present.

Archetype   An image or character representative of some greater, more common element that recurs constantly and variously in literature.

Aside   Lines in a play that are delivered not to another character but to the audience or to the speaker himself or herself.

Assonance   The use of similar vowel sounds in adjacent or closeby words (for example, *slide* and *mind*).

Avant garde   A term used to describe writing that is strikingly different from the dominant writing of the age—in its form, style, content, and attitude.

Ballad   A poem originally sung or singable, recounting some domestic or heroic story, usually within a four-line stanza alternating three-beat and four-beat lines.

Bathos   An unsuccessful attempt to arouse great emotion, becoming not grand but absurd or silly.

Blank verse   Unrhymed lines of iambic pentameter.

Caesura   A pause within a line of poetry, often created through punctuation.

Canto   A division of certain long poems, such as Dante's *Divine Comedy* and Byron's *Don Juan*.

Carpe diem   Latin for "seize the day," used in literature to describe poetry that examines temporary human pleasures against the backdrop of eternity—as in Marvell's "To His Coy Mistress."

Catharsis   Exhaustion and cleansing of an audience member's emotions through participation in the events of a tragedy.

Character   A person created by an author for use in a work of fiction, poetry, or drama.

Chorus   A group of singers or actors who comment on and respond to the action in a play of classical Greece; also, a refrain in a song or poem.

Classicism   A term deriving from the era of the ancient Greeks and Romans, used in English literature to describe the outlook of the eighteenth century, where writers celebrated the "classical" values of restraint, order, and stylistic elegance.

Cliché   A phrase so overused that it has lost its original punch (for example, "beating a dead horse").

Climax   A point at which the events in a play or story reach their crisis, where the maximum emotional reaction of the reader is created.

Closed poetry   Closed poetry possesses certain structural patterns, notably rhyme and rhythm, that are clearly discernible.

Coda   A closing section of some literary works, occurring after the main action has been resolved.

Colloquialism   A term used in speech but not acceptable in formal writing.

Colloquy   A debate or conversation among characters.

Comedy   A work of literature, often a play, whose first intention is to amuse and that ordinarily has a happy ending.

Comic relief   A light, amusing section of a play or story that relieves tension and often comments by its humor on the surrounding serious action.

Complication   A part of a plot in which the conflict among characters or forces is engaged.

Conceit   A metaphor extended to great lengths in a poem (for example, Donne's "The Flea").

Conflict   A struggle among opposing forces or characters in fiction, poetry, or drama.

Connotation   Implications of words or sentences, beyond their literal, or denotative, meanings.

Consonance   Repetition of consonant sounds within words.

Couplet   Two lines of verse that have unity within themselves, often because they rhyme.

Cue   In a play, words or action from one character that signal the start of another character's words or action.

Dactyl   A metrical foot containing an accented syllable followed by two unaccented syllables ($'\smile\smile$), as in the word "craziness."

Denotation   Literal meaning of a word or of sentences.

Denouement   The final action of a plot, in which the conflict is resolved; the outcome.

Deus ex machina   Literally, "God from a machine"—the improbable intervention of an outside force that arbitrarily resolves a conflict.

Dialogue   Conversation between two people in fiction, drama, or poetry.

Diction   The use of words; good diction is accurate and appropriate to the subject.

Dimeter   A line of poetry composed of two metrical feet.

Dionysian   A term referring to the ancient Greek values embraced by the god Dionysius and his worshipers—faith in the irrational and in the primacy of human emotions; often a descriptive term in literature.

Dramatic irony   A term used to describe the effect of words of a character in a play that have more significance than they appear to have.

Dramatic monologue   A poem spoken by a character other than the author (for example, Browning's "My Last Duchess").

Elegy   A poetic meditation on death, often occasioned by the death of a specific individual.

End-stopped lines   Lines of poetry completed with the pause of punctuation.

Enjambment   Lines of poetry whose sense and grammar continue without a pause from one line into the next.

Epic   A long poem, usually narrative, recounting the trials and victories of a great hero, a hero usually important to an entire nation or people.

Epigram   A sharp, witty saying, such as Oscar Wilde's "I can resist everything but temptation."

Epigraph   A short inscription at the start of a literary work.

Epilogue   A concluding portion of a literary work, occurring after the main action has been completed.

Epithet   A descriptive word or phrase pointing out a specific quality—as when Shakespeare is referred to as "the Bard." The word is often used to describe terms of contempt.

Epode   The third portion of the comments of the Chorus in a classical Greek play, following the strophe and the antistrophe.

Essay   Literally, "attempt"—any short piece of nonfiction prose that makes specific points and statements about a limited topic.

Euphemism   A word or phrase substituting indirect for direct statement (for example, "passed away" in place of "died").

Euphony   A use of words to pleasant musical effect.

Exposition   A portion of a narrative or dramatic work that establishes the tone, setting, and basic situation.

Fable   A short tale that presents a specific moral and whose characters are often animals.

Fantasy   A work that takes place in a world that does not exist.

Farce   A broadly comic play relying for its humor on unlikely situations and characters.

Feminine ending   An additional syllable at the end of a line that has no metrical stress.

Figurative language   Language that deliberately departs from everyday phrasing, with dramatic and imagistic effects that move the reader into a fresh mode of perception.

Foot   A metrical unit of a line of poetry that contains at least one stressed syllable and one or more unstressed syllables.

Foreshadowing   In a plot, an indication of something yet to happen.

Form   The structure and organization of a work of art; form expresses its content.

Free verse   Poetry that relies more on rhythm than on regular meter for its effectiveness.

Genre   A distinct kind of writing, such as mystery, gothic, farce, or black comedy.

Gothic fiction   Novels, often historical, in which weird, grotesque activity takes place; Mary Shelley's *Frankenstein* is an example of gothic fiction.

Haiku   A form of Japanese poetry now also practiced by Westerners, which in three lines of five, seven, and then five syllables presents a sharp picture and a corresponding emotion or insight.

Heptameter   A line of poetry composed of seven metrical feet.

Heroic couplet   Two lines of rhyming iambic pentameter.

Hero (or heroine)   The central character of a literary work; he or she often has great virtues and faults, and his or her trials and successes form the main action of the plot.

Hexameter   A line of poetry containing six metrical feet.

Hubris   Overbearing or insolent pride; in Greek drama, the arrogance toward the gods that leads to a character's downfall.

Humours   The four Renaissance divisions of human temperament, corresponding to the liquids of the human body—blood, yellow bile, black bile, and phlegm—which are often associated with the personalities of dramatic characters.

Hyperbole   Deliberately overstated, exaggerated figurative language, used either for comic or great emotional effect.

Iamb   A metrical foot composed of one unaccented syllable followed by one stressed syllable ($\smile$ ′), as in the word "undone."

Iambic pentameter   A line containing five iambic feet, the most widely used meter in English-language poetry.

Image, imagism   A concrete expression of something perceived by the senses, using simile, metaphor, and figurative language.

Internal rhyme   Rhyme that occurs within a single line of poetry.

Irony   An effect associated with statements or situations in which something said or done is at odds with how things truly are.

Line   The fundamental element of a poem—a set of words that ends at a specific point on the page and has a unity independent of what goes before and after.

Lyric   A short, personal poem marked by strong feeling, musicality, and vivid language.

Masculine ending   The last stressed syllable in a line of poetry.

Meditative poetry   Verse with a strong and personal expression of religious feeling, especially as practiced by John Donne and others in the seventeenth century; also, a form of poetry in which the poet muses quietly and personally on a particular scene or emotion.

Metafiction   A contemporary form of fiction in which an author makes the process of writing fiction part of his or her subject.

Metaphor An implicit comparison of an object or feeling with another unlike it, as when Eliot's "Prufrock" says, "I have measured out my life with coffee spoons."

Metaphysical poetry Thoughtful, often religious, intellectually vigorous poetry, as practiced by John Donne and others in the seventeenth century.

Meter A rhythmic pattern in a poem created by the regular alternation of stressed and unstressed syllables.

Metonymy A figure of speech in which an object or person is not mentioned directly but suggested by an object associated with it, as when a reference to "the White House" means "the President."

Mock heroic A form of long poem in which the structures and values of the epic are used to burlesque a trivial subject (for example, Pope's "The Rape of the Lock").

Monometer A line of poetry composed of only one metrical foot.

Mood The emotional tone or outlook an author brings to a subject.

Muse Originally any one of nine Greek goddesses presiding over the arts; "the muse" usually refers to an abstract being that inspires poets to write.

Myth Ancient stories of unknown origin involving the supernatural; myths have provided cultures and writers with interpretations of the world's events.

Narrative A story that consists of an account of a sequence of events.

Naturalism Literature in which the author attempts to represent the world in a realistic and often harsh and hopeless way.

Novel A long fictional narrative that represents human events, characters, and actions.

Novella A short novel or tale.

Octameter A line of poetry composed of eight metrical feet.

Octave An eight-line stanza of poetry, often part of a sonnet.

Ode A lyric meditation, usually in elevated figurative language, upon some specific object, event, or theme.

Off rhyme A form of rhyme employing not-quite-identical sounds, such as "slip" and "slap."

Omniscient narrator A speaker or implied speaker of a work of fiction who can tell the story, shift into the minds of one or more characters, be in various places, and comment on the meaning of what is happening in the story.

Onomatopoeia An effect in which a word or phrase sounds like its sense (for example, Tennysons's "murmuring of innumerable bees").

Open poetry Related to free verse, it is not structurally restricted by rhyme or rhythm.

Ottava rima An eight-line stanza whose end-words usually rhyme in an *abababcc* pattern; used by many English poets (for example, Byron in *Don Juan*).

Pacing Narrative or linguistic devices that keep literary works moving and interesting.

Parable A story illustrating a moral, in which every detail parallels the moral situation.

Paradox A statement that seems contradictory but actually points out a truth (for example, Wordsworth's line, "The Child is father of the Man").

Parody A literary work that deliberately makes fun of another literary work or of a social situation.

Pathetic fallacy The fallacy of attaching human feelings to nature.

Pathos The qualities in a work of art that arouse pity or sadness, especially the helpless feeling caused by undeserved bad luck.

Persona   The mask through which a writer gives expression to his or her own feelings or participates in the action of a story, poem, or play.

Personification   A literary strategy giving nonhuman things human characters or attitudes, as in Aesop's fables or Keats's poem "To Autumn."

Plot   The sequence of events in a story, poem, or play; the events build upon each other toward a convincing conclusion.

Poetry   A form of writing in which the author writes in lines, with either a metrical pattern or a free-verse rhythm.

Point of view   The angle from which a writer tells a story. Point of view can be either omniscient, limited, or through the eyes of one or more characters.

Prologue   A preface or introduction setting the scene for what is to follow.

Prose   Any form of writing that does not have the rhythmic patterns of metrical verse or free verse. Good prose is characterized by tightness, specificity, and a sense of style.

Protagonist   The leading character; the protagonist engages the main concern of readers or audience.

Proverb   A statement putting forth a great truth (for example, the Biblical proverb "Go to the ant, thou sluggard; consider his ways and be wise").

Pun   A form of word play, often serious, that relies on the double meaning of words or sounds for its effect (for example, the dying Mercutio's words to Romeo, "ask for me tomorrow and you shall find me a grave man").

Quatrain   A four-line stanza.

Realism   An approach to writing that emphasizes recording everyday experience.

Refrain   A line or group of lines repeated several times in a poem.

Resolution   The dramatic action occurring after the climax of a play, before the events themselves are played out.

Rhetoric   The study and practice of language in action—presenting ideas and opinions in the most effective way.

Rhyme   Similarity of sound between words.

Rhythm   In poetry, the regular recurrence of stressed syllables; in literature in general, the overall flow of language, having a sensory effect on the reader.

Romance   Any work of fiction that takes place in an extravagent world remote from daily life.

Romanticism   A powerful literary movement beginning in the late eighteenth century; it shook off classical forms and attitudes, embracing instead the power, promise, and political dignity of the imaginative individual.

Satire   A literary work using wit, irony, anger, and parody to criticize human foibles and social institutions.

Scansion   The act of counting out the meter of a poem.

Scene   A portion of a drama, poem, or work of fiction that occurs within one time and setting.

Science fiction   Fantasy in which scientific facts and advances fuel the plot.

Sestet   A six-line stanza of poetry, often part of a sonnet.

Setting   The background of a literary work—the time, the place, the era, the geography, and the overall culture.

Short story   A brief fictional narrative.

Simile   A comparison of two things via the word "like" or "as."

Situational irony   The contrast between what a character wants and what he or she receives, arising not through the character's fault but from other circumstances.

Soliloquy   A speech by a character who is alone on stage, talking to himself or herself or to the audience.

Sonnet   A poem of fourteen lines using some kind of metrical form and rhyme scheme and always unified with a concentrated expression of a large subject.

Sound   In literature, the combination of sensations perceived by the ear or the mind's ear.

Spondee   A metrical foot containing two stressed syllables, as in the phrase "time out."

Sprung rhythm   A form of meter defined by the poet Gerard Manley Hopkins that emphasizes only the number of stresses in a line, thus making a kind of tense meter of accentual irregularity.

Stanza   A portion of a poem set off by blank space before and after; more formally, a stanza may have rhyme and metrical regularity matching that of stanzas before and after.

Stereotype   Widely believed and oversimplified attitudes toward a person, an issue, a style, and so on.

Stream of consciousness   Writing that attempts to imitate and follow a character's thought processes.

Stress   The emphasis a syllable or word naturally receives within a line of poetry, or in human speech.

Strophe   In an ancient Greek play, the comments of that portion of the Chorus speaking first during a scene.

Style   The property of writing that gives form, expression, and individuality to the content.

Subject   The person, place, idea, situation, or thing with which some piece of literature most immediately concerns itself.

Subplot   A complication within a play or piece of fiction that is not part of the main action but often complements it.

Subtext   Significant communication, especially in dialogue, that gives motivation for the words being said.

Surrealism   Art that values and expresses the unconscious imagination by altering what is commonly seen as reality.

Suspense   Those literary qualities that leave a reader breathlessly awaiting further developments with no clear idea of what those developments will be.

Symbol   Something that represents something else, the way a flag represents a country or a rose may stand for love—implying not only another physical thing but an associated meaning.

Synecdoche   A kind of metaphor in which the mention of a part stands for the whole (for example, "head" refers not only to the heads of cattle but to each animal as a whole).

Synesthesia   A subjective sensation or image (as of color) that is felt in terms of another sense (as of sound).

Synopsis   A summary of the main points of a plot.

Syntax   The arrangement of words to form sentences.

Tercet   A three-line stanza, often one in which each line ends with the same rhyme.

Terza rima   A series of three-line stanzas that rhyme *aba, bcb, cdc, ded*, and so on; used by Dante in the *Divine Comedy* and by Shelley, among others.

Tetrameter   A line of verse composed of four metrical feet.

Theater of the absurd   Avant-garde, post-World War II drama representing the hopelessness of the human condition by abandoning realistic characters, language, and plot.

Theme   The main idea of a literary work created by its treatment of its immediate subject.

Tone   The expression of a writer's attitudes toward a subject; the mood the author has chosen for a piece.

Tour de force   A display of literary skill that is very impressive, but often empty.

Tragedy   A literary work, usually a play, where the main characters participate in events that lead to their destruction.

Tragicomedy   A work of literature, usually a play, that deals with potentially tragic events that are finally avoided, leading to a happy ending.

Trimeter   A line of poetry containing three metrical feet.

Trochee   A metrical foot consisting of an accented syllable followed by an unaccented one ($\prime$ $\smile$), as in the word "salty."

Understatement   A passage that deliberately and ironically states or implies that something is less than it really is.

Utopia   An ideal social and political state created by an author (for example, Plato, Thomas More, H. G. Wells, and Paul Goodman wrote utopias).

Verbal irony   The discrepancy between things as they are stated and as they really are.

Verse   A unit of poetry, usually a line or stanza; in general, any kind of literary work written in poetic lines.

Wit   Originally a word that meant "intelligence," "wit" now refers to a facility for quick, deft writing that usually employs humor to make its point.

Permissions Acknowledgments

Lawrence Ferlinghetti, "In Goya's Greatest Scenes." From Lawrence Ferlinghetti: *A Coney Island of the Mind*. Copyright © 1958 by Lawrence Ferlinghetti. Reprinted by permission of New Directions Publishing Corporation.

Gisele Fong, "Corrosion." © 1990 by Gisele Fong, from *Making Face, Making Soul/Haciendo Caras*. © 1990 by Gloria Anzaldúa. Reprinted by permission of Aunt Lute Books. (415) 558-8116.

Carolyn Forché, "Dulcimer Maker" from *Gathering the Tribes* by Carolyn Forché. © 1976 Carolyn Forché. Reprinted by permission of Yale University Press.

Robert Frost, "Mending Wall," "Once by the Pacific," "Stopping by Woods on a Snowy Evening," and "Tree at My Window" by Robert Frost from *The Poetry of Robert Frost* edited by Edward Connery Lathem. Copyright 1923, 1928, © 1969 by Holt, Rinehart and Winston, Copyright 1936, 1951, 1956 by Robert Frost, Copyright © 1964 by Lesley Frost Ballantine. Reprinted by permission of Henry Holt and Co., Inc.

Gabriel García Márquez, "A Very Old Man With Enormous Wings" from *Leaf Storm and Other Stories* by Gabriel García Márquez. English translation copyright © 1972 by Gabriel García Márquez. Reprinted by permission of HarperCollins Publishers.

Nikki Giovanni, "Knoxville, Tennessee" from *Black Feeling, Black Talk, Black Judgement* by Nikki Giovanni. Copyright © 1968, 1970 by Nikki Giovanni. By permission of William Morrow & Company, Inc.

Nikki Giovanni, "Mothers" from *My House* by Nikki Giovanni. Copyright © 1972 by Nikki Giovanni. By permission of William Morrow & Company, Inc.

Susan Glaspell, *Suppressed Desires*—A Comedy in Two Episodes by Susan Glaspell, in collaboration with George Cram Cook. Copyright 1920 by Small, Maynard & Co., Inc. Copyright 1951 by Walter H. Baker Company. Reprinted by permission of Baker's Plays, Boston, MA 02111. All rights reserved and held by Baker's Plays.

Nadine Gordimer, "The Train from Rhodesia" from *The Soft Voice of the Serpent and Other Stories*. Reprinted by permission of Russell & Volkening as agents for the author. Copyright © 1952 by Nadine Gordimer, © copyright renewed 1980 by Nadine Gordimer.

Lady Gregory, "The Rising of the Moon" from *The Collected Plays of Lady Gregory*, Coole Edition, published by Colin Smythe Limited, Buckinghamshire, UK.

Anthony Grooms, "Homespace" from *Ice Poems*. Poetry Atlanta Press, copyright © Anthony Grooms, 1988. Reprinted by permission of the author.

Thom Gunn, "On the Move" from *Selected Poems 1950–1975* by Thom Gunn. Copyright © 1979 by Thom Gunn. Reprinted by permission of Farrar, Straus & Giroux, Inc., and Faber and Faber Ltd.

Lorraine Hansberry, *A Raisin in the Sun*. Copyright © 1958 by Robert Nemiroff, as an unpublished work. Copyright © 1959 by Robert Nemiroff, as Executor of the Estate of Lorraine Hansberry. Copyright renewed 1987 by Robert Nemiroff. Reprinted by permission of Random House, Inc. In *A Raisin in the Sun*, "Harlem" ("Dream Deferred") is from *The Panther and the Lash* by Langston Hughes. Copyright 1951 by Langston Hughes. Reprinted by permission of Alfred A. Knopf, Inc. Caution: Professionals and amateurs are hereby warned that *A Raisin in the Sun*, being fully protected under the copyright Laws of the United States of America, the British Empire, including the Dominion of Canada, and all other countries of the Universal Copyright and Berne Conventions, is subject to royalty. All rights, including professional, amateur, motion picture, recitation, lecturing, public reading, radio and television broadcasting, and the rights of translation into foreign languages, are strictly reserved. Particular emphasis is laid on the question of readings, permission for which must be secured in writing. All inquiries should be addressed to the William Morris Agency, 1350 Avenue of the Americas, New York, NY 10019, authorized agents for the Estate of Lorraine Hansberry and for Robert Nemiroff, Executor.

Joy Harjo, "Fishing," *The New York Times* (June 21, 1991). Copyright © 1991 by The New York Times Company. Reprinted by permission.

Audre Lorde, "Oya" from *New York Head Shop and Museum.* Permission granted by Broadside Press.

Robert Lowell, "Children of Light" from *Lord Weary's Castle,* copyright 1946 and renewed 1974 by Robert Lowell, reprinted by permission of Harcourt Brace Jovanovich, Inc.

Mairi MacInnes, "VJ Day," in *Quarterly Review of Literature,* Poetry Series #3, Vol. XXII (1981). Reprinted by permission of *Quarterly Review of Literature.*

Bobbie Ann Mason, "Big Bertha Stories" from *Love Life* by Bobbie Ann Mason. Copyright © 1988 by Bobbie Ann Mason. Reprinted by permission of HarperCollins Publishers.

Annette M'Baye, "Silhouette," in *New Sum of Poetry from the Negro World* (Paris: Présence Africaine, 1966, No. 57). Trans. Kathleen Weaver, in *The Penguin Book of Women Poets,* ed. Carol Cosman, Joan Keefe, and Kathleen Weaver (New York: Viking Press, 1979). Translation © Kathleen Weaver, Berkeley, California. Reprinted by permission of Présence Africaine and Kathleen Weaver.

Claude McKay, "America" and "Outcast." By permission of The Archives of Claude McKay, Carl Cowl, Administrator. See *Selected Poems of Claude McKay* published 1981 by Harcourt Brace Jovanovich.

Josephine Miles, "Housewife." In Josephine Miles, *Collected Poems, 1930–83,* p. 62. Urbana: University of Illinois 1983. Reprinted by permission of the University of Illinois Press, and the University of California at Berkeley.

Czeslaw Milosz, "On Prayer" © 1988 by Czeslaw Milosz Royalties, Inc. From *The Collected Poems, 1931–1987* by Czeslaw Milosz, first published by The Ecco Press in 1988. Reprinted by permission.

Janice Mirikitani, "Prisons of Silence" from *Shedding Silence,* Copyright © 1987 by Janice Mirikitani. Reprinted by permission of Celestial Arts, Berkeley, CA.

Janice Mirikitani, "Sing with Your Body." © copyright by Janice Mirikitani, San Francisco, Ca. Reprinted from *Awake in the River* (Isthmus Press, 1978) by permission of the author.

Yukio Mishima, "Patriotism," trans. Geoffrey W. Sargent. From Yukio Mishima: *Death in Midsummer and Other Stories.* Copyright © 1966 by New Directions Publishing Corporation. Reprinted by permission of New Directions Publishing Corporation.

Marianne Moore, "The Steeple-Jack," copyright 1951 © 1970 by Marianne Moore, © renewed 1979 by Lawrence E. Brinn and Louise Crane, Executors of the Estate of Marianne Moore, from *The Complete Poems of Marianne Moore* by Marianne Moore. Used by permission of Viking Penguin, a division of Penguin Books USA Inc.

Pat Mora, "Elena," by Pat Mora is reprinted with permission of the publisher from *Chants* (Houston: Arte Publico Press–University of Houston, 1984).

Bharati Mukherjee, "Hindus" from *Darkness* by Bharati Mukherjee, Penguin: New York. Copyright © Bharati Mukherjee, 1985. Reprinted by permission of Penguin Books Canada Limited and Bharati Mukherjee.

Alice Munro, "The Found Boat" from *Something I've Been Meaning to Tell You.* Copyright © 1974 by Alice Munro. Reprinted by arrangement with Virginia Barber Literary Agency, Inc. All rights reserved.

David Mura, "Grandfather and Grandmother in Love" from *After We Lost Our Way* by David Mura (New York: E.P. Dutton, 1989; Brownsville, Oregon: Story Line Press, 1994). Reprinted by permission of the author.

R. K. Narayan, "Mother and Son," from *Malgudi Days* by R. K. Narayan. Copyright © 1972, 1975, 1978, 1980, 1981, 1982 by R. K. Narayan. Used by permission of Viking Penguin, a division of Penguin Books USA Inc.

Gloria Naylor, "Kiswana Browne," from *The Women of Brewster Place* by Gloria Naylor. Copyright © 1980, 1982 by Gloria Naylor. Used by permission of Viking Penguin, a division of Penguin Books USA Inc.

Carlos Nejar, "Oil Lamps," in *Quarterly Review of Literature*, Poetry Series #3, Vol. XXII (1981). Reprinted by permission of *Quarterly Review of Literature*.

Pablo Neruda, "The United Fruit Co.," trans. Robert Bly, from *Neruda and Vallejo: Selected Poems*, translated by James Wright, John Knoepfle and Robert Bly (Boston: Beacon Press, 1971). Reprinted with the permission of Robert Bly.

Flannery O'Connor, "A Good Man Is Hard to Find" from *A Good Man Is Hard to Find and Other Stories*, copyright 1953 by Flannery O'Connor and renewed 1981 by Regina O'Connor, reprinted by permission of Harcourt Brace Jovanovich, Inc.

Simon J. Ortiz, "Speaking." Permission granted by author, Simon J. Ortiz.

Wilfred Owen, "Anthem for Doomed Youth" and "Dulce et Decorum Est." From Wilfred Owen: *Collected Poems of Wilfred Owen*. Copyright © 1963 by Chatto & Windus, Ltd. Reprinted by permission of New Directions Publishing Corporation.

Grace Paley, "A Conversation With My Father" from *Enormous Changes at the Last Minute* by Grace Paley. Copyright © 1972, 1974 by Grace Paley. Reprinted by permission of Farrar, Straus & Giroux, Inc.

Papyrus Harris, "Beginning of the songs of delight." In Miriam Lichtheim, *Ancient Egyptian Literature. Three Volumes*, Volume II, p. 192. Copyright © 1976 Regents of the University of California. Reprinted by permission of the University of California Press.

Nicanor Parra, "Piano Solo." From Nicanor Parra: *Poems and Antipoems*. Copyright © 1958 by Florence H. Williams and Nicanor Parra. Reprinted by permission of New Directions Publishing Corporation.

Octavio Paz, "Engaged," trans. Muriel Rukeyser: Copyright © 1963, 1973 by Octavio Paz and Muriel Rukeyser. Reprinted by permission of New Directions Publishing Corporation.

Pepi I Pyramid Text, "The king prays to the sky-goddess" and "The sky-goddess protects the king." In Miriam Lichtheim, *Ancient Egyptian Literature. Three Volumes*, Volume I, pp. 44, 46. Copyright © 1973 Regents of the University of California. Reprinted by permission of the University of California Press.

Luigi Pirandello, "War" from *Better Think Twice About It and Other Short Stories*. Reprinted by permission of the Pirandello Estate and Toby Cole, Agent.

Sylvia Plath, "The Applicant" and "Daddy." Copyright © 1963 by Ted Hughes. From *The Collected Poems of Sylvia Plath*, edited by Ted Hughes. Reprinted by permission of HarperCollins Publishers, and Faber and Faber Ltd.

Estela Portillo, *Day of the Swallows.* Reprinted by permission of the author.

Ezra Pound, "The River-Merchant's Wife: A Letter" and "A Virginal." From Ezra Pound: *Personae*. Copyright 1926 by Ezra Pound. Reprinted by permission of New Directions Publishing Corporation.

Alexander Pushkin, "To My Old Nurse" and "A sower went out to sow his seed." From *Poems of Pushkin* by Alexander Pushkin, translated by Henry Jones. Copyright © 1965 by Henry Jones. Published by arrangement with Carol Publishing Group. A Citadel Press Book.

Ibn Quzman, "The Radish," in *Moorish Poetry*, trans. A. J. Arberry (Cambridge, UK: Cambridge University Press, 1953). Reprinted by permission.

Rahel, "To My Country," trans. Diane J. Mintz, in *The Penguin Book of Women Poets*, ed. Carol Cosman, Joan Keefe, and Kathleen Weaver (New York: Viking Press, 1979). Translation copyright Diane J. Mintz. Reprinted by permission of Diane J. Mintz.

Dylan Thomas, "Fern Hill." From Dylan Thomas: *Poems of Dylan Thomas.* Copyright 1945 by The Trustees for the Copyrights of Dylan Thomas. Reprinted by permission of New Directions Publishing Corporation, and J. M. Dent.

Joyce Carol Thomas, "Black Child" copyright © 1993 by Joyce Carol Thomas.

James Thurber, "The Catbird Seat." Copr. © 1945 James Thurber. Copr. © 1973 Helen Thurber & Rosemary A. Thurber. From *The Thurber Carnival,* published by Harper & Row.

Mohamud S. Togane, "Arfaye" from *The Bottle and the Bushman,* copyright © Mohamud S. Togane, 1986. Reprinted by permission of The Muses' Company.

Melvin B. Tolson, "A Legend of Versailles." Reprinted with permission of Twayne Publishers, an imprint of Macmillan Publishing Company, from *Harlem Gallery* by Melvin B. Tolson. Copyright © 1965 by Twayne Publishers, Inc.

John Updike, "Ex-Basketball Player." From *The Carpentered Hen and Other Tame Creatures* by John Updike. Copyright © 1957, 1982 by John Updike. Reprinted by permission of Alfred A. Knopf, Inc.

Luisa Valenzuela, "The Censors," trans. David Unger. From *Open Door* by Luisa Valenzuela, North Point Press, U.S.A., 1988; Serpent's Tail, England, 1992. Reprinted by permission of the author.

César Vallejo, "To My Brother Miguel," trans. Kathleen Ross and Richard Schaaf. Reprinted by permission of the publisher, from *The Black Heralds,* Latin American Literary Review Press 1990, Pittsburgh, Pennsylvania.

Gerald Vizenor, "Family Photograph." Reprinted by permission of the author.

David Wagoner, "A Valedictory to Standard Oil of Indiana" from *Collected Poems 1956–1976* by David Wagoner. Indiana University Press, copyright 1976 by David Wagoner. Reprinted by permission of the author.

Diane Wakoski, "To an Autocrat." Copyright © 1970 by Diane Wakoski. Reprinted from *Emerald Ice: Selected Poems 1962–1987* with the permission of Black Sparrow Press.

Derek Walcott, "Nearing La Guaira" from *Selected Poems* by Derek Walcott. Copyright © 1964 by Derek Walcott. Reprinted by permission of Farrar, Straus & Giroux, Inc.

Alice Walker, "Roselily" from *In Love & Trouble: Stories of Black Women,* copyright © 1972 by Alice Walker, reprinted by permission of Harcourt Brace Jovanovich, Inc.

Margaret Walker, "Lineage" and "Poppa Chicken," from *This Is My Century: New and Collected Poems* © 1989 by Margaret Walker Alexander, Published by University of Georgia Press.

Chad Walsh, "Port Authority Terminal: 9 A.M. Monday" from *The End of Nature* by Chad Walsh. Ohio University Press, copyright © 1969 by Chad Walsh. Reprinted by permission.

James Welch, "The Only Bar in Dixon" from *Riding the Earthboy 40* by James Welch. Reprinted by permission of James Welch. Copyright 1970.

Eudora Welty, "A Worn Path" from *A Curtain of Green and Other Stories,* copyright 1941 and renewed 1969 by Eudora Welty, reprinted by permission of Harcourt Brace Jovanovich, Inc.

John A. Williams, *August Forty-Five.* © 1981 by John A. Williams. Used by permission of the Author.

John A. Williams, "Son in the Afternoon." © 1965 by John A. Williams. Used by permission of the Author.

William Carlos Williams, "Danse Russe" and "To Waken an Old Lady." From William Carlos Williams: *The Collected Poems of William Carlos Williams, 1909–1939,* vol. I. Copyright 1938 by New Directions Publishing Corp. Reprinted by permission of New Directions Publishing Corporation.

Index

1039